2

U.S.

GAAP Guide

Richard H. Gesseck, CPA, and
Lawrence Gramling, Ph.D., CPA

Wolters Kluwer

Editorial Staff

Editor . . . . Sandra Lim
Production . . . . Jennifer Schencker, Vijayalakshmi Suresh, and Anbarasu Anbumani

This publication is designed to provide accurate and authoritative information in regard to the subject matter covered. It is sold with the understanding that the publisher is not engaged in rendering legal, accounting or other professional service and that the author is not offering such advice in this publication. If legal advice or other expert assistance is required, the services of a competent professional person should be sought.

—From a *Declaration of Principles* jointly adopted by a Committee of the American Bar Association and a Committee of Publishers and Associations

ISBN: 978-0-8080-4708-7

2700 Lake Cook Road
Riverwoods, IL 60015
800 344 3734
CCHGroup.com

Portions of this work were published in a previous edition.

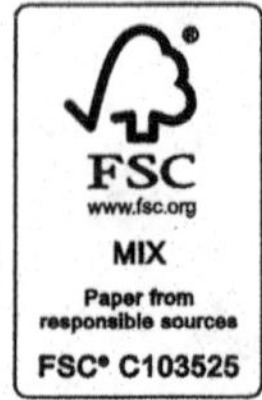

Printed in the United States of America

2018 U.S. Master GAAP Guide

by Richard H. Gesseck and Lawrence Gramling

Highlights

The *2018 U.S. Master™ GAAP Guide* helps accountants solve many complex accounting and disclosure problems. Superior technical analysis and practical explanations of accounting principles are provided. The *Guide* uses a helpful three-step approach for each topic covered. First, flowcharts illustrate the decision process and accounting procedures. Then, general discussion of the major provisions provides a context for understanding; and, finally, detailed examples show the specific computations and accounting requirements.

The *Guide* provides summaries, explanations, and applications of U.S. generally accepted accounting principles (U.S. GAAP) for nongovernmental entities in the United States of America, as authoritatively documented in the Financial Accounting Standards Board's (FASB's) *Accounting Standards Codification®* (ASC). It is organized along the major sections of the FASB Codification with a separate chapter devoted to each of the nine sections. This comprehensive approach allows easy reference to the Codification along with the many helpful examples that are presented in this volume.

2018 Edition

The 2018 edition of the *U.S. Master GAAP Guide* features the following:

- Twenty-two new Accounting Standards Updates (ASUs) (see Appendix B).
- A discussion of Topic 842, *Leases*, which was created under ASU 2016-02 issued in February 2016 and supersedes the guidance in Topic 840.
- Analysis of ASU 2017-05, *Other Income—Gains and Losses from the Derecognition of Nonfinancial Assets (Subtopic 610-20): Clarifying the Scope of Asset Derecognition Guidance and Accounting for Partial Sales of Nonfinancial Assets*, which provides guidance for recognizing gains and losses from the transfer of nonfinancial assets in contracts with noncustomers.
- A summary of the amendments in ASU 2016-15, *Statement of Cash Flows (Topic 230): Classification of Certain Cash Receipts and Cash Payments*, which gives specific guidance on how certain cash receipts and cash payments are presented and classified in the statement of cash flows.
- A review of ASC 321, which specifies the accounting and reporting requirements for all investments in equity securities and applies to all entities, including cooperatives and mutual entities and trusts that do not report substantially all of their debt securities at fair value.

Preface

The *2018 U.S. Master™ GAAP Guide* provides summaries, explanations, and applications of U.S. generally accepted accounting principles (U.S. GAAP) for nongovernmental entities in the United States of America, as authoritatively documented in the Financial Accounting Standards Board's (FASB's) *Accounting Standards Codification®* (ASC).

This book is organized into nine chapters that correspond to the areas of the ASC. The ASC topics within each area are listed on the detailed contents page at the beginning of each chapter. Each topic is then addressed individually within the chapter.

Within each topic, three levels of explanation and analysis are generally offered. This three-level approach includes flowchart material, where appropriate; general discussion; and detailed example material, where appropriate. First, a flowchart illustrates the general decision process and accounting procedures required by U.S. GAAP. Next, a general discussion of the major provisions of the standards is presented. This discussion is more detailed than the material presented in the flowchart, but it does not attempt to incorporate computational aspects of the standards. The third level of explanation and analysis consists of detailed examples that show the reader specific computational and accounting requirements of the standards. The example material is designed to progress from simple to complex considerations. Specific implementation problems are discussed in this section of the analysis.

In cases where ASC topics have been significantly changed by recent updates, a list of the applicable FASB Accounting Standards Updates (ASUs) appears at the conclusion of the topic's coverage under the heading "Recent Changes." Additionally, Appendix B of this book provides a chronological listing of all recent ASUs and indicates the ASC topics that they significantly changed. Appendix C lists proposed ASUs that the FASB has issued in the form of Exposure Drafts (EDs). The list indicates the ASC topic(s) that each ED would significantly change.

Appendix D explains how readers can cross-reference specific ASC content with the historical pronouncements the Codification was originally derived from. This will help experienced practitioners in making the transition to codified GAAP. Readers should keep in mind that all ASC content is uniformly authoritative, unlike prior pronouncements of GAAP.

Readers are encouraged to refer to authoritative standards in conjunction with reading the corresponding portions of this book. The ASC and, where appropriate, Securities and Exchange Commission (SEC) guidance should always be considered as the final authority on accounting, reporting, and disclosure matters.

Accounting practitioners should view this book as a working guide for solving complex accounting problems. CPA examination candidates will also benefit from this book because a high percentage of the financial accounting questions are directly related to specific standards of U.S. GAAP. Candidates ar encouraged to pay particular attention to the computational notes and journal entries associated with the detailed example material.

This book has also proven to be invaluable when used by accounting students as an interpretative instrument. Many accounting students become confused by the concise and technical presentation found in the original standards. Interpretative material included in the standards often does little to overcome this obstacle. The use of this book will minimize classroom time devoted to explanations of the technical provisions of U.S. GAAP and free instructors to spend more time dealing with the many conceptual issues of accounting. In undergraduate courses, this book may be used as a supplement (e.g., in Intermediate Accounting) or as a main text (e.g., in Advanced Financial Accounting). Additionally, MBA and other graduate students can benefit from the technical detail in this book that may otherwise be missing from their coursework.

It is the authors' hope that the *U.S. Master™ GAAP Guide* will provide you with new insights into, and practical understanding of, the standards that constitute U.S. GAAP. Readers' comments and suggestions for improvements in subsequent editions are welcome. Comments and suggestions should be sent to tony.powell@WoltersKluwer.com.

Acknowledgments

The authors thank the American Institute of Certified Public Accountants, the Financial Accounting Standards Board, and the Securities and Exchange Commission for use of their publications, and the editors of the *CPA Journal* for permission to reproduce certain flowchart materials.

About the Authors

Richard H. Gesseck, CPA, has more than 40 years of public accounting experience, including 20 years as an audit partner with Ernst & Young and almost 10 years as an audit partner with regional firms. Dick now provides accounting and auditing training to CPA firms and public and privately held entities. Previously he served middle-market, public and privately held manufacturing, distribution, and hi-tech entities.

Dick has served as the lead audit partner to numerous publicly held companies, including two *Fortune* 500 companies. He has had key roles in several significant M&A transactions. He also has significant experience with registration statements, comfort letters, communications with the SEC, and solving numerous technical audit and accounting (A&A) and SEC issues.

Dick has served as a conference leader for more than 300 technical accounting and auditing seminars for numerous state CPA societies and the AICPA and has provided customized A&A training for MasterCard International and Discovery Communications (SEC Reporting), BET Networks, Inc., and Corning, Inc. (FASB Update), RadioShack (revenue recognition), the United States Postal Service Office of Inspector General and Defense Contractor Audit Agency (Audit risk assessment), and several CPA firms (GAAP and GAAS updates).

Dick has also authored several auditing and accounting courses for the AICPA, including:

- *Auditors Risk Assessment Process: Tackling the New Risk Assessment SASs*
- *Detecting Misstatements: Integrating SAS 99 with the new Risk Assessment Standards*
- *Applying the PCAOB Audit Risk Standards to Smaller Issuers*
- *Applying Risk Assessment Procedures to Smaller Business Audits*
- *Alternatives to GAAP – Using Special Purpose Frameworks*
- *Applying the Risk Assessment Standards Using a Case Study Approach*
- *Financial Reporting Framework for SMEs*
- *Applying Risk Assessment Procedures to Smaller Business Audits*

Dick has been honored by the Connecticut Society of Certified Public Accountants (CTCPA) and AICPA with multiple outstanding discussion leader awards. In 2013, he received the CTCPA Jack Brooks Leadership Award for his contributions to the CPA profession.

Dick received a bachelor of science degree in business administration from the University of New Haven, and was the recipient of that University's 2002 Distinguished Alumni Award. He is currently a member of the FASB's Small Business Advisory Committee. In 2014, he completed a 10-year term as a member of the Connecticut State Board of Accountancy. He is a past president of the CTCPA and New Haven Country Club and has served on several other board (including chairing audit committees of public and privately entities), and is an active member of the AICPA and the CTCPA.

Lawrence Gramling, Ph.D., CPA, is an accounting professor and Associate Dean for Undergraduate Programs at the School of Business of the University of Connecticut, in Storrs, Connecticut. Dr. Gramling has published articles in various academic and professional journals, including *Issues in Accounting Education, The CPA Journal,* and *Connecticut CPA Quarterly.* Larry has developed and taught professional education courses for over 30 years, including webinars throughout the country on topics ranging from financial accounting, auditing, ethics, and quality control at CPA firms. He has been a consultant to CPA firms concerning their quality of practice. Larry was formerly the president of the Connecticut Society of Certified Public Accountants (CTCPA), has chaired the CTCPA's Peer Review and Strategic Planning Committees, and has served on the CTCPA's Board of Governors and the CTCPA Educational Trust. Larry continues to be an active member of the CTCPA and the AICPA.

Larry received his B.S. in Accounting, cum laude, from the University of Scranton and his MBA from Northeastern University. He earned his Ph.D. in Accounting from the University of Maryland. His research interests include CPE methods and CPA firm regulation, fraud and forensic accounting, CPA firm peer review results, disclosures of estimates in public corporation financial statements, and communications in footnotes to financial statements.

Contents

Chapter		Page
1	General Principles	1001
2	Presentation	2001
3	Assets	3001
4	Liabilities	4001
5	Equity	5001
6	Revenue	6001
7	Expenses	7001
8	Broad Transactions	8001
9	Industry	9001
	Appendix A: Conceptual Framework	10,001
	Appendix B: Accounting Standards Updates	11,001
	Appendix C: Exposure Drafts	12,001
	Appendix D: Cross-Referencing the Codification and Pre-Codification Standards	13,001
	Appendix E: Present Value Factors	14,001
	Index	15,001

Table of Contents

Chapter	Page
1 General Principles	1001
105 Generally Accepted Accounting Principles	1001
2 Presentation	2001
205 Presentation of Financial Statements	2001
210 Balance Sheet	2009
215 Statement of Shareholder Equity	2022
220 Comprehensive Income	2022
225 Income Statement	2043
230 Statement of Cash Flows	2044
235 Notes to Financial Statements	2073
250 Accounting Changes and Error Corrections	2079
255 Changing Prices	2100
260 Earnings per Share	2100
270 Interim Reporting	2148
272 Limited Liability Entities	2160
274 Personal Financial Statements	2160
275 Risks and Uncertainties	2161
280 Segment Reporting	2162
3 Assets	3001
305 Cash and Cash Equivalents	3001
310 Receivables	3001
320 Investments—Debt Securities	3041
321 Investments—Equity Securities	3041
323 Investments—Equity Method and Joint Ventures	3064
325 Investments—Other	3081
326 Financial Instruments—Credit Losses	3083
330 Inventory	3083
340 Other Assets and Deferred Costs	3095
350 Intangibles—Goodwill and Other	3096
360 Property, Plant, and Equipment	3113
4 Liabilities	4001
405 Liabilities	4001
410 Asset Retirement and Environmental Obligations	4009
420 Exit or Disposal Cost Obligations	4022
430 Deferred Revenue	4027
440 Commitments	4027
450 Contingencies	4035
460 Guarantees	4041
470 Debt	4043
480 Distinguishing Liabilities from Equity	4104

Chapter		Page
5 Equity		5001
	505 Equity	5001
6 Revenue		6001
	605 Revenue Recognition	6001
	606 Revenue from Contracts with Customers	6009
	610 Other Income	6040
7 Expenses		7001
	705 Cost of Sales and Services	7001
	710 Compensation—General	7002
	712 Compensation—Nonretirement Postemployment Benefits	7009
	715 Compensation—Retirement Benefits	7014
	718 Compensation—Stock Compensation	7152
	720 Other Expenses	7180
	730 Research and Development	7184
	740 Income Taxes	7195
8 Broad Transactions		8001
	805 Business Combinations	8001
	808 Collaborative Arrangements	8025
	810 Consolidation	8025
	815 Derivatives and Hedging	8047
	820 Fair Value Measurements and Disclosures	8086
	825 Financial Instruments	8092
	830 Foreign Currency Matters	8104
	835 Interest	8139
	840 Leases	8191
	842 Leases	8302
	845 Nonmonetary Transactions	8327
	850 Related Party Disclosures	8343
	852 Reorganizations	8345
	853 Service Concession Arrangement	8345
	855 Subsequent Events	8346
	860 Transfers and Servicing	8346
9 Industry		9001
	905 Agriculture	9001
	908 Airlines	9002
	910 Contractors—Construction	9002
	912 Contractors—Federal Government	9003
	915 Development Stage Entities	9003
	920 Entertainment—Broadcasters	9004
	922 Entertainment—Cable Television	9006
	924 Entertainment—Casinos	9008

Chapter	Page
926 Entertainment—Films	9009
928 Entertainment—Music	9009
930 Extractive Activities—Mining	9013
932 Extractive Activities—Oil and Gas	9014
940 Financial Services—Broker and Dealers	9015
942 Financial Services—Depository and Lending	9015
944 Financial Services—Insurance	9016
946 Financial Services—Investment Companies	9024
948 Financial Services—Mortgage Banking	9025
950 Financial Services—Title Plant	9028
952 Franchisors	9029
954 Health Care Entities	9039
958 Not-for-Profit Entities	9040
960 Plan Accounting—Defined Benefit Pension Plans	9050
962 Plan Accounting—Defined Contribution Pension Plans	9067
965 Plan Accounting—Health and Welfare Benefit Plans	9068
970 Real Estate—General	9069
972 Real Estate—Common Interest Realty Associations	9072
974 Real Estate—Real Estate Investment Trusts	9072
976 Real Estate—Retail Land	9072
978 Real Estate—Time-Sharing Activities	9079
980 Regulated Operations	9080
985 Software	9087
995 U.S. Steamship Entities	9105
Appendix A: Conceptual Framework	10,001
Appendix B: Accounting Standards Updates	11,001
Appendix C: Exposure Drafts	12,001
Appendix D: Cross-Referencing the Codification and Pre-Codification Standards	13,001
Appendix E: Present Value Factors	14,001
Index	15,001

CHAPTER 1
GENERAL PRINCIPLES

CONTENTS

The *General Principles* area of the FASB *Accounting Standards Codification®* contains one topic:

105 Generally Accepted Accounting Principles

Topic 105: Generally Accepted Accounting Principles

Topic 105, *Generally Accepted Accounting Principles,* contains one subtopic:

10 Overall

This Topic establishes the Financial Accounting Standards Board (FASB) *Accounting Standards Codification®* as the source of authoritative generally accepted accounting principles (GAAP) for nongovernmental entities in the United States of America.

CHAPTER 2
PRESENTATION

CONTENTS

The *Presentation* area of the FASB *Accounting Standards Codification* contains 15 topics:

205	Presentation of Financial Statements
210	Balance Sheet
215	Statement of Shareholder Equity
220	Comprehensive Income
225	Income Statement
230	Statement of Cash Flows
235	Notes to Financial Statements
250	Accounting Changes and Error Corrections
255	Changing Prices
260	Earnings per Share
270	Interim Reporting
272	Limited Liability Entities
274	Personal Financial Statements
275	Risks and Uncertainties
280	Segment Reporting

Topic 205: Presentation of Financial Statements

Topic 205, *Presentation of Financial Statements*, contains the following subtopics:

10 Overall

20 Discontinued Operations

905 Agriculture*

946 Financial Services—Investment Companies*

954 Health Care Entities*

958 Not-For-Profit Entities*

960 Plan Accounting—Defined Benefit Pension Plans*

962 Plan Accounting—Defined Contribution Pension Plans*

965 Plan Accounting—Health and Welfare Benefit Plans*

972 Real Estate—Common Interest Realty Associations*

* See the corresponding topic in Chapter 9 for coverage of this shared subtopic.

Discontinued Operations

ASC 205-20 provides guidance on the presentation and disclosure requirements for discontinued operations. Discontinued operations may include a component of an entity or a group of components or a business or nonprofit activity that has either been disposed of or is classified as held for sale. The component may be a reportable or operating segment, a reporting unit, a subsidiary, or an asset group, as defined in ASC 205-20-20. Disposal of a component or group of components is reported in discontinued operations when the disposal results from (1) a classification of a disposal as "held for sale" (ASC 205-20-45-1E), (2) a disposal through sale, or (3) a disposal by other than sale, such as by abandonment.

Strategic Shift

ASU 2014-08, *Presentation of Financial Statements (Topic 205) and Property, Plant, and Equipment (Topic 360): Reporting Discontinued Operations and Disclosures of Disposals of Components of an Entity*, revised the Accounting Standards Codification to define a "discontinued operation" as a "strategic shift" that has (or will have) a major effect on an entity's operations and financial results. Considerable judgment is required to determine whether a strategic shift has occurred or will occur as a result of the discontinued operations. One example of a strategic shift would be a consumer products manufacturer with five major product lines that decides to sell off one of its product lines. This would represent a strategic shift that is reported in discontinued operations. Another example would be a sports equipment manufacturer that traditionally has sold to both football and baseball markets but decides to dispose of 80% of the group of components that serves its baseball market. This would also be considered a strategic shift that is reported as a discontinued operation. On the other hand, one discontinued brand within one of many multi-brand product lines that are still continuing would not be considered a discontinued operation.

Classification as "Held for Sale"

Similar to other U.S. GAAP requirements, for a component or a group of components to be classified as "held for sale," the following criteria must be met (ASC 205-20-45-1E):

a. Management commits to a plan to sell
b. The entity to be sold is available for immediate sale in its present condition
c. An active program to locate a buyer or buyers has been initiated
d. The sale is probable and is expected to be a completed sale within one year in most cases
e. The sale price being marketed is reasonable in relation to its fair value
f. It is unlikely that there will be significant changes to the plan to sell or that the plan would be withdrawn

A business or nonprofit activity that, on acquisition, meets the above criteria to be classified as held for sale is a discontinued operation. If the one-year requirement in d., above, is met (except as permitted by paragraph 205-20-45-1G—events and circumstances beyond the entity's control), a business or nonprofit activity shall be classified as held for sale as a discontinued operation at the acquisition date if the other criteria above are probable of being met within a short period following the acquisition (usually within three months).

Accounting and Disclosure Requirements for Discontinued Operations

Once an enterprise has determined that a disposition or expected sale is classified as a discontinued operation, the appropriate accounting and disclosures must be made in the financial statements. In the accounting period that a disposition occurs or a sale is expected, the results of operations for the component and any gain or loss expected on the disposition must be included in a separate section of the income statement after income from continuing operations. The results of operations must be presented not only for the current year, but for all prior periods, presented with current year statements. The amount of any gain or loss expected on disposition included in the total results of operations must be separately disclosed either on the face of the statements or in related notes (ASC 205-20-45-3B). For an expected sale classified as discontinued operations, the results of operations are reported in the accounting period or periods that generated the results of operations. The loss, if any, reported as part of the gain or loss from discontinued operations is computed, when fair value is less than the carrying value, as the difference between the carrying value and fair value after reducing fair value for the cost to sell using the provisions of ASC 360-10-35-40. If fair value increases, a gain may be reported, but not in excess of the cumulative losses reported from prior write-downs. Any gains and losses from the disposal group should be used to adjust only long-lived assets and the long-lived assets should be reported in the balance sheet at the lower of carrying amount or fair value after reducing fair value by the cost to sell.

Assets and liabilities from discontinued operations for which the disposition has not occurred should not be offset, but should be reported separately as assets and liabilities on the balance sheet. In addition, major classes of assets and liabilities subject to disposition should be reported separately or disclosed in related notes.

In accounting periods subsequent to reporting discontinued operations, adjustments may be required for amounts previously reported. Such adjustments should be reported in discontinued operations in the accounting period that the adjustments occur. In addition, the enterprise should disclose the nature and amount of any adjustments. Examples of adjustments that may require subsequent reporting are resolution of contingencies that arose in connection with the disposition and contingencies that relate to the operation of the component before the disposition and settlement of employee benefits (ASC 205-20-45-5).

If an entity decides not to dispose of the component of an enterprise because circumstances have changed, the disposal group should be reclassified as held for use. The long-lived assets should be reclassified at the lower of the fair value on the date that the entity decides not to dispose of the component and the carrying amount of the disposal group prior to the time that the group was classified as held for sale adjusted for any depreciation expense that would have been taken if the group had never been reported as held-for-sale. Any adjustment from the reclassification is reported as a component of income from continuing operations. In addition, results of operations reported as discontinued operations should be reclassified in the income statement for accounting periods presented (ASC 360-10-45-7).

ASC 205-20-45, paragraphs 6 through 8, address the allocation of interest to discontinued operations. Interest shall be allocated to discontinued operations when it is for debt that is to be assumed by the buyer in a sale transaction or debt that is required to be repaid as a result of a disposal transaction. The reporting entity also has the option to allocate to discontinued operations other consolidated debt interest not directly related to other operations.

ASC 205-20-45-9 states that general corporate overhead shall not be allocated to discontinued operations.

Required disclosures vary depending on the nature of the discontinued operation, but for all types of discontinued operations the disclosures should include (a) a description of the facts, circumstances, timing and manner of disposal; (b) if not separately disclosed on the face of the income statement, the gain or loss on discontinuation; and (c) if applicable, the segment in which the discontinued operation is recorded. To illustrate the accounting requirements for a discontinued operation, one example will be used. Assumptions for Example 2-1 are as follows.

Example 2-1
Assumptions for Discontinued Operations

1. During 20X6 Johnson Enterprises, a highly diversified enterprise with a December 31 year-end, decided to dispose of Operating Segment A on February 1, 20X7.
2. This disposal of Operating Segment A represented a strategic shift in Johnson Enterprise's operations and financial results.
3. Results of operations for Operating Segment A for 20X6 and 20X5 are losses of $4,000,000 and $2,000,000, respectively. The carrying value of the assets of the operating segment is $10,000,000 and fair value less cost to sell of the assets of the operating segment is $9,000,000.
4. Johnson Enterprises reported income from continuing operations, after tax, of $25,000,000 for 20X6 and $20,000,000 for 20X5.
5. The tax rate applicable to Johnson Enterprises is 40% and the rate related to the disposal is also 40%.

Because the discontinued operations will not be completed until 20X7, the disposal group is reported as held for sale and the assets and liabilities of Operating Segment A must be reported separately in the asset and liability sections of the balance sheet. The assets of the operating segment must be reported at the lower of carrying value or fair value less cost to sell.

Because fair value less cost to sell of $9,000,000 is less than the carrying value of $10,000,000, the assets will be reported at $9,000,000 and a $1,000,000 loss on disposal will be reported as part of the results of operations from the discontinued operations. Therefore, results of operations for 20X6 for discontinued operations are $5,000,000 ($4,000,000 operations for 20X6 + $1,000,000 loss on disposal).

Because comparative statements for 20X5 are included with the 20X6 statements, results of operations for Operating Segment A for 20X5 of $2,000,000 must be reclassified as discontinued operations. Because Johnson Enterprises has a tax rate of 40%, the tax benefit for 20X6 is $2,000,000 ($5,000,000 × 40%) and the tax benefit for 20X5 is $800,000 ($2,000,000 × 40%). A partial income statement illustrating the discontinued operation reporting is presented below:

Johnson Enterprises
Partial Income Statement
For the Years Ended December 31, 20X5 and 20X6

		20X6		20X5
Income from continuing operations		$25,000,000		$20,000,000
Discontinued operations:				
Loss from operations of discontinued Component A (including loss on disposal of $1,000,000)	$(5,000,000)		$(2,000,000)	
Tax Benefit	2,000,000		800,000	
Loss on discontinued Operations		(3,000,000)		(1,200,000)
Net Income		$22,000,000		$18,800,000

In addition to the financial presentation shown above, Johnson Enterprises is required to provide certain information in the notes to the financial statements. ASC 205-20-50, paragraphs 1 through 3, specify the following disclosures:

- The facts and circumstances that led to the disposal or expected disposal and the expected manner and timing of the disposition.
- The loss or gain reported for the write down to fair value or recovery of losses computed using the provisions of ASC 360-10-35-40 and the location of the gain or loss on the income statement, if not separately reported on the face of the statement.
- The segment where the assets and liabilities are reported in accordance with ASC 280, if applicable.
- If an entity changes the plan to dispose of the discontinued operations or removes an asset from the disposal group, describe the circumstances and facts leading to the change in plans and disclose in the circumstances and facts leading to the change in plans and disclose in the same accounting period the impact of the change on operations for the current and prior periods presented.

Additionally, ASC 205-20-50-4 states that an entity must disclose the following information for each discontinued operation when there is continuing involvement with a discontinued operation:

1. Nature of the activities that give rise to continuing involvement.
2. The period of time during which the involvement is expected to be continued.
3. The amount of any cash flows related to the discontinued operations after the disposal transaction as well as any revenues or expenses in continuing operations that would have been eliminated in consolidation before the disposal transaction.
4. If the entity maintains an equity method interest in the disposal after the disposal (investee), information that enables the users of financial statements to compare the performance from period to period assuming the entity held the same equity method investment in all periods; these disclosures are to include the following:
   a. pretax income of the investee for each period for which the net income is presented after the period of the disposal
   b. ownership interest in the discontinued operation before the disposal
   c. ownership interest in the investee after the disposal
   d. the share of the income or loss of the investee in the period after the disposal and the line item that includes that income or loss

Also, ASC 205-20-50-5 states that an entity must disclose the following information if it is not presented in the financial statements:

1. Pretax profit or loss (or change in net assets for a not-for-profit entity) of the discontinued operation for the periods in which the results of operations of the discontinued operation are presented in the statement where net income is reported (or statement of activities for a not-for-profit entity).
2. The major classes of line items constituting the pretax profit or loss (or change in net assets for a not-for-profit entity) of the discontinued operation (for example, revenue, cost of sales, depreciation and amortization, and interest expense) for the periods in which the results of operations of the discontinued operation are presented in the statement where net income is reported (or statement of activities for a not-for-profit entity).
3. Either of the following:
   a. The total operating and investing cash flows of the discontinued operation for the periods in which the results of operations of the discontinued operation are presented in the statement where net income is reported (or statement of activities for a not-for-profit entity).
   b. The depreciation, amortization, capital expenditures, and significant operating and investing noncash items of the discontinued operation for the periods in which the results of operations of the discontinued operation are presented in the statement where net income is reported (or statement of activities for a not-for-profit entity).

4. If the discontinued operation includes a noncontrolling interest, the pretax profit or loss (or change in net assets for a not-for-profit entity) attributable to the parent for the periods in which the results of operations of the discontinued operation are presented in the statement where net income is reported (or statement of activities for a not-for-profit entity).
5. The carrying amount(s) of the major classes of assets and liabilities included as part of a discontinued operation classified as held for sale for the period in which the discontinued operation is classified as held for sale and all prior periods presented in the statement of financial position. Any loss recognized on the discontinued operation classified as held for sale in accordance with ASC paragraphs 205-20-45-3B through 45-3C are not to be allocated to the major classes of assets and liabilities of the discontinued operation.

Liquidation Basis of Accounting

ASU 2013-06, *Not-for-Profit Entities (Topic 958): Services Received from Personnel of an Affiliate*, which is effective for periods beginning after December 15, 2013, requires an entity to prepare its financial statements using the liquidation basis of accounting when liquidation is imminent. Liquidation is considered imminent when a remote likelihood exists that an entity can return from liquidation and either (1) the liquidation plan is approved by whomever has authority to make the plan effective and there is a remote likelihood that the execution of the plan will be blocked by others or (2) a liquidation plan is being imposed by others, such as in an involuntary bankruptcy. If a liquidation plan was specified in the entity's governing documents from inception (e.g., a limited-life entity), the liquidation basis of accounting should be applied only if the approved liquidation plan differs from the liquidation plan that was specified at the entity's inception.

Liquidation basis—assets. Liquidation basis of accounting financial statements should present relevant information about an entity's expected resources in liquidation by measuring and presenting assets at the amount of the expected cash proceeds from liquidation. This may require the entity to include items not previously recognized under U.S. GAAP that it expects to sell in liquidation, such as trademarks.

Liquidation basis—liabilities. An entity using liquidation basis accounting should recognize and measure its liabilities following U.S. GAAP and should not anticipate being legally released from being the primary obligor. The entity is required to accrue and present separately costs and income during the liquidation, including any costs associated with the sale of those assets and liabilities.

Financial statements for liquidation. An entity that applies the liquidation basis of accounting is to prepare (1) a statement of net assets in liquidation and (2) a statement of changes in net assets in liquidation.

Disclosures. As a minimum an entity in liquidation is required to disclose (1) that the statements are prepared using the liquidation basis of accounting, including the facts and circumstances surrounding this basis of accounting; (2) a description of the liquidation plan, including the manner of disposing of assets and settling liabilities and the expected date to complete the liquidation; (3)

methods and significant measurement assumptions for assets and liabilities; and (4) the type and amount of costs and income accrued in the statement of net assets in liquidation and the period over which the costs are expected to be paid or the income is to be earned.

Going Concern Disclosures

ASU 2014-15, *Presentation of Financial Statements—Going Concern (Subtopic 205-40): Disclosure of Uncertainties about an Entity's Ability to Continue as a Going Concern*, is the first time that the financial accounting standards have provided detailed guidance about management's responsibility to evaluate whether there is substantial doubt about an entity's ability to continue as a going concern and to provide the related note disclosures. Auditors have relied on guidance from Generally Accepted Auditing Standards for many years but since the fair presentation of financial reporting is the responsibility of management, this recent guidance should allow management to determine the impact of conditions or events that could raise substantial doubt about the entity's ability to continue as a going concern.

Conditions or events. The main provisions of ASU 2014-15 require management to base their evaluation of the entity's ability to continue as a going concern on conditions or events that are known, or at least reasonably knowable, at the date of the financial statements.

Probable. The term *probable* is used consistently throughout the ASU to be the standard by which management evaluates the conditions and events: is it *probable* that the entity will be unable to meet its obligations as they become due within one year after the balance sheet date?

Annual assessment. Because management must assess the identified conditions or events within one year of the balance sheet date, the assessment of the going concern is an annual exercise by management.

Mitigating effect. Once management has identified conditions or events that raise substantial doubt about the ability to continue as a going concern, management should consider whether its plans that are intended to alleviate those conditions or events would alleviate the substantial doubt. Management should determine whether its plans will be effectively implemented and would in fact mitigate the effect of the conditions or events.

Disclosures. If management concludes that its plans would mitigate the conditions or events, management should make disclosures of three things:

1. The conditions or events that raised the substantial doubt about an entity's ability to continue as a going concern before consideration of management's plans.
2. Management's evaluation of the significance of those conditions or events in relation to the entity's ability to meet its obligations.
3. Management's plans that alleviated the substantial doubt about an entity's ability to continue as a going concern.

On the other hand, if management concludes that its plans would not alleviate the substantial doubt about an entity's ability to continue as a going concern, the entity should include a statement in the notes to the financial statements indicating that there is *substantial doubt about the entity's ability to continue as a going concern*, as well as make disclosures similar to the three items above:

1. The conditions or events that raised the substantial doubt about an entity's ability to continue as a going concern;
2. Management's evaluation of the significance of those conditions or events in relation to the entity's ability to meet its obligations; and
3. Management's plans that are intended to mitigate the conditions or events that raise substantial doubt about an entity's ability to continue as a going concern.

Recent Changes

ASU 2013-07, *Presentation of Financial Statements (Topic 205): Liquidation Basis of Accounting*, is effective for entities that determine that liquidation is imminent during annual reporting periods beginning after December 15, 2013 and interim reporting periods therein.

ASU 2014-08, *Presentation of Financial Statements (Topic 205) and Property, Plant, and Equipment (Topic 360): Reporting Discontinued Operations and Disclosures of Disposals of Components of an Entity*, is effective prospectively to (1) disposals of components of an entity that occur within annual reporting periods beginning on or after December 15, 2014 and interim periods within those years and (2) all business or nonprofit activities that on acquisition are classified as held for sale that occur within annual periods beginning on or after December 15, 2014 and interim periods within those years. For most nonpublic business entities, the prospective application is delayed one year (until December 15, 2015) only for the interim reporting period requirements.

ASU 2014-15, *Presentation of Financial Statements—Going Concern (Subtopic 205-40): Disclosure of Uncertainties about an Entity's Ability to Continue as a Going Concern*, is effective for annual reporting periods ending after December 15, 2016, and for annual periods and interim periods thereafter. Early adoption of the standard is permitted.

Topic 210: Balance Sheet

Topic 210, *Balance Sheet*, contains the following subtopics:

10 Overall

20 Offsetting

912 Contractors—Federal Government*

942 Financial Services—Depository and Lending*

944 Financial Services—Insurance*

946 Financial Services—Investment Companies*

954 Health Care Entities*

958 Not-For-Profit Entities*

* See the corresponding topic in Chapter 9 for coverage of this shared subtopic.

Current Assets and Liabilities

Definition of a "Current Asset"

A current asset is cash or an asset that will be turned into cash or consumed within one year or the normal operating cycle, whichever is longer. The normal operating cycle is the period of time involved in turning cash into a product by buying or producing a product and then turning that product back into cash (the time period from cash to cash). For example, a retail firm would use cash to buy inventory, the inventory would be converted to accounts receivable, and accounts receivable would be converted to cash. Several of these cycles may be completed within one year and, in such cases, the longer time period of one year is used for classifying assets. However, in some industries, such as the tobacco industry, the aging process causes the operating cycle to exceed one year. In industries where the operating cycle exceeds one year, the longer operating cycle is used when classifying assets as current or long-term (ASC 210-10-45, paragraphs 1 through 4).

Examples of Current Assets and Their Bases of Reporting

Several assets are considered current assets according to the definition above. Examples include cash and cash equivalents, accounts receivable, short-term notes receivable, inventory, certain marketable securities, and prepaid expenses. The basis used for reporting current assets varies depending upon the type of current asset. For example, receivables are generally reported at net realizable amounts (i.e., the amount of the receivable less uncollectible amounts). Trading securities are reported at fair market value and short-term prepaid expenses, such as insurance expense, are reported at the unamortized cost basis. Inventory is reported in the current asset section of the balance sheet using the lower-of-cost-or-market rule and a cost flow method, such as last-in-first-out (LIFO) or first-in-first-out (FIFO).

Definition of a "Current Liability"

A current liability is defined as an obligation meeting the following requirements: the obligation is due within one year or one normal operating cycle, whichever is longer, and the obligation will be satisfied by something classified as current (either a current asset or the incurrence of another current liability). The normal operating cycle is the average period of time between the commitment of cash to acquire economic resources to be resold or used in production and the final realization of cash from the sale of products or services that are or are made from the acquired resources. For example, a retail firm would commit cash to buy inventory, the inventory would be converted to accounts receivable, and accounts receivable would be converted to cash. Several of these cycles may be completed within one year and, in such cases, the longer time period of one year is used for classifying liabilities. However, in some industries, such as the liquor industry, the aging process causes the operating cycle to exceed one year. In industries where the operating cycle exceeds one year, the longer operating cycle is used when classifying liabilities as current or long-term.

The second part of the definition, satisfaction of the obligation with something classified as current, requires additional discussion. The obligation due within one year or one normal operating cycle may be settled by paying cash or another current asset. However, the obligation also may be settled by incurring another current liability, such as a short-term note payable. If the obligation is due within one year and is to be paid by a long-term asset, long-term liability, or stockholders' equity item, the obligation generally is not classified as a current liability.

Examples of Current Liabilities

Several liabilities meet the preceding definition for classification as current liabilities. Examples include accounts payable, salaries payable, taxes payable, warranty liabilities, premium liabilities, short-term notes payable, current portions of long-term debt, and contingent liabilities. Some current liabilities are a result of normal operating activities, such as accounts payable and salaries payable. For some current liabilities, such as warranties and premiums, the recipients of the cash payment or services to be provided are unknown. Other liabilities, such as notes payable or current portions of long-term debt, may relate to financing issues, such as the acquisitions of long-term assets. In addition, there may be some uncertainty that an actual liability exists with some current liabilities, such as liabilities resulting from litigation, where the amount and whether there is an actual liability will be determined in future years.

Specific provisions of U.S. GAAP address certain aspects of accounting for current liabilities, including debt due on demand (ASC 470), short-term debt expected to be refinanced on a long-term basis (ASC 470), and contingent liabilities (ASC 450).

Offsetting

ASC 210-20 covers the concept of offsetting (or "netting") of assets and liabilities in the balance sheet, more commonly referred to as a right of setoff. It defines a right of setoff and addresses the issue of when an entity can use it. ASC 210-20 also specifies when certain receivables and payables from repurchase and reverse repurchase agreements can be offset. A right of setoff exists when the debtor has the legal right to release or eliminate an obligation owed to a counterparty by offsetting that obligation with an obligation owed to the debtor by the same counterparty.

Flowchart 2-1 identifies when an entity's assets and liabilities can be offset. The decision blocks in Flowchart 2-1 are numbered for easy reference and are referred to in the discussion. Assets and liabilities can be offset when the four conditions in Flowchart 2-1 are met:

1. Two entities to the transaction each owe the other amounts that can be determined (Block 1).
2. The entity has the intent to offset assets and liabilities (Block 2).
3. The entity preparing the financial statements has the right to offset receivables against payables (Block 3).
4. The right of offset legally can be enforced (Block 4).

If all of the preceding four conditions are met, the debtor can offset related assets and liabilities and report the net amount in the statement of financial position. However, if any one of the conditions is not met, the entity cannot offset assets and liabilities.

Flowchart 2-1

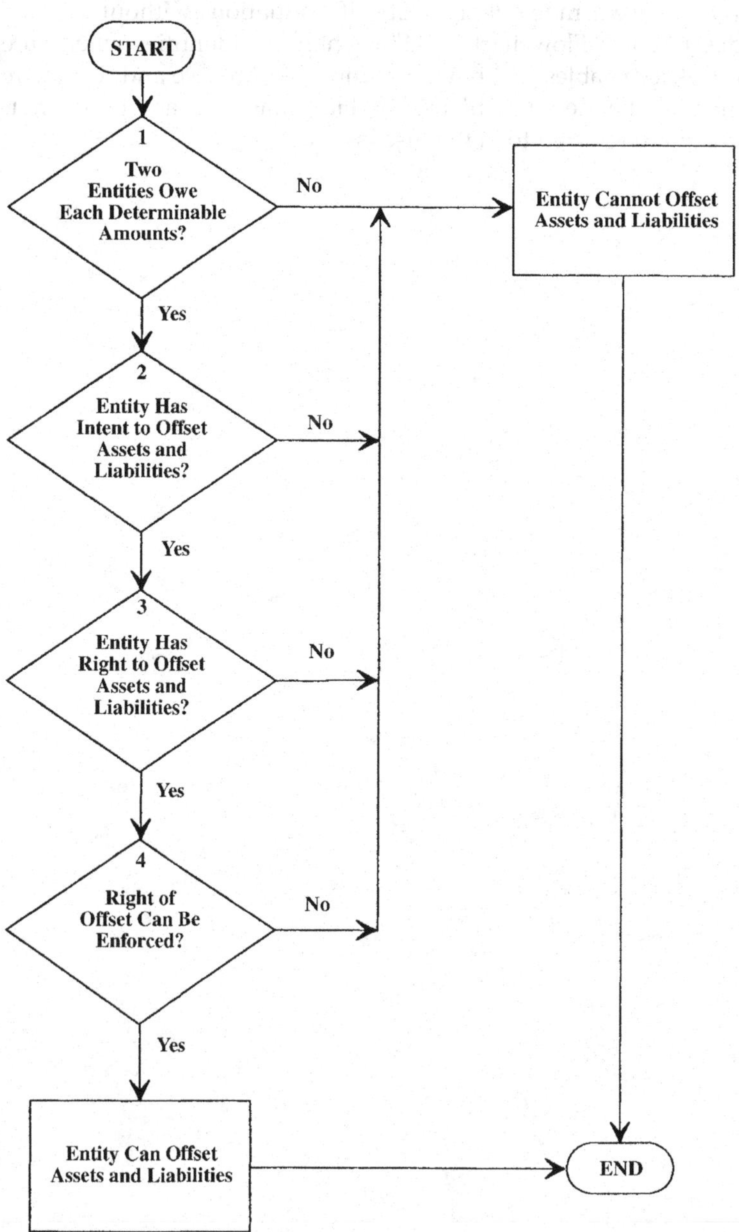

Generally, accrued receivables and accrued payables related to changes in market values of option, forward, swap, and similar type contracts are not offset unless there is a right of offset as illustrated above. However, an entity may offset changes in market values of such contracts when a master netting arrangement is involved with the same counterparties, even though the four conditions described above are not met.

ASC 210-20 allows offsetting of receivables and payables in repurchase and reverse repurchase arrangements in specific situations without meeting the conditions described in Flowchart 2-1. Flowchart 2-2 identifies when an entity can elect to offset receivables and payables under repurchase and reverse repurchase arrangements. The decision blocks in Flowchart 2-2 are numbered for easy reference and are referred to in the discussion.

Flowchart 2-2

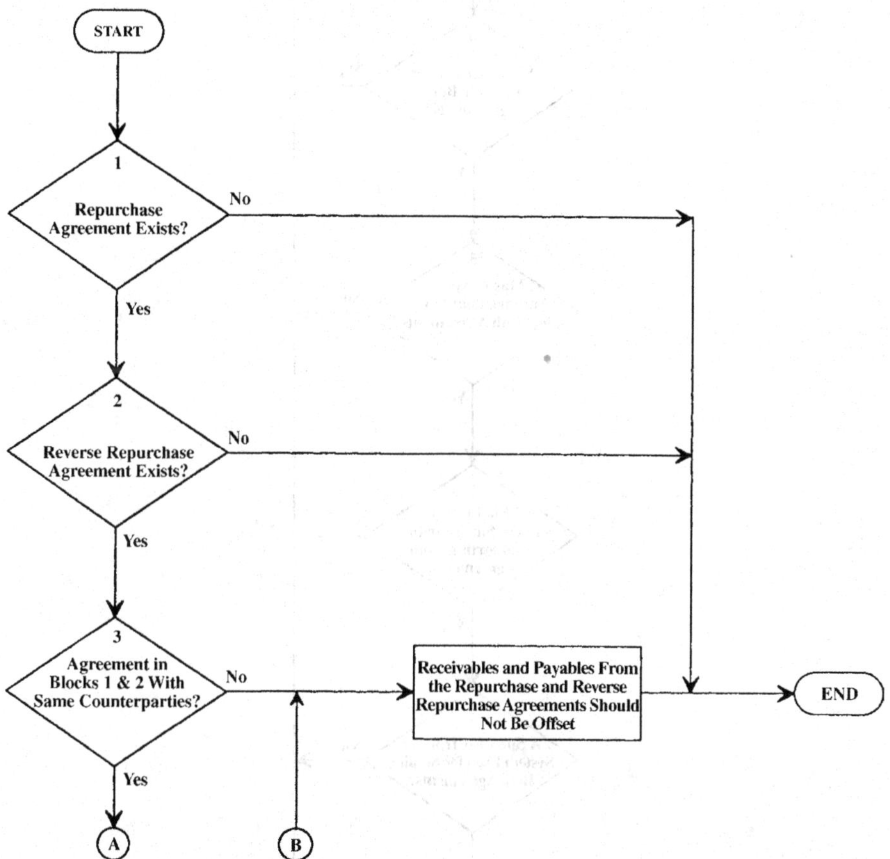

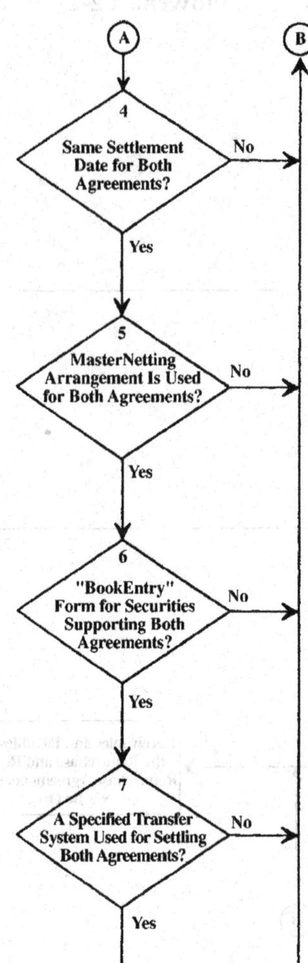
A
B
4
Same Settlement Date for Both Agreements?
No
Yes
5
MasterNetting Arrangement Is Used for Both Agreements?
No
Yes
6
"BookEntry" Form for Securities Supporting Both Agreements?
No
Yes
7
A Specified Transfer System Used for Settling Both Agreements?
No
Yes

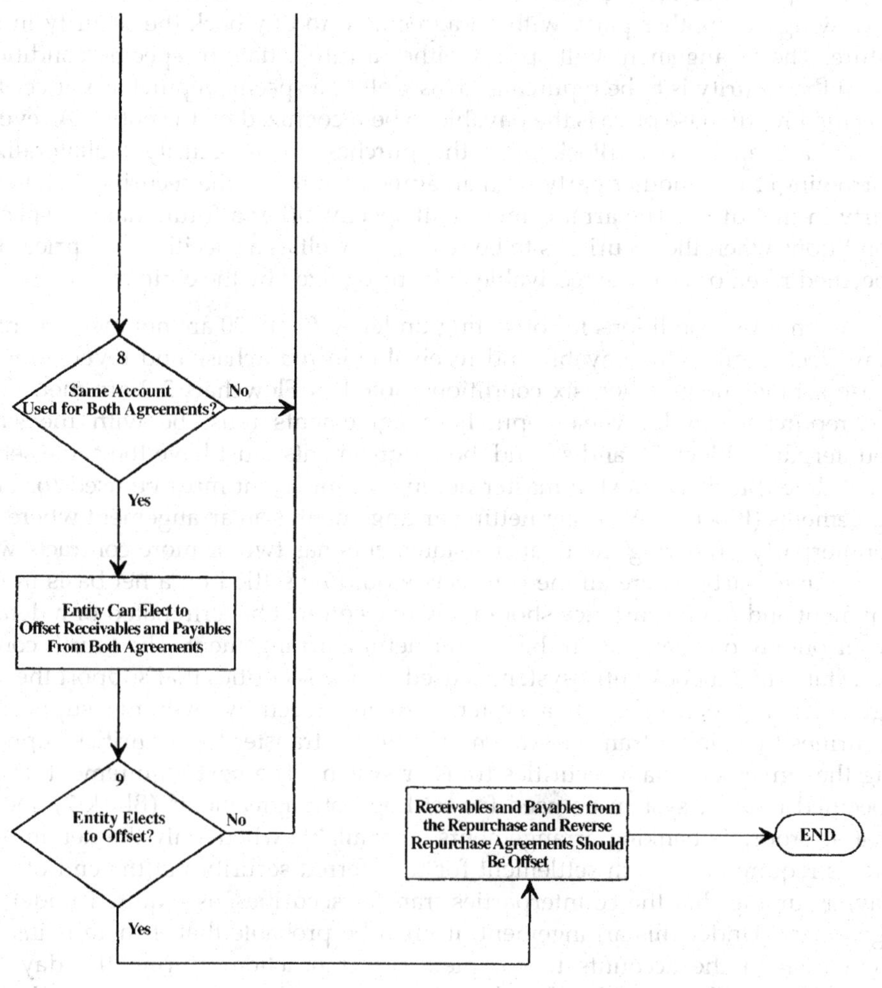
8
Same Account Used for Both Agreements?
No
Yes
Entity Can Elect to Offset Receivables and Payables From Both Agreements
9
Entity Elects to Offset?
No
Yes
Receivables and Payables from the Repurchase and Reverse Repurchase Agreements Should Be Offset
END

A repurchase arrangement (Block 1) is a sale of a security (collateralized borrowing) to another party with an agreement to buy back the security in the future. The arrangement will specify either a future date or specific conditions when the security is to be repurchased, as well as a specific repurchase price. The specified repurchase price is the payable to be recognized by the entity. A reverse repurchase agreement (Block 2) is the purchase of a security (collateralized borrowing) from another party with an agreement to sell the security back to the party in the future. The arrangement will specify either a future date or specific conditions when the security is to be resold, as well as a specific resell price. The specified resell price is the receivable to be recognized by the entity.

Even if the conditions for offsetting under ASC 210-20 are not met, an entity may elect to offset the payable and receivable in repurchase and reverse repurchase arrangements when six conditions noted in Flowchart 2-2 are met. First, the repurchase and reverse repurchase agreements must be with the same counterparty (Block 3), and second, both agreements must have the same settlement date (Block 4). Next, a master netting arrangement must be used for both agreements (Block 5). A master netting arrangement is an arrangement where the counterparty preparing the financial statements has two or more contracts with one counterparty where all the contracts would be settled on a net basis in one payment and in one currency should any one contract be terminated or a default occur on any one contract in the master netting arrangement. The fourth condition states that a book entry system is used for the securities that support the two agreements (Block 6). Such a system provides security over the supporting securities by using a transfer system operator to transfer the securities supporting the agreement via a securities transfer system. The next requirement, that a specified transfer system be used for settling both agreements (Block 7), means that appropriate banking arrangements be available where only the net amount due is required as a cash settlement for transferred securities at the end of each day, assuming that the counterparties transfer securities, as required under the agreement. Under this arrangement, it must be probable that if there is insufficient cash in the accounts to complete the transactions during the day, the transactions will be completed under the banking arrangement as long as there is sufficient cash in the accounts at the end of the day. This procedure is commonly referred to as daylight overdraft or some other form of intraday credit. The last requirement (Block 8) states that the same account will be used by the entity to pay cash under the repurchase agreement and to receive cash under the reverse repurchase agreement. If all six requirements are met, the entity may elect (Block 9), but is not required, to offset the payable under the repurchase agreement and the receivables under the reverse repurchase agreement. The method selected by the entity should be applied on a consistent basis.

Disclosure Requirements

Effective for annual reporting periods beginning on or after January 1, 2013, entities should provide disclosures required by the amendments of ASU 2011-11, *Balance Sheet (Topic 210): Disclosures about Offsetting Assets and Liabilities*, to enable the users of financial statements to evaluate the effects or potential effects of netting arrangements on its financial position for recognized assets and liabilities. These new disclosures are required for both financial instruments and derivatives that are either offset or subject to enforceable netting arrangements if not offset. ASU 2013-01, *Balance Sheet (Topic 210): Clarifying the Scope of Disclosures about Offsetting Assets and Liabilities*, clarified the original requirements to include (1) recognized derivative instruments accounted for in accordance with ASC 815, including bifurcated embedded derivatives and reverse repurchase agreements, and securities lending transactions that are offset in accordance with either ASC 210 or ASC 815; and (2) recognized derivative instruments accounted in accordance with ASC 815, including bifurcated embedded derivatives, repurchase agreements and reverse purchase agreements, and securities borrowing and securities lending transactions that are subject to an enforceable master netting arrangement or similar agreement irrespective of whether they are offset in accordance with either ASC 210 or ASC 815.

The following quantitative information is to be reported separately for assets and liabilities that are within the scope of the foregoing discussion:

a. The gross amount of those recognized assets and those recognized liabilities
b. The amounts offset in accordance with the guidance in ASC 210 or ASC 815 to determine the net amounts presented in the statement of financial position
c. The net amounts presented in the statement of financial position
d. The amounts subject to an enforceable master netting arrangement or similar agreement that is not otherwise included in b, above
    1. The amounts related recognized financial instruments and other derivative instruments that either:
        i. Management decided not to offset as an accounting policy election or
        ii. Do not meet the guidance in ASC 210 or ASC 815
    2. The amounts related to financing collateral (including cash collateral)
e. The net amount after deducting d from c.

All of this information must be presented in a tabular format, separately for assets and liabilities. See Example 2-2, below, for an example of the tabular disclosure of quantitative information for assets and liabilities.

Example 2-2
Offsetting Tabular Disclosures

Wolf Company has a derivative asset with a fair value of $2,000,000 and a derivative liability with a fair value of $1,600,000 with Counterparty X. Wolf has also received $200,000 of cash collateral from Counterparty X for a portion of the net derivative asset.

The instruments qualify for offsetting and Wolf elects to offset. Consequently, the balance sheet includes a net derivative asset of $200,000.

Wolf also entered a sale and repurchase agreement with Counterparty Y that is accounted for as a collateralized borrowing. Under this arrangement:

- The carrying value of investments in bonds (financial asset) held and used as collateral by Wolf is $1,380,000, and their fair value is $1,500,000.
- The carrying value of the collateralized borrowing (repo payable) is $1,400,000.
- Wolf also has a reverse sale and repurchase agreement with Counterparty Y, accounted for as a collateralized lending. The fair value of the related asset (bonds) received as collateral (not carried on the balance sheet) is $1,900,000, and the carrying value of the secured lending (reverse repo receivable) is $1,600,000.
- The transactions with Counterparty Y are not offset.

The resulting tabular disclosure for these two arrangements might be as follows:

Wolf Company: Offsetting of Financial Assets and Derivative Assets
As of December 31, 20X3

	(1)	(2)	(3) = (1) - (2)
DESCRIPTION:	**Gross Amounts of Recognized Assets**	**Gross Amounts Offset in the Statement of Financial Position**	**Net Amounts of Assets Presented in the Statement of Financial Position**
Derivatives	$2,000,000	$(1,800,000)	$ 200,000
Reverse repurchase, securities borrowing and similar arrangements	1,600,000	-0-	1,600,000
Other financial instruments	-0-	-0-	-0-
Total	$3,600,000	$(1,800,000)	$1,800,000

Wolf Company: Financial Assets, Derivative Assets, and Collateral Held by Counterparty
As of December 31, 20X3

	(3)	(4)		(5) = (3) - (4)
		Gross Amounts Not Offset in the Statement of Financial Position		
	Net Amounts of Assets Presented in the Statement of Financial Position	Financial Instruments	Cash Collateral Received	Net Amount
Counterparty X	$ 200,000	$-0-	$-0-	$200,000
Counterparty Y	1,600,000	(1,600,000)	-0-	-0-
Other				
Total	$1,800,000	$(1,600,000)	$-0-	$200,000

Wolf Company: Offsetting of Financial Liabilities and Derivative Liabilities
As of December 31, 20X3

	(1)	(2)	(3) = (1) - (2)
DESCRIPTION:	**Gross Amounts of Recognized Liabilities**	**Gross Amounts Offset in the Statement of Financial Position**	**Net Amounts of Liabilities Presented in the Statement of Financial Position**
Derivatives	$1,600,000	$(1,600,000)	$-0-
Repurchase, securities lending and similar arrangements	1,400,000	-0-	1,400,000
Other financial instruments	-0-	-0-	-0-
Total	$3,000,000	$(1,600,000)	$1,400,000

Wolf Company: Financial Liabilities, Derivative Liabilities, and Collateral Pledged by Counterparty
As of December 31, 20X3

	(3)	(4)		(5) = (3) - (4)
		Gross Amounts Not Offset in the Statement of Financial Position		
	Net Amounts of Liabilities Presented in the Statement of Financial Position	Financial Instruments	Cash Collateral Pledged	Net Amount
Counterparty X	$-0-	$-0-	$-0-	$-0-
Counterparty Y	1,400,000	(1,400,000)	-0-	-0-

	(3)	(4)		(5) = (3) - (4)
		Gross Amounts Not Offset in the Statement of Financial Position		
	Net Amounts of Liabilities Presented in the Statement of Financial Position	Financial Instruments	Cash Collateral Pledged	Net Amount
Other				
Total	$1,400,000	$(1,400,000)	$-0-	$-0-

Several other accounting standards allow an offsetting presentation in the financial statements similar to the requirements of ASC 210-20. Examples of standards that allow a form of offsetting are ASC 840, related to leveraged leases; ASC 944, related to reinsurance; ASC 715, related to pension asset and liabilities; and ASC 740 on reporting of net tax assets and liabilities.

Comparative Information

When a set of basic financial statements is presented in an annual report, it is desirable that one or more prior years set of basic statements be presented with the current year statements for comparison purposes. In addition, if prior year statements are included in the current year annual report, related prior year notes or explanations should also be included if they are significant.

Topic 215: Statement of Shareholder Equity

Topic 215, *Statement of Shareholder Equity*, contains the following subtopic:

10 Overall

This ASC topic contains no detailed content. It merely directs the reader to ASC 505 for further information.

Topic 220: Comprehensive Income

Topic 220, *Comprehensive Income*, contains one subtopic:

10 Overall

Recent Changes

ASU 2013-02, *Comprehensive Income (Topic 220): Reporting of Amounts Reclassified out of Accumulated Other Comprehensive Income*, is effective prospectively for reporting periods beginning after December 15, 2012. For nonpublic entities, amendments are prospectively effective for reporting periods beginning after December 15, 2013.

Introduction

In general, ASC 220-10 requires an entity issuing a full set of financial statements to prepare an income statement using a comprehensive income approach. Comprehensive income is the increase or decrease in equity of an entity for an accounting period from all sources other than from owners (FASB Statement of Financial Accounting Concepts (SFAC) No. 6, paragraph 70). Examples of changes in equity other than from owners include items such as change in retained earnings from net income or net loss, change in other equity from unrealized holding gains and losses from debt and equity investments, prior period adjustments, and other paid-in-capital adjustments. All of the preceding examples represent elements of comprehensive income as defined by SFAC No. 6; however, not all such items are included in a comprehensive income statement using the provisions of ASC 220-10. Under ASC 220-10, a comprehensive income statement will include net income or loss and selected other elements of comprehensive income, such as those defined in ASC 220-10-55-2. Other elements of comprehensive income are gains and losses from events or transactions that previously have been reported as a component of stockholders' equity because specific accounting principles require such reporting.

ASC 220-10 is applicable to every entity that presents a full set of basic financial statements when the entity has elements of other comprehensive income. ASC 220-10 does not have to be applied by not-for profit entities and entities with no other comprehensive income.

ASC 220-10 (as amended by ASU 2011-05, *Comprehensive Income (Topic 220): Presentation of Comprehensive Income*) requires entities within its scope to present the total of comprehensive income, the components of net income, and the components of other comprehensive income either in a single çontinuous statement of comprehensive income or in two separate but consecutive statements. In both choices, an entity is required to present each component of net income along with total net income, each component of other comprehensive income along with a total for other comprehensive income, and a total amount for comprehensive income. In a single continuous statement, the entity is required to present the components of net income and total net income, the components of other comprehensive income, and a total for other comprehensive income, along with the total of comprehensive income in that statement. In the two-statement approach, an entity is required to present components of net income and total net income in the statement of net income. The statement of other comprehensive income should immediately follow the statement of net income and include the components of other comprehensive income and a total for other comprehensive income, along with a total for comprehensive income. Regardless of whether an entity chooses to present comprehensive income in a single continuous statement or in two separate but consecutive statements, the entity is required to present on the face of the financial statements reclassification adjustments for items that are reclassified from other comprehensive income to net income in the statement(s) where the components of net income and the components of other comprehensive income are presented. However, ASC 220-10 does not address the issues of when and how to measure or recognize comprehensive income.

When consolidated financial statements are presented where the subsidiary or subsidiaries are not wholly owned (a noncontrolling interest), in addition to presenting consolidated comprehensive income on the face of the statements the amount of comprehensive income assigned to the parent and the amount assigned to the noncontrolling interest must also be disclosed.

General Discussion

As noted above, comprehensive income consists of both net income and other comprehensive income. Other comprehensive income includes all gains and losses, revenues, and expenses excluded by accounting principles from net income and designated as comprehensive income by ASC 220-10. Elements of other comprehensive income may change with changes in U.S. generally accepted accounting principles (U.S. GAAP). However, based on current U.S. GAAP, the following items are examples of other comprehensive income included in a comprehensive income statement (ASC 220-10-45-10A):

a. Foreign currency translation adjustments (see paragraph 830-30-45-12)
b. Gains and losses on foreign currency transactions that are designated as, and are effective as, economic hedges of a net investment in a foreign entity, commencing as of the designation date (see paragraph 830-20-35-3(a))
c. Gains and losses on intra-entity foreign currency transactions that are of a long-term-investment nature (that is, settlement is not planned or anticipated in the foreseeable future), when the entities to the transaction are consolidated, combined, or accounted for by the equity method in the reporting entity's financial statements (see paragraph 830-20-35-3(b))
d. Gains and losses (effective portion) on derivative instruments that are designated as, and qualify as, cash flow hedges (see paragraph 815-20-35-1(c))
e. Unrealized holding gains and losses on available-for-sale debt securities (see paragraph 320-10-45-1)
f. Unrealized holding gains and losses that result from a debt security being transferred into the available-for-sale category from the held-to-maturity category (see paragraph 320-10-35-10(c))
g. Amounts recognized in other comprehensive income for debt securities classified as available-for-sale and held-to-maturity related to an other-than-temporary impairment recognized in accordance with Section 320-10-35 if a portion of the impairment was not recognized in earnings
h. Subsequent decreases (if not an other-than-temporary impairment) or increases in the fair value of available-for-sale debt securities previously written down as impaired (see paragraph 320-10-35-18)
i. Gains or losses associated with pension or other postretirement benefits (that are not recognized immediately as a component of net periodic benefit cost) (see paragraph 715-20-50-1(j))
j. Prior service costs or credits associated with pension or other postretirement benefits (see paragraph 715-20-50-1(j))

k. Transition assets or obligations associated with pension or other postretirement benefits (that are not recognized immediately as a component of net periodic benefit cost) (see paragraph 715-20-50-1(j))

l. Changes in fair value attributable to instrument-specific credit risk of liabilities for which the fair value option is elected (see paragraph 825-10-45-5)

Revenues and expenses that comprise net income are reported and displayed in the comprehensive income statement. In addition, net income must be reported as a separate amount in the comprehensive income statement.

Other comprehensive income should be reported or classified in the comprehensive income statement using the nature of the comprehensive income element. For example, an entity might have two or more subdivisions or categories of other comprehensive income as follows: items related to foreign currency, and items related to unrealized gains and losses from equity and debt securities (ASC 220-10-55-2). Items of other comprehensive income may be reported in the statement using a gross (before tax) or a net-of-tax (after tax) basis. If a gross method is used, a single total for tax expense or tax benefit related to the total other comprehensive income items should be reported on the face of the statement. If the tax expense or tax benefit for each element of comprehensive income is not reported on the face of the statement, such information must be reported in the notes to the financial statements (ASC 220-10-45, paragraphs 11 and 12). In some cases, gains and losses reported as part of comprehensive income may be realized and reported as part of net income during a current accounting period. When this situation occurs, the amount reported in the income statement, referred to as reclassification adjustments, must be removed from other comprehensive income. For example, assume an enterprise has available-for-sale securities and an unrealized loss has been reported as part of other comprehensive income. Further assume that in the current accounting period, the company sells part or all of the securities. The gain or loss from the sale is realized and is reported as a component of net income. The amount reported as a component of net income is used as the reclassification adjustment to adjust the related element in comprehensive income. Reclassification adjustments are required in these other comprehensive income elements: when unrealized gains and losses on debt and equity securities are reported as part of net income, when gains and losses from foreign currency translation are realized upon liquidation of part or all of the investment in the foreign enterprise, and when gains and losses related to foreign currency or futures transactions are reported as a component of net income (ASC 220-10-45, paragraphs 15 through 17).

ASC 220 does not require a specific format in the preparation of a comprehensive income statement; however, the general format should be a one- or two-statement approach. If one statement is used, net income, other comprehensive income, and comprehensive income are reported in the same statement. If a two-statement format is used, net income is reported in one statement and other comprehensive income, beginning with net income from the first statement and ending with comprehensive income, is reported in the second statement. The FASB suggests but does not require that net income be reported first, followed by other comprehensive income. Both net income and other comprehensive income elements should be displayed with equal prominence in the statements. In addition, the FASB does not require that terms such as "other comprehensive income," "comprehensive income," etc. be used. Other terms that appropriately describe the income elements may be used (ASC 220-10-45, paragraphs 8 and 9).

A reconciliation of the beginning and ending carrying amounts of equity divided between amounts assigned to the parent and amounts assigned to any noncontrolling interest in less than wholly owned subsidiaries is required. This reconciliation includes each component of other comprehensive income.

When an entity prepares interim financial statements, a total for comprehensive income must be reported in summary statements prepared and distributed to shareholders (ASC 220-10-45-18).

Retained earnings in the balance sheet are increased/decreased for the amount of net income/net loss reported in the comprehensive income statement. However, a separate stockholders' equity account, such as unrealized other comprehensive income (commonly referred to as "accumulated other comprehensive income"), is increased/decreased for the total of the other comprehensive income reported in the comprehensive income statement. The unrealized other comprehensive income account would usually be reported after retained earnings in the balance sheet. The total of the unrealized other comprehensive income account reported in stockholders' equity must be subdivided into components equivalent to the components reported in the comprehensive income statement, such as items related to foreign currency and items related to unrealized gains and losses from equity and debt securities. This required disclosure may be made on the face of the balance sheet, in a statement reporting changes in stockholders' equity or in related notes to the financial statements (ASC 220-10-45-14).

Reclassifications

In some cases, gains and losses reported as part of comprehensive income may be realized and reported as part of net income during a current accounting period. When this situation occurs, the amount reported in the income statement, referred to as reclassification adjustments, must be removed from other comprehensive income. For example, assume an enterprise has available-for-sale securities and an unrealized loss has been reported as part of other comprehensive income. Further assume that in the current accounting period, the company sells part or all of the securities. The gain or loss from the sale is realized and is reported as a component of net income. The amount reported as a component of net income is used as the reclassification adjustment to adjust the related element in comprehensive income.

Reclassification adjustments are required in these other comprehensive income elements: when unrealized gains and losses on debt and equity securities are reported as part of net income, when gains and losses from foreign currency translation are realized upon liquidation of part or all of the investment in the foreign enterprise, and when gains and losses related to foreign currency or futures transactions are reported as a component of net income (ASC 220-10-45, paragraphs 15 through 17, as amended).

An entity is to separately provide information about the effects of significant amounts reclassified out of each component of accumulated other comprehensive income if those amounts are all required under other ASC Topics to be reclassified to net income in their entirety in the same reporting period either (1) on the face of the statement where net income is presented or (2) as a separate disclosure in the notes to the financial statements. If an entity chooses 1, the entity is to present parenthetically the effect of significant reclassification amounts, including the aggregate tax effect, on the respective line item of net income by component of other comprehensive income. If an entity chooses 2, it is to present the significant amounts by each component of accumulated other comprehensive income and provide a subtotal of each component of comprehensive income. Both before-tax and net-of-tax presentations are permitted. See Example 2-3, below, for an example of the disclosure in the notes to the financial statements.

Example 2-3

Entity XYZ
Notes to the Financial Statements
Changes in Accumulated Other Comprehensive Income by Component[1]
For the period ended December 31, 20XX

	Gains and Losses on Cash Flow Hedges	Unrealized Gains and Losses on Available-for-Sale Securities	Total
Beginning balance	(10,000)	16,000	6,000
Other comprehensive income before reclassifications	14,000	16,000	30,000
Amounts reclassified from accumulated other comprehensive income	(4,500)	(6,000)	(10,500)
Net current-period other comprehensive income	9,500	10,000	19,500
Ending balance	(500)	26,000	25,500

[1] All amounts are net of tax. Amounts in parentheses indicate debits.

Technical Considerations

Three examples will be used to illustrate the accounting and reporting requirements for comprehensive income. Assumptions for Example 2-4 are as follows.

Example 2-4
Assumptions for Comprehensive Income

1. Emerson Inc. (Emerson), a December 31 year-end company, prepared the following basic income statement for 20X6.

Sales		$10,000,000
Cost of sales		6,000,000
Gross profit		$4,000,000
Operating expenses		(1,000,000)
Other income and expenses		100,000
Income from continuing operations before tax		$3,100,000
Income tax expense		930,000
Income from continuing operations		$2,170,000
Discontinued operations:		
Loss from operations of discontinued Company XYZ (including loss on disposal of $2,000,000)	$(1,000,000)	
Income tax benefit	300,000	
Loss on discontinued operations		(700,000)
Net Income		$1,470,000

2. In addition to the income statement items in Assumption 1, above, Emerson had these other comprehensive income elements for 20X6:

Gains from foreign currency translation	$1,500,000
Loss from hedge of net investment in a foreign entity	(200,000)
Gain from intercompany foreign currency transaction of a long-term investment nature	400,000
Gain from change in market value of futures contract	250,000
Unrealized holding loss from available-for-sale securities	(400,000)
Unrealized holding gain—transfer to available-for-sale securities from held-to-maturity securities	500,000
Unrealized holding loss from decrease in fair value of available-for-sale securities written down for impairment	(150,000)
Total other comprehensive income elements before taxes	$1,900,000

3. Emerson has a 30% tax rate for 20X6.
4. There were no reclassification adjustments for other comprehensive income elements for 20X6.
5. There were no beginning balances in unrealized other comprehensive income at the beginning of 20X6.

Using the information from Example 2-4, a statement of income and comprehensive income with all required disclosures is presented for Emerson for 20X6. Preparation of the statement is illustrated below using a single statement format with a net-of-tax approach for presentation of the other comprehensive income elements. The tax impact of each element of other comprehensive income is reported on the face of the statement. Revenues and expenses that constitute traditional net income of $3,570,000 are presented first in the statement followed by other comprehensive income of $1,330,000 after tax. Other comprehensive income is divided into two subgroups or categories based on the nature of the income elements. Using both net income and other comprehensive income, comprehensive income for Emerson for 20X6 is $4,900,000.

Because Emerson has no reclassification adjustments and a net-of-tax approach is used for each element of other comprehensive income with the tax impact of each item presented on the face of the statement, the only other disclosure required by Emerson is an analysis of the changes in unrealized other comprehensive income reported in the balance sheet. Table 2-1 shows this required disclosure. The elements are analyzed using the same three categories as presented in the income statement. Because there were no beginning balances (Assumption 5), the ending balance of $1,330,000 in the unrealized other comprehensive income is equal to the amount of other comprehensive income after tax as reported in the comprehensive income statement. The $1,330,000 other comprehensive income increases unrealized other comprehensive income reported in the balance sheet after retained earnings.

Emerson Inc.
Statement of Income and Comprehensive Income For the Year Ended December 31, 20X6

Sales		$10,000,000
Cost of sales		6,000,000
Gross profit		$4,000,000
Operating expenses		(1,000,000)
Other income and expenses		100,000
Income from continuing operations before tax		$3,100,000
Income tax expense		930,000
Income from continuing operations		$2,170,000
Discontinued operations:		
Loss from operations of discontinued Company XYZ (including loss on disposal of $2,000,000)	$(1,000,000)	
Income tax benefit	300,000	
Loss on discontinued operations		(700,000)
Net Income		$1,470,000
Other Comprehensive Income:		
Gains and losses related to foreign currency:		
Gains from foreign currency translation, less tax of $450,000	$1,050,000	
Loss from hedge of net investment in a foreign entity, less tax benefit of $60,000	(140,000)	
Gain from intercompany foreign currency transaction of a long-term investment nature, less tax of $120,000	280,000	
Gain from change in market value of futures contract, less tax of $75,000	175,000	
Gains and losses related to debt and equity securities:		
Unrealized holding loss from available-for-sale securities, less tax benefit of $120,000	(280,000)	

Unrealized holding gain—transfer to available-for-sale securities from held-to-maturity securities, less tax of $150,000	350,000	
Unrealized holding loss from decrease in fair value of available-for-sale securities written down for impairment, less tax benefit of $45,000	(105,000)	
Other comprehensive income		1,330,000
Comprehensive Income		$2,800,000

Table 2-1 Changes in Unrealized Other Comprehensive Income[1]

	Foreign Currency Items[2]	Unrealized Gains/ (Losses) on Securities[3]	Unrealized Other Comprehensive Income[4]
Beginning 20X6 Balance	$0	$0	$0
Change in Current Period	1,365,000	(35,000)	1,330,000
Ending 20X6 Balance	$1,365,000	$(35,000)	$1,330,000

[1] Information for preparation of this required disclosure taken from Assumption 5 and the 20X6 comprehensive income statement.
[2] $1,050,000 + $(140,000) + $280,000 + $175,000 = $1,365,000.
[3] $(280,000) + $350,000 + $(105,000) = (35,000).
[4] $1,190,000 + $175,000 + (35,000) = $1,330,000.

Emerson could elect to present the other comprehensive income items on a gross basis instead of using a net-of-tax approach. The comprehensive income statement, below, illustrates the gross method. Elements for net income are presented the same as in the previous statement. The change in presentation of other comprehensive income does not change the presentation of net income. The other comprehensive net income items are presented using the same three categories as in the prior statement, but gross amounts are used instead of net-of-tax amounts. A single tax expense of $570,000 ($1,900,000 × 30% tax rate) is presented on the face of the statement similar to tax expense on income from continuing operations for net income.

Because Emerson has elected the gross method of presentation of other comprehensive income, the tax impact of each element of other comprehensive income must be disclosed in the notes to the financial statements. Table 2-2 shows the required disclosure. In addition, when using the gross method, Emerson also would need to disclose the changes in the unrealized other comprehensive income as presented in Table 2-1.

Emerson Inc.
Statement of Income and Comprehensive Income
For the Year Ended December 31, 20X6

Sales	$10,000,000
Cost of sales	6,000,000
Gross profit	$4,000,000

Operating expenses		(1,000,000)
Other income and expenses		100,000
Income from continuing operations before tax		$3,100,000
Income tax expense		930,000
Income from continuing operations		$2,170,000
Discontinued operations:		
Loss from operations of discontinued Company XYZ (including loss on disposal of $2,000,000)	$(1,000,000)	
Income tax benefit	300,000	
Loss on discontinued operations		(700,000)
Net Income		$1,470,000
Other Comprehensive Income:		
Gains and losses related to foreign currency:		
Gains from foreign currency translation	$1,500,000	
Loss from hedge of net investment in a foreign entity	(200,000)	
Gain from intercompany foreign currency transaction of a long-term investment nature	400,000	
Gain from change in market value of futures contract	250,000	
Gains and losses related to debt and equity securities:		
Unrealized holding loss from available-for-sale securities	(400,000)	
Unrealized holding gain—transfer to available-for-sale securities from held-to-maturity securities	500,000	
Unrealized holding loss from decrease in fair value of available-for-sale securities written down for impairment	(150,000)	
Other comprehensive income	1,900,000	
Tax expense for other comprehensive income	(570,000)	
Other comprehensive income after tax		1,330,000
Comprehensive Income		$2,800,000

Table 2-2 Tax Impact of Each Element of Other Comprehensive Income[1]

	Other Comprehensive Income Before Tax	Tax (Expense) Benefit	Other Comprehensive Income After Tax
Other Comprehensive Income:			
Gains and losses related to foreign currency:			
Gains from foreign currency translation	$1,500,000	$(450,000)	$1,050,000
Loss from hedge of net investment in a foreign entity	(200,000)	60,000	(140,000)
Gain from intercompany foreign currency transaction of a long-term investment nature	400,000	(120,000)	280,000

Gain from change in market value of futures contract	250,000	(75,000)	175,000
Gains and losses related to debt and equity securities:			
Unrealized holding loss from available-for-sale securities	(400,000)	120,000	(280,000)
Unrealized holding gain—transfer to available-for-sale securities from held-to-maturity securities	500,000	(150,000)	350,000
Unrealized holding loss from decrease in fair value of available-for-sale securities written down for impairment	(150,000)	45,000	(105,000)
Other comprehensive income	$1,900,000	$(570,000)	$1,330,000

[1] Information taken from Assumptions 2 and 3.

Emerson has the option of using a two-statement approach instead of using one statement as presented above. To illustrate the two-statement approach, a statement of income and a statement of other comprehensive income are presented below. The statement of other comprehensive income must start with net income reported in the statement of income. Emerson elects the net-of-tax approach for presentation of other comprehensive income. Because a net-of-tax approach is used with tax amounts reported on the face of the statement, the only other disclosure required with the two-statement approach is an analysis of the accumulated other comprehensive income. This analysis is the same as presented in Table 2-1 and is not repeated here.

Emerson Inc.
Statement of Income For the Year Ended December 31, 20X6

Sales		$10,000,000
Cost of sales		6,000,000
Gross profit		$4,000,000
Operating expenses		(1,000,000)
Other income and expenses		100,000
Income from continuing operations before tax		$3,100,000
Income tax expense		930,000
Income from continuing operations		$2,170,000
Discontinued operations:		
Loss from operations of discontinued Company XYZ (including loss on disposal of $2,000,000)	$(1,000,000)	
Income tax benefit	300,000	
Loss on discontinued operations		(700,000)
Net Income		$1,470,000

Emerson Inc.
Statement of Comprehensive Income For the Year Ended December 31, 20X6

Net Income		$1,470,000
Other Comprehensive Income:		
Gains and losses related to foreign currency:		
Gains from foreign currency translation, less tax of $450,000	$1,050,000	
Loss from hedge of net investment in a foreign entity, less tax benefit of $60,000	(140,000)	
Gain from intercompany foreign currency transaction of a long-term investment nature, less tax of $120,000	280,000	
Gain from change in market value of futures contract, less tax of $75,000	175,000	
Gains and losses related to debt and equity securities:		
Unrealized holding loss from available-for-sale securities, less tax benefit of $120,000	(280,000)	
Unrealized holding gain—transfer to available-for-sale securities from held-to-maturity securities, less tax of $150,000	350,000	
Unrealized holding loss from decrease in fair value of available-for-sale securities written down for impairment, less tax benefit of $45,000	(105,000)	
Other comprehensive income		1,330,000
Comprehensive Income		$2,800,000

The second example illustrates computations for reclassification adjustments for other comprehensive income. Assumptions for Example 2-5 are as follows.

Example 2-5

Assumptions for Reclassification Adjustments

1. Farmer Enterprises (Farmer), a December 31 year-end company, is preparing reclassification adjustments for the 20X6 comprehensive income statement related to available-for-sale debt and equity securities sold during 20X6.

2. Farmer purchased 10,000 shares of Nelson Enterprise (Nelson) common stock on September 1, 20X4, and sold 6,000 shares on July 1, 20X6. The cost of the stock was $5 per share and the market price of the stock was as follows: December 31, 20X4—$8; December 31, 20X5—$6; July 1, 20X6—$10; December 31, 20X6—$12. The stock was classified as available-for-sale securities. No dividends were paid on the equity investment.

3. Farmer purchased a $3,000,000, 6%, five-year debt security of Johnson Enterprises on January 1, 20X5. The debt security pays interest annually on December 31. The debt was purchased at a price of $2,760,438, which is an effective yield of 8%. At December 31, 20X5, the fair value of the debt is 96.6% of par value, or $2,898,000, and on December 31, 20X6 the fair value of the debt is 102.7% of par value, or

$3,081,000. Farmer sold the $3,000,000 debt investment on December 31, 20X6 at 102.7. The debt investment was classified as available-for-sale securities.

4. Farmer has a 30% tax rate for 20X4–20X6.

Example 2-5 illustrates the accumulation of information, including reclassification adjustments for debt and equity securities, that is reported in a comprehensive income statement. This process involves computation of holding gains and losses and related tax impacts on equity securities for the years 20X4–20X6, and the computation of holding gains and losses for debt securities and related tax impact for 20X5 and 20X6, calculation of gain or losses and related tax impact on the sale of both debt and equity securities in 20X6, reclassification adjustments for both debt and equity securities from the sale of the securities, and interest income from the debt investment. In addition, journal entries are prepared to illustrate the proper accounting for each event.

The following two journal entries are required to record purchase of the $50,000 (10,000 shares × $5 cost) equity investment on September 1, 20X4 and the debt investment on January 1, 20X5.

Investment in Nelson Enterprise Common Stock	50,000	
Cash		50,000
To record $50,000 equity investment.		
Investment in Johnson Enterprise debt	2,760,438	
Cash		2,760,438
To record investment in debt securities.		

Table 2-3 illustrates computation of holding gains and losses for equity securities for 20X4–20X6. Holding gains are reported in each year, except for 20X5, which has a holding loss of $20,000. Because 6,000 shares were sold on July 1, the holding gain for 20X6 is computed in two parts. The holding gain of $40,000 was computed for all 10,000 shares through July 1, and an $8,000 holding gain is computed for the remaining 4,000 shares from July 1 through December 31, the balance sheet date. The net holding gain for the entire three-year period is $58,000.

Table 2-3 Computation of Holding Gains/(Losses) on Equity Investment

(a) Time Period	(b) Beginning Fair Value	(c) Ending Fair Value	(d) = (c)–(b) Holding Gain/(Loss)
9/1/X4 – 12/31/X4	10,000 shares × $5 = $50,000	10,000 shares × $8 = $ 80,000	$30,000
1/1/X5 – 12/31/X5	10,000 shares × $8 = $80,000	10,000 shares × $6 = $ 60,000	(20,000)
1/1/X6 – 7/1/X6	10,000 shares × $6 = $60,000	10,000 shares × $10 = $100,000	40,000
7/1/X6 – 12/31/X6	4,000 shares × $10 = $40,000	4,000 shares × $12 = $ 48,000	8,000
12/31/X6 Balance			$58,000

Journal entries for 20X4–20X6 to record the holding gains and losses are as follows:

20X4 Holding Gain Journal Entry:

Investment in Nelson Enterprise Common Stock	30,000	
Unrealized Holding Gain on Equity Securities		30,000

20X5 Holding Loss Journal Entry:

Unrealized Holding Loss on Equity Securities	20,000	
Investment in Nelson Enterprise Common Stock		20,000

20X6 Holding Gain Journal Entry:

Investment in Nelson Enterprise Common Stock	48,000	
Unrealized Holding Gain on Equity Securities		48,000

The $40,000 holding gain from January 1 to July 1 is combined with the $8,000 holding gain from July 1 to December 31 to compute the total $48,000 holding gain for 20X6. In addition, the holding loss for 20X5 is recorded as a reversal of the holding gain reported in 20X4. The unrealized holding gains and losses are reported as part of other comprehensive income in the comprehensive income statement.

Table 2-4 shows computation of the tax expense or benefit from the holding gains and losses and the after-tax holding gains and losses.

Table 2-4 Computation of Tax and After-Tax Amounts of Holding Gains and Losses on Equity Securities

(a) Year	(b) Holding Gain/(Loss)	(c) Tax Rate	(d) = (c) × (b) Tax Expense (Benefit)	(e) = (b) – (d) After Tax Holding Gain/(Loss)
20X4	$30,000	30%	$9,000	$21,000
20X5	(20,000)	30%	(6,000)	(14,000)
20X6	48,000 [a]	30%	14,400	33,600
Total	$58,000		$17,400	$40,600

[a] $40,000 1/1/X6 – 7/1/X6 holding gain + $8,000 7/1/X6 – 12/31/X6 holding gain = $48,000.

Using information from Table 2-4, journal entries for 20X4–20X6 for the tax impact of the holding gains and losses and to close the after-tax holding gains and losses to unrealized other comprehensive income are as follows:

20X4 Entry:

Income Tax Expense	9,000	
Deferred Tax Liability		9,000
Unrealized Holding Gain on Equity Securities	30,000	
Unrealized Other Comprehensive Income		21,000
Income Tax Expense		9,000

20X5 Entry:

Deferred Tax Liability	6,000	
Income Tax Expense		6,000
Income Tax Expense	6,000	

Unrealized Other Comprehensive Income	14,000	
Unrealized Holding Loss on Equity Securities		20,000
20X6 Entry July 1:		
Income Tax Expense	12,000	
Deferred Tax Liability		12,000
$40,000 holding gain × 30% = $12,000		
20X6 Entry from July 1 to December 31:		
Income Tax Expense	2,400	
Deferred Tax Liability		2,400
$8,000 holding gain × 30% = $2,400		

20X6 Entry to Close Unrealized Holding Gain to Unrealized Other Comprehensive Income

Unrealized Holding Gain on Equity Securities	48,000	
Unrealized Other Comprehensive Income		33,600
Income Tax Expense		14,400

The holding loss in 20X5 creates a tax benefit of $6,000 that is a reversal of part of the deferred tax liability established for the holding gain in 20X4. The unrealized other comprehensive income account is reported as a separate account in stockholders' equity after retained earnings. The balance in this account at the end of 20X6 prior to any reclassification adjustments is $40,600, which represents the unrealized holding gains and losses from 20X4–20X6.

The gain and tax impact of the gain on the sale of the 6,000 shares of equity securities on July 1, 20X6 is computed in Table 2-5. The gain on the sale of the equity securities and the related tax expense is used as the reclassification adjustment in the other comprehensive income presentation.

Table 2-5 Computation of Gain and Tax Impact from Sale of Equity Securities

6,000 shares × $10 selling price	$60,000
6,000 shares × $5 cost	30,000
Gain on sale of equity securities	$30,000
Tax rate	× 30 %
Tax expense on gain	$9,000
Gain on sale of equity securities[a]	$30,000
Tax expense on gain	9,000
After-tax gain on sale of equity securities	$21,000

[a] This gain is also the reclassification adjustment for 20X6 for equity securities. In addition, the tax expense and after-tax gain shown in this table are also the tax benefit and after-tax amounts for the reclassification adjustment

The journal entry required on July 1, 20X6 for the sale of the equity investment and the reclassification adjustment for holding gains and losses reported in prior years is:

Cash	60,000	
Reclassification Adjustment for Equity Investment	30,000	
Investment in Nelson Enterprise Common Stock		60,000
Gain on Sale of Equity Investment		30,000

The reclassification adjustment is reported as part of other comprehensive income and offsets holding gains and losses reported in current and prior periods relative to the equity securities sold. The gain on the sale of the equity investment is reported as part of net income.

Next, the deferred tax liability established for the holding gains and losses related to the equity securities sold and reported prior to the sale of the equity securities is removed, and the tax benefit of $9,000 related to the reclassification adjustment is reported. The following entry is required for this information:

Deferred Tax Liability	9,000	
Income Tax Expense		9,000

The deferred tax liability balance at the time of sale of the equity investment is $15,000 ($9,000 – $6,000 + 12,000 from preceding journal entries). The deferred tax liability should be reduced by 60%, or $9,000 ($15,000 × 60%), because 60% (6,000 shares ÷ 10,000 shares) of the investment is sold. Last, the following journal entry records the tax impact of the gain from the sale of the equity securities.

Income Tax Expense	9,000	
Income Tax Payable		9,000

The net reclassification adjustment of $21,000 ($30,000 adjustment – $9,000 tax benefit) and tax benefit is closed to unrealized other comprehensive income to remove the holding gains and losses closed to this account in current and prior years related to equity securities sold during the current accounting period. The required entry is as follows:

Income Tax Expense	9,000	
Unrealized Other Comprehensive Income	21,000	
Reclassification Adjustment for Equity Investment		30,000

Last, the entry to close the gain on sale of the investment and related tax impact to retained earnings is presented as follows:

Gain on Sale of Equity Investment	30,000	
Income Tax Expense		9,000
Retained Earnings		21,000

Table 2-6 shows the calculation of the carrying value of the debt investment, including the amount of cash interest received; the amount of interest income reported as part of net income; and the amount of discount amortized each accounting period. An 8% effective interest rate is used in the computation of interest income and the 6% stated rate is used when computing the cash interest received.

Table 2-6 Computation of Carrying Value of Bond Investment

Year	Cash Received	Interest Income	Discount Amortization	Carrying Value of Investment
				$2,760,438
12/31/X5	$180,000 [a]	$220,835 [b]	$40,835 [c]	2,801,273 [d]
12/31/X6	180,000	224,102	44,102	2,845,375

[a] $3,000,000 face of debt × 6% stated interest rate = $180,000 annual cash interest.
[b] $2,760,438 × 8% effective interest rate = $220,835.
[c] $220,835 annual interest income – $180,000 annual cash interest = $40,835.
[d] $2,760,438 + $40,835 = $2,801,273.

Journal entries to record recognition of annual interest income and amortization of the discount are as follows:

20X5 Entry

Cash	180,000	
Investment in Johnson Enterprise Debt	40,835	
Interest Income		220,835

20X6 Entry

Cash	180,000	
Investment in Johnson Enterprise Debt	44,102	
Interest Income		224,102

The discount is amortized directly by increasing the investment account. Interest income is reported as part of net income in the comprehensive income statement and is closed after tax impact to retained earnings.

Once the carrying value is computed, Table 2-7 illustrates the computation of holding gains for the debt investment. The holding gains for each year are computed by comparing the fair value of the debt investment at the end of each year with the carrying value of the debt at the end of the same year (computed in Table 2-6), less cumulative holding gains and losses reported in prior periods.

Table 2-7 Computation of Holding Gains and Losses for Bond Investment

(a)	(b)	(c)	(d) =(c)–(b)	(e)	(f)=(d)–(e)
Time Period	Ending Carrying Value[a]	Ending Fair Value[b]	Total Holding Gain/(Loss)	Holding Gain/(Loss) Reported in Prior Periods[c]	Holding Gain/(Loss) Current Period
1/1/X5–12/31/X5	$2,801,273	$2,898,000	$96,727	$0	$96,727
1/1/X6–12/31/X6	2,845,375	3,081,000	235,625	96,727	138,898
Total					$235,625

[a]Carrying value information taken from Table 2-6.

[b]Fair value information taken from Assumption 3.

[c]Prior years' holding gains and losses is the sum of all holding gains and losses for all prior years.

Journal entries for the unrealized holding gains for debt securities are similar to the entries for equity securities and are not repeated. (See the preceding holding gain entries for debt securities.)

Once the holding gains on the debt investment are computed, the tax impact of the holding gains and related after-tax amounts can be calculated. Table 2-8 shows these computations.

Table 2-8 Computation of Tax and After-Tax Amounts of Holding Gains and Losses on Debt Securities

(a)	(b)	(c)	(d)=(b)×(c)	(e)=(b)–(d)
Year	Holding Gain/(Loss)	Tax Rate	Tax Expense (Benefit)	After-Tax Holding Gain/ (loss)
20X5	$96,727	30%	$29,018	$67,709
20X6	138,898	30%	41,670	97,228
Total	$235,625		$70,688	$164,937

Journal entries for the tax impact, after-tax amounts, and closing entries to unrealized other comprehensive income are similar to those used for equity securities and are not repeated here.

Table 2-9 illustrates calculation of the gain and tax effect from sale of the debt investment on December 31, 20X6. This information is also used as the reclassification adjustment when preparing the other comprehensive income section of the comprehensive income statement.

Table 2-9 Computation of Gain and Tax Impact from Sale of Debt Securities

Selling price of debt securities (Assumption 3)	$3,081,000
Carrying value of debt securities (Table 2-6)	2,845,375
Gain on sale of debt securities	$235,625
Tax rate	30%
Tax expense on gain	$70,688
Gain on sale of debt securities[a]	$235,625
Tax expense on gain	70,688
After-tax gain on sale of debt securities[a]	$164,937

[a] This gain is also the reclassification adjustment for 20X6 for equity securities. In addition, the tax expense and after-tax gain shown in this table are also the tax benefit and after-tax amounts for the reclassification adjustment.

See the journal entries for gains on sale of investment and reclassification entries for equity securities because the entries for debt securities are similar in nature.

Table 2-10 shows a summary of all information from the debt and equity investments for the years 20X4–20X6 as reported in a comprehensive income statement.

Table 2-10 Information about Debt and Equity Securities Reported in Comprehensive Income Statement

	20X4	20X5	20X6
Information Reported in Net Income:			
Gain on sale of equity investment (Table 2-5)			$30,000
Gain on sale of debt investment (Table 2-9)			235,625
Interest income on debt investment (Table 2-6)		$220,835	224,102
Tax expense:			
On equity investment (Table 2-5)		9,000	
On debt investment (Table 2-9)			70,688
On interest income		66,251	67,231
Information Reported in Other Comprehensive Income:			
Holding gain/(loss) from equity securities, net of tax of $9,000, $(6,000) and $14,000, respectively (Table 2-4)	$21,000	(14,000)	33,600
Holding gain from debt securities, net of tax of $29,018 and $41,670, respectively (Table 2-8)		67,709	97,228
Reclassification Adjustments:			
On equity securities, net of tax of $9,000 (Table 2-5)	21,000		
On debt securities, net of tax of $70,688 (Table 2-9)			164,937

This completes the analysis of Example 2-5. Example 2-6 illustrates preparation of a comprehensive income statement when an entity has reclassification adjustment. Assumptions for Example 2-6 are as follows.

Example 2-6
Assumptions for Comprehensive Income with Reclassification Adjustments

1. Lane Enterprises (Lane), a December 31 year-end company, prepared the following basic income statement for 20X6:

Sales	$15,000,000
Cost of sales	8,000,000
Gross profit	$7,000,000
Operating expenses	(1,500,000)

Other income and expenses:		
Interest expense	$(100,000)	
Interest income	224,102	
Gain on sale of equity investment	30,000	
Gain on sale of debt investment	235,625	389,727
Income before extraordinary items and tax		$5,889,727
Income tax expense		1,766,918
Net Income		$4,122,809

2. In addition to the income statement items in Assumption 1, above, Lane had the following other comprehensive income elements for 20X6:

Loss from foreign currency translation	$(1,200,000)
Gain from change in market value of futures contract	400,000

   Lane had no reclassification adjustments for the other comprehensive items listed above.

3. Assume that Lane had other comprehensive income items, including reclassification adjustments from Example 2-5, Table 2-10.
4. Beginning balances in unrealized other comprehensive income at the beginning of 20X6 were as follows:

Unrealized holding gains from equity securities	$7,000
Unrealized holding gains from debt securities	67,709

5. Lane has a 30% tax rate for 20X6.
6. Lane elects to present a single-statement format for the comprehensive income statement, to show both other comprehensive income and reclassification adjustments on a net-of-tax basis, and to present the analysis of accumulated other comprehensive income as a separate disclosure.

Using the information from Example 2-6, a comprehensive income statement for 20X6 can be prepared. The statement is prepared using a single statement format, and both other comprehensive income items and reclassification adjustments are presented net of related tax impacts with the tax amount reported on the face of the statement. In addition, the reclassification adjustments are presented on a net basis as an offset to the related other comprehensive income item, with the amount of the reclassification adjustment presented on the face of the statement. Therefore, given this method of presentation, the only additional disclosure required is an analysis of unrealized other comprehensive income. A comprehensive income statement for 20X6 for Lane is presented below.

Lane Enterprises Statement of Income and Comprehensive Income for the Year Ending December 31, 20X6

Sales	$15,000,000
Cost of sales	8,000,000
Gross profit	$7,000,000
Operating expenses	(1,500,000)

Other income and expenses:			
Interest expense		$(100,000)	
Interest income		224,102	
Gain on sale of equity investment		30,000	
Gain on sale of debt investment		235,625	389,727
Income before extraordinary items and tax			$5,889,727
Income tax expense			1,766,918
Net Income			$4,122,809
Other Comprehensive Income:			
Gains and losses related to foreign currency:			
Loss from foreign currency translation, less tax benefit of $360,000		$(840,000)	
Gain from change in market value of futures contract, less tax of $120,000		280,000	
Gains and losses related to debt and equity securities:			
Unrealized holding gain from available-for-sale equity securities, less tax of $14,000	$33,600		
Less: Reclassification adjustment for gain included in net income, net of tax of $9,000	(21,000)	12,600	
Unrealized holding gain from available-for-sale debt securities, less tax of $41,670	$97,228		
Less: Reclassification adjustment for gain included in net income, net of tax of $70,688	(164,937)	(67,709)	
Other comprehensive income			(615,109)
Comprehensive Income			$3,507,700

Using the information from the Example 2-6 assumptions and the 20X6 comprehensive income statement, the required disclosure of unrealized other comprehensive income is presented in Table 2-11.

Table 2-11 Changes in Unrealized Other Comprehensive Income[a]

	Foreign Currency Items	Unrealized Gains/(Losses) on Securities	Unrealized Other Comprehensive Income[b]
Beginning 20X6 Balance	$0	$74,709 [d]	$74,709
Change in Current Period	(560,000)[c]	(55,109)[e]	(615,109)
Ending 20X6 Balance	$(560,000)	$(19,600)	$(540,400)

[a] Information for preparation of this required disclosure taken from Assumptions 4 and 6 and the 20X6 comprehensive income statement.
[b] Column represents a summation of all components of unrealized other comprehensive income.
[c] $(840,000) + $280,000 = $(560,000)—information taken from the 20X6 comprehensive income statement.
[d] $7,000 + $67,709 = $74,709—information taken from Assumption 4.
[e] $12,600 + $(67,709) = $(55,109)—information taken from the 20X6 comprehensive income statement.

Topic 225: Income Statement

Topic 225, *Income Statement*, contains the following subtopics:

10 Overall

20 Unusual or Infrequently Occurring Items

30 Business Interruption Insurance

912 Contractors—Federal Government*

932 Extractive Activities—Oil and Gas*

942 Financial Services—Depository and Lending*

944 Financial Services—Insurance*

946 Financial Services—Investment Companies*

954 Health Care Entities*

958 Not-For-Profit Entities*

* See the corresponding topic in Chapter 9 for coverage of this shared subtopic.

Unusual or Infrequently Occurring Items

ASC 225-20 addresses the presentation and disclosure of unusual and infrequently occurring items. Certain transactions or events may be unusual in nature or infrequent in occurrence, or both. A transaction or event of this nature should be reported as a one-line item in income from continuing operations. The item is not presented net of tax and an earnings per share amount is not reported for an unusual or infrequent item. The nature and effect of the item should be disclosed in the notes to the financial statements. If there is more than one unusual or infrequent item, it would be appropriate to report similar items in the aggregate, providing that none of the items is individually material (ASC 225-20-45-16).

Business Interruption Insurance

ASC 225-30 states that an entity may use judgment when classifying business interruption insurance recoveries in the income statement as long as the classification elected does not violate current generally accepted accounting principles. In addition, ASC 225-30 specifies that the following disclosures are required for business interruption insurance recoveries: the nature of the event that caused the loss and where the insurance recoveries are reported (such as an extraordinary item) and the amount of the recovery reported in the current accounting period.

Recent Changes

ASU 2015-01, *Income Statement—Extraordinary and Unusual Items (Subtopic 225-20): Simplifying Income Statement Presentation by Eliminating the Concept of Extraordinary Items*, eliminates the concept of extraordinary items from generally accepted accounting principles effective for fiscal years, and interim periods within those fiscal years, beginning after December 15, 2015. A reporting entity may apply the amendments prospectively. A reporting entity also may apply the amendments retrospectively to all prior periods presented in the financial statements. Early adoption is permitted provided that the guidance is applied from the beginning of the fiscal year of adoption. The effective date is the same for all entities, including public business entities.

Topic 230: Statement of Cash Flows

Topic 230, *Statement of Cash Flows*, contains the following subtopics:

10 Overall

830 Foreign Currency Matters [See the corresponding topic in Chapter 8 for coverage of this shared subtopic]

926 Entertainment—Films*

942 Financial Services—Depository and Lending*

946 Financial Services—Investment Companies *

958 Not-For-Profit Entities*

970 Real Estate—General*

978 Real Estate—Time-Sharing Activities*

* See the corresponding topic in Chapter 9 for coverage of this shared subtopic.

General Discussion

A complete set of general-purpose financial statements includes a statement of cash flows. The primary objective of the statement of cash flows is to provide users of financial statements with information about the cash receipts and cash payments of a reporting entity. More specifically, the statement explains why cash and cash equivalents increased or decreased during an accounting period. Such information about the receipts and payments of cash and cash equivalents should help users of financial statements to assess the following (ASC 230-10-10-2):

1. The entity's ability to generate positive cash flows in the future;
2. The entity's ability to pay its obligations and dividends;
3. The entity's need for outside financing;

4. The reasons for the differences between net income and associated cash receipts and payments; and
5. The effects of noncash investing and financing activities on the entity's financial position.

ASC 230-10 applies to all entities, including both business entities and not-for-profit entities, with certain exceptions. The following entities are not required to provide a statement of cash flows (ASC 230-10-15-4):

1. A defined benefit pension plan or other employee benefit plan that presents financial information in accordance with ASC 960.
2. An investment company that is within the scope of Topic 946.
3. A fund (such as a common trust fund or a variable annuity fund) maintained by a guardian, administrator, or trustee (such as a bank or insurance company) for the purpose of investing and reinvesting money on a collective basis.

For an investment company, as described in 2., above, to be exempt from providing a statement of cash flows, it must meet all of the following three conditions:

1. Significantly all of the investments held by the company are reported at fair value and classified as Level 1 or Level 2 measurements in Topic 820.
2. As related to average total assets, the company had little or no debt. Average outstanding debt is used for the comparison.
3. A statement of changes in net assets is provided by the company.

Cash and Cash Equivalents

As noted in the preceding discussion, the statement of cash flows explains why cash, cash equivalents, and amounts generally described as restricted cash or restricted cash equivalents increased or decreased during a reporting period. Cash is currency on hand, demand deposits, and other kinds of accounts that have the same characteristics as demand deposits. Cash equivalents are highly liquid, short-term securities that meet the following two conditions:

1. They can be converted readily into known amounts of cash.
2. Their maturity dates are so close that there is no significant risk of a change in fair value from interest rate changes.

Normally, a security that meets the preceding criteria must have an original maturity to the entity holding the security of not more than three months in order to be classified as a cash equivalent. Examples of cash equivalents include money market funds, treasury bills, and commercial paper.

Not all securities meeting the preceding definition of cash equivalents must be treated as such. An entity should establish a policy that is consistently followed regarding what items meeting the preceding definition of cash equivalency are included as cash equivalents (ASC 230-10-45-6). The policy of determining which items are cash equivalents should be disclosed (e.g., in a note to the financial statements), and any change in policy should be accounted for as a change in accounting principle (ASC 230-10-50-1). The change in accounting principle should be accounted for by restating all financial statements presented in the period of change.

If cash or cash equivalents are restricted, an entity shall disclose information about the nature of restrictions. For example, restricted cash in current assets may represent amounts required to be set aside by a contractual agreement with an insurer for the payment of specific workers' compensation claims. Restricted cash included in long-term assets may include amounts pledged as collateral for long-term financing arrangements as contractually required by the lender. (ASC 230-10-55-12A)

Gross vs. Net Amounts

In the preparation of the statement of cash flows, gross cash flow amounts are assumed to be more relevant than net amounts; therefore, the statement generally is prepared using gross cash inflows and gross cash outflows. However, ASC 230-10-45, paragraphs 8 and 9, provide certain exceptions to this general rule. For example, net change in cash flows for a reporting period may be used for selected items that have quick turnovers, large amounts, and short maturities. Examples include cash inflows and outflows related to loans receivable, demand deposits of a bank, customer accounts payable of a broker-dealer, investments, and debt with an original maturity of not more than three months. In addition, savings institutions, credit unions, and banks are exempt from reporting gross cash flows related to customer loans, time deposits, and deposits with other financial institutions (ASC 942-230-45-1).

Organization/Structure

The statement of cash flows should be divided into three basic activities sections with related note disclosures. The three activities sections are as follows:

1. Operating activities section.
2. Investing activities section.
3. Financing activities section.

Each section of the statement of cash flows is discussed in detail below.

Operating Activities Section

The operating activities section of the statement of cash flows contains cash flows related to income or the income statement and includes all transactions and events not defined as investing or financing transactions. Examples of cash inflows and cash outflows included in the operating activities section of the statement are presented in Chart 2-1.

Chart 2-1 Examples of Cash Inflows and Outflows Included in the Operating Activities Section

Cash Inflows (ASC 230-10-45, paragraphs 16, 20, and 21)	Cash Outflows (ASC 230-10-45, paragraphs 17, 20, and 21)
1. Cash received from the sale of goods and services.	1. Cash payments for cost of sales.
2. Cash received from the collection of accounts and notes receivable related to the sale of goods and services.	2. Cash payments to employees and suppliers.
3. Cash received from earnings on investments in debt and equity securities and loans, such as interest and dividends.	3. Cash payments to government agencies such as payment of taxes, fines and duties.
4. Cash received from sale of loans and other debt instruments of other entities, acquired for the purpose of resale, that were carried at fair value or the lower of cost or market.	4. Cash paid for securities and other assets acquired for the purpose of resale that are carried in a trading account at fair value.
5. Cash received from other transactions not classified as investing and financing transactions.	5. Cash paid for loans, acquired for the purpose of resale, that are carried at fair value or the lower of cost or market.
	6. Cash payments made to settle asset retirement obligations.
	7. Cash payments for interest, and payments related to other transactions not classified as investing or financing transactions.

When preparing the operating activities section of the cash flow statement, a direct or indirect method may be used.

Direct Method

The direct method, preferred by the FASB, uses gross cash operating inflows and outflows to compute cash-basis income. Cash-basis income is computed directly using major classes of gross cash receipts and gross cash payments. Chart 2-2 lists the minimum major classes of gross cash receipts and payments that must be presented in the operating activities section when the direct method is used (ASC 230-10-45-25).

Chart 2-2 Minimum Major Classes of Gross Receipts and Payments

1. Cash inflows from customers including cash from sales, lessees, licensees and similar transactions;
2. Cash inflows from dividends and interest;
3. Cash inflows from other operating activities, if appropriate;

4. Cash outflows paid employees and suppliers, such as for inventory advertising and insurance;
5. Cash outflows for interest;
6. Cash outflows for income taxes; and
7. Cash outflows for other operating activities, if appropriate.

An entity may elect to present more detailed classes of gross cash receipts and payments than are required in Chart 2-2.

When an entity uses the direct method in the preparation of the operating activities section of the cash flow statement, a reconciliation of accrual basis accounting income to net cash flows from operating activities is required to be presented in a supplemental schedule. That is, if the direct method is used, the reconciliation reported for the indirect method must be disclosed in the statement.

Indirect Method

An enterprise may elect to use an indirect method in the preparation of the operating activities section of the cash flow statement. The indirect method converts accrual-basis income to cash-basis income by adding and deducting noncash items. Basically, the indirect method is a reconciliation of accrual basis accounting income to net cash flows from operations. The indirect method begins with either income from continuing operations or net income, depending upon whether or not a company elects to show certain net-of-tax items separately in the statement. Separate disclosure is not required of such items under ASC 230-10. Noncash expense items, such as depreciation expense, are added back to income, and noncash revenue items, such as equity in investee companies, are deducted from income when using the indirect method. In the indirect method, the reconciliation of accrual-basis income to net cash from operations includes separate reporting of all major classes of reconciling items. This requires adjusting accrual-basis net income for the impact of the following (ASC 230-10-45-28):

- Deferrals related to prior operating cash inflows and outflows, such as changes in inventory, and accruals related to future operating cash inflows and outflows, such as changes in receivables and payables (Type 1 Reconciling Items); and
- Items whose cash impact is included in either the investing or financing section of the statement, such as depreciation and gains and losses on debt extinguishment (Type 2 Reconciling Items).

Chart 2-3 provides examples of major classes of reconciling items for the indirect method.

Chart 2-3 Examples of Reconciling Items Used in the Indirect Approach

Type 1 Reconciling Items

Additions Back to Accrual-Basis Income:

1. Decrease in accounts receivable.
2. Decrease in other operating receivables.
3. Decrease in inventory.

4. Decrease in prepaid expenses, such as insurance and advertising.
5. Increase in accounts payable.
6. Increase in salaries payable.
7. Increase in income taxes payable.
8. Increase in deferred tax liability.

Deductions from Accrual-Basis Income:

1. Increase in accounts receivable.
2. Increase in other operating receivables.
3. Increase in inventory.
4. Increase in prepaid expenses, such as insurance and advertising.
5. Decrease in accounts payable.
6. Decrease in salaries payable.
7. Decrease in income taxes payable.
8. Decrease in deferred tax liability.

Type 2 Reconciling Items

Additions Back to Accrual-Basis Income:

1. Depreciation expense.
2. Amortization of intangible assets, such as amortization of patents.
3. Unrealized losses from write-down of current marketable equity securities.
4. Losses on transactions, such as losses on sale of property, plant and equipment and investments.
5. Amortization of bond and note discounts.
6. Losses related to discontinued operations.
7. Decreases in income from changes in accounting principles.

Deductions from Accrual-Basis Income:

1. Equity in earnings of investee companies.
2. Unrealized gains from market recovery of current marketable equity securities.
3. Gains on transactions, such as gains on sale of property, plant and equipment and investments.
4. Amortization of bond and note premiums.
5. Gains related to segment dispositions.
6. Increases in income from changes in accounting principles.

When the indirect method is used, the amount of interest paid, after deducting the amount capitalized, and the amount of income taxes paid must be disclosed. Also, the reconciliation of accrual-basis income to net cash from operations required by the indirect method may be reported on the face of the statement or in a separate schedule.

Investing Activities Section

The second section of the cash flow statement is the investing activities section and includes cash inflows and outflows related to investing activities. More specifically, the investing activities section includes cash inflows and outflows from investment transactions related to the acquisition and disposition of assets, such as property, plant, and equipment; investment securities; intangibles; and other assets of an investment nature. Examples of cash inflows and cash outflows included in the investing activities section of the cash flow statement are presented in Chart 2-4.

Chart 2-4 Examples of Cash Inflows and Outflows Included in the Investing Activities Section

Cash Inflows (ASC 230-10-45-12)	Cash Outflows (ASC 230-10-45-13)
1. Cash received from the collection or sales of loans made by the enterprise.	1. Cash payments for loans made by the enterprise.
2. Cash received from the sale of other entities' debt instruments.	2. Cash payments for acquisition of debt of other entities.
3. Cash received from the sale of property, plant and equipment.	3. Cash payments for equity securities of other entities.
4. Cash received from the sale of tangible assets other than property, plant and equipment.	4. Cash payments made at the time of purchase, or shortly after purchase for property, plant and equipment.
5. Cash received from the sale of equity securities of other entities and the return on those securities.	5. Cash payments made at the time of purchase, or shortly after purchase for tangible assets, other than property, plant and equipment.

Cash payments related to items 4 and 5 in Chart 2-4 require further explanation. Only payments made at the time of purchase, shortly before, or shortly after the purchase of property, plant, and equipment and other tangible assets are considered investing activities. Examples include the down payment or advance payments on the tangible assets. If a note is used for all or part of the purchase price of a tangible asset, future payments on the note are financing activities, not investing activities. Interest capitalization incurred in connection with the acquisition of a tangible asset is an investing activity and is included in the investing activities section of the cash flow statement.

Cash inflows and outflows from the sale and purchase of securities or other assets acquired for the purpose of resale and carried in a trading account at market value and classified as trading securities are classified in the cash flow statement based on the nature and purpose of the acquisition of the securities. In addition, cash inflows and outflows from the sale or purchase of loans, carried at the lower of cost or market or fair market value, acquired for the purpose of resale are classified as operating activities in the cash flow statement.

Cash inflows from disposing of loans, debt or equity instruments, or property, plant, and equipment include directly related proceeds of insurance settlements, such as the proceeds of insurance on a building that is damaged or destroyed.

Financing Activities Section

The third section of the cash flow statement includes cash receipts and cash payments related to financing activities. More specifically, the financing activities section includes cash inflows and outflows from financing transactions related to liability and stockholders' equity items and includes transactions such as the borrowing and repaying of borrowed funds, sale and reacquisition of company stock, and payment of dividends. Examples of cash inflows and cash outflows included in the financing activities section of the cash flow statement are presented in Chart 2-5.

Chart 2-5 Examples of Cash Inflows and Outflows Included in the Financing Activities Section

Cash Inflows (ASC 230-10-45-14)	Cash Outflows (ASC 230-10-45-15)
1. Cash received from issuing equity securities.	1. Cash payments for dividends and other payments to owners.
2. Cash received from issuing bonds, notes and mortgages.	2. Cash payments to reacquire equity securities of the enterprise.
3. Cash received from issuing other short and long-term borrowings, other than those noted in 2 above.	3. Cash payments for amounts borrowed.
	4. Cash payments for principal payments to creditors for long-term borrowings.

Cash payments in item 3 generally relate to repayments of notes where cash was initially borrowed by the enterprise. However, cash payments in item 4 generally relate to principal payments on notes that were initially issued for purchases of tangible assets, such as property, plant, and equipment.

Gross cash inflows and gross cash outflows for both the investing and financing sections of the cash flow statement should be reported separately. For example, gross cash inflows from the sale of common stock should be reported separately from gross cash outflows to reacquire shares of the company's common stock.

Cash receipts and cash payments should be classified in one of the three sections, discussed above, based on the nature of the item rather than its origin. For example, cash borrowed is a financing activity regardless of whether the borrowing is intended as a hedge of an investment, and a transaction involving a futures contract is an investing activity whether or not the contract is a hedge of an existing asset or a firm commitment.

It may be difficult to classify some cash receipts and cash payments, because they have aspects of more than one activity. In some cases, an asset purchased may be viewed as inventory or as a productive asset. If the asset is viewed as inventory, related cash flows are included in the operating activities section of the cash flow statement. However, if the asset is viewed as a productive asset, related cash flows are included in the investing activities section of the statement. For example, an asset may be purchased and then sold after it is used or leased for a short period of time. Such a transaction could be viewed as an operating activity. Generally, assets purchased and used by the entity are considered investing activities. When a transaction has aspects of more than one activity, cash flows from that transaction should be classified in the section that predominantly relates to their source. In order to reduce the amount of variability in practice, in August 2016, FASB issued ASU 2016-15, *Statement of Cash Flows (Topic 230): Classification of Certain Cash Receipts and Cash Payments,* to give specific guidance on how certain cash receipts and cash payments are presented and classified in the statement of cash flows. U.S. GAAP was either unclear or did not include guidance on classifying these items. The amendments are effective for public business entities for fiscal years beginning after December 15, 2017 and interim periods within those fiscal years. For all other entities, the amendments are effective for fiscal years beginning after December 15, 2018 and interim periods within fiscal years beginning after December 15, 2019.

Summary of Amendments

The amendments in ASU 2016-15 provide guidance on eight specific cash flow issues.

1. **Debt Prepayment or Debt Extinguishment Costs**

Cash payments for debt prepayment or debt extinguishment costs should be classified as cash outflows for financing activities.

2. **Settlement of Zero-Coupon Debt Instruments or Other Debt Instruments with Coupon Interest Rates That Are Insignificant in Relation to the Effective Interest Rate of the Borrowing**

At the settlement of zero-coupon debt instruments or other debt instruments with coupon interest rates that are insignificant in relation to the effective interest rate of the borrowing, the issuer should classify the portion of the cash payment attributable to the accreted interest related to the debt discount as cash outflows for operating activities, and the portion of the cash payment attributable to the principal as cash outflows for financing activities.

3. **Contingent Consideration Payments Made after a Business Combination**

Cash payments not made soon after the acquisition date of a business combination by an acquirer to settle a contingent consideration liability should be separated and classified as cash outflows for financing activities and operating activities. Cash payments up to the amount of the contingent consideration liability recognized at the acquisition date (including measurement-period adjustments) should be classified as financing activities; any excess should be classified as operating activities. Cash payments made soon after the acquisition date of a business combination by an acquirer to settle a contingent consideration liability should be classified as cash outflows for investing activities.

4. **Proceeds from the Settlement of Insurance Claims**

Cash proceeds received from the settlement of insurance claims should be classified on the basis of the related insurance coverage (i.e., the nature of the loss). For insurance proceeds that are received in a lump-sum settlement, an entity should determine the classification on the basis of the nature of each loss included in the settlement.

5. **Proceeds from the Settlement of Corporate-Owned Life Insurance Policies, including Bank-Owned Life Insurance Policies**

Cash proceeds received from the settlement of corporate-owned life insurance policies should be classified as cash inflows from investing activities. The cash payments for premiums on corporate-owned policies may be classified as cash outflows for investing activities, operating activities, or a combination of investing and operating activities.

6. **Distributions Received from Equity Method Investees**

When a reporting entity applies the equity method, it should make an accounting policy election to classify distributions received from equity method investees using either of the following approaches:

a. Cumulative earnings approach: Distributions received are considered returns on investment and classified as cash inflows from operating activities, unless the investor's cumulative distributions received less distributions received in prior periods that were determined to be returns of investment exceed cumulative equity in earnings recognized by the investor. When such an excess occurs, the current-period distribution up to this excess should be considered a return of investment and classified as cash inflows from investing activities.

b. Nature of the distribution approach: Distributions received should be classified on the basis of the nature of the activity or activities of the investee that generated the distribution as either a return on investment (classified as cash inflows from operating activities) or a return of investment (classified as cash inflows from investing activities) when such information is available to the investor.

If an entity elects to apply the nature of the distribution approach and the information to apply that approach to distributions received from an individual equity method investee is not available to the investor, the entity should report a change in accounting principle on a retrospective basis by applying the cumulative earnings approach in (1) for that investee. In such situations, an entity should disclose that a change in accounting principle has occurred with respect to the affected investee(s) due to the lack of available information and should provide the disclosures required in paragraphs 250-10-50-1(b) and 250-10-50-2, as applicable. This amendment does not address equity method investments measured using the fair value option.

7. **Beneficial Interests in Securitization Transactions**

A transferor's beneficial interest obtained in a securitization of financial assets should be disclosed as a noncash activity, and cash receipts from payments on a transferor's beneficial interests in securitized trade receivables should be classified as cash inflows from investing activities.

8. **Separately Identifiable Cash Flows and Application of the Predominance Principle**

The classification of cash receipts and payments that have aspects of more than one class of cash flows should be determined first by applying specific guidance in U.S. generally accepted accounting principles (U.S. GAAP). In the absence of specific guidance, an entity should determine each separately identifiable source or use within the cash receipts and cash payments on the basis of the nature of the underlying cash flows. An entity should then classify each separately identifiable source or use within the cash receipts and payments on the basis of their nature in financing, investing, or operating activities. In situations in which cash receipts and payments have aspects of more than one class of cash flows and cannot be separated by source or use, the appropriate classification should depend on the activity that is likely to be the predominant source or use of cash flows for the item.

Noncash Investing and Financing Activities

Some items that are of either an investing or a financing nature do not appear in any of the preceding sections of the cash flow statement, because no cash is involved in the transaction. For example, the purchase of a building by exchanging a note or the purchase of equipment by issuing common stock is a noncash investing or financing activity. Noncash investing or financing activities should be included in the statement either in a note or summarized in a separate schedule to the cash flow statement.

The cash flow statement should be prepared in such a way as to show the beginning and ending cash and cash equivalent balances. This may be accomplished by adding the beginning cash balance to the change in cash for the period to compute the ending cash balance.

If an entity has foreign transactions or foreign operations, the impact of changes in exchange rates on assets and liabilities will affect cash flow reporting. Therefore, the cash flow statement should report the reporting currency (e.g., the U.S. dollar) equivalent of cash payments and cash receipts related to the foreign currency. When converting foreign cash flows to the reporting currency, the exchange rates in effect on the dates that the cash flows occurred should be used. However, the ASC allows the use of an appropriate weighted average exchange rate for the accounting period if the cash flow results are not substantially different from that produced using actual exchange rates on the dates of the cash flows. The impact of exchange rates on cash flows should be reported as a separate component of the reconciliation of changes in cash flow for the accounting period under consideration. The impact of the exchange rate changes may be placed as a last item in the cash flow statement just prior to the net increase or decrease in cash for the accounting period. (See Topic 830 in Chapter 8 for a more detailed discussion of foreign currency transactions and foreign currency translation).

Derivative instruments classified as cash flow or fair value hedges are reported in the same place in the cash flow statement as the items hedged.

Technical Considerations

Three examples will be used to illustrate the technical aspects of the cash flow statement. Before addressing a comprehensive application of a cash flow statement, the operating activities section of a statement is illustrated, because either a direct or an indirect approach to the preparation of this section may be selected. Therefore, the first example explains the preparation of the operating section using both a direct and indirect approach. The second example is a comprehensive example that is used to illustrate the preparation of the cash flow statement using a T-account approach, and the third example is a comprehensive example illustrating the worksheet approach to the preparation of a cash flow statement. Assumptions for Example 2-7 are as follows.

Example 2-7

Assumptions for the Preparation of the Operating Activities Section of the Cash Flow Statement

1. Johnson Enterprises (Johnson) had the following income statement for 20X6.

Johnson Enterprises
Income Statement
For the Year Ended December 31, 20X6

Revenues:		
Sales	$4,320,000	
Interest revenue	148,500	
Dividend revenue	60,750	
Gain on sale of investments	40,500	
Equity in earnings of investee	54,000	
Gain on extinguishment of debt	81,000	
Other revenue	13,500	
Total revenue		$4,718,250
Expenses:		
Cost of goods sold	$1,485,000	
Salary expense	1,282,500	
Depreciation expense	236,250	
Patent amortization	13,500	
Interest expense	81,000	
Income tax expense	418,500	
Other expenses	33,750	
Loss on sale of property, plant and equipment	135,000	
Goodwill impairment	101,250	
Total expenses		3,786,750
Net income		$931,500

2. Balance sheet amounts at 12/31/X5 and 12/31/X6, and changes in the amounts, for balance sheet accounts that relate to the preceding income statement, are presented below:

	12/31/X6	12/31/X5	Increase/ (Decrease)
Accounts receivable	$325,000	$200,000	$125,000
Interest receivable	61,500	50,000	11,500
Inventory	201,000	255,000	(54,000)
Accounts payable	298,000	200,000	98,000

	12/31/X6	12/31/X5	Increase/ (Decrease)
Salary payable	100,000	127,000	(27,000)
Interest payable	56,750	50,000	6,750
Income taxes payable	105,000	180,000	(75,000)

Indirect Method of Reporting Cash Flows from Operating Activities

The indirect method of preparing the operating activities section of the cash flow statement is illustrated first. The indirect method begins with accrual-basis net income. Noncash items are added to or deducted from net income to convert the accrual-basis net income amount to a cash-basis amount. The operating activities section using the indirect method is presented as follows:

Johnson Enterprises
Partial Statement of Cash Flows
For the Year Ended
December 31, 20X6

Cash Flows from Operating Activities:		
Net income		$931,500
Adjustments to reconcile net income to net cash provided by operating activities:		
Gain on sale of investment	$(40,500)	
Equity in earnings of investee	(54,000)	
Gain on extinguishment of debt	(81,000)	
Depreciation expense	236,250	
Goodwill impairment	101,250	
Patent amortization	13,500	
Loss on sale of property, plant and equipment	135,000	
Increase in accounts receivable	(125,000)	
Increase in interest receivable	(11,500)	
Decrease in inventory	54,000	
Increase in accounts payable	98,000	
Decrease in salaries payable	(27,000)	
Increase in interest payable	6,750	
Decrease in income taxes payable	(75,000)	
Total net income adjustments		230,750
Net cash provided by operating activities		$1,162,250

Depreciation expense, goodwill impairment, and patent amortization are noncash expenses that were deducted when accrual-basis income was computed. Because they are noncash expenses, they should not be deducted when computing cash-basis income and, therefore, the impact of the noncash expenses is eliminated from accrual-basis income when converting to the cash basis by adding the noncash expenses back to income. Equity in the earnings of an investee is a noncash revenue item that was included in the computation of accrual-basis income. It is deducted from accrual-basis income when computing cash-basis income. The gain on sale of investment, the gain on extinguishment of debt, and the loss on sale of property, plant, and equipment represent the income statement impact of the gain or loss, but not the cash flow impact. The cash inflow impact of the sale of the property, plant, and equipment and the investment is included in the investing activities section of the cash flow statement, and the cash outflow impact of the extinguishment of debt is included in the financing activities section of the statement. Therefore, the impact on accrual-basis income of all gains and losses with cash flow implications in other sections of the statement is eliminated when accrual-basis income is converted to cash-basis income. If the gains and losses were not eliminated by deducting the gains and adding back the losses to accrual-basis income, the gains and losses would be counted twice in the cash flow statement—once in the operating section and once in either the investing or financing activities section.

Most current assets and liabilities on the balance sheet have a corresponding impact on the income statement. For example, the corresponding account on the income statement for accounts receivable is sales, and the corresponding account on the income statement for inventory and accounts payable is cost of goods sold. Therefore, when converting items, such as sales and cost of sales, from the accrual basis to a cash basis, the corresponding account or accounts on the balance sheet must be considered. Increases in current assets related to the income statement, such as the $125,000 increase in accounts receivable, are deducted when computing cash-basis income. Decreases in current assets, such as the decrease in inventory of $54,000, are added when converting accrual-basis income to a cash-basis amount. Increases in current liabilities related to income statement items, such as the increase in accounts payable of $98,000, are added to accrual-basis income and decreases in current liabilities are deducted when converting accrual income to a cash-basis amount.

Direct Method of Reporting Cash Flows from Operating Activities

The direct method can now be used to compute the $1,162,250 cash flow from operating activities using the same information in Example 2-7. The direct method uses a different approach of computing cash flows from operating activities than is used by the indirect method. The indirect method begins with accrual-basis income and noncash items are added and deducted to convert accrual-basis income to a cash basis. The direct approach uses each income statement revenue and expense item that has at least some cash impact and ignores all noncash revenue and expense items, such as equity in earnings of investee and depreciation expense. Each income statement item with some cash impact is converted to a complete cash basis, if it is not already on a complete cash basis, by adjusting the income item for its related balance sheet account. Table 2-12, shows the conversion of each accrual-basis income item with some cash flow impact to a complete cash basis.

Table 2-12
Computation of Cash Flows for the Direct Method

Account	Debit	Credit	Account	Debit	Credit	Account	Debit	Credit	Cash Collected/ (Paid)
Accounts Receivable			**Sales**			**Cash Collected from Customers**			
	125,000				4,320,000		(a) 4,320,000	(b) 125,000	→ $4,195,000
	(b) 125,000				(a) 4,320,000				
Interest Receivable			**Interest Revenue**			**Cash Collected for Interest**			
	11,500				148,500		(c) 148,500	(d) 11,500	
	(d) 11,500				(c) 148,500				→ 137,000
			Dividend Revenue			**Cash Collected for Dividends**			
					60,750		(e) 60,750		
					(e) 60,750				→ 60,750
			Other Revenue			**Cash Collected for Other Revenue**			
					13,500		(f) 13,500		
					(f) 13,500				→ 13,500

Account	Debit	Credit	Account	Debit	Credit	Account	Debit	Credit	Account	Debit	Credit	Cash Collected/ (Paid)
Accounts Payable			**Inventory**			**Cost of Sales**			**Cash Paid to Suppliers**			
		98,000			54,000		1,485,000			(g) 98,000	(i) 1,485,000	→ (1,333,000)
		(g) 98,000			(h) 54,000		(i) 1,485,000			(h) 54,000		
Salary Payable						**Salary Expense**			**Cash Paid to Employees**			
	27,000						1,282,500				(j) 27,000	
	(j) 27,000						(k) 1,282,500				(k) 1,282,500	→ (1,309,500)
Interest Payable						**Interest Expense**			**Cash Paid for Interest**			
		6,750					81,000			(l) 6,750	(m) 81,000	→ (74,250)
		(l) 6,750					(m) 81,000					
Income Tax Payable						**Income Tax Expense**			**Cash Paid for Income Taxes**			
	75,000						418,500				(n) 75,000	
	(n) 75,000						(o) 418,500				(o) 418,500	→ (493,500)
						Other Expenses			**Cash Paid for Other Expenses**			
							33,750				(p) 33,750	→ (33,750)
							(p) 33,750					$1,162,250

Only balance sheet accounts that relate to income statement items are used in Table 2-12 for the conversion to the cash basis, and all noncash income statement items, such as depreciation expense and gains and losses, have been removed from revenues and expenses. Table 2-12 is prepared in this manner in an effort to simplify the conversion to the cash basis and illustrate the direct method of preparing the operating section of the cash flow statement. Example 2-8 provides a complete worksheet using the direct method with all income statement and all balance sheet items used in the preparation.

A T-account approach is used to convert the individual accrual basis revenue and expense items to a cash basis. The change for the year in each current asset and current liability that impacts the income statement is posted to a T-account. In addition, the amount earned or incurred for each revenue and expense item is placed in a T-account. The amounts in the T-accounts are posted directly to a separate cash account for each revenue and expense balance, as illustrated in Table 2-12.

Using the cash-basis revenue and expense items in Table 2-12, the operating section of the cash flow statement can be prepared using the direct method.

Johnson Enterprises
Partial Statement of Cash Flows
For the Year Ended December 31, 20X6

Cash Flows from Operating Activities:	
Cash collected from customers	$4,195,000
Cash collected from dividends and interest	197,750
Cash collected from other revenues	13,500
Cash paid to suppliers and employees	(2,642,500)
Cash interest paid	(74,250)
Cash paid for income taxes	(493,500)
Cash paid for other operating expenses	(33,750)
Net cash provided from operating activities	$1,162,250

Cash received from dividends and interest of $197,750 is interest revenue of $137,000 and dividend revenue of $60,750. Cash paid to suppliers and employees of $2,642,500 consists of cost of sales of $1,333,000 and $1,309,500 of salary expense. When the direct method is used in the preparation of the operating activities section of the cash flow statement, in addition to the preceding computation of cash provided from operating activities, a reconciliation of accrual-basis net income to net cash derived from operating activities must be provided. The reconciliation of accrual-basis income to net cash provided by operating activities is the same as in the indirect method. The reconciliation is provided as follows:

Reconciliation of Net Income to Net Cash Provided by Operating Activities:		
Net income		$931,500
Adjustments to reconcile net income to net cash provided by operating activities:		
Gain on sale of investment	$(40,500)	
Equity in earnings of investee	(54,000)	
Gain on extinguishment of debt	(81,000)	
Depreciation expense	236,250	
Goodwill impairment	101,250	
Patent amortization	13,500	
Loss on sale of property, plant and equipment	135,000	
Increase in accounts receivable	(125,000)	
Increase in interest receivable	(11,500)	
Decrease in inventory	54,000	
Increase in accounts payable	98,000	
Decrease in salaries payable	(27,000)	
Increase in interest payable	6,750	
Decrease in income taxes payable	(75,000)	
Total net income adjustments		230,750
Net cash provided by operating activities		$1,162,250

Example 2-7 illustrated preparation of the operating section of a cash flow statement using both the direct and indirect methods. Example 2-8 illustrates the preparation of a complete cash flow statement using a T-account approach. Assumptions for Example 2-8 are as follows.

Example 2-8
Assumptions for Preparation of Cash Flow Statement

Comparative balance sheets and a current year income statement for Peterson Enterprises are provided below.

Peterson Enterprises
Comparative Balance Sheets December 31, 20X5 and 20X6

	12/31/X6	12/31/X5	Change in Balance Sheet Account
Cash and cash equivalents	$1,075,000	$400,000	$675,000
Accounts receivable	575,000	550,000	25,000
Notes receivable	100,000	100,000	0
Interest receivable	5,000	20,000	(15,000)
Inventory	720,000	680,000	40,000
Investment	700,000	800,000	(100,000)
Land	875,000	750,000	125,000
Property, plant and equipment	1,700,000	1,250,000	450,000
Accumulated depreciation	(238,125)	(200,000)	(38,125)
Goodwill	76,000	80,000	(4,000)
Patent	27,000	30,000	(3,000)
Total assets	$5,614,875	$4,460,000	$1,154,875
Accounts payable	$600,000	$575,000	$25,000
Notes payable-current	75,000	75,000	0
Interest payable	40,000	35,000	5,000
Salaries payable	50,000	40,000	10,000
Income taxes payable	185,000	300,000	(115,000)
Notes payable	200,000	0	200,000
Deferred taxes	140,000	150,000	(10,000)
Bonds payable	580,000	1,000,000	(420,000)
Total liabilities	$1,870,000	$2,175,000	$(305,000)
Common stock	$1,140,000	$800,000	$340,000
Paid-in-capital in excess of par	1,680,000	1,000,000	680,000
Retained earnings	924,875	485,000	439,875
Total stockholders' equity	$3,744,875	$2,285,000	$1,459,875
Total liabilities and stockholders' equity	$5,614,875	$4,460,000	$1,154,875

The income statement for 20X6 is as follows:

Peterson Enterprises
Income Statement
For the Year Ended December 31, 20X6

Sales		$3,200,000
Cost of Sales		(1,560,000)
Gross Profit		$1,640,000
Operating Expenses:		
Salary Expense	$(600,000)	
Selling Expense	(120,000)	
Administration Expense	(100,000)	
Depreciation Expense	(78,125)	
Goodwill impairment	(4,000)	
Patent Amortization	(3,000)	
Total Operating Expenses		(905,125)
Other Income and Expense:		
Interest Expense	$(75,000)	
Interest Income	60,000	
Gain on Sale of Investment	50,000	
Gain on Sale of Land	25,000	
Gain on Extinguishment of Bonds	30,000	
Loss on Sale of Property, Plant and Equipment	(10,000)	
Total Other Income and Expense		80,000
Income Before Tax		$814,875
Income Tax Expense:		
Current	$(335,000)	
Deferred	10,000	
		(325,000)
Net Income		$489,875

Other information about Peterson Enterprises for 20X6 is as follows:

1. Peterson sold investments with a cost basis of $200,000 for a gain of $50,000.
2. Property, plants, and equipment with a cost of $100,000 and accumulated depreciation of $40,000 were sold for $50,000. Additional property, plant, and equipment were purchased for $400,000 cash.
3. Land with a cost of $75,000 was sold for $100,000 cash.
4. Peterson issued 50,000 shares of $5 par common stock for $15 per share.
5. Bonds with a carrying value of $300,000 were extinguished at a cost of $270,000.
6. Ten thousand shares of common stock with a fair value of $15 were exchanged for property, plant, and equipment.
7. Land with a fair value of $200,000 was purchased by issuing a $200,000 long-term note.

8. Eight thousand shares of common stock were exchanged for $120,000 of bonds payable.
9. Cash dividends of $50,000 were paid in 20X6.
10. Investments were purchased at a cost of $100,000.
11. Peterson considers cash equivalents to be all highly liquid securities with an original maturity of three months or less.

When using the T-account approach in the preparation of the cash flow statement, all accounts other than cash and cash equivalents are analyzed to explain why cash and cash equivalents have increased or decreased. T-accounts are created for each account other than cash and cash equivalents and the increase or decrease in each account from the prior year represents a debit or credit to the account. All transactions for the accounting period that impact the balance sheet accounts are recreated, and each account impacted is either debited or credited for the transaction until the change in the account for the year is explained. When recreating the transactions, all debits and credits to cash and cash equivalents are placed in a cash and cash equivalent T-account divided into operating, investing, financing, and noncash sections. The debits and credits in the cash and cash equivalent T-account provide the information for preparation of the formal cash flow statement.

The balance sheet T-accounts presented below provide the necessary information for preparation of the cash flow statement for Peterson for 20X6. The T-accounts are followed by an explanation of how the system works.

Accounts Receivable	
25,000	
(p) 25,000	

Notes Receivable	

Interest Receivable	
	15,000
	(q) 15,000

Inventory	
40,000	
(r) 40,000	

Investment	
	100,000
(o) 100,000	(e) 200,000

Land	
125,000	
(l) 200,000	(d) 75,000

Property, Plant and Equipment	
450,000	
(i) 400,000	(c) 100,000
(k) 150,000	

Accumulated Depreciation	
	38,125
(c) 40,000	(h) 78,125

Goodwill	
	4,000
	(g) 4,000

Patent	
	3,000
	(f) 3,000

Accounts Payable	
	25,000
	(s) 25,000

Notes Payable-Current	

Interest Payable	
	5,000
	(t) 5,000

Salaries Payable	
	10,000
	(u) 10,000

Income Taxes Payable	
115,000	
(v) 115,000	

Notes Payable	
	200,000
	(l) 200,000

Deferred Taxes	
10,000	
(w) 10,000	

Bonds Payable	
420,000	
(b) 300,000	
(m) 120,000	

Common Stock	
	340,000
	(j) 250,000
	(k) 50,000
	(m) 40,000

Paid-In-Capital In Excess of Par	
	680,000
	(j) 500,000
	(k) 100,000
	(m) 80,000

Retained Earnings	
	439,875
(n) 50,000	(a) 489,875

Cash and Cash Equivalents

Operating Activities:		Cash Receipts		Cash Payments	
Net income	(a)	489,875	(b)	30,000	Gain on extinguishment of bonds
Loss on sale of property	(c)	10,000			
Patent amortization	(f)	3,000	(d)	25,000	Gain on sale of land
Goodwill impairment	(g)	4,000	(e)	50,000	Gain on sale of investment
Depreciation expense	(h)	78,125	(p)	25,000	Increase in accounts receivable
Decrease in interest receivable	(q)	15,000	(r)	40,000	Increase in inventory
Increase in accounts payable	(s)	25,000	(v)	115,000	Decrease in taxes payable
Increase in interest payable	(t)	5,000	(w)	10,000	Decrease in deferred taxes
Increase in salaries payable	(u)	10,000			
Investing Activities:					
Sale of property	(c)	50,000	(i)	400,000	Purchase of property, plant and equipment
Sale of land	(d)	100,000			
Sale of investment	(e)	250,000	(o)	100,000	Purchase of investments
Financing Activities:			(b)	270,000	Extinguishment of bonds
Sale of common stock	(j)	750,000	(n)	50,000	Payment of dividends

Noncash Investing and Financing Activities

1. Issued 10,000 shares of common stock with a par value of $5 and a fair value of $150,000 for property, plant, and equipment with a fair value of $150,000.

2. Issued a long-term note with a fair value of $200,000 for land with a fair value of $200,000.

3. Issued 8,000 shares of common stock with a par value of $5 and a fair value of $120,000 in exchange for bonds with a carrying value of $120,000.

The T-account approach makes it very easy to prepare the cash flow statement. For example, the bonds payable account in the Example 2-8 assumptions decreased by $420,000 from 12/31/X5 to 12/31/X6. Therefore, the $420,000 decrease is placed on the debit side of the liability account. Next, by using journal entry (b) below, the manner in which the approach works can be seen. Entry (b) represents a recreation of the transaction related to the extinguishment of bonds. The bonds payable T-account is debited for $300,000, which explains part of the $420,000 decrease. The gain on extinguishment of bonds is credited to the cash and cash equivalents T-account, because all gains and losses are adjustments to net income when converting from accrual-basis income to cash-basis income. The $270,000 cash credit is a credit to the cash and cash equivalent T-account in the financing section and represents the cash payment for transaction (b). The gain on extinguishment of bonds is grossed up to its before-tax amount of $30,000; it is grossed up to properly reflect cash from operations and to remove all the noncash gain from the operating section. In addition, the $489,875 income amount already includes a deduction for taxes paid on the gain. Next, entry (m) also causes a change in the bonds payable account. The bonds payable account is debited for $120,000, which explains the remaining $120,000 of the $420,000 decrease. Common stock is credited for $40,000 and paid-in-capital is credited for the remaining $80,000. Because this transaction is a noncash financing transaction, a narrative comment must be placed in the noncash investing and financing section of the cash and cash equivalent T-account. After entry (m), the change in the bonds payable account of $420,000 has been fully explained.

No journal entries are provided for current assets and current liabilities that have an impact on the income statement, such as accounts receivable and accounts payable. The entries for these items were made directly in the T-accounts when converting accrual income to cash-basis income. A review of the comparative balance sheets in Example 2-8 reveals that accounts receivable for the year, which relates to sales on the income statement, increased by $25,000. This increase is placed on the debit side of the accounts receivable T-account. In entry (p), which is made directly to the T-accounts, accounts receivable is debited for $25,000 and the cash and cash equivalents account is credited in the operating section for the same amount as an increase in receivables. Therefore, the increase in receivables represents a decrease in cash from operations because part of the sales for the year on the accrual basis has not been collected. Accounts payable increased for the year, and accounts payable relates to cost of sales on the income statement. The accounts payable T-account is credited for the increase, and the cash and cash equivalents T-account is debited in the operations section. The increase in accounts payable represents an increase in cash from operations. The purchase of merchandise for the year on the accrual basis is greater than the amount actually paid because of the increase in accounts payable. Therefore, cash is greater on a cash basis than on the accrual basis. This T-account approach represents a simple, but effective, method of converting accrual-basis income to a cash basis.

Listed below are the journal entries that support the information used in the T-account approach. All entries are provided except for changes in current assets and current liabilities that have an impact upon the income statement. Entries for changes in current assets and current liabilities are made directly in the T-accounts.

Journal Entries:

	Debit	Credit
(a) Cash and Cash Equivalents	489,875	
Retained Earnings		489,875
Recognition of Accrual Income		

	Debit	Credit
(b) Bonds Payable	300,000	
Gain on Extinguishment of Bonds		30,000
Cash		270,000
Retirement of Bonds and Included in the $30,000 is the Tax Payment of $14,100 on the Gain		
(c) Cash	50,000	
Accumulated Depreciation	40,000	
Loss on Sale of Property	10,000	
Property, Plant and Equipment		100,000
Sale of Property, Plant and Equipment		
(d) Cash	100,000	
Land		75,000
Gain on Sale of Land		25,000
Sale of Land		
(e) Cash	250,000	
Investments		200,000
Gain on Sale of Investment		50,000
Sale of Investments		
(f) Patent Amortization	3,000	
Patent		3,000
Patent Amortization for the Year		
(g) Goodwill Impairment	4,000	
Goodwill		
Goodwill Impairment for the Year		4,000
(h) Depreciation Expense	78,125	
Accumulated Depreciation		78,125
Depreciation Expense for the Year		
(i) Property, Plant and Equipment	400,000	
Cash		400,000
Purchase of Property, Plant and Equipment		
(j) Cash	750,000	
Common Stock		250,000
Paid-In-Capital in Excess of Par		500,000
Sale of Common Stock		
(k) Property, Plant and Equipment	150,000	
Common Stock		50,000
Paid-In-Capital in Excess of Par		100,000
Exchange of Stock for Property		
(l) Land	200,000	
Notes Payable		200,000
Purchase of Land by Issuing Note		
(m) Bonds Payable	120,000	
Common Stock		40,000
Paid-In-Capital in Excess of Par		80,000
Exchanged Stock for Bonds		

(n) Retained Earnings	50,000	
Cash		50,000
Payment of Dividends		
(o) Investment	100,000	
Cash		100,000
Purchase of an Investment		

Using the information from the Cash and Cash Equivalent T-account, the cash flow statement for 20X6 can be prepared.

Peterson Enterprises
Statement of Cash Flows
For the Year Ended December 31, 20X6

Cash Flows from Operating Activities:		
Net Income		$489,875
Adjustments to reconcile net income to cash provided by operating activities:		
Gain on extinguishment of bonds	$(30,000)	
Gain on sale of land	(25,000)	
Gain on sale of investment	(50,000)	
Loss on sale of property, plant and equipment	10,000	
Patent amortization	3,000	
Goodwill impairment	4,000	
Depreciation expense	78,125	
Increase in accounts receivable	(25,000)	
Increase in inventory	(40,000)	
Decrease in taxes payable	(115,000)	
Decrease in deferred taxes	(10,000)	
Decrease in interest receivable	15,000	
Increase in accounts payable	25,000	
Increase in interest payable	5,000	
Increase in salaries payable	10,000	
Total net income adjustments		(144,875)
Net cash provided by operating activities		$345,000
Cash Flows from Investing Activities:		
Purchase of property, plant and equipment	$(400,000)	
Purchase of investments	(100,000)	
Sale of property, plant and equipment	50,000	
Sale of land	100,000	
Sale of investments	250,000	
Net cash flows from investing activities		(100,000)
Cash Flows from Financing Activities:		
Extinguishment of bonds	$(270,000)	
Payment of cash dividends	(50,000)	
Sale of common stock	750,000	
Net cash flows from financing activities		430,000

Net increase in cash and cash equivalents		$675,000
Cash and cash equivalents at beginning of year		400,000
Cash and cash equivalents at end of year		$1,075,000
Supplemental Schedule of Disclosures of Cash Flow Information:		
Cash paid during the year for:		
Interest (net of capitalized amounts)	$70,000	
Income taxes	450,000	

Supplemental Schedule of Noncash Investing and Financing Activities

1. Peterson issued 10,000 shares of common stock with a par value of $5 and a market value of $150,000 for property, plant, and equipment with a market value of $150,000.
2. Peterson exchanged a long-term note with a fair value of $200,000 for land with a fair value of $200,000.
3. Peterson issued 8,000 shares of common stock with a par value of $5 and a fair value of $120,000 in exchange for bonds with a carrying value of $120,000.

Disclosure of Accounting Policy

For the purpose of the statement of cash flows, Peterson considers cash equivalents to be all highly liquid securities with an original maturity of three months or less.

The cash flow statement is divided into three major sections—an operating activities section, an investing activities section, and a financing activities section. In addition, the statement contains two supplemental schedules and a disclosure of Peterson's accounting policy relative to what is included in cash equivalents. The supplemental schedule of disclosures of cash flow information shows the amount of interest and income taxes paid for the year. The amounts disclosed are computed as follows:

		Income tax expense	$320,900
Interest expense	$75,000	Taxes paid on extraordinary gain	14,100
Increase in interest payable	(5,000)	Decrease in taxes payable	115,000
Cash paid for interest	$70,000	Cash paid for income taxes	$450,000

The second supplemental schedule is a schedule of noncash investing and financing transactions. The section contains transactions of an investing or financing nature where cash is not involved. Also, the cash flow statement is prepared in such a way as to reconcile beginning cash and cash equivalents of $400,000 with ending cash and cash equivalents of $1,075,000.

Example 2-8 illustrated the preparation of a cash flow statement using the T-account approach with the indirect method being used in the preparation of the operating section of the statement. Assuming the same information as in Example 2-8, a worksheet approach is used in the preparation of the statement, and the direct method is used for the operating section of the statement.

The worksheet is prepared using all balance sheet account balances for December 31, 20X5, and December 31, 20X6. The 20X5 and 20X6 columns have been reversed from the order presented in the Example 2-8 assumptions. In addition, debit and credit columns are used to recreate the transactions occurring during 20X6 that caused the increase or decrease in the account balances except for the change in cash and cash equivalents. The change in cash and cash equivalents is included at the bottom of the assets so that the worksheet will balance. Next, the income statement for 20X6 is included as part of the worksheet, and is placed just below the balance sheet accounts. The income statement is designated as the operating activities section of the cash flow statement. For purposes of computing the information for the cash flow statement, revenue items are viewed as debits (cash inflows) and expense items (the items with brackets) are considered credits (cash outflows). Therefore, when transactions for the year are recreated to explain changes in balance sheet accounts, certain income statement items are debited or credited. A credit to a revenue item, such as the credit to sales, is a deduction to arrive at cash-basis sales. A debit to a revenue item, such as interest income, is an addition to the revenue account to arrive at cash-basis revenue because revenue items are viewed as debits. Expense items are viewed as credits; a credit to an expense, such as the $40,000 credit to cost of sales, is a deduction, and a debit is an addition. Below the income statement are the investing and financing sections of the cash flow statement, as well as a noncash investing and financing section. As transactions for the year are recreated, entries involving cash or cash equivalents are not debited or credited to cash, but the cash impact of the transaction is placed either in the investing or financing section of the worksheet. For example, notice in (d) that land with a cost basis of $75,000 was sold for $100,000 and a gain of $25,000 was reported in the income statement. When recreating the transaction, land is credited for $75,000, the gain of $25,000 is removed from the income statement by crediting the gain on sale of land, and the $100,000 cash receipt is included under the investing section as a debit or a $100,000 increase in cash. Debits under the investing, and financing sections represent cash inflows and credits represent cash outflows. The gain of $25,000 is removed from the income statement because it increases income and overstates cash from sale of the land. Cash from the land sale was $100,000 and was included in the investing section of the worksheet. If the gain of $25,000 was not removed from the income statement, it would be included as cash from operations and cash from the land sale would be overstated by $25,000. All transactions for the year are recreated and debited or credited in the worksheet in a similar manner. The column to the far right on the worksheet under the operating, investing, and financing sections represents cash flow for the year, and the formal cash flow statement can be prepared directly from the right column. However, if the direct method is used for the operating section, the cash flow from operations is taken directly from the right-hand column. When the direct method is used, a separate schedule showing the reconciliation of accrual-basis income to net cash provided by operations, which is the same as the indirect method, must be presented. The operating activities section using the indirect method or the reconciliation for the direct method may be prepared directly from the worksheet by beginning with net income of

$489,875 and adding all items in the debit column under the operating activities section and deducting all credit items under the operating section.

At the very bottom of the worksheet is a section for noncash investing and financing transactions, such as the exchange of stock for property, plant, and equipment. When one of the transactions related to property, plant, and equipment was recreated, property, plant, and equipment was debited and common stock and paid-in-capital were credited. There was no impact upon cash, but the transaction was an investing activity. Such transactions are included at the bottom of the worksheet in narrative format.

The worksheet for the preparation of the cash flow statement is presented as follows:

Peterson Enterprises
Worksheet for Preparation of Cash Flow Statement

	12/31/X5		Debits		Credits	12/31/X6
Cash and Cash Equivalents	$400,000					$1,075,000
Accounts Receivable	550,000	(p)	25,000			575,000
Notes Receivable	100,000					100,000
Interest Receivable	20,000			(q)	15,000	5,000
Inventory	680,000	(r)	40,000			720,000
Investment	800,000	(o)	100,000	(e)	200,000	700,000
Land	750,000	(l)	200,000	(d)	75,000	875,000
Property, Plant and Equipment	1,250,000	(k) (i)	150,000 400,000	(c)	100,000	1,700,000
Accumulated Depreciation	(200,000)	(c)	40,000	(h)	78,125	(238,125)
Goodwill	80,000			(g)	4,000	76,000
Patent	30,000			(f)	3,000	27,000
Increase in Cash and Cash Equivalents			675,000			
Totals	$4,460,000		$1,630,000		$475,125	$5,614,875
Accounts Payable	$575,000			(s)	25,000	$600,000
Notes Payable—Current	75,000					75,000
Interest Payable	35,000			(t)	5,000	40,000
Salaries Payable	40,000			(u)	10,000	50,000
Income Taxes Payable	300,000	(v)	115,000			185,000
Notes Payable	0			(l)	200,000	200,000
Deferred Taxes	150,000	(w)	10,000			140,000
Bonds Payable	1,000,000	(b) (m)	300,000 120,000			580,000
Common Stock	800,000			(j) (m) (k)	40,000 50,000 250,000	1,140,000
Paid-in-Capital in Excess of Par	1,000,000			(j) (m) (k)	500,000 80,000 100,000	1,680,000
Retained Earnings	485,000	(n)	50,000	(a)	489,875	924,875
Total Liabilities and Stockholders' Equity	$4,460,000		$595,000		$1,749,875	$5,614,875
Operating Section						
Sales	$3,200,000			(p)	25,000	$3,175,000
Interest Income	60,000	(q)	15,000			75,000
Gain on Sale of Investment	50,000			(e)	50,000	0
Gain on Sale of Land	25,000			(d)	25,000	0
Gain on Extinguishment of Bonds	30,000			(b)	30,000	0
Cost of Sales	(1,560,000)	(s)	25,000	(r)	40,000	(1,575,000)
Salary Expense	(600,000)	(u)	10,000			(590,000)
Selling Expense	(120,000)					(120,000)
Administration Expense	(100,000)					(100,000)
Depreciation Expense	(78,125)	(h)	78,125			0

	12/31/X5		Debits		Credits	12/31/X6
Goodwill Impairment	(4,000)	(g)	4,000			0
Patent Amortization	(3,000)	(f)	3,000			0
Interest Expense	(75,000)	(t)	5,000			(70,000)
Loss on Sale of Property, Plant and Equipment	(10,000)	(c)	10,000			0
Income Tax Expense:						
Current	(320,900)			(v)	115,000	
Tax on Bond Extinguishment	(14,100)					(450,000)
Deferred	10,000			(w)	10,000	0
Net Income	$489,875	(a)	489,875			0
Net Cash from Operating Activities						$345,000
Investing Section						
Sale of Property, Plant and Equipment		(c)	50,000			50,000
Sale of Land		(d)	100,000			100,000
Sale of Investments		(e)	250,000			250,000
Purchase of Property, Plant and Equipment				(i)	400,000	(400,000)
Purchase of Investments				(o)	100,000	(100,000)
Net Cash from Investing Activities						$(100,000)
Financing Section						
Extinguishment of Bonds				(b)	270,000	$(270,000)
Sale of Common Stock		(j)	750,000			750,000
Payment of Dividends				(n)	50,000	(50,000)
Net Cash from Financing Activities						$430,000
Total Adjustments			$1,790,000		$1,115,000	
Increase in Cash						$675,000

Noncash Investing and Financing Section

1. Peterson issued 10,000 shares of common stock with a par value of $5 and a market value of $150,000 for property, plant, and equipment with a market value of $150,000.
2. Peterson exchanged a long-term note with a fair value of $200,000 for land with a fair value of $200,000.
3. Peterson issued 8,000 shares of common stock with a par value of $5 and a fair value of $120,000 in exchange for bonds with a carrying value of $120,000.

The gain from bond extinguishment is grossed up to $30,000 and the tax of $14,100 is placed with the income tax expense in order to compute the total tax paid in cash. (See the prior discussion on why the gain is grossed up to a pretax amount.)

Information from the worksheet can now be used to prepare the formal cash flow statement for Peterson for 20X6. The direct approach is used for the operating section and, therefore, information for the preparation is taken directly from the right-hand column of the worksheet. Cash paid to suppliers and employees of $2,165,000 consists of cost of sales of $1,575,000 and salary expense of $590,000. Cash paid for other operating expenses of $220,000 is composed of the $120,000 selling expense and the $100,000 administrative expense.

Because the direct method is used in preparing the operating section, a reconciliation of accrual basis income to cash from operations must be prepared.

It is prepared below in a separate schedule using income of $489,875 and the debits and credits from the operating section of the worksheet.

Peterson Enterprises Statement of Cash Flows For the Year Ended December 31, 20X6

Cash Flows from Operating Activities:		
Cash collected from customers	$3,175,000	
Cash collected from interest	75,000	
Cash paid to suppliers and employees	(2,165,000)	
Cash interest paid	(70,000)	
Cash paid for income taxes	(450,000)	
Cash paid for other operating expenses	(220,000)	
Net cash provided from operating activities		$345,000
Cash Flows from Investing Activities:		
Purchase of property, plant and equipment	$(400,000)	
Purchase of investments	(100,000)	
Sale of property, plant and equipment	50,000	
Sale of land	100,000	
Sale of investments	250,000	
Net cash flows from investing activities		(100,000)
Cash Flows from Financing Activities:		
Extinguishment of bonds	$(270,000)	
Payment of cash dividends	(50,000)	
Sale of common stock	750,000	
Net cash flows from financing activities		430,000
Net increase in cash and cash equivalents		$675,000
Cash and cash equivalents at beginning of year		400,000
Cash and cash equivalents at end of year		$1,075,000
Reconciliation of Net Income to Net Cash Provided by Operating Activities:		
Net income		$489,875
Adjustments to reconcile net income to cash provided by operating activities:		
Gain on extinguishment of bonds	$(30,000)	
Gain on sale of land	(25,000)	
Gain on sale of investment	(50,000)	
Loss on sale of property, plant and equipment	10,000	
Patent amortization	3,000	
Goodwill impairment	4,000	
Depreciation expense	78,125	
Increase in accounts receivable	(25,000)	
Increase in inventory	(40,000)	
Decrease in taxes payable	(115,000)	
Decrease in deferred taxes	(10,000)	
Decrease in interest receivable	15,000	
Increase in accounts payable	25,000	

Increase in interest payable	5,000	
Increase in salaries payable	10,000	
Total net income adjustments		(144,875)
Net cash provided by operating activities		$345,000

Supplemental Schedule of Noncash Investing and Financing Activities:

1. Peterson issued 10,000 shares of common stock with a par value of $5 and a market value of $150,000 for property, plant, and equipment with a market value of $150,000.
2. Peterson exchanged a long-term note with a fair value of $200,000 for land with a fair value of $200,000.
3. Peterson issued 8,000 shares of common stock with a par value of $5 and a fair value of $120,000 in exchange for bonds with a carrying value of $120,000.

Disclosure of Accounting Policy

For the purpose of the statement of cash flows, Peterson considers cash equivalents to be all highly liquid securities with an original maturity of three months or less.

Recent Changes

ASU 2016-15 gives specific guidance on how certain cash receipts and cash payments are presented and classified in the statement of cash flows. U.S. GAAP was either unclear or did not include guidance on classifying these items. The amendments are effective for public business entities for fiscal years beginning after December 15, 2017 and interim periods within those fiscal years. For all other entities, the amendments are effective for fiscal years beginning after December 15, 2018 and interim periods within fiscal years beginning after December 15, 2019.

Topic 235: Notes to Financial Statements

Topic 235, *Notes to Financial Statements*, contains the following subtopics:

10 Overall

910 Contractors—Construction*

912 Contractors—Federal Government*

932 Extractive Activities—Oil and Gas*

942 Financial Services—Depository and Lending*

944 Financial Services—Insurance*

946 Financial Services—Investment Companies*

962 Plan Accounting—Defined Contribution Pension Plans*

972 Real Estate—Common Interest Realty Associations*

* See the corresponding topic in Chapter 9 for coverage of this shared subtopic.

Flowchart and General Discussion

ASC 235 establishes disclosure requirements for significant accounting policies used by a reporting entity in the preparation of basic financial statements. This topic provides for some uniformity and comparability of accounting information by providing guidelines for the content and format of disclosures relating to accounting policies.

Flowchart 2-3 outlines the basic decision process involved in determining if a particular accounting policy must be disclosed. Accounting policies of a business enterprise need be disclosed only if the financial statements to be issued are prepared in conformance with U.S. generally accepted accounting principles (U.S. GAAP) (Block 1). The policies must be disclosed, even though *all* basic financial statements (income statement, balance sheet, and cash flow statement) are *not* prepared. As long as at least one basic statement is presented in conformance with U.S. GAAP, accounting policies must be disclosed.

Flowchart 2-3

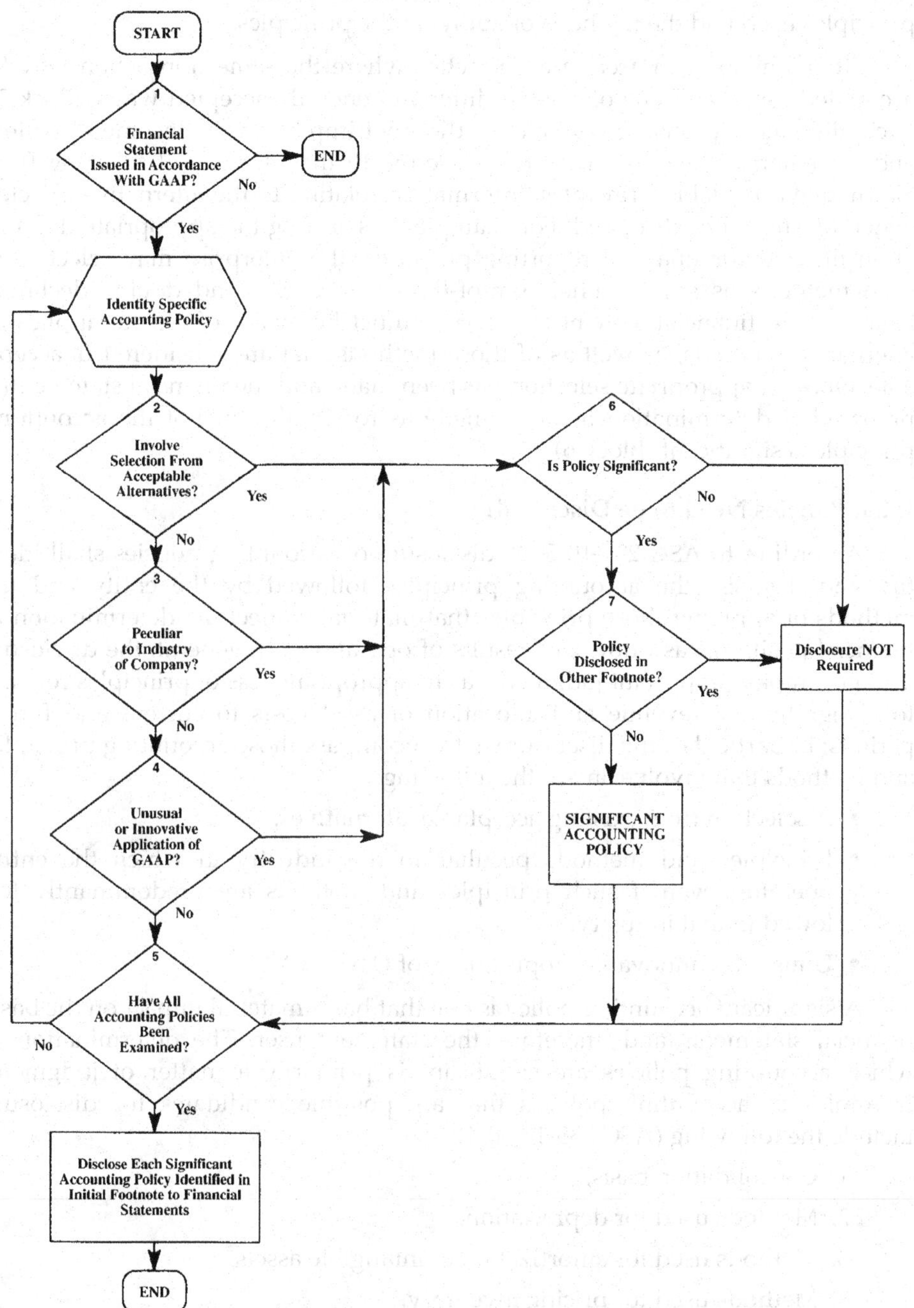

Accounting policies are generally accepted accounting principles used in the preparation of financial reports. These policies include both the accounting principles used and the methods of applying the principles.

Situations exist in accounting practice where the same transaction may be accounted for in any one of several different generally accepted ways (Block 2). Each alternative principle may have a different impact on the income statement and the balance sheet. If an entity is faced with the situation of selecting from alternative acceptable principles, information relating to the alternative selected generally should be disclosed. For example, in selecting the appropriate depreciation method for financial reporting purposes, the enterprise may select from such methods as straight-line, sum-of-the-years' digits, and double declining balance. The financial statement preparer must be aware of all the applicable alternative methods, as well as of those methods that are considered unacceptable. Once an appropriate selection has been made and the financial statement(s) prepared, a determination must be made as to whether or not the accounting principle is significant (Block 6).

What Policies Need to be Disclosed?

According to ASC 235-10-50-3, disclosure of accounting policies shall identify and describe the accounting principles followed by the entity and the methods of applying those principles that materially affect the determination of financial position, cash flows, or results of operations. In general, the disclosure is to encompass important judgments as to appropriateness of principles relating to recognition of revenue and allocation of asset costs to current and future periods; in particular, the disclosure is to encompass those accounting principles and methods that involve any of the following:

- A selection from existing acceptable alternatives.
- Principles and methods peculiar to the industry in which the entity operates, even if such principles and methods are predominantly followed in that industry.
- Unusual or innovative applications of U.S. GAAP.

A significant accounting policy is one that has a material impact on the basic financial statements and, therefore, the statement user. The determination of which accounting policies are significant is primarily a matter of judgment. Examples of accounting policies that are possible candidates for disclosure include the following (ASC 235-10-50-4):

1. Consolidation basis,
2. Methods used for depreciation,
3. Methods used for amortization of intangible assets,
4. Methods used for pricing inventory,
5. Methods of recognizing profit on long-term construction contracts, and
6. Recognition of revenue from franchising and leasing operations.

This list includes only examples and is not meant to be all-inclusive or to apply to every entity. There may be situations where an enterprise has a policy relating to one of the items listed above, yet disclosure may not be required if the policy is not considered significant. The list is helpful in providing some guidance as to the determination of significant accounting policies.

Selection from Existing Acceptable Alternative Accounting Principles

The impact of the accounting policy on the user of the financial information is difficult to assess. However, if entity A has a material amount of inventory and uses LIFO inventory pricing, and entity B, in a similar situation, uses FIFO inventory pricing, the inventory costs and the cost of goods sold during the period would not be comparable. The lack of comparison is due to the difference in the accounting policy regarding inventory pricing. Each entity has selected a different acceptable accounting procedure for determining the cost of inventory. If each entity disclosed the accounting policy used, the informed reader would be able to assess more clearly the performance of each entity. In this case, disclosure of the accounting policy would provide some measure of uniformity and comparability between the two entities.

If a specific accounting policy results from the selection among acceptable alternatives and is determined to be a significant policy, it will require disclosure under the provisions of ASC 235 if it is not disclosed elsewhere in the notes or in the financial statements (Block 7). The intent of ASC 235 is to avoid duplication of information presented.

Policies Relating to Particular Industries

Some industries use specialized accounting principles and procedures in recording and reporting financial information (Block 3). A specialized accounting principle or procedure may be common to the entity's industry, but it differs from those normally followed by the majority of other industries. If the specialized accounting principle or procedure is significant (Block 6), and is not disclosed elsewhere in the notes or in the financial statements (Block 7), appropriate disclosure is required.

An example of a specialized industry policy is where the operating cycle is considered to be longer than one year. This allows the inclusion in current assets of items that will not be converted into cash or consumed within one year. Most industries assume an operating cycle of one year and classify assets as current on this basis.

Even though entities in a particular industry use a given specialized accounting principle or procedure, it is necessary to disclose the policy, because the statement user may not be aware of the fact that the policy is peculiar to the industry. From a broad viewpoint, specialized accounting principles and procedures are, in effect, a selection from alternative acceptable accounting policies. An entity in an industry with specialized practices may elect not to follow those practices.

Unusual or Innovative Accounting Policy Application

ASC 235 specifies that any generally accepted accounting principle that is applied in an unusual or innovative manner (Block 4) should be disclosed if the application is significant (Block 6) and is not disclosed elsewhere in the notes or financial statements (Block 7). By their very nature, unusual or innovative accounting policies are few in number. One example might be an unusual method of accounting for work-in-process inventory for a manufacturing entity. Accounting for work-in-process inventory can be a complex problem in cost accounting, especially when the manufacturing process is sophisticated. In an effort to simplify the accounting process, some manufacturing entities have adopted the policy of an instantaneous production process (i.e., inventories are either raw materials or finished goods, but there is never a work-in-process inventory). Under this system, goods that are in process are considered merely to be raw materials in a different form. Labor and overhead costs are accumulated in a clearing account, rather than applied to work-in-process inventory. The balance in the clearing accounts at any balance sheet date is considered current assets and is classified with inventories. When applied appropriately, this accounting policy is certainly unusual and innovative; and disclosure may be required if work-in-process inventory is considered to be material.

Format of Disclosures

ASC 235 allows for some flexibility in the method of disclosure, but requires that any significant accounting policy be presented in such a manner as to be an integral part of the basic financial statements. It is recommended that disclosures be identified under the heading "Summary of Significant Accounting Policies" and be located as the first note to the financial statements, or preceding the first note.

Recent Changes

ASU 2014-09, *Revenue from Contracts with Customers*, supersedes most revenue recognition requirements in ASC 605, Revenue Recognition. ASU 2014-09 applies to all contracts to provide goods or services to customers except for leases, insurance contracts, financial instruments, and certain guarantees and nonmonetary exchanges.

Underlying ASU 2014-09 is the following core principle: Recognize revenue to depict the transfer of promised goods or services to customers in an amount that reflects the consideration to which the selling entity expects to be entitled to receive in exchange for those goods or services.

Public entities are required to adopt ASU 2014-09 for annual reporting periods beginning after December 15, 2016, including interim reporting periods within that reporting period; early application is not permitted. Nonpublic entities are required to adopt ASU 2014-09 for annual reporting periods beginning after December 15, 2017, and for interim and annual reporting periods after those reporting periods. Nonpublic entities may elect early application, but no earlier than the effective date for public entities. On April 1, 2015, the FASB voted to extend the effective dates for public and nonpublic entities for an additional year but permit early adoption as of the original effective dates.

Topic 250: Accounting Changes and Error Corrections

Topic 250, *Accounting Changes and Error Corrections*, contains three subtopics:

10 Overall

978 Real Estate—Time-Sharing Activities *

980 Regulated Operations *

* See the corresponding topic in Chapter 9 for coverage of this shared subtopic.

ASC 250 deals with reporting and disclosing accounting changes and accounting errors. The major accounting changes addressed in ASC 250 are changes in accounting principles, changes in accounting estimates, and changes in reporting entities. The reporting of errors in previously issued financial statements is not an accounting change, but it is also addressed in ASC 250.

Flowchart 2-4 depicts the general accounting principles and reporting requirements of ASC 250. The major decision points have been numbered for reference in the discussions that follow.

Flowchart 2-4

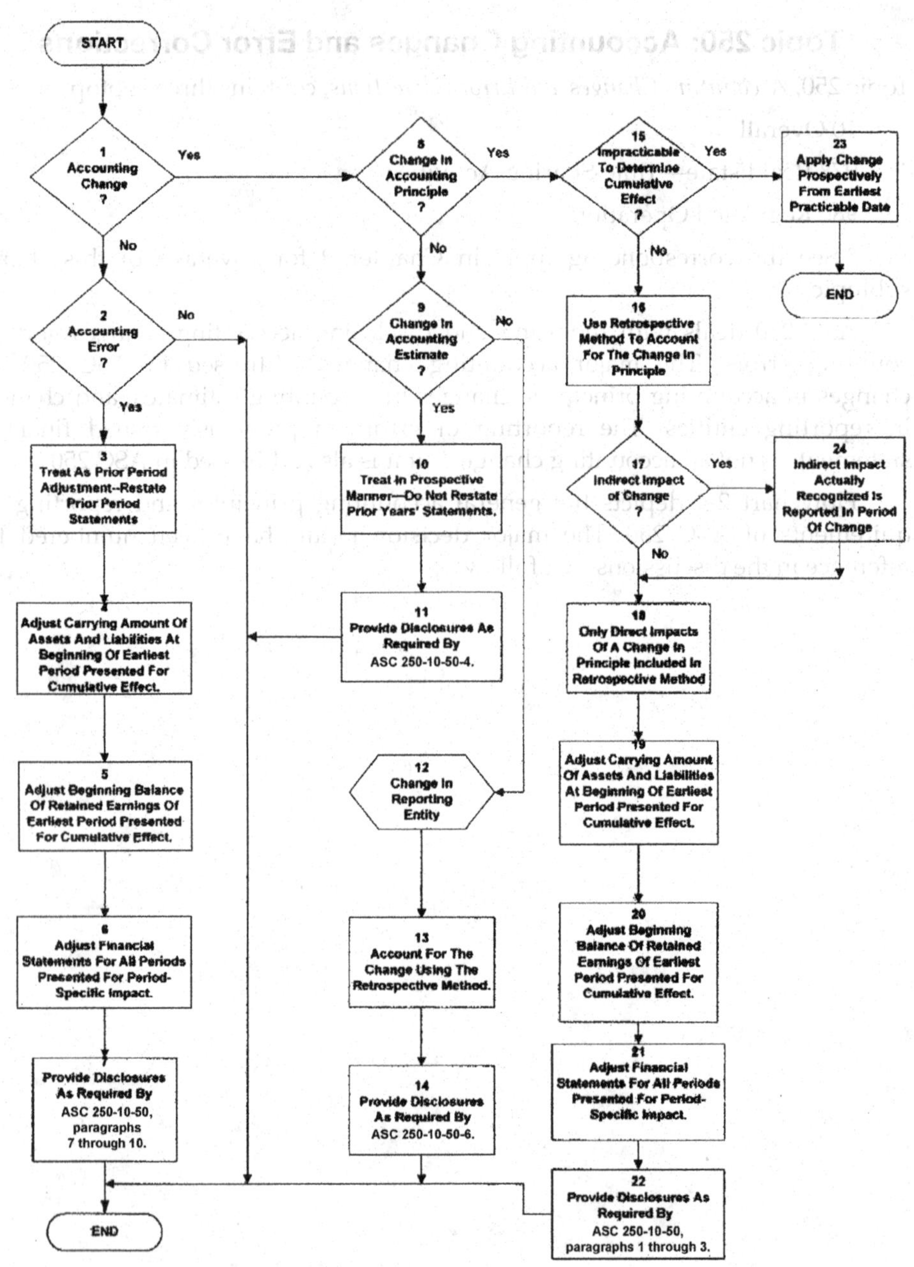

Changes in Accounting Principles—General Discussion

A change in accounting principle (Block 8) is a change from one generally accepted accounting principle to another. Examples include a change from specific identification to a first-in-first-out inventory method, changes in the computation of the cost elements included in inventory, and changes in the method of revenue recognition. A change from an accounting principle that is *not* generally accepted to one that *is* generally accepted is treated as an error correction rather than as a change in accounting principle. In addition, the following are not treated as changes in accounting principles: adoption of an accounting principle for transactions that occur for the first time, such as adopting the leasing standard for a lease when the company has no other lease activities, and modification or adoption of an accounting principle for transactions or events that are clearly different from those that have occurred in the past. An accounting principle may be changed when one of the following two conditions are met: a new generally accepted accounting standard that requires the change is issued or the reporting entity can justify that a change to an alternative accounting principle is preferable (ASC 250-10-45-2).

A private company that makes an accounting policy election to apply the guidance in the "Accounting Alternative Subsections" for the first time need not justify that the use of the accounting alternative is preferable.

When a newly issued standard requiring a change in accounting principle does not specify the method of transition to the new principle, the provisions of ASC 250 should be used when making the transition (ASC 250-10-45-3).

Retrospective Method of Reporting a Change in Accounting Principles

If it is practicable to apply the retrospective method, a change in accounting principle is accounted for by using a retrospective application (Block 16) to all prior periods. The retrospective method is applied in the following manner:

1. Compute the cumulative effect of changing to the new accounting method for accounting periods prior to the earliest accounting period presented and report the impact of the change in the beginning balances of assets and/or liabilities affected by the change at the beginning of the first accounting period presented (Block 19),

2. Adjust the beginning balance of retained earnings (or similar component of equity, such as the unrestricted net assets of a not-for-profit entity) in the same accounting period in which the assets and/or liabilities are adjusted (Block 20), and

3. Restate all prior accounting periods presented using period-specific application to reflect the impact of the change in individual accounting periods presented (Block 21) (ASC 250-10-45-5).

The cumulative effect adjustment reported in the earliest period presented is computed as the difference between what the balances are in assets, liabilities, and retained earnings using the old method versus what the balances would have been if the new method had been used prior to the earliest period presented. The period-specific application is the adjustments to assets, liabilities, equity, and/or income as a result of applying the new accounting method to a specific accounting period presented. Only the direct effects (Block 18) of applying the new accounting standards, including any effects on tax, should be used when applying the retrospective application. Indirect effects (Block 17), such as the impact of a change in a bonus in a prior accounting period as a result of a change in income from a retrospective application of a changed accounting principle, are not included in the retrospective application. If the indirect effects are actually reported—for example, the bonus in prior years is recomputed and recognized as a result of the change in accounting principle—they are reported in the accounting period that the change is made (Block 24) (ASC 250-10-45-8).

If it is impracticable to determine the period-specific impact on prior periods presented, but the cumulative effect on prior periods can be computed, the cumulative effect adjustment to the assets and liabilities and beginning retained earnings should be reported as described in 1 and 2 above. However, the restatement of prior accounting periods using a period-specific application as noted in 3 above would not be used, as it is impracticable to make that determination. When it is impracticable to determine the cumulative impact (Block 15) of a change in accounting principle on prior accounting periods, the change in principle should be applied in a prospective manner using the earliest date that is practicable (Block 23). A typical example of the prospective reporting of a change in accounting principle is a change to the last-in, first-out (LIFO) method of reporting inventory from another acceptable inventory method. ASC 250 provides guidelines as to when an entity may apply the impracticability option when accounting for a change in accounting principle using the retrospective method. An entity may apply the impracticability option when one of the following criteria is met:

1. The entity is unable to apply the method after making all reasonable effort,
2. The entity cannot independently substantiate assumptions about intent of management in prior accounting periods, or
3. The entity cannot distinguish information about:
    a. Estimates as they relate to availability at the date of the prior period, and
    b. Evidence of circumstances in existence on the dates that amounts would be measured, reported, or disclosed because the method requires significant estimates (ASC 250-10-45-9).

A change in accounting principle must be justified by the entity making the change on the basis that an alternative acceptable accounting principle selected is preferable to the acceptable accounting principle previously used. The preferability requirement is satisfied when a new accounting principle is created, a preference is expressed for an existing accounting principle, or an accounting principle is rejected by the issuance of a new accounting principle. All other types of changes in accounting principles must be justified by the entity making the change. However, it is not acceptable to change an accounting principle for a single nonrecurring event or for situations that will be terminated or discontinued (ASC 250-10-45, paragraphs 12 and 13).

When an entity makes a change in accounting principle during an interim accounting period, the change is accounted for using the retrospective method, as discussed above, with one exception: the entity cannot apply the impracticability option to interim accounting periods prior to the interim period when the change is made within the same fiscal year. If the entity cannot apply the retrospective method to pre-change interim periods in the same fiscal year, the entity is required to wait and apply the accounting change at the beginning of the next fiscal year. When an entity changes an accounting principle in the fourth quarter of an annual period and does not provide the disclosures for such a change as specified by ASC 270-10-50-1 (see Topic 270 later in this chapter) in either annual or fourth-quarter reports, the disclosures listed in ASC 250-10-50-1 should be provided in the annual report of the year in which the change is made (ASC 250-10-45, paragraphs 14 and 15).

Changes in Accounting Principles—Technical Considerations

One example will be used to illustrate the technical aspects of changes in accounting principles. Assumptions for Example 2-9 are as follows.

Example 2-9
Assumptions for Change in Accounting Principle

1. Financial Enterprises, a December 31 year-end company, has used the average cost method of inventory valuation since January 1, 20X4, the date of inception of the firm. During 20X6, the company elects to change to the FIFO inventory method and can justify the change to FIFO because FIFO better matches revenues and expenses. Financial Enterprises has a 30% tax rate for all years.
2. The impact of the change in principle on inventory and cost of sales is as follows:

	Inventory Value Using		Cost of Sales Amount Using	
Date	**FIFO**	**Average Cost**	**FIFO**	**Average Cost**
1/1/20X4	$0	$0	$0	$0
12/31/20X4	80,000	70,000	270,000	280,000
12/31/20X5	200,000	184,100	528,000	533,900
12/31/20X6	240,000	212,600	520,000	531,500

3. Income statements for 20X4–20X6 using both FIFO and average cost are as follows:

	20X4 Income Statement Using		20X5 Income Statement Using		20X6 Income Statement Using	
	FIFO	Average Cost	FIFO	Average Cost	FIFO	Average Cost
Sales	$1,000,000	$1,000,000	$2,000,000	$2,000,000	$2,000,000	$2,000,000
Cost of Sale	270,000	280,000	528,000	533,900	520,000	531,500
Gross Profit	$730,000	$720,000	$1,472,000	$1,466,100	$1,480,000	$1,468,500
Expenses	400,000	400,000	600,000	600,000	600,000	600,000
Income Before Tax	$330,000	$320,000	$872,000	$866,100	$880,000	$868,500
Tax Expense	99,000	96,000	261,600	259,830	264,000	$260,550
Net Income	$231,000	$224,000	$610,400	$606,270	$616,000	$607,950

4. Statements of financial position (balance sheets) for 20X4–20X6 using both FIFO and average cost are as follows:

	20X4 Statement of Financial Position Using		20X5 Statement of Financial Position Using		20X6 Statement of Financial Position Using	
	FIFO	Average Cost	FIFO	Average Cost	FIFO	Average Cost
Cash	$8,250,000	$8,250,000	$8,803,000	$8,806,000	$9,231,400	$9,236,170
Inventory	80,000	70,000	200,000	184,100	240,000	212,600
Property	2,000,000	2,000,000	2,000,000	2,000,000	2,000,000	2,000,000
Total Assets	$10,330,000	$10,320,000	$11,003,000	$10,990,100	$11,471,400	$11,448,770
Taxes Payable	$99,000	$96,000	$261,600	$259,830	$264,000	$260,550
Dividends Payable	100,000	100,000	150,000	150,000	200,000	200,000
Common Stock	1,000,000	1,000,000	1,000,000	1,000,000	1,000,000	1,000,000
Paid-in-Capital	9,000,000	9,000,000	9,000,000	9,000,000	9,000,000	9,000,000
Retained Earnings	131,000	124,000	591,400	580,270	1,007,400	988,220
Total Liabilities & Equity	$10,330,000	$10,320,000	$11,003,000	$10,990,100	$11,471,400	$11,448,770

5. Retained earnings statements for 20X6 and 20X5 using both the FIFO and average cost method are as follows:

Financial Enterprises
Retained Earnings Statement
For the Years Ending December 31, 20X6 and 20X5

	20X6		20X5	
	FIFO	Average Cost	FIFO	Average Cost
Beginning Retained Earnings	$591,400	$580,270	$131,000	$124,000
Income	616,000	607,950	610,400	606,270
Dividends	200,000	200,000	150,000	150,000
Ending Retained Earnings	$1,007,400	$988,220	$591,400	$580,270

6. Cash flow statements for 20X6 and 20X5 using both the FIFO and average cost methods are as follows:

Financial Enterprises Cash Flow Statements For the Years Ending December 31, 20X6 and 20X5

	20X6		20X5	
	FIFO	Average Cost	FIFO	Average Cost
Net Income	$616,000	$607,950	$610,400	$606,270
Increase in Inventory	(40,000)	(28,500)	(120,000)	(114,100)
Increase in Taxes Payable	2,400	720	162,600	163,830
Cash Flow from Operating Activities	$578,400	$580,170	$653,000	$656,000
Cash Dividends	(150,000)	(150,000)	(100,000)	(100,000)
Increase in Cash	$428,400	$430,170	$553,000	$556,000
Beginning Cash Balance	8,803,000	8,806,000	8,250,000	8,250,000
Ending Cash Balance	$9,231,400	$9,236,170	$8,803,000	$8,806,000

7. Financial Enterprises is reporting comparative financial statements for 20X6 and 20X5. Earnings per share information is not required and there is no indirect impact of the change from average cost to FIFO.

Because Financial Enterprises has changed from the average cost method to the FIFO method of inventory costing and can justify the change as a preferable accounting principle, the change is accounted for as a change in principle. Financial Enterprises must account for the change in principle using the retrospective method, which requires a presentation of the 20X6 statements using FIFO and a restatement of the 20X5 financial statements as if the FIFO method had been used, because 20X5 is the earliest year presented. In addition, beginning 20X5 balances in assets, liabilities, and equity items in the balance sheet that are affected by the change are adjusted to reflect the cumulative effect of the change and an adjustment for the change is presented as an adjustment to beginning retained earnings of 20X5. Comparative 20X6 and 20X5 retained earnings statements that reflect the change in principle are shown below. Basic retained earnings statements are taken from Assumption 4.

Financial Enterprises Retained Earnings Statement For the Years Ending December 31, 20X6 and 20X5

	20X6	20X5 as Restated Note 1
Beginning Retained Earnings	$591,400	$124,000
Prior-Period Adjustment: Change in Accounting Principle, Net of Tax of $3,000		7,000
Adjusted Beginning Retained Earnings		$131,000
Income	616,000	610,400
Dividends	200,000	150,000
Ending Retained Earnings	$1,007,400	$591,400

Though the 20X5 retained earnings statement is restated as if FIFO had been used during 20X5, the beginning retained earnings balance is the beginning balance that was originally presented using an average cost basis (Assumption 4). The $7,000 net of tax change is the cumulative effect difference between using average cost and what the amount would have been if FIFO had been used for all periods prior to 20X5. Because Financial had only one year of operations (20X4) prior to 20X5, the earliest year presented, the difference in the inventory valuation for that one year is used in the cumulative effect computation for 20X5 ($80,000 inventory under FIFO – $70,000 under average cost = $10,000 × 1.00 – 30% tax rate = $7,000) (Assumption 2). The $131,000 adjusted beginning retained earnings balance shown for 20X5 is the beginning retained earnings balance that would have been presented if FIFO had been used in all prior periods (Assumption 5). The $610,400 income and the ending retained earnings balance of $591,400 represent the balances that would have been presented if FIFO had been used in 20X4 and 20X5 (Assumptions 3 and 5). In addition, the beginning retained earnings balance of $591,400 has been restated to show what the beginning balance would have been if the FIFO method had been used for all prior periods. The actual ending retained balance presented in the issued 20X5 statements of $580,270 was computed using average cost because the change was not made until 20X6. This balance would have been the beginning 20X6 retained balance if Financial Enterprises had not changed to FIFO. Therefore, the $591,400 balance represents the balance as if FIFO had been used in prior accounting periods (Assumption 5).

Comparative income statements are presented below as if the FIFO method of inventory had been used in both 20X6 and 20X5. Note 1 presents the items in the 20X5 income statement that were changed as a result of applying period-specific changes to all items affected by the change. In addition, Assumption 5 shows the difference between statements presented using FIFO and average cost for both 20X6 and 20X5. (See Note 1 for the changes in the 20X5 restatement and the impact of the change on specific items in the 20X5 statement.)

Financial Enterprises
Income Statement
For the Years Ending December 31, 20X6 and 20X5

	20X6	20X5 as Restated Note 1
Sales	$2,000,000	$2,000,000
Cost of Sale	520,000	528,000
Gross Profit	$1,480,000	$1,472,000
Expenses	600,000	600,000
Income Before Tax	$880,000	$872,000
Tax Expense	264,000	261,600
Net Income	$616,000	$610,400

Presented below are the 20X6 statement of financial position and the restated FIFO 20X5 statement of financial position restated to reflect specific-period adjustments for the change from average cost to FIFO. Note 1 presents the items in the 20X5 income statement that were changed as a result of applying period-specific changes to all items impacted by the change. In addition, Assumption 4 shows the difference between statements presented using FIFO and average cost for both 20X6 and 20X5. (See Note 1 for the changes in the 20X5 restatement and the impact of the change on specific items in the 20X5 statement.)

Financial Enterprises Statement of Financial Position December 31, 20X6 and 20X5

	20X6	20X5 as Restated Note 1
Cash	$9,231,400	$8,803,000
Inventory	240,000	200,000
Property	2,000,000	2,000,000
Total Assets	$11,471,400	$11,003,000
Taxes Payable	264,000	261,600
Dividends Payable	200,000	150,000
Common Stock	1,000,000	1,000,000
Paid-in-Capital	9,000,000	9,000,000
Retained Earnings	1,007,400	591,400
Total Liabilities & Equity	$11,471,400	$11,003,000

Presented below are the 20X6 statement of cash flow and the FIFO 20X5 statement of cash flow restated to reflect specific-period adjustment for the change from average cost to FIFO. Note 1 presents the items in the 20X5 statement of cash flows that were changed as a result of applying period-specific changes to all items affected by the change. In addition, Assumption 6 shows the difference between statements presented using FIFO and average cost for both 20X6 and 20X5. (See Note 1 for the changes in the 20X5 restatement and the impact of the change on specific items in the 20X5 statement.)

Financial Enterprises
Cash Flow Statements
For the Years Ending December 31, 20X6 and 20X5

	20X6	20X5 as Restated Note 1
Net Income	$616,000	$610,400
Increase in Inventory	(40,000)	(120,000)
Increase in Taxes Payable	2,400	162,600
Cash Flow from Operating Activities	578,400	653,000
Cash Dividends	(150,000)	(100,000)
Increase in Cash	428,400	$553,000
Beginning Cash Balance	8,803,000	8,250,000
Ending Cash Balance	$9,231,400	$8,803,000

Note 1 shows the required disclosures for a change in accounting principle using the technical aspects from Example 2-9. Only the line items that were affected by the change are shown; however, the entire financial statement could be presented to show the impact of the change in principle. All information for the disclosure was taken from the assumptions in Example 2-9.

Note 1: Financial elected to change its method of inventory valuation from the average cost method to the first-in-first-out (FIFO) method during 20X6. The average cost method had been used in all prior accounting periods. The inventory valuation method was changed to the FIFO method because the FIFO method more fairly matches revenues and expenses. Financial statements for all prior periods presented have been adjusted by applying the FIFO method retrospectively. Comparative financial statements for the years 20X6 and 20X5 have been presented in this set of financial statements, therefore the financial statement line items for 20X6 and 20X5 that are impacted by the change in accounting principle are presented below:

Income Statement Impact

	20X6			20X5		
Line Item	FIFO	Average Cost	Impact of Change	FIFO	Average Cost	Impact of Change
Cost of Sales	$520,000	$531,500	$11,500	$528,000	$533,900	$5,900
Tax Expense	264,000	260,550	3,450	261,600	259,830	1,770
Net Income	616,000	607,950	8,050	610,400	606,270	4,130

Balance Sheet Impact

	20X6			20X5		
Line Item	**FIFO**	**Average Cost**	**Impact of Change**	**FIFO**	**Average Cost**	**Impact of Change**
Cash	$9,231,400	$9,236,170	$4,770	$8,803,000	$8,806,000	$3,000
Inventory	240,000	212,600	27,400	200,000	184,100	15,900
Tax Payable	264,000	260,550	3,450	261,600	259,830	1,170
Retained Earnings	1,007,400	988,220	19,180	591,400	580,270	11,130

Cash Flow Impact

	20X6			20X5		
Line Item	**FIFO**	**Average Cost**	**Impact of Change**	**FIFO**	**Average Cost**	**Impact of Change**
Net Income	$616,000	$607,950	$8,050	$610,400	$606,270	$4,130
Increase In Inventory	(40,000)	(28,500)	(11,500)	(120,000)	(114,100)	(5,900)
Increase In Taxes Payable	2,400	720	1,680	162,600	163,830	(1,230)
Change in Cash From Operations	$578,400	$580,170	$1,770	$653,000	$656,000	$3,000

The cumulative effect adjustment at the beginning of 20X5 on retained earnings is $10,000 before tax and $7,000 after tax adjustment.

Changes in Accounting Principles—Disclosure Requirements

ASC 250-10-50, paragraphs 1 through 3 (Block 22), specify the disclosure requirements for changes in accounting principles:

- The reason for and the nature of the change including an explanation of why the alternative accounting principle adopted is a preferable accounting standard.
- The method of applying the change in principle:
  - Describe information in prior accounting periods that has been adjusted retrospectively.
  - Disclose the effect of the accounting change on income from continuing operations, net income, and related earnings-per-share amounts (or other performance measurements if applicable).
  - As of the beginning of the earliest accounting period presented, disclose the cumulative effect computed as a result of the accounting change on retained earnings (or other equity amounts or net assets).
  - Disclose the reason that the retrospective method is impracticable when the retrospective method is not used and describe the alternative method used to report the accounting change.
- Disclose the following information when the indirect effects of the change in accounting principle are reported:

— Describe the indirect impact of the principle change and report the amounts and related per-share amounts, if appropriate, recognized in the current accounting period.

— Report the total indirect impact and related per-share amounts, where appropriate, for all prior periods presented, if it is practicable to report this information.

- The impact of the change in principle on income from continuing operations, net income, and related earnings per share (or other appropriate performance measurements) for each post-change interim accounting period in the fiscal year of the change.

Changes in Accounting Estimates—General Discussion

Much of the accounting information presented in the financial statements is based on judgments of future events. These judgments involve estimates for items such as warranty costs to be incurred in the future, the amount of bad debts associated with accounts receivable and the useful life and residual value of depreciable assets. With the passage of time, new information may be obtained that requires a change in assessment about a previous estimate. If the original estimate was the best possible one based on available evidence at the time, and if new information is obtained that indicates the original estimate is not currently a proper assessment of the facts, a change in an accounting estimate (Block 9) has occurred. However, if an original estimate was *not* the best estimate based on then available facts, and if later information indicates that the original estimate was improper, an accounting error has occurred. (See the section headed "Accounting Errors—General Discussion," below.)

A change in an accounting estimate is handled differently from a change in an accounting principle. The change in accounting estimate is accounted for on a prospective basis (i.e., any adjustment is charged to the current or current and future periods) (Block 10). The financial statements of prior periods are not restated.

An accounting change that incorporates elements of both a change in accounting principle and a change in accounting estimate is accounted for as a change in estimate. The FASB decided to account for this type of change as a change in estimate because of the inability of separating the cumulative effect of the change in accounting principle from the impact of the change in estimate.

A change in depreciation, depletion, or amortization methods is not accounted for as a change in principle, but is treated as a change in estimate effected by a change in principle (ASC 250-10-45-18). When a change in accounting estimate is effected by a change in principle, the change must be justified as preferable just as an entity would justify a change in accounting principle (ASC 250-10-45-19). See the general discussion on changes in accounting principles earlier in this chapter for determining when an alternative accounting principle is preferable.

A change in depreciation methods that is planned when the asset is purchased and represents company policy, such as a change from an accelerated method to straight line at some point in the asset's life to fully depreciate the asset over its useful life, would not be treated as a change in principle when the policy is applied on a consistent basis (ASC 250-10-45-20).

Changes in Accounting Estimates—Technical Considerations

Two examples are used to illustrate the technical aspects of changes in accounting estimates. Assumptions for Example 2-10 are as follows.

Example 2-10
Assumptions for Change in Accounting Estimate

1. Hudson Enterprises (Hudson), a December 31 year-end company, purchased equipment on January 1, 20X4, for $110,000. The equipment has a useful life of 10 years and an estimated residual value of $10,000. Hudson used straight-line depreciation.

2. During 20X6, after two years of depreciation have been charged to income, new information is available that indicates that the useful life of the equipment should have been eight years, rather than the 10 years originally used.

This change in the estimated useful life of the equipment qualifies as a change in an accounting estimate. The depreciation charged to income in 20X6 and future years will be affected by this change.

The undepreciated asset balance will be depreciated over the remaining useful life of the equipment. The computations necessary to determine the appropriate charge for depreciation for 20X6 and subsequent periods, assuming straight-line depreciation is used, would be:

Original cost of equipment	$110,000
Estimated residual value	(10,000)
Amount to be depreciated	$100,000
Useful life	÷ 10
Annual depreciation charge	$10,000
Original amount to be depreciated	$100,000
Less: Depreciation for 20X4 and 20X5 ($10,000 × 2)	20,000
Undepreciated balance at beginning of 20X6	$80,000
Revised remaining life (8 years – 2 years)	÷ 6
Current and future period depreciation charge	$13,333

The undepreciated equipment balance at the beginning of the year of change was $80,000, and there were six years remaining in the revised useful life of the asset; therefore, depreciation for years three to eight of the asset's life would be $13,333. The only entry in 20X6 would be the annual depreciation charge, determined by using the new estimated useful life. The entry would be as follows:

Depreciation Expense	13,333	
Accumulated Depreciation—Equipment		13,333

This completes the discussion of Example 2-10 material. Example 2-11 illustrates the accounting for a change in accounting estimate that is affected by a change in accounting principle. Assumptions for Example 2-11 are as follows.

Example 2-11
Assumptions for Change in Accounting Estimate Affected by a Change in Principle

1. Peterson Enterprises (Peterson), a December 31 year-end company, purchased equipment on January 1, 20X4, for $220,000. The equipment has a useful life of 10 years and an estimated residual value of $20,000. Peterson elected to use sum-of-the-years' depreciation for the equipment.
2. During 20X6, after two years of depreciation have been charged to income, Peterson changes from sum-of-the-years' digits depreciation to straight-line. Peterson can justify that straight-line depreciation is a preferable accounting principle.

The change in depreciation methods from sum-of-the-years' digits to straight-line is accounted for as a change in accounting estimate effected by a change in accounting principle. Peterson, in changing from one generally accepted accounting principle for depreciation to another, can justify the change as a preferable accounting principle. In Example 2-11, the carrying value of the asset at the beginning of 20X6 will be depreciated over the remaining eight-year useful life using the straight-line method. Computation of the new amount of depreciation over the remaining eight-year useful life is presented below:

Original cost of equipment	$220,000
Estimated residual value	(20,000)
Amount to be depreciated 1/1/20X4	$200,000

Computation of sum-of-the-years' digit fractions for 20X4 and 20X5 is as follows:

10 (10 + 1)/2 = 55

20X4 fraction = 10/55

20X5 fraction = 9/55

See Topic 360 in Chapter 3 for a detailed discussion of the computation of the fractions for sum-of-the-years'-digits depreciation.

Computation of book value as of 1/1/20X6 is as follows:	
Amount to be depreciated 1/1/20X4	$200,000
Depreciation for 20X4—10/55 X $200,000	(36,364)
Depreciation for 20X6—9/55 X $200,000	(32,727)
Book value 1/1/20X6	$130,909
Remaining useful life	8
Current and future period depreciation charge	$ 16,364

At the beginning of 20X6, the carrying value of the equipment or the undepreciated amount is $130,909. The $130,909 is written off over the remaining eight-year remaining useful life using the straight-line method because Peterson changed from sum-of-the-years'-digits depreciation to straight-line during 20X6. The annual depreciation charge over the remaining eight-year time period is $16,634. There is no catch-up entry for a change in accounting estimate; therefore, the only entry for 20X6 is the normal adjusting entry for depreciation expense. The 20X6 depreciation entry is presented below:

Depreciation Expense	16,364	
Accumulated Depreciation		16,364

Changes in Accounting Estimates—Disclosure Requirements

ASC 250-10-50-4 (Block 11) specifies the disclosure requirements for a change in accounting estimate and a change in accounting estimate effected in the form of a change in principle. The disclosures are as follows:

1. For a change in estimate that affects several accounting periods, such as a change in the useful life of an asset, the impact on income from continuing operations, net income, and related earnings per share (or other performance measures) should be disclosed.
2. For a change in estimate that is made in the ordinary course of business, such as a change in bad debts or warranty costs, the disclosures listed in 1 above are not required unless the change is considered material in nature.
3. Disclosures that may be required by other accounting standards.
4. Provide the disclosures specified by ASC 250 for a change in principle when a change in estimate is a change in estimate affected by a change in principle (see the disclosure requirements for changes in accounting principles earlier in this chapter).
5. Provide a description of the change in estimate in the period of change when the change in estimate does not have a material impact in the period of change but is expected to have a material impact in future accounting periods.

Changes in Reporting Entities—General Discussion

A company is faced with accounting for a change in reporting entity (Block 12) when the financial statements to be issued reflect a different group of entities than was shown in previous financial statements. A change in reporting entity may result from the preparation of consolidated statements rather than individual entity statements, or from a change in the composition of subsidiaries or companies making up the consolidated or combined group.

Proper accounting for a change in reporting entity requires a restatement of financial statements for all prior periods presented, using a retrospective method (Block 13). In addition, the retrospective method should be applied to interim financial statements that have been previously issued. However, any interest capitalized using the provisions of ASC 835-20 related to equity method of accounting is not changed when applying the retrospective method (ASC 250-10-45-21).

When a change in reporting entity is a result of a business combination, the provisions of ASC 805 should be used for the reporting and for disclosures (ASC 250-10-50-6).

Changes in Reporting Entities—Disclosure Requirements

ASC 250-10-50-6 (Block 14) specifies the disclosure requirements for changes in reporting entities. The disclosures are as follows:

1. The nature of the change and the reasons for the change in reporting entity.
2. The impact on income from continuing operations, net income, other comprehensive income, and related earnings per share (or other performance measures) for all accounting periods presented.
3. Provide a description of the nature of the change in reporting entity and the reason for the change in the period of change when the change in reporting entity does not have a material impact in the period of change but is expected to have a material impact in future accounting periods.
4. Any appropriate disclosures specified in ASC 805 (Business Combinations).

Accounting Errors—General Discussion

Accounting errors (Block 2 of Flowchart 2-4) exist at the time financial statements are prepared and result from mistakes such as the following: mistakes of a mathematical nature, mistakes made when applying accounting principles, mistakes from facts that are misused, or mistakes from facts that are overlooked. If an error was made in a period and discovered before the financial statements were distributed, it should be corrected in that period. ASC 250 deals with errors that were made in one period and not discovered until a subsequent period. Therefore, previously issued financial statements contain an error. The definition of "error in previously issued financial statements" in ASC 250-10-20 is: "An error in recognition, measurement, presentation, or disclosure in financial statements resulting from mathematical mistakes, mistakes in the application of U.S. generally accepted accounting principles (U.S. GAAP), or oversight or misuse of facts that existed at the time the financial statements were prepared. A change from an accounting principle that is not generally accepted to one that is generally accepted is a correction of an error."

The correction of an error is reported as a prior-period adjustment (Block 3) by restating the financial statements of all prior periods presented using the following method (ASC 250-10-45-23):

1. Compute the cumulative effect of the error for accounting periods prior to the earliest accounting period presented and report the impact, if any, of the error in the beginning balances of assets or liabilities affected by the error at the beginning of the first accounting period presented (Block 4).

2. Adjust the beginning balance of retained earnings in the same accounting period in which the assets and/or liabilities are adjusted (Block 5).
3. Restate all prior accounting periods presented using period-specific application to reflect the impact of the error in individual accounting periods presented (Block 6).

For entities that are SEC registrants, ASC 250-10-S99-2 discusses the process that should be used when quantifying misstatements in financial statements. When considering whether a misstatement is material to the financial statements, an entity should not only consider the misstatements that arise in the current year but the impact of misstatements in the financial statements not corrected at the end of the prior accounting period. ASC 250-10-S99-2 states that the "rollover" and "iron curtain" methods are commonly used to correct misstatements. The rollover method corrects only the current accounting period error and the iron curtain method corrects not only the current year but all prior-year misstatements. For example, if an entity misstates expenses and liabilities every year for three years by $100 each year, the current-year misstatement would only be $100. However, the total error would be $400, $300 from the prior three years and $100 for the current year. If the rollover method is used, financial statements are corrected only for $100. If the iron curtain method is used, current year financial statements are corrected for $400. ASC 250-10-S99-2 states that generally a combination of the rollover and the iron curtain methods should be used. In this example, the $100 current-year misstatement should be corrected and the $300 carryover misstatement should be corrected. If the total correction is material to current-year operations, ASC 250-10-S99-2 suggests that prior-year statements be corrected.

Accounting Errors—Technical Considerations

One example is used to illustrate the accounting and reporting for an accounting error. Assumptions for Example 2-12 are as follows.

Example 2-12
Assumptions for Change in Error Correction

1. Johnson Enterprises (Johnson), a December 31 year-end company, purchased equipment on January 1, 20X4, for $100,000. The equipment has a useful life of 10 years and no residual value. Johnson elected to use straight-line depreciation for the equipment.
2. At the beginning of year 20X6, it was discovered that the equipment had never been recorded and/or depreciated.
3. Johnson has a 30% tax rate.

At the beginning of 20X6, it was discovered that the equipment had never been recorded or depreciated. This failure to record the asset and related depreciation constituted an accounting error. The company had understated the value of its depreciable assets and depreciation expense of 20X4 and 20X5. The amount of the error will be treated as a prior period adjustment and is calculated below:

Cost of asset	$100,000
Estimated useful life	÷10
Annual depreciation expense	$10,000
Number of years omitted	× 2
Depreciation expense not recorded	$20,000

In addition to correcting for the depreciation not recorded, the company must also record the asset acquired. The entry to accomplish this in 20X6 is:

Prior Period Adjustment—Accounting Error	20,000	
Equipment	100,000	
Accumulated Depreciation		20,000
Cash		100,000

Assuming that the beginning retained earnings balance previously reported for 20X6 was $150,000, and that, during 20X6, net income amounted to $50,000 and dividends were $20,000, the following correction to retained earnings is required:

Retained earnings previously reported	$150,000
Adjustment:	
Prior period adjustment for accounting error in recording depreciation, net of tax of $6,000	(14,000)
Adjusted beginning retained earnings	$136,000
Net income	50,000
Dividends	(20,000)
Retained earnings 12/31/X6	$166,000

If 20X6 and 20X5 comparative statements were presented, the correction for the failure to record the asset and depreciation would be shown through a retroactive restatement of 20X5 financial statements.

The 20X5 beginning-of-year balance in equipment would be increased by $100,000, cash would be decreased by $100,000, accumulated depreciation would be increased $10,000 (depreciation expense from 20X4), and the beginning balance in retained earnings would be adjusted for a prior-period adjustment of $6,000 ($10,000 pretax depreciation expense for 20X4 × 100% - 30% tax rate). Depreciation expense for 20X5 would be increased by $10,000 (depreciation expense for 20X5), income tax expense decreased by $3,000 ($10,000 depreciation expense × 30% tax rate), and net income is decreased by $6,000 ($10,000 depreciation expense × 100% - 30% tax rate).

Accounting Errors—Disclosure Requirements

ASC 250-10-50, paragraphs 7 through 10 (Block 7), specify the disclosure requirements for accounting errors. The disclosures are as follows:

1. Describe the nature of the error and disclose that prior-period statements have been restated.
2. For each prior accounting period, disclose the impact of the correction on each line item in the financial statements and appropriate per-share amounts.

3. As of the beginning of the earliest accounting period presented, disclose the cumulative effect of the change on retained earnings or other appropriate component.

4. Disclose in the year of the prior-period adjustment the impact on both a gross and net basis of the prior-period adjustment on the net income of prior accounting periods presented. If only the current year is presented without prior years' statements included with the current year, disclosure of the impact of the prior-period adjustment on beginning retained earnings of the current year should be provided and the impact on income of the preceding accounting period should also be disclosed.

Prior Period Adjustments

Only accounting error corrections may be accounted for as prior period adjustments under the provisions of ASC 250-10. Items that do not qualify as prior period adjustments will be treated as items of profit or loss and will flow through income. Prior period adjustments do not affect income, but are treated as direct adjustments to beginning retained earnings. In addition, both the gross and net impact of a prior period adjustment must be disclosed in financial statements in the accounting period in which the adjustment is reported.

If prior year statements are issued with the current statements for comparison purposes, the impact of the adjustment (including tax impact) must be disclosed for each period included in the statements. If only current year statements are presented, the impact of the adjustment on current year beginning retained earnings and net income of the most recent prior accounting period is required.

ASC 250-10-45-28 requires that when summary financial information, such as five- or 10-year summaries, is presented in financial statements, and any of the summary years include prior period adjustments, income and other impacted items in the summaries must be restated and an appropriate disclosure must be made in the first summary subsequent to the adjustment.

To illustrate the proper accounting and reporting for a prior period adjustment, classified as such by the provisions of ASC 250-10, the assumptions listed in Example 2-13 are used.

Example 2-13
Prior Period Adjustments

1. Book-It, Inc. (Book-It) purchased a piece of equipment on January 1, 20X4, for $100,000. The equipment has a useful life of 10 years, and there is assumed to be no residual value associated with the equipment.

2. On the purchase date, the accountant at Book-It charged the entire cost of the equipment to expense.

3. Book-It uses straight-line depreciation for all owned assets.
4. Book-It is preparing financial statements for the year ended December 31, 20X6. Income reported for the year is $260,000. Book-It paid dividends during the year of $100,000. The beginning balance in retained earnings is $85,000.

The event described in Example 2-13 is an accounting error, and qualifies for treatment, under the provisions of ASC 250-10, as a prior period adjustment. Assume that the error was discovered at the end of 20X6. To simplify the solution to Example 2-13, income tax consequences of the error will be ignored. The entire cost of the equipment was charged to income in 20X4, and the amounts properly charged to income should have been the depreciation for the years 20X4 through 20X6. The depreciation for 20X6 will be charged to income of the period and will not enter into the determination of the amount of the prior period adjustment. The prior period adjustment is equal to the difference between the cost of the equipment, improperly charged to income, and the depreciation for years 20X4 and 20X5. The computation of the amount of the prior period adjustment would be determined as follows:

Depreciation expense for 20X4 and 20X5 ($100,000/10 years = $10,000 × 2 years)	$20,000
Cost of equipment improperly charged to income	100,000
Prior Period Adjustment	$80,000

The correcting journal entry required by Book-It, Inc. at the end of 20X6 would be:

Equipment	100,000	
Depreciation Expense (for 20X6)	10,000	
Accumulated Depreciation—Equipment		30,000
Prior Period Adjustment		80,000

As a result of this entry, the equipment is properly recorded as a part of property, plant, and equipment; depreciation expense for 20X6 has been recognized, and the accumulated depreciation account has been properly established at $30,000 (depreciation for the years 20X4 through 20X6). Because the error was discovered prior to the issuance of the financial statement, corrected income for 20X6 would be $250,000 ($260,000 as previously reported - $10,000 depreciation expense for 20X6).

The proper presentation of Book-It's Statement of Retained Earnings for 20X6 would be as follows:

Book-It, Inc.
Statement of Retained Earnings For the Year Ended December 31, 20X6

Retained Earnings, January 1, 20X6	$85,000
Adjustment:	
Prior period adjustment—error in recording equipment	80,000
Adjusted Retained Earnings, January 1, 20X6	$165,000

Net Income for 20X6	250,000
Dividends for 20X6	(100,000)
Retained Earnings, December 31, 20X6	$315,000

The prior period adjustment was treated as a direct charge to the beginning retained earnings balance, and did not flow through the income statement. The only income effect of the correction was to record the proper depreciation for 20X6. The account "Prior Period Adjustment" will be closed directly to the retained earnings account.

Adjustments Required in Interim Periods

For an item to be classified as an adjustment to a preceding interim period of the current annual period, each of the following conditions (ASC 250-10-45-25) must be met:

1. The adjustment must be considered to be material;
2. The adjustment must be directly related to the activities of preceding interim periods of the current annual period; and
3. The amount of the adjustment could not be reasonably estimated in preceding interim periods, but can be estimated in the current interim period.

Examples of transactions or events that might meet these conditions would include cases involving litigation, public utility rate-making proceedings, renegotiation of government contracts, and final settlement of income tax matters, except for the effects of retroactive tax legislation.

When faced with a transaction or event meeting these three conditions, the company first must determine the amount of the adjustment applicable to the current interim period. This adjustment will be included in the income of the current interim period. Next, the amount of the adjustment associated with each preceding interim period of the current annual period must be determined. Income of each of these preceding interim periods should be restated to reflect the adjustments so determined. Finally, income of the first interim period of the current annual period should be restated to give effect to the amount of the adjustment relating to all prior annual periods.

To illustrate the proper accounting for adjustments to preceding interim periods, the assumptions listed in Example 2-14 are used.

Example 2-14
Adjustments to Preceding Interim Periods

1. Energy, Inc. is a public utility providing electric service to the towns of Ross and Prior and the surrounding area.
2. The state regulatory authority permits the company to increase its rates to customers as soon as an application for a rate increase is filed with the authority. The revenue collected as a result of the pending rate case is subject to refund, depending upon the findings of the authority.

3. In the middle of 20X5, Energy, Inc. filed an application for a rate increase and immediately increased its rates to customers. Revenues collected, subject to refund, are as follows:

Collected during 20X5	$110,000
Collected in First Quarter of 20X6	58,000
Collected in Second Quarter of 20X6	47,000
Collected in Third Quarter of 20X6	52,000

4. In the third quarter of 20X6, the regulatory authority rules that the rate increases were not justified, and the amounts collected must be refunded to the customers. The revenue earned as a result of the rate increase is considered to be material.

5. Energy, Inc. is in the process of preparing interim financial statements for the third quarter of 20X6.

The facts presented in Example 2-14 indicate that the events qualify for treatment as adjustments to preceding interim periods. The revenue collected is material, the amounts can be associated with preceding interim periods of the current annual period, and the amounts could not be reasonably estimated prior to the settlement of the rate-making proceedings.

An adjustment will be required to income of the third quarter of 20X6, the second quarter of 20X6 and the first quarter of 20X6. The adjustment in the first quarter of 20X6 must reflect amounts relating to the preceding annual period (20X5). Table 2-13 shows the effect of the required adjustment on the income of the interim periods of 20X6.

Table 2-13 Adjustments to Prior Interim Periods

	Interim Period—20X6		
Adjustment	**3rd Quarter**	**2nd Quarter**	**1st Quarter**
Overstatement of 20X5 revenues			$110,000
Overstatement in first quarter of 20X6			58,000
Overstatement in second quarter of 20X6		$47,000	
Overstatement in third quarter of 20X6	$52,000		
Adjustment to income for each quarter of 20X6	$52,000	$47,000	$168,000

Income for the first quarter of 20X6 must be restated by $168,000, the effect of the adjustment relating to the first quarter and the preceding annual period. The adjustments to income for the second and third quarters of 20X6 reflect the amounts specifically related to those periods.

In addition to the restatement of the income amounts, the following disclosures are required by ASC 250-10-50-11:

1. The interim report prepared for the period containing the adjustment should disclose the impact of the adjustment on income from continuing operations, net income and related earnings per share amounts for each preceding interim period of the current annual period; and
2. The interim report prepared for the interim period containing the adjustment should disclose income from continuing operations, net income and related earnings per share amounts, restated as discussed in this section and as shown in the Example 2-14.

Recent Changes

ASU 2016-03, *Intangibles—Goodwill and Other (Topic 350), Business Combinations (Topic 805), Consolidation (Topic 810), Derivatives and Hedging (Topic 815): Effective Date and Transition Guidance,* removed the effective dates for all of the PCC accounting alternatives, making them effective immediately and indefinitely.

Topic 255: Changing Prices

Topic 255, *Changing Prices,* contains two subtopics:

10 Overall

912 Contractors—Federal Government [See the corresponding topic in Chapter 9 for coverage of this shared subtopic]

ASC 255-10 encourages, but does not require, entities that prepare their financial statements in accordance with U.S. generally accepted accounting principles (U.S. GAAP) and in U.S. dollars to disclose supplementary information about the impact of inflation. Should an entity elect to disclose information about changing prices, ASC 255-10 provides appropriate guidelines for measurement and presentation. However, the FASB does not discourage companies from experimenting with other disclosure formats.

Because entities are not required to present supplementary disclosures of Current Cost/Constant Purchasing Power information, the disclosure requirements are not presented here.

Topic 260: Earnings per Share

Topic 260, *Earnings per Share,* contains one subtopic:

10 Overall

Approach to Calculating Earnings per Share

ASC 260-10 provides guidelines for the calculation of earnings per share (EPS). Overall, ASC 260-10 is quite complex. In attempting to explain and analyze ASC 260-10, the basic problem is one of approach. Each component part of the calculation will be broken down into its essential features, and those features will be analyzed in detail. Once the analysis of a particular feature is completed, additional features will be discussed. This type of analysis enables each important area of the earnings per share calculation to be addressed individually and the various pieces to be put together into a complete computation of EPS. The discussion and related examples should provide the reader with an in-depth understanding of the EPS calculation.

Two flowcharts are used in the presentation of the earnings per share requirements. Flowchart 2-5 covers the accounting requirements for basic earnings per share and Flowchart 2-6 addresses the issues related to diluted earnings per share. All decision blocks have been numbered for referencing during the discussion.

Flowchart 2-5
Basic Earnings per Share

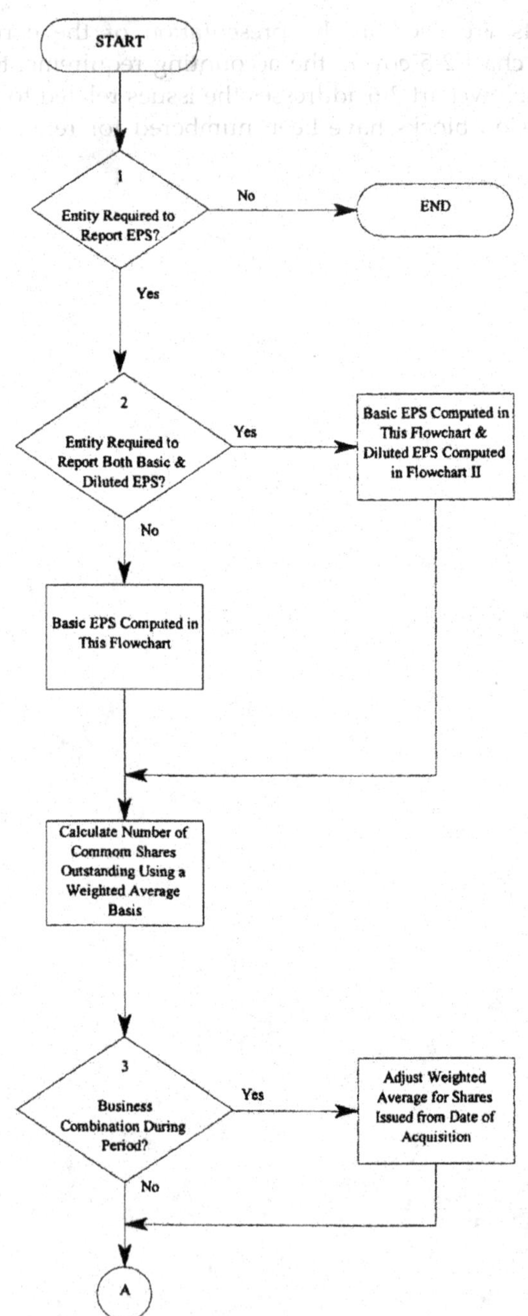

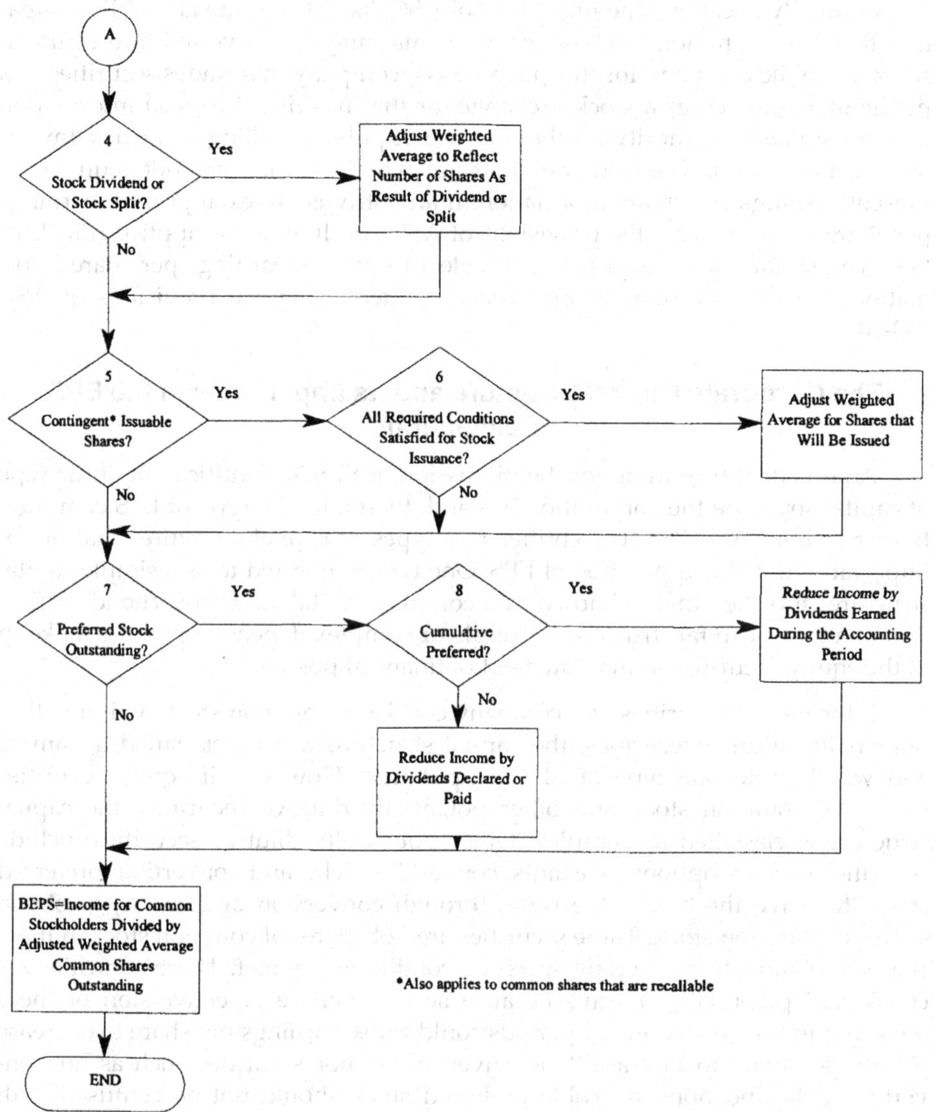
A
4
Stock Dividend or Stock Split?
Yes
Adjust Weighted Average to Reflect Number of Shares As Result of Dividend or Split
No
5
Contingent* Issuable Shares?
Yes
6
All Required Conditions Satisfied for Stock Issuance?
Yes
Adjust Weighted Average for Shares that Will Be Issued
No
No
7
Preferred Stock Outstanding?
Yes
8
Cumulative Preferred?
Yes
Reduce Income by Dividends Earned During the Accounting Period
No
Reduce Income by Dividends Declared or Paid
No
BEPS=Income for Common Stockholders Divided by Adjusted Weighted Average Common Shares Outstanding
*Also applies to common shares that are recallable
END

Generally speaking, the provisions of ASC 260-10 apply to all public companies that have common stock or securities that may be converted into common stock. A public company for this purpose is a company that trades securities in a public market, such as a stock exchange, or that has filed financial information with a regulatory authority for the purpose of publicly selling securities. Investment companies and subsidiaries that are wholly owned are not required to present earnings per share information. If an entity is not exempt from earnings per share computations, the provisions of ASC 260-10 must be applied (Block 1); however, should an exempt enterprise elect to present earnings per share information, the EPS information must be presented using the provisions of ASC 260-10.

The Corporate Capital Structure and Its Importance in the EPS Calculation

An excellent beginning for the discussion of EPS is identification of the type of capital structure the corporation has and, therefore, the type of EPS computations required. ASC 260-10 identifies two types of capital structures that are of importance to the computation of EPS. One type is referred to as a simple capital structure, and the other is known as a complex capital structure. The identification of a given capital structure as simple or complex depends upon the makeup of the equity securities in the statement of financial position.

If the equity securities of a company consist of common stock with no other potentially dilutive securities, the capital structure will be classified as simple and will lead to one type of EPS computation. However, if equity securities consist of common stock and other potentially dilutive securities, the capital structure is classified as complex. Other potentially dilutive securities include securities such as options, warrants, convertible debt, and convertible preferred stock that give the holder the right, through conversion or exercise, to obtain shares of common stock. These securities are not shares of common stock, but are rights to obtain stock if certain specified conditions are met. These securities are considered potentially dilutive because actual exercise or conversion of these securities in future accounting periods could cause earnings per share to decrease or loss per share to increase. Nonconvertible senior securities such as nonconvertible debt and nonconvertible preferred stock should not be confused with other potentially dilutive securities. Nonconvertible senior securities are not used when determining capital structure. A company may have many types of sophisticated nonconvertible senior securities and still have a simple capital structure.

An enterprise with a simple capital structure, as defined above, is required to report only one earnings per share computation. Basic earnings per share is used as the designation in ASC 260-10; however, other terminology may be used in place of basic earnings per share.

If an enterprise has a complex capital structure, a dual presentation of earnings per share is required. The suggested terminology for the dual presentation is basic earnings per share and diluted earnings per share. However, other designations are acceptable. The remainder of the discussion will focus on how to calculate basic earnings per share and diluted earnings per share.

Basic Earnings Per Share

Basic earnings per share (BEPS) (Block 2) is used to evaluate the performance of an enterprise over a specific accounting period. For purposes of the following discussion, basic earnings per share is defined as the computation of earnings per share, ignoring all potentially dilutive securities, such as options, warrants, convertible debt, and convertible preferred stock. Basic earnings per share is income for common stockholders divided by common shares outstanding computed using a weighted-average basis. The outstanding common shares must also be adjusted for any contingently issuable common shares of stock. Contingently issuable common shares are shares of common stock that will be issued in the future when specific conditions are met and no cash or very little cash will be received from the issuance. Contingently issuable common shares are used in the basic earnings per share computation only when all specific conditions for issuance have been fulfilled. BEPS can be computed using the following formula:

$$\text{BEPS} = \frac{\text{I - PD}}{\text{WACS + CIS}}$$

BEPS	= Basic earnings per share
I	= Income
PD	= Preferred dividends
WACS	= Weighted–average shares of common stock
CIS	= Contingently issuable common shares

Both the numerator and denominator of the preceding equation require more detailed discussion.

Computation of Weighted Average Number of Shares—The Denominator

The first step in the computation of BEPS is to calculate the common shares outstanding during the accounting period under consideration using a weighted-average basis. Each share of common stock must be weighted for the portion of time it is outstanding during the period. Some shares of common stock may be outstanding for the entire accounting period, and others may be outstanding for only a few days, weeks, or months. The use of a weighted average takes this fact into consideration, whereas a simple average would ignore it. The question that an enterprise computing earnings per share must address is what type of weighted average amount is appropriate. A daily weighted average would provide the greatest amount of precision; however, another method, such as a weekly or monthly average, is acceptable as long as the results produced are reasonable.

To show the computation of the weighted-average shares of common stock outstanding during an accounting period, assume the facts in Example 2-15.

Example 2-15
Weighted-Average Shares—General

1. Lowe Enterprises (Lowe), a December 31 year-end company, had 2,400,000 common shares outstanding on January 1, 20X6 and 3,000,000 shares outstanding on December 31, 20X6.
2. During 20X6 the following common shares were sold or repurchased by Lowe:
   a. 600,000 shares were sold on June 1.
   b. 100,000 shares were sold on July 1.
   c. 100,000 shares were repurchased on October 1.
3. The 100,000 shares repurchased on October 1 were from shares outstanding from the beginning of the year and are accounted for as treasury shares.
4. Lowe uses a monthly average to compute the weighted-average shares outstanding during the period, and the computation is for an annual accounting period.

Table 2-14 represents the computation of the number of common shares outstanding for 20X6 using a monthly weighted-average basis.

Table 2-14 Calculation of Weighted-Average Shares—Monthly Basis

Assumptions from Example 2-15 (1)	*Number of Shares (2)*	*Months Outstanding (3)*	*Fraction of Year (4)*	*Weighted-Average Shares (5)=(2)×(4)*
1	2,400,000	12	12/12	2,400,000
2(a)	600,000	7	7/12	350,000
2(b)	100,000	6	6/12	50,000
2(c)	(100,000)	3	3/12	(25,000)
	Weighted-Average Shares Outstanding			2,775,000

The actual number of shares outstanding at the end of 20X6 is 3,000,000 (2,400,000 + 600,000 + 100,000 - 100,000), compared with the weighted-average number of 2,775,000 used in the earnings per share computation. The 100,000 shares of treasury shares repurchased were outstanding from January 1 through October 1 (nine months), and were deducted for the three months that they were not outstanding (3 = 12 - 9). The 100,000 treasury shares were included in the 2,400,000 shares outstanding shares at the beginning of the year. Because the treasury shares were included in the 2,400,000 shares and the 2,400,000 were weighted for the entire year, the 100,000 treasury shares must be deducted for the three months that they are not outstanding. The shares actually issued during the year were weighted for the number of months each issue was actually outstanding during 20X6.

An alternative approach to the weighting of the treasury shares would have been to weight the original 2,400,000 shares for the nine months all shares were outstanding and then weight 2,300,000 (2,400,000 - 100,000 treasury shares) shares for the remaining three months of the year. Another alternative to weighting the treasury shares would be to weight 2,300,000 (2,400,000 - 100,000 shares of treasury stock) of the 2,400,000 shares outstanding at the beginning of the year for 12 months, or the entire year, and weight the 100,000 shares that were repurchased on October 1 for nine months. Regardless of the techniques used for treasury stock, the results are the same.

Example 2-14 illustrated the computation of weighted-average shares using a monthly basis for an annual accounting period. Example 2-16 shows the use of a daily average for an interim accounting period. The facts for Example 2-16 are as follows.

Example 2-16
Weighted-Average Shares—General

1. Reed Enterprises (Reed), a December 31 year-end company, had 6,000,000 common shares outstanding on January 1, 20X6 and 6,700,000 shares outstanding on March 31, 20X6, the end of the first quarter.
2. During the first quarter of 20X6, the following common shares were sold or repurchased by Reed:
   a. 600,000 shares were sold on January 30.
   b. 500,000 shares were sold on February 14.
   c. 400,000 shares were repurchased on March 22.
3. The 400,000 shares repurchased on March 22 were from shares outstanding from the beginning of the year and are accounted for as treasury shares.
4. Reed uses a daily average to compute the weighted-average shares outstanding during the period, and the computation is for the first quarter of 20X6.

Table 2-15, below, represents the computation of the number of common shares outstanding for the first quarter of 20X6 using a daily weighted-average basis.

Table 2-15 Calculation of Weighted-Average Shares—Daily Basis

Assumptions from Example 2-16 (1)	*Number of Shares (2)*	*Days Outstanding (3)*	*Fraction of Quarter (4)*	*Weighted-Average Shares (5)=(2)×(4)*
1	6,000,000	90	90/90	6,000,000
2(a)	600,000	60	60/90	400,000
2(b)	500,000	45	45/90	250,000
2(c)	(400,000)	9	9/90	(40,000)
	Weighted-Average Shares Outstanding		6,610,000	

The actual number of shares outstanding on March 31, the end of the first quarter, is 6,700,000 (6,000,000 + 600,000 + 500,000 - 400,000), compared with a weighted-average number of shares of 6,610,000.

Flowchart 2-5 identifies some additional adjustments that may be required in the calculation of the weighted-average shares to be included in the denominator of the basic earnings per share computation.

If, during the accounting period under consideration, a business combination (Block 3) is consummated, the weighted-average shares to use in the EPS computation will include the common shares issued to effect the combination weighted from the date of acquisition.

To illustrate the proper calculation of the weighted-average shares when a business combination has occurred during the accounting period, assume the facts in Example 2-17.

Example 2-17
Weighted-Average Shares—Business Combination

1. The Johnson Company (Johnson), a December 31 year-end entity, had 3,000,000 common shares outstanding on January 1, 20X6.
2. During 20X6 Johnson had the following common stock transactions:
    a. 400,000 shares were sold on April 1.
    b. 300,000 shares of common stock of Johnson were used to effect a business combination on July 1, 20X6.
3. Johnson uses a monthly average to compute the weighted-average shares outstanding during the period, and the computation is for the 20X6 annual accounting period.

Table 2-16 presents the computation of the number of common shares outstanding for 20X6 using a monthly weighted-average basis.

Table 2-16 Calculation of Weighted-Average Shares—Business Combination—Monthly Weighting

Assumptions from Example 2-17 (1)	*Number of Shares* (2)	*Months Outstanding* (3)	*Fraction of Year* (4)	*Weighted-Average Shares* (5)=(2)×(4)
1	3,000,000	12	12/12	3,000,000
2(a)	400,000	9	9/12	300,000
2(b)	300,000	6	6/12	150,000
	Weighted-Average Shares Outstanding			3,450,000

The 3,000,000 shares were outstanding for 12 months, and the 400,000 shares sold on April 1 were outstanding for nine months; both were weighted accordingly. Johnson issued 300,000 shares to effect the acquisition of a business combination. These shares should be weighted from the date of acquisition to the balance sheet date, or six months. The reason for this weighting is that, in a business combination, income of the acquired company prior to the date of combination is not incorporated with the income of the acquiring company.

The next adjustment to the denominator in the BEPS calculation is required when there has been a stock dividend, stock split, or reverse split distributed during the period (Block 4). When the number of common shares outstanding changes as a result of splits or stock dividends, the weighted-average number of shares should be adjusted to reflect the change, and the adjustment should be on a retroactive basis for all periods presented. If the stock dividend or stock split occurs after the balance sheet date, but before the financial statements are issued, the adjustment still is required on a retroactive basis. The effects of stock dividends and stock splits and the computation of weighted-average number of shares outstanding is illustrated using the assumptions listed in Example 2-18.

Example 2-18
Weighted Average Shares—Stock Dividends and Splits

1. Larson Enterprises (Larson), a December 31 year-end entity, had 1,500,000 common shares outstanding on January 1, 20X6.
2. During 20X6 Larson had the following common stock transactions:
   a. 300,000 shares were sold on April 1.
   b. 200,000 shares were sold on July 1.
   c. A 10% stock dividend was declared and paid September 1.
   d. 2-for-1 stock split occurred on January 15, 20X7, and the 12/31/X6 financial statements were not released until March 3, 20X7.
3. The weighted-average number of shares calculated for 20X5, before considering any stock splits or dividends, was 1,200,000. Larson is presenting comparative financial statements for 20X6 and 20X5.
4. Because the results are not materially different from a daily average, Larson uses a monthly average to compute the weighted-average shares outstanding during the period, and the computation is for the 20X6 annual accounting period.

Table 2-17 presents the computation of the number of common shares outstanding for 20X6 and 20X5 using a monthly weighted-average basis.

Table 2-17 Calculation of Weighted-Average Shares—Stock Dividends and Splits—Monthly Weighting

Computation of Weighted-Average Shares for 20X6:

Assumptions from Example 2-17 (1)	*Number of Shares* (2)	*Months Outstanding* (3)	*Fraction of Year* (4)	*Weighted-Average Shares* (5)=(2)×(4)
1	1,500,000	12	12/12	1,500,000
2(a)	300,000	9	9/12	225,000

Computation of Weighted-Average Shares for 20X6:

Assumptions from Example 2-17 (1)		*Number of Shares (2)*	*Months Outstanding (3)*	*Fraction of Year (4)*	*Weighted-Average Shares (5)=(2)×(4)*
2(b)		200,000	6	6/12	100,000
	Weighted-average shares before dividend and split				1,825,000
2(c)	10% stock dividend (1,825,000 × 10%)				182,500
	Weighted-average shares before stock split				2,007,500
2(d)	2-for-1 stock split				2,007,500
	Weighted-Average Shares Outstanding				4,015,000

Computation of Weighted-Average Shares for 20X5:

Weighted-average shares outstanding for 20X5 (Assumption 3)		1,20,000
10% stock dividend (1,200,000 × 10%)		120,000
Weighted average before split		1,320,000
2–for–1 stock split		1,320,000
	Weighted-average shares outstanding, retroactively restated for 20X5	2,640,000

Computation of the weighted-average number of shares prior to the stock dividend and split have been discussed at length in previous examples. According to Example 2-18's assumptions, the stock dividend was distributed after the sale of additional shares was completed. The dividend will be paid on these additional shares. Therefore, the number of weighted shares issued in connection with the dividend is equal to 10% of the total weighted shares (1,825,000) prior to the dividend. The dividend percentage would not apply to any increases or decreases in the number of shares after the date of record of the dividend. This requires an additional step in the calculation of the weighted average number of shares outstanding at the date of record for the stock dividend.

In this example, the stock split occurred after the end of the year but prior to the financial statement release date. When this occurs, the weighted-average shares must give recognition to the split as if the split had occurred in the period under consideration (in this case, in 20X6). The 2-for-1 split results in a doubling of the previously calculated weighted-average number of shares outstanding of 2,007,500. The final total weighted-average number of shares outstanding then is 4,015,000. This number will be used as the denominator of the BEPS calculation.

Because Larson plans to present comparative financial statement for the years 20X6 and 20X5, a restatement of the weighted-average number of shares outstanding in 20X5 is required to reflect the distribution of the stock dividend and the stock split. The determination of the new weighted-average number of shares for 20X5 will be made as if the dividend and split occurred at the end of

20X5. At the end of 20X5, Larson calculated the weighted-average number of shares to be 1,200,000 for purposes of computing BEPS. Because the stock dividend occurred prior to the split, it must be considered first. The 10% stock dividend will add an additional 120,000 weighted-shares to the previous total of 1,200,000. The stock split then is applied to this new total of 1,320,000, to give a total weighted-average number of shares in 20X5 of 2,640,000. This is the value of the denominator that will be used to compute BEPS for 20X5.

This completes the discussion about stock dividends and splits. However, other items, such as prior period adjustments and stock rights, may require a retroactive restatement of the weighted-average number of shares used in earnings per share computations similar to dividends and splits. Some prior period adjustments require a restatement of income in one or more prior accounting periods. This restatement may impact the number of shares used in the denominator in the prior periods, especially in the diluted earnings per share computation, which is discussed in the next section. Stock rights also may impact the number of shares used in the computation of basic earnings per share. An issuance of stock rights is like a stock dividend when there is a bonus component attached to the stock rights. There is a bonus component attached to the stock rights when the fair value of the stock exceeds the exercise price of the right. The weighted-average number of shares outstanding will have to be adjusted for all prior periods that earnings per share is presented when stock rights have a bonus component and the rights are offered to all shareholders. The adjustment to the denominator in the EPS calculation for all prior accounting periods presented with current year statements, for an issuance of stock rights, is equal to the number of outstanding shares just before issuance of the stock rights times a stock rights factor.

The last adjustment to the denominator in the basic earnings per share computation is required when there are contingent issuable shares (Block 5) and the shares meet all required conditions for issuance of the stock (Block 6). Shares of common stock that are contingently issuable are shares that will be issued for little, if any, cash when specific conditions are met. When all required conditions have been met, the shares are included in the weighted-average number of shares outstanding when computing basic earnings per share.

This completes the discussion of items affecting the denominator in the basic earnings per share computation. Consideration has not been given to any potentially dilutive securities in the preceding examples because such securities are used only in the computation of diluted earnings per share. Items that affect the numerator in the BEPS calculation will now be discussed.

Calculation of Net Income Available to Common Shareholders—The Numerator

The numerator of the equation for the calculation of BEPS may require adjustment for certain senior securities. The impact of debt securities already has been included in the numerator (i.e., interest expense has been deducted to arrive at the net income figure). However, there will be an adjustment necessary if the company has preferred stock outstanding (Block 7). Dividends on preferred stock are not shown on the income statement as a reduction in income because such dividends are considered as distributions to equity holders. However, the earnings per share computation is based upon the common shares outstanding and must be based upon earnings available to the common shareholders. Therefore, it is necessary to reduce reported net income by an amount equal to dividends on preferred stock. If the preferred stock is cumulative (Block 8), net income is to be reduced by current year dividends, even if they are not paid or declared. If the preferred stock is noncumulative, net income will be reduced by dividends paid or declared. The discussion pertains to preferred dividends only; cash dividends on common stock are not deducted from income in the computation of EPS.

To illustrate the adjustments to the numerator required for preferred stock outstanding, assume that Duncan Enterprises (Duncan) had net income of $5,000,000 for the year 20X6. Duncan has 100,000 shares of 8%, $100 par value cumulative preferred stock outstanding during the year. Dividends have not been paid in 20X6. The adjustment to reported net income is computed below:

Reported net income before adjustment	$5,000,000	
Adjustment for dividends ($100 × 8% × 100,000 shares)	(800,000)	
Net income for BEPS calculation		$4,200,000

If the preferred stock had been noncumulative, there would be no adjustment to net income for purposes of the computation because the dividend had not been paid or declared.

Example 2-19 illustrates the complete calculation of BEPS by including items that affect both the numerator and the denominator.

Example 2-19
Basic Earnings per Share

1. Hughes Enterprises (Hughes), a December 31 year-end company, had 5,000,000 common shares outstanding on January 1, 20X6.
2. During 20X6 the following common shares were sold by Hughes:
   a. 500,000 shares were sold on July 1.
   b. 400,000 shares were sold on October 1.
3. A business combination in a prior year requires Hughes to issue an additional 10,000 shares of common stock for each additional mini storage facility placed in operation during 20X6. Hughes opened two new storage facilities on January 1, 20X6.
4. Hughes had 200,000 shares of 10%, $50 par value cumulative preferred stock. All dividends have been paid, including the dividends for 20X6.
5. After-tax income amounts for 20X6 are as follows: income from continuing operations—$6,000,000, loss from discontinued operations—$200,000, and increase in income from change in accounting principle—$550,000.
6. Hughes uses a monthly average to compute the weighted average shares outstanding during the period, and the computation is for an annual accounting period.

Table 2-18 shows the computation of the number of common shares outstanding for 20X6 using a monthly weighted-average basis.

Table 2-18 Calculation of Numerator and Denominator for Basic Earnings per Share

Computation of Numerator:

Income from continuing operations	$6,000,000
Preferred dividends paid ($50 par × 10% × 200,000 shares)	(1,000,000)
Income for common stockholders	$5,000,000
Loss from discontinued operations	(200,000)
Increase from change in accounting principle	550,000
Net income for common stockholders	$5,350,000

Computation of Denominator:

Assumptions from Example 2-15 (1)	*Number of Shares (2)*	*Months Outstanding (3)*	*Fraction of Year (4)*	*Weighted-Average Shares (5)=(2)×(4)*
1	5,000,000	12	12/12	5,000,000
2(a)	500,000	6	6/12	250,000
2(b)	400,000	3	3/12	100,000
3	20,000	12	12/12	20,000
	Weighted-Average Shares Outstanding			5,370,000

Basic earnings per share is computed by dividing the relevant income amounts by the weighted-average shares outstanding. Using the information from Table 2-18, the calculations are presented below:

	Income (1)	*Number of Shares (2)*	*Basic EPS (3)=(1)/(2)*
Income for common stockholders	$5,000,000	5,370,000	$.93
Loss from discontinued operations	(200,000)	5,370,000	(.03)
Change in accounting principle	550,000	5,370,000	.10
Net income for common stockholders	$5,350,000	5,370,000	$1.00

Basic earnings per share for income from continuing operations of $.93 and net income of $1.00 must be presented on the face of the income statement. Basic earnings per share related to discontinued operations, and the change in accounting principles may be presented on the face of the income statement or disclosed in related notes.

This completes the discussion of basic earnings per share, which is the first major building block in the process of computing earnings per share information, in accordance with the provisions of ASC 260-10. The goal of this first discussion was to illustrate the computation of basic earnings per share and to provide background information on adjustments to income for common stockholders. In addition, the discussion covered the computation of weighted-average number of shares to use in the EPS computation prior to considering potentially dilutive securities. Consideration of potentially dilutive securities will further complicate calculation of the numerator and denominator, discussed above. All information used in the calculation of basic earnings per share will also be used in the computation of diluted earnings per share.

Diluted Earnings Per Share

Diluted earnings per share (DEPS) is used to evaluate the performance of an enterprise over a specific accounting period, assuming maximum dilution of earnings per share from all potentially dilutive securities. For purposes of the following discussion, DEPS is defined as the computation of earnings per share, considering all potentially dilutive securities, such as options, warrants, convertible securities, and contingent agreements. DEPS is income for common stockholders adjusted where appropriate for potentially dilutive securities divided by common shares outstanding computed using a weighted-average basis. The outstanding common shares must also be adjusted for any contingently issuable common shares of stock and other potentially dilutive securities. The reader may wish to review the discussion of contingently issuable shares and other potentially dilutive securities discussed earlier in this chapter. All income and shares used in the computation of basic earnings per share also are used in the dilutive EPS calculation. In addition, income and weighted-average shares may be adjusted for the impact of other potentially dilutive securities. Dilutive earnings per share can be computed using the following formula:

$$DEPS = \frac{I - PD + APDS}{WACS + CIS + APDS}$$

DEPS	= Diluted earnings per share	WACS	= Weighted–average shares of common stock
I	= Income	CIS	= Contingently issuable common shares
PD	= Preferred dividends	APDS	= Adjustment for potentially dilutive securities

A review of the formula used in the computation of dilutive earnings per share indicates that the only new items used in the dilutive computation are potentially dilutive securities. For potentially dilutive securities to be used in DEPS computations, such securities must be dilutive (i.e., decrease earnings per share or increase a loss per share).

Flowchart 2-6 outlines the major tests and related procedures to be followed when covering potentially dilutive securities in the computation of diluted earnings per share. Flowchart 2-6 divides the discussion of potentially dilutive securities into the following three basic categories: options, warrants, and securities that are equivalent to options and warrants; convertible securities; and contingent agreements.

Flowchart 2-6

Diluted Earnings per Share

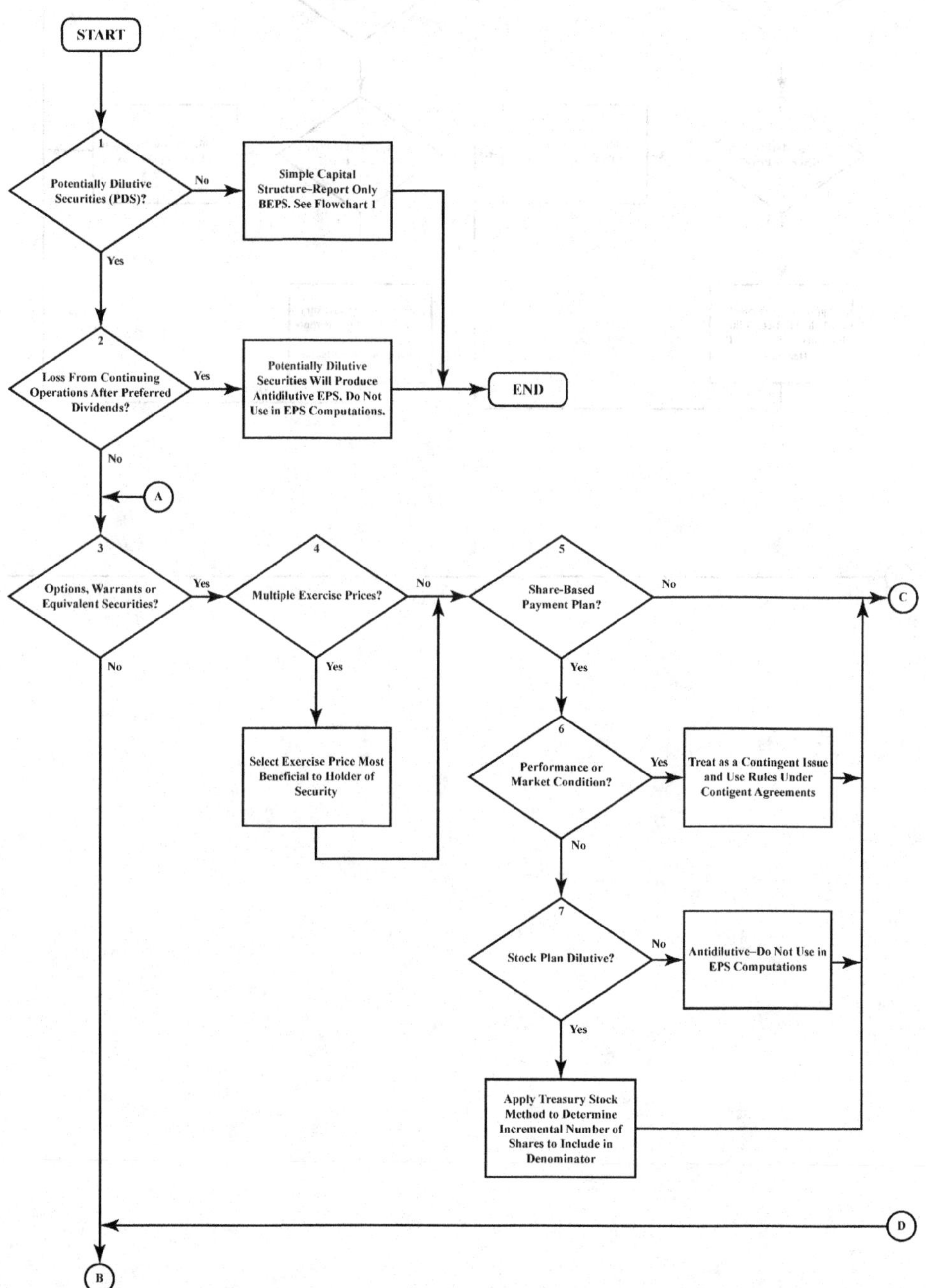

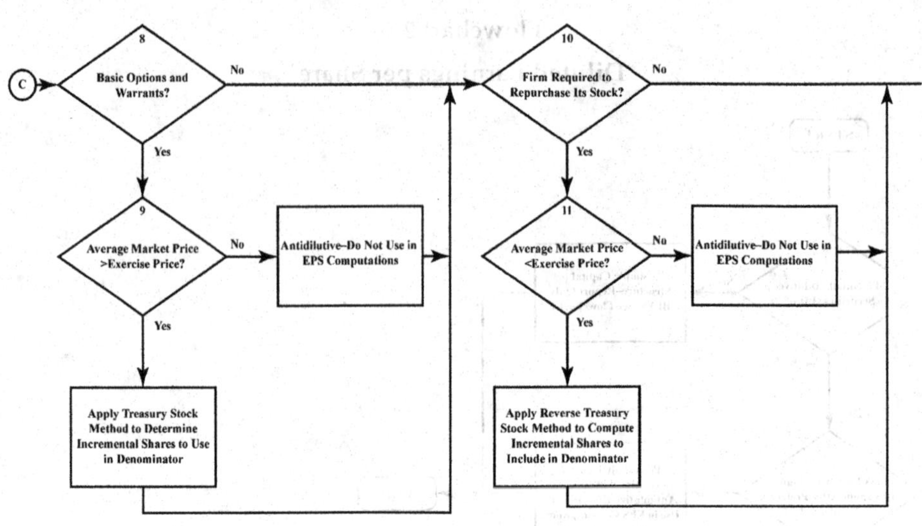
C
8
Basic Options and Warrants?
No
Yes
9
Average Market Price >Exercise Price?
No
Antidilutive–Do Not Use in EPS Computations
Yes
Apply Treasury Stock Method to Determine Incremental Shares to Use in Denominator
10
Firm Required to Repurchase Its Stock?
No
Yes
11
Average Market Price <Exercise Price?
No
Antidilutive–Do Not Use in EPS Computations
Yes
Apply Reverse Treasury Stock Method to Compute Incremental Shares to Include in Denominator

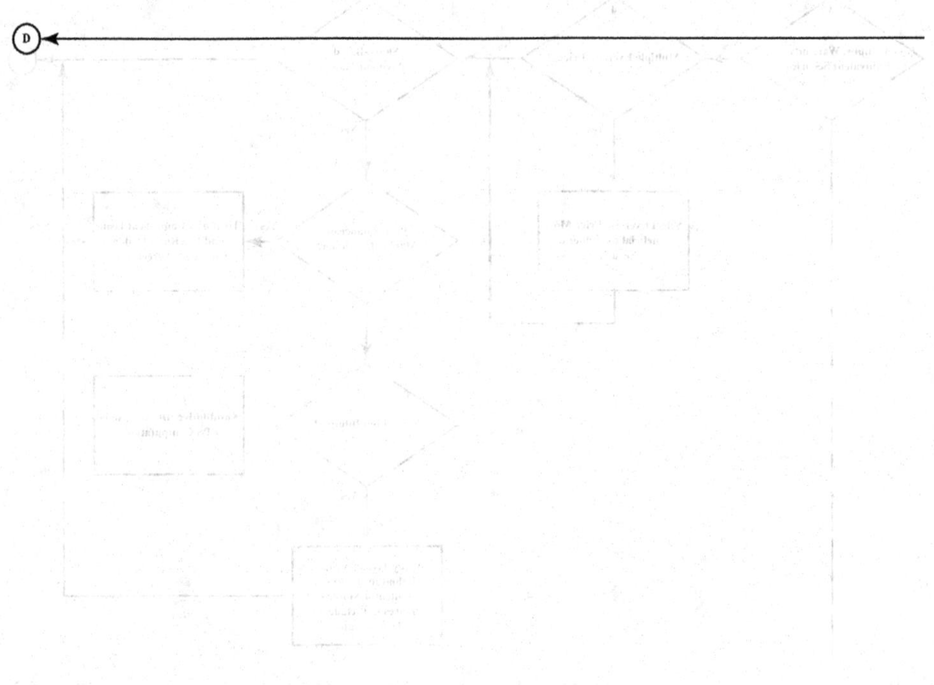
D

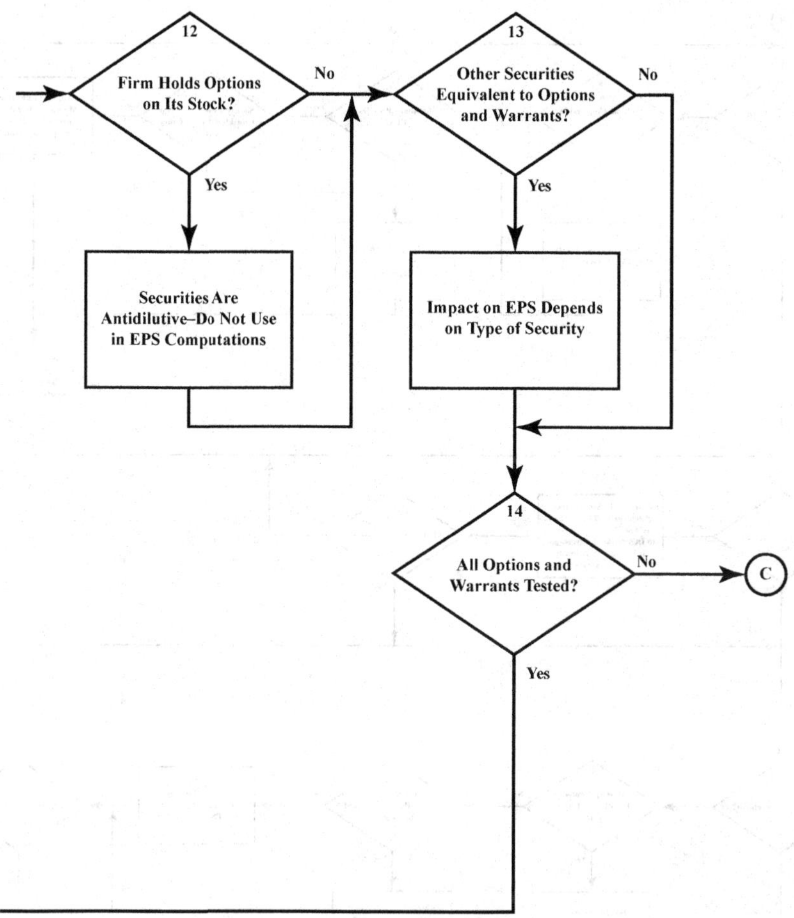
12
Firm Holds Options on Its Stock?
No
Yes
Securities Are Antidilutive–Do Not Use in EPS Computations
13
Other Securities Equivalent to Options and Warrants?
No
Yes
Impact on EPS Depends on Type of Security
14
All Options and Warrants Tested?
No
C
Yes

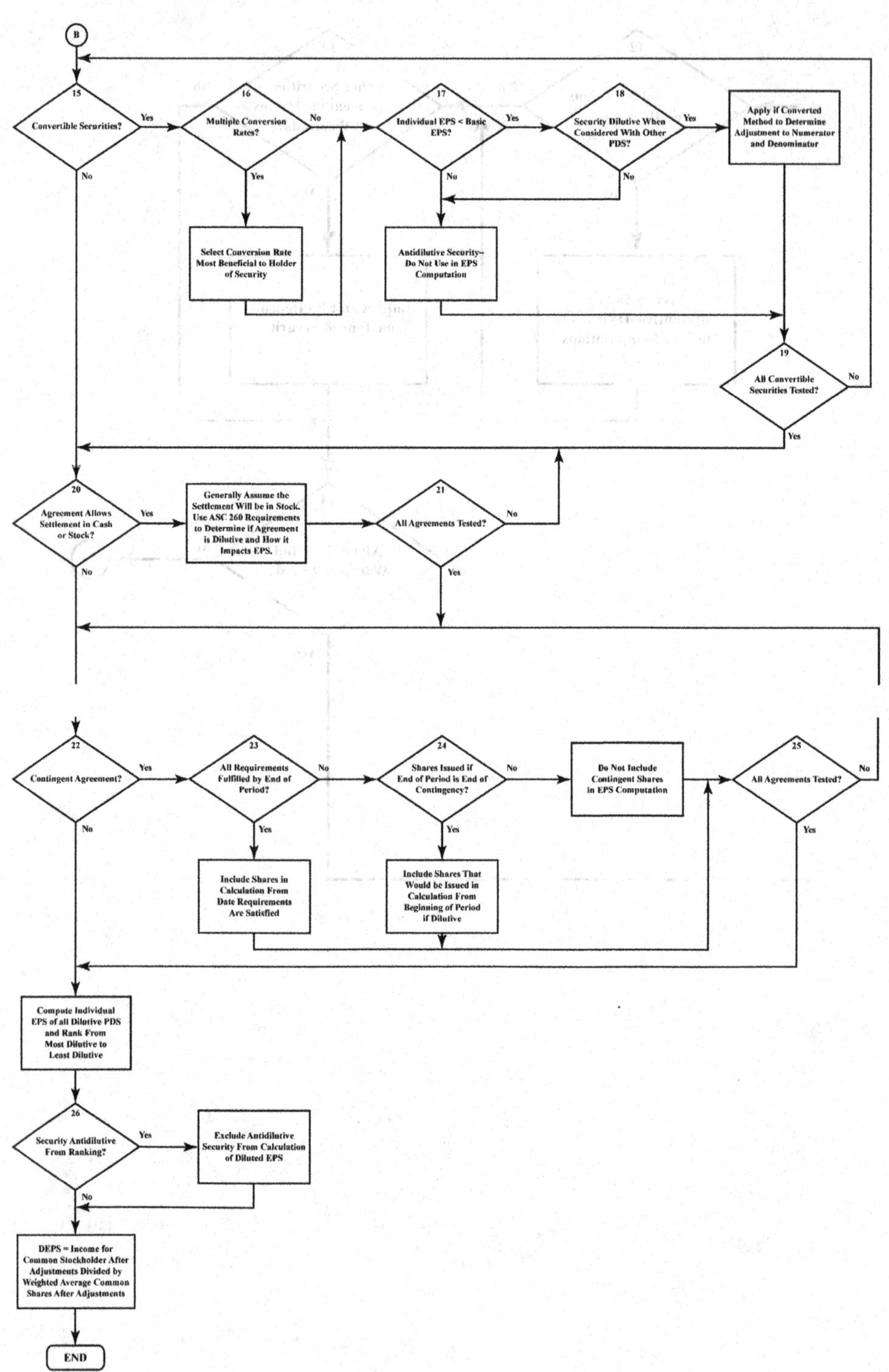
B
15
Convertible Securities?
Yes
No
16
Multiple Conversion Rates?
No
Yes
Select Conversion Rate Most Beneficial to Holder of Security
17
Individual EPS < Basic EPS?
Yes
No
Antidilutive Security-- Do Not Use in EPS Computation
18
Security Dilutive When Considered With Other PDS?
Yes
No
Apply if Converted Method to Determine Adjustment to Numerator and Denominator
19
All Convertible Securities Tested?
No
Yes
20
Agreement Allows Settlement in Cash or Stock?
Yes
No
Generally Assume the Settlement Will be in Stock. Use ASC 260 Requirements to Determine if Agreement is Dilutive and How it Impacts EPS.
21
All Agreements Tested?
No
Yes
22
Contingent Agreement?
Yes
No
23
All Requirements Fulfilled by End of Period?
No
Yes
Include Shares in Calculation From Date Requirements Are Satisfied
24
Shares Issued if End of Period is End of Contingency?
No
Yes
Include Shares That Would be Issued in Calculation From Beginning of Period if Dilutive
Do Not Include Contingent Shares in EPS Computation
25
All Agreements Tested?
No
Yes
Compute Individual EPS of all Dilutive PDS and Rank From Most Dilutive to Least Dilutive
26
Security Antidilutive From Ranking?
Yes
No
Exclude Antidilutive Security From Calculation of Diluted EPS
DEPS = Income for Common Stockholder After Adjustments Divided by Weighted Average Common Shares After Adjustments
END

If an enterprise has in its capital structure potentially dilutive securities (Block 1), the assumed conversion or exercise of the securities must decrease earnings per share or increase a loss per share, as noted above. If an entity reports a loss from continuing operations (after deducting any preferred dividends) for the period under consideration, whether interim or annual period, no potentially dilutive securities would be used in the computation of dilutive EPS because the use of such securities would be antidilutive. Therefore, the income benchmark for considering dilution is income from continuing operations after adjustment for preferred dividends (Block 2). If an enterprise has a net loss for the period, but has income from continuing operations because of gains and losses from transactions such as discontinued operations, potentially dilutive securities would be considered for use in the dilutive EPS computation because income is reported from continuing operations, which is the benchmark for considering dilution. In this case, the EPS number reported for the overall net loss is antidilutive. However, if there is a loss from continuing operations, but an overall net income number reported in the income statement, potentially dilutive securities would not be considered in the computation because it would cause EPS to be antidilutive for the loss from continuing operations. Each of the three categories of potentially dilutive securities will be discussed in detail.

Options, Warrants, and Equivalent Securities

Options and warrants are securities that allow the holder to purchase shares of common stock for a specified price. The number of shares that may be purchased depends upon the terms of the option or warrant. The following securities may not be in the form of a basic call option or warrant, but, for purposes of earnings per share computations, may be treated as options or warrants or may be the equivalent of options or warrants:

1. Share-based payment plans,
2. Agreements requiring the enterprise to repurchase its common stock,
3. Agreements where an entity has a put or call option on its common stock,
4. Warrants or options to acquire convertible securities,
5. Convertible securities requiring a cash payment at the date of conversion,
6. Convertible securities allowing a cash payment at the date of conversion,
7. Warrants specifying that the proceeds from exercise must be used to retire debt or other securities,
8. Warrants requiring that debt of the issuing entity, instead of cash, must be tendered as part or all of the total exercise price,
9. Warrants permitting the holder to tender cash or debt or other securities of the issuing entity in payment of the exercise price,
10. Stock purchase agreements,
11. Nonvested employee stock options, and
12. Unpaid stock subscriptions.

Options, warrants, and equivalent securities (here-in-after referred to as options and warrants) give the holder the right to become a common shareholder, and, therefore, these securities represent an equivalent number of common shares that may be issued if the holder exercises the right. If certain tests are met, earnings per share is computed on the assumption that the securities are converted into actual common shares. The actual exchange into common stock has not taken place, but it is assumed that it has. Provided that the appropriate tests are met, holders of options and warrants are treated like common shareholders for purposes of the diluted earnings per share computation.

To begin the process of determining if and how options and warrants enter into the computation of dilutive earnings per share, all such securities must be identified (Block 3). Next, the enterprise must determine whether any of the securities have multiple exercise prices (Block 4), and, if so, the entity must select the exercise price that is most beneficial to the holder of the security when considering the security in the computation of earnings per share. If the enterprise has a share-based payment plan (Block 5) and it relates to performance or market condition (Block 6), the share-based payment plan is treated as a contingent agreement (discussed later in this chapter). However, if the share-based payment plan is not related to performance or market conditions, the treasury stock method is used to determine the number of incremental shares to add to the denominator when computing diluted EPS, if the share-based payment plan is dilutive (Block 7). The treasury stock method assumes that dilutive options and warrants are exercised at the beginning of the accounting period, or later if issued after the beginning of the period. The proceeds assumed to be received from the assumed exercise of the securities, in excess of any required use of those proceeds, such as the retirement of debt, are assumed to be used to repurchase shares of common stock at the average market price for the accounting period. The difference between the shares issuable under the option or warrant agreement and the number of shares repurchased with the assumed proceeds represents the number of incremental shares to add to the denominator in the computation of diluted earnings per share. The proceeds assumed to be received in the case of a share-based payment plan are composed of the following:

1. Cash the employee will pay the employer when the options are exercised,

2. Compensation expense *that has not been reported* as a reduction of income (relates to future accounting periods), and

3. Tax benefit (excess of the compensation expense deducted for tax purposes over deduction for financial purposes) taken to paid-in-capital if the options were exercised.

The share-based payment plan is dilutive if the number of common shares assumed to be repurchased at the average market price using the proceeds in 1–3, above, is less than the number of shares assumed issued if the options were exercised. If the stock plan is dilutive, the excess of the number of shares assumed issued over the number assumed to be repurchased is the incremental number of shares to add to the denominator in the EPS computation.

If an entity has basic options or warrants (Block 8), the options or warrants are dilutive and used in the diluted EPS computation when the average market price exceeds the exercise price (Block 9) during the accounting period (i.e., when the options or warrants are in the money). If the average market price is less than the exercise price, the options and warrants are antidilutive and are not used in the EPS calculation. If the options or warrants are dilutive, the treasury stock method is used to determine the number of incremental shares to use in the EPS calculation. For basic options and warrants, the incremental number of shares can be determined easily using the following formula:

$$S = \frac{AMP - EP}{AMP} \times NS$$

Where:	S	=	Incremental shares
	AMP	=	Average market price for the accounting period
	EP	=	Exercise price of the option or warrant
	NS	=	Number of shares issuable upon exercise of option or warrant

In ASC 260-10-55, paragraphs 4 and 5, the FASB provides general guidelines for determining the average market price of the stock during an accounting period. Technically, every stock transaction during a period should be included in the average market price, but generally an average of closing prices on a weekly or monthly basis may be used. If there is a great deal of volatility in prices of the entity's common stock, the use of an average of the high and low prices, as opposed to closing pricing, may be more appropriate.

An enterprise may have an agreement (put option or forward purchase contract) that requires it to repurchase its common stock at a specified price (Block 10). If the average market price during the accounting period is less than the exercise price (Block 11), the agreement is dilutive, and incremental shares from use of the reverse treasury stock method are included as an adjustment to the weighted average number of shares outstanding. If, however, the exercise price is less than the average market price, the agreement is antidilutive and is not used in the EPS computation. The reverse treasury stock method assumes that sufficient common shares are sold at the beginning of the accounting period at a price equal to the average market price for the accounting period to collect adequate funds to repurchase the required shares under the agreement. The adjustment to the denominator in the EPS computation is the difference between the number of shares issued and the number of shares repurchased based on the contract.

An enterprise also may have an agreement (purchased call option) that allows it to buy its common stock at a specified price for a specified period of time (Block 12). These types of agreements are not included in the computation of diluted EPS, because they are antidilutive.

There are many other types of securities that are treated the same as or are equivalent to options and warrants (Block 13). These securities have been listed in the discussion dealing with securities that are equivalent to options and warrants. The securities may impact the computation of diluted EPS in different ways.

Once all options, warrants, and equivalent securities have been tested for dilution (Block 14), the next step is to illustrate the technical aspects of options and warrants in the calculation of diluted earnings per share. Two examples are used to illustrate the impact of options and warrants on the computation of diluted earnings per share. Assumptions for Example 2-20 are as follows.

Example 2-20
Options and Warrants

1. Reed Enterprises (Reed), a December 31 year-end company, had 4,000,000 common shares outstanding on January 1, 20X6.

2. Reed had the following options and warrants during 20X6;

   a. On July 1, 20X5, 1,500,000 options were issued giving the holders the right to purchase 1,500,000 shares of common stock at $30 per share.

   b. On December 1, 20X5, 600,000 options were issued giving the holder the right to purchase 600,000 shares of common stock at $25 per share. All 600,000 options were exercised on December 1, 20X6.

   c. On May 1, 20X6, 900,000 warrants were issued giving the holder the right to purchase 900,000 shares of common stock at $34 per share.

3. Average market prices for Reed's common stock during 20X6 were: Quarter 1—$32; Quarter 2—$33; Quarter 3— $35; Quarter 4—$40; May 1–June 30, 20X6—$34; and October 1–November 30, 20X6—$38.

4. Reed had no preferred stock during 20X6, and there were no changes in common shares during 20X6 except for the exercise of the 600,000 options on December 1.

5. The after-tax income amounts for 20X6 were as follows:

	Quarter 1	*Quarter 2*	*Quarter 3*	*Quarter 4*	*Annual*
Income/(loss) from continuing operations	$1,500,000	$(500,000)	$2,000,000	$2,500,000	$5,500,000
Gain/(loss) from discontinued operations	(3,000,000)				(3,000,000)
Unusual gain		900,000			900,000
Net income/ (loss)	$(1,500,000)	$400,000	$2,000,000	$2,500,000	$3,400,000

Using the information from the Example 2-20 assumptions, incremental shares of common stock to add to the denominator in the computation of diluted earnings per share are computed in Tables 2-19 and 2-20. Table 2-19 shows the calculation of the incremental shares for the 1,500,000 options issued in 20X5. All options were outstanding for the entire year, and none were exercised during the year. The computation is made for each quarter and averaged for the annual accounting period. Because the average market price of $32 is in excess of the $30 exercise price during the first quarter, the options are dilutive, and application of the treasury stock method produces 93,750 incremental shares to use in diluted EPS. Computation of the incremental shares in Table 2-19 uses the shortcut formula presented in the general discussion of options and warrants. No incremental shares are used in the Quarter 2 computation of diluted earnings per share. The options are dilutive for the second quarter because the average market price of $33 is in excess of the $30 exercise price; however, because there is a loss from continuing operations (Example 2-20, Assumption 5), all potentially dilutive securities would be antidilutive, and no incremental shares are used in Quarter 2 computation of diluted earnings per share. There is a total net loss in Quarter 1, but Reed has income from continuing operations. Because the benchmark for determining dilution is income from continuing operations, as long as there is income from continuing operations, incremental shares will be used for options and warrants when dilutive, even if there is a total net loss for the enterprise. Such is the case for Quarter 1, which means that the *required* presentation of diluted earnings per share for the total net loss is antidilutive. The 136,364 incremental shares from Quarter 2 are not used in Quarter 2 earnings per share calculations, but are used in the annual computation because there is income from continuing operations for the annual time period.

Table 2-19 Calculation of Incremental Shares from Options and Warrants for Diluted Earnings Per Share

1,500,000 Options (Assumption 2(a)):

Quarter	*Are Options and Warrants Dilutive?*	*Computation*	*Incremental Shares*
1	Yes	$\frac{\$32 - \$30}{\$32} \times 1{,}500{,}000$	93,750
2	No	Loss Reported	0
3	Yes	$\frac{\$35 - \$30}{\$35} \times 1{,}500{,}000$	214,286
4	Yes	$\frac{\$40 - \$30}{\$40} \times 1{,}500{,}000$	375,000
Totals for Quarters 1, 3 and 4			683,036
2		$\frac{\$33 - \$30}{\$33} \times 1{,}500{,}000$	136,364
Totals for Quarters 1–4			819,400

1,500,000 Options (Assumption 2(a)):

Quarter	*Are Options and Warrants Dilutive?*	*Computation*	*Incremental Shares*
Number of Quarters			4
Incremental shares for annual calculation			204,850

Table 2-20 shows the computation of incremental shares for the 600,000 options in Assumption 2b. This computation is similar to the calculations shown in Table 2-19 with two exceptions. All of the 600,000 options were actually exercised on November 30, 20X6 and, therefore, were not outstanding all of 20X6. When the incremental shares are computed for Quarter 4, the Quarter 4 average market price is not used. The average market price of $38 is computed for the period actually outstanding (October and November). In addition, because the options were only outstanding for two of the three months of the last quarter, the incremental shares are weighted for two-thirds of the quarter.

Table 2-20 Calculation of Incremental Shares from Options and Warrants for Diluted Earnings per Share

600,000 Options (Assumption 2(b)):

Quarter	*Are Options and Warrants Dilutive?*	*Computation*	*Incremental Shares*
1	Yes	$\frac{\$32 - \$25}{\$32} \times 600{,}000$	131,250
2	No	Loss Reported	0
3	Yes	$\frac{\$35 - \$25}{\$32} \times 600{,}000$	171,429
4	Yes	$\frac{\$38 - \$25}{\$38} \times 600{,}000 \times 2/3$	136,842
Totals for Quarters 1, 3 and 4			439,521
2		$\frac{\$33 - \$25}{\$33} \times 600{,}000$	145,455
Totals for Quarters 1–4			584,976
Number of Quarters			4
Incremental shares for annual calculation			146,244

Calculations of the incremental shares for the 900,000 warrants are shown in Table 2-21. Because these warrants were not issued until May 1, there would be no incremental shares to use in the Quarter 1 computation of diluted earnings per share. Because the warrants were only outstanding two of the three months in Quarter 2, any incremental shares would be weighted for two-thirds of the quarter. However, the warrants are antidilutive for the second quarter because the average market price of $33 is less than the $34 exercise price. In addition, even if the warrants were dilutive, they would not be used in Quarter 2 because a loss from continuing operations is reported in that quarter. Computations for Quarters 3 and 4 are similar to prior computations. However, there are no incremental shares from Quarter 2 added back for the annual computation because the warrants were antidilutive for the second quarter. In computations for the 1,500,000 and 600,000 options, the second quarter incremental shares were always added back for the annual computation. However, these options were actually dilutive but were not used in the second quarter computations only because a loss was reported in Quarter 2.

Table 2-21 Calculation of Incremental Shares from Options and Warrants for Diluted Earnings per Share

900,000 Warrants (Assumption 2(c)):

Quarter	*Are Options and Warrants Dilutive?*	*Computation*	*Incremental Shares*
1	N/A		0
2	No	Not dilutive—Exercise price exceeds average market price and loss reported for quarter	0
3	Yes	$\frac{\$35 - \$34}{\$35} \times 900{,}000$	25,714
4	Yes	$\frac{\$40 - \$34}{\$40} \times 900{,}000$	135,000
Totals for Quarters 1–4			160,714
Number of Quarters			4
Incremental shares for annual calculation			40,179

Using information on incremental shares from the computations in Tables 2-19 through 2-21, the adjustments to the weighted-average shares outstanding from options and warrants is summarized in Table 2-22. There is no adjustment for Quarter 2 and both basic and diluted earnings per share will be the same for that quarter.

Table 2-22 Summary of Incremental Shares from Options and Warrants for Diluted Earnings per Share

	Quarter 1	*Quarter 2*	*Quarter 3*	*Quarter 4*	*Annual*
1,500,000 Options (Table 2-19)	93,750	0	214,286	375,000	204,850
600,000 Options (Table 2-20)	131,250	0	171,429	136,842	146,244
900,000 Warrants (Table 2-21)	0	0	25,714	135,000	40,179
Adjustment To Denominator	225,000	0	411,429	646,842	391,273

Table 2-23 uses information from Assumption 5 in Example 2-20 and summary information from Table 2-22 to compute any adjustments to the numerator and denominator for computation of diluted earnings per share.

Table 2-23 Calculation of Numerator and Denominator for Diluted Earnings per Share

Computation of Numerator for Diluted EPS:

No adjustment required to numerator. The numerator would be the income amounts shown in Assumption 5 of Example 2-20.

Computation of Denominator for Diluted EPS:

	Quarter 1	*Quarter 2*	*Quarter 3*	*Quarter 4*	*Annual*
Weighted-Average Shares	4,000,000	4,000,000	4,000,000	4,200,000	4,050,000
Option & Warrant Adjustment (Table 2-22)	225,000	0	411,429	646,842	391,273
Denominator for Diluted EPS	4,225,000	4,000,000	4,411,429	4,846,842	4,441,273

There is no adjustment to the numerator for options and warrants because options and warrants generally require adjustments only to the denominator. The 4,000,000 weighted average shares shown for Quarters 1–3 equals the shares actually outstanding during that period because no common shares were sold or repurchased and no potentially dilutive securities were exercised or converted during the first three quarters. However, the weighted-average shares for Quarter 4 and the annual period are greater than the 4,000,000 shares reported for the first three quarters. The 200,000 additional shares for Quarter 4 came from exercise of the 600,000 warrants on December 1, 20X6. Because 600,000 warrants were converted into 600,000 shares of common stock, the 600,000 shares were outstanding for one month. Therefore, for Quarter 4, weighted-average shares would increase by 200,000 (600,000 × 1/3), which is computed by weighting the shares for one-third of the quarter that they were outstanding. The 4,050,000 weighted-average shares for the annual period is computed by averaging the weighted-average shares from all four quarters ((4,000,000 + 4,000,000 + 4,000,000 + 4,200,000) ÷ 4).

Because Reed has income from continuing operations for the annual accounting period ($5,500,000), the denominator used in the computation of diluted earnings per share is 4,441,273 (4,050,000 + 391,273). If the $5,500,000 income had been a loss of $5,500,000, the 391,273 incremental shares would not have been used in the computation, and basic and diluted EPS for the annual accounting period would have been the same. This procedure would apply even if some of the quarters had income and used incremental shares in the EPS computation that caused basic and diluted EPS in those quarter to be different.

This completes the discussion of Example 2-20 on the calculation of incremental shares from options and warrants. Example 2-21 covers issues related to stock-based compensation. Assumptions for Example 2-21 are as follows.

Example 2-21
Stock-Based Compensation Plans

1. Smith Enterprises (Smith), a December 31 year-end company, granted 200,000 options to purchase 200,000 shares of common stock to five employees on January 1, 20X6.
2. Terms of the options were as follows: exercise price of the options was $20, all options vested at the end of two years, forfeitures were 3% per year, and the service period for amortization purposes was two years, the same as the vesting period.
3. Average market price for Smith's common stock during 20X6 was $29.
4. The grant-date fair value of the options is $10 using appropriate option pricing model.
5. Actual forfeitures during 20X6 were 4,000 and were ratably forfeited during the year.
6. Smith had income from continuing operations, and its tax rate for 20X6 was 40%.

A review of the assumptions from Example 2-21 indicates that Smith has a share-based payment plan that is not related to performance or market conditions, therefore the plan is treated like options and warrants for purposes of computing diluted earnings per share. The treasury stock method is used to compute the number of incremental shares to add to the denominator in the computation of diluted earnings per share. The first step is to compute the amount of assumed proceeds that would be available to repurchase common shares if all of the options had been exercised. Under a share-based payment plan, proceeds will generally consist of three components. This example has all three types of proceeds: from exercise of the options by the employees, from unamortized compensation expense, and from the tax benefit deficiency. Table 2-24 shows the computation of the assumed proceeds from all three components. The first part illustrates the calculations of the proceeds from the assumed exercise of the options. If the options were exercised by the employees, the company would receive $20 per option or share of common stock issued. The options are assumed to be exercised (common stock is assumed to be issued) at the beginning of the period or later if issued later. In this example, the options were issued January 1, 20X6, the beginning of the first accounting period, and, therefore, they are assumed to be exercised at the beginning of the period and common stock is assumed to be outstanding from the beginning of the accounting period. The computation must be made on an average option balance for the period. Accordingly, the beginning and ending balance is totaled and divided by two to obtain the average balance for the period. In this example, the only difference in the beginning and ending balance is the number of options actually forfeited by employees during the year. Example 2-21, Assumption 5, states that 4,000 options are actually forfeited during the year and the ending balance is reduced by 4,000 options to 196,000 (200,000 beginning option balance – 4,000 options forfeited). The average option balance is adjusted for the number of options actually forfeited during the year, regardless of the number of forfeitures used when computing compensation expense. The average option balance during the year times the $20 option price is the proceeds assumed to be received by Smith from exercise of the options.

The second part of Table 2-24 shows the computation of the assumed proceeds from the unrecognized compensation cost. This component exists when the entity has compensation expense for financial accounting purposes. Because a fair value model is required for estimating the fair value of share-based payments using the provisions of ASC 718, compensation cost is computed by using an appropriate option pricing model on the date of grant. In this example the grant-date fair value is computed as $10 using an option pricing model. The number of options less the number expected to be forfeited times the $10 grant-date fair value is the total compensation cost to be reported. The total compensation cost is amortized over the service period using a straight-line method. In this example, the service period is two years. The assumed proceeds from the unamortized compensation cost also must be computed on an average basis. The actual beginning option balance of 200,000 times the grant-date fair value option price equals the beginning of period unrecognized compensation cost. The beginning unrecognized compensation cost plus the ending balance divided by two equals the average unrecognized compensation cost for 20X6 that is part of the assumed proceeds from the share-based payment plan. Computing the ending unrecognized compensation balance requires three separate computations. The beginning unrecognized balance is adjusted for the compensation cost reported for 20X6, annual compensation cost not reported related to options at the end of the year, and compensation cost related to actual forfeitures.

The last computation in Table 2-24 represents the tax benefit deficiency, which is the difference between the amount of compensation cost expected to be reported for tax purposes and the amount expected to be reported for financial accounting purposes. According to ASC 718, when the amount deducted as compensation cost for financial reporting purposes exceeds the amount expected to be deducted for tax purposes, the deferred tax asset related to the difference is deducted from paid-in-capital when the options are actually exercised. This difference is considered a reduction of assumed proceeds when applying the treasury stock method to share-based payment plans when computing diluted earnings per share. In Table 2-24, the compensation cost reported for financial accounting purposes is computed as $1,980,000 using the average option balance of 198,000 and the grant-date fair value option price of $10. The $1,782,000 compensation cost for tax purpose is determined using an intrinsic approach, which is the difference between the fair value of the stock and the option price on the date of exercise. Because the options have not actually been exercised, the average market price for the accounting period is used for the fair value or selling price of the stock on the date of exercise. The pretax deficiency is $198,000, and because Smith has a 40% tax rate, the after-tax deficiency used to reduce the assumed proceeds is $79,200.

Table 2-24 Computation of Assumed Proceeds in Share–Based Payment Plan

Amount Employees Pay Assuming Exercise of Options:			
Actual beginning option balance		200,000	
Actual ending option balance (200,000 - 4,000 Forfeitures)		196,000	
Total		396,000	
Divided by 2		2	
Average option balance		198,000	
Option price		× $20	
Amount employees paid assuming exercise			$3,960,000
Unrecognized Compensation Cost in 20X6: Beginning of period cost:			
Beginning of period options	200,000		
Grant-date fair value of options ×	$10		
Beginning of period compensation cost		$2,000,000	
End of period cost:			
Beginning of period compensation cost	$2,000,000		
Compensation cost for 20X6	(940,000)[1]		
Annual compensation cost not reported related to options at end of year	(40,000)[2]		
Compensation cost related to actual forfeited options	(40,000)[3]		
End of period unrecognized compensation cost		980,000	
Total		$2,980,000	
Divided by 2		2	
End of period average unrecognized compensation cost			1,490,000

Tax Benefit Deficiency Computation:			
Average end of year option balance (see above)	198,000		
Grant-date fair value options	× 10		
Total compensation cost of outstanding options		$1,980,000	
Average end of year option balance (see above)	198,000		
$29 average market price –$20 option price =	× $9		
Intrinsic value of outstanding options		1,782,000	
Total compensation expense in excess of tax deduction		$198,000	
Tax rate		× 40%	
Tax benefit deficiency			(79,200)
Assumed proceeds used in treasury stock method			$5,370,800

[1]200,000 options × 3% = 6,000

200,000 options × 3% = 6,000

Total estimated forfeitures 12,000

200,000 options – 12,000 forfeitures = 188,000 × $10 grant-date fair value=$1,880,000/2 year service period = $940,000.

[2]200,000 beginning of period options - 4,000 actual forfeitures = 196,000 end of period option - 188,000 beginning of period estimated options = 8,000 × $10 grant-date fair value = $80,000/2 year service period = $40,000.

[3]4,000 actual forfeited options during 20X6 × $10 grant-date fair value = $40,000.

In Table 2-25, using the information from Table 2-24, the total proceeds of $5,370,800 are assumed to be used to buy back all the common shares possible at the average market price. The difference between the number of shares of 185,200 that can be repurchased using the assumed proceeds and the 198,000 average number of shares assumed issued upon exercise of the options is the incremental shares to use in the computation of diluted earnings per share. The number of shares assumed issued is the average balance outstanding for the accounting period.

Table 2-25 Computation of Incremental Shares from Share-Based Payment Plan Used in Diluted Earnings per Share Computation

Average number of shares at end of year (Table 2-24)		198,000
Computation of Number of Shares Assumed Repurchased:		
Assumed proceeds used in the treasury stock method (Table 2-24)	$5,370,800	
Average market price for 20X6	$29	

Number of shares assumed repurchased using average market price	185,200
Incremental number of shares to be used in diluted earnings per share	12,800

This completes the discussion of options, warrants, and equivalent securities. The next section covers convertible securities.

Convertible Securities

Convertible securities (Block 15) are securities that may be exchanged for common stock, based upon some predetermined agreement. The most common types of convertible securities are convertible debt and convertible preferred stock. The issuing company uses the conversion privilege to make the security offering more attractive to the investor. The holder of the convertible security may become a common shareholder by trading in the debt or preferred stock for a specified number of common shares. These types of securities could have a dilutive effect upon earnings per share if converted. This is the reason they must be considered in the computation of diluted earnings per share. Some convertible securities may have multiple conversion rates (Block 16) available to the holder of the security. When multiple conversion rates are available, the entity should select the rate that is most beneficial to the holder of the security when considering the security in the computation of diluted earnings per share.

For a convertible security to enter into the computation of diluted earnings per share, it must be dilutive. To be dilutive, the individual earnings per share effect of the convertible security must be less than basic earnings per share (Block 17). A convertible security may be dilutive when compared to basic EPS, but antidilutive when considered with all other potentially dilutive securities (Block 18). A convertible security is used in the computation of earnings per share only if it is individually dilutive and dilutive in relation to the group of potentially dilutive securities. To determine if a convertible security is dilutive in relation to the group of securities, the convertible security must be dilutive in relation to the previous calculation of diluted earnings per share. To be dilutive in relation to the group, the individual EPS of a convertible security must be less than the previously calculated diluted earnings per share amount. The individual earnings per share effect of a convertible security is determined by dividing the number of shares obtainable upon conversion into the annual dividend or after-tax interest and nondiscretionary requirements associated with the security. Nondiscretionary requirements are items that are tied to income, such as bonuses, and will change if income changes. If there is more than one potentially dilutive security, the individual earnings per share effect for all potentially dilutive securities is computed separately for each individual security, and the test for dilution will begin with the security that has the lowest individual earnings per share. A new DEPS will be computed, using the previous DEPS and the earnings per share effect determined to be the lowest. Each successive security is compared to the new DEPS amount to determine whether it is dilutive. The process continues on an individual security basis until all securities have been tested.

When convertible debt is found to have a dilutive impact on earnings per share, the number of shares issuable upon conversion is included in the denominator of the diluted earnings per share computation, using the "if converted" method. The "if converted" method assumes that the debt was converted at the beginning of the accounting period (or later if issued after the beginning of the accounting period), and it is necessary to adjust the numerator of the equation for the after-tax effect of the interest expense recorded during the accounting period. If there is a discount or premium associated with the convertible debt, it must be taken into consideration in the determination of interest expense and the after-tax effect of the expense. In addition, the numerator must be adjusted for the after-tax effect of items tied to income, because income has increased from the assumed elimination of the interest expense on the debt.

It is also assumed that dilutive convertible preferred stock was converted at the beginning of the accounting period (or later, if issued later). The number of common shares issuable upon conversion should be included in the denominator of the diluted EPS equation. There may be an adjustment necessary for the preferred dividend declared or paid. In an earlier discussion, preferred dividends were deducted from net income to arrive at net income available for common shareholders. If the assumption is made that the preferred stock is converted into common shares, this deduction is not appropriate, and the preferred dividends must be added back to net income. If preferred dividends were not previously deducted from net income, no adjustment is required.

Once all convertible securities have been tested for dilution (Block 19), the next step is to illustrate the technical aspects of convertible securities in the calculation of diluted earnings per share. One example is used to illustrate the impact of convertible securities. Assumptions for Example 2-22 are as follows.

Example 2-22
Convertible Securities

1. Lowe Enterprises (Lowe), a December 31 year-end company, is reviewing its convertible securities for the impact of the securities on the computation of earnings per share for 20X6.

2. Lowe had the following convertible securities:

    a. On July 1, 20X5, $1,000,000, 8% convertible bonds were sold at par. Each $1,000 bond is convertible into 100 shares of common stock.

    b. On April 1, 20X6, 100,000 shares of $20 par, 6% cumulative convertible preferred stock was sold. The preferred stock is convertible into 30,000 shares of common stock. Quarterly dividends are 1.5% of par value and are paid at the end of each quarter.

3. The after-tax income from continuing operations, preferred dividends, weighted-average shares outstanding, and basic earnings per share amounts for 20X6 was as follows:

	Quarter 1	*Quarter 2*	*Quarter 3*	*Quarter 4*	*Annual*
Income from continuing operations	$1,000,000	$2,040,000	$2,050,000	$2,500,000	$7,590,000
Preferred dividends		(30,000)	(30,000)	(30,000)	(90,000)
Income for common share-holders	$1,000,000	$2,010,000	$2,020,000	$2,470,000	$7,500,000
Weighted-average shares	2,000,000	2,000,000	2,000,000	2,000,000	2,000,000
Basic earnings per share	$.50	$1.01	$1.01	$1.24	$3.75

4. Lowe had no preferred stock other than the stock listed in Assumption 2b and no potentially dilutive securities other than the securities in Assumption 2.
5. Lowe paid a bonus equal to 5% of income before taxes and before the bonus.
6. Lowe's tax rate for 20X6 was 40%.

The first step in incorporating convertible securities into the dilutive earnings per share computation is to determine the adjustment to income (numerator) and the adjustment to the weighted-average shares outstanding. Next, an individual earnings per share is computed for each convertible security for each time period to determine whether the convertible security is individually dilutive. A convertible security is individually dilutive if its individual earnings per share is less than basic earnings per share. Last, if the convertible security is individually dilutive, the security also must be dilutive as a group. That is, if the security is assumed to be converted to common stock, the impact on earnings and common shares must cause the earnings per share to decrease or loss per share to increase from the previous earnings per share computation. Each convertible security must be taken in sequence, using the one with the most dilution (smallest individual EPS) first and the security with the least amount of dilution (largest individual EPS) last. Computation of individual earnings per share for both convertible debt and convertible preferred stock is presented in Tables 2-26 and 2-27. Table 2-26 shows the numerator and denominator adjustments for the convertible debt. Income is increased each quarter by $20,000, the amount of the interest expense that was reported. If the debt is assumed to be converted into common stock at the beginning of the period, that interest expense does not exist since the debt was converted. Therefore, before-tax income increases by $20,000 each quarter and by $80,000 for the annual period. The numerator also includes nondiscretionary adjustments, and because Lowe provides a bonus equal to 5% of income before tax and before the bonus, an additional $1,000 ($20,000 × 5%) bonus for each quarter is computed as a result of the increase in income of

$20,000. As a result, the net increase in the numerator is $19,000 ($20,000 – $1,000) before tax. Lowe has a 40% tax rate and an after-tax rate of 60% for 20X6. The after-tax increase in income is $11,400, and the numerator for the diluted earnings per share computation will increase by $11,400 per quarter, or $45,600 for the annual EPS computation, if the convertible debt is dilutive. If the debt is converted into common stock, an additional 100,000 common shares would be issued. Therefore, because it is assumed that the debt is converted at the beginning of the period, 100,000 shares would be added to the denominator. Using this information, the individual EPS for the convertible debt is $.114 per quarter and $.456 for the annual accounting period.

Table 2-26 Computation of Individual Earnings per Share for Convertible Debt

Time Period (a)	*Before-Tax Interest (b)*[1]	*Bonus Adjustments (c)*[2]	*Total (d)=(b)-(c)*	*After-Tax Rate (1-Tax Rate) (e)*	*After-Tax Interest (f)=(d)× (e)*	*Shares Issued Upon Conversion (g)*	*Individual EPS =(f)/(g)*
Quarter 1	$20,000	$1,000	$19,000	60%	$11,400	100,000	$.114
Quarter 2	$20,000	$1,000	$19,000	60%	$11,400	100,000	$.114
Quarter 3	$20,000	$1,000	$19,000	60%	$11,400	100,000	$.114
Quarter 4	$20,000	$1,000	$19,000	60%	$11,400	100,000	$.114
Annual	$80,000	$4,000	$76,000	60%	$45,600	100,000	$.456

[1] $1,000,000 par value × 8% annual interest rate = $80,000 annual interest ÷ 4 quarters = $20,000 interest expense per quarter.
[2] $20,000 increase in before-tax income × 5% = $1,000.

Next, the individual EPS for the convertible preferred stock is computed (Table 2-27). Because the stock was not issued until April 1, the assumed conversion occurs on April 1, the date the preferred stock is issued. Therefore, the preferred stock does not enter into the EPS computations for Quarter 1. Lowe paid $30,000 in dividends each quarter; therefore the individual earnings per share for each quarter is $1.00 and $4.00 for the annual period. The 22,500 common shares used in the annual accounting period are the 30,000 shares from assumed conversion of the preferred stock weighted only for three-quarters of the year because the shares were outstanding only from April 1 to December 31.

Table 2-27 Computation of Individual Earnings per Share for Convertible Preferred Stock

Time Period (a)	*Preferred Dividend (b)*[1]	*Shares Issued Upon Conversion (c)*	*Individual EPS (d)=(b)/(c)*
Quarter 1	[2]$0	0	N/A
Quarter 2	$30,000	30,000	$1.00
Quarter 3	$30,000	30,000	$1.00
Quarter 4	$30,000	30,000	$1.00
Annual	[3]$90,000	[4]22,500	$4.00

[1] 100,000 preferred shares × $20 par value = $2,000,000 × 1.5% = $30,000 quarterly dividend.

[2] The preferred stock was not issued until April 1, 20X6; therefore the dividends were not paid until Quarter 2.
[3] $30,000 + $30,000 + $30,000 = $90,000 annual dividends.
[4] 0 + 30,000 + 30,000 + 30,000 = 90,000 ÷ 4 quarters = 22,500.

After computing the individual earnings per share for each quarter and for the annual accounting period, the individual earnings per share are compared to basic earnings per share to determine whether the convertible securities are dilutive on an individual basis. Table 2-28 presents a comparison of basic earnings per share with the individual earnings per share of both the debt and the preferred stock. Table 2-28 shows that all convertible securities are dilutive for all periods, except for the preferred stock for the annual accounting period. A convertible security that is individually dilutive may not be included in the final earnings per share computation, because when all potentially dilutive securities, including convertible securities, are considered as a group, some may be antidilutive. Only convertible securities are included in this example; however, all potentially dilutive securities are considered when assessing dilution as a group. Table 2-29 shows the test for dilution as a group. The convertible security with the smallest individual earnings per share is considered first. The convertible debt is used first because its individual EPS of $.114 is less than the $1.00 individual earnings per share of the convertible preferred stock. In Quarter 2, the debt is used to compute an earnings per share amount equal to $.9626 and that this amount is less than the prior earnings per share computation of $1.01; therefore, the debt is dilutive in Quarter 2 on a group basis. Next, the preferred stock is assumed to be converted to common stock and used in the earnings per share computation. After including the preferred stock, a new EPS number of $.9631 is computed. Because the $.9631 EPS number is greater than the prior computation of $.9626, the preferred stock is antidilutive on a group basis and would not be used in diluted EPS computation even though the preferred stock is dilutive on an individual basis for Quarter 2. Using this same procedure for the remaining time periods, the debt is dilutive for all time periods, but the preferred stock is antidilutive for all time periods except for Quarter 4. The preferred stock was not tested on a group basis for the annual time period, because it was antidilutive on an individual basis. The convertible preferred stock would only be used in the diluted earnings per share computation for Quarter 4 and would be excluded for all other time periods.

Table 2-28 Determination of Individual Dilution of Convertible Securities

Time Period (a)	*Basic EPS (Example 2-22, Assumption 3) (b)*	*Individual EPS for Debt (Table 2-26) (c)*	*Individual EPS for Preferred Stock (Table 2-27) (d)*	*Debt Dilutive on Individual Basis (e)=(c)<(b)*	*Preferred Stock Dilutive on Individual Basis (f)=(d)<(b)*
Quarter 1	$ .50	$.114	N/A	Yes	N/A
Quarter 2	$1.01	$.114	$1.00	Yes	Yes
Quarter 3	$1.01	$.114	$1.00	Yes	Yes

Time Period (a)	Basic EPS (Example 2-22, Assumption 3) (b)	Individual EPS for Debt (Table 2-26) (c)	Individual EPS for Preferred Stock (Table 2-27) (d)	Debt Dilutive on Individual Basis (e)=(c)<(b)	Preferred Stock Dilutive on Individual Basis (f)=(d)<(b)
Quarter 4	$1.24	$.114	$1.00	Yes	Yes
Annual	$3.75	$.456	$4.00	Yes	No

Table 2-29 Determination of Group Dilution of Convertible Securities

Time Period (a)		Income (Numerator) (b)	Number of Shares (Denominator) (c)	EPS (d)=(b)/(c)	Dilutive In Total (e)
Quarter 1					
	Basic	$1,000,000	2,000,000	$.5000	
	Debt	11,400	100,000		
	Total	$1,011,400	2,100,000	.4816	Yes
Quarter 2					
	Basic	$2,010,000	2,000,000	1.0100	
	Debt	11,400	100,000		
	Total	$2,021,400	2,100,000	.9626	Yes
	Preferred Stock	30,000	30,000		
	Total	$2,051,400	2,130,000	.9631	No
Quarter 3					
	Basic	$2,020,000	2,000,000	1.0100	
	Debt	11,400	100,000		
	Total	$2,031,400	2,100,000	.9673	Yes
	Preferred Stock	30,000	30,000		
	Total	$2,061,400	2,130,000	.9678	No
Quarter 4					
	Basic	$2,470,000	2,000,000	1.2350	
	Debt	11,400	100,000		
	Total	$2,481,400	2,100,000	1.1820	Yes
	Preferred Stock	30,000	30,000		
	Total	$2,511,400	2,130,000	1.1790	Yes
Annual					
	Basic	$7,500,000	2,000,000	3.7500	
	Debt	45,600	100,000		
	Total	$7,545,600	2,100,000	3.5931	Yes

This completes the discussion of convertible securities. The next section covers agreements that allow settlement in either cash or stock.

Agreements That Allow Settlement in Cash or Stock

Some agreements allow the holder of a security or the enterprise the right to settle the agreement in either cash or common stock of the entity (Block 20). For example, a stock appreciation right (SAR) agreement might allow the holder of the SAR to receive stock or cash upon exercise of the agreement. Generally, agreements that allow settlement in cash or stock are assumed to be settled for stock for purposes of EPS computations, unless the entity can provide information that would support the assumption that the agreement would be settled in cash. Each agreement should be evaluated to determine if it will impact earnings per share computations, whether it will be dilutive, and how the agreement will enter into the earnings per share computation. Each agreement is evaluated separately until all agreements have been tested (Block 21). This completes the discussion of agreements that allow settlement in cash or stock. The next section covers contingent agreements.

Contingent Agreements

For any one of several reasons, an enterprise may enter into an agreement that requires the issuance of shares of common stock if some future condition is realized. These types of agreements are referred to as contingent agreements (Block 22) or contingently issuable shares because the consideration (stock) involved will be paid if some future event takes place (i.e., the consideration is contingent upon the future event). When the contingent agreement involves the issuance of common stock, it will affect the computation of earnings per share. An infinite variety of contingent agreements is possible, and the discussion here cannot cover all types of contingent agreements. However, most contingent agreements can be classified into three categories. The first basic type of agreement specifies that shares of common stock will be issued, provided a certain level of earnings is achieved and maintained. A second type of agreement specifies that shares of common stock will be issued, depending upon the future market price of the stock. The third type of agreement covers other contingent issues (e.g., a specified number of common shares will be issued to shareholders for the opening of each new retail store).

Whether common shares under a contingent agreement are included in the earnings per share computation depends on the circumstances of the contingency and whether inclusion of the shares would be dilutive. If all requirements of the contingent agreement have been fulfilled by the end of the accounting period (Block 23), the common shares are included in the earnings per share computation from the beginning of the period in which the requirements are fulfilled. However, if the contingent requirements are not fulfilled by the end of the accounting period, assume that the time period for the contingency ends with the end of the current accounting period. Determine the number, if any, of common shares that would be issued assuming the contingency ends at the end of the current accounting period (Block 24). Any shares that would be issued in such a situation would be included in the earnings per share calculation from the beginning of the accounting period. For example, if the contingency is tied to achieving a required level of earnings, the level of earnings achieved in the current accounting period is assumed to remain the same until the end of the contingency period. To illustrate, assume that 100,000 additional common shares will be issued to shareholders if earnings exceed $5,000,000 for two consecutive years. During 20X6, the first year, earnings were $6,500,000, and 100,000 shares would be used in the calculation because it is assumed that the $6,500,000 level will be maintained in 20X7. If income of $4,000,000 had been reported for 20X6, the contingency would not be used in the earnings per share calculation.

Once it has been determined that common shares related to a contingent agreement will be assumed issued, the impact on the diluted earnings per share computation will be accounted for as options or warrants, convertible securities, or an agreement that allows settlement in cash or stock. The procedure used will depend on the elements of the contingency. Once all contingently issuable common shares have been tested for dilution (Block 25), the next step is to illustrate the technical aspects of contingent agreements in the calculation of diluted earnings per share.

The assumptions in Example 2-23 are used to illustrate the technical aspects of contingent agreements.

Example 2-23
Contingent Agreements

1. Main Enterprises (Main), a December 31 year-end company, had the following contingent agreements during 20X6:
    a. On January 1, 20X6, Main acquired a subsidiary in a business combination. As part of the agreement to combine, Main agreed to issue an additional 50,000 shares of common stock to the previous owners of the acquired company on December 31, 20X7 if the acquired company's earnings exceeded $150,000 for each of the years 20X6 and 20X7. The acquired company had the following earnings during 20X6: Quarter 1—$60,000, Quarter 2—$100,000, Quarter 3—$60,000, and Quarter 4—$45,000.
    b. On January 1, 20X6, Main acquired a company through another business combination. As part of the agreement to combine, Main agreed to issue an additional 75,000 shares of common stock to the previous owners of the acquired company on December 31, 20X7 if the market value of Main's common stock fell below $45 per share. The market price of Main's common stock exceeded $50 per share during the entire year of 20X6.
2. Main had no other potentially dilutive securities other than the contingent agreements in Assumption 1.
3. Main reported income from continuing operations for all four quarters and the annual accounting period during 20X6.

Neither of the contingent agreements would be used in the computation of basic earnings per share because the conditions for issuance of the shares have not been fulfilled. However, the common shares may be assumed issued for diluted EPS if the conditions would be met assuming the end of the accounting period is the end of the contingency period.

The earnings contingency requires an earnings level of $150,000. The subsidiary earned only $60,000 in Quarter 1; therefore, the condition is not met assuming that the end of Quarter 1 is the end of the contingency period. The contingent shares would not be included in Quarter 1 computation of diluted EPS. However, in Quarter 2 the earnings level is $160,000 ($60,000 from Quarter 1 + $100,000 from Quarter 2). Accordingly, the 50,000 shares would be assumed issued in Quarter 2 under the assumption that the end of Quarter 2 is the end of the contingency period. The 50,000 contingent shares would also be included in Quarters 3 and 4 computations, and 37,500 (0 + 50,000 + 50,000 + 50,000 = 150,000 ÷ 4) would be include in the annual diluted EPS computation.

No common shares would be included in either basic or diluted earnings per share from the market price contingency. The market price exceeds $50 per share for the entire year of 20X6. The 75,000 contingent shares would only have to be issued if the market price fell below $45 per share. Table 2-30 shows the computation of the number of contingent shares to include in diluted EPS.

Table 2-30 Summary of Contingent Agreements

	Quarter 1	*Quarter 2*	*Quarter 3*	*Quarter 4*	*Annual*
Earnings Contingency	0	50,000	50,000	50,000	37,500
Market Price Contingency	0	0	0	0	0

After all potentially dilutive securities have been tested for individual dilution, individual earnings per share is computed for each security by dividing the adjustment to the numerator by the adjustment for the denominator. Next, the individual earnings per share impacts are ranked from the lowest individual EPS (most dilutive) to the highest individual EPS (least dilutive). The security with the most dilutive EPS is used first in the EPS computation. If any security's individual EPS amount is greater than the prior EPS computation, that security is assumed to be antidilutive, even though it was individually dilutive, and is excluded from the diluted EPS computation (Block 26). See a more detailed discussion of this process in the analysis of convertible securities, because these securities would be most impacted by this sequencing procedure.

Other Considerations

Several other issues related directly or indirectly to earnings per share computations require further discussion, including securities that participate in dividends with common stock, capital structures that have two or more classes of common stock, and securities issued by a subsidiary of an entity currently computing earnings per share.

Securities that participate in dividend distributions with common stockholder, such as fully participating or partially participating preferred stock, should be included in the earnings per computation, if dilutive, using the assumed converted (if converted) procedure. See a detailed discussion of the "if-converted" procedure in the analysis of convertible securities.

When a company has two or more classes of common stock (or common stock and participating nonconvertible preferred stock) with different rates of dividends, and no class of stock has senior rights over the other class of stock, such as dividend preferences or preferences upon liquidation, the two-class procedure should be used when computing earnings per share. The two-class procedure is applied as follows: dividends from all classes of stock are used to reduce income from continuing operations, and the remaining income after deducting dividends is allocated to each class of stock based on it right of participation in the income, assuming that all income is distributed. Both basic and diluted earnings per share is computed, if required, for each class of stock by following the earnings per share procedures discussed in the previous sections.

To illustrate the two-class procedure, assume the facts in Example 2-24.

Example 2-24
Two-Class Common

1. Ward, Inc. (Ward), a December 31 year-end company, is computing earnings per share for 20X6.
2. Ward has 10,000 shares of 8%, $50 par value fully participating non-convertible preferred stock.
3. Ward had 100,000 common shares with a par value of $10 outstanding on January 1, 20X6. No common or preferred shares were sold or repurchased during 20X6.
4. Ward had no potentially dilutive securities during 20X6.
5. Ward paid $150,000 in dividends to both preferred and common share-holders, and income after tax for 20X6 was $450,000.

Ward has a simple capital structure and will only report basic earnings per share, because it has no potentially dilutive securities. The first step in determining the allocation of earnings to preferred and common stocks in the EPS computation is to determine the allocation of the $150,000 in dividends declared for 20X6. Because the preferred stock is fully participating, both common and preferred receive an equal percentage times their par value times the number of shares. First, dividends of $40,000 ($50 × 8% × 10,000 shares) will be allocated to the preferred stock. Second, dividends of $80,000 ($10 × 8% × 100,000 shares) will be allocated to common. The balance of the dividends of $30,000 ($150,000 – $40,000 – $80,000) will be allocated one-third to preferred and two-thirds to common. The one-third and two-thirds allocation is based on the ratio of the balance in the capital accounts of the stock. Preferred has a balance of $500,000 ($50 par × 10,000 shares) and common has a balance of $1,000,000 ($10 par value × 100,000 shares). Therefore, the $30,000 remaining dividend balance is allocated $10,000 (1/3 × $30,000) to preferred and $20,000 ($30,000 × 2/3) to common. The allocation of the $150,000 in dividends is computed as follows:

	Preferred Stock	Common Stock
\$50 par × 8% = \$4.00 × 10,000 shares	\$40,000	
\$10 par × 8% = \$ .80 × 100,000 shares		\$80,000
1/3 to preferred (\$30,000 × 500,000/1,500,000)	10,000	
2/3 to common (\$30,000 × 1,000,000/1,500,000)		20,000
Total	\$50,000	\$100,000

Ward had earnings of \$450,000 for 20X6 and distributed \$150,000 in dividends, leaving undistributed earnings of \$300,000. The \$300,000 in undistributed earnings must be allocated to preferred and common based on the fully participating feature. Therefore, the undistributed earnings should be allocated to preferred and common using the one-third and two-thirds allocation process determined above. The allocation is computed as follows:

	Preferred Stock	Common Stock
Allocation to preferred (1/3 × \$300,000)	\$100,000	
Allocation to common (2/3 × \$300,000)		\$200,000
Undistributed earnings	\$100,000	\$200,000
Distributed earnings (from above)	50,000	100,000
Total 20X6 earnings	\$150,000	\$300,000
Weighted average number of shares	10,000	100,000
Basic earnings per share	\$15.00	\$3.00

When a subsidiary has potentially dilutive securities that can be turned into common stock of the parent company, the securities, if dilutive, should be used in the computation of the parent earnings per share. However, if the securities can be turned into common stock of the subsidiary, the potentially dilutive securities should enter into the computation of the earnings per share of the subsidiary, and EPS of the subsidiary then will be used in the parent's earnings per share computation. These procedures also would apply to investments accounted for using the equity method of accounting as required by ASC 323.

Disclosures

Earnings per share should be reported for each accounting period that an income statement or income summary is presented. When an enterprise has a simple capital structure, only basic earnings per share is reported. If an entity has a complex capital structure, the reporting of both basic and diluted earnings per share is required. An entity has some flexibility in the terms used for basic and diluted EPS. The terms "basic" and "diluted" do not have to be used. Companies are free to develop other appropriate terms as long as they are descriptive of the EPS numbers. ASC 260-10-45-4 suggests that terms such as "earnings per common share" and "earnings per common share—assuming dilution," respectively, are appropriate. Earnings per share amounts (basic or basic and diluted) must be presented on the face of the income statement for income from continuing operations and for net income. In addition, EPS amounts also must be reported for discontinued operations, and accounting changes. However, these EPS amounts may be presented on the face of the income statement or disclosed in related notes. A dual presentation of basic and diluted earnings per share must be reported for all accounting periods presented if diluted earnings per share is required for a minimum of one accounting period, and both must be reported for all periods presented even if EPS is the same for both diluted and basic.

In addition to the presentation described above, ASC 260-10-50 requires companies to disclose the following earnings per share information:

1. The numerator and denominator used in the basic and diluted earnings per share computations must be reconciled. The reconciliation must include each individual income and common share adjustment used for EPS for income from continuing operations.
2. The impact of preferred dividends when computing income to use in the earnings per share computation.
3. Potentially dilutive securities that were not used in the EPS computation because such securities were antidilutive, but could be dilutive in future accounting periods.
4. Any transactions that occurred after the most recent balance sheet date, but prior to the release of the financial statements, which would have a material impact on the number of common shares or potentially dilutive securities if the transaction had occurred prior to the balance sheet date.

One comprehensive example is used to illustrate computation of both basic and diluted earnings per share and the disclosures required by ASC 260-10-50. Assumptions for Example 2-25 are as follows.

Example 2-25
Comprehensive Example of Earnings per Share

1. Burch Enterprises (Burch), a December 31 year-end company, had 2,400,000 common shares outstanding on January 1, 20X6 and 3,000,000 shares outstanding on December 31, 20X6.
2. During 20X6, the following common shares were sold or repurchased by Burch:
   a. 600,000 shares were sold on June 1.
   b. 100,000 shares were sold on July 1.
   c. 100,000 shares were repurchased on October 1.
   d. The 100,000 shares repurchased on October 1 were from shares outstanding from the beginning of the year and are accounted for as treasury shares.
3. Burch uses a monthly average to compute the weighted-average shares outstanding during the period, and the computation is for the annual accounting period of 20X6.
4. Burch had the following options and warrants during 20X6:
   a. On July 1, 20X5, 1,500,000 options were issued giving the holders the right to purchase 1,500,000 common shares at a price of $30 per share.
   b. On December 1, 20X5, 600,000 options were issued giving the holder the right to purchase 600,000 shares of common stock at a price of $25 per share. All 600,000 options were exercised on December 1, 20X6.

c. On May 1, 20X6, 900,000 warrants were issued giving the holder the right to purchase 900,000 shares of common stock at a price of $34 per share.

5. Burch had the following convertible securities:

   a. On July 1, 20X5, $1,000,000, 8% convertible bonds were sold at par. Each $1,000 bond is convertible into 100 shares of common stock.

   b. On April 1, 20X6, 100,000 shares of $20 par, 6% cumulative convertible preferred stock was sold. The preferred stock is convertible into 30,000 shares of common stock. Quarterly dividends are 1.5% of par value and are paid at the end of each quarter. Dividends of $90,000 were paid on the preferred stock during 20X6.

6. Burch had the following contingent agreements during 20X6:

   a. On January 1, 20X6, Burch acquired a subsidiary in a business combination. As part of the agreement to combine, Burch agreed to issue an additional 50,000 shares of common stock to the previous owners of the acquired company on December 31, 20X7 if the acquired company's earnings exceeded $150,000 for each of the years 20X6 and 20X7. The acquired company had the following earnings during 20X6: Quarter 1—$60,000, Quarter 2—$100,000, Quarter 3—$60,000, and Quarter 4—$45,000.

   b. On January 1, 20X6, Burch acquired a company through another business combination. As part of the agreement to combine, Burch agreed to issue an additional 75,000 shares of common stock to the previous owners of the acquired company on December 31, 20X7 if the market value of Burch's common stock fell below $45 per share. The market price of Burch's common stock exceeds $50 per share during the entire year of 20X6.

7. Burch pays a bonus equal to 5% of income before taxes and before the bonus.

8. Burch reported after tax income amounts for 20X6 as follows: Income from continuing operations—$5,000,000, loss from discontinued operations—$1,000,000, and increase in income from change in accounting principle—$600,000.

9. Burch's tax rate for 20X6 was 40%.

10. Burch issued 500,000 common shares on February 15, 20X7 at a price of $53 per share prior to the release of the 20X6 financial statements.

The potentially dilutive securities used in this example were taken from prior examples in this chapter. Given the length of some of the computations, the incremental shares or adjustments to income are taken directly from those examples and not recomputed in the analysis of this problem. The numerator and denominator adjustments will be referenced to the tables where the calculations were made. The reader may wish to refer to these tables as the problem is analyzed.

The first step in the analysis of the assumptions in Example 2-25 is to determine the numerator and denominator for use in computing basic earnings per share. Table 2-31 shows the computation of the number of common shares outstanding for 20X6 using a monthly weighted-average basis.

Table 2-31 Calculation of Numerator and Denominator for Basic Earnings per Share Computation of Numerator:

Income from continuing operations	$5,000,000
Preferred dividends paid (Assumption 5(b))	(90,000)
Income for common stockholders	$4,910,000
Loss from discontinued operations	(1,000,000)
Income from change in accounting principle	600,000
Net income for common stockholders	$4,510,000

Computation Of Denominator:

Assumptions from Example 2-25 (a)	*Number of Shares (b)*	*Months Outstanding (c)*	*Fraction of Year (d)*	*Weighted-Average Shares (e)=(b)×(d)*
1	2,400,000	12	12/12	2,400,000
2(a)	600,000	7	7/12	350,000
2(b)	100,000	6	6/12	50,000
2(c)	(100,000)	3	3/12	(25,000)
Weighted-Average Shares Outstanding			2,775,000	

Basic earnings per share is computed by dividing the relevant income amounts by the weighted-average shares outstanding. Using the information from Table 2-31, the basic earnings per share calculations for each element of income for 20X6 are presented below.

Table 2-32 Calculation of Basic Earnings per Share

	Income (a)	*Number of Shares (b)*	*Basic EPS (c)=(a)/(b)*
Income for common stockholders	$4,910,000	2,775,000	$1.77
Loss from discontinued operations	(1,000,000)	2,775,000	(.36)
Income from change in accounting principle	600,000	2,775,000	.22
Net income for common stockholders	$4,510,000	2,775,000	$1.63

The next step in the earnings per share process is to compute diluted EPS. When computing diluted EPS, the individual EPS amounts for all potentially dilutive securities must be compared to basic EPS to determine whether they are individually dilutive. If they are individually dilutive, then the securities must be ranked beginning with the security with the lowest individual EPS to the security with the highest individual EPS. Table 2-33 shows the individual EPS of all potentially dilutive securities and a comparison of the individual EPS to basic EPS used to determine dilution on an individual basis.

Table 2-33 Computation of Individual EPS and Determination of Dilution

Security (a)	*Adjustment to Numerator (b)*	*Adjustment to Denominator (c)*	*Individual EPS (d)=(b)/(c)*	*Basic EPS (e)*	*Is Security Dilutive? (f)=(d)<(e)*
1,500,000 Options (Table 2-19)	$0	204,850	$0	$1.77	Yes
600,000 Options (Table 2-20)	$0	146,244	$0	$1.77	Yes
900,000 Warrants (Table 2-21)	$0	40,179	$0	$1.77	Yes
Earnings Contingency (Table 2-30)	$0	37,500	$0	$1.77	Yes
Convertible Debt (Table 2-26)	$45,600	100,000	$.456	$1.77	Yes
Convertible Preferred Stock (Table 2-27)	$90,000	22,500	$4.00	$1.77	No
Market Price Contingency	No common shares were assumed to be issued because the $50 market price of the stock was greater than the $45 required market price.				

Using the information from Table 2-33, all the potentially dilutive securities are dilutive on an individual basis, except for the convertible preferred stock. In addition, the contingency related to market price will not be used in diluted EPS computations because the required market price maintenance has been exceeded for all of 20X6. Because the market price has been maintained during 20X6, no additional shares would be assumed to be issued. Of the seven potentially dilutive securities, five will be used in diluted EPS computation if they are dilutive on a group basis. Because there is no income adjustment for the options, warrants and the earnings contingency, they are automatically dilutive on a group basis. Therefore, because these securities have a $0 individual EPS (these securities are the most dilutive on an individual basis), they would be used first in the computation of diluted EPS. If the earnings per share computation after using the options, warrants, and earnings contingency is greater than the $.456

individual EPS of the convertible debt, the convertible debt is dilutive on a group basis. The computation of diluted EPS is presented in Table 2-34.

Table 2-34 Computation of Dilution on a Group Basis

	Numerator (Income) (a)	*Denominator (Number of Shares) (b)*	*EPS (c)=(a)/(b)*
Income for common shareholders (Table 2-31)	$4,910,000		
Weighted average number of shares (Table 2-31)		2,775,000	
1,500,000 options (Table 2-33)		204,850	
600,000 options (Table 2-33)		146,244	
900,000 warrants (Table 2-33)		40,179	
Earnings contingency (Table 2-33)		37,500	
Totals	$4,910,000	3,203,773	$1.53
Convertible debt (Table 2-33)	45,600	100,000	
Totals	$4,955,600	3,303,773	1.50

Because the earnings per share of $1.50 after considering the convertible debt is less than the previous earnings per share of $1.53, the convertible debt is dilutive on a group basis and will be used in diluted EPS computations. Using information from Table 2-34 and Assumption 8 of Example 2-25, diluted earnings per share is computed in Table 2-35.

Table 2-35 Computation of Diluted Earnings per Share

	Income (a)	*Number of Shares (b)*	*Diluted EPS (c)=(a)/(b)*
Income after adjustment for potentially dilutive securities (Table 2-34)	$4,955,600	3,303,773	$1.50
Loss from discontinued operations	(1,000,000)	3,303,773	(.30)
Income from change in accounting principle	600,000	3,303,773	.18
Net income for common stockholders	$4,555,600	3,303,773	$1.38

Presentation of both basic and diluted earnings per share must be presented on the face of the income statement for both income from continuing operations and net income. In addition, EPS for the discontinued operations and the change in accounting principle reported by Burch for 20X6 may be reported on the face of the income statement or in related notes. Burch is electing to present all earnings per share amounts on the face of the statement. The presentation may be made as follows (information is taken from Tables 2-31 and 2-35):

	For the Year Ended 20X6	
	Basic EPS	***Diluted EPS***
Income for common stockholders	$1.77	$1.50
Loss from discontinued operations	(.36)	(.30)
Income from change in accounting principle	.22	.18
Net income for common stockholders	$1.63	$1.38

The required earnings per share note disclosure is presented below.

NOTE: Reconciliation of the numerator and denominator used in the computation of basic and diluted earnings per share is presented below:

	For the Year Ended 20X6			
	Numerator (Income)	*Denominator (Number of Shares)*	*Basic EPS*	*Diluted EPS*
Income from continuing operations (Assumption 8)	$5,000,000			
Preferred dividends (Assumption 5(b)	(90,000)			
Income for common shareholders (Basic EPS)	$4,910,000	2,775,000	1.77	
Impact of Dilutive Securities				
1,500,000 options (Table 2-33)		204,850		
600,000 options (Table 2-33)		146,244		
900,000 warrants (Table 2-33)		40,179		
Earnings contingency (Table 2-33)		37,500		
Convertible debt (Table 2-33)	45,600	100,000		
Income for common shareholders and impact of assumed conversion (Diluted EPS)	$4,955,600	3,303,773		1.50

Convertible preferred stock convertible into 30,000 shares of common stock was outstanding from April 1–December 31, 20X6. The convertible preferred stock was not used in the computation of diluted earnings per share because the securities were antidilutive. In addition, a contingency requiring the issuance of 75,000 of common stock if the market price of the common stock falls below $45 per share was not used in the computation because the price of the common stock was greater than $45 during all of 20X6. Burch issued 500,000 common shares at a price of $53 per share on February 15, 20X7.

Recent Changes

ASU 2015-01, *Income Statement—Extraordinary and Unusual Items (Subtopic 225-20): Simplifying Income Statement Presentation by Eliminating the Concept of Extraordinary Items*, eliminates the concept of extraordinary items from generally accepted accounting principles effective for fiscal years, and interim periods within those fiscal years, beginning after December 15, 2015. A reporting entity may apply the amendments prospectively. A reporting entity also may apply the amendments retrospectively to all prior periods presented in the financial statements. Early adoption is permitted provided that the guidance is applied from the beginning of the fiscal year of adoption. The effective date is the same for all entities, including public business entities.

ASU 2015-06, *Earnings Per Share (Topic 260): Effects on Historical Earnings per Unit of Master Limited Partnership Dropdown Transactions*, specifies that for the purposes of calculating historical earnings per unit under the two-class method, the earnings (losses) of a transferred business before the date of a dropdown transaction should be allocated entirely to the general partner. In that circumstance, the previously reported earnings per unit of the limited partners (which is typically the earnings per unit measure presented in the financial statements) would not change as a result of the dropdown transaction. Qualitative disclosures about how the rights to the earnings (losses) differ before and after the dropdown transaction occurs for purposes of computing earnings per unit under the two-class method also are required. The amendments in this Update are effective for fiscal years beginning after December 15, 2015, and interim periods within those fiscal years. Earlier application is permitted. The amendments in this Update should be applied retrospectively for all financial statements presented.

Topic 270: Interim Reporting

Topic 270, *Interim Reporting*, contains three subtopics:

10 Overall

740 Income Taxes [See the corresponding topic in Chapter 7 for coverage of this shared subtopic]

932 Extractive Activities—Oil and Gas [See the corresponding topic in Chapter 9 for coverage of this shared subtopic]

Flowchart and General Discussion

The two primary objectives of ASC 270 are to develop accounting principles and disclosure requirements that are appropriate for interim statements and to specify minimum guidelines for reporting of interim information by publicly traded companies. Interim financial reporting refers to the issuing of financial information for some time period less than an entire year. An interim period may be, for example, a month, a quarter of a year, or a half of a year.

ASC 280 specifies the disclosures about each reportable segment that must be presented in interim reports.

The flowchart of ASC 270 depicts, in a general way, the major decisions and related accounting considerations specified by ASC 270. The discussion that follows is organized around Flowchart 2-7, and reference to Flowchart 2-7 is made during the discussion of each major subject area. ASC 270 addresses the interim income statement in some detail; therefore, the discussion below begins with the reporting of revenues in the interim period and continues down the income statement until all major items have been covered.

Flowchart 2-7

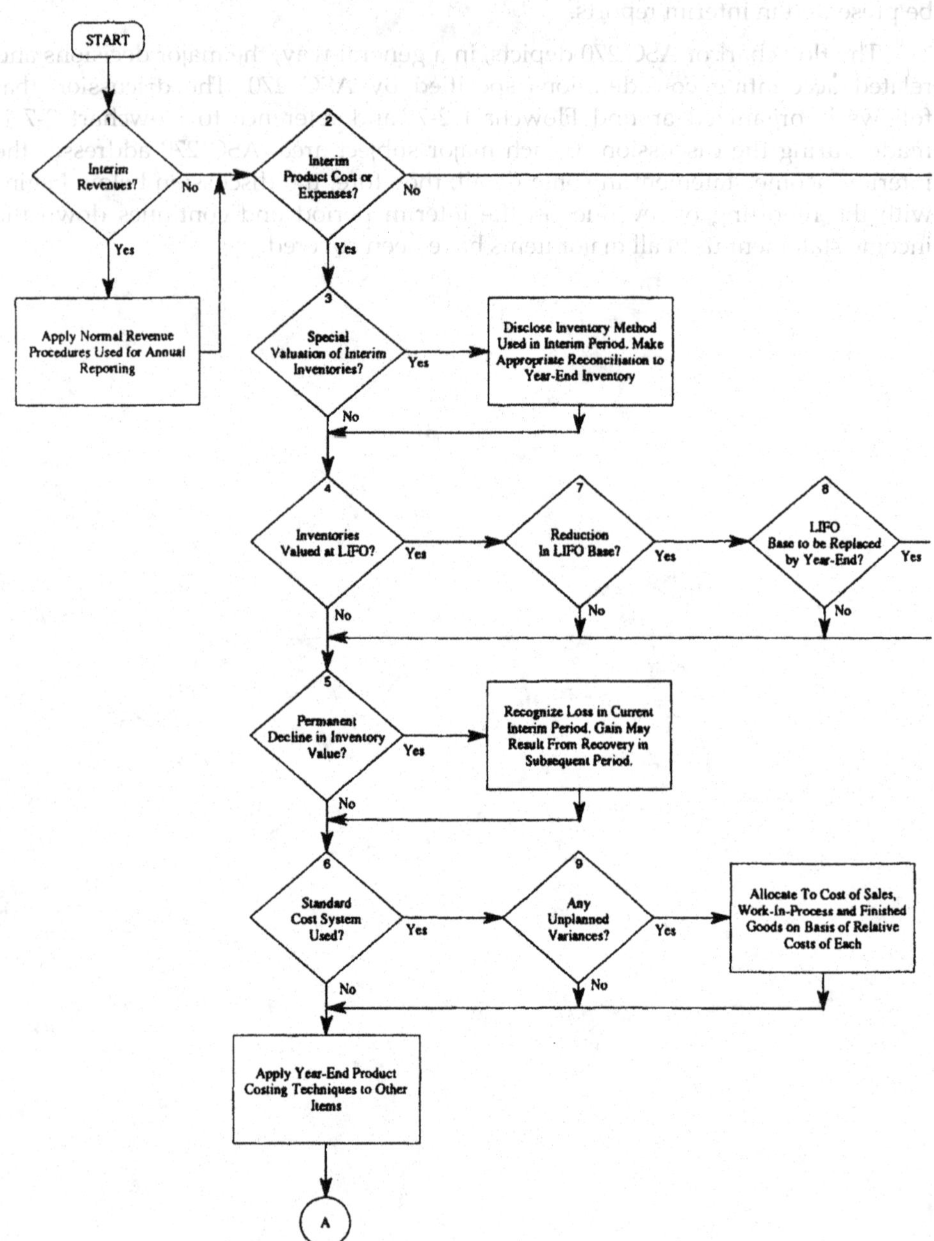

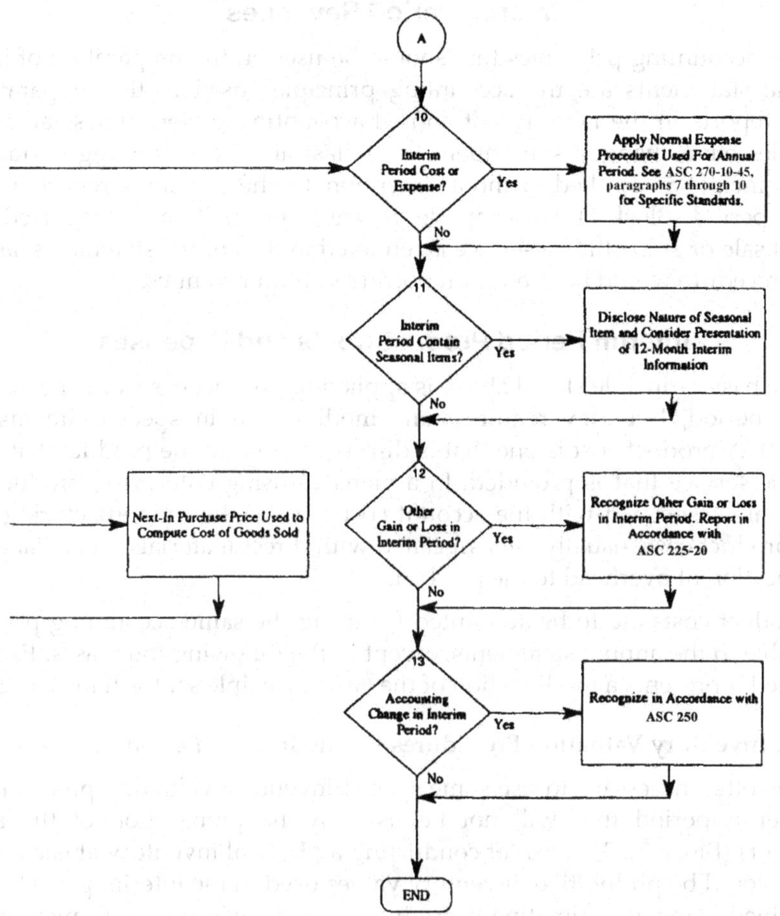
A
10
Interim Period Cost or Expense?
Yes
Apply Normal Expense Procedures Used For Annual Period. See ASC 270-10-45, paragraphs 7 through 10 for Specific Standards.
No
11
Interim Period Contain Seasonal Items?
Yes
Disclose Nature of Seasonal Item and Consider Presentation of 12-Month Interim Information
No
Next-In Purchase Price Used to Compute Cost of Goods Sold
12
Other Gain or Loss in Interim Period?
Yes
Recognize Other Gain or Loss in Interim Period. Report in Accordance with ASC 225-20
No
13
Accounting Change in Interim Period?
Yes
Recognize in Accordance with ASC 250
No
END

Interim Period Revenues

The accounting principles that should be used in the preparation of interim financial statements are the accounting principles used in the preparation of annual reports in the most recent annual accounting period, unless accounting principles have changed subsequent to the last annual accounting period. This basic principle is applied without exception to the revenues reported in the interim period (Block 1). For example, revenues normally are recognized at the point of sale or at the time a service is rendered in the annual statements, and this same procedure would be used for reporting interim revenues.

Interim Period Product Costs and Expenses

The basic principle stated above is applied to product costs or expenses of an interim period, but may require some modification in special circumstances (Block 2). A product cost is one that is directly related to the product that is sold or to the service that is provided. In a merchandising enterprise, product costs usually are associated with the account cost of sales. In a manufacturing enterprise, product costs usually are associated with direct materials, direct labor, and the allocation of overhead to the product.

Product costs are to be accounted for using the same accounting principles applicable to the annual statements, except in the following four cases. Each case discussed represents a modification of the basic principle set forth in ASC 270.

Special Inventory Valuation Procedures for the Interim Period

It is often necessary to use some special inventory valuation procedures for the interim period that will not be used in the preparation of the annual statements (Block 3). The cost of conducting a physical inventory at each interim period would be prohibitive. Inventory values used in the interim period may be determined using an estimating procedure such as the gross profit method. This procedure will not be used for the annual statements, as a physical inventory probably will be taken. When a special inventory valuation procedure is used in the interim period, the nature of the method must be disclosed. In addition, if any adjustments are required to reconcile the interim inventories to the annual inventories, this information must be disclosed.

Last-In, First-Out (LIFO) Inventory Valuation in Interim Period

There is the possibility of modification of the basic principle relating to product costs when the LIFO inventory valuation technique is used by the company (Block 4). If sales and purchases during the interim period are such that a reduction in the LIFO base occurs (Block 7), but it is assumed that the base will be replaced before the annual statements are prepared (Block 8), a modification to the basic principle is required.

In the situation described above, cost of sales should include the price *expected* to be paid for the next inventory items purchased (Next-In Purchase Price), rather than the costs associated with the LIFO base. To illustrate the proper accounting in the interim period for this situation, assume that a company uses the LIFO inventory valuation process and that the LIFO base consists of

10,000 units, at a cost of $10 per unit ($100,000 LIFO base). Prior to the last sale in the second quarter of 20X6, the *total* inventory consists of the LIFO base of 10,000 units, plus one layer of 3,000 units, at a cost of $45 per unit ($135,000 Cost of Layer). The last sale of the second quarter of 20X6 was for 5,000 units. The company has determined that the price of the *next* units purchased will be $50 per unit. Further, the company expects the layer to be replaced prior to the preparation of the annual statements.

Under normal circumstances, the LIFO base would be reduced by 2,000 units. However, ASC 270 specifies that, under these conditions, the next purchase price, rather than the costs assigned to the LIFO base, should be used to determine the cost of sales. The following amounts would be used to reflect the cost of the last sale in the second quarter of 20X6.

Cost of Goods Sold:	
3,000 units from the layer × $45	$135,000
2,000 units at next purchase price × $50	100,000
Cost of 5,000 Units Sold	$235,000
Reduction in Inventory:	
3,000 units from the layer × $45	$135,000
2,000 units from LIFO base × $10	20,000
Total Inventory Reduction	$155,000

Based upon this information, the following journal entry is required to record the cost of the sale.

Cost of Goods Sold	235,000	
Inventory		155,000
LIFO Base Inventory Liquidation		80,000

The LIFO base inventory liquidation account would be classified as a current liability and would be removed when the next purchase is made.

If the purchase price of the next units purchased is $50 per unit, and 10,000 units are purchased at this price, the determination of the amount to assign to inventory would be as follows:

Cost of 10,000 Units Purchased (10,000 × $50)	$500,000
LIFO Base Inventory Liquidation	(80,000)
Cost Assigned to Units Purchased	$420,000

The journal entry required to record the purchase of the additional units would be:

Inventory	420,000	
LIFO Base Inventory Liquidation	80,000	
Accounts Payable		500,000

The units just purchased are made up of 8,000 units at a cost of $50 per unit, and 2,000 units at a cost of $10 per unit. This entry, in effect, replaces the 2,000 units removed in the preceding sale. The LIFO base is restored to 10,000 units at $10 per unit, and the layer is made up of 8,000 units at $50 per unit.

Permanent Decline in Inventory Value During the Interim Period

If there is a permanent decline in the value of inventory during the interim period (Block 5), the resulting loss should be recognized in the interim period and not deferred to the end of the year. No recognition is to be given to temporary declines in the value of inventory. If a permanent inventory decline occurs in an interim period and a loss is recognized, but there is a subsequent recovery in value before the end of the year, a gain should be recognized. The gain recognized may not exceed the amount of the loss previously recognized.

To illustrate the proper accounting for permanent inventory declines in an interim period, assume that a company has inventory of 10,000 units carried at a purchase price of $24 per unit ($240,000). The company expects to sell the units at a price of $30 per unit. The company has estimated that the cost to sell the units amounts to 10% of the selling price, and the normal profit margin is 20% of the selling price. At the end of the first quarter of 20X6, the cost to replace the 10,000 units is determined to be $22 per unit. The decrease in value from $24 to $22 per unit is assumed to represent a permanent decline in value.

Because the decline is assumed to be permanent, a loss must be recognized in the first quarter of 20X6. Before the amount of the loss can be determined, the floor and ceiling values must be computed to find the appropriate market price. This technique is required by ASC 330. The ceiling should not be greater than net realizable value. Net realizable value is equal to the expected selling price, less the cost to complete and sell a unit of inventory. The floor is equal to the net realizable value, reduced by the normal profit margin. For this particular case, the ceiling and floor would be computed as follows:

Ceiling:	
Expected Selling Price	$30
Cost to Sell ($30 × 10%)	(3)
Ceiling	$27
Floor:	
Expected Selling Price	$30
Cost to Sell	(3)
Normal Profit ($30 × 20%)	(6)
Floor	$21

The cost to replace the inventory item is $22 per unit, which falls between the ceiling of $27 per unit and the floor of $21 per unit. Therefore, $22 per unit becomes the market value of the inventory item. The market value of $22 per unit is compared with the cost of $24 per unit; and, because market is lower, the inventory item must be written-down by $2 per unit ($22–$24). A loss of $20,000 (10,000 units × $2 per unit) will be recognized. The entry to record the permanent decline in inventory value would be:

Loss on Decline in Market Value of Inventory	20,000	
Inventory		20,000

This loss would be recognized in the first quarter of 20X6.

To extend the example, assume that, at the end of the fourth quarter of 20X6, the 10,000 units were not sold, and the cost to replace the units rose from $22 to $23.50 per unit (i.e., there was a recovery in an assumed permanent decline in inventory value). Assuming no change in the expected selling price, cost to sell and normal profit margin, a gain of $15,000 ($23.50 – $22.00 = $1.50 × 10,000 units) would be recognized in the fourth quarter of 20X6. The journal entry to record the gain would be:

Inventory	15,000	
Gain on Market Recovery of Inventory Decline		15,000

Regardless of the recovery in value of the inventory item, the gain may never exceed $20,000, the amount of the loss recorded in the first quarter of 20X6.

Practices vary in determining costs of inventory. For example, cost of goods produced may be determined based on standard or actual cost, while cost of inventory may be determined on an average, first-in, first-out (FIFO), or last-in, first-out (LIFO) cost basis. While entities generally shall use the same inventory pricing methods and make provisions for writedowns at interim dates on the same basis as used at annual inventory dates, the following exceptions are appropriate at interim reporting dates:

a. Some entities use estimated gross profit rates to determine the cost of goods sold during interim periods or use other methods different from those used at annual inventory dates. These entities shall disclose the method used at the interim date and any significant adjustments that result from reconciliations with the annual physical inventory.

b. Entities that use the LIFO method may encounter a liquidation of base period inventories at an interim date that is expected to be replaced by the end of the annual period. In those cases the inventory at the interim reporting date shall not give effect to the LIFO liquidation, and cost of sales for the interim reporting period shall include the expected cost of replacement of the liquidated LIFO base.

c. Inventory losses from the application of the guidance on subsequent measurement shall not be deferred beyond the interim period in which the decline occurs. Recoveries of such losses on the same inventory in later interim periods of the same fiscal year through market value recoveries (for inventory measured using LIFO or the retail inventory method) or net realizable value recoveries (for all other inventory) shall be recognized as gains in the later interim period. Such gains shall not exceed previously recognized losses. Some declines in the market value (for inventory measured using LIFO or the retail inventory method) or net realizable value (for all other inventory) of inventory at interim dates, however, can reasonably be expected to be restored in the fiscal year. Such temporary declines need not be recognized at the interim date since no loss is expected to be incurred in the fiscal year.

d. Entities that use standard cost accounting systems for determining inventory and product costs should generally follow the same procedures in reporting purchase price, wage rate, usage, or efficiency variances from standard cost at the end of an interim period as followed at the end of a fiscal year. Purchase price variances or volume or capacity cost variances that are planned and expected to be absorbed by the end of the annual period, should ordinarily be deferred at interim reporting dates. The effect of unplanned or unanticipated purchase price or volume variances, however, shall be reported at the end of an interim period following the same procedures used at the end of the fiscal year.

Standard Cost Systems and Interim Reporting

A final situation that may require a modification of the basic principle of recording product costs relates to a company that employs a standard cost accounting system (Block 6). Any variances from standard existing at year-end for annual statement presentation will be allocated among finished goods, work-in-process, raw materials inventory and cost of sales, based upon the relative balances in these accounts. Variances from standard can be divided into planned variances and unplanned variances. In the interim period any *planned* variances will be accounted for as assets or liabilities, and any *unplanned* variances will be allocated using the procedures described for year-end handling variances.

To illustrate the proper handling of *unplanned* variances in the interim period, the information developed in Example 2-26 is used. The information presented in Example 2-26 relates to the third quarter of 20X6.

Example 2-26
Inventory and Variance Information

	Dollars	Percent
Cost of Sales	$200,000	66.67
Work-In-Process Inventory	35,000	11.67
Finished Goods Inventory	65,000	21.66
Total	$300,000	100.00

	Planned Variance	Unplanned Variance
Material Price	1,000U	2,000U
Material Quantity	4,000F	500F
Labor Rate	3,000F	4,000F
Labor Efficiency	1,000U	3,000U
Budget	500U	5,000U
Volume	6,000U	1,000U

U = Unfavorable variance
F = Favorable variance

The unplanned variances will be allocated to cost of sales, work-in-process inventory and finished goods inventory, based upon the percentages developed in Example 2-26. The allocation process is shown in Table 2-36.

Table 2-36 Allocation of Unplanned Variances

	Total	Cost of Sales (66.67%)	Allocated to: Work-In-Process (11.67%)	Finished Goods (21.66%)
Material Price	$2,000	$1,333	$233	$434
Material Quantity	(500)	(333)	(58)	(109)
Labor Rate	(4,000)	(2,667)	(467)	(866)
Labor Efficiency	3,000	2,000	350	650
Budget	5,000	3,333	584	1,083
Volume	1,000	667	117	216
Total	$6,500	$4,333	$759	$1,408

The journal entry required to eliminate the unplanned variances at the end of the third quarter of 20X6 would be:

Cost of Sales	4,333	
Work-In-Process Inventory	759	
Finished Goods Inventory	1,408	
Material Quantity Variance	500	
Labor Rate Variance	4,000	
Material Price Variance		2,000
Labor Efficiency Variance		3,000
Budget Variance		5,000
Volume Variance		1,000

The planned variances would be carried forward to the year-end.

Other product costs or expenses not described above would be handled in the interim period the same way they would be handled at year-end. The next major category of income statement items deals with period costs or expenses.

Period Costs or Expenses in Interim Statements

A period cost or expense is a cost that is not directly related to the product or service (Block 10). These costs generally are expensed when incurred or are assigned to the period on the basis of some allocation process.

Accounting for period costs and expenses presents few accounting difficulties. ASC 270-10-45, paragraphs 7 through 10, establish specific guidelines or standards for the treatment of period costs in the interim statements. The standards identified are:

- Period costs are to be charged to interim periods as the expense is incurred, or allocated to interim periods based upon some predetermined allocation method. For example, rent may be allocated based on the passage of time, which implies a straight-line allocation process.

- Certain costs incurred in an interim period cannot be determined to benefit any other interim period and should be charged to income in the interim period incurred.
- Costs may not be allocated to interim periods on a discretionary basis.
- Gains and losses in an interim period should be taken to income in that period and *not* deferred to future interim periods. This standard applies only to gains or losses that would not normally be deferred at year-end, when an annual presentation is to be made.
- Costs that are normally year-end adjustments or that cannot be determined until the year-end, such as bonuses and bad debts, should be estimated and allocated to the interim period.

Additional Considerations of Interim Period Items

Seasonal Influences on Interim Reporting

Many business enterprises experience seasonal fluctuations in operations (Block 11). Interim reports of such an enterprise may be misleading if the user is not aware of the seasonal nature of the company's business. As a result, interim reports of businesses with seasonal fluctuations in operations should disclose the seasonal nature of the business and consideration should be given to the presentation of 12-month statements ending with the current interim period. If the company elects to present 12-month interim information, it should include the current and immediately preceding year.

Other Gains and Losses in Interim Periods

Certain gains and losses should be reported in the interim accounting period when they occur (Block 12). Currently, such gains and losses include the following:

1. Gains or losses that are either unusual in nature *or* infrequent in occurrence, but *not* both; and
2. Gains and losses from discontinued operations.

These gains or losses, if material, should be included in income in the interim period and should not be deferred or allocated to subsequent interim periods. Materiality should be determined on the relationship between the gain or loss and total *estimated* income for the entire year. Materiality should not be determined in relation to the interim period income. Each of the items shown above should be classified separately in the interim period income statement.

The disclosure requirements in interim reports for business combinations are covered by ASC 805.

In addition to the gains and losses identified above, contingent items may exist at the interim reporting date. Contingent items for interim periods should be accounted for in the same manner as in the annual report.

Income Taxes in the Interim Period

Income taxes must be accrued in each interim accounting period using an estimate of the annual effective tax rate. The estimated annual effective tax is applied to year-to-date income to compute the year-to-date tax. Prior interim period tax is subtracted from the year-to-date tax to compute the tax for the interim period under consideration. For example, assume that an entity is computing taxes for the second quarter accounting period. The company would estimate the annual effective tax rate and apply that rate to income for the first six months (year-to-date) of income to compute the tax expense for the first six months. Tax expense for the second quarter is the tax expense for the first six months less the tax expense reported for the first quarter.

The determination of the effective tax rate under ASC 740 involves two computations and should give adequate consideration to all available tax credits, tax alternatives and tax systems. An enterprise must estimate the effective tax rate for the current tax provision and also for the deferred tax provision to arrive at the total effective tax rate for interim reporting purposes.

In determining the appropriate amount of taxes for an interim period, the provisions of ASC 740 should be applied.

Accounting Changes in Interim Periods

ASC 250 specifies the appropriate accounting and disclosures for reporting a change in an accounting principle during an interim period. When an entity makes a change in accounting principle (Block 13) during an interim period, the provisions of ASC 250 should be applied.

When an entity makes a change in accounting principle during an interim accounting period, the change is accounted for using the retrospective method as specified in ASC 250. The entity cannot apply the impracticability option to interim accounting periods within the same fiscal year prior to the interim period when the change is made. If the entity cannot apply the retrospective method to pre-change interim periods in the same fiscal year, the entity must apply the accounting change at the beginning of the next fiscal year. When an entity changes an accounting principle in the fourth quarter of an annual period and does not provide the disclosures for such a change as specified by ASC 270 (see the disclosures below) in either annual or fourth quarter reports, the disclosures specified by ASC 250 should be provided in the annual report of the year in which the change is made.

Change in Accounting Principle Made in the Fourth Quarter

Special accounting treatment is required for a publicly held company that makes a change in accounting principles in the fourth quarter of an annual period. If the company provides information concerning the effects of the change in accounting principles in either fourth quarter interim statements or the annual statements, the disclosures shown below are required. If the effects of the change are not disclosed according to the guidelines provided below, they must be disclosed in the notes to the annual statements using the disclosure requirements for accounting changes specified in ASC 250.

Disclosures

ASC 270-10-50 specifies the minimum financial reporting and disclosure guidelines for a company that is publicly traded. The minimum reporting and disclosures are as follows:

1. Gross revenues or sales;
2. Income tax expense;
3. Accounting principle changes or changes in estimates;
4. Gains and losses from discontinued operations;
5. Items that are unusual *or* infrequent, but not both;
6. Earnings per share;
7. Revenues, costs, and expenses that are seasonal in nature;
8. Significant changes in income tax provisions or estimates;
9. Contingencies;
10. Balance sheet and cash flow changes that are significant in nature;
11. Net income and comprehensive income;
12. Provide disclosures about any measurement of asset and liabilities at fair value included in the balance sheet using ASC 820;
13. The information about fair value of financial instruments;
14. The information about certain investments in debt and equity securities;
15. The information about other-than-temporary impairments; and
16. The amount of foreclosed residential real estate property and the amount of loans in the process of disclosure.

ASC 715-20 specifies the disclosure requirements related to pensions and other postretirement benefit plans for interim accounting periods.

In addition to the disclosures listed above, ASC 280 specifies disclosures about segments that must be presented in interim reports. Other accounting standards in other chapters in this book, including ASC 820, specify disclosure requirements that may be required when presenting interim reports.

Topic 272: Limited Liability Entities

Topic 272, *Limited Liability Entities*, contains one subtopic:

10 Overall

This topic is not covered in this book.

Topic 274: Personal Financial Statements

Topic 274, *Personal Financial Statements*, contains one subtopic:

10 Overall

This topic is not covered in this book.

Topic 275: Risks and Uncertainties

Topic 275, *Risks and Uncertainties*, contains two subtopics:

10 Overall

912 Contractors—Federal Government [See the corresponding topic in Chapter 9 for coverage of this shared subtopic]

Disclosures

The central feature of this subtopic's disclosure requirements is selectivity: specified criteria serve to screen the host of risks and uncertainties that affect every entity so that required disclosures are limited to matters significant to a particular entity. The disclosures focus primarily on risks and uncertainties that could significantly affect the amounts reported in the financial statements in the near term or the near-term functioning of the reporting entity.

The risks and uncertainties this subtopic addresses can stem from any of the following:

1. The nature of the entity's operations, including the activities in which the entity is currently engaged if principal operations have not commenced.
2. The use of estimates in the preparation of the entity's financial statements.
3. Significant concentrations in certain aspects of the entity's operations.

All of the disclosures required by this subtopic shall be included in the basic financial statements. In order to operationalize this required disclosure, reporting entities shall make disclosures in their financial statements about the risks and uncertainties existing as of the date of those statements in the following four areas:

1. Nature of operations, including the activities in which the entity is currently engaged if principal operations have not commenced.
2. Use of estimates in the preparation of financial statements.
3. Certain significant estimates.
4. Current vulnerability due to certain concentrations.

These four areas of disclosure are not mutually exclusive. The information required by some may overlap. Accordingly, the disclosures required by this subtopic may be combined in various ways, grouped together, or placed in diverse parts of the financial statements, or included as part of the disclosures made pursuant to other requirements.

Recent Changes

ASU 2014-10, *Development Stage Entities (Topic 915): Elimination of Certain Financial Reporting Requirements, Including an Amendment to Variable Interest Entities Guidance in Topic 810, Consolidation*, amendments related to the elimination of the inception–to-date information and the other remaining disclosure requirements of Topic 915 should be applied retrospectively except for the clarification to Topic 275, shown above, which shall be applied prospectively. For public business entities, those amendments are effective for annual reporting periods beginning after December 15, 2014, and interim periods therein. For other entities, the amendments are effective for annual reporting periods beginning after December 15, 2014, and interim reporting periods beginning after December 15, 2015.

ASU 2015-11, *Inventory (Topic 330): Simplifying the Measurement of Inventory*, an amendment of the FASB is effective for public business entities. The amendments in this Update are effective for fiscal years beginning after December 15, 2016, including interim periods within those fiscal years. For all other entities, the amendments in this Update are effective for fiscal years beginning after December 15, 2016, and interim periods within fiscal years beginning after December 15, 2017. The amendments in this Update should be applied prospectively with earlier application permitted as of the beginning of an interim or annual reporting period.

Topic 280: Segment Reporting

Topic 280, *Segment Reporting*, contains five subtopics:

10 Overall

908 Airlines*

924 Entertainment—Casinos*

932 Extractive Activities—Oil and Gas*

954 Health Care Entities*

* See the corresponding topic in Chapter 9 for coverage of this shared subtopic.

Flowchart and General Discussion

ASC 280-10 specifies the reporting requirements for operating segments of companies. The intent of ASC 280-10 is to require companies, under appropriate circumstances, to report selected information about operating segments and information about foreign operations, major customers, and products and services. The subtopic is meant to apply to cases where companies issue complete sets of financial statements using generally accepted accounting principles and to situations where companies issue condensed interim statements. The basic information to be disclosed is a disaggregation by operating segments of the consolidated financial information of the reporting entity.

Generally speaking, the provisions of ASC 280-10 apply to all public companies. A public company is a company trading debt or equity securities in a public market, such as a stock exchange, that publishes financial reports in an effort to publicly sell securities, or that must file financial information with the Securities and Exchange Commission (SEC). The subtopic does not apply to nonpublic companies and not-for-profit companies. In addition, ASC 280-10 does not apply to parent companies, subsidiaries, equity method investee companies, and joint ventures when separate financial statements are included in a consolidated report containing both separate company statements and the consolidated statements. However, if financial statements are presented separately for the aforementioned entities, the provisions of ASC 280-10 apply. All entities are encouraged to provide disclosures in accordance with ASC 280-10.

Two flowcharts are used to illustrate the decision requirements of ASC 280-10. Flowchart 2-8 provides information about determination of operating segments and when such segments are reportable. Flowchart 2-9 covers the requirements related to foreign operations, product and service information, and major customer requirements. Both flowcharts are designed to help the reader determine when separate reporting is required under the provisions of ASC 280-10.

Flowchart 2-8

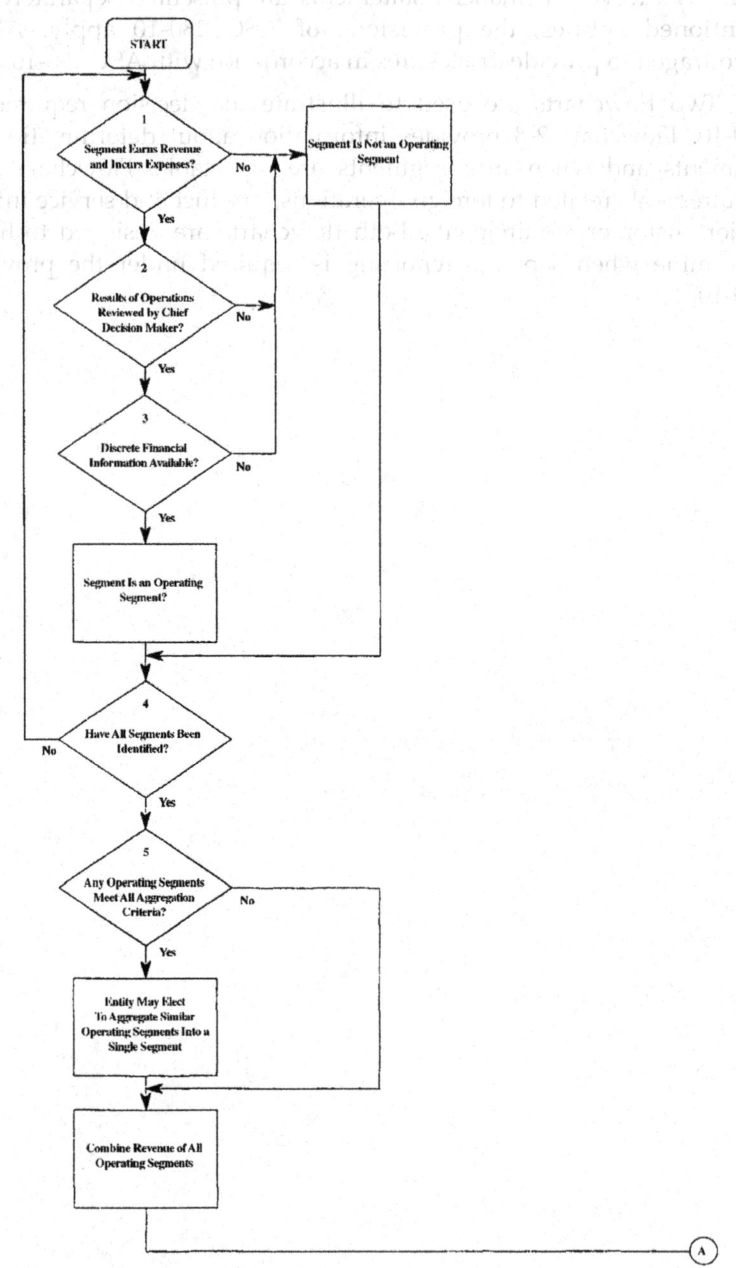

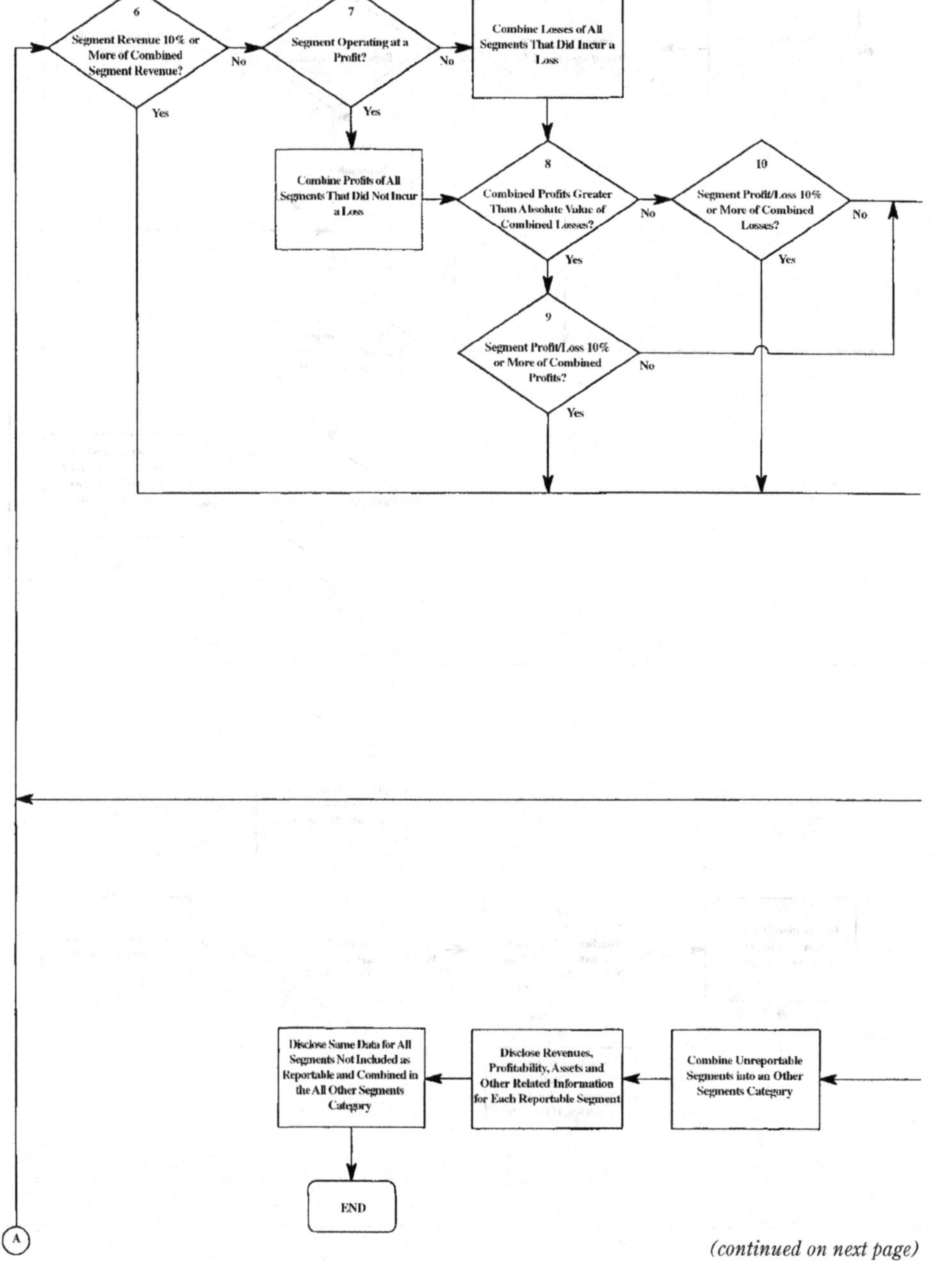

(continued on next page)

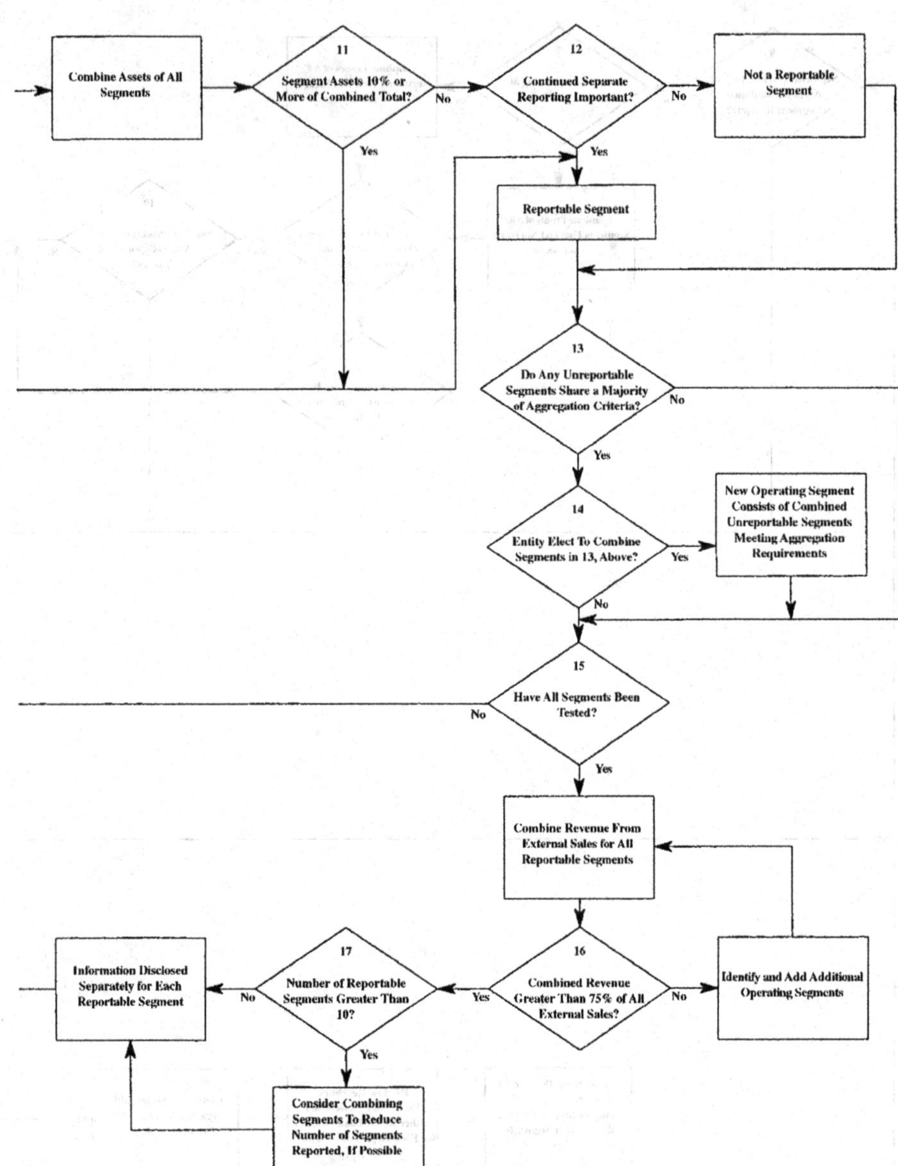
Combine Assets of All Segments
11
Segment Assets 10% or More of Combined Total?
No
Yes
12
Continued Separate Reporting Important?
No
Yes
Not a Reportable Segment
Reportable Segment
13
Do Any Unreportable Segments Share a Majority of Aggregation Criteria?
No
Yes
14
Entity Elect To Combine Segments in 13, Above?
Yes
No
New Operating Segment Consists of Combined Unreportable Segments Meeting Aggregation Requirements
15
Have All Segments Been Tested?
No
Yes
Combine Revenue From External Sales for All Reportable Segments
16
Combined Revenue Greater Than 75% of All External Sales?
Yes
No
Identify and Add Additional Operating Segments
17
Number of Reportable Segments Greater Than 10?
No
Yes
Information Disclosed Separately for Each Reportable Segment
Consider Combining Segments To Reduce Number of Segments Reported, If Possible

Before determining whether various industry operations must be disclosed separately, the company must divide its operations into separate operating segments and then determine whether each operating segment is reportable. To be classified as a separate operating segment, the segment must be a component of an entity that meets all of the following requirements as illustrated in Flowchart 2-8, Blocks 1–3 (Paragraph 10):

1. The segment earns revenues and incurs expenses through business activity (Block 1).
2. The person or persons in charge of decision making (the decision maker over the operating segments) conducts periodic reviews of the results of operations to assess performance and allocate assets (Block 2).
3. The segment provides separate financial information (Block 3).

Each operating segment identified using the three criteria noted above may or may not be reported separately, depending upon certain conditions established in ASC 280-10. However, if some of the identified operating segments are similar, an entity may want to combine one or more of the similar segments into one operating segment. For an entity to elect to combine operating segments, the segments must be similar in all of the following areas (ASC 280-10-50-11): economic aspects, products and services, process for production of the products or services, customers (by class or type), distribution methods, and, where appropriate, regulation requirements. If one or more operating segments meet all of the aggregation requirements, the entity can elect to combine such operating segments into one segment for purposes of applying the provisions of ASC 280-10 (Block 5).

Once all operating segments have been identified (Block 4), each operating segment is tested to determine whether selected information about the segment should be reported separately.

A brief review of Flowchart 2-8 indicates that there are three major tests associated with the process of identifying a reportable operating segment. An individual operating segment may be reported separately if that segment constitutes a significant portion of the enterprise's revenue (the revenue test), profits or losses (the profitability test), or assets (the asset test). In addition to a segment meeting any one of these three tests, management, in certain situations, must be convinced that separate reporting will be of continued importance in the financial statements. If the conditions are met, generally, the operating segment will be reported separately.

As shown in Flowchart 2-8, the first major accounting task is to combine the revenue of all operating segments. Segment revenue includes revenue from external customers and intersegment sales and transfers. Once segment revenue has been determined for each operating segment, the revenue of all operating segments is combined to compute total operating segment revenues. The revenue test is based on combined revenue, not on consolidated revenue. Intersegment items would be eliminated to get from combined to consolidated revenues.

Once combined revenue has been determined, the revenue test can be conducted. If an individual operating segment's revenue is 10% or more of the total of all combined operating segment revenue (Block 6), that operating segment will be reported separately.

If an individual operating segment fails to meet the revenue test, the next step is to determine whether it meets the profitability test. To conduct this test, it is necessary to separate those operating segments earning a profit from those incurring a loss (Block 7). For purposes of the profitability test, an operating segment's profit or loss is the profit or loss used in performance assessment and resource allocation for that operating segment. Some typical items that may be included in operating segment profit or loss computations are (ASC 280-10-50-22):

1. Revenue from transactions with customers external to the entity;
2. Revenue from intersegment transactions;
3. Interest income;
4. Expenses related to depreciation, depletion and amortization;
5. Interest expense;
6. Investor company's share of earnings of investment in investee company, where the equity method is used to account for the investment;
7. Unusual gains or losses;
8. Income tax expense/benefit; and
9. Noncash items considered significant, excluding items in item 4 above.

The profits of all operating segments that earned a profit should be combined into one total, and the losses for all operating segments that incurred a loss should be combined into another total. For purposes of the profitability test, the greater of the combined profits or the absolute value of the combined losses will be used as the base (Block 8). If the combined profits are greater than the combined losses, all segment profits or losses will be compared to the combined profits (Block 9). In this case, it will be necessary to compare the absolute value of the loss with the combined profits for those segments incurring a loss. If the combined losses exceed the combined profits, all segment profits and losses will be compared to combined losses (Block 10). If a particular operating segment's profit or loss is 10% or more of the combined profits or losses, whichever is appropriate in the circumstances, that operating segment is a reportable segment. For the 10% profit or loss test used to determine reportable segments, an entity should use consistent profit and loss amounts for the test even if the chief decision maker uses different measures of profit and loss for different segments for decision making purposes (ASC 280-10-55, paragraphs 12 through 15).

If an operating segment fails both the revenue and profitability tests, it still may qualify for separate reporting, depending upon the dollar value of its assets. Operating segment assets used in the asset test are the assets used in allocation of resources to the segment and segment performance assessment.

If the assets of an operating segment are 10% or more of the combined total assets of all operating segments (Block 11), separate reporting for the segment is appropriate.

If an individual operating segment fails to meet any of the three major tests, it still may be reported separately if, in the accounting period prior to the current reporting period, the operating segment was a reportable segment and the enterprise believes that continued separate reporting of the segment is important (Block 12). When individual operating segments fail to meet any of the requirements for separate reporting, an entity may elect to combine information for two or more operating segments for purposes of retesting using the revenue, profitability, or asset test when most of the criteria for aggregation, discussed above, are met (Blocks 13 and 14). Operating segments that do not meet the quantitative tests for reportable segments may be aggregated with other segments when such aggregation is consistent with the objective of ASC 280-10, meets the majority of the aggregation criteria discussed in this chapter, and have similar economic characteristics (ASC 280-10-50-13). Each individual operating segment must be tested separately or in some combination if aggregation is allowed or elected, to determine whether it should be classified as reportable or non-reportable (Block 15). Once the testing for all operating segments has been completed and all reportable segments have been isolated, two tests are imposed by ASC 280-10 to insure that the information to be disclosed in the financial statements is meaningful.

First, the revenue from sales to external customers of all reportable operating segments should be combined. The combined total from reportable operating segments must be 75% or more of consolidated revenue (Block 16). If the combined revenues do not meet this test, additional operating segments must be added as reportable segments until the test is met. The additional operating segments to be added should come from the group of segments that failed to meet any of the tests described above. Although ASC 280-10 does not provide guidance on how to select the additional segments for inclusion, it is logical to select those segments that came nearest to meeting the three major tests. For example, assume that one segment was excluded because its revenue, profitability, and assets were about 8% of the respective totals and that another excluded segment had revenues, profitability, and assets of about 5% of the same totals. Logic would dictate inclusion of the 8% segment before the 5% segment for purposes of meeting the 75% revenue test.

The final test identified in ASC 280-10 involves the number of separately reportable segments. The purpose of this test is to keep the reporting and disclosure of operating segment information from becoming too detailed. If the number of reportable segments is greater than 10, the enterprise should consider whether a limit on the number of reportable operating segments has been reached, and the enterprise may wish to make an effort to combine segments in order to reduce the total reportable segments to 10 or less (Block 17). When combining reportable operating segments, logic suggests that those segments meeting more of the aggregation criteria should be combined first.

After all tests and other considerations, all operating segments that are classified as reportable segments should provide, by segment, the disclosure information required by ASC 280-10 for reportable segments. Any operating segment not meeting the requirements to be reported separately may be separately disclosed if the company feels that separate reporting would be helpful to the users of the financial statements. Otherwise, all operating segments classified as non-reportable segments should be combined into one category, and information reported separately for this category.

Reportable operating segments may not be structured in such a way as to report information about individual enterprise products or services or groups of related products and services, or the operating segments of an enterprise may not be structured such that operations of the segment are in one geographic area. For example, an individual operating segment may have several different products or services, and when disclosure information is provided by the operating segment, it is not possible for the users of such information to determine information about individual products or services and to assess risk related to such products and services. In addition, an operating segment may have operations in several different foreign countries and, because information is not provided by specific foreign countries, a user of the disclosure information provided by that reportable operating segment might not be able to assess the risk related to operations in one specific foreign country or geographic area. Therefore, ASC 280-10 requires disclosures on an enterprise basis of information about products and services, geographic areas, and major customers on a total company basis if such information is not reported by the operating segment (ASC 280-10-50-38).

Flowchart 2-9 depicts the decision making process and general reporting requirements for products and services, geographic areas, and major customer information. If the operating segments of an entity are structured using individual products or services or related products or services (Block 1), product and service information is already included in the disclosures for reportable segments and no additional disclosures are required for products or services. However, if operating segments are not structured by products or services, the entity must disclose the amount of revenue for each product or service or related products or services generated from external customers, unless it is not possible for the enterprise to report such information.

If reportable operating segments are structured around foreign countries (e.g., one operating segment might cover all operations in Canada) (Block 2), then foreign country information may already be disclosed, and no additional disclosures will be required. Operations in areas under U.S. sovereignty or jurisdiction, such as Puerto Rico, the Virgin Islands, and American Samoa, should be considered domestic when an enterprise is separating domestic and foreign operations (ASC 280-10-55-25). If operating segments are not structured using foreign countries as a basis, additional revenue and asset information about the home country and foreign countries must be disclosed.

The following information should be reported for both the home country and all foreign countries: revenue from sales to customers outside the company; long-lived assets, excluding financial instruments; a financial company's relationships with customers that are of a long-term nature; servicing rights, such as rights to service mortgages; deferred taxes classified as assets; and policy acquisition costs that are deferred. In addition, to the preceding disclosures, an entity must disclose the method of allocating revenues to the various countries. Generally, the foreign country revenue and asset information is reported on a total basis. However, when revenue or asset information from a single foreign country is significant, the information is reported separately for that foreign country. When reporting both product and service and geographic information, the information reported is based on the data used in the preparation of basic financial statements for direct and indirect users. In addition, if it is not possible for an entity to provide product and service information or geographic information, that information should be reported in the financial statements (ASC 280-10-50, paragraphs 40 and 41).

Flowchart 2-9

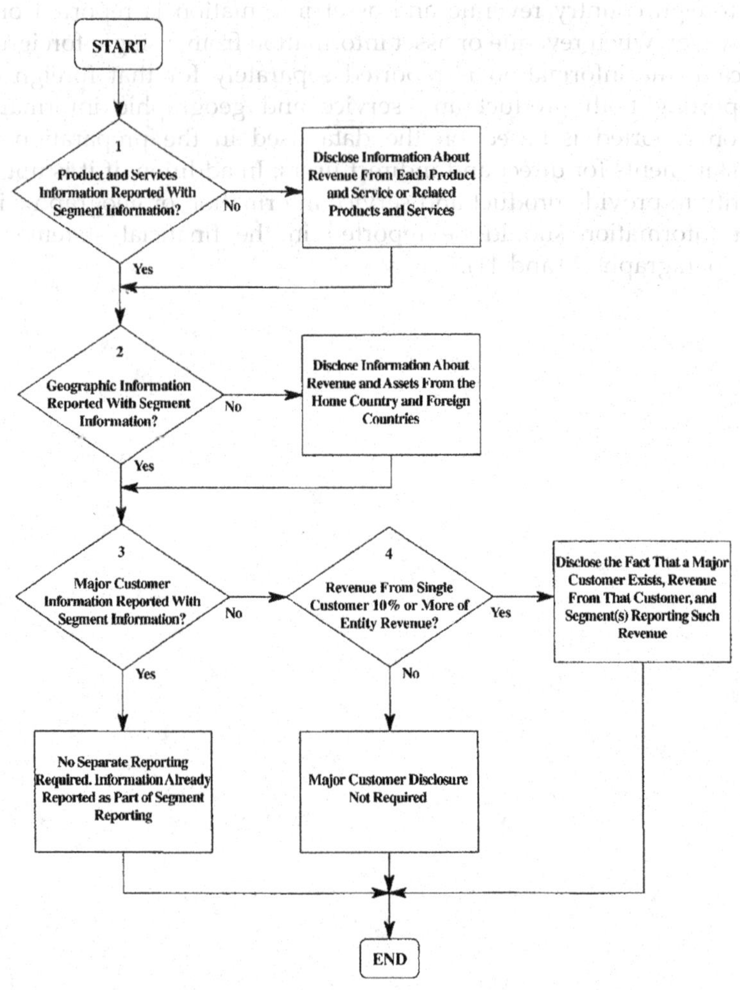

As shown in Flowchart 2-9, if 10% or more of the revenue of an enterprise results from sales to an external customer, this information should be disclosed (Blocks 3 and 4). The amount of revenue received from each major customer should be identified, along with the operating segment(s) making the sale, but disclosure of the customers' identity is not required. In most cases, identification of a single customer is very straightforward. However, when dealing with government agencies, it is sometimes difficult to determine whether a single customer is simply the specific government agency or the entire government. In such cases, the single customer would be the entire federal or state government. Also, when two or more companies are controlled by the same company, all the companies are considered a single customer (ASC 280-10-50-42).

Disclosure Requirements

ASC paragraphs 280-10-50-20 through 50-36 specify the disclosure requirements for reportable operating segments. Required disclosures are discussed below, except for information about products, services, geographic areas, and major customers. (Disclosure requirements for products and services, geographic areas, and major customers were covered in the general discussion of these issues.) When financial statements are presented in a financial report for the current accounting period with prior year statements presented for comparative purposes, the disclosures discussed below should be presented for each period that an income statement is presented:

1. Disclose the items used to determine reportable segments of the entity, including how the segments are organized (paragraph 21).
2. For each reportable segment, disclose the products and services, classified by type, that were used to generate revenue for the segment (paragraph 21).
3. For each reportable segment, disclose total assets and the elements of profit and loss reported by the segment, or the profit and loss used by the person or persons responsible for segment performance evaluation and resource allocation (paragraph 22). Amortization and depreciation expense should be disclosed for each segment determined to be reportable if it is not included in segment profit or loss calculations reviewed by the chief decision maker but is provided with the profit or loss computation as supplemental information for review by the chief decision maker (ASC 280-10-55, paragraphs 12 through 15). (Many elements of profit and loss are listed in the prior discussion of the profitability test. Please review these for disclosure requirements.)
4. For each reportable segment, disclose interest income and interest expense for the segment, unless net interest is used in the segment's performance evaluation and resource allocation. If net interest is used, that information should be disclosed (paragraph 22).
5. For each reportable segment, explain how profit and loss was measured, and disclose at least the following information: the cause or nature of differences, such as company policies regarding allocation, between measurement of company before-tax consolidated income from continuing operating and segment profit or loss; accounting used for intersegment transactions; and changes in methods used to compute segment profit and loss and the impact of such changes (paragraph 29).
6. For each reportable segment, disclose: the investment amount in investees accounted for using the equity method; expenditures for long-lived assets, excluding financial instruments, a financial company's relationships with customers that are of a long-term nature, servicing rights (such as rights to service mortgages), deferred taxes classified as assets, and policy acquisition costs that are deferred; an explanation of how assets were measured and, at least, the cause or nature of differences, such as company policies regarding allocation between measurement of

company consolidated assets and segment assets, accounting used for intersegment transactions, and disproportionate allocation of items to operating segments (such as allocation of patent amortization to the segment without an allocation of the related patent asset) (paragraphs 25 and 29).

7. Disclose a reconciliation of: (a) total revenues from reportable operating segments with consolidated revenue of the company, (b) total profits and losses from reportable operating segments with consolidated before-tax income from continuing operations, (c) total assets of reportable operating segments with total consolidated assets of the company, and (d) total of all significant items, other than in 7(a)–(c), from reportable operating segments with related consolidated amounts (paragraph 30). Balance sheet reconciliations are required for each period that a balance sheet is presented.
8. Disclose each significant item used in the reconciliation, identifying and describing each item.
9. Disclose whether prior period information has been restated when there is a change in the structure of an organization that causes a change in reportable operating segments, and if prior period information is not restated, disclose information in the current accounting period using both the new and old composition, unless it is not possible to disclose such information (paragraphs 34 and 35).
10. For each reportable segment, disclose the following information when interim financial statements are presented: revenue from sales to customers outside the company, revenues from intersegment sales, profit or loss reported by the segment, total assets in the interim period that differ materially from the corresponding amount reported in a prior annual report, differences in the way segments are determined or profits and losses measured if different from a prior annual report, and reconciliation of total profits and losses from reportable operating segments with consolidated before-tax income from continuing operations (paragraph 32).

Technical Considerations

One example is used to illustrate the technical aspects of segment reporting. Assumptions for Example 2-27 are as follows.

Example 2-27

Assumptions for Segment Reporting

1. World-Wide Enterprises (the company), a domestic December 31 year-end company, is presenting segment information in accordance with the requirements of ASC 280-10 in its 20X8 annual financial statements. The Company's operations are divided into operating segments using individual products or services or groups of related products and services. Each segment has a manager that reports to a person that makes decisions about performance assessment and resource allocation for all segments.

2. The Company has six operating segments: furniture manufacturing, motels, restaurants, theaters, construction, and real estate. The furniture segment manufactures top-of-the-line furniture for sale to retail furniture stores and large office buildings. The Company owns and operates a chain of low-priced motels, a chain of medium-priced steak restaurants, and a chain of first-run movie theaters. The construction segment builds major office buildings on a contract basis. The real estate segment owns and operates several large ranches that are used to feed cattle and produce a variety of crops. None of the segments meets a majority of the aggregation criteria in ASC 280-10; therefore, all operating segments will have to be considered separately.

3. Each operating segment uses the same accounting principles as reported in the company's annual report and the Company evaluates the performance of each segment using before-tax income or loss from continuing operations. Transactions between segments are accounted for as if each segment is an external customer.

4. Schedule 1, below, presents worksheet information about revenues, profits and losses, and assets for each operating segment. The Company had no significant noncash items, except for depreciation and amortization, and income taxes and unusual items are not allocated to segment profits and losses. In addition, there are no discontinued operations, or accounting changes in the 20X8 income statement. For 20X8, the Company had intersegment profit of $1,500,000 and $1,000,000 of expenses at the corporate level that were not allocated to operating segments. The Company had $10,000,000 of assets at the corporate level that were not allocated to operating segments. Other significant items at the corporate level were interest revenue of $800,000, interest expense of $600,000, depreciation and amortization of $1,000,000, and expenditures for assets of $5,000,000.

5. The Company had operations in the United States and six foreign countries. Revenue and asset information for each country is as follows:

	Revenue	Assets
United States	$300,000,000	$475,000,000
Mexico	90,000,000	125,000,000
Canada	80,000,000	100,000,000
Australia	70,000,000	95,000,000
Argentina	25,000,000	40,000,000
New Zealand	20,000,000	35,000,000
Venezuela	15,000,000	30,000,000
Total	$600,000,000	$900,000,000

Revenues and assets from Mexico, Canada, and Australia were considered material. Revenue is allocated to each country using the location of the customer.

6. The Company had sales to one customer of $85,000,000. The sales were made from the construction and furniture segments.

Schedule 1
Operating Segment Information at the End of 20X8

	Furniture Manufacturing	*Motels*	*Restaurants*	*Theaters*	*Construction*	*Real Estate*	*Combined*
Sales to external customers	$200,000,000	$50,000,000	$25,000,000	$15,000,000	$250,000,000	$60,000,000	$600,000,000
Intersegment sales	75,000,000					25,000,000	100,000,000
	$275,000,000	$50,000,000	$25,000,000	$15,000,000	$250,000,000	$85,000,000	$700,000,000
Interest revenue	10,000,000	4,000,000	2,500,000	2,000,000	20,000,000	6,000,000	44,500,000
Interest expense	8,000,000	2,500,000	2,000,000	1,000,000	18,000,000	5,200,000	36,700,000
Depreciation and amortization	20,000,000	5,000,000	8,000,000	2,500,000	35,000,000	7,000,000	77,500,000
Profit/(Loss)	65,000,000	10,000,000	15,000,000	(3,000,000)	78,000,000	(40,000,000)	125,000,000
Assets	275,000,000	68,000,000	100,000,000	32,000,000	350,000,000	75,000,000	900,000,000
Asset expenditures	20,000,000	6,000,000	10,000,000	2,000,000	18,000,000	4,000,000	60,000,000

Using the information from the assumptions in Example 2-27, the first step is to determine whether any operating segments can be combined using the aggregation criteria in ASC 280-10-50-11. As indicated in Assumption 2, none of the operating segments meet the criteria for aggregation. Therefore, all six operating segments will have to be tested separately for reporting. The first test for reporting is the revenue test. Schedule 1 shows that the combined revenue from sales to external customers and intersegment sales is $700,000,000. Therefore, any operating segment with revenue of $70,000,000 ($700,000,000 × 10%) or more will qualify for separate reporting. The furniture manufacturing segment with revenues of $275,000,000, the construction segment with revenues of $250,000,000, and the real estate segment with revenues of $85,000,000 are the only segments that qualify under the revenue test for separate reporting.

The next test to determine whether any additional segments should be reported separately is the profitability test. Schedule 1 shows that the theaters and real estate segments incurred operating losses, and that all other segments experienced operating profits. Therefore, it is necessary to divide the segments into two groups: those with losses and those with profits. The operating profit and operating loss groups are made up of the following segments:

	Operating Profits	Operating Losses
Furniture Manufacturing	$65,000,000	
Motels	10,000,000	
Restaurants	15,000,000	
Construction	78,000,000	
Theaters		$(3,000,000)
Real Estate		(40,000,000)
Total	$168,000,000	$(43,000,000)

Next, the $168,000,000 total profits are compared with the $43,000,000 absolute value of the combined losses. In Example 2-27, the combined profits are greater than the combined losses; therefore, the $168,000,000 becomes the basis for comparison in the profitability test. For an operating segment to be considered for separate reporting, its operating profit or loss must be at least $16,800,000 ($168,000,000 × 10%). Based on this information, the furniture manufacturing, construction, and real estate segments qualify as reportable operating segments. Although the real estate segment incurred an operating loss, the absolute value of its loss was more than $16,800,000; thus it too would qualify as a reportable operating segment under the profitability test.

The last major test for inclusion deals with the assets of each operating segment. The combined assets of all operating segments are $900,000,000. To meet the asset test, an operating segment must have at least $90,000,000 ($900,000,000 × 10%) of assets. Again, the furniture manufacturing and construction segments meet the asset test, but already are included on the basis of the revenue test. Of the remaining segments only the restaurants segment meets the asset test ($100,000,000 in assets).

As a result of the three major tests, the furniture manufacturing, restaurants, construction, and real estate segments meet the criteria for separate reporting. The motels and theaters segments met neither any of the quantitative tests for separate reporting, nor any of the tests in the immediately preceding accounting period. Because none of the tests were met in the prior accounting period, the two segments cannot be reported separately, because of the concept that continued separate reporting would be important. In addition, the motels and theaters segments cannot be combined for retesting, because a majority of the aggregation criteria are not met; therefore, the two segments will be combined into an "other segments" category unless separate reporting is required to meet the 75%-of-revenue test.

The combined revenues of the reportable segments must be tested to determine whether the revenues from external customers of all reportable segments is equal to 75% or more of the revenues from external customers of all operating segments. The combined revenue from external customers for all reportable segments is computed as follows:

	Reportable Segments Revenue from Sales to External Customers
Furniture manufacturing	$200,000,000
Restaurants	25,000,000
Construction	250,000,000
Real estate	60,000,000
Total	$535,000,000

Revenue from sales to all external customers is $600,000,000 (Schedule 1). The reportable segments' revenue from this source is 89% ($535,000,000 ÷ $600,000,000) of the total. Therefore, the 75% rule is met, and no additional segments need be added. Because the 75% rule has been met, the motels and theaters segments are excluded as possible reportable segments and should be reported in combined form in the "other segments" category.

World-Wide has less than 10 reportable segments, so no combination of reportable segments is required. Based on the information presented in Example 2-27, World-Wide would report furniture manufacturing, restaurants, construction, and real estate separately and would combine motels and theaters into one reporting group.

Because World-Wide's operations are divided into operating segments using products and services and groups of related products and services, no separate disclosures about products and services are required. Because the Company operates in several different countries, geographic information must be provided. The Company has operations in six foreign countries and the United States. However, revenue and asset information from only Mexico, Canada, and Australia are considered material; therefore, information for these three countries should be disclosed separately and information for Argentina, New Zealand, and Venezuela should be reported as one total amount.

The Company had sales of $85,000,000 to one single customer during 20X8. Sales to this customer equal 14.2% ($85,000,000 ÷ $600,000,000) of total sales of the enterprise. Because sales to this customer account for more than 10% of all sales, major customer information must be presented.

Using the information from Example 2-27, note disclosures can now be prepared for the reportable operating segments. The required note is as follows:

NOTE: Segment Reporting

The Company's operations are divided into operating segments using individual products or services or groups of related products and services. Each segment has a manager that reports to a person that makes decisions about performance assessment and resource allocation for all segments. The Company has six operating segments: furniture manufacturing, motels, restaurants, theaters, construction, and real estate. The furniture segment manufactures top-of-the-line furniture for sale to retail furniture stores and large office buildings. The Company owns and operates a chain of low-priced motels, a chain of medium-priced steak restaurants, and a chain of first-run movie theaters. The construction segment builds major office buildings on a contract basis. The real estate segment owns and operates several large ranches that are used to feed cattle and produce a variety of crops. Each operating segment uses the same accounting principles as reported in the company's annual report, and the Company evaluates the performance of each segment using before-tax income or loss from continuing operations. Transactions between segments are accounted for as if each segment is an external customer.

Table 2-37 presents profit or loss and asset information for all reportable segments. The only significant noncash items are depreciation and amortization. Taxes are not allocated to segment operations, and for 20X8, the Company had no discontinued operations. The "Other Segments" category shown in Table 2-37 consists of two segments: motels and theaters—which have never met the revenue, profit, or asset tests for reportable segments.

Table 2-37

	Furniture Manufacturing	*Restaurants*	*Construction*	*Real Estate*	*Other Segments*	*Total*
Sales to External Customers	$200,000,000	$25,000,000	$250,000,000	$60,000,000	$65,000,000	$600,000,000
Intersegment sales	75,000,000			25,000,000		100,000,000
	$275,000,000	$25,000,000	$250,000,000	$85,000,000	$65,000,000	$700,000,000
Interest Revenue	10,000,000	2,500,000	20,000,000	6,000,000	6,000,000	44,500,000
Interest Expense	8,000,000	2,000,000	18,000,000	5,200,000	3,500,000	36,700,000
Depreciation and Amortization	20,000,000	8,000,000	35,000,000	7,000,000	7,500,000	77,500,000
Profit/(Loss)	65,000,000	15,000,000	78,000,000	(40,000,000)	7,000,000	125,000,000
Assets	275,000,000	100,000,000	350,000,000	75,000,000	100,000,000	900,000,000
Asset Expenditures	20,000,000	10,000,000	18,000,000	4,000,000	8,000,000	60,000,000

Reconciliations of reportable segment assets, revenue, profit or loss, and other items of significance to consolidated amounts are presented as follows:

Assets:

Assets of reportable segments	$800,000,000
Assets of nonreportable segments	100,000,000
Assets not allocated to operating segments	10,000,000
Consolidated assets	$910,000,000

Revenues:

Revenue from reportable segments	$635,000,000
Revenue from nonreportable segments	65,000,000
Revenue from intersegment sales	(100,000,000)
Consolidated revenue	$600,000,000

Profit or Loss:

Profit from reportable segments	$118,000,000
Profit from nonreportable segments	7,000,000
Income from intersegment transactions	(1,500,000)
Expenses at corporate level not allocated to segments	(1,000,000)
Income before tax	$122,500,000

Other Items of Significance:

	Amounts reported by Segments	Amounts Not Reported at Segment Level	Consolidated Amounts
Interest revenue	$44,500,000	$800,000	$45,300,000
Interest expense	36,700,000	600,000	37,300,000
Depreciation and amortization	77,500,000	1,000,000	78,500,000
Asset expenditures	60,000,000	5,000,000	65,000,000

Listed below are revenue and long-lived asset information for all geographic areas. (Information from Mexico, Canada, and Australia is considered material, and such information is presented separately for each of the three countries. Operations in Argentina, New Zealand, and Venezuela are not material when evaluated separately; therefore, information for these three countries is combined in one amount. Revenue is allocated to each country using customer location.)

	Revenue	Assets
United States	$300,000,000	$475,000,000
Mexico	90,000,000	125,000,000
Canada	80,000,000	100,000,000
Australia	70,000,000	95,000,000
Other foreign countries	60,000,000	105,000,000
Total	$600,000,000	$900,000,000

The furniture manufacturing and construction segments received revenues of $85,000,000 from one customer.

CHAPTER 3
ASSETS

CONTENTS

The *Assets* area of the FASB *Accounting Standards Codification* contains 11 topics:

305	Cash and Cash Equivalents
310	Receivables
320	Investments—Debt Securities
321	Investments—Equity Securities
323	Investments—Equity Method and Joint Ventures
325	Investments—Other
326	Financial Instruments—Credit Losses
330	Inventory
340	Other Assets and Deferred Costs
350	Intangibles—Goodwill and Other
360	Property, Plant, and Equipment

Topic 305: Cash and Cash Equivalents

Topic 305, *Cash and Cash Equivalents,* contains four subtopics:

10 Overall

942 Financial Services—Depository and Lending*

946 Financial Services—Investment Companies*

954 Health Care Entities*

* See the corresponding topic in Chapter 9 for coverage of this shared subtopic.

This topic is not covered in this book.

Topic 310: Receivables

Topic 310, *Receivables,* contains 20 subtopics:

10 Overall

20 Nonrefundable Fees and Other Costs

30 Loans and Debt Securities Acquired with Deteriorated Credit Quality

40 Troubled Debt Restructurings by Creditors

905 Agriculture*

910 Contractors—Construction*

912 Contractors—Federal Government*

920 Entertainment—Broadcasters*

940 Financial Services—Brokers and Dealers*

942 Financial Services—Depository and Lending*

944 Financial Services—Insurance*

946 Financial Services—Investment Companies*

948 Financial Services—Mortgage Banking*

954 Health Care Entities*

958 Not-For-Profit Entities*

960 Plan Accounting—Defined Benefit Pension Plans*

962 Plan Accounting—Defined Contribution Pension Plans*

965 Plan Accounting—Health and Welfare Benefit Plans*

976 Real Estate—Retail Land*

978 Real Estate—Time-Sharing Activities*

* See the corresponding topic in Chapter 9 for coverage of this shared subtopic.

Accounting and Reporting Impairment of Loans and Receivables

ASC 310-10-35 specifies accounting and reporting standards for loan impairment (i.e., how much of an allowance should be reported for receivables classified as loans and how the amounts should be determined). The terms "loan" and "receivable" will be used interchangeably in this discussion.

A loan is a right under contract to receive an amount of money on a specified date, on demand, or on a date that can be determined, and the right is reported as an asset in the balance sheet of the creditor. Examples of loans that meet this definition are long-term notes receivable and accounts receivable that are not collectible within one year. Unless specifically exempt, the provisions of ASC 310-10-35 apply to all creditors, and includes both loans that are collateralized and those that are not. ASC 310-10-35 does not cover the following situations (ASC 310-10-35-13):

1. Loans related to leases as accounted for under ASC 840, *Leases.*
2. Debt securities covered by ASC 320, *Investments—Debt Securities.*
3. Loans carried at fair value or the lower of cost or market, such as those covered by ASC 948, *Financial Services—Mortgage Banking.*
4. Large groups of homogeneous loans with small balances, such as credit card loans.

The impairment of loans associated with a troubled debt restructuring is covered in detail under ASC 310-40 as it relates to creditor accounting for a modification of terms.

ASC 310-10-S99-4 specifies the methodology, documentation, and written policies and procedures for SEC registrants determining loan loss allowances.

Flowchart 3-1 identifies the major accounting requirements for loan impairments. The decision blocks are numbered for easy reference and are referred to in the discussion.

Flowchart 3-1

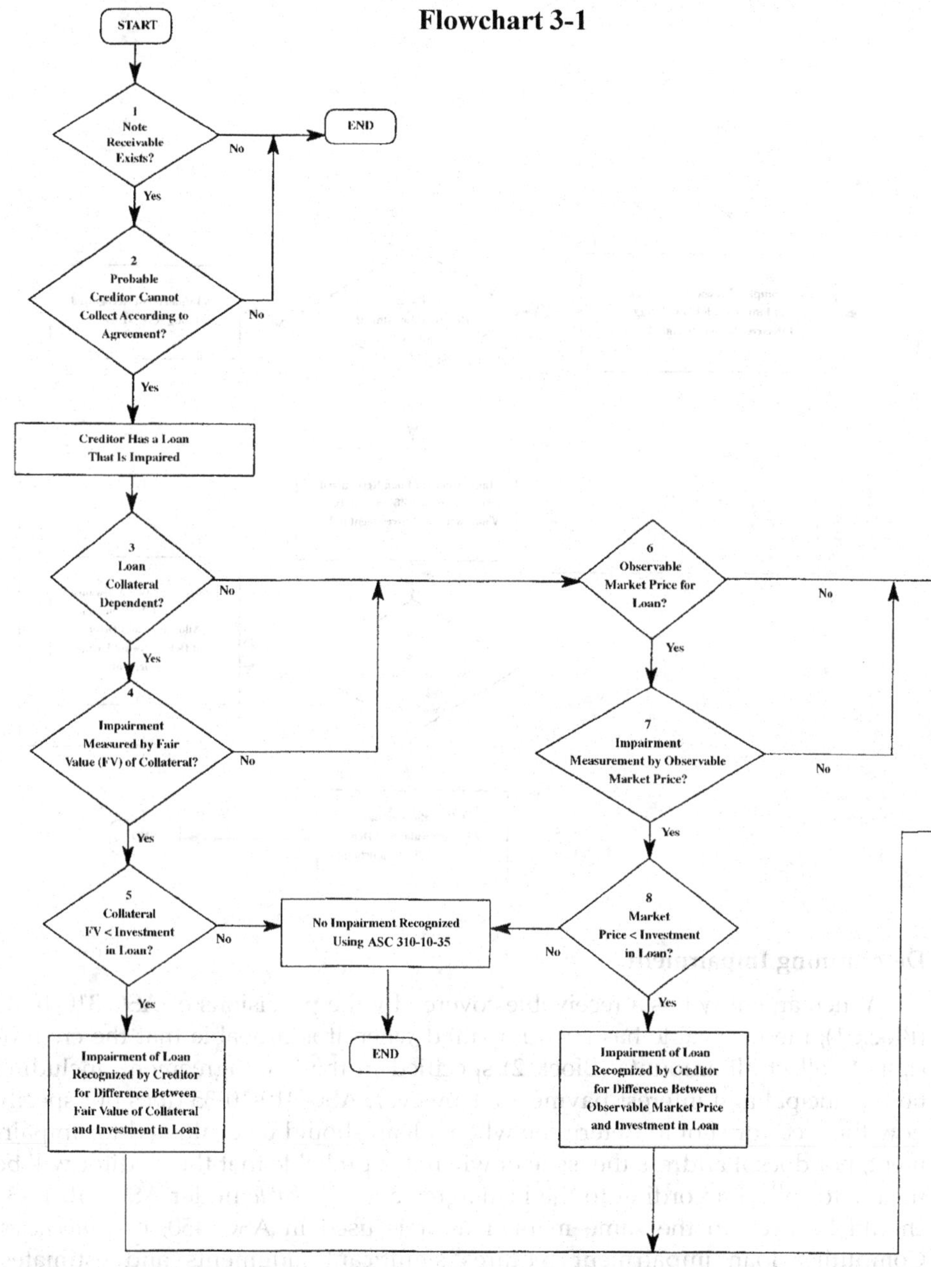

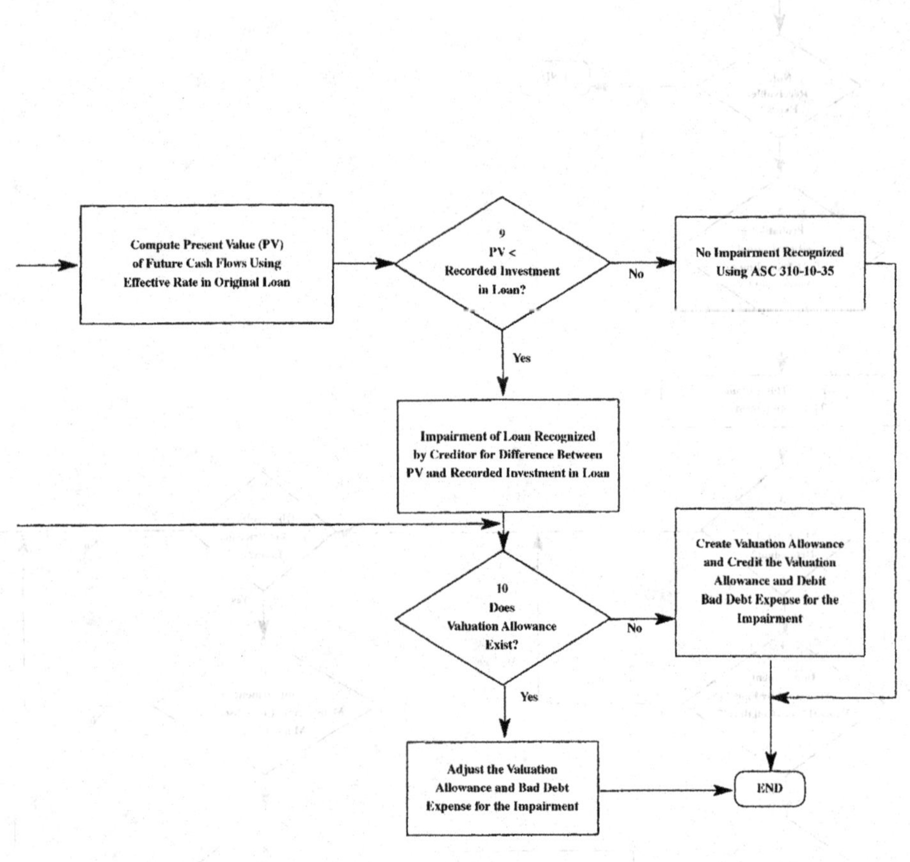

Determining Impairment

When an entity has a receivable covered by the provisions of ASC 310-10-35 (Block 1), the receivable has been impaired when it is probable that the creditor cannot collect all amounts (Block 2) specified in the loan agreement, including both principal and interest payments. However, ASC 310-10-35 does not specify how the creditor should determine when a loan should be evaluated for impairment, nor does it address the issue of when it is probable that the creditor will be unable to collect according to the loan agreement. *Probable* under ASC 310-10-35 should be used in the same manner as it is used in ASC 450, *Contingencies*. Computing loan impairment requires significant judgments and estimates. Therefore, creditors may assess impairment on a loan-to-loan basis or they may aggregate loans with similar risk characteristics.

Generally, the creditor should use the present value of future cash flows to measure impairment; however, the ASC allows the creditor to elect to use observable market prices, when available, or the fair value of collateral when the loan is "collateral dependent," i.e., is to be repaid by the underlying collateral. If a loan is collateral dependent (Block 3), impairment of the loan may be measured by the fair market value of the collateral. When the creditor elects to use the collateral to measure impairment (Block 4), the loan is considered impaired if the fair value of the collateral is less than the recorded investment in the loan (Block 5). The amount of the impairment is equal to the excess of the recorded investment in the loan over the fair value of the collateral. If the fair value of the collateral is greater than the recorded investment in the loan, no impairment is recognized. For collateral dependent loans, if the probability of foreclosure has been determined by the creditor, loan impairment must be measured by the fair value of the underlying collateral. If the loan is not collateral dependent, the creditor may use an observable market price, if available, when measuring loan impairment (Block 6). If the creditor uses an observable market price to measure impairment (Block 7), and the market price is less than the recorded investment in the loan (Block 8), an impairment of the loan equal to the excess of the recorded investment in the loan over the market price is recognized. If the market price exceeds the recorded investment in the loan, no impairment is recognized. When the creditor does not use the fair value of collateral or an observable market price for computing loan impairment, the present value of future cash receipts must be used for the computation. A comparison should be made between the recorded investment in the loan and the present value of estimated future cash receipts using the provisions of ASC 310-10-35. If the present value of the future cash receipts is less than the recorded investment in the loan (Block 9), an impairment of the loan must be recognized by the creditor for the excess of the recorded investment in the loan over the present value of the cash receipts.

Under certain situations, a loan could be impaired as discussed above but no impairment should be recognized. Use of the cash-basis method, cost recovery method, or some combination of the two methods for recognition of interest income may cause the recorded investment in the loan to be less than the fair value of the loan, even though the conditions for impairment under ASC 310-10-35 are met. When such a condition exists, additional impairment should not be recognized. In addition, if the conditions for impairment are met under ASC 310-10-35, but the creditor previously has written off part of the loan causing the recorded investment in the loan to be less than the fair value of the loan, no additional impairment is recognized. Fair value of the loan in this situation refers to all of the following situations: fair value of the collateral when the loan is collateral dependent, observable market price when such a price is used, and present value of the future cash receipts when present value is used for fair value.

When a loan impairment is recognized by the creditor, the amount of the impairment is an adjustment to bad debt expense and the allowance for bad debts. If a valuation allowance has not been established (Block 10) in a prior period for the impaired loan, bad debt expense is debited and a valuation allowance is credited for the amount of the impairment. If a valuation allowance has been established in a prior accounting period, the valuation allowance and bad debt expense are adjusted in such a way that the valuation allowance will equal the amount of the impairment. Estimated cash receipts used in the present value computation are based on the creditor's best estimate using projections and all evidence that is reasonable and supportable. These cash flows should be reduced by any costs that might be incurred over the remaining life of the loan, such as the cost to resell the loan, if appropriate. The discount rate used in the computation of the present value is the effective interest rate used in the original loan. No consideration is given to change in risk or rate changes as a result of the loan impairment. However, if the original contractual rate is allowed to vary because it is tied to an independent rate, such as the prime rate, the rate to use in the present value computations may require special accounting. When the rate varies over the remaining life of the loan, the creditor has the option of computing the effective rate in the following manner: use an effective rate equal to the rate in effect when the loan is impaired or adjust the effective rate based on changes in the variable rate over the life of the receivable. However, the creditor should not try to estimate changes in the variable rate for purposes of computing the effective rate. The method that the creditor selects should be applied on a consistent basis for all variable interest loans. Therefore, the only item requiring an estimate in computation of the present value amount is future cash flows.

Because cash flows are based on the best estimate by the creditor, changes in either the amount or timing of the cash flows may occur subsequent to the date of impairment. When there is a significant change in either the amount or timing of future cash receipts, the loan impairment should be recomputed using the procedures described above. Any adjustments should be made to the allowance account, but the carrying amount of the loan should always be less than the recorded investment in the loan. Additionally, if the fair value of collateral or observable market price is used in the computation of loan impairment and if the fair value of the items change, loan impairment should be recomputed as described above.

ASC 310-10-35 does not specify the appropriate accounting for interest income for a loan that has been impaired. Because the method for recognition, measurement, and presentation of interest income in the financial statement is not prescribed by ASC 310-10-35, the creditor may use any valid method(s) for interest income accounting.

Example 3-1, Example 3-2, and Example 3-3 illustrate the accounting and reporting requirements of loan impairment. Assumptions for Example 3-1 are as follows.

Example 3-1
Assumptions for Loan Impairment

1. Creditor, Inc., a December 31 year-end enterprise, has a $4,000,000, 8%, six-year note receivable from Debtor, Inc. that was issued January 1, 20X4. The note was issued at par value; therefore, the effective rate is 8%.

2. On January 1, 20X6, because of financial problems of Debtor, Inc., Creditor, Inc. estimates that only $3,200,000 of the principal amount of the loan will be collected.

3. Creditor, Inc. has no allowance for bad debts related to this note.

4. Creditor, Inc. uses the effective interest method for recognition of interest income.

Using the information from Example 3-1, the impairment loss and the adjustment to bad debt expense and related allowance account are computed in Table 3-1-A.

Table 3-1-A Computation of Loan Impairment Loss

Recorded investment in loan			$4,000,000
Present value of cash receipts:			
Present value of interest:			
Principal amount		$4,000,000	
Stated interest rate		8%	
Annual cash interest		$320,000	
Present value of ordinary annuity factor—4 periods at 8%		3.31213	
Present value of cash interest		$1,059,882	
Present value of principal:			
Estimated principal collection	$3,200,000		
Present value of $1 factor—4 periods at 8%	.73503		
Present value of principal		2,352,096	
Present value of future cash receipts			3,411,978
Impairment loss on loan			$588,022
Balance in bad debt allowance account			0
Adjustment to bad expense & allowance			$588,022

Using the information from Table 3-1-A, the following journal entry is required on January 1, 20X6 to recognize the impairment loss from the loan.

Bad Debt Expense	588,022	
Allowance for Bad Debts		588,022

The allowance for bad debts is a contra account to the note receivable, and if the allowance balance is not used to write off a portion of the note receivable in future years, the allowance account will be reversed against the note receivable at the end of the life of the note.

Interest income will be recognized each accounting period using the effective interest method (i.e., an application of a constant effective interest rate (8%, which is the effective rate in the original note) to the unrecovered present value of the future cash receipts). The difference between the cash interest received and interest income will be an adjustment to the note receivable account. Table 3-1-B shows the cash interest, interest income, and receivable adjustment for the remaining four-year life of the note.

Table 3-1-B Computation of Interest Income and Receivable Adjustment

	Cash Interest	Interest Income	Receivable Adjustment	Present Value Balance
				[a]$3,411,978
December 31, 20X6	[b]$320,000	[c]$272,958	[d]$47,042	[e]3,364,936
December 31, 20X7	320,000	269,195	50,805	3,314,131
December 31, 20X8	320,000	265,130	54,870	3,259,261
December 31, 20X9	320,000	[f]260,739	59,261	3,200,000
Totals	$1,280,000	$1,068,022	$211,978	

[a] Present value amount taken from Table 3-1-A.
[b] $4,000,000 × 8% = $320,000.
[c] $3,411,978 × 8% = $272,958.
[d] $320,000 – $272,958 = $47,042.
[e] $3,411,978 – $47,042 = $3,364,936.
[f] Rounded.

In Table 3-1-B, interest income is computed using the effective interest rate of 8%. The difference in interest income recognized using the 8% effective rate and cash interest is a decrease in the note receivable balance. The entry required for 20X6 for recognition of interest income and receivable adjustment is as follows:

Cash	320,000	
Note Receivable		47,042
Interest Income		272,958

Entries for the remaining three years will be the same except for the amounts. The amounts for the entries for 20X7–20X9 are shown in Table 3-1-B. Assuming Creditor, Inc. is correct and the debtor only pays $3,200,000 of the principal at the end of the life of the note, Creditor, Inc. must remove the allowance for bad debts of $588,022 (Table 3-1-A) established at the date of impairment because it was not used for any write-offs subsequent to impairment. In addition, the balance in the note receivable account of $3,788,022 ($4,000,000 original balance – $211,978 receivable adjustment from Table 3-1-B) must be removed. The entry required at the end of the life of the note is presented below.

Cash	3,200,000	
Allowance for Bad Debts	588,022	
Note Receivable		3,788,022

Example 3-1 was a straightforward loan impairment situation with no existing discounts, premiums, accrued interest or other unamortized items. Example 3-2 illustrates accounting for loan impairment when unamortized items exist. Assumptions for Example 3-2 are as follows.

Example 3-2
Assumptions for Loan Impairment

1. Creditor, Inc. (Creditor), a December 31 year-end enterprise, has a $1,000,000, 7%, four-year note receivable from Debtor, Inc. that was issued January 1, 20X6. The market rate of interest on the date the note was issued was 10%. Amortization of the note receivable discount from 20X6–20X9 is presented below.

Date	Cash Interest	Interest Income	Discount Amortization	Investment in Note Receivable
				$904,903
December 31, 20X6	$70,000	$90,490	$20,490	925,393
December 31, 20X7	70,000	92,539	22,539	947,932
December 31, 20X8	70,000	94,793	24,793	972,725
December 31, 20X9	70,000	97,275 [a]	27,275	1,000,000
Totals	$280,000	$375,097	$95,097	

[a] Rounded.

2. On January 1, 20X8, as a result of changing economic situations, Creditor, Inc. estimates that only $700,000 of the principal amount will be collected. In addition, Creditor, Inc. also estimates that the equivalent of $28,000 of interest per year will be collected from the loan over the loan's remaining life. On this date, the note has a $52,068 ($1,000,000 – $947,932) unamortized discount.

3. Creditor, Inc. has a $40,000 allowance for bad debts related to this note that was established in a prior accounting period.

4. Creditor, Inc. uses the effective interest method for recognition of interest income.

Using the information from Example 3-2, the impairment loss and the adjustment to bad debt expense and related allowance account are computed in Table 3-2-A.

Table 3-2-A Computation of Loan Impairment Loss

Face amount of receivable		$1,000,000
Unamortized discount (Example 3-2, Item 2, above)		(52,068)
Recorded investment in receivable		$947,932
Present value of cash receipts:		
Present value of interest:		
Estimated annual cash interest	$28,000	
Present value of ordinary annuity factor—2 periods at 10%	1.73554	
Present value of estimated cash interest	$48,595	

Present value of principal:		
Estimated principal collection	$700,000	
Present value of $1 factor—2 periods at 10%	.82645	
Present value of principal	578,515	
Present value of future cash receipts		627,110
Impairment loss on loan		$320,822
Balance in bad debt allowance account		40,000
Adjustment to bad expense & allowance		$280,822

Using the information from Table 3-2-A, the following journal entry is required on January 1, 20X8 to recognize the loan impairment loss.

Bad Debt Expense	280,822	
Allowance for Bad Debts		280,822

The amount credited to the allowance account is $280,822, but the balance in the allowance account after this entry is $320,822.

Interest income is recognized each accounting period using the effective interest method (i.e., an application of a constant effective interest rate (10%, which is the effective rate in the original note) to the unrecovered present value of the future cash receipts). The difference between the cash interest received and interest income is an adjustment to the note receivable account. Table 3-2-B shows the cash interest, interest income, and receivable adjustment for the remaining two-year life of the note.

Table 3-2-B Computation of Interest Income and Receivable Adjustment

Date	Cash Interest	Interest Income	Receivable Adjustment	Present Value Balance
				[a]$627,110
December 31, 20X8	[b]$28,000	[c]$62,711	[d]$34,711	[e]661,821
December 31, 20X9	28,000	[f]66,179	38,179	700,000
Totals	$56,000	$128,890	$72,890	

[a] Present value amount taken from Table 3-2-A.
[b] Information taken from Example 3-2, Item 2.
[c] $627,110 × 10% = $62,711.
[d] $62,711 − $28,000 = $34,711.
[e] $627,110 + $34,711 = $661,821.
[f] Rounded.

In Table 3-2-B, interest income is computed using the effective interest rate of 10%. The difference in the interest income recognized using the 10% effective rate and the $28,000 estimated annual cash interest payments is an increase in notes receivable. However, this does not consider the $52,068 unamortized discount from the original issuance of the note. This discount can be accounted for in different ways because it will not have an impact on the amount of interest income recognized by the creditor. For example, it could be written off against the receivable at the time of impairment, or it could be amortized to the receivable over the remaining life of the note. In this example, the unamortized discount is amortized to notes receivable over the remaining life of the note. Using the discount amortization from the assumptions in Example 3-2 and the amount of note receivable adjustment from Table 3-2-B, the amount of annual change in the notes receivable account is presented in Table 3-2-C.

Table 3-2-C Computation of Notes Receivable Adjustment

Date	Discount Amortization[a]	Receivable Adjustment[b]	Total Adjustment	Receivable
December 31, 20X8	$24,793	$34,711	$9,918	
December 31, 20X9	27,275	38,179	10,904	
Totals	$52,068	$72,890	$20,822	

[a] Information taken from Example 3-2, Item 1.
[b] Information taken from Table 3-2-B.

Using the information from Tables 3-2-B and 3-2-C, and assuming the creditor is correct relative to its interest collection, the entry required for 20X8 for recognition of interest income and receivable adjustment is as follows:

Cash	28,000	
Discount on Notes Receivable	24,793	
Notes Receivable	9,918	
Interest Income		62,711

The amount of the discount amortization of $24,793 decreases notes receivable, and the receivable adjustment of $34,711 from the present value computations increases notes receivable. Therefore, the net increase in notes receivable for 20X8 is $9,918.

The entry for the last year is the same as the preceding entry except for the amounts. The amounts for the entry for 20X9 are shown in Tables 3-2-B and 3-2-C. Assuming that Creditor, Inc. is correct about the estimated interest payments and principal collection, at the end of the life of the note, Creditor, Inc. must remove the allowance for bad debts of $320,822 (Table 3-2-A) established at the date of impairment and prior years because it was not used for any write-offs subsequent to the impairment. In addition, the balance in the notes receivable account of $1,020,822 ($1,000,000 original balance + $20,822 receivable adjustment from Table 3-2-C) must be removed at the end of the life of the loan. The entry required at the end of the life of the note is presented below.

Cash	700,000	
Allowance for Bad Debts	320,822	
Notes Receivable		1,020,822

This completes the discussion of Example 3-2. Example 3-3 covers a situation where significant changes in cash flows occurred subsequent to the year the loan impairment was computed. Assumptions for Example 3-3 are as follows.

Example 3-3
Assumptions for Loan Impairment

1. Creditor, Inc., a December 31 year-end enterprise, has a $5,000,000, 6%, six-year note receivable from Debtor, Inc. that was issued January 1, 20X4. The note was issued at par value; therefore, the effective rate is 6%.
2. On January 1, 20X6, as a result of financial problems facing the debtor, Creditor, Inc. estimates that $1,000,000 of the principal will not be collectible at the end of the life of the loan.
3. On January 1, 20X7, because of new financial problems of Debtor, Inc., Creditor, Inc. estimates that an additional $1,000,000 of the principal will be uncollectible.
4. Creditor, Inc. has a $100,000 allowance for bad debts related to this note that was established in a prior accounting period.
5. Creditor, Inc. uses the effective interest method for recognition of interest income.

Using the information from Example 3-3, the impairment loss and the adjustment to bad debt expense and related allowance account are computed in Table 3-3-A.

Table 3-3-A Computation of Loan Impairment Loss

Recorded investment in loan			$5,000,000
Present value of cash receipts:			
Present value of interest:			
Principal amount		$5,000,000	
Stated interest rate		6%	
Annual cash interest		$300,000	
Present value of ordinary annuity factor—4 periods at 6%		3.46511	
Present value of cash interest		$1,039,533	
Present value of principal:			
Estimated principal collection	$4,000,000		
Present value of $1 factor—4 periods at 6%	.792094		
Present value of principal		3,168,376	
Present value of future cash receipts			4,207,909

Impairment loss on loan	$792,091
Balance in bad debt allowance account	100,000
Adjustment to bad expense & allowance	$692,091

Using the information from Table 3-3-A, the following journal entry is required on January 1, 20X6 to recognize the loan impairment loss.

Bad Debt Expense	692,091	
Allowance for Bad Debts		692,091

Table 3-3-B shows the cash interest, interest income, and receivable adjustment for the remaining four-year life of the note.

Table 3-3-B Computation of Interest Income and Receivable Adjustment

	Cash Interest	Interest Income	Receivable Adjustment	Present Value Balance
				[a]$4,207,909
December 31, 20X6	[b]$300,000	[c]$252,475	[d]$47,525	[e]4,160,384
December 31, 20X7	300,000	249,623	50,377	4,110,007
December 31, 20X8	300,000	246,600	53,400	4,056,607
December 31, 20X9	300,000	[f]243,393	56,607	4,000,000
Totals	$1,200,000	$992,091	$207,909	

[a] Present value amount taken from Table 3-3-A.
[b] $5,000,000 × 6% =$300,000.
[c] $4,207,909 × 6% =$252,475.
[d] $300,000 – $252,475 =$47,525.
[e] $4,207,909 – $47,525 =$4,160,384.
[f] Rounded.

In Table 3-3-B, interest income is computed using the effective interest rate of 6%. The difference in the interest income recognized using the 6% effective rate and the cash interest is a decrease in the note receivable balance. The entry required for 20X6 for recognition of interest income and receivable adjustment is as follows:

Cash	300,000	
Note Receivable		47,525
Interest Income		252,475

At the beginning of 20X7, Creditor, Inc. estimates that an additional $1,000,000 of the loan from Debtor, Inc. will not be collected. Therefore, Creditor, Inc. must recompute any impairment loss because of the significant change in estimated future cash receipts. The additional impairment loss is computed in Table 3-3-C.

Table 3-3-C Computation of Additional Loan Impairment Loss

Recorded investment in loan	$5,000,000	
Receivable adjustment from 20X6 impairment—see 12/31/X6 entry	47,525	
Revised recorded investment in loan	$4,952,475	
Present value of cash receipts:		
Present value of interest:		
Principal amount		$5,000,000
Stated interest rate		6%
Annual cash interest		$300,000
Present value of ordinary annuity factor—3 periods at 6%		2.67301
Present value of cash interest	$801,903	
Present value of principal:		
Estimated principal collection	$3,000,000	
Present value of $1 factor—3 periods at 6%	.83962	
Present value of principal	2,518,860	
Present value of future cash receipts		3,320,763
Impairment loss on loan	$1,631,712	
Balance in bad debt allowance account	792,091	
Adjustment to bad expense & allowance	$839,621	

Using the information from Table 3-3-C, the following journal entry is required on January 1, 20X7 to recognize the additional loan impairment loss.

Bad Debt Expense	839,621	
Allowance for Bad Debts		839,621

The balance in the allowance for bad debt account is now $1,631,712, as shown in Table 3-3-C. Because the creditor has estimated that an additional $1,000,000 of the principal will not be collected, interest income, cash interest, and the receivable adjustment for the remaining three-year life of the loan will also change. The amortization schedule presented in Table 3-3-B is replaced with the following amortization schedule in Table 3-3-D.

Table 3-3-D Computation of Interest Income and Receivable Adjustment

Date	Cash Interest	Interest Income	Receivable Adjustment	Present Value Balance
				[a]$3,320,763
December 31, 20X7	[b]$300,000	[c]$199,246	[d]$100,754	[e]3,220,009
December 31, 20X8	300,000	193,201	106,799	3,113,210

Date	Cash Interest	Interest Income	Receivable Adjustment	Present Value Balance
December 31, 20X9	300,000	[f]186,790	113,210	3,000,000
Totals	$900,000	$579,237	$320,763	

[a] Present value amount taken from Table 3-3-C.
[b] $5,000,000 × 6% =$300,000.
[c] $3,320,763 × 6% =$199,246.
[d] $300,000 –$199,246 =$100,754.
[e] $3,320,763 –$100,754 =$3,220,009.
[f] Rounded.

Interest income, cash interest, and the receivable adjustment will now be taken from the amortization schedule in Table 3-3-D for the remaining life of the loan unless other significant changes in future cash flows require an additional adjustment. The entry required for 20X6 for recognition of interest income and receivable adjustment as of December 31, 20X7 is as follows:

Cash	300,000	
Notes Receivable		100,754
Interest Income		199,246

The entries for cash, note receivable, and interest income would have been $300,000, $50,377, and $249,623 (Table 3-3-B), respectively, if the additional $1,000,000 estimated reduction in cash receipts on January 1, 20X7 had not occurred. Entries for 20X8 and 20X9 can be taken directly from Table 3-3-D. Assuming that no additional changes in estimated cash flow occur during the remaining life of the loan, the following entry is required at the end of the life of the loan to remove the balance in the allowance account of $1,631,712 (Table 3-3-C) and the $4,631,712 ($4,952,475 (Table 3-3-C) – $320,763 (Table 3-3-D)) balance in the notes receivable account.

Cash	3,000,000	
Allowance for Bad Debts	1,631,712	
Notes Receivable		4,631,712

Impairment Based on Observable Market Price

Example 3-4 covers loan impairments when an observable market price is used for the impairment computation. Assumptions for Example 3-4 are as follows.

Example 3-4
Assumptions for Loan Impairment

1. Creditor, Inc., a December 31 year-end enterprise, has a $3,000,000, 7%, five-year note receivable from Debtor, Inc. that was issued January 1, 20X4. The note was issued at par value; therefore, the effective rate is 7%.
2. On December 31, 20X6, because of financial difficulties faced by Debtor, Inc., Creditor, Inc. estimates that only $2,500,000 of the $3,000,000 principal amount of the loan will be collected.

3. The observable market price of the loan on December 31, 20X6 is $2,100,000, and on December 31, 20X7 it is $2,500,000.

4. Creditor, Inc. has no allowance for bad debts related to this note.

5. Creditor, Inc. uses the effective interest method for recognition of interest income.

Using the information from Example 3-4, the impairment loss on the loan can be computed at December 31, 20X6. In addition, because there was a significant change in the observable market price on December 31, 20X7, one year later, an adjustment must be made to the allowance account to reflect this additional impairment. The impairment loss on December 31, 20X6 and the required adjustment at December 31, 20X7 are computed in Table 3-4-A.

Table 3-4-A Computation of Loan Impairment Loss

	12/31/X6	12/31/X7
Recorded investment in loan	$3,000,000	$3,000,000
Observable market price	2,100,000	2,500,000
Impairment loss on loan	$900,000	$500,000
Balance in bad debt allowance account	0	900,000
Adjustment to bad expense & allowance	900,000	$(400,000)

Using the information from Table 3-4-A, the entry to record the impairment at December 31, 20X6 is as follows:

Bad Debt Expense	900,000	
Allowance for Bad Debt Expense		900,000

In addition, Creditor, Inc. should recognize the annual receipt of interest, which is $210,000 ($3,000,000 × 7%). The required entry for interest income for 20X6 is:

Because there was a significant change in the observable market price during 20X7, the change must be reflected as an adjustment to the allowance account. Because the market price increased by $400,000, the allowance for bad debts will be reduced by $400,000. The journal entries on December 31, 20X7 to record the interest income and the change in the observable market price are as follows (see Table 3-4-A and Example 3-4):

Cash	210,000	
Interest Income		210,000
Cash	210,000	
Interest Income		210,000
Allowance for Bad Debt Expense	400,000	
Bad Debt Expense		400,000

Assuming the creditor was correct in the cash receipt estimate and the debtor only pays $2,500,000 of the principal amount of the loan, and assuming no other change in the observable market price of the loan, the following entries are required at the end of 20X8 to reflect receipt of the $2,500,000 principal amount of the loan, recognize $210,000 of interest income and remove the $500,000 allowance balance.

Cash	2,500,000	
Allowance for Bad Debts	500,000	
Notes Receivable		3,000,000
Cash	210,000	
Interest Income		210,000

Loan Impairment Disclosures

For creditors, the loan impairment information below should be reported. This information may be reported in the face of the statements or in related notes.

1. For each period that a balance sheet is presented, the following information is reported for receivables that have recorded impairments:
   a. The total recorded investment in the receivables.
   b. The amount of the receivable for which an allowance for losses has been computed.
   c. The amount of the receivable for which no allowance for losses has been computed.
2. For each period that an income statement is presented, the following information should be disclosed:
   a. Average amount of receivables impaired.
   b. Amount of interest income related to impaired loans.
   c. Amount of interest income reported on a cash basis related to impaired loans, if practicable.
   d. The following information should be disclosed for the allowance for losses account related to impaired loans:
      (1) Beginning balance.
      (2) Ending balance.
      (3) Additions charged to income.
      (4) Recoveries of prior write-offs.
      (5) Amount of direct write-offs charged against the allowance account.
3. The policy that the creditor uses for reporting interest income from loans that are impaired, including the method for reporting cash receipts.

Disclosure—Foreclosures

Foreclosed and repossessed assets included in other assets on the statement of financial position shall disclose the carrying amount of foreclosed residential real estate properties held at the reporting date as a result of obtaining physical possession. The recorded investment of consumer mortgage loans secured by residential real estate in the process of foreclosure shall be disclosed.

Nonrefundable Fees and Other Costs—Introduction

ASC 310-20 specifies the accounting and reporting requirements for certain types of fees and costs related to lending activities. In addition, it addresses the issue of initial direct costs for leasing activities.

The discussion of ASC 310-20 is divided into three major categories. The first category addresses the issue of fees and costs related to lending activities, the second category discusses initial direct costs as they relate to leases, and the third category covers disclosure issues.

Fees and Costs Related to Lending Activities

ASC 310-20 covers the accounting and reporting for different types of fees and costs related to loans that are originated or purchased by an entity. The types of fees and costs covered by ASC 310-20 include commitment, loan origination syndication, and others. Each type of fee or cost will be covered in detail in the following discussion.

Commitment Fees and Costs

When a lender grants to a potential borrower a commitment to provide a loan to the borrower for a fee, the fee is referred to as a commitment fee. The lender should account for the commitment fee by deferring the fee, after deducting any direct costs incurred to grant the commitment (net commitment fee), on the date of commitment and by recognizing the fee as revenue in the future, depending on the outcome of the potential loan. If the loan is not granted, the net deferred fee is reported as income in the accounting period that the commitment expires. If the loan is granted, the net commitment fee is reported in income over the life of the loan by adjusting the yield on the loan. However, there are two exceptions to the preceding general rule of accounting for commitment fees.

First, if experience of the entity indicates that it is remote that the commitment will be exercised, the net commitment fee is charged to income as a service fee over the period of the commitment using a straight-line method. If, however, the commitment is later exercised prior to the end of the commitment period, any net commitment fee that has not been amortized on the date that the commitment is exercised is reported in income over the life of the loan by adjusting the yield on the loan.

Second, an entity may retrospectively determine the amount of the commitment fee by using a percentage of a prior period's unused line of credit. The commitment fee so determined is recognized as service fee income on the date the amount of the commitment fee is determined if the following two conditions are met:

1. The percentage of the prior period unused line of credit is nominal compared to the interest rate on related borrowings, and
2. The stated rate of interest on the related loan is equal to the market rate of interest on the date the loan is granted.

Commitment fees also include charges made on credit cards for lines of credit. Commitment fees on credit cards are deferred on the date they are charged to the card and reported in income over the time period that the card holder is expected to have the card using a straight-line method.

This completes the section on commitment fees and commitment costs. The next section covers the proper accounting for loan origination fees and costs.

Origination Fees and Costs

Loan origination fees, such as points and buy-down costs, are fees charged to an entity borrowing money when a loan is originated by the lender. In addition, the lender may incur certain costs, such as those for preparation of loan documents, when originating a loan. Such costs are referred to as loan origination costs. Loan origination costs should include the following: costs directly incurred in loan transactions with third parties and costs incurred for functions that the lender performs.

An entity that receives loan origination fees should defer the fees on the date of the transaction and report the fees as income over the time period of the loan by adjusting the loan yield (i.e., reporting as interest income). Any loan origination cost incurred on a loan with origination fees should first be offset against the fees, and only the net fees or net costs should be deferred and reported in income as an adjustment of the loan yield over the time period of the loan. If loan origination costs are incurred on loans with no loan origination fees, the costs should be deferred and reported in income as a reduction of the loan yield over the time period of the loan. Costs, other than loan origination costs, incurred to generate a loan should be expensed as incurred.

Any loan origination fees related to troubled debt restructuring classified as a modification of terms are accounted for by reducing the investment in the loan.

This completes the discussion of loan origination fees and origination costs. The next section covers syndication fees.

Syndication Fees

An entity, commonly referred to as a syndicator, that manages a syndication of loans will receive fees for the management activities. The fees received by the syndicator should be accounted for on the date of completion of the loan syndication unless the syndicator retains a part of the loans. If a part of the loans is retained by the syndicator, a part of the fees will be deferred under certain situations. The fees are deferred when the average yield to other parties in the syndication is greater than the yield received by the syndicator adjusted for pass-through fees by the syndicator. The amount of the fee deferred is equal to an amount that would allow the yield to the syndicator to be not less than the average yield to other parties in the syndication.

Restructuring and Refinancing Fees and Costs

When a lender restructures or refinances an existing loan, the lender must determine whether the restructuring or refinancing is accounted for as if the existing loan continues or as if a new loan is issued. When the restructuring or refinancing terms to the lender are not as favorable as terms on similar existing loans with other entities or, more specifically, if the effective yield of the new terms is less than existing loans, the restructuring or refinancing is accounted for as if the existing loan continues. If, however, the new terms are as favorable to the lender or the effective yield for the new terms is not less than the yield of existing loans, the restructuring or refinancing is accounted for as a new loan.

When the restructuring or refinancing is accounted for as if the existing loan continues, all costs or fees that have not been amortized and any penalties for prepayments should be carried forward and included in the new loan's net investment. Therefore, the net investment in the new loan would then consist of the net investment in the loan prior to refinancing plus any additional funds loaned, fees paid by the debtor, and direct loan origination costs.

When the restructuring or refinancing is accounted for as if it is a new loan, all costs or fees that have not been amortized and any penalties for prepayments should be reported as part of interest income when the lender grants the new loan. Fees and costs incurred to consummate the new loan, such as commitment and origination fees, should be accounted for using the provisions previously discussed for such fees and costs.

Restructuring or refinancing of loans in a troubled debt situation is excluded from ASC 310-20 and is covered by ASC 310-40, *Troubled Debt Restructuring by Creditors*.

Purchase of a Loan or a Group of Loans

An entity may purchase an existing loan or a group of loans in a lump-sum acquisition. The amount reported for the investment in the loan(s) purchased is equal to the amount paid for the loans adjusted for net fees paid or received by the buyer. The difference between the amount reported for the investment and the principal amount of the loans is treated as a loan yield adjustment over the remaining loan period. Any additional costs paid by the entity to consummate the loan purchase are expensed in the accounting period incurred.

Accounting for the purchase of loans is more complex when an entity purchases a group of loans for a lump-sum price. The entity may account for the loan investment (which is computed in the same manner as discussed above) by using an aggregate method or the entity can allocate to individual loans the amount of the investment.

The interest method should be applied when recognizing income on the loans purchased by using cash flows from the loans, except as noted in ASC 310-20-35-26. If changes occur in the loan, such as a sale of a part of the loan(s) or a prepayment is received by the creditor, part of the unamortized loan items should be taken to income to keep the effective yield on the loans constant.

Many of the fees and costs covered in the preceding discussion of lending activities are accounted for as adjustments to the yield on the loan. Generally, the adjustment to the yield on the loan is accomplished by using the interest method. In some cases, the interest method is difficult to apply because of factors such as increases or decreases in stated interest rates, interest rates tied to variable factors, and lack of scheduled term of payments. The FASB provides some guidance in the application of the interest method in ASC 310-20-35.

Initial Direct Costs Related to Leases

ASC 310-20 defines initial direct costs. In addition, ASC 310-20 requires that initial direct costs for direct financing leases be included as a component of the net investment of the lease.

Nonrefundable Fees and Other Costs—Disclosure Requirements

ASC 310-20 provides disclosure requirements for both the income statement and the statement of financial position. According to ASC 310-20-45-3, the following information should be reported in the current period income statement:

1. Report as interest income adjustments to yield from fees and costs, such as origination, commitment, and other adjustments.
2. Include in service fees income fee amortization where amortization is computed using a straight-line method.

ASC 310-20-45-1 specifies the disclosure requirements for the statement of financial position: the reporting of unamortized related loan items that are yield adjustments, such as premiums, discounts, origination fees and costs, and commitment fees and costs as an increase or decrease to the related loan amount.

Loans and Debt Securities Acquired with Deteriorated Credit Quality

ASC 310-30 specifies the accounting for the difference between contractual and expected to be collected cash flows from an initial investment in debt securities or loans by the investor when the difference or part of the difference relates to the quality of credit and the investment is acquired in a transfer. The contractual cash flows in excess, if any, of the anticipated cash flows from the loan investment, commonly referred to as the nonaccretable difference, cannot be used to adjust the yield, as a valuation allowance or as an accrued loss. However, the accretable yield on the investment in loans is limited to the amount that the estimated anticipated interest, principal, and any other cash flows exceed the initial investment of the investor.

Troubled Debt Restructuring—Flowchart and General Discussion

ASC 310-40 specifies the accounting and reporting standards for a restructuring of troubled debt from the creditor's perspective. Not all debt restructurings qualify for treatment as a troubled debt restructuring. Debt restructuring, troubled or otherwise, involves the modification or elimination of a debt instrument before, at, or after maturity date by means other than those required in the debt instrument. A troubled debt restructuring exists when the debtor is unable to meet current debt requirements and the creditor grants to the debtor a concession that normally would not be provided. In effect, the creditor is making the concession in hopes that he will receive more from the debtor than he would if the concession were not made.

Although there are many types of troubled debt restructurings, ASC 310-40-15-9 identifies the following:

1. Transfer from the debtor to the creditor of receivables from third parties, real estate, or other assets to satisfy fully or partially a debt (including a transfer resulting from foreclosure or repossession).
2. Issuance or other granting of an equity interest to the creditor by the debtor to satisfy fully or partially a debt unless the equity interest is granted pursuant to existing terms for converting the debt into an equity interest.
3. Modification of terms of a debt, such as one or a combination of any of the following:
    a. Reduction (absolute or contingent) of the stated interest rate for the remaining original life of the debt.
    b. Extension of the maturity date or dates at a stated interest rate lower than the current market rate for new debt with similar risk.
    c. Reduction (absolute or contingent) of the face amount or maturity amount of the debt as stated in the instrument or other agreement.
    d. Reduction (absolute or contingent) of accrued interest.

This list is not meant to be all-inclusive, and other types of troubled debt restructurings will have to be evaluated on their merits. Flowchart 3-2 is designed to illustrate the major accounting and reporting consequences of these four types of troubled debt restructurings from the viewpoint of the creditor.

Flowchart 3-2

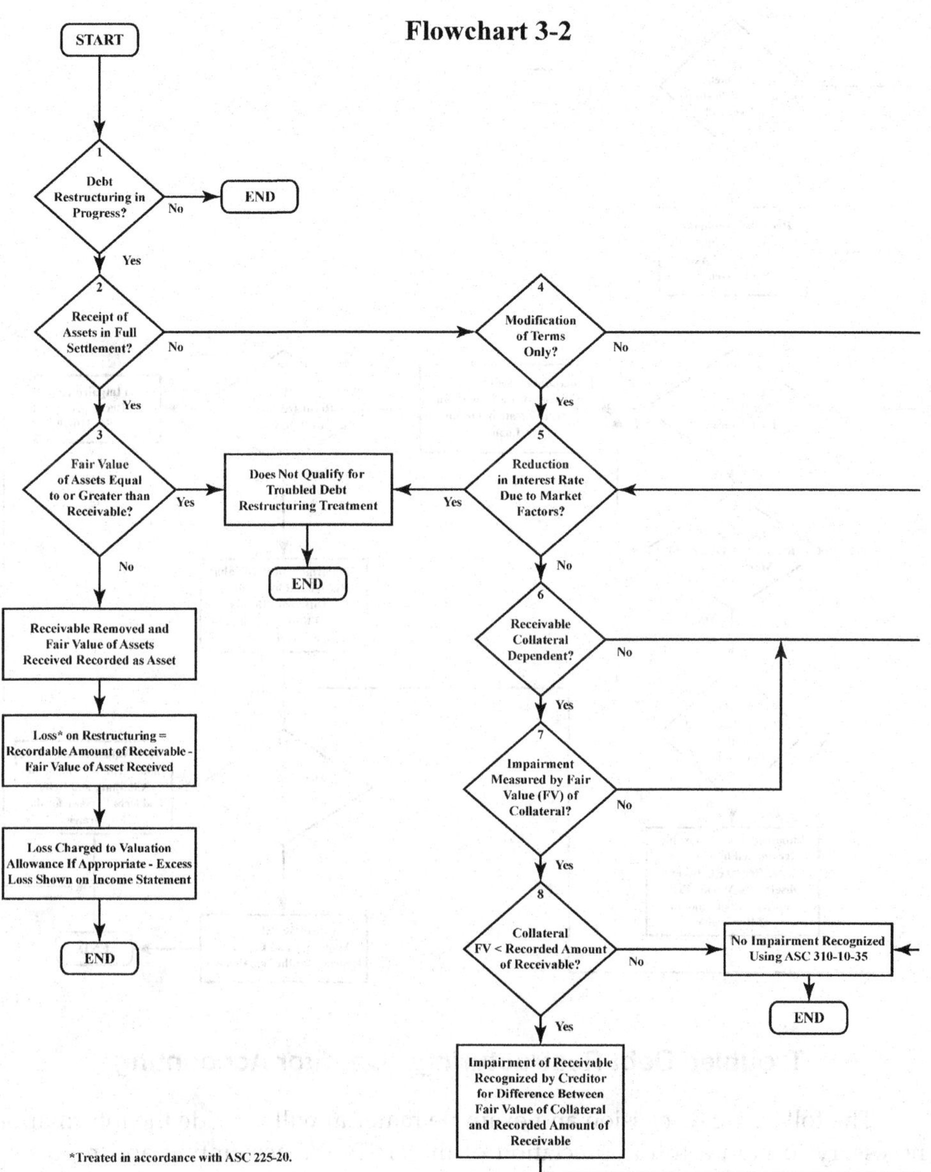
START
1
Debt Restructuring in Progress?
No
END
Yes
2
Receipt of Assets in Full Settlement?
No
Yes
3
Fair Value of Assets Equal to or Greater than Receivable?
Yes
No
Receivable Removed and Fair Value of Assets Received Recorded as Asset
Loss* on Restructuring = Recordable Amount of Receivable - Fair Value of Asset Received
Loss Charged to Valuation Allowance If Appropriate - Excess Loss Shown on Income Statement
END
Does Not Qualify for Troubled Debt Restructuring Treatment
END
4
Modification of Terms Only?
No
Yes
5
Reduction in Interest Rate Due to Market Factors?
Yes
No
6
Receivable Collateral Dependent?
No
Yes
7
Impairment Measured by Fair Value (FV) of Collateral?
No
Yes
8
Collateral FV < Recorded Amount of Receivable?
No
Yes
No Impairment Recognized Using ASC 310-10-35
END
Impairment of Receivable Recognized by Creditor for Difference Between Fair Value of Collateral and Recorded Amount of Receivable
*Treated in accordance with ASC 225-20.

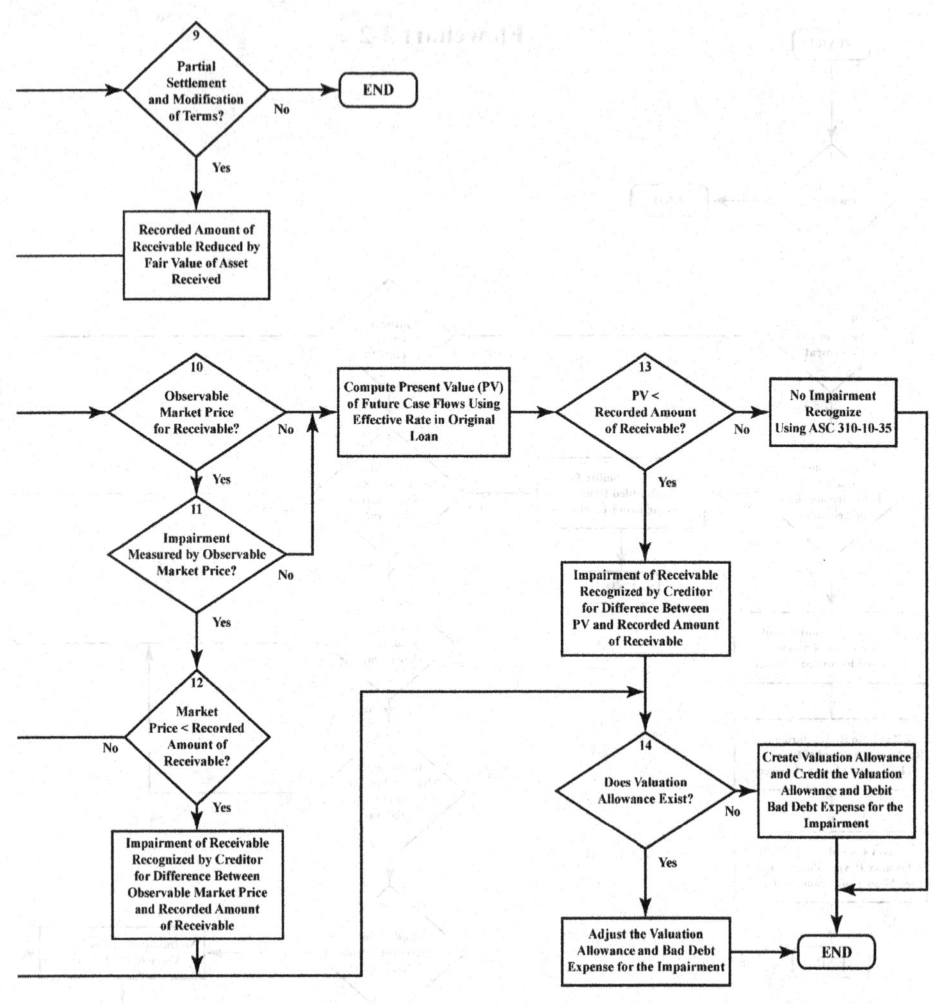

Troubled Debt Restructuring—Creditor Accounting

The following discussion and example material will provide the information necessary to gain a full appreciation of the creditor's accounting and reporting requirements.

There are three major types of troubled debt restructurings from the standpoint of the creditor. These include receipt of asset(s) in full settlement of the debt, modification of the terms of the agreement, and a partial settlement of the debt, coupled with a modification of terms. After each of these three topics has been considered in detail, some accounting complexities of ASC 310-40 are taken up, followed by a listing of the required disclosures.

Flowchart 3-2 shows the major accounting decisions and related procedures that are identified in ASC 310-40. Specific references to Flowchart 3-2 are made as the various types of restructurings are discussed.

Receipt of Assets in Full Settlement

In a troubled debt restructuring, a creditor may receive assets or stock of the debtor in full settlement of the obligation (Block 2). In this case, the transaction will qualify as a *troubled* debt restructuring only if the fair value of the assets received are not greater than the recorded investment in the receivable (Block 3). The recorded amount of the receivable is the face of the receivable adjusted for the following items: unamortized discounts or premiums on the date of restructuring, accrued interest as of the date of restructuring, and any acquisition or financial costs. The recorded investment in the receivable does not give consideration to any valuation allowances related to the receivable. The *carrying amount* of the receivable is the recorded investment in the receivable, reduced by any related valuation allowance. Careful attention must be given to the difference between the two terms. For the most part, the following discussion will deal with the recorded investment in the receivable.

If the fair value of the assets received is less than the recorded investment in the receivable, the creditor has made a concession to the debtor. This is one of the essential requirements of ASC 310-40. If no such concession has been made, the transaction will not qualify for troubled debt restructuring accounting. When it has been determined that the fair value of the assets received is less than the recorded investment in the receivable, the creditor will recognize a loss on the restructuring. The loss to be recognized is equal to the difference between the recorded investment in the receivable and the fair value of the assets received. However, if a valuation allowance, such as allowance for uncollectible accounts, has been established in connection with the receivable, the loss may be partially or fully offset against the valuation allowance. Losses on restructuring should be applied first to the valuation allowance, and any loss in excess of the allowance will be reported on the current period income statement. Any losses resulting from restructuring that appear on the income statement must be handled in accordance with the provisions of ASC 225-20. ASC 225-20 provides three different classifications for the loss, depending on the environment of the creditor. The loss may be classified as a one-line item in the nonoperating section of the income statement, or an expense of normal operations, such as general and administrative expenses. For example, a financial institution might treat the loss as a general and administrative expense (charged to a bad debt account), whereas a nonfinancial creditor may treat the loss as a one-line item in the nonoperating section. The offset of the loss against the valuation allowance is recognition that previous adjusting entries relating to the allowance represented a partial (or complete) recognition of the loss on restructuring. Therefore, the loss should be charged against the valuation allowance, if appropriate. If no valuation allowance has been established in connection with the receivable, the entire loss would be reported in the current period income statement.

Any assets received by the creditor in a troubled debt restructuring will be recorded and accounted for in subsequent periods as if the creditor had purchased the assets for cash. The assets received are to be recorded at their fair value on the date of restructuring.

To illustrate the situation where a creditor receives assets in full settlement of a troubled debt, the assumptions listed in Example 3-5 are used.

Example 3-5
Receipt of Assets in Full Settlement of Debt

1. Creditor, Inc. has a $3,000,000 note receivable from Debtor, Inc., which is payable in full in two years.
2. The note bears interest at the rate of 12% per annum, and there is $100,000 of unamortized discount on the books of Creditor, Inc. in connection with the note.
3. Because of economic problems faced by Debtor, Inc., Creditor Inc. is willing to accept a parcel of land owned by Debtor, Inc. in full settlement of the note. At the date of settlement, the land had a fair value of $2,300,000.
4. In previous years, Creditor, Inc. had established a $50,000 allowance for uncollectible notes, which was related directly to the note of Debtor, Inc.

To determine if the provisions of troubled debt restructuring accounting apply to this transaction, a comparison of the fair value of the asset received with the recorded investment in the receivable must be made. This comparison is shown below:

Face Amount of the Note Receivable	$3,000,000
Unamortized Discount	(100,000)
Recorded Investment in the Receivable	$2,900,000
Fair Value of Land Received	(2,300,000)
Excess of Recorded Investment over Fair Value	$600,000

In this case, the fair value of the land is less than the recorded investment in the receivable; therefore, the transaction qualifies for troubled debt restructuring accounting. A loss on restructuring will be recognized for the difference between fair value of the assets received and the recorded investment in the receivable, or $600,000, as calculated above.

The entry required to record the troubled debt restructuring is presented below:

Loss on Restructuring of Receivable	600,000	
Discount on Notes Receivable	100,000	
Land	2,300,000	
Notes Receivable		3,000,000

The loss of $600,000 should be offset against the $50,000 allowance for uncollectibles because $50,000 of the loss has been recognized in the period when the allowance was established. The entry to accomplish this would be:

Allowance for Uncollectibles	50,000	
Loss on Restructuring of Receivable		50,000

After this entry has been made, Creditor, Inc. would report the excess loss of $550,000 ($600,000 – $50,000) in accordance with ASC 225-20. The two preceding entries could have been combined into one entry, but were shown separately for purposes of illustration.

Modification of Terms

Recall that modification of terms involves some adjustment to the existing debt, such as a change in interest rate, maturity value, maturity date, or some combination of these items (Block 4). If a debt restructuring involves a reduction in the interest rate originally specified, the transaction will qualify for *troubled* debt restructuring accounting only if the reduction was not due merely to market factors (Block 5). Once it has been determined that the transaction involves a modification of term, the creditor must determine if the receivable has been impaired as required by the provisions of ASC 310-10-35. A receivable has been impaired when the creditor cannot collect all principal and interest payments, as specified by the loan agreement. Generally, the creditor should use the present value of cash flows to be received in the future to compute the amount of the impairment. However, the creditor may elect to use a market price for impairment if that price is available to the creditor, or, if the receivable is supported by collateral, the fair value of the collateral. A receivable is supported by collateral (i.e., collateral dependent) when the creditor expects the loan to be repaid from the collateral that supports the receivable. If a receivable is supported by collateral (Block 6), impairment of the receivable may be measured by the fair market value of the collateral. When the creditor elects to use the collateral to measure impairment (Block 7), the loan is considered impaired if the fair value of the collateral is less than the recorded amount of the receivable (Block 8). The amount of the impairment is equal to the excess of the recorded amount of the receivable over the fair value of the collateral. If the fair value of the collateral is greater than the recorded amount of the receivable, no impairment is recognized under ASC 310-10-35. If the receivable is not supported by collateral, the creditor may use a market price, if available, when measuring receivable impairment (Block 10). If the creditor uses a market price to measure impairment (Block 11), and the market price is less than the recorded amount of the receivable (Block 12), an impairment of the receivable equal to the excess of the recorded amount of the receivable over the market price is recognized. If the market price exceeds the recorded amount of the receivable, no impairment is recognized. When the creditor does not use the fair value of collateral or a market price for computing receivable impairment, the present value of future cash receipts must be used for the computation. A comparison should be made between the recorded amount of the receivable and the present value of estimated future cash receipts using the provisions of ASC 310-10-35. If the present value of the future cash receipts is less than the recorded amount of the receivable (Block 13), an impairment of the receivable must be recognized by the creditor for the excess of the recorded investment of the receivable in excess of the present value of the cash receipts.

Under certain situations, a loan could be impaired as discussed above but no impairment should be recognized. Use of the cash-basis method, cost recovery method, or some combination of the two methods for recognition of interest income may cause the recorded investment in the loan to be less than the fair value of the loan, even though the conditions for impairment under ASC 310-10-35 are met. When such a condition exists, additional impairment should not be recognized. In addition, if the conditions for impairment are met under ASC 310-10-35, but the creditor previously has written off part of the loan causing the recorded investment in the loan to be less than the fair value of the loan, no additional impairment is recognized. Fair value of the loan in this situation refers to all of the following situations: fair value of the collateral when the loan is collateral dependent, observable market price when such a price is used, and present value of the future cash receipts when present value is used for fair value.

When an impairment is recognized by the creditor, the amount of the impairment is an adjustment to bad debt expense and the allowance for bad debts. If a valuation allowance has not been established (Block 14) in a prior period for the impaired receivable, bad debt expense is debited and a valuation allowance is credited for the amount of the impairment. If a valuation allowance has been established in a prior accounting period, the valuation allowance and bad debt expense are adjusted in such a way that the valuation allowance will equal the amount of the impairment. Estimated cash receipts used in the present value computation are based on the best estimate by the creditor using projections and all evidence that is reasonable and can be supported. The discount rate used in the computation of the present value is the effective interest rate used in the original loan. No consideration is given to change in risk or rate changes as a result of the troubled debt restructuring. Therefore, the only item requiring an estimate in computation of the present value amount is the future cash flows.

ASC 310-10-35 does not specify the appropriate accounting for interest income for a loan that has been impaired. Because the method for recognition, measurement, and presentation of interest income in the financial statement is not prescribed by ASC 310-10-35, the creditor may use any valid method(s) for interest income accounting.

To begin the illustration of the concepts identified above, the assumptions listed in Example 3-6 are used.

Example 3-6
Modification of Terms

1. Creditor, Inc., a December 31 year-end enterprise, has a $2,000,000, 10%, six-year note receivable from Debtor, Inc. that was issued January 1, 20X4. The note was issued at par value; therefore, the effective rate is 10%.
2. On January 1, 20X6, because of economic problems faced by Debtor, Inc., Creditor, Inc. is willing to forgive $200,000 of the principal and reduce the interest rate from 10% to 6% on the new principal. It is probable that Creditor, Inc. will be able to collect the new $1,800,000 principal and 6% interest over the next four years.
3. Creditor, Inc. has a $50,000 allowance for bad debts related to this note that was established in a prior accounting period.

4. Creditor, Inc. uses the effective interest method for recognition of interest income.
5. All present value computations are assumed to be in accordance with ASC 310-40.

Using the information from Example 3-6, the impairment loss on the restructuring can be computed. The impairment loss and the adjustment to bad debt expense and related allowance account are computed in Table 3-6-A.

Table 3-6-A Computation of Impairment Loss from Restructuring

Recorded investment in receivable			$2,000,000
Present value of cash receipts:			
Present value of interest:			
Principal amount		$2,000,000	
Less: Forgiveness		200,000	
Revised principal amount		$1,800,000	
Stated interest rate		6 %	
Annual cash interest		$108,000	
Present value of ordinary annuity factor—4 periods at 10%		3.1699	
Present value of cash interest	$342,349		
Present value of principal:			
Principal amount	$1,800,000		
Present value of $1 factor—4 periods at 10%	.68301		
Present value of principal	1,229,418		
Present value of future cash receipts			1,571,767
Impairment loss on debt restructuring			$428,233
Balance in bad debt allowance account			50,000
Adjustment to bad expense & allowance			$378,233

Using the information from Table 3-6-A, the following journal entry is required on January 1, 20X6 to recognize the impairment loss from the troubled debt restructuring.

Bad Debt Expense	378,233	
Allowance for Bad Debts		378,233

The entry to the allowance account is for $378,233, but the balance in the allowance account after this entry is $428,233. The allowance for bad debts is a contra account to the note receivable, and if the allowance balance is not used to write off a portion of the note receivable in future years, the allowance account will be reversed against the note receivable at the end of the life of the note.

Interest income will be recognized each accounting period using the effective interest method (i.e., an application of a constant effective interest rate (10%, which is the effective rate in the original note) to the unrecovered present value of the future cash receipts). The difference between the cash interest received and interest income will be an adjustment to the note receivable account. Table 3-6-B shows the cash interest, interest income, and receivable adjustment for the remaining four-year life of the note.

Table 3-6-B Computation of Interest Income and Receivable Adjustment

	Cash Interest	Interest Income	Receivable Adjustment	Present Value Balance
				[a]$1,571,767
December 31, 20X6	[b]$108,000	[c]$157,177	[d]$49,177	[e]1,620,924
December 31, 20X7	108,000	162,095	54,095	1,675,039
December 31, 20X8	108,000	167,504	59,504	1,734,543
December 31, 20X9	108,000	173,457	65,457	1,800,000
Totals	$432,000	$660,233	$228,233	

[a] Present value amount taken from Table 3-6-A.
[b] $1,800,000 × 6% = $108,000.
[c] $1,571,767 × 10% = $157,177.
[d] $157,177 − $108,000 = $49,177.
[e] $1,571,767 + $49,177 = $1,620,944.

In Table 3-6-B, interest income is computed using the effective interest rate of 10%. The difference in the interest income recognized using the 10% effective rate and the cash interest using the revised 6% rate is an increase in the note receivable balance. The entry required for 20X6 for recognition of interest income and receivable adjustment is as follows:

Cash	108,000	
Note Receivable	49,177	
Interest Income		157,177

Entries for the remaining three years will be the same except for the amounts. The amounts for the entries for 20X7–20X9 are shown in Table 3-6-B. Upon receipt of the principal amount of $1,800,000 at the end of the life of the note, Creditor, Inc. must remove the allowance for bad debts of $428,233 (Table 3-6-A) established at the date of restructuring and prior years because it was not used for any write-offs subsequent to restructuring. In addition, the balance in the note account of $2,228,233 ($2,000,000 original balance + $228,233 receivable adjustment from Table 3-6-B) must be removed. The entry required at the end of the life of the note is presented below.

Cash	1,800,000	
Allowance for Bad Debts	428,233	
Note Receivable		2,228,233

Example 3-6 related to a modification of terms and was a straightforward situation with no existing discounts, premiums, accrued interest or other unamortized items. Example 3-7 incorporates some of these unamortized items into the computation. Assumptions for Example 3-7 are as follows.

Example 3-7
Modification of Terms

1. Creditor, Inc., a December 31 year-end entity, has a $350,000, 8%, six-year note receivable from Debtor, Inc. that was issued January 1, 20X4. The market rate of interest on the date the note was issued was 10%. Amortization of the note receivable discount from 20X4–20X9 is presented below.

	Cash Interest	Interest Income	Discount Amortization	Investment in Note Receivable
December 31, 20X4	$28,000	$31,951	$3,951	323,464
December 31, 20X5	28,000	32,346	4,346	327,810
December 31, 20X6	28,000	32,781	4,781	332,591
December 31, 20X7	28,000	33,259	5,259	337,850
December 31, 20X8	28,000	33,785	5,785	343,635
December 31, 20X9	28,000	34,365	6,365	350,000
Totals	$168,000	$198,487	$30,487	

2. On January 1, 20X6, because of economic problems faced by Debtor, Inc., Creditor, Inc. is willing to accept the payment of $100,000 per year for the next four years in place of the original note. On this date, there is $28,000 of accrued interest on the note, and as noted from the preceding table, the note has a $22,190 ($350,000 – $327,810) unamortized discount.
3. Creditor, Inc. has a $15,000 allowance for bad debts related to this note that was established in a prior accounting period.
4. Creditor, Inc. uses the effective interest method for recognition of interest income.
5. All present value computations are assumed to be in accordance with ASC 310-40.

Using the information from Example 3-7, the impairment loss on the restructuring can be computed. The impairment loss and the adjustment to bad debt expense and related allowance account are computed in Table 3-7-A.

Table 3-7-A Computation of Impairment Loss from Restructuring

Face amount of receivable	$350,000
Accrued interest	28,000
Unamortized discount (Item 2 in Example 3-7)	(22,190)
Recorded investment in receivable	$355,810

Present value of cash receipts:		
Future cash receipts	$100,000	
Present value of ordinary annuity factor—4 periods at 10%	3.16986	
Present value of cash receipts		316,986
Impairment loss on debt restructuring		$38,824
Balance in bad debt allowance account		15,000
Adjustment to bad expense & allowance		$23,824

Using the information from Table 3-7-A, the following journal entry is required on January 1, 20X6 to recognize the impairment loss from the troubled debt restructuring.

Bad Debt Expense	23,824	
Allowance for Bad Debts		23,824

The entry to the allowance account is for $23,824, but the balance in the allowance account after this entry is $38,824. The allowance for bad debts is a contra account to the note receivable, and if the allowance balance is not used to write off a portion of the note receivable in future years, the allowance account will be reversed against the note receivable at the end of the life of the note. In addition to the entry to recognize the impairment loss, the following entry is used to write off the accrued interest to the note receivable account.

Note Receivable	28,000	
Interest Receivable		28,000

Other methods of accounting for the interest receivable could be used; however, this represents an easy way of removing the accrued interest, and allows all future payments to be a reduction of notes receivable.

Interest income is recognized each accounting period using the effective interest method (i.e., an application of a constant effective interest rate (10%, which is the effective rate in the original note) to the unrecovered present value of the future cash receipts). The difference between the cash interest received and interest income is an adjustment to the note receivable account. Table 3-7-B shows the cash interest, interest income and receivable adjustment for the remaining four-year life of the note.

Table 3-7-B Computation of Interest Income and Receivable Adjustment

	Cash Interest	Interest Income	Receivable Adjustment	Present Value Balance
				[a]$316,986
December 31, 20X7	[b]$100,000	[c]$31,699	[d]$68,301	[e]248,685
December 31, 20X8	100,000	17,355	82,645	90,909
December 31, 20X9	100,000	9,091	90,909	0
Totals	$400,000	$83,014	$316,986	

[a] Present value amount taken from Table 3-7-A.
[b] $100,000 taken from Example 3-7, Item 2.

[c] $316,986 × 10% = $31,699.
[d] $100,000 – $31,699 = $68,301.
[e] $316,986 – $68,301 = $248,685.

In Table 3-7-B, interest income is computed using the effective interest rate of 10%. The difference in the interest income recognized using the 10% effective rate and the $100,000 annual cash payments is a decrease in notes receivable. However, this does not consider the $22,190 unamortized discount from the original issuance of the note. This discount can be accounted for in different ways because it will not have an impact on the amount of interest income recognized by the creditor. For example, it could be written off against the receivable at the time of restructuring, or it could be amortized to the receivable over the remaining life of the note. In Example 3-7, the unamortized discount is amortized to notes receivable over the remaining life of the note. Using discount amortization from the assumptions in Example 3-7 and the amount of note receivable reduction from Table 3-7-B, the amount of annual change in the notes receivable account is presented in Table 3-7-C.

Table 3-7-C Computation of Notes Receivable Adjustment

	Discount Amortization[a]	Receivable Adjustment[b]	Total Receivable Adjustment
December 31, 20X6	$4,781	$68,301	$73,082
December 31, 20X7	5,259	75,131	80,390
December 31, 20X8	5,785	82,645	88,430
December 31, 20X9	6,365	90,909	97,274
Totals	$22,190	$316,986	$339,176

[a] Information taken from Example 3-7, Item 1.
[b] Information taken from Table 3-7-B.

Using the information from Tables 3-7-B and 3-7-C, the entry required for 20X6 for recognition of interest income and receivable adjustment is as follows:

Cash	100,000	
Discount on Notes Receivable	4,781	
Interest Income		31,699
Notes Receivable		73,082

Entries for the remaining three years will be the same except for the amounts. The amounts for the entries for 20X7–20X9 are shown in Tables 3-7-B and 3-7-C. At the end of the life of the note, Creditor, Inc. must remove the allowance for bad debts of $38,824 (Table 3-7-A) established at the date of restructuring and prior years because it was not used for any write-offs subsequent to restructuring. The entry required at the end of the life of the note is presented below.

Allowance for Bad Debts	38,824	
Notes Receivable		38,824

Partial Settlement and Modification of Terms

Troubled debt restructurings may take on many different forms, two of which have been illustrated in the sections above. In addition to these types of restructurings, it is possible to have a combination of the two. In this case, the creditor is faced with a partial settlement of the receivable and some modification of the terms of the remaining settlement (Block 9). When faced with this type of restructuring, the creditor first must reduce the recorded investment in the receivable by the fair value of the assets received in partial settlement. Once this has been accomplished, the balance in the receivable account is referred to as the remaining or revised investment in the receivable. This remaining investment in the receivable will be used for purposes of all subsequent testing of the transaction. No loss on restructuring is recognized when the receivable is reduced by the fair value of the asset received.

Once this step has been completed, the creditor must determine if the receivable under the modified terms has been impaired. Generally, the creditor should use the present value of cash flows to be received in the future to compute the amount of the impairment. However, the creditor may elect to use a market price for impairment if that price is available to the creditor, or, if the receivable is supported by collateral, the fair value of the collateral. A receivable is supported by collateral (i.e., collateral dependent) when the creditor expects the loan to be repaid from the collateral that supports the receivable. If a receivable is supported by collateral (Block 6), impairment of the receivable may be measured by the fair market value of the collateral. When the creditor elects to use the collateral to measure impairment (Block 7), the loan is considered impaired if the fair value of the collateral is less than the recorded amount of the receivable (Block 8). The amount of the impairment is equal to the excess of the recorded amount of the receivable over the fair value of the collateral. If the fair value of the collateral is greater than the recorded amount of the receivable, no impairment is recognized under ASC 310-10-35. If the receivable is not supported by collateral, the creditor may use a market price, if available, when measuring receivable impairment (Block 10). If the creditor uses a market price to measure impairment (Block 11), and the market price is less than the recorded amount of the receivable (Block 12), an impairment of the receivable equal to the excess of the recorded amount of the receivable over the market price is recognized. If the market price exceeds the recorded amount of the receivable, no impairment is recognized. When the creditor does not use the fair value of collateral or a market price for computing receivable impairment, the present value of future cash receipts must be used for the computation. A comparison should be made between the recorded amount of the receivable and the present value of estimated future cash receipts using the provisions of ASC 310-10-35. If the present value of the future cash receipts is less than the recorded amount of the receivable (Block 13), an impairment of the receivable must be recognized by the creditor for the excess of the recorded investment of the receivable in excess of the present value of the cash receipts.

If a valuation allowance has not been established (Block 14) in a prior period for the impaired receivable, bad debt expense is debited and a valuation allowance is credited for the amount of the impairment. If a valuation allowance has been established in a prior accounting period, the valuation allowance and bad debt expense is adjusted in such a way that the valuation allowance will equal the amount of the impairment. Estimated cash receipts used in the present value computation are based on the best estimate by the creditor using projections and all evidence that is reasonable and can be supported. The discount rate used in the computation of the present value is the effective interest rate used in the original loan. No consideration is given to change in risk or rate changes as a result of the troubled debt restructuring. Therefore, the only item requiring an estimate in computation of the present value amount is the future cash flows.

To illustrate application of a partial settlement and modification of terms, the assumptions listed in Example 3-8 are used.

Example 3-8
Assumptions for Partial Settlement and a Modification of Terms

1. Creditor, Inc., a December 31 year-end enterprise, has a $6,000,000, 8% note receivable from Debtor, Inc., which is payable in full in six years. The note was issued at par value; therefore, the effective rate is 8%.
2. On January 1, 20X6, one year after the note was issued, Debtor, Inc. is no longer able to pay all of the interest and principal in the future. As a result, Creditor, Inc. has agreed to accept, in partial settlement of the note, a parcel of land with a fair value of $3,000,000 at the date of restructuring; forgive $1,000,000 of the principal amount of the note; and reduce the interest rate from 8% to 5% on the new maturity value of the note.
3. Creditor, Inc. has not established an allowance for bad debts related to this note in a prior accounting period.
4. Creditor, Inc. uses the effective interest method for recognition of interest income.
5. All present value computations are assumed to be in accordance with ASC 310-40.

Assuming that the reduction in interest rate was not due merely to market factors, the transaction would qualify for troubled debt restructuring. The exchange of land represents a partial settlement of the note, and the forgiveness of principal, reduction in interest rate, and acceptance of land in partial settlement represent modifications of the original terms of the note.

The first step in the accounting process is to reduce the recorded investment in the receivable by the fair value of the land received. This computation is shown below:

Recorded investment in the note receivable	$6,000,000
Fair value of land received	3,000,000
Revised investment in the note receivable	$3,000,000

The journal entry to record the reduction in the receivable is as follows:

Land	3,000,000	
Notes Receivable		3,000,000

Once the revised recorded investment in the receivable has been determined, the next step is to compute any required impairment loss by comparing the revised investment in the receivable with the present value of the future cash receipts specified under the new terms using the effective interest related to the original note agreement. Computation of the impairment loss is shown in Table 3-8-A.

Table 3-8-A Computation of Impairment Loss from Restructuring

Revised recorded investment in receivable			$3,000,000
Present value of cash receipts:			
Present value of interest:			
Principal amount		$3,000,000	
Less: Forgiveness		1,000,000	
Revised principal amount		$2,000,000	
Revised stated interest rate		5%	
Annual cash interest		$100,000	
Present value of ordinary annuity factor—5 periods at 8%		.99271	
Present value of cash interest		$399,271	
Present value of principal:			
Principal amount	$2,000,000		
Present value of $1 factor—5 periods at 8%	.680583		
Present value of principal			
Present value of future cash receipts			1,760,437
Impairment loss on debt restructuring			$1,239,563

Using the information from Table 3-8-A, the following journal entry is required to recognize the impairment loss from the troubled debt restructuring.

Bad Debt Expense	1,239,563	
Allowance for Bad Debts		1,239,563

Interest income will be recognized each accounting period using the effective interest method (i.e., an application of a constant effective interest rate (8%, which is the effective rate in original note agreement) to the unrecovered present value of the future cash receipts). The difference between the cash interest received and interest income will be an adjustment to the note receivable account. Table 3-8-B shows the cash interest, interest income and receivable adjustment for the remaining five-year life of the note.

Table 3-8-B Computation of Interest Income and Receivable Adjustment

	Cash Interest	Interest Income	Receivable Adjustment	Present Value Balance
				[a]$1,760,437
December 31, 20X6	[b]$100,000	[c]$140,835	[d]$40,835	[e]1,801,272
December 31, 20X7	100,000	144,102	44,102	1,845,374
December 31, 20X8	100,000	147,630	47,630	1,893,004
December 31, 20X9	100,000	151,440	51,440	1,944,444
December 31, 2010	100,000	155,556	55,556	2,000,000
Totals	$500,000	$739,563	$239,563	

[a] Present value amount taken from Table 3-8-A.
[b] $2,000,000 × 5% = $100,000.
[c] $1,760,437 × 8% = $140,835.
[d] $140,835 – $100,000 = $40,835.
[e] $1,760,437 + $40,835 = $1,801,272.

In Table 3-8-B, interest income is computed using the effective interest rate of 8%. The difference in the interest income recognized using the 8% effective rate and the cash interest using the revised 5% rate is an increase in the note receivable. The entry required for 20X6 for recognition of interest income and receivable adjustment is as follows:

Cash	100,000	
Note Receivable	40,835	
Interest Income		140,835

Entries for the remaining four years will be the same except for the amounts. The amounts for the entries for 20X7–2010 are shown in Table 3-8-B. Upon receipt of the principal amount of $2,000,000 at the end of the life of the note, Creditor, Inc. must remove the allowance for bad debts of $1,239,563 (Table 3-8-A) established at the date of restructuring and prior years because it was not used for any write-offs subsequent to restructuring. In addition, the balance in the note account of $3,239,563 ($3,000,000 original balance + $239,563 receivable adjustment from Table 3-8-B) must be removed. The entry required at the end of the life of the note is presented below.

Cash	2,000,000	
Allowance for Bad Debts	1,239,563	
Note Receivable		3,239,563

This completes the discussion and examples for the three major types of troubled debt restructurings.

Troubled Debt Restructuring—Other Considerations

A debt restructuring may involve changing cash receipt amounts or other indeterminate items. For example, a cash receipt may be based on the debtor maintaining a specific profit level in future periods. Another situation may involve the interest rate on the restructured receivable being linked to some variable factor, such as the bank prime rate of interest. The creditor should use all available evidence to arrive at a best estimate of future cash receipts based on reasonable assumptions and projections that can be supported. However, if subsequent to the date an impairment has been determined, there is a significant change in the estimate of amount or timing of future cash receipts, the creditor must recalculate the impairment using the same procedures as illustrated in the preceding pages. Any change in impairment should be an adjustment to the valuation allowance account.

If the terms of the restructuring allow the interest rate to vary, the interest rate at the date of restructuring is used in the computation of the present value of the future cash receipts. Subsequent changes in the interest rate may require special accounting treatment. If the stated interest rate varies over the remaining life of the receivable, the creditor has the option of computing the effective rate of interest in the following manner: fix the rate based on the rate in effect when the loan is restructured or adjust the effective rate based on changes in the variable rate over the life of the receivable. However, the creditor should not try to estimate changes in the variable for purposes of computing the effective rate. The method that the creditor selects should be applied on a consistent basis and for all variable interest loans.

Any legal fees or direct costs incurred by a creditor related to a debt restructuring should be charged to expense in the period incurred. According to ASC 310-20-35-12, fees received by a creditor in a modification of terms should be used to reduce the recorded amount of the receivable.

One final item in ASC 310-40 deals with the substitution or addition of debtors in a troubled debt restructuring. A debt restructuring may involve a substitution of the existing debt with debt of another entity; additional debtor (s) may be added without removing the original debtor. When faced with this situation, the substance of the transaction should dictate the necessary accounting treatment. If the debtors involved in a substitution or addition agreement are related or under common control (e.g., parent and subsidiary), the transaction should be treated as a modification of terms for purposes of applying the provisions of ASC 310-40. If the debtors are not related or under common control, the transaction should be handled as a receipt of assets in full settlement and a combination of restructuring types.

Troubled Debt Restructuring—Foreclosures

In January 2014, FASB issued new guidance clarifying when a creditor should derecognize from its balance sheet a consumer mortgage loan that was collateralized by residential real estate and recognize "other real estate owned." Previously existing guidance provided that a creditor should make this change upon an "in-substance" repossession or foreclosure. Such a foreclosure is deemed to occur when the creditor receives physical possession of the debtor's assets, regardless of whether formal foreclosure proceedings take place. However, the terms "in-substance repossession or foreclosure" and "physical possession" were not clearly defined in the accounting literature before the January 2014 guidance.

The new guidance clarified that derecognition of a consumer mortgage loan and recognition of other real estate owned should occur when either:

- The creditor has obtained legal title to the residential real estate property through foreclosure, *or*
- The borrower has conveyed all interests in the residential property through a deed in lieu of foreclosure or through a similar legal agreement.

This new guidance also includes additional requirements to disclose consumer mortgage loans for which formal foreclosure proceedings are in process.

In August 2014, FASB further clarified troubled debt restructurings that are deemed to be foreclosures. Under certain government-sponsored loan guarantee programs, such as the programs sponsored by the Federal Housing Authority (FHA), creditors can extend mortgage loans to borrowers with a guarantee that entitles the creditor to recover all or a portion of the unpaid principal and interest balances from the government if the borrower defaults. The new guidance clarifies that the loan should be derecognized and a separate receivable from the guarantor (e.g., FHA) should be recorded upon foreclosure if the following criteria are met:

- The government guarantee is not separable from the loan before foreclosure.
- The creditor has the intent to convey the real estate to the guarantor and make a claim on the guarantee, and the creditor has the ability to recover under that claim.
- Any amount of the claim that is based on the fair value of the real estate is fixed.

Disclosures of Troubled Debt Restructuring

ASC 310-40-50 presents the disclosures that are required by the creditor in the preparation of the basic financial statements. For troubled debt restructurings involving some modification of terms, the information below should be reported. This information may be reported in the face of the statements or in related notes.

1. For each period that a balance sheet is presented, the following information is reported for receivables that have recorded impairments:
   a. The total recorded investment in the receivables.
   b. The amount of the receivable for which an allowance for losses has been computed per ASC 310-40.
   c. The amount of the receivable for which no allowance for losses has been computed.

2. For each period that an income statement is presented, the following information should be disclosed:
   a. Average amount of receivables impaired.
   b. Amount of interest income related to impaired loans.
   c. Amount of interest income reported on a cash basis related to impaired loans, if practicable.
   d. The following information should be disclosed for the allowance for losses account related to impaired loans:
      (1) Beginning balance.
      (2) Ending balance.
      (3) Additions charged to income.
      (4) Recoveries of prior write-offs.
      (5) Amount of direct write-offs charged against the allowance account.
3. The policy that the creditor uses for reporting interest income from restructured loans, including the method for reporting cash receipts.
4. Obligations to lend money to debtors involved in a troubled debt restructuring classified as a modification of terms.

For years subsequent to the year that a troubled debt restructuring involving a modification of terms is reported in the financial statements, the disclosures in 1 and 2(a)–(c), above, are not required when the following two conditions are met:

1. There is no loan impairment under the restructured agreement.
2. The interest rate specified in the restructured agreement is greater than what the creditor would require for a comparable new loan at the time of restructuring.

Recent Changes

ASU 2017-08, *Receivables—Nonrefundable Fees and Other Costs (Subtopic 310-20): Premium Amortization on Purchased Callable Debt Securities,* shortens the amortization period for certain callable debt securities held at a premium. Specifically, the amendments require the premium to be amortized to the earliest call date. The amendments do not require an accounting change for securities held at a discount; the discount continues to be amortized to maturity. For public business entities, the amendments in this Update are effective for fiscal years, and interim periods within those fiscal years, beginning after December 15, 2018. For all other entities, the amendments are effective for fiscal years beginning after December 15, 2019, and interim periods within fiscal years beginning after December 15, 2020. Early adoption is permitted, including adoption in an interim period. If an entity early adopts the amendments in an interim period, any adjustments should be reflected as of the beginning of the fiscal year that includes that interim period. An entity should apply the amendments in this Update on a modified retrospective basis through a cumulative-effect adjustment directly to retained earnings as of the beginning of the period of adoption. Additionally, in the period of adoption, an entity should provide disclosures about a change in accounting principle.

Investments

The FASB Codification contains several Topics for investments due to the different accounting treatment for various forms of investment. These Topics include:

Topic 320, Investments—Debt Securities

Topic 321, Investments—Equity Securities

Topic 323, Investments—Equity Method and Joint Ventures

Topic 325, Investments—Other

Topic 320: Investments—Debt Securities

Topic 321: Investments—Equity Securities

NOTE: These two Topics were formerly discussed as one Topic, *Investments—Debt and Equity Securities.* See Recent Changes, immediately below. As a result of an extensive revision to the financial instruments topic (Topic 825), the codification has split Topic 320, into two topics: Topic 320, *Investments—Debt Securities*, and Topic 321, *Investments—Equity Securities*. This change will not be reflected in the FASB Codification until either 2018 or 2019, depending on the type of entity, as explained in the effective date discussion, below. The authors have chosen to reflect all discussion of investments in both debt and equity securities under this combined "Investments" section. The FASB Codification will change the discussion of investments as of December 15, 2017 for public entities.

Recent Changes

Topic 825, *Financial Instruments,* will be amended by ASU 2016-01, *Financial Instruments—Overall (Subtopic 825-10): Recognition and Measurement of Financial Assets and Financial Liabilities.*

Some of the key provisions of ASU 2016-01 follow.

1. Equity investments (except those accounted for under the equity method of accounting or those that result in consolidation of the investee) are required to be measured at fair value, with changes in fair value recognized in net income. However, an entity may choose to measure equity investments that do not have readily determinable fair values at cost minus impairment, if any, plus or minus changes resulting from observable price changes in orderly transactions for the identical or a similar investment of the same issuer.
2. The impairment assessment of equity investments without readily determinable fair values has been simplified by requiring a qualitative assessment to identify impairment. When a qualitative assessment indicates that impairment exists, an entity is required to measure the investment at fair value.

3. Entities that are not public business entities are no longer required to disclose the fair value of financial instruments measured at amortized cost.
4. The requirement for public business entities to disclose the method(s) and significant assumptions used to estimate the fair value that is required to be disclosed for financial instruments measured at amortized cost on the balance sheet has been eliminated.
5. Require public business entities to use the exit price notion when measuring the fair value of financial instruments for disclosure purposes.
6. Require an entity to present separately in other comprehensive income the portion of the total change in the fair value of a liability resulting from a change in the instrument-specific credit risk when the entity has elected to measure the liability at fair value in accordance with the fair value option for financial instruments.
7. Require separate presentation of financial assets and financial liabilities by measurement category and form of financial asset on the balance sheet or the accompanying notes to the financial statements.
8. Clarify that an entity should evaluate the need for a valuation allowance on a deferred tax asset related to available-for-sale securities in conjunction with the entity's other deferred tax assets.

For public business entities, the amendments in ASU 2016-01 are effective for fiscal years beginning after December 15, 2017, including interim periods within those fiscal years. For all other entities, including not-for-profit entities and employee benefit plans within the scope of Topics 960 through 965 on plan accounting, the amendments in ASU 2016-01 are effective for fiscal years beginning after December 15, 2018, and interim periods within fiscal years beginning after December 15, 2019. All entities that are not public business entities may adopt the amendments in ASU 2016-01 earlier, as of the fiscal years beginning after December 15, 2017, including interim periods with those fiscal years. The standards under ASU 2016-01 are not reflected in the discussion of Topic 825, *Financial Instruments*.

Early application by public business entities to financial statements of fiscal years or interim periods that have not yet been issued or, by all other entities, that have not yet been made available for issuance, the following amendments in ASU 2016-01 are permitted as of the beginning of the fiscal year of adoption. In connection therewith:

1. An entity should present separately in other comprehensive income the portion of the total change in the fair value of a liability resulting from a change in the instrument-specific credit risk if the entity has elected to measure the liability at fair value in accordance with the fair value option for financial instruments.
2. Entities that are not public business entities are not required to apply the fair value of financial instruments disclosure guidance in the "General" subsection of Section 825-10-50.

Except for the early application guidance discussed above, early adoption of ASU 2016-01 is not permitted.

An entity should apply ASU 2016-01 by means of a cumulative-effect adjustment to the balance sheet as of the beginning of the fiscal year of adoption. Further, for equity securities without readily determinable fair values, the standard should be applied prospectively to equity investments that exist as of the date of adoption of ASU 2016-01.

Topic 320, *Investments—Debt Securities,* contains eight subtopics:

10 Overall

940 Financial Services—Brokers and Dealers*

942 Financial Services—Depository and Lending*

944 Financial Services—Insurance*

946 Financial Services—Investment Companies*

954 Health Care Entities*

958 Not-For-Profit Entities*

965 Plan Accounting—Health and Welfare Benefit Plans*

Topic 321, *Investments—Equity Securities,* contains two subtopics:

10 Overall

958 Not-For-Profit Entities*

* See the corresponding topic in Chapter 9 for coverage of this shared subtopic.

Debt Securities—ASC 320 specifies the accounting and reporting requirements for all investments in debt securities, including those resulting from the securitization of other financial instruments and all loans that meet the definition of a security. Topic 320 applies to all entities, including cooperatives and mutual entities (e.g., credit unions and mutual insurance entities) and trusts that do not report substantially all of their debt securities at fair value. Topic 320 guidance does not apply to the following situations (ASC 320-10-15):

1. Brokers and dealers in securities (Topic 940).
2. Defined benefit pension and other postretirement plans (Topics 960, 962, and 965).
3. Investment companies (Topic 946).

The guidance in Topic 320 does not apply to:

1. Derivative instruments that are subject to the requirements of Topic 815, including those that have been separated from a host contract as required by Section 815-15-25. If an investment would otherwise be in the scope of this topic and it has within it an embedded derivative that is required by that section to be separated, the host instrument (as described in that section) remains within the scope of this topic.
2. Investments in consolidated subsidiaries.

In addition, transaction gains and losses from held-to-maturity debt securities classified as foreign-currency-denominated debt are accounted for using the provisions of ASC 830-20.

A debt security under ASC 320-10 is any security representing a creditor relationship with an entity. Examples of debt securities include: corporate bonds, debt convertible into other securities, preferred stock that is redeemable, and securities of the U.S. Treasury. Examples of instruments not treated as debt securities are: leases, trade accounts receivable, forward contracts, financial futures contracts, and option contracts.

Classifications of Debt Securities—Once it has been determined that an entity has securities that are covered under ASC 320-10, the first step is to classify the debt securities into three categories: held-to-maturity, trading, and available-for-sale.

Held-to-maturity—Debt securities are classified as held-to-maturity only if the enterprise has the positive intent and ability to hold the securities until maturity. (Debt securities having certain types of held-to-maturity provisions should be reviewed to determine whether they contain embedded derivatives that should be accounted for using the provisions of ASC 815.)

Trading securities—Debt securities are classified as securities acquired with the intent of selling it within hours or days are classified as trading securities. However, an entity is not precluded from classifying as a trading security a security it plans to hold for a longer period. In other words, entity is not precluded from classifying a security as a trading security simply because it does not intend to sell it in the near term.

Available-for-Sale Securities—Debt securities that not classified as held-to-maturity or trading are classified as available-for-sale.

On each balance sheet date, the enterprise must review its investment security classification to determine whether a change in classification is appropriate. Next, fair value of the securities must be determined using the provisions of ASC 820, *Fair Value Measurement*. According to ASC 820, fair value is the amount that would be received on the measurement date from the sale of property, or the amount paid to transfer a liability between sellers and buyers (market participants) in an orderly transaction. In addition, it is assumed that the sellers and buyers are unrelated parties on the measurement date (see a detailed discussion of ASC 820 in Chapter 8).

Held-to-maturity debt securities are a highly restrictive classification. The mere lack of an intent to sell does not make the held-to-maturity classification relevant for a given investment in a debt security. Further, the intent to hold a debt security for an indefinite period would not enable an investment in a debt security to be classified as a held-to-maturity debt security. ASC 320-10-25-5 gives a number of specific examples where the held-to-maturity classification would not be appropriate.

Valuation of Classifications of Securities:

Held-to-maturity securities are reported in the statement of financial position at amortized cost. Amortized cost refers to instances when a debt security may be issued at a discount or premium because the stated rate on the security and market rate differ at the time of issuance. Discounts and premiums on debt securities for all classifications are amortized to income over the outstanding life of the investment using the interest method as specified in ASC 835, *Interest*. See Chapter 8 for a detailed analysis of the interest method.

Debt investments classified as trading securities are reported on the statement of financial position at fair value. If fair value is different from cost or carrying value, an unrealized holding gain or loss is reported in earnings.

Available-for-sale debt securities are reported on the statement of financial position at fair value. Unrealized holding gains and losses shall be excluded from earnings and reported in other comprehensive income until realized except for the portion if the unrealized gain or loss that that is designated as being hedged in a fair value hedge; such a fair value hedge would be recognized in earnings during the period of the hedge.

In addition to discounts and premiums being charged to income, an entity may receive interest from an investment in a debt security. Interest from all three classifications of securities are included in earnings in the accounting period earned.

Two specific issues require additional discussion. First, the impact on classification of securities when a held-to-maturity debt security is sold or transferred should be addressed. As discussed above, an enterprise must have the positive intent and ability to hold a security to maturity to place that security in the held-to-maturity category. However, the concept of maturity of a debt security is defined in a broad manner. Maturity is assumed to occur in all of the following situations (ASC 320-10-25-14):

1. The security is due, and the face or call amount is receivable by the investor.
2. The security is sold so close to the maturity or call date (generally three months) that a change in fair value is not likely as a result of a change in interest rates.
3. The security is sold after the investor has collected a major part of the principal (85% or more) that existed on the date the debt was acquired.

An entity, under specific situations, may transfer or sell investments classified as held-to-maturity before the maturity date as specified above and not compromise its position with respect to the original classification of the investment or classification of future investments in the held-to-maturity category. If one of the following situations or events causes an entity to sell or transfer a security classified as held-to-maturity, the sale or transfer does not affect how the entity originally classified the investment nor will it affect how the entity classifies investments in the future (ASC 320-10-25, paragraphs 6 through 9):

- Evidence of a significant deterioration in the issuer's creditworthiness (e.g., a downgrading of an issuer's published credit rating).
- A change in tax law that eliminates or reduces the tax-exempt status of interest on the debt security (but not a change in tax law that revises the marginal tax rates applicable to interest income).

- A major business combination or major disposition (such as sale of a component of an entity) that necessitates the sale or transfer of held-to-maturity securities to maintain the entity's existing interest rate risk position or credit risk policy.
- A change in statutory or regulatory requirements significantly modifying either what constitutes a permissible investment or the maximum level of investments in certain kinds of securities, thereby causing an entity to dispose of a held-to-maturity security.
- A significant increase by the regulator in the industry's capital requirements that causes the entity to downsize by selling held-to-maturity securities.
- A significant increase in the risk weights of debt securities used for regulatory risk-based capital purposes.

The second area that requires additional discussion is the transfer of investments between classifications. According to ASC 320-10-35-10, when securities are transferred between categories, the transfer is made at fair market value and any unrealized gains or losses should be accounted for using the information from Chart 3-1.

Chart 3-1 Transfer Investments in Debt Securities between Categories

Category From	To	Accounting Requirements
Trading[1]	A-F-S[2]	Do not reverse unrealized gains and/or losses already recognized.
Trading	H-T-M[3]	Do not reverse unrealized gains and/or losses already recognized.
A-F-S	Trading	Take to income the unrealized gain or loss included in accumulated or unrealized other comprehensive income on the date of transfer.
A-F-S	H-T-M	The unrealized gain or loss reported as unrealized other comprehensive income in stockholders' equity while classified as A-F-S should remain in stockholders' equity. The gain or loss should be written off over the remaining life of the investment using a method that is consistent with the discount or premium amortization. The gain or loss amortization should be accounted for as an adjustment to the security's yield.
H-T-M[4]	Trading	The unrealized gain or loss should be computed and included in income on the date of transfer.
H-T-M	A-F-S	The unrealized gain or loss should be computed and included as a separate component of other comprehensive income.

[1] Transfers to or from the trading category would be rare.
[2] A-F-S = available-for-sale.
[3] H-T-M = held-to-maturity.
[4] Transfers from the held-to-maturity category would be rare.

Impairment of an available-for-sale or held-to-maturity security occurs when the fair value is less than its cost. Management of the investing entity must determine whether a decline in fair value below the cost is either temporary or other than temporary. (NOTE: ASC 320-35-30 explains that "other than temporary" does not mean permanent.)

Equity Securities—An equity security is a security that meets one of the following conditions: represents an interest in the ownership of an entity, represents a right of disposition of an interest in the ownership of an entity at an amount that is either fixed or can be determined, or represents a right of acquisition of an interest in the ownership of an entity at an amount that is either fixed or can be determined. Examples of equity securities include: common and preferred stock, options, rights, and warrants. ASC 321 specifies the accounting and reporting requirements for all investments in equity securities. Topic 321 applies to all entities, including cooperatives and mutual entities (e.g., credit unions and mutual insurance entities) and trusts that do not report substantially all of their debt securities at fair value. Topic 321 does not apply to the following entities (ASC 321-10-15):

1. Brokers and dealers in securities (Topic 940).
2. Defined benefit pension and other postretirement plans (Topics 960, 962, and 965).
3. Investment companies (Topic 946).

The guidance of Topic 321 does not apply to:

1. Derivative instruments that are subject to the requirements of Topic 815, including those that have been separated from a host contract as required by Section 815-15-25. If an investment would otherwise be in the scope of this Topic and it has within it an embedded derivative that is required by that section to be separated, the host instrument (as described in that section) remains within the scope of this Topic.
2. Equity securities accounted for under the equity method (Topic 323).
3. Investments in consolidated subsidiaries.
4. An exchange membership that has the characteristics specified in paragraph 940-340-25-1(b) for an ownership interest in the exchange.
5. Federal Home Loan Bank and Federal Reserve Bank Stock (Subtopic 942-325).

The term equity security does not include any of the following:

1. Written equity options because they represent obligations of the writer, not investments.
2. Cash-settled options on equity securities or options on equity-based indexes (because those instruments do not represent ownership interests in an entity).
3. Convertible debt or preferred stock that by its terms must be redeemed by the issuing entity or is redeemable at the option of the investor.

Equity Securities covered—Once it has been determined that an entity has equity securities to be covered under ASC 321-10, the fair value of the security must be readily determinable. Equity securities are assumed to have fair values that can be readily determined if the securities are quoted on a U.S. stock exchange or a foreign stock exchange that is equivalent to a U.S. exchange. In addition, fair value is determinable for mutual funds that have published quotes and ready markets.

Some equity securities do not have readily determinable fair values. In these cases, the equity securities investment is recorded at cost less impairment. The recorded amount should be subsequently adjusted up for down for observable price changes. ASC 321-10-35 defines readily observable price changes as prices in orderly transactions for the identical investment or similar investment of the same issuer. The adjustments would be recorded in net income.

An ongoing assessment is needed to determine whether an equity security investment without a readily determinable fair value has been impaired. This analysis of impairment is based on qualitative assessment of impairment indicators. Some impairment indicators include (ASC 321-10-35:3):

1. Significant deterioration in the earnings performance, credit ratings, asset quality, or business prospects of the investee.
2. Significant adverse change in the regulatory, economic, or technological environment of the investee.
3. Significant adverse change in the general market condition of either the geographical area or the industry in which the investee operates.
4. A bona fide offer to purchase, offer by the investee to sell or a completed auction process for the same or similar investment for an amount less than the carrying amount of that investment.
5. Factors that raise significant concerns about the investee's ability to continue as a going concern (e.g., negative cash flows from operations, working capital deficiencies, or noncompliance with statutory capital requirements or debt covenants).

Disclosure and Financial Statement Requirements

Investments classified as trading, held-to-maturity, or available-for-sale should be classified based on when an entity expects to turn an investment into cash. Investments in debt securities in the categories of trading, held-to-maturity, or available-for-sale securities should be classified as current assets if the investments are expected to be turned into cash within one year or the normal operating cycle, whichever is longer. Otherwise, the investments should be classified as long-term assets in the investment section of the statement of financial position.

Classification of cash inflows and outflows in the cash flow statement from buying and selling investments in debt and equity securities depends on the category of the security. Cash flows from securities in the trading category are placed in the operating section of the cash flow statement. Cash flows from securities in the held-to-maturity and available-for-sale categories are placed in the investing section of the statement.

ASC 320-10-50 specifies the disclosure requirements for investments in debt and ASC 321-10-50 specifies the disclosure requirements for investments in equity securities. As of each date for which a statement of financial position is presented, reporting entities must disclose by major security type (based on the nature and risks of the securities): amortized cost basis, aggregate fair value, total other-than-temporary impairment recognized in accumulated other comprehensive income, total gains for securities with net gains in accumulated other comprehensive income, and total losses for securities with net losses in accumulated other comprehensive income for securities classified as available-for-sale. Additionally, for securities classified as held-to-maturity, disclosure is required by major security type of amortized cost basis, aggregate fair value, gross unrecognized holding gains, gross unrecognized holding losses, the net carrying amount, total other-than-temporary impairment recognized in accumulated other comprehensive income, and gross gains and losses in accumulated other comprehensive income for any derivatives that hedged the forecasted acquisition of the held-to-maturity securities. Financial institutions must include in their disclosures specified major security types; additional types also may be necessary.

Separately for investments in debt securities classified as available-for-sale and securities classified as held-to-maturity, reporting enterprises must disclose information about the contractual maturities of those securities as of the date of the most recent statement of financial position presented. Maturity information may be combined in appropriate groupings. Financial institutions must disclose the fair value and the net carrying amount (if different from fair value) of debt securities based on at least four maturity groupings: (1) within one year, (2) after one year through five years, (3) after five years through 10 years, and (4) after 10 years. Securities not due at a single maturity date, such as mortgage-backed securities, may be disclosed separately rather than allocated over several maturity groupings; if securities are allocated, the basis for allocation must also be disclosed.

For each period for which the results of operations are presented, ASC 320-10-50 and ASC 321-10-50 require reporting entities to disclose the following:

1. The proceeds from sales of available-for-sale securities and the gross realized gains and gross realized losses that have been included in earnings as a result of those sales.

2. The basis on which the cost of a security sold or the amount reclassified out of accumulated other comprehensive income into earnings was determined.

3. The gross gains and gross losses included in earnings from transfers of securities from the available-for-sale category into the trading category.

4. The amount of the net unrealized holding gain or loss on available-for-sale securities for the period that has been included in accumulated

other comprehensive income and the amount of gains and losses reclassified out of accumulated other comprehensive income into earnings for the period.

5. The portion of trading gains and losses for the period that relates to trading securities still held at the reporting date.
6. For any sales of or transfers from securities classified as held-to-maturity, the net carrying amount of the sold or transferred security, the net gain or loss in accumulated other comprehensive income for any derivative that hedged the forecasted acquisition of the held-to-maturity security, the related realized or unrealized gain or loss, and the circumstances leading to the decision to sell or transfer the security.

Additional quantitative, narrative, and tabular disclosures are required for investments in an unrealized loss position, cost-method investments, and debt securities for which other-than-temporary impairment was recognized when only the amount related to a credit loss was recognized in earnings.

For equity securities with readily determinable fair values, an entity's financial statements for each period presented shall disclose the portion of unrealized gains and losses that relates to equity securities still held at the reporting date. (ASC 321-10-50-4)

For equity securities without readily determinable fair values, an entity shall disclose all of the following:

1. The carrying amount of investments without readily determinable fair value.
2. The amount of impairments and downward adjustments, if any, both annual and cumulative.
3. The amount of upward investments, if any, both annual and cumulative.
4. As of the date of the most recent statement of position, additional information (in narrative form) that is sufficient to permit financial statement users to understand the quantitative disclosures and the information that the entity considered in reaching the carrying amounts and upward and downward adjustments resulting from observable price changes.

Three examples are used to illustrate the technical application of ASC 320-10 and ASC 321-10. Assumptions for Example 3-9 are as follows.

Example 3-9
Assumptions for Debt and Equity Investments

1. The Hudson Company (Hudson), a December 31 year-end company, has three investments—two bonds and one common stock. Hudson is using the cost method to account for the common stock investment because ownership in the stock is less than 20% of the outstanding stock.

2. All stock and bond investments were purchased on January 1, 20X6, except for Best Company bonds. Investment in Best Company was purchased on November 1, 20X6. Purchase and fair value information for each investment is as follows:

	Cost	Interest Rates	Life of Debt	Fair Value 12/31/X6	Fair Value 12/31/X7
Best Company Bonds	$100,000	6%	8 Years	$97,000	NA
Max, Inc. Bonds	400,000	7%	10 Years	408,000	$380,000
Wood, Inc. Common Stock	200,000	NA	NA	205,000	198,000

All bonds pay interest on an annual basis, and the bonds were purchased at par value. Therefore, the stated and market rates of interest are the same and there is no discount or premium on the bond transactions. No dividends were paid on the common stock.

3. Best Company bonds are classified as a trading security, Max, Inc. bonds are classified as a held-to-maturity security, and Wood, Inc. common stock is classified as an available-for-sale security. The decline in fair value of Max, Inc. bonds in 20X7 is assumed to be other-than-temporary, and the entire decline is attributed to a credit loss. All other changes in fair value for all securities are assumed to be temporary.
4. The Best Company bonds were sold on July 1, 20X7 for $95,000. All securities other than the trading security are classified as noncurrent.
5. All fair value amounts were determined using the provisions of ASC 820.

The investment in Wood, Inc. common stock is covered by the provisions of ASC 321-10 because it is accounted for using the cost method, and the fair value of the stock can be readily determined. In addition, both bond investments are covered by the ASC 320-10 because they both meet the definition of a debt security outlined in the general discussion. Using the information from Example 3-9, unrealized holding gains and losses can be computed for the investments classified as trading (Best Company bonds) and as available-for-sale (Wood, Inc. common stock). As previously stated, held-to-maturity securities are carried at cost and no unrealized holding gains or losses are computed. However, because there was a decline in fair value of Max, Inc. bonds below cost that is considered to be an other-than-temporary decline, a loss will be recognized and a new cost basis will be established for the bonds. In addition, interest income must be computed for both bond investments. Because the bonds were purchased at par value, there is no discount or premium amortization. Computation of the unrealized holding gains and losses for Best Company and Wood, Inc. and calculation of interest income for Best Company and Max, Inc. are presented in Table 3-9-A. The loss from the other-than-temporary decline of Max, Inc. is computed later.

Table 3-9-A Computation of Unrealized Holding Gain/Loss for Trading and Available-for-Sale Securities

Trading Security—Best Company

	20X6
Fair market value	$97,000
Cost or carrying value	(100,000)
Difference between fair value & cost	$(3,000)
(Gain)/loss recognized in prior period	0
Unrealized holding gain/(loss) recognized	$(3,000)

Available-for-Sale Security—Wood, Inc.

	20X6	20X7
Fair market value	$205,000	$198,000
Cost or carrying value	(200,000)	(200,000)
Difference between fair value & cost	$5,000	$(2,000)
(Gain)/loss recognized in prior period	0	(5,000)
Unrealized holding gain/(loss) recognized	$5,000	$(7,000)

Computation of Interest Income—Best Company

	20X6	20X7
Face of bonds	$100,000	$100,000
Stated interest rate	6%	6%
Annual interest income	$6,000	$6,000
Part of year outstanding	100%	50%
Interest income reported for the year	$6,000	$3,000

Computation of Interest Income—Max, Inc.

	20X6	20X7
Face of bonds	$400,000	$400,000
Stated interest rate	7%	7%
Annual interest income	$28,000	$28,000

Using the information from Table 3-9-A, journal entries for both 20X6 and 20X7 can be prepared for each category of investments. Journal entries for the trading category are presented first. The investment in Best Company bonds was sold on July 1, 20X7 at a loss of $2,000 (selling price of $95,000 – $97,000 carrying value).

Trading Category—Journal Entries

December 31, 20X6 Journal Entries (Information Taken from Table 3-9-A)

Unrealized Investment Holding Loss	3,000	
Investment in Best Bonds		3,000
To record holding loss for 20X6.		
Cash	6,000	
Interest Income		6,000
To record interest income for 20X6.		

July 1, 20X7 Journal Entry for Sale of Investment and Recognition of Interest Income (Information Taken from Example 3-9 Assumptions, Item 4 and Table 3-9-A)

Cash	95,000	
Loss on Sale of Trading Securities	2,000	
Investment in Best Company Bonds		97,000[a]
To record sale of trading securities.		

[a] $97,000 = $100,000 purchase price – $3,000 write-down in 20X6.

Cash	3,000	
Interest Income		3,000
To record interest income for 20X7.		

The investment in Best Company bonds is classified as a current asset in the financial statements at the end of 20X6. In addition, the investment account is written down directly to reflect the $3,000 unrealized loss and that the unrealized investment holding loss is reported as a component of income. The loss from the sale of the trading securities in 20X7 is also reported as a component of income.

Next, journal entries for the available-for-sale category for both 20X6 and 20X7 are presented as follows:

Available-for-Sale Category—Journal Entries

December 31, 20X6 Journal Entries (Information Taken from Table 3-9-A)

Allowance for Market Change in Noncurrent Investment	5,000	
Unrealized Investment Holding Gain		5,000
To record unrealized holding gain for 20X6.		

December 31, 20X7 Journal Entries (Information Taken from Table 3-9-A)

Unrealized Investment Holding Loss	7,000	
Allowance for Market Change in Noncurrent Investment		7,000
To record unrealized holding loss for 20X7.		

The $5,000 unrealized holding gain reported in 20X6 is reported as a separate component of other comprehensive income, and the $5,000 allowance account is reported as an addition to the investment in Wood, Inc. common stock. In 20X7, fair value declined below the original cost basis of Wood, Inc. stock, the $5,000 unrealized holding gain is recovered from and a $2,000 net holding loss is included as unrealized other comprehensive income in stockholders' equity, and a $7,000 unrealized holding loss is now reported as a component of other comprehensive income. The $2,000 credit balance in the allowance account ($5,000 debit – $7,000 credit) is reported as a contra long-term asset to the investment in Wood, Inc.'s stock, and the net balance presented in the balance sheet is $198,000 ($200,000 – $2,000). The Wood, Inc. investment is classified as a noncurrent asset based on the assumptions in Example 3-9.

Next, journal entries for held-to-maturity securities are presented for both 20X6 and 20X7.

Held-to-Maturity—Journal Entries

December 31, 20X6 Journal Entry (Information Taken from Table 3-9-A)

Cash	28,000	
Interest Income		28,000
To record interest income for 20X6.		

December 31, 20X7 Journal Entries (Information Taken from Example 3-9 and Table 3-9-A)

Loss on Held-to-Maturity Securities	20,000[a]	
Investment in Max, Inc. Bonds		20,000
To record other than temporary decline in fair value of Max, Inc. Bonds		

[a] $20,000 = $380,000 fair value – $400,000 cost.

Cash	28,000	
Interest Income		28,000
To record interest income for 20X7.		

The only entry for 20X6 is the entry to recognize $28,000 of interest income. No changes are made for temporary declines in the fair value of held-to-maturity securities. However, in 20X7, the $20,000 decline in fair value is assumed to be other than temporary and a $20,000 loss must be reported and a new cost basis of $380,000 is established for the investment. The loss of $20,000 is reported in the income statement. The investment account is classified as noncurrent in the balance sheet, as specified in the assumptions for Example 3-9.

Investments with Discounts or Premiums

Example 3-9 was a straightforward situation where bonds were sold at par value and the cost basis was not amortized for discounts or premiums. Example 3-10 incorporates discounts and premiums into the investment computations. Assumptions for Example 3-10 are as follows.

Example 3-10
Assumptions for Debt and Equity Investments

1. Johnson Enterprises, a December 31 year-end company, has three bond investments and two stock investments. The company is using the cost method to account for the two common stock investments because ownership in each company's common stock is less than 20% of the outstanding stock.
2. All stock and bond investments were purchased on January 1, 20X6. Purchase information for each bond investment is as follows:

	Face Amount	Selling Price	Stated Rate	Market Rate	Life of Debt
McDonald Company Bonds	$1,000,000	$924,183	8%	10%	5 years
Henry Company Bonds	2,000,000	2,086,598	6%	5%	5 years
Russell Company Bonds	500,000	432,897	6%	8%	10 years

All bonds pay interest on an annual basis. The cost of the investments in Williams Company common stock and Hope Company common stock was $500,000 and $1,000,000, respectively. Dividend income received from the investment in Williams Company common stock for 20X6 is $30,000. Dividend income for 20X6–20X8 from the investment in the common stock of Hope Company is $50,000, $65,000 and $70,000, respectively.

3. All changes in market values are assumed to be temporary. No stocks or bonds were sold or transferred during the three-year period, except for the trading securities. The amortized cost and fair market values of all investments at the end of 20X6, 20X7, and 20X8 are presented below.

4. All trading securities were sold on January 5, 20X7 for $1,450,000.

5. All fair value amounts were determined using the provisions of ASC 820.

The analysis of the Example 3-10 assumptions will address individually each category of securities.

Trading Securities

The qualifying debt security included in the trading category is covered by the provisions of ASC 320-10 and the other investment is an equity security that is accounted for under the cost method and the fair value can be reasonably determined is covered by the provisions of ASC 321-10. Because fair value was less than cost or amortized cost for both trading securities, an unrealized holding loss of $13,601 is recognized for 20X6. The change in amortized cost for the bonds is the amortization of the discount from year to year. The unrealized holding loss is reported as a separate item on the income statement. The investments are written down directly and the balances are reported in the balance sheet as current assets. In addition to computation of the holding gain or loss, interest income of $92,418 is computed for 20X6. The $92,418 interest income includes cash interest of $80,000 plus $12,418 of discount amortization. The unrealized loss and interest income are computed in Table 3-10-A.

	20X6		20X7		20X8	
	Amortized Cost	Fair Value	Amortized Cost	Fair Value	Amortized Cost	Fair Value
Trading Securities						
Investment in:						
McDonald Company bonds	$936,601	$925,000				
Williams Company common stock	500,000	498,000				
Available-for-Sale Securities						
Investment in:						
Henry Company bonds	2,070,928	2,065,000	$2,054,474	$2,052,000	$2,037,198	$2,040,000
Hope Company common stock	1,000,000	995,000	1,000,000	998,000	1,000,000	1,005,000
Held-to Maturity Securities						
Investment in:						
Russell Company bonds	437,529	430,000	442,531	440,000	447,933	450,000

Table 3-10-A Computation of Unrealized Holding Gain/Loss and Income for Trading Securities

Computation of Holding Gain/Loss Cost or Carrying Value:		
		20X6
Investment in:		
McDonald Company bonds	$936,601	
Williams Company common stock	500,000	$1,436,601
Fair Market Value:		
Investment in:		
McDonald Company bonds	$925,000	
Williams Company common stock	498,000	1,423,000
Difference between fair value & cost		$(13,601)
(Gain)/loss recognized in prior period		0
Unrealized holding gain/(loss) recognized		$(13,601)

Computation of Income and Discount Amortization:	
	20X6
Carrying value of bonds end of year	$936,601
Carrying value of bonds beginning of year	(924,183)
Discount amortization for current year	$12,418
Cash interest ($1,000,000 × 8%)	80,000
Annual interest income	$92,418
Dividend income (Example 3-10, Assumption 2)	$30,000

Using the information from Table 3-10-A, journal entries at the end of 20X6 are presented as follows for the trading category.

Trading Category—Journal Entries

	Debit	Credit
Unrealized Investment Holding Loss	13,601	
Investment in McDonald Company Bonds		[a]11,601
Investment in Williams Company Common Stock		[b]2,000
To record holding loss for 20X6.		

[a] $936,601 cost – $925,000 fair market value = $11,601.
[b] $500,000 cost – $498,000 fair market value = $2,000.

	Debit	Credit
Cash	80,000	
Investment in McDonald Company Bonds	12,418	
Interest Income		92,418
To record interest income and discount amortization for 20X6.		
Cash	30,000	
Dividend Income		30,000
To record dividend income for 20X6.		

The investment in McDonald Company bonds is debited for $12,418, the amount of the discount amortization for 20X6. In addition, the entry for $30,000 represents dividend income received on Williams Company common stock.

On January 5, 20X7, both investments in the trading category were sold for $1,450,000. After the write-down at December 31, 20X6, the carrying values of McDonald Company bonds and Williams Company common stock were $925,000 (Table 3-10-A) and $498,000 (Table 3-10-A), respectively. Using this information, the journal entry required for the sale is as follows:

Cash	1,450,000	
Investment in McDonald Company Bonds		925,000
Investment in Williams Company Common Stock		498,000
Gain on Sale of Trading Securities		27,000

Available-for-Sale Securities

The next category of investments to be considered is available-for-sale securities. Both investments qualify for accounting under ASC 320-10 and ASC 321-10, respectively. The first is a corporate debt security and the second is an equity security where fair value can be determined and the investment is accounted for using the cost method. The change in the amortized cost basis for the debt security is amortization of the premium created at the time of purchase. Table 3-10-B shows computation of any unrealized holding gains and losses for 20X6–20X8. In addition, Table 3-10-B also presents computation of interest income on the bonds for 20X6–20X8 and shows the amount of dividend income for all three years.

Table 3-10-B
Computation of Unrealized Holding Gain/Loss and Income for Available-for-Sale Securities

Computation of Holding Gain/Loss	*20X6*		*20X7*		*20X8*	
Cost or Carrying Value:						
Investment in:						
Henry Company bonds	$2,070,928		$2,054,474		$2,037,198	
Hope Company common stock	1,000,000	$3,070,928	1,000,000	$3,054,474	1,000,000	$3,037,198
Fair Market Value:						
Investment in:						
Henry Company bonds	$2,065,000		$2,052,000		$2,040,000	
Hope Company common stock	995,000	3,060,000	998,000	3,050,000	1,005,000	3,045,000
Difference between fair value & cost		$(10,928)		$(4,474)		$7,802
(Gain)/loss in prior period		0		10,928		4,474
Unrealized holding gain/(loss)		$(10,928)		$6,454		$12,276

Computation of Income and Discount Amortization	*20X6*	*20X7*	*20X8*
Carrying value of bonds beginning of year	$(2,086,598)	$(2,070,928)	$(2,054,474)
Carrying value of bonds end of year	2,070,928	2,054,474	2,037,198
Premium amortization for current year	$(15,670)	$(16,454)	$17,276
Cash interest ($2,000,000 × 6%)	120,000	120,000	120,000
Annual interest income	$104,330	$103,546	$102,724
Dividend income (Example 3-10, Assumption 2)	$50,000	$65,000	$70,000

Using the information from Table 3-10-B, journal entries at December 31, 20X6, 20X7, and 20X8 are presented below.

20X6 Journal Entries

Unrealized investment holding loss	10,928	
Allowance for market change in noncurrent investment		10,928
To record unrealized holding loss for 20X6.		
Cash	120,000	
Investment in Henry Company bonds		15,670
Interest income		104,330
To record interest income and premium amortization for 20X6.		
Cash	50,000	
Dividend income		50,000
To record dividend income for 20X6.		

20X7 Journal Entries

Allowance for market change in noncurrent investment	6,454	
Unrealized investment holding gain		6,454
To record unrealized holding gain for 20X7.		
Cash	120,000	
Investment in Henry Company bonds		16,454
Interest income		103,546
To record interest income and premium amortization for 20X7.		
Cash	65,000	
Dividend income		65,000
To record dividend income for 20X7.		

20X8 Journal Entries

Allowance for market change in noncurrent investment	12,276	
Unrealized investing holding gain		12,276
To record unrealized holding gain for 20X8.		
Cash	120,000	
Investment in Henry Company bonds		17,276
Interest income		102,724
To record interest income and premium amortization for 20X8.		
Cash	70,000	
Dividend income		70,000
To record dividend income for 20X8.		

The entries to close the unrealized holding gains and losses included as a component of other comprehensive income to unrealized other comprehensive income in stockholders' equity are not shown.

The credit to the investment in Henry Company bonds is the premium amortization for the premium that was created at the time of the bond purchase. Information about the remaining entries has been covered in detail in the journal entries from Example 3-9.

Held-to-Maturity Securities

The last category to consider is the held-to-maturity category. The debt security included in the held-to-maturity category is covered by ASC 320-10, because the security is corporate debt. There were no declines in the debt security that were considered to be other than temporary; therefore, the difference in cost and fair value cannot be reported in the financial statements for the held-to-maturity category. The only accounting required is the reporting of interest income. Because the bonds were purchased at a discount, the amortized cost basis is increasing over time from amortization of the discount. The amount of interest income reported each accounting period is the cash interest plus the discount amortization. Interest income for the held-to-maturity category for 20X6–20X8 is calculated in Table 3-10-C.

Table 3-10-C Computation of Income and Discount Amortization for Held-to-Maturity Securities

	20X6	20X7	20X8
Carrying value of bonds at end of year	$437,529	$442,531	$447,933
Carrying value of bonds at beginning of year	(432,897)	(437,529)	(442,531)
Discount amortization for current year	$4,632	$5,002	$5,402
Cash interest ($500,000 × 6%)	30,000	30,000	30,000
Annual interest income	$34,632	$35,002	$35,402

Using the information computed in Table 3-10-C, journal entries for 20X6–20X8 for the held-to-maturity category are prepared as follows:

December 31, 20X6 Journal Entry

Cash	30,000	
Investment in Russell Company bonds	4,632	
Interest income		34,632
To record interest income and discount amortization for 20X6.		

December 31 20X7 Journal Entry

Cash	30,000	
Investment in Russell Company bonds	5,002	
Interest income		35,002
To record interest income and discount amortization for 20X7.		

December 31 20X8 Journal Entry

Cash	30,000	
Investment in Russell Company bonds	5,402	
Interest income		35,402
To record interest income and discount amortization for 20X8.		

Transfers between Securities Classification Categories

Example 3-11 covers situations where investments are transferred between categories. Assumptions for Example 3-11 are as follows.

Example 3-11
Assumptions for Debt and Equity Investments

1. Micro Enterprises, a December 31 year-end company, has determined that several transfers of investments have been made between categories.
2. The investment transfers are presented below. Information provided is as of the date of transfer.

Investment in:	Amortized Cost	Fair Value	Transfer
Johnson Company Common Stock	$200,000	$250,000	From T[1] to A-F-S[2]
Jones Company Common Stock	500,000	400,000	From A-F-S to T
Financial Company Bonds	350,000	375,000	From H-T-M[3] to T
Jackson Enterprise Bonds	800,000	740,000	From H-T-M to A-F-S
Forest Company Bonds	386,139	360,255	From A-F-S to H-T-M

[1] T = trading.
[2] A-F-S = available-for-sale.
[3] H-T-M = held-to-maturity.

3. At the date of transfer, Jones Company common stock has a $100,000 balance in the valuation allowance and unrealized loss accounts. The investment in Forest Company bonds has a 5% stated rate (interest paid annually) and an effective rate of 6%. The face of the bonds is $400,000. At the date of transfer the bonds have a four-year remaining life, and the transfer is made on January 1. On the date of transfer, Forest Company bonds have a $13,861 balance in the valuation allowance and unrealized loss accounts.
4. All investment accounts, except trading, are classified a noncurrent.
5. All fair value amounts were determined using the provisions of ASC 820.

There is no entry for the transfer of the investment in Johnson Company common stock. The stock is transferred to the available-for-sale category at the $250,000 fair market value, the amount recorded for the investment. The $50,000 gain has already been recognized in income. The investment is just reclassified as an available-for-sale security.

The transfer of the investment in Jones Company common stock is made at fair market value and the $100,000 ($500,000 – $400,000) unrealized holding loss is taken to income in the period of the transfer. The following entry is required for the transfer:

Allowance for Market Change in Noncurrent Investment	100,000	
Unrealized Holding Loss on Trading Securities	100,000	
Unrealized Holding Loss on Available-for-Sale Securities		100,000
Investment in Jones Company Common Stock		100,000

The transfer of the Financial Company bonds from the held-to-maturity category to the trading category is made at fair market value. Because none of the change in market value has been recognized as a held-to-maturity security, the entire $25,000 ($375,000 – $350,000) unrealized holding gain is taken to income in the period that the transfer is made. The journal entry required for the transfer is as follows:

Investment in Financial Company Bonds	25,000	
Unrealized Holding Gain on Trading Securities		25,000

The transfer of Jackson Enterprise bonds from the held-to-maturity category to the available-for-sale category is made at fair market value of $740,000. Because the Jackson Enterprise bonds have never been written down to fair value, an entry is required to establish an unrealized holding loss of $60,000 ($800,000 – $740,000) and an allowance for $60,000. The unrealized holding loss is included as a component of other comprehensive income and the allowance is a contra asset to the investment account. The entry to record the transfer is shown below:

Unrealized Holding Loss on Available-for-Sale Securities	60,000	
Allowance for Market Change in Noncurrent Investment		60,000

The transfer of Forest Company bonds from the available-for-sale category to the held-to-maturity category is made at fair market value. The allowance for market change in the investment of $13,861 is removed, and the bonds are written down by $13,861. The unrealized holding loss included in stockholders' equity as unrealized other comprehensive income is not removed, but is amortized over the remaining life of the bonds as an adjustment to the bond yield in the same manner as the discount. The entry to record the transfer is as follows:

Allowance for Market Change in Noncurrent Investment	13,861	
Investment in Forest Company Bonds		13,861

The entry to recognize income and record amortization of the investment discount and unrealized holding loss remaining in stockholders' equity is presented below:

Cash	20,000	
Investment in Forest Company Bonds	3,168	
Interest Income		20,000
Unrealized Other Comprehensive Income from Available-for-Sale Securities		3,168

Cash of $20,000 in the preceding entry is computed as the face amount of the debt of $400,000 times the stated rate of 5%. The increase in the investment of $3,168 is the amortization of the discount on the investment ($386,139 carrying value × 6% effective rate = $23,168 interest expense – $20,000 cash interest = $3,168). Because the unrealized holding loss is amortized over the remaining life of the bonds as an adjustment to yield, interest income will be adjusted for the loss amortization. The unrealized loss amortization can be determined by adding the unrealized loss of $13,861 to the carrying value of the debt of $386,139 and computing a new effective rate that will equate the $400,000 amount ($386,139 +

$13,861) with the future interest cash flows of $20,000 and the future bond maturity cash flows of $400,000. The rate that equates these two amounts is 5%. Using the current effective rate of 6% and the new effective rate of 5%, interest income and amortization of the unrealized holding loss is computed in Table 3-11-A.

Table 3-11-A Computation of Interest Income and Amortization of Unrealized Holding Loss

Carrying value of the bond	$386,139	
Effective interest rate	6%	
Interest income before unrealized loss		$23,168
Carrying value of the bond	$386,139	
Unrealized holding loss	13,861	
Carrying value with loss	$400,000	
New effective rate	5%	
Interest income with unrealized loss		20,000
Amortization of unrealized loss		$3,168

Topic 323: Investments—Equity Method and Joint Ventures

Topic 323, *Investments—Equity Method and Joint Ventures,* contains seven subtopics:

10 Overall

30 Partnerships, Joint Ventures, and Limited Liability Entities

740 Income Taxes

932 Extractive Activities—Oil and Gas*

946 Financial Services—Investment Companies*

970 Real Estate—General*

974 Real Estate—Real Estate Investment Trusts*

* See the corresponding topic in Chapter 9 for coverage of this shared subtopic.

Flowchart and General Discussion

Perhaps the most important decision the accountant must make to determine if ASC 323-10 is applicable involves the computation of the percentage of ownership of the investor in the investee company's voting stock. Note that ASC 323-10 is not applicable to common stock investments of the following: entities of a nonbusiness nature, investment companies covered by the Investment Company Act of 1940, and entities that would be covered by the Investment Company Act of 1940 if certain conditions were met.

Chart 3-2 depicts the major points of ASC 323-10-15, which tells the reader if ASC 323-10 is applicable.

Chart 3-2
Percentage of Ownership

Applicable Accounting		Percentage Ownership
		100
Can use equity or cost when consolidation is not appropriate under **ASC 810.**	Consolidate	
		50
Can use cost method if it can be demonstrated that significant influence does not exist.	Equity	
		20
Can use equity method if significant influence can be demonstrated.	Cost	
		0

Chart 3-2 shows that if an investor company owns 20% or more of the voting stock (voting common and voting preferred) of the investee company, the investment qualifies for equity method accounting because the presumption is that the investor company can exert significant influence over the operating or financial policies of the investee. If the investor company owns less than 20% of the voting stock of the investee, the equity method is not applicable because the presumption is that the investor cannot exert significant influence over the investee. This presumption of significant influence can be overcome by the facts of a particular situation. There are situations where investor companies own less than 20% of the voting stock of an investee and can exert significant influence over the operating or financial policies of the investee. A company owning less than 20% of the voting stock can demonstrate significant influence by membership on the board of directors or participation in policy making. Consult ASC 323-10-15 for a more complete discussion of the demonstration of significant influence.

It is also possible for an investor company owning more than 20%, but less than 50%, of the voting stock to be unable to exert significant influence over the policies of the investee. The following examples are situations where the presumption of significant influence may fail (ASC 323-10-15-10):

1. Using channels such as litigation or complaints to regulatory authorities, the investee company opposes the investor's efforts to exert significant influence.
2. The investor relinquishes rights to exert significant influence through an agreement between the investee and investor.
3. Other investors have sufficient ownership to operate the investee company and can disregard the wishes of the investor.
4. The investor is unsuccessful in its attempts to acquire more financial data from the investee company than is available to other owners of the investee company.
5. The investor is unsuccessful in its efforts to get representation on the board of directors of the investee company.

As explained in ASC 323-10-15-11, the preceding list does not cover all cases where an investor owning more than 20% of the voting stock of the investee fails to exercise significant influence. The key point to remember is that investor companies that are able to exert significant influence should use the equity method regardless of the percentage of ownership. The 20% ownership criterion is merely an attempt to quantify the concept of significant influence.

As shown in Chart 3-2, if ownership in the voting stock of an entity exceeds 50%, the entity is viewed as a subsidiary of the parent company and consolidation generally is appropriate. All majority-owned subsidiaries must be consolidated except for two situations. The two situations are as follows:

1. A parent company should not consolidate the financial statements of a subsidiary when the majority owners do not have control of the subsidiary.
2. A parent company should not consolidate the financial statements of a subsidiary when temporary control of the subsidiary is likely.

If a subsidiary is not consolidated because of one of the two preceding reasons, the investment in the subsidiary must be accounted for by either the cost method or the equity method. The rules used for determining whether the cost method or the equity method is used for investments of 50% or less ownership should be used to determine which method is used for unconsolidated subsidiaries. That is, if a parent company can exert significant influence over the operating policies of the subsidiary, the equity method should be used. If significant influence cannot be demonstrated, the cost method is appropriate. Because the only reason a subsidiary is not consolidated is lack of control, generally the cost method would be used. However, there are situations where a parent company does not have control, but can exert significant influence.

Flowchart 3-4 illustrates the percentage of ownership criteria and goes on to show the general provisions of ASC 323-10. As shown in Blocks 1 and 2 of Flowchart 3-4, if the investor company previously held an equity investment of less than 20%, but subsequently has increased its percentage ownership to more than 20%, a retroactive adjustment will be necessary before equity accounting treatment is begun. Naturally, if the percentage of ownership falls below 20% (and significant influence cannot be demonstrated), the investor would discontinue the equity accounting treatment (Blocks 5, 6, and 7).

Flowchart 3-4

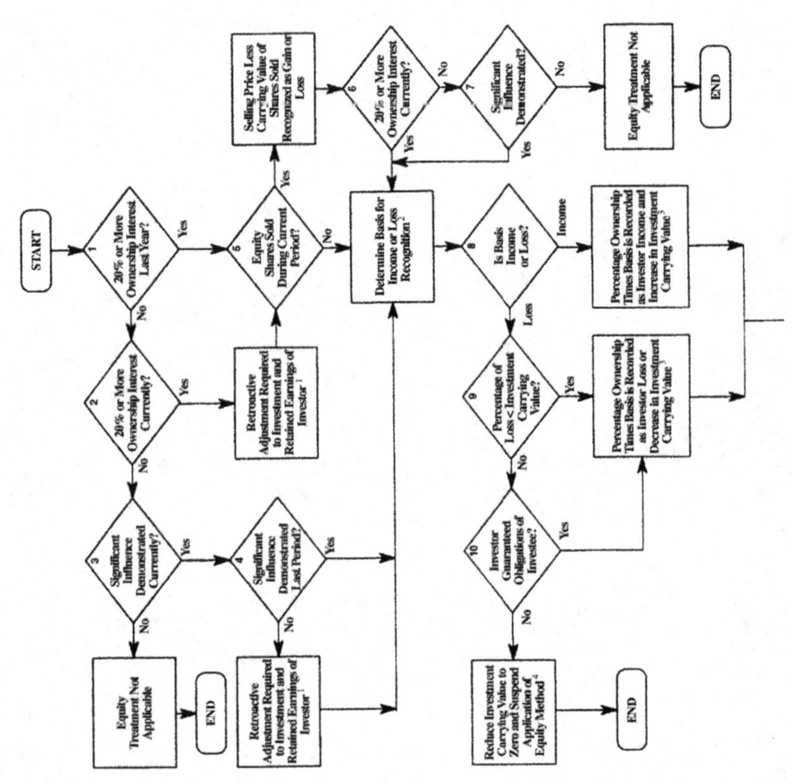

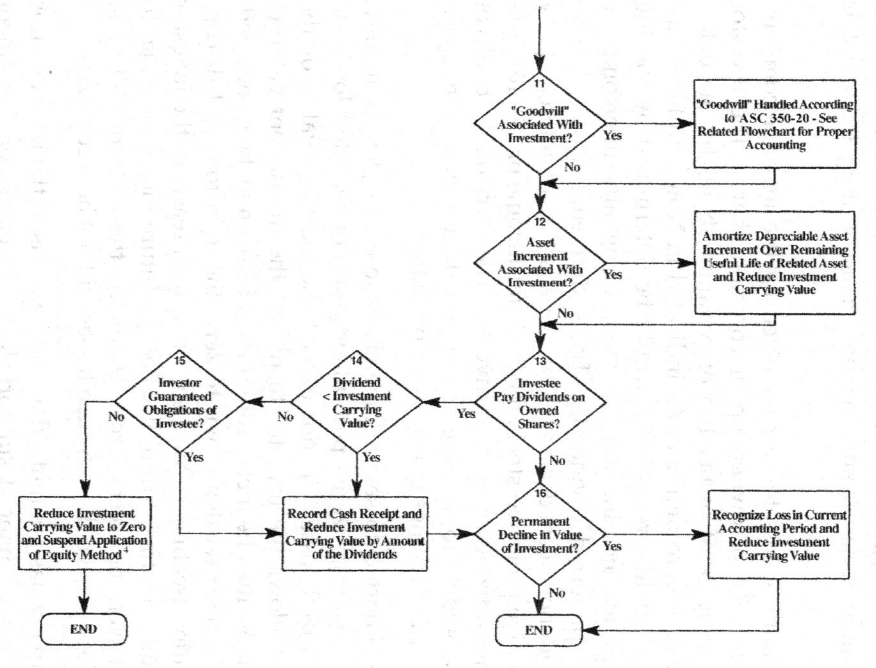
11
"Goodwill" Associated With Investment?
Yes
No
"Goodwill" Handled According to ASC 350-20 - See Related Flowchart for Proper Accounting
12
Asset Increment Associated With Investment?
Yes
No
Amortize Depreciable Asset Increment Over Remaining Useful Life of Related Asset and Reduce Investment Carrying Value
13
Investee Pay Dividends on Owned Shares?
Yes
No
14
Dividend < Investment Carrying Value?
Yes
No
15
Investor Guaranteed Obligations of Investee?
Yes
No
Reduce Investment Carrying Value to Zero and Suspend Application of Equity Method⁴
END
Record Cash Receipt and Reduce Investment Carrying Value by Amount of the Dividends
16
Permanent Decline in Value of Investment?
Yes
No
Recognize Loss in Current Accounting Period and Reduce Investment Carrying Value
END

[1] Adjustment amount determined in a manner consistent with accounting for a step-by-step acquisition of a subsidiary.
[2] Basis for income recognition is equal to current investee income (loss) less any intercompany profits and less any cumulative preferred dividends.
[3] Extraordinary items and prior period adjustments are reported separately by investor, if material.
[4] Subsequent losses will not be recorded. Subsequent income only recognized if it is in excess of accumulated losses. See a discussion of ASC 323-10-35, paragraphs 23 through 26, regarding the impact of other investments in the investee on suspending the equity method when losses reduce the investment to zero later in this chapter.

When equity method accounting is found to be applicable, the investor company will initially measure its investment at cost in accordance with ASC 805-50-30, *Business Combinations, Initial Measurement*, and recognize income from the investment as the income is earned by the investee. Likewise, losses from investee operations will be recognized, within certain limits, as such losses are incurred. Recognition of income or loss will be reflected as adjustments to the carrying value of the investment account. Recognized income will increase the carrying value and losses will decrease the carrying value of the investment. One problem that is created by this treatment occurs when recognizable losses accumulate in an amount greater than the carrying value of the investment. This is likely to happen only in rare cases, and the proper accounting treatment is discussed below.

The amount of income or loss to be recognized by the investor company depends upon the percentage of ownership of common shares. The investor would multiply the percentage of ownership of common shares by the determined basis for income or loss recognition. As indicated in Note 2 to Flowchart 3-4, this basis for income or loss recognition would be determined by starting with the investee's reported net income and subtracting any intercompany profits and cumulative preferred dividends. (These dividends would be deducted even if they had not been declared.) In the absence of intercompany transactions and cumulative preferred stock, the basis for income or loss recognition would be equal to reported income of the investee. The entry on the books of the investor company would be to increase its investment account and to credit an account such as Equity in Earnings of Investee Company.

The recognition of reported losses is somewhat more complex. Generally, the investor company can recognize its percentage share of reported losses so long as the total recognized losses do not exceed the carrying value of the investment. ASC 323-10 allows the investor to reduce the investment value to zero, but special conditions must be met before further losses may be recognized. Once the investment has been written down to zero, the investor must discontinue the equity accounting treatment. After such a state is reached, the investor will not resume the equity treatment until its share of future income is equal to the share of losses that were not recognized. Therefore, the investor still must keep track of reported losses, even though such losses will not be recognized.

If the investor company has guaranteed any obligations of the investee or is committed to provide future financial support, losses in excess of investment carrying value may be recognized. In this case, the investment carrying value could become negative. The above-described accounting procedures are shown in Flowchart 3-4 (Blocks 9 and 10).

The next major accounting problem shown on Flowchart 3-4 deals with the existence of goodwill. Such an excess should be allocated to specific assets, allocated to assets and goodwill, or allocated to goodwill. Subsequent to the allocation, the amount will be tested for impairment using the provisions of ASC 350-20. Any excess of book value over cost first should be assigned to noncurrent assets other than long-term marketable securities, and any unassigned excess should be amortized.

Under the equity method of accounting for investments in common stock, dividends received from the investee company are treated as a reduction in the investment value rather than as income. Again, there is the potential problem of receiving dividends in excess of the carrying value of the investment. If this were to happen, the dividends would be treated the same as the previously discussed losses. Flowchart 3-4, Blocks 14 and 15, illustrate the accounting for dividends received.

The final accounting consideration relates to declines in the value of the investment. If a decline is determined to be permanent, the investment value should be reduced currently, and a loss recognized.

This general discussion of Flowchart 3-4 and the equity method of accounting lays the foundation for the more detailed analysis that follows.

Technical Considerations

From a technical accounting standpoint, certain paragraphs of ASC 323-10 provide the basic outline for applying the equity method. Because of their importance, those paragraphs are discussed in detail, with example material to illustrate the points made in the paragraphs. The reader is encouraged to make frequent references to Flowchart 3-4 in order that each technical consideration may be kept in perspective.

Intra-entity Gains and Losses (ASC 323-10-35, Paragraphs 7 through 12)

Until realized, income and losses between the investee and investor companies should be eliminated, just as if the companies were consolidated.

The treatment of unrealized intra-entity income and losses depends upon whether or not the transaction between the investor and investee is considered to be an arm's-length transaction. An "arm's-length" transaction is a transaction that would be negotiated between an independent buyer and an independent seller.

When the investor has a majority interest in the voting stock of the investee company, income and losses from non-arm's-length transactions between the investee and investor companies should not be recognized until the profits or losses have been realized through an outside party transaction.

In this particular case, any unrealized income or losses would be eliminated in their entirety. To illustrate, assume Jar, Inc. holds a 75% ownership interest in the common shares of Book-It, Inc., an unconsolidated subsidiary. Assume that Jar, Inc. sold merchandise to Book-It, Inc. and recorded a gross profit of $50,000. It was determined that this was not an arm's length transaction. At the balance sheet date of Book-It, Inc., none of the merchandise purchased from Jar, Inc. had been sold. Therefore the entire $50,000 unrealized profit would be eliminated, and Book-It, Inc. would determine its net income on the basis of the new inventory cost.

Where an arm's-length transaction can be demonstrated between the investee and investor, only the allocated share of the unrealized income or losses would be eliminated. Assume, for illustrative purposes, the same facts as above (a sale to the investee by the investor, a downstream transaction), except that Jar, Inc. holds a 25% (rather than 75%) ownership interest in Book-It, Inc. Ignoring income tax considerations, $12,500 of unrealized intercompany profits would be eliminated ($50,000 × .25 = $12,500). If we assume a 50% tax rate, the elimination would be calculated as follows:

Total unrealized profits	$50,000
Tax consequence of profits	25,000
After tax unrealized profits	$25,000
Proportionate share of profits (25%)	$ 6,250

In this case, the investor's net income would be reduced by $6,250. Had the sale been made to the investor by the investee (an upstream transaction), the investee would have reduced income by $25,000 and thereby reduced the investor's equity interest by $6,250 (25% of $25,000).

Basis Difference (ASC 323-10-35, Paragraphs 13 and 14)

When an investor acquires an interest in an investee company and pays more or less than the equity in the net assets, accounting for the difference is the same as if the investee company were consolidated.

Assuming excess of cost over equity, the difference should be accounted for in one of the following manners:

1. Allocated to specific assets,
2. Allocated to both assets and goodwill, or
3. Allocated to goodwill.

To illustrate the application of this guidance, consider the following example: On January 1, 20X6, Jar, Inc. purchased 1,000 shares (25%) of the 4,000 shares of Book-It, Inc. for $400,000 cash. The relevant values of Book-It, Inc., at acquisition date, are shown in Table 3-12.

Table 3-12

	Book Value	Fair Value
Nondepreciable assets	$400,000	$600,000
Depreciable assets (20 year life straight-line depreciation)	900,000	1,500,000
Total	$1,300,000	$2,100,000
Liabilities	$500,000	$500,000
Stockholders' equity	800,000	
Total	$1,300,000	
Situation 1—Allocation of Excess to Specific Assets		
Cost of investment	$400,000	
Book value of net assets purchased (25% × ($1,300,000 – $500,000))	200,000	
Excess of cost over book value	$200,000	

	Book Value	Fair Value
Asset Readjustment:		
Allocated to nondepreciable assets:		
$600,000 fair value – $400,000 book value = $200,000 × 25% ownership	(50,000)	
Allocated to depreciable assets:		
$1,500,000 fair value – $900,000 book value × 25% ownership	(150,000)	
Unassigned excess	$0	

Situation 2—Allocation of Excess to Both Assets and Goodwill

Assume the same information as in Situation 1 except the fair values of Book-It,

Inc. were:

Nondepreciable assets	$500,000
Depreciable assets	1,200,000
Total	$1,700,000

The allocation would be made as follows:

Cost of investment	$400,000
Book value of net assets purchased (25% × ($1,300,000 – $500,000))	200,000
Excess of cost over book value	$200,000
Asset Readjustment:	
Allocated to nondepreciable assets:	
($500,000 – $400,000 = $100,000 × 25%)	(25,000)
Allocated to depreciable assets:	
($1,200,000 – $900,000 = $300,000 × 25%)	(75,000)
Unallocated excess = goodwill	$100,000

Situation 3—Allocation to Goodwill

Assume the same facts as in Situation 1, except that fair value is equal to book value at date of acquisition. The allocation would be made as follows:

Cost of investment	$400,000
Book value of net assets purchased (25% × ($1,300,000 – $500,000))	200,000
Excess of cost over book value or goodwill	$200,000

The journal entries needed to record the purchase and subsequent amortization under each of the three situations are reflected in Table 3-13. Goodwill is not amortized but tested for impairment.

The only difference in the journal entries in Table 3-13 is in the amount of amortization periodically charged against income. The difference in the amortization amounts is due to the different amortization periods effective under each situation.

The examples reflect the fact that the investment account contains elements other than the book value of assets purchased. Therefore, the investor is required to keep a record of the different elements in order to properly to expense each item in the appropriate accounting period.

Table 3-13

	Situation 1		Situation 2		Situation 3	
Purchase[a]						
Investment in Book-It, Inc. Common Stock	400,000		400,000		400,000	
Cash		400,000		400,000		400,000
Amortization						
Equity in Earnings of Book-It, Inc. (Ordinary)	[b]7,500		[c]3,750		0	
Investment in Book-It, Inc. Common Stock		7,500		3,750		0

[a] The allocation process has no effect on the entry to record the investment.
[b] Allocated to depreciable assets $150,000/20 year useful life = $7,500
[c] Depreciable assets $ 75,000/20 year useful life = $3,750

The various elements shown in Situation 2 may be reflected in a T-account as follows:

Investment in Book-It, Inc., Common Stock

Purchased Book Value	$200,000
Nondepreciable Asset Increment	25,000
Depreciable Asset Increment	75,000
Goodwill	100,000
Total	$400,000

An entity with an investment accounted for using the equity method may have one additional element in the investment account not shown in the T-account or in Situation 2. That additional element is interest capitalization. Using the provisions of ASC 835-20, *Capitalization of Interest*, interest may be capitalized on the investment balance in specific situations. See Chapter 8 for a detailed analysis of capitalization of interest on an investment balance.

A problem arises when the investor has allocated a portion of the excess of cost over book value to assets that later are sold by the investee. The investor must adjust his share of the unamortized increment previously reflected in the investment account. To illustrate, assume the nondepreciable and depreciable assets as reflected in Situation 1 (allocation of $50,000 to nondepreciable, and $150,000 to depreciable, assets) above are sold by the investee for a gain of $400,000 and a loss of $200,000, respectively, after the investment has been owned for two years. The investor's share of the gain is $100,000 ($400,000 × 25%) and $50,000 ($200,000 × 25%), respectively. The investor's adjusted gain or loss would be reflected in the investment account as shown in Table 3-14.

Table 3-14 Allocation to Assets

	Nondepreciable		Depreciable	
Investor's share of investee gain or (loss)—25%		$100,000		$(50,000)
Asset increment	$(50,000)		$(150,000)	
Amortization (2 years)	0		[a]15,000	
Unamortized increment		(50,000)		(135,000)
Gain or (loss) reported by investor		$50,000		$(185,000)

[a] $150,000 ÷ 20 years: $7,500 × 2 = $15,000

Situations 1, 2, and 3 are concerned with instances when cost exceeds the fair value of the net assets purchased. If the fair value of the net assets purchased exceeds the cost, negative goodwill exists. This excess is recognized in earnings as a gain under ASC 805.

The Equity Method—Overall Guidance (ASC 323-10-45, Paragraphs 1 and 2)

An investor with an investment in the common stock of an investee company should report the investment in its balance sheet as one amount. Similarly, the investor's percentage of income or loss from the investment should be presented as one amount in the income statement of the investor, unless some of the income or loss relates to items other than income from continuing operations. Material income or loss not related to income from continuing operations should be classified as discontinued operations or prior period adjustments.

To illustrate, assume that Jar, Inc. purchased 1,000 shares (25%) of the 4,000 shares of Book-It, Inc. for $400,000 on January 1, 20X6. During 20X6, Jar, Inc.'s income from continuing operations was $500,000. The tax rate for Jar, Inc. is 40%. Book-It, Inc.'s income statement is reflected below:

Income from continuing operations		$200,000
Discontinued operations		
Loss from operations of discontinued company	$(20,000)	
Loss on disposal	(10,000)	
Loss on discontinued operations		(30,000)
Net Income		$170,000

Jar, Inc.'s income statement would be constructed as illustrated below:

Income before nonoperating items	$500,000	
Nonoperating items:		
Equity in continuing operations of Book-It, Inc. ($200,000 × .25)	50,000	
Income from continuing operations before tax	$550,000	
Provision for income tax	220,000	
Income from continuing operations		$330,000
Discontinued operations:		
Equity in loss from operations of discontinued company (including loss on disposal of $2,500)[a]	$(7,500)	
Income tax benefit	(600)	(6,900)
Net Income		$323,100

[a] $20,000 × 25% (ownership) = $5,000 × 80% (dividend received deduction) = $4,000.
$5,000 – $4,000 = $1,000 subject to income tax.
$1,000 × 40% = $400.
$10,000 × 25% = $2,500 × 80% = $2,000.
$2,500 – $2,000 = $500 × 40% tax rate = $200.
$5,000 + $2,500 = $7,500.
$400 + $200 = $600.

For an in-depth study of taxes on undistributed earnings of investee companies, see Topic 740 in Chapter 7. Topic 260 in Chapter 2 illustrates the proper per-share disclosure of the above amounts.

Equity Method Losses, Investee Losses if the Investor Has Other Investments in the Investee, and Percentage Used to Determine the Amount of Equity Method Losses (ASC 323-10-35, Paragraphs 19 through 28)

The investor company should discontinue using the equity method of accounting for an investment in an investee company when the investor's share of losses of the investee reduces the investment account to zero, unless one of the following is met: the investor has investments other than common stock in the investee or the investor has an agreement to provide continued support to the investee or an agreement that guarantees investee obligations. If an investor has other investments, in addition to the common stock investment, in an investee and losses from the investee reduced the common stock investment account to zero, the equity method should continue to be applied by the investor. The investor's share of investee losses should be reported in the income statement of the investor and the basis of the other investments should be adjusted by the investor's share of the losses. If the investor has more than one other investment in the investee, the adjustment to the basis of the other investments should follow the order of liquidation. That is, the security that is most senior or that would be considered first in order of liquidation of the investee should first be adjusted for the investor's share of investee losses. Once the security is adjusted for the investor's share of investee losses, the provisions of ASC 320-10 or ASC 321-10, if applicable, should be applied to the security. Examples of investments other than common stock include investee loans, preferred stock, and debt securities of the investee. In addition, guidelines are provided on how the investor should compute its share of the investee losses and its share of subsequent income. The investor percentage interest in the common stock of the investee should not be used as a basis for making the determination. Common stock includes in-substance common stock and the requirements should be applied when an entity can exercise significant influence only when the entity has an investment in common stock and/or in-substance common stock.

If the investments other than common stock in the investee company are securities that fall under the provisions of ASC 321-10, the following procedures should be used to determine the amount of the loss from equity investments to report in the investor's income statement for the accounting period under consideration: (1) the investor should first apply the provisions of ASC 323-10 to determine the total amount of the investor's share of the investee loss using the equity method, (2) the basis of investments other than common stock with positive balances are adjusted for the amount of the loss using the order of seniority, and (3) if appropriate, the provisions of ASC 321-10 should be applied to the adjusted basis of the investments. When the basis of all the other investments in (2) above is reduced to zero, the investor should stop reporting its share of investee losses. However, the investor should continue to accumulate the amount of the unreported losses to use in the application of ASC 323-10-35, paragraphs 19 through 22. If the investor sells one of the other investments where investee losses were used to reduce the basis of the security and the adjusted basis is less than the carrying value of the security, the amount of the investee losses used in the adjustment process should be reversed at the time of the sale of the security.

Investee Capital Transactions (ASC 323-10-35, Paragraphs 15 through 17)

When an investee company has a transaction that is capital in nature, and the transaction impacts the investor's share of the investee stockholders' equity, the transaction should be accounted for using a step-by-step basis.

Dividends on cumulative preferred stock of the investee company should be deducted from investee income/loss before the investor company computes its share of investee income/loss, even if the dividends are not paid or are not declared. To illustrate, assume that Jar, Inc. purchased 1,000 shares (25 percent) of the 4,000 outstanding shares of Book-It, Inc. for $400,000, on January 1, 20X6. During 20X6 and 20X7, Book-It, Inc. had earnings (losses) of $400,000 and ($200,000), respectively. No dividends were declared in 20X6 or 20X7. A partial stockholders' equity section for Book-It appears as follows:

Preferred stock ($200 par, cumulative, 8%, 1,000 shares)	$200,000
Common stock ($100 par, 4,000 shares outstanding)	400,000

Table 3-15 reflects Jar, Inc.'s share of Book-It, Inc.'s earnings after considering preferred dividends.

Table 3-15

Year	Income (Loss)	Preferred Dividends	Income (Loss) After Preferred Dividends	% of Ownership	Jar. Inc.'s Share of Book-It, Inc.'s Income (Loss) After Preferred Dividends
20X6	$400,000	[a]$16,000	$384,000	25	[b]$96,000
20X7	$(200,000)	16,000	(216,000)	25	(54,000)

[a] $200 par × .08 = $16 × 1,000 shares = $16,000.
[b] Consideration must be given to preferred dividends whether declared or not.

Therefore, Jar, Inc., after considering the preferred dividends, would report earnings of $96,000 in 20X6, instead of $100,000 ($400,000 × 25%), and would report a loss of $54,000 in 20X7, instead of $50,000 ($200,000 × 25%).

Decrease in Level of Ownership or Degree of Influence (ASC 323-10-35, Paragraphs 35 and 36)

When the investor's percentage ownership in an investee falls below the 20% requirement for equity method accounting or when, for some reason, the investor can no longer exercise significant influence over the investee company, the equity method should be discontinued, but no adjustment to the investment account is required for the discontinuation. If cumulative dividends subsequent to discontinuation of the equity method exceed cumulative earnings, the excess dividends should be used to reduce the investment account balance.

Once the investor's ownership interest falls below 20%, or if it is determined that significant influence is not exerted, the investor must discontinue application of the equity method and start applying the cost method. A change from the equity method to the cost method is illustrated by the following example. Assume that Jar, Inc. purchased 1,000 shares (25%) of the 4,000 outstanding shares of Book-It, Inc. common stock for $400,000 on January 1, 20X6. The purchase price was $100,000 in excess of the fair value of the net assets at that date. The $100,000 goodwill is to be tested for impairment. Table 3-16 reflects the operations of Book-It, Inc. for the years 20X6 through 20Y1. Assume that, on January 1, 20X8, Book-It, Inc. sold 2,667 shares of common stock to other companies, thereby reducing the ownership interest of Jar, Inc. from 25% to 15%. This sale would require a switch from the equity to the cost method for Jar, Inc. The income recognized by Jar, Inc., and the balance in the investment account, are shown in Table 3-17.

Table 3-16

Year	Income (Loss)	Dividends
20X6	$100,000	$70,000
20X7	200,000	150,000
20X8	75,000	60,000
20X9	15,000	20,000
20Y0	(20,000)	10,000
20Y1	(10,000)	5,000

Table 3-17

Year	Equity in Earnings	Dividends Recognized	Goodwill Impairment	Investment Account Balance
Jan. 1, 20X6	$ 0	$ 0	$ 0	$400,000
20X6	[a]25,000	[b]$17,500	[c]$2,500	405,000
20X7	50,000	37,500	2,500	415,000
20X8	[d]11,250	9,000	0	415,000
20X9	2,250	3,000	0	[e]415,500
20Y0	(3,000)	1,500	0	413,500
20Y1	(1,500)	750	0	412,750

[a]$100,000 × 25% = $25,000.
[b]$70,000 × 25% = $17,500.
[c]Goodwill impairment was computed as $2,500 for both 20X6 and 20X7.
[d]Percentage ownership is now 15%.
[e]No change in investment account because the change was made January 1, 20X8 to the cost method and cumulative earnings exceed cumulative dividends.

It is necessary for the investor to keep a record of the cumulative earnings and cumulative dividends from the time of change from the equity to the cost method, because the investor must reduce the investment account by the amount that the cumulative dividends exceed the cumulative earnings from the time of the change. However, the amount of the reduction is limited to the *dividends paid* in the year that the cumulative dividends exceed cumulative earnings. This is illustrated by Table 3-18, which also provides support for the investment account balance for years 20Y0 and 20Y1.

Table 3-18 Jar, Inc.'s Share of Cumulative Earnings and Dividends of Book-It, Inc. from 20X8–20Y1 and Investment Reduction

Year	Earnings	Cumulative Earnings	Dividends	Cumulative Dividends	Excess of Cumulative Dividends over Cumulative Earnings	Investment Reduction	Excess of Cumulative Dividends over Cumulative Earnings After Investment Reduction
20X8	$11,250	$11,250	$9,000	$9,000	0	0	0
20X9	2,250	13,500	3,000	12,000	0	0	0
20Y0	(3,000)	10,500	1,500	13,500	$3,000	[a]1,500	$1,500
20Y1	(1,500)	9,000	750	14,250	5,250	750	3,000

[a]Investment reduction is limited to dividends received.

The year 20Y0 is the first year in which cumulative dividends exceed cumulative earnings. The excess of cumulative dividends over cumulative earnings since the change from equity to cost is $3,000, but the investment reduction is only $1,500—the amount of the dividends received in 20Y0. The reduction in the investment account is treated in a prospective manner (i.e., the account is reduced in current and future periods, but limited only to the amount of dividends paid in those periods).

Increase in Level of Ownership or Degree of Influence (ASC 323-10-35, Paragraphs 33 and 34)

The equity method of accounting for an investment in an investee company may be required for an investment that was previously accounted for using a different method, such as the cost method, because the investor company can now exercise significant influence as a result of an increase in percentage of ownership or other reasons. ASU 2016-07, *Investments—Equity Method and Joint Ventures (Topic 323): Simplifying the Transition to the Equity Method of Accounting,* eliminated the previous requirement that when an investment qualifies for use of the equity method as a result of an increase in the level of ownership interest or degree of influence, an investor had been required to adjust the investment, results of operations, and retained earnings retroactively on a step-by-step basis as if the equity method had been in effect during all previous periods that the investment had been held. But this has changed: Under this Update, the equity method investor shall simply add the cost of acquiring any additional interest in the investee to the current basis of the investor's previously held interest and adopt the equity method of accounting as of the date the investment becomes qualified for equity method accounting prospectively. Therefore, upon qualifying for the equity method of accounting, no retroactive adjustment of the investment is required. When the change is made to the equity method of accounting, the investment carrying value may be more or less than the equity in the net assets of the investee. This difference should be accounted for as goodwill unless the investor can allocate the difference to other investee accounts.

Disclosure Requirements

ASC 323-10-50-3 identifies the disclosure requirements for investments carried on the equity method. The disclosures required can be divided into four major categories as follows:

1. The investor should disclose the name, percentage ownership, accounting policy, and any difference between investment carrying value and the equity in the net assets of the investee for each investment accounted for under the equity method.
2. For investments, other than subsidiaries, where a market price is available, the aggregate value of each investment should be shown.

3. The investor should supply summary information in separate statements or notes concerning the investee's assets, liabilities, and results of operations for joint ventures and other investments, if material.
4. Any material effects of possible conversion of convertible securities, exercise of options, and warrants or any other contingent issuances of an investee should be disclosed in the notes to the financial statements.

Recent Changes

ASU 2016-07 eliminates the requirement that when an investment qualifies for use of the equity method as a result of an increase in the level of ownership interest or degree of influence, an investor must use a step-by-step basis as if the equity method had been in effect during all previous periods that the investment had been held. Instead, this update requires that the equity method investor add the cost of acquiring the additional interest in the investee to the current basis of the investor's previously held interest and adopt the equity method of accounting as of the date the investment becomes qualified for equity method accounting; no retroactive adjustment of the investment is required. The provisions of this Update shall be effective for all entities for fiscal years, and interim periods within those fiscal years, beginning after December 15, 2016. Earlier application is permitted.

Topic 325: Investments—Other

Topic 325, *Investments—Other*, contains 13 subtopics:

10 Overall

20 Cost Method Investments

30 Investments in Insurance Contracts

40 Beneficial Interests in Securitized Financial Assets

905 Agriculture*

940 Financial Services—Brokers and Dealers*

942 Financial Services—Depository and Lending*

944 Financial Services—Insurance*

954 Health Care Entities*

958 Not-For-Profit Entities*

960 Plan Accounting—Defined Benefit Pension Plans*

962 Plan Accounting—Defined Contribution Pension Plans*

965 Plan Accounting—Health and Welfare Benefit Plans*

* See the corresponding topic in Chapter 9 for coverage of this shared subtopic.

Accounting for Purchases of Life Insurance

ASC 325-30 addresses the issue of how an entity should account for a purchase of life insurance when the company is either the owner or beneficiary of the insurance contract. The life insurance contract should be accounted for as an investment and reported in the statement of financial position at the amount that could be realized from the contract on the balance sheet date. A change in contract value or cash surrender value of the insurance policy is an adjustment to the premiums paid when computing income or expense for the accounting period. A company holding life insurance on its employees may not recognize income from death benefits until the actual death of the insured.

Either the fair value method or the investment method may be used to account for investments in life settlement contracts. The fair value method initially reports the investment at an amount equal to the transaction price. The investment should be remeasured each accounting period and changes in fair value of the investment reported in earnings. The investment method reports the investment at the transaction price plus initial direct external costs. Continuing policy costs required to keep the policy in force should be capitalized. Any gain would be reported in earnings in the accounting period during which the insured dies equal to the difference between the proceeds of the policy and the carrying value of the policy. Policies reported using the fair value method should be reported separately from those using the investment method and investment income from fair value method policies and investment method policies should be reported separately. Cash inflows and outflows from the life settlement contracts are reported in the cash flow statement according to the nature and purpose of the life settlement contracts.

A liability for future benefits should be reported using the provisions of ASC 715-60 for endorsement split-dollar life insurance agreements if the agreement is an in-substance postretirement benefit plan. However, if the endorsement split-dollar life insurance agreement is an in-substance deferred compensation plan, the provisions of ASC 710 should be used for the appropriate accounting.

A liability for future benefits should be reported using the provisions of ASC 715-60 for collateral assignment split-dollar life insurance agreements if the agreement is an in-substance postretirement benefit plan. However, if the collateral assignment split-dollar life insurance agreement is an in-substance deferred compensation plan, the provisions of ASC 710 should be used for the appropriate accounting.

When an employer agrees to maintain a life insurance policy or provide an employee with death benefits using a substantive arrangement during the retirement of the employee, a liability for future benefits should be reported using the provisions of ASC 715-60 for collateral assignment split-dollar life insurance agreements if the agreement is an in-substance postretirement benefit plan. However, if the collateral assignment split-dollar life insurance agreement is an in-substance deferred compensation plan, the provisions of ASC 710 should be used for the appropriate accounting. In addition, the asset related to collateral assignment split-dollar life insurance agreements should be measured and reported using the nature and substance of the life insurance agreement.

Contractual amounts, in addition to the cash surrender value of the life insurance should be used when the policyholder determines the amount to realize under the life insurance arrangement. When amounts that a policyholder could recover from the insurance arrangement are subject to insurance company discretion, the amounts should not be included in the realizable amount. In addition, contract limitations should be considered when determining realizable amounts when it is probable, using the provisions of ASC 450, that contract terms limit the amounts that the policyholder could realize. Amounts that can be realized under the insurance arrangement should be determined using an individual life–by–individual life policy-surrender assumption. The cash surrender value element in the insurance policy should not be discounted using the provisions of ASC 835-30 when participation in changes in the cash surrender value does not change as a result of the request to surrender the policy.

Topic 326 Financial Instruments—Credit Losses

This Topic applies to all entities and most financial assets that are not measured at fair value through net income. This Topic requires a financial asset measured at amortized cost basis be presented at the net amount expected to be collected. The allowance for credit losses is a valuation account that is deducted from the amortized cost basis of the financial asset to present the net carrying value at the amount expected to be collected on the financial asset. The allowance should reflect management's current estimate of credit losses that are expected to occur over the remaining life of a financial asset. This approach is in contrast with previous guidance whereby credit losses were not recognized until they occurred.

Recent Changes

ASU 2016-13, *Financial Instruments—Credit Losses (Topic 326): Measurement of Credit Losses on Financial Instruments,* was issued in June 2016. The amendments in this Update require a financial asset measured at amortized cost basis should be presented at the net amount expected to be collected through an allowance for credit losses that is deducted from the amortized cost basis. These changes will not come into effect until fiscal years beginning after December 15, 2019 (i.e., 2020 for most companies), these changes are not reflected in this edition of the *GAAP Guide* but will be reflected in subsequent annual editions.

Topic 330: Inventory

Topic 330, *Inventory*, contains 11 subtopics:

10 Overall

905 Agriculture*

908 Airlines*

910 Contractors—Construction*

912 Contractors—Federal Government*

926 Entertainment—Films*

930 Extractive Activities—Mining*

932 Extractive Activities—Oil and Gas*

976 Real Estate—Retail Land*

978 Real Estate—Time-Sharing Activities*

985 Software*

* See the corresponding topic in Chapter 9 for coverage of this shared subtopic.

Inventory: General

Inventory is reported in the current asset section of the balance sheet and consists of the following three items: (1) items held for sale (finished goods), (2) items in process that will be held for sale (goods in process), and (3) items that will be used in the production process (raw materials). Inventory is initially recorded at cost with the cost of the inventory equal to all amounts incurred to get the product to its appropriate condition and location for sale. However, some items that constitute cost of inventory require additional discussion. Production costs should be allocated to inventory cost. Variable production cost is allocated to inventory based on production facility actual use and fixed production cost is allocated using normal capacity of the production facility. Normal capacity is the production that an entity anticipates achieving over a number of periods under normal conditions taking into consideration factors such as planned maintenance that would cause loss of capacity. Ranges in capacity will occur from period to period, which will establish the normal capacity range. Production levels may be abnormally low or abnormally high depending on events that occur during the period under consideration. Examples that cause abnormally low production levels include items such as unanticipated downtime of plant and equipment, labor shortage, material shortage, and reduction in demand for product. If actual production approximates normal capacity, the actual production may be used for the allocation of fixed overhead. If production levels are abnormally low or the entity has an idle plant, the amount of fixed overhead allocated to each unit should not be increased. However, if production is abnormally high, the entity should decrease the amount of fixed overhead allocated to each unit of production to prevent measurement of inventory above its cost. Some inventory related costs are not allocated to inventory, but are expensed in the accounting period incurred. Examples include unallocated overheads, abnormal freight, abnormal handling costs, and spoilage (wasted materials). In addition, general and administrative costs generally are expensed in the accounting period incurred unless the cost directly relates to the production of the inventory and selling costs are not included as part of the inventory cost. When using the completed contract inventory method, general and administrative costs may be accounted for as contract costs (ASC 330-10-30, paragraphs 1 through 8).

Accounting Approaches

An entity may use either a perpetual or a periodic approach when accounting for inventory and cost of sales. When using a perpetual system, an inventory account is increased for the purchase of merchandise, and reduced for the cost of the sale when merchandise is sold. There is no purchases account, and cost of items sold is recorded in a cost of goods sold account.

Under a periodic system, purchase of merchandise is recorded in a purchases account, and there is no entry to record the cost of merchandise sold. Ending inventory is reported in the balance sheet each accounting period at the lower of cost or market. Cost of inventory is determined using an acceptable cost flow method, such as first-in-first-out (FIFO) or last-in-first-out (LIFO), and market value is the current cost to replace the inventory item. Market cannot exceed an upper limit and cannot be less than a lower limit. The upper limit is equal to net realizable value, or the selling price of the inventory less the cost to complete and dispose of the item. The lower limit is net realizable value less a normal profit.

Cost Flow Assumptions

When costing ending inventory, several cost flow methods are available including first-in, first-out (referred to as "FIFO"), last-in, first-out (referred to as "LIFO"), weighted average method, and specific identification. Other, more complex methods used to determine ending inventory relate to a specific industry or represent a method to estimate inventory and include: the dollar value LIFO method, the retail method, the LIFO retail method, the dollar value retail method, and the gross profit method.

Computations under Each Cost Flow Assumption

Using the FIFO method, cost of goods sold is computed using the cost related to the earlier purchases and ending inventory is calculated using the later costs.

The LIFO method uses the later costs when computing cost of goods sold and the early costs for costing ending inventory.

Under the weighted average method, one average cost amount is computed for use in calculating both ending inventory and cost of sales. The specific identification method identifies the specific item sold or the specific item included in ending inventory, and the cost of that specific item is charged to cost of sales or used in the computation of ending inventory.

Dollar value LIFO is a method of computing ending inventory using pools of products and price indexes instead of individual products and unit prices. A single pool of products under dollar value LIFO would consist of all related products. For example, a manufacturer might have only one pool for its entire inventory consisting of raw materials, work in process, and finished goods, assuming that the manufacturer either has only one product line or that all of its product lines are related (i.e., all inventory for a "natural business unit"). However, if a manufacturer has two unrelated product lines (two natural business units), two inventory pools generally are required under dollar value LIFO accounting. Some industries, such as the retail industry, may have multiple pools of products, because a pool of products is determined using classes or types of products or major lines, as opposed to using the natural business unit concept in the pooling decision. Under dollar value LIFO, a base inventory and a base price are computed using the beginning inventory at the time of a change to LIFO. At the end of each accounting period, ending inventory is computed using a method such as FIFO. A price index is computed by dividing ending inventory computed using current prices by ending inventory computed using base prices. A layer of inventory is computed for the current year by comparing ending inventory in base year dollars with base year ending inventory. The price index is then applied to the layer of inventory to compute the layer in terms of current dollars. The layer of inventory in current dollars is added to the base inventory to compute ending inventory in terms of dollar value LIFO. This process is repeated at the end of each accounting period, and additional layers of inventory are added or deducted as required.

The retail method of inventory computation is a method for estimating inventory in retail stores. Using this method, beginning inventory, purchases, and merchandise available for sale are computed at both cost and retail. An average markup percentage is computed by dividing the merchandise available at cost by the merchandise available at retail. Ending inventory at retail is computed by deducting sales at retail from the merchandise available at retail. The average percentage computed above is applied to the ending inventory at retail to compute ending inventory at cost.

The LIFO retail method incorporates the procedures in the retail method with the concepts from LIFO to calculate inventory. The dollar value LIFO retail method uses concepts from both the retail method and the dollar value LIFO method, as discussed above, to compute ending inventory.

The gross profit method is another method used to estimate the cost of inventory. Under the gross profit method, purchases at cost are added to beginning inventory at cost to compute goods available for sale. Sales are decreased to a cost basis by applying a gross profit percentage to sales to determine the amount of profit included in total sales. Total sales less the estimated gross profit produces sales on a cost basis. Goods available for sale less sales on a cost basis equals an estimate of ending inventory. The gross profit percentage applied to sales to reduce sales to a cost basis is computed by dividing the profit or markup on inventory items by the selling price.

Two examples are used to illustrate accounting for inventory. Assumptions for Example 3-12 are as follows.

Example 3-12
Assumptions for Inventory

1. James, Inc., a December 31 year-end company, had the following transactions for 20X6:
   a. The purchase of merchandise on credit for $10,000.
   b. The sale for $12,000 of merchandise with a cost basis of $6,000.

c. The return of merchandise that sold for $6,000 and had a cost basis of $3,000.

d. January 1, 20X6 inventory of $12,000 and December 31, 20X6 inventory of $19,000.

e. The cost of sales for 20X6 of $3,000.

2. There was no theft, loss, or shrinkage of inventory during 20X6.

When a perpetual inventory system is used to account for inventory, the purchase of merchandise is recorded directly into an inventory account; when the merchandise is sold, the sale is reported at an amount equal to the selling price and cost of goods sold is recorded for the cost of the merchandise sold. When merchandise is returned to the company, sales are indirectly reduced for the selling price of the goods and the cost of the returned merchandise is included in inventory. At the end of the accounting period, cost of goods sold is closed to income summary, and income summary is closed to retained earnings.

When a periodic inventory system is used, the purchase of merchandise is recorded in a purchases account. When the merchandise is sold, a sale is recorded for the selling price of the merchandise, but there is no entry to record cost of sales at the time of the sale. When merchandise is returned to the company, sales are reduced for the selling price of the returned merchandise, but no entry is made for the cost of the returns. At the end of the accounting period, purchases and beginning inventory are closed to income summary. Ending inventory is recorded by debiting inventory and crediting income summary. The balance in income summary is closed to retained earnings. Using the preceding discussion for the perpetual and periodic methods and the assumptions in Example 3-12, journal entries for 20X6 can be prepared to illustrate each method.

Perpetual Method

Purchase of Merchandise on Credit for $10,000		
Inventory	10,000	
Accounts Payable		10,000
Sale of Merchandise for $12,000 with a cost of $6,000		
Accounts Receivable	12,000	
Cost of Sales	6,000	
Sales		12,000
Inventory		6,000
Returned Merchandise with a Cost of $3,000 that Sold for $6,000		
Sales Returns and Allowances	6,000	
Inventory	3,000	
Accounts Receivable		6,000
Cost of Goods Sold		3,000
Closing Entry for Cost of Sales of $3,000		
Income Summary	3,000	
Cost of Goods Sold		3,000

Retained Earnings	3,000	
Income Summary		3,000

Periodic Method

Purchase of Merchandise on Credit for $10,000

Purchases	10,000	
Accounts Payable		10,000

Sale of Merchandise for $12,000 with a Cost of $6,000

Accounts Receivable	12,000	
Sales		12,000

Returned Merchandise with a Cost of $3,000 that Sold for $6,000

Sales Returns and Allowances	6,000	
Accounts Receivable		6,000

To Close Out Beginning Inventory

Income Summary	12,000	
Inventory		12,000

To Set Up Ending Inventory

Inventory	19,000	
Income Summary		19,000

To Close Purchases

Income Summary	10,000	
Purchases		10,000

To Close Income Summary to Retained Earnings

Retained Earnings	3,000	
Income Summary		3,000

Sales returns and allowances is a contra sales account and is reported as a deduction from sales. Compare the related journal entries for both inventory systems to note the difference for each entry. This completes the discussion of Example 3-12.

Illustrations of Cost Flow Methods

Example 3-13 illustrates different cost flow methods for costing ending inventory. Assumptions for Example 3-13 are as follows.

Example 3-13
Assumptions for Inventory

1. The Ryan Company, a December 31 year-end entity, is computing ending inventory at December 31, 20X6.

2. The Company had the following purchases and sales during 20X6:

Date	Number of Items Purchased	Per Unit Cost	Total Cost	Items Sold
Beginning Balance	50,000	$10	$500,000	
1/15/X6	10,000	12	120,000	
2/20/X6				12,000
3/25/X6				15,000
4/18/X6	30,000	15	450,000	

Date	Number of Items Purchased	Per Unit Cost	Total Cost	Items Sold
5/25/X6				40,000
6/29/X6	20,000	16	320,000	
7/10/X6	15,000	18	270,000	
8/22/X6				20,000
9/12/X6				33,000
10/3/X6	30,000	20	600,000	
11/9/X6	10,000	23	230,000	
12/6/X6	15,000	26	390,000	
Totals	180,000		$2,880,000	120,000

3. The ending inventory is 60,000 units (180,000 – 120,000).
4. Average cost per unit is $16 ($2,880,000 ÷ 180,000).

Assume that Ryan Company uses the FIFO inventory method with, first, a perpetual inventory system and, second, a periodic inventory system. Using the assumptions from Example 3-13, ending inventory is computed in Table 3-13-A.

Table 3-13-A Computation of Ending Inventory Using FIFO with Perpetual and Periodic Systems

Perpetual			*Periodic*		
(a) Number of Units	(b) Cost Per Unit	(c)=(a)×(b) Total	(a) Number of Units	(b) Cost Per Unit	(c)=(a)×(b) Total
15,000	$26	$390,000	15,000	$26	$390,000
10,000	23	230,000	10,000	23	230,000
30,000	20	600,000	30,000	20	600,000
5,000	18	90,000	5,000	18	90,000
60,000		$1,310,000	60,000		$1,310,000

Notice that when the FIFO costing method is used, costs of the first purchases are charged to cost of goods sold and the last costs are used to determine the cost basis of the inventory. When using the periodic system, the assumption is made that all sales are taken out after all purchases for the accounting period are made, but, when using the perpetual system, sales are taken from purchases as the sale is made. For example in this situation, using the periodic system, it is assumed that all 180,000 units are purchased before a sale is made. If the perpetual system is used, it is assumed that 10,000 units are purchased on 1/15/X6 and then sales from 2/20/X6 and 3/25/X6 are taken from the existing inventory balance. Unlike the LIFO and average methods, both the perpetual and periodic systems always provides the same ending inventory of $1,310,000 using FIFO.

Using the information from Table 3-13-A and Example 3-13, Assumption 2, cost of goods sold for Ryan for 20X6 is computed for both the perpetual and periodic systems as follows:

Cost of Goods Available for Sale (Assumption 2)	$2,880,000
Ending Inventory (Table 3-13-A)	1,310,000
Cost of Goods Sold	$1,570,000

This completes the discussion of the FIFO method of accounting for inventory.

Now, assume that Ryan uses the LIFO method of inventory accounting. Using the information from Example 3-13, ending inventory using LIFO for both the perpetual and periodic systems is presented in Table 3-13-B.

Table 3-13-B Computation of Ending Inventory Using LIFO with Perpetual and Periodic Systems

Perpetual Units		Perpetual Unit Price		Perpetual Total	Periodic Units		Periodic Unit Price		Periodic Total
50,000	×	$10	=	$500,000	50,000	×	$10	=	$500,000
10,000	×	12	=	120,000	10,000	×	12	=	120,000
60,000				$620,000	60,000				$620,000
(10,000)	×	12	=	(120,000)					
(2,000)	×	10	=	(20,000))					
(15,000)	×	10	=	(150,000)					
33,000	×	10	=	$330,000					
30,000	×	15	=	450,000					
63,000				$780,000					
(30,000)	×	15	=	(450,000)					
(10,000)	×	10	=	(100,000)					
23,000	×	10	=	$230,000					
20,000	×	16	=	320,000					
15,000	×	18	=	270,000					
58,000				$820,000					
(15,000)	×	18	=	(270,000)					
(5,000)	×	16	=	(80,000)					
(15,000)	×	16	=	(240,000)					
(18,000)	×	10	=	(180,000)					
5,000	×	10		$50,000					
30,000	×	20		600,000					
10,000	×	23		230,000					
15,000	×	26		390,000					
60,000				$1,270,000					

As presented in Table 3-13-B, the cost of ending inventory of $620,000 determined using the periodic system is significantly less than the $1,270,000 cost determined using the perpetual system. Note the difference in computations. Under the periodic system, because it is assumed that all purchases are made before any sales are reported, the ending inventory of 60,000 units is costed using the $10 unit price for the 50,000 units in beginning inventory and the $12 unit cost from the first purchase. The perpetual system provides a different cost because a unit sold is assumed to come from the most recent cost of purchases at the time that the sale is made.

Cost of goods sold for both systems is computed below using information from Assumption 2 and Table 3-13-B.

	Perpetual	Periodic
Cost of Goods Available for Sale (Assumption 2)	$2,880,000	$2,880,000
Ending Inventory (Table 3-13-B)	1,270,000	620,000
Cost of Goods Sold	$1,610,000	$2,260,000

This completes the discussion of the LIFO method of inventory costing.

Next, the average cost method is used to illustrate costing of ending inventory. The average cost per unit of $16 is provided in Example 3-13, Assumption 4. Table 3-13-C, below shows the computation of ending inventory using the average cost method when both the periodic and perpetual systems are used.

Table 3-13-C Computation of Ending Inventory Using the Average Method with Perpetual and Periodic Systems

Units		Periodic Unit Price	Total
60,000	×	$16	$960,000

Units		Perpetual Unit Price		Total
50,000	×	$10.00000	=	$500,000
10,000	×	12.00000	=	120,000
60,000	×	10.33333	=	$620,000
(12,000)	×	10.33333	=	(124,000)
(15,000)	×	10.33333	=	(155,000)
33,000	×	10.33333	=	$341,000
30,000	×	15.00000	=	450,000

Units		Perpetual Unit Price		Total
63,000	×	12.55555	=	$791,000
(40,000)	×	12.55555	=	502,222
23,000	×	12.55555	=	$288,778
20,000	×	16.00000	=	320,000
15,000	×	18.00000	=	270,000
58,000	×	15.15134	=	$878,778
(20,000)	×	15.15134	=	(303,027)
(33,000)	×	15.15134	=	(499,994)
5,000	×	15.15134	=	$75,757
30,000	×	20.00000	=	600,000
10,000	×	23.00000	=	230,000
15,000	×	26.00000	=	390,000
60,000	×	21.59595	=	$1,295,757

[a] In some cases numbers were rounded when making computations.

When the periodic system is used with the average cost method, ending inventory is computed by applying the average cost of $16 (computed using beginning inventory and all purchases for the accounting period) to the ending inventory balance of 60,000 units. The $16 average cost is computed by dividing total merchandise cost of $2,880,000 by the total units for the year of 180,000. Calculation of ending inventory using the perpetual system is more complex because a moving average unit price must be used in the computation. After each purchase of merchandise, a new average unit price is computed and then used for all future sales until another purchase is made. Notice that average unit prices used to determine the cost of sales ranges from a low of $10.33333 to a high of $21.59595.

With the information from Table 3-13-C and Assumption 2, Example 3-13, cost of goods sold is computed below for both the perpetual and periodic systems.

	Perpetual	Periodic
Cost of Goods Available for Sale (Assumption 2)	$2,880,000	$2,880,000
Ending Inventory (Table 3-13-C)	1,295,757	960,000
Cost of Goods Sold	$1,584,243	$1,920,000

Subsequent Measurement of Inventory: Adjustments to Lower of Cost or Market

The cost basis of recording inventory ordinarily achieves the objective of a proper matching of costs and revenues when the inventory is sold. However, whenever the cost of goods is impaired because of damage, deterioration, obsolescence, changes in price levels, or other causes, the cost of the inventory may not be the proper amount to recognize as the cost of goods sold at the time that the inventory is sold. A loss of utility (i.e., a decrease in value) shall be reflected as a charge against the revenues of the period in which the loss of utility occurs.

The subsequent measurement of inventory depends on the cost method that is being used and is different for the following categories of inventory:

1. Inventory measured using any method other than LIFO or the retail inventory method, and
2. Inventory measured using LIFO or the retail inventory method.

Inventory Measured Using Any Method Other Than LIFO or the Retail Inventory Method

Inventory measured using any method other than LIFO or the retail inventory method (e.g., inventory measured using FIFO or average cost) shall be measured at the lower of cost and net realizable value. Net realizable value is the estimated selling prices in the ordinary course of business less predictable costs of completion, disposal, and transportation. When evidence exists that the net realizable value of inventory is lower than its cost, the difference shall be recognized as a loss in earnings in the period in which it occurs.

Inventory Measured Using LIFO or the Retail Inventory Method

A departure from the cost basis of pricing the inventory measured using LIFO or the retail inventory method is required when the utility of the goods is no longer as great as their cost. Where there is evidence that the utility of goods, in their disposal in the ordinary course of business, will be less than cost, the difference shall be recognized as a loss of the current period. This is generally accomplished by stating such goods at a lower level commonly designated as market. The term *market* is therefore to be interpreted as indicating utility on the inventory date and may be thought of in terms of the equivalent expenditure, which would have to be made in the ordinary course at that date to procure corresponding utility. Therefore, the measurement of losses for inventory measured using LIFO or the retail inventory method shall be accomplished by applying the rule of pricing inventories at the lower of cost or market. This provides a practical means of measuring utility and thereby determining the amount of the loss to be recognized and accounted for in the current period.

As a general guide, utility is indicated primarily by the current cost of replacement of the goods as they would be obtained by purchase or reproduction. In applying the rule, however, judgment must always be exercised and no loss shall be recognized unless the evidence indicates clearly that a loss has been sustained. There are therefore exceptions to such a standard. Replacement or reproduction prices would not be appropriate as a measure of utility when the estimated sales value, reduced by the costs of completion and disposal, is lower, in which case the realizable value so determined more appropriately measures utility.

Furthermore, when the evidence indicates that cost will be recovered with an approximately normal profit upon sale in the ordinary course of business, no loss shall be recognized even though replacement or reproduction costs are lower. This might be true, for example, in the case of production under firm sales contracts at fixed prices or when a reasonable volume of future orders is assured at stable selling prices.

Because of the many variations of circumstances encountered in inventory pricing, the definition of market is intended as a guide rather than a literal rule. It shall be applied realistically in light of the objectives expressed in this subtopic and with due regard to the form, content, and composition of the inventory. For example, the retail inventory method, if adequate markdowns are currently taken, accomplishes the objectives described herein. It is also recognized that, if a business is expected to lose money for a sustained period, the inventory shall not be written down to offset a loss inherent in the subsequent operations.

Subsequent Measurement Guidance Applicable to All Inventory

If inventory has been the hedged item in a fair value hedge, the inventory's cost basis for purposes of subsequent measurement shall reflect the effect of the adjustments of its carrying amount made pursuant to Chapter 8.

Depending on the character and composition of the inventory, the guidance in paragraphs that is applicable to the inventory being measured may properly be applied either directly to each item or to the total of the inventory (or, in some cases, to the total of the components of each major category). The method shall be that which most clearly reflects periodic income.

The purpose of reducing the carrying amount of inventory is to reflect fairly the income of the period. The most common practice is to apply the applicable subsequent measurement guidance separately to each item of the inventory. However, if there is only one end-product category, the application of the applicable subsequent measurement guidance to inventory in its entirety may have the greatest significance for accounting purposes. Accordingly, the remeasurement of individual items may not always lead to the most useful result if the market value (for inventory measured using LIFO or the retail inventory method) or net realizable value (for all other inventory) of the total inventory is not below its cost. This might be the case for example, if selling prices are not affected by temporary or small fluctuations in current costs of purchase or manufacture.

Similarly, where more than one major product or operational category exists, the application of the applicable subsequent measurement guidance to the total of the items included in such major categories may result in the most useful determination of income. When no loss of income is expected to take place as a result of a reduction of cost prices of certain goods because others forming components of the same general categories of finished products have a market value (for inventory measured using LIFO or the retail inventory method) or net realizable value (for all other inventory) equally in excess of cost, such components need not be adjusted to the extent that they are in balanced quantities. Thus, in such cases, the guidance on subsequent measurement may be applied directly to the totals of the entire inventory, rather than to the individual inventory items, if they enter into the same category of finished product and if they are in balanced quantities, provided the procedure is applied consistently from year to year.

To the extent, however, that the stocks of particular materials or components are excessive in relation to others, the more widely recognized procedure of applying the guidance on subsequent measurement to the individual items constituting the excess shall be followed. This would also apply in cases in which the items enter into the production of unrelated products or products having a material variation in the rate of turnover. Unless an effective method of classifying categories is practicable, the rule shall be applied to each item in the inventory.

Recent Changes

ASU 2015-11, *Inventory (Topic 330): Simplifying the Measurement of Inventory,* an amendment of the FASB, is effective for public business entities. The amendments in this Update are effective for fiscal years beginning after December 15, 2016, including interim periods within those fiscal years. For all other entities, the amendments in this Update are effective for fiscal years beginning after December 15, 2016, and interim periods within fiscal years beginning after December 15, 2017. The amendments in this Update should be applied prospectively with earlier application permitted as of the beginning of an interim or annual reporting period.

Topic 340: Other Assets and Deferred Costs

Topic 340, *Other Assets and Deferred Costs,* contains the following subtopics:

10 Overall

20 Capitalized Advertising Costs

30 Insurance Contracts that Do Not Transfer Insurance Risk

910 Contractors—Construction*

928 Entertainment—Music*

940 Financial Services—Brokers and Dealers*

944 Financial Services—Insurance*

948 Financial Services—Mortgage Banking*

952 Franchisors*

954 Health Care Entities*

970 Real Estate—General*

978 Real Estate—Time-Sharing Activities*

980 Regulated Operations*

* See the corresponding topic in Chapter 9 for coverage of this shared subtopic.

This topic is not covered in this book.

Topic 350: Intangibles—Goodwill and Other

Topic 350, *Intangibles—Goodwill and Other*, contains 12 subtopics:

10 Overall

20 Goodwill

30 General Intangibles Other than Goodwill

40 Internal-Use Software

50 Website Development Costs

908 Airlines*

920 Entertainment—Broadcasters*

922 Entertainment—Cable Television*

932 Extractive Activities—Oil and Gas*

950 Financial Services—Title Plant*

980 Regulated Operations*

985 Software*

* See the corresponding topic in Chapter 9 for coverage of this shared subtopic.

Introduction

Intangibles may be purchased individually, purchased as part of a group, acquired as part of a business combination, or developed internally. ASC 350 specifies the accounting and reporting requirements at the date of acquisition for intangible assets acquired individually or as a group purchase, except for intangible assets acquired in a business combination. ASC 805 specifies the accounting and reporting requirements on the date of acquisition for intangibles and goodwill acquired in a business combination. ASC 350 specifies the accounting and reporting requirements for all goodwill and other intangibles subsequent to the date of acquisition, regardless of how acquired. Additionally, ASC 350 specifies the accounting and reporting requirements for internally developed intangibles. ASC 350 does not apply to intangible assets reported as part of insurance contracts acquired using the provisions of ASC 944, *Financial Services—Insurance.*

Acquired intangible assets are recorded at fair value and amortized over their useful lives if the assets are deemed to have a finite life. In addition, intangible assets with finite lives are tested for impairment. Intangible assets with indefinite lives are not amortized, but are tested for impairment. Goodwill acquired in a business combination is not amortized but is allocated to reporting units and tested for impairment.

Intangible Assets Acquired Individually or in a Group

An intangible asset acquired individually, such as the purchase of a patent, Internet domain name or customer lists, or within a group of assets should be reported as an asset at fair value (ASC 350-30-30). The fair value of an intangible asset is the amount that would be determined if the entity used the assumptions that market participants would use if they were pricing the intangible asset. The intangible asset should be measured at fair value even if the entity does not expect to use it or expects to use it in a manner that is not considered its highest and best use. When an intangible asset is purchased as part of a group of assets (acquisition of an intangible asset in a business combination is excluded), the fair value of the intangible asset is determined by allocating the acquisition price to all the assets acquired based on the relative fair values of all the assets purchased. No goodwill is to be recognized in such a group acquisition.

Useful Life of an Intangible Asset

An intangible asset acquired individually or in a group purchase may have a finite or indefinite useful life. An intangible asset with a finite life should be amortized over its estimated useful life and an intangible with an indefinite life should not be amortized, but tested for impairment when appropriate. The useful life of an intangible asset is determined by using the time period that an intangible is estimated to contribute directly or indirectly to an enterprise's future cash flows. Factors that should be considered when determining the useful life of an intangible asset are (ASC 350-30-35-3) expected asset use, useful life of related assets, contract, regulatory or legal aspects that limit useful life, the entity's past experience in renewing or extending similar arrangements (or, in the absence of such experience, the assumptions that market participants would use about renewal or extension consistent with the highest and best use of the asset), impact of obsolescence, competition, demand and other economic and political factors, and relationship between level of expenditures for maintenance and future cash flows. The useful life of a reacquired right classified as an intangible asset is the remaining contract time period, and if the entity sells the right, the gain or loss on the sale should be determined using the unamortized asset. Once the useful life has been determined, the amount recorded for the intangible less any residual value is amortized over its useful life using the method that would best reflect the pattern of use of the asset. For example, if the asset is used up faster in early years and is used up less in later years, some form of an accelerated amortization method should be used. However, if the asset is used up equally each accounting period, the straight-line method is appropriate. If it is not reasonable to determine the pattern of use, the straight-line method should be used. The intangible should not be written off in the year of acquisition unless an impairment test indicates such write off is appropriate. However, ASC 730-10 specifies that an acquired intangible asset (not acquired in a business combination) should be expensed in the period of acquisition if it is used for a specific research and development activity and does not have an alternative future use.

An entity should review the estimated useful life of an intangible each accounting period. If a change in useful life is indicated, the change should be treated as a change in accounting estimate and accounted for in a prospective manner by amortizing the remaining carrying amount over the new revised estimated useful life (ASC 350-30-35-9). The residual value to use in the amortization process is the asset's fair value at the end of its useful life less any disposition cost. The residual value is assumed to be zero unless the asset is expected to have a useful life to another enterprise at the end of the useful life of the current reporting entity and a third party has committed to purchase the intangible at the end of its useful life or a residual value can be determined by reviewing existing market transactions for the asset and that market is anticipated to exist at the end of the asset's life (ASC 350-30-35-8).

When an intangible asset that is assumed to have a finite life and is subject to amortization is deemed by an entity to now have an indefinite life, amortization should cease and the asset should be tested for impairment. Future accounting for the intangible would be the same as the accounting for an intangible not subject to amortization. In addition to amortization each accounting period, an entity should test the intangible asset for impairment.

Testing an Intangible Asset for Impairment

An intangible asset that is not subject to amortization (i.e., an indefinite-lived intangible asset) shall be tested for impairment annually and more frequently if events or changes in circumstances indicate that it is more likely than not that the asset is impaired.

Qualitative Assessment An entity may first perform a qualitative assessment to determine whether it is necessary to perform the quantitative impairment test described below. An entity has an unconditional option to bypass the qualitative assessment for any indefinite-lived intangible asset in any period and proceed directly to performing the quantitative impairment test. An entity may resume performing the qualitative assessment in any subsequent period. If an entity elects to perform a qualitative assessment, it first shall assess qualitative factors to determine whether it is more likely than not that an indefinite-lived intangible asset is impaired.

In assessing whether it is more likely than not that an indefinite-lived intangible asset is impaired, an entity shall assess all relevant events and circumstances that could affect the significant inputs used to determine the fair value of the indefinite-lived intangible asset. Examples of such events and circumstances include the following (this list is not meant to be all-inclusive):

a. Cost factors such as increases in raw materials, labor, or other costs that have a negative effect on future expected earnings and cash flows that could affect significant inputs used to determine the fair value of the indefinite-lived intangible asset;

b. Financial performance such as negative or declining cash flows or a decline in actual or planned revenue or earnings compared with actual and projected results of relevant prior periods that could affect significant inputs used to determine the fair value of the indefinite-lived intangible asset;

c. Legal, regulatory, contractual, political, business, or other factors, including asset-specific factors, that could affect significant inputs used to determine the fair value of the indefinite-lived intangible asset;

d. Other relevant entity-specific events such as changes in management, key personnel, strategy, or customers; contemplation of bankruptcy; or litigation that could affect significant inputs used to determine the fair value of the indefinite-lived intangible asset;

e. Industry and market considerations such as a deterioration in the environment the entity operates in; an increased competitive environment; a decline in market-dependent multiples or metrics (in both absolute terms and relative to peers); or a change in the market for the entity's products or services due to the effects of obsolescence, demand, competition, or other economic factors (such as the stability of the industry, known technological advances, legislative action that results in an uncertain or changing business environment, and expected changes in distribution channels) that could affect significant inputs used to determine the fair value of the indefinite-lived intangible asset; and

f. Macroeconomic conditions such as deterioration in general economic conditions, limitations on accessing capital, fluctuations in foreign exchange rates, or other developments in equity and credit markets that could affect significant inputs used to determine the fair value of the indefinite-lived intangible asset.

In addition, an entity shall consider other relevant events and circumstances that could affect the significant inputs used to determine the fair value of the indefinite-lived intangible asset. An entity shall consider the extent to which each of the adverse events and circumstances identified could affect the significant inputs used to determine the fair value of an indefinite-lived intangible asset. An entity shall also consider the following to determine whether it is more likely than not that the indefinite-lived intangible asset is impaired:

a. Positive and mitigating events and circumstances that could affect the significant inputs used to determine the fair value of the indefinite-lived intangible asset;

b. If an entity has made a recent fair value calculation for an indefinite-lived intangible asset, the difference between that fair value and the then carrying amount; and

c. Whether there have been any changes to the carrying amount of the indefinite-lived intangible asset.

An entity shall evaluate, on the basis of the weight of the evidence, the significance of all identified events and circumstances that could affect the significant inputs used to determine the fair value of the indefinite-lived intangible asset for determining whether it is more likely than not that the indefinite-lived intangible asset is impaired. None of the individual examples of events and circumstances described above is intended to represent standalone events and circumstances that necessarily require an entity to calculate the fair value of an intangible asset. Also, the existence of positive and mitigating events and circumstances is not intended to represent a rebuttable presumption that an entity should not perform the quantitative impairment test described below.

If after assessing the totality of events and circumstances and their potential effect on significant inputs to the fair value determination an entity determines that it is not more likely than not that the indefinite-lived intangible asset is impaired, then the entity is not required to calculate the fair value of the intangible asset and perform the quantitative impairment test.

If after assessing the totality of events and circumstances and their potential effect on significant inputs to the fair value determination an entity determines that it is more likely than not that the indefinite-lived intangible asset is impaired, then the entity shall calculate the fair value of the intangible asset and perform the quantitative impairment test described below.

Quantitative impairment test. The quantitative impairment test for an indefinite-lived intangible asset shall consist of a comparison of the fair value of the asset with its carrying amount. If the carrying amount of an intangible asset exceeds its fair value, an entity shall recognize an impairment loss in an amount equal to that excess. After an impairment loss is recognized, the adjusted carrying amount of the intangible asset shall be its new accounting basis.

Internally Generated Intangibles

In addition to purchasing intangible assets, a company may incur costs to develop, restore, or maintain an intangible asset. Some of these types of costs may, in fact, be research and development costs and subject to the provisions of ASC 730-10, *Research and Development*. All costs referred to in the subsequent discussion are costs other than those of research and development.

For the costs incurred in connection with internally generated intangible assets to be capitalized, they first must meet three specific conditions. First, the costs must be related to an intangible asset that can be specifically identified, such as legal fees in connection with obtaining a patent. Second, the identifiable asset must have a determinable life. Third, the intangible must not be one that is inherent in a going concern and related to the enterprise as a whole. Internally created goodwill would fail to meet all three of these conditions because it is not specifically identifiable, it lacks a determinable life, and it is inherent to a going concern. Therefore, the costs associated with the creation of goodwill may not be capitalized as an asset. However, it is acceptable to assume that internally generated goodwill replaces goodwill acquired in a business combination if the company maintains the overall value of goodwill.

An example of costs that would meet all three of the conditions specified above would be the costs incurred to defend a patent held by the company. These costs would be identifiable with the patent, have a determinable life and not be related to the enterprise as a whole. These costs were incurred to restore or maintain the patent. The costs to defend a patent should be capitalized and amortized over the remaining finite useful life of the patent to the reporting entity based on how the expected benefits are used or consumed. The intangible asset should be reviewed for impairment.

Accounting for Goodwill

Goodwill is defined in ASC 350-10-20 as an asset acquired in a business combination representing the future economic benefit of acquired assets that could not be separately recognized and identified individually.

Goodwill is generally not amortized but is tested at least annually for impairment at a level of reporting referred to as a reporting unit. However, for private companies, a 2014 ASU allows an accounting alternative for the subsequent measurement of goodwill to allow the amortization of goodwill on a straight-line basis over a maximum of 10 years. A period shorter than 10 years may be elected if the entity can demonstrate that a shorter useful life is more appropriate. An entity that elects this alternative must make an accounting policy election to test goodwill for impairment at either the entity or the reporting unit level. This alternative still requires the private company entity or reporting unit to test goodwill for impairment whenever a triggering event occurs. As described below, an entity may first use a qualitative option to determine whether there are qualitative factors make it more likely than not that goodwill is impaired.

Testing Goodwill for Impairment

Goodwill is assigned to a reporting unit using the provisions of ASC 805-20. Goodwill is impaired when the carrying amount of a reporting unit that includes goodwill exceeds its fair value. An entity may first use a qualitative assessment to determine whether it is more likely or not that goodwill impairment exists by evaluating factors such as macroeconomic conditions (e.g., deterioration of the economy, foreign exchange rate fluctuations, etc.), industry or market affecting the entity, cost factors impacting the entity, negative financial performance, and the loss of key personnel.

If it is concluded that goodwill is more likely than not impaired, goodwill must then be tested for impairment using a two-step reporting level basis.

Step 1: the carrying amount of the reporting unit to which the goodwill is assigned is compared with the fair value of the reporting unit, including goodwill. If the carrying value of the unit is less than its fair value, no impairment exists and Step 2 of the impairment test is not required. However, if fair value of the reporting unit is less than the carrying amount, the second step of the impairment test must be performed to determine the amount of the impairment loss.

Step 2: the carrying amount of the goodwill is compared to the implied fair value of the goodwill in the reporting unit. If the implied fair value of the goodwill is less than the related carrying amount, an impairment loss is reported for the difference but not in excess of the carrying amount of the goodwill. Goodwill impairment losses create a new accounting basis for the goodwill equal to the adjusted carrying amount, and reversal of prior impairment losses is not allowed once an entity completes the measurement loss. The implied fair value of goodwill is an estimate of the fair value because the fair value of goodwill cannot directly be determined. The implied fair value of goodwill is computed using the same procedures that would be used by an entity when initially computing goodwill in a business combination. The fair value of a reporting unit is assigned to all assets (include any unrecognized intangibles) and liabilities of the reporting unit using the same process as required in a business combination. Any excess of the fair value of the reporting unit over the fair value assigned to the assets and liabilities is the implied fair value of the goodwill of the reporting unit. The process described above is only for determining the implied fair value of goodwill and no changes in the assets and liabilities of the reporting should be made.

ASU 2017-04, *Intangibles—Goodwill and Other (Topic 350): Simplifying the Test for Goodwill Impairment,* allows entities in 2017 to early adopt a simplifying approach to testing goodwill impairment. Under the simplified approach, entities still compare the fair value of the reporting unit with its carrying amount. The impairment loss is simply computed as the difference by which the carrying amount exceeds the fair value of the reporting unit but may not exceed the total amount of goodwill allocated to the reporting unit. This approach is simpler because the entity will no longer be required to determine the implied fair value of goodwill using the same procedures that would be used by an entity when initially computing goodwill in a business combination, as explained in the preceding paragraph.

If an entity has one or more reporting units with zero or negative carrying amounts but it concluded that Step 1 was met because the fair value was greater than the carrying amount, Step 2 of the impairment test must still be performed to measure the amount of impairment loss, if any, when it is more likely than not that a goodwill impairment exists. (NOTE: ASU 2017-04 also eliminates the requirements for any reporting unit with a zero or negative carrying amount to perform this qualitative assessment. Thus, the same impairment test is used for all reporting units. The entity is required to disclose that amount of goodwill allocated to each reporting unit with a zero or negative carrying amount of net assets.)

If the financial statements of an entity are issued before the goodwill impairment test is completed, an estimated impairment loss is presented in the financial statements, if it is probable that a loss will be computed and the amount of the loss can be estimated using the provisions of ASC 450. The next accounting period should report any differences between the estimated impairment loss and the amount actually computed. (NOTE: By simplifying the previously complex calculations under Step 2, ASU 2017-04 eliminates the possibility of recording a preliminary estimated impairment in one period and then a final amount of impairment in a later period.)

The fair value of the reporting unit used in the determination of goodwill impairment is the amount that would be received from selling the unit on the measurement date between sellers and buyers (market participants) in an orderly transaction. In addition, on the measurement date, the sellers and buyers are unrelated parties. ASC 820 states that measuring the collection of asset and liabilities at fair value where an entity has sufficient interest to control the entity is different from determining fair value of individual securities. Therefore, the fair value of a controlled entity may exceed the market capitalization of the entity because there may be a premium for the control feature. Fair value may not have to be computed each accounting period but carried forward from one accounting period to the next. Fair value may be carried forward when the following conditions are met: no significant changes in reporting unit assets and liabilities occurred since the last fair value determination, fair value substantially exceeded carrying value in the last fair value determination, and it is remote that fair value of the reporting unit would be less than the unit's carrying value.

The reporting unit used in the impairment test is the operating segment (as defined in ASC 280) or a component of a business, which is one level below the operating segment. The operating segment is the reporting unit if all components are similar, none of the components in the segment are reporting units, and the segment has only one component. The component is the reporting unit when the following conditions are met: the component constitutes a business, discrete financial information is provided by the component, and management of the segment reviews the component's operating results.

To test for goodwill impairment, an entity must assign assets, liabilities, and goodwill to reporting units. Assets and liabilities are assigned to reporting units on the date of acquisition when the asset or liability relate to the reporting unit operations and they will be used in computing fair value of the unit. Corporate level assets and liabilities are assigned to the reporting unit if they meet the requirements specified above. The assets and liabilities assigned may be part of a business combination, purchased separately, or purchased as part of a group. Assets or liabilities related to more than one reporting unit may be assigned to the various reporting units using some method that is reasonable and is applied on a consistent basis. The method and basis of assignment and other relevant factors used in the assignment process should be documented at the date of acquisition.

Goodwill acquired in a business combination should be assigned to reporting units that will benefit from the goodwill on the acquisition date. The method used when assigning goodwill to one or more reporting units should be supportable, reasonable and applied on a consistent basis. Conceptually, goodwill is assigned to a reporting unit by determining the fair value of the acquired business included in the reporting unit (the fair value of the business acquired or part acquired). The fair value is then assigned to individual acquired assets and liabilities and if the fair value exceeds the amount assigned to the assets and liabilities, the excess is the amount of goodwill assigned to that reporting unit. Goodwill may be assigned to a reporting unit that did not receive an assignment of assets and liabilities from the business combination. In that situation, the amount of goodwill assigned is determined by comparing the fair value of the reporting unit before and after the acquisition. The difference is the amount of goodwill assigned to that reporting unit.

The reporting unit fair value and the goodwill implied fair value of a less than wholly owned reporting unit (one with a noncontrolling interest) should be determined the same way as the determination would be for a business combination covered by the provisions of ASC 805. When an impairment loss is computed using the second step of the impairment testing process, a rational basis should be used to assign the impairment loss to the parent and the noncontrolling interest, assuming the reporting unit having goodwill was assigned to both the parent and the noncontrolling interest. If the reporting unit allocates goodwill only to the parent, the impairment loss would be assigned only to the parent.

Any gain or loss from the disposal of a less than wholly owned reporting unit is assigned to both the parent and the noncontrolling interest.

An entity should test goodwill for impairment at least on an annual basis and during the annual accounting period if information warrants earlier testing. The annual testing may be performed anytime during the annual accounting period, but the testing must be performed the same time every year. In addition, impairment testing may be performed at different times during the accounting period for different reporting units. ASC 350-20-35-30 provides examples of situations that would indicate that goodwill should be tested for impairment between accounting periods, including when the carrying amount of the reporting unit is zero or negative. Also, goodwill should be tested for impairment if a part of goodwill has been allocated to a business disposition.

When goodwill and other assets of the same reporting unit are tested for impairment at the same time, a two-step process should be used for the impairment testing. First, the other assets should be tested for impairment and any impairment loss should be reported prior to testing for goodwill impairment. Second, goodwill should be tested for impairment using the provisions discussed above.

Goodwill computed using the equity method should not be amortized but tested for impairment using the provisions of ASC 323-10-35-32.

Other Considerations

Several issues related to goodwill accounting and reporting require additional discussion. When testing for goodwill impairment, the fair value of a reporting unit and the implied fair value of goodwill from a business combination with a noncontrolling interest (less than wholly owned) is determined using the same process as for a business combination in ASC 805. When applying the second step of the goodwill impairment test, a rational basis should be used to attribute any impairment loss to the parent and the noncontrolling interest. For example, if goodwill is related only to the parent, any goodwill impairment loss is attributed only to the parent. However, if goodwill is related to both the parent and the noncontrolling interest, the goodwill impairment loss should be attributed to both.

When an entity disposes of all or a part of a reporting unit, goodwill should be considered when computing the gain or loss on the disposition. For example, goodwill should be included in the carrying value of the reporting unit if the transaction is a disposition of the entire reporting unit. However, if the transaction is a disposition of only part of a reporting unit and the part disposed of is classified as a business, goodwill related to the business part is include in the carrying value of the business when computing the gain or loss on the disposition. The amount of goodwill to include is based on a relative fair value approach. The fair value of the business and the fair value of the remaining part of the reporting unit are used in the relative fair value approach to compute the amount of the goodwill allocation. For example, if goodwill is $1,000 and the fair value of the business and remaining part of the reporting unit are $100,000 and $400,000, respectively, the amount of goodwill allocated to the disposition is $200

($100,000 + $400,000 = $500,000. $100,000 ÷ $500,000 × $1,000 = $200). When the disposition relates to less than a wholly owned reporting unit, the gain or loss on the disposition should be distributed to both the noncontrolling interest and the parent.

Subsidiary goodwill (goodwill of a subsidiary that is reported in the subsidiary's separate financial statements) is tested for impairment at the subsidiary level using reporting units of the subsidiary. When an impairment loss is reported at the subsidiary level, the reporting unit at the consolidated level that includes the reporting unit at the subsidiary level with the impaired goodwill must test for goodwill impairment. Only if goodwill is impaired at the consolidated reporting unit level is the impairment loss reported in the consolidated financial statements.

If the reporting units of an entity are reorganized, the assets and liabilities of the reporting units should be reallocated using the same procedures as discussed above for the initial assignment to reporting units. However, goodwill is reallocated to the reporting units using a relative fair value method similar to that used when disposing of reporting units. To illustrate, assume that a company with three reporting units reorganizes its reporting units such that Reporting Unit 1 is integrated with Reporting Units 2 and 3. Goodwill from Reporting Unit 1 is allocated to Reporting Units 2 and 3 using the fair value of the two part of Reporting Unit 1 allocated to Reporting Units 2 and 3 before allocation occurs.

Technical Considerations

Four examples are used to illustrate the technical aspects of intangible assets and goodwill. Assumptions for Example 3-14 are as follows.

Example 3-14
Intangible Asset Assumptions

1. On January 1, 20X6, Technology Company (Technology), a December 31 year-end company, purchases Patent No. 1 for $50,000 cash. Patent No. 1 expires in 10 years and it is expected to produce cash flows for the next 10 years. At the end of the 10-year time period, the patent is expected to have a zero residual value. Benefit from the patent is expected to be received equally over the 10-year time period.
2. Patent No. 2 was purchased on January 1, 20X6 by Technology for $100,000 cash. Patent No. 2 expires in 10 years and is expected to produce cash flows for the next 10 years. However, Technology has a commitment from Johnson Enterprises (Johnson) to purchase the patent at the end of six years for $40,000 or 40% of the original $100,000 fair value, and Technology intends to sell the patent at the end of six years. Benefit from the patent is expected to be received equally over the six-year time period.
3. On July 1, 20X6, Technology purchased a trademark at a cash cost of $500,000. The remaining legal life of the trademark is eight years but the trademark can be renewed every 10 years with little cost to the company. All analysis indicates that this trademark will provide future cash flows to Technology indefinitely.

Patent No. 1 should be reported at the $50,000 fair value and amortized over its 10-year useful life using the straight-line method. The straight-line method is used because benefit from the patent is expected to be received equally over the life of the patent. Journal entries for acquisition of the patent on January 1 and amortization on December 31 are as follows:

Patent	50,000	
Cash		50,000
Amortization of Patent	5,000	
Patent		5,000
$50,000/10 years = $5,000.		

Patent No. 2 should be reported at the $100,000 fair value. Patent No. 2 should be amortized over the six-year useful life to Technology using the straight-line method. The amount to amortize is $60,000 ($100,000 – $40,000 residual value). The residual value used in the amortization process is the amount to be received at the end of the six-year time from Johnson. Journal entries for acquisition of the patent on January 1 and amortization on December 31 are as follows:

Patent	100,000	
Cash		100,000
Amortization of Patent	10,000	
Patent		10,000
$60,000/6 years = $10,000.		

Both Patent No. 1 and Patent No. 2 should be tested for impairment.

The trademark should be recorded at its fair value of $500,000 and should not be amortized, because it is assumed to have an indefinite life. It is assumed to have an indefinite life because the trademark is expected to produce future cash flows indefinitely for the firm. The trademark should be tested for impairment.

This completes the discussion of Example 3-14. Assumptions for Example 3-15 are as follows.

Example 3-15
Assumptions for Intangible Assets

1. The Peterson Company (Peterson), a December 31 calendar year-end company, issued 5,000 shares of its $10 par value stock for a patent with an estimated fair value of $140,000. The stock is currently selling for $30 per share. The estimated useful life of the patent is five years, which is the time period that the company expects to receive cash flows from the patent. Benefit from the patent is expected to be received equally over its remaining life.
2. Peterson acquired a trademark by exchanging a piece of equipment for the trademark. The equipment has a cost basis of $200,000 and $75,000 of accumulated depreciation has been recorded to the date of the transfer. The equipment has a fair market value of $160,000. All analysis indicates that this trademark will provide future cash flows to the company indefinitely.

The purchase of the patent by exchanging stock is recorded using the provisions of ASC 505-50, which states that the patent should be recorded at the fair value of the item received or given up, whichever is more clearly determinable. Because the stock has a current quoted market price and the value of the patent is only an estimated value, the $30 selling price of the stock or $150,000 ($30 × 5,000 shares) is used as the fair value to record for the patent received. The entry to record the patent is as follows:

Patent	150,000	
Common Stock		50,000
Contributed Capital in Excess of Par		100,000
$10 Par Value × 5,000 shares = $50,000		
$150,000 – $50,000 = $100,000		

The patent is amortized over its useful of five years using the straight-line method. The journal entry to record the amortization was shown above and will not be repeated again. In addition, the patent must be tested for impairment when appropriate.

Acquisition of the trademark by exchanging equipment is an exchange of nonmonetary assets and the provisions of ASC 845-10. Because this is not an exchange of inventory for inventory, or an exchange of similar productive assets, it can be assumed that the earnings process has culminated and any gain or loss resulting from the transaction may be recognized. The trademark received will be valued at the fair value ($160,000) of the equipment given up. The asset and related depreciation will be removed from the books and any gain or loss will be recognized. In this case, a gain of $35,000 will be recognized. The amount of the gain is determined by the difference between the fair value of the asset given up and the carrying value of that asset ($200,000 cost – $75,000 accumulated depreciation = $125,000 carrying value of the asset – $160,000 fair value = $35,000 gain). The entry required to reflect the exchange is shown below:

Trademark	160,000	
Accumulated Depreciation	75,000	
Equipment		200,000
Gain on Asset Transfer		35,000

The Gain on Asset Transfer is reported in the income statement in other income and expense. Because the trademark has an indefinite life, no amortization of the trademark is required. However, the trademark must be tested for impairment. This completes the discussion of Example 3-15. Assumptions for Example 3-16 are as follows.

Example 3-16
Assumptions for Intangible Assets Purchased as a Group

1. Technology, Inc. (Technology), a December 31 calendar year-end company, acquired a group of assets on January 1, 20X6 at a cost of $1,400,000.
2. Fair value of the assets acquired are as follows:

Total Tangible Assets	$950,000
Intangible Assets:	
Patent	25,000
Trademark	400,000
Total Tangible and Intangible Assets	$1,375,000

The $1,400,000 purchase price is allocated to the assets using a relative fair value approach. The computation is presented below:

Total Tangible Assets ($950,000/$1,375,000 × $1,400,000)	=	$ 967,273
Patent ($25,000/$1,375,000 × $1,400,000)	=	5,455
Trademark ($400,000/$1,375,000 × $1,400,000)	=	407,272
Total		$1,400,000

No goodwill can be reported in a group purchase of assets that is not a business combination. The entry to record the purchase of the assets is as follows.

Tangible Assets	967,273	
Patent	25,455	
Trademark	407,272	
Cash		1,400,000

This completes the discussion of Example 3-16. Assumptions for Example 3-17 are as follows:

Example 3-17
Assumptions for Goodwill

1. Ace Enterprises, a December 31 calendar year-end company, computed $1,000,000 of goodwill in a business combination on January 1, 20X6. The $1,000,000 was allocated to Reporting Units 1 and 2.
2. At December 31, 20X7 fair value of Reporting Units 1 and 2 was $20,000,000 and $18,000,000, respectively. The carrying value of goodwill for Reporting Units 1 and 2 was $600,000 and $400,000, respectively.
3. The carrying value of Reporting Units 1 and 2, including goodwill, at December 31, 20X7 was $16,000,000 and $19,500,000, respectively.
4. The implied fair value of goodwill for Reporting Unit 1 and 2 is $700,000 and $375,000, respectively.

The first step in determining goodwill impairment is to compare the fair value of the reporting unit with its carrying value. If the fair value of the reporting unit exceeds the carrying value, there is no goodwill impairment and no further testing is required. The $20,000,000 fair value of Reporting Unit No. 1 exceeds the $16,000,000 carrying value and, therefore, goodwill is not impaired and no further testing is required. The $18,000,000 fair value for Reporting Unit 2 is less than the $19,500,000 carrying value and goodwill must be tested further for possible impairment. The second step is to compare the $375,000 implied fair value of goodwill with the $400,000 carrying value of goodwill assigned to Reporting Unit 2. Because the implied fair value of goodwill is less than the goodwill carrying value, a goodwill impairment loss of $25,000 ($400,000 carrying value – $375,000 implied fair value) is reported. The following journal entry is required for the impairment loss.

Goodwill Impairment Loss	25,000	
Goodwill		25,000

The account Goodwill Impairment Loss is reported as a line item in the income statement prior to the subtotal, income from continuing operations, and the new goodwill carrying value of $975,000 ($375,000 new carrying value + $600,000) is reported as a line item in the balance sheet.

If the carrying value of a reporting unit is zero or negative, the second step of the impairment test shall be performed to measure the amount of impairment loss, if any, when it is more likely than not that a goodwill impairment exists. The impairment loss is recognized in an amount equal to the excess and cannot exceed the carrying amount of the goodwill.

Financial Statement Presentation and Disclosures

Intangible assets should be aggregated and reported as a line item in the balance sheet. However, an enterprise may elect to report individual intangibles separately or by classes of intangibles in the balance sheet. Also, goodwill should be reported as a separate line item in the balance sheet. Impairment losses and amortization expense related to intangible assets should be reported in the income statement as line items in income from continuing operations. Goodwill impairment losses should be aggregated and reported as the last item in income from continuing operations. If the goodwill impairment loss relates to a discontinued operation, the impairment loss should be included as part of discontinued operations. For guidance on reporting discontinued operations, see Chapter 2.

Disclosure requirements for goodwill are provided in ASC 350-20-50. Disclosure requirements for other intangible assets are provided in ASC 350-30-50. The disclosure information should be provided for each business combination that is material when intangible asset fair values (excluding goodwill) are significant. All business combinations that are immaterial should be aggregated and if they are material in the aggregate, the aggregated business combinations should be treated as a material business combination. Listed below are the required disclosures:

1. The following information is required in the year of acquisition for intangibles acquired separately or as part of a group (this included a business combination or an asset acquisition):

a. The following information in total and by intangible asset class is required for intangible assets that require amortization: amount assigned, significant residual value, and weighted-average amortization period.

b. Total amount assigned to intangibles and amount assigned to major intangible asset classes for intangibles not subject to amortization.

c. The following information is required for acquired research and development assets (excludes business combination transactions): amount acquired, amount written off in the accounting period, and location in the income statement where aggregate amounts written off are reported.

d. For intangible assets with renewal or extension terms, the weighted-average period prior to the next renewal or extension (both explicit and implicit), by major intangible asset class.

2. For each period that a balance sheet is presented, disclose the following information either in the face of the statements or in related notes:

a. The following information in total and by intangible asset class is required for intangible assets that require amortization: gross carrying amount, accumulated amortization, total amortization expense reported for the accounting period, and expected total amortization expense for each of the next five years subsequent to the current accounting period.

b. Total carrying amount for intangibles and carrying amount for major intangible asset classes for intangibles not subject to amortization.

c. The entity's accounting policy on the treatment of costs incurred to renew or extend the term of a recognized intangible asset.

d. For intangible assets that have been renewed or extended in the period for which a statement of financial position is presented: (1) For entities that capitalize renewal or extension costs, the total amount of costs incurred in the period to renew or extend the term of a recognized intangible asset, by major intangible asset class (2) The weighted-average period prior to the next renewal or extension (both explicit and implicit), by major intangible asset class.

e. The following changes (shown separately) in the carrying amount of goodwill for the accounting period are required: (a) beginning-of-period and end-of-period accumulated impairment losses and gross amounts, (b) additional amount of goodwill reported for the accounting period (excluding goodwill related to a disposal group that is classified as held for sale), (c) goodwill adjustments from deferred tax recognition using the provisions of ASC 805-740, (d) goodwill included in a disposal group that is classified as held for sale, (e) amount of derecognized goodwill not reported in a disposal group that is held for sale, (f) amount of impairment losses reported, (g) net exchange differences using the provisions of ASC 830, and (h) any other changes in goodwill carrying amount.

3. Disclose the same information in 2 above for each reportable segment and in total when an entity reports segment information in accordance with ASC 280. Disclose any significant goodwill allocation changes involving reportable segments.
4. Disclose the amount of goodwill, if any, that has not been allocated to reporting units and explain why it has not been allocated.
5. In the accounting period in which an intangible asset impairment loss is reported, disclose the following: facts and circumstances causing the impairment and describe the impaired intangible, method used to calculate fair value, amount of impairment loss, caption where the loss is reported in the income statement or statement of activities, and operating segment where loss is reported.
6. In the accounting period in which a goodwill impairment loss is reported, disclose the following: facts and circumstances causing the impairment, method used to calculate fair value of the related reporting unit, amount of impairment loss, and if appropriate, the fact and reason that the loss is estimated and is not final and adjustments made to the original estimate in subsequent accounting periods.

Accounting for Goodwill: Accounting Alternative

ASU 2014-02, *Intangibles—Goodwill and Other (Topic 350): Accounting for Goodwill,* is a consensus of the Private Company Council (PCC). As a PCC amendment, ASU 2014-02 does not apply to public business entities, not-for-profit entities, or employee benefit plans within the scope of ASC 960 through ASC 965 on plan accounting.

The amendment of this ASU allows an accounting alternative for the subsequent measurement of goodwill to allow the amortization of goodwill on a straight-line basis over a maximum of 10 years. A period shorter than 10 years may be elected if the entity can demonstrate that a shorter useful life is more appropriate. An entity that elects this alternative must make an accounting policy election to test goodwill for impairment at either the entity or the reporting unit level. This would require the entity or reporting unit to test goodwill for impairment whenever a triggering event occurs. As described earlier, an entity may first use a qualitative option to determine whether there are qualitative factors make it more likely than not that goodwill is impaired.

Disclosures required are similar to existing U.S. GAAP as detailed earlier in this section. However, if an entity elects the accounting alternative, it is not required to present changes in goodwill in a tabular reconciliation.

Upon adoption of the guidance in this accounting alternative section, that guidance shall be effective prospectively for new goodwill recognized after the adoption of that guidance. For existing goodwill, that guidance shall be effective as of the beginning of the first fiscal year in which the accounting alternative is adopted. Goodwill existing as of the beginning of the period of adoption shall be amortized prospectively on a straight-line basis over 10 years, or less than 10 years if an entity demonstrates that another useful life is more appropriate.

Internal-Use Software

Entities often license internal-use software from third parties. A software license within shall be accounted for as the acquisition of an intangible asset and the incurrence of a liability (i.e., to the extent that all or a portion of the software licensing fees are not paid on or before the acquisition date of the license) by the licensee.

ASU 2015-05, *Intangibles—Goodwill and Other—Internal-Use Software (Subtopic 350-40): Customer's Accounting for Fees Paid in a Cloud Computing Arrangement,* addresses a customer's accounting for its fees paid to the cloud service provider in a cloud computing (or "hosting") arrangement. These arrangements include software as a service, infrastructure as a service or other similar arrangements.

The guidance indicates that if a cloud computing arrangement includes a software license, the customer should account for the software license element of the arrangement consistent with the acquisition of other software licenses. If a cloud computing arrangement does *not* include a software license, the customer should account for the arrangement as a service contract. The guidance does not change existing U.S. GAAP for a customer's accounting for service contracts.

For public business entities, the ASU should be applied in annual periods, including interim periods within those annual periods, beginning after December 15, 2015. For all other entities, the ASU should be applied for annual periods beginning after December 15, 2015, and for interim periods in annual periods beginning after December 15, 2016. Early adoption is permitted for all entities. Entities may elect to adopt the amendments either (a) prospectively to all arrangements entered into or materially modified after the effective date, or (b) retrospectively.

Recent Changes

ASU 2014-02, *Intangibles—Goodwill and Other (Topic 350): Accounting for Goodwill,* a consensus of the Private Company Council is discussed immediately above. (Note: ASU 2016-03, *Intangibles—Goodwill and Other (Topic 350), Business Combinations (Topic 805), Consolidation (Topic 810) Derivatives and Hedging (Topic 815): Effective Date and Transition Guidance,* removed the effective dates for all of the PCC accounting alternatives, making them effective immediately and indefinitely.)

ASU 2015-05, *Intangibles—Goodwill and Other—Internal-Use Software (Subtopic 350-40): Customer's Accounting for Fees Paid in a Cloud Computing Arrangement,* an amendment to the FASB Codification is described, above.

ASU 2017-04, *Intangibles—Goodwill and Other (Topic 350): Simplifying the Test for Goodwill,* eliminates Step 2 from the goodwill impairment test. In computing the implied fair value of goodwill under Step 2, an entity had to perform procedures to determine the fair value at the impairment testing date of its assets and liabilities following the procedure that would be required in determining the fair value of assets acquired and liabilities assumed in a business combination. An entity still has to perform the qualitative assessment (Step 1) for a reporting unit to determine if the quantitative impairment test is necessary. An entity should apply the amendments in this Update on a prospective basis. An entity is required to disclose the nature of and reason for the change in accounting principle upon transition. That disclosure should be provided in the first annual period and in the interim period within the first annual period when the entity initially adopts the amendments in this Update.

A public business entity that is a U.S. Securities and Exchange Commission (SEC) filer should adopt the amendments in this Update for its annual or any interim goodwill impairment tests in fiscal years beginning after December 15, 2019. A public business entity that is not an SEC filer should adopt the amendments in this Update for its annual or any interim goodwill impairment tests in fiscal years beginning after December 15, 2020. All other entities, including not-for-profit entities, that are adopting the amendments in this Update should do so for their annual or any interim goodwill impairment tests in fiscal years beginning after December 15, 2021. Early adoption is permitted for interim or annual goodwill impairment tests performed on testing dates after January 1, 2017.

Topic 360: Property, Plant, and Equipment

Topic 360, *Property, Plant, and Equipment,* contains 16 subtopics:

10 Overall

905 Agriculture*

908 Airlines*

910 Contractors—Construction*

922 Entertainment—Cable Television*

930 Extractive Activities—Mining*

932 Extractive Activities—Oil and Gas*

942 Financial Services—Depository and Lending*

944 Financial Services—Insurance*

954 Health Care Entities*

958 Not-For-Profit Entities*

960 Plan Accounting—Defined Benefit Pension Plans*

965 Plan Accounting—Health and Welfare Benefit Plans*

970 Real Estate—General*

972 Real Estate—Common Interest Realty Associations*

980 Regulated Operations*

* See the corresponding topic in Chapter 9 for coverage of this shared subtopic.

Depreciation—General Discussion

Once a productive tangible asset is purchased and recorded as an asset in the financial statements, it generally is removed from the accounting records over time using a system of depreciation. Depreciation is the allocation of the historical cost of the asset over its useful life. The allocation of the asset's cost is made in such a way that the cost of the asset is allocated to each accounting period that related services from the asset are provided.

Methods of Depreciation

Several acceptable methods have been developed that allocate the cost in different ways. Examples of methods include straight-line, sum-of-the-years'-digits, double-declining-balance, and units-of-production. All of these methods are considered generally accepted accounting principles.

Under the straight-line method, the asset is assumed to be used up in equal amounts each accounting period over the estimated useful life of the asset; therefore, the cost of the asset less any expected residual value is allocated equally to each accounting period over the useful life of the asset. The useful life is the number of years that the asset is expected to provide service prior to its disposition. Residual value is the expected value of the asset at the end of its useful life. Under both the sum-of-the-years'-digits and the double-declining-balance methods, the asset is assumed to be used up more in the early years of the asset's life. Under these two methods, more depreciation is reported in accounting periods in the earlier years of the asset's life and less in later years. The straight-line, sum-of-the-years'-digits, and double-declining-balance methods all assume that the usefulness of the asset declines based on a passage of time.

The units-of-production method is used when the usefulness of the asset declines based on activity of the asset. In this case, the cost of the asset is allocated to each accounting period based on the level of activity in that accounting period. Activity may be tied to factors such as number of hours used, number of units produced, or number of miles driven. Therefore, if the amount of depreciation (allocation of cost) is tied to the number of hours used, depreciation for a specific accounting period is equal to the number of hours used in that accounting period over the total estimated hours of life of the asset times the cost of the asset. When depreciation is tied to activity, estimated useful life is expressed in terms of total estimated activity as opposed to use during a specific time period. The amount of cost allocated each accounting period is debited to depreciation expense and credited to accumulated depreciation. Depreciation expense is reported on the income statement as an operating expense or as part of the cost of inventory, if the asset is involved in the production of inventory. Accumulated depreciation is a contra asset account and is reported as an offset to the related asset.

One example is used to illustrate the various depreciation methods described above. Assumptions for Example 3-18 are as follows.

Example 3-18
Assumptions for Depreciation

1. The Johnson Company (Johnson), a December 31 year-end entity, purchased equipment for $1,600,000 on January 1, 20X6. The equipment has a 5-year useful life and an estimated residual value of $100,000.

2. Johnson estimated that 200,000 units can be produced by the equipment over the next five years with yearly production as follows: 20X6: 50,000 units; 20X7: 40,000 units; 20X8: 20,000 units; 20X9: 60,000 units; and 2010: 30,000 units.

The following formula is used to compute annual depreciation by the straight-line method.

AD = C – RV/UL
AD = Annual depreciation
C = Cost of asset
RV = Residual value
UL = Useful life

Using the information from Example 3-18 and this formula, annual depreciation is computed as follows using the straight-line method:

AD = ($1,600,000 – $100,000)/5 years
AD = $300,000

When depreciation is computed using the sum-of-the-years'-digits method, a decreasing fraction is applied in each accounting period to the cost of the asset less the estimated residual value. The denominator of the fraction may be computed using the following formula:

D = UL(UL + 1)/2
D = Denominator
UL = Useful life

Using the information from Example 3-18 and the preceding formula, the denominator to use in the sum-of-the-years'-digits method is computed as follows:

D = 5(5 + l)/2
D = 15

The numerator used in the sum-of-the-years'-digits computation is the life of the asset in reverse order. In Example 3-18, the first year's depreciation is 5/15 of the amount to depreciate, the fourth year is 4/15, the third year is 3/15, the fourth year is 2/15, and the last year is 1/15. Using this information and the asset information from Example 3-18, depreciation for the years 20X6–20Y0 is computed as follows using sum-of-the-years'-digits:

20X6 Depreciation – 5/15	×	($1,600,000 – $100,000)	=	$500,000
20X7 Depreciation – 4/15	×	($1,600,000 – $100,000)	=	$400,000
20X8 Depreciation – 3/15	×	($1,600,000 – $100,000)	=	$300,000
20X9 Depreciation – 2/15	×	($1,600,000 – $100,000)	=	$200,000
20Y0 Depreciation – 1/15	×	($1,600,000 – $100,000)	=	$100,000

Notice that under the sum-of-the-years digits method, more depreciation is allocated in 20X6 and 20X7 and less depreciation is allocated in 20X9 and 20Y0 than under the straight-line method. In addition, there is an equal decline ($100,000) between each year of depreciation using sum-of-the-years'-digits.

The next method, double-declining-balance, also allocates more of the cost of the asset to the early years. The double-declining-balance method allocates the cost of the asset using total cost. Residual value is not deducted from cost when using the double-declining-balance method. The following formula is used to compute depreciation by the double-declining-balance method:

AD = 2 (1/UL) × DB
AD = Annual depreciation
UL = Useful life
DB = Declining balance, which is the cost of the asset – all prior year's depreciation

Using the formula and information from Example 3-18, allocation of the cost of the asset for 20X6–20Y0 is computed below.

20X6 Allocation

AD = 2 (1/5) × $1,600,000
AD = $640,000

20X7 Allocation

AD = 2 (1/5) × ($1,600,000 – $640,000)
AD = $384,000

20X8 Allocation

AD = 2 (1/5) × ($1,600,000 – $640,000 – $384,000)
AD = $230,400

20X9 Allocation

AD = 2 (1/5) × ($1,600,000 – $640,000 – $384,000 – $230,400)
AD = $138,240

20Y0 Allocation

$1,600,000 – $640,000 – $384,000 – $230,400 – $138,240 = 207,360
$207,360 amount left to depreciate – $100,000 residual value = § 107,360
AD = $107,360

The allocation formula was not used in 2010. Because this is the last year for depreciation and the asset cannot be depreciated below its residual value, the depreciation for 20Y0 of $107,360 was computed by taking the remaining amount left to depreciate of $207,360 less the estimated residual value of $100,000.

The last method, the units-of-production method, is based on activity rather than the passage of time that was used in the methods discussed above. The allocation of depreciation can be computed for the units-of-production method by using the following formula:

AD = (CU/TEU) × (C – RV)
AD = Annual depreciation
CU = Current year units
TEU = Total estimated units over life of asset
C = Cost of asset
RV = Residual value

Using the preceding formula and the information from Example 3-18, allocation of the cost of the asset for 20X6–20Y0 is computed as follows by the units-of-production method:

20X6 Allocation

$$AD = (50{,}000/200{,}000) \times (\$1{,}600{,}000 - \$100{,}000)$$
$$AD = \$375{,}000$$

20X7 Allocation

$$AD = (40{,}000/200{,}000) \times (\$1{,}600{,}000 - \$100{,}000)$$
$$AD = \$300{,}000$$

20X8 Allocation

$$AD = (20{,}000/200{,}000) \times (\$1{,}600{,}000 - \$100{,}000)$$
$$AD = \$150{,}000$$

20X9 Allocation

$$AD = (60{,}000/200{,}000) \times (\$1{,}600{,}000 - \$100{,}000)$$
$$AD = \$450{,}000$$

20Y0 Allocation

$$AD = (30{,}000/200{,}000) \times (\$1{,}600{,}000 - \$100{,}000)$$
$$AD = \$225{,}000$$

The amount of depreciation varies from accounting period to accounting period because the number of units actually produced are not the same from year to year.

Using the depreciation information computed from all the different allocation methods, the amount computed each year for each method is summarized below in Table 3-18-A.

Table 3-18-A Summary of Depreciation Methods

Method	20X6	20X7	20X8	20X9	20Y0
Straight-Line	$300,000	$300,000	$300,000	$300,000	$300,000
Sum-of-the-Years Digits	$500,000	$400,000	$300,000	$200,000	$100,000
Double-Declining-Balance	$640,000	$384,000	$230,400	$138,240	$107,360
Units-of-Production	$375,000	$300,000	$150,000	$450,000	$225,000

Depreciation—Disclosure Requirements

ASC 360-10-50-1 specifies the disclosure requirements for depreciation as follows:

1. Describe, in a general manner, the method(s) used when calculating depreciation.
2. Disclose, on the balance sheet date, the amount of accumulated depreciation. This may be disclosed in total or by primary classes of assets.
3. Disclose the amount of depreciation expense for the accounting period under consideration.
4. Disclose, on the balance sheet date, the balances in the primary classes of assets. This disclosure may be made by function or by nature of the assets.

Impairment and Disposal of Long-Lived Assets—General Discussion

ASC 360-10 specifies the accounting and reporting requirements for long-lived assets held for use and long-lived assets held for disposition. ASC 360-10 covers recognized long-lived assets of both for-profit and not-for-profit entities. Examples of long-lived assets include property, plant and equipment, right-of-use assets of lessees, long-lived assets of lessors subject to operating leases, prepaid assets classified as long-term, and proved oil and gas properties when the successful efforts accounting is used (ASC 360-10-15-4). However, selected long-lived assets are excluded from the provisions of ASC 360-10-15-5:

1. Goodwill.
2. Intangible assets not subject to amortization.
3. Financial instruments.
4. Equity investments accounted for using either the cost or equity method.
5. Deferred tax assets.
6. Servicing assets.
7. Costs of policy acquisitions that are deferred.
8. Unproven oil and gas properties when successful efforts accounting is used.
9. Long-lived assets covered by ASC 920, 928, 980-360, or 985-20.

When a long-lived asset covered by ASC 360 is part of a group of assets, some of which are not covered by ASC 360, ASC 360 applies to the entire group, commonly referred to as the asset group. When the asset group is held for use, the group should be the lowest level of assets that generate independent cash flows. If the asset group is held for disposition, the disposal group represents an asset disposition that will occur in a single transaction and includes liabilities that will be transferred in the disposition.

ASC 360 must be applied if an entity has recognized long-lived assets. The following discussion on long-lived assets is divided into two parts: long-lived assets held for disposition and long-lived assets held for use.

Long-Lived Assets Held for Disposition

When a long-lived asset is held for disposition, an enterprise must determine if the expected disposition is classified as a discontinued segment of a business, disposition of assets by abandonment, disposition by exchange or in a spin-off, or disposition by sale. If the proposed asset disposition meets the requirements for discontinued operations using ASC 205-20-45-1, review the detailed discussion of discontinued operations in Chapter 2.

If the proposed asset disposition is not classified as discontinued operations, and the disposition is to be accomplished by abandonment, the long-lived asset should continue to be accounted for as an asset that is held for use. See a detailed discussion of assets held for use later in this chapter. Disposition by abandonment of a long-lived asset is assumed to occur when the asset is no longer used. When a company has a specified plan for disposition that indicates a time period for abandonment that is less than the useful life used to compute current depreciation amounts, the depreciation amounts should be adjusted to reflect the shorter useful life of the asset. An asset should not be accounted for as abandoned when it is temporarily not in use (ASC 360-10-35, paragraphs 47 through 49).

Long-lived assets expected to be disposed of by exchanging them for similar productive assets or assets that will be disposed of in a spin-off to owners should be accounted for as held for use until the actual exchange or spin-off occurs. When future expected cash flows are used in the computation of any impairment loss while accounted for as held for sale, an entity must assume that the assets will not be exchanged or distributed. If the fair value of the asset is less than its carrying amount on the date of exchange or distribution, an impairment loss is reported for the difference. This impairment loss is in addition to any impairment loss reported while accounted for as held for use. See a detailed discussion of ASC 845-10 in Chapter 8 as it relates to the type of transaction that is considered an exchange or spin off.

Long-lived assets expected to be disposed of by sale must meet certain conditions before the assets can be classified as held for sale. When all of the following conditions are met, the asset or asset group should be classified as held for sale (ASC 360-10-45-9):

a. Management commits to a plan to sell
b. The asset to be sold is available for immediate sale in its present condition
c. An active program to locate a buyer or buyers has been initiated
d. The sale is probable and is expected to be a completed sale within one year in most cases
e. The sale price being marketed is reasonable in relation to its fair value
f. It is unlikely that there will be significant changes to the plan to sell or that the plan would be withdrawn

If all the conditions are not met, the asset shall be classified as held for use (ASC 360-10-45-10).

Once an asset or asset group meets the preceding requirements, the asset is classified as held for sale. However, when assets no longer meet all held-for-sale conditions prior to a sale, the assets or asset group is reclassified as held-for-use, unless the assets meet the exception condition allowed in ASC 360-10-45-11.

ASC 360-10-45-11 allows an exception to the rule that an asset must be sold within one year of classification as held for sale as noted in item d, above. This one-year requirement can be overcome in the following situations:

1. The entity expects third parties (other than the buyer) to impose conditions on the sale of the asset or asset group that will require an extension of the time needed to complete the transaction, a firm purchase commitment must exist prior to responding to the conditions, and it is probable that a firm purchase commitment will be obtained within one year.

2. Conditions are placed on the entity by the buyer or others after a firm purchase commitment is obtained that will require an extension of time to complete the transaction, actions to address the issue have been initiated on a timely basis, and the entity expects a favorable outcome.
3. An entity does not sell an asset or asset group during the one year time period because conditions occur that were considered unlikely at the inception preventing the sale, actions were initiated by the seller during the one year time period to respond to the changed conditions, the entity is actively marketing the asset or asset group, given the change in conditions, and the conditions for sale as specified in ASC 360-10-45-9 are met, as discussed above.

An entity may acquire a long-lived asset or asset group with the intent of selling the asset rather than using the asset. Such an asset is classified as held for sale at the acquisition date if it is probable that the asset will be sold and the sale will be completed within one year and will qualify as a completed sale unless an exception is allowed by ASC 360-10-45-11, which is discussed above, and all other conditions as specified in ASC 360-10-45-9, as discussed above, have been met or will be met in a "short period" of time. "Short period" of time is usually within three months (ASC 360-10-45-12).

When the conditions for classifying an asset as held for sale (ASC 360-10-45-9 conditions) are not met on the balance sheet date, but are met prior to the release of the financial statements, the asset or asset group is classified and accounted for as held and used. However, when the asset is tested for impairment at the balance sheet date, estimates of future expected cash flows should take into consideration the anticipated future sale of the asset or asset group. An impairment loss is reported for the amount that fair value is less than the carrying value of the asset. Any impairment determination made at the balance sheet date should not be changed because the conditions for held for sale are met prior to the release of the financial statements. However, the required disclosures for held for sale assets should be reported in notes to the financial statements. See the required disclosures in the disclosure section (ASC 360-10-50-3).

Assets or asset groups (disposal groups, but not qualifying as a discontinued operation in accordance with ASC 205-20-45-10) are reported separately in the balance sheet at an amount equal to fair value less the cost to sell the asset (adjusted fair value) or carrying value, whichever is lower.

A long-lived asset to be disposed of other than by sale (e.g., by abandonment, in an exchange measured based on the recorded amount of the nonmonetary asset relinquished, or in a distribution to owners in a spinoff) is required to continue to be classified as held and used until it is disposed of. The guidance on long-lived assets to be held and used in ASC 360-10-35, 360-10-45, and 360-10-50 is to apply while the asset is classified as held and used. If a long-lived asset is to be abandoned or distributed to owners in a spinoff together with other assets (and liabilities) as a group and that disposal group meets the conditions in ASC paragraphs 205-20-45-1A through 45-1C to be reported in discontinued operations, ASC paragraphs 205-20-45-3 through 45-5 are to apply to the disposal group at the date it is disposed of.

Fair value used in the computation of the adjusted fair value is defined by ASC 820 as the amount that would be received on the measurement date from the sale of property or the amount paid to transfer a liability between sellers and buyers (market participants) in an orderly transaction. In addition, it is assumed that the sellers and buyers are unrelated parties on the measurement date. One way to determine fair value is to use quoted market prices. In many cases, however, quoted market prices are not available and an enterprise must estimate fair value. One way that fair value may be estimated is by using future cash flows on a present-value basis. One present-value method is referred to as the expected-present-value concept.

The expected-present-value concept uses multiple cash flows situations to reflect the possible cash flow outcomes for a specific asset or asset group and a risk free interest rate. The traditional present value concept uses a single set of cash flows and an interest rate equal to the risk of the situation. ASC 360-10-35-36 states that the expected-present-value concept may be more appropriate when long-lived assets have uncertainties related to both timing and amount of future cash flows. Costs to sell the asset or asset group are additional direct costs that would be incurred because the entity has made the decision to sale the asset or asset group. If the sale is estimated to occur after one year, the selling costs should be discounted. Examples of direct costs to sale are closing costs, legal costs, title transfer costs, and broker commissions. However, estimates of future losses from use of the asset should not be include in costs to sell. If the asset is acquired for resale, the fair value less the cost to sell should be determined at the date of acquisition. Disposal groups held for sale should be reported separately as assets and liabilities in the balance sheet. The assets and liabilities should not be offset. Assets and liabilities included in the disposal group not covered by ASC 360 should be accounted for using other appropriate standards prior to determining fair value. No depreciation should be reported for assets or disposal groups classified as held for sale. However, any expenses related to liabilities in a disposal group should be accrued in the normal manner. Assets and disposal groups held for sale should be reported on the face of the financial statements or in related note disclosures by major classes of assets.

If the adjusted fair market value (fair value less cost to sell) is less than the carrying amount of the asset, a loss is recognized in an amount equal to the difference between the adjusted fair market value and the carrying amount of the asset, and the related asset or asset group is written down to equal the adjusted fair value (fair value less cost to sell) (ASC 360-10-35-40). The loss is reported before tax in the income statement as part of income from continuing operations. If a separate caption, such as income from operations, is used, the impairment loss or gain should be included in the caption. A not-for-profit entity would report the loss in a statement of activities. If fair market value or expected costs of disposition require adjustments prior to actual asset disposition, the carrying value of the asset should be increased or decreased and a gain or loss reported. However, a gain should not be reported for more that the cumulative losses previously reported. The individual asset's carrying value should be adjusted regardless if it is an individual asset or a long-lived asset that is part of an asset group.

In some cases, assets or disposal groups that are classified as held for sale are reclassified as assets held and used because conditions that were considered unlikely at the time of original classification changed and the assets are no longer held for sale. When assets are reclassified from held for sale to held and used, the asset or disposal group should be measured at the lower of the following amounts (ASC 360-10-35-44): fair value on the date that the entity decides not to sell the asset or carrying amount on the date the asset was classified as held for sale less depreciation that would have been taken if the asset had not been classified as held for sale. If an adjustment is made in the carrying amount of the asset because of the reclassification, the amount of the change is reported in the income statement as a component of income from continuing operations in the accounting period when the decision is made to reclassify the asset. In addition, the adjustment should be reported in the same income caption as used for impairment losses.

An individual asset or liability may be removed from a disposal group that is classified as held for sale. The remaining group of assets and liabilities should only be classified as held for sale if the conditions in ASC 360-10-45-9, as discussed above, are met. Should the group not meet the criteria, individual long-lived assets should be remeasured at the lower of the following: fair value less cost to sell or the asset's carrying amount. If any of the individual long-lived assets of the group is no longer expected to be sold, the asset should be reclassified using the procedures for reclassification as discussed above (ASC 360-10-45-7).

Any loss reported from a write down to fair value less cost to sell of an asset or disposal group is reported in the income statement as a component of income from continuing operations before tax. For not-for-profit entities, the loss should be reported in the statement of activities as a component of income from continuing operations.

Disclosure: Long-Lived Assets Classified as Held for Sale or Disposed Of

For any period in which a long-lived asset (disposal group) either has been disposed of or is classified as held for sale (see ASC 360-10-45-9), an entity is to disclose all of the following in the notes to financial statements (ASC 360-10-50-3):

a. A description of the facts and circumstances leading to the disposal or the expected disposal.

b. The expected manner and timing of that disposal.

c. The gain or loss recognized in accordance with ASC paragraphs 360-10-35-37 through 35-45 and 360-10-40-5.

d. If not separately presented on the face of the statement where net income is reported (or in the statement of activities for a not-for-profit entity), the caption in the statement where net income is reported (or in the statement of activities for a not-for-profit entity) that includes that gain or loss.

e. If not separately presented on the face of the statement of financial position, the carrying amount(s) of the major classes of assets and liabilities included as part of a disposal group classified as held for sale. Any loss recognized on the disposal group classified as held for sale in accordance with ASC paragraphs 360-10-35-37 through 35-45 and 360-10-40-5 is not to be allocated to the major classes of assets and liabilities of the disposal group.

f. If applicable, the segment in which the long-lived asset (disposal group) is reported under ASC 280 on segment reporting.

In addition to the disclosures above, if a long-lived asset (disposal group) includes an individually significant component of an entity that either has been disposed of or is classified as held for sale (see ASC 360-10-45-9) and does not qualify for presentation and disclosure as a discontinued operation (see ASC 205-20 on discontinued operations):

a. For a public business entity and a not-for-profit entity that has issued, or is a conduit bond obligor for, securities that are traded, listed, or quoted on an exchange or an over-the-counter market, both of the following:

    1. The pretax profit or loss (or change in net assets for a not-for-profit entity) of the individually significant component of an entity for the period in which it is disposed of or is classified as held for sale and for all prior periods that are presented in the statement where net income is reported (or statement of activities for a not-for-profit entity) calculated in accordance with ASC 205-20-45-6 through 45-9 and

    2. If the individually significant component of an entity includes a noncontrolling interest, the pretax profit or loss (or change in net assets for a not-for-profit entity) attributable to the parent for the period in which it is disposed of or is classified as held for sale and for all prior periods that are presented in the statement where net income is reported (or statement of activities for a not-for-profit entity).

b. For all other entities, both of the following:

    1. The pretax profit or loss (or change in net assets for a not-for-profit entity) of the individually significant component of an entity for the period in which it is disposed of or is classified as held for sale calculated in accordance with ASC 205-20-45-6 through 45-9; and

    2. If the individually significant component of an entity includes a noncontrolling interest, the pretax profit or loss (or change in net assets for a not-for-profit entity) attributable to the parent for the period in which it is disposed of or is classified as held for sale.

This completes the discussion of assets held for disposition. The next section covers the accounting and reporting requirements for assets held and use.

Long-Lived Assets Held and Used

When long-lived assets are held and used, situations or circumstances may indicate that the carrying amount of the assets may not be recovered over future accounting periods. ASC 360-10-35-21 provides examples that might indicate when an asset's carrying amount would not be recoverable. Some of the examples include a major decline in the market value of the asset or asset group, a significantly greater than anticipated increase in costs of a constructed asset or asset group, a current period loss, cash flow loss with a history of losses, or expectations of future losses, and a change in the manner or extent of physical condition or use.

Testing for Impairment

If circumstances indicate that an asset carrying value may not be recovered, the asset or asset group must be further tested for possible impairment. Impairment is considered to be a condition where the fair value of an asset or asset group is less than the related carrying amount (ASC 360-10-35-17). To test for impairment, the long-lived asset or assets should be placed in asset groups using the lowest level of assets and liabilities that generate independent cash flows (ASC 360-10-35-23). For example, if an enterprise has five retail stores, the entity most likely would have five asset groups because each store would have cash inflows and outflows independent of the other four retail outlets. However, if the enterprise cannot group a long-lived asset into asset groups, because independent cash flows cannot be generated, impairment should be tested at the enterprise level (ASC 360-10-35-24). Goodwill is not included in the asset group unless the asset group is a reporting unit that has an allocation of goodwill. In addition, cash flows should not be adjusted for the fact that goodwill is not included in an asset grouping that is less than a reporting unit.

Once the assets are divided into appropriate groups, the enterprise should estimate future net cash flows (cash inflows less cash outflows) for each group. The cash flows would include any cash flows directly related to use and disposition of the group but would not include interest. The cash flows should be computed on a gross basis (i.e., the cash flows should not be discounted for present value). The enterprise should use its own assumptions regarding the use of the asset or assets and the assumptions should be reasonable in relation to other assumptions used when developing information for other purposes such as budgets and projects. If ranges of cash flows are possible and/or if alternatives are under consideration for use of the asset(s), a probability-weighted cash flow estimate may be the best approach when estimating future expected cash flows for the asset(s) (ASC 360-10-35, paragraphs 29 and 30).

For example, an entity may assume that the asset will be used for five years and sold, or used for 10 years and sold with a 30% probability that it will be sold in five years and a 70% probability that it will be sold in 10 years. In addition, there may be possible ranges of cash flows in each of the years for each of the alternatives. As an example, the cash flows for the five year alternative may be as follows: 30% probability that the cash flows will be $10 million, 20% probability that the cash flows will be $15 million, and 50% probability that the cash flows will be $25 million. Therefore, the entity would have to weight both the cash flows and the alternatives to arrive at an appropriate estimate of future cash flows for impairment testing. The time period used for the cash flow estimate is the remaining life of the asset or asset group. When an asset group is used, the remaining life of the primary asset in the asset group is the time period to use for the cash flow estimate.

The primary asset is assumed to be the most significant intangible or tangible asset subject to amortization or depreciation that provides the cash flow generating ability of the asset group (ASC 360-10-35, paragraphs 31 and 32). The criteria that may be used when determining the primary asset are: investment level required for asset replacement, the asset's remaining life compared to the remaining lives of the other assets, and whether the other assets would have been acquired if the asset under consideration were not acquired (ASC 360-10-35, paragraphs 31 and 32). When the primary asset does not have the longest remaining useful life, the asset group is assumed to be sold at the end of the life of the primary asset when computing cash flows. When estimating future cash flows, the cash flows should be based on the existing service potential of the asset, including those that are substantially complete, on the test date. The existing service potential includes the following (ASC 360-10-35, paragraphs 31 and 32): remaining useful life of the asset, the asset's cash-flow-generating ability, and physical output capacity when considering tangible assets. When estimating future cash flows, an entity should include not only normal cash inflows and outflows, but also cash flows needed to maintain the existing service potential of the assets including component replacement such as roof replacement. However, the cash flows should not include cash expenditures that increase the service potential of the asset. If the asset is under development, the estimated future cash flows should be based on the expected service potential of the assets once the asset(s) are substantially complete. In addition, cash flows should include all payments required for development of the asset including interest payments that are capitalized as part of the cost of the asset using the provisions of ASC 835-20. When the asset under development is part of an asset group, estimated cash flows include both the cash flows to maintain service potential of the asset group and the cash flows to complete the long-lived asset (ASC 360-10-35, paragraphs 34 and 35). Prior to estimating cash flows for purposes of testing for recoverability, an entity may need to review depreciation and amortization estimates to determine if they are appropriate. If adjustments are required, this information should be taken into consideration prior to determining cash flows for recoverability.

Once the estimated future cash flows have been determined, the carrying amount of the asset group should be compared to its undiscounted net cash flow. If the cash flow is less than the carrying value of the asset or asset group, the asset should be tested for possible impairment. If cash flows exceed the related carrying amount of the asset, the asset or group is not tested for impairment, but the entity may wish to review depreciation policies and methods for the asset and make any needed adjustments.

When undiscounted net cash flows are less than the carrying amount of an asset or group, the asset or group must be further tested for impairment. The fair value of the asset group is compared to the related carrying amount of the asset. Fair value is determined in the same manner as discussed in the section on long-lived assets held for disposition. If the fair value of the group is greater than the related carrying amount, an impairment loss is not reported.

When impairment must be recognized, only the long-lived assets are reduced for the impairment loss. Other assets in the asset and liability group, such as accounts receivable and accounts payable, are not adjusted for the impairment loss, but are adjusted prior to impairment testing using other accounting standards, because ASC 360 does not include these assets and liabilities within its scope. The impairment loss is allocated to all long-lived assets in the asset group using a relative carrying value basis, except that a long-lived asset's carrying value cannot be reduced below its fair value as long as fair value can be determined with reasonable effort and cost. To apply the relative carrying value basis, all carrying values of all long-lived assets subject to impairment is totaled. The carrying value of each long-lived asset over the total times the impairment loss is the amount of the loss allocated to that long-lived asset as long as the remaining carrying amount is not less than the fair value of that asset. The recognition of the impairment loss establishes a new cost basis for the long-lived asset and for depreciable assets, the new basis is depreciated over its remaining useful life. If a long-lived asset increases in value, the impairment loss cannot be restored (ASC 360-10-35-20). The loss on impairment is reported before tax in the income statement as part of income from continuing operations. A not-for-profit entity would report the loss in a statement of activities. If the caption, income from operations, is used in the income statement, the impairment loss should be included as part of that caption.

Impairment and Disposal of Long-Lived Assets—Technical Considerations

To illustrate the provisions of ASC 360, six examples are developed. The first two examples relate to assets held for use and the last four examples covers assets held for sale. Unless otherwise stated in the assumptions, the sale is probable and will be completed in one year. The assumptions for Example 3-19 are as follows.

Example 3-19
Assumptions for Long-Lived Assets Held for Sale

1. Johnson Enterprises (Johnson) has the following anticipated transactions involving the possible sale of long-lived assets:

    a. Johnson plans to sell a plant facility and has action in place to find a buyer. The plant will be transferred to the new buyer as soon as Johnson vacates the facility. The time period for moving is normal under the circumstances.

b. Johnson plans to sell its office building but will continue to use the building until the new building is complete. Johnson has initiated actions to find a buyer and will transfer title when the new building is complete.

c. Johnson acquires real estate property that it intends to resale. However, renovations must be made to the property prior to sale and the property will not be sold until the renovations are complete.

d. Johnson enters into a contract to sell a manufacturing plant. When the buyers had the property inspected, ground water contamination was discovered. Johnson agreed to clean up the contamination and has initiated plans for the cleanup. However, the cleanup will take longer than one year but it is probable that the cleanup will be completed on a timely basis.

e. Johnson plans to sell one of its office buildings and has initiated plans to find a buyer. However, during the year economic conditions changed such that the building has not been sold. Johnson continues to market the building and is actively trying to find a buyer.

2. Johnson is preparing December 31, 20X6 financial statements and all preceding events occurred during 20X6.

The issue for all events a through e is whether the transaction should be accounted for as long-lived assets held for sale using ASC 360-10-45-9 or held and used. If the transaction meets all requirements of ASC 360-10-45-9, as discussed in the preceding material, the long-lived asset is accounted for as held for sale. If it fails to meet the criteria, the asset is accounted for as held and used. Table 3-19-A illustrates the accounting for each transaction and provides justification for the proper accounting treatment.

Table 3-19-A Determination of Accounting Treating for Long-Lived Assets

Transaction	*Accounting Treatment*	*Justification*
A	Held for Sale	Meets all criteria in ASC 360-10-45-9
B	Held and Used	The delay in the transfer of the building indicates that the building is not available for immediate sale
C	Held and Used	The delay in selling the property because of the renovations indicates that the property is not available for immediate sale.

Transaction	*Accounting Treatment*	*Justification*
D	Held for Sale	Sale will take longer than one year, which is a violation of ASC 360-10-45-9; however, this exception would be allowed because the seller is taking action to solve the problem and it is probable that the problem will be solved.
E	Held for Sale	Sale will take longer than one year, which is a violation of ASC 360-10-45-9; but this exception will be allowed because the seller is actively marketing the property and the company was not aware at the time the property was placed on the market for sale that economic conditions would change.

Notice that transactions d and e do not meet the requirements of ASC 360-10-45-9 for treatment as held for sale because the one-year rule is not met. However, ASC 360-10-45-11 provides exceptions to the one-year rule and Items d and e qualify for an exception.

This completes the discussion of Example 3-19. Assumptions for Example 3-20 are as follows:

Example 3-20
Assumptions for Long-Lived Assets Held for Sale

1. The Jones Company (Jones), a December 31 year-end entity, is reviewing its long-lived assets using the provisions of ASC 360, and has found that certain long-lived assets are being held for disposition at the end of 20X6.

2. Jones has equipment for sale and has accumulated the following information related to the equipment:

	Carrying Amount	Fair Value	Estimated Direct Costs of Disposition
Equipment	$2,000,000	$1,800,000	$100,000

The equipment held for sale is covered by the provisions of ASC 360, and the equipment should be reported in the statement of financial position at December 31, 20X6 at the lower of fair value less cost to sell or carrying amount. Fair value less cost to sale of $1,700,000 is computed below and compared to the $2,000,000 carrying amount of the equipment to compute a $300,000 loss from the expected disposition. Table 3-20-A shows computation of the fair value less cost to sell and the loss on expected disposition of the equipment.

Table 3-20-A Computation of Fair Value Less Cost to Sell and Loss on Expected Disposition

Fair value of equipment	$1,800,000
Less: Direct costs of disposition	100,000
Fair value less cost to sell	$1,700,000
Carrying amount of equipment	2,000,000
Loss from expected disposition	$300,000

Using information from Table 3-20-A, the loss reported on the expected disposition of the equipment, and the equipment write down are presented in the following journal entry:

Estimated Loss from Long-Lived Assets Held for Sale	300,000	
Equipment		300,000

The estimated loss of $300,000 is reported in the income statement as a part of income from continuing operations. Because the equipment is held for sale, Jones should not record depreciation expense or accumulated depreciation on the equipment.

This completes the discussion of Example 3-20. Assumptions for Example 3-21 are as follows:

Example 3-21
Assumptions for Long-Lived Assets Held for Use

1. Three companies with December 31 year-ends are reviewing their long-lived assets using the provisions of ASC 360 because the companies have current year operating losses, a history of operating losses, and anticipated future losses. The companies each have one major asset, for which cash flows can be identified independent of cash flows of other assets and liabilities.
2. The companies accumulated the following information for long-lived assets at December 31, 20X6:

	Carrying Amount	Estimated Net Future Cash Flow	Fair Value
Company 1	$10,000,000	$8,000,000	$7,500,000
Company 2	8,000,000	9,000,000	8,200,000
Company 3	5,000,000	4,950,000	5,050,000

The provisions of ASC 360 are applicable to all three companies because all three have long-lived assets. In addition, the companies must assess long-lived assets for impairment because the current year operating losses, history of operating losses, and expectations of future operating losses could indicate that the carrying amount of the long-lived assets may not be recoverable. All three companies grouped their long-lived assets into one group and consider recoverability at the entity level because each company has only one asset, with cash flows that can be identified and are independent of cash flows of other assets. The estimated undiscounted future net (cash inflows-cash outflows) cash flows are compared to carrying amounts of long-lived assets to determine whether an impairment loss should be considered. Because the undiscounted cash flow of the long-lived asset of Company 1 of $8,000,000 is less than the carrying amount of $10,000,000, the second step of testing for impairment must be taken for the asset. Next, the fair value of Company 1's long-lived asset of $7,500,000 is compared to the $10,000,000 carrying amount of asset. Because the $7,500,000 fair value is $2,500,000 ($10,000,000 – $7,500,000) less than the carrying amount of the asset, an impairment loss of $2,500,000 is reported for Company 1. The following journal entry is required to report the impairment loss on the books of Company 1.

Estimated Loss From Impairment of Long-Lived Assets	2,500,000	
Assets of Company 1		2,500,000

The impairment loss should be reported in the income statement as a part of income from continuing operations. A new cost basis of $7,500,000 is established for the long-lived asset and this amount is depreciated over the remaining life of the asset.

There is no impairment loss for Company 2 because the undiscounted cash flows of $9,000,000 exceed the carrying amount of the long-lived asset of $8,000,000. This indicates that the carrying value of the asset will be recovered, and the second step of comparing fair value to carrying amount is not required.

There is no impairment loss reported for Company 3. The undiscounted cash flows of $4,950,000 are less than the carrying amount of $5,000,000. But the assets do not meet the second test, because the carrying value of $5,000,000 is less than the fair value of the assets of $5,050,000.

This completes the discussion of Example 3-21. Example 3-22 covers a situation where weighted average probability of expected cash flows is used when testing for impairment. Assumptions for Example 3-22 are as follows.

Example 3-22
Assumptions for Long-Lived Assets Held for Use

1. Technology, Inc. (Technology), a company with a December 31 year-end, is reviewing its long-lived assets using the provisions of ASC 360 because it has current year cash flow losses, a history of cash flow losses, and anticipated future losses. Technology has one major asset, for which cash flows can be identified independent of cash flows of other assets and liabilities.
2. Technology accumulated the following information for its long-lived asset at December 31, 20X6:

a. The company has identified two options for the asset: a 20% probability that the asset will be sold in three years, or an 80% probability that the asset will be sold in five years.

b. If the asset is sold in three years, the estimated expected cash flows are as follows: a 30% probability of $10 million, a 20% probability of $12 million, a 40% probability of $15 million, and a 10% probability of $20 million.

c. If the asset is sold in five years, the estimated expected cash flows are as follows: a 30% probability of $16 million, a 20% probability of $20 million, a 40% probability of $25 million, and a 10% probability of $35 million.

d. The present value of the cash flows is as follows: $2.02 million if the asset is sold in three years, and $11.08 million if the asset is sold in five years.

3. The carrying value of the asset at December 31, 20X6 is $25 million.

Technology must review its long-lived asset for possible impairment because cash flow results indicate that the carrying amount of the asset may not be recoverable. Because Technology has identified alternative cash flow options, it should use a probability weighted average method when computing cash flows for impairment testing. The weighted average cash flow computation weights different assumptions about cash flows based on the probability of occurrence. Table 3-22-A shows the computation of cash flows and the present value of the cash flows using a probability weighted average method as specified by ASC 360.

Table 3-22-A Computation of Probability Weighted Average Cash Flows Present Value

Options	*Net Cash Flows*	*Probability Assessment*	*Probability Weighted Average Cash Flows*	*Probability Assessment*	*Probability Weighted Average Cash Flows*	*Present Value of Cash Flows (Fair Value)*
Sell In Three Years	$10	30 %	$3.0			
	$12	20 %	2.4			
	$15	40 %	6.0			
	$20	10 %	2.0			
Total		100 %	$13.4	20%	$2.68	$2.02
Sell In Five Years	$16	30 %	$4.8			
	$20	20 %	4.0			
	$25	40 %	10.0			
	$35	10 %	3.5			

Options	Net Cash Flows	Probability Assessment	Probability Weighted Average Cash Flows	Probability Assessment	Probability Weighted Average Cash Flows	Present Value of Cash Flows (Fair Value)
Total		100 %	$22.3	80%	17.84	11.08
Total					$20.52	$13.10

In Table 3-22-A, Technology has presented two options for the long-lived asset. One option is to sell in three years and the second option is to sell in five years. In addition, within each sell option, Technology has determined that there are four different cash flow options. There is a 20% probability that the asset will be sold in three years and an 80% probability that the asset will be sold in five years. Within each sell option the four cash flow options have a 30%, 20%, 40%, and 10% probability of occurring. Each cash flow option within each sell option is weighted based on its probability. Then the sum of each sell option is weighed based on its probability. The present value of the cash flows is then computed using the weighted average cash flow amounts as illustrated in Table 3-22-A.

Because the undiscounted cash flows on a probability weighted average basis of $20.52 million is less than the carrying value of $25 million, the asset must be tested for impairment by comparing fair value, which in this case is the present value of the cash flows using a risk-free interest rate, with the carrying amount of the asset. Therefore, because the present value of $13.10 million is less than the $25 million carrying value, an impairment loss of $11.90 million must be reported. This creates a new cost basis of $13.10 million for the long-lived asset, which is depreciated over its remaining useful life.

Using this information, the following journal entry is required at December 31, 20X6 (in millions).

Estimated Loss From Impairment of Long-Lived Assets	11.9	
Long-Lived Assets		11.9

This completes the discussion of Example 3-22. Example 3-23 illustrates the allocation of an impairment loss to several long-lived assets. Assumptions for Example 3-23 are as follows.

Example 3-23
Assumptions for Long-Lived Assets Held for Use

1. Peterson Enterprises (Peterson), a December 31 year-end company, is reviewing its long-lived assets using the provisions of ASC 360 because it has current year cash flow losses, a history of cash flow losses, and anticipated future losses. Peterson has five long-lived assets included in an asset group for which cash flows can be identified independent of cash flows of other assets and liabilities.

2. The carrying values, in millions of dollars, of the assets and liabilities in the asset group are listed below:

a. Current assets $200
b. Liabilities 125
c. Long-lived asset 1 600
d. Long-lived asset 2 500
e. Long-lived asset 3 700
f. Long-lived asset 4 300
g. Long-lived asset 5 900

3. The company computed an impairment loss of $800 million for 20X6.

The provisions of ASC 360 are applicable to Peterson, because it has long-lived assets. In addition, Peterson must assess long-lived assets for impairment, because the current year operating cash flows, history of cash flow losses, and expectations of future cash flow losses could indicate that the carrying amount of the long-lived assets may not be recoverable. Peterson has five long-lived assets and both current assets and liabilities in the group that was used to test for impairment. There is no impairment loss for the current assets and liabilities because the provisions of ASC 360 do not cover these items. However, the carrying value of the current assets and liabilities were adjusted in accordance with other standards prior to applying the impairment provisions of ASC 360. The company has computed an impairment loss of $800 million, and the loss must be allocated among the five long-lived assets using a relative carrying value approach. In Table 3-23-A, the $800 million is allocated to each long-lived asset based on the relationship of the carrying value of that specific asset to the total carrying value of all long-lived assets. That percentage is then applied to the $800 million loss to determine the allocation to the specific asset. For example, Asset 1, with a carrying value of $600 million, is divided by the $3,000 million total carrying value of all assets to produce a 20% allocation to Asset 1. This 20% allocation applied to the $800 million impairment loss provides a $160 million impairment loss allocation to Asset 1.

Table 3-23-A Allocation of Impairment Loss to Long-Lived Assets

Asset (a)	*Carrying Value (b)*	*Fraction of Impairment Loss (c)*	*Impairment Loss (d)*	*Allocation of Impairment Loss (e)=(c)×(d)*
Asset 1	$600	$600/$3,000=20%	$800	$160
Asset 2	500	$500/$3,000=17%	800	136
Asset 3	700	$700/$3,000=23%	800	184
Asset 4	300	$300/$3,000=10%	800	80
Asset 5	900	$900/$3,000=30%	800	240
Total	$3,000			$800

Using the impairment loss allocations from Table 3-23-A, Table 3-23-B shows the computation of the new carrying values for each long-lived asset.

Table 3-23-B Computation of New Carrying Value for Long-Lived Assets

Asset (a)	Original Carrying Value (b)	Allocation of Impairment Loss (c)	New Carrying Value (d) = (b) – (c)
Current Assets	$200		$200
Liabilities	125		125
Asset 1	600	$160	440
Asset 2	500	136	364
Asset 3	700	184	516
Asset 4	300	80	220
Asset 5	900	240	660
Total	$3,325	$800	$2,525

This completes the discussion of Example 3-23. Example 3-24 uses the same assumptions as used in Example 3-23 to illustrate a situation that may require a reallocation of impairment losses when several long-lived assets are in one testing group. Assumptions for Example 3-24 are as follows.

Example 3-24
Assumptions for Long-Lived Assets Held for Use

1. Assume the same facts as in Example 3-23 except that Peterson determined that the fair value of Asset 5 was $750 million.

The assumptions from Example 3-24 indicate that the fair value of Asset 5, which the entity is able to determine without significant cost, of $750 million is in excess of the new carrying value of $660 million (Table 3-23-B). The allocation of an impairment loss to various long-lived assets should not reduce the carrying value of the asset below its fair value. Because the fair value of $750 exceeds the new carrying value of Asset 5 by $90 million ($750 – $660), a reallocation of this $90 difference must be made to the other long-lived assets. The same allocation procedure used in Example 3-23 is used for the reallocation. Table 3-24-A shows the reallocation procedure and the amount of impairment loss reallocated to each asset. Notice that the revised carrying value of each long-lived asset is used in the reallocation process.

Table 3-24-A Reallocation of Impairment Loss

Asset (a)	New Carrying Value (from Table 3-39) (b)	Fraction of Impairment Loss (c)	Impairment Loss (d)	Allocation of Impairment Loss (e)=(c)×(d)
Asset 1	$440	$440/$1,540=29%	$90	$26
Asset 2	364	$364/$1,540=24%	90	22

Asset (a)	New Carrying Value (from Table 3-39) (b)	Fraction of Impairment Loss (c)	Impairment Loss (d)	Allocation of Impairment Loss (e)=(c)×(d)
Asset 3	516	$516/$1,540=33%	90	30
Asset 4	220	$220/$1,540=14%	90	12
Total	$1,540			$90

Using the loss allocation from Table 3-24-A, the new carrying values for the long-lived assets can now be computed. Table 3-24-B shows this computation. Asset 5 is now stated at it $750 million fair value.

Table 3-24-B Computation of Revised Carrying Value of Long-Lived Assets

Asset (a)	Carrying Value Prior To Reallocation (b)	Reallocation of Impairment Loss (c)	New Carrying Value (d)=(b) – (c)
Current Assets	$200		$200
Liabilities	125		125
Asset 1	440	$26	414
Asset 2	364	22	342
Asset 3	516	30	486
Asset 4	220	12	208
Asset 5	660	(90)	750
Total	$2,525	$0	$2,525

Impairment and Disposal of Long-Lived Assets—Disclosure Requirements

The ASC requires significant disclosures for long-lived assets where an impairment loss is reported in the financial statements and for long-lived assets that are held for disposition. The disclosure requirements are divided into long-lived assets with an impairment loss and long-lived assets held for sale.

Long-Lived Assets with an Impairment Loss

The following disclosures should be reported for long-lived assets with an impairment loss (ASC 360-10-50):

1. Describe the long-lived assets that were impaired and the situation that caused the impairment.
2. The amount of the loss on impairment reported in the income statement or statement of activities.
3. The loss on impairment is reported as part of income from continuing operations when presented in the income statement and if income from

operations is used in the statements, the impairment loss should be included as part of that caption.

4. If the loss on impairment is not reported as a separate line item or parenthetically in the statement, the caption where the loss is reported must be disclosed.

5. The method of determining fair value that was used in computing the loss on impairment.

6. The segment of the business impacted by the impairment loss, if appropriate.

Long-Lived Assets Held for Sale

The following disclosures should be reported for long-lived assets sold or held for sale (ASC 205-20-50):

1. Describe the assets held for disposition and the conditions and details generating the following:

   a. Anticipated disposition

   b. Anticipated disposition date

   c. Asset and liability carrying amounts.

2. The amount of the gain or loss on sale or anticipated sale of long-lived assets reported in the income statement or statement of activities.

3. The loss on anticipated asset disposition is reported as part of income from continuing operations when presented in the income statement.

4. If the loss on the anticipated asset disposition is not reported as a separate line item or parenthetically in the statement, the caption where the loss is reported must be disclosed.

5. The amount of the gain or loss generated from changes in estimates about anticipated asset dispositions.

6. The segment of the business impacted by the anticipated asset disposition, if appropriate.

7. If assets subject to an anticipated disposition have results of operations reported in the operations of the total entity, those results should be separately disclosed when results can be determined.

Foreclosure Properties Held for Sale

See the section "Troubled Debt Restructuring—Foreclosures," above, for guidance related to foreclosed and repossessed assets.

Planned Major Maintenance Activities—General Discussion

When accounting for planned major maintenance activities (e.g., the overhaul of an aircraft engine), an entity may not use the accrue-in-advance method in the preparation of either interim or annual financial statements (ASC 360-10-25-5).

CHAPTER 4
LIABILITIES

CONTENTS

The *Liabilities* section of the FASB *Accounting Standards Codification* contains these topics:

405	Liabilities
410	Asset Retirement and Environmental Obligations
420	Exit or Disposal Cost Obligations
430	Deferred Revenue
440	Commitments
450	Contingencies
460	Guarantees
470	Debt
480	Distinguishing Liabilities from Equity

Topic 405: Liabilities

Topic 405, *Liabilities*, contains the following subtopics:

- 10 Overall
- 20 Extinguishments of Liabilities
- 30 Insurance-Related Assessments
- 40 Obligations Resulting from Joint and Several Liability Arrangements
- 905 Agriculture*
- 910 Contractors—Construction*
- 912 Contractors—Federal Government*
- 920 Entertainment—Broadcasters*
- 924 Entertainment—Casinos*
- 926 Entertainment—Films*
- 928 Entertainment—Music*
- 940 Financial Services—Brokers and Dealers*
- 942 Financial Services—Depository and Lending*
- 944 Financial Services—Insurance*
- 946 Financial Services—Investment Companies*
- 954 Health Care Entities*
- 958 Not-For-Profit Entities*
- 980 Regulated Operations*

* See the corresponding topic in Chapter 9 for coverage of this shared subtopic.

Topic 405: Liabilities

Topic 405 includes the following subtopics:

10 Overall

20 Extinguishments of Liabilities

30 Insurance-Related Assessments

40 Obligations Resulting from Joint and Several Liability Arrangements.

Extinguishment of Liabilities

Subtopic 20 under ASC 405 addresses extinguishments of liabilities but does not address debt conversions or troubled debt restructurings.

An entity may settle a liability by transferring assets to the creditor or otherwise obtaining an unconditional release. Alternatively, an entity may enter into other arrangements designed to set aside assets dedicated to eventually settling a liability.

The guidance in ASC 405-20 applies to extinguishments of all liabilities, including both financial liabilities and nonfinancial liabilities.

A debtor shall derecognize a liability when it has been extinguished. A liability has been extinguished if:

1. The debtor pays the creditor and is relieved of its obligation for the liability. Paying the creditor includes:
   a. Delivering cash,
   b. Delivering other financial assets,
   c. Delivering goods or services, and
   d. Reacquiring by the debtor of its outstanding debt securities.
2. The debtor is legally released from being the primary obligor under the liability, either judicially or by the creditor. For purposes of applying this Subtopic, a sale and related assumption effectively accomplish a legal release if nonrecourse debt (such as certain mortgage loans) is assumed by a third party in conjunction with the sale of an asset that serves as sole collateral for that debt.

If a creditor releases a debtor from primary obligation on the condition that a third party assumes the obligation and that the original debtor becomes secondarily liable, that release extinguishes the original debtor's liability. However, in those circumstances, whether or not explicit consideration was paid for that guarantee, the original debtor becomes a guarantor. As a guarantor, it shall recognize a guarantee obligation in the same manner as would a guarantor that had never been primarily liable to that creditor, with due regard for the likelihood that the third party will carry out its obligations. The guarantee obligation shall be initially measured at fair value, and that amount reduces the gain or increases the loss recognized on extinguishment.

Recent Update to ASC 405-20

Liabilities related to the sale of prepaid stored-value products within the scope of ASU 2016-04, *Liabilities—Extinguishments of Liabilities (Subtopic 405-20): Recognition of Breakage for Certain Prepaid Stored-Value Products (a consensus of the FASB Emerging Issues Task Force),* are financial liabilities. ASU 2016-04 provides a narrow scope exception to the guidance in Subtopic 405-20 to require that breakage for those liabilities be accounted for consistent with the breakage guidance in Topic 606.

ASU 2016-04 is effective for public business entities, certain not-for-profit entities, and certain employee benefit plans for financial statements issued for fiscal years beginning after December 15, 2017, and interim periods within those fiscal years. For all other entities, it is effective for financial statements issued for fiscal years beginning after December 15, 2018, and interim periods within fiscal years beginning after December 15, 2019. Earlier application is permitted, including adoption in an interim period.

ASU 2016-04 should be applied either using a modified retrospective transition method by means of a cumulative-effect adjustment to retained earnings as of the beginning of the fiscal year in which the guidance is effective or retrospectively to each period presented.

Insurance-Related Assessments

Subtopic 30 under ASC 405 addresses accounting for insurance-related assessments. The subtopic applies to insurance entities as well as noninsurance entities that are subject to a variety of assessments related to insurance activities, including those by state guaranty funds and workers' compensation second-injury funds. Some entities may be subject to insurance-related assessments because they self-insure against loss or liability.

State Guaranty Funds

States have enacted legislation establishing guaranty funds. The state guaranty funds assess entities licensed to sell insurance in the state to provide for the payment of covered claims or to meet other insurance obligations—subject to prescribed limits—of insolvent insurance entities. The assessments are generally based on premium volume for certain covered lines of business. Most state guaranty funds assess entities for costs related to a particular insolvency after the insolvency occurs.

State guaranty funds use a variety of methods for assessing entities, including retrospective-premium-based assessments, prospective-premium-based assessments, prefunded-premium-based assessments, and administrative-type assessments.

ASC 405-30 applies to assessments mandated by statute or regulatory authority that are related directly or indirectly to underwriting activities (including self-insurance), except for income taxes and premium taxes.

ASC 405-30 does not apply to the following transactions and activities:

1. Amounts payable or paid as a result of reinsurance contracts or arrangements that are in substance reinsurance.
2. Assessments of depository institutions related to bank insurance and similar funds.
3. The annual fee imposed on health insurers by the Patient Protection and Affordable Care Act as amended by the Health Care and Education Reconciliation Act (the Acts).

Entities subject to assessments shall recognize liabilities for insurance-related assessments when all of the following conditions are met:

1. *Probability of assessment.* An assessment has been imposed or information available before the financial statements are issued or are available to be issued indicates it is probable that an assessment will be imposed.
2. *Obligating event.* The event obligating an entity to pay (underlying cause of) an imposed or probable assessment has occurred on or before the date of the financial statements.
3. *Ability to reasonably estimate.* The amount of the assessment can be reasonably estimated.

Additional guidance for the probability of assessment follows.

Premium-based guaranty-fund assessments, except those that are prefunded, are presumed probable when a formal determination of insolvency occurs and presumed not probable before a formal determination of insolvency. For these purposes, a formal determination of insolvency occurs when an entity meets a state's (ordinarily the state of domicile of the insolvent insurer) statutory definition of an insolvent insurer. In most states, the entity must be declared to be financially insolvent by a court of competent jurisdiction. In some states, there must also be a final order of liquidation.

Prefunded guaranty-fund assessments and premium-based administrative-type assessments are presumed probable when the premiums on which the assessments are expected to be based are written. Loss-based administrative-type and second-injury fund assessments are presumed probable when the losses on which the assessments are expected to be based are incurred.

Additional guidance for determining the obligating event follows.

Because of the fundamental differences in how assessment mechanisms operate, the event that makes an assessment probable (e.g., an insolvency) may not be the event that obligates an entity. The following defines the event that obligates an entity to pay an assessment for each kind of assessment identified in ASC 405-30:

1. For premium-based assessments, the event that obligates the entity is generally writing the premiums or becoming obligated to write or renew (such as multiple-year, noncancelable policies) the premiums on which the assessments are expected to be based. Some states, through law or regulatory practice, provide that an insurance entity cannot avoid paying a particular assessment even if that insurance entity reduces its premium writing in the future. In such circumstances, the event that

obligates the entity is a formal determination of insolvency or similar triggering event. For example, in certain states, an insurance entity may remain liable for assessments even though the insurance entity discontinues the writing of premiums. In this circumstance, the underlying cause of the liability is not the writing of the premium, but the insolvency. Regulatory practice would be determined based on the stated intentions or prior history of the insurance regulators.

2. For loss-based assessments, the event that obligates an entity is an entity's incurring the losses on which the assessments are expected to be based.

Additional guidance for determining whether the entity has the ability to reasonably estimate the liability follows.

One of the conditions for recognizing a liability is that the amount can be reasonably estimated. Some amount of loss can be reasonably estimated when available information indicates that the estimated amount of the loss is within a range of amounts. If no amount within the range is a better estimate than any other amount, the minimum amount in the range should be accrued.

Recognition of Liability for Assessments

Guaranty-fund assessments and other insurance-related assessments, as referred to above, should be recognized as follows:

1. A liability for retrospective-premium-based guaranty-fund assessments should be recognized for the entire amount of future assessments related to a particular insolvency when a formal determination of insolvency is rendered.
2. A liability for prospective-premium-based guaranty-fund assessments should be recognized when the entity is writing or becoming obligated to write or renew, the premiums on which the expected future assessments are to be based (e.g., multiple-year contracts under which an insurance entity has no discretion to avoid writing future premiums). Therefore, the event that obligates the entity generally will not have occurred at the time of the insolvency. Law or regulatory practice affects the event that obligates the entity in either of the following ways:
   a. In states that, through law or regulatory practice, provide that an entity cannot avoid paying a particular assessment in the future (even if the entity reduces premium writings in the future), the event that obligates the entity is a formal determination of insolvency or a similar event. An entity that has the ability to reasonably estimate the amount of the assessment shall recognize a liability for the entire amount of future assessments that cannot be avoided related to a particular insolvency when a formal determination of insolvency occurs.
   b. In states without such a law or regulatory practice, the event that obligates the entity is the writing of, or becoming obligated to write, the premiums on which the expected future assessments are to be

based. An entity that has the ability to reasonably estimate the amount of the assessments shall recognize a liability when the related premiums are written or when the entity becomes obligated to write the premiums.

3. A liability for refunded-premium-based guaranty-fund assessments should be recognized when the related premiums are written.
4. A liability for other premium-based assessments should be recognized in the same manner as prefunded-premium-based guaranty-fund assessments.
5. A liability for loss-based assessments should be recognized as the related loss is incurred.
6. A liability for administrative-type assessments are generally recognized (expensed) in the period assessed.

Asset for Premium Tax Offsets and Policy Surcharges

When it is probable that a paid or accrued assessment will result in an amount that is recoverable from premium tax offsets or policy surcharges, an asset shall be recognized for that recovery.

For retrospective-premium-based assessments, to the extent that it is probable that paid or accrued assessments will result in a recoverable amount in a future period from business currently in force considering appropriate persistency rates for long-duration contracts, an asset shall be recognized at the time the liability is recorded.

An asset shall not be established for paid or accrued assessments that are recoverable through future premium rate structures.

Policy surcharges that are required as a pass-through to the state or other regulatory bodies shall be accounted for in a manner such that amounts collected or receivable are not recorded as revenues and amounts due or paid are not expensed (meaning, similar to accounting for sales tax).

Estimating the Liability

Entities subject to assessments may be able to obtain information to assist in estimating the total guaranty-fund cost or the following years' assessments, as appropriate, for an insolvency from entities such as the state guaranty fund associations, the National Organization of Life and Health Insurance Guaranty Associations, and the National Conference of Insurance Guaranty Funds.

An entity need not be able to compute the exact amounts of the assessments or be formally notified of such assessments by a guaranty fund to make a reasonable estimate of its liability. Entities subject to assessments may have to make assumptions about future events, such as when the fund will incur costs and pay claims that will determine the amounts and the timing of assessments.

The best available information about market share or premiums by state and premiums by line of business shall be used to estimate the amount of an insurance entity's future assessments.

If a noninsurance entity's assessments are based on premiums, it may be necessary to consider the amount of premium the self-insurer would have paid if it had insured its liability with an insurer. If a noninsurance entity's assessments are based on losses, it shall consider the losses that have been incurred by the entity when determining the liability. Most often, assessments that have an impact on noninsurance entities that self-insure workers' compensation obligations are for second-injury funds. Second-injury funds generally assess insurance entities and self-insurers based on paid losses.

A noninsurance entity may develop an accrual for its second-injury liability based on any of the following methods:

1. The ratio of the entity's prior-period paid workers' compensation claims to aggregate workers' compensation claims in the state that was used as a basis for previous assessments.
2. Total fund assessments in prior periods.
3. Known changes in the current period to either the number of employees self-insured by the entity or the number of workers who are the subject of recoveries from the second-injury fund that might alter total fund assessments and the entity's proportion of the total fund assessments.

Estimates of loss-based assessments shall be consistent with estimates of the underlying incurred losses and shall be developed based on enacted laws or regulations and expected assessment rates.

Estimates of some insurance-related assessment liabilities may be difficult to derive. The development or determination of estimates is particularly difficult for guaranty-fund assessments because of uncertainties about the cost of the insolvency to the guaranty fund and the portion that will be recovered through assessment. Examples of uncertainties include the following:

- Limitations, as provided by statute, on the amount of individual contract liabilities that the guaranty fund will assume, that cause the guaranty fund associations' liability to be less than the amount by which the entity is insolvent.
- Contract provisions (e.g., credited rates) that may be modified at the time of the insolvency or alternative payout options that may be offered to contract holders that affect the level and payout of the guaranty fund's liability.
- The extent and timing of available reinsurance recoveries, which may be subject to significant uncertainties.
- Alternative strategies for the liquidation of assets of the insolvent entity that affect the timing and level of assessments.
- Certain liabilities of the insolvent insurer that may be particularly difficult to estimate (e.g., asbestos or environmental liabilities).

Because of the uncertainties surrounding some insurance-related assessments, the range of assessment liability may have to be reevaluated regularly during the assessment process. For some ranges, there may be amounts that appear to be better estimates than any other within the range. If this is the case, the liability recorded shall be based on the best estimate within the range. For ranges in which there is no such best estimate, the liability that should be recorded shall be based on the amount representing the minimum amount in the range.

Present Value Measurement of the Obligation

Current practice in the insurance industry is to allow, but not require (with limited exceptions, such as pensions and postretirement benefits), the discounting of liabilities to reflect the time value of money when the aggregate amount of the obligation and the amount and timing of the cash payments are fixed or reliably determinable for a particular liability.

Similarly, for assessments that meet those criteria, the liability may be recorded at its present value by discounting the estimated future cash flows at an appropriate interest rate.

Asset for Premium Tax Offsets and Policy Surcharges

The asset recognized for premium tax offsets and policy surcharges shall be measured based on current laws and projections of future premium collections or policy surcharges from in-force policies. In determining the asset to be recorded, in-force policies do not include expected renewals of short-duration contracts but do include assumptions as to persistency rates for long-duration contracts.

The time value of money need not be considered in the determination of the recorded amount of a potential recovery if the liability is not discounted. In instances in which the recovery period for an asset is substantially longer than the payout period for the liability, it may be appropriate to record the asset on a discounted basis regardless of whether the liability is discounted.

The recognition of such assets related to prospective-premium-based assessments is limited to the amount of premium an entity has written or is obligated to write and to the amounts recoverable over the life of the in-force policies. The expected premium tax offset or policy surcharge asset related to the accrual of prospective-premium-based assessments shall be based on and limited to the amount recoverable as a result of premiums the insurer has written or is obligated to write.

Subsequent Measurement for Asset for Premium Tax Offsets and Policy Surcharges

The asset recorded for premium tax offsets and policy surcharges shall be subject to a valuation allowance to reflect any portion of the asset that is no longer probable of realization. Considering expected future premiums other than on in-force policies in evaluating the recoverability of premium tax offsets or policy surcharges is not appropriate.

Disclosures

In general, the disclosures related to loss contingencies apply to this topic under ASU 405-30. Additionally, if amounts have been discounted, the entity shall disclose in the financial statements the undiscounted amounts of the liability and any related asset for premium tax offsets or policy surcharges as well as the discount rate used. If amounts have not been discounted, the entity shall disclose in the financial statements the amounts of the liability, any related asset for premium tax offsets or policy surcharges, the periods over which the assessments are expected to be paid, and the period over which the recorded premium tax offsets or policy surcharges are expected to be realized.

Obligations Resulting from Joint and Several Liability

Subtopic 40 under ASC 405 includes in its scope obligations resulting from joint and several liability arrangements under debt agreements, contracts, settled litigation, and court decisions. For an obligation for which the amount is "fixed" as of the reporting date, the entity records a liability equal to the sum of the amount the entity has agreed to pay based on the arrangement with its co-obligors plus any additional amount the entity expects to pay on behalf of its co-obligors representing the "best estimate" if there is one or the minimum amount within a range following the contingent loss rules. The entity is required to disclose the following:

a. The total amount of the outstanding obligation under the arrangement, without regard to any amounts that may be recoverable from other entities.
b. The carrying amount of the liability and the receivable recognized.
c. The nature of any recourse provisions that would result in the recovery of amounts paid, including any limitations.
d. The entry initially recorded and any significant subsequent changes, including the financial statement line items.

Topic 405 does not contain any other accounting guidance. Instead, it identifies the locations in the ASC that provide guidance for specific types of liabilities. The following topics directly address the recognition of specific liabilities and are also discussed below in this chapter.

- Asset Retirement and Environmental Obligations, see Topic 410
- Exit or Disposal Cost Obligations, see Topic 420
- Deferred Revenue, see Topic 430
- Commitments, see Topic 440
- Contingencies, see Topic 450
- Guarantees, see Topic 460
- Debt, see Topic 470
- Distinguishing Liabilities from Equity, see Topic 480

Topic 410: Asset Retirement and Environmental Obligations

Topic 410, *Asset Retirement and Environmental Obligations*, contains four subtopics:

10 Overall

20 Asset Retirement Obligations

30 Environmental Obligations

980 Regulated Operations [See the corresponding topic in Chapter 9 for coverage of this shared subtopic.]

General Discussion—Asset Retirement Obligations

ASC 410-20 specifies the accounting and reporting requirements for liabilities related to the retirement of tangible long-lived assets and the related asset retirement cost. Examples of assets covered by ASC 410-20 include assets related to nuclear power plants, mining and landfill operations, offshore oil platforms and oil fields. Also, lease agreements often contain requirements that the lessee return the leased property to its original state as of the inception of the lease. If the lessee made leasehold improvements, then the lessee should record an asset retirement obligation, as discussed below.

ASC 410-20 applies to all enterprises that have legal obligations related to the retirement of long-lived assets of a tangible nature that are a result of the development, acquisition, or construction of long-lived tangible assets, and/or the normal operations of the assets. Legal obligation related to the retirement is defined in a broad manner by the ASC and includes an obligation that an entity must settle because of an existing law, an enacted law, a statute, an ordinance, an oral contract, a written contract, or a contract under the doctrine of promissory estoppel. The doctrine of promissory estoppel states that an obligation related to asset retirement may exist even though no consideration was provided for the promise to reclaim the property, because the entity making the promise should have expected the entity receiving the promise to rely on the promise.

ASC 410-20 does not apply to an obligation that is created solely from a plan to dispose of a tangible long-lived asset under the provisions of ASC 360 or to an obligation created from using the asset improperly. In addition, ASC 410-20 does not apply to certain types of lessee obligations. Lessee obligations generally should be accounted for using the provisions of ASC 840. However, if a lessee obligation meets the requirements of a legal obligation for retirement as discussed above, and the lease obligation does not meet the definition of minimum lease payments or contingent rental payments using the provisions of ASC 840, then the provisions of ASC 410-20 would apply. In addition, if the lease obligation of the lessor meets the requirements of ASC 840, the obligation should be accounted for using the provisions of ASC 410-20 instead of ASC 840.

Once an entity determines that a retirement obligation for tangible long-lived assets should be reported, a liability for the asset retirement obligation is to be reported at an amount equal to the fair value of the liability in the accounting period that the liability is incurred, if it is reasonable to determine fair value. When it is not reasonable to determine fair value in the accounting period incurred, the liability should be reported in the accounting period when it is first possible to reasonably determine the fair value of the liability (ASC 410-20-25-4). FASB Statement of Financial Accounting Concepts (SFAC) No. 6 addresses liability recognition and ASC 410-20 addresses fair value measurements.

ASC 410-20-25-6 provides additional information about fair value measurement and states that the fair value of the asset retirement obligation generally can be estimated when any of the following conditions exist:

- Information indicates that the obligation's fair value is embodied in the purchase price of the asset;
- An active market is available for the transfer of the obligation; or
- Information is available that allows for the application of a present value model that incorporates uncertainty and timing into the fair value estimate.

Generally, it is assumed that information is available for application of present value techniques when others have specified the method and timing of the settlement of the asset retirement obligation such as by contract, law, or regulation and information is available to estimate the date of settlement or range of dates, method of settlement, or potential methods of settlement and the probabilities related to dates and methods of settlement. When an entity has a conditional asset retirement obligation (the timing and/or method of settlement are dependent upon some future event), the liability should be reported when the fair value of the obligation can reasonably be estimated. ASC 410-20-55, paragraphs 47 through 62, provide several examples illustrating when an entity is able to estimate the fair value of the asset retirement obligation.

Once the asset retirement liability has been computed, the related long-lived asset should be increased by an amount equal to the amount of the liability in the same accounting period that the liability is reported.

ASC 820 provides guidance on the determination of fair value. Fair value is the amount that would be received on the measurement date from the sale of property or the amount paid to transfer a liability between sellers and buyers (market participants) in an orderly transaction. In addition, it is assumed that the sellers and buyers are unrelated parties on the measurement date. One way to determine fair value is to use quoted market prices. In many cases, however, quoted market prices are not available and an enterprise must estimate fair value. Fair value may be estimated using future cash flows on a present-value basis. One present-value method is referred to as the expected-present-value technique. The expected-present-value technique uses multiple cash flows situations to reflect the possible cash flow outcomes for a specific asset retirement obligation and a credit-adjusted risk-free interest rate. The traditional present value technique uses a single set of cash flows and an interest rate equal to the risk of the situation. ASC 410-20-30-1 states that the expected-present-value technique will usually be the only one that would be appropriate for asset retirement liabilities because of the uncertainties related to both timing and amount of future cash flows.

When estimating cash flows to determine fair value of the retirement liability, the enterprise should normally use the same assumptions that the market place would use if the information is available without significant effort or cost to the entity. If the market place information is not available, the enterprise should use its own assumptions that are reasonable and can be supported when computing cash flow information. In addition, when discounting cash flows using the expected cash flow approach, the entity should use a credit-adjusted risk-free discount rate that reflects the entity's credit standing.

An asset retirement liability may be incurred in more than one accounting period because the obligation is created over more than one time period, such as in the case of nuclear power plants or landfills. If the obligation is incurred over more than one accounting period, each liability incurred is accounted for as a separate liability layer and each layer is measured at fair value (ASC 410-20-35-1).

Once an asset retirement liability is recorded, increases and decreases in the liability may occur in subsequent accounting periods. The changes in the liability account generally occur for two reasons: (1) increases in the liability from passage of time, and (2) increases and decreases in the liability from changes in estimates of cash flows. The entity should always adjust the liability for increases due to the passage of time prior to adjustments resulting from changes in cash flow estimates. Increases in the liability from the passage of time, referred to as accretion in ASC 410-20, are computed by using the interest method of amortization. The interest method is the application of the discount rate used in the computation of the present value amount to the beginning liability balance. An expense will be debited and the retirement liability will be credited for the amount of the accretion. The expense is reported in the income statement as an operating expense; however, the amount of the accretion cannot be used as part of interest expense for purposes of applying the provisions of ASC 835-20 related to interest capitalization. Increases and decreases in the amount or timing of cash flows should be used to increase or decrease both the retirement liability and the related long-lived asset. Increases in cash flows should be discounted at the current risk-adjusted discount rate and decreases in cash flows should be discounted using the discount rate that was used when the cash flows were originally discounted if it is possible to determine the rate used. If the rate is not determinable, a weighted average discount rate should be used for cash flow decreases. Any increase or decrease in the long-lived asset should be treated as a change in accounting estimate in accordance with the provisions of ASC 250.

The increase in the long-lived asset from the recognition of an asset retirement liability is allocated over its remaining useful life using a systematic and rational method. However, in some situations, an enterprise may capitalize and expense the same amount in a specific accounting period. To illustrate, assume an enterprise has a long-lived asset with a five-year remaining life where 20% of the asset retirement liability is capitalized each accounting period. The entity generally would not violate the systematic and rational method rule by expensing in the same accounting period the 20% of the liability capitalized.

When testing the long-lived assets for impairment using the provisions of ASC 360, the carrying amount of the long-lived asset used in the testing process should include the amount of the asset retirement liability. However, cash flows related to the asset retirement liability should be excluded from the computation of fair value and the undiscounted cash flows used in testing recoverability of the asset. The fair value of the asset retirement liability is used to increase the fair value of long-lived assets if a quoted market price is used instead of cash flows to determine fair value and the quoted price incorporates the costs of asset retirement (ASC 360-10-35, paragraphs 18 and 19).

An entity may acquire insurance policies, guarantees by other companies, surety bonds, or other items to provide assurance for the asset retirement obligation. Acquisition of assurance or other funding does not satisfy the asset retirement obligation or allow retirement of the related liability. However, such assurances may impact the credit-adjusted risk-free discount rate used in the present value computations. Changes in assurances also may impact the credit-adjusted risk-free rate used in the discounting of the increases in cash flows. Any cost incurred by the entity related to assurances is not accounted for as part of the asset retirement obligation.

A regulated entity subject to the provisions of ASC 980 may have costs related to asset retirement obligations that will be recovered from customers. There may be a difference in the timing of amounts used for rate-making purposes and the amounts reported in the financial statements using ASC 410-20. When a regulated entity meets the requirements of ASC 980 and reports different amounts for rate-making purposes as compared to the amounts reported on the financial statements resulting from a timing difference, a regulatory asset or liability should be reported for this difference (ASC 980-410-25-2).

Technical Considerations

Three examples are used to illustrate the technical aspects of asset retirement obligations. Assumptions for Example 4-1 are as follows.

Example 4-1
Assumptions for Asset Retirement Obligations

1. Fischer, Inc. (Fischer) a December 31 year-end company, placed an offshore oil platform in service on January 1, 20X6. Fischer has a legal requirement to remove the platform at the end of its five-year useful life.

2. On January 1, Fischer incurred an asset retirement liability and the company measures the fair value of the liability using expected cash flows; this fair value measurement is assumed to be in accordance with ASC 410-20. The expected cash flows adjusted for market risk related to the asset retirement obligation is $1,000,000. The credit-adjusted risk-free rate of interest is 7%.

3. The increase in the long-lived asset from the asset retirement obligation is depreciated over the five-year life using a straight-line method.

4. Fischer used an outside contractor to settle the asset retirement obligation at a cost of $921,000.

Because Fischer has a legal requirement to remove the offshore oil platform at the end of its useful life of five years, it has incurred an asset retirement obligation on January 1, 20X6. Next, Fischer should determine the expected cash flows related to the obligation and then estimate fair value of the liability by computing the present value of expected cash flows using a credit-adjusted risk-free rate of interest. Fischer has determined that expected cash flows adjusted for market risk are equal to $1,000,000, and the credit-adjusted risk-free rate of interest is 7%. Using this information and the expected life of five years, the fair value of the liability can be computed as below:

Expected cash flows	$1,000,000
Present value of $1 factor (5 periods at 7%)(Appendix E)	.712986
Present value of expected cash flows (fair value)	$712,986

Using the fair value amount of $712,986, the journal entry required to record the liability on January 1, 20X6, is as follows:

Long-Lived Asset	712,986	
Liability For Asset Retirement		712,986

The liability for asset retirement will increase over the five-year useful life based on the passage of time. This annual increase (accretion expense) is computed using the interest method, which is the application of the 7% discount rate to the beginning balance of the asset retirement liability. The annual accretion expense is computed in Table 4-1.

Table 4-1 Computation of Accretion Expense for Asset Retirement Obligation

Date	*Accretion Expense*	*Liability Balance*
Beginning Balance		$712,986
20X6	$49,909 [a]	762,895
20X7	53,403	816,298
20X8	57,141	873,439
20X9	61,141	934,580
2010	65,420	1,000,000
Total Accretion	$287,014	

[a] $712,986 × 7% = $49,909.

In Table 4-1, the increase in the asset retirement liability from the accretion expense causes the liability to equal $1,000,000 at the end of the life of the asset. The $1,000,000 liability balance is the amount of the expected cash flows adjusted for market risk. Next, the depreciation of the asset retirement obligation added to the long-lived asset must be computed. The component is depreciated using a straight-line method over a five-year useful life. Table 4-2 shows the computation of the annual depreciation amount.

Table 4-2 Computation of Annual Depreciation Expense

Date	*Depreciation Expense*	*Liability Balance*
Beginning Balance		$712,986
20X6	$142,597 [a]	570,389
20X7	142,597	427,792
20X8	142,597	285,195
20X9	142,597	142,598
20Y0	142,598 [b]	0
Total	$712,986	

[a] $712,986/5 Years = $142,597.
[b] Rounded

Using the information from Tables 4-1 and 4-2, journal entries at December 31, 20X6 to record accretion and depreciation expense are presented below:

Accretion Expense	49,909	
Liability For Asset Retirement		49,909
Depreciation Expense	142,597	
Accumulated Depreciation		142,597

Accretion and depreciation expense are reported in the income statement as operating expenses. Journal entries for accretion and depreciation expense for the remaining four years are the same as show above, except for amounts. Amounts for the remaining four years for accretion and depreciation expense can be taken directly from Tables 4-1 and 4-2.

At the end of 2010, the asset retirement obligation is settled by an outside contractor for $921,000, which is $79,000 ($1,000,000 – $921,000) less than the entity expected to incur to eliminate the liability. Therefore, Fischer has a $79,000 gain from settlement of the obligation. The entry to settle the asset retirement obligation and to report the gain at the end of 2010 is as follows.

Liability For Asset Retirement	1,000,000	
Accounts Payable		921,000
Gain On Settlement Of Liability For Asset Retirement		79,000

The gain on settlement of the asset retirement liability is reported in the income statement as a line item in income from continuing operations. This completes the discussion of Example 4-1. Example 4-2 covers issues related to the computation of an asset retirement obligation using expected cash flows. Assumptions for Example 4-2 are as follows.

Example 4-2
Assumptions for Asset Retirement Obligations

1. Lang Enterprises (Lang), a December 31 year-end company, placed a long-lived asset in service on January 1, 20X6. Lang has a legal requirement to remove the long-lived asset at the end of its five-year useful life.

2. On January 1, Lang incurred an asset retirement liability, and it measures fair value of the liability using expected cash flows. Lang has estimated expected cash flows for labor costs as follows: a 10% probability that cash flows will be $250,000, a 30% probability that cash flows will be $325,000, a 40% probability that cash flows will be $400,000, and a 20% probability that cash flows will be $450,000.

3. Lang allocates overhead and equipment usage to labor at a 75% rate, which is equivalent to the percentage used by outside contractors. A profit margin of 15% is added to labor and allocated costs, and a risk premium of 4% of inflation adjusted expected cash flows is included in the cash flow computations.

4. A rate of inflation of 2% is assumed for the five-year life of the long-lived asset. The risk-free discount rate is 6%; 2% is added to the risk free rate to reflect Lang's credit standing.

5. This fair value measurement is assumed to be in accordance with ASC 820's fair value measurement requirements.

Because Lang has a legal requirement to remove the long-lived asset at the end of its useful life of five years, it has incurred an asset retirement obligation on January 1, 20X6. Next, Lang will determine the fair value of the liability by using expected cash flows. Lang should determine the expected cash flows related to labor cost for the obligation. Because Lang has estimated four possible streams or options of cash flows for labor costs with specific probabilities for each option, each cash flow option will be weighted based on its percentage of probability of occurring. After each option has been weighted, all weighted options are totaled to arrive at a $372,500 probability weighted average cash flow for the labor cost as shown in Table 4-3.

Table 4-3 Computation of Probability Weighted Average Cash Flows

Cash Flow Options	*Net Cash Flows*	*Probability Assessment*	*Probability Weighted Average Cash Flows*
1	$250,000	10%	$25,000
2	$325,000	30%	97,500
3	$400,000	40%	160,000
4	$450,000	20%	90,000
Total		100%	$372,500

Once cash flows for labor costs have been computed, cash flows adjusted for market risk may be computed. After cash flows adjusted for market risk have been determined, the present value of the market risk adjusted cash flows using Lang's credit-adjusted risk-free rate of interest of 8% can be calculated to arrive at fair value of the asset retirement liability. Table 4-4 shows these calculations.

Table 4-4 Computation of Expected Cash Flow Adjusted for Market Risk and Present Value of Cash Flows

Cash flows for labor costs (from Table 4-3)		$372,500
Allocation of equipment and overhead ($372,500 × 75%)		279,375
Total cash flows for labor and allocated costs . .		$651,875
Markup ($651,875 × 15%)		97,781
Cash flows prior to inflation adjustment		$749,656
2% inflation adjustment:		
Cash flows prior to adjustment	$749,656	
Future Value of $1 (2% for 5 periods)	1.10408	
Cash flows with inflation adjustment	$827,680	
Cash flows prior to adjustment	749,656	
2% inflation adjustment		78,024
Expected cash flow adjusted for inflation		$827,680
Adjustment for market risk premium ($827,680 × 4%)		33,107
Expected cash flows after market risk adjustment		$860,787
Present value of $1 factor (8% for 5 periods) (Appendix E)		.680583
Expected present value of expected cash flows (fair value)		$585,837

The computation of expected cash flows after adjustment of market risk includes all items that an outside contractor would normally use to compute an estimate for asset retirement. It incorporates an allocation of equipment and overhead costs, profit margin, inflation adjustment, and a premium for market risk. Using information from Table 4-4, the journal entry to record the asset retirement liability and the related increase in the long-lived asset at January 1, 20X6 is presented below:

Long-Lived Asset	585,837	
Liability For Asset Retirement		585,837

Once the liability is recorded, it must be increased each year for the accretion due to passage of time. Because the company's credit-adjusted risk-free rate of interest of 8% was used to compute the fair value of the liability, the 8% rate will be used to compute the annual accretion expense. The ending balance in the liability account will equal the market risk adjusted expected cash flows shown in Table 4-4 because this is the amount that normally would be paid at the time the asset is actually retired. Table 4-5 shows this computation.

Table 4-5 Computation of Accretion Expense for Asset Retirement Obligation

Date	*Accretion Expense*	*Liability Balance*
Beginning Balance		$585,837
20X6	$46,867 [a]	632,704
20X7	50,616	683,320
20X8	54,666	737,986
20X9	59,039	797,025
2010	63,762	860,787
Total	$274,950	

[a] $585,837 × 8% = $46,867.

Journal entries for the accretion expense are illustrated in Example 4-1 material and will not be repeated for Example 4-2. The reader is encouraged to review the accretion journal entries from Example 4-1. Next, the increase in the long-lived asset from the asset retirement obligation must be depreciated. Lang uses a straight-line method over the five-year useful life of the asset to depreciate the asset component. The amount of annual depreciation is $117,167 ($585,837 ÷ 5 Years). Journal entries for annual depreciation are illustrated in Example 4-1. Please review the depreciation journal entries from Example 4-1 material. This completes the explanation of Example 4-2. Example 4-3 uses the same assumptions as in Example 4-2, but illustrates a change in cash flows after two years of operation. Assumptions for Example 4-3 are as follows.

Example 4-3
Assumptions for Asset Retirement Obligations

1. Assume the same facts as in Example 4-2, except after two years, Lang increases by 5% its estimate for labor costs but did not change the probability assessment relative to cash flow patterns.

2. At the time of the change in labor costs, the credit-adjusted risk-free discount rate is 7%.

The increase in labor cost by 5% causes a revision in cash flows related to labor cost, which will cause all aspects of the valuation of the asset retirement obligation to change. This change will cause an increase in both the asset retirement liability and the related long-lived asset. Any increase in cash flows requires that the present value of the cash flows be revised using the then current credit-adjusted risk-free discount rate, which is 7%. The first step is to revise cash flows associated with labor cost. Table 4-6 shows the revised cash flows labor cost.

Table 4-6 Computation of Probability Weighted Average Cash Flows

Cash Flow Options	*Net Cash Flows*	*Probability Assessment*	*Probability Weighted Average Cash Flows*
1 . . .	$250,000 × 1.05% = $262,500	10%	$26,250
2 . . .	$325,000 × 1.05% = $341,250	30%	102,375
3 . . .	$400,000 × 1.05% = $420,000	40%	168,000
4 . . .	$450,000 × 1.05% = $472,500	20%	94,500
Total		100%	$391,125

Table 4-6 shows that the 5% increase in labor costs caused the cash flow labor cost to increase to $391,125. The difference in the prior cash flow labor cost of $372,500 and the new cash flow labor costs of $391,125 is the increase in cash flow labor costs of $18,625 ($391,125 – $372,500 from Table 4-4) that will be used to compute the market risk adjusted expected cash flows. Table 4-7 shows the market risk adjusted cash flows and the new present value computation for the expected cash flows for the cash flow increase.

Table 4-7 Computation of Present Value of the Increase in Market Risk Adjusted Expected Cash Flows

Increase in cash flows for labor costs		$18,625
Allocation of equipment and overhead ($18,625 × 75%)		13,969
Total cash flows for labor and allocated costs . .		$32,594
Markup ($32,594 × 15%)		4,889
Cash flows prior to inflation adjustment		$37,483
2% inflation adjustment:		
Cash flows prior to adjustment	$37,483	
Future value of $1 (2% for 3 periods)	1.0612	
Cash flows with inflation adjustment	$39,777	
Cash flows prior to adjustment	37,483	
2% inflation adjustment		2,294
Expected cash flow adjusted for inflation		$39,777
Adjustment for market risk premium ($39,777 × 4%)		1,591

Expected cash flows after market risk adjustment	$41,368
Present value of $1 factor (7% for 3 periods) . . .	.816298
Expected present value of expected cash flows (fair value)	$33,769

Using the information from Table 4-7, the journal entry to show the increase in the asset retirement liability and the related long-lived asset on January 1, 20X8 is presented below.

Long-Lived Asset	33,769	
Liability For Asset Retirement		33,769

The amount of depreciation expense for 20X8–20X10 will increase because of the increase in the long-lived asset and the amount of accretion expense for the same time period will also increase.

Disclosure Requirements

ASC 410-20-50 specifies the disclosure requirements for asset retirement obligations. The required disclosures follow:

1. Describe the asset retirement obligation and the related long-lived asset.
2. Disclose the fair value of assets legally restricted for settling obligations related to asset retirements.
3. Roll forward the beginning asset retirement obligation to the ending balance showing accretion expense reported in the income statement, the settlement of retirement obligations during the current accounting period, retirement obligations incurred during the current accounting period, and changes in the retirement obligations due to estimated cash flow revisions.
4. If fair value cannot be reasonably estimated, disclose that fact and the reasons.

Environmental Obligations

Environmental remediation obligations under environment remediation liability laws are loss contingencies. ASC 450-20-25-2 requires the accrual of a liability if information becomes available before the financial statements are issued or are available to be issued that indicates that: (1) it is probable that an asset has been impaired or a liability has been incurred at the date of the financial statements; and (2) the amount of the loss can be reasonably estimated.

In the context of environmental remediation liabilities, the probability criterion consists of two elements that must be met on or before the date the financial statements are issued or are available to be issued. First, litigation has commenced or a claim or an assessment has been asserted, or, based on available information, commencement of litigation or assertion of a claim or an assessment is probable. Second, based on available information, it is probable that the outcome of such litigation, claim, or assessment will be unfavorable. There is a presumption that the outcome of such litigation, claim, or assessment will be unfavorable if (1) litigation has commenced or a claim or an assessment has been asserted, or commencement of litigation or assertion of a claim or assessment is probable; and (2) the reporting entity is associated with the site subject to remediation. Association results from arranging for the disposal of hazardous substances found at a site or transporting hazardous substances to the site or being the current or previous owner or operator of the site.

Estimating liabilities for environmental remediation obligations may be difficult because of uncertainties. Uncertainties relating to the reporting entity's share of an environmental remediation liability shall not preclude it from recognizing its best estimate of its share of the liability or, if no best estimate can be made, the minimum estimate of its share of the liability, if the liability is probable and the total remediation liability associated with the site is reasonably estimable within a range.

The reporting entity's estimate of the remediation liability shall include its allocable share of the liability for a specific site and its share of amounts related to the site that will not be paid by other parties potentially associated with the site (i.e., responsible parties) or the government. Costs to be included are incremental direct costs of the remediation effort and costs of compensation and benefits for those employees who are expected to devote a significant amount of time directly to the remediation effort. The costs of services related to routine environmental compliance matters and litigation costs involved with potential recoveries are not part of the remediation effort.

In certain situations, such as those described in ASC 410-30-25-18 through 25-21, it may be appropriate to capitalize environmental remediation costs.

Potential recoveries may be claimed from a number of different parties or sources, including insurers. The amount of an environmental remediation liability should be determined independently from any potential claim for recovery. An asset relating to the recovery shall be recognized only when realization of the claim for recovery is deemed probable.

ASC 450-20 on contingencies provides the primary guidance applicable to disclosures of environmental remediation loss contingencies. ASC 410-30-50 includes disclosures that are required, disclosures that are encouraged, and disclosures that are related to loss contingencies. Among them, reporting entities with environmental remediation obligations are required to disclose whether the accrual for environmental remediation liabilities is measured on a discounted basis. If so, additional disclosures are required including the undiscounted amount of the obligation and the discount rate used. Reporting entities are also required to disclose the amounts for assets for probable recoveries from third parties.

Topic 420: Exit or Disposal Cost Obligations

Topic 420, *Exit or Disposal Cost Obligations*, contains one subtopic:

10 Overall

ASC 420-10 specifies the accounting and reporting requirements for costs of exit or disposal activities. An exit activity generally is a restructuring but may include other activities. In general, an exit activity is a plan or program that management controls and changes in a material manner the scope of the business or the way that the business is conducted. Costs associated with an exit activity may include, among others, the following:

- One-time termination benefits to employees that are involuntarily terminated,
- Contract termination costs other than capital leases, and
- Facility consolidation costs or employee relocation costs.

ASC 420-10 applies to costs associated with an exit activity, including exit activities related to newly acquired entities in a business combination and disposal activities covered by ASC 360-10. However, costs associated with long-lived asset retirements under the provisions of ASC 410-20 are not covered by ASC 420-10.

A liability and expense is reported for costs related to an exit activity in the accounting period incurred, except for one-time termination benefits that are incurred over future time periods. The exit activity liability is initially reported at fair value. If fair value cannot be determined in the accounting period that the liability is incurred, the liability is reported in the first accounting period that fair value can be determined. A liability is assumed to be incurred when the definition of a liability, as specified in FASB Statement of Financial Accounting Concepts No. 6, has been met.

Generally, a liability is a present obligation to transfer assets or provide services resulting from past events or transactions. The fact that an entity has an exit or disposal plan does not necessarily create a liability. A present obligation to others must exist to have an exit or disposal liability. A present obligation exists if an entity has little, if any, ability to avoid a transfer of assets or services in the future to settle the obligation.

The definition of "fair value" for an exit or disposal activity is defined as the amount that would be received on the measurement date from the sale of property or the amount paid to transfer a liability between sellers and buyers (market participants) in an orderly transaction. In addition, it is assumed that the sellers and buyers are unrelated parties on the measurement date. One way to determine fair value is to use quoted market prices. In many cases, however, quoted market prices are not available and an enterprise must estimate fair value.

One way that fair value may be estimated is by using a present-value model. ASC 420-10 states that a present-value model is most likely the best one to estimate the fair value of exit or disposal liabilities. Because exit or disposal activities generally have uncertainty in timing and amounts of cash flows, the expected-present-value model would generally be the best one to use when determining fair value.

Changes in fair value subsequent to the initial measurement of the exit or disposal liability should be determined using the same credit-adjusted, risk-free rate that was used when the liability was initially measured. Any changes in cash flow timing or amounts is reported as a cumulative change and the liability and an expense is adjusted for the revision in the accounting period of the change. The expense is reported in the income statement in the same financial statement line item as the expense for the initial exit or disposal liability. In addition, the exit or disposal liability should be increased for changes resulting from the passage of time and an equal amount should be charged to accretion (interest) expense.

ASC 420-10 divides most costs related to exit or disposal activities into three categories: (1) one-time termination benefits, (2) contract termination costs, and (3) other associated costs.

One-Time Termination Benefits

One-time termination benefits are benefits that are given to employees that are involuntarily terminated under a one-time agreement or arrangement. A one-time agreement or arrangement relates to a specific termination event or future period. The termination benefits are recognized as of the date communicated to the employee (i.e., the communication date) provided that:

1. The plan of termination has been approved by management with the proper authority.
2. The plan of termination identifies the number of employees, employee function or job classification, location, and anticipated date of completion.
3. The terms of the plan of termination are established and the benefits are specified in sufficient detail to allow employees involuntarily terminated to determine the amount and type of benefits to be received.
4. The withdrawal or making significant changes to the plan are unlikely given its status.

The measurement and recognition of a liability related to one-time termination benefits depends on the agreement with the employees to be terminated. A liability should be reported at fair value at the communication date if the employees can receive the benefits regardless of when they leave employment (i.e., they are not required to provide service to receive the benefits). Any changes after the initial measurement should be accounted for using the provisions of ASC 420-10-35. However, if services are required to be provided by the employees, a liability should be determined at the communication date using fair value at the termination date. The liability should then be reported ratably over the future service period of the employees. Any changes after the initial measurement in cash flow timing or amounts should be accounted for using the same credit-adjusted, risk-free rate used in the initial liability measurement. Any cumulative impact related to the change is reported in the accounting period of the change as an adjustment to the liability. Changes in termination plans where employees are retained longer than the minimum retention period requires an adjustment to the termination liability using the process described above. A termination plan that contains both involuntary and voluntary termination benefits should be accounted using the provisions of ASC 420-10 for the involuntary benefits and ASC 715-30 for the voluntary termination benefit that are offered for a short time period.

Contract Termination Costs

Contract termination costs include costs to terminate an operating lease or other type of contract. Such costs include those related to terminating a contract prior to the end of the contract period and those that will be incurred during the remaining contract time period when the entity is not receiving any economic benefit. The costs for contracts terminated prior to the end of the contract period are reported in the accounting period that the contract is terminated in accordance with the contract agreement. When a contract is terminated, but costs will continue to be incurred by the entity without any economic benefit, the liability should be reported on the cease-use date for those costs. (The cease-use date is the date that the entity stops using the rights conveyed by the contract.)

Other Associated Costs

Other associated costs related to exit activities may include costs related to relocating employees, or closing or consolidating facilities. The liability for exit costs related to these types of activities should be reported in the accounting period that the liability is incurred.

The expense for the initial liability recognized is reported in the income statement in income from continuing operations. In a not-for-profit entity, the expense is reported in income from continuing operations in the statement of activities. If an income category, such as income from operations, is reported in an income statement, the exit or disposal expense should be included in that subtotal. Accretion or interest expense on the liability due to the passage of time should be reported in the income statement in the same location as interest expense on other debt. When exit or disposal costs relate to a discontinued operation, such costs should also be included in the discontinued operations section of the income statement. When the requirement for an exit or disposal liability, established in a prior accounting period, is removed because certain circumstance or events occur, the liability is reversed and a credit is reported in the income statement in the same financial statement line item as the original exit expense. The exit or disposal liability is classified as current or long-term based on the same criteria used for other liabilities.

Technical Considerations

One example is used to illustrate the technical aspects of costs related to exit or disposal activities. Assumptions for Example 4-4 are presented below.

Example 4-4
Assumptions for Exit Activity

1. Jones Enterprises (Jones), a December 31 year-end company, plans to cease operations in a specific location (not a discontinued operation). Jones has determined that 200 employees will be involuntarily termi-

nated in 60 days and the employees were notified of this information on January 1, 20X6. Each employee will receive a $10,000 cash payment as a termination benefit on the date that the employee ceases employment with the firm and employment may cease anytime within the 60 day time frame. For purposes of this example, it is assumed that there is no material difference in the $10,000 cash payment and the fair value of the payment because of the short time period involved in the transaction.

2. Jones also leased a facility (related to the operations in 1, above) that is accounted for as an operating lease. Lease payments, which are made in advance on the property, are $1,000,000 per year. Jones will cease using the facility on January 1, 20X6, with three years left under the lease agreement. There are no sublease rentals that could reasonably be obtained for the facility. The credit-adjusted, risk-free interest rate is 5%.
3. All present value computations are assumed to be in accordance with ASC 420-10.

The plan to stop operations is considered an exit activity under the provisions of ASC 420-10 and involves two types of costs. First, the $10,000 payment to employees for involuntary termination is a one-time termination benefit and cancellation of the operating lease represents a contract termination cost. The liability for the one-time termination cost is computed and reported at fair value on January 1, 20X6, the date that the employees were notified of the termination (the communication date), because the employees can receive the benefits regardless of when they leave employment. The one-time termination benefit liability is computed as $2,000,000 ($10,000 cash payment × 200 employees) on January 1, 20X6.

Next, the contract termination liability should be reported on January 1, 20X6, because this is the date that the operating lease contract is terminated. Because no sublease rentals could reasonably be obtained for the facility, the entire $1,000,000 should be used when determining the contract termination liability. The present value of $1,000,000 future cash flows should be computed using the 5%, credit-adjusted, risk-free interest rate for the remaining three years of the lease. The computation is shown below:

Future cash flows	$1,000,000
Present value factor for an annuity due at 5% for 3 periods	2.85941
Contract termination liability	$2,859,410

The total exit liability on January 1, 20X6 for Jones is $4,859,410 ($2,000,000 one-time termination cost + $2,859,410 contract termination cost). The journal entry to record the exit cost liability on January 1 is as follows:

Exit Activity Expense	4,859,410	
Exit Liability		4,859,410

The Exit Activity Expense is reported in the income statement as a component of income from continuing operations.

Each accounting period subsequent to the exit activity, interest expense (accretion expense) must be computed on the exit liability related to the lease contract due to the passage of time. The interest expense is computed by applying the 5%, credit-adjusted, risk-free interest rate to the carrying balance of the related contract liability. The interest expense computation for 20X6 is presented below:

Contract termination liability balance-lease contract	$2,859,410
Discount rate	5%
20X6 interest expense	$142,971

Using the $142,971 interest expense computation, the journal entry required at the end of 20X6 is as follows:

Interest Expense	142,971	
Exit Liability		142,971

Disclosure Requirements

ASC 420-10-50 specifies the disclosure requirements for an exit or disposal activity. The following disclosures should be reported in the accounting period that the activity is initiated and all subsequent accounting periods until the activity is completed.

1. Describe the exit or disposal activity. The description should include the anticipated completion date and the circumstances and facts that caused the anticipated activity.
2. Disclose for each major class of exit costs (see the preceding discussion for each class of cost):
   a. The amount of costs incurred in current accounting period, the cumulative amount of costs incurred and the total costs expected to be incurred.
   b. A reconciliation of the beginning and ending liability balance and changes for costs incurred and reported as an expense, adjustments with explanations of the reasons, and costs settled or paid.
3. Disclose the financial statement line item in the income statement or activity statement where the activity costs are aggregated.
4. When an exit liability is not reported in the financial statements because fair value could not be determined, that fact should be disclosed as well as the reasons why.
5. For each reportable segment disclose the amount of the costs incurred in the current accounting period, the cumulative amount of costs incurred to date, the total costs expected to be incurred, and net adjustments with explanations to the activity liability.

Topic 430: Deferred Revenue

Topic 430, *Deferred Revenue*, contains six subtopics:

10 Overall

922 Entertainment—Cable Television*

926 Entertainment—Films*

928 Entertainment—Music*

954 Health Care Entities*

972 Real Estate—Common Interest Realty Associations*

* See the corresponding topic in Chapter 9 for coverage of this shared subtopic.

This topic is not covered in this book.

Topic 440: Commitments

Topic 440, *Commitments*, contains five subtopics:

10 Overall

920 Entertainment—Broadcasters*

928 Entertainment—Music*

952 Franchisors*

954 Health Care Entities*

* See the corresponding topic in Chapter 9 for coverage of this shared subtopic.

Flowchart and General Discussion

ASC 440-10 addresses the financial accounting and reporting of unconditional purchase obligations. An unconditional purchase obligation is an obligation of an entity for a future exchange of money for goods or services in fixed amounts at fixed prices. The fixed amounts and fixed prices can also be minimum amounts and minimum prices. *Take-or-pay* contracts and *throughput* contracts as examples of unconditional purchase obligations. ASC 440-10 provides that, under specified conditions, information concerning unconditional purchase obligations should be disclosed in the financial statements.

Take-or-Pay Contracts

Take-or-pay and throughput contracts are specialized enough to require definition. A take-or-pay contract is one in which the purchaser and seller of goods or services agree that the purchaser is to pay certain amounts periodically in return for the right to receive the product or service of the seller. The amount that will be paid by the buyer is set at a minimum, and that amount must be paid even if the purchaser does not take delivery of the goods or services. If the buyer takes delivery of items in excess of the minimum required amount, the additional quantity must be paid for and, generally, does not apply against future minimum purchase quantities. The buyer would be motivated to enter into a take-or-pay contract to be reasonably confident that a minimum quantity of the goods desired would be available on a regular basis. The seller would be motivated by the steady cash flows and assured market for its product.

Throughput Contracts

Throughput contracts may involve an owner of materials to be processed and the owner of a manufacturing facility that has the capability of performing the desired processing. The owner of the materials would agree to pay certain amounts periodically to the owner of the facility in return for the processing of the product. The owner of the materials would be obligated to pay the owner of the facility even if the contracted quantities were not delivered for processing. Throughput contracts also may involve shippers of materials and the owners of the transportation facilities. In this case, the shipper of the material would agree to pay certain specified amounts periodically in return for transporting the materials. The contracts usually specify a minimum quantity that must be processed or shipped within the agreed-upon period of time. The owner of the materials would be motivated to enter into a throughput contract to be sure that transportation, or processing facilities were available as needed. The shipper or processor would be motivated by the stable pattern of the cash flows and the required payment for the utilization of their facilities.

Financing Arrangements

Unconditional purchase obligations may be associated with financing arrangements because they specify that certain minimum cash flows will take place between the parties to the contract. A lender may be called upon to provide project financing for a particular borrower. Under a project financing arrangement, the lender looks to the cash flows and earnings of the specific project as the source for repayment of the loan. The reason for this type of financing is that the project may be a corporation with no other assets, or the financing may be without recourse to the general assets of the borrower.

With these definitions and explanations in mind, attention may be turned to Flowchart 4-1 for an overview of the disclosure requirements specified by ASC 440-10.

Flowchart 4-1

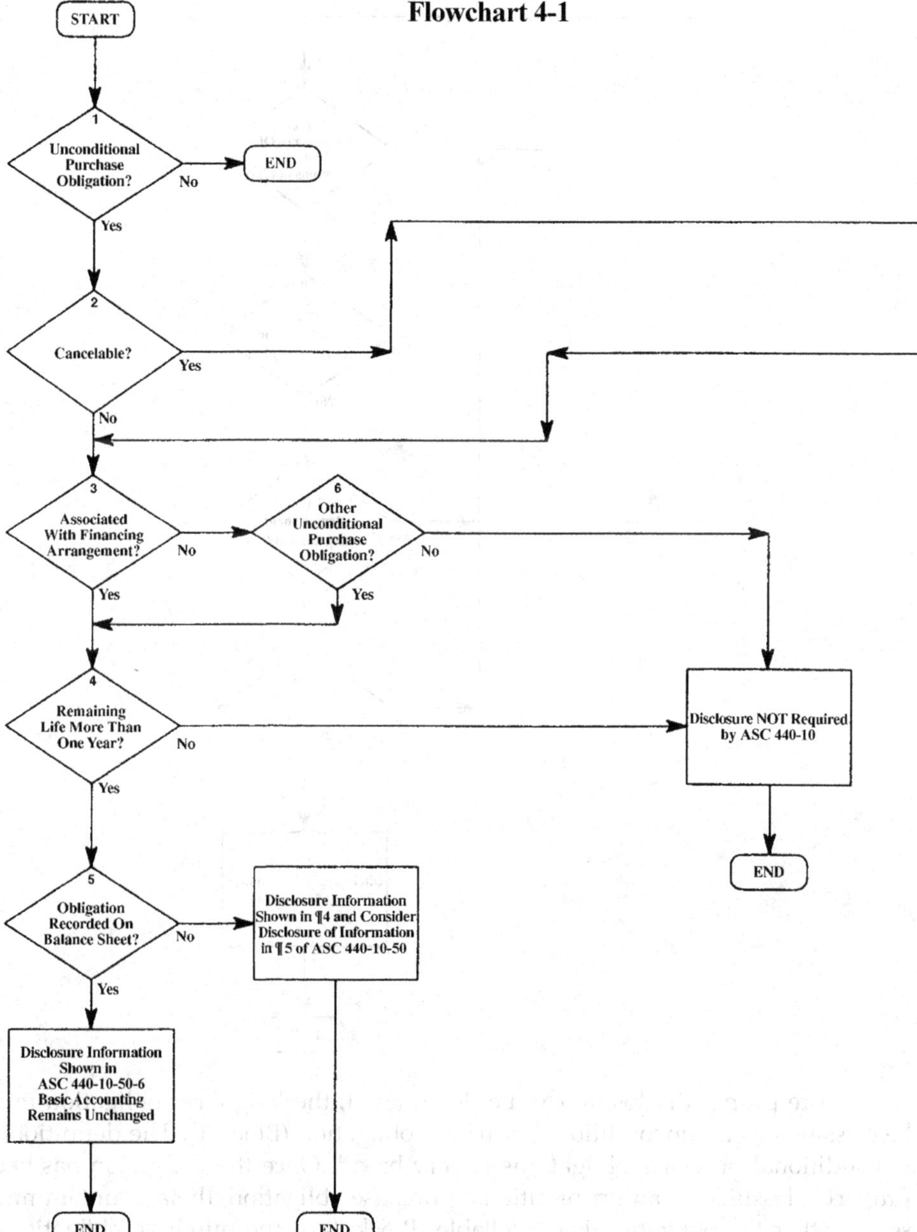

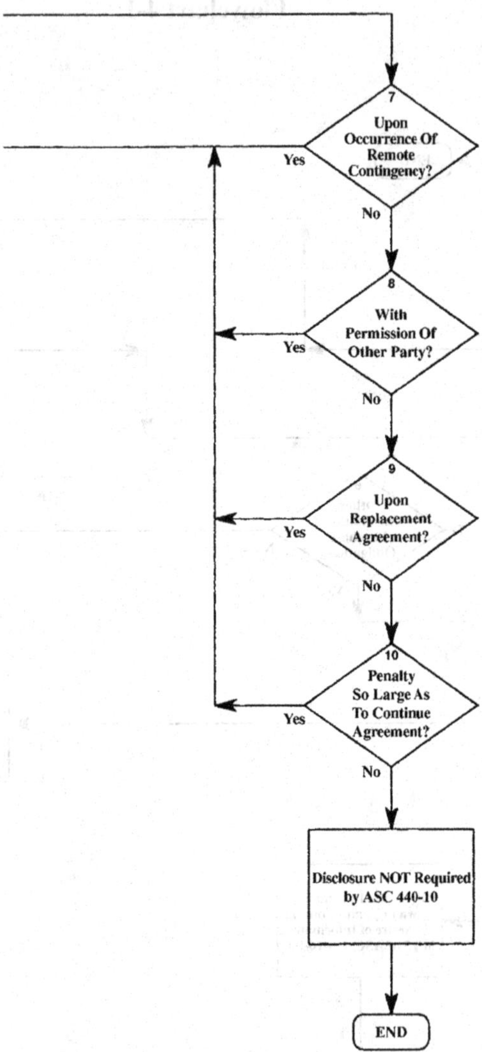

Before proper disclosure can be determined, the long-term obligation must be classified as an unconditional purchase obligation (Block 1). The definition of unconditional purchase obligations is very broad. Once the obligation has been properly classified as an unconditional purchase obligation, the accountant must see whether the obligation is cancellable (Block 2). If the purchase obligation is *noncancellable,* the next step in the accounting process is to determine whether it is associated with a financing arrangement (Block 3). If the obligation is cancellable, disclosure will not be required by ASC 440-10. If the obligation is cancellable, but meets any one of the following four conditions, it is to be treated as if it were *noncancellable.*

The obligation is cancellable (1) in the event of a remote contingency (Block 7), (2) if the other party to the transaction gives permission (Block 8), (3) if the two parties sign an agreement that replaces the existing agreement (Block 9), or

(4) it is reasonably assured that the agreement will continue because the penalty for cancellation is significant (Block 10). These four conditions indicate that the contract may be cancelled, but the likelihood of cancellation is very remote at the current time.

If the obligation is noncancellable *or* may be treated as noncancellable, it may be associated with a financing arrangement. When it has been determined that the obligation is associated with a financing arrangement, it must have a remaining useful life of more than one year before the provisions of ASC 440-10 apply (Block 4). If the obligation is *not* associated with a financing agreement, it still may require disclosure. Other unconditional purchase obligations (Block 6) include long-term debt and redeemable capital stock. The disclosures required by ASC 440-10 depend on whether the obligation has been recorded in a balance sheet (Block 5).

For unconditional purchase obligations that previously have been recorded in the balance sheet, the purchaser is required to disclose under ASC 440-10-50 the aggregate amounts of the payments required by unconditional purchase obligations for each of the next five years following the date of the latest balance sheet.

For those unconditional purchase obligations that meet the conditions described above, but have not been recorded in the balance sheet, the following disclosures are required under ASC 440-10-50:

1. The obligation's nature and terms,
2. The amount of the aggregate obligation that is fixed, or can be determined, for the current year and each of the next five years,
3. The nature of the obligation's variable parts, and
4. The amount of goods and services purchased under the unconditional purchase obligation for each accounting period that an income statement is presented.

ASC 440-10 permits the combining of similar or related types of unconditional purchase obligations. In addition to the required disclosures listed above, the FASB encourages, but does not require, entities to report the amount of imputed interest related to the obligation.

If an entity elects to disclose the amount of imputed interest, the discount rate should be the interest rate associated with the project financing arrangement, if known, or the purchaser's incremental borrowing rate if the project financing rate is not known.

The provisions of ASC 440-10 are much more extensive than they appear at first reading. With this discussion complete, the technical presentation below should be easier to understand.

Unconditional Purchase Obligations—Technical Considerations

To illustrate the provisions of ASC 440-10, two examples are developed. Information relating to Example 4-5 follows.

Example 4-5
Unconditional Purchase Obligations

1. On January 1, 20X4, Selby Enterprises (Selby) entered into an agreement with Avery Chemical Corporation (Avery). The agreement was a take-or-pay contract with Avery under which Selby is obligated to purchase 25% of the output of Avery's Chemical 127A for the period of time the debt used to finance the chemical plant is outstanding. The debt is scheduled to be retired after December 31, 2013. The agreement between Selby and Avery was negotiated as part of the financing arrangement for the chemical plant.
2. The agreement is noncancellable and requires the following minimum annual payments by Selby to Avery:

   20X4 to 20X7—$2,000,000
   20X8 to 2013—$3,000,000

   The payments are required even if Selby does not take delivery of its 25% share of Chemical 127A.
3. The annual payment is computed at an amount equal to 25% of the sum of the following items: operating expenses; depreciation; raw material costs; interest on debt financing; and a reasonable profit. The obligation resulting from this contract has not been recorded on the books of Selby.
4. The interest rate on funds borrowed to finance the chemical plant is 12%, and the incremental borrowing rate of Selby is 14%.
5. Purchases of Chemical 127A under the contract were as follows:

   20X4—$2,500,000
   20X5—$2,100,000
   20X6—$2,050,000
6. Selby is in the process of preparing its financial statements for the year ended December 31, 20X6.

Selby has entered into a take-or-pay contract, an unconditional purchase obligation as defined by ASC 440-10. The contract is noncancellable by agreement and is associated with the financing arrangement relating to the chemical plant of Avery. The contract does not expire until 2013, which is more than one year from December 31, 20X6, the date of Selby's financial statements. The obligation is subject to the provisions of ASC 440-10; and Selby must disclose the information described in ASC 440-10-50, because the obligation is not recorded on its books. Selby may elect to disclose information about the imputed interest associated with the obligation as outlined in ASC 440-10-50-5. Assuming that Selby elects to disclose the imputed interest on the obligation, the first step in the accounting process is to calculate the present value of the minimum payments required by the contract. The computation is shown below:

Minimum 20X7 payment		$2,000,000
Present value factor for annuity of $1 for 1 period at 12%		.89286
Present value of payment		$1,785,720
Minimum payment 20X8—2013		$3,000,000
Present value factor for annuity of $1 for 7 periods at 12%	4.56376	
Present value factor for annuity of $1 for 1 period at 12%	.89286	3.67090
Present value of payments		$11,012,700
Total present value of payments		$12,798,420

The interest rate used in the present value computation was 12% because it was the rate associated with the financing of the chemical plant and it was known by Selby.

The present value computation is made difficult by the fact that a change in the minimum contract payments from $2,000,000 to $3,000,000 is made in 20X8. There will be a change in the annuity stream of $1,000,000 ($3,000,000 – $2,000,000), beginning in 20X8, and this calls for the adjustment shown in the computation for the years 20X8 through 2013. Based upon this information, the following footnote may be prepared:

Note 1: On January 1, 20X4, Selby entered into a long-term contract for the purchase of 25% of the output of a chemical product of Avery Chemical Corporation. The contract runs through 2013 and requires the following minimum annual payments by Selby to Avery:

20X7	$2,000,000
20X8	3,000,000
20X9	3,000,000
2010	3,000,000
2011	3,000,000
Later Years	6,000,000
Total Amount	$20,000,000
Imputed Interest	7,201,580
Total Present Value	$12,798,420

Selby is responsible for 25% of the cost of raw materials and operating costs of the chemical plant owned by Avery. Selby made the following purchases under the contract: $2,500,000 in 20X0; $2,100,000 in 20X4; and $2,050,000 in 20X6.

With the preparation of this footnote, Selby would have complied with the provisions of ASC 440-10 as they relate to the take-or-pay contract. Example 4-6 is designed to illustrate additional implications of ASC 440-10. Example 4-6 information is shown below.

Example 4-6
Unconditional Purchase Obligation

1. On January 1, 20X5, Ladd Company (Ladd), a December 31 year-end entity, entered into a throughput contract with Bird Chemical Corporation (Bird). The agreement allows Ladd to submit 200,000 tons of sulfur for processing at Bird's plant annually for the next 10 years.
2. The contract is cancelable only if a replacement agreement has been signed between Ladd and Bird. In addition, the contract states that, if Bird is unable to meet its financial responsibilities, Ladd is required to advance funds to Bird equal to 30% of processing and debt service costs. Funds advanced in this manner will be applied to future processing charges. Ladd's obligation for the funds is related to the operations of the plant owned by Bird.
3. The throughput contract was negotiated as part of a financing arrangement for construction of the chemical processing plant by Bird. The contract requires the following minimum annual payments from Ladd to Bird for the processing of the sulfur:

   20X5 to 20X9—$15,000,000
   2010 to 2014—$12,000,000
4. The interest rate on funds borrowed to finance the chemical plant is not known to Ladd. Ladd's incremental borrowing rate is determined to be 10%.
5. Total processing charges by Bird under the contract have been $17,000,000 in each of the last two years.
6. Ladd is in the process of preparing financial statements for the year ended December 31, 20X6.

Ladd has entered into a throughput contract, an unconditional purchase obligation. The contract is cancelable, but only upon the signing of a replacement agreement, and should be treated as noncancellable for purposes of applying the provisions of ASC 440-10. The unconditional purchase obligation is associated with the financing arrangement for the construction of the chemical plant by Bird. The contract expires in 2014, which is more than one year from December 31, 20X6. The obligation is not recorded on the books of Ladd at December 31, 20X6, and is subject to the disclosure requirements of ASC 440-10-50.

The following footnote disclosure would meet the reporting requirements specified in ASC 440-10 for the throughput contract:

Note 1: On January 1, 20X5, Ladd entered into a throughput contract with Bird Chemical Corporation, allowing Ladd to submit 200,000 tons of sulfur annually for processing for the next 10 years. If Bird is not able to meet its financial responsibilities, Ladd is required to advance funds to Bird that will be applied to future processing charges. At December 31, 20X6, the minimum required annual payments are:

20X7	$15,000,000
20X8	15,000,000
20X9	15,000,000
2010	12,000,000
2011	12,000,000
Later Years	48,000,000
Total	$117,000,000

Ladd has incurred processing costs of $17,000,000 in each of the last two years.

Ladd did not reduce the $117,000,000 obligation to present value, even though the information to carry out the computation was available. ASC 440-10 encourages, but does not require, the determination of imputed interest.

Topic 450: Contingencies

Topic 450, *Contingencies*, contains seven subtopics:

10 Overall

20 Loss Contingencies

30 Gain Contingencies

912 Contractors—Federal Government*

954 Health Care Entities*

958 Not-For-Profit Entities*

980 Regulated Operations*

* See the corresponding topic in Chapter 9 for coverage of this shared subtopic.

General Discussion

ASC 450 identifies accounting principles and reporting requirements for contingencies. A contingency is defined in ASC 450-10-20 as the possibility of a gain or loss resulting from a situation, set of circumstances, or condition that currently exists where the outcome of the gain or loss will be determined at some future date by the occurrence or lack of occurrence of an event. Where a contingency may involve a gain, it is referred to as a gain contingency; where the possibility of a loss exists, it is referred to as a loss contingency.

ASC 450 identifies different probabilities for the occurrence of a loss contingency. The probabilities range from probable to reasonably possible to remote. It is helpful to think of the range of probabilities as a continuum:

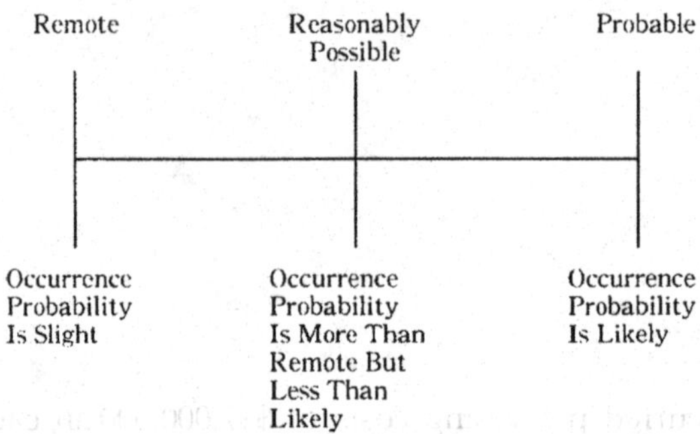

As indicated by the continuum, when a loss contingency exists, and it is determined that the probability of the future event occurring or failing to occur is slight, the loss contingency is referred to as remote. When the probability of the future event occurring is more than remote, but less than likely, the loss contingency is considered to be reasonably possible. It naturally follows that, when the probability of the occurrence of the future event is likely, the loss contingency is referred to as probable. The classification scheme is directly related to the accounting and disclosure requirements for the loss contingency.

The estimated amount of the loss from a loss contingency should be charged to income if the following two conditions are met (ASC 450-20-25-2):

1. On the balance sheet date, it is probable, from information available before the issuance of the financial statements, that an entity has incurred a liability or that an asset of the entity has been impaired and
2. The entity can reasonably estimate the amount of the loss.

Before the estimated loss resulting from the loss contingency can be charged to income, *both* of the preceding conditions must be met.

The first condition limits the accounting considerations to probable loss contingencies (i.e., to situations in which the future event is likely to occur). However, if the loss contingency is considered probable, but the amount of the loss cannot be reasonably estimated, there will be no charge to income. If the amount of probable loss falls within a range, the minimum amount will be accrued unless another amount within the range is considered more likely. Loss contingencies that are considered reasonably possible, or that fail to meet one of the conditions specified above, generally will be disclosed in the footnotes to the financial statements. Loss contingencies that are remote generally will not require disclosures.

Under ASC 450, gain contingencies are not recorded until such time as the gain is realized. Although footnote disclosure of gain contingencies is allowed, care should be exercised in the disclosure so as not to mislead the reader.

Chart 4-1 is a summary of some possible loss contingencies, along with the appropriate accounting and disclosure requirements. A given loss contingency may be placed in one of three categories for accounting purposes:

1. Those loss contingencies that typically are accrued, with a resulting charge to income,
2. Those loss contingencies that should be accrued if they meet the two conditions stated above (contingency is classified as probable and amount of loss can be estimated), and
3. Those loss contingencies for which accrual is unnecessary.

Chart 4-1 Treatment of Certain Loss Contingencies

Contingency Losses:	Typically Accrued	Accrual[a] Possible	Accrual Unnecessary	Disclose	Not Disclosed
1. Collectibility of receivables	X			X[b]	
2. Obligations related to product warranties and product defects, and customers premiums	X			X[b]	
3. Threat of expropriation		X		X[c]	
4. Litigation, claims and assessments		X		X[c]	
5. Guarantees of indebtedness of others		X		X	
6. Obligations of commercial banks under standby letters of credit		X		X	
7. Guarantees to repurchase receivables that have been sold		X		X	
8. Risk of loss or damage of entity's property			X	X[c]	
9. Catastrophe losses of property and casualty insurance companies			X	X[c]	
10. General or unspecified business risks			X		X

[a] Accrual is required if *both* the loss contingency is probable and the amount of the loss can be reasonably estimated.

[b] Disclose through an accrual if both conditions are met, or through a footnote to the financial statements.

[c] No disclosure is necessary *unless* it is considered probable that a claim will be asserted and there is a reasonable possibility that the outcome will be unfavorable. If the occurrence is slight (remote), there is no requirement to disclose.

For purposes of disclosure, a given loss contingency may be placed in one of three categories:

1. Those that do not require disclosure in the footnotes to the financial statements,
2. Those that do require disclosure in the footnotes, and
3. Those that may require disclosure if certain conditions are met.

As shown in Chart 4-1, companies are not permitted to disclose loss contingencies relating to general or unspecified business risks. Generally, loss contingencies that meet one of the two criteria necessary for accrual, but fail to meet both, will be disclosed in the footnotes to the financial statements.

Other loss contingencies, such as litigation, claims, and assessments, may be disclosed in the footnotes, if it is probable that a claim associated with these items will be asserted, and if there is a *reasonable possibility* of an adverse outcome. However, if the possibility of an adverse outcome is considered to be *remote,* no disclosure is required.

Certain types of loss contingencies that have a remote possibility of resulting in an actual loss should be disclosed in the footnotes. These specifically identified loss contingencies include guarantees of debts of other entities (including indirect guarantees, such as an agreement to advance funds if another entity's income drops below a stated minimum), guarantees to buy back receivables that were sold, and payables of banks with standby letters of credit.

ASC 450 allows for the appropriation of retained earnings for loss contingencies, but the appropriation must be included in the stockholders' equity section of the balance sheet. No portion of the appropriation is allowed to be charged to income.

Classification and Accounting—Loss Contingencies

To illustrate the specific provisions of ASC 450, the assumptions listed in Example 4-7 are used.

Example 4-7
Loss Contingencies

1. Worldwide Enterprises, Inc. (Worldwide) is in the process of preparing its financial statements for the year ended December 31, 20X6. The statements will be issued on or about March 5, 20X7.

2. At year-end, Worldwide has estimated that its product warranty costs relating to items sold in 20X6 amount to $125,000. It is probable that customers will make claims for services in connection with products they purchased in 20X6.

3. Worldwide is involved in three lawsuits relating to charges of patent infringement. The first suit was initiated on October 3, 20X6, followed almost immediately by a second suit on October 8, 20X6. The third suit was not initiated until January 27, 20X7. The first suit was settled on February 18, 20X7, and required Worldwide to pay $75,000 in damages. The third suit, initiated in 20X7, also was settled on this date, and required the payment of damages amounting

to $35,000. The second suit is considered to be a nuisance suit, and the likelihood of an adverse outcome is deemed to be remote.

4. Due to severe economic conditions in the industry in which Worldwide operates, management wishes to accrue a loss contingency in the amount of $250,000. Management believes that this accrual will provide a more conservative income statement and balance sheet.

5. Because of political unrest in a foreign country in which Worldwide operates, management believes that there is a real threat of expropriation of its operations in that country. Other companies operating in the same foreign country recently have had their assets expropriated. The range of potential loss could be anywhere from $1,000,000 to as high as $4,000,000.

A description of the accounting and reporting requirements for each of these items will be given. First, the product warranty costs estimated on the basis of 20X6 sales should be accrued through a charge to income of that period. It is probable that a liability has been incurred in connection with the sales of 20X6, and the amount of the liability can be reasonably estimated. The journal entry required to accrue the loss contingency would be:

Estimated Product Warranty Expense	125,000	
Estimated Liability Under Product Warranty		125,000

The expense will appear as an operating expense in the 20X6 income statement, and the liability will appear on the 20X6 balance sheet.

The first lawsuit was initiated in 20X6, but settled prior to the issuance of the financial statements. Under the provisions of ASC 450, an accrual should be made for the loss contingency in the 20X6 financial statements. The entry to record the settlement would be similar to the entry shown above.

The second lawsuit is considered to be a nuisance suit, and the possibility of an adverse outcome has been assessed to be remote. No accrual or disclosure is required in this matter.

The third lawsuit was initiated in 20X7 (after the balance sheet date), but settled prior to the issuance of the financial statements. Because the event giving rise to the lawsuit did not occur in 20X6, an accrual is not appropriate. Information relating to this lawsuit should be disclosed in the footnotes to the 20X6 financial statements of Worldwide as a subsequent event.

ASC 450 expressly prohibits an accrual for general or unspecified business risks. Due to this fact, the loss contingency relating to the general economic conditions of the industry should not be accrued or disclosed. Worldwide may wish to appropriate retained earnings to reflect this loss contingency. Any appropriation made must be included in the stockholders' equity section of the 20X6 balance sheet and clearly labeled as an appropriation.

The last item deals with the threat of expropriation of certain foreign operations of Worldwide. Because assets of other companies doing business in the same foreign country have been expropriated, it is reasonable to assume that an asset expropriation loss contingency of Worldwide is probable. The estimate of probable loss ranges between $1,000,000 and $4,000,000, so there is some uncertainty as to whether or not the loss can be reasonably estimated. If the loss can be reasonably estimated, an accrual should be prepared for the loss contingency. Where a range of potential loss can be determined but no single value is more probable than any other value, then the minimum amount within the range should be accrued. In this case, Worldwide should accrue $1,000,000, and disclose in the notes to the financial statements the probable loss ranging from $1,000,000 to $4,000,000.

The loss contingency established for the threat of expropriation probably would be classified as an unusual or infrequent item in Worldwide's 2006 income statement.

Loss Contingency Disclosures

For loss contingencies that are accrued, the entity should disclose the nature of the accrual and, in some cases, the amount. The entity may wish to disclose the amount of the accrual if such disclosure is required so as not to make the financial statements misleading. For loss contingencies not accrued, the company should disclose the nature of the contingency and, if possible, an estimate of the range of possible loss or a statement that such estimate cannot be made. Disclosure is preferable to accrual when a reasonable estimate of loss cannot be made. Disclosure is required if it is considered probable that a claim will be asserted and there is a reasonable possibility that the outcome will be unfavorable.

Gain Contingencies and Insured Loss Contingencies

The accounting models for loss contingencies and gain contingencies in ASC 450, *Contingencies*, differ. However, the key consideration for each is timing of recognition and providing appropriate forewarning disclosures.

Contingent gains should not be recognized prior to when they are realized or realizable. The term "realized" means that cash (or other assets such as claims to cash) has been received without expectation of repayment or refund. The term "realizable" means that the assets expected to be received or held are readily convertible to known amounts of cash or claims to cash. The assessment of whether a gain is realized or is realizable requires significant judgment and thorough and robust documentation.

For example, if a settlement is reached in a lawsuit and the entity is only waiting to receive the cash award, the entity may record the gain (assuming collectability is not an issue) because it is realizable. However, if a settlement is in discussion, but has not yet been agreed to by both parties, it would generally not be appropriate to record a gain until such settlement is reached. Similarly, if a favorable verdict has been received in a lawsuit, but the other party still has the opportunity to appeal, it generally would not be appropriate to recognize the gain until all appeals have been exhausted. At that point, it may also still be necessary to assess the enforceability of the judgment if the other party does not have assets (or sufficient assets) in the jurisdiction in which the verdict was rendered.

Contingent gains related to insurance recoveries warrant special consideration. To the extent that recovery is probable (a lower threshold than realized or realizable), the portion of an insurance claim that relates to recovery of an incurred loss may be recognized when the loss is recognized. For this purpose, a "loss" does not include lost revenue. If the insurance claim is in dispute (i.e., the carrier has denied coverage), a rebuttable presumption exists that recoverability of the claim is not probable and should not be recognized.

Claims for insurance recoveries in excess of recorded book losses are considered gain contingencies, and require the gain to be realizable or realized prior to recognition. For example, an insurance policy might provide for payment of the "replacement cost" of fixed assets in excess of book value or recovery of "lost profits."

Topic 460: Guarantees

Topic 460, *Guarantees*, contains two subtopics:

10 Overall

954 Health Care Entities [See the corresponding topic in Chapter 9 for coverage of this shared subtopic]

ASC 460 provides accounting and disclosure requirements for guarantees including indirect guarantees of indebtedness of others in both interim and annual financial reports. ASC 460 applies to guarantee contracts that meet any of the following (ASC 460-10-15-4):

1. A contract that requires, on a contingent basis, the guarantor to pay the guaranteed party if another entity fails to perform under contract requirements. This is a performance guarantee and payments may consist of cash, financial instruments, stocks, other assets or services.
2. A contract that requires, on a contingent basis, the guarantor to pay the guaranteed party an amount that is based on changes of an underlying. The underlying may be related to an asset, liability, or equity item of the guaranteed party. Payments may consist of the items listed in item 1, above. Examples include irrevocable financial standby letter of credit that guarantees payment of a specific obligation that is financial in nature, market value guarantee of a nonfinancial or financial asset, market price guarantee of common stock of the guaranteed party, a contingent contract based on an underlying that includes a business or owner guarantee that states that business revenue (or part of the business revenue) will be at least a specific amount for a specified period of time, and a collection guarantee of contractual scheduled cash flows from a special purpose entity's financial assets.
3. An indirect guarantee of another party's indebtedness.
4. An indemnification contract where the guarantor, on a contingent basis, must make payments to the guaranteed party using changes in an underlying. The underlying may be related to an asset, liability, or equity item of the guaranteed party. Examples include adverse lawsuit judgments and additional tax requirements resulting from adverse interpretations or changes in tax law.

Selected guarantee contracts are excluded from the provisions of ASC 460. These include (ASC 460-10-15-7):

1. Guarantees of the future performance of entity issuing the guarantee.
2. Indemnification or guarantee excluded by ASC 450-20-15-2.

3. Guaranteed residual value of leased property by the lessee when the lease is classified as a capital lease.
4. Guarantees accounted for as a contingent rent using the provisions of ASC 840-30 even if it meets the requirements of ASC 460.
5. Insurance or reinsurance company guarantees or indemnification covered by the provisions of ASC 944.
6. Contracts meeting ASC 460 requirements, but represents a vendor rebate based on units sold or revenue generated by the guaranteed party.
7. Contracts providing payments constituting a vendor rebate based on volume of purchases by the buyer.
8. Guarantees or indemnifications that do not allow the guarantor to report a transaction as a sale of an asset related to an underlying of the guarantee or report the profit in earnings.
9. Registration payment arrangements within the scope of ASC 825-20.
10. Guarantees accounted for as credit derivative instruments at fair value under ASC 815.

A guarantee that meets the measurement requirements of ASC 460 must be reported as a liability in the balance sheet at the inception of the guarantee using fair value. The amount reported as fair value depends on the type of guarantee. ASC 460-10-30-2 provides guidelines as to what constitutes fair value for different types of guarantees. For example, the premium received by the guarantor should be used in a stand-alone, arm's length transaction with an unrelated party. The premium should also be used as a practical expedient in transactions with multiple elements where there are not available fair value measurements.

If a contingent loss must be reported using the provisions of ASC 450, because it is probable there is loss related to the guarantee and it can reasonably be estimated, the amount of liability reported at the inception of the guarantee is the larger of the liability requirement of ASC 460, or the contingent liability reported using the provisions of ASC 450.

Once a liability has been determined for a guarantee, the debit side of the transaction must be determined. The debit could be to cash, a receivable, prepaid asset, or expense, depending on the circumstance of the guarantee. ASC 460-10-55-23 provides examples of different debits for different types of guarantees. ASC 460 does not provide specific guidelines for measuring the liability subsequent to its initial recording. However, the liability generally would be reduced as the risk related to the guarantee is removed. Generally, this occurs using one of three methods: when the guarantee has been settled, amortization using some systematic and rational method, or change as fair value changes (ASC 460-10-35-2).

Costs incurred for extended warranty and product maintenance agreements that are priced separately from the price of the product are either expensed as incurred or deferred and amortized in proportion to the revenue recognized. Costs incurred to directly consummate the contract are deferred and amortized to expense. Other costs, such as general and administrative and cost of contract performance are expensed as incurred. An entity should recognize a loss on extended warranty and product maintenance contracts when a loss is indicated. A loss is indicated when all future expenses, including those that are deferred, exceed the estimated future revenues. For purposes of determining losses, expenses and revenues from the contracts are computed by aggregating the contracts in some consistent manner. If a loss is indicated, any unamortized deferred cost is charged to expense and a liability is recorded for any loss in excess of the deferred costs.

Disclosures are required for each guarantee; similar guarantees may be grouped and disclosures provided for each group of similar guarantees (ASC 460-10-50). Required disclosures are as follows:

1. The nature of the guarantee, including its length or term of guarantee, how the guarantee developed, what would cause performance by the guarantor under the agreement, and the status of the payment/performance risk of the guarantee as of the date of the statement of financial position.
2. The guarantor's maximum possible undiscounted amount of payments that could be required by the agreement.
3. The amount of guarantor's liability (current carrying amount) including any amount required by ASC 450. The amount should be reported even if the guarantee is embedded in other contracts.
4. The nature of any recourse options against third parties or assets held as collateral or by third parties that could be liquidated to cover possible payments under the guarantee.

If the guarantee is a product warranty or similar guarantee (referred to collectively as product warranties) not requiring liability measurement, the disclosure in 2 above is not required, but the following additional disclosures are required for such guarantees (ASC 460-10-50-8):

1. The accounting policy and methodology used by the guarantor in determining the warranty liability (this would also apply to extended warranties).
2. Reconciliation in tabular format of the changes in the aggregate of the liability for product warranty.

The disclosures described in ASC 460 also relate to guarantees associated with related parties as defined in ASC 850 and these disclosures would be in addition to the disclosures required by ASC 850.

Topic 470: Debt

Topic 470, *Debt*, contains 13 subtopics:

10 Overall

20 Debt with Conversion and Other Options

30 Participating Mortgage Loans

40 Product Financing Arrangements

50 Modifications and Extinguishments

60 Troubled Debt Restructurings by Debtors

932 Extractive Activities—Oil and Gas*

942 Financial Services—Depository and Lending*

944 Financial Services—Insurance*

954 Health Care Entities*

958 Not-For-Profit Entities*

970 Real Estate—General*

980 Regulated Operations*

* See the corresponding topic in Chapter 9 for coverage of this shared subtopic.

Overall—Flowchart and General Discussion

ASC 470-10-45, paragraphs 12A through 20, are concerned with a rather common classification problem. How should the entity classify short-term obligations that its management intends to refinance on a long-term basis? Normally, short-term obligations are thought of as current liabilities. In certain cases, short-term obligations may be excluded from the current liabilities portion of the balance sheet.

The short-term obligations referred to in ASC 470-10-45, paragraphs 12A through 20, may be thought of as debt that is due within one year, or within the operating cycle of the business if for a period longer than one year. Short-term obligations do not include obligations incurred in the normal course of generating revenues (e.g., accounts payable, accrued wages payable).

Flowchart 4-2 illustrates the major provisions of ASC 470-10-45, paragraphs 12A through 20. The left side of Flowchart 4-2 reflects the decisions required to determine whether a given short-term obligation may be classified as other than a current liability, and the right side aids in the determination of the proper amount to be reclassified. The decision blocks are numbered and are referred to in the discussion that follows.

Flowchart 4-2

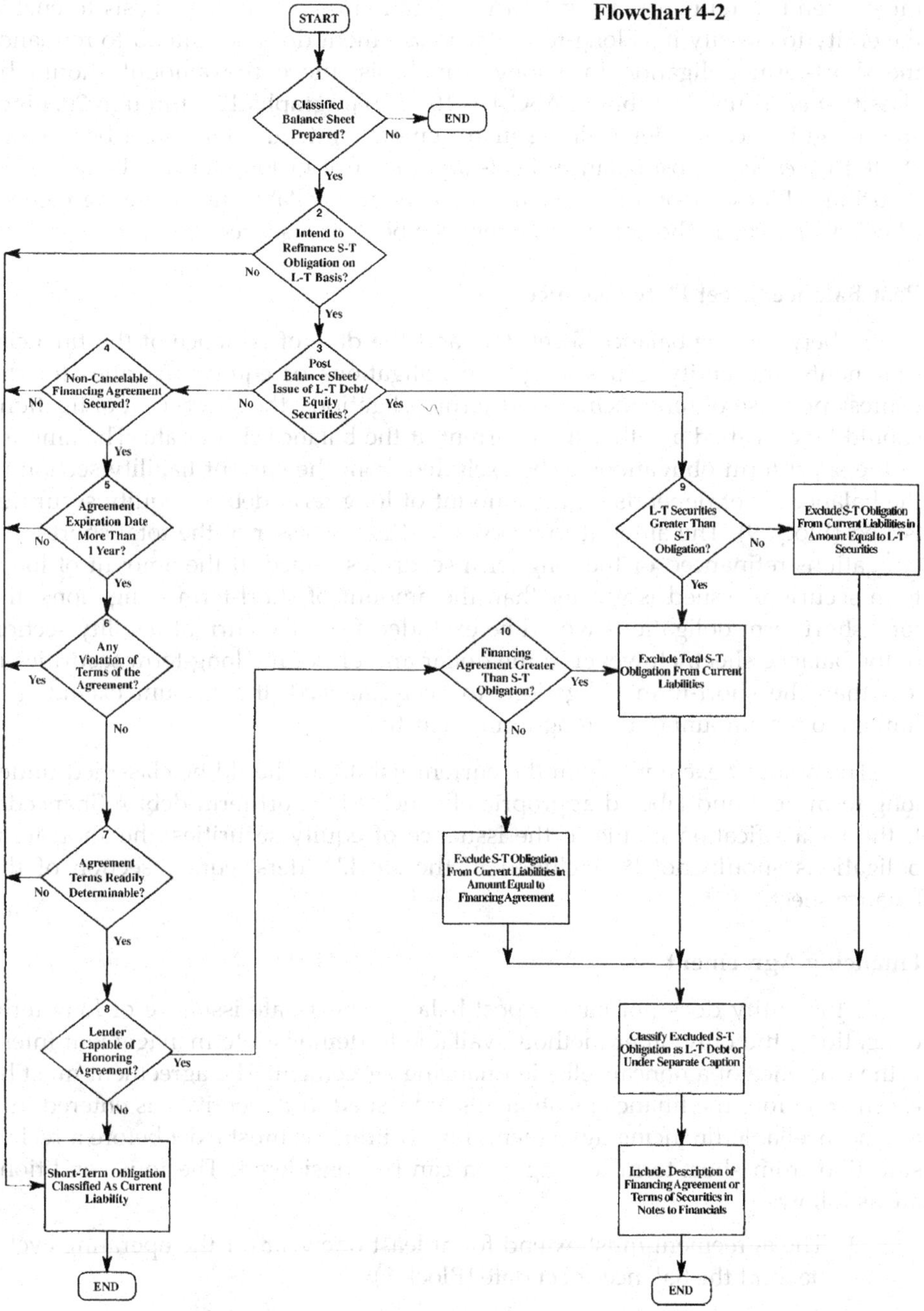

START

1 Classified Balance Sheet Prepared? — No → END; Yes ↓

2 Intend to Refinance S-T Obligation on L-T Basis? — No → Short-Term Obligation Classified As Current Liability; Yes ↓

3 Post Balance Sheet Issue of L-T Debt/ Equity Securities? — No → 4; Yes → 9

4 Non-Cancelable Financing Agreement Secured? — No → Short-Term Obligation Classified As Current Liability; Yes ↓

5 Agreement Expiration Date More Than 1 Year? — No → Short-Term Obligation Classified As Current Liability; Yes ↓

6 Any Violation of Terms of the Agreement? — Yes → Short-Term Obligation Classified As Current Liability; No ↓

7 Agreement Terms Readily Determinable? — No → Short-Term Obligation Classified As Current Liability; Yes ↓

8 Lender Capable of Honoring Agreement? — Yes → 10; No ↓

Short-Term Obligation Classified As Current Liability → END

9 L-T Securities Greater Than S-T Obligation? — No → Exclude S-T Obligation From Current Liabilities in Amount Equal to L-T Securities; Yes → Exclude Total S-T Obligation From Current Liabilities

10 Financing Agreement Greater Than S-T Obligation? — Yes → Exclude Total S-T Obligation From Current Liabilities; No → Exclude S-T Obligation From Current Liabilities in Amount Equal to Financing Agreement

Classify Excluded S-T Obligation as L-T Debt or Under Separate Caption

Include Description of Financing Agreement or Terms of Securities in Notes to Financials

END

For the provisions of ASC 470-10-45, paragraphs 12A through 20, to apply, the entity must prepare a classified balance sheet (Block 1). (Certain industries have specialized accounting practices that preclude the preparation of classified balance sheets. In these cases, ASC 470-10-45, paragraphs 12A through 20, would not be applicable.) If the entity prepares a classified balance sheet, management must intend to refinance a short-term obligation on a long-term basis to enable the entity to classify it as long-term. If management does not intend to refinance the short-term obligation to a long-term basis, the entire amount should be classified as a current liability. ASC 470-10-45, paragraphs 12A through 20, gives specific guidance for determining management's intent. Intent must be demonstrated by *either* a post-balance-sheet-date issuance of long-term debt or equity securities (Block 3) or the existence of a noncancellable financing agreement (Block 4). These are the only ways intent can be demonstrated.

Post-Balance Sheet-Date Issuance

If, between the balance sheet date and the date of issuance of the financial statements, the entity issues long-term obligations or equity securities for the express purpose of refinancing short-term obligations, the short-term obligations should be classified as other than current at the balance sheet date. The amount of the short-term obligations to be excluded from the current liability section of the balance sheet depends on the amount of long-term debt or equity securities issued (Block 9). The amount to be excluded is the lesser of the total short-term obligations refinanced or the long-term securities issued. If the amount of long-term securities issued is greater than the amount of short-term obligations, the total short-term obligations would be excluded from the current liability section of the balance sheet. However, if the dollar amount of the long-term securities is less than the short-term obligations to be refinanced, the amount excluded is limited to the amount of the long-term securities.

The amount excluded from the current liabilities should be classified under long-term debt and labeled appropriately such as "Short-term debt refinanced." If the reclassification is due to the issuance of equity securities, the short-term obligations should not be included in the stockholders' equity section of the balance sheet.

Financing Agreement

If the entity does not have a post-balance sheet-date issuance of long-term obligations, the only other method available to demonstrate management intent is the existence of a noncancellable financing agreement. The agreement must be executed before the financial statements are issued. If the entity has entered into a noncancellable financing agreement, four conditions must exist before a reclassification from short-term to long-term can be considered. The four conditions are as follows:

1. The agreement must extend for at least one year (or the operating cycle) beyond the balance sheet date (Block 5);
2. There must be no violations of any of the terms of the financing agreement up to the date of issuance of the financial statements; or, if a violation has occurred, a waiver has been obtained (Block 6);
3. The terms of the agreement must be readily determinable (Block 7); and
4. The lender or prospective lender must be capable of honoring the financing agreement (Block 8).

If the agreement fails to meet any of these four conditions, the obligations must continue to be classified as current regardless of management intent.

Provided that all the conditions outlined above are met, the amount of the short-term obligations to be excluded from current liabilities is the lesser of the total short-term obligations to be refinanced or the minimum amount expected to be available to the entity under the financing agreement (Block 10). If the dollar amount of the financing agreement is greater than or equal to the amount of the short-term obligations to be refinanced, the total amount of the short-term obligations should be excluded from current liabilities. If the minimum amount available under the agreement is less than the amount of the short-term obligations, then only that amount may be reclassified. In this case, part of the short-term obligations may be reclassified to long-term, and part will remain in the current liability section of the balance sheet.

As indicated above, the amount to be excluded from current liabilities may be classified under either long-term debt or a separate caption. When the separate caption option is used, a title such as "Short-term debt expected to be refinanced" or "Interim debt" should be placed below current liabilities but before long-term debt.

Additional Considerations

There are two additional considerations that must be discussed to gain a full understanding of ASC 470-10-45, paragraphs 12A through 20. The basic thrust of ASC 470-10-45, paragraphs 12A through 20, deals with refinancing on a long-term basis; however, there are situations where short-term obligations may be continually replaced by new short-term obligations, with the short-term debt appropriately classified as long-term. This might be the case when an entity makes use of a revolving credit agreement or a stand-by credit agreement. An entity has not demonstrated specifically the ability to refinance short-term debt on a long-term basis if, after the date of the financial statements but before the statements are released, an entity replaces short-term debt with other short-term debt. Before the short-term obligations may be classified as other than current, the revolving credit agreement or the stand-by credit agreement must meet the same conditions as any other financing agreement (see Blocks 4 through 8 of Flowchart 4-2). If the conditions are met, it would be appropriate to consider reclassification.

The second consideration deals with the case where the amount that may be obtained under the financing agreement is subject to change. For example, the amount available under the agreement may be limited by the amount of collateral offered at any time (i.e., the amount of the loan agreement may be tied directly to the value of inventory or outstanding accounts receivable). In cases where the amount available under the financing agreement changes, the amount that is used to determine the excludable amount would be a reasonable estimate of the minimum funds available from the date of maturity of the short-term obligations to the end of the fiscal year. For example, assuming that the funds available are linked to inventory, the maximum amount of the short-term obligation that could be reclassified would be the minimum inventory at any time during the next year. If it is not possible to determine the amount available under the financing agreement, no reclassification is allowed. For example: Assume Company A has a revolving credit agreement that expires 15 months after the current balance-sheet date. Further, under this agreement the Company may borrow up to $2,000,000. At the current balance-sheet date $1,800,000 is outstanding. Over the next 12 months Company A expects that a minimum of $1,500,000 will be outstanding at any time. For these reasons, the company would classify that amount as long-term as of the current balance-sheet date.

Technical Considerations—Post-Balance Sheet-Date Issuance

Example 4-8 lists the refinancing assumptions that are used to illustrate reclassification under a post-balance sheet-date issuance of long-term obligations.

Example 4-8
Refinancing Assumptions

1. Jar, Inc. has a year-end of December 31, 20X6, and prepares a classified balance sheet for issuance on or about April 10, 20X7.
2. At December 31, 20X6, Jar, Inc. has $10,000,000 of 8% short-term obligations that mature on March 31, 20X7.
3. Jar, Inc. intends to refinance the $10,000,000 on a long-term basis.
4. On March 30, 20X7 Jar, Inc. sold $12,000,000 of debenture bonds with the express purpose of using the proceeds to retire the short-term obligations. The debentures mature in five years and have a stated interest rate of 9%.

Using Flowchart 4-2 to aid in the decision process, the first condition is met (Block 1), because Jar, Inc. prepares a classified balance sheet. Assumption 3 indicates that Jar, Inc. intends to refinance the short-term obligations on a long-term basis; therefore, the second condition (Block 2) also is met. Assuming that $10,000,000 of the proceeds from the sale of the debentures were, in fact, used to retire the short-term obligations on March 31, 20X7, the transaction would qualify as a post-balance sheet-date issuance (Block 3). Actual retirement of the short-term debt may or may not occur before the balance sheet is released. In Example 4-8, the maturity date of the short-term debt is prior to the release of the financial statements. However, the maturity date of the short-term obligation may be after the release of the statements.

The next step in the process would be to compare the amount of the debt issue with the total amount of the short-term obligations refinanced (Block 9). The total amount ($12,000,000) of the debt issued is greater than the amount ($10,000,000) of the short-term obligations; therefore, the entire amount of the short-term obligations would be reclassified as other than current on the December 31, 20X6 balance sheet. Jar, Inc. could elect to classify the $10,000,000 as either long-term debt or short-term debt expected to be refinanced. Appropriate disclosures will be illustrated later in this discussion.

Assuming that $8,000,000 of debentures were issued, rather than the original $12,000,000, and that the proceeds of $8,000,000 and $2,000,000 of internally generated cash were used to retire the short-term obligations, Jar, Inc. would reclassify only $8,000,000 of the short-term obligations. In this case, Jar, Inc. is limited by the amount of the debt that was issued to refinance the short-term obligations. The remaining $2,000,000 ($10,000,000 – $8,000,000) would continue to be classified as current liabilities.

For Example 4-9, assume all information in Example 4-8 is the same except that the maturity date for the short-term obligations is May 1, 20X7. In this case, the debentures will be sold on March 30, 20X7, and the proceeds will be used to retire the short-term obligations on May 1, 20X7. Assume that $10,000,000 of the proceeds from the sale of the debentures was used to make a temporary investment in government securities, and that the maturity date of the securities was May 1, 20X7 (the same as the maturity date of the short-term obligations). Based upon these assumptions, the $10,000,000 of short-term obligations would be reclassified as other than current.

This concludes the technical discussion of post-balance sheet-date issuance of securities. The next section will deal with the technical considerations involved when the company has entered into a financing agreement for the purpose of refinancing short-term obligations.

Technical Considerations—Financing Agreements

Example 4-9 lists the assumptions to be used in illustrating reclassification under a financing agreement. The assumptions are somewhat more complex than those presented above, because it is necessary to know the details of the agreement before any determination can be made about the propriety of reclassification.

Example 4-9
Refinancing Assumptions

1. Jar, Inc. has a year-end of December 31, 20X5, and prepares a classified balance sheet for issuance on or about April 10, 20X6.
2. At December 31, 20X5, Jar, Inc. has $10,000,000 of 8% short-term obligations that mature on August 15, 20X6.
3. Jar, Inc. intends to refinance the $10,000,000 on a long-term basis.
4. Prior to April 10, 20X6, Jar, Inc. entered into a financing agreement with a local bank that allows the company to borrow up to $12,000,000 at any time during the next two years. Any amount borrowed is due in full five years from the date the funds are received and bears interest at the rate of 11%.
5. It has been determined that the local bank is financially capable of honoring the agreement. The agreement may not be canceled unless Jar, Inc. is in violation of any of the terms of the agreement.
6. As of April 10, 20X6, there is no evidence of any violation of the provisions of the agreement.

Flowchart 4-2 may be used to aid in the decision-making process for this set of assumptions. Jar, Inc. issues a classified balance sheet (Block 1), and intends to refinance certain short-term obligations on a long-term basis (Block 2). The method of refinancing is through the use of a financing agreement. The terms of the agreement specify that it is noncancellable (Block 4), and assumption number 4 indicates that the term of the agreement is more than one year (Block 5). There are no known violations of the financing agreement as of April 10, 20X6 (Block 6), and the terms of the agreement are readily determinable (i.e., the amount, interest rate, lender, and maturity date are all known (Block 7)). Finally, it has been determined that the lending institution is capable of honoring the agreement (Block 8). Because the conditions in Blocks 4 through 8 have been met, reclassification of the short-term obligations is appropriate.

To determine the proper amount to be reclassified, it is necessary to compare the minimum amount available to Jar, Inc. under the financing agreement with the total amount of the short-term obligations expected to be refinanced. The amount available ($12,000,000) is greater than the amount of the short-term obligations ($10,000,000); therefore, it is appropriate to exclude the entire amount of the short-term obligations from the current liability section of the December 31, 20X5 balance sheet. Jar, Inc. may elect to classify the $10,000,000 as either long-term debt or short-term debt expected to be refinanced. If the latter is chosen, the amount should appear after current liabilities, but before long-term debt, on the balance sheet for 20X5.

In Example 4-9, if the amount available under the financing agreement had been less than the amount of the short-term obligations that Jar, Inc. expected to refinance, Jar, Inc. would have been limited to excluding short-term obligations in the amount of the financing agreement. If this situation were to arise, part of the short-term obligations would be reclassified, and part would remain in the current liability section of the balance sheet.

A final example is presented to illustrate the reclassification process when the amount available to the borrower under a financing agreement varies. Assume that all of the provisions listed in Example 4-9 are the same, except that the financing agreement specifies that Jar, Inc. may borrow up to 90% of the value of its trade accounts receivable. In this case, the amount available under the financing agreement will vary directly with the value of accounts receivable. Assume Jar, Inc. estimates that accounts receivable will reach a high of $15,000,000 in the first quarter of the year and a low of $10,000,000 in the third quarter of the year. The short-term obligations to be refinanced mature in the third quarter of the year. During this period the best estimate of the amount available under the financing agreement is $9,000,000 ($10,000,000 × .9). Therefore, only $9,000,000 of the short-term obligations may be reclassified on the December 31, 20X1 balance sheet.

Disclosure Requirements

If an entity has excluded short-term obligations from current liabilities on the basis of the provisions of ASC 470-10-45, paragraphs 12A through 20, it must disclose in the notes to the financial statements a general description of either the financing agreement or the debt or equity securities issued. The disclosure should contain the amounts involved, a description of the financing agreement (including conditions and terms), restrictions imposed by the financing agreement, and a description of the stock issued (including number of shares and amounts).

Obligations That Are Callable or Due on Demand—Flowchart and General Discussion

ASC 470-10-45, paragraphs 9 through 12, require obligations that are either due on demand or callable by the creditor to be classified on the balance sheet as current liabilities. However, obligations that are callable and obligations that are due on demand that are expected to be refinanced on a long-term basis are accounted for using the provisions of ASC 470-10-45, paragraphs 12A through 20.

Flowchart 4-3 illustrates the major provisions of ASC 470-10-45, paragraphs 9 through 12. The decision blocks have been numbered and will be referred to in the discussion.

Flowchart 4-3

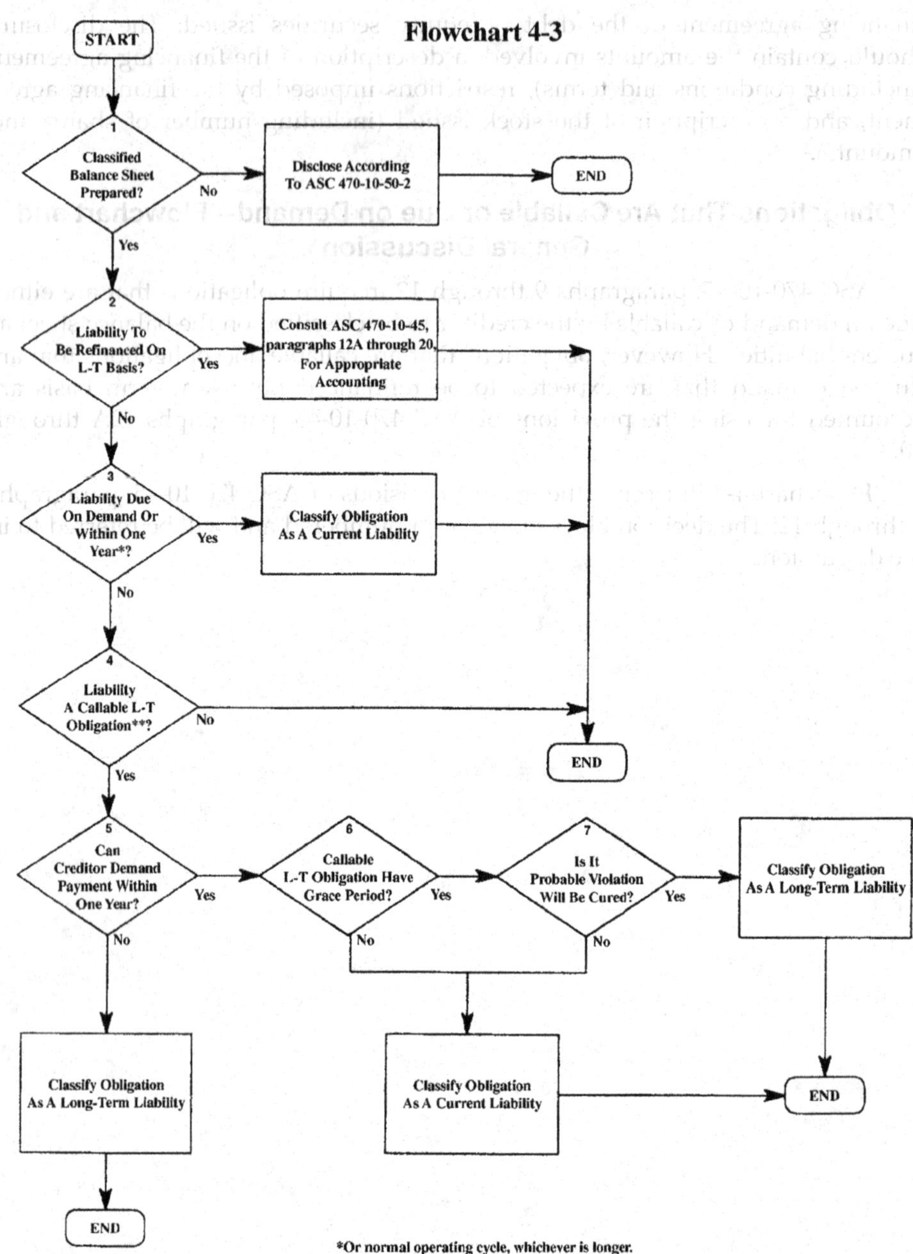

For the classification provisions of ASC 470-10-45, paragraphs 9 through 12, to be applicable, the entity must prepare a classified balance sheet (Block 1). However, if the entity does not prepare a classified balance sheet, certain disclosures are required. The required disclosures are discussed below. If a classified balance sheet is prepared and the entity has a liability that is expected to be refinanced on a long-term basis whether or not callable or due on demand (Block

2), the provisions of ASC 470-10-45, paragraphs 12A through 20, are applied. If the entity has an obligation that is due on demand or within one year of the balance sheet date (or normal operating cycle, whichever is longer) (Block 3), the obligation should be classified as a current liability.

In certain cases, an entity may violate a provision of a debt agreement. As a result of the violation, the entity may have a long-term obligation that becomes callable (Block 4) or becomes callable if the violation is not cured within a specified period of time. The classification of the long-term obligation is dependent on the circumstances.

If the creditor cannot demand payment for more than one year (Block 5) or the normal operating cycle, whichever is longer, the obligation is classified as long-term. The creditor may not be able to demand payment for more than one year, because the right of collection has been waived or because the debtor has cured the violation before the financial statements are issued.

If the creditor can demand payment within one year (or the normal operating cycle, whichever is longer), further analysis is required to determine the proper balance sheet classification. If the long-term obligation has a grace period (Block 6) and if it is probable (likely to occur) that the debtor will cure the violation within the grace period (Block 7), the long-term obligation continues to be classified as long-term. However, if the obligation has no grace period or if there is a grace period and it is other than probable that the violation will be cured within the grace period, the long-term obligation is classified as a current liability.

The grace period is a period of time provided to the debtor by the creditor to cure any violation that may exist in the debt instrument. For example, assume the debtor is required to make interest and principal payments on the last day of each quarter. If the payment is not made on the due date, the debtor has 20 days after the end of the quarter to make the payment or the loan will be callable at the option of the creditor. The 20-day time period is the grace period. The probable concept noted above is discussed in more detail in ASC 450.

Technical Considerations

Example 4-10 illustrates some of the technical considerations under ASC 470.

Example 4-10 Assumptions for Liability Classification

Listed below are several obligations that are outstanding on December 31, 20X6, the date of the financial statements. Assume that each transaction or debt is treated as an independent situation and each company prepares a classified balance sheet unless otherwise noted.

1. Cramer Enterprises has $3,000,000 in debt that is due April 1, 20X7. The Company intends to refinance the debt on a long-term basis.
2. The Pearson Company has $575,000 of debt that is due on September 15, 20X7. Pearson expects to pay the debt off in cash when due.
3. Johnson, Inc. has $2,500,000 in long-term obligations. During 20X6, Johnson, Inc. violated one of the provisions of the debt agreement. On

February 10, prior to the release of the financial statements for 20X6, Johnson cured the violation.

4. Financial Enterprises has a $200,000 note that is due on demand.
5. The Robertson Company has $5,000,000 in long-term obligations. During 20X6, Robertson violated a provision of the debt agreement. The debt agreement allows for a grace period that extends to March 15, 20X7. It is probable that Robertson will cure the violation within the grace period. Robertson prepares an unclassified balance sheet.
6. Miller, Inc. has a $6,500,000 long-term obligation. During 20X6, Miller violated a provision of the debt agreement. The debt agreement provides for a grace period until February 15, 20X7. Miller is not expected to cure the violation within the grace period.
7. White Enterprises has a $1,250,000 long-term obligation that is callable because of a violation of the debt agreement. The debt agreement provides for a grace period of 60 days. The grace period expires on February 10, 20X7. It is probable that White will cure the violation within the grace period. White's 20X6 financial statements are released on February 2, 20X7.

Each of the obligations is classified and discussed in Table 4-8.

Table 4-8 Classification and Discussion of Obligations

Obligation	Obligation Classification	Reason for Classification and Flowchart 4-3 Reference
$3,000,000 Debt (Item 1)	Classified Using ASC 470-10-45, paragraphs 12A through 20	The debt is due within one year and is expected to be refinanced on a long-term basis. (Block 2)
$575,000 Debt (Item 2)	Current Liability	The debt is due within one year and is to be paid with current assets. (Block 3)
$2,500,000 Debt (Item 3)	Long-Term Liability	The debt is a long-term obligation for which the violation was cured before the statements were released. (Blocks 5, 6 and 7)
$200,000 Debt (Item 4)	Current Liability	The note is due on demand. (Block 3)
$5,000,000 Debt (Item 5)	Disclose Using ASC 470-10-50-2. See Discussion Below	The Company prepares an unclassified balance sheet. (Block 1)

Obligation	Obligation Classification	Reason for Classification and Flowchart 4-3 Reference
$6,500,000 Debt (Item 6)	Current Liability	A provision of the long-term debt agreement has been violated and the company is not expected to cure the violation within the grace period. (Blocks 5, 6 and 7)
$1,250,000 Debt (Item 7)	Long-Term Liability	The debt agreement contains a grace period and it is probable that the company will cure the violation within the grace period. (Blocks 5, 6 and 7)

Disclosure Requirements

ASC 470-10-50-2 specifies the required disclosures for obligations that are callable or are due on demand and includes the following:

1. The circumstances surrounding a callable long-term obligation classified as a long-term liability. This would include only those long-term obligations where the debt agreement has a grace period and it is probable that the debtor will cure the violation within the grace period.

2. The circumstances surrounding a callable long-term obligation when the enterprise prepares an unclassified balance sheet.

Additional disclosures for long-term debt are required by ASC 440-10-50.

Debt with Conversion and Other Options—Flowchart and General Discussion

ASC 470-20 deals with the problem of accounting for securities that contain both debt and equity elements. Securities with features of both debt and equity provide the safeguard of debt—periodic interest payments—and allow the holder to participate in the long-term growth of the entity by converting the debt security to an equity interest. Some securities may be debt during their entire life, and be retired as debt. Other securities may begin as debt instruments and eventually be converted into an equity interest. Still other securities may begin as debt instruments and, at some time, be divided into a debt *and* equity interest.

Flowchart 4-4 is designed around the three types of debt securities identified in ASC 470-20. The types of securities identified contain both debt and equity features and include convertible debt, debt with non-detachable stock purchase warrants, and debt with detachable stock purchase warrants. The basic thrust of ASC 470-20 is to determine when it is appropriate to account for the debt and equity elements of these securities on an individual basis.

The discussion that follows will treat separately each of the securities specifically identified in ASC 470-20.

Flowchart 4-4

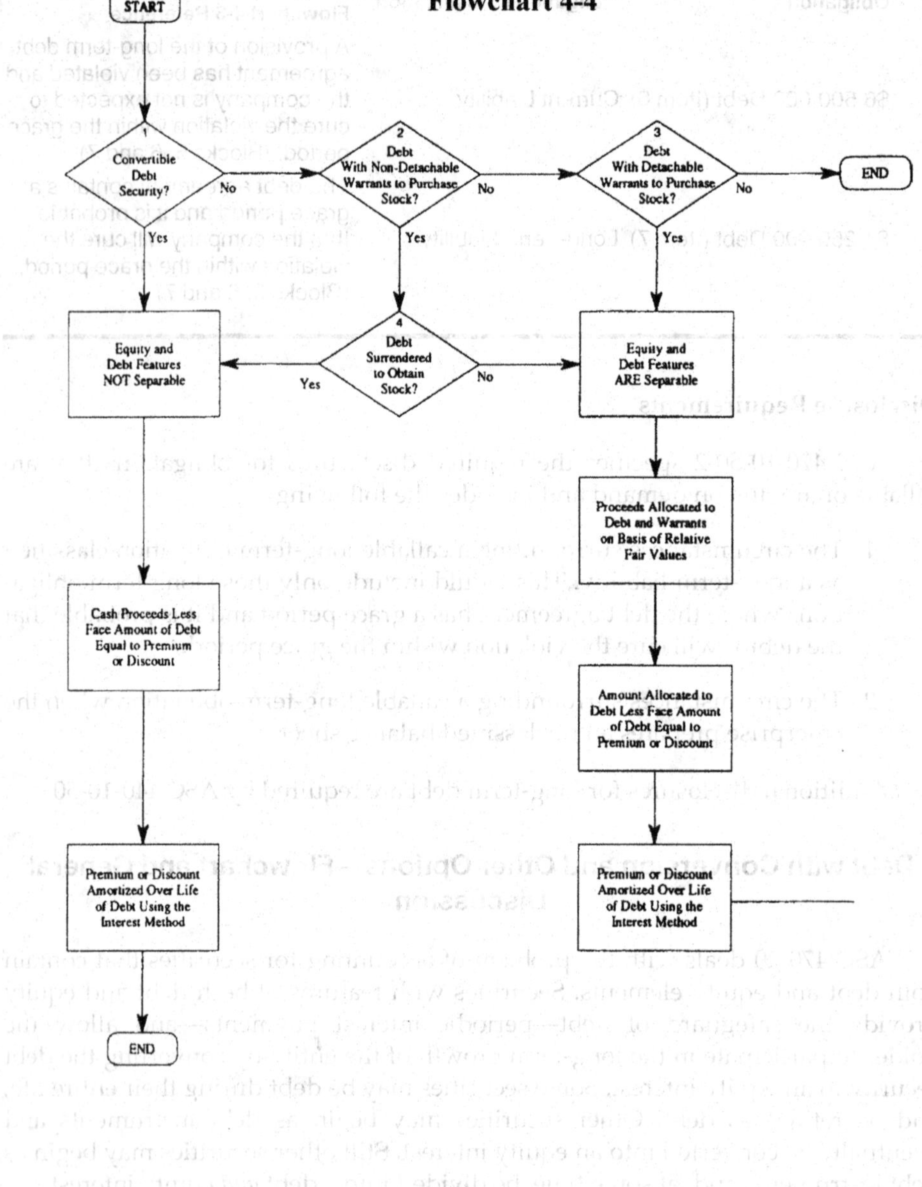

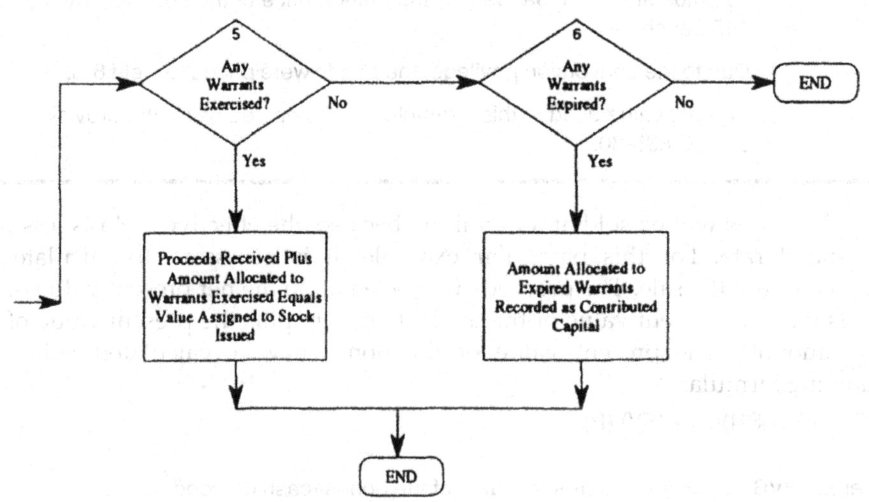

Convertible Debt

Convertible debt is debt that can be converted into common stock of the entity issuing the debt security, or an affiliated enterprise, and generally is issued at a price that is not materially greater than the face of the debt. The conversion option is an option of the holder of the debt and, generally, the debt is converted at a price specified at the date of issuance of the debt. Debt that is convertible into common stock may be sold at a lower yield (through a lower interest rate or a more substantial premium) than may similar debt without the conversion privilege. If the conversion privilege is exercised, the debt is surrendered to the issuer, and common stock is issued in its place.

When an entity has convertible debt (Block 1), the security should be accounted for solely as debt unless at the date of issuance the conversion feature is "in the money." The difference between the cash proceeds from the sale of the convertible debt and the face amount should be recorded as a discount or premium. The discount or premium thus recorded should be amortized over the life of the debt, using the interest method. (The interest method is the application of the effective interest rate to the unrecovered obligation balance—face of the bonds, plus or minus the unamortized premium or discount.)

To illustrate the accounting for convertible debt which is not "in the money," the assumptions listed in Example 4-11 are used.

Example 4-11
Convertible Debt Assumptions

1. On January 1, Seller Company, Inc. issued 1,000, five-year, 10%, $1,000 face-value convertible bonds.
2. Interest is payable semiannually on January 1 and July 1.

3. Each $1,000 bond is convertible into 20 shares of $10 par value common stock. On January 1, the market price of the common stock is $45 per share.
4. Due to the conversion privilege, the bonds were priced to yield 8%.
5. Present value used in this example was computed using the provisions of ASC 835-30.

The bonds will be sold at a premium, because the effective yield is less than the stated rate. For this particular example, it is necessary to calculate the proceeds from the sale. The proceeds will be equal to the net present value of the bonds (i.e., the present value of the interest annuity plus the present value of the face amount). The present value of the bond may be calculated using the following formula:

PVB = (FV × SR)(A) + (FV) (P)

Where:	PVB	=	Present value of the bonds (cash proceeds).
	FV	=	Face value of the bonds.
	SR	=	Stated interest rate per interest payment period.
	A	=	Present value of an annuity, using the effective interest rate per interest payment period.
	P	=	Present value of $1, using the effective interest rate per interest payment period.

For the bond example, there are 10 interest payment periods (5 years × 2 interest payments per year = 10 payments); therefore, the stated interest rate to be used in the above formula will be 5% (10% ÷ 2) and the effective rate will be 4% (8% ÷ 2). The interest rates must be expressed as a rate per interest payment period. With this in mind—and using 8.11090 as the present value factor for an ordinary annuity for 10 periods at 4%, and .67556 as the present value factor for $1 for 10 periods at 4%—the formula will provide the following result:

PVB = ($1,000,000 × .05) (8.11090) + ($1,000,000) (.67556) = $1,081,105

The difference between the proceeds of $1,081,105 and the $1,000,000 face amount of the bonds is recorded as the premium on the bonds. The entry to record the issuance of the convertible bonds is as follows:

Cash	1,081,105	
Bonds Payable		1,000,000
Premium on Bonds		81,105

If, in the above example, the proceeds were known, but the effective interest rate was not known, the formula could be used on a trial-and-error approach to determine the effective interest. This is a very time-consuming task, and one that can be handled quite easily through the use of a computer.

Once the bond proceeds have been determined, a premium amortization schedule similar to that in Table 4-9 may be prepared. Table 4-9 itemizes the cash interest paid, interest expense, premium amortization, and bond carrying value for each interest payment period. The interest method has been used to amortize the bond premium.

Table 4-9 Schedule of Interest and Premium Amortization

	Period	*Cash Interest*	*Interest Expense*	*Premium Amortization*	*Carrying Value of Bonds*
Initial Value					
	—	—	—	—	$1,081,105
	1	[a]$50,000	[b]$43,244	[c]$6,756	[d]1,074,349
	2	50,000	42,974	7,026	1,067,323
	3	50,000	42,693	7,307	1,060,016
	4	50,000	42,401	7,599	1,052,417
	5	50,000	42,097	7,903	1,044,514
	6	50,000	41,781	8,219	1,036,295
	7	50,000	41,452	8,548	1,027,747
	8	50,000	41,110	8,890	1,018,857
	9	50,000	40,754	9,246	1,009,611
	10	50,000	*40,389	9,611	[e]1,000,000
		$500,000	$418,895	$81,105	

[a] $1,000,000 × 5% = $50,000.
[b] $1,081,105 × 4% = $43,244.
[c] $50,000 - $43,244 = $6,756.
[d] $1,081,105 - $6,756 = $1,074,349.
[e] Represents the maturity value of the bonds at the end of five years.
* Rounded.

Using the information in Table 4-9, the journal entry required on July 1 (the first interest payment period) would be:

Interest Expense	43,244	
Premium on Bonds	6,756	
Cash		50,000

To complete the example, assume that, just after the third interest payment, all the bonds were converted into common stock. At the time of conversion, the bonds have a carrying value of $1,060,016. Each bond will be converted into 20 shares of $10 par value common stock; therefore, 20,000 (1,000 × 20) shares of common will be issued for the bonds. Assuming that fair value is equal to book value, the journal entry to record the conversion would be as follows:

Bonds Payable	1,000,000	
Premium on Bonds	60,016	

Common Stock (20,000 shares × $10 par)	200,000
Additional paid-in capital	860,016

The debt securities have now all been converted into equity. If only part of the bonds had been converted, a proportionate share of the premium would have been removed from the account.

If convertible debt is in the money as of the date of issuance, recognition is given to the beneficial conversion feature, or BCF. For example: Assume that $1,000 principal amount of 6% debt, convertible into 100 shares of the issuer's common stock in five years is issued for cash of $1,000. At the date of issuance the fair value of the issuer's common stock is $11 a share. In this case, the issuer would allocate a portion of proceeds to the BCF (i.e., excess of fair value of common stock into which the debt is convertible over proceeds) to additional paid-in capital and accrete discount. The entry to record this transaction would be a debit to cash for $1,000, a credit to debt for $900, and a credit to additional paid-in capital of $100. The discount on the debt of $100 would be accreted over five years using the effective interest rate method and recording a debit to interest expense and credit to debt. The effective interest rate would be in excess of the stated rate of 6% because of the BCF.

Debt with Non-Detachable Stock Purchase Warrants

A review of Flowchart 4-4 indicates that debt with non-detachable stock purchase warrants (Block 2) will be treated as either convertible debt or as debt with detachable stock purchase warrants. The appropriate treatment of the security is determined by whether or not the debt must be surrendered to obtain the stock (Block 4). If the debt must be surrendered, the security will be accounted for as if it were convertible debt. Accounting for convertible debt has been discussed above. If the debt does not have to be surrendered to obtain the stock, the security will be accounted for in the same manner as debt with detachable stock purchase warrants. Accounting for debt with detachable stock purchase warrants is discussed next.

Debt with Detachable Stock Purchase Warrants

Generally, detachable warrants may be removed from the debt and used to purchase shares of stock, or they may be sold to a third party interested in acquiring shares. The debt and warrants usually trade separately in the market. This means that the two are independent securities that carry individual values. If a company has debt with detachable stock purchase warrants, ASC 470-20 requires that separate recognition be given to the value of the debt and the warrants (Block 3). The value to be assigned to the debt and equity elements of the security is based on the relative fair values of the debt and warrants. Because the two trade separately, the relative fair values may be determined. However, in some cases, the fair values may have to be estimated.

The total proceeds from the sale of the securities should be allocated to the debt and warrants on the basis of actual or estimated fair market values. The portion of the proceeds that is allocated to the warrants is considered to be paid-in or contributed capital of the issuer company. An account, such as stock warrants outstanding, should be used to record the value assigned to the warrants. The difference between the proceeds allocated to the debt and the face of the debt should be recorded as a discount or premium. The discount or premium is amortized over the life of the debt, using the interest method.

As the warrants are exercised, the value assigned to the stock issued is equal to the proceeds allocated to the warrants exercised, plus any additional proceeds received from the exercise of the warrants (Block 5). Unexercised warrants generally expire after a period of time (Block 6). The amount allocated to warrants that have expired is considered to be paid-in or contributed capital of the company. Warrants may be allowed to expire because there is no economic advantage to be gained from their exercise.

To illustrate the accounting for debt with detachable stock purchase warrants, the assumptions listed in Example 4-12 are used.

Example 4-12
Assumptions for Debt with Detachable Stock Purchase Warrants

1. On January 1, Seller Company, Inc. issued 200, four-year, 10%, $1,000 face value bonds with detachable warrants.
2. Interest is paid annually on December 31.
3. Each $1,000 bond has a detachable warrant that can be used to purchase one share of Seller Company, Inc. common stock for $50. The par value of the common stock is $30 per share.
4. The debt with detachable warrants was priced to yield 11%.
5. At the time of sale, it is estimated that the bonds would sell for $958.975, independent of the warrants, and that the warrants would sell for $10, independent of the bonds.
6. Present value used in this example was computed using the provisions of ASC 835-30.

The proceeds from the sale may be calculated using the preceding formula. The formula—using 3.10245 as the present value factor for an ordinary annuity for four periods at 11% and .65873 as the present value factor for $1 for four periods at 11%—will yield the following results:

PVB = ($200,000 × .10) (3.10245) + ($200,000) (.65873) = $193,795

The proceeds now must be allocated to the debt and warrants on the basis of their relative fair values. The first step in the process is to determine the total fair value of the two securities. This is accomplished in the following manner:

Bonds (200 bonds × $958.975)	$191,795
Warrants (200 warrants × $10)	2,000
Total fair value	$193,795

In this example, the total value of the bonds and warrants is equal to the proceeds received from the sale. Therefore, allocation based on the relative fair values of each would provide results equal to their individual fair values, making it unnecessary to complete the allocation process.

The discount or premium on the bonds is determined by the difference between the proceeds allocated to the bonds and the face amount of the bonds. For this example, a discount would result because the effective yield is greater than the stated yield. The discount is calculated as follows:

Face Value of Bonds	
(200 bonds × $1,000)	$200,000
Proceeds Allocated to Bonds	191,795
Discount on Bonds	$8,205

Based upon this information, the following journal entry is required to record the issuance of the bonds and warrants.

Cash	193,795	
Discount on Bonds Payable	8,205	
Bonds Payable		200,000
Stock Warrants Outstanding		2,000

The discount of $8,205 is amortized over the life of the bonds using the interest method. Because $2,000 of the proceeds were allocated to the warrants, the effective discount on the bonds was increased by $2,000. Without considering the warrants, the discount on the bonds would have been $6,205 ($200,000 – $193,795). With the allocation of the proceeds to the warrants, the discount is determined to be $8,205. This difference will affect the determination of the interest rate used to amortize the discount, using the interest method. The 11% interest rate used above resulted in the $6,205 discount, and cannot be used to amortize a discount of $8,205. The problem now is to determine the interest rate that will allocate the $8,205 discount over the life of the debt.

The correct interest rate may be determined by the trial-and-error method or by the use of a computer program. The trial-and-error method is very time-consuming because present value factors must be found for both an annuity and the present value of $1. Determining the effective interest through the use of a computer program is an excellent way to solve this problem. The typical computer program is both efficient and quick in the solution of this type of problem.

The appropriate interest rate to use to amortize the discount in this example is 11.3318%. Once this rate has been determined, an amortization schedule similar to Table 4-10 can be developed. Table 4-10 summarizes the cash interest paid, interest expense, discount amortization, and the bond carrying value for the life of the security.

Convertible debt with a beneficial conversion feature may also be issued with detachable warrants. For example, assume that $1,000 principal amount of 6% debt convertible into 100 shares of the issuer's common stock in five years and a warrant with a fair value of $50 to purchase common stock are collectively issued for cash of $1,000. At the date of issuance the fair value of the issuer's common stock is $11 a share. In this case, the issuer would apply a two-step process:

Step 1: Allocate the proceeds between debt and the warrant based on their relative fair values: Allocate $950 to debt and $50 to the warrant based on their relative fair values of $1,000 (95%) and $50 (5%). This allocation results in discount on the debt of $50.

Step 2: Allocate the excess of the fair value of the common stock over the proceeds allocated to the debt to the BCF: The excess of the fair value of common stock of $1,100 (100 shares × $11) over proceeds allocated to debt of $950 (Step 1) is in turn allocated to the BCF, resulting in additional debt discount of $150.

The entry to record this transaction would be a debit to cash for $1,000, a credit to debt for $800 and a credit to additional paid-in capital of $200. The discount on the debt of $200 would be accreted over five years using effective interest rate method as a debit to interest expense and credit to debt. The effective interest rate would be in excess of the stated rate of 6%.

Table 4-10 Schedule of Interest Expense and Discount Amortization

	Period	*Cash Interest*	*Interest Expense*	*Premium Amortization*	*Carrying Value of Bonds*
Initial Value	—	—	—	—	[a]$191,795
	1	[b]$20,000	[c]$21,734	[d]$1,734	[e]193,529
	2	20,000	21,930	1,930	195,459
	3	20,000	22,149	2,149	197,608
	4	20,000	22,392	2,392	[f]200,000
		$80,000	$88,205	$8,205	

[a] Proceeds allocated to the bonds.
[b] $200,000 × 10% = $20,000.
[c] $191,795 × 11.3318% = $21,734.
[d] $21,734 - $20,000 = $1,734.
[e] $191,795 + $1,734 = $193,529.
[f] Represents the maturity value of the bonds.

Using the information in Table 4-10, the journal entry required for the first annual interest payment and discount amortization would be as follows:

Interest Expense	21,734	
Discount on Bonds Payable		1,734
Cash		20,000

Table 4-10 contains the information to prepare the above journal entry for each year of the life of the bonds.

To continue with the example, assume that 190 warrants were exercised for the purchase of 190 shares of common stock. The proceeds from the exercise of the warrants would be $9,500 (190 warrants × $50 exercise price). The following entry would be required to reflect the exercise of the warrants:

Cash	9,500	
Stock Warrants Outstanding	[a]1,900	
Common Stock		[b]5,700
Contributed Capital in Excess of Par		[c]5,700

[a] 190 warrants/200 warrants × $2,000 = $1,900.
[b] 190 common shares × $30 par value = $5,700.
[c] ($9,500 proceeds + $1,900 value of warrants) - ($5,700 amount assigned to common stock) = $5,700.

Assuming that the remaining warrants were allowed to expire, the journal entry shown below would be required.

Stock Warrants Outstanding	[a]100	
Contributed Capital from Warrants		100

[a] $2,000 - $1,900 = $100.

In Example 4-12, the proceeds received from the sale of the bonds were equal to the value of the bonds and warrants. This is a simple example, designed to illustrate the basic accounting required for debt with detachable stock purchase warrants. For a more complex example, the assumptions listed in Example 4-13 are used.

Example 4-13
Assumptions for Debt with Detachable Stock Purchase Warrants

1. On January 1, Seller Company, Inc. issued 500, four-year, 9%, $1,000 face value bonds with detachable warrants.
2. Interest is paid annually on December 31.
3. Each $1,000 bond has a detachable warrant that can be used to purchase one share of Seller Company, Inc. common stock for $100. The par value of the common stock is $75 per share.
4. The debt with detachable warrants was priced to yield 8%.
5. At the time of sale, it is estimated that the bonds will sell for $1,020, independent of the warrants; and that the warrants will sell for $20, independent of the bonds.
6. Present value used in this example was computed using the provisions of ASC 835-30.

Using the formula given, the following proceeds may be calculated:
PVB = ($500,000 × .09) (3.31213[a]) + ($500,000) (.73503[b]) = $516,561

[a] Present value factor for an ordinary annuity for four periods at 8%. See Appendix E, Table II.
[b] Present value factor for $1 for four periods at 8%. See Appendix E, Table I.

These particular bonds were sold at a premium, because the effective yield of 8% is less than the stated yield of 9%. The proceeds of $516,561 must be allocated to the bonds and warrants on the basis of their relative fair values. The total fair values would be determined as follows:

Bonds (500 bonds × $1,020 fair value)	$510,000
Warrants (500 warrants × $20 fair value)	10,000
Total fair value	$520,000

Because there is a difference between the proceeds of $516,561 and the total fair value of $520,000, the proceeds must be allocated to the bonds and warrants. The allocation would be accomplished as follows:

Bonds ($510,000/$520,000 × $516,561)	$506,627
Warrants ($10,000/$520,000 × $516,561)	9,934
Total proceeds allocated	$516,561

The premium relating to the bonds may be determined, once the allocation process is complete. The premium is equal to the difference between the amount allocated to the bonds and the face amount of the bonds, and is calculated below:

Amount allocated to bonds	$506,627
Face amount of bonds	500,000
Premium on bonds payable	$6,627

Based upon the information generated above, the journal entry to record the issuance of the bonds would be as follows:

Cash	516,561	
Bonds Payable		500,000
Premium on Bonds Payable		6,627
Stock Warrants Outstanding		9,934

The premium will be amortized over the life of the bonds, using the interest method. As in Example 4-12, a new effective interest rate must be determined to properly amortize the premium. The appropriate rate to use in the amortization process is 8.5945%, and was determined by the use of a computer program. With the calculation of this rate, an amortization table may be prepared. Table 4-11 summarizes relevant information relating to the example bond issue.

Table 4-11 Schedule of Interest Expense and Premium Amortization

	Period	*Cash Interest*	*Interest Expense*	*Premium Amortization*	*Carrying Value of Bonds*
Initial Value	—	—	—	—	[a]$506,627
	1	[b]$45,000	[c]$43,542	[d]$1,458	[e]505,169
	2	45,000	43,417	1,583	503,586
	3	45,000	43,281	1,719	501,867
	4	45,000	43,133	1,867	[f]500,000
		$180,000	$173,373	$6,627	

[a] Proceeds allocated to the bonds.
[b] $500,000 × 9% = $45,000.

[c] $506,627 × 8.5945% = $43,542.
[d] $45,000 - $43,542 = $1,458.
[e] $506,627 - $1,458 = $505,169.
[f] Represents the maturity value of the bonds.

The entry required for the first annual interest payment and premium amortization is presented below:

Interest Expense	43,542	
Premium on Bonds Payable	1,458	
Cash		45,000

Entries to record the exercise of warrants and the expiration of warrants would be similar to those presented above and need not be repeated.

Induced Conversions—General Discussion

ASC 470-20-40, paragraphs 13 through 17, specify the accounting for convertible debt converted into equity securities that is induced by sweeteners for the convertible debt. A sweetener for the convertible debt is additional consideration paid to a debt holder in an effort to induce the debtor to convert into equity securities. Sweeteners for the convertible debt include consideration such as additional shares of stock, warrants, and cash. The provisions of ASC 470-20-40, paragraphs 13 through 17, are applicable if a conversion meets the following criteria:

1. The conversion occurred because of changes in the conversion requirements.
2. The time period for exercise of the changed conversion requirements is limited.
3. For all debt that is converted to stock, all the required stock is issued.

If the conversion meets all three preceding requirements, it is accounted for using the provisions of ASC 470-20-40, paragraphs 13 through 17. If all conditions are not met, the conversion is accounted for using either the provisions of ASC 470-50 or other provisions of ASC 470-20.

When convertible debt is converted under the provisions of ASC 470-20-40, paragraphs 13 through 17, the debtor company should recognize an expense equal to the fair value of all securities and other consideration transferred in the conversion in excess of the fair value of the securities that would have been issued using the original conversion terms. Fair value is determined and the expense is recognized on the date that the offer is accepted by the debtor (i.e., when the debtor either converts the securities or enters into a binding agreement to convert).

Technical Considerations

Two examples are used to illustrate the technical considerations of accounting for induced conversions of convertible debt. Assumptions for Example 4-14 are presented below.

Example 4-14
Assumptions for Induced Conversions of Convertible Debt

1. Micro Enterprises, a December 31 calendar year-end company, issued $1,000,000, 9%, convertible bonds on January 1, 20X6. The bonds are due December 31, 2014 and were sold at a discount. The debt is convertible into $5 par common stock at a conversion price of $20 per share.
2. On January 1, 2011, the fair value of the bonds is $1,100,000 and the bonds have an unamortized discount of $150,000. Micro Enterprises, in order to induce conversion, offered bond holders $50 cash for each $1,000 bond converted within 60 days.
3. All bond holders accepted the offer and on the date of acceptance, the market price of the Micro Enterprises' common stock is $30 per share.

The first step in the analysis of the Example 4-14 assumptions is to determine whether the offer qualifies as an induced conversion of convertible debt. The inducement offer by Micro Enterprises does qualify under the provisions of ASC 470-20-40, paragraphs 13 through 17, because the original conversion privilege is changed by offering $50 per $1,000 bond to convert, the changed privilege is available for only 60 days, and all equity securities related to the bonds converted are issued.

The additional consideration paid by Micro Enterprises and the expense incurred for the induced conversion is $50 per $1,000 bond, or $50,000. The $50,000 conversion expense is computed as follows:

Face value of bonds	$1,000,000
Face of one bond	÷ $1,000
Number of $1,000 bonds	1,000
Consideration per $1,000 bond	× $50
Total conversion expense	$50,000

Next, the number of common shares issued on conversion and the addition to the common stock account are computed:

Total face of bonds	$1,000,000
Conversion price	÷ $20
Number of shares issued on conversion	50,000
Par value of common stock	× $5
Addition to common stock	$ 250,000

Using information from the Example 4-14 assumptions and the preceding calculations, the following journal entry is required for the conversion:

Convertible Bonds Payable	1,000,000	
Debt Conversion Expense	50,000	
Discount on Bonds Payable		150,000

Common Stock	250,000
Additional Paid-in Capital	600,000
Cash	50,000

The $600,000 credit to additional paid-in capital is the amount needed to balance the entry. The debt conversion expense is reported on the income statement in the nonoperating section of income from continuing operations.

Example 4-14 illustrated accounting requirements when additional consideration for the inducement is cash. Example 4-15 covers a situation where the conversion rate is changed to induce conversion. Assumptions for Example 4-15 are presented below.

Example 4-15
Assumptions for Induced Conversions of Convertible Debt

1. On January 1, 20X6, Jones Enterprises (Jones) issued $500,000, 14%, convertible bonds due December 31, 2014. The bonds were sold at a premium and are convertible into $15 par common stock at a conversion price of $25 per share.
2. On December 31, 20X8, Jones, in an effort to induce conversion of the bonds into common stock, reduced the conversion price from $25 to $20 per share for shareholders that converted within 40 days. On this date, the market value of the bonds is $525,000, and the bonds have an unamortized premium of $50,000.
3. All bond holders accepted the offer on December 31, 20X8. On the date of conversion, the market price of the Jones' common stock is $28 per share.

The transaction in Example 4-15 qualifies as an induced conversion of convertible debt because Jones reduced the conversion privilege from $25 to $20 per share for 40 days as an inducement to convert to equity securities, and all equity shares related to bonds converted are issued.

Because the conversion is classified as an induced conversion of debt securities, the cost of the conversion must be computed. The cost of the debt conversion is computed in Table 4-12.

Table 4-12 Calculation of Debt Conversion Expense

Face amount of debt securities converted	$500,000
New conversion price	$20
Number of shares issued upon conversion	25,000
Fair value of shares on conversion date	× $28
Fair value of shares converted	$700,000
Face amount of debt securities converted	$500,000
Old conversion price	÷ $25

Number of shares under original conversion	20,000
Fair value of shares on conversion date	× $28
Fair value of shares under original conversion	560,000
Debt Conversion Expense	$140,000

Using the information from Table 4-12 and Example 4-15, the following journal entry is required for the conversion transaction.

	Debit	Credit
Convertible Bonds Payable	500,000	
Premium on Bonds Payable	50,000	
Debt Conversion Expense	140,000	
		375,000
Common Stock		375,000
Additional Paid-in Capital		315,000

The credit to additional common stock of $375,000 is computed as follows:

Number of shares issued in conversion	25,000
Par value	× $15
Common stock	$375,000

The credit to additional paid-in capital is the amount required to balance the entry.

Product Financing Arrangements—General Discussion

Product financing arrangements generally, but not always, involve three parties to the accounting transaction. The first party is one that attempts to seek financing of a product pending its future use or resale. This party is often referred to as the sponsor of the product financing arrangement. The second party is the one through which the financing will flow. The second party generally holds title to the goods that are subject to the financing arrangement, but has agreed to resell the goods to the sponsor at some point in the future. The second party may use the goods and/or the agreement with the sponsor to secure financing. The third party is the one providing the financing. The financing arrangement may be viewed as a vehicle through which the sponsor is able to finance the product and still retain control over its ultimate disposition.

Many product financing arrangements do not transfer the risks and rewards of ownership of the product to other parties. Under ASC 470-40, such arrangements are not to be treated as sales.

Charts 4-2 and 4-3 illustrate two examples of common product financing arrangements. These pictorial representations are helpful aids in understanding the accounting implications of product financing arrangements.

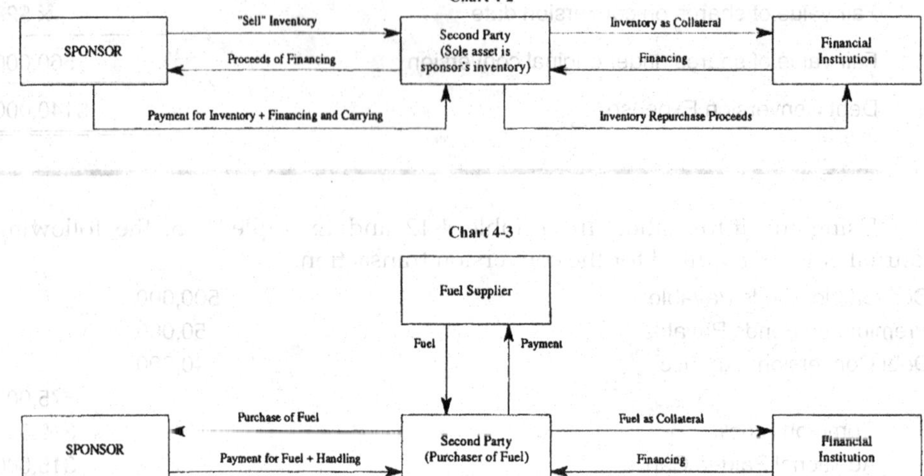

The first example, Chart 4-2, illustrates a financing arrangement where the sponsor uses its inventory as the basis for providing the arrangement. To begin the process, the sponsor sells all or a part of its inventory to the second party. Generally, the inventory represents the sole asset of the second party. As part of the sale, the sponsor agrees to repurchase the inventory in the future at the same price paid by the second party. The second party agrees not to encumber the inventory in any matter except to use it as a basis for obtaining necessary financing at the bank. In addition, the sponsor would agree to pay all inventory storage and holding costs as well as bank finance charges. The financing obtained from the bank is used to pay for the inventory purchased from the sponsor. The sponsor will repurchase the inventory in the future, and the second party will use the proceeds from the repurchase to pay the principal obligations to the bank. Interest payments from the sponsor to the second party may be handled at the time of repurchase of inventory or at some other specified date.

The second example, Chart 4-3, is a variation of the one discussed above. In the second example, inventory is not the subject of the financing arrangement. In this case, the second party would arrange to purchase needed fuel from a supplier on behalf of the sponsor. The second party would use the fuel as collateral to secure financing from the bank. The proceeds from the financing would be used to pay the supplier for the fuel. The sponsor would purchase the fuel from the second party as needed. The payments made for the fuel acquired would include the costs to storage and handle the fuel as well as the financing charges incurred by the second party. The second party would use the proceeds from the sale to the sponsor to repay the obligation to the bank.

In both of these examples, the second party serves as a surrogate for the sponsor. This party could be removed from the transaction, and one could view the agreement as being between the sponsor and the financial institution. Although the form of the product financing arrangements may appear very complex, its substance is quite clear.

The product financing arrangements covered by ASC 470-40 must meet two conditions. First, the arrangement must require the sponsor to purchase the product (or a product that is almost identical or a product containing the product as a component) at a price that has been specified. The price paid for the product must not be subject to change except to the extent of changes in the financing or holding costs incurred by the second party. Second, the payments to be received by the second party are designed to cover substantially all costs associated with the product itself and the holding and financing of the product. The payments received may be adjusted for changes in the costs of holding and financing the product.

ASC 470-40-25-2 describes the accounting required for product financing arrangements meeting the conditions outlined above. If the arrangement is similar to the one shown in Example 4-16 (i.e., where the sponsor uses inventory as the basis for the arrangement), the liability incurred to finance the arrangement must be recorded by the sponsor when the proceeds are received from the second party. In addition, no sale is to be recorded, and inventory is not to be removed from the balance sheet of the sponsor. However, inventory should be transferred to a special account to indicate that it is involved in a product financing arrangement.

If the arrangement is similar to the one shown in Example 4-17 (i.e., the second party acquires a product on behalf of the sponsor), the sponsor must record the asset and related liability when the product is acquired by the second party.

The costs incurred in connection with holding the product and financing it through a financial institution are to be accounted for using those policies established by the sponsor for normal holding and financing costs. The provisions of ASC 835-20 would apply to the financing charges associated with the product financing arrangement.

Product Financing Arrangements—Technical Considerations

To demonstrate the specific problems encountered in the application of ASC 470-40, two examples are presented. Information for Example 4-16 is presented below.

Example 4-16
Product Financing Arrangement

1. The Cooper Company (Cooper), the sponsor company, was involved in several sales, sale and repurchase, and/or product financing arrangements during 20X6.
2. On January 21, 20X6, Cooper sold $200,000 of merchandise to Russell Enterprises at a price of $250,000. Cooper did not agree to repurchase the merchandise or to arrange for another business entity to purchase the product.

3. On March 15, 20X6, Cooper sold $150,000 of merchandise to Mitchell, Inc. (Mitchell). The merchandise sold had a cost basis to Cooper of $125,000. Mitchell may return any or all of the merchandise purchased within 45 days of the date of sale. Cooper is not responsible for any holding or financing costs incurred by Mitchell in connection with the sale.
4. On July 1, 20X6, Cooper sold $320,000 of routinely manufactured merchandise to Larson Enterprises (Larson). The merchandise sold had a cost basis to Cooper of $300,000. Larson, using the merchandise as collateral, borrowed $320,000 from the Second National Bank to pay for the inventory purchased. Cooper agreed to repurchase the merchandise if Larson was unable to resell the merchandise for $320,000. In addition, Cooper agreed to pay all handling, storage, and financing costs relating to the purchased merchandise.
5. On October 15, 20X6, it was determined that Larson was able to resell the merchandise for $320,000. Larson incurred the following costs relating to the purchase:

Interest charges	$10,000
Handling and storage costs	3,000
Insurance costs	1,000
Total	$14,000

The handling, storage, and insurance costs are not considered to be inventory costs.

The first step in the accounting process is to determine if any of the sales transactions qualify as product financing arrangements. The sale on January 21, to Russell Enterprises, is *not* a product financing arrangement, because Cooper did not agree to a repurchase of the merchandise or arrange for a third party to purchase the merchandise from Russell. The provisions of ASC 470-40 do not apply to this sales transaction.

The sale on March 15, to Mitchell does not qualify as a product financing arrangement. Cooper, the sponsor entity, is *not* required to pay Mitchell for any costs incurred to hold or finance the merchandise purchased. However, this transaction does qualify as a sale with right of return, and the provisions of ASC 605-15-25, paragraphs 1 through 4, would be applicable.

The sale on July 1, to Larson, does qualify as a product financing arrangement. Cooper, the sponsor entity, has agreed to repurchase the merchandise if Larson is unable to resell the goods. In addition, Cooper has agreed to pay Larson for the cost of handling, storage, and financing the merchandise purchased.

Because the sale to Larson Enterprises qualifies as a product financing arrangement, Cooper must treat the transfer of merchandise as a borrowing, and not as a sale of inventory. Cooper must establish a liability account in an amount equal to the repurchase guarantee of $320,000. This liability account should be established when Cooper receives the transaction proceeds from Larson *or* when a receivable for the proceeds is established. The liability account will be removed when the product is actually resold by Larson or when Cooper is obliged to repurchase the merchandise. In addition to the liability account, Cooper must reduce its inventory by an amount equal to the *cost* of the merchandise subject to the borrowing. In this example, inventory would be reduced by $300,000. The cost of the inventory subject to the arrangement should be transferred to a separate asset account to indicate that it is subject to a product financing arrangement. This new asset account will be transferred to cost of goods sold when Larson sells the merchandise or when the inventory is transferred back to Cooper.

The general journal entries required to reflect the provisions of ASC 470-40 would be:

Accounts Receivable	320,000	
Liability—Product Financing Arrangement		320,000
Inventory—Product Financing Arrangement	300,000	
Inventory		300,000

The account receivable would be removed when Cooper receives the proceeds from Larson. The liability account should be classified as a current liability on the balance sheet. The special inventory account would be classified as a current asset and appear just below the inventory account on the balance sheet.

The Example 4-16 material states that Larson was able to resell the merchandise to a third party. When this information becomes known, Cooper will record a sale and the related cost of sales associated with the product financing arrangement. The following general journal entries would be made on the books of Cooper, the sponsor:

Liability—Product Financing Arrangement	320,000	
Sales		320,000
Cost of Goods Sold	300,000	
Inventory—Product Financing Arrangement		300,000

Under the terms of the product financing arrangement, Cooper is required to pay all handling and financing costs incurred by Larson. Larson's interest costs of $10,000 cannot be capitalized as part of the cost of the inventory. ASC 835-20 does not allow the capitalization of interest on routinely produced inventory that would be ready for resale by the purchaser. The interest costs should be expensed by Cooper as the amounts become known. In addition to interest costs, Cooper must pay Larson for the storage and handling costs and insurance costs associated with the purchased merchandise. The costs shown in this example are assumed to be period costs as opposed to inventory costs. Cooper would prepare the following general journal entry to reflect its payments to Larson:

Interest Expense	10,000	
Storage and Handling Expense	3,000	
Insurance Expense	1,000	
Cash		14,000

With this last journal entry, the analysis of the Example 4-16 material is complete. Additional insights into the provisions of ASC 470-40 are illustrated in Example 4-17, the information for which is presented below.

Example 4-17
Product Financing Arrangement

1. On November 1, 20X6, the Sponsor Company, a December 31 year-end entity, arranged for Purchaser Company to purchase routinely manufactured merchandise from Johnson Enterprises for $500,000.
2. Sponsor Company agreed to purchase the merchandise from Purchaser Company within the next year for $500,000 plus the costs incurred to store, handle, and finance the merchandise.
3. Purchaser Company, using the purchase agreement and the merchandise as collateral, obtained a loan from First National Bank for $500,000.
4. On December 31, 20X6, Purchaser Company reported the following costs relating to the merchandise purchased:

(a) Interest costs	$16,200
(b) Storage and handling	1,200
(c) Insurance costs	600
Total	$18,000

The storage and insurance costs are not considered to be part of the cost of the inventory.

5. On October 1, 20X7, Sponsor Company purchased the merchandise from Purchaser Company for the agreed upon price. From January 1, 20X7 to October 1, 20X7, Purchaser Company incurred the following costs in relation to the merchandise:

(a) Interest costs	$72,900
(b) Storage and handling	5,400
(c) Insurance costs	2,700
Total	$81,000

The purchase of merchandise by Purchaser Company for the benefit of Sponsor Company qualifies as a product financing arrangement. The agreement between the two entities calls for the purchase of merchandise at a specified price and requires the sponsor to pay all costs of handling, storing, and financing the merchandise.

On November 1, 20X6, Purchaser Company borrowed $500,000 from the First National Bank and used the proceeds to purchase the merchandise from Johnson Enterprises. On this date, Sponsor Company will record an asset and obligation in the amount of $500,000. The following journal entry would be made on the books of the Sponsor Company:

Inventory—Product Financing Arrangement	500,000	
Liability—Product Financing Arrangement		500,000

In addition to recording the asset and obligation, Sponsor Company must accrue the costs associated with storing, handling and financing the inventory of merchandise. On December 31, 20X6, Purchaser Company reports the costs incurred that must be paid by Sponsor Company. Once these costs are known to Sponsor Company, a decision must be made as to whether the costs are period costs or inventory costs. The interest expense of $16,200 must be treated as a period cost, because ASC 835-20 does not permit the capitalization of interest on routinely produced inventory that is ready for resale by the purchaser. The storage, handling, and insurance costs are not considered product costs and will be expensed in the current accounting period. The journal entry necessary to record the accrued liability at year-end would be:

Interest Expense	16,200	
Storage and Handling Expense	1,200	
Insurance Expense	600	
Liability—Product Financing Arrangement		18,000

On October 1, 20X7, Sponsor Company purchased the merchandise associated with the product financing arrangement from Purchaser Company for $500,000. In addition, Sponsor Company paid all handling, storage, and financing costs incurred by Purchaser Company in relation to the merchandise. Because Sponsor Company had accrued handling, storage, and financing costs at the end of 20X6, the amount expensed for such costs for 20X7 would include expenses only for the period January 1, 20X7 through October 1, 20X7. The journal entries required to record the purchase and payment of associated costs are shown below:

Liability—Product Financing Arrangement	518,000	
Interest Expense	72,900	
Storage and Handling Expense	5,400	
Insurance Expense	2,700	
Cash		599,000
Inventory	500,000	
Inventory—Product Financing Arrangement		500,000

The $518,000 shown as a reduction in the liability account is composed of the following elements:

Cost of merchandise	$500,000
Interest (Nov.–Dec. 20X6)	16,200
Storage and handling (Nov.–Dec. 20X6)	1,200
Insurance (Nov.–Dec. 20X6)	600
Total costs	$518,000

The $599,000 cash payment to Purchaser Company represents the cost of the merchandise plus all associated costs. A review of the journal entry to record the inventory on the books of Sponsor Company shows that the amount recorded as inventory, $500,000, is the cost basis of the merchandise. All the associated handling, storage, and financing costs are treated as period costs and charged to income.

Modifications and Extinguishments—Flowchart and General Discussion

ASC 470-50 provides guidelines for debtors to determine when debt issues have been extinguished, and specifies the appropriate accounting for extinguished debt. ASC 470-50 applies to all debt extinguishments whether early, at maturity, or after maturity, unless otherwise exempt. ASC 470-50 does not apply to extinguishments under troubled debt situations nor does it apply to accounting for convertible debt. Extinguishments under troubled debt restructurings are covered by ASC 470-60 (debtor's accounting) and ASC 310-40 (creditor's accounting). ASC 470-20 addresses accounting for convertible debt.

Flowchart 4-5 identifies the classification, general accounting, and reporting of debt extinguishments. The left side of Flowchart 4-5 deals with the problem of classification, and the right side addresses the major accounting and reporting problems. The decision blocks have been numbered for easy reference and are referred to in the discussion.

Flowchart 4-5

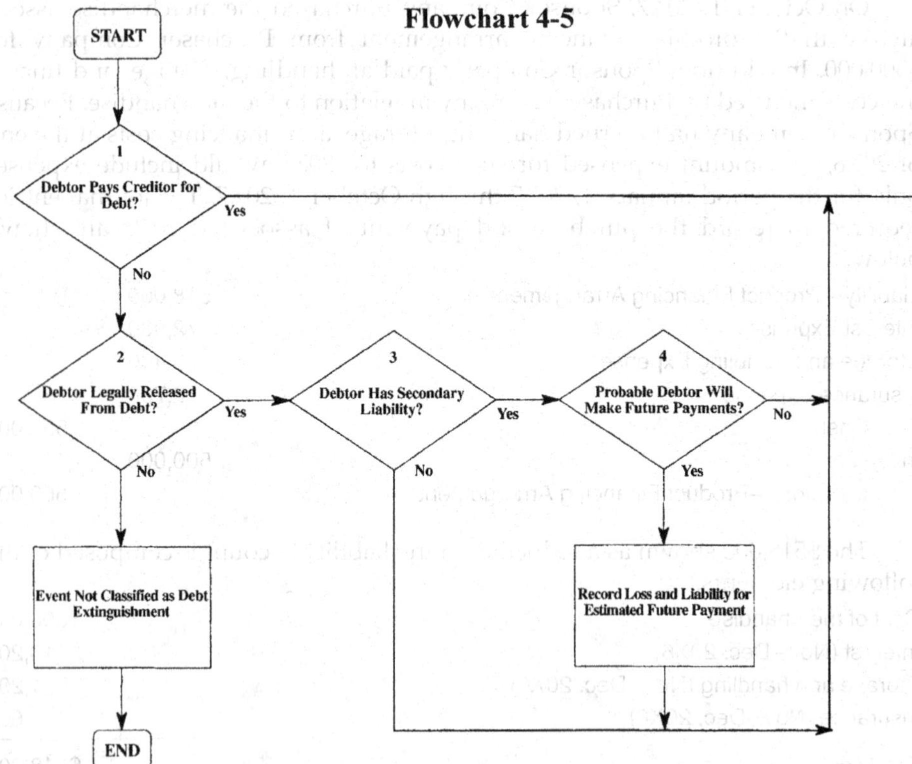

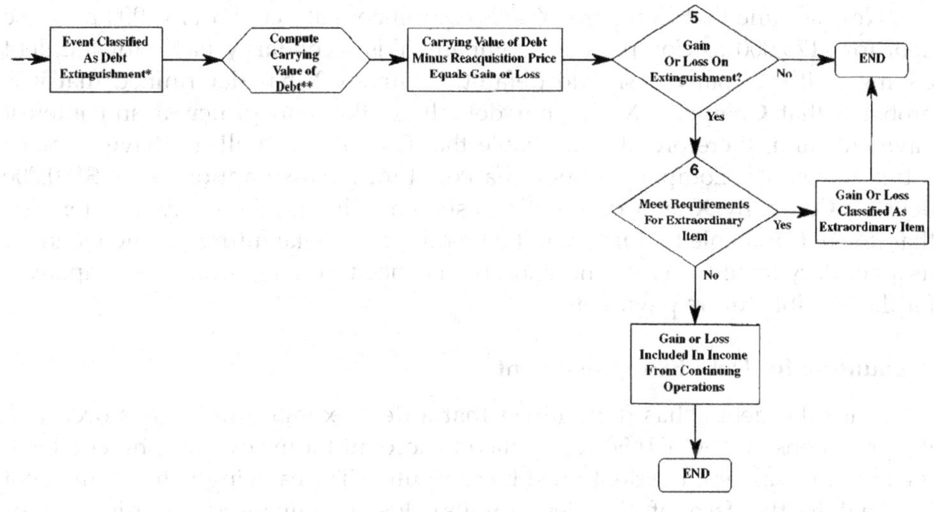

* For debt extinguishment classified as troubled debt, see ASC 470-60 (debtor) or ASC 310-40 (creditor).
** Carrying value of debt is equal to the face of the debt -/+ unamortized discount or premium - unamortized issue costs.

Classification as Debt Extinguishment

ASC 470-50 identifies two situations when a transaction may be classified as a debt extinguishment. These situations are shown in decision Blocks 1 and 2. Debt is considered extinguished (Block 1) when the debtor pays the creditor and no longer has any responsibility or obligation for the debt issue. This includes direct payments to entities and the repurchase of debt securities in the market. Securities purchased in the market may either be retired or held in treasury.

Debt also may be extinguished when the debtor is relieved of primary obligation under the debt agreement, either judicially or legally (Block 2). When primary obligation for payment of the debt has been removed, the debtor may have secondary liability (Block 3). When the debtor has secondary liability, the probability of making future payments must be determined. ASC 450 must be consulted when determining the probability of future payment. However, if it is probable that the debtor will have to make future payments because of the secondary liability (Block 4), an estimated loss and estimated liability must be reported for the expected amount of the future payments.

To illustrate a situation in which the debtor is relieved of primary obligation under a debt agreement, assume that Company A sells a computer that is subject to a $25,000 nonrecourse loan to Company XYZ for $35,000. Because the debt is nonrecourse, the only collateral for the debt is the asset. Consequently, the debtor is legally relieved of both primary obligation and secondary liability as a result of the asset sale. Assumption of the $25,000 nonrecourse loan by Company XYZ qualifies as a debt extinguishment.

Next assume that Company Y sells equipment subject to a $150,000 recourse debt for $175,000 to Company X. Company Y is secondarily liable for the debt payments if Company X should default. Company Y has determined that it is probable that Company X will not default on the loan principal and interest payments and, therefore, it is probable that Company Y will not have to make future payments. Company Y should account for the assumption of the $150,000 debt by Company X as a debt extinguishment. Should Company Y determine that it is not probable that it will not be required to make future payments under its secondary liability, a loss and liability may need to be reported by Company Y for the possible future payments.

Accounting for Debt Extinguishment

Once the debtor has determined that a debt extinguishment has occurred, the provisions of ASC 470-50 are applied to account for the extinguishment. First, the carrying value of the debt must be computed. The carrying value of the debt is equal to the face of the debt minus/plus any unamortized discount or unamortized premium less any unamortized issue costs. Second, the difference between the reacquisition price and the carrying value of the debt, if any, is accounted for as a gain or loss (Block 5).

The repurchase of debt may be accomplished through the use of internally generated funds, funds obtained from the sale of equity securities, or funds obtained from the sale of other debt securities. This latter type of repurchase is commonly referred to as "debt refunding." The difference between the repurchase price and the carrying value of the debt refunded should be recognized immediately as a gain or loss.

The gain or loss on extinguishment of debt is reported in income from continuing operations.

Modifications and Extinguishments—Technical Considerations

Three examples will be used to illustrate accounting and reporting of debt extinguishment. Assumptions for Example 4-18 are as follows.

Example 4-18
Assumptions for Debt Extinguishment

1. Carlow Enterprises (Carlow) has $20,000,000 outstanding in bonds that will mature in five years. At the date of refunding, there was $160,000 in unamortized bond premium and $20,000 in unamortized bond issue costs associated with the issue.
2. Carlow was able to repurchase the bonds for $19,500,000. The $19,500,000 needed for the repurchase was obtained through the issue of $20,000,000 of new debt. The new bond issue was sold at 98 (i.e., $98 for every $100 of face value).
3. The refunding of the $20,000,000 debt issue was not for sinking-fund purposes.

Because Carlow paid the creditor and is no longer responsible for future debt principal and interest payments, the refunding is classified as a debt extinguishment.

The journal entry required to record the sale of the new bond issue is as follows:

Cash ($20,000,000 × .98)	19,600,000	
Bond Discount	400,000	
Bonds Payable		20,000,000

The proceeds received from this bond issue will be used to retire the old bond issue. The journal entry required to record the retirement of the old bond issue is as follows:

Bonds Payable	20,000,000	
Bond Premium	160,000	
Bond Issue Costs		20,000
Cash		19,500,000
Gain on Extinguishment of Debt		640,000

The Gain on Extinguishment of Debt is classified using the provisions of ASC 225-20 and is computed as follows:

Bond Face Value	$20,000,000
Unamortized Bond Premium	160,000
Unamortized Bond Issue Costs	(20,000)
Bond Carrying Value	$20,140,000
Bond Repurchase Price	19,500,000
Gain on Extinguishment of Debt	$ 640,000

To illustrate additional provisions of the debt extinguishment pronouncements, the assumptions listed in Example 4-19 are used.

Example 4-19
Assumptions for Debt Extinguishment

1. Financial Enterprises (Financial), a December 31 year-end company, was involved in two unrelated transactions that may or may not be classified as debt extinguishments.
2. On March 1, 20X6, Financial retired $500,000 of a $1,000,000, 8% debt issue, due in five years, for $462,500. On this date the debt had a $50,000 unamortized discount and $15,000 in unamortized issue costs.
3. On July 1, 20X6, Financial sold a computer for $125,000. The buyer paid $25,000 in cash and assumed a $100,000, 10% nonrecourse note. On July 1 the note had a $10,000 unamortized discount. Book value of the computer is $125,000.

Each debt issue is analyzed below in Table 4-13 to determine which is classified as a debt extinguishment.

Table 4-13 Debt Classification

Debt Issue	Classify as Debt Extinguishment	Reason for Classification
$500,000 of the $1,000,000, 8% debt issue	Yes	Debtor paid creditor and is relieved of all obligation under the debt agreement for $500,000 or of the principal.
$100,000, 10% nonrecourse debt	Yes	Debtor is relieved of primary obligation when the buyer of the asset assumes the debt. The debtor is not secondarily liable because the debt is nonrecourse.

Each of the two events is classified as a debt extinguishment. Next, the required accounting for each extinguishment is illustrated. The retirement of half of the $1,000,000, 8% debt issue is considered first. Because only half of the principal is being repurchased, only half of the unamortized discount and issue costs will be removed at the date of extinguishment. The carrying value of the portion of the debt extinguished and the gain or loss on extinguishment is computed as:

Face Value of Debt Extinguished ($1,000,000 × .5)	$500,000
Unamortized Discount ($50,000 × .5)	(25,000)
Unamortized Issue Costs ($15,000 × .5)	(7,500)
Carrying Value of Debt	$467,500
Repurchase Price	462,500
Gain on Extinguishment of Debt	$5,000

The journal entry required at the date of extinguishment is as follows:

Bonds Payable	500,000	
Bond Discount		25,000
Bond Issue Costs		7,500
Cash		462,500
Gain on Extinguishment of Debt		5,000

The carrying value and gain or loss on extinguishment for the $100,000, 10% nonrecourse debt issue is computed below:

Face of Nonrecourse Debt	$100,000
Unamortized Discount	(10,000)
Carrying Value of Note	$90,000
Repurchase Price (Assumption of Face of Note)	100,000
Loss on Debt Extinguishment	$10,000

The entry required to record the sale of the computer and the assumption of the note by the buyer is:

Cash	25,000	
Loss on Debt Extinguishment	10,000	
Note Payable	100,000	
Note Discount		10,000
Computer		125,000

Examples 4-18 and 4-19 were relatively straightforward, but involved all aspects of debt extinguishment. Example 4-20 illustrates the computation of unamortized discounts and premiums and issue costs using the interest method. Assumptions for Example 4-20 are as follows.

Example 4-20
Assumptions for Debt Extinguishment

1. Dataline, Inc. sold a $1,500,000, 12%, six-year bond issue on January 1, 20X6, for $1,380,857 (a 14% market rate of interest). The bonds are dated January 1 and pay interest semiannually on January 1 and July 1. Cost of issuing the bonds amounted to $20,000.
2. On May 1, 20X8, the bonds were retired by repurchasing them in the market at 96. On the date of retirement unamortized bond issue cost was $11,000.

The repurchase of the bonds in the market qualifies as an extinguishment of debt because the debtor has paid the creditors and is not required to make any future payments. The first step in accounting for the debt retirement is to compute the carrying value of the debt. The following amortization schedule will easily provide the carrying value of the debt and the unamortized discount.

Table 4-14 Amortization Schedule for Debt

Period	Cash Interest	Interest Expense	Amortization	Balance
				$1,380,857
July 1, 20X6	[1]$90,000	[2]$96,660	[3]$6,660	1,387,517
January 1, 20X7	90,000	97,126	7,126	1,394,643
July 1, 20X7	90,000	97,625	7,625	1,402,268
January 1, 20X8	90,000	98,159	8,159	1,410,427
July 1, 20X8	90,000	98,730	8,730	1,419,157
January 1, 20X9	90,000	99,341	9,341	1,428,498
July 1, 20X9	90,000	99,995	9,995	1,438,493
January 1, 2010	90,000	100,695	10,695	1,449,188
July 1, 2010	90,000	101,443	11,443	1,460,631
January 1, 2011	90,000	102,244	12,244	1,472,875

Period	Cash Interest	Interest Expense	Amortization	Balance
July 1, 2011	90,000	103,101	13,101	1,485,976
January 1, 2012	90,000	[4]104,024	14,024	1,500,000

[1] $1,500,000 × .06 (semiannual stated rate) = $90,000.
[2] $1,380,857 × .07 (semiannual market rate) = $96,660.
[3] $96,660 – $90,000 = $6,660.
[4] Rounded.

Several items in Table 4-14 require explanation. First, the cash interest of $90,000 is computed using the 6% semiannual interest rate. However, interest expense must reflect the market rate of interest in effect when the bonds were issued. Therefore, the market rate of 7% is used in the computation of the interest expense using the interest method.

Because the bonds were retired on May 1, a date between interest payment dates, interest expense and the unamortized discount must be computed up to the date of retirement. The next interest payment date, after retirement of the debt, is July 1, 20X8. Because the debt is retired on May 1, four months since the last interest payment, 4/6 of the payments on July 1, 20X8, must be computed and recorded. The calculation is made below:

Cash Interest (Table 4-14) $90,000 × 4/6 =	$60,000
Interest Expense (Table 4-14) $98,730 × 4/6 =	65,820
Discount Amortization (Table 4-14) $8,730 × 4/6 =	$5,820

Using this information the following journal entry can be made:

Interest Expense	65,820	
Bond Discount		5,820
Cash		60,000

Next, the carrying value of the debt, unamortized discount and the gain or loss on extinguishment can be computed.

Total Discount ($1,500,000 × $1,380,857)	$119,143
Discount Amortization:	
July 1, 20X6	(6,660)
January 1, 20X7	(7,126)
July 1, 20X7	(7,625)
January 1, 20X8	(8,159)
January 1—May 1, 20X8	(5,820)
Unamortized Discount on May 1, 20X8	$83,753
Face of Debt Issue	$1,500,000
Unamortized Discount	(83,753)
Unamortized Bond Issue Costs (Example 3, Item 2)	(11,000)
Carrying Value of Debt	$1,405,247
Repurchase Price of Debt ($1,500,000 × .96)	1,440,000
Loss on Debt Extinguishment	($34,753)

The journal entry required to record the debt extinguishment on May 1, 20X8, is presented below:

Bonds Payable	1,500,000	
Loss on Extinguishment of Debt	34,753	
Cash		1,440,000
Bond Discount		83,753
Bond Issue Costs		11,000

The Loss on Debt Extinguishment is classified in the income statement using the provisions of ASC 225-20.

Modifications and Extinguishments—Disclosure Requirements

To illustrate the reporting requirements of debt extinguishment, the assumptions in Example 4-21 are used.

Example 4-21
Assumptions for Disclosure Requirements

1. The Borrower Company, a December 31 year-end entity, reported income before non-operating items of $300,000 for 20X6, a year when several debt issues were extinguished.
2. Aggregate gains and losses from the retirement of debt to satisfy sinking fund requirements for one year were $50,000. Aggregate gains and losses from the extinguishment of debt not related to sinking fund requirements were $100,000. The composition of the $100,000 aggregate gain is shown below:

	Gain (Loss)	Source of Funds
Extinguishment of 8% Debt	$(25,000)	Internal
Extinguishment of 10% Convertible Bonds	140,000	Sale of Equity Securities
Extinguishment of 9% Debt	(15,000)	Bond Issue
Aggregate Gain	$100,000	

3. In addition to the income items noted above, Borrower Company reported a $50,000 extraordinary gain. The change resulted in an increase in income.
4. The tax rate applicable to all income during the period is 50%. Borrower Company had 500,000 shares of common stock outstanding during the period.

A partial income statement for Borrower Company is presented below.

Partial Income Statement

Income before non-operating items	$300,000
Gain from extinguishment of debt	150,000
Income before taxes and extraordinary item	$450,000
Income taxes	225,000
Income before extraordinary item	$225,000
Extraordinary:	
gain (net of taxes of $25,000)	25,000
Net Income	$250,000

ASU 2015-01, *Income Statement—Extraordinary and Unusual Items (Subtopic 225-20): Simplifying Income Statement Presentation by Eliminating the Concept of Extraordinary Items,* is effective for fiscal years, and interim periods within those fiscal years, beginning after December 15, 2015. A reporting entity may apply the amendments prospectively. A reporting entity also may apply the amendments retrospectively to all prior periods presented in the financial statements. Early adoption is permitted provided that the guidance is applied from the beginning of the fiscal year of adoption. The effective date is the same for all entities, including public business entities. As such, the partial income statement in Example 4-21 above is for a single period prior to the effective date of ASU 2015-01.

Troubled Debt Restructuring—Flowchart and General Discussion

ASC 470-60 specifies the accounting and reporting standards for a restructuring of troubled debt from the debtor's perspective. Not all debt restructurings qualify for treatment as a troubled debt restructuring. Debt restructuring, troubled or otherwise, involves the modification or elimination of a debt instrument before, at, or after maturity date by means other than those required in the debt instrument. A troubled debt restructuring exists when the debtor is unable to meet current debt requirements and the creditor grants to the debtor a concession that normally would not be provided. In effect, the creditor is making the concession in hopes that he will receive more from the debtor than he would if the concession were not made.

Although there are many types of troubled debt restructurings, ASC 470-60 identifies and treats in detail the following:

1. Transfer of assets from the debtor to the creditor in full settlement of the debt;
2. Transfer of an equity interest in the debtor to the creditor in full settlement of the debt;
3. Modification of the terms of the debt through a change in the interest rate, maturity date, face or maturity value of the debt, and accrued interest, or some combination of these items;
4. Transfer of assets or an equity interest in partial settlement of the debt, *and* modification of the terms as described in 3 above.

This list is not meant to be all-inclusive, and other types of troubled debt restructurings will have to be evaluated on their merits. Flowchart 4-6 is designed to illustrate the major accounting and reporting consequences of these four types of troubled debt restructurings from the viewpoint of the debtor.

Flowchart 4-6

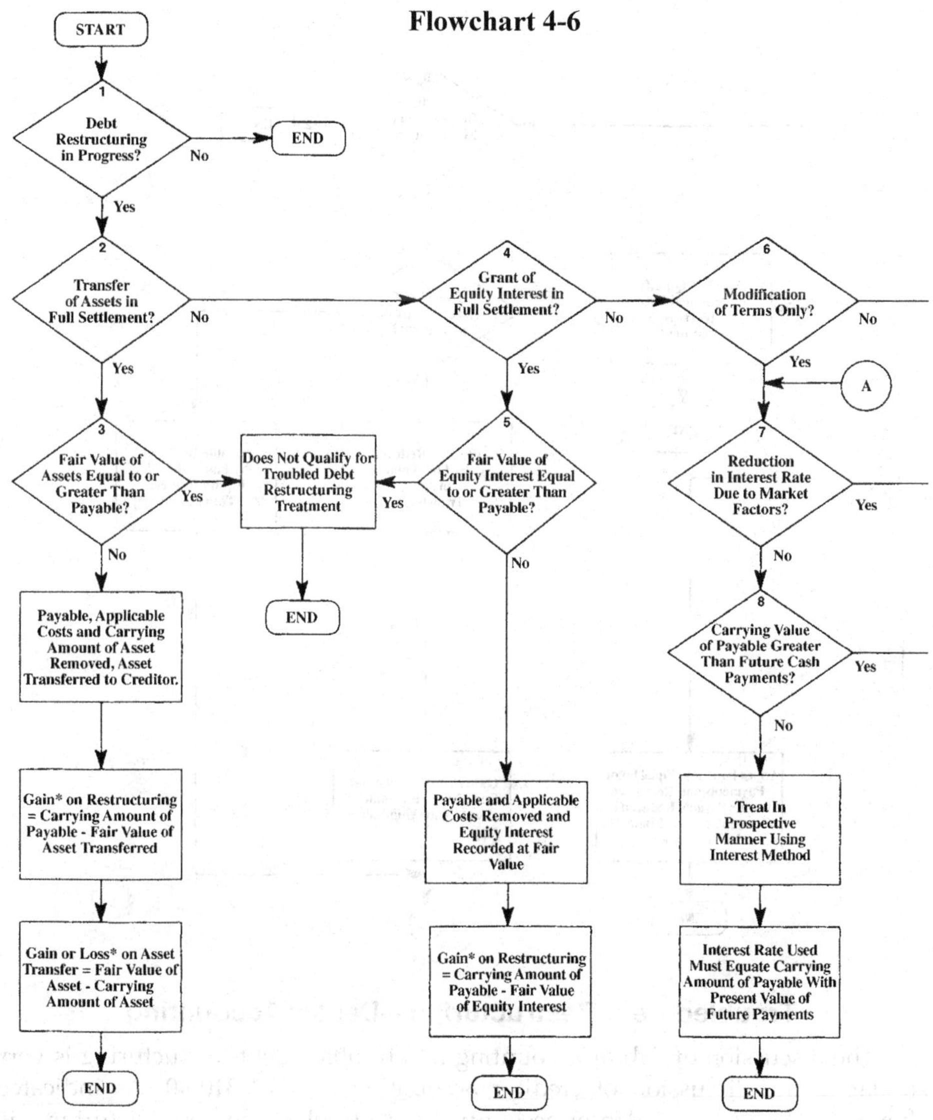

***Accounted for in Accordance with ASC 225-20.**

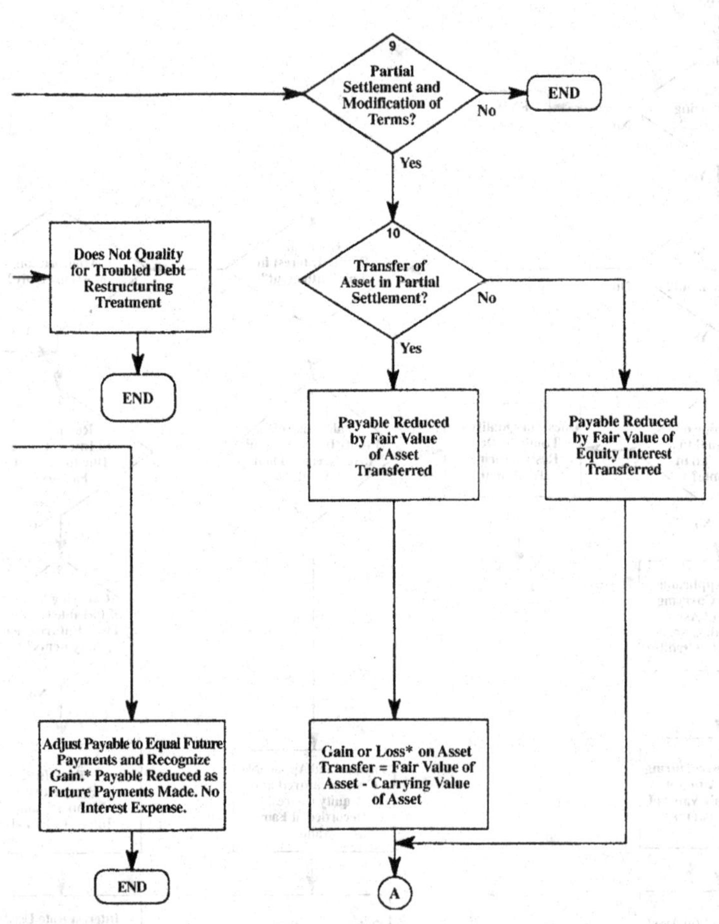

Troubled Debt Restructuring—Debtor Accounting

The discussion of debtor accounting in a troubled debt restructuring is very similar to the discussion of creditor accounting in ASC 310-40. As indicated above, the discussion of debtor accounting for a troubled debt restructuring will incorporate the four basic types of restructurings. Each type of restructuring will be treated separately. After the four general types have been discussed, some additional accounting complications will be addressed, followed by the required disclosures specified in ASC 470-60.

Transfer of Assets in Full Settlement

One possible way to effect a debt restructuring is for the debtor to transfer assets to the creditor (Block 2). When such a restructuring occurs, it still is necessary to determine if the transaction qualifies for *troubled* debt restructuring treatment. The transaction will be considered a troubled debt restructuring only if the fair value of the assets transferred is not equal to or greater than the carrying amount of the payable (Block 3). When the fair value of the asset transferred is less than the carrying amount of the payable, the creditor has made a concession to the debtor. This is a basic requirement of troubled debt restructuring.

The determination of fair value of the asset transferred is discussed by ASC 470-60. ASC 820 states that fair value is the amount that would be received on the measurement date from the sale of property or the amount paid to transfer a liability between sellers and buyers (market participants) in an orderly transaction. In addition, it is assumed that the sellers and buyers are unrelated parties on the measurement date. The carrying amount of the payable is equal to the face of the payable plus or minus any adjustments for items such as unamortized discounts or premiums, unamortized debt issue costs, and accrued interest.

Once it has been determined that the fair value of the assets transferred are not equal to or greater than the carrying amount of the payable, the transaction will be accounted for as a troubled debt restructuring. In such a case, the debtor always will recognize a gain on the restructuring itself and, in most cases, also will recognize a gain or loss on the transfer of the assets. The difference between the fair value of the asset transferred and the carrying amount of the payable is to be recognized as the gain on restructuring of debt. This gain is classified in accordance with the provisions of ASC 225-20. When the asset is removed from the books of the debtor, the difference between the book value of the asset and its fair value represents the gain or loss on the asset transfer. Any gain or loss on the asset transfer should be classified according to ASC 225-20. ASC 225-20 specifies that the gain or loss may be classified as a one-line item in the non-operating section of the income statement, or as a part of ordinary operations of the company. The appropriate classification in any particular case will depend upon the circumstances faced by the company in that year.

To illustrate the technical aspects of troubled debt restructuring where assets are transferred to the creditor in full settlement of the debt, the assumptions listed in Example 4-22 are used.

Example 4-22
Asset Transfer in Full Settlement of Debt

1. Debtor, Inc. has a $5,000,000 note payable to Creditor, Inc.
2. The note bears interest at the rate of 10% per annum, and there is $200,000 of unamortized discount and $100,000 of accrued interest on the books of Debtor, Inc.
3. Due to severe economic conditions, Creditor, Inc. is willing to accept equipment of Debtor, Inc., with a fair value of $4,000,000, in full

settlement of the note. Creditor, Inc. believes that, in the absence of such a concession, it is not likely to collect on the note.

4. The equipment had a cost basis to Debtor, Inc. of $4,500,000; and, at the date of transfer, accumulated depreciation of $1,000,000 had been recorded.

Based on this information, the first step is to determine if the fair value of the asset transferred is equal to or greater than the carrying amount of the payable. This computation is shown below:

Face Amount of Payable	$5,000,000
Unamortized Discount	(200,000)
Accrued Interest	100,000
Carrying Amount of Payable	$4,900,000
Fair Value of Asset Transferred	4,000,000
Excess of Carrying Amount over Fair Value	$900,000

In this case, the fair value of the assets is less than the carrying amount of the payable. Therefore, troubled debt accounting is appropriate.

The gain on restructuring is equal to the difference between the fair value of the asset and the carrying amount of the payable, which is the $900,000 determined above.

The next step is to see if there is a gain or loss associated with the transfer of the asset. The gain or loss is the difference between the book value and the fair value of the asset transferred, and is determined as follows:

Cost of Equipment Transferred	$4,500,000
Accumulated Depreciation	(1,000,000)
Book Value of Equipment Transferred	$3,500,000
Fair Value of Equipment Transferred	4,000,000
Gain on Transfer of Asset	$500,000

With this information known, the asset and payable must be removed from the books of Debtor, Inc., and the various gains recognized. The entry required to accomplish this is presented below:

Notes Payable	5,000,000	
Accumulated Depreciation	1,000,000	
Accrued Interest Payable	100,000	
Discount on Notes Payable		200,000
Equipment		4,500,000
Gain on Restructuring of Debt		900,000
Gain on Transfer of Assets		500,000

The gain on restructuring would be reported in accordance with the provisions of ASC 225-20 in the current period income statement. The gain on asset transfer would be classified also according to the provisions of ASC 225-20.

Transfer of Equity Interest in Full Settlement

A transfer of equity interest in full settlement of existing debt may be accomplished through the issuance of stock of the debtor company to the creditor. As in the case of asset transfers, the fair value of the equity interest transferred must *not* be equal to or greater than the carrying amount of the debt (Block 5). If the fair value of the equity interest transferred is less than the payable, the transaction qualifies for treatment as a troubled debt restructuring. Unlike the asset transfer situation, there will be no gain or loss resulting from the transfer of the equity interest. There will, however, be a gain from the restructuring. The equities transferred should be recorded on the books of the debtor at fair value. The gain from restructuring will be the difference between the fair value of the stock and the carrying value of the payable. Again, the gain should be classified in accordance with ASC 225-20.

The assumptions listed in Example 4-23 are used to illustrate accounting for a transfer of equity interest in full settlement of debt.

Example 4-23
Equity Transfer in Full Settlement of Debt

1. Debtor, Inc. has $8,000,000 in bonds payable that are held by Creditor, Inc.
2. The bonds pay interest at the rate of 12% per annum, and there is $300,000 of unamortized premium and $100,000 of unamortized bond issue costs on the books of Debtor, Inc.
3. Due to severe economic conditions, Creditor, Inc. is willing to accept 600,000 common shares of Debtor, Inc. in full settlement of the bonds. Creditor, Inc. believes that, in the absence of such a concession, it is not likely to collect on the bonds.
4. The common stock has a par value of $2 per share and is currently selling for $10 per share.

To determine if the transaction qualifies for troubled debt restructuring accounting, the fair value of the stock transferred must be compared with the carrying amount of the bonds. The computation is shown below:

Face Value of Bonds	$8,000,000
Unamortized Bond Issue Costs	(100,000)
Unamortized Premium	300,000
Carrying Amount of Bonds	$8,200,000
Fair Value of Stock Transferred	
(600,000 shares × $10 per share)	6,000,000
Excess of Carrying Amount over Fair Value	$2,200,000

Because the fair value of the stock is less than the carrying amount of the bonds, the transaction qualifies for troubled debt accounting.

The only gain to be recognized is the gain resulting from the restructuring. The gain is equal to the difference between the fair value of the stock and the carrying amount of the bonds, and is the $2,200,000 computed above. Based upon this information, the following entry is needed to record the transfer:

		Debit	Credit
Bonds Payable		8,000,000	
Premium on Bonds Payable		300,000	
	Common Stock		[a]1,200,000
	Contributed Capital in Excess of Par		[b]4,800,000
	Bond Issue Costs		100,000
	Gain on Restructuring of Debt		2,200,000

[a] 600,000 shares × $2 par value per share = $1,200,000.
[b] 600,000 shares × $10 fair value = $6,000,000 × $1,200,000 = $4,800,000.

It is impossible to have a loss on restructuring, because if the fair value of the asset or equity interest transferred is greater than the carrying amount of the debt, the transaction does not qualify for troubled debt restructuring accounting.

Modification of Terms

A modification of terms consists of some adjustment to the existing debt, such as a change in interest rate, maturity value, maturity date or some combination of these items (Block 6). However, not all modification of terms will result in troubled debt restructuring accounting. For example, if the modification resulted in a reduction in the stated interest rate, and that reduction were due to market factors (Block 7), this agreement would not qualify for troubled debt restructuring accounting. If the modification of terms is due to reasons other than this, the transaction will be treated as a troubled debt restructuring.

Before proper accounting can be determined, the debtor must compare the future *gross cash outlays* (principal and interest) under the new terms with the carrying value of the existing payable (Block 8). If the carrying value of the payable is greater than the future cash payments, a gain on restructuring will result. The gain is equal to the difference between the carrying value of the payable and the total future cash payments. In this case, the creditor has made a concession as to the total amount of cash to be received under the new terms. In addition to recognizing the gain from restructuring, the payable is to be written down by an amount that will equate the carrying amount of the payable with the future cash payments. Subsequent payments during the life of the debt will be principal payments only, with no interest being recognized.

If the carrying value of the payable does not exceed the future cash payments, the transaction is to be treated in a prospective manner. The carrying amount of the payable will *not* be adjusted, and no gain will be recognized. It will be necessary to adjust current and future interest expense through the calculation of a new effective interest rate, based upon the new terms. The effective rate will be the rate of interest that equates the present value of the future payments (under the new terms) with the carrying value of the payable. Current and future interest expense will be computed using the interest method at the new effective rate.

The following examples are used to illustrate the various possibilities identified above. Example 4-24 lists the assumptions that are used to demonstrate proper accounting in a situation where the carrying value of the payable exceeds the future cash payments.

Example 4-24
Modification of Terms

1. Debtor, Inc. has a $3,000,000 note, payable in full to Creditor, Inc. in 10 years.
2. The note bears interest at the rate of 10% per annum, and there is $150,000 of unamortized discount on the books of Debtor, Inc.
3. Due to economic conditions, Creditor, Inc. believes that it must grant some type of concession to Debtor, Inc. to collect on the note. Creditor, Inc. is willing to accept the payment of $250,000 a year for the next 10 years in place of the existing note.

The agreement represents a modification as to the terms and amount of repayment of the note. Therefore, the agreement qualifies for troubled debt restructuring accounting. The first step is to compare the carrying value of the note with the gross future cash payments. This computation is shown below:

Face Amount of Note	$3,000,000
Unamortized Discount	(150,000)
Carrying Value of Note	2,850,000
Future Cash Payments ($250,000 × 10 years)	2,500,000
Excess of Carrying Value over Cash Payments	$350,000

In this case, the carrying value of the note is greater than the gross future cash payments, and a gain from restructuring of $350,000 must be recognized. The payable is reduced to $2,500,000, an amount equal to the future cash payments. The entry required to reflect the write-down is as follows:

Notes Payable	500,000	
Discount on Notes Payable		150,000
Gain on Restructuring of Debt		350,000

All subsequent payments will represent repayment of principal, and no interest expense will be recognized. This is the reason for the elimination of the discount on the note in the above entry. Discounts and premiums normally are associated with interest expense; and, in this case, no interest expense will be recognized. The entry necessary to show subsequent annual note payments is shown below:

Notes Payable	250,000	
Cash		250,000

A more complex situation exists when the debtor must calculate a new effective rate of interest as the result of some modification of terms. This would be the case where the total future cash payments are greater than the carrying value of the payable. To illustrate the accounting under these circumstances, the assumptions listed in Example 4-25 are used.

Example 4-25
Modification of Terms

1. Debtor, Inc. has a $3,000,000 note, payable in full to Creditor, Inc., in four years.
2. The note bears interest at the rate of 10% per annum, and there is no unamortized discount or premium associated with the note.
3. Due to economic conditions, Creditor, Inc. has agreed to make certain concessions to Debtor, Inc. in order to insure collectibility of the note. Creditor, Inc. has agreed to accept $2,500,000 at the end of four years *and* to reduce the interest rate from 10% to 8% on the new balance.

This agreement represents a modification as to the amount of repayment and the rate of interest to be paid. Assuming that the reduction in interest was not due to market factors, the agreement qualifies for troubled debt restructuring accounting. As before, the first step is to compare the carrying value of the payable with the total future cash payments. This computation is shown below:

Note Principal Repayment	$2,500,000
Interest Payments ($2,500,000 × 8% × 4 years)	800,000
Total Future Cash Payments	$3,300,000
Cash Value of Note	3,000,000
Excess of Cash Payments over Carrying Value	$300,000

In this case, the total future cash payments exceed the carrying value of the note, and the effects of the modification of terms will be accounted for on a prospective basis. It is now necessary to determine the interest rate that will equate the present value of the $3,300,000 future cash payments with the $3,000,000 carrying value of the note.

The rate may be determined through the trial-and-error method, using the present value of $1 for the principal repayment, and the present value of an ordinary annuity for the interest payments. The new effective rate was calculated to be 2.6628%. Once the new rate has been determined, an amortization schedule, such as that presented in Table 4-15, can be prepared.

Table 4-15 Amortization Schedule for Interest Expense and Note

	Year	Cash Interest	Interest Expense	Amortization of Note	Note Carrying Value
Initial Value		-	-	-	$3,000,000
	1	[a]$200,000	[b]$79,884	[c]$120,116	[d]2,879,884
	2	200,000	76,686	123,314	2,756,570
	3	200,000	73,402	126,598	2,629,972
	4	200,000	*70,028	129,972	[e]2,500,000
		$800,000	$300,000	$500,000	

[a] \$2,500,000 × 8% = \$200,000.
[b] \$3,000,000 × 2.6628% = \$79,884.
[c] \$200,000 – \$79,884 = \$120,116.
[d] \$3,000,000 – \$120,116 = \$2,879,884.
[e] Represents the modified maturity value at the end of 4 years.
* Rounded.

Table 4-15 shows the cash interest paid, the interest expense to be recognized and the amortization of the note over the four-year period. Because the effects of the restructuring are to be accounted for on a prospective basis, no gain or loss is recognized. The entry required for the first year's interest payment is shown below:

Note Payable	120,116	
Interest Expense	79,884	
Cash		200,000

At the date of restructuring, no entry would be required, because no gain is recognized and there is no write-down of the payable.

Partial Settlement and Modification of Terms

A troubled debt settlement may take on a combination of forms or types. For example, a transfer of assets may be combined with a modification of terms. By definition, any time there is a partial settlement of a debt, there has been a modification of terms. If a troubled debt restructuring is to be accomplished through a partial settlement and a modification of terms, the transfer of assets or equity interest is accounted for first, and then the modification of terms is handled. The carrying amount of the payable is reduced by the fair value of the assets or equity interest transferred to the creditor (Block 10). No gain from restructuring is recognized at this point; but, if the settlement involved the transfer of assets, the gain or loss from such transfer should be recognized. After this has been accomplished, the *remaining* carrying value of the payable is compared to the total future cash payments under the new terms. If the remaining carrying value of the payable is greater than the future cash payments, a gain on restructuring will be recognized (Block 8). The gain is equal to the difference in the remaining carrying value of the payable and the future cash payments under the new terms. The payable is to be reduced by an amount that will equate the payable with the future cash payments. No interest expense will be recognized over the remaining life of the payable. Subsequent payments are merely a reduction of the revised carrying value of the payable. If the remaining carrying value of the payable is *not* greater than the future cash payments, a new effective rate of interest must be determined. This rate must equate the present value of the future cash payment under the new terms with the revised carrying value of the payable. No gain is recognized at the time of restructuring. Future interest expense will be recognized, using the interest method based upon the new effective rate.

To illustrate a straightforward example of accounting for a troubled debt restructuring that involves a partial settlement and a modification of terms, the assumptions listed in Example 4-26 are used.

Example 4-26
Partial Settlement and Modification of Terms

1. Debtor, Inc. has a $4,000,000 note, payable in full to Creditor, Inc., in four years.

2. The note bears interest at the rate of 10% per annum, and there is $100,000 of unamortized discount on the books of Debtor, Inc.

3. Debtor, Inc. is not able to pay the interest on the note, and it is not likely that it will be able to repay the principal amount when due. Therefore, Creditor, Inc. has agreed to accept a parcel of land owned by Debtor, Inc. and reduce the maturity value of the note to $2,000,000. In addition, the interest rate is reduced from 10% to 6% on the new maturity value of the note.

4. The parcel of land had an original cost to Debtor, Inc. of $700,000 and a fair value of $1,000,000 at the date of restructuring.

This transaction represents a troubled debt restructuring with a partial settlement, represented by the payment of land, and a modification of terms, represented by the reduction in interest rate. The first step is to reduce the carrying value of the note by the fair value of the land transferred. This calculation is shown below:

Face Amount of Note	$4,000,000
Unamortized Discount	(100,000)
Carrying Amount of the Note	3,900,000
Fair Value of Asset Transferred	1,000,000
Revised Carrying Amount of Note	$2,900,000

Because the partial settlement is effected by the transfer of an asset, the gain or loss resulting from the asset transfer must be recognized. The gain or loss is equal to the difference between the fair value and the carrying value of the asset transferred, and is computed below:

Fair Value of Asset Transferred	$1,000,000
Carrying Value of Asset Transferred	700,000
Gain on Asset Transfer	$300,000

The journal entry required to reflect the reduction in the carrying value of the note is as follows:

Notes Payable	1,000,000	
Land		700,000
Gain on Transfer of Assets		300,000

No gain on restructuring is recognized at this point, and there has been no reduction in the unamortized discount.

Once the revised carrying value has been determined, it is necessary to evaluate the accounting problems posed by the modification of terms. Assuming that the reduction in interest rate was not due to market factors, the next step is to compare the revised carrying value of the note with the future total cash payments, under the modified terms of the agreement. This comparison is shown below:

Revised Carrying Amount of Note (per above)	$2,900,000
Future Cash Payments:	
Principal	$2,000,000
Interest (at 6% for 4 years)	480,000
Total Future Cash Payments	2,480,000
Excess of Carrying Amount over Cash Payments	$420,000

Because the revised carrying value of $2,900,000 is greater than the future cash payments of $2,480,000, the carrying value of the note must be written down, and a gain of $420,000 must be recognized. The carrying value of the note will then be equal to the future cash payments, and no interest will be recognized over the remaining life of the note. Because no interest is to be recognized, the unamortized discount also must be removed at the time of restructuring. The journal entry to accomplish this is:

Notes Payable	520,000	
Discount on Notes Payable		100,000
Gain on Restructuring of Debt		420,000

The two preceding entries could have been combined into one journal entry, but were shown separately for illustrative purposes. This example resulted in a gain on restructuring because the carrying value of the payable, as revised, was greater than the future cash payments under the new terms.

To illustrate a somewhat more complex example of a partial settlement and modification of terms, the assumptions listed in Example 4-27 are used.

Example 4-27
Partial Settlement and Modification of Terms

1. Debtor, Inc. has a $2,000,000 note, payable in full to Creditor, Inc. in four years.

2. The note bears interest at the rate of 10% per annum, and there is no unamortized discount or premium associated with the note.

3. Debtor, Inc. is not able to pay the interest on the note, and it is not likely that it will be able to repay the principal amount when due. Therefore, Creditor,

Inc. has agreed to accept 50,000 common shares of Debtor, Inc. in partial settlement of the note. In addition, Creditor, Inc. has agreed to forgive $200,000 of the note and reduce the interest rate to 8% on the new maturity value.

4. The common stock of Debtor, Inc. has a par value of $1 per share and a fair value of $10 per share on the date of restructuring.

The acceptance of stock represents a partial settlement of the debt and the forgiveness of $200,000 represents modification of the terms of the note. The first step in the process is to reduce the carrying value of the note by the fair value of the common stock transferred. Remember that no gain or loss results from the transfer of an equity interest, and it is not appropriate to recognize a gain on restructuring at this point. The calculation of the revised carrying value is shown below:

Carrying Amount of the Note	$2,000,000
Fair Value of Common Stock Transferred (50,000 shares × $10 fair value)	500,000
Revised Carrying Amount of the Note	$1,500,000

The journal entry necessary to reflect the reduction in carrying value of the payable and the issuance of the stock is:

Notes Payable	500,000	
Common Stock (50,000 shares × $1 par)		50,000
Contributed Capital in Excess of Par		450,000

Now the revised carrying amount of the note must be compared with the total future cash payments under the modified terms. This comparison is shown below:

Future Cash Payments:	
Principal ($1,500,000 – $200,000 forgiveness)	$1,300,000
Interest ($1,300,000 × 8% × 4 years)	416,000
Total Future Cash Payments	$1,716,000
Revised Carrying Amount of the Note	1,500,000
Excess of Cash Payments over Carrying Amount	$216,000

The forgiveness of $200,000 does not affect the revised carrying value of the note, because no asset or equity interest was transferred to obtain the $200,000 concession.

Because the $1,716,000 total future cash payments are greater than the $1,500,000 revised carrying amount of the note, it is necessary to determine a new effective interest rate. The rate must equate the present value of the $1,716,000 with the $1,500,000 carrying amount of the note. The calculation of the rate may be accomplished through the trial-and-error method, using the present value of $1 for the principal amount and the present value of an ordinary annuity for the interest payments. The new effective rate was calculated to be 3.7832%. Once the new rate has been determined, an amortization schedule can be prepared. Table

4-16 below shows the amortization of the note and resulting interest expense for the note used in this case.

Table 4-16 Amortization Schedule for Interest and Note

	Year	Cash Interest	Interest Expense	Note Amortization	Note Carrying Value
Initial Value					$1,500,000
	1	[a]$104,000	[b]$56,748	[c]$47,252	[d]1,452,748
	2	104,000	54,960	49,040	1,403,708
	3	104,000	53,105	50,895	1,352,813
	4	104,000	*51,187	52,813	[e]1,300,000
		$416,000	$216,000	$200,000	

[a] $1,300,000 × 8% = $104,000.
[b] $1,500,000 × 3.7832% = $56,748.
[c] $104,000 – $56,748 = $47,252.
[d] $1,500,000 – $47,252 = $1,452,748.
[e] Represents the maturity value of the note with the modified terms.
* Rounded.

Given the information in Table 4-16, the journal entry to record the first annual interest payment is shown below:

Interest Expense	56,748	
Notes Payable	47,252	
Cash		104,000

The forgiveness of $200,000 is amortized over the four-year period as the interest payments are made. The total of the "Note Amortization" column is equal to the amount of the forgiveness. The new effective rate of interest insured a proper amortization of both interest expense and the note payable. At the end of the four-year period, the carrying value of the note is equal to the maturity value.

Although Example 4-27 is somewhat complex, the solution was highly structured. However, when there is an unamortized discount or premium, or unamortized debt issue costs associated with the note, the solution to the problem becomes quite complicated. In Example 4-27, once the effective interest rate was determined, it was relatively easy to divide the cash interest payment into interest expense and amortization of the principal amount of the note. When the debtor has unamortized discount, premium or issue costs (hereafter referred to as "unamortized items"), the problem becomes, How does one divide the cash interest payment into interest expense, amortization of note principal, *and* amortization of unamortized items?

In cases where the future cash payments *exceed* the carrying amount of the debt, ASC 470-60 prohibits the write-down of the debt or other unamortized items. In these cases, a new effective rate of interest must be calculated that equates the present value of the future payments with the carrying amount of the note. The carrying amount of the note is equal to the face amount, plus or minus related unamortized items. The new effective rate, when there are unamortized items, is applied against the unrecovered balance, and the resulting principal amortization is actually made up of two elements. One element of the amortization is the part that applies to the forgiveness granted by the creditor, and the other element is the amortization of the original unamortized items. How does one separate these two elements?

ASC 835-30 requires that discounts and premiums on notes be established and reported as a reduction or addition to the related note. Because a separate account will be established for the related unamortized items, it is necessary to determine the amortization applicable to these items. ASC 470-60 requires the use of the interest method in the determination of amounts to be amortized, unless another method provides results that are not materially different from the interest method. ASC 470-60 provides no guidance in making the division between the two elements discussed above.

In an effort to resolve this problem, a logical method has been devised to separate the two elements. The first step is to determine the effective rate, *without* consideration being given to the unamortized items; and the note principal then is amortized, using this rate. Next, the effective rate is determined, giving full consideration to the unamortized items; and the note principal again is amortized, using this rate. The difference between the two principal amortization schedules must be the amortization that is applicable to the discount or premium. Other approaches may be just as logical and acceptable.

To illustrate the basic problem and solution, assume the same facts as listed in Example 4-27, except that there is an unamortized discount of $50,000 associated with the note. The only *new* element added to the problem is the unamortized discount.

Given this added assumption, the new revised carrying amount of the note would be determined as follows:

Face Amount of the Note	$2,000,000
Unamortized Discount	(50,000)
Carrying Amount of the Note	$1,950,000
Fair Value of Common Stock Transferred	500,000
Revised Carrying Amount of the Note	$1,450,000

The entry to reduce the note by the fair value of the stock transferred is identical to that used in the previous example and need not be repeated. The future cash payments of $1,716,000 exceed the revised carrying amount of $1,450,000; therefore, it is necessary to determine the effective interest rate that will equate the present value of the cash payments with the revised carrying value of the payable. The rate required to equate these two amounts is 4.76385%.

Once the effective rate has been determined, an amortization schedule similar to that shown in Table 4-17 can be developed.

Table 4-17 Amortization Schedule for Interest and Note

	Year	Cash Interest	Interest Expense	Note Amortization	Note Carrying Value
Initial Value					$1,450,000
	1	[a]$104,000	[b]$69,076	[c]$34,924	[d]1,415,076
	2	104,000	67,412	36,588	1,378,488
	3	104,000	65,669	38,331	1,340,157
	4	104,000	63,843	40,157	[e]1,300,000
		$416,000	$266,000	$150,000	

[a] $1,300,000 × 8% = $104,000.
[b] $1,450,000 × 4.76385% = $69,076.
[c] $104,000 – $69,076 = $34,924.
[d] $1,450,000 – $34,924 = $1,415,076.
[e] Represents the maturity value of the note under the modified terms.

If one were to use the information in Table 4-17 to prepare the entry to record the annual interest payment, it would be as follows:

Interest Expense	69,076	
Notes Payable	34,924	
Cash		104,000

However, this entry is not sufficient, because it fails to record the amortization of the note discount. In effect, the note principal amortization of $34,924 is a *net* amount, which includes the amortization of the principal and the amortization of the discount. If the problem is to be solved correctly, it is necessary to gross up the principal amortization shown in Table 4-17. The principal amortization in Table 4-16 amounted to $200,000, and the same amortization in Table 4-17 amounted to $150,000. Therefore, the difference between the two numbers ($50,000) must be the amortization of the discount related to the note. Based upon this information, Table 4-18 develops a year-by-year analysis of the difference between the principal amortizations shown in the two tables.

Table 4-18 Schedule for Discount Amortization

Year	Table 4-16 Note Amortization	Table 4-17 Note Amortization	Difference Discount Amortization
1	$47,252	$34,924	[a]$12,328
2	49,040	36,588	12,452
3	50,895	38,331	12,564
4	52,813	40,157	12,656
	$200,000	$150,000	$50,000

[a] $47,252 – $34,924 = $12,328.

With the information in Tables 4-17 and 4-18, it now is possible to prepare the correct journal entry to record the first annual interest payment. This entry is shown below:

Interest Expense	69,076	
Notes Payable	47,252	
Discount on Notes Payable		12,328
Cash		104,000

This entry accomplishes all the necessary amortizations. Anything less would result in an error. The difference between the $47,252 note principal amortization and the $12,328 discount amortization is the $34,924 net amortization shown in Table 4-17. The purpose of Tables 4-16 and 4-18 is to find the individual amortization amounts of $47,252 and $12,328, rather than the net amount of $34,924.

With the solution to this problem, the discussion of the major types or troubled debt restructurings is completed. Attention now is turned to some special considerations relating to restructuring.

Other Considerations

An agreement in a troubled debt restructuring may be such that the cash payments to be made depend upon some indeterminate or contingent future event. Or it could be that the rate of interest on the debt varies, depending upon some factor such as the bank prime rate.

In cases where the future payments are contingent upon some future event, ASC 450-30-23-1 should apply. That paragraph specifies that a gain should not be recognized until it is *realized.* This being the case, the maximum possible payments or amounts should be included in the future cash payments. This total then will be compared with the carrying amount of the debt to determine if there is a gain on restructuring. In other words, a gain should not be recognized at the time of restructuring if it is possible to offset the gain with contingent future payments.

An interest rate that is allowed to vary after the date of restructuring is not given recognition at the date of restructuring, but is treated as a change in an accounting estimate in subsequent periods when the rate actually changes. The applicable rate to use in determining the future cash payments is the rate that prevails on the date of restructuring.

Any contingent agreement should be reviewed every statement date to determine if a liability and expense should be recorded consistent with the provisions of ASC 450. If it is probable that the contingent amount will now be paid, and that amount can be reasonably estimated, a two-step accounting process is necessary. First, a determination must be made of the amount of the contingent payment included in the future cash payments. Next, the amount that can be reasonably estimated and will probably be paid (hereafter referred to as the liability) must be compared to the contingent payments included in the future cash payments. The excess of the liability over the contingent amounts included in the future cash payments is recorded as interest expense and as a payable. The carrying amount of the restructured payable is reduced by the lesser of the contingent payments included in the future cash payments or the liability.

One final consideration deals with legal fees and direct costs associated with a troubled debt restructuring. Legal fees and other direct costs associated with the transfer of an equity interest should be used to reduce the recorded amount of the equity interest. Other direct costs incurred by the debtor should be offset against any gain on restructuring. Any direct costs that exceed the gain on restructuring should be charged to expense in the period of restructuring.

To illustrate the accounting for a troubled debt restructuring where a contingent agreement is present, the assumptions set forth in Example 4-28 are used.

Example 4-28
Contingent Agreement

1. Debtor, Inc. has a $4,000,000 note, payable to Creditor, Inc., which requires principal repayments of $400,000 at the end of each of the next 10 years.
2. The note bears interest at the rate of 10% per annum, and there is no unamortized discount or premium associated with the note.
3. Debtor, Inc. is in financial difficulty and may not be able to make the required interest and principal payments. As a result, Creditor, Inc. is willing to accept 500,000 shares of common stock of Debtor, Inc. and the payment of $250,000 at the end of each of the next 10 years. In addition, Creditor, Inc. specifies that it will receive an additional $25,000 payment for each year in which the earnings of Debtor, Inc. exceed $200,000.
4. The common stock of Debtor, Inc. has a par value of $1 per share and a fair value of $2 per share on the date of restructuring.
5. Debtor, Inc. incurs $10,000 of direct costs in connection with the restructuring. Of that total, $2,500 is directly related to the equity issue.

In this particular case, the first step is to reduce the carrying amount of the note by the fair value of the equity interest transferred. The revised carrying amount is calculated below:

Carrying Amount of the Note	$4,000,000
Fair Value of the Common Stock Transferred (500,000 shares × $2 per share)	1,000,000
Revised Carrying Amount of the Note	$3,000,000

Because $2,500 of the direct costs were associated with the issue of the common stock, the contributed capital will be reduced by this amount. The journal entry necessary to reflect the reduction in the carrying amount of the note and the direct costs related to the stock issue is shown below:

Notes Payable	1,000,000	
Common Stock		[a]500,000

Contributed Capital in Excess of Par	[b]497,500
Cash	2,500

[a] 500,000 shares × $1 par value = $500,000.
[b] $1,000,000 – $500,000 – $2,500 = $497,500.

The next step is to compare the expected future cash payments with the revised carrying amount of the note. In order to make this comparison, the future cash flows must be calculated. Contingent payments are included in the future cash payments, based on an estimate of the maximum amount expected to be paid. The expected future cash payments would be calculated as follows:

Future Cash Payments:	
Required Payments—$250,000 × 10 years	$2,500,000
Contingent Payments—$25,000 × 10 years	250,000
Expected Future Cash Payments	$2,750,000

The revised carrying amount of $3,000,000 is greater than the expected future cash payments of $2,750,000; therefore, a gain on restructuring will be recognized for the difference of $250,000. However, this gain must be reduced by the direct costs not directly associated with the stock issue, which amounts to $7,500. A gain of $242,500 therefore will be recognized. The entry required to record the gain and the direct costs not related to the stock issue is presented below:

Notes Payable	250,000	
Gain on Restructuring of Debt		242,500
Cash		7,500

The $7,500 represents the payment of the direct costs. The note now has been written-down to the amount of the expected future cash payments, and no interest expense will be recognized over the remaining life of the note. The two preceding entries could have been combined, but were shown separately for purposes of illustration.

The assumptions listed in Example 4-29 are used to illustrate the proper accounting for a troubled debt restructuring that involves a variable interest rate.

Example 4-29
Variable Interest Rate

1. Debtor, Inc., a December 31 year-end enterprise, has a $3,500,000 note payable to Creditor, Inc., which is payable in full in five years.
2. The note bears interest at the rate of 12% per annum, and there is no unamortized discount or premium associated with the note.
3. Debtor, Inc. is unable to pay the current interest, and it appears that it will not be able to repay the principal amount when due. As a result, Creditor, Inc. has agreed to forgive $1,000,000 of principal amount of the note and to charge interest on the new maturity value at the 9% bank prime rate in effect on the last day of the year.

The analysis of this situation is begun with the computation of the expected future cash payments. The interest rate used in the computation is the 9% prime rate in effect on the date of restructuring. The computation of the expected future cash payments is shown below:

Carrying value of the payable	$3,500,000
Forgiveness of principal amount	(1,000,000)
Maturity value of revised payable	2,500,000
Interest ($2,500,000 × 9% × 5 years)	1,125,000
Expected future cash payments	$3,625,000

Because the $3,625,000 in total future cash payments under the modified terms of the agreement is greater than the $3,500,000 carrying value of the debt, it is necessary to determine a new effective interest rate. The rate must equate the present value of $3,625,000 with the debt of $3,500,000. The rate was determined to be .80563%. Once the rate has been computed, an amortization schedule can be prepared. Table 4-19 shows the cash payments, the interest expense to be recognized using the new effective interest rate, the amortization of the principal forgiveness of $1,000,000, and the balance in the payable.

Table 4-19 Amortization Schedule for Interest and Note

	Year	Cash Interest	Interest Expense	Note Amortization	Note Carrying Value
Initial Value					$3,500,000 [a]
	1	$225,000 [b]	$28,197 [c]	$196,803 [d]	3,303,197 [e]
	2	225,000	26,612	198,388	3,104,809
	3	225,000	25,013	199,987	2,904,822
	4	225,000	23,402	201,598	2,703,224
	5	225,000	21,776 [f]	203,224	2,500,000 [g]
		$1,125,000	$125,000	$1,000,000	

[a] $3,500,000 taken from above.
[b] $2,500,000 × 9% = $225,000.
[c] $3,500,000 × .80563% = $28,197.
[d] $225,000 – $28,197 = $196,803.
[e] $3,500,000 – $196,803 = $3,303,197.
[f] Rounded.
[g] Revised maturity value at the end of the life of the note.

Based upon the information in Table 4-19, the following journal entry is required to record the interest expense and note amortization on the date of the first interest payment.

Interest Expense	28,197	
Note Payable	196,803	
Cash		225,000

Now assume that the bank prime rate changed from 9% to 7% two years after the restructuring (i.e., at the beginning of Year 3). In this case, the expected cash payments must be recalculated, based upon the new bank prime rate of 7%. The computation will be made from the end of Year 2 through Year 5, and would be as follows:

Maturity value of the payable	$2,500,000
Interest ($2,500,000 × 7% × 3 years)	525,000
Expected future cash receipts	$3,025,000

The carrying value of the payable at the end of Year 2 is $3,104,809 (see Table 4-19), which is greater than the expected future cash payments of $3,025,000. Generally, it is appropriate to recognize a gain on restructuring in such a situation; however, because future cash flows could fluctuate and eliminate the current gain, no gain should be recognized at this point. According to ASC 470-60, the carrying amount of the payable should not change and no gain should be recognized until the gain cannot be offset by future cash payments.

Disclosures

The disclosures required to be presented by the debtor in the preparation of the basic financial statements in the period of restructuring include the following (ASC 470-60-50):

1. Any modification of terms and settlements must be described for each debt restructured;
2. The gains on debt restructuring must be aggregated and reported along with related earnings per share information; and
3. The gains and losses on asset transfers must be aggregated and reported in income.

For periods subsequent to the reporting period of the restructuring, the debtor should disclose information concerning contingent payments included in the carrying amount of the payable.

Topic 480: Distinguishing Liabilities from Equity

Topic 480, *Distinguishing Liabilities from Equity*, contains one subtopic:

10 Overall

General Discussion

ASC 480-10 provides accounting and reporting requirements for selected financial instruments with both liability and equity characteristics. A financial instrument is cash, an ownership interest in an enterprise, or a contractual right or contractual obligation of one entity to receive or deliver cash or another financial instrument or to exchange financial instruments on potentially favorable terms or unfavorable terms with the other entity.

ASC 480-10 covers three categories of free-standing financial instruments that create obligations for the issuer of the instruments. A free-standing financial instrument is a financial instrument that an entity enters into that is not part of any of the other financial instruments of the entity (it is entered into separate and apart from any other financial instruments or equity transaction), or that an entity enters into with another transaction and it can be exercised separately and detached legally. The three categories of free-standing financial instruments are: mandatorily redeemable financial instruments, financial instruments that require the repurchase of equity shares of the issuing company by transferring assets, and financial instruments that require the issuance of a variable number of shares.

ASC 480-10 does not apply to obligations under share-based compensation plans accounted for under ASC 718. However, it applies to such obligations when ASC 718 or related guidelines are no longer applicable, and to mandatorily redeemable shares that are issued to satisfy an exercise by the employee of an employee stock option. ASC 805 should be used to determine the accounting for the initial measurement and recognition of consideration provided in a business combination. The accounting requirements also apply to contingent consideration issued in a business combination. If the contingent consideration was classified as a liability using the provisions of ASC 480-10, ASC 805 should be used to subsequently measure the consideration at fair value.

Generally, mandatorily redeemable financial instruments are accounted for as liabilities. However, this rule does not apply to redemptions that are required only upon termination or liquidation of the enterprise. If the redemption relates to equity shares, ASC 480-10 applies if there is an unconditional obligation to redeem the shares by transferring assets to the holder upon an event that will occur at a specified date or a date that can be determined. Examples of financial instruments that could meet the requirements of ASC 480-10 include mandatorily redeemable preferred stock, trust-preferred shares, and shares of stock that must be redeemed upon the death of the holder of the shares.

A financial instrument that contains an obligation to repurchase equity shares of the issuer by transferring assets is classified as a liability when the instrument meets the following two criteria: (1) it requires a transfer of assets by the issuer to settle the obligation and (2) it contains a requirement to repurchase the equity shares of the issuer or is indexed to such a requirement. Examples of instruments that meet these requirements are written put options or forward purchase contracts that require physical or net cash settlement. Physical settlement indicates that the buyer delivers the full amount of cash or other financial instruments to the seller and the seller provides to the buyer the full amount of the stock, financial instruments, or nonfinancial instruments. Net cash settlement indicates that the party with a loss provides to the party with a gain an amount of cash equal to the gain.

A financial instrument is accounted for as a liability if it contains an unconditional obligation or a conditional obligation whereby the issuer can or is required to issue a variable number of equity shares to settle the obligation if the monetary value of the obligation at inception is primarily based on one of the following: (1) a monetary amount that is fixed and known at inception; (2) the variation associated with the instrument is based on other than fair value of the equity shares of the issuing entity (e.g., the S&P); or (3) the variation related to the instrument is inversely related to the fair value of the equity shares of the issuing entity. An example of this type of financial instrument may include the receipt of $500,000 with a promise to issue equity shares of the entity at a future date worth $550,000.

Financial instruments meeting the requirements of ASC 480-10 are presented in the liability section of the balance sheet and should not be presented between liabilities and equity. However, if an entity has only mandatorily redeemable financial instruments classified as liabilities under the provisions of ASC 480-10 and no other equity instruments, the financial instruments should be described in the statement of financial position as shares subject to mandatory redemption in an effort to differentiate them from other liabilities. In addition, any accruals or payments included in the financial statements related to such financial instruments should be reported separately from other accruals and payments related to normal liabilities.

Liabilities associated with financial instruments meeting the requirements of ASC 480-10 should be reported at fair value initially and should be measured at fair value subsequent to initial measurement with the change in fair value reported in the income statement, except for derivatives covered by ASC 815 and certain forward contracts as discussed below. ASC 820 should be used when determining fair value. Financial instruments classified as derivatives and covered by ASC 815 should be measured using the provisions of ASC 815. Measurement of forward contracts depends on the situation or structure of the instrument. Forward contracts that require physical settlement by exchanging cash for the equity shares are measured at fair value after adjustment for any consideration or unstated privileges or rights. Stockholders' equity should be reduced at the inception of the contract for an amount equal to the fair value of the shares. Forward contracts that require physical settlement by exchanging cash and mandatorily redeemable financial instruments for the equity shares should be measured as follows: (1) if there is a fixed settlement date and a fixed amount to be paid, the instruments should be measured using the present value of the amount to be paid at settlement, and interest should be accrued using the implicit rate at inception; or (2) if either the settlement date or amount to be paid varies, the instruments should be measured using the amount of cash that would be paid at the reporting date assuming the conditions specified in the contract and assuming settlement at the reporting date. Any changes at subsequent reporting dates should be reported as interest cost.

Common shares related to mandatorily redeemable shares or forward contracts requiring physical settlement by the repurchase of a fixed number of shares should be excluded from the computation of both basic and diluted earnings per share. In addition, any amounts, such as dividends or participation rights, not included in interest cost must be deducted when computing income available to the common shareholders.

Technical Considerations

Two examples are used to illustrate the technical aspects of ASC 480-10. Assumptions for Example 4-30 are presented below.

Example 4-30
Assumptions for Mandatorily Redeemable Financial Instruments

1. First National Bank establishes the First Trust, which is consolidated with First National Bank financial statements. The First Trust issues $10,000,000 in preferred stock and then uses the proceeds to buy $10,000,000 of loans due in 10 years from the First National Bank. Interest paid to First Trust on the loans will be distributed to the shareholders of the preferred stock. The preferred stock must be redeemed by First Trust at the end of the 10-year loan period.
2. Financial Enterprises, a December 31 year-end company, issues $8,000,000 of common stock on July 1, 20X6, that must be redeemed by the company four months after any change in control of the company. Control of the company changed December 1, 20X7. The fair value of the stock on December 1, 20X7 is $8,200,000.
3. On January 1, 20X6, Central Enterprises issued 100,000 shares of common stock (200,000 shares authorized), par value $1 to Jim Holder with the requirement that the shares be redeemed upon the death of Holder. Central Enterprises issued no other stock. On December 31, 20X6, the balance sheet date, the following amounts are available for presentation in the financial statements: total assets—$10,000,000, total liabilities—$6,000,000, common shares—$4,000,000, retained earnings related to common shares—$3,700,000, and accumulated other comprehensive income related to the stock—$200,000.

Because the preferred stock must be redeemed by First Trust at the end of the 10-year, loan period by transferring assets to the holders of the stock, the securities are classified as mandatorily redeemable preferred shares. The preferred stock is classified as a liability in the consolidated financial statements of First National Bank because First Trust is considered a variable interest entity. Any dividend payment on the preferred stock is treated as interest expense in the financial statements rather than dividends.

In the second situation, the $8,000,000 issuance of common stock by Financial Enterprises is not considered a mandatorily redeemable financial instrument until December 1, 20X7, the date of change in control. The shares of common stock are considered to be conditionally redeemable until control has been changed. On December 1, 20X7 the common stock meets the requirements to be classified as a mandatorily redeemable financial instrument under the provisions of ASC 480-10, because the stock will have to be redeemed on March 31, 20X8. Therefore, the common stock should be reclassified as a liability and transferred from equity to the liability section of the statement of changes in financial position at the fair value of $8,200,000 by increasing liabilities and reducing equity. No gain or loss is reported on the transfer.

In situation 3, Central Enterprises must treat the 100,000 shares of common stock as a liability because the death of Jim Holder is certain and the stock meets the definition of a mandatorily redeemable financial instrument under the provisions of ASC 480-10. Because 100,000 shares of common stock is the only stock that Central has issued, the stock liability should be presented in the liability section as *shares subject to mandatory redemption.* In addition, certain equity disclosures are required when the only equity is classified as a liability. Presented below is a partial statement of financial position and partial note for the mandatorily redeemable financial instrument for Central Enterprises.

Central Enterprises Statement of Financial Position
December 31, 20X6

Assets	$10,000,000
Liabilities:	
Liabilities Other Than Redeemable Financial Instruments	$ 6,000,000
Shares Subject To Mandatory Redemption	4,000,000
Total Liabilities	$10,000,000
Stockholders' Equity	0
Total Liabilities and Equity	$10,000,000

Notes to the Financial Statements

Note X: Common shares are classified as a liability in the statement of financial position because they are subject to mandatory redemption at book value upon the death of the holder of the stock. They are composed of:

Common Stock, $1 par value, 200,000 shares authorized, 100,000 shares issued and outstanding	$ 100,000
Retained earnings	3,700,000
Accumulated other comprehensive income	200,000
Total	$4,000,000

This completes the discussion of Example 4-30. Assumptions for Example 4-31 are presented below.

Example 4-31

Assumptions for Obligation to Repurchase Shares and Issue Variable Number of Shares

1. On January 1, 20X6, Major Enterprises entered into a forward contact to repurchase 500,000 shares of common stock, par value $1 from another entity for cash on January 1, 20X9, at a price of $15 per share. The current price of the stock is $10 per share.
2. On January 1, 20X6, Agency, Inc. entered into a contract to purchase 10,000 shares of its common stock on January 1, 20X8, for $10 if the price of the stock falls below $10. The contract also allows the Com-

pany, on the same date, to purchase 10,000 shares for $11 if the stock price is greater than $11.

3. On January 1, 20X6, Touch Master, Inc. entered into a contract to receive $2,000,000 with the agreement that it will issue a number of common stock equal to $2,400,000 on January 1, 2010.

The forward purchase contract of Major Enterprises is classified as a liability under the provisions of ASC 480-10 because there is an unconditional obligation to transfer a specified amount of cash ($15 per share) to the holders of the stock on January 1, 20X9. On January 1, 20X6, Major Enterprises should reduce equity by $5,000,000 (500,000 shares × $10 current per share price) and establish a liability for $5,000,000. The $5,000,000 liability is the present value of the $7,500,000 (500,000 shares × $15 acquisition price) amount that will have to be paid to acquire the stock in 20X9. The $2,500,000 difference ($7,500,000 – $5,000,000) is the amount of interest to be reported over the time period until the stock is repurchased. The interest will increase the liability from the $5,000,000 amount to the $7,500,000 amount that is required for the acquisition.

In the second situation, Agency, Inc. has both a written put option and a purchased call option. Agency should report a liability for the put and call option contract.

Touch Master, in situation 3, must report a liability for the shares that will be issued on January 1, 2010 to settlement the contract entered into on January 1, 20X6. Touch Master will issue a variable number of shares equal to a market price of $2,400,000 that will be determined on January 1, 2010.

Disclosure Requirements

ASC 480-10-50 provides the disclosures required for financial instruments that meet its provisions as follows:

1. The terms and nature of the financial instruments and obligations and rights included in the instruments. Also, include information about settlement alternatives and provide identification of the entity with control of the settlement alternatives.
2. Disclose the components of mandatorily redeemable financial instruments that would normally relate to shareholders equity and other comprehensive income classified as liabilities under ASC 480-10 when the entity has no other equity subject to the redemption feature. Examples include par value and other paid-in amounts disclosed separately from retained earnings or the accumulated deficit.
3. Disclose the following as if the settlement of the instruments occurs at the reporting date using the terms specified in the contract: number of shares that would be issued and fair value of the shares and the amount that would be paid.
4. The impact on the settlement amounts for changes in the fair value of the equity shares, such as the entity is required to issue how many additional shares for each $1 decrease in the fair value of the stock.

5. If applicable, the maximum amount required to be paid by the issuer for redemption of the instrument by physical settlement.
6. If applicable, the maximum number of shares that the issuer could be required to issue.
7. If applicable, specify that the contract does not limit the amount that an issuer could have to pay or the number of shares that the issuer could have to issue.
8. Disclose the following for a forward contract or an option that is indexed to the equity shares of the issuer: option strike price or forward price, the number of shares of the issuer to which the contract is indexed, and contract or settlement date.

Disclosures 3–8 should be provided for each settlement alternative.

This completes the discussion of ASC 480-10-25.

CHAPTER 5
EQUITY

CONTENTS

The *Equity* area of the FASB *Accounting Standards Codification* contains one topic:

505 Equity

Topic 505: Equity

Topic 505, *Equity*, contains nine subtopics:

10 Overall

20 Stock Dividends and Stock Splits

30 Treasury Stock

50 Equity-Based Payments to Non-Employees

60 Spinoffs and Reverse Spinoffs

905 Agriculture *

942 Financial Services—Depository and Lending *

944 Financial Services—Insurance *

946 Financial Services—Investment Companies *

* See the corresponding topic in Chapter 9 for coverage of this shared subtopic.

Overall

ASC 505-10-25-2 states that the net income (or results of operations) of a company would not include adjustments resulting from transactions in its capital stock, changes in appropriated retained earnings, or adjustments associated with a quasi-reorganization.

When an income statement and a balance sheet are presented, a company should disclose changes in its stockholders' equity accounts for the most recent annual accounting period and for any subsequent interim accounting period, if presented. In addition, the increase or decrease in the number of equity shares should also be disclosed for the same time periods. Such disclosure may be made in separate statements or in related notes to the financial statements.

ASC 505-10-50 requires all entities with debt or equity securities (or the rights to these securities) to provide certain disclosures about its capital structure.

The required disclosures about an entity's capital structure follow:

1. For outstanding securities disclose the related privileges and rights such as:
   a. Liquidation and dividend rights.
   b. Rights of participation.
   c. Conversion or exercise information, such as prices, rates, and dates.
   d. Voting rights that are unusual.
   e. Requirements for sinking-fund purposes.
   f. Significant contract terms when the contract requires additional shares to be issued.
2. For the latest annual period and any interim periods subsequent to the annual period for which financial statements are presented, disclose the shares issued from the following: exercise, conversion, or other requirements.
3. Disclose liquidation preferences of senior stock, such as preferred stock, if the preference exceeds the par or stated value by a considerable amount. This information should be disclosed on the face of the balance sheet on an aggregate basis and presented in short or parenthetically.
4. Disclose call amounts for preferred stock on either an aggregate or per share basis.
5. Disclose cumulative preferred dividends in arrears on both an aggregate and per share basis.
6. The redemption requirement amounts for each of the next five years for capital stock that can be redeemed at prices that are fixed or can be determined. This information may be disclosed by issue or all issues may be combined.

Stock Dividends and Stock Splits

ASC 505-20 addresses stock dividends and stock splits. Stock dividends are distributions of shares of the company's own stock to existing shareholders in an effort to provide additional evidence of ownership interest without the shareholders paying consideration for the dividend distribution. Accounting for stock dividends depends on the size of the dividend. Stock dividends are divided into small and large dividends. A dividend that is less than 20%–25% of the outstanding shares is classified as a small dividend, and a dividend that is greater than 20%–25% of the outstanding shares is classified as a large stock dividend. A small stock dividend is accounted for by capitalizing (debit) retained earnings for the fair value of the stock on the date of declaration of the stock dividend and increasing the capital stock and related additional paid-in-capital accounts. A large stock dividend is accounted for by capitalizing retained earnings and increasing the stock account by an amount determined by the legal requirements in the state in which the company is incorporated (generally the par value of the stock). The reader is encouraged to consult state legal requirements when determining what amount to capitalize.

Stock splits may be classified as stock splits or reverse splits. A stock split is an increase in the number of shares and a corresponding reduction in the par value of the stock with no change in the total stock account. A reverse stock split is a decrease in the number of shares outstanding with a corresponding increase in the par value of the stock with no change in the total stock account. A stock split is used to decrease the trading price of the stock, and a reverse stock split is used to increase the trading price. There is no formal accounting entry for stock splits and reverse splits other than a memorandum entry. The balance in the stock account is the same before and after the splits. In some cases, an entity may issue a stock split effected in the form of a stock dividend. In this situation, the company would generally debit a paid-in-capital account and credit the related stock account, such as common stock, for the par value of the stock times the number of shares issued.

Treasury Stock

ASC 505-30 addresses treasury stock. Treasury stock is the company's own shares of stock acquired by the company either to be reissued for specific or nonspecific purposes in future accounting periods or to be retired. Two methods are available to account for treasury stock acquisitions, the cost method, and the par value method. The cost method is the method most commonly used and generally should be used when the company does not expect to formally or constructively retire the stock. When the cost method is used, the cost of the acquired shares is included in a treasury stock account, and the treasury stock account is reported as a deduction from stockholders' equity. When treasury stock is reissued in future accounting periods, the cost of the treasury stock is removed and, if there is a difference between the price received and the cost basis of the stock, the difference is used as an adjustment to stockholders' equity. When the price received exceeds the basis of the stock, paid-in-capital from treasury stock transactions is increased. If the price received is less than the basis of the stock, additional paid-in-capital from treasury stock transactions for the same class of stock is reduced and, if reduced to zero, any excess difference is charged to retained earnings.

When the par value method is used to account for the acquisition of treasury shares, treasury stock is increased by an amount equal to the par value times the number of shares acquired, and additional paid-in-capital in excess of par is reduced by an amount equal to the excess of the selling price over the par value from the original sale of the reacquired shares. When cash paid for the acquisition exceeds the amounts for the treasury shares and the additional paid-in-capital, the excess is used to increase additional paid-in-capital from treasury stock transactions. When the cash paid for the stock is less than the amounts included for additional paid-in-capital and treasury shares, additional paid-in-capital from treasury stock transactions is increased for the difference and, if reduced to zero, retained earnings is charged for the remaining difference. If the treasury shares are reissued, the difference between the par value (which is the amount in the treasury stock account) and the cash received is used to increase additional paid-in-capital from treasury stock transactions or additional paid-in-capital in excess of par. Should the cash received be less than the par value of the stock, additional paid-in-capital from treasury stock transactions is reduced and, if reduced to zero, any excess difference is charged to retained earnings. When the par value method is used, the balance in the treasury stock account is reported as a reduction of the stock account to which it relates (such as common stock).

Accounting for Share-Based Transactions with Parties Other Than Employees

ASC 505-50 specifies the accounting and reporting requirements for share-based transactions with parties other than employees. ASC 718 specifies the requirements for share-based transactions with employees.

When an entity purchases goods or services by issuing a share-based instrument such as common stock, the goods or services received should be recorded at the fair value of the item received unless the fair value of the instrument issued can be measured more reliably.

The fair value provisions of ASC 820 exclude share-based payment transactions. Fair value used in share-based transactions is defined as the price that would be paid in a transaction between a willing buyer and a willing seller. Fair value should be determined using quoted market prices of identical or similar items. However, in many cases, such prices are not available, and an enterprise must estimate fair value. Fair value may be estimated using an acceptable valuation technique that is consistent with the fair value requirements of ASC 505-50; incorporates established principles of financial economic theory; and incorporates all substantive elements of the instrument. When fair value of the share-based instrument is used instead of the fair value of the item received, fair value of the share-based instrument on a specific date, referred to as the measurement date, is used as fair value. The measurement date should be the earlier of the commitment date for performance to earn the instrument, or the date that performance by the party receiving the equity instrument has been completed.

In some cases, an entity may purchase goods and services from nonemployees with an equity instrument that, under current GAAP, must be classified as a liability. Therefore, the exchange of an equity instrument is an exchange of a liability for goods and services. ASC 480-10 states the following three categories of free-standing financial instruments are classified as liabilities when certain conditions are met: mandatorily redeemable financial instruments, requirement to repurchase equity shares of the issuing company by transferring assets, and specific requirements to issue a variable number of shares.

Three examples are used to illustrate the technical aspects of stock exchanged for goods and services when the exchange is with nonemployees. Assumptions for Example 5-1 are as follows.

Example 5-1
Assumptions for Purchase of Goods with Stock

1. Johnson Enterprises (Johnson), a December 31 year-end company, purchased $500,000 of merchandise on September 10, 20X6 by exchanging 30,000 shares of $5 par value common stock.
2. A quoted market price for the stock is not currently available.
3. Johnson states that the $500,000 cost of the merchandise is a reliable measure of its value.

Because a reliable measure is not available for the common stock used in the exchange and a price is available for the merchandise, the $500,000 cost of the merchandise is the most reliable measure of fair value and should be used to record the cost of the merchandise involving the exchange of stock. Therefore, the merchandise should be recorded at $500,000, common stock at $150,000 (30,000 shares × $5 par value), and paid-in capital at $350,000 ($500,000 – $150,000). The following entry should be made on September 10 to record the purchase of merchandise:

Merchandise	500,000	
Common Stock		150,000
Paid-in Capital in Excess of Par		350,000

Example 5-2 covers a situation where common stock is issued for services. Assumptions for Example 5-2 are as follows.

Example 5-2
Assumptions for Purchase of Services with Stock

1. Financial Enterprises, a December 31 year-end company, had significant legal work performed by one attorney during 20X6 related to a patent infringement case.
2. The attorney agreed, at the beginning of the case, to accept 50,000 shares of $10 par value common stock in full payment for the legal work.
3. The 50,000 shares were distributed to the attorney on December 15, 20X6. On this date, the stock was quoted on a U.S. stock exchange for $25 per share. The average daily volume for the stock is 500,000 shares.

A quoted market price on a U.S. stock exchange is available for the common stock, and the average daily volume on the stock exchange for this stock is significantly larger than the number of shares exchanged. Therefore, the quoted market price represents a reliable measure for the cost of the legal services. Because the attorney did not provide Financial Enterprises with the cost of the legal services performed and the stock price represents a reliable fair value amount, the quoted market price of the stock is assumed to be the most reliable measure of the cost of the services. The legal costs for 20X6 should be expensed for $1,250,000 (50,000 shares × $25), the fair value of the stock on December 15,

20X6, which is the date of exchange. In addition, common stock and paid-in capital should be increased by $500,000 (50,000 × $10) and $750,000 ($1,250,000 – $500,000), respectively. The journal entry required on December 15 to record the exchange of stock for legal fees is presented as follows:

Legal Costs	1,250,000	
Common Stock		500,000
Paid-in Capital in Excess of Par		750,000

Example 5-3 covers a situation where an equity instrument is issued for services, but the equity instrument meets the requirements for liability accounting under the provisions of ASC 480-10. Assumptions for Example 5-3 are as follows.

Example 5-3
Assumptions for Purchase of Services with Stock Classified As A Liability

1. Master Enterprises, a December 31 year-end company, had significant work performed by a law firm during 20X6 at an amount equal to $100,000.

2. The law firm agreed to accept 10,000 shares of mandatorily redeemable preferred stock in full payment for the legal work. The preferred stock is related to a debt issue due in five years. The stock must be redeemed by Master Enterprises at the maturity date of the debt issue—in five years.

3. The 10,000 shares were distributed to the law firm on November 1, 20X6. There is no quoted market price for the stock.

A quoted market price is unavailable for the redeemable preferred stock, therefore, the stock does not provide a reliable measure for the cost of the legal services. Because the law firm provided Master Enterprises with a cost of the legal services performed and the stock price does not represents a reliable fair value amount, the cost of the legal services performed is assumed to be the most reliable measure of the cost of the services. The legal costs for 20X6 should be expensed for $100,000, the fair value of the legal services. In addition, the preferred stock is classified as mandatorily redeemable preferred stock because it must be redeemed at the end of the five-year loan period and reported as a liability in the 20X6 balance sheet. The journal entry required on November 1 to record the exchange of stock for legal fees is presented as follows:

Legal Costs	100,000	
Redeemable Preferred Stock		100,000

This completes the discussion of stock transactions involving parties other than employees.

CHAPTER 6
REVENUE

CONTENTS

This chapter includes the following FASB *Accounting Standards Codification* topics:

605 Revenue Recognition
606 Revenue from Contracts with Customers
610 Other Income

Topic 605: Revenue Recognition

Products—Flowchart and General Discussion

It is a very common business practice to permit the buyer of a product to return it to the seller. The right of return may exist for a wide variety of reasons. For example, the product may have been damaged or the customer may not be satisfied with its appearance or performance. In some cases, the seller may permit the buyer to return unsold products. For example, in the book publishing industry, sellers often allow purchasers to return a certain percentage of the books purchased. This practice reduces the risk of loss to the purchaser. And revenue on such sales may be recognized if the seller is able to make a reliable estimate of products to be returned.

ASC 605-15-25 provides guidance on recognizing revenue from sales of products when a right of return exists. This section outlines certain conditions that are designed to ensure that the sales transaction between the seller and purchaser is an arm's-length transaction between two independent parties. Sellers are precluded from recognizing revenue on sales transactions with parties that the sellers have established primarily for the purpose of recognizing such sales revenue.

The provisions of ASC 605-15-25 do not apply to sales transactions where products may be returned by the purchaser under a warranty arrangement nor do they apply to transactions involving real estate or leases. In addition, ASC 605-15-25 does not apply to service industry cancellation privileges.

Flowchart 6-1 depicts the criteria of ASC 605-15-25 and the resulting impact on revenue recognition. Block 1 of Flowchart 6-1 indicates that the basic transaction must involve a sale with right of return before the other provisions of ASC 605-15-25 are applicable.

Flowchart 6-1

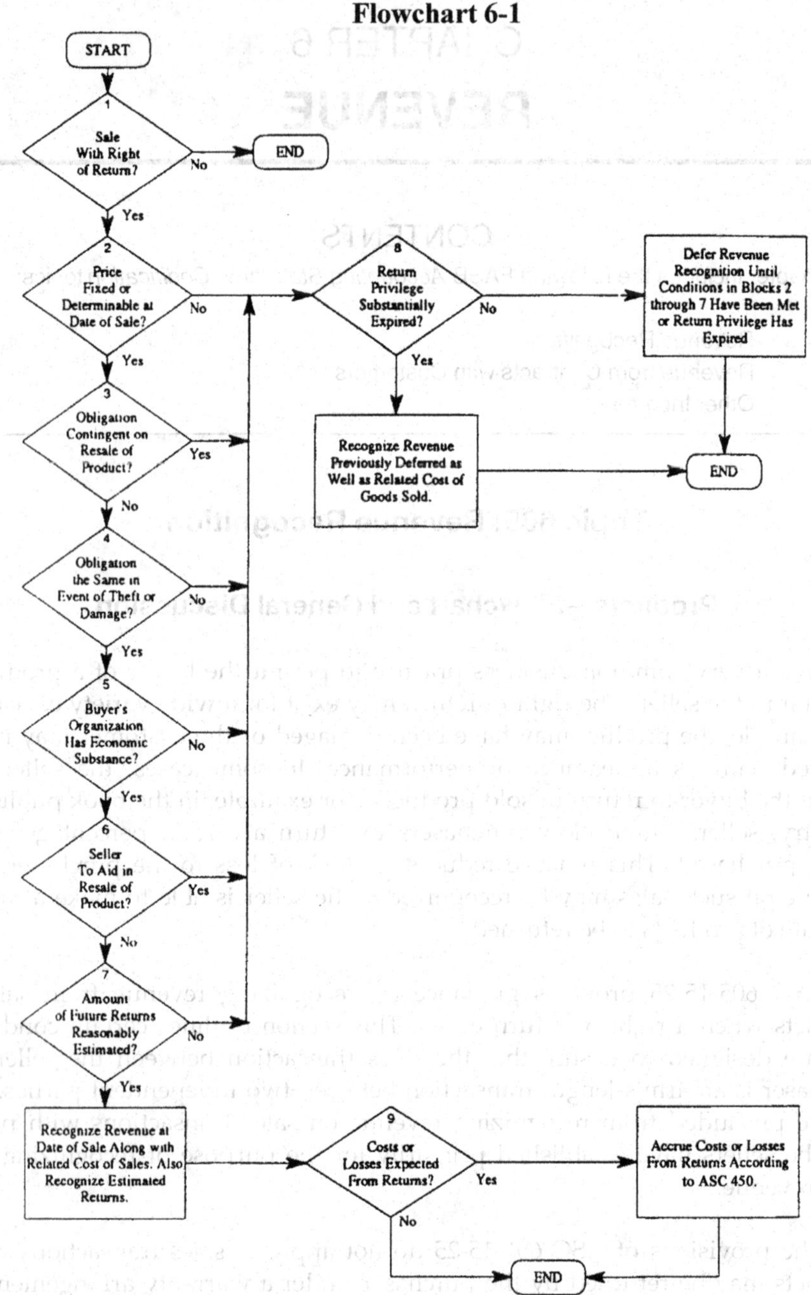

ASC 605-15-25-1 includes six conditions that must be met to recognize revenue (Blocks 2 through 7).

1. The first condition specifies that the sales price must be fixed or determinable at the date of the sale (Block 2).
2. The second condition is that, the buyer must have paid for the product purchased or have an obligation to pay that does not depend on the product being resold (Block 3). If the obligation of the purchaser to pay for the merchandise is contingent upon its subsequent resale, it would be inappropriate for the seller to recognize revenue until such time as the purchaser was obligated to pay (i.e., the product had been sold).
3. Third, the obligation of the purchaser to pay the seller must not be altered as a result of theft of the merchandise or its physical destruction (Block 4).
4. Fourth, the merchandise is the property of the purchaser, and any risk of theft or destruction must be borne by that party.
5. Fifth, the purchaser's organization must have real economic substance separate from the sale transaction in question (Block 5). This condition prohibits immediate revenue recognition from transactions with "paper" organizations that have been created merely for the purpose of facilitating revenue recognition. The fifth condition prohibits the seller from having a liability that ensures that the product will be resold (Block 6). If such an obligation exists, immediate revenue recognition is not deemed proper.
6. The sixth and final condition (Block 7) specifies that the amount of any future returns must be susceptible to reasonable estimation.

If all six conditions are met, the seller should recognize revenue from the sales transaction at the time of the sale and provide for any reasonable costs or losses associated with the sale according to the provisions of ASC 450. The conditions specified in Blocks 2 through 7 may not be met on the date of the sale but may be met subsequent to that date. If the conditions listed in Blocks 2 through 7 are met subsequent to the date of the sale, and prior to the expiration of the return privilege, revenue from the sale should be recognized on the date the identified conditions have been met.

If the agreement between the purchaser and seller fails to meet any one of the conditions listed above, revenue recognition will be postponed until the return privilege has substantially expired or all the conditions have been met (Block 8). When the right of return has expired, revenue from the transaction should be recognized. If it can be demonstrated that all the conditions specified by ASC 605-15-25-1 have been met prior to the expiration of the right of return, it would be proper to recognize revenue at the time the conditions are met.

ASC 605-15-25-1 specifies that the amount of any future returns must be susceptible to reasonable estimation before immediate revenue recognition is permitted. ASC 605-15-25-3 provides guidance in the area of estimating the future returns and specifies four situations that may impair the ability of accountants to make a reasonable estimate of the returns. These situations would include products that are subject to demand changes or technological obsolescence or products that may be returned over reasonably long periods of time. In addition, the lack of experience with products that have similar characteristics may impair an accountant's ability to make a reasonable estimate. Finally, if the volume of homogeneous transactions is not large, it may be extremely difficult to estimate the potential returns with any degree of accuracy.

Technical Considerations

To illustrate the specific accounting requirements of ASC 605-15-25, two examples are presented. Information relating Example 6-1 is presented below.

Example 6-1
Revenue Recognition When Right of Return Exists

1. Outwest Enterprises (Outwest) sells merchandise to Southmost, Inc. (Southmost), an unrelated company, on January 1, 20X6, for $50,000. The cost basis of the merchandise sold is $40,000, which is 80% of the selling price.
2. Title or ownership to the merchandise passes on January 1, the day Southmost takes possession of the merchandise.
3. Southmost is required to pay for the merchandise in 30 days. The goods may be returned anytime up to 15 days after the date of sale.
4. Outwest estimates sales returns to be 3% of net credit sales. Southmost actually returned merchandise with a selling price of $1,500.
5. Outwest utilizes a perpetual inventory system.

The first step in the accounting process is to determine if the provisions of ASC 605-15-25 are applicable to the Example 6-1 information. The basic transaction involves a sale with the right of return. In addition, the price of the merchandise is fixed at the date of the sale, and the obligation to pay is not contingent upon the sale of the merchandise by the buyer. Title to the merchandise and the risks and rewards of ownership has transferred to Southmost. The two parties are not related, and Southmost's business has economic substance beyond this particular transaction. Outwest is under no obligation to assist Southmost in the sale of the merchandise. And Outwest is in a position to make a reasonable estimate of future returns. As such, all the conditions for revenue recognition have been met under the provisions of ASC 605-15-25, and revenue will be recognized at the date of sale. If any one of the conditions had not been met, revenue recognition would have been deferred until a future date. The journal entry to record the sale and related cost of sales would be as follows:

Accounts Receivable	50,000	
Costs of Goods Sold	40,000	
Inventory		40,000
Sales		50,000

The sales agreement contains a return privilege that permits Southmost to return any or all of the merchandise purchased within 15 days of the date of the sale. Based upon past experience, Outwest would estimate that goods with a selling price of $1,500 ($50,000 sale × 3% estimated return rate) would be returned from this sales transaction. As a result, the entry to record the estimated returns would be as follows:

Sales Returns and Allowances	1,500	
Allowance for Sales Returns		1,500

In addition to this entry, the impact on inventory and cost of sales of the estimated return must be reflected in the financial statements. The impact will be disclosed by establishing an inventory adjustment account and a cost of goods sold adjustment account at the cost basis of the merchandise sold. The cost basis of the expected returns from the transaction between Outwest and Southmost is \$1,200 (\$1,500 selling price of estimated returns × 80% cost-to-sales percentage). Outwest would record the following entry to reflect the inventory and costs of goods sold adjustment accounts:

Inventory Adjustment for Estimated Returns	1,200	
Costs of Sales Adjustment for Estimated Returns		1,200

The sales returns and allowances account is a contra account to sales and would be reflected in the income statement as a reduction in sales. The allowance for sales returns is a contra asset account and would appear on the balance sheet as a reduction in accounts receivable. The inventory adjustment account would be reflected on the balance sheet as a part of inventory. And the cost of sales adjustment account would be reflected on the income statement as a reduction of cost of sales.

The last step in Example 6-1 is to account for the merchandise actually returned by Southmost. The selling price of the goods returned amounted to \$1,500. Outwest needs to reduce the previously established contra sales account and contra receivable account for the selling price of the merchandise returned. The journal entry to accomplish this reduction would be as follows:

Allowance for Sales Returns	1,500	
Accounts Receivable		1,500

The cost of sales and the contra cost of sales account must be reduced for the cost of the merchandise returned. The cost basis of the merchandise returned is \$1,200 (\$1,500 × 80% cost-to-sales percentage). Finally, the returned merchandise must be returned to inventory, and the inventory adjustment account must be reduced for the cost of the merchandise returned. The journal entry required would be:

Inventory	1,200	
Cost of Sales Adjustment for Estimated Returns	1,200	
Cost of Goods Sold		1,200
Inventory Adjustment for Estimated Returns		1,200

If Outwest is unable to resell the returned merchandise at a price equal to or greater than the original selling price, a loss would be accrued. Accounting for the potential loss should be made at the date of the *original sale* in accordance with the provisions of ASC 450.

The journal entries shown above are meant to be illustrative; the account titles used in a particular situation may vary, and the periodic inventory system would require the use of other accounts not shown above.

The purpose of Example 6-2 is to demonstrate the proper accounting for revenue when it is not recognized at the date of sale. Information for Example 6-2 is presented below.

Example 6-2
Revenue Recognition When Right of Return Exists

1. On January 1, 20X6, Palmer Enterprises sells merchandise to Miller, Inc. for $200,000. The cost basis of the merchandise sold is $170,000.
2. Miller, Inc. is required to pay for the merchandise in 20 days. The merchandise may be returned for up to 30 days after the date of the sale.
3. All conditions for recognition of revenue at the time of sale are *not* met. In addition, the conditions are *not* met prior to the expiration of the return period.
4. Palmer Enterprises uses the perpetual inventory method of accounting for its inventory.

In Example 6-2, Palmer Enterprises sells merchandise with the right of return, but all the conditions have not been met for immediate revenue recognition. Refer to Flowchart 6-1, Blocks 2 through 7, to review the necessary conditions for immediate revenue recognition. In this example, revenue from the sale and the related cost of goods sold must be deferred until some future date. The journal entry needed to reflect the transaction would be as follows:

Accounts Receivable	200,000	
Deferred Cost of Goods Sold	170,000	
Unearned Revenue		200,000
Inventory		170,000

The deferred cost of goods sold account should be classified as a current asset, and the unearned revenue is properly classified as a current liability. These accounts will remain unchanged until all the conditions specified by ASC 605-15-25-1 have been met or the return privilege has expired. In the example given, the conditions are never met; and, at the end of 30 days, the right of return will expire. At the end of the return period, the following journal entry is needed to reflect the sale and cost of sales:

Unearned Revenue	200,000	
Cost of Goods Sold	170,000	
Sales Revenue		200,000
Deferred Cost of Goods Sold		170,000

Sales and cost of sales should be recognized at the earlier of the date that all conditions for recognition of revenue are met or the date of expiration of the return privilege. In Example 6-2, the return privilege expired before all the conditions for revenue recognition had been met.

Services

ASC 605-20 addresses accounting for revenues from extended warranties and product maintenance agreements that are priced separately from the price of the product, among other service arrangements. Generally, revenues from warranty or product maintenance contracts should be deferred and recognized as income over the life of the contract using a straight-line method. A method other than straight-line may be used for revenue recognition when an entity can provide evidence that the pattern of costs incurred under the contract is not on a straight-line basis. An entity should recognize a loss on extended warranty and product maintenance contracts when a loss is indicated. A loss is indicated when all future expenses, including those that are deferred, exceed the estimated future revenues. For purposes of determining losses, expenses and revenue from the contract are computed by aggregating the contract in some consistent manner. If a loss is indicated, any unamortized deferred cost is charged to expense, and a liability is recorded for any loss in excess of the deferred costs.

Multiple-Element Arrangements

ASC 605-25 discusses revenue recognition issues when there are multiple deliverables by an entity to its customers, such as multiple products, performances, or services that may be delivered at different times.

Milestone Method

ASC 605-28 provides guidance on the application of the milestone method of revenue recognition in arrangements that include research or development deliverables.

Long-Term Contracts

ASC 605-35 contains accounting and reporting requirements for long-term construction contracts (hereinafter referred to as long-term contracts). Accounting for long-term contracts applies to entities that are involved in the contracting business.

Two methods are available to entities in accounting for long-term contracts: (1) the completed contract method; and (2) the percentage-of-completion method.

Under the completed contract method, income is reported on the completion date of the contract or when the contract is substantially complete. Because no income is reported prior to the completion of the contract, generally costs are accumulated, but not recognized, until income is reported. However, should a loss be anticipated on a long-term contract, the loss should be reported in the accounting period in which it is determined that a loss will occur. When using the completed contract method, costs incurred are accumulated and offset against the billings on the contract. If the accumulated costs exceed the billings, a current asset is reported in the statement of financial position for the excess. When billings exceed accumulated costs, a liability is reported for the excess. The liability generally is classified as a current item. When an entity has more than one long-term contract and some contracts have billings in excess of costs and other contracts have costs in excess of billings, each group of contracts (i.e., those with billings in excess of costs and those with costs in excess of billings) are aggregated for presentation purposes in the statement of financial position.

When an entity uses the percentage-of-completion method, income is reported as work is performed on the contract. The amount of income that should be reported each accounting period is based on one of the following methods.

1. Income is computed by multiplying the estimated total income by the following percentage: cost incurred during the current accounting period divided by the total estimated costs to be incurred for the contract. Costs included in the percentage determination should include all costs that provide a meaningful income allocation.
2. Any other method that might be appropriate if it reflects progress toward completion considering the work completed to date.

If in any accounting period, a loss on the entire contract is indicated, the loss should be recognized. When billings exceed costs and reported profit, a liability should be reported for the excess. Generally, the liability is classified as a current item. When costs and reported profit exceed billings, a current asset is reported for the excess. Contracts are aggregated for presentation purposes in the same manner as discussed above for contracts accounted for using the completed contract method.

Principal-Agent Considerations

ASC 605-45 addresses whether an entity should record revenue using a gross approach (i.e., principal) or net approach (i.e., agent).

Under the gross approach, an entity reports revenue equal to an amount that was billed to the customer (e.g., it recognizes sales and cost of sales). Under the net approach, the entity reports net revenue (e.g., commissions).

There are eight indicators that may support the use of the gross approach by the selling entity, as follows:

1. The entity is the primary obligor responsible for providing the product or service.
2. The entity has the unmitigated general inventory risk (i.e., it has the risks and rewards of ownership).
3. The entity has latitude in establishing the selling price.
4. The entity changes the product or performs part of the service.
5. The entity has discretion in the selection of the supplier.
6. The entity is involved in the determination of the product or service specifications.
7. The entity assumes the risk of the physical loss of inventory after the customer orders the product or during shipping.
8. The entity assumes the credit risk.

There are three indicators that may support the use of the net approach by the selling entity, as follows:

1. The entity's supplier is the primary obligor responsible for providing the product or service.
2. The amount the entity earns is fixed.
3. The supplier assumes the credit risk.

Reimbursements for out-of-pocket expenses incurred. ASC 605-45-45 specifies that reimbursements for out-of-pocket expenses should be reported as revenue in the income statement.

Shipping and handling costs. Under ASC 605-45-45, shipping and handling costs billed to customers should be classified as revenue in the income statement. Further, shipping and handling costs incurred by the seller should be classified in accordance with a designated accounting policy (such as included in cost of sales) and disclosed in accordance with the provisions of ASC 235 along with the line item in the income statement and the amount. Shipping and handling costs incurred should not be deducted from revenues.

Taxes collected from customers. Under ASC 605-45-50 taxes collected from customers and remitted to government authorities may be reported on either a gross or net basis. Taxes collected from customers may include sales taxes, value added taxes, and use taxes. The accounting policy elected by the entity should be disclosed in accordance with ASC 235. If the entity follows the gross method, it should disclose the amount of such taxes for each period for which an income statement is presented.

Participants in a collaborative arrangement (as defined in ASC 808-10) should report revenue earned and costs incurred from sales to third parties in accordance with ASC 605-45. In general, the party to the collaborative arrangement that is classified as the principal participant should report transactions on a gross basis. However, if other authoritative accounting requirements apply to payments related to collaborative arrangements, those requirements should be used. Other issues, including disclosure requirements for collaborative arrangements, are discussed under Topic 808 in Chapter 8.

Topic 606: Revenue from Contracts with Customers

Topic 606, *Revenue Recognition*, contains a single subtopic—10 Overall. Under that subtopic are the following topics:

05 General

10 Objectives

15 Scope and Scope Exceptions

25 Recognition

32 Measurement

45 Other Presentation Matters

50 Disclosure

55 Implementation Guidance and Illustrations

60 Costs Related to a Contract with a Customer

65 Transition and Open Effective Date Information

Overview of New Topic 606

ASU 2014-09, *Revenue from Contracts with Customers*, supersedes most of the previous revenue recognition requirements in ASC 605, *Revenue Recognition*. ASU 2014-09 applies to sellers' contracts to provide goods or services to customers and created new ASC Topic 606.

ASU 2014-09 is intended to:

- Remove inconsistencies and weaknesses under ASC Topic 605;
- Provide a more robust framework to address revenue;
- Improve comparability among entities and industries;
- Require more useful information and improved disclosures; and
- Simplify financial statement preparation by reducing the number of requirements.

Excluded, as amended, from the scope of ASU 2014-09 (ASC 606) are:

- Lease contracts,
- All contracts within the scope of ASC 944, *Financial Services—Insurance*,
- Financial instruments and other contractual rights or obligations that are within the scope of other ASC topics,
- Guarantees but not product or service guarantees, that are within the scope of other ASC topics (ASC 460 and 815), and
- Nonmonetary exchanges between sellers in the same business to facilitate sales to customers.

Some contracts may be within scope of ASC 606 and other ASC topics (e.g., a lease with a specified service). In such situations, the other ASC topics should be applied first if they specify how to separate and/or initially measure parts of a contract before applying ASC 606.

ASU 2014-09 may affect several financial statement line items in the selling entity's financial statements, including:

- Sales, accounts receivable, contract assets and contract liabilities (including refunds due customers for the amounts and the timing of revenue recognition), and performance obligations;
- Other assets for contract-acquisition costs;
- Income taxes on additional temporary differences;
- Selling, general, and administrative costs for commissions and bonuses based on sales; and
- Interest income and/or interest expense on the financing component of contract

Effective Dates, As Amended

The effective dates of ASU 2014-09 were amended by ASU 2015-14, *Revenue from Contracts with Customers (Topic 606): Deferral of the Effective Date*.

For public entities, as amended, the new revenue standards are required for annual reporting periods beginning after December 15, 2017, including interim reporting periods within that reporting period. Regardless, public entities are permitted to adopt the new revenue standards for annual reporting periods beginning after December 15, 2016, including interim reporting periods within that reporting period, under the original effective date. Any earlier application is not permitted.

For nonpublic entities the new revenue standards are required for annual reporting periods beginning after December 15, 2018, and interim reporting periods within annual reporting periods beginning after December 15, 2019. Regardless, nonpublic entities are permitted to adopt the new revenue standards for annual reporting periods beginning after December 15, 2016, including interim reporting periods within that reporting period, under the original effective date. Any earlier application is not permitted

Key Terms

Some key terms under ASC 606 follow:

- Contract—An agreement that creates enforceable rights and obligations
- Contract asset—A right to consideration in exchange for goods or services that the seller has transferred to a customer
- Contract liability—A seller's obligation to transfer goods or services to a customer for which the seller has received consideration (or the amount is due) from the customer
- Performance obligation—A seller's promise in the contract to provide distinct goods or services
- Revenue—An inflow of assets from ongoing or central operations of delivering or producing goods or services
- Standalone selling price—The price for the specific goods or services
- Transaction price—The consideration a seller expects to be entitled to in exchange for transferring promised goods or services

Core Principle

Underlying ASU 2014-09 is the following core principle:

> Recognize revenue to depict the transfer of promised goods or services to customers in an amount that reflects the consideration to which the selling entity expects to be entitled to receive in exchange for those goods or services.

Steps to Recognizing Revenue

There are five steps to applying the core principle under ASC 606 as follows:

1. Identify the existence of a contract with customer.
2. Identify the separate performance obligation(s) [or promise(s)].
3. Determine the transaction price.
4. Allocate the transaction price to performance obligations.
5. Recognize revenue as each performance obligation is satisfied.

Step 1: Identify the Contract

The definition of a contract is based on the common legal definition of contract in the United States. A contract creates enforceable rights and obligations. A contract may be written, oral, or evidenced otherwise (e.g., an electronic offer/acceptance). Examples of a contract may include an electronic "Add to cart"; a formal executed document; an accepted PO; or past business practices, among others.

A contract exists if it:

1. Has commercial substance (i.e., cash flows result from contract);
2. Has been approved by both parties, and both parties are committed to satisfying their obligations;
3. Identifies each party's rights regarding the goods or services to be transferred;
4. Identifies the payment terms (even if amount is uncertain); and
5. It is probable that the vendor/seller will collect the consideration it will be entitled to in exchange for the goods or services transferred to the customer.

ASU 2014-09 applies only if all of the above 5 criteria are met.

A contract does not exist if:

- The buyer or seller many terminate contract without compensating the other party, and/or
- The collectability from the customer is not probable when due.

If the agreement (contract) meets the criteria to apply ASU 2014-09 at inception, then no reassessment is required unless there is a significant change in the facts/circumstances, e.g., the customer's ability to pay deteriorates significantly

If the agreement does not meet the criteria to apply ASU 2014-09, then the seller/vendor continues to reassess subsequent facts and circumstances to determine if the criteria are met.

A seller accounts for consideration received from a customer when there is no contract as a liability until the required criteria under ASU 2014-09 are met. Ultimately the seller would recognize the consideration received as revenue only when the seller has no remaining obligations to transfer goods/services and substantially all consideration has been received from the customer and is nonrefundable. ASU 2016-12, *Revenue from Contracts with Customers (Topic 606): Narrow-Scope Improvements and Practical Expedients*, clarifies that the seller recognizes revenue in such circumstances to be the amount of consideration received when the seller has transferred control of the goods or services, the seller has stopped transferring goods or services (if applicable) and has no obligation under the contract to transfer additional goods or services, and the consideration received from the customer is nonrefundable.

So under ASU 2014-09, collectability is a factor when determining whether a valid contract exists, whereas collectability of consideration must be reasonably assured for revenue to be recognized under the ASC prior to the effective date of ASU 2014-09. Under ASU 2016-12, the objective of the collectability assessment is to determine whether the contract is valid and represents a substantive transaction on the basis of whether a customer has the ability and intention to pay the promised consideration in exchange for the goods or services that will be transferred to the customer.

When one party to a contract has performed, but not the other, a contract asset or contract liability is presented in the seller's balance sheet.

A contract asset is the seller's right to consideration for the goods or services. The seller's unconditional right to receive consideration for the goods or services is as an account receivable. Accounts receivable are shown separately from contract assets in the seller's balance sheet.

A contract liability is the seller's obligation to transfer goods or services to the customer for which consideration has been received (or amount is due).

An example of a transaction resulting in a contract asset and liability follows:

Assume that on January 1, a seller enters into a non-cancellable contract to transfer a product to a customer on March 31. The contract requires the customer to pay the cash consideration of $1,000 in advance on January 31. The customer pays on February 15 and the seller transfers the product on March 31.

What entries would the seller make?

January 31		
Accounts receivable	$1,000	
Contract liability		$1,000
February 15		
Cash	1,000	
Accounts receivable		1,000
March 31		
Contract liability	1,000	
Contract sales		1,000

Assume the same facts as above, except that the contract was cancellable. What entries would the seller make?

January 31		
No entry.		
February 15		
Cash	$1,000	
Contract liability		$1,000
March 31		
Contract liability	1,000	
Contract sales		1,000

A portfolio, rather than a contract-by-contract, approach may be used for a large number of contracts when:

- The contracts and their underlying performance obligations have similar characteristic;
- The effects on the financial statements will not differ materially; and
- The estimates and/or assumptions reflect the size and composition of the portfolio.

An example of the portfolio approach follows.

The seller enters into 100 contracts with different customers. Each contract includes the sale of a single product for $100. The seller collects cash upon the transfer of control of the product to the customer. The seller customarily permits a customer to return any unused product within 30 days and receive a full refund. The seller applies the portfolio approach because it reasonably expects that the effects on its financial statements of applying the portfolio approach would not differ materially from applying revenue recognition standards on a contract by contract basis.

Combining Contracts

A seller should combine two or more contracts entered into at or near the same time with same customer (or related parties of the customer) and account for them as single contract if:

- The contracts are negotiated as package with a single commercial objective; or
- The amount of consideration to be paid under one contract depends on price or performance on the other contract; or
- The goods/services promised in the contracts are a single performance obligation.

Contract Modifications

A contract modification may change the contract scope or price or both. Once approved by the parties to the contract the modification creates new or changes existing enforceable rights/obligations. A modification may be approved in writing, orally, or implied by customary business practices.

A contract modification may result in a dispute about scope and price. If so, the seller should continue to apply ASU 2014-09 to the approved, existing contract until approval of the modification. If the modification is approved as to the change in scope, but not price, then the seller should estimate the price using the guidance on estimating variable consideration and constraining estimates of variable consideration as discussed under Step 3 below.

The seller accounts for a contract modification as a separate contract if the contract scope increases with the addition of a distinct promised good or service and the price increases by the standalone selling price of that new good or service. The concept of a distinct good or service is discussed under Step 2 below.

If the contract modifications do not result in a separate contract, the seller accounts for the additional goods or services not yet transferred (i.e., the remaining promised goods or services) at date of the contract modification using one of three options based on the facts and circumstances as follows:

1. As a termination of existing contract and creation of new contract;
2. As a continuation of existing contract; or
3. As a combination of the two.

Option 1: The seller allocates consideration to distinct remaining goods/services as sum of the promised consideration included in the estimated transaction price not yet recognized from original contract (including any deferred revenue) and the additional promised consideration from the modification.

Option 2: The seller reflects the effect of the modification on a cumulative catch-up basis to the revenue at date of contract modification.

Option 3: The seller considers the remaining goods or services as a combination of Options 1 and 2. Further, the seller accounts for effects on unsatisfied obligations consistent with the objectives of the other two options as relevant.

An example of applying Options 1 and 2 follows.

Seller enters into a contract to provide services over three years for $100 a year, payable at the beginning of the year. In year 3, after the payment of $100 for that year, the contract is renegotiated (modified). As modified, the contract is extended for an additional three years at $80 a year. The table below shows the effects of applying, as appropriate based on the facts and circumstances, Option 1 or Option 2. Option 1 assumes the services are distinct and the modification is accounted for prospectively. Option 2 assumes the services are not distinct and the modification is accounted for as a cumulative catch-up.

	Cash	Revenue Recognized	
Year	Collected	Option 1	Option 2
1	$ 100	$ 100	$ 100
2	100	100	100
3	100	80	60
4	60	80	87
5	80	80	87
6	80	80	86
Total	$ 520	$ 520	$ 520

Two examples of contract modifications for additional goods follow. In Example 6-3, the price for the additional goods reflects their standalone selling price. In Example 6-4, the price for the additional goods does not reflect their standalone selling price.

Example 6-3
Price for Additional Products Reflects Their Standalone Price

Under a contract, the seller promises to sell 100 products to customer for $12,000 ($100 per product).The products are transferred at various points in time over six-months. The contract is modified after 75 products have been transferred. As modified, the seller promises to deliver an additional 25 products (i.e., 125 products in total) for an additional $2,375 ($95 per product).

The pricing for the additional products reflects their standalone selling price at the time of the contract modification. The additional products are distinct from the original products because the seller regularly sells such products separately.

Conclusion: The contract modification for the additional 25 products is, in effect, a new and separate contract and the performance obligation with the customer for future products does not affect the accounting for the existing contract.

Example 6-4
Price for Additional Products Does Not Reflect Their Standalone Price

Assume the same facts as in Example 6-3, above, except that the standalone price for the additional products is $100 rather than $95 per product. Because the pricing for the additional products does not reflect their standalone selling price, the seller would allocate the modified transaction price (less the amounts allocated to products transferred at or before the date of the modification) to all of the remaining products to be transferred.

As such, the amount recognized as revenue for each of the remaining products would be a blended price of $97.50 per product determined as follows:

$100 × 25 products not yet transferred under original contract plus

$95 × 25 products to be transferred under the contract modification
÷ 50 remaining products equals a blended $97.50 per product.

Step 2: Identify the Separate Performance Obligation(s)

The seller's performance obligation is the seller's promise to transfer (provide) a distinct good or service to the customer. That promise may be explicit, implicit, or implied by seller's customary business practice.

ASU 2016-10, *Revenue from Contracts with Customers (Topic 606): Identifying Performance Obligations and Licensing,* provides guidance that a seller is not required to assess whether promised goods or services are performance obligations if they are immaterial in the context of the contract with the customer.

A promise may be a bundle of goods or services, or a series of them, that are substantially the same and have the same pattern of transference to the customer. Examples of performance obligations include: (1) a contract to sell and install specialized equipment; (2) a contract to design, procure, and construct a building; and (3) a contract for cleaning services.

A good or service is distinct if:

- It is separately identifiable from other promises in the contract, and
- The customer can benefit from the good or service either on its own or together with other readily available goods or services.

Factors to consider in determining whether the good or service is separately identifiable include:

- Whether or not the good or service is an input to produce or deliver an output specified by customer. (A good or service is not separately identifiable if it is an input to an output.)
- Whether or not the good or service does or does not significantly modify another good/service. (A good or service is not separately identifiable it if significantly modifies another good or service.)
- Whether or not the good or service is highly dependent on or otherwise interrelated with other goods and services. (A good or service is not separately identifiable if it is highly dependent on or otherwise interrelated with other goods or services.)

A seller accounts for a bundle of promises to provide goods/services as a single performance obligation if the risks of transferring the goods/providing the services are inseparable, that is:

- The goods/services are highly interrelated, and the seller provides a significant integration service to provide a combined item; and
- The seller significantly modifies the goods/services as negotiated specifically with the customer.

The seller accounts for all other bundled goods/services performance obligations separately if:

- They are distinct; and
- They have different patterns of risks associated with transferring them among the goods/services in the contract with the customer.

Contracts with customers typically state the goods/services the seller promises to transfer to the customer. Implicit promises can also create valid expectations by customers that the seller will transfer goods/services at the time of entering into contract based on the seller's:

- Customary business practices;
- Published policies; and
- Specific statements.

An example of an implicit promise follows.

The seller has historically provided maintenance service for no additional consideration to end customers that purchase its product. The seller does not explicitly promise maintenance service during the negotiations, and final contract does not specify such service. Since the seller has established a customary business practice, the customer has a valid expectation of such service. The customary business practice is an implicit promise to provide maintenance service. As such, the seller identifies the implicit promise to provide maintenance service as a performance obligation and allocates a portion of transaction price to it which is discussed below under Step 4.

If a good/service is not distinct, it is combined with other goods/services until a bundle of goods/services is distinct. Such combining could result in the seller accounting for all of the goods/services in a contract as a single performance obligation.

The seller accounts for a series of distinct goods or services as a single performance obligation if:

- Each distinct good/service in the series has a similar pattern of transfer and is considered to be a performance obligation satisfied over time (e.g., cleaning service); and
- The same method would be used to measure the seller's progress toward completely satisfying its performance obligation to transfer each distinct good or service in the series to the customer.

Two examples of identifying the separate performance obligations under Step 2 follow:

Example 6-5
Whether Software Company Has a Single Performance Obligation

A software company (seller) licenses time management software to a customer. It also promises to provide consulting services to that customer to customize the software to the customer's specifications. As negotiated, the software requires significant customization.

Question: Does the software company have a single performance obligation?

Answer: Since the software company is providing a significant service integrating the goods (software) and services (consulting) it would account for the software goods and consulting services as a single performance obligation.

Example 6-6
Contractor's Accounting for the Goods and Services to Be Provided

A general contractor enters into a contract to design and build an office building. The contractor is responsible for the overall management of the project and identifies the various goods and services to be provided, including engineering, site work, foundation work, procurement of materials, construction of the structure, installation of certain specified equipment, and finishing.

Questions: How would the contractor account for the goods and services to be provided under the contract? Why?

Answer: The contractor would account for the goods and services to be provided as a single performance obligation since they are highly interrelated and require significant integration into a single product output (i.e., the office building). Further, all the goods and services transferred and services provided are significantly modified and customized to fulfill the contract.

Step 3: Determine the Contract Price

The contract's transaction price is the amount of consideration the seller is reasonably assured to be entitled to receive in exchange for transferring or providing the promised goods or services.

The transaction price may include fixed and/or variable (uncertain) amounts. Variable consideration may be explicitly stated in contract. Variable amounts may relate to discounts, customer rebates, incentives, performance bonuses/penalties, price concessions, refunds, credits, etc. The amount of variable consideration is dependent on the occurrence/nonoccurrence of future event. ASU 2016-12 clarifies that the variable consideration guidance applies only to variability resulting from reasons other than the form of the consideration.

Consideration is also variable if the customer has a valid expectation of a price concession based on the seller's:

- Customary business practices, published policies, or specific statements that the seller will accept an amount less than stated contract price; or
- On other facts and circumstances that indicate the seller's intention when entering into the contract its intent to offer a price concession to the customer.

Some portion of consideration received by the seller may be a liability (e.g., an advance deposit, a refund liability, or a contract liability). (A contract liability is discussed separately below.)

The seller estimates the variable amount to be included in the transaction price using a method that is most predictive of the outcome. Two estimation methods are available as follows:

1. Expected value method (i.e., probability-weighted amount).
2. The most likely amount method.

Expected Value Method

The expected value method reflects the sum of the probability-weighted amounts within a range of possible consideration amounts. This method is generally used when there are a large number of possible outcomes.

Most Likely Amount Method

The most likely amount method reflects the single most likely amount in a range of possible consideration amounts (i.e., the most likely outcome). This method is used when the contract has only two possible outcomes (i.e., the seller will either earn a performance bonus or not).

Estimates of variable consideration reflect certain constraints. Specifically, the seller would not include in an estimate of the transaction price any amount that is so uncertain that it may not faithfully depict the consideration the seller will ultimately be entitled to receive. Also, the seller would only include as variable consideration in the transaction price an amount only to the extent that a significant reversal in the amount of cumulative revenue recognized will not occur when the uncertainty associated with variable consideration is ultimately resolved. In summary, sellers will generally recognize more revenue sooner under ASU 2014-09.

An example of the accounting for variable consideration for a volume discount incentive follows.

Seller enters into a contract with a customer to sell it Product G for $100 a unit. If the customer purchases more than 500 units of Product G in a calendar year, the price per unit is retroactively reduced to $90 per unit (a volume rebate).

For the first quarter ended March 31, 20X1, the seller sells 50 units of Product G to the customer and estimates that the customer's purchases will not exceed the 500-unit threshold required for the volume rebate in the calendar year. Therefore, the seller recognizes revenue of $5,000 (50 units × $100 per unit) for the period ending March 31, 20X1, because the seller is reasonably assured to be entitled to that amount.

In June 20X1, the seller's customer triples its sales capacity. As a result, the seller now estimates that the customer's purchases of Product G will exceed the 500-unit threshold for the calendar year. For the second quarter ended June 30, 20X1, the seller sells an additional 300 units of Product G to the customer.

Question: How much revenue would the seller recognize in the quarter ended June 30, 20X1? How much was billed in that quarter?

Answer: The seller recognizes revenue of $26,500 for the quarter ended June 30, 20X1, determined as follows:

$27,000 for the sale of 300 units (300 units × $90 per unit) less $500 (50 units × $10 price reduction) for the reduction of revenue relating to units sold for the quarter ended March 31. The entity is reasonably assured to be entitled to $11,500

Billed: 300 units x $100 = $30,000

The transaction price does not include estimates of consideration from the future exercise of options for additional goods/services or future change orders.

Time Value of Money

The seller discounts the transaction price only if there is a significant financing component. Judgment is required. The seller considers:

- Whether the cash price is substantially different from aggregate amount of payments.
- The difference between the timing of the transfer of the good(s) or service(s) and their payment. (Generally, as a specified practical expedient, the seller would not discount the contract price if payment is expected within one year from the transfer.)
- Whether the difference between the interest rate in the contract and the market interest rate is significant.

Any interest income or expense from the financing component of the contract is shown separately from revenue from contracts with customers in the income statement.

An example of applying the time value of money to a transaction without and with financing follows.

The seller enters into a contract to transfer control of equipment to the customer upon the execution of the contract by both parties. The contract price for the equipment is $500,000, payable in monthly installments of $9,666, including interest at 6% for five years. Assume the contractual rate of interest is indicative of the market rate for the credit worthiness of the customer. As such, the market terms of the transaction indicate that the cash selling price of the equipment is $500,000. And, the seller would recognize sales (revenue) and a loan receivable for that amount. Interest at 6% would be accrued and recognized separately from sales on the loan receivable

However, assume that an interest of 12% would be more indicative of the credit worthiness of the customer. As such, the cash selling price of the equipment would be $434,535. (Sixty monthly payments of $9,666 discounted at 12%.) And, the seller would recognize sales (revenue) and a loan receivable for that amount. Interest at 12% would be accrued and recognized separately from sales on the loan receivable

A significant financing component does not exist if:

- The customer paid in advance, and the timing of transfer of the good/service is at customer's discretion.
- A substantial amount of the consideration is variable, and amount or timing of collection varies based on the occurrence or nonoccurrence of a future event that is not substantially within control of either the customer or seller.
- The difference between the consideration and cash selling price arises for reasons other than providing financing to either the customer or seller, and the difference between the amounts is proportional to reason for difference.

An example of the latter condition follows.

A contractor enters into a contract for the construction of a building. The contract specifies that the customer will retain 5% of each payment. Such retainage will be paid to the contractor only when the building is complete. If the retainage is intended to protect the customer from the contractor failing to adequately complete some or all of its obligations under the contract rather than to provide financing, the contractor will likely conclude that the contract does not include a significant financing component and, therefore, will not reflect the time value of money in the transaction price.

Refund Liability

The seller may receive consideration but expects to refund some or all of it to the customer. The portion of the amount received [or receivable] that is expected to be refunded is not included in transaction price and is shown as a liability. That liability is updated each reporting period for changes in circumstances. An example follows of a refund liability resulting from a right of return.

The seller enters into 100 contracts to sell 100 units of Product A to several individual customers for $100 each. The cost per unit is $60. The seller simultaneously transfers the product and collects the consideration in cash. Under the contracts, the customer may return any unused product for any reason within 30 days for a full refund. Based on historical information, three products are expected to be returned and re-sold at the normal selling price. The seller makes the following entry, which recognizes a liability for the expected refund.

Cash (100 units x $100 a unit)	$10,000	
Refund liability (3 units x $100 a unit)		$300
Sales (97 units x $100 a unit)		9,700
Cost of sales (97 units x $60 a unit)	5,820	
Inventory (100 units x $60 a unit)		6,000
Contract asset* (3 units X $60 a unit)	180	

In some cases, the seller may receive noncash consideration under the contract with the customer. The seller measures such consideration at its fair value. ASU 2016-12 specifies that the measurement date for noncash consideration is the contract inception date. If the fair value cannot be reasonably estimated directly, then its fair value is measured indirectly by reference to standalone selling prices of goods or services promised. If a customer contributes goods/services (e.g., materials or labor) to facilitate the fulfillment of contract, the seller assesses whether it obtains control of those contributed goods/services. If the seller obtains control, then the seller accounts for contributed goods/services as noncash consideration.

Step 4: Allocate the Transaction Price

The allocation of the transaction price to the performance obligations should depict the amount the seller is reasonably assured to be entitled to receive in exchange for satisfying each separate performance obligation. The seller's allocation reflects standalone prices, discounts, contingent consideration, etc. Judgment is required to select the best method of allocation. The seller uses standalone selling prices of the goods or services, or estimates them, if necessary, as of the contract's inception. Any subsequent changes in transaction price are allocated in the period of change using the same basis as at the contract's inception.

The standalone price is the price the seller would sell the goods/services separately to customer at the contract's inception. Observable standalone prices are those that are contractually stated or the list price.

Estimation methods used by the seller to determine the selling price include:

- Cost plus margin,
- Adjusted market, and
- Residual technique.

The adjusted market method reflects the amount the customer is willing to pay or a competitor's price.

The residual technique method is used for highly variable selling price.

Discounts are allocated entirely to one or more performance obligations if:

- The seller regularly sells each good/service (or each bundle of goods/services) in the contract on a standalone basis;
- The seller also regularly sells on a standalone basis bundles of some of those distinct goods/services at a discount;
- The discount attributable to each bundle is substantially the same as the discount in contract; and
- An analysis of the goods/services in each bundle provides observable evidence of performance obligations to which the entire discount in the contract belongs.

An example of allocating a discount to the performance obligations under the contract follows.

The seller enters into a contract with a customer to sell products X, Y, and Z for $45. The seller regularly sells those products on a standalone basis as follows:

Product X	$ 10
Product Y	15
Product Z	25
Total	$ 50

Question: How would you allocate the discount?

Answer: The customer receives a $5 discount ($50, the sum of standalone selling prices – $45 transaction price) for buying the bundle of three products. The discount would be allocated based on the relative selling prices.

However, assume Products X and Y are regularly sold as a bundle and transferred at the same time. As such, the seller then accounts for two separate performance obligations: (1) Products X and Y combined; and (2) the Product Z.

If the seller regularly sells Products X and Y for $20 (i.e., at a $5 discount) and regularly sells Product Z for $25, then the seller has observable prices as evidence that the $5 discount in the contract should be allocated solely to Products X and Y.

Therefore, the seller would allocate the transaction price of $45 as follows:

Product X and Y	$ 20
Product Z	25
Total	$ 45

The seller allocates the variable amount of consideration (and subsequent changes) entirely to a performance obligation, or to a distinct good/service that forms part of a single performance obligation, if:

- The terms of the variable payment relate specifically to the seller's efforts to satisfy the performance obligation or transfer a distinct good/service; and

- Allocating the variable amount entirely is consistent with the objective to depict the amount of consideration the seller expects to be entitled to when considering all performance obligations and the payment terms in contract.

Changes in the contract price are allocated on the same basis as at contract inception. The amounts allocated to a satisfied performance obligation recognized as revenue (or reduction of revenue) are allocated in period in which transaction price changes. The seller does not reallocate the transaction price to reflect changes in the standalone selling prices after the contract's inception.

Step 5: Recognize Revenue

Revenue is recognized when (or as) the seller satisfies each performance obligation. A performance obligation is satisfied by transferring goods/services. The transfer occurs when (or as) the customer obtains control of the goods/ services either at a point in time or over time.

Control is the ability to direct use of and obtain substantially all remaining benefits from an asset. Control includes the ability to prevent others from directing the use of and/or obtaining the benefits from the asset, which is sometimes referred to as "defensive control." Control considers any agreement to repurchase the promised asset or any component thereof.

Indicators that a customer obtains control of a promised asset at a point in time include the following:

- The seller has the present right to receive payment for the asset.
- The customer has legal title to the asset.
- The seller has transferred physical possession of the asset.
- The customer has the significant risks and rewards of ownership of the asset.
- The customer has accepted the asset.

Not all of the indicators need to be present to demonstrate that the customer has control. Judgment is required.

An example of satisfying a performance obligation and recognizing revenue at a point in time follows.

Seller enters into a contract to sell band instruments to a customer. The delivery terms include free on board (FOB) shipping point. The seller uses a third-party carrier to deliver the product.

In accordance with the seller's past business practices for this customer, it will provide the customer with a replacement band instrument, at no additional cost, if it is damaged or lost while in transit. This arrangement has been commonly referred to as a "synthetic FOB destination." The seller has determined that its past business practices of replacing damaged band instruments has implicitly created a performance obligation.

Question: How many performance obligations are there?

Answer: The seller has two performance obligations: (1) to provide the customer with a band instrument, and (2) to cover the risk of loss during transit.

Question: When does the customer obtain control of the band instruments?

Answer: The customer obtains control of the band instruments at the point of shipment. Even though it does not have physical possession of them at that point, it does have legal title and, therefore, can sell the instruments to or exchange them with another party. Also, the seller is precluded from selling the band instruments to another customer.

In this example, the additional performance obligation for risk coverage does not affect when the customer obtains control of the product.

However, it does result in the customer receiving a service from the seller while the band instruments are in transit. As such, the seller has not satisfied all of its performance obligations at the point of shipment and would not recognize all of the revenue at that time. Instead, the seller would allocate a portion of the transaction price to the performance obligation to provide risk coverage and would recognize revenue as that performance obligation is satisfied.

Control may be transferred over time. In such situations, the performance obligation is satisfied and revenue recognized over time. Control is considered transferred over time if:

- The customer simultaneously receives and consumes the benefits provided by seller's performance as seller performs;
- The seller's performance creates or enhances an asset that the customer controls as the asset is created or enhanced; or
- The seller's performance does not create an asset with an alternative use to the seller, and seller has an enforceable right to payment for the seller's performance completed to date.

Question: How does the seller measure its progress toward satisfying a performance obligation over time?

Answer: Progress may be measured using either output methods or input methods.

Output Methods

Output methods are based on the direct measurements of the value to the customer of goods or services transferred to date if the seller has a right to invoice the customer for the amount that corresponds directly with the value of the performance completed to date which is the amount recognize as revenue.

Input Methods

Input methods are based on the efforts or inputs in satisfying the performance obligation (e.g., the ration of costs incurred over the total expected costs to satisfy performance obligation). The seller may use a straight-line method if the efforts or inputs are expended evenly throughout the performance period.

The seller is required to have reliable information to reasonably measure its progress toward satisfying a performance obligation. In the early stages of a contract, the seller may not be able to make a reasonably measurement other than expecting to recover all costs incurred in satisfying the performance obligation. In such situations, the seller recognizes revenue only to the extent of costs incurred until such time when the seller can reasonably measure its progress toward satisfying the performance obligation.

In summary, the seller must determine whether a contract performance obligation has been satisfied before revenue can be recognized. Revenue under that contract may only be recognized when or as control of the asset is transferred to customer.

An example of measuring progress toward completion satisfaction of a performance obligation for uninstalled materials follows.

Contractor-seller enters into a contract with a customer to construct a manufacturing plant for $1,000,000 over two years. The contract also requires the contractor-seller to procure specialized equipment from a third party and integrate that equipment into the plant. The contractor-seller expects to transfer control of the specialized equipment within six months from the date the project begins. The installation and integration of the equipment will continue throughout the contract.

Question: Is the contract a single performance obligation?

Answer: The contract is a single performance obligation because all of the promised goods or services in the contract are highly interrelated. The contractor also provides significant services modifying and/or integrating those goods or services into the single output, i.e., a manufacturing plant for which the customer has contracted.

Question: How might the contractor measure its progress toward satisfying its performance obligation?

Answer: The contractor measures progress toward the complete satisfaction of its performance obligation on the basis of costs incurred relative to total costs expected to be incurred.

At contract's inception, the contractor expects the following:

Transaction price	$ 1,000,000
Expected cost of the specialized equipment	200,000
Expected other costs	600,000
Total expected costs	$ 800,000

The contractor concludes that the best depiction of its performance is to recognize revenue for the specialized equipment in an amount equal to the cost of the specialized equipment upon the transfer of control to the customer. Therefore, the contractor would exclude the cost of the specialized equipment from its measurement of its progress toward completion on a cost-to-cost basis as follows:

During the first six months, the contractor incurs $150,000 of costs of the total $600,000 of expected costs (excluding the $200,000 cost of the specialized equipment). As such, the contractor estimates that the performance obligation is 25% complete ($150,000 ÷ $600,000) and recognizes revenue of $200,000 [25% × ($1,000,000 total transaction price − $200,000 revenue for the specialized equipment)].

Upon transfer of control of the specialized equipment, the contractor recognizes revenue and costs of $200,000.

Subsequently, the contractor continues to recognize revenue on the basis of costs incurred to total expected costs (excluding the revenue and cost of the specialized equipment).

A final example of recognizing revenue follows.

The seller enters into a contract to produce a significantly customized product for a customer. The seller has determined that the contract is a single performance obligation. The contract has the following characteristics:

- The customization is significant, and customer's specifications may be changed at the customer's request during the contract term.
- Nonrefundable, interim progress payments are required to finance the contract.
- The customer can cancel the contract at any time (with a termination penalty); any work in process has no alternative use to the seller.
- Physical possession and title do not pass until completion of the contract.

Question: How should the seller recognize revenue?

Answer: The terms of the contract, in particular the customer specifications (and ability to change the specifications), indicate that the work in process has no alternative use to the seller, and the nonrefundable progress payments suggest that control of the product is being transferred over the contract term. Revenue is therefore recognized over time as the products are produced. The seller will need to select the most appropriate measurement model (either an input or output method) to measure the revenue arising from the transfer of control of the product over time.

Some Special Revenue Recognition Issues

Some special revenue recognition issues addressed under ASU 2014-09 include the following:

- Breakage
- Nonrefundable upfront fees
- Principal versus agent considerations
- Repurchase agreements
- Consignment arrangements
- Bill-and-hold arrangements
- Warranties
- Shipping and handling costs
- Sales and similar taxes

Breakage

Breakage is the customer's unexercised contractual right, e.g., the right to redeem a gift card. If the seller expects to be entitled to the unexercised amount (i.e., there is no escheatment), then the seller recognizes such amount as revenue in proportion to the pattern of rights exercised by the customer. On the other hand, if the seller does not expect to be entitled to the unexercised amount (i.e., there is escheatment which requires the seller to remit consideration to a third party, such as a government body responsible for unclaimed property, based on a customer's unexercised rights), then the seller should not recognize revenue related to unexercised rights.

An example of accounting for breakage follows:

Country Store sells 100 gift cards for $50 each in 20X1. Based on historical data, it expects 10% breakage. The unused gift card balances are not subject to escheatment. To date, customers have redeemed 45 cards for $2,250 worth of merchandize. As such, Country Store recognizes revenue of $2,500 determined as follows:

Cards redeemed ($2,250) plus the breakage in proportion to the total rights exercised ($250) [Total expected breakage ($500) times the proportion of cards redeemed ($2,250) divided by the expected amount to be redeemed ($4,500)].

Nonrefundable Upfront Fees

Upfront fees may be charged to customer at or near contract inception. Such fees may be identified as joining fees, activation fees, setup fees, etc. Generally, the upfront fee is for a necessary activity to fulfill the contract but does not result in the seller either transferring a good or service to the customer. As such, that form of upfront fee is really an advance payment for future goods or services and recognized as revenue when those future goods or services are provided to the customer.

Principal and Agent Considerations

ASU 2014-09 has been amended by ASU 2016-08, *Revenue from Contracts with Customers (Topic 606): Principal versus Agent Considerations (Reporting Revenue Gross versus Net)*. ASU 2016-08 becomes effective concurrently with the effective date of ASU 2014-09. The following discussion reflects the amendments under ASU 2016-08.

Sellers that are classified as a principal report sales and cost of sales, i.e., gross reporting. Those that are classified as an agent report commissions, i.e., net reporting.

Following are indicators that the reporting entity is an agent:

a. Another party is responsible for fulfilling the contract promise for goods or services.

b. The reporting entity has no risk of inventory loss.

c. The reporting entity has no discretion in setting the selling price.

d. The reporting entity receives consideration in the form of a commission for compensation of its services.

e. The reporting entity bears no credit risk.

The above indicators may be more or less relevant to the assessment of classifying the reporting entity as an agent depending on the nature of the specified goods or services and the terms and conditions of the contract. In addition, different indicators may provide more persuasive evidence in different contracts. Judgment is required.

Repurchase Agreements

A seller may sell an asset and also promise to repurchase it. The repurchase may be:

- An obligation (i.e., a forward contract);
- A right (i.e., a call option); or
- An obligation at the customer's request (i.e., a put option).

The seller accounts for the transaction as either a lease or debt under a forward contract or call option. If the repurchase price is less than the selling price, the seller accounts for the transaction as a lease. If the repurchase price greater than the selling price, the seller accounts for the transaction as debt.

Put options are a little more complicated. If the repurchase price is less than the original selling price and the customer has a significant incentive to "put it to the seller," then the seller accounts for the transaction as a sale with a right of return. Absent such an incentive, the seller accounts for the transaction as a lease. If the repurchase price under the put option is equal to or greater than the original selling price, then the seller accounts for the transaction as a financing.

Consignment Arrangements

Indicators of a consignment arrangement between the reporting entity seller or vendor and the other party that holds the asset include the following:

- The product held by the other party is controlled by the reporting entity seller or vendor until a specified event occurs or a period of time elapses.
- The reporting entity seller or vendor is able to require the return of the product from the other party holding the asset or the transfer of it to yet another different party.
- The third-party holder or consignee does not have the unconditional obligation to pay for the product.

No revenue is recognized under any consignment arrangement.

Bill-and-Hold Arrangements

Under a bill-and-hold arrangement, the seller or vendor may bill customer for the asset but maintains physical possession of it. The seller may recognize revenue only when customer is deemed to have control of the asset. If the following criteria are met, the seller may recognize revenue under a bill-and-hold arrangement.

- There must be substantive reason for the arrangement initiated by the buyer.
- The product must be identified separately as belonging to the customer by the seller.
- The product must be ready for immediate transfer to the customer.
- The seller cannot have the ability to use or otherwise direct the product to another customer.

Warranties

A seller accounts for a warranty as a separate performance obligation if the customer has the option to purchase the warranty separately. If the warranty is not sold separately, the seller accounts for the warranty as a cost accrual, unless the warranty is to provide the customer with a service in addition to assurance that the product complies with agreed-upon specifications.

The seller should consider factors such as whether the warranty is required by law, the length of the warranty period, and the nature of the tasks the seller has promised to perform as part of the warranty to determine whether the warranty provides the customer with an additional service. Judgment will be required. The portion of a warranty that provides a service in addition to assurance that the product complies with specifications is accounted for as a separate performance obligation. A seller that cannot reasonably separate the obligation to provide an additional service from the rest of the warranty should account for both together as a single performance obligation providing a service.

An example of the accounting for a warranty follows.

The seller's sale of a product includes a 90-day standard warranty, whereby the seller replaces defective components of the product. The warranty does not provide any additional service to the customer. As such, the seller accounts for the warranty as a cost accrual.

Shipping and Handling

Under ASU 2016-10, the seller is permitted, as an accounting policy election, to account for shipping and handling activities that occur after the customer has obtained control of a good as an activity to fulfill the promise to transfer the good rather than as an additional promised service.

Sales and Similar Taxes

ASU 2016-12 permits a seller, as an accounting policy election, to exclude amounts collected from customers for all sales (and other similar taxes) from the transaction price.

Incremental, Fulfillment, and Contract Costs

ASU 2014-09 created guidance relating to contract costs in newly created ASC 340-40, *Other Assets and Deferred Costs—Contracts with Customers.* ASC 340-40 provides accounting guidance for:

- Incremental costs of obtaining a contract with a customer; and
- Costs incurred in fulfilling a contract with a customer that are not within the scope of another ASC Topic (e.g., inventory or property, plant and equipment).

For convenience, these matters are discussed briefly below, as well as in more detail elsewhere herein.

Incremental costs of obtaining a contract include those incurred that would not have been incurred if contract had not been obtained (e.g., sales commission). Such costs are recognized as an asset if the seller expects to recover the costs and amortized over the performance period that the related goods or services are provided or transferred. Recoverable incremental costs of obtaining a contract are presented separately from other contract assets in the seller's balance sheet. Regardless, as a practical expedient, sellers may expense these costs as incurred if the amortization period is one year or less.

Costs to fulfill a contract are recognized as an asset only if those costs:

- Relate directly to a contract/anticipated contract that the seller can specifically identify;
- Such costs generate or enhance resources of the seller that will be used in satisfying or continuing to satisfy the contract performance obligations in the future; and
- Such costs are expected to be recovered by the seller.

Under ASU 2016-20, *Technical Corrections and Improvements to Topic 606, Revenue from Contracts with Customers*, a loss is required to be recorded when the expected contract costs exceed the total anticipated contract revenue. That ASU requires that the provision for losses be determined at least at the contract level. Further, ASU 2016-20 allows an entity to determine the provision for losses at the performance obligation level as an accounting policy election.

Amortization and Impairment

Amortize the asset capitalized on a basis consistent with transfer of goods of services to which the asset relates.

Also, recognize any impairment loss to the extent the carrying amount of the asset exceeds the remaining amount of consideration that the seller expects to receive, less costs relating directly to providing the contracted goods or services not recognized as expense. When performing impairment testing, ASU 2016-20 specifies that the entity should (a) consider expected contract renewals and extensions, and (b) include both the amount of consideration it already has received but has not recognized as revenue and the amount it expects to receive in the future.

Costs incurred within scope of another ASC Topic are accounted for in accordance with that ASC Topic.

An example of accounting for incremental, fulfillment and contract costs follows.

Seller enters into a contract to operate a customer's information technology center for four years. The customer promises to pay a fixed fee of $20,000 per month under the contract.

Seller incurs a selling commission of $10,000 to obtain the contract. It also incurred $15,000 of legal fees for due diligence work and travel costs of $25,000 to deliver the proposal for the contract.

Before providing the services, the seller designs and builds a technology platform that interfaces with the customer's systems; that platform is not transferred to the customer. The following initial costs are incurred related to the technology platform:

Design services	$ 25,000
Hardware	100,000
Software	75,000
Migration and testing	100,000
Total costs	$ 300,000

Question: How should the seller account for the above costs?

Answer: The seller would capitalize the selling commission of $10,000 to obtain the contract and amortize such costs over the four-year term of the contract.

The seller would expense the legal fees ($15,000) and travel costs ($25,000) since they would have been incurred regardless of whether the contract was obtained.

The initial setup costs relate primarily to activities to fulfill the contract but do not transfer goods or services to the customer. As such, the seller would account for these costs as follows:

- The hardware costs would be accounted for in accordance with ASC 360, *Property, Plant, and Equipment*.
- The software costs would be accounted for in accordance with ASC 350, *Intangibles—Goodwill and Other*.
- The design, migration, and testing costs would be capitalized and amortized over the four-year term of the contract.

Disclosure Requirements

As amended by ASU 2014-09, ASC 606-10-50 specifies the disclosure requirements related to revenue from contracts with customers. Presented below are those disclosures.

1. The objective of these disclosure requirements is to disclose sufficient information to enable users of financial statements to understand the nature, amount, timing, and uncertainty of revenue and cash flows arising from contracts with customers. To achieve that objective, the seller shall disclose qualitative and quantitative information about all of the following:

a. Its contracts with customers (see paragraphs 606-10-50-4 through 50-16).

b. The significant judgments, and changes in the judgments, made in applying the guidance in this Topic to those contracts (see paragraphs 606-10-50-17 through 50-21).

c. Any assets recognized from the costs to obtain or fulfill a contract with a customer in accordance with paragraph 340-40-25-1 or 340-40-25-5 (see paragraphs 340-40-50-1 through 50-6).

2. The seller shall consider the level of detail necessary to satisfy the disclosure objective and how much emphasis to place on each of the various requirements. The seller shall aggregate or disaggregate disclosures so that useful information is not obscured by either the inclusion of a large amount of insignificant detail or the aggregation of items that have substantially different characteristics.

3. Amounts disclosed are for each reporting period for which a statement of comprehensive income (statement of activities) is presented and as of each reporting period for which a statement of financial position is presented. The seller need not disclose information in accordance with the guidance with Topic 606 if it has provided the information in accordance with another ASU Topic.

Contracts with Customers

4. An entity shall disclose all of the following amounts for the reporting period unless those amounts are presented separately in the statement of comprehensive income (statement of activities) in accordance with other ASU Topics:

   a. Revenue recognized from contracts with customers, which the seller shall disclose separately from its other sources of revenue

   b. Any impairment losses recognized (in accordance with Topic 310 on receivables) on any receivables or contract assets arising from the seller's contracts with customers, which the seller shall disclose separately from impairment losses from other contracts.

Disaggregation of Revenue

5. The seller shall disaggregate revenue recognized from contracts with customers into categories that depict how the nature, amount, timing, and uncertainty of revenue and cash flows are affected by economic factors. (The seller shall apply the guidance in paragraphs 606-10-55-89 through 55-91 when selecting the categories to use to disaggregate revenue.)

6. In addition, the seller shall disclose sufficient information to enable users of financial statements to understand the relationship between the disclosure of disaggregated revenue (in accordance with paragraph 606-10-50-5) and revenue information that is disclosed for each reportable segment if the seller applies ASU Topic 280 on segment reporting.

7. The seller, except for a public business entity, a not-for-profit entity that has issued, or is a conduit bond obligor for, securities that are traded, listed, or quoted on an exchange or an over-the-counter market, or an employee benefit plan that files or furnishes financial statements with or to the Securities and Exchange Commission (SEC), may elect not to apply the quantitative disaggregation disclosure guidance in paragraphs 606-10-50-5 through 50-6 and 606-10-55-89 through 55-91.
8. If the seller elects not to provide those disclosures, it shall disclose, at a minimum, revenue disaggregated according to the timing of transfer of goods or services (e.g., revenue from goods or services transferred to customers at a point in time and revenue from goods or services transferred to customers over time) and qualitative information about how economic factors (such as type of customer, geographical location of customers, and type of contract) affect the nature, amount, timing, and uncertainty of revenue and cash flows.

Contract Balances

9. The seller shall disclose all of the following:
    a. The opening and closing balances of receivables, contract assets, and contract liabilities from contracts with customers if not otherwise separately presented or disclosed.
    b. Revenue recognized in the reporting period that was included in the contract liability balance at the beginning of the period.
    c. Revenue recognized in the reporting period from performance obligations satisfied (or partially satisfied) in previous periods (e.g., changes in transaction price).
10. The seller shall explain how the timing of satisfaction of its performance obligations (see paragraph 606-10-50-12(a)) relates to the typical timing of payment (see paragraph 606-10-50-12(b)) and the effect that those factors have on the contract asset and the contract liability balances. (The explanation provided may use qualitative information.)
11. The seller shall provide an explanation of the significant changes in the contract asset and the contract liability balances during the reporting period. The explanation shall include qualitative and quantitative information. Examples of changes in the seller's balances of contract assets and contract liabilities include any of the following:
    a. Changes due to business combinations
    b. Cumulative catch-up adjustments to revenue that affect the corresponding contract asset or contract liability, including adjustments arising from a change in the measure of progress, a change in an estimate of the transaction price (including any changes in the assessment of whether an estimate of variable consideration is constrained), or a contract modification
    c. Impairment of a contract asset

d. A change in the time frame for a right to consideration to become unconditional (i.e., for a contract asset to be reclassified to a receivable)

e. A change in the timeframe for a performance obligation to be satisfied (i.e., for the recognition of revenue arising from a contract liability)

12. The seller, except for a public business entity, a not-for-profit entity that has issued, or is a conduit bond obligor for, securities that are traded, listed, or quoted on an exchange or an over-the-counter market, or an employee benefit plan that files or furnishes financial statements with or to the SEC, may elect not to provide any or all of the disclosures in paragraphs 606-10-50-8 through 50-10. However, if the seller elects not to provide the disclosures in paragraphs 606-10-50-8 through 50-10, it shall provide the disclosure in paragraph 606-10-50-8(a), which requires the disclosure of the opening and closing balances of receivables, contract assets, and contract liabilities from contracts with customers if not otherwise separately presented or disclosed.

Performance Obligations

13. The seller shall disclose information about its performance obligations in contracts with customers, including a description of all of the following:

a. When the seller typically satisfies its performance obligations (e.g., upon shipment, upon delivery, as services are rendered, or upon completion of service), including when performance obligations are satisfied in a bill-and-hold arrangement

b. The significant payment terms (e.g., when payment typically is due, whether the contract has a significant financing component, whether the consideration amount is variable, and whether the estimate of variable consideration is typically constrained in accordance with paragraphs 606-10-32-11 through 32-13)

c. The nature of the goods or services that the seller has promised to transfer, highlighting any performance obligations to arrange for another party to transfer goods or services (i.e., if the entity is acting as an agent)

d. Obligations for returns, refunds, and other similar obligations

e. Types of warranties and related obligations.

Transaction Price Allocated to the Remaining Performance Obligations

14. The seller shall disclose the following information about its remaining performance obligations:

a. The aggregate amount of the transaction price allocated to the performance obligations that are unsatisfied (or partially unsatisfied) as of the end of the reporting period

b. An explanation of when the seller expects to recognize as revenue the amount disclosed in accordance with paragraph 606-10-50-13(a), which the seller shall disclose in either of the following ways:

(1) On a quantitative basis using the time bands that would be most appropriate for the duration of the remaining performance obligations

(2) By using qualitative information

15. As a practical expedient, the seller need not disclose the information in paragraph 606-10-50-13 for performance obligations if either of the following conditions is met:

a. The performance obligation is part of a contract that has an original expected duration of one year or less

b. The seller recognizes revenue from the satisfaction of the performance obligation in accordance with paragraph 606-10-55-18

16. The seller shall explain qualitatively whether it is applying the practical expedient in paragraph 606-10-50-14 and whether any consideration from contracts with customers is not included in the transaction price and, therefore, not included in the information disclosed in accordance with paragraph 606-10-50-13. For example, an estimate of the transaction price would not include any estimated amounts of variable consideration that are constrained (see paragraphs 606-10-32-11 through 32-13).

17. The seller, except for a public business entity, a not-for-profit entity that has issued, or is a conduit bond obligor for, securities that are traded, listed, or quoted on an exchange or an over-the-counter market, or an employee benefit plan that files or furnishes financial statements with or to the SEC, may elect not to provide the disclosures in paragraphs 606-10-50-13 through 50-15.

Significant Judgments in the Application of the Guidance in This Topic

18. The seller shall disclose the judgments, and changes in the judgments, made in applying the guidance in this Topic 606 that significantly affect the determination of the amount and timing of revenue from contracts with customers. In particular, the seller shall explain the judgments, and changes in the judgments, used in determining both of the following:

a. The timing of satisfaction of performance obligations (see paragraphs 606-10-50-18 through 50-19)

b. The transaction price and the amounts allocated to performance obligations (see paragraph 606-10-50-20)

Determining the Timing of Satisfaction of Performance Obligations

19. For performance obligations that the seller satisfies over time, it shall disclose both of the following:

a. The methods used to recognize revenue (e.g., a description of the output methods or input methods used and how those methods are applied)

b. An explanation of why the methods used provide a faithful depiction of the transfer of goods or services

20. For performance obligations satisfied at a point in time, an entity shall disclose the significant judgments made in evaluating when a customer obtains control of promised goods or services.

Determining the Transaction Price and the Amounts Allocated to Performance Obligations

21. The seller shall disclose information about the methods, inputs, and assumptions used for all of the following:

    a. Determining the transaction price, which includes, but is not limited to, estimating variable consideration, adjusting the consideration for the effects of the time value of money, and measuring noncash consideration

    b. Assessing whether an estimate of variable consideration is constrained

    c. Allocating the transaction price, including estimating standalone selling prices of promised goods or services, and allocating discounts and variable consideration to a specific part of the contract (if applicable)

    d. Measuring obligations for returns, refunds, and other similar obligations

22. The seller, except for a public business entity, a not-for-profit entity that has issued, or is a conduit bond obligor for, securities that are traded, listed, or quoted on an exchange or an over-the-counter market, or an employee benefit plan that files or furnishes financial statements with or to the SEC, may elect not to provide any or all of the following disclosures:

    a. Paragraph 606-10-50-18(b), which states that an entity shall disclose, for performance obligations satisfied over time, an explanation of why the methods used to recognize revenue provide a faithful depiction of the transfer of goods or services to a customer

    b. Paragraph 606-10-50-19, which states that the seller shall disclose, for performance obligations satisfied at a point in time, the significant judgments made in evaluating when a customer obtains control of promised goods or services

    c. Paragraph 606-10-50-20, which states that the seller shall disclose the methods, inputs, and assumptions used to determine the transaction price and to allocate the transaction price. However, if the seller elects not to provide the disclosures in paragraph 606-10-50-20, the it shall provide the disclosure in paragraph 606-10-50-20(b), which states that the seller shall disclose the methods, inputs, and assumptions used to assess whether an estimate of variable consideration is constrained

Practical Expedients

23. If the seller elects to use the practical expedient in either paragraph 606-10-32-18 (about the existence of a significant financing component) or paragraph 340-40-25-4 (about the incremental costs of obtaining a contract), the seller shall disclose that fact.

24. The seller, except for a public business entity, a not-for-profit entity that has issued, or is a conduit bond obligor for, securities that are traded, listed, or quoted on an exchange or an over-the-counter market, or an employee benefit plan that files or furnishes financial statements with or to the SEC, may elect not to provide the disclosures in paragraph 606-10-50-22.

Transitioning to ASU 2014-09

Two methods are available to reflect the adoption of ASU 2014-09:

1. Full retrospective method.
2. Simplified transition or modified retrospective method.

Under the full retrospective method, the reporting entity restates the financial statements for each prior reporting period presented. However, entities can elect to apply certain practical expedients.

Under the simplified transition method, the reporting entity shows the cumulative effect of initially applying ASU 2014-09 recognized as of the date of initial application (e.g., January 1, 2019, for a calendar-year private entity). Entities electing the modified retrospective method would apply the new guidance only to contracts that are not completed at the adoption date and would not adjust prior reporting periods.

ASU 2016-12, issued in May 2016, clarifies that a completed contract for purposes of transition is a contract for which all (or substantially all) of the revenue was recognized under legacy GAAP before the date of initial application. Accounting for elements of a contract that do not affect revenue under legacy GAAP are irrelevant to the assessment of whether a contract is complete. In addition, ASU 2016-12 permits an entity to apply the modified retrospective method either to all contracts or only to contracts that are not completed contracts.

An example of applying the simplified transition method follows.

Private Company A's normal sales terms are FOB shipping point via a third-party carrier. However, for certain customers it provides the customer with a replacement product at no cost if a product is damaged or lost in transit. As of December 31, 2017, Company A reversed certain sales under these arrangements since they were considered to be the equivalent of FOB destination shipping terms. The amount of these sales was $10,000, and the amount of the cost of the products was $7,000.

Under ASU 2014-09, this arrangement results in two performance obligations: (1) deliver products, and (2) provide a service (risk of loss coverage). As such, Company A would allocate the contract price to these two obligations.

The customer obtains control of the product at the point of shipment. Even though the customer does not have physical possession of the product at that point, it does have legal title and, therefore, can sell the product to or exchange it with another party. Company A is also precluded from selling the product to another customer.

The customer also receives a benefit (i.e., protection from loss) from the service from Company A while the products are in transit.

Under ASU 2014-09, Company A recognizes the revenue from products at the point of shipment (FOB shipping point) and the service revenue when the product arrives at the customer's location.

Assume Company A has elected to adopt ASU 2014-09 on January 1, 2019, using the simplified transition method. Further, the estimated standalone selling price of the risk coverage service is $500.

Prepare the required journal entry to record the adoption of ASU 2014-09 under the simplified transition method as of January 1, 2019.

Sales	$ 10,000	
Cost of sales		$ 7,000
Service revenues		500
Cumulative effect		2,500

To record adoption of ASU 2014-09 as of January 1, 2018.

Retrospective Application and Practical Expedients

Entities are permitted to adopt the revenue standard by restating all prior periods (i.e., full retrospective adoption) following ASC 250, *Accounting Changes and Error Corrections.* Entities electing full retrospective application are permitted to use any combination of several practical expedients.

Any of the expedients used must be applied consistently to all contracts in all reporting periods presented. Entities that choose to use any practical expedients must disclose that they have used the expedients and provide a qualitative assessment of the estimated effect of applying each expedient, to the extent reasonably possible.

The practical expedients excerpted from ASC 606-10-65-1 permitted for use by entities using the full retrospective method follow:

1. An entity need not restate contracts that begin and are completed within the same annual reporting period.
2. For completed contracts that have variable consideration, an entity may use the transaction price at the date the contract was completed rather than estimating variable consideration amounts in the comparative reporting periods.
3. For all reporting periods presented before the date of initial application, an entity need not disclose the amount of the transaction price allocated to the remaining performance obligations and an explanation of when the entity expects to recognize that amount as revenue . . .

4. For contracts that were modified before the beginning of the earliest reporting period presented, an entity need not retrospectively restate the contract for contract modifications. Instead, an entity is permitted under ASU 2016-12 to reflect the aggregate effect of all contract modifications that occur before the beginning of the earliest period presented when:
   a. Identifying the satisfied and unsatisfied performance obligations;
   b. Determining the transaction price; and
   c. Allocating the transaction price to the satisfied and unsatisfied performance obligations.

Recent Changes

Reflected in the above discussion of ASC Topic 606 are ASU 2014-09, 2015-14, 2016-08, 2016-10, 2016-12, and 2016-20.

Topic 610: Other Income

Topic 610 specifies standards of financial accounting and reporting for income recognized that is not in a contract with a customer within the scope of Topic 606, *Revenue from Contracts with Customers,* or in accordance with other specific revenue or income recognition guidance.

Topic 610 was updated by ASU 2017-05, *Other Income—Gains and Losses from the Derecognition of Nonfinancial Assets (Subtopic 610-20): Clarifying the Scope of Asset Derecognition Guidance and Accounting for Partial Sales of Nonfinancial Assets.* ASU 2017-05 was issued in February 2017 as complementary update to ASU 2017-01, *Business Combinations (Topic 805): Clarifying the Definition of a Business.* ASU 2017-05 provides guidance for recognizing gains and losses from the transfer of nonfinancial assets in contracts with noncustomers. ASC 610-20, as amended by ASU 2017-05 eliminates rules specifically addressing sales of real estate. As a result, sales and partial sales of real estate will now be subject to the same derecognition model as all other nonfinancial assets. The nonfinancial asset measurement guidance in ASC 610-20 is substantially aligned with existing measurement guidance for transferring a business or a financial asset, thus reducing the number of models that exist today. Also, ASU 2017-05 substantially reduces the guidance under ASC Topic 845, *Nonmonetary Transactions.*

Essentially, there are four main categories of derecognition models that are applied in order as follows:

1. *Revenue from Contracts with Customers*—ASC 606

If the counterparty in the transaction is a customer and the assets being transferred are an output of the entity's ordinary activities, the transaction is within the scope of new ASC Topic 606.

2. *Businesses*—ASC 810

If the transferred set of assets and activities meets the definition of a business, the transaction is within the scope of the derecognition guidance in ASC 810, *Consolidation.* The new definition of a business (as included in ASU 2017-01) must be used when applying ASC 610-20, regardless of whether the entity has adopted the new definition of a business. With the new definition of a business, more transactions will likely be treated as dispositions of nonfinancial assets (rather than dispositions of businesses), which will increase the number of transactions subject to the new disposition guidance.

3. *Financial Assets*—ASC 860

If the transaction is entirely within the scope of ASC 860, *Transfer and Servicing* (of Financial Assets), then apply ASC 860. This includes the transfer of investments accounted for under ASC 323, *Investments—Equity Method and Joint Ventures.* Entities will no longer look through these investments to determine if the underlying assets should be accounted for under other guidance, as previously required under the real estate-specific guidance.

4. *Nonfinancial Assets*—ASC 610-20

If the transaction is not within the scope of ASC 606, 810, or 860, and no other specified scope exceptions apply (e.g., sale leasebacks, conveyances of oil and gas mineral rights, certain nonmonetary exchanges, leases), the transaction for the transfer of nonfinancial assets and "in-substance nonfinancial assets" will be accounted for under ASC 610-20. An in-substance nonfinancial asset is defined as "a financial asset (e.g., a receivable) promised to a counterparty in a contract if substantially all of the fair value of the assets (recognized and unrecognized) that are promised to the counterparty in the contract is concentrated in nonfinancial assets." (Substantially all is typically interpreted to mean 90% or greater.) For example, if an entity transfers a building and receivables that do not comprise a business to a non-customer and 95% of the fair value is concentrated in the building, then the receivables would be considered in substance nonfinancial assets. As such, both the building and the receivables would be derecognized.

ASC 610-20 may require the application of other guidance. Additional comments related to ASU 2017-05 are presented below.

Recognizing and Measuring a Gain or Loss

To derecognize nonfinancial assets and recognize a gain or loss, the transferor entity must lose control of the assets while also satisfying the criteria for the transfer of control to another party under the new revenue recognition guidance. If these criteria are not met, an entity would continue to recognize the asset and record a liability for the consideration received.

A transferor entity must assess whether the transferee has gained control of the nonfinancial assets under ASC 810. This assessment will differ based on whether the transferor sold the nonfinancial assets directly or indirectly through the transfer of a controlled subsidiary. If the nonfinancial assets are transferred directly, the transferor must not have a controlling financial interest in the transferee. If transferred indirectly through a controlled subsidiary, the transferor must relinquish control of the subsidiary to demonstrate loss of control.

The criteria (e.g., payment terms, rights) for a contract as discussed in the new revenue recognition guidance must exist to assess whether the transferee has gained control of the nonfinancial asset. The indicators of a transfer of control of a nonfinancial asset to a buyer include the transferor's right to payment and physical possession of the asset, and the transferee's legal title to the asset, risks and rewards of ownership of the asset and acceptance of the asset.

A full gain or loss is recognized by the transferor for the transfer of nonfinancial assets to a joint venture that results in a loss of control in such assets by the transferor and a gain in control by the joint venture transferee.

For transactions involving the transfer of multiple assets, control of each asset may not transfer at the same time. As a result, some assets may be derecognized at the transaction date and others may be derecognized at later dates. If derecognition occurs at different times, consideration will need to be allocated to each distinct asset using the relative standalone selling price method.

The gain/loss on the transfer is the difference between the consideration allocated to each distinct nonfinancial asset and its carrying amount. Since nonfinancial assets are generally subject to impairment, significant losses on derecognition are unlikely.

In a partial sales transaction, an entity usually transfers control of a nonfinancial asset in exchange for a noncontrolling interest in the counterparty. Alternatively, when the nonfinancial asset is held in a subsidiary and control is lost, a partial interest in the subsidiary is typically transferred in exchange for cash, and a noncontrolling interest in the subsidiary is retained. An example for a partial sale of real estate follows:

Background: Entity A owns 100% of an office building carrying value of $50 and a fair value of $100. The office building does not meet the new definition of a business. Entity A transfers 100% of its interest in the office building to Entity C for $60 and a 40% noncontrolling interest in Entity C. Entity C held no assets or liabilities other than the cash required to purchase a 60% interest in the office building. As a result, the fair value of Entity C is $100 after the transfer. Prior to the transfer, Entity C is owned by an unrelated third party that is not a customer in this transaction.

Conclusion: Entity A's effective ownership interest in the office building is reduced from 100% to 40% as a result of the transaction. The noncontrolling interest (accounted for under the equity method) that Entity A has accepted as partial consideration for the transfer is valued at $40 ($100 for the fair value of Entity C times Entity A's 40% ownership interest in Entity C). The total consideration transferred is $100 ($60 in cash plus a noncontrolling interest with a fair value of $40). Since the consideration received is $100 and the building's carrying value was $50, a gain of $50 would be recognized. The equity investment in Entity C would be recognized at its fair value of $40.

Gains or losses on disposals on nonfinancial assets not qualifying as discontinued operations are included in income from continuing operations before income taxes. Disclosures include the facts and circumstances leading to the disposal, the amount of gain or loss, and the financial statement line item that includes the gain or loss, if not presented separately.

Effective Dates of and Transitioning to ASU 2017-05

The amendments to the nonfinancial asset guidance are effective at the same time an entity adopts the new revenue guidance in ASC 606. Therefore, for public business entities with calendar year-ends, the standard is effective on January 1, 2018. All other entities have an additional year to adopt the guidance. Early adoption is permitted beginning January 1, 2017, for calendar year-end entities, provided adoption coincides with the adoption of the revenue standards. Entities may transition to ASU 2017-05 using either the full retrospective approach or the modified retrospective approach, regardless of the transition approach elected for the new revenue standard.

CHAPTER 7
EXPENSES

CONTENTS

The *Expenses* area of the FASB *Accounting Standards Codification* contains the following topics:

705	Cost of Sales and Services
710	Compensation—General
712	Compensation—Nonretirement Postemployment Benefits
715	Compensation—Retirement Benefits
718	Compensation—Stock Compensation
720	Other Expenses
730	Research and Development
740	Income Taxes

Topic 705: Cost of Sales and Services

Topic 705, *Cost of Sales and Services*, contains six subtopics:

10 Overall

20 Accounting for Consideration

905 Agriculture*

912 Contractors—Federal Government*

926 Entertainment—Films*

976 Real Estate—Retail Land*

985 Software*

* See the corresponding topic in Chapter 9 for coverage of this shared subtopic.

ASU 2014-09, *Revenue from Contracts with Customers,* is discussed in Chapter 6. That pronouncement includes amendments to ASC 705-20 for guidance on accounting for consideration received by an entity from a vendor. The following discussion reflects the adoption of ASU 2014-09.

Consideration from a vendor includes cash amounts that an entity receives or expects to receive from a vendor. Consideration from a vendor also includes credit or other items (e.g., a coupon or voucher) that the entity can apply against amounts owed to the vendor. The entity shall account for consideration from a vendor as a reduction of the purchase price of the goods or services acquired from the vendor unless the consideration from the vendor is:

1. In exchange for a distinct good or service that the entity transfers to the vendor;
2. A reimbursement of costs incurred by the entity to sell the vendor's products; or
3. Consideration for sales incentives offered to customers by manufacturers.

If the amount of consideration from the vendor exceeds the standalone selling price of the distinct good or service that the entity transfers to the vendor, then the entity shall account for such excess as a reduction of the purchase price of any goods or services acquired from the vendor. If the standalone selling price is not directly observable, the entity shall estimate it.

If the cash consideration represents a reimbursement of a specific, incremental, identifiable cost incurred by the entity in selling the vendor's products or services, such consideration is accounted for as a reduction in costs. If the amount of cash consideration paid by the vendor exceeds the cost being reimbursed, that excess amount shall also be accounted for as a reduction of cost of sales when recognized in the entity's income statement.

An entity with sales incentive arrangements that meet all of the criteria described in paragraph ASC 705-20-25-7 shall not account for consideration received from a vendor as a reduction of the purchase price of the goods or services acquired from the vendor. It shall consider the guidance in Topic 606, *Revenue from Contracts with Customers.* Sales incentives that do not meet all of the criteria in ASC 705-20-25-7 shall be accounted for as a reduction of the purchase price of the goods or services acquired from the vendor.

Topic 710: Compensation—General

Topic 710, *Compensation—General,* contains three subtopics:

10 Overall

908 Airlines*

980 Regulated Operations*

* See the corresponding topic in Chapter 9 for coverage of this shared subtopic.

General Discussion and Flowchart

Most employers have plans for compensating employees who are absent from work for any one of a variety of reasons. Examples include illnesses, vacations, sabbaticals, and holidays. ASC 710-10 addresses accounting for the costs of these compensated absences. In addition, ASC 710-10 applies to certain postretirement benefits as described in ASC 710-10-15-4. The following items are specifically excluded from the provisions of ASC 710-10 by ASC 710-10-15-5:

1. Certain postretirement benefits as described in ASC 710-10-15-5.
2. Deferred compensation.
3. Share-based payments given to employees.

The right to receive compensation when the employee is absent from work must be demonstrated in some positive manner. The right exists if payment for future absence vests or accumulates. Vested rights are those rights that are not contingent upon continued employment of the employee. That is, even if the employee terminates employment with the employer, the employer has an obligation to pay the employee the amount of the earned benefit. An accumulated benefit can be carried forward to future periods if it has not used. There may be limits placed on the amount of the benefit that can be carried forward or the length of the carry forward period.

To illustrate the difference between a vested and accumulated right, assume that a company has a policy of compensating employees for a two-week vacation each year. The employee earns .833 (10 paid vacation days/12 working months) days of vacation for each month worked in the current year. If the employee terminates employment with the company during the year, he/she is entitled to compensation for each vacation day earned. This feature of the vacation pay policy indicates that the employee's right to receive future compensation *vests* as earned. The company may allow employees to carry forward unused vacation days earned. This would mean that the earned vacation rights *accumulate* as well as vest.

The general provisions of ASC 710-10 are outlined in Flowchart 7-1. Some of the key terms and concepts, discussed above, appear in Flowchart 7-1. As demonstrated in Flowchart 7-1, the basic accounting issue in ASC 710-10 is whether to accrue a liability and expense in connection with certain compensated absences.

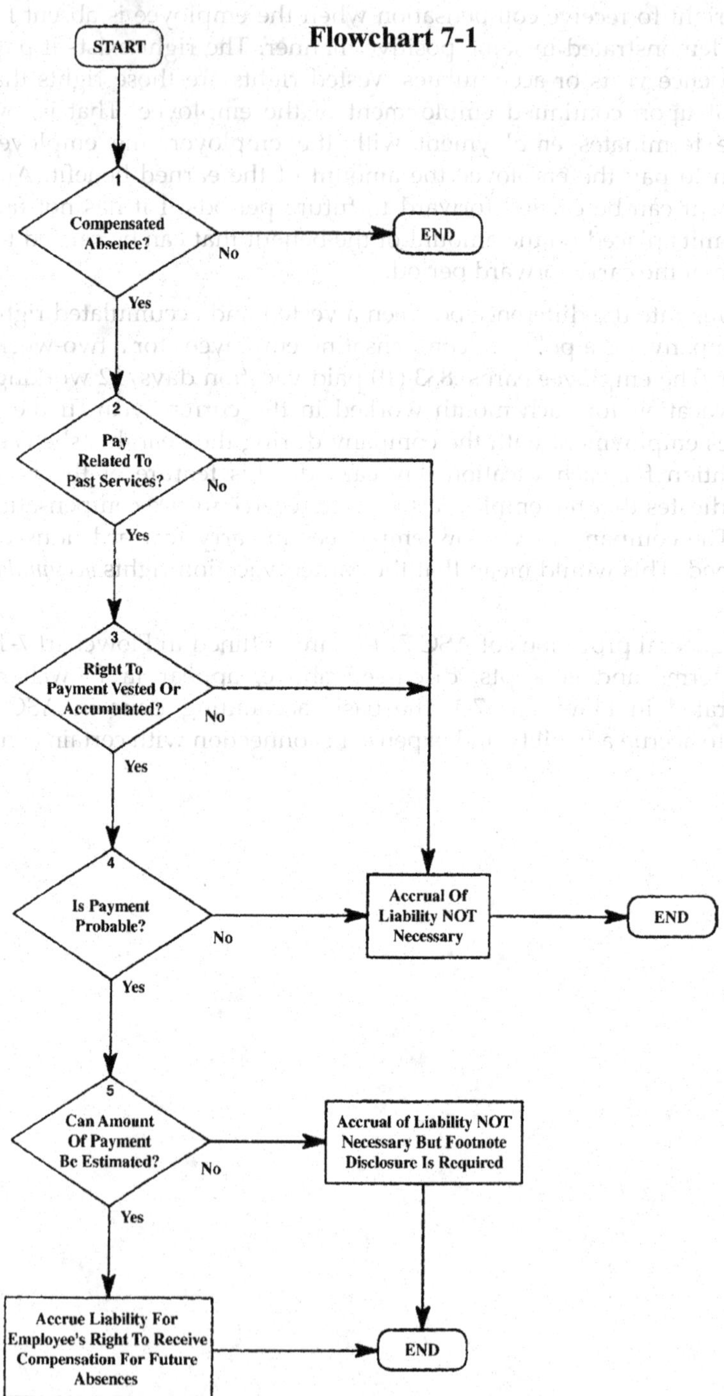
Flowchart 7-1
START
1
Compensated Absence?
No
END
Yes
2
Pay Related To Past Services?
No
Yes
3
Right To Payment Vested Or Accumulated?
No
Yes
4
Is Payment Probable?
No
Accrual Of Liability NOT Necessary
END
Yes
5
Can Amount Of Payment Be Estimated?
No
Accrual of Liability NOT Necessary But Footnote Disclosure Is Required
Yes
Accrue Liability For Employee's Right To Receive Compensation For Future Absences
END

The employer entity is required to accrue for compensated absences (Block 1), if four criteria are met:

1. The employer entity must be obligated to pay for future absences relating to services already rendered by the employee (Block 2).
2. The employee's right to receive payment for future absences must vest or accumulate (Block 3).
3. The future payment to the employee by the employer entity is *probable* (Block 4).
4. The amount of the future payment must be *reasonably estimated* (Block 5).

If *all* these four conditions are met, the employer entity is required to record a liability and expense for the compensated absences as they are earned by the employee. If the conditions described in Blocks 2 through 4 have been met, but the amount of the future payment cannot be reasonably estimated, footnote disclosure is required. If the particular compensated absence does not meet all of the conditions described in Blocks 2 through 5, the employer entity does not record a liability.

These general provisions appear easy to understand, but the application of them in specific cases may prove difficult. Chart 7-1 summarizes the accounting treatment required for various types of compensated absences. The footnotes to the chart explain the reason for the accounting treatment.

Chart 7-1 Compensated Future Absences

Type of Absence	Accrual[1] Necessary	Accrual Not Necessary
Vacation Pay	X	
Sick Leave—No Vesting/No Accumulating		X
Sick Leave—Vesting	X	
Sick Leave—Accumulates/No vesting	X[2]	X[2]
Holidays		X[3]
Jury Duty		X
Sabbatical Leave	X[4]	X[4]
Military Leave Benefits		X
Overtime Bank	X[5]	

[1] The accrual requirement is based on the assumption that all four basic conditions described in Flowchart 7-1 have been met.

[2] An accrual is permitted but is not required.

[3] Accrual is required if all conditions for accrual are met.

[4] If the leave is for the purpose of research or other service that enhances the reputation of the employer, the sabbatical should not be accrued. However, if the leave is for past services, the sabbatical should be accrued. ASC 710-10-25-5 further clarifies the issue of sabbatical leaves and similar benefits by stating that the cost related to the sabbatical leave meets the definition of "accumulates" and must be accrued (assume that all other accrual conditions are met) over the required service period when a minimum service period must be completed and the sabbatical benefit does not increase with additional service years. The provisions of ASC 710-10-25-5 do not apply when the employee must perform research or public service that enhances the reputation of the employer.

[5] The overtime bank constitutes earned overtime that employees can elect to take as vacation leave or additional compensation.

When accounting for compensated absences, the substance of the arrangement takes priority over its form. For example, if an employer normally pays employees for sick leave, even though the absence is not the result of illness, the amounts involved should be accrued, assuming that all the other conditions are met. The concept of substance over form dictates the accounting.

The pay rate to use for the accrual of compensated absences is not addressed in ASC 710-10. The author believes that the proper pay rate would be the employee's current rate. Consideration should be given to the possibility of future adjustments as future pay rates change. If the amounts involved are material enough to require a future adjustment, the amount of the adjustment should be treated as a change in an accounting estimate and accounted for on a prospective basis in accordance with ASC 250. The author does not believe that estimated future pay rates should be used to accrue the liability nor would it be appropriate to discount the liability to present value.

Compensated Absences—Technical Considerations

To illustrate the basic provisions of ASC 710-10, two examples are presented. The first example also serves as an introduction to the second, and more complex, example. Information relating to Example 7-1 follows.

Example 7-1
Compensated Absence Information

1. The Northland Company (Northland), a December 31 year-end enterprise, provides employees with paid vacations, sick leave, holidays, and other types of paid absences.
2. Vacations, which vest, can be taken only in the year subsequent to the year in which the services were performed.
3. Sick leave neither vests nor accumulates.
4. At December 31, 20X6, the estimated cost of compensated absences earned in 20X6 and payable in 20X7 are as follows:

Vacation pay	$25,000
Sick pay	10,000
Holiday pay	5,000
Jury duty	1,000
	$41,000

The first step in the accounting process is to analyze each type of compensated absence to determine whether the four criteria have been met to require an accrual of a liability. Refer to Flowchart 7-1 to identify the four criteria. The vacation pay is a compensated absence (Block 1), and the amount of pay is related to past services; vacation time earned in 20X6 cannot be taken until 20X7 (Block 2). The employee's right to receive the vacation pay vests but does not accumulate (Block 3). Because the vacation pay vests, the employee is entitled to be paid for earned days not taken in the subsequent year. It is probable that a payment for vacation pay will be made by Northland (Block 4), and the amount of the payment has been reasonably estimated at $25,000 (Block 5). Because the vacation pay meets all the criteria specified in ASC 710-10, a liability is required to be accrued at December 31, 20X6.

The amounts associated with the sick pay, holiday pay, and jury duty should not be accrued at year-end, because they are not related to past services of the employee.

The journal entry required at December 31, 20X6, would be:

Estimated Expense for Compensated Absences	25,000	
Estimated Liability for Compensated Absences		25,000

The compensated absences for sick pay, holiday pay, and jury duty will be expensed as incurred.

The Estimated Expense for Compensated Absences account will be classified on the income statement as an operating expense. The Estimated Liability for Compensated Absences account will be classified as a current liability because all earned vacation time must be taken in the period following the year in which it was earned by the employee.

This completes the discussion of the Example 7-1 material. The information presented in Example 7-2 is designed to illustrate some of the complexities of ASC 710-10.

Example 7-2
Compensated Absence Information

1. Savage Enterprises (Savage), a December 31 year-end company, provides employees with paid vacations, sick leave, paid holidays, and other types of paid absences after certain minimum employment conditions have been met.

2. The sick leave policy of the company indicates that the earned sick leave of an employee vests and that employees may use sick leave even when their absence from work is not the result of illness. Sick leave must be earned in one fiscal period and taken in the next (e.g., sick leave earned in 20X6 may not be taken until 20X7).

3. Savage's vacation pay policy indicates that earned vacation leave vests and that employees must earn their vacation leave in one fiscal period and take the time off in the next fiscal period.

4. In certain cases, sabbatical leave is granted to an employee as a result of valuable past services rendered to the company. Employees are notified in one fiscal period that they may take a sabbatical leave in the next fiscal period.

5. At December 31, 20X6, estimated compensated absences earned during 20X6 and expected to be paid in 20X7 (or subsequent periods) have been estimated by the company and are shown below:

	Based on Current Pay Rates	Based on Estimated Future Rates
a. Vacation leave	$125,000	$135,000
b. Sick leave	50,000	55,000
c. Paid holidays	20,000	23,000
d. Sabbatical leave	40,000	50,000
e. Jury duty	3,000	4,000
	$238,000	$267,000

The information presented in Example 7-2 represents all of the criteria necessary for accrual of a liability. The future benefits to be paid to employees represent payment for past services, the right to receive payment vests as earned, the future payment for sick leave and vacation leave is probable, and the amount of the payment can be reasonably estimated.

The sabbatical leave shown in Example 7-2 is the result of past services to Savage; and, assuming that it meets all the other criteria described above, the accrual of a liability is appropriate using the provisions of ASC 710-10.

The compensated absences associated with the paid holidays and jury duty should not be accrued because the amounts involved do not represent payment for past services.

The amount of the accrual is $215,000 ($125,000 vacation leave plus $50,000 sick leave plus $40,000 sabbatical leave). The accrual should be based on the existing current pay rates, rather than on estimated future pay rates. This accounting may require an adjustment in 20X7 if the future pay rates are realized. The adjustment should be treated as a change in an accounting estimate in accordance with the provisions of ASC 250. The journal entry to record the accrual would be:

Estimated Expense for Compensated Absences	215,000	
Estimated Liability for Compensated Absences		215,000

This completes the example material relating to accounting for compensated absences.

Topic 712: Compensation—Nonretirement Postemployment Benefits

Topic 712, *Compensation—Nonretirement Postemployment Benefits,* contains one subtopic:

10 Overall

General Discussion and Flowchart

ASC 712-10 specifies the accounting and reporting requirements for postemployment benefits.

Postemployment benefits are benefits paid after employment, and before retirement, to employees who have worked for the entity or employees who currently are not active and to dependents and beneficiaries of such employees. Examples of postemployment benefits include workers' compensation, short- and long-term disability benefits, health care and life insurance benefits, severance pay, wage continuation, and unemployment benefits that are considered supplemental. However, not all postemployment benefits are covered by ASC 712-10. The following four items are specifically excluded from the provisions of ASC 712-10:

1. Postretirement and pension plans that contain postemployment benefits that are accounted for using the provisions of ASC 715.
2. Contractual and special terminations benefits that are accounted for using the provisions of ASC 715.
3. Stock plans that are covered by ASC 718.
4. Plans classified as deferred compensation that are covered by the provisions of ASC 710.

The overall objective of ASC 712-10 is to determine whether to accrue a liability and expense or loss in connection with postemployment benefits. In an effort to determine if and when an accrual is required, the FASB uses the provisions of both ASC 710-10-25 on compensated absences and ASC 450 on contingencies to account for such postemployment benefits. If a postemployment benefit meets the conditions of ASC 710-10-25-1, a liability and expense must be accrued. However, if the conditions of ASC 710-10-25-1 are not met, a liability and loss will be accrued if the conditions of ASC 450 are met. If the provisions of ASC 710-10-25-1 or ASC 450 are not met, no accrual is required.

The integration of ASC 450 and ASC 710-10-25-1 is outlined in Flowchart 7-2. Once it has been determined that an entity provides postemployment benefits (Block 1), the benefits should be tested for accrual first using the four criteria in ASC 710-10-25-1. The first criterion specifies that the employer must be obligated to pay for postemployment benefits relating to services that have been performed by the employee (Block 2). That is, the employee must have provided services for the benefit. Next, the right to receive payment for the benefits must vest or accumulate (Block 3). Vested benefits or rights are those rights that are not dependent upon continued employment of the employee. That is, even if the employee terminates employment with the employer, the employer has an obligation to pay the employee for the amount of the benefit earned. An accumulated benefit is an earned benefit that can be carried forward to future periods if it has not been used. There may be limits on the amount of the benefit that can be carried forward or on the length of the carry forward period. Postemployment benefits generally do not meet the concept of vesting as intended under ASC 710-10-25-1 since they would not be paid if an employee terminated. However, some postemployment benefits do accumulate. For example, if an employee is provided disability benefits equal to 50% of his or her annual salary for one to five years of service, 65% for six to ten years of service and 80% for 10 years or more of service, the requirement that benefits accumulate has been met under ASC 710-10-25-1. The final two criteria for accrual under ASC 710-10-25-1 are very similar to the criteria required under ASC 450 on contingencies. Specifically, it must be probable that the future payments will be made for the postemployment benefit (Block 4); and, the amount of the future payment can be estimated (Block 5). If all of these conditions are met, the entity must record a liability and expense for the postemployment benefits. If the conditions in Blocks 2 through 4 have been met, but the amount of the future payment cannot be estimated, a footnote disclosure is required. If the particular benefit does not meet all of the conditions described in Blocks 2 through 5, the entity must determine if an accrual is required under the provisions of ASC 450 on contingencies.

Flowchart 7-2

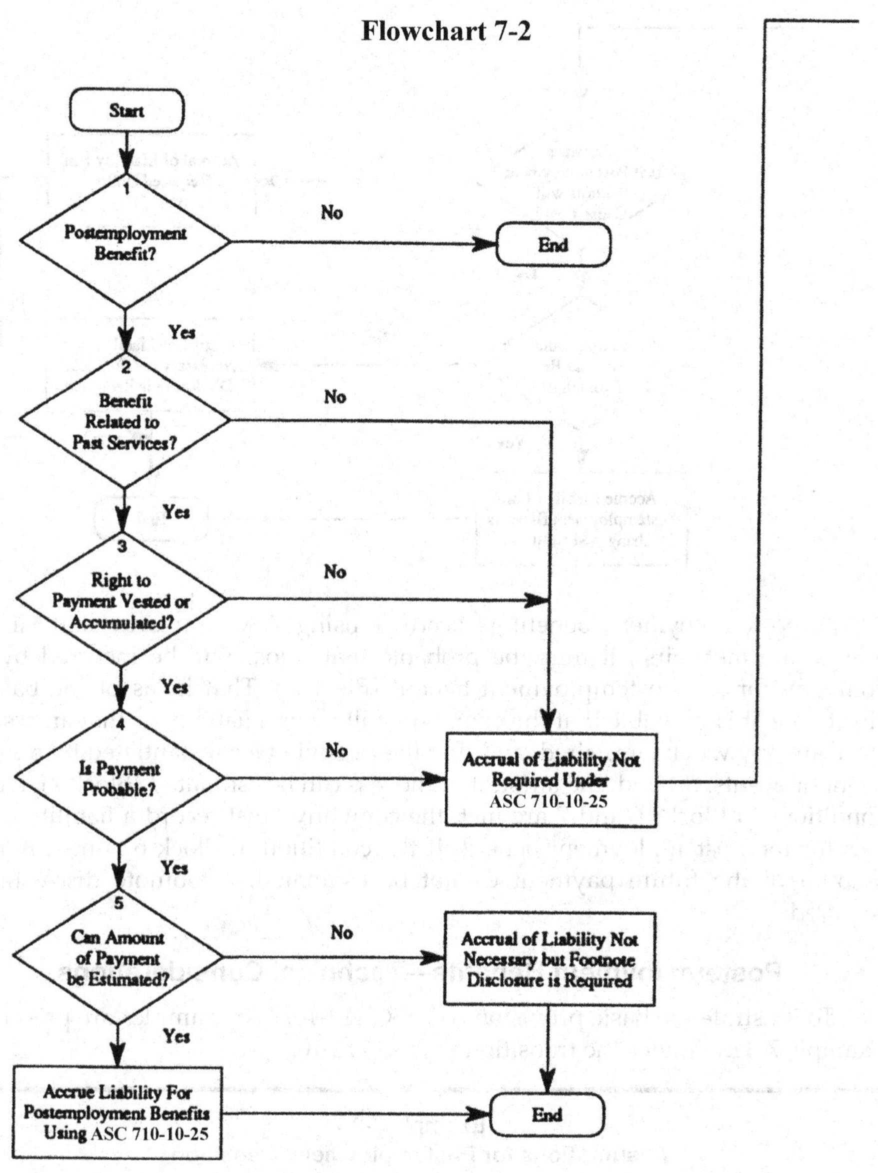

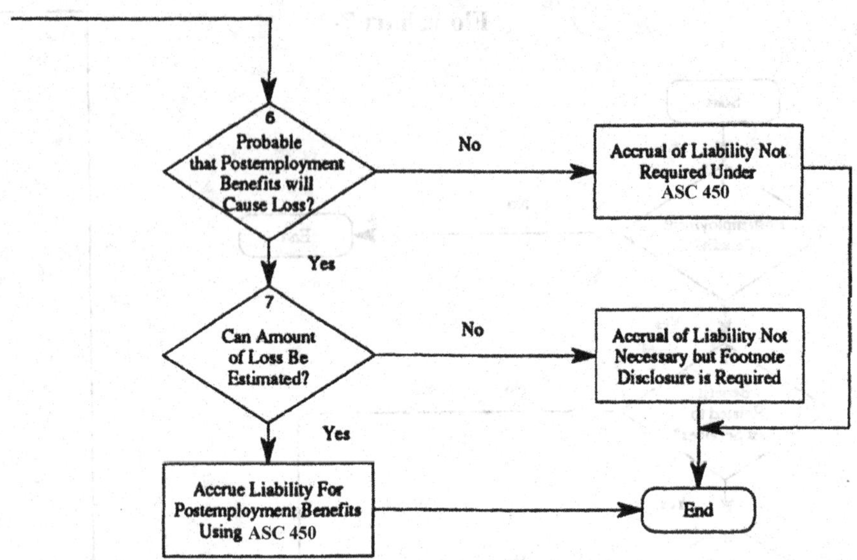

A postemployment benefit is accrued using ASC 450 provisions if two criteria are met. First, it must be probable that a loss will be incurred by the company for the postemployment benefit (Block 6). That is, as of the balance sheet date, it is probable that the company will incur a liability or that an asset of the company will be impaired, and that the loss will be substantiated by a future event or events. Second, the amount of the loss can be estimated (Block 7). If both conditions in Blocks 6 and 7 are met, the company must record a liability and a loss for the postemployment benefit. If the condition in Block 6 is met, but the amount of the future payment cannot be estimated, a footnote disclosure is required.

Postemployment Benefits—Technical Considerations

To illustrate the basic provisions of ASC 712-10, two examples are presented. Example 7-3 illustrates the transition to ASC 712-10.

Example 7-3
Assumptions for Postemployment Transition

1. The Johnson Company (Johnson), a December 31 year-end enterprise, provides employees with a variety of postemployment benefits such as workers' compensation, short-and long-term disability, and severance pay.
2. Johnson adopted ASC 712-10 on January 1, 20X6. At the time of adoption, company personnel determined that $15,000,000 of unrecorded postemployment benefits met the requirements for accrual under the provisions of either ASC 450 or ASC 710-10-25-1.

Using the information from Example 7-3, Johnson has $15,000,000 of unrecognized postemployment benefits that should be reported in its financial statements. When an enterprise adopts ASC 712-10, the transition is accounted for as a change in accounting principle.

This completes the discussion of the Example 7-3 material. The information presented in Example 7-4 illustrates the annual accounting issue related to postemployment benefits. Assumptions for Example 7-4 are as follows.

Example 7-4
Assumptions for Postemployment Benefits

1. Peterson Enterprises (Peterson), a December 31 year-end company, provides employees with several types of postemployment benefits. At December 31, 20X6, Peterson is reviewing its postemployment benefits to determine the amount of liability to record.
2. Employees are provided two weeks of severance pay for each year of employment. At the end of 20X6 it is probable that unrecorded severance pay of $1,500,000 will be paid in future years.
3. Peterson provides disability benefits to employees after two years of service. Disability payments are as follows: 60% of annual salary for employment years 3–10, 70% of annual salary for employment years 11–20, and 80% of annual salary for employment years 21 until retirement. At December 31, it is probable that $1,000,000 of unrecorded disability benefits will be paid in future years.
4. Medical insurance coverage is provided to all former employees who are permanently disabled. The insurance is continued until the employees are eligible for retirement. The level of benefits provided is the same regardless of years of service or salary levels. It is probable that $1,200,000 of recorded insurance benefits will be paid.
5. All employees are covered by workers' compensation. At the end of 20X6, it is probable that Peterson will incur $2,500,000 in workers' compensation claims filed during 20X6.

The information from Example 7-4 indicates that the unrecorded severance pay and the disability benefits meet the conditions for accrual under ASC 710-10-25-1. The severance pay and disability benefits are a result of services provided by the employees, the benefits accumulate, it is probable that payments will be made, and the amount of the payments can be estimated. The medical insurance coverage and workers' compensation do not meet the conditions of ASC 710-10-25-1 for accrual. The two benefits are not a result of services provided by the employees and the benefits do not vest or accumulate. The amount of the liability recorded for severance pay and disability benefits is $2,500,000 ($1,500,000 + $1,000,000). The following journal entry is required at December 31 to record the postemployment benefits:

Postemployment Benefit Expense	2,500,000	
Estimated Liability for Postemployment Benefits		2,500,000

Because the medical insurance coverage and workers' compensation did not meet the requirements for accrual under ASC 710-10-25-1, the two benefits should be checked to determine if they meet the requirements of ASC 450.

Because it is probable that Peterson will suffer a loss from the insurance coverage and the workers' compensation, and the amount of the loss can be estimated, an accrual is required under ASC 450. The amount of the loss to recognize in 20X6 is \$3,700,000 (\$1,200,000 + \$2,500,000). The journal entry required to record the loss at the end of 20X6 is as follows:

Estimated Loss from Postemployment Benefits	3,700,000	
Estimated Liability from Postemployment Benefits		3,700,000

Topic 715: Compensation—Retirement Benefits

Topic 715, *Compensation—Retirement Benefits*, contains 10 subtopics:

10 Overall

20 Defined Benefit Plans—General

30 Defined Benefit Plans—Pension

60 Defined Benefit Plans—Other Postretirement

70 Defined Contribution Plans

80 Multiemployer Plans

912 Contractors—Federal Government*

930 Extractive Activities—Mining*

958 Not-For-Profit Entities*

980 Regulated Operations*

* See the corresponding topic in Chapter 9 for coverage of this shared subtopic.

General Discussion and Definition of Important Terms

ASC 715 provides accounting and reporting guidance for entities that compensate their employees with pensions and other postretirement benefits. A pension plan is an agreement or arrangement with an entity and employees of the entity whereby the entity agrees to provide retired employees with benefits. Generally, the benefits are periodic cash payments, but may consist of lump-sum distributions such as death benefits.

ASC 715 applies to both written and well-defined unwritten pension plans. In addition, it is applicable to plans that are in substance equivalent to a pension plan and plans that provide health and welfare benefits after retirement. However, ASC 715 does not apply to plans that provide for life insurance not within a pension plan.

Before discussing Flowchart 7-3 and general aspects of accounting for pensions, it is important to define some of the terms that appear in Flowchart 7-3 and later in the example material. ASC 715 defines several specialized terms of which some are defined below and others later. Some explanation and supportive illustrations aid in the understanding of the meaning of the following terms contained in ASC 715:

1. *Defined Benefit Pension Plan.* A pension plan that defines the benefits to be received by employees or the method of determining the amount.

2. *Defined Contribution Plan.* A pension plan that specifies the method of determining contributions made to employees' accounts, but does not specify the benefits to be paid or the method of determining the benefits. Future benefits depend upon contributions to the plan and return earned on those contributions.

3. *Multiemployer Pension Plan.* A pension plan that is either a defined benefit or a defined contribution plan for two or more employers, each making contributions to the same plan determined by formula usually under a collective bargaining arrangement.

4. *Multiple-Employer Pension Plan.* A pension plan where two or more unrelated employers contribute to a pension plan that generally is not under a collective bargaining arrangement. The plan is not classified as a multiemployer plan, but is in substance an aggregation of single employer plans.

5. *Service Cost.* Cost to an employer for credit for pension benefits given to employees for services provided during the current year.

6. *Projected Benefit Obligation.* The obligation of an enterprise on a specified date, based on services provided by employees prior to that date, for the present value of pension benefits to be paid to employees in future years. The projected benefit obligation considers future salary levels in its computation, if the benefit formula is based on future salary levels.

7. *Accumulated Benefit Obligation.* The obligation of an enterprise on a specified date, based on services provided by employees prior to the date, for the present value of pension benefits to be paid to employees in future years. The accumulated benefit obligation amount does not reflect any consideration for future salary levels.

8. *Prior Service Cost.* The increase or decrease in pension cost for benefits granted or reduced on a retroactive basis resulting from an amendment or initiation of a pension plan.

9. *Market-Related Value of Pension Plan Assets.* The market-related value of plan assets is either the fair value of the plan's assets or a computed value. A computed value is determined using a method that recognizes changes in fair value of the assets over a period of time not to exceed five years in a systematic and rational manner. The market-related value of plan assets is the basis used to calculate the expected return on plan assets.

10. *Measurement Date.* The date on which the fair value of plan assets and the pension obligation are computed. Generally, the measurement date is the balance sheet date.

With this introduction to the preceding terms, the reader should be able to understand the features in Flowchart 7-3.

Flowchart and General Discussion

Flowchart 7-3 identifies the general accounting and reporting requirements for pension plans as specified in ASC 715. The decision blocks have been numbered for referencing in the discussion below.

Flowchart 7-3

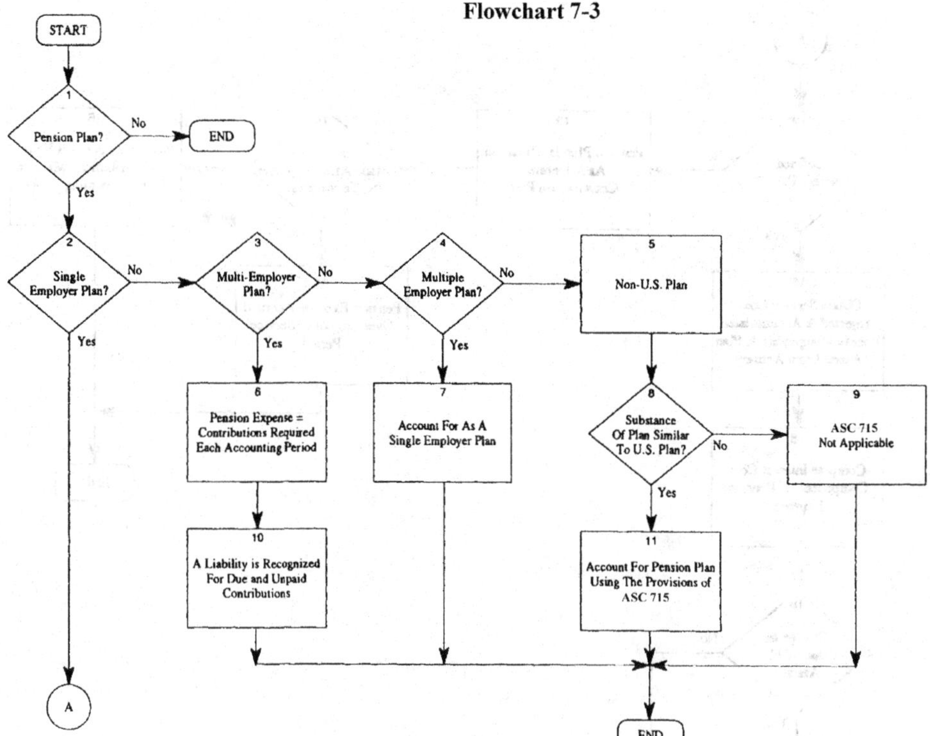

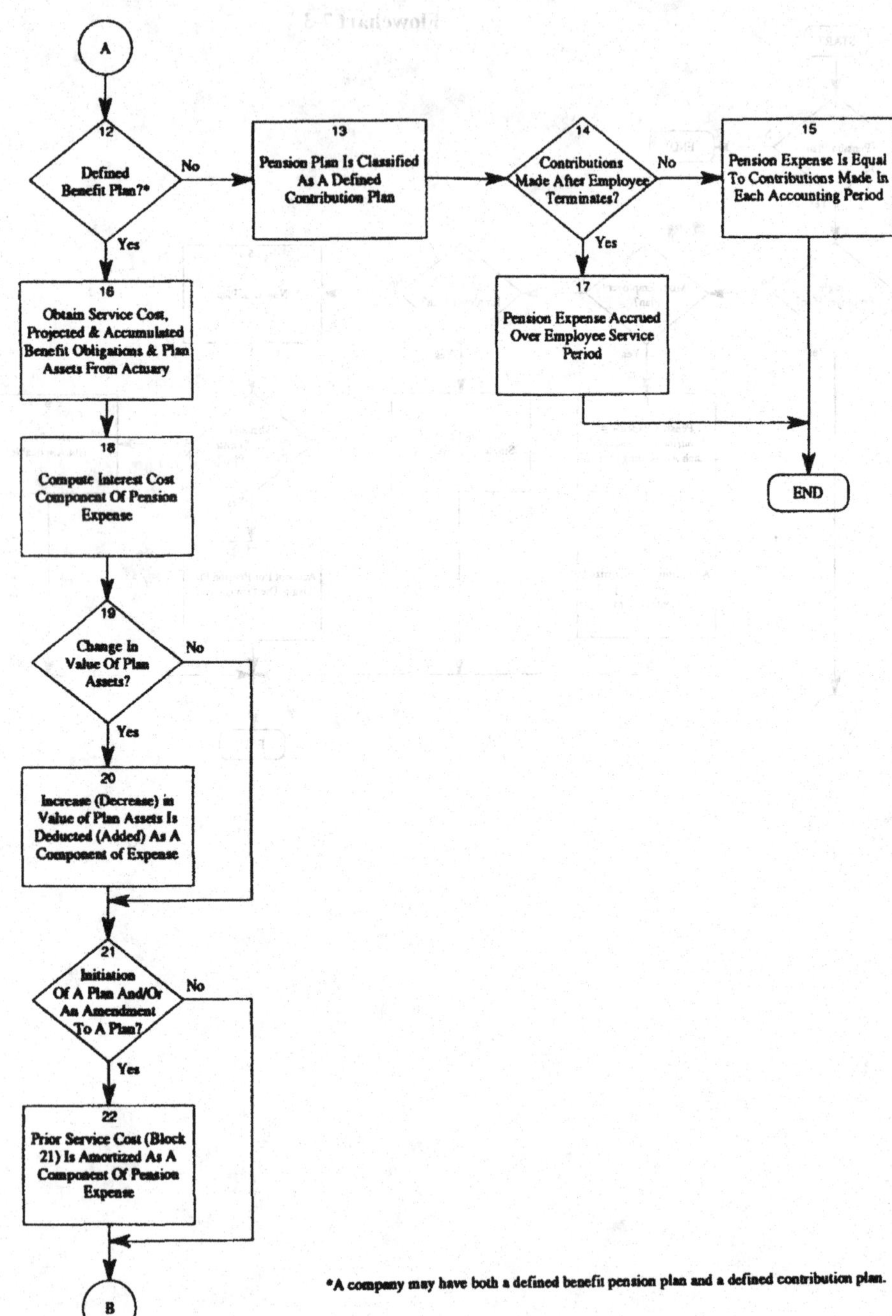

*A company may have both a defined benefit pension plan and a defined contribution plan.

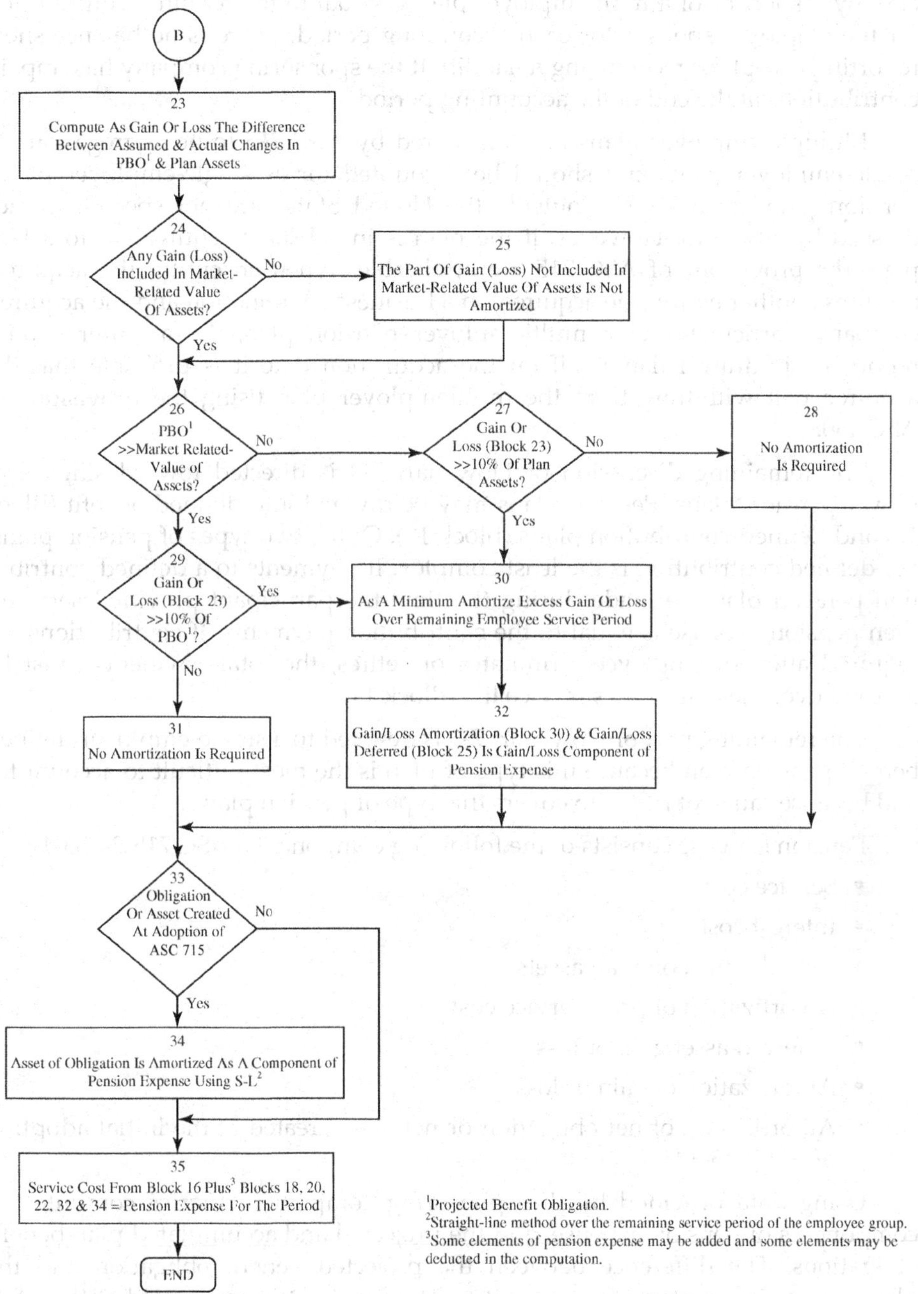
B
23
Compute As Gain Or Loss The Difference Between Assumed & Actual Changes In PBO[1] & Plan Assets
24
Any Gain (Loss) Included In Market-Related Value Of Assets?
No
25
The Part Of Gain (Loss) Not Included In Market-Related Value Of Assets Is Not Amortized
Yes
26
PBO[1] >>Market Related-Value of Assets?
No
27
Gain Or Loss (Block 23) >>10% Of Plan Assets?
No
28
No Amortization Is Required
Yes
Yes
29
Gain Or Loss (Block 23) >>10% Of PBO[1]?
Yes
30
As A Minimum Amortize Excess Gain Or Loss Over Remaining Employee Service Period
No
31
No Amortization Is Required
32
Gain/Loss Amortization (Block 30) & Gain/Loss Deferred (Block 25) Is Gain/Loss Component of Pension Expense
33
Obligation Or Asset Created At Adoption of ASC 715
No
Yes
34
Asset of Obligation Is Amortized As A Component of Pension Expense Using S-L[2]
35
Service Cost From Block 16 Plus[3] Blocks 18, 20, 22, 32 & 34 = Pension Expense For The Period
END
[1]Projected Benefit Obligation.
[2]Straight-line method over the remaining service period of the employee group.
[3]Some elements of pension expense may be added and some elements may be deducted in the computation.

Pension plans can be divided into single-employer plans (Block 2), multiemployer plans (Block 3), multiple-employer plans (Block 4), and non-U.S. plans (Block 5).

Accounting and reporting by single-employer plans is discussed later; most of ASC 715 is concerned with single-employer plans. Pension expense for an employer sponsor of a multiemployer plan is equal to the required contribution for the employer sponsor for each accounting period. There is no balance sheet reporting except for recognizing a liability if the sponsoring company has unpaid contributions at the end of the accounting period.

Multiple-employer plans are considered by ASC 715 to be aggregations of single-employer plans and should be accounted for as single-employer plans. Pension plan arrangements outside the United States are not specifically addressed by ASC 715. However, if the plan is in substance equivalent to a U.S. plan, the provisions of ASC 715 are applicable. When an entity (the acquirer) acquires another entity (the acquiree) in a business combination and the acquired company participates in a multiemployer pension plan, the acquirer should report a withdrawal liability if on the acquisition date it is probable that the acquiree will withdraw from the multiemployer plan using the provisions of ASC 450.

The remaining discussion of Flowchart 7-3 is directed toward single-employer pension plans. Pension plans may be divided into defined benefit (Block 12) and defined contribution plans (Block 13). Of the two types of pension plans, the defined contribution is the least complex. If payments to a defined contribution pension plan are made during the time the participant provided services, then pension expense is equal to the contribution payments. If contributions are required after an employee terminates or retires, the total payments must be accrued over the employee's service life (Block 14).

The remaining part of Flowchart 7-3 is devoted to a single-employer defined benefit pension plan because this type of plan is the most difficult to account for and because much of ASC 715 covers this type of pension plan.

Pension expense consists of the following components (ASC 715-30-35-4):

- Service cost
- Interest cost
- Actual return on plan assets
- Amortization of prior service cost
- Deferred asset gain or loss
- Amortization of gain or loss
- Amortization of net obligation or net asset created at the initial adoption of ASC 715-30

Using data provided by the sponsoring company, actuaries compute the components of pension expense, and the projected and accumulated plan benefit obligations. The difference between the projected benefit obligation and the plan's assets is the plan's funded status. The plan's assets are stated at their fair value (Block 16).

The service cost component of pension cost is determined by the actuary based on the plan's benefit formula. The interest cost component represents the increase in the projected benefit obligation as a result of the passage of time. The interest cost component may be computed (Block 18) using the following formula:

IC = APBOB × ADR

IC	= Interest cost component of pension expense.
APBOB	= Actual projected benefit obligation at the beginning of the accounting period.
ADR	= Assumed discount rate.

The interest cost component is computed as of the end of the accounting period using the beginning-of-period balance of the projected benefit obligation.

The expected rate of return on plan assets is reflected in the determination of pension cost but the actual rate of return is disclosed. The difference between the actual rate of return and the expected rate of return is reflected in the deferred asset gain or loss component of pension cost as discussed below. The actual return on plan assets is the difference between the beginning- and end-of-period balances in the fair value of plan assets, adjusted for contributions and benefit payments (Blocks 19 and 20). The actual return on plan assets may be computed using the formula below:

APRA = (AFPAE – C + B) – AFPAB

ARPA	= Actual return on plan assets.
AFPAE	= Actual fair value of plan assets at end of accounting period.
C	= Contributions to pension plan during accounting period.
B	= Benefit payments from pension plan.
AFPAB	= Actual fair value of plan assets at beginning of accounting period.

If the fair value of plan assets is greater at the end of the period, the actual return is deducted as a component of the pension cost, i.e., deferred asset gain. If fair value is less at the end of the period, the actual return is added to pension cost, i.e., deferred asset loss. Combining the actual return with the deferred asset gain or loss equals the expected return on plan assets.

For purposes of applying the provisions of ASC 715-30, plan assets include assets that have been segregated and restricted, such as those in a trust, for the purpose of paying pension benefits. Included in such assets are investments in bonds, stocks, real estate, and contracts with insurance companies. Assets that are not restricted from use by the employer are not considered plan assets. In addition, contributions accrued by the employer but not paid to the trust are not considered plan assets.

The fair value of plan assets used in computing the actual return on the assets is defined as the amount that would be received on the measurement date from the sale of property between sellers and buyers (market participants) in an orderly transaction. In addition, the sellers and buyers are unrelated parties on the measurement date.

Another component of pension cost is amortization of any prior service cost (Blocks 21 and 22). Prior service cost is the retroactive change in pension cost (increase or decrease in the projected benefit obligation) from an amendment to a pension plan. In addition, prior service cost includes costs related to the initiation of a pension plan. For example, if a pension plan is initiated during the current year, the cost to the company for credit given to employees for services provided in periods prior to the inception of the plan is prior service cost.

Increases in prior service cost during the accounting period from the amendment or initiation of a pension plan are debited to other comprehensive income and credited to either a pension liability or pension asset. Decreases in prior service cost are debited to either a pension liability or pension asset and credited to other comprehensive income.

Prior service cost that is an increase in the projected benefit obligation is amortized over the future service periods of employees who:

- Are active on the date of the amendment or initiation of the pension plan, and
- Expect to receive benefits under the pension plan.

If most of the participants in the pension plan are inactive on the date of amendment or initiation, the amortization period should be the remaining life expectancy of the pension plan participants. Alternatively, the plan sponsor may elect to amortize prior service cost more rapidly. If an alternative method is elected, the method should be disclosed.

If an amendment decreases the projected benefit obligation, the decrease is used to reduce any existing unamortized balance of prior service cost. As a result of amendments that decrease benefits, the unamortized balance of prior service cost may be negative. Such a negative balance would be amortized as discussed above.

The amount of prior service cost amortized to pension cost during the accounting period is also removed from other comprehensive income. In the statement of comprehensive income, such amortization will be shown as a reclassification adjustment. (Note: Each component of other comprehensive income amount is closed to accumulated other comprehensive income. Therefore, when the prior service cost is amortized to pension cost, the reclassification adjustment requires a credit to other comprehensive income that then reduces the original debit that is included in accumulated other comprehensive income.) Prior service cost is included in other comprehensive income when it is created through a plan amendment or plan initiation and is removed from other comprehensive income when the prior service cost is amortized to pension cost. Frequently, deferred income taxes are associated with items of other comprehensive income, such as prior service cost and related amortization. The provisions of ASC 740 should be reviewed to determine whether there is a tax impact related to prior service cost.

The next component of pension cost to consider is the gain or loss to extent recognized (Block 23). Gains and losses, including both realized and unrealized gains and losses, are the differences between (1) assumed or expected rates of return on plan assets (i.e., asset gains and losses) and (2) the actual and expected projected benefit obligation (i.e., liability or actuarial gains or losses). For example, the projected benefit obligation may have been based upon certain assumptions about employee turnover, among other things, and future events may indicate that the assumed turnover was substantially different than the actual turnover. Another example would be where the contributions invested in the plan earned a higher or lower rate of return than anticipated.

The net gain or loss consists of the following three parts:

1. The difference between actual and expected returns on the projected benefit obligation.
2. The difference between actual and anticipated returns on plan assets.
3. The part of the gain or loss not included in the market-related value of plan assets and not subject to amortization (Block 24).

Using the preceding information, computation of the net gain or loss seems relatively straightforward. However, the calculation is very complex. Three formulas are presented to explain the calculations. The first two formulas compute the net gain or loss that is subject to amortization (Items 1 and 2, above). The third formula calculates the asset gain or loss that is not subject to amortization (Item 3). The two formulas to compute the net gain or loss subject to amortization are presented below:

(G)/L = (APBOB – AFPAB) – (EPBOB – EFPAB) + P(G)/L

(G)/L	= Gain or loss at beginning of accounting period.
APBOB	= Actual projected benefit obligation at the beginning of the accounting period.
AFPAB	= Actual fair value of plan assets at the beginning of the accounting period.
EPBOB	= Estimated projected benefit obligation at the beginning of the accounting period.
EFPAB	= Estimated fair value of plan assets at the beginning of the accounting period.
P(G)/L	= Gain or loss at end of prior year after deducting any required amortization in prior year.

(G)/LSA = (G)/L + (AFPAB – MRPAB)

(G)/LSA	= Gain or loss subject to amortization.
(G)/L	= Gain or loss at beginning of accounting period.
AFPAB	= Actual fair value of plan assets at the beginning of the accounting period.
MRPAB	= Market-related value of plan assets at the beginning of the accounting period.

The two preceding formulas may be turned into a tabular format so as to make computations easier to visualize and understand. A tabular format of the two formulas is presented in Chart 7-2.

Chart 7-2 Tabular Format for Computation of Net Gain or Loss Subject to Amortization

Actual Projected Benefit Obligation		$00000000
Actual Fair Value of Plan Assets		(00000000)
Excess		$000000
Estimated Projected Benefit Obligation	$(0000000)	
Estimated Fair Value of Plan Assets	0000000	(000000)
(Gain)/Loss Before Prior Years' (Gain)/Loss		$000000
(Gain)/Loss from Prior Periods		000000
(Gain)/Loss at Beginning of Period		$000000
Fair Value of Plan Assets	$0000000	

Market-Related Value of Plan Assets	(0000000)
Gain/(Loss) Not Included in Market-Related Value of Plan Assets	000000
(Gain)/Loss Subject to Amortization	$000000

Using the preceding two formulas and the tabular format above, it can be seen that the difference between actual projected benefit obligation and actual fair value of plan assets and the estimated or projected amounts is the gain or loss for the year. However, this gain or loss does not consider any carryover of gains or losses from previous years. The end-of-period balance from the prior year, if any, after deducting proper amortization is added/deducted from the current gain or loss. The carryover gain or loss from the previous period does not include the gain or loss not included in the market-related value of plan assets (i.e., the part of the gain or loss that is the difference between fair value of plan assets and market-related value of plan assets). After the gain or loss at the beginning of the period has been computed, the gain or loss is adjusted for the gain or loss not included in the market-related value of plan assets. The ending gain or loss is the gain or loss subject to amortization.

Incorporating the market-related value concept into the computation of the gain or loss subject to amortization is another effort by the FASB to reduce the possible volatility in the pension expense computation. Increases in the gain or loss during the accounting period are debited to other comprehensive income and credited to either a pension liability or pension asset. Decreases in the gain or loss are debited to either a pension liability or pension asset and credited to other comprehensive income.

After the gain or loss subject to amortization has been computed, a test must be made to determine if amortization is required. First, the projected benefit obligation at the beginning of the year is compared to the market-related value of the plan assets at the beginning of the year (Block 26). Second, the larger of these two amounts is selected. The gain or loss subject to amortization is compared to 10% of the larger of the beginning-of-year market-related value of the assets of the pension plan or the projected benefit obligation (Blocks 27 and 29). If the gain or loss exceeds 10% of the larger amount, amortization is required. If the gain or loss is less than 10%, no amortization is required (Block 28). If amortization is required, only the excess of the gain or loss over 10% of the larger number is amortized. The excess gain or loss is amortized in the following manner:

1. The excess gain or loss is amortized by dividing the excess gain or excess loss by the average service years remaining for all participants who are active and anticipate receiving pension plan benefits.

2. If most of the participants in the pension plan are not active, the excess gain or excess loss should be divided by the average life expectancy remaining for those employees who are not active.

3. As an alternative to 1 or 2, above, any systematic amortization method is appropriate, as long as the following conditions are met:

a. The amortization in 1 or 2, above, is used any time the alternative method produces annual amortization less than what would be computed in 1 or 2, above;

b. The alternative amortization procedure is applied on a consistent basis;

c. The alternative amortization procedure is applied in the same manner to gains and losses; and

d. The alternative amortization procedure is disclosed in the financial statements.

The amount of the gain or loss amortized to pension cost during the accounting period is removed from other comprehensive income using a reclassification adjustment. For example, if a gain is amortized to pension expense, a gain was reported as a credit to other comprehensive income in the accounting period that the gain originated. The other comprehensive income amount was closed to accumulated other comprehensive income as a credit balance. Therefore, when the gain is amortized to pension expense, the reclassification adjustment requires a debit to other comprehensive income that then reduces the original credit that is included in accumulated other comprehensive income. The gain or loss is included in other comprehensive income when it is created and is removed from other comprehensive income when the gain or loss is amortized to pension cost. The provisions of ASC 740 should be reviewed to determine whether there is a tax impact related to the gain or loss.

The third formula is used to compute the amount of the asset gain or loss that is deferred (i.e., the amount of the gain or loss that is not amortized, but is included in total in the gain or loss component of the pension expense). The formula is presented below:

$$DAG/(L) = ((AFPAE - C + B) - AFPAB)) - (EROR \times MRPAB)$$

DAG/(L)	= Deferred asset gain or loss.
AFPAE	= Actual fair value of plan assets at end of accounting period.
C	= Contributions to pension plan during accounting period.
B	= Benefit payments from pension plan during accounting period.
AFPAB	= Actual fair value of plan assets at beginning of accounting period.
EROR	= Expected long-term rate of return on plan assets.
MRPAB	= Market-related value of plan assets at the beginning of the accounting period.

The deferred gain or loss computed by the formula is the excess of the actual return on plan assets over the expected rate of return on plan assets. A deferred gain is added as part of the gain or loss component of pension expense, and a deferred loss is deducted.

By adding the deferred asset gain and deducting the deferred asset loss, the volatility of the pension expense or pension income created by using the actual return on plan assets in the pension expense calculation is reduced. A deferred asset gain is added in the computation of pension expense and the combination of the deferred asset gain and the actual return equal the expected return on plan assets. A deferred asset loss is deducted in the computation of pension expense, and the combination of the deferred asset loss and the actual return equal the expected return on plan assets.

The last component of pension expense to consider is amortization of the pension obligation or asset created at the adoption of ASC 715-30 (Block 33). The asset or obligation is computed on the measurement date for the first year in which ASC 715-30 is applied. The asset or obligation is computed below:

(A)/O = APBOT – (AFPAT + APC – PPC)

(A)/O	= Net asset or net obligation established at initial adoption of ASC 715-30.
APBOT	= Actual projected benefit obligation on the date of transition to ASC 715-30.
AFPAT	= Actual fair value of plan assets on the date of transition to ASC 715-30.
APC	= Balance in the pension liability account on the date of transition to ASC 715-30.
PPC	= Balance in the pension asset account on the date of transition to ASC 715-30.

If the projected benefit obligation exceeds the fair value of plan assets and related accounts, an obligation is recognized. However, if plan assets and related accounts exceed the projected benefit obligation, an asset is recognized.

The asset or obligation created at the adoption of ASC 715-30 is amortized (Block 34) in the following manner (Paragraph 77):

1. The transitional asset or obligation is amortized by dividing the asset or obligation by the average service years remaining for all participants who are active and anticipate receiving pension plan benefits (a straight-line method).
2. If the service period in 1, above, is less than 15 years, 15 years may be selected by the entity for the amortization period.
3. If most of the participants in the pension plan are not active, the transitional asset or obligation should be divided by the average life expectancy remaining for those employees who are not active.

The amount of the transitional asset or transitional obligation amortized to pension cost during the accounting period is removed from other comprehensive income using a reclassification adjustment. For example, if the transitional item is an obligation, amortization of the transitional obligation increases pension expense and requires a credit to other comprehensive income for the amount of the obligation amortization to pension expense. The credit to other comprehensive income will be closed to accumulated other comprehensive income to reduce the original amount of the transitional obligation that was reported as a debit to accumulated other comprehensive income. Therefore, when a transitional obligation is amortized to pension expense, the reclassification adjustment requires a credit to other comprehensive income that then reduces the original debit that is included in accumulated other comprehensive income. If the transitional item is an asset, the accounting is reversed. Amortization of the transitional asset requires a debit to other comprehensive income as a reclassification adjustment that then reduces the original credit that is included in accumulated other comprehensive income. Therefore, transitional assets or obligations are removed from accumulated other comprehensive income when the transitional items are amortized to pension cost. The provisions of ASC 740 should be reviewed to determine whether there is a tax impact related to the transitional asset or obligation.

This completes the explanation of the computation of the annual pension expense or pension income. The final pension cost is equal to the accumulation of the components as indicated in the preceding discussion of prior service cost, actuarial gains and losses, and transitional assets and obligations. However, three items used in the computation of the gain or loss subject to amortization require further discussion. The three items are estimated projected benefit obligation, estimated fair value of plan assets, and market-related value of plan assets when a computed amount is used instead of fair value. The method of computing each of these elements is presented below using a tabular format. Chart 7-3 shows the calculation of the estimated projected benefit obligation.

Chart 7-3 Computation of Estimated Projected Benefit Obligation

Actual beginning projected benefit obligation (PBO)	$0000000000
Service cost for period	000000
Interest Cost:	
Actual beginning PBO	$0000000000
Assumed discount rate	0%
Interest cost for period	000000
Benefit payments for period	(000000)
Prior service cost	0000000
Ending Estimated PBO	$0000000000

Next, the estimated fair value of plan assets is computed. Chart 7-4 shows the calculation.

Chart 7-4 Computation of Estimated Fair Value of Plan Assets (FVOPA)

Actual beginning FVOPA		$0000000000
Expected Return:		
Market-related value of plan assets	$0000000000	
Long-term rate of return	00%	
Expected return		000000
Contributions during period		000000
Benefit payments during period		(000000)
Ending estimated FVOPA		$0000000000

Chart 7-5 illustrates the computation of the market-related value of plan assets.

Chart 7-5 Computation of Market-Related Value of Plan Assets (MRPA)

Beginning MRPA		$0000000000
Expected Return:		
Beginning MRPA	$000000000	
Long-term rate of return	00%	
Expected return	000000	
Contributions during period	000000	
Benefit payments during period	(000000)	
Amortization of deferred asset gain or (loss) (from Chart 7-6)	0000	
Ending MRPA	$0000000000	

The amortization of the deferred asset gain or loss used in the computation of the market related value of plan assets is computed in Chart 7-6.

Chart 7-6 Calculation and Amortization of the Deferred Asset Gain/(Loss)

Calculation of Deferred Asset Gain/(Loss)		
Ending fair value of plan assets		$0000000000
Add: Benefit payments		000000
Deduct: Contributions		(000000)
Adjusted ending fair value		$0000000000
Beginning fair value of plan assets		(0000000000)
Actual return		$00000
Expected Return:		
Market-related value of plan assets	($0000000000)	
Long-term rate of return	00%	
Expected return		(00000)
Deferred asset gain (loss)		$ 0000

Amortization of Deferred Asset Gain/(Loss)

Deferred asset gain/(loss)	
Year	
1	$00000
2	00000
3	(00000)
4	00000
5	(00000)
Total	$00000
Amortization period (in years)	÷ 0
Amount of amortization	$ 000

The deferred asset gain or loss is amortized to the market related value of plan assets over a period of time not to exceed five years.

Next the enterprise must determine the proper journal entry to make for the pension cost computed for the accounting period. If the pension cost computation includes amortization of items included in accumulated other comprehensive income (such as prior service cost, actuarial gains, or losses, and transitional assets or obligations), a debit or credit to other comprehensive income (a reclassification adjustment) is required for the amount of the amortization included in the pension cost computation. Cash is credited for any contributions and pension cost is debited for any pension expense or credited if the entity reports pension income in the computation. Any difference between the pension cost (assuming pension expense) plus any debits to other comprehensive income and cash contributions plus any credits to other comprehensive income is an adjustment to a pension asset or a pension liability account. In addition, an entry is required to record any change (other than amounts amortized) in the amount of prior service cost or actuarial gains and losses during the accounting period. The change in prior service cost or actuarial gains and losses is included in other comprehensive income with an adjustment to either a pension asset or pension liability. For example, if prior service cost is increased from a plan amendment during the accounting period, the entity increases other comprehensive income for the increase that is not included in the current year pension cost and either a pension liability or a pension asset is increased or decreased for a corresponding amount.

An entity must report in its statement of financial position a pension asset or pension liability for the amount of any overfunded or underfunded pension plan. The funded status of all overfunded plans should be aggregated and one pension asset amount is reported for all overfunded plans. The funded status of all underfunded pension plans should be aggregated and one pension liability amount is reported for all underfunded pension plans. The pension asset or liability is computed as the difference between the projected benefit obligation and the fair value of plan asset on the measurement date, which is the date of the statement of financial position. A pension plan asset from an overfunded pension plan is classified as a noncurrent asset in the balance sheet; however, a pension plan liability is classified as either current, noncurrent, or a combination of current and noncurrent. A plan-by-plan approach is used to determine the pension liability classification. The present value of the benefits determined on an actuarial basis included in the pension plan obligation meeting the definition of a current item is classified as a current liability (payable within one year or the normal operating cycle, whichever is longer). The provisions of ASC 740 should be used to determine any tax impact.

This completes the discussion of Flowchart 7-3 and general application of ASC 715-30. However, for a complete understanding of the standard, other considerations should be addressed.

- First, consideration should be given to the difference between projected benefit obligation and accumulated benefit obligation. Before continuing with the material, review the definitions of projected and accumulated benefit obligations in the preceding discussion. The accumulated benefit obligation uses no assumption about future salary levels, and the projected benefit obligation considers future salary levels if the pension benefit formula is based on future levels. The projected benefit obligation may be based on a pay-related plan or a non-pay-related plan. An example of a pay-related plan is a final-pay plan. A final-pay plan is a pension plan benefit formula where the benefits that an employee will receive are computed using a participant's salary over a specified number of years. An example of a non-pay-related plan is a flat-benefit plan. A flat-benefit plan is a pension benefit formula where the benefits that an employee will receive are computed using a specific fixed amount for each service year. If the projected benefit obligation uses a non-pay-related plan, the accumulated and projected benefit obligations are the same, because the accumulated benefit obligation uses a non-pay-related plan.

- Second, the measurement date as defined in the introduction section requires further explanation. The measurement date for purposes of computing the pension obligation and the fair value of the plan assets is the date of the statement of financial position, unless one of the following conditions is met: (1) a subsidiary is consolidated with a parent company when the subsidiary has a year-end that is different from the parent and the pension plan is sponsored by the subsidiary and (2) an investee company that is accounted for by using the equity method of accounting has a different year-end from the investor company and the pension plan is sponsored by the investee company. Under the foregoing two situations, pension plan assets and obligations should be measured on the date used to consolidate the subsidiary's statement of financial position for the subsidiary and the date used to apply the equity method for the investee company. Also, under ASU 2015-04, *Compensation—Retirement Benefits (Topic 715): Practical Expedient for the Measurement Date of an Employer's Defined Benefit Obligation and Plan Assets*, as a practical expedient, the reporting entity may make an accounting policy election to measure defined benefit plan assets and obligations using the month-end closest to the reporting entity's fiscal year-end. Once adopted, this practical expedient should be consistently followed from year to year and consistently applied to all plans. For public entities, ASU 2015-04 is effective for years beginning after December 15, 2015, and for interim periods within those years. For other entities, ASU 2015-04 is effective for years beginning after December 15, 2016, and interim periods within years beginning after December 15, 2017. Earlier application is permitted for both public and private entities. This standard is to be applied prospectively.

When preparing interim financial statements, the entity should use the funded status of the pension plan at the most recent fiscal year-end statement of position date and adjust the funded status for the following: (1) contributions or benefit payments and (2) accrual of benefit cost elements (such as service cost, interest cost, and return on assets), excluding amortized items, that occurred subsequent to the statement of position date. If an entity remeasures its pension assets and obligations during a fiscal year for events (such as plan amendments settlements or curtailments), it should use those remeasurement amounts in subsequent interim accounting periods.

The next item to consider is the attribution method. The service component of pension expense and the projected and accumulated benefit obligation should be measured using a single method. The method assigns the benefits or costs of the pension plan to the time periods during which employees provide services, using the formula prescribed in the pension plan arrangement. The benefits assigned to specific years of employee service are based on the present value of actuarial assumptions. Each actuarial assumption used in the measurement process reflects an estimate solely with respect to that assumption, and all assumptions are estimated assuming a going concern for the pension plan.

Another item to consider is accounting for pension benefits when an entity (the acquirer) is involved in a business combination using the provisions of ASC 805. When an entity (the acquirer) acquires a company (the acquiree) that sponsors a single-employer defined benefit pension plan, an asset or liability should be recorded for the difference between fair value of plan assets and the projected benefit obligation (the funded status). If the obligation exceeds the fair value of the plan assets, a liability is recorded and if the assets exceed the obligation, an asset is recorded. When the funded status is determined, the impact of expected plan amendments, curtailments, or terminations should be excluded by the acquirer if the acquirer does not have an obligation to make the changes. The projected benefit obligation assumed by the acquirer should include any changes of assumptions that the acquiring company determines to be appropriate using all future events considered relevant by the acquirer.

Not-for-profit entities may have defined-benefit pension plans. A not-for-profit entity must report in its statement of financial position a pension asset or pension liability for the amount of any overfunded or underfunded pension plan. The funded status of all overfunded plans should be aggregated and one pension asset amount is reported for all overfunded plans. The funded status of all underfunded pension plans should be aggregated and one pension liability amount is reported for all underfunded pension plans. The pension asset or liability is computed as the difference between the projected benefit obligation and the fair value of plan assets on the measurement date, which is the date of the statement of financial position. If the not-for-profit entity prepares a classified statement of financial position, a pension plan asset from an overfunded pension plan is classified as a noncurrent asset in the balance sheet; however, a pension plan liability is classified as either current, noncurrent, or a combination of current and noncurrent. A plan-by-plan approach is used to determine the pension liability classification. The present value of the benefits determined on an actuarial basis that are included in the pension plan obligation meeting the definition of a current item is classified as a current liability (payable within one year or the normal operating cycle, whichever is longer. Gains or losses and prior service cost or credits that arise during the accounting period that are not used in the computation of pension expense are included as a separate line item(s) within changes in unrestricted net assets. In addition, the amount of the gain or loss, prior service cost or credits, and transitional assets or obligations amortized to pension cost during the accounting period are removed from the unrestricted net assets using a reclassification adjustment. The provisions of ASC 740 should be used to determine any tax impact. The measurement date for a defined benefit pension plan for a not-for-profit entity is the same as for a profit entity and the interim reporting information is the same as for a business entity.

Technical Considerations

Three examples are used to illustrate the technical considerations related to pensions. Assumptions for Example 7-5 are presented below.

Example 7-5
Assumptions for Defined Benefit Pension Plan

1. The Johnson Company (Johnson), a public enterprise with a calendar year end, has a defined benefit pension plan that covers substantially all employees. Johnson has only U.S. operations and elects to adopt all provisions of ASC 715-30 on January 1, 20X6.

2. On January 1, 20X6, the date of transition to ASC 715-30, Johnson's actuary provided the following information:

(a) Projected benefit obligation	$1,200,000
(b) Fair value of plan assets	1,025,000
(c) Market-related value of plan assets	1,025,000
(d) Average remaining service life of employees at date of transition (majority of employees are active).	14 years

3. On December 31, 20X6, 20X7, and 20X8 (the balance sheet date and the measurement date for the pension plan), the following information was provided by Johnson's actuary or by its personnel:

	20X6	20X7	20X8
(a) Service cost	$150,000	$180,000	$225,000
(b) Actual projected benefit obligation	1,500,000	1,650,000	1,800,000
(c) Estimated projected benefit obligation	1,300,250	1,606,092	1,770,093
(d) Actual fair value of plan assets	1,100,000	1,325,000	1,450,000
(e) Estimated fair value of plan assets	1,137,750	1,224,322	1,464,382
(f) Market-related value of plan assets	1,130,200	1,267,108	1,416,199
(g) Accumulated benefit obligation	1,200,000	1,515,000	1,600,000
(h) Contributions to trust	169,750	223,908	269,907
(i) Assumed discount rate	10%	10%	10%
(j) Expected long-term rate of return on plan assets	11%	11%	11%

4. The future service life for all amortization, except amortization related to the initial adoption of ASC 715-30, is 10 years.

5. Benefit payments and contributions to the pension trust are the same for all years.

6. Deferred asset gains and losses are amortized to the market-related value of plan assets over the maximum period allowed, which is five years.

7. This example assumes that any transitional asset or obligation is included in accumulated other comprehensive income.

The first step in analyzing the assumptions in Example 7-5 is to compute the pension expenses for 20X6, 20X7, and 20X8. The pension expense calculation requires six complex computations. Several pages are needed to analyze the assumptions in the example, and the reader is encouraged to refer frequently to the assumptions in Example 7-5 to fully understand the analysis. Each element of pension expense for each year is computed separately and then all elements are summarized to compute total pension expense.

The first element of pension expense is service cost. The service cost component is provided by the actuary and requires no computation. The service costs for 20X6, 20X7, and 20X8 are shown in Table 7-1.

Table 7-1 Service Cost Component of Pension Expense

Year	Service Cost[1]
20X6	$150,000
20X7	180,000
20X8	225,000

[1] Information taken from Example 7-5, Item 3.

The interest cost component of pension expense is the second element of the pension provision. The interest cost components for 20X6, 20X7, and 20X8 are computed in Table 7-2.

Table 7-2 Computation of Interest Cost for Pension Expense

	20X6	20X7	20X8
Projected Benefit Obligation			
At Beginning of Year[1]	$1,200,000	$1,500,000	$1,650,000
Assumed Discount Rate[1]	10%	10%	10%
Interest Cost Component	$120,000	$150,000	$165,000

[1] Information was taken from Example 7-5, Item 3.

Regarding the computations in Table 7-2, the measurement date for purposes of computing pension expense and other pension computations is December 31. The balance sheet date also is December 31. The computation is made for December 31, but the projected benefit obligation used in the calculation is a January 1 balance.

The third component of pension expense is the actual return on pension plan assets. Table 7-3 illustrates the calculation of the returns on plan assets for 20X6, 20X7, and 20X8.

Table 7-3 Calculation of Return on Plan Assets

	20X6	20X7	20X8
Fair Value of Plan Assets at End of Year	$1,100,000	$1,325,000	$1,450,000
Plus: Benefit payments	169,750	223,908	269,907
Less: Contributions	(169,750)	(223,908)	(269,907)
Adjusted Fair Value of Plan Assets at End of Year	$1,100,000	$1,325,000	$1,450,000
Fair Value of Plan Assets at Beginning of Year	(1,025,000)	(1,100,000)	(1,325,000)
Actual Return on Assets	$75,000	$225,000	$125,000

As shown in Table 7-3, the actual returns on plan assets used in the pension expense computation are $75,000, $225,000, and $125,000 for 20X6, 20X7, and 20X8, respectively. Because the fair value of the plan assets has been increasing, the actual return on assets is deducted in the pension expense calculation.

The fourth component of pension expense is amortization of prior service cost. Because there is no amendment to the pension plan during 20X6, 20X7, or 20X8, there is no prior service cost to amortize.

The next component of pension expense is the net gain or loss. The net gain or loss calculation is very complex and requires frequent reference to the Example 7-5 assumptions. The net gain or loss is composed of two parts: (1) the net gain or loss subject to amortization and (2) the net gain or loss that is deferred. The gain or loss subject to amortization is addressed first, and is computed using the tabular format developed in the general discussion of pensions. The reader may wish to refer to the formulas and tabular format in the general discussion.

Using the tabular format and information from Example 7-5, Items 2 and 3, the net gain or loss subject to amortization for 20X6, 20X7, and 20X8 can be calculated. There is no gain or loss computed for 20X6. The gain or loss subject to amortization is the gain or loss computed at the beginning of the accounting period under consideration. By definition, there is no gain or loss on the date of initial adoption of ASC 715-30. Therefore, because January 1, 20X6, is the date of initial adoption of ASC 715-30 for Johnson, no gain or loss is computed for 20X6. The computations for 20X7 and 20X8 are shown in Table 7-4.

Table 7-4 Calculation of Net Gain or Loss Subject to Amortization[1]

		20X7		20X8
Actual Projected Benefit Obligation		$1,500,000		$1,650,000
Actual Fair Value of Plan Assets		(1,100,000)		(1,325,000)
Excess		$400,000		$325,000
Estimated Projected Benefit Obligation	$(1,300,250)		$(1,606,092)	
Estimated Fair Value of Plan Assets	1,137,750	(162,500)	1,224,322	(381,770)
(Gain)/Loss Before Prior Years' (Gain)/Loss		$237,500		$(56,770)
(Gain)/Loss from Prior Years		0		231,770[2]
(Gain)/Loss at Beginning of Period		$237,500		$175,000
Fair Value of Plan Assets	$1,100,000		$1,325,000	
Market-Related Value of Plan Assets	(1,130,200)	(30,200)	(1,267,108)	57,892
(Gain) Loss Subject to Amortization		$207,300		$232,892

[1] All information used in Table 7-4 is taken from Example 7-5, Item 3.
[2] Loss of $237,500 – $5,730, 20X7 amortization (Table 7-5) = $231,770.

The losses computed in Table 7-4 for 20X7 and 20X8 are subject to amortization. However, unless the loss for each year exceeds 10% of the greater of the beginning of year projected benefit obligation or market-related value of plan assets, no amortization is required. Table 7-5 shows the computation and amortization of any excess loss.

Table 7-5 Computation and Amortization of Excess Net Loss

	20X7	20X8
Net Loss (Table 7-4)	$207,300	$232,892
Greater of Projected Benefit Obligation or Market-Related Value of Plan Assets[1]	$(1,500,000)	$(1,650,000)
Percentage	× 10%	× 10%
Total	(150,000)	(165,000)
Excess Loss Subject to Amortization	$57,300	$67,892
Average Remaining Service Life (Years)[2]	÷ 10	÷ 10
Amortization of Net Loss	$5,730	$6,789

[1] Information taken from Example 7-5, Item 3.
[2] Average remaining service life taken from Example 7-5, Item 4.

Table 7-5 shows that the excess loss for 20X7 is $57,300, which is amortized at a rate of $5,730 over the remaining service life of 10 years. The amortization for 20X8 of the $67,892 excess loss is $6,789.

Amortization of net losses from Table 7-5 is combined with gains or losses not subject to amortization. Gains or losses not subject to amortization may be computed using the formula provided in the general discussion. The formula is:

DAG/(L) = ((AFPAE – C + B) – AFPAB)) – (EROR × MRPAB)

DAG/(L)	= Deferred asset gain or loss.
AFPAE	= Actual fair value of plan assets at end of accounting period.
C	= Contributions to pension plan during accounting period.
B	= Benefit payments from pension plan during accounting period.
AFPAB	= Actual fair value of plan assets at the beginning of the accounting period.
EROR	= Expected long-term rate of return on plan assets.
MRPAB	= Market-related value of plan assets at the beginning of the accounting period.

Using the preceding formula and the assumptions from Example 7-5, Item 3, deferred asset gains or losses (gains and losses not subject to amortization) are computed in Table 7-6.

Table 7-6 Calculation of Deferred Asset Gains or Losses

20X6

DAG/(L)	= (($1,100,000 – $169,750 + $169,750) – $1,025,000) – (11% × $1,025,000)
DAG/(L)	= $75,000 – $112,750
DAG/(L)	= $37,750 (loss)

20X7

DAG/(L)	= ((($1,325,000 – $223,908) + $223,908) – $1,100,000) – (11% × $1,130,200)
DAG/(L)	= $225,000 – $124,322
DAG/(L)	= $100,678 (gain)

20X8

DAG/(L)	= (($1,450,000 – $269,907 + $269,907) – $1,325,000) – (11% × $1,267,108)
DAG/(L)	= $125,000 – $139,382
DAG/(L)	= $14,382 (loss)

As shown in Table 7-6, the actual return on plan assets exceeds the expected long-term rate of return on market-related value of plan assets only for 20X7. When the actual return exceeds the expected return on the market-related value of plan assets, a deferred gain is recognized. In years 20X6 and 20X8, the expected return on assets exceeded the actual return and a deferred loss is recognized for both years.

By using the information from Tables 7-5 and 7-6, the net gain or loss component of pension expense can be computed, as shown in Table 7-7.

Table 7-7 Calculation of Net Gain or Loss Component of Pension Expense

	20X6	20X7	20X8
Amortization of Net Loss from Table 7-5	$0[1]	$5,730	$6,789
Deferred Gain/(Loss) from Table 7-6	(37,750)	100,678	(14,382)
Net Gain/(Loss) Component of Pension Expense	$(37,750)	$106,408	$(7,593)

[1] The net loss subject to amortization for 20X6 was not computed in Table 7-5, because by definition there is no gain or loss on the initial adoption of ASC 715-30.

The net gain or loss component of pension expense for 20X6 consists of only the deferred asset loss of $37,750. Because the deferred asset loss is the part of the loss not included in the market related value of plan assets, the deferred loss is deducted in the computation of pension expense. In 20X7 the deferred asset gain of $100,678 is added to the amortization of net loss of $5,730. Deferred asset gains (the part of the asset gain or loss not included in the market related value of plan assets) are added to net loss amortizations and deducted from net gain amortizations. Deferred asset losses are accounted for in the opposite manner. The net gain or loss component of $106,408 is added as a component of pension expense in 20X7. In 20X8 the deferred asset loss of $14,382 is deducted from the net loss amortization of $6,789. The net gain or loss component of $7,593 is deducted as a component of pension expense. The deferred asset gain or loss when combined with the actual return in the pension expense computation causes the actual return to equal the expected return on plan assets.

The last component of pension expense to consider is amortization of the pension obligation or asset created at the adoption of ASC 715-30. The pension asset or obligation is calculated using the information from Example 7-5, Item 2, and the formula developed in the general discussion. The formula is:

$$(A)/O = APBOT - (AFPAT + APC - PPC)$$

(A)/O	= Net asset or net obligation established at initial adoption of ASC 715-30.
APBOT	= Actual projected benefit obligation on the date of transition to ASC 715-30.
AFPAT	= Actual fair value of plan assets on the date of transition to ASC 715-30.
APC	= Balance in the pension liability account on the date of transition to ASC 715-30.
PPC	= Balance in the pension asset account on the date of transition to ASC 715-30.

The computation of the asset or obligation at initial adoption of ASC 715-30 is made below:

(A)/O = $1,200,000 – ($1,025,000 + $0 – $0)
(A)/O = $1,200,000 – $1,025,000
(A)/O = $175,000 (obligation)

There is no balance sheet asset or obligation at the time of initial adoption of ASC 715-30, as noted by the zeros in the preceding formula. Therefore, because the projected benefit obligation of $1,200,000 exceeds the fair value of the plan assets, the $175,000 difference is a pension obligation. The obligation is amortized over the average remaining service life of the employee group of 14 years. The average remaining service life is given in Example 7-5, Item 2(d). The amortization for 20X6, 20X7, and 20X8 is computed in Table 7-8.

Table 7-8 Calculation of Amortization of Pension Obligation

		(c) = (a)/(b) Amortization		
(a) Pension Obligation	(b)Service Life	20X6	20X7	20X8
$175,000	14 Years	$12,500	$12,500	$12,500

Using information from Tables 7-1, 7-2, 7-3, 7-7, and 7-8, pension expense for 20X6, 20X7, and 20X8 is summarized below in Table 7-9.

Table 7-9 Computation of Pension Expense

Pension Expense Component	20X6	20X7	20X8
1. Service Cost (Table 7-1)	$150,000	$180,000	$225,000
2. Interest Cost (Table 7-2)	120,000	150,000	165,000
3. Actual Return on Pension Plan Assets (Table 7-3)	(75,000)	(225,000)	(125,000)
4. Amortization of Prior Service Cost	0	0	0
5. (Gain) or Loss (Table 7-7)			
• Deferred Asset Gain/(Loss)	(37,750)	100,678	(14,382)
• Amortization of (Gain)/Loss	0	5,730	6,789
6. Amortization of Net Obligation Created at Adoption of ASC 715-30 (Table 7-8)	12,500	12,500	12,500
Total Pension Expense	$169,750	$223,908	$269,907

Using the information from Tables 7-4 and 7-9 and the funding information from Example 7-7, Item 3, journal entries for 20X6, 20X7, and 20X8 can be prepared. The journal entries for the pension expense are as follows:

20X6

Pension Expense	169,750	
Pension Liability	12,500	

Other Comprehensive Income—		
Transitional Obligation		12,500
Cash		169,750
20X7		
Pension Expense	223,908	
Pension Liability	18,230	
Other Comprehensive Income—		
Gain/Loss Amortization		5,730
Other Comprehensive Income—		
Transitional Obligation		12,500
Cash		223,908
20X8		
Pension Expense	269,907	
Pension Liability	19,289	
Other Comprehensive Income—		
Gain/Loss Amortization		6,789
Other Comprehensive Income—		
Transitional Obligation		12,500
Cash		269,907

Notice in the journal entries that the amount of the pension expense and contributions to the trust are the same. However, amortization of the gain or loss and the transitional obligation require a reclassification adjustment to remove them from accumulated other comprehensive income. Then pension liability is adjusted for the difference.

Table 7-4 computes the amount of the actuarial gain or loss that is used in the 20X7 and 20X8 pension expense computation. A $237,500 loss was computed for 20X7 and $56,770 gain was computed for 20X8. The amounts represent beginning-of-year numbers, which means that the computations used end-of-year amounts from the prior years. Therefore, the 20X7 amount of $237,500 is based on December 31, 20X6 information, and the 20X8 amount of $56,770 is based on December 31, 20X7 information. When actually recording the actuarial loss and gain in the financial statements, the $237,500 loss is reported as of December 31, 20X6 and the $56,770 gain is reported as of December 31, 20X7. The December 31, 20X8 gain or loss, which is used in the 20X9 pension expense computation is not computed, but the computations and entries are similar to the 20X6 and 20X7 computations. The increase in the loss and the increase in the gain must be reported in other comprehensive income in the accounting period in which the gain or loss occurs. The amount of the gain or loss included in other comprehensive income is closed to accumulated other comprehensive income. The gain or loss is then removed from accumulated other comprehensive income as a reclassification adjustment when it is amortized to pension expense. The required entries are as follows:

20X6		
Other Comprehensive Income	237,500	
Pension Liability		237,500

20X7

Pension Liability	56,770	
Other Comprehensive Income		56,770

This completes the actual analysis of Example 7-5; however, it is beneficial to see the computations of three items assumed in this example to be provided by the actuary. These items may be provided by the actuary or they may be computed by the enterprise. The three items are the market-related value of plan assets, the estimated projected benefit obligation, and the estimated fair value of plan assets. These three items are computed only for the first year, 20X6.

The first item to consider is the market-related value of plan assets. Using the tabular format developed in the general discussion and information provided in Example 7-5, the market-related value of plan assets is computed for 20X6 in Table 7-10.

Table 7-10 Computation of Market-Related Value of Plan Assets[1]

Beginning-of-period market-related value of plan assets	$1,025,000
Expected Return:	
Beginning-of-period market-related value of plan assets	$1,025,000
Expected long-term rate of return	11%
Expected return on plan assets	112,750
Contributions to trust during period	169,750
Benefits paid during period	(169,750)
Amortization of deferred gain or (loss)	(7,550)[2]
End of period market-related value of plan assets	$1,130,200

[1] Information for construction of Table 7-10 taken from Example 7-5, Items 2(c), 3(f), (h), and (j), and 5.
[2] Information computed in Table 7-11.

The amortization of the gain or loss in the computation of the market-related value of plan assets is the cumulative unamortized deferred asset gain or loss used in the computation of pension expense. The deferred asset gain or loss is amortized to the market-related value of plan assets over a period of time not to exceed five years. The amortization of the deferred asset loss for 20X6 included in Table 7-10 is computed in Table 7-11.

Table 7-11 Computation of Deferred Gain or Loss Amortization[1]

Deferred Asset (Loss) for 20X6	$(37,750)
Net Deferred Gain (Loss)	$(37,750)
Amortization Period (Years)[2]	÷ 5
Amortization of Deferred Gain (Loss)	$(7,550)

[1] Deferred asset gains and losses are computed in Table 7-6.
[2] The five-year amortization period is from Example 7-5, Item 6.

The second item to be computed is the estimated projected benefit obligation for 20X6. Using the format provided for the computation in the general discussion and information provided or computed in the preceding analysis, the computations are made in Table 7-12.

Table 7-12 Computation of Estimated Projected Benefit Obligation

Beginning-of-period actual projected benefit obligation (Example 7-5, Item 2)	$1,200,000
Service cost component of pension expense (current year) (Table 7-1)	150,000
Interest cost component of pension expense (current year) (Table 7-2)	120,000
Benefits paid (Example 7-5, Items 3(h) and 5)	(169,750)
Prior service cost	0
Estimated projected benefit obligation December 31	$1,300,250

The next item to compute is the estimated fair value of plan assets. The estimated fair value of plan assets for 20X6 is computed in Table 7-13 using the format provided in the general discussion.

Table 7-13 Computation of the Estimated Fair Value of Plan Assets[1]

Actual fair value of plan assets at beginning of accounting period	$1,025,000
Expected Return:	
Market-related value of plan assets at beginning of accounting period	$1,025,000[2]
Expected long-term rate of return	11%
Expected rate of return on plan assets	112,750
Contributions made to trust	169,750
Less: Benefits paid	(169,750)
Estimated fair value of plan assets on December 31	$1,137,750

[1] Information for construction of Table 7-13 is taken from Example 7-5, Items 2(b) and (c), 3(h) and (j), and 5.
[2] Market-related value taken from Table 7-10.

This completes the analysis of Example 7-5, which was a straightforward defined benefit pension problem. Example 7-6 incorporates complex issues into a defined benefit plan and considers such items as:

- Asset or liability existing at date of transition.
- Existence of prior service cost.
- Contributions different from pension expense.

Assumptions for Example 7-6 are provided below.

Example 7-6
Assumptions for Defined Benefit Pension Plan

1. Micro Enterprises (Micro), a public company with a December 31 year-end, has a defined benefit plan that covers substantially all employees. The company has only U.S. operations and elects to adopt all provisions of ASC 715-30 on January 1, 20X6.

2. On the date of initial adoption, January 1, 20X6, Micro received the following information from its actuary.

(a) Projected benefit obligation	$2,450,000
(b) Fair value of plan assets	2,050,000
(c) Market-related value of plan assets	2,050,000
(d) Pension liability	100,000
(e) Average remaining service life of employees at date of transition (majority of employees are active)	12 years

3. On December 31, 20X6, 20X7, and 20X8 (the balance sheet date and the measurement date), the following information was provided by Micro's actuary.

	20X6	20X7	20X8
(a) Service cost	$250,000	$290,000	$300,000
(b) Actual projected benefit obligation	3,300,000	3,900,000	4,250,000
(c) Estimated projected benefit obligation	3,190,500	3,457,000	4,151,000
(d) Actual fair value of plan assets	2,300,000	2,675,000	2,950,000
(e) Estimated fair value of plan assets	2,425,000	2,459,375	2,932,578
(f) Market-related value of plan assets	2,393,750	2,575,781	2,860,371
(g) Accumulated benefit obligation	3,100,000	3,500,000	3,750,000
(h) Prior service cost from plan amendment	400,000		
(i) Payments to trust	300,000	350,000	400,000
(j) Assumed discount rate	9%	9%	9%
(k) Expected long-term rate of return on plan assets	10%	10%	10%

4. On the date of amendment of the pension plan, Micro had 200 active employees. It is estimated that 10% of the employees will retire or leave Micro each year. The future service life for all other amortization is 12 years.

5. The amendment to the pension plan in 3(h) was made on December 31, 20X6.

6. Benefits paid during 20X6–20X8 were $130,000, $430,000, and $400,000, respectively.

7. Deferred asset gains and losses are amortized to the market-related value of plan assets using a four-year period.

8. This example assumes that any transitional asset or obligation is included in accumulated other comprehensive income.

The first step in analyzing the assumptions in Example 7-6 is to compute the pension expense for each of the years listed. Computation of pension expense requires six different complex calculations, and several pages are needed for the analysis. Refer frequently to the assumptions in Example 7-6 to follow the analysis. Each element for each of the three years is computed separately and then all elements are summarized to compute pension expense.

The first element of pension expense is service cost. The service cost component requires no computation because it is provided by the actuary. Table 7-14 shows the service costs for 20X6, 20X7, and 20X8.

Table 7-14 Service Cost Component of Pension Expense[1]

Year	Service Cost
20X6	$250,000
20X7	290,000
20X8	300,000

[1] Information given in Example 7-6, Item 3.

The second element of the pension provision is the interest cost component. The interest costs for 20X6, 20X7, and 20X8 are computed in Table 7-15.

Table 7-15 Computation of Interest Cost for Pension Expense

	20X6	20X7	20X8
Projected Benefit Obligation at Beginning of Year[1]	$2,450,000	$3,300,000	$3,900,000
Assumed Discount Rate[1]	9%	9%	9%
Interest Cost Component	$220,500	$297,000	$351,000

[1] Information taken from Example 7-6, Item 3(b) and (j).

In Table 7-15, the measurement date for purposes of pension expense and other pension computations is December 31. The balance sheet date is also December 31. The computation is made for December 31, but the projected benefit obligation used in the calculation is a January 1 balance.

The third component of pension expense is the actual return on pension plan assets. Table 7-16 shows the calculation of the return on plan assets for 20X6, 20X7, and 20X8.

Table 7-16 Calculation of Return on Plan Assets[1]

	20X6	20X7	20X8
Fair Value of Plan Assets at End of Year	$2,300,000	$2,675,000	$2,950,000
Plus: Benefit Payments	130,000	430,000	400,000
Less: Contributions	(300,000)	(350,000)	(400,000)
Adjusted Fair Value of Plan Assets at End of Year	$2,130,000	$2,755,000	$2,950,000
Fair Value of Plan Assets at Beginning of Year	(2,050,000)	(2,300,000)	(2,675,000)
Actual Return on Assets	$80,000	$455,000	$275,000

[1] Information from Example 7-6, Items 2(b), 3(d) and (i), and 6.

As shown in Table 7-16, the actual returns on plan assets to be used in the pension expense computations are $80,000, $455,000, and $275,000 for 20X6, 20X7, and 20X8, respectively. Because fair values of the plan assets have increased in each of the three years, the actual return is positive and is deducted in the computation of pension expense. For any year that fair value decreases, actual return on assets is negative and is added as a component of pension expense.

The fourth component of pension expense is amortization of unrecognized prior service cost. The $400,000 prior service cost resulting from an amendment on December 31, 20X6 is amortized over the remaining service life of the active employee group on the date of amendment. As noted in Item 4 of Example 7-6, there are 200 employees on December 31, 20X6, the date of the amendment. In addition, it is estimated that 10% of the 200 employees will retire or leave Micro each year. Adding employees after the amendment date does not have an impact on the amortization process because the amortization process for each amendment is based on the employee group's remaining service life on the date of amendment. Before amortization of prior service cost is computed information for computing amortization ratios is gathered, the amortization ratios are computed, and the amortization ratios are applied to the prior service cost to determine prior service cost amortization. This information is calculated in Tables 7-17, 7-18, and 7-19.

Table 7-17 shows the computation of the information for amortization ratios for the remaining years of service for the employee group on December 31, 20X6.

Table 7-17 Computation of Information for Annual Amortization Ratios for Prior Service Cost Amortization

Active Employees	Year										Total Service Years
	20X7	20X8	20X9	2010	2011	2012	2013	2014	2015	2016	
1–20	20										20
21–40	20	20									40
41–60	20	20	20								60
61–80	20	20	20	20							80
81–100	20	20	20	20	20						100
101–120	20	20	20	20	20	20					120
121–140	20	20	20	20	20	20	20				140
141–160	20	20	20	20	20	20	20	20			160
161–180	20	20	20	20	20	20	20	20	20		180
181–200	20	20	20	20	20	20	20	20	20	20	200
Service Years	200	180	160	140	120	100	80	60	40	20	1,100

Several items in Table 7-17 require further explanation. Because 10% of the 200 employees (20 employees) will leave Micro each year, the 200 employees are divided into groups of 20. For example, in the first column, the 20 employees to leave at the end of the first year are numbered 1–20, and the 20 employees to leave at the end of the second year are numbered 21–40 and so on until the entire 200 employees have terminated. In addition, 200 service years are available for 20X7 computations because all 200 employees are employed during 20X7. However, the number of service years declines to 180 for 20X8 because 20 employees were removed from the computations at the end of 20X7. The number of service years declines by 20 each year until 2016, which is the last year of amortization. In 2016, only 20 employees (20 service years) are left in the original employee group existing on December 31, 20X6. At the end of 2016, the entire 200 original employees are no longer with Micro. The last column, total service years, is a cross-footing of the service lives for all 10 years of amortization and represents the total service life for all employees for the 10 years of amortization.

Using the information in Table 7-17, annual amortization ratios are computed in Table 7-18 for each year from 20X7 to 2016. The ratios are used for amortizing the $400,000 prior service cost.

Table 7-18 Annual Amortization Ratios for Prior Service Cost

Year	Ratio[1]
20X7	200/1,100
20X8	180/1,100
20X9	160/1,100
2010	140/1,100
2011	120/1,100

Year	Ratio[1]
2012	100/1,100
2013	80/1,100
2014	60/1,100
2015	40/1,100
2016	20/1,100

[1] Information was taken from Table 7-17.

The ratios for each year in Table 7-18 are computed by dividing each year's service lives by the total service life (1,100) for all employees for the entire 10-year period.

Using the ratios in Table 7-18 and the prior service cost of $400,000 from Item 3, Example 7-6, amortization of prior service cost for 20X6–2016 is computed in Table 7-19.

Table 7-19 Amortization of Prior Service Cost

(a) Year	(b) Amount of Plan Amendment[1]	(c) Amortization Ratio[2]	(d) = (b) × (c) Amortization of Prior Service Cost	(e) Prior Service Cost Balance at 12/31
20X6	$0	—	$—	$—
20X7	400,000	200/1,100	72,727	327,273
20X8	400,000	180/1,100	65,455	261,818
20X9	400,000	160/1,100	58,182	203,636
2010	400,000	140/1,100	50,909	152,727
2011	400,000	120/1,100	43,636	109,091
2012	400,000	100/1,100	36,364	72,727
2013	400,000	80/1,100	29,091	43,636
2014	400,000	60/1,100	21,818	21,818
2015	400,000	40/1,100	14,545	7,273
2016	400,000	20/1,100	7,273	0
Total			$400,000	

[1] Information taken from Example 7-6, Item 3(f).
[2] Information came from Table 7-18.

As shown in Table 7-19, the pension expense component from prior service cost amortization for 20X6–20X8 is $0, $72,727, and $65,455, respectively. There is no amortization for 20X6, because the amendment did not occur until December 31, 20X6.

Micro may elect a less complex method of amortization of prior service cost so long as it is applied on a consistent basis. For example, Micro could amortize the prior service cost over the average remaining service life of the active employee group on the date of amendment using a straight-line basis. To illustrate the simplified method, 5.5 years (1,100 service years ÷ 200 employees) is used as the time period for the straight-line method, assuming the facts in Table 7-17. Using the $400,000 prior service cost, the annual amortization of prior service cost is $72,727 ($400,000 ÷ 5.5 years).

The next component of pension expense is the net gain or loss. The net gain or loss calculation is a very complex computation and requires frequent reference to the Example 7-6 assumptions. The net gain or loss is composed of two parts: (1) the net gain or loss subject to amortization and (2) the net gain or loss that is deferred. The gain or loss subject to amortization is addressed first, and is computed using the tabular format developed in the general discussion of pensions. The reader may wish to review the formulas and tabular format in the general discussion.

Using the tabular format and the information from Example 7-6, Items 2 and 3, the net gain or loss subject to amortization for 20X6, 20X7, and 20X8 can be calculated. There is no gain or loss computed for 20X6. The gain or loss subject to amortization is the gain or loss computed at the beginning of the accounting period under consideration. By definition, there is no gain or loss subject to amortization on the date of initial adoption of ASC 715-30. Therefore, because January 1, 20X6 is the date of initial adoption of ASC 715-30 for Micro, no gain or loss is computed for 20X6. The computations for 20X7 and 20X8 are made in Table 7-20.

Table 7-20 Calculation of Net Gain or Loss Subject to Amortization[1]

		20X7		20X8
Actual Projected Benefit Obligation		$3,300,000		$3,900,000
Actual Fair Value of Plan Assets		(2,300,000)		(2,675,000)
Excess		$1,000,000		$1,225,000
Estimated Projected Benefit Obligation	$(3,190,500)		$(3,457,000)	
Estimated Fair Value of Plan Assets	2,425,000	(765,500)	2,459,375	(997,625)
(Gain)/Loss Before Prior Years'		$234,500		$227,375
(Gain)/Loss				
(Gain)/Loss From Prior Years		0		234,500[2]
(Gain)/Loss At Beginning of Period		$234,500		$461,875
Fair Value of Plan Assets	$2,300,000		$2,675,000	
Market-Related Value of Plan Assets	(2,393,750)	(93,750)	(2,575,781)	99,219
(Gain)/Loss Subject to Amortization		$140,750		$561,094

[1] All information used in Table 7-20 taken from Example 7-6, Item 3.

[2] Loss at beginning of 20X7 of $234,500 – $0 amortization (Table 7-21) for 20X7 = $234,500.

The losses computed in Table 7-20 for 20X7 and 20X8 are subject to amortization. However, unless the loss for each year exceeds 10% of the greater of the beginning-of-year projected benefit obligation or market-related value of plan assets, no amortization is required. Table 7-21 shows the computation of any excess loss and the proper amortization.

Table 7-21 Computation of Amortization of Net Loss

	20X7	20X8
Net Loss (Table 7-20)	$140,750	$561,094
Greater of Projected Benefit Obligation or Market-Related Value of Plan Assets[1]	$(3,300,000)	$(3,900,000)
Percentage	× 10%	× 10%
Total	$(330,000)	$(390,000)
Excess Loss Subject to Amortization	$0	$171,094
Average Remaining Service Life (Years)[2]	÷ 12	÷ 12
Amortization of Net Loss	$0	$14,258

[1] Information taken from Example 7-6, Item 3.
[2] Average remaining service life taken from Example 7-6, Item 4.

As shown in Table 7-21, there is no gain or loss for 20X6. The gain or loss subject to amortization is the gain or loss computed at the beginning of the accounting period under consideration. Because ASC 715-30 was adopted on January 1, 20X6, there is by definition no gain or loss at the beginning of 20X6. This fact was illustrated in the computation of the gain or loss in Table 7-20. There is no amortization of the net loss for 20X7 because the $140,750 loss does not exceed 10% of the projected benefit obligation. However, $14,258 of the $561,094 net loss for 20X8 is amortized because the net loss exceeds 10% of the projected benefit obligation by $171,094.

Amortization of the net loss from Table 7-21 is combined with any gain or loss not subject to amortization. Computation of any gain or loss not subject to amortization may be calculated using the formula developed in the general discussion. The formula is:

$$DAG/(L) = ((AFPAE - C + B) - AFPAB) - (EROR \times MRPAB)$$

DAG/(L) = Deferred asset gain or loss.
AFPAE = Actual fair value of plan assets at end of accounting period.
C = Contributions to pension plan during accounting period.

B	= Benefit payments from pension plan during accounting period.
AFPAB	= Actual fair value of plan assets at the beginning of the accounting period.
EROR	= Expected long-term rate of return on plan assets.
MRPAB	= Market-related value of plan assets at the beginning of the accounting period.

Using the preceding formula and the assumptions from Example 7-6, Item 3, the deferred asset gain or loss is computed in Table 7-22.

Table 7-22 Calculation of Deferred Asset Gain or Loss

20X6

DAG/(L)	= (($2,300,000 – $300,000 + $130,000) – $2,050,000) – (10% × $2,050,000)
DAG/(L)	= $80,000 – $205,000
DAG/(L)	= $125,000 (loss)

20X7

DAG/(L)	= (($2,675,000 – $350,000 + $430,000) – $2,300,000)) – (10% × $2,393,750)
DAG/(L)	= $455,000 – $239,375
DAG/(L)	= $215,625 (gain)

20X8

DAG/(L)	= (($2,950,000 – $400,000 + $400,000) – $2,675,000)) – (10% × $2,575,781)
DAG/(L)	= $275,000 – $257,578
DAG/(L)	= $17,422 (gain)

As shown in Table 7-22, the actual return on plan assets exceeds the expected long-term rate of return on market-related value of plan assets for 20X7 and 20X8. Because the actual return exceeds the expected return on the market-related value of plan assets, a deferred gain is recognized for 20X7 and 20X8 and a deferred loss is reported for 20X6.

By using the information from Table 7-21 and Table 7-22, the net gain or loss component of pension expense can now be computed, as shown in Table 7-23.

Table 7-23 Calculation of Net Gain or Loss Component of Pension Expense

	20X6	20X7	20X8
Amortization of Net Loss from Table 7-21	$0	$0	$14,258
Deferred Gain/(Loss) from Table 7-22	(125,000)	215,625	17,422
Net Gain/(Loss) Component of Pension Expense	$(125,000)	$215,625	$31,680

Deferred asset gains (gains not included in the market related value of plan assets) are added to loss amortizations and are deducted from gain amortizations. Therefore, the $17,442 deferred asset gain in 20X8 is added to the $14,258 amortization of net loss in 20X8. A deferred asset gain is added as a component of pension expense, and a deferred asset loss is deducted. A net loss amortization is added as a component of pension expense and a net gain amortization is deducted. Therefore, the $125,000 loss component is deducted in the pension expense computation, and the $215,625 and the $31,680 gain components are added in the computation of pension expense. The deferred asset gain or loss when combined with the actual return in the pension expense computation causes the actual return to equal the expected return on plan assets.

The last component of pension expense to consider is amortization of the pension obligation or asset created at the adoption of ASC 715-30. The pension asset or obligation can be calculated using the information from Example 7-6, Item 2, and the formula developed in the general discussion. The formula is

(A)/O = APBOT – (AFPAT + APC – PPC)

(A)/O	= Net asset or net obligation established at initial adoption of ASC 715-30.
APBOT	= Actual projected benefit obligation on the date of transition to ASC 715-30.
AFPAT	= Actual fair value of plan assets on the date of transition to ASC 715-30.
APC	= Balance in the pension liability account on the date of transition to ASC 715-30.
PPC	= Balance in the pension asset account on the date of transition to ASC 715-30.

The computation of the asset or obligation at initial adoption of ASC 715-30 is made as follows:

(A)/O	= $2,450,000 – ($2,050,000 + $100,000 – $0)
(A)/O	= $2,450,000 – $2,150,000
(A)/O	= $300,000 (obligation)

Because the projected benefit obligation of $2,450,000 exceeds the fair value of the plan assets and the pension liability, the $300,000 is a pension obligation. The obligation is amortized over the average remaining service life of the employee group of 12 years (Example 7-6, Item 2). The amortization for 20X6, 20X7, and 20X8 is computed in Table 7-24.

Table 7-24 Calculation of Amortization of Unrecognized Pension Obligation

(a)Pension Obligation	(b)Service Life	(c) = (a)/(b) Amortization 20X6	20X7	20X8
$300,000	12 Years	$25,000	$25,000	$25,000

Using the information from Tables 7-14, 7-15, 7-16, 7-19, 7-22, and 7-23, pension expenses for 20X6, 20X7, and 20X8 are summarized below in Table 7-25.

Table 7-25 Computation of Pension Expense

Pension Expense Component	20X6	20X7	20X8
Service Cost (Table 7-14)	$250,000	$290,000	$300,000
Interest Cost (Table 7-15)	220,500	297,000	351,000
Actual Return on Pension Plan Assets (Table 7-16)	(80,000)	(455,000)	(275,000)
Amortization of Prior Service Cost (Table 7-19)	0	72,727	65,455
Gain or Loss (Table 7-23)			
a. Deferred Asset Gain/(Loss)	(125,000)	215,625	17,422
b. Amortization of (Gain)/Loss	0	0	14,258
Amortization of Net Obligation Created at Adoption of ASC 715-30 (Table 7-24)	25,000	25,000	25,000
Total Pension Expense	$290,500	$445,352	$498,135

Using the information from Tables 7-20 and 7-25, and the funding information from Example 7-6, Item 3, journal entries for 20X6, 20X7, and 20X8, can be prepared. The journal entries for the pension expense are as follows:

20X6

Pension Expense	290,500	
Pension Liability	34,500	
Other Comprehensive Income—Transitional Obligation		25,000
Cash		300,000

20X7

Pension Expense	445,352	
Pension Liability	2,375	
Other Comprehensive Income—Prior Service Cost Amortization		72,727
Other Comprehensive Income—Transitional Obligation		25,000
Cash		350,000

20X8

Pension Expense	498,135	
Pension Liability	6,578	
Other Comprehensive Income—Prior Service Cost Amortization		65,455
Other Comprehensive Income—Gain/Loss Amortization		14,258
Other Comprehensive Income—Transitional Obligation		25,000
Cash		400,000

Amortization of the prior service cost, the gain or loss, and the transitional obligation require a reclassification adjustment to remove them from accumulated other comprehensive income. Then, pension liability is adjusted for the difference.

Table 7-20 computes the amount of the actuarial loss that is used in the 20X7 and 20X8 pension expense computation as $234,500 and $227,375, respectively. The amounts represent beginning-of-year numbers, which means that the computations used end-of-year amounts from the prior years. Therefore, the 20X7 amount of $234,500 is based on December 31, 20X6 information, and the 20X8 amount of $227,375 is based on December 31, 20X7 information. When actually recording the actuarial losses in the financial statements, the $234,500 loss is reported as of December 31, 20X6 and the $227,375 loss is reported as of December 31, 20X7. The December 31, 20X8 gain or loss, which is used in the 20X9 pension expense computation is not computed, but the computations and entries are similar to the 20X6 and 20X7 computations. In addition, an amendment to the pension plan at December 31, 20X6 increases prior service cost by $400,000 (Example 7-6, Assumption 5). The increase in the actuarial loss and the increase in the prior service cost must be reported in other comprehensive income in the accounting period in which the loss occurs and in the accounting period that the pension plan is amended. The amount of the loss and prior service cost that is included in other comprehensive income is closed to accumulated other comprehensive income. The loss and prior service cost are then removed from accumulated other comprehensive income as a reclassification adjustment when they are amortized to pension expense. The required entries are as follows:

20X6

Other Comprehensive Income—Actuarial Loss	234,500	
Pension Liability		234,500
Other Comprehensive Income—Prior Service Cost	400,000	
Pension Liability		400,000

20X7

Other Comprehensive Income—Actuarial Loss	227,375	
Pension Liability		227,375

This completes the technical application of defined benefit pension plans. Example 7-7 illustrates the accounting requirements for a defined contribution pension plan. Assumptions for Example 7-7 are presented below.

Example 7-7
Assumptions for Defined Contribution Pension Plan

1. Investor Enterprises (Investor), a public company with only U.S. operations, has a defined contribution pension plan that covers substantially all employees. Investor has a December 31 year-end.
2. Investor's contribution is made for periods in which the employees provide service. The contribution is equal to 6% of the employees' annualized salaries. Annualized salaries for eligible employees during 20X6 are $4,500,000.

Because Investor has a defined contribution plan and contributions are made for periods in which the employees provide services, its pension expense for 20X6 is equal to the pension contribution. The 20X6 contribution is $270,000 ($4,500,000 annualized salaries × 6%). The following journal entry is required at December 31, 20X6.

Pension Expense	270,000	
Cash		270,000

The footnote disclosure required for the defined contribution plan is presented below:

Note: Investor has a defined contribution pension plan and pension cost is $270,000 for 20X6.

This completes the technical application of pension plans. The next section covers pension plan disclosure requirements.

Disclosures

The disclosure requirements for pension plans are divided into the following categories: disclosures for defined contribution plans, disclosures for multiemployer plans, disclosures for defined benefit plans, disclosures when an entity has two or more plans, disclosures for nonpublic companies, disclosures for interim periods, and disclosures for not-for-profit entities. Disclosures for both pensions and postretirement plans are essentially the same and disclosures for both plans are disclosed together in the financial statements, generally in a column format. However, pension disclosures are presented at the end of the pension discussion and disclosures for postretirement plans are presented at the end of the discussion on postretirement plans.

Disclosures for Defined Contribution Pension Plans

ASC 715-70-50 specifies the following disclosures for defined contribution pension plans:

1. Pension costs reported in the financial statements for the accounting period reported separately from any defined benefit pension cost.
2. Identification, including impact and nature, of any material item(s) that would prevent interperiod comparability of the information presented.

The disclosures for defined contribution pension plans should be presented for all accounting periods presented.

Disclosures for Multiemployer Pension Plans

ASC 715-80-50 covers disclosures for multiemployer plans and include the following:

1. Contribution amounts made to the plan for all annual accounting periods for which an income statement is included. The employer may, but is not required, to separately disclose the amount of the contribution that relates to pension plans and the amount that relates to postretirement plans.

2. Identification, including impact and nature, of any material item(s) that would prevent interperiod comparability of the information presented.

3. When an employer withdraws from a multiemployer plan and a situation exists that gives rise to an obligation that is either reasonably possible or probable, or it is probable or reasonably possible that employer contributions would be increased over the remaining contract period, the provisions of ASC 450 should be applied.

Disclosures for Defined Benefit Pension Plans

The disclosures for defined benefit pension plans are covered in ASC 715-30-50, and include the following:

1. Amount of pension cost reported for the accounting period divided into the following categories: service cost, interest cost, expected return on assets, prior service cost/credit component, gain or loss component, transitional obligation or asset component, and settlement or curtailment gain or loss recognized.

2. Beginning balance in the projected benefit obligation reconciled with the ending balance reporting the following items separately in the reconciliation, where appropriate: service cost component, interest cost component, gains and losses from actuarial assumptions, amount of benefits paid, amount of contributions by participants of the plan, amounts from amendments to the plan, impact of special termination benefits, settlements and curtailments, impact of business combinations, impact of divestitures, and impact of changes in foreign currency exchange rates.

3. Beginning balance for fair value of plan assets reconciled with the ending balance reporting the following items separately in the reconciliation, where appropriate: actual return on plan assets, amount of employer contributions, amount of contributions by participants of the plan, amount of benefits paid, impact of settlements of pension plans, impact of business combinations, impact of divestitures, and impact of changes in foreign currency exchange rates.

4. Disclosures about plan assets:

   a. As of the latest statement of financial position presented (on a weighted-average basis for employers with more than one plan), a narrative description of the plan's investment policies and strategies along with other factors that are pertinent to an understanding of the policies and strategies. Examples of other factors include but are not limited to investment goals, risk-management practices, permitted and prohibited investments (including the use of derivatives), diversification, and the relationship between plan assets and benefit obligations. For each major category of plan assets (see 4b, below), the narrative is to include

(1) Target allocation percentages (or ranges of percentages), and

(2) A description of the significant investment strategies of investment funds if those funds are disclosed as one or more major categories of plan assets.

b. As of each date for which a statement of financial position is presented, the fair value of each major category of plan assets. Asset categories are to be based on the nature and risks of assets in an employer's plans, such as cash and cash equivalents; equity securities (segregated by industry type, company size, or investment objective); debt securities issued by national, state, and local governments; corporate debt securities; asset-backed securities; structured debt; derivatives on a gross basis (segregated by type of underlying risk in the contract, for example, interest rate contracts, foreign exchange contracts, equity contracts, commodity contracts, credit contracts, and other contracts); investment funds (segregated by type of fund); and real estate.

c. Considering the major categories of assets as described in 4b, above, a narrative description of the basis used to determine the assumed overall expected long-term rate of return on assets. The narrative could include, for example, the general approach used, the extent to which the overall rate-of-return-on-assets assumption was based on historical returns, the extent to which adjustments were made to the historical returns in order to reflect expectations of future returns, and how the adjustments were determined.

d. Information that enables financial-statement users to assess the valuation techniques and inputs that were used to develop the fair value measurements of plan assets at the reporting date. For fair value measurements using significant observable inputs (Level 1 or Level 2), an employer must disclose how the measurements affected changes in plan assets during the period, further disclosing the following information for each major category of plan assets (see 4b, above) for each annual period:

(1) The level within the fair value hierarchy in which the fair value measurements in their entirety fall. The levels are to correspond to fair value measurements using quoted prices in active markets for identical assets or liabilities (Level 1), significant other observable inputs (Level 2), and significant unobservable inputs (Level 3).

(2) For fair value measurements of plan assets using significant unobservable inputs (Level 3), a reconciliation of the beginning and ending balances that separately presents changes during the period attributable to the following: Actual Return on Plan Assets (Component of Net Periodic Pension Cost), separating the amount related to assets still held at the reporting date and the amount related to assets sold during the period; purchases, sales, and settlements (net); and transfers in or out of Level 3 (such as transfers due to changes in the observability of significant inputs).

(3) Information about the inputs and valuation techniques used to measure fair value, along with a discussion of changes in inputs and valuation techniques, if any, during the period.

e. In providing the foregoing information about plan assets, an employer is to consider the overall objectives of providing users of financial statements with an understanding of the following:

(1) How investment allocation decisions are made, including the factors that are pertinent to an understanding of investment policies and strategies

(2) The major categories of plan assets

(3) The valuation techniques and inputs used to measure the fair value of plan assets

(4) How fair value measurements using significant unobservable inputs (Level 3) affected changes in plan assets for the period

(5) Significant concentrations of risk within plan assets

5. Disclose the pension accumulated benefit obligation.

6. Using the date of the last balance sheet presented, disclose for each of the next five years and in the aggregate for the subsequent five years, the benefits anticipated to be paid. The same assumptions used to determine the pension benefit obligation at year end should be used when determining estimated benefits. In addition, the benefit estimate should include benefits related to expected future employee service.

7. An estimate of the contributions anticipated to be paid to the plan for the next year beginning after the date of the last balance sheet presented. The estimates can be aggregated into the following categories: contributions that are discretionary, contributions required by law or regulations, and contributions that are noncash.

8. Disclose the funded status of the pension plan and amounts reported in the statement of financial position. The assets, current liabilities, and noncurrent liabilities should be shown separately.

9. The following rates used in the computation of pension information should be disclosed (indicate in a tabular format, assumptions used when determining net benefit cost and the benefit obligation):

   a. Discount rate on a weighted-average basis assumed in the computations.

   b. If appropriate, rate of increase in compensation used in computing the obligations on a weighted-average basis.

   c. Long-term weighted-average interest rate assumed for the return on assets of the pension plan.

10. For each accounting period that an income statement is provide, pension amounts included in the income statement.

11. For each accounting period that a balance sheet is provided, pension amounts included in the balance sheet.
12. Employer and related party securities (including type and amount) included in pension plan assets, where appropriate.
13. The future yearly pension benefits to be paid to participants from related party and employer-issued insurance contracts, where appropriate.
14. During the accounting period, any employer and/or related party transactions with the pension plan, where appropriate.
15. If an alternative method is used to amortize net gains or losses or prior service cost, the method should be identified.
16. Description, nature, and cost of any contractual or special termination benefits provided during the accounting period.
17. When appropriate, explain changes in plan assets or pension obligation of a significant nature not evident by other pension disclosures.
18. When appropriate, any commitment of a substantive nature used when accounting for the pension obligation, such as a practice of increasing benefits on a regular basis.
19. The amount of actuarial gain or loss, prior service cost or credit reported in other comprehensive income for the accounting period, presented separately, and the amount of the reclassification adjustment for these items, as well as any transitional asset or obligation included as components in pension cost.
20. The amount of actuarial gain or loss, prior service cost or credit, and transitional asset or obligation, separately presented, included in accumulated other comprehensive income that has not yet been included in pension cost.
21. The amount of actuarial gain or loss, prior service cost or credit, and transitional asset or obligation, separately presented, included in accumulated other comprehensive income that will be included in pension cost in the fiscal year subsequent to the most recent annual statement of financial position.
22. For the fiscal year following the most recent annual statement of financial position, disclose plan assets, separated by amount and timing, that are expected to be returned to the employer during that 12-month period or operating cycle, whichever is longer.

Disclosures When an Entity Has Two or More Plans

ASC 715-20-50 specifies accounting and disclosure requirements when an entity has two or more pension plans (the following disclosures are presented as of the measurement date for each balance sheet presented):

1. When an employer has two or more defined benefit pension plans, the pension expense, pension assets, and pension liabilities are determined by applying the provisions of ASC 715-30 to each plan separately.

2. When an employer has two or more pension plans, aggregation is required for disclosure purposes. However, disaggregation of the plans may be appropriate if it provides more useful information.
3. Generally, aggregation of overfunded and underfunded plans is appropriate. When such disclosures are aggregated, separate disclosure of the following is required:
   a. Fair value of plan assets and projected benefit obligations on an aggregate basis for plans with fair value of assets less than the benefit obligation.
   b. Fair value of plan assets and accumulated pension benefit obligations on an aggregate basis for plans where the fair value of the plan assets are less than the accumulated pension benefit obligations.
4. Pension assets and liabilities (current and noncurrent) should be disclosed separately in the balance sheet.
5. Disclosures for U.S. and non-U.S. plans may be combined unless the benefit obligation of the non-U.S. plans is significant compared to the total benefit obligation and the plans use different assumptions that are significant.
6. The disclosure guidelines listed above should be used when a foreign enterprise prepares its statement in accordance with generally accepted accounting principles for its foreign and domestic plans.

Disclosures for Non-Public Companies

Non-public companies may elect reduced disclosures for pension plans. Disclosures related to the balance sheet of an entity should be presented for each balance sheet date presented and disclosures related to the income statement should be presented for each period that an income statement is presented. The reduced disclosures for non-public companies are covered in ASC 715-20-50-5 and include the following:

1. Amount of pension cost reported for the accounting period.
2. Fair value of plan assets, pension obligation and funded status of the pension plan.
3. Disclosures about plan assets:
   a. As of the latest statement of financial position presented (on a weighted-average basis for employers with more than one plan), a narrative description of the plan's investment policies and strategies along with other factors that are pertinent to an understanding of the policies and strategies. Examples of other factors include but are not limited to investment goals, risk-management practices, permitted and prohibited investments (including the use of derivatives), diversification, and the relationship between plan assets and benefit obligations. For each major category of plan assets (see 3b, below), the narrative is to include

(1) Target allocation percentages (or ranges of percentages) and

(2) A description of the significant investment strategies of investment funds if those funds are disclosed as one or more major categories of plan assets.

b. As of each date for which a statement of financial position is presented, the fair value of each major category of plan assets. Asset categories are to be based on the nature and risks of assets in an employer's plan(s), such as cash and cash equivalents; equity securities (segregated by industry type, company size, or investment objective); debt securities issued by national, state, and local governments; corporate debt securities; asset-backed securities; structured debt; derivatives on a gross basis (segregated by type of underlying risk in the contract, for example, interest rate contracts, foreign exchange contracts, equity contracts, commodity contracts, credit contracts, and other contracts); investment funds (segregated by type of fund); and real estate.

c. Considering the major categories of assets as described in 3b, above, a narrative description of the basis used to determine the assumed overall expected long-term rate of return on assets. The narrative could include, for example, the general approach used, the extent to which the overall rate-of-return-on-assets assumption was based on historical returns, the extent to which adjustments were made to the historical returns in order to reflect expectations of future returns, and how the adjustments were determined.

d. Information that enables financial-statement users to assess the valuation techniques and inputs that were used to develop the fair value measurements of plan assets at the reporting date. For fair value measurements using significant observable inputs (Level 1 or Level 2), an employer must disclose how the measurements affected changes in plan assets during the period, further disclosing the following information for each major category of plan assets (see 3b, above) for each annual period:

(1) The level within the fair value hierarchy in which the fair value measurements in their entirety fall. The levels are to correspond to fair value measurements using quoted prices in active markets for identical assets or liabilities (Level 1), significant other observable inputs (Level 2), and significant unobservable inputs (Level 3).

(2) For fair value measurements of plan assets using significant unobservable inputs (Level 3), a reconciliation of the beginning and ending balances that separately presents changes during the period attributable to the following: Actual Return on Plan Assets (Component of Net Periodic Pension Cost), separating the amount related to assets still held at the reporting date and the amount related to assets sold during the period; purchases,

sales, and settlements (net); and transfers in or out of Level 3 (such as transfers due to changes in the observability of significant inputs).

(3) Information about the inputs and valuation techniques used to measure fair value, along with a discussion of changes in inputs and valuation techniques, if any, during the period.

e. In providing the foregoing information about plan assets, an employer is to consider the overall objectives of providing users of financial statements with an understanding of the following:

(1) How investment allocation decisions are made, including the factors that are pertinent to an understanding of investment policies and strategies

(2) The major categories of plan assets

(3) The valuation techniques and inputs used to measure the fair value of plan assets

(4) How fair value measurements using significant unobservable inputs (Level 3) affected changes in plan assets for the period

(5) Significant concentrations of risk within plan assets

4. Disclose the pension accumulated benefit obligation.
5. Using the date of the last balance sheet presented, disclose for each of the next five years and in the aggregate for the subsequent five years, the benefits anticipated to be paid. The same assumptions used to determine the pension benefit obligation at year end should be used when determining estimated benefits. In addition, the benefit estimate should include benefits related to expected future employee service.
6. An estimate of the contributions anticipated to be paid to the plan for the next year beginning after the date of the last balance sheet presented. The estimates can be aggregated into the following categories: contributions that are discretionary, contributions required by law or regulations, and contributions that are noncash.
7. Amounts of the following: benefit payments, and contributions made by the employer and participants, separately disclosed.
8. Disclose the amounts reported in the statement of financial position. The assets, current liabilities, and noncurrent liabilities should be shown separately.
9. The following rates used in the computation of pension information should be disclosed:

   a. Discount rate on a weighted-average basis assumed in the computations.

   b. If appropriate, rate of increase in compensation used in computing the obligations on a weighted-average basis.

c. Long-term weighted-average interest rate assumed for the return on assets of the pension plan.

d. Include in tabular format the assumptions used to determine both the net benefit cost and the benefit obligation.

10. Employer and related party securities (including type and amount) included in pension plan assets, where appropriate.
11. The future yearly pension benefits to be paid to participants from related party and employer-issued insurance contracts, where appropriate.
12. During the accounting period, any employer and/or related party transactions with the pension plan, where appropriate.
13. Significant events that are not routine (both nature and impact) including events such as settlements, curtailments, and amendments.
14. The amount of actuarial gain or loss, prior service cost or credit reported in other comprehensive income for the accounting period, presented separately, and the amount of the reclassification adjustment for these items, as well as any transitional asset or obligation included as components in pension cost.
15. The amount of actuarial gain or loss, prior service cost or credit, and transitional asset or obligation, separately presented, included in accumulated other comprehensive income that has not yet been included in pension cost.
16. The amount of actuarial gain or loss, prior service cost or credit, and transitional asset or obligation, separately presented, included in accumulated other comprehensive income that will be included in pension cost in the fiscal year subsequent to the most recent annual statement of financial position.
17. For the fiscal year following the most recent annual statement of financial position, disclose plan assets, separated by amount and timing, that are expected to be returned to the employer during that 12-month period or operating cycle, whichever is longer.

Disclosures for Interim Accounting Periods

Paragraphs 6 and 7 of ASC 715-20-50 specify the disclosure requirements for interim accounting periods:

Public Entity (ASC 715-20-50-6)

1. For each accounting period that an income statement is presented, disclose the amount of pension cost divided into the following categories: service cost, interest cost, expected return on plan assets, prior service cost/credit component, gain or loss component, transitional obligation or asset component, and settlement or curtailment gain or loss recognized.

2. If employer contributions paid or expected to be paid are significantly different from that reported in ASC 715-20-50-1(g) for annual reports, disclose the amount of contributions paid or expected to be paid. Estimated contributions can be aggregated into the following categories: contributions that are discretionary, contributions required by law or regulations, and contributions that are noncash.

Nonpublic Entity (ASC 715-20-50-7)

1. In interim periods with a complete set of financial statements, if employer contributions paid or expected to be paid are significantly different from that reported in ASC 715-20-50-5(f) for annual reports, disclose the amount of contributions paid or expected to be paid. Estimated contributions can be aggregated into the following categories: contributions that are discretionary, contributions required by law or regulations, and contributions that are noncash.

Disclosures for Not-for-Profit Entities

ASC 958-715-50 specifies the disclosure requirements for not-for-profit entities:

1. The amount of actuarial gain or loss, prior service cost or credit reported in the statement of activities, presented separately, for each annual period that a statement of activities is presented, and the amount of the reclassification adjustment for these items.
2. The amount of net transitional asset or obligation reported in pension expense for each statement of activities presented.
3. The amount of actuarial gain or loss, prior service cost or credit, and transitional asset or obligation, separately presented that has not yet been included in pension cost for each statement of financial position presented.
4. The amount of actuarial gain or loss, prior service cost or credit, and transitional asset or obligation that will be included in pension cost in the fiscal year subsequent to the most recent annual statement of financial position.
5. For the fiscal year following the most recent annual statement of financial position, disclose plan assets, separated by amount and timing, that are expected to be returned to the not-for-profit entity during that 12-month period or operating cycle, whichever is longer.

Flowchart and General Discussion

Settlements and Curtailments

ASC 715-30 specifies the accounting procedures to be followed when a defined benefit pension plan is settled or curtailed. In addition, it provides the accounting and reporting requirements for special and contractual termination benefits.

The general discussion, Flowchart 7-4, and technical application of the settlement and curtailment provisions of ASC 715-30 assume that the reader has a complete understanding of the general accounting and reporting requirements specified by ASC 715-30. The reader is encouraged to read and work the ASC 715-30 example material presented earlier in this chapter before proceeding.

Before a discussion of Flowchart 7-4 can begin, the reader must understand when pension plan transactions are classified as settlements and curtailments.

A settlement of a defined benefit pension plan is a transaction that meets all of the following criteria:[1]

- The transaction is an action that is irrevocable.
- The employer or the pension plan no longer has primary responsibility for the benefit obligation of the pension plan.
- Any major risk relative to the pension assets or obligation used in the settlement has been eliminated.

The payment of lump-sum amounts to employees in return for their rights to receive specific pension benefits is considered a settlement of a defined benefit pension plan. In addition, the purchase of a participating or nonparticipating annuity contract that covers the vested benefits of a pension plan is considered a settlement of a part or all of the plan when the same plan or a successor plan continues to provide pension benefits for future service.

A nonparticipating annuity contract is a contract with an insurance company in which the insurance company agrees to pay pension benefits to the participants of the pension plan in return for a fixed premium.

A participating annuity contract is a contract with an insurance company in which the company agrees to pay pension benefits to pension plan participants, but the pension plan or company shares in the experience of the insurance company. If the substance of the contract is such that the company or pension plan has not transferred all risks to the insurance company, the contract with the insurance company is not considered a settlement of the pension plan.

A curtailment of a defined benefit pension plan is a transaction or event where the future service years of the current employees are reduced significantly or where benefits for part or all of the future service are eliminated for a significant number of participants. An example of a curtailment is the termination of employees because of the disposal of a segment of a business. The termination of the employees causes a reduction in the years of future service, but the pension plan stays in effect and continues to operate. When a pension plan is terminated and the plan no longer exists, the company has both a settlement and curtailment.

Given the definitions of settlements and curtailments, attention is now directed to a discussion of Flowchart 7-4. All blocks in Flowchart 7-4 have been numbered for referencing in the discussion that follows.

Flowchart 7-4

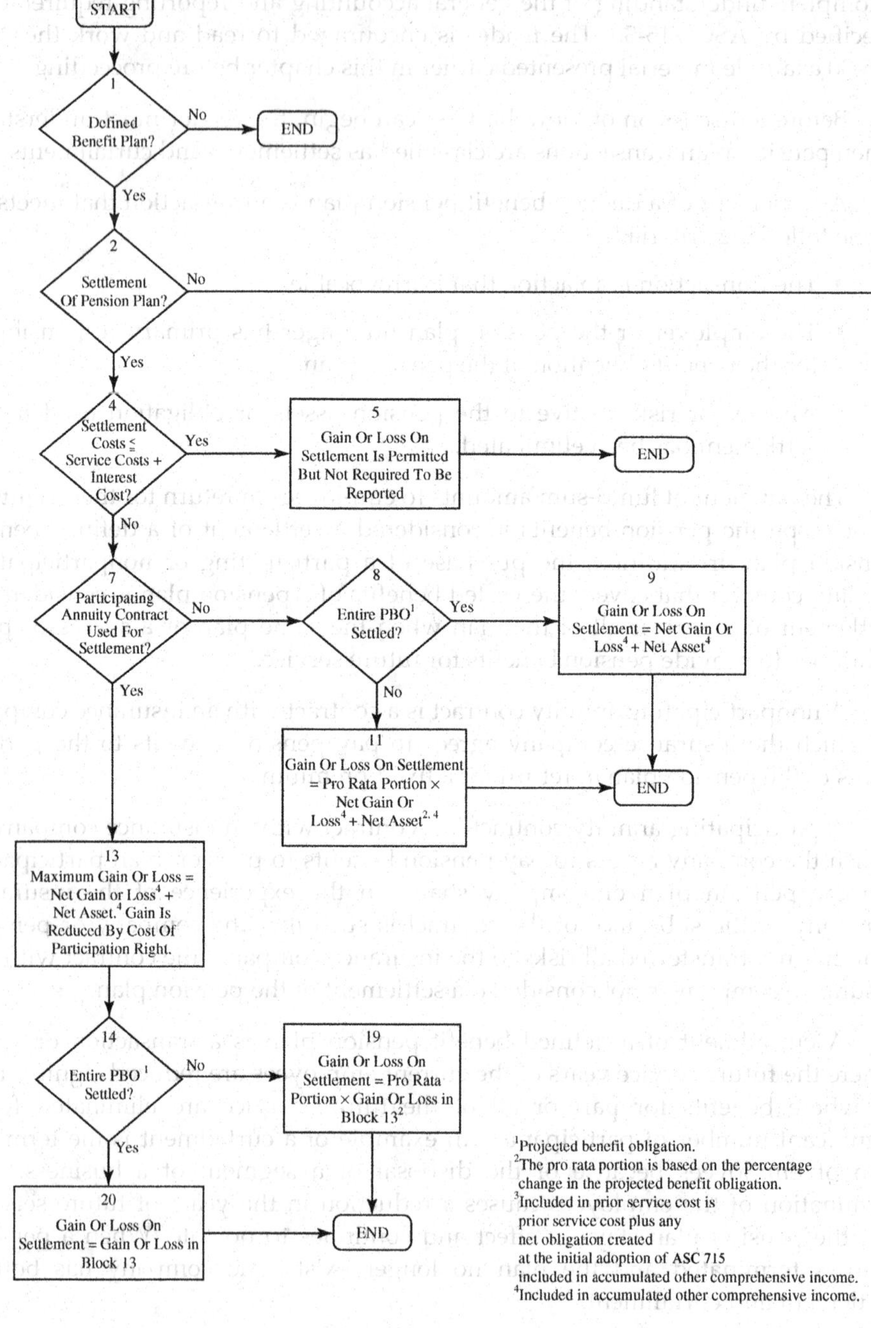
START
1
Defined Benefit Plan?
No
END
Yes
2
Settlement Of Pension Plan?
No
Yes
4
Settlement Costs ≤ Service Costs + Interest Cost?
Yes
5
Gain Or Loss On Settlement Is Permitted But Not Required To Be Reported
END
No
7
Participating Annuity Contract Used For Settlement?
No
8
Entire PBO[1] Settled?
Yes
9
Gain Or Loss On Settlement = Net Gain Or Loss[4] + Net Asset[4]
No
11
Gain Or Loss On Settlement = Pro Rata Portion × Net Gain Or Loss[4] + Net Asset[2, 4]
END
Yes
13
Maximum Gain Or Loss = Net Gain or Loss[4] + Net Asset.[4] Gain Is Reduced By Cost Of Participation Right.
14
Entire PBO[1] Settled?
No
19
Gain Or Loss On Settlement = Pro Rata Portion × Gain Or Loss in Block 13[2]
Yes
20
Gain Or Loss On Settlement = Gain Or Loss in Block 13
END

[1]Projected benefit obligation.
[2]The pro rata portion is based on the percentage change in the projected benefit obligation.
[3]Included in prior service cost is prior service cost plus any net obligation created at the initial adoption of ASC 715 included in accumulated other comprehensive income.
[4]Included in accumulated other comprehensive income.

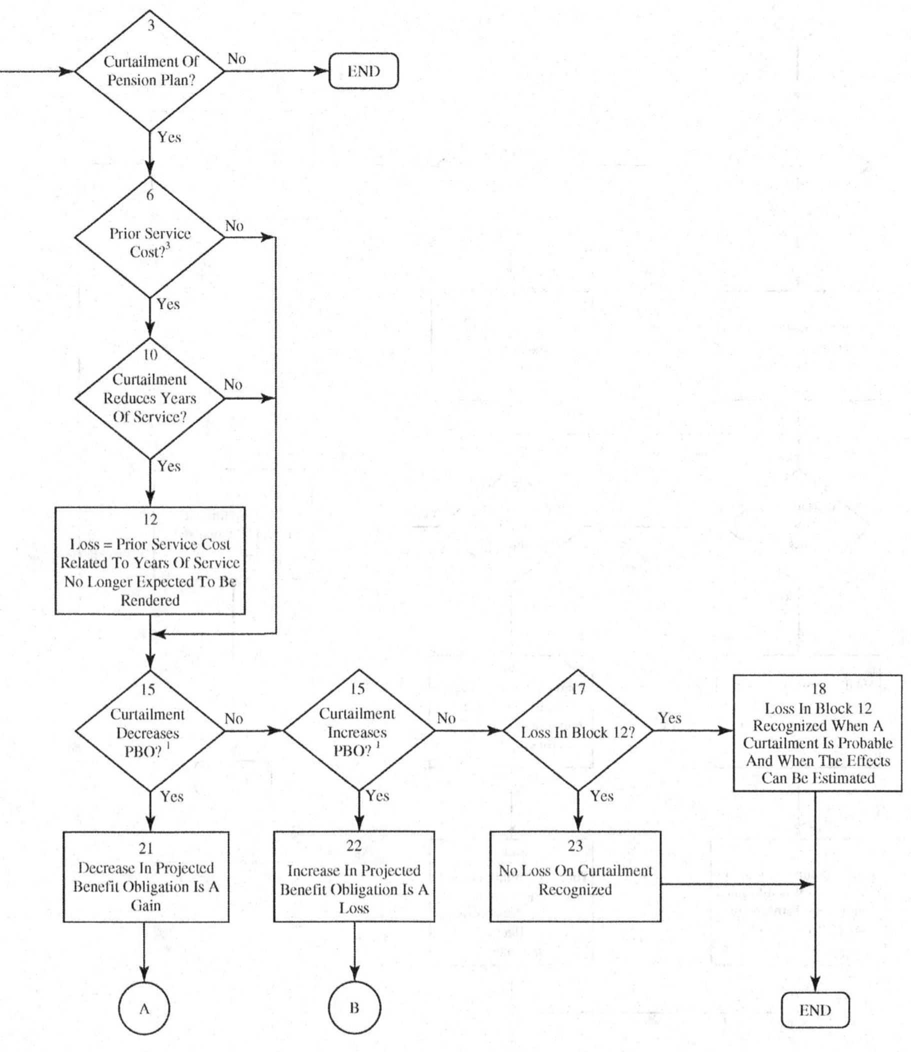
3
Curtailment Of Pension Plan?
No
END
Yes
6
Prior Service Cost?[3]
No
Yes
10
Curtailment Reduces Years Of Service?
No
Yes
12
Loss = Prior Service Cost Related To Years Of Service No Longer Expected To Be Rendered
15
Curtailment Decreases PBO?[1]
No
Yes
15
Curtailment Increases PBO?[1]
No
Yes
17
Loss In Block 12?
Yes
Yes
18
Loss In Block 12 Recognized When A Curtailment Is Probable And When The Effects Can Be Estimated
21
Decrease In Projected Benefit Obligation Is A Gain
22
Increase In Projected Benefit Obligation Is A Loss
23
No Loss On Curtailment Recognized
A
B
END

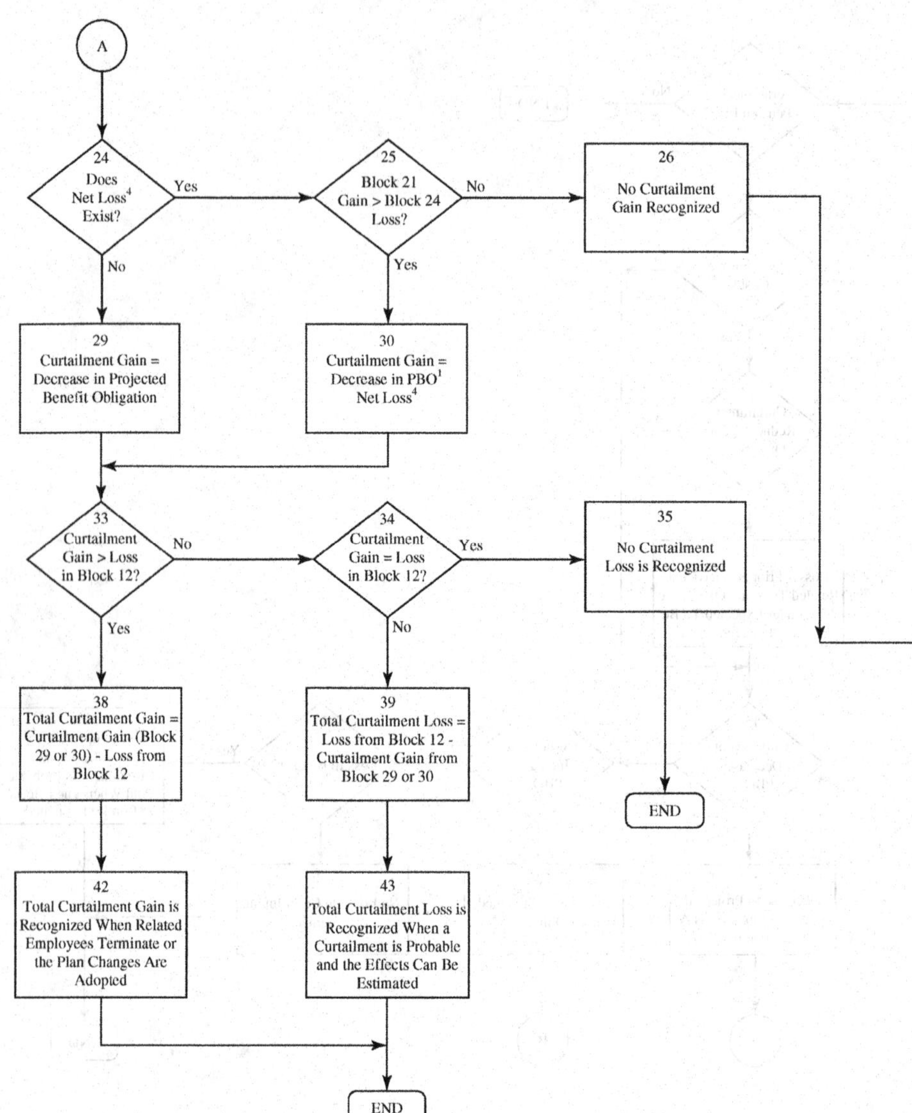
A
24
Does
Net Loss4
Exist?
Yes
No
25
Block 21
Gain > Block 24
Loss?
No
Yes
26
No Curtailment
Gain Recognized
29
Curtailment Gain =
Decrease in Projected
Benefit Obligation
30
Curtailment Gain =
Decrease in PBO1
Net Loss4
33
Curtailment
Gain > Loss
in Block 12?
No
Yes
34
Curtailment
Gain = Loss
in Block 12?
Yes
No
35
No Curtailment
Loss is Recognized
END
38
Total Curtailment Gain =
Curtailment Gain (Block
29 or 30) - Loss from
Block 12
39
Total Curtailment Loss =
Loss from Block 12 -
Curtailment Gain from
Block 29 or 30
42
Total Curtailment Gain is
Recognized When Related
Employees Terminate or
the Plan Changes Are
Adopted
43
Total Curtailment Loss is
Recognized When a
Curtailment is Probable
and the Effects Can Be
Estimated
END

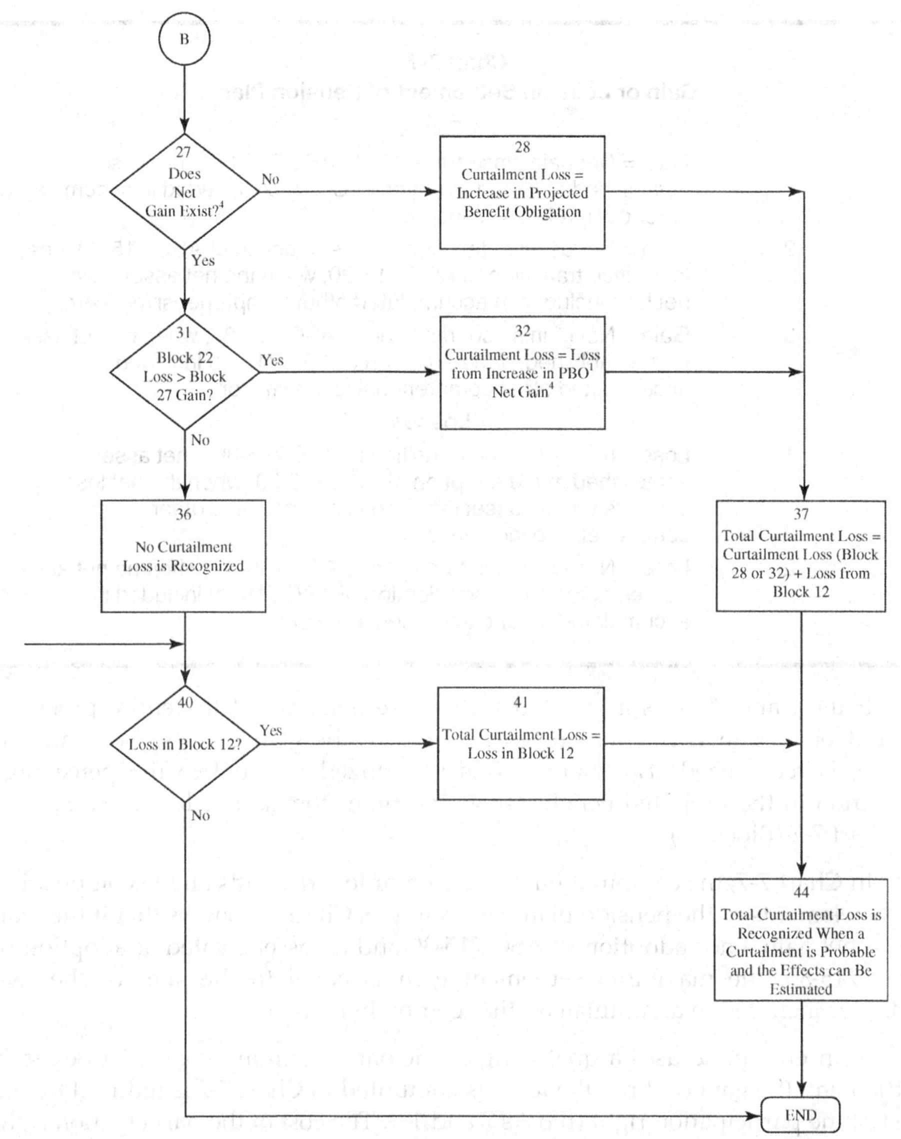

Once a transaction or event has been identified as a settlement or curtailment of a defined benefit pension plan, the enterprise must compute any gain or loss related to the settlement or curtailment. Computation of the gain or loss on a pension plan settlement is addressed in Flowchart 7-4. If the cost to settle a pension plan is equal to or less than the summation of the service cost and the interest cost components of pension expense (Blocks 4 and 5), the enterprise is permitted, but is not required, to report a gain or loss on the settlement.

If an enterprise uses a lump-sum payment or purchases a nonparticipating annuity contract (Block 7), and the entire projected benefit obligation is settled (Block 8), the gain or loss on the settlement is computed as shown in Chart 7-7 (Block 9).

Chart 7-7
Gain or Loss on Settlement of Pension Plan

Gains

1. Gain = Net gain since transition to ASC 715-30 + net asset established at the adoption of ASC 715-30 included in accumulated other comprehensive income, or
2. Gain = Net asset established at the adoption of ASC 715-30 – net loss since transition to ASC 715-30, when the net asset exceeds the net loss included in accumulated other comprehensive income, or
3. Gain = Net gain since transition to ASC 715-30, when no net asset was established at the adoption of ASC 715-30 included in accumulated other comprehensive income, or

Losses

1. Loss = Net loss since transition to ASC 715-30 – net asset established at the adoption of ASC 715-30, when the net loss exceeds the net asset included in accumulated other comprehensive income, or
2. Loss = Net loss since transition to ASC 715-30, when no net asset was established at the adoption of ASC 715-30 included in accumulated other comprehensive income.

If the transaction is accounted for as a settlement but the entire projected benefit obligation is not settled, only a part of the gain or loss, as computed above, is recognized. The gain or loss recognized is equal to the percentage reduction in the projected benefit obligation times the gain or loss as computed in Chart 7-7 (Block 11).

In Chart 7-7, the computation of the gain or loss depends on the composition of the elements of the pension plan. For example, Chart 7-7 shows that if the plan has a net gain since adoption of ASC 715-30 and an asset created at adoption of ASC 715-30, the maximum settlement gain is equal to the sum of the two balances included in accumulated other comprehensive income.

If an enterprise uses a qualifying participating annuity contract to effect a settlement, the gain (but not the loss) as computed in Chart 7-7 is reduced by the cost of the participation right (Blocks 7 and 13). The cost of the participation right is the difference between the cost of a participating and a nonparticipating annuity contract. If the entire projected benefit obligation is not settled (Block 14), the gain or loss reported in the income statement is equal to the percentage decrease in the projected benefit obligation times the loss or the gain after reduction of the cost of the participation right.

Next, gains and losses on curtailment of defined benefit pension plans are considered. The computation of the gain or loss on curtailment is divided into a three-step process. The first step is to calculate the loss from prior service cost, if any (Block 6). For purposes of this computation, prior service cost consists of prior service cost from plan amendments and any net obligation from transition to ASC 715-30 included in accumulated other comprehensive income. If the enterprise has prior service cost and the curtailment reduces employee years of service (Block 10), the loss recognized is equal to the prior service cost included in accumulated other comprehensive income times the percentage decrease in employee years of service (Block 12).

The second step is to compute the gain or loss from the decrease or the increase in the projected benefit obligation (Blocks 15 and 16). A decrease in the projected benefit obligation is a gain and an increase is a loss (Blocks 21 and 22). If the curtailment causes a decrease in the projected benefit obligation, the gain from the decrease is accounted for as follows:

- The gain is recognized in total if the plan has no net loss included in accumulated other comprehensive income since transition to ASC 715-30 (Blocks 24 and 29), or
- If the gain is greater than the net loss included in accumulated other comprehensive income, the excess is recognized as a gain (Block 30), or
- If the gain is less than the net loss included in accumulated other comprehensive income, no gain or loss is recognized (Blocks 25 and 26).

If the curtailment causes an increase in the projected benefit obligation, the loss from the decrease is accounted for as follows:

- The loss is recognized in total if the plan has no net gain included in accumulated other comprehensive income since transition to ASC 715-30 (Blocks 27 and 28), or
- If the loss is greater than the net gain included in accumulated other comprehensive income, the excess is recognized as a loss (Blocks 31 and 32), or
- If the loss is less than the net gain included in accumulated other comprehensive income, no loss or gain is recognized (Block 36).

When computing the curtailment gain or loss, the balance of the net asset created at transition to ASC 715-30 is added to the gain or loss since transition to ASC 715-30 (balances in accumulated other comprehensive income).

The third step of the three-step process is to combine the loss from the decrease in employee service years with the gain or loss from the decrease or increase in the projected benefit obligation. Combination of steps 1 and 2 will result in a final net gain or net loss (Blocks 33–41). If the result is a net gain, the gain is recognized in the income statement when the related employees terminate or the plan changes are adopted (Block 42). If the result is a net loss, the loss is reported in the income statement when the curtailment is probable and the effects of the curtailment can be estimated (Blocks 43 and 44). The net gain or net loss is classified in the income statement using the provisions of ASC 225-20. Generally, the net gain or loss is classified as a line item in income from continuing operations.

If an enterprise entered into a transaction classified as an asset reversion prior to ASC 715-30, a deferred gain was reported from the prior reversion. At the date of transition to ASC 715-30, any deferred gain remaining would be reported as a gain and classified in the income statement as the cumulative effect of an accounting principle change. The amount reported as the cumulative effect is the smaller of the following:

- The deferred gain balance from the asset reversion that has not been amortized.
- The net asset from the initial adoption of ASC 715-30 that has not been amortized.

An asset reversion transaction is one in which an enterprise settles a pension obligation and plan assets in excess of the obligation are transferred back to the enterprise.

Technical Considerations—Settlements and Curtailments

Five examples are used to illustrate the technical considerations for settlements and curtailments of defined benefit pension plans. It is important that the general technical provisions of ASC 715-30 be understood before reviewing the following examples. Assumptions for Example 7-8 are presented below.

Example 7-8

Assumptions for Settlement of Defined Benefit Pension Plan

1. Taylor Enterprises (Taylor) has a final-pay noncontributory defined benefit pension plan that covers substantially all employees. Taylor adopted all provisions of ASC 715-30 on January 1, 20X6.
2. During 20X9, Taylor settled 75% of the projected benefit obligation (the vested benefit portion). The vested benefits were settled by entering into a nonparticipating annuity contract with an insurance company.
3. At the date of settlement, the following information related to the pension plan is provided by the actuary:

•	Net loss included in accumulated other comprehensive income	$200,000
•	Net asset created at adoption of ASC 715-30 included in accumulated other comprehensive income	100,000
•	Prior service cost from plan amendment included in accumulated other comprehensive income	75,000
•	Pension liability	150,000

The first step in the analysis of the assumptions in Example 7-8 is to determine if the transaction qualifies as a settlement under the provisions of ASC 715-30. The transaction qualifies as a settlement because the purchase of the nonparticipating annuity contract is an irrevocable action that transfers primary responsibility for the plan obligation to an insurance company and eliminates any significant risks to the plan for the pension obligation.

Because the transaction qualifies as a settlement, the company may have a gain or loss on the settlement. The gain or loss on plan settlement is computed as follows:

Net Loss included in accumulated other comprehensive income	$200,000
Net Asset Created at Adoption of ASC 715-30 included in accumulated other comprehensive income	100,000
Percent Change in Projected Benefit Obligation	75%
Loss on Settlement	$75,000

The journal entry required on the date of settlement to record the settlement loss is as follows:

Loss on Settlement of Defined Benefit Pension Plan	75,000	
Other Comprehensive Income		75,000

The loss on settlement of the pension plan is classified on the income statement using the provisions of ASC 225-20.

The prior service cost included in accumulated other comprehensive income is not used in the computation of the settlement loss. Only the net gain or loss included in accumulated other comprehensive income and the asset included in accumulated other comprehensive income created at the initial adoption of ASC 715-30 are used in the calculation. Because only 75% of the projected benefit obligation is settled, only 75% of the maximum loss can be recognized.

This completes the analysis of Example 7-8. Assumptions for Example 7-9 are presented below.

Example 7-9
Assumptions for Settlement of Defined Benefit Plan

1. The Denton Company (Denton) and Buckeye Enterprises (Buckeye) both have final-pay noncontributory defined benefit pension plans that cover substantially all employees. Both companies adopted all provisions of ASC 715-30 on January 1, 20X6.
2. During 20X8 both companies settled portions of the projected benefit obligation (the vested part). Denton entered into a nonparticipating annuity contract with an insurance company. Buckeye settled its vested part of the benefit obligation using a participating annuity contract.
3. The net loss, net gain, net asset, net obligation, and prior service cost amounts listed below are the balances included in accumulated other comprehensive income. On the date of settlement, the following information relates to the pension plans of the companies:

	Denton Company	Buckeye Enterprises
• Net loss	$175,000	
• Net gain		$225,000
• Net asset created at adoption of ASC 715-30		350,000
• Net obligation created at adoption of ASC 715-30	400,000	
• Prior service cost from plan amendment	200,000	250,000

	Denton Company	Buckeye Enterprises
• Percentage of projected benefit obligation settled	70%	80%
• Pension Liability		240,000
• Pension asset	210,000	

4. Buckeye paid $2,750,000 for the participating annuity contract to settle a $2,525,000 vested benefit obligation. A nonparticipating annuity contract would have cost Buckeye $2,525,000.

The first step in analysis of the pension plans in Example 7-9 is to determine whether the transactions for both companies qualify as pension plan settlements under the provisions of ASC 715-30. Both transactions qualify as settlements because the purchase of the nonparticipating and participating annuity contracts are irrevocable actions that transfer primary responsibility for the plan obligation to insurance companies and eliminate any significant risks to the plans for the pension obligation.

The second step in the analysis is to compute any gain or loss on the pension plan settlement. The gain or loss for Denton is computed below:

Net Loss Included in Accumulated Other Comprehensive Income	$175,000
Maximum Loss on Settlement	$175,000
Percentage of Projected Benefit Obligation Settled	70%
Loss on Settlement	$122,500

The journal entry required for the settlement is as follows:

Loss on Settlement of Defined Benefit Pension Plan	122,500	
Other Comprehensive Income		122,500

The prior service cost from the plan amendment and the net obligation created at the initial adoption of ASC 715-30 are not used in the calculation of the settlement gain or loss.

Buckeye used a participating annuity contract to settle the projected benefit obligation. When an enterprise uses a participating annuity contract to settle a plan obligation, the maximum gain (but not the loss) is reduced by the cost of the participation right. The cost of the participation right for Buckeye is computed as follows:

Cost of the participating annuity	$2,750,000
Cost of a nonparticipating annuity to settle the same benefit obligation	2,525,000
Cost of participation right	$225,000

Next the gain or loss on settlement for Buckeye is computed.

Net Gain	$225,000
Net Asset Created at the Initial Adoption of ASC 715-30	350,000
Maximum Gain on Settlement	575,000

Cost of Participation Right	225,000
Maximum Gain After Participation Right	$350,000
Percentage of Projected Benefit Obligation Settled	80%
Gain on Settlement	$280,000

The cost of the participation right is a reduction of the gain before applying the percentage of projected benefit obligation settled. The journal entry required to record the settlement is as follows:

Other Comprehensive Income	280,000	
Gain on Settlement of Defined Benefit Pension Plan		280,000

The first two examples covered settlements of defined benefit pension plans. Examples 7-10 and 7-11 illustrate curtailments of defined benefit pension plans and Example 7-12 illustrates a transaction that is classified as both a settlement and a curtailment. Assumptions for Example 7-10 are provided below.

Example 7-10
Assumptions for the Curtailment of a Defined Benefit Plan

1. Nelson Enterprises (Nelson) has a final-pay noncontributory defined benefit pension plan that covers substantially all employees. All provisions of ASC 715-30 were adopted on January 1, 20X6.
2. In October of 20X8, Nelson determined that it is probable that during early 20X9, Nelson will terminate a significant number of employees because of declining business. Nelson has determined that the following facts relative to the pension plan will be available on the date of termination. The net obligation, net loss, and prior service cost amounts listed below are the balances included in accumulated other comprehensive income:

• Reduction in nonvested pension benefit related to employees terminated	$20,000
• Reduction in projected benefit obligation based on estimated future levels of compensation of terminated employees	120,000
• Net obligation from transition to ASC 715-30	100,000
• Net loss since adoption of ASC 715-30	160,000
• Prior service cost from plan amendment	50,000
• Pension liability	100,000
• Percentage reduction in service years of those employees present at date of adoption of ASC 715-30	25%
• Percentage reduction in service years of those employees present at time of plan amendment	15%

The first step in analyzing the Example 7-10 material is to determine if the expected termination of employees qualifies as a pension plan curtailment. Because the expected future years of service of current employees will be reduced as a result of the termination of a significant number of employees, the termination is classified as a curtailment. Because the termination is classified as a pension plan curtailment, the gain or loss on curtailment must be computed. The gain or loss is computed in Table 7-26.

Table 7-26 Computation of Gain or Loss on Curtailment

Net obligation	$(100,000)	
Percentage reduction in service years of those employees present at date of adoption of ASC 715-30	25%	$(25,000)
Prior service cost	$(50,000)	
Percentage reduction in service years of those employees present at date of plan amendment	15%	(7,500)
Loss		$(32,500)
Gain from reduction in nonvested pension benefits related to employee termination	$20,000	
Gain from reduction in projected benefit obligation based on future levels of compensation of terminated employees	120,000	
Total	$140,000	
Net loss since adoption of ASC 715-30	(160,000)	0
Loss on pension curtailment		$(32,500)

Table 7-26 is divided into two parts. First, a $32,500 loss on prior service cost is computed, because the years of service expected to be rendered by the employees has been reduced. For purposes of this computation, prior service cost includes prior service cost included in accumulated other comprehensive income from plan amendments and any net obligation included in accumulated other comprehensive income established at the date of initial adoption of ASC 715-30. If a net asset had been established at the initial adoption of ASC 715-30, it would be added to the net gain or loss since transition to ASC 715-30. The reduction in the expected service years of the employee group existing at the adoption of ASC 715-30 as a result of the termination is 25%. Therefore, 25%, or $25,000, of the net obligation is recognized as a loss, and $75,000 ($100,000 – $25,000) is amortized over the remaining life of the employee group.

The reduction in the expected service years of the employee group existing at the date of amendment of the plan is 15%. Consequently, 15% of the prior service cost ($7,500) is recognized as a loss at the time of curtailment. The remaining $42,500 ($50,000 – $7,500) is amortized over the remaining employee service life.

The second part of Table 7-26 focuses on the possible gain from the reduction in the projected benefit obligation. The reduction in the projected benefit obligation is caused by the elimination of nonvested benefits and estimates of future salary levels for terminated employees. The projected benefit obligation is computed based on an assumption of increasing or decreasing salary levels in future periods. The future increases in salaries will not occur for the employees who are terminated. Removing the estimates of future salary increases from the projected benefit obligation causes the obligation to decrease, resulting in a gain. In addition, because the terminated employees will not receive the nonvested benefits, the removal of such benefits from the projected benefit obligation causes the obligation to decrease and results in a gain. As shown in Table 7-26, the gain from both items is $140,000. Because a net loss is available, the loss is offset against the gain. The loss of $160,000 exceeds the gain of $140,000 and no gain is recognized. If the $160,000 loss had been a gain, the entire $140,000 would have been recognized as a gain. Therefore, Nelson must recognize a loss on pension plan curtailment of $32,500, as shown in Table 7-26.

Using the information from Table 7-26, the entry to record the loss on the curtailment of the pension plan in October 20X8 is:

Other Comprehensive Income	32,500	
Pension Liability		32,500

The preceding entry is made in 20X8, even though the termination is not expected to occur until 20X9, because it is probable that the termination will happen and the facts can be estimated.

The account, Loss on Pension Plan Curtailment, is classified in the income statement using the provisions of ASC 225-20. Generally, the account is classified as a line item in the nonoperating section of income from continuing operations.

Example 7-10 illustrated a curtailment that required the recording and reporting of a loss. Example 7-11 contains assumptions about two different companies' pension plans that are used to compute gains on curtailment. Assumptions for Example 7-11 are presented below.

Example 7-11
Assumptions for the Curtailment of Defined Benefit Plans

1. Newland Enterprises and the Powell Company have final-pay noncontributory defined benefit pension plans that cover substantially all employees. Both companies adopted all provisions of ASC 715-30 on January 1, 20X6.

2. On December 1, 20X9, both companies terminated a significant number of employees because of declining business. On the date of termination, the following information relates to the companies' pension plans. The net loss, net gain, net asset, net obligation, and prior service cost amounts listed below are the remaining balances included in accumulated other comprehensive income that have not been amortized to pension expense.

	Newland Enterprises	Powell Company
• Reduction in nonvested pension benefit related to employees terminated	$100,000	$60,000
• Reduction in projected benefit obligation based on estimated future levels of compensation of terminated employees	600,000	400,000
• Net obligation from transition to ASC 715-30	150,000	
• Net asset from transition to ASC 715-30		100,000
• Net loss since adoption of ASC 715-30	200,000	
• Net gain since adoption of ASC 715-30		250,000
• Prior service cost from plan amendment	100,000	75,000
• Pension liability	300,000	
• Pension asset		250,000
• Percentage reduction in service years of those employees present at date of adoption of ASC 715-30	40%	20%
• Percentage reduction in service years of those employees present at time of plan amendment	30%	25%

The termination of employees by both firms qualifies as a curtailment because the expected service years of the employee groups are significantly reduced.

Because the employee terminations are classified as curtailments, the gain or loss on curtailment must be computed. The gain or loss for Newland Enterprises is computed in Table 7-27.

Table 7-27 Computation of Gain or Loss on Curtailment for Newland Enterprises

Net obligation	$(150,000)	
Percentage reduction in service years of those employees present at date of adoption of ASC 715-30	40%	$(60,000)
Prior service cost	$(100,000)	
Percentage reduction in service years of those employees present at date of plan amendment	30%	(30,000)
Loss		$(90,000)

Gain from reduction in nonvested pension benefits related to employee termination	$100,000	
Gain from reduction in projected benefit obligation based on future levels of compensation of terminated employees	600,000	
Total	$700,000	
Net loss since adoption of ASC 715-30	(200,000)	500,000
Gain on pension curtailment		$410,000

The calculation of the curtailment gain is similar to the computation of the loss in Table 7-26 and requires very little explanation. The reader may wish to review the explanation of Table 7-26 before proceeding with Table 7-27. One point in Table 7-27 should be explained. The loss of $200,000 is offset against the $700,000 gain from the reduction in the projected benefit obligation, leaving a net gain of $500,000. The $90,000 loss from reduction in service years is offset against the $500,000 net gain, leaving a $410,000 gain on curtailment. The curtailment gain is recognized in earnings when the employees are terminated. The entry for the gain is made on December 1, 20X9, because the employees are terminated on this date. The following journal entry is required to record the gain on curtailment of the pension plan.

Other Comprehensive Income	410,000	
Gain on Pension Plan Curtailment		410,000

Next, the gain or loss on curtailment for the Powell Company is computed. Table 7-28 shows the gain or loss computation.

Table 7-28 Computation of Gain or Loss on Curtailment for Powell Company

Prior service cost		$(75,000)
Percentage reduction in service years of those employees present at date of plan amendment		25%
Loss		$(18,750)
Gain from reduction in nonvested pension benefits related to employee termination	$60,000	
Gain from reduction in projected benefit obligation based on future levels of compensation of terminated employees	400,000	
Total		460,000
Gain on pension curtailment		$441,250

Computation of the gain on curtailment in Table 7-28 is similar to the computations in Tables 7-26 and 7-27 and requires very little discussion. However, two points need to be noted. First, in the computation of the loss in the top part of Table 7-28, only prior service cost is used. At the date of transition to ASC 715-30, an asset was established. The asset is not used in the computation of the loss. Last, because the Powell Company has a net gain of $350,000 ($250,000 remaining net gain balance since transition to ASC 715-30 + $100,000 remaining net asset balance created at adoption of ASC 715-30), the gain of $460,000 from the decrease in the projected benefit obligation is recognized in total and then offset against the loss from the prior service cost.

Using the information from Table 7-28, the following journal entry is required to record the gain on pension curtailment for the Powell Company.

Other Comprehensive Income	441,250	
Gain on Pension Plan Curtailment		441,250

This completes the analysis of Example 7-11. Example 7-12 illustrates both a settlement and a curtailment in the same pension plan. Assumptions for Example 7-12 are presented below.

Example 7-12
Assumptions for a Settlement and Curtailment

1. On January 1, 20X6, Richard Enterprises terminated its final-pay noncontributory defined benefit pension plan by purchasing a nonparticipating annuity contract for $2,000,000. Any excess assets were withdrawn by the company, and no benefits were provided under any other plan.
2. The following information relates to Richard Enterprises' pension plan on the date of termination. The net asset, net gain, and prior service cost amounts listed below are the remaining balances included in accumulated other comprehensive income that have not been amortized as part of pension expense:

• Projected benefit obligation	$2,300,000
• Accumulated benefit obligation	2,000,000
• Fair value of plan assets	2,600,000
• Estimates of future compensation levels included in the projected benefit obligation	300,000
• Net asset established at adoption of ASC 715-30	225,000
• Net gain since adoption of ASC 715-30	200,000
• Prior service cost from plan amendment	50,000
• Pension liability	75,000

The termination of the pension plan in Example 7-12 is accounted for both as a settlement and a curtailment. The plan benefits are settled by the purchase of a $2,000,000 nonparticipating annuity contract, and the remaining assets of $600,000 ($2,600,000 – $2,000,000) are distributed to Richard Enterprises in the form of cash. The gain or loss on the termination is composed of two parts: (1) a settlement gain or loss and (2) a curtailment gain or loss. Computation of settlement and curtailment gains and losses is discussed in detail in Examples 7-8 through 7-11. The reader may wish to review the explanation of these examples before continuing with the computations of Example 7-12. The gain or loss on termination of the pension plan is computed in Table 7-29.

Table 7-29 Computation of Settlement and Curtailment Gain or Loss

Settlement Gain		
Net Asset Established At Adoption of ASC 715-30	$225,000	
Net Gain Since Adoption of ASC 715-30	200,000	
Gain on Settlement of Plan		$425,000
Curtailment Gain		
Reduction in Projected Benefit Obligation from Removal of Expected Future Salary Levels	$300,000	
Prior Service Cost from Plan Amendment	(50,000)	
Gain from Curtailment of Plan		250,000
Gain on Termination of Pension Plan		$675,000

Using the information in Table 7-29, the following journal entry is required to record the termination:

Cash	600,000	
Other Comprehensive Income	75,000	
Gain on Termination of Pension Plan		675,000

The gain on the termination of the pension plan is classified the same as the gain or loss on settlement or curtailment (i.e., using the provisions of ASC 225-20).

This completes the technical considerations related to settlements and curtailments of defined benefit pension plans. The next section discusses the general considerations and technical aspects of termination benefits.

General Considerations—Termination Benefits

Many enterprises offer benefits to certain employees, usually employees nearing retirement age, for a short period of time as an incentive to terminate their employment with the firm. These benefits are commonly referred to as special termination benefits. In addition, some firms have entered into agreements with selected employees who provide them with termination benefits in case of the occurrence of a specific event, such as the closing of a plant. Such benefits are called contractual termination benefits.

ASC 715-30 specifies the accounting for both special and contractual termination benefits. Such benefits may take the form of future payments, lump-sum payments, or a combination of both and may be paid from the enterprise's (1) existing assets, (2) established pension plan, (3) newly formed plan, or (4) a combination of (1)–(3). In addition, a situation causing termination benefits may result in a curtailment of a pension plan as discussed in the preceding section.

When an enterprise offers certain employees special termination benefits, a loss and a liability are recognized when the following conditions are met:

- The offer is accepted by the employee.
- The employer can reasonably estimate the amount of the payment(s).

If contractual termination benefits are involved, an enterprise should record a loss and a liability when the following two conditions are met:

1. It is probable that the employee will receive the contractual termination benefit.
2. The employer can reasonably estimate the amount of the payment(s).

The loss from termination benefits is classified in the income statement in accordance with the provisions of ASC 225-20, which generally requires classification of the loss as a line item in income from continuing operations. The liability is classified as current and/or long-term depending on when the liability is expected to be paid.

Technical Considerations—Termination Benefits

To illustrate accounting for termination benefits, the assumptions in Example 7-13 are used.

Example 7-13
Assumptions for Termination Benefits

1. Financial Enterprises (Financial), a December 31 year-end company, offered special termination benefits to five selected employees during 20X6. All employees except one accepted the offer. In addition, Financial decided in November 20X6 to dispose of a division in July 20X7. Three employees in the division have contractual termination benefit agreements.

2. The following estimated costs are available at December 31, 20X6 for the special termination benefits.

Costs Related to Four Employees Accepting Offer:	
a. Lump-sum payments	$125,000
b. Annuity payment for 5 years	50,000
Costs Related to One Employee Rejecting Offer:	
a. Lump-sum payments	$20,000
b. Annuity payment for 5 years	12,000

3. The estimated costs listed below relate to the three employees who are to receive benefits under the contractual agreement.

a. Lump-sum payments	$300,000
b. Annuity payment for 3 years	100,000

4. Financial uses an eight-percent interest rate for returns on employee benefit plans. All payments are assumed to be made at the end of the year, and it is probable that employees under the contractual agreement will receive the benefits.

Using the information in Example 7-13, the first step in the analysis is to determine whether Financial has incurred a liability and a loss. In regard to the special termination benefits, because four employees accepted the special benefit offer and Financial can reasonably estimate the amount of the payments, a loss and a liability must be recorded for the cost associated with the four employees. The costs related to the one employee not accepting the offer are ignored. In addition, a loss and a liability must be recorded in 20X6 for the contractual termination benefits because it is probable that the employees will receive the benefits and Financial can reasonably estimate the amount of the payments.

Next, the total cost of the special and contractual termination benefits must be computed, as shown in Table 7-30.

Table 7-30 Computation of Special and Contractual Termination Benefits

Special Termination Benefits Lump-sum payments		$125,000
Present value of annuity payments ($50,000 × 3.99271)		199,636
Total		$324,636
Contractual Termination Benefits		
Lump-sum payments	$300,000	
Present value of annuity payments ($100,000 × 2.57710)	257,710	
Total		557,710
Loss on Termination Benefits		$882,346

Total cost to Financial for termination benefits in 20X6 is $882,346. The present value of the $50,000 five-year annuity payment is $199,636 and the $100,000 three-year annuity payment is $257,710. The 3.99271 factor is the present value factor for an ordinary annuity at 8% for five periods. The 2.57710 factor is the present value factor for an ordinary annuity at 8% for three periods.

The entry required by Financial on December 31, 20X6 for termination benefits is:

Loss on Termination Benefits	882,346	
Estimated Liability for Termination Benefits		882,346

Disclosures

Settlement and curtailment disclosures have been integrated with the regular pension plan disclosures in accordance with ASC 715-30. Please review the pension plan disclosures in this chapter for current settlement and curtailment disclosure requirements.

General Discussion and Definition of Important Terms

A postretirement benefit plan is a form of deferred compensation where an employer pays health care and welfare benefits to employees in return for services. More specifically, a postretirement benefit plan is an agreement between an enterprise and employees of the enterprise whereby the company agrees to provide retirees of the company with postretirement benefits in return for services of the employees during some specified period of time. Examples of postretirement benefits are health care, legal services, day care, life insurance not provided through a pension plan, and tuition assistance.

ASC 715-60 requires a complex postretirement benefit cost calculation similar to what is required by ASC 715-30 for pension accounting. ASC 715-60 applies to both written and well-defined unwritten plans that in substance provide postretirement benefits. An unwritten plan may be considered a postretirement plan when an entity has a practice of paying benefits or has stated orally to employees (current or former) that postretirement benefits will be paid. Generally, it is assumed that an entity will pay postretirement benefits in the future if benefits are currently being paid and have been paid in the past. In addition, ASC 715-60 applies to deferred compensation plans to individuals when a combination of all the plans constitutes a postretirement plan. ASC 715-60 does not apply to the following:

1. Separate contracts to individual employees where terms of the contracts are determined on a case-by-case basis.
2. Pension benefits provided through a pension plan.
3. Life insurance benefits provided through a pension plan.

Before discussing Flowchart 7-5 and general aspects of accounting for postretirement plans, it is important to define some of the terms that appear in Flowchart 7-5 and the example material. Following are definitions of some of the specialized terms defined in ASC 715-60:

1. *Defined Benefit Postretirement Benefit Plan.* A postretirement benefit plan that defines the benefits to be received by employees or the method of determining the benefits expressed in monetary amounts or amounts of coverage.
2. *Defined Contribution Postretirement Benefit Plan.* A postretirement benefit plan that specifies the amount of contribution or the method of determining contributions made to employees' accounts, but does not specify the benefits to be paid or the method of determining benefits. Future employee benefits depend upon the amount of contributions, return earned on the contributions, and any forfeited benefits.
3. *Multiemployer Postretirement Benefit Plan.* A postretirement benefit plan that is either a defined benefit or defined contribution plan where two or more employers make contributions to the same plan usually under collective bargaining arrangements. The plan is sometimes referred to as a union plan. When an entity (the acquirer) acquires another entity (the acquiree) in a business combination and the company acquired participates in a multiemployer postretirement plan, the acquirer should report a withdrawal liability if on the acquisition date it is probable that the acquiree will withdraw from the multiemployer plan using the provisions of ASC 450.
4. *Multiple-Employer Postretirement Benefit Plan.* A postretirement benefit plan that is either a defined benefit or a defined contribution plan where

two or more unrelated employers make contributions to the same postretirement plan that is generally not under a collective bargaining arrangement. The plan is not classified as a multiemployer plan, but is in substance an aggregation of single employer plans.

5. *Non-U.S. Postretirement Benefit Plan.* A non-U.S. postretirement benefit plan is a plan outside the United States.

6. *Expected Postretirement Benefit Obligation.* The present value of the plan obligation to pay future benefits under the postretirement plan as of a specific date (measurement date) computed using proper actuarial methods. The future benefits to be paid may be paid to the employee, beneficiaries, or dependents.

7. *Accumulated Postretirement Benefit Obligation.* The obligation of an enterprise on a specific date, based on services provided by employees prior to that date, for the present value of postretirement benefits to be paid to employees in future years. The accumulated benefit obligation is a percentage of the expected benefit obligation, based on the plan benefit formula, until plan participants reach full eligibility. The expected and accumulated benefit obligations are equal once full eligibility is achieved.

8. *Service Cost.* The cost to an entity for benefits to be paid to plan participants for services rendered during the current accounting period.

9. *Prior Service Cost.* The increase or decrease in the postretirement benefit obligation as a result of plan amendments and/or plan initiations.

10. *Market-Related Value of Plan Assets.* Market-related value of plan assets is either fair market value or a computed amount. When a computed amount is elected, the amount is determined using a method that recognizes changes in fair value of the plan assets over a period of time not to exceed five years in a systematic and rational manner. The market-related value is used in the computation of the expected return and in the gain or loss calculation when a computed amount is elected for market-related value.

11. *Measurement Date.* The measurement date is the date on which the postretirement obligation and the fair value of plan assets are determined. Generally, the measurement date is the balance sheet date.

12. *Substantive Postretirement Plan.* A mutually understood agreement between the employer that is providing the benefits and the employees who are providing services regarding the terms of the postretirement benefit plan. The plan used for accounting purposes is the substantive plan, and it may be the existing written plan or one that differs from the written plan.

Other terms are introduced later in the discussion. With this introduction to the preceding terms, the reader should be able to understand Flowchart 7-5.

Flowchart and General Discussion

Flowchart 7-5 identifies the general accounting and reporting requirements established by ASC 715-60. The decision blocks have been numbered for referencing in the discussion that follows.

Flowchart 7-5

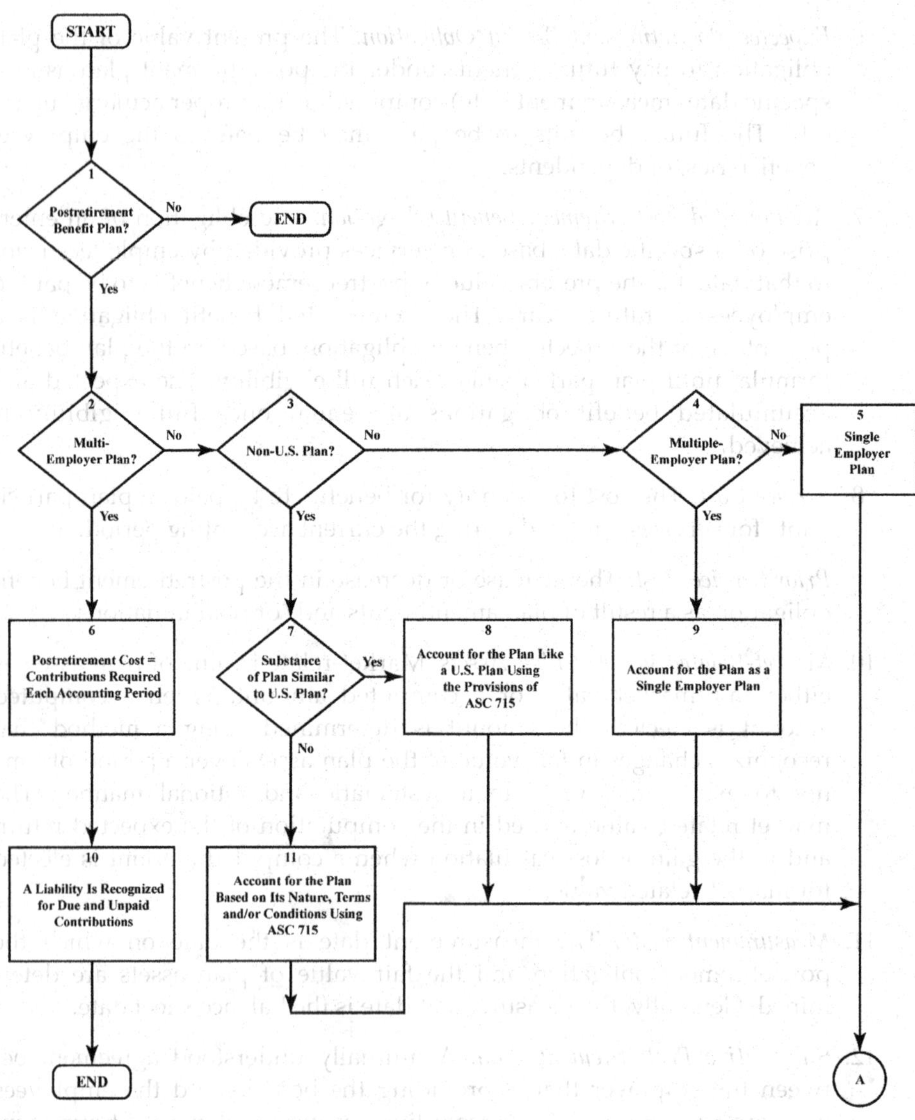

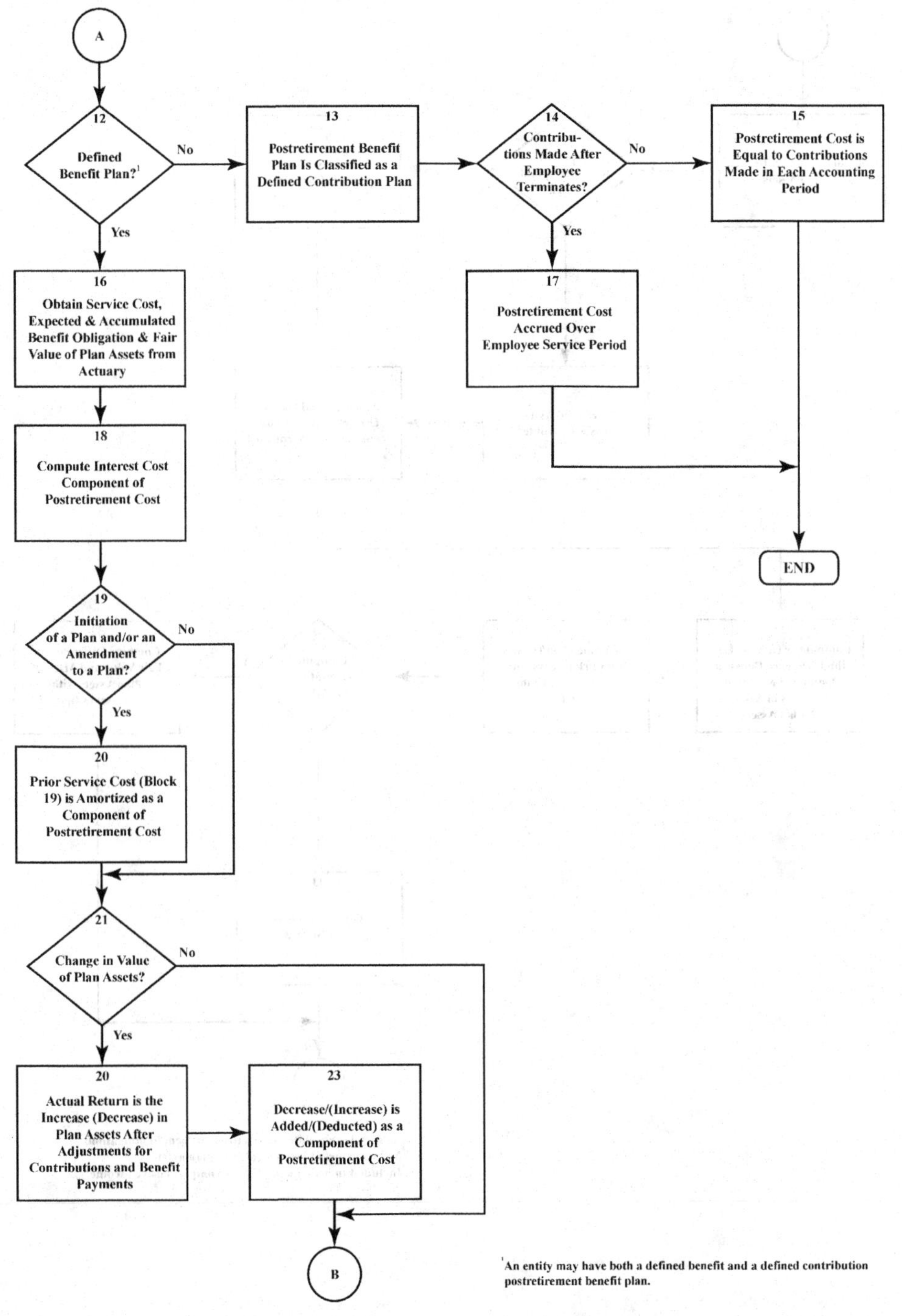

[1] An entity may have both a defined benefit and a defined contribution postretirement benefit plan.

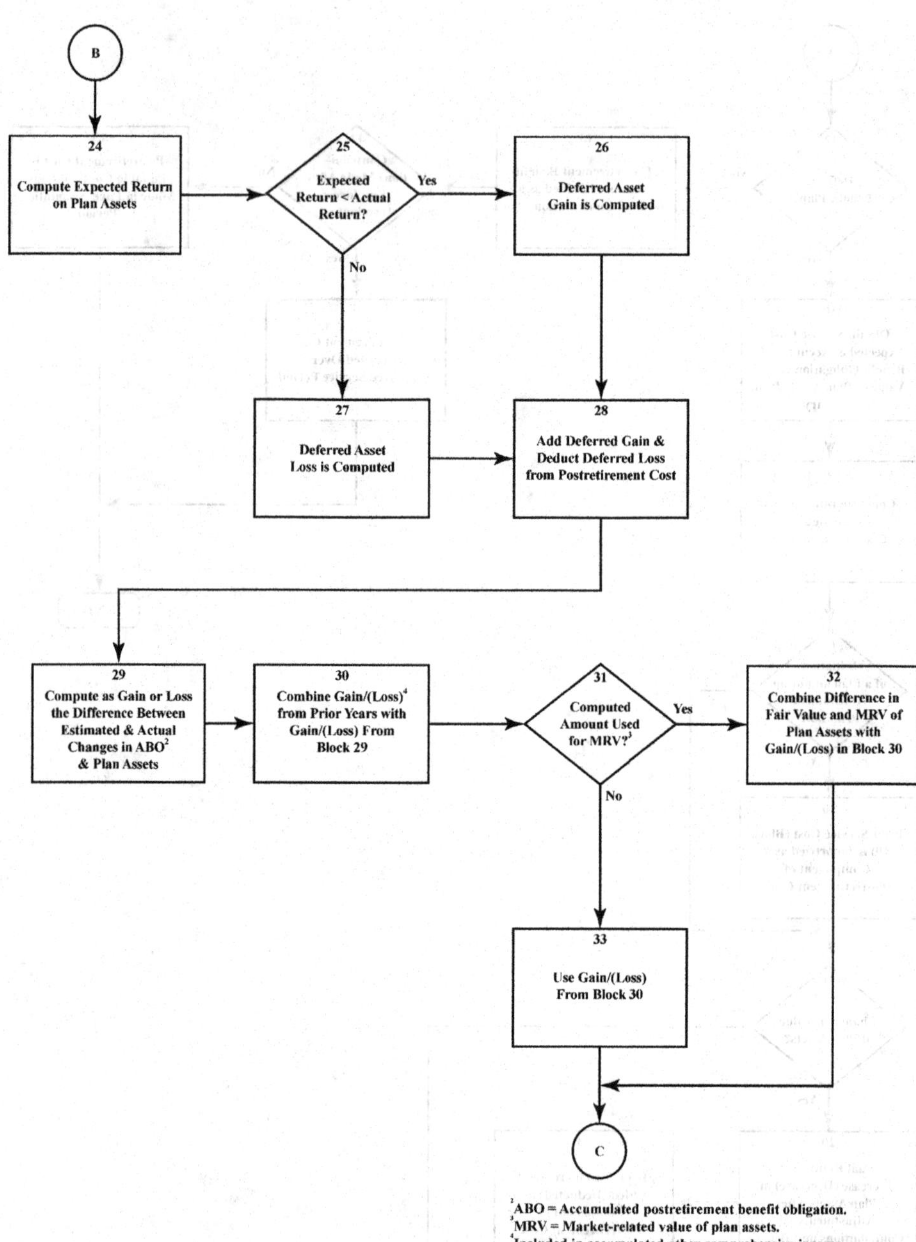

[2]ABO = Accumulated postretirement benefit obligation.
[3]MRV = Market-related value of plan assets.
[4]Included in accumulated other comprehensive income.

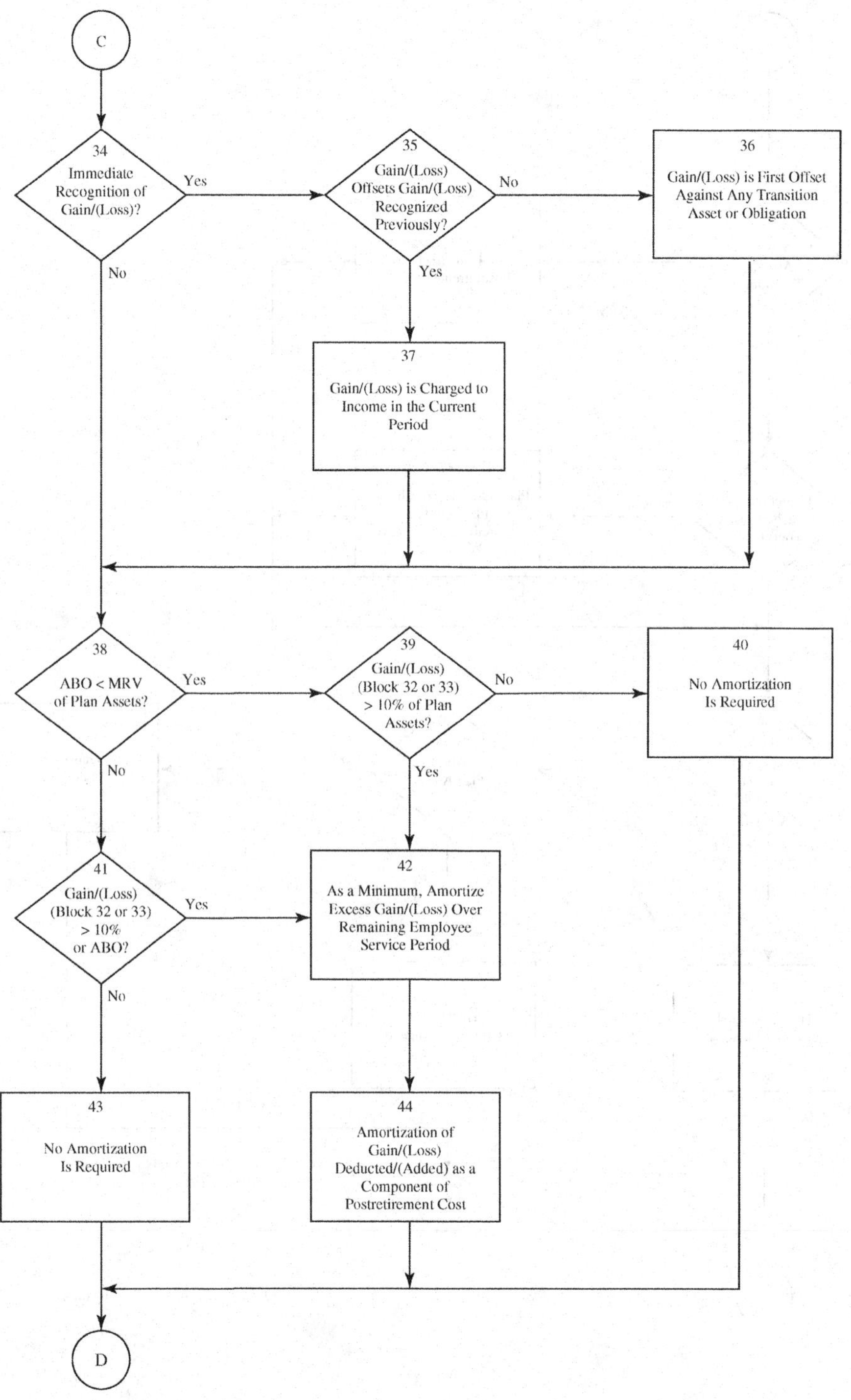
C
34
Immediate Recognition of Gain/(Loss)?
Yes
No
35
Gain/(Loss) Offsets Gain/(Loss) Recognized Previously?
No
Yes
36
Gain/(Loss) is First Offset Against Any Transition Asset or Obligation
37
Gain/(Loss) is Charged to Income in the Current Period
38
ABO < MRV of Plan Assets?
Yes
No
39
Gain/(Loss) (Block 32 or 33) > 10% of Plan Assets?
No
Yes
40
No Amortization Is Required
41
Gain/(Loss) (Block 32 or 33) > 10% or ABO?
Yes
No
42
As a Minimum, Amortize Excess Gain/(Loss) Over Remaining Employee Service Period
43
No Amortization Is Required
44
Amortization of Gain/(Loss) Deducted/(Added) as a Component of Postretirement Cost
D

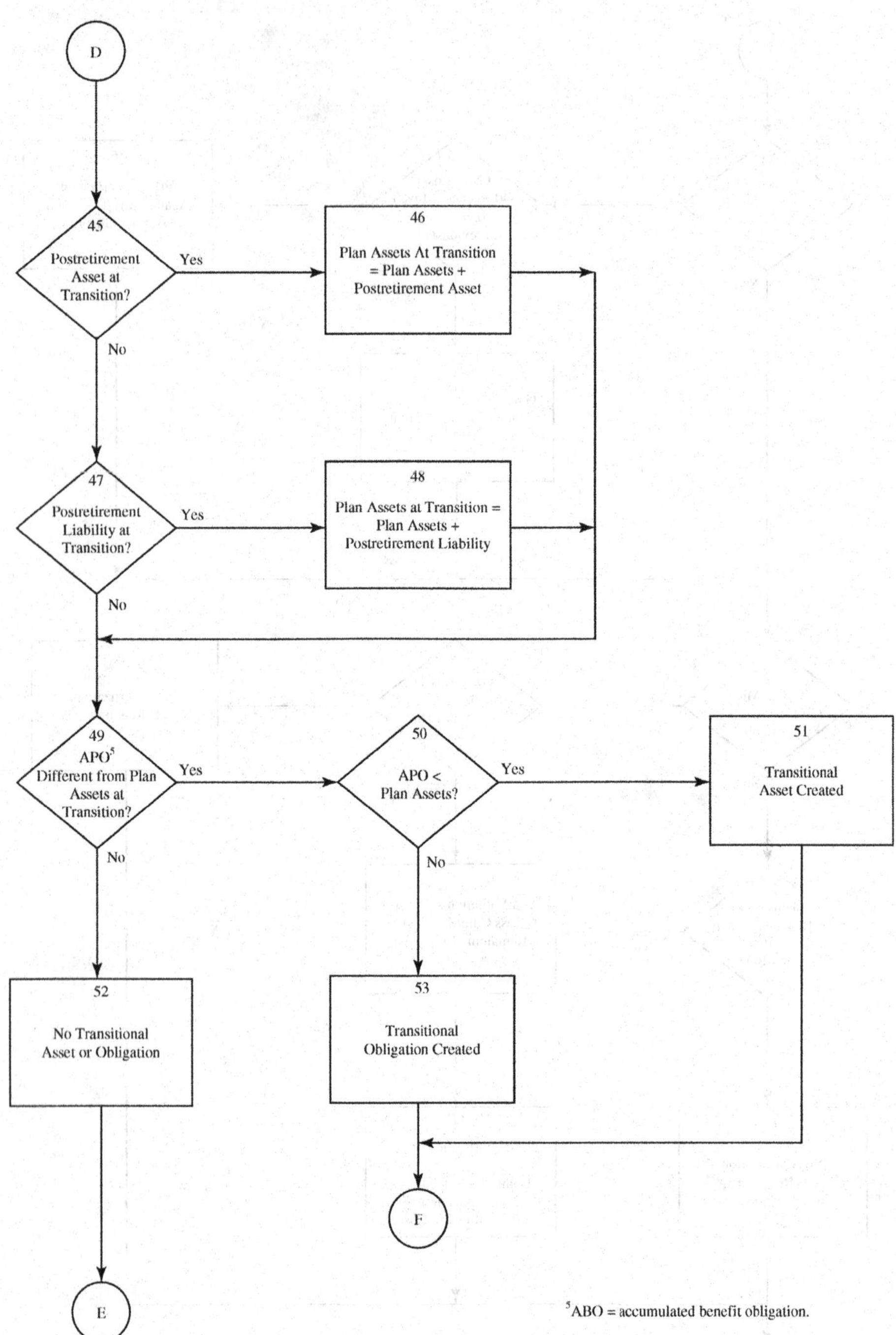

[5]ABO = accumulated benefit obligation.

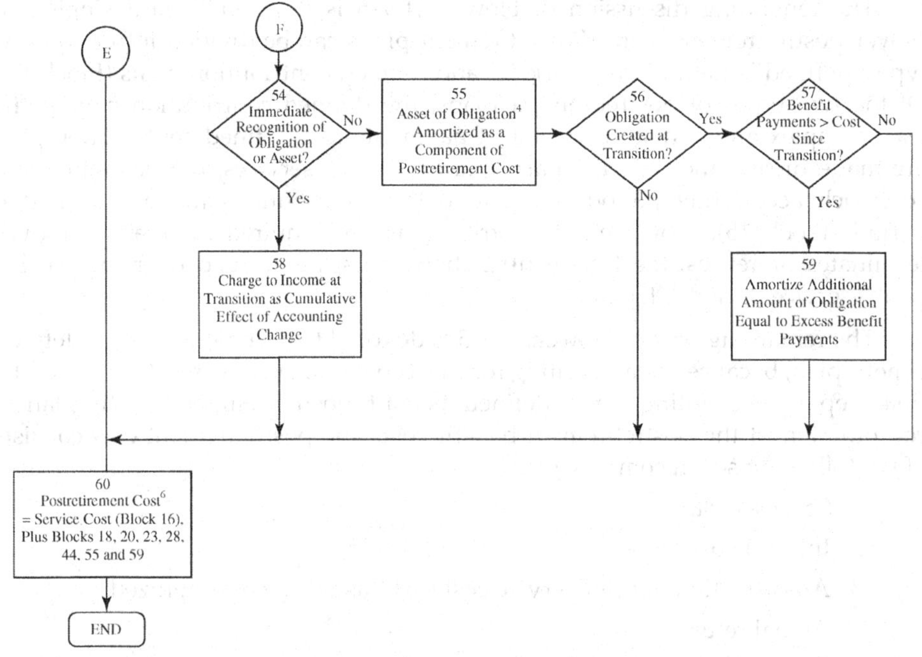

[6]Some elements of postretirement cost may be added and some elements may be deducted in the computation.

Postretirement benefit plans can be divided into multiemployer plans (Block 2), non-U.S. plans (Block 3), multiple-employer plans (Block 4), or single-employer plans (Block 5).

Multiemployer plans, commonly referred to as union plans, are plans where unrelated employers, with a common bond such as the same labor union or same industry, contribute to the same postretirement plan. All assets contributed by the various employers are placed in a common pool for the payment of benefits for all participants of all employers. Postretirement cost for an employer of a multiemployer plan is equal to the required contribution to the plan (Block 6). A liability is recorded for any unpaid contribution at the end of the accounting period (Block 10) (Paragraph 81).

Non-U.S. plans are postretirement plan arrangements outside the United States. ASC 715-60 does not provide requirements for non-U.S. plans. However, the provisions of ASC 715-60 must be applied to the non-U.S. plans. If the non-U.S. plan is in substance like a U.S. plan, the plan is accounted for as if it is a U.S. plan using the provisions of ASC 715-60 (Blocks 7 and 8). If the foreign plan is not like a U.S. plan, it is accounted for under ASC 715-60 based on an analysis of the plan's obligation and benefits (Block 11).

Multiple-employer plans are plans where unrelated employers contribute to the same plan with the objective of reducing costs or for investment purposes. Such plans are assumed to be aggregations of single-employer plans and should be accounted for as single-employer plans based on the interest of each employer (Block 9).

The remaining discussion of Flowchart 7-5 is directed toward single-employer postretirement plans. Postretirement plans can be divided into two basic types: defined benefit plans (Block 12) and defined contribution plans (Block 13). Of the two types of postretirement plans, the defined contribution plan is the least complex and is discussed first. If payments to a defined contribution plan are made during the time the participant provides services, the postretirement cost each accounting period is equal to the contributions made during that period (Block 15). However, if contributions are required after an employee terminates or retires, the total contributions must be accrued over the participant's service period (Block 17).

The remaining part of Flowchart 7-5 is devoted to a single-employer defined benefit plan, because the accounting for this type of plan is the most difficult. The first step in accounting for a defined benefit postretirement benefit plan is computation of the postretirement benefit cost. The postretirement cost consists of the following seven components:

1. Service cost.
2. Interest cost.
3. Amortization of prior service cost that has not been recognized.
4. Actual return.
5. Deferred asset gain or loss (gain is added and loss is deducted).
6. Amortization of gain or loss (loss is added and gain is deducted).
7. Amortization of transitional net obligation or transitional net asset, created at the initial adoption of ASC 715-60, that has not been recognized if immediate recognition is not elected.

Before computing postretirement cost for a company, certain information must be obtained from an actuary. As a minimum the actuary must provide the company with service cost, expected and accumulated benefit obligations and fair value of plan assets (Block 16). The first component of postretirement cost, service cost, is provided by the actuary and requires no computation. Service cost is added in the calculation of postretirement cost.

The second component of postretirement cost is interest cost. Interest cost is the increase in the accumulated postretirement benefit obligation from the passage of time, because the accumulated benefit obligation is measured on a present value basis. The interest cost component (Block 18) may be computed using the following formula:

$$IC = BAAPBO \times ADR$$

IC = Interest cost component.

BAAPBO = Beginning-of-period actual accumulated postretirement benefit obligation.

ADR = Assumed discount rate.

The interest cost component is added in the computation of the postretirement cost.

The next component is amortization of any prior service cost (Blocks 19 and 20). Prior service cost is the increase or decrease in the accumulated postretirement benefit obligation from either a plan amendment or the initiation of a postretirement plan. The change in plan benefits may relate to periods prior to the amendment or initiation and be assigned to services provided by plan participants in such periods, or the change in benefits may relate to periods subsequent to the amendment or initiation and benefits may be assigned to such future periods. Increases in prior service cost during the accounting period from the amendment or initiation of a postretirement plan are debited to other comprehensive income and credited to either a postretirement liability or postretirement asset. Decreases in prior service cost are debited to either a postretirement liability or postretirement asset and credited to other comprehensive income.

Prior service cost that increases the postretirement obligation is amortized to future periods in the following manner:

1. For each active participant who has not reached full eligibility on the date of amendment or initiation, amortize an equal amount to each year of service remaining from the date of amendment or initiation to the date of full eligibility.
2. For plans where most participants have reached full eligibility, divide the cost by the life expectancy remaining for those employees who are not active.
3. A more rapid alternative method may be elected, such as a straight-line method, by writing off the cost over the average service years remaining to the date of full eligibility for all participants who are active.

If historical evidence indicates that benefits from plan amendments are shorter than the remaining service life, the entity may accelerate amortization of prior service cost that increases the postretirement obligation.

When a plan amendment decreases the postretirement obligation, the following amortization step process should be used:

1. Use the decrease to reduce any unamortized prior service cost from prior years that increased the obligation.
2. Reduce any unamortized transitional obligation with the excess from Step 1.
3. Any excess prior service cost from Step 2 is amortized using the same methods as discussed for amendments or initiations that result in an increase in the accumulated postretirement benefit obligation.

The amount of prior service cost amortized to postretirement cost during the accounting period is removed from other comprehensive income using a reclassification adjustment. For example, when amortization of prior service cost increases postretirement expense, the original amount of the prior service cost created from a plan amendment or the initiation of a new plan was reported as a debit to other comprehensive income in the accounting period that the plan was amended or initiated. The other comprehensive income amount was closed to accumulated other comprehensive income as a debit balance. Therefore, when the prior service cost is amortized to postretirement expense, the reclassification adjustment requires a credit to other comprehensive income that then reduces the original debit that is included in accumulated other comprehensive income. The prior service is included in other comprehensive income when it is created through a plan amendment or plan initiation and is removed from other comprehensive income when the prior service cost is amortized to postretirement cost. The provisions of ASC 740 should be reviewed to determine whether there is a tax impact related to prior service cost.

The fourth component, the actual return on plan assets, is computed as the difference between beginning and ending fair value of plan assets, after adjustments for contributions and benefit payments made during the accounting period (Blocks 21–23). In addition, when the entity responsible for plan assets is taxable, the return on assets is adjusted for any tax expense or tax benefit. Fair value is defined as the amount that would be received on the measurement date from the sale of property between sellers and buyers (market participants) in an orderly transaction. In addition, the sellers and buyers are unrelated parties on the measurement date. The actual return may be computed using the following formula:

$$ARPA = ((AFPAE - C + B) - AFPAB) \pm TEB$$

ARPA	= Actual return on plan assets.
AFPAE	= Actual fair value of plan assets at end of accounting period.
C	= Contributions to postretirement plan during accounting period.
B	= Benefit payments from postretirement plan during accounting period.
AFPAB	= Actual fair value of plan assets at beginning of accounting period.
TEB	= Income tax expense or benefit when the entity responsible for the plan is taxable.

The next component of postretirement cost is the deferred asset gain or loss (Blocks 24–28). The deferred asset gain or loss is not amortized as part of the postretirement cost, but is included in total in the computation. The deferred asset gain or loss is the difference between the actual return (Block 25) and the expected return (Block 24). The expected return is the beginning-of-period market-related value of plan assets times the long-term rate of return on plan assets. The definition of market-related value of plan assets may be reviewed at this time. The expected long-term rate of return on plan assets is the expected average rate of return on plan assets and contributions for the year. The deferred asset gain or loss can be computed using the following formula:

$$DAG/(L) = (((AFPAE - C + B) - AFPAB) + TEB) - (EROR \times MRPAB)$$

DAG/(L)	= Deferred asset gain or loss.
AFPAE	= Actual fair value of plan assets at end of accounting period.
C	= Contributions to postretirement plan during accounting period.
B	= Benefit payments from postretirement plan during accounting period.
AFPAB	= Actual fair value of plan assets at beginning of accounting period.
TEB	= Income tax expense or benefit when the entity responsible for the plan is taxable.
EROR	= Expected long-term rate of return on plan assets.
MRPAB	= Market-related value of plan assets at beginning of accounting period.

A deferred asset gain is computed (Block 26) when the expected return is less than the actual return, and a deferred asset loss is computed (Block 27) when the expected return exceeds the actual return. A deferred asset gain is added as part of the postretirement cost and a deferred loss is deducted (Block 28). By adding the deferred asset gain and deducting the deferred asset loss, volatility of the postretirement cost created by using the actual return on plan assets in the computation is reduced. A deferred asset gain reduces an increase or a gain from the actual return on plan assets, and a deferred asset loss reduces a decrease or a loss from the actual return on plan assets. The combination of the deferred asset gain or loss and the actual return equal the expected return on plan assets.

The sixth component of postretirement cost is amortization of gain or loss (Block 29). Gains and losses, including both realized and unrealized gains and losses, are the difference between projected results and actual results. For example, the accumulated postretirement benefit obligation may have been based upon certain assumptions such as employee turnover, among other things, and future events may indicate that the assumptions used were different than anticipated. In addition, the actual return on plan assets may be higher or lower than projected. The net gain or loss subject to amortization may be divided into the following four components:

1. The difference between the projected and actual beginning-of-period accumulated postretirement benefit obligation (Block 29).
2. The difference between the projected and actual beginning-of-period fair value of plan assets (Block 29).
3. The unamortized gain or loss carried forward to the current year from prior years, if any (Block 30).
4. The market-related value of plan assets not included in fair value when a computed amount is used for market-related value (the difference between beginning-of-period fair value and market-related value of plan assets) (Blocks 31 and 32).

Computation of the gain or loss subject to amortization (Blocks 32 and 33) may be made using the tabular format in Chart 7-8.

Chart 7-8 Format for Computation of Net Gain or Loss Subject to Amortization

Actual Accumulated Benefit Obligation		$ XXXXXXX
Projected Accumulated Benefit Obligation		(XXXXXXX)
(Gain)/Loss		$XXXXXXX
Actual Fair Value of Plan Assets	$(XXXXXX)	
Projected Fair Value of Plan Assets	XXXXXX	
(Gain)/Loss		XXXXXX
(Gain)/Loss Before Prior Years' (Gain)/Loss		$ XXXXXXX
Unrecognized (Gain)/Loss from Prior Periods		XXXXXXX
Unrecognized (Gain)/Loss at Beginning of Period		$ XXXXXXX
Fair Value of Plan Assets at Beginning of Period	$ XXXXXX	

Market-Related Value at Beginning of Period	(XXXXXX)	
Gain/(Loss) Not Included in Market-Related Value		XXXXX
(Gain)/Loss Subject to Amortization		$ XXXXXXX

The difference between the actual and projected accumulated postretirement benefit obligation is an actuarial gain or loss, and when the actual obligation exceeds the projected obligation, a loss is computed. When the actual obligation is less than the projected, a gain is calculated. The difference between the actual and projected fair value of plan assets is a gain or loss from investments of plan assets. When actual fair value exceeds projected fair value, a gain is reported, and when actual is less than projected, a loss is calculated. The gain or loss from the obligation is combined with the gain or loss from plan assets to compute the gain or loss at the beginning of the year. However, this gain or loss does not consider any carryovers from prior years. The end-of period balance from the prior year, if any, after deducting proper amortization for the prior year, is added/deducted from the current year gain or loss. The carryover gain or loss from the previous accounting period does not include the gain or loss not included in the market-related value of plan assets (i.e., the part of the gain or loss that is the difference between fair value of plan assets and market-related value of plan assets). The use of a computed amount for market-related value of plan assets in the computation of the gain or loss subject to amortization is another effort by the FASB to reduce volatility in the postretirement cost computation. After the gain or loss at the beginning of the accounting period has been computed, it is adjusted for the gain or loss not included in the market-related value of plan assets. The ending gain or loss is the gain or loss subject to amortization.

Increases in the gain or loss during the accounting period are debited to other comprehensive income and credited to either a postretirement liability or postretirement asset. Decreases in the gain or loss are debited to either a postretirement liability or postretirement asset and credited to other comprehensive income.

An enterprise may elect immediate recognition of the gain or loss subject to amortization (Block 34) instead of deferring and amortizing the gain or loss over future accounting periods. When an entity elects immediate recognition of gains and losses, the following procedure is required (Blocks 35–37):

1. Gains that offset losses recognized in prior accounting periods shall be included in income in the current period.

2. Losses that offset gains recognized in prior accounting periods shall be charged to income in the current period.

3. Gains that do not offset losses recognized in prior accounting periods shall be used first to offset any unamortized transitional obligation and any excess gain is included in income in the current period.

4. Losses that do not offset gains recognized in prior accounting periods shall be used first to offset any unamortized transitional asset and any excess loss is charged to income in the current period.

If an entity does not elect immediate recognition of the gain or loss subject to amortization, a test must be made to determine if amortization is required. First, the accumulated postretirement benefit obligation at the beginning of the year is compared to the beginning of the year market-related value of plan assets (Block 38). Second, the larger of the two amounts is selected. The gain or loss subject to amortization is compared to 10% of the larger of these two amounts (Blocks 39 and 41). If the gain or loss exceeds 10% of the larger amount, amortization is required. If the gain or loss is less than 10%, no amortization is required (Blocks 40 and 43). When amortization is required, only the excess of the gain or loss over 10% of the larger number is amortized. The excess gain or loss is amortized in the following manner (Paragraphs 59 and 60):

1. The excess gain or loss is amortized by dividing the excess gain or excess loss by the average service years remaining for all participants who are active.
2. If most of the participants in the postretirement plan are not active, the excess gain or excess loss should be divided by the average life expectancy remaining for those employees who are not active.
3. As an alternative to 1 or 2, above, any appropriate amortization method is acceptable as long as the following conditions are met:
   a. The amortization in 1 or 2, above, is used any time the alternative method produces annual amortization less than what would be computed in 1 or 2, above;
   b. The alternative amortization procedure is applied on a consistent basis;
   c. The alternative amortization procedure is applied in the same manner to gains and losses; and
   d. The alternative amortization procedure is disclosed in the financial statements.

An entity will not have a gain or loss subject to amortization in the year of transition to ASC 715-60 because amortization of gains and losses is based on a beginning-of-year balance. All gains and losses existing on the date of transition are automatically absorbed into the transitional asset or transitional obligation.

The amount of the gain or loss amortized to postretirement cost during the accounting period is removed from other comprehensive income using a reclassification adjustment. For example, if a gain is amortized to postretirement expense, a gain was reported as a credit to other comprehensive income in the accounting period that the gain originated. The other comprehensive income amount was closed to accumulated other comprehensive income as a credit balance. Therefore, when the gain is amortized to postretirement expense, the reclassification adjustment requires a debit to other comprehensive income that then reduces the original credit that is included in accumulated other comprehensive income. The gain or loss is included in other comprehensive income when it is created and is removed from other comprehensive income when the gain or loss is amortized to postretirement cost. The provisions of ASC 740 should be reviewed to determine whether there is a tax impact related to the gain or loss.

In addition to the gain or loss subject to amortization, an entity may have another gain or loss to include in the postretirement cost. If an enterprise elects to deviate temporarily from the substantive postretirement plan, a gain or loss will result from the deviation. Such gains and losses are taken to income in the period of the gain or loss.

The last component of postretirement cost is amortization of the transitional asset or obligation (Blocks 45–59). The transitional asset or obligation is computed on the measurement date for the first year in which the statement is applied. The asset or obligation may be computed using the following formula:

(A)/O = AAPBOT – (AFPAT + APC – PPC)

(A)/O	= Net transitional asset or obligation established at initial adoption of ASC 715-60.
AAPBOT	= Actual accumulated postretirement benefit obligation on the date of transition to ASC 715-60.
AFPAT	= Actual fair value of plan assets on the date of transition to ASC 715-60.
APC	= Balance in the postretirement liability account on the date of transition to ASC 715-60.
PPC	= Balance in the postretirement asset account on the date of transition to ASC 715-60.

When the accumulated postretirement benefit obligation exceeds the fair value of the plan assets after adjustment for any balance sheet account, a transitional obligation is created (Block 53). However, if adjusted plan assets exceed the accumulated benefit obligation, an asset is recognized (Block 51). Any remaining unamortized postretirement transitional asset or transitional obligation balance should be included in accumulated other comprehensive income.

An entity may elect to recognize immediately the transitional asset or obligation. If immediate recognition is elected, the asset or obligation is included in income in the period of transition as the cumulative effect of a change in accounting principle. The cumulative effect change is reported in the income statement before net income. If an entity does not elect immediate recognition, the asset or obligation is amortized over future accounting periods in the following manner (Block 55):

1. The transitional asset or obligation is amortized by dividing the asset or obligation by the average service years remaining for all participants who are active (a straight-line method).

2. If most of the participants in the postretirement plan are not active, the transitional asset or obligation should be divided by the average life expectancy remaining for those employees who are not active.

3. If the service period in 1, above, is less than 20 years, 20 years may be selected by the entity for the amortization period.

In addition to amortization in 1–3, above, amortization of the transitional obligation may be increased or accelerated when cumulative benefit payments since transition exceeds cumulative postretirement cost since transition (Block

57). When this situation occurs, an additional amount of the transitional obligation equal to the excess of benefit payments over postretirement cost is amortized (Block 59).

The amount of the transitional asset or transitional obligation amortized to postretirement cost during the accounting period is removed from other comprehensive income using a reclassification adjustment. For example, if the transitional item is an obligation, amortization of the transitional obligation increases postretirement expense and requires a credit to other comprehensive income for the amount of the obligation amortization to postretirement expense. The credit to other comprehensive income will be closed to accumulated other comprehensive income to reduce the original amount of the transitional obligation that was reported as a debit to accumulated other comprehensive income. Therefore, when a transitional obligation is amortized to postretirement expense, the reclassification adjustment requires a credit to other comprehensive income that then reduces the original debit that is included in accumulated other comprehensive income. If the transitional item is an asset, the accounting is reversed. Amortization of the transitional asset requires a debit to other comprehensive income as a reclassification adjustment that then reduces the original credit that is included in accumulated other comprehensive income. Therefore, transitional assets or obligations are included in accumulated other comprehensive income and are removed from other comprehensive income when the transitional items are amortized to postretirement cost. The provisions of ASC 740 should be reviewed to determine whether there is a tax impact related to the transitional asset or obligation.

This completes the explanation of each of the components that make up the annual postretirement cost. The final postretirement cost is equal to the accumulation of the components in the preceding discussion (Block 60).

As indicated in the preceding discussion of prior service cost, actuarial gains and losses, and transitional assets and obligations, any unrecognized balances in these items are included in accumulated other comprehensive income. The adjustment is made to the ending balance of accumulated other comprehensive income.

Three items used in the computation of the gain or loss subject to amortization component of postretirement cost requires further explanation. The three items are: (1) projected accumulated postretirement benefit obligation, (2) projected fair value of plan assets, and (3) market-related value of plan assets. The method of computing each of the items is presented in tabular format. Chart 7-9 shows how the projected accumulated postretirement obligation is computed.

Chart 7-9 Computation of Projected Accumulated Postretirement Benefit Obligation (APBO)

Actual beginning APBO		$0000000
Service cost for period		00000
Interest Cost:		
Actual beginning APBO	$0000000	
Assumed Discount Rate	0%	

Interest cost for period		00000
Benefit payments for period		(00000)
Prior service cost		000000
Ending Projected APBO		$00000000

The projected fair value of plan assets can be computed using the format in Chart 7-10.

Chart 7-10 Computation of Projected Fair Value of Plan Assets (FVOPA)

Actual beginning FVOPA		$00000000
Expected Return:		
Market-related value of plan assets	$0000000	
Long-term rate of return	0%	
Expected return		000000
Contributions during period		000000
Benefit payments during period		(000000)
Ending projected FVOPA		$00000000

Chart 7-11 shows the calculation of the market-related value of plan assets.

Chart 7-11 Computation of Market-Related Value of Plan Assets (MRPA)

Beginning MRPA		$00000000
Expected Return:		
Beginning MRPA	$0000000	
Long-term rate of return	0%	
Expected return		000000
Contributions during period		000000
Benefit payments during period		(000000)
Amortization of deferred asset gain or (loss) (from Chart 7-12)		0000
Ending MRPA		$00000000

Amortization of the deferred asset gain or loss used in the market-related value computation is calculated in Chart 7-12.

Chart 7-12 Computation and Amortization of Deferred Asset Gain/(Loss)

Calculation of Deferred Asset Gain/(Loss):

Actual Return:	
Ending fair value of plan assets	$00000000
Deduct: Contributions	(00000)

Calculation of Deferred Asset Gain/(Loss):

Add: Benefit payments		00000
Adjusted ending fair value		$00000000
Beginning fair value of plan assets		(00000000)
Actual return on plan assets		$0000
Expected Return:		
Beginning market-related value of plan assets	$(0000000)	
Expected long-term rate of return	00%	
Expected return on plan assets		(0000)
Deferred asset gain or (loss)		$0000

Amortization of Deferred Asset Gain/(Loss):

Deferred asset gain/(loss)	
Year	
1	$000000
2	000000
3	(000000)
4	000000
5	(000000)
Total	$000000
Amortization period (in years)	÷ 0
Amount of amortization	$000

The deferred asset gain or loss is amortized to the market-related value of plan assets over a period not to exceed five years.

Next the enterprise must determine the proper journal entry to make for the postretirement cost computed for the accounting period. If the postretirement cost computation includes amortization of items included in accumulated other comprehensive income (such as prior service cost, actuarial gains or losses, and transitional assets or obligations), a debit or credit to other comprehensive income (a reclassification adjustment) is required for the amount of the amortization included in the postretirement cost computation. Cash is credited for any contributions and postretirement cost is debited for any postretirement expense or credited if the entity reports postretirement income in the computation. Any difference between the postretirement cost and any debits to other comprehensive income and cash contributions plus any credits to other comprehensive income is an adjustment to a postretirement asset or a postretirement liability account. In addition, an entry is required to record any change (other than amounts amortized) in the amount of prior service cost or actuarial gains and losses during the accounting period. The change in prior service cost or actuarial gains and losses is included in other comprehensive income with an adjustment to either a postretirement asset or postretirement liability. For example, if prior service cost is increased from a plan amendment during the accounting period, the entity increases other comprehensive income for the increase that is not included in the current year postretirement cost and either a postretirement liability or a postretirement asset is increased or decreased for a corresponding amount.

An entity must report in its statement of financial position a postretirement asset or postretirement liability for the amount of any overfunded or underfunded postretirement plan. The funded status of all overfunded plans should be aggregated, and one postretirement asset amount is reported for all overfunded plans. The funded status of all underfunded postretirement plans should be aggregated and one postretirement liability amount is reported for all underfunded postretirement plans. The postretirement asset or liability is computed as the difference between the accumulated postretirement benefit obligation and the fair value of the plan asset on the measurement date, which is the date of the statement of financial position. A postretirement plan asset from an overfunded postretirement plan is classified as a noncurrent asset in the balance sheet; however, a postretirement plan liability is classified as either current, noncurrent, or a combination of current and noncurrent. A plan-by-plan approach is used to determine the postretirement liability classification. The present value of the benefits determined on an actuarial basis included in the postretirement plan obligation meeting the definition of a current item is classified as a current liability (payable within one year or the normal operating cycle, whichever is longer). The provisions of ASC 740 should be used to determine any tax impact.

This completes the general discussion of accounting for postretirement cost for defined benefit and defined contribution plans; however, for a complete understanding of postretirement benefit accounting, other considerations should be addressed.

First, the measurement date as defined in the introduction requires further explanation. The measurement date for purposes of computing the postretirement obligations and plan assets is the date of the statement of financial position, unless one of the following conditions is met: (1) a subsidiary is consolidated with a parent company when the subsidiary has a year-end different from the parent and the postretirement plan is sponsored by the subsidiary or (2) an investee company accounted for using the equity method of accounting has a different year-end from the investor company and the postretirement plan is sponsored by the investee company. Under these two situations, postretirement plan assets and obligations should be measured on the date used to consolidate the subsidiary's statement of financial position for the subsidiary and the date used to apply the equity method for the investee company.

When preparing interim financial statements, the entity should use the funded status of the postretirement plan at the most recent fiscal year-end statement of position date and adjust the funded status for the following: (1) contributions or benefit payments and (2) accrual of benefit cost elements (such as service cost, interest cost, and return on assets), excluding amortized items, that occurred subsequent to the statement of position date. If an entity remeasures its postretirement assets and obligations during a fiscal year for events such as plan amendments, settlements, or curtailments, it should use those remeasurement amounts in subsequent interim accounting periods.

Second, the determination of fair value of plan assets on the measurement date requires additional discussion. Fair value of plan assets used in the computation is determined on the measurement date and includes assets that have been restricted and segregated for the postretirement plan. Plan assets consist of employer and employee contributions plus earnings on invested assets less benefit payments and all expenses. Plan assets usually are invested in items such as stocks, bonds and real estate. Fair value of plan assets determined on the measurement date is defined as the amount that would be received on the measurement date from the sale of property between sellers and buyers (market participants) in an orderly transaction. In addition, the sellers and buyers are unrelated parties on the measurement date.

The next item to consider for further discussion is the attribution method used in the computation. The service cost component of postretirement cost, and the expected and accumulated postretirement benefit obligation should be measured using a single attribution method. This method assigns postretirement benefits to each year of service in the period of attribution or in accordance with the benefit formula for plans with certain types of benefit formulas. The period of attribution is the time period from the date of employment or credited period, if later, to the date that the participant reaches full eligibility. When assigning benefits to years of service, certain actuarial assumptions must be used. The FASB concluded that an explicit approach should be used with respect to actuarial assumptions. An estimate should be computed for each actuarial assumption used in the measurement process, and all assumptions are estimated assuming a going concern for the postretirement plan.

Another item to consider is insurance contracts. An entity may enter into a contract with an insurance company whereby the insurance company agrees to assume the responsibility for payment of specific benefits to participants for a fee. In this case, risk is transferred from the employer to the insurance company. In such cases, the benefits assumed by the insurance company should not be included in the accumulated postretirement benefit obligation and the insurance contract should not be included in plan assets.

The next element to consider is accounting for postretirement benefits when an entity is involved in a business combination using the provisions of ASC 805. When an entity (the acquirer) acquires a company (the acquiree) that sponsors a single-employer defined benefit postretirement plan, an asset or liability should be recorded for the difference between fair value of plan assets and the accumulated postretirement benefit obligation (funded status). If the obligation exceeds fair value of plan assets, a liability is recorded and if the assets exceed the obligation, an asset is recorded. When the funded status is determined, the impact of expected plan amendments, curtailments, or terminations should be excluded by the acquirer if the acquirer does not have an obligation to make the changes. The accumulated postretirement benefit obligation assumed by the acquirer should include any changes of assumptions that the acquiring company determines to be appropriate using all future events considered relevant by the acquirer.

Not-for-profit entities may have defined benefit postretirement plans. A not-for-profit entity must report in its statement of financial position a postretirement asset or postretirement liability for the amount of any overfunded or underfunded postretirement plan. The funded status of all overfunded plans should be aggregated and one postretirement asset amount is reported for all overfunded plans. The funded status of all underfunded postretirement plans should be aggregated and one postretirement liability amount is reported for all underfunded postretirement plans. The postretirement asset or liability is computed as the difference between the projected benefit obligation and the fair value of plan asset on the measurement date, which is the date of the statement of financial position. If the not-for-profit entity prepares a classified statement of financial position, a postretirement plan asset from an overfunded pension plan is classified as a noncurrent asset in the balance sheet; however, a postretirement plan liability is classified as either current, noncurrent, or a combination of current and noncurrent. A plan-by-plan approach is used to determine the postretirement liability classification. The present value of the benefits determined on an actuarial basis included in the postretirement plan obligation meeting the definition of a current item is classified as a current liability (payable within one year or the normal operating cycle, whichever is longer). Gains or losses and prior service cost or credits that arise during the accounting period that are not used in the computation of postretirement expense are included as a separate line item(s) within changes in unrestricted net assets. In addition, the amount of the gain or loss, prior service cost or credits, and transitional assets or obligations amortized to postretirement cost during the accounting period is removed from the unrestricted net assets using a reclassification adjustment. The provisions of ASC 740 should be used to determine any tax impact. The measurement date for a defined benefit postretirement plan for a not-for-profit entity is the same as for a profit entity and the interim reporting information is the same as for a business entity.

Postretirement Plans—Technical Considerations

Six examples are used to illustrate the technical considerations related to postretirement benefits. Assumptions for Example 7-14 are as follows.

Example 7-14
Assumptions for Defined Benefit Postretirement Plan

1. Peterson Enterprises (Peterson), a public company with a December 31 year-end, has a defined benefit postretirement plan that covers substantially all employees. Peterson elects to adopt all provisions of ASC 715-60 on January 1, 20X6.

2. On the date of initial adoption, January 1, 20X6, Peterson received the following information from its actuary.

(a) Accumulated postretirement benefit obligation	$1,470,000
(b) Fair value of plan assets	1,230,000
(c) Market-related value of plan assets	1,230,000

(d) Pension liability	60,000
(e) Average remaining service life of participants at date of transition (majority of participants are active)	25 years

3. On December 31, 20X6, 20X7, and 20X8 (the balance sheet date and the measurement date) the following information was provided by Peterson's actuary.

	20X6	20X7	20X8
(a) Service cost	$150,000	$174,000	$180,000
(b) Actual accumulated postretirement benefit obligation	1,980,000	2,340,000	2,550,000
(c) Projected accumulated postretirement benefit obligation	1,914,300	2,074,200	2,490,600
(d) Actual fair value of plan assets	1,380,000	1,605,000	1,770,000
(e) Projected fair value of plan assets	1,455,000	1,475,625	1,719,547
(f) Market-related value of plan assets	1,436,250	1,545,469	1,686,223
(g) Prior service cost from plan amendment	240,000		
(h) Payments to trust	180,000	210,000	200,000
(i) Benefit payments	78,000	258,000	240,000
(j) Assumed discount rate	9%	9%	9%
(k) Expected long-term rate of return on plan assets	10%	10%	10%

4. The postretirement plan amendment on December 31, 20X6 increased the accumulated postretirement benefit obligation. The prior service cost is amortized over the average remaining service life to full eligibility of 20 years, and the future service period for all other amortization is also 20 years.
5. Deferred asset gains and losses are amortized to the market-related value of plan assets using a four-year time period.
6. Peterson elects to amortize any transitional asset or obligation rather than using immediate recognition.
7. This example assumes that any transitional asset or obligation is included in accumulated other comprehensive income.

The first step in analyzing the assumptions in Example 7-14 is to compute the postretirement cost for each of the three years. Computation of postretirement cost requires seven different complex calculations, and the analysis will take several pages. The reader is encouraged to frequently refer to the assumptions in Example 7-14 to follow the analysis. Each element for each of the three years is computed separately and then all elements are summarized to compute postretirement cost.

The first element is service cost. The service cost component requires no computation because it is assumed to be provided by the actuary. Table 7-31, shows the service cost for 20X6, 20X7, and 20X8.

Table 7-31 Service Cost Component of Postretirement Cost[1]

Year	Service Cost
20X6	$150,000
20X7	174,000
20X8	180,000

[1] Information given in Example 7-14, Item 3.

The second element of the postretirement provision is the interest cost component. The interest cost for 20X6, 20X7, and 20X8 is computed in Table 7-32.

Table 7-32 Computation of Interest Cost for Postretirement Cost

	20X6	20X7	20X8
Accumulated Postretirement Benefit Obligation at Beginning of Year[1]	$1,470,000	$1,980,000	$2,340,000
Assumed Discount Rate[1]	9%	9%	9%
Interest Cost Component	$132,300	$178,200	$210,600

[1] Information taken from Example 7-14, Items 2, 3(b), and (j).

The interest cost calculation is made for December 31, but the accumulated postretirement benefit obligation used in the calculation is a January 1 balance (beginning-of-period balance).

The next element of postretirement cost is amortization of unrecognized prior service cost. The $240,000 prior service cost resulting from an amendment on December 31, 20X6 is amortized over the 20-year average remaining service life to full eligibility of the active employee group on the date of amendment. The $240,000 prior service cost is put in other comprehensive income (closed to accumulated other comprehensive income) in the period of the amendment and is removed as it is amortized to postretirement cost. There is no amortization in 20X6 because the plan was not amended until year-end. Table 7-33 shows prior service cost amortization over the three-year period.

Table 7-33 Calculation of Amortization of Prior Service Cost[1]

(a) Prior Service Cost	(b) Service Life	(c) = (a)/(b) Amortization 20X6	20X7	20X8
$240,000	20 Years	$0	$12,000	$12,000

[1] Information taken from Example 7-14, Items 3(g) and 4.

Because the prior service cost increased the accumulated benefit obligation, the $12,000 annual amortization is added when computing the postretirement cost.

The fourth element of postretirement cost is the actual return on postretirement plan assets. Table 7-34 shows the calculation of the return on plan assets for the three years under consideration.

Table 7-34 Calculation of Return on Plan Assets[1]

	20X6	20X7	20X8
Fair Value of Plan Assets at End of Year	$1,380,000	$1,605,000	$1,770,000
Plus: Benefit Payments	78,000	258,000	240,000
Deduct: Contributions	(180,000)	(210,000)	(200,000)
Adjusted Fair Value of Plan Assets at End of Year	$1,278,000	$1,653,000	$1,810,000
Fair Value of Plan Assets at Beginning of Year	(1,230,000)	(1,380,000)	(1,605,000)
Actual Return on Assets	$48,000	$273,000	$205,000

[1] Information taken from Example 7-14, Items 2, 3(d), (h), and (i).

Because fair values of plan assets have increased in each of the three years, the actual return is positive (a gain) and is deducted in the computation of postretirement cost. For any year that fair value decreases, actual return on assets is negative (a loss) and is added as a component of postretirement cost.

The fifth component of postretirement cost is the deferred asset gain or loss. The reader may wish to review the formula for computation of the deferred asset gain or loss in the general discussion before reviewing this calculation. The deferred asset gain or loss is computed in Table 7-35 using a tabular format.

Table 7-35 Computation of Deferred Asset Gain or Loss[1]

	20X6	20X7	20X8
Actual Return on Plan Assets (Table 7-34)	$48,000	$273,000	$205,000
Expected Return:			
Market-Related Value of Plan Assets	$1,230,000	$1,436,250	$1,545,469
Expected Long-Term Rate of Return	10%	10%	10%
Expected Return	(123,000)	(143,625)	(154,547)
Deferred Asset Gain/(Loss)	$(75,000)	$129,375	$50,453

[1] Information taken from Example 7-14, Items 2(c), 3(f), and (k).

The $75,000 deferred loss in 20X6 is deducted in the postretirement cost calculation and the deferred gains in 20X7 and 20X8 are added in the computation. Gains and losses related to the market-related value concept are handled in reverse to normal gains and losses, because the purpose of the market-related value concept is to reduce volatility of the postretirement cost. The deferred asset gain or loss when combined with the actual return in the postretirement expense computation causes the actual return to equal the expected return on plan assets.

The next component of postretirement cost is amortization of the net gain or loss. The net gain or loss calculation is a very complex computation and will require frequent reference back to the Example 7-14 assumptions and may require reference back to the formula and tabular format in the general discussion. The net gain or loss is composed of four parts: (1) the difference between the projected and actual beginning-of-period accumulated postretirement benefit obligation, (2) the difference between the projected and actual beginning-of-period fair value of plan assets, (3) the unamortized gain or loss (included in accumulated other comprehensive income) carried forward to the current year from prior years, and (4) the difference between the beginning-of-period fair value and market-related value of plan assets. The gain or loss is computed for 20X7 and 20X8 in Table 7-36 using the tabular format developed in the general discussion and is divided into the four components listed, above. No gain or loss is computed for 20X6, the year of transition. By definition, there is no gain or loss on the date of initial adoption of ASC 715-60, because any gain or loss at date of transition is included in the transitional asset or obligation. Because the date of transition is January 1, 20X6 and the gain or loss is computed as of the beginning of the accounting period, there is no gain or loss for 20X6.

Table 7-36 Calculation of Net Gain or Loss Subject to Amortization[1]

		20X7		20X8
Actual APBO[2]	$1,980,000		$2,340,000	
Projected APBO	(1,914,300)		(2,074,200)	
(Gain)/Loss		$65,700		$265,800
Actual Fair Value of Plan Assets	$(1,380,000)		$(1,605,000)	
Projected Fair Value of Plan Assets	1,455,000		1,475,625	
(Gain)/Loss		75,000		(129,375)
(Gain)/Loss Before Prior Years' (Gain)/Loss		$140,700		$136,425
(Gain)/Loss from Prior Years		0		140,700[3]
(Gain)/Loss at Beginning of Period		$140,700		$277,125
Fair Value of Plan Assets	$1,380,000		$1,605,000	
Market-Related Value of Plan Assets	(1,436,250)		(1,545,469)	
Gain/(Loss) Not Included in Market-Related Value		(56,250)		59,531
(Gain)/Loss Subject to Amortization		$84,450		$336,656

		20X7		20X8
Greater of Actual APBO or Market-Related Value of Plan Assets	$(1,980,000)		$(2,340,000)	
Percentage	× 10%		× 10%	
Total		(198,000)		(234,000)
Excess Loss Subject to Amortization		$0		$102,656
Average Remaining Service Life (Years)[4]		÷ 20		÷ 20
Amortization of Net Loss		$0		$5,133

[1] All information used taken from Example 7-14, Item 3, and is based on beginning-of-period numbers.
[2] APBO = Accumulated Postretirement Benefit Obligation.
[3] Loss at beginning of 20X7 of $140,700 • $0 amortization (Table 7-37) for 20X7 = $140,700.
[4] Average remaining service life taken from Example 7-14, Item 4.

The losses computed in Table 7-36 for 20X7 and 20X8 are subject to amortization. However, unless the loss for each year exceeds 10% of the greater of the beginning of year actual accumulated postretirement benefit obligation or market-related value of plan assets, no amortization is required. Table 7-36 also shows the computation of any excess loss and the proper amortization. The loss carried over to 20X8 is $140,700 and not $84,450. The part of the gain or loss related to the market-related value of plan assets is not carried forward but is recomputed each year. The loss from 20X8 that is carried forward to 20X9 is $271,992 ($277,125 – $5,133). As illustrated in Table 7-36, there is no amortization of the net loss for 20X7 because the $84,450 loss does not exceed 10% of the accumulated postretirement benefit obligation. However, $5,133 of the $336,656 net loss for 20X8 is amortized over the service period of 20 years because the net loss exceeds 10% of the accumulated postretirement benefit obligation by $102,656.

The last component of postretirement cost is amortization of the transitional obligation or asset created at inception of ASC 715-60. The postretirement asset or obligation can be calculated using the information from Example 7-14, Item 2, and a tabular format developed from the formula in the general discussion. The reader is encouraged to review the formula and general discussion before proceeding. The transitional asset or obligation is computed in Table 7-37.

Table 7-37 Computation of Postretirement Transitional Asset/Obligation[1]

Accumulated Postretirement Benefit Obligation at Transition		$1,470,000
Fair Value of Plan Assets at Transition	$1,230,000	
Postretirement Asset	0	
Postretirement Liability	60,000	

Adjusted Fair Value of Plan Assets	1,290,000
Transitional (Asset)/Liability	$180,000

[1] Information taken from Example 7-14, Item 2.

Because the accumulated postretirement benefit obligation of $1,470,000 exceeds fair value of plan assets after adjustment for the postretirement liability, the $180,000 excess is a transitional obligation. The obligation is amortized over the average remaining service life of the employee group of 25 years (Example 7-14, Item 2). Amortization of the transitional obligation for 20X6, 20X7, and 20X8 is computed in Table 7-38.

Table 7-38 Calculation of Amortization of Transitional Postretirement Obligation

(a) Transitional Obligation[1]	(b) Service Life[2]		(c) = (a)/(b) Amortization	
		20X6	20X7	20X8
$180,000	25 Years	$7,200	$7,200	$7,200

[1] Transitional postretirement obligation taken from Table 7-37.
[2] Service life taken from Example 7-14, Item 2.

Peterson will amortize $7,200 a year for 25 years. Peterson does not have the alternative option of amortization over 20 years, because the average remaining service period exceeds 20 years. In addition, according to Example 7-14 (Item 6), Peterson elected not to immediately recognize the transitional obligation.

Next, it must be determined if an additional amount of the transitional obligation should be amortized. An additional amount of the obligation should be amortized when cumulative benefit payments exceeds cumulative postretirement cost since transition. Cumulative benefit payments are adjusted for any plan assets or postretirement liability existing at the date of transition. Plan assets on the date of transition of $1,290,000 ($1,230,000 + $60,000) after adjustment for the postretirement liability on date of transition exceed benefit payments for all three years of $576,000 ($78,000 + $258,000 + $240,000). Therefore, at the end of any accounting period, the adjusted plan assets are in excess of the benefit payments. There can be no additional amortization of the transitional obligation, because the benefit payments after adjustment for plan assets cannot exceed the postretirement cost.

Using the information from Tables 7-31 through 7-36 and 7-38, postretirement cost for 20X6, 20X7, and 20X8 is summarized in Table 7-39.

Table 7-39 Computation of Postretirement Cost

Postretirement Cost Component	20X6	20X7	20X8
1. Service Cost (Table 7-31)	$150,000	$174,000	$180,000
2. Interest Cost (Table 7-32)	132,300	178,200	210,600
3. Amortization of Prior Service Cost (Table 7-33)	0	12,000	12,000
4. Actual Return on Postretirement Plan Assets (Table 7-34)	(48,000)	(273,000)	(205,000)
5. Deferred Asset Gain/(Loss) (Table 7-35)	(75,000)	129,375	50,453
6. Gain or Loss (Table 7-36)	0	0	5,133
7. Amortization of Transitional Obligation Created at Adoption of ASC 715-60 (Table 7-38)	7,200	7,200	7,200
8. Additional Amortization of Transitional Obligation	0	0	0
Total Postretirement Cost	$166,500	$227,775	$260,386

Using the information from Tables 7-36 and 7-39, funding information from Example 7-14, Item 3, and prior service cost information from Example 7-14, Item 4, and journal entries for 20X6, 20X7, and 20X8 can be prepared. The journal entries for the postretirement expense are as follows:

20X6

	Debit	Credit
Postretirement Expense	166,500	
Postretirement Liability	20,700	
Other Comprehensive Income— Transitional Obligation		7,200
Cash		180,000

20X7

	Debit	Credit
Postretirement Expense	227,775	
Postretirement Liability	1,425	
Other Comprehensive Income— Prior Service Cost Amortization		12,000
Other Comprehensive Income— Transitional Obligation		7,200
Cash		210,000

20X8

	Debit	Credit
Postretirement Expense	260,386	
Postretirement Liability	36,053	
Other Comprehensive Income— Prior Service Cost Amortization		12,000
Other Comprehensive Income— Gain/Loss Amortization		5,133
Other Comprehensive Income— Transitional Obligation		7,200
Cash		200,000

Amortization of the loss, prior service cost, and the transitional obligation require a reclassification adjustment to remove them from accumulated other comprehensive income. The postretirement liability is adjusted to balance the entry for the difference between postretirement cost, cash contributions, and the reclassification adjustments.

Table 7-36 computes the amount of the actuarial loss that is used in the 20X7 and 20X8 pension expense computation as $140,700 and $136,425, respectively. The amounts represent beginning-of-year numbers, which means that the computations used end-of-year amounts from the prior years. Therefore, the 20X7 amount of $140,700 is based on December 31, 20X6 information, and the 20X8 amount of $136,425 is based on December 31, 20X7 information. When actually recording the actuarial losses in the financial statements, the $140,700 loss is reported as of December 31, 20X6 and the $136,425 loss is reported as of December 31, 20X7. The December 31, 20X8 gain or loss, which is used in the 20X9 pension expense computation is not computed, but the computations and entries are similar to the 20X6 and 20X7 computations. Addition to the actuarial losses reported, there is an increase in prior service cost of $240,000 resulting from a plan amendment that occurred on December 31, 20X6 (Example 7-14, Item 4). The increase in the loss for both years and the increase in prior service cost must be reported in other comprehensive income in the accounting period in which the items occur. The amount of the loss and prior service cost included in other comprehensive income is closed to accumulated other comprehensive income. The loss and prior service cost are then removed from accumulated other comprehensive income as a reclassification adjustment when they are amortized to postretirement expense. The required entries are as follows:

20X6

Other Comprehensive Income-Actuarial Loss	140,700	
Postretirement Liability		140,700
Other Comprehensive Income-Prior Service Cost	240,000	
Postretirement Liability		240,000

20X7

Other Comprehensive Income—Actuarial Loss	136,425	
Postretirement Liability		136,425

A postretirement asset would have been adjusted for the change in the actuarial loss or prior service cost if the plan had been an overfunded postretirement plan.

This completes the actual analysis of Example 7-14, but it may be helpful for the reader to see how three items of information used in the computation and assumed to be provided by the actuary are computed. These items are projected accumulated postretirement benefit obligation, market-related value of plan assets, and projected fair value of plan assets. This information may be computed by the enterprise or may be provided by the actuary. Table 7-40 shows the computation of the projected accumulated postretirement benefit obligation.

Table 7-40 Computation of Projected Accumulated Postretirement Benefit Obligation[1]

	20X6	20X7	20X8
Actual APBO[2] at Beginning of Period	$1,470,000	$1,980,000	$2,340,000
Service Cost (Table 7-31)	150,000	174,000	180,000
Interest Cost (Table 7-32)	132,300	178,200	210,600
Benefits Paid	(78,000)	(258,000)	(240,000)
Prior Service Cost	240,000	0	0
Projected APBO at December 31	$1,914,300	$2,074,200	$2,490,600

[1] Information taken from Example 7-14, Items 2 and 3, unless otherwise indicated.
[2] APBO—Accumulated Postretirement Benefit Obligation.

Table 7-41 shows the calculation of the market-related value of plan assets.

Table 7-41 Computation of Market-Related Value of Plan Assets[1]

	20X6	20X7	20X8
MRVPA[2] at Beginning of Period	$1,230,000	$1,436,250	$1,545,469
Expected Return:			
MRVPA at Beginning of Period	$1,230,000	$1,436,250	$1,545,469
Expected Long-Term Rate of Return	10%	10%	10%
Expected Return on Plan Assets	123,000	143,625	154,547
Contributions to Trust	180,000	210,000	200,000
Benefits Paid	(78,000)	(258,000)	(240,000)
Amortization of Deferred Asset Gain/(Loss)[3]	(18,750)	13,594	26,207
MRVPA at End of Period	$1,436,250	$1,545,469	$1,686,223

[1] Information taken from Example 7-14, Items 2 and 3, unless otherwise indicated.
[2] MRVPA = Market-related value of plan assets.
[3] Information taken from Table 7-42.

Amortization of the deferred asset gain or loss is the cumulative unamortized deferred gain or loss used in the computation of the postretirement cost. It is amortized to the market-related value of plan assets over a period of time not to exceed five years. In Example 7-14, four years was elected. Table 7-42 shows the computation.

Table 7-42 Computation of Amortization of Deferred Asset Gain/(Loss)

Deferred Asset Gain/(Loss)[1]	**20X6**	**20X7**	**20X8**
20X6 Loss	$(75,000)	$(75,000)	$(75,000)
20X7 Gain		129,375	129,375

Deferred Asset Gain/(Loss)[1]	20X6	20X7	20X8
20X8 Gain			50,453
Net Deferred Gain/(Loss)	$(75,000)	$54,375	$104,828
Amortization Period[2]	÷ 4	÷ 4	÷ 4
Amortization of Gain/(Loss)	$(18,750)	$13,594	$26,207

[1] Deferred asset gain or loss taken from Table 7-35.
[2] Amortization period is 4 years and is taken from Example 7-14, Item 5.

The last item is the projected fair value of plan assets, and the calculation for this item is shown in Table 7-43.

Table 7-43 Computation of Projected Fair Value of Plan Assets[1]

	20X6	20X7	20X8
FMVPA[2] at Beginning of Period	$1,230,000	$1,380,000	$1,605,000
Expected Return:			
MRVPA at Beginning of Period	$1,230,000	$1,436,250	$1,545,469
Expected Long-Term Rate of Return	10%	10%	10%
Expected Return on Plan Assets	123,000	143,625	154,547
Contributions to Trust	180,000	210,000	200,000
Benefits Paid	(78,000)	(258,000)	(240,000)
FMVPA at End of Period	$1,455,000	$1,475,625	$1,719,547

[1] Information taken from Example 7-14, Items 2 and 3, unless otherwise indicated.
[2] FMVPA = Fair market value of plan assets.

This completes the analysis of Example 7-14, which was a postretirement benefit plan with plan assets. Example 7-15 is a postretirement benefit plan that considers items such as no plan assets and additional amortization of the transitional obligation. Assumptions for Example 7-15 are as follows.

Example 7-15
Assumptions for Defined Benefit Postretirement Plan

1. The Thompson Company (Thompson), a public company with a December 31 year-end, has a defined benefit postretirement plan that covers substantially all salaried and non-salaried employees. Thompson elects to adopt all provisions of ASC 715-60 on January 1, 20X6. Prior to the adoption of ASC 715-60, Thompson had used a pay-as-you-go basis. There are no plan assets or postretirement balance sheet asset or liability at date of transition.
2. On the date of initial adoption, January 1, 20X6, Thompson had a $3,000,000 accumulated postretirement benefit obligation. The remaining service period for the plan participants at date of transition is 15 years.

3. On December 31, 20X6 and 20X7 (the balance sheet date and the measurement date), the following information was provided by Thompson's actuary.

	20X6	20X7
(a) Service cost	$200,000	$250,000
(b) Actual accumulated postretirement benefit obligation	3,100,000	3,200,000
(c) Projected accumulated postretirement benefit obligation	2,890,000	2,898,000
(d) Payments to trust	550,000	700,000
(e) Benefit payments	550,000	700,000
(f) Assumed discount rate	8%	8%

4. Thompson elects to amortize any transitional obligation over the alternative 20-year time period. The future service period for all other amortization is 18 years.

5. This example assumes that any transitional asset or obligation is included in accumulated other comprehensive income.

The first step in analyzing the assumptions in Example 7-15 is to compute the postretirement cost for 20X6 and 20X7. There are no plan assets for 20X6 and 20X7, because Thompson has no plan assets at transition and the payments to the trust for 20X6 and 20X7 are the same as the benefit payments for the same time period. Assume that all contributions by Thompson and all benefit payments are made at the same time. Because there are no assets, no actual return or deferred asset gain or loss component is calculated for the postretirement cost.

The first element, service cost, is provided by the actuary and is $200,000 for 20X6 and $250,000 for 20X7. Interest cost, the second element, is computed in Table 7-44.

Table 7-44 Calculation of Interest Cost Component[1]

	20X6	20X7
Accumulated Postretirement Benefit Obligation at Beginning of Year	$3,000,000	$3,100,000
Assumed Discount Rate	8%	8%
Interest Cost Component	$240,000	$248,000

[1] Information taken from Example 7-15, Items 2 and 3.

The net gain or loss subject to amortization is computed next. There is no gain or loss computed for 20X6, because it is the year of transition. Because there are no plan assets, the gain or loss is the difference between the actual and projected accumulated benefit obligation. The gain or loss is computed in Table 7-45.

Table 7-45 Calculation of Net Gain or Loss Subject to Amortization for 20X7[1]

Actual APBO[2]		$3,100,000
Projected ABPO		(2,890,000)
(Gain)/Loss Before Prior Years' (Gain)/Loss		$210,000
(Gain)/Loss from Prior Years		0
(Gain)/Loss Subject to Amortization		$210,000
Greater of Actual APBO or Market-Related Value of Plan Assets	$3,100,000	
Percentage	10%	
Total		310,000
Excess Loss Subject to Amortization		$0

[1] All information taken from Example 7-15, Item 3, and is based on beginning-of-period numbers.
[2] APBO = Accumulated Postretirement Benefit Obligation.

As illustrated in Table 7-45, there is no amortization of the net loss for 20X7 because the $210,000 loss does not exceed 10% of the accumulated postretirement benefit obligation.

The last component of postretirement cost is amortization of the transitional obligation or asset created at adoption of ASC 715-60. The postretirement asset or obligation can be calculated using the information from Example 7-15, Item 2, and a tabular format developed from the formula in the general discussion. Table 7-46 shows the computation and amortization of the transitional obligation.

Table 7-46 Computation and Amortization of Postretirement Transitional Obligation[1]

Accumulated Postretirement Benefit Obligation at Transition		$3,000,000
Fair Value of Plan Assets at Transition	$0	
Postretirement Asset	0	
Postretirement Liability	0	
Adjusted Fair Value of Plan Assets		0
Transitional Obligation		$3,000,000
Amortization Period (Years)		÷ 20
Annual Amortization		$150,000

[1] Information taken from Example 7-15, Item 2 and 4.

Because there are no plan assets or postretirement balance sheet asset or liability, the transitional obligation is equal to the accumulated postretirement benefit obligation at the beginning of 20X6. The obligation is amortized at a rate of $150,000 over the optional 20-year time period. Thompson can elect 20 years because the remaining service period for the plan participants at date of transition (15 years) is less than 20.

Using the information from Tables 7-44 through 7-46, the postretirement cost for 20X6 and 20X7 can be computed as per Table 7-47.

Table 7-47 Computation of Postretirement Cost

Postretirement Cost Component	20X6	20X7
1. Service Cost (Example 7-15, Item 3)	$200,000	$250,000
2. Interest Cost (Table 7-44)	240,000	248,000
3. Gain or Loss (Table 7-45)	0	0
4. Amortization of Net Obligation Created at Adoption of ASC 715-60 (Table 7-46)	150,000	150,000
Postretirement Cost Before Additional Amortization	$590,000	$648,000
5. Additional Amortization of Net Obligation (Table 7-48)	0	12,000
Total Postretirement Cost	$590,000	$660,000

As noted in Table 7-47, it must be determined if an additional amount of the transitional obligation should be amortized. An additional amount of the obligation is amortized when cumulative benefit payments exceeds cumulative postretirement cost since transition. Cumulative benefit payments are adjusted for any plan assets or postretirement liability existing at the date of transition. There are no plan assets or postretirement liability on date of transition and, therefore no adjustments need to be made. Any additional amortization of the transitional obligation is computed in Table 7-48.

Table 7-48 Calculation of Additional Amortization of Transitional Obligation[1]

		20X6		20X7
Benefit Payments—20X6	$550,000		$550,000	
Benefit Payments—20X7	—		700,000	
Cumulative Benefit Payments		$550,000		$1,250,000
Postretirement Cost—20X6	$(590,000)		$(590,000)	
Postretirement Cost—20X7	—		(648,000)	
Cumulative Postretirement Cost		(590,000)		(1,238,000)

	20X6	20X7
Excess of Benefit Payment Over Postretirement Cost	$0	$12,000

[1] Information taken from Example 7-15, Item 3(d) and (e), and Table 7-49.

Using the information from Tables 7-47 and 7-48, and the funding information from Example 7-15, Item 3, journal entries for 20X6 and 20X7 can be prepared. The journal entries for the postretirement expense are as follows:

20X6		
Postretirement Expense	590,000	
Postretirement Liability	110,000	
Other Comprehensive Income—Transitional Obligation		150,000
Cash		550,000
20X7		
Postretirement Expense	660,000	
Postretirement Liability	202,000	
Other Comprehensive Income—Transitional Obligation		162,000
Cash		700,000

The $162,000 transitional obligation is the $150,000 amortization of the transitional obligation and the $12,000 additional transitional obligation amortization computed in Table 7-48. Amortization of the transitional obligation requires a reclassification adjustment to remove the amounts amortized from accumulated other comprehensive income. This completes the analysis of Example 7-15. Example 7-16 covers a variety of situations involving the initial adoption of ASC 715-60 and additional amortization of transitional obligations. Assumptions for Example 7-16 are as follows:

Example 7-16
Assumptions for Initial Adoption of ASC 715-60

1. Listed below are several different situations related to the initial adoption of ASC 715-60. Assume that each situation is independent and the transition to ASC 715-60 was made on January 1, 20X6.

	Situation				
	1	2	3	4	5
Accumulated Postretirement Benefit Obligation	$3,150,000	$4,100,000	$3,500,000	$1,600,000	$4,000,000
Fair Value of Plan Assets	2,200,000	3,850,000	4,000,000	860,000	0
Postretirement Liability	0	450,000	25,000	0	0

	Situation				
	1	2	3	4	5
Postretirement Asset	320,000	0	0	200,000	0
Remaining Service Life	15 Years	18 Years	15 Years	25 Years	12 Years

2. Situations 4 and 5 reported the following postretirement costs and benefit payments:

	Situation 4	Situation 5
Postretirement Cost—20X6	$200,000	$285,000
Postretirement Cost—20X7	225,000	290,000
Benefit Payments—20X6	205,000	275,000
Benefit Payments—20X7	275,000	325,000

3. Immediate recognition of the transitional asset or obligation is elected for Situations 1 and 2, and delayed recognition (amortization) is elected for Situations 3–5.

4. A 15-year time period is elected for any transitional amount in Situation 3 and the longer 20-year period is elected for Situation 5.

The first issue to be addressed in the Example 7-16 material is what is the transitional obligation or asset, if any, on the date of initial adoption of ASC 715-60 for each of the five independent situations? The transitional obligation or asset is computed for each situation in Table 7-49.

Table 7-49 Computation of Transitional Obligation or Asset[1]

	Situation				
	1	2	3	4	5
Fair Value of Plan Assets	$2,200,000	$3,850,000	$4,000,000	$860,000	$0
Postretirement Liability	0	450,000	25,000	0	0
Postretirement Asset	(320,000)	0	0	(200,000)	0
Adjusted Fair Value	$1,880,000	$4,300,000	$4,025,000	$660,000	$0
Accumulated Postretirement Benefit Obligation	(3,150,000)	(4,100,000)	(3,500,000)	(1,600,000)	(4,000,000)
Transitional (Obligation)/Asset	$(1,270,000)	$200,000	$525,000	$(940,000)	$(4,000,000)

[1] All information taken from Example 7-16 assumptions.

In the computations, the postretirement liability existing on the date of transition increases the fair value of plan assets for purposes of computing the transitional obligation or asset and the postretirement asset decreases the fair value of the plan assets.

Based on the assumptions, immediate recognition was elected for the transitional obligation in Situation 1 and the transitional asset in Situation 2.

As a result of the write-off of the transitional obligation in Situation 1, the postretirement asset existing at date of transition is reduced to zero and a postretirement liability account is created for $950,000. In Situation 2 the postretirement liability at date of transition is reduced by $200,000 leaving a $250,000 balance ($450,000 – $200,000). The transitional asset in Situation 3 is amortized over 15 years at a rate of $35,000 ($525,000/15) per year. The $35,000 amortization is deducted when computing postretirement cost. The transitional obligations in Situations 4 and 5 are amortized at a rate of $37,600 ($940,000/25 years) and $200,000 ($4,000,000/20 years) per year, respectively. In Situation 5, the longer alternative 20-year amortization period was elected. Because the transitional amounts are obligations and the delayed method (amortization) is elected, additional amortization is required when cumulative benefit payments exceed cumulative postretirement cost. Table 7-50 shows the computation of any excess benefit payments for the amount of additional amortization, if any.

Table 7-50 Calculation of Excess Benefit Payments for Additional Obligation Amortization[1]

	20X6	
	Situation 4	**Situation 5**
Benefit Payments—20X6	$205,000	$275,000
Adjustment for Plan Assets and/or Obligation at Transition[2]	(660,000)	(0)
Cumulative Adjusted Benefit Payments	$0	$275,000
Postretirement Cost—20X6	(200,000)	(285,000)
Excess Benefit Payments	$0	$0

	20X7			
	Situation 4		**Situation 5**	
Benefit Payments—20X6	$205,000		$275,000	
Benefit Payments—20X7	275,000	$480,000	325,000	$600,000
Adjustment for Plan Assets and/ or Obligation at Transition		(660,000)		(0)
Cumulative Adjusted Benefit Payments		$0		$600,000
Postretirement Cost—20X6	$(200,000)		$(285,000)	
Postretirement Cost—20X7	(225,000)	(425,000)	(290,000)	(575,000)
Excess Benefit Payments		$0		$25,000

[1] Information taken from Example 7-16, Item 2, unless otherwise indicated.
[2] Adjusted fair value of plan assets taken from Table 7-49.

Based on the computations in Table 7-50, there is no additional amortization of the transitional obligation in Situation 4 for 20X6 or 20X7. In 20X7 the transitional obligation in Situation 5 should be amortized for an additional $25,000. Therefore, total amortization for 20X7 for Situation 5 is $225,000 ($200,000 over 20 years + $25,000 additional amortization). The cumulative benefit payments in Situation 4 are reduced for the adjusted fair value of plan assets at date of transition to ASC 715-60. The adjusted fair value of plan assets is plan assets plus any balance sheet postretirement liability or minus any balance sheet postretirement asset at transition date.

Example 7-17 illustrates amortization of prior service cost. All previous examples involving prior service cost used the alternative accelerated straight-line method over the average remaining service life to full eligibility of active participants on the date of amendment. The minimum requirement for prior service cost amortization is more complex than the straight-line method and requires an allocation from the amendment date to the date of full eligibility of an equal amount of the prior service cost to each year of remaining service for each active employee (Paragraph 52). Example 7-17 provides assumptions that illustrate the application of the minimum amortization for prior service cost.

Example 7-17
Assumptions for Minimum Prior Service Cost Amortization

1. Bismack Enterprises (Bismack) amended its postretirement benefit plan on December 31, 20X6, and the accumulated postretirement benefit obligation was increased by $500,000.
2. Bismack provides health care benefits to employees who provide 15 years of service after age 40. On the date of amendment, Bismack had 200 active employees. Of the 200 employees, 50 are not considered in the prior service cost amortization because of the following: 20 employees are under age 40, 20 are expected to terminate before reaching full eligibility, and 10 have reached full eligibility.
3. The following information is provided about years of service to full eligibility for the 150 employees eligible for prior service cost amortization.

Number of Employees	Years to Full Eligibility
10	1
5	2
11	3
4	4
8	5
6	6
4	7
2	8
15	9
20	10

Number of Employees	Years to Full Eligibility
10	11
7	12
28	13
15	14
5	15

Based on the assumptions in Example 7-17, there are 150 active employees who can be used in the computation. Item 3 also lists the number of years of service to full eligibility for each active employee. Adding employees after the amendment date does not have an impact on the amortization process, because the amortization process for each amendment is based on the active employee group's remaining service life to full eligibility on the date of amendment. Before amortization of prior service cost is computed, the following information is required: information for computing amortization ratios is calculated, amortization ratios are computed, and amortization ratios are applied to prior service cost to determine prior service cost amortization. This information is calculated in Tables 7-51 through 7-53.

Table 7-51 illustrates computation of the information for amortization ratios for the remaining years of service to full eligibility for the employee group on January 1, 20X7.

Table 7-51 Computation of Information for Annual Amortization Ratios for Prior Service Cost Amortization

Active Employees	Year															Total Service Years
	20X7	20X8	20X9	2010	2011	2012	2013	2014	2015	2016	2017	2018	2019	2020	2021	
1–10	10															10
11–15	5														5	10
16–26	11	11													11	33
27–30	4	4	4												4	16
31–38	8	8	8	8											8	40
39–44	6	6	6	6	6										6	36
45–48	4	4	4	4	4	4									4	28
49–50	2	2	2	2	2	2	2								2	16
51–65	15	15	15	15	15	15	15	15							15	135
66–85	20	20	20	20	20	20	20	20	20						20	200
86–95	10	10	10	10	10	10	10	10	10	10					10	110
96–102	7	7	7	7	7	7	7	7	7	7	7				7	84
103–130	28	28	28	28	28	28	28	28	28	28	28	28			28	364
131–145	15	15	15	15	15	15	15	15	15	15	15	15	15		15	210
146–150	5	5	5	5	5	5	5	5	5	5	5	5	5	5	5	75
Service Years	150	140	135	124	120	112	106	102	100	85	65	55	48	20	5	1,367

Several items in Table 7-51 require further explanation. Because employees reach full eligibility at different times within the next 15 years, the employees are divided into groups that reach full eligibility at the same time, and their service years are scheduled to future years until full eligibility is achieved. For example, employees 1–10 reach full eligibility in one year, and employees 11–15 reach full eligibility in two years; therefore, 10 service years are scheduled to 20X7 for employees 1–10 and five service years are scheduled to both 20X7 and 20X8 for employees 11–15. This process is continued until all active employees' service years are scheduled to all future years. One hundred and fifty service years are available for 20X7 computations because all 150 employees have not reached full eligibility until the end of 20X7. However, the number of service years declines to 140 for 20X8 because 10 employees were removed from the computations at the end of 20X7, because they reached full eligibility at the end of 20X7. The number of service years will decline each year as full eligibility is achieved for each employee until the end of 2021 when all participants active on the amendment date reach full eligibility. The last column, total service years, is a cross-footing of the service lives to full eligibility for all 15 years and represents the total service life for all employees for the 15 years of amortization.

Using the information in Table 7-51, annual amortization ratios are computed for each year from 20X7–2021. The ratios are used for amortizing the $500,000 prior service cost. The computations are made in Table 7-52.

Table 7-52 Annual Amortization Ratios for Prior Service Cost

Year	Ratio[1]
20X7	150/1,367
20X8	140/1,367
20X9	135/1,367
2010	124/1,367
2011	120/1,367
2012	112/1,367
2013	106/1,367
2014	102/1,367
2015	100/1,367
2016	85/1,367
2017	65/1,367
2018	55/1,367
2019	48/1,367
2020	20/1,367
2021	5/1,367

[1] Information taken from Table 7-51.

The ratio for each year in Table 7-52 is computed by dividing each year's service lives by the total service life (1,367) for all employees for the entire 15-year period.

Using the ratios in Table 7-52 and the prior service cost of $500,000 from Item 3, Example 7-17, amortization of prior service cost for 20X7–2021 is computed in Table 7-53.

Table 7-53 Amortization of Prior Service Cost

(a) Year	(b) Amount of Plan Amendment[1]	(c) Amortization Ratio[2]	(d) = (b) × (c) Amortization of Prior Service Cost	(e) Prior Service Cost Balance at 12/31
20X7	$500,000	150/1,367	$54,865	$445,135
20X8	500,000	140/1,367	51,207	393,928
20X9	500,000	135/1,367	49,378	344,550
2010	500,000	124/1,367	45,355	299,195
2011	500,000	120/1,367	43,891	255,304
2012	500,000	112/1,367	40,966	214,338
2013	500,000	106/1,367	38,771	175,567
2014	500,000	102/1,367	37,308	138,259
2015	500,000	100/1,367	36,576	101,683
2016	500,000	85/1,367	31,090	70,593
2017	500,000	65/1,367	23,775	46,818
2018	500,000	55/1,367	20,117	26,701
2019	500,000	48/1,367	17,556	9,145
2020	500,000	20/1,367	7,316	1,829
2021	500,000	5/1,367	1,829	0
Total			$500,000	

[1] Information taken from Example 7-17, Item 1.
[2] Information taken from Table 7-52.

Bismack could elect a less complex method of amortization of prior service cost, as used in prior examples, as long as it is applied on a consistent basis. For example, Bismack could amortize the prior service cost over the average remaining service life to full eligibility of the active employee group on the date of amendment using a straight-line basis. Using the information from Table 7-51 Bismack could amortize the prior service cost over 9.11 years (1,367 service years ÷ 150 employees) using the simplified straight-line method. Using the $500,000 prior service cost, the annual amortization of prior service cost is $54,885 ($500,000 ÷ 9.11 years).

Example 7-18 illustrates computation of the expected and accumulated postretirement benefit obligations. The assumptions for Example 7-18 are as follows.

Example 7-18
Assumptions for Expected and Accumulated Postretirement Benefit Obligation

1. A company has a postretirement plan whereby employees who reach age 60 with at least 15 years of service with the company receive health care benefits.

2. For purposes of this illustration, assume that the company has one employee who was hired by the company at age 35. It is expected that the employee will retire at age 65 and will live 10 years after retirement. A 10% rate is used by the company when computing the present value of the estimated benefits.

3. The obligation is computed assuming that, first the employee is age 46, and second, the employee is age 56.

4. The employee is estimated to have the following claims after retirement: age 66—$1,000, age 67—$1,500, age 68—$2,000, age 69—$1,400, age 70—$3,000, age 71—$3,200, age 72—$4,000, age 73—$4,500, age 74—$4,700, and age 75—$5,000.

Using the information from Example 7-18, the expected and accumulated postretirement benefit obligation may be computed as per Table 7-54.

Several items in Table 7-54 require further explanation. The expected postretirement benefit obligation is the present value of the estimated claims to be paid after retirement using a 10% assumed rate. The time period used for computation depends upon the age of the employee. In the first computation, the employee is assumed to be age 46. At age 46 it is 20 years (periods) until the first estimated claim will be paid, 21 periods until the second one is paid and so forth. Therefore, the time period for the present value of the claims is the time period from the employees' age to the date of the claim. At age 56 it is only 10 years until the first claim is paid, and the present value computation is based on certain periods (e.g., 10 periods, 11 periods). The accumulated postretirement benefit obligation is the expected postretirement benefit obligation times the number of years of service actually rendered divided by the number of years of service from date of hire to date of full eligibility. This employee was hired at age 35 and will reach full eligibility at age 60 or 25 years. In the first computation, the employee has worked for 11 years (46 – 35 = 11). Therefore, the accumulated postretirement benefit obligation at age 46 is times the expected obligation. At age 56 it is times the expected obligation.

The five preceding examples covered defined benefit postretirement plans. Example 7-19 illustrates the accounting for a defined contribution plan.

Table 7-54 Computation of Expected and Accumulated Postretirement Benefit Obligation[1]

Expected and Accumulated Benefit Obligation at Age 46				Expected and Accumulated Benefit Obligation at Age 56			
Age at Date of Claim	Estimated Claims	Present Value Factor for $1	Present Value of Estimated Claims	Age at Date of Claim	Estimated Claims	Present Value Factor for $1	Present Value of Estimated Claims
66	$1,000	.1486[2]	$149	66	$1,000	.3855[3]	$386
67	1,500	.1351[4]	203	67	1,500	.3505[5]	526
68	2,000	.1228	246	68	2,000	.3186	637
69	1,400	.1117	156	69	1,400	.2897	406
70	3,000	.1015	305	70	3,000	.2633	790
71	3,200	.0923	295	71	3,200	.2394	766
72	4,000	.0839	336	72	4,000	.2176	870
73	4,500	.0763	343	73	4,500	.1978	890
74	4,700	.0693	326	74	4,700	.1799	846
75	5,000	.0630	315	75	5,000	.1635	818
Expected PBO[6]			$2,674				$6,935
Percentage			× 11/25				× 21/25
Accumulated PBO			$1,177				$5,825

[1] Information taken from Example 7-18.
[2] Present value factor of $1 for 20 periods at 10%.
[3] Present value factor of $1 for 10 periods at 10%.
[4] Present value factor of $1 for 21 periods at 10%.
[5] Present value factor of $1 for 11 periods at 10%.
[6] PBO = Postretirement benefit obligation.

Example 7-19
Assumptions for Defined Contribution Postretirement Plan

1. The Jones Company (Jones), a public company with a December 31 year-end, has a defined contribution postretirement health care plan that covers substantially all employees. Jones adopted all provisions of ASC 715-60 on January 1, 20X6.
2. Annual contributions and cost of the plan are 3% of employees annualized salaries. Annualized salaries for covered employees during 20X6 are $3,000,000.

Because Jones has a defined contribution plan, and contributions and cost of the plan are 3% of employee annual salaries, postretirement cost for 20X6 is $90,000 ($3,000,000 annual salaries × 3%). The following journal entry is required at December 31, 20X6:

Postretirement Cost	90,000	
Cash		90,000

The footnote disclosure required for the defined contribution plan is presented below:

Note: Jones has a defined contribution postretirement health care plan that covers substantially all employees. Contributions and cost of the plan are 3% of covered employees' annualized salary. Postretirement cost for 20X6 is $90,000.

This completes the technical application of postretirement plans. The next section covers settlements and curtailments of postretirement benefit plans.

Settlements and Curtailments of Defined Benefit Postretirement Plans—General Discussion

The general discussion, Flowchart 7-6, and technical application of settlements and curtailments of defined benefit postretirement benefit plans assumes that the reader has a complete understanding of the accounting and reporting requirements for defined benefit postretirement plans. The reader is encouraged to review the accounting for such plans in the prior section before proceeding with this material.

Before a discussion of Flowchart 7-6 and technical material begins, a definition of settlements and curtailments is provided.

A settlement of a defined benefit postretirement plan is a transaction that meets all of the following requirements:

- The transaction is an action that is irrevocable.
- The employer or the postretirement plan no longer has primary responsibility for the benefit obligation of the postretirement plan.
- Any major risk relative to the postretirement assets or obligation used in the settlement has been eliminated.

The purchase of participating or nonparticipating annuity contracts for all or part of the accumulated postretirement obligation and lump-sum payments of cash to employees in return for their right to receive future benefits represent examples of transactions that qualify as settlements. A participating annuity contract is a contract with an insurance company in which the company agrees to pay postretirement benefits to postretirement plan participants, but the postretirement plan or company shares in the experience of the insurance company. If the substance of the contract is such that the company or plan has not transferred all risks to the insurance company, the participating contract is not considered a settlement. A nonparticipating annuity contract is a contract with an insurance company in which the insurance company agrees to pay postretirement benefits to the participants of the postretirement plan in return for a fixed premium.

A curtailment of a defined benefit postretirement plan is a transaction or event where the future service years of the current employees are reduced significantly or where benefits for part or all of the future service are eliminated for a significant number of active participants.

The closing of a plant or division where expected future years of service are eliminated or the termination of a postretirement plan where future benefits cannot be earned are examples of curtailments of postretirement plans.

Now that both settlements and curtailments have been defined, attention can be directed to a discussion of Flowchart 7-6. All blocks in Flowchart 7-6 have been numbered for referencing in the discussion that follows.

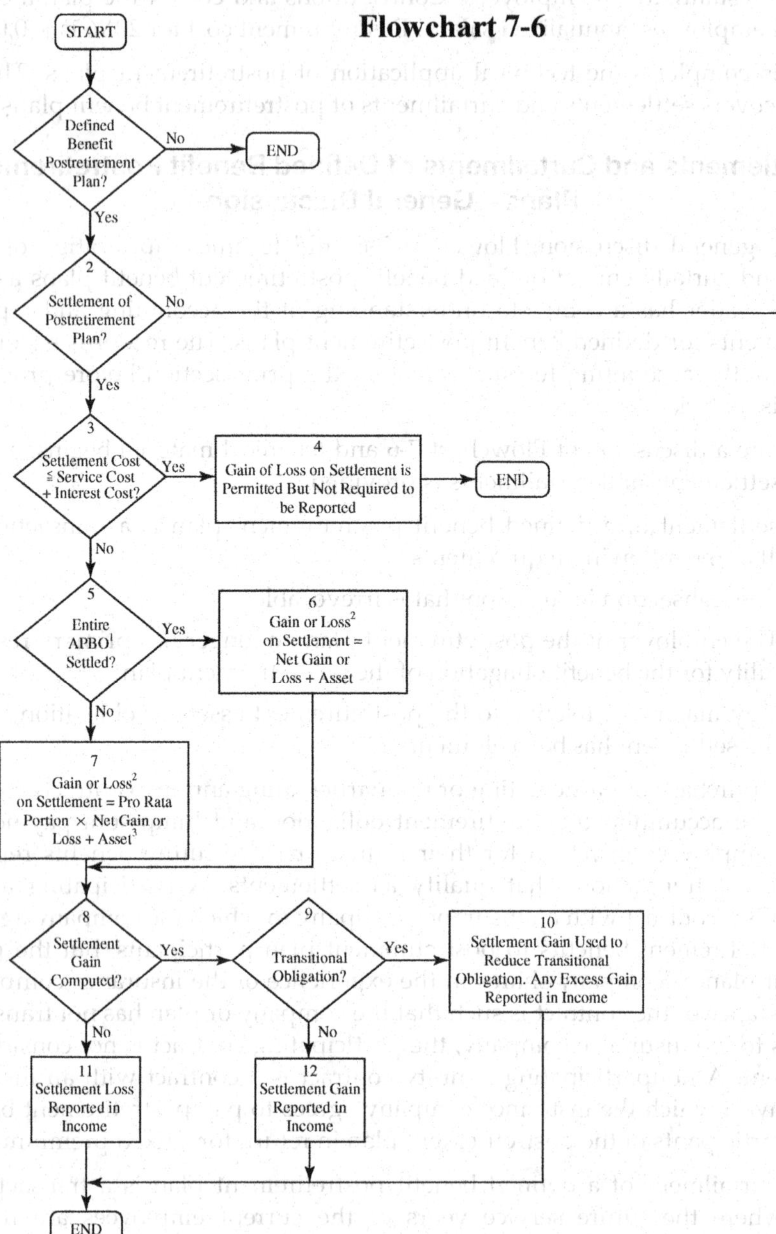

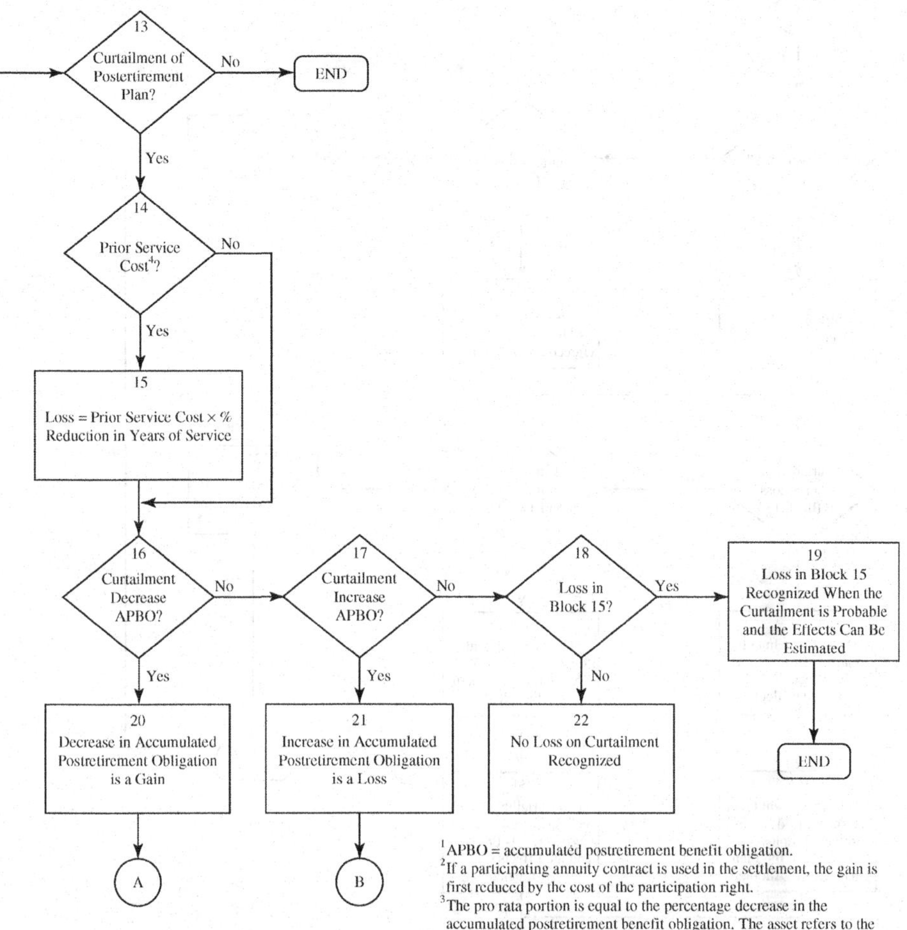

[1] APBO = accumulated postretirement benefit obligation.

[2] If a participating annuity contract is used in the settlement, the gain is first reduced by the cost of the participation right.

[3] The pro rata portion is equal to the percentage decrease in the accumulated postretirement benefit obligation. The asset refers to the remaining balance of the transitional asset in accumulated other comprehensive income.

[4] Prior service cost includes prior service cost from plan amendments and transitional obligation in accumulated other comprehensive income.

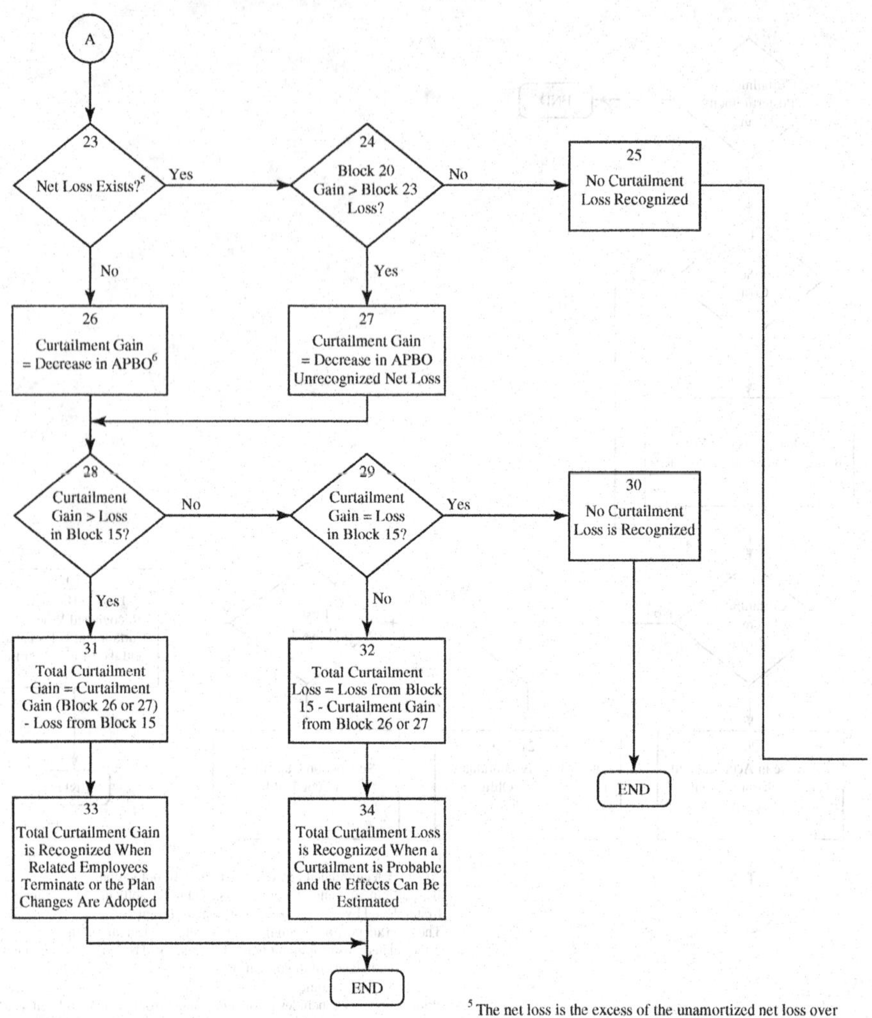

[5] The net loss is the excess of the unamortized net loss over any transitional asset in accumulated other comprehensive income.

[6] APBO = accumulated postretirement benefit obligation.

[7] The unrecognized net gain is the net gain + any transitional asset or the excess of the transitional asset over a net loss in accumulated other comprehensive income.

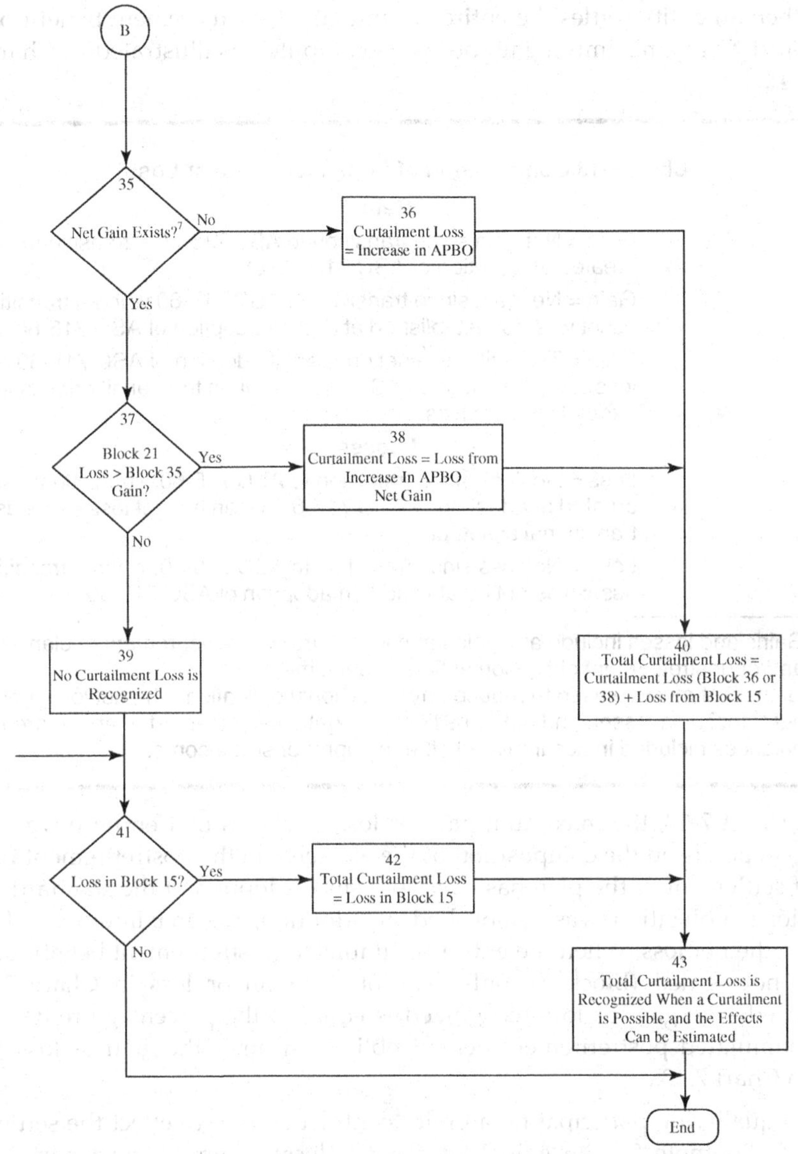

Once a transaction or event has been identified as a settlement (Block 2) or curtailment (Block 13), an entity must compute the settlement or curtailment gain or loss. Computation of the gain or loss is the entire focal point in the accounting for settlements and curtailments. Accounting for settlements is addressed in Flowchart 7-6. If the cost to settle the obligation of the postretirement plan is equal to or less than the summation of the service cost and the interest cost components of postretirement cost (Blocks 3 and 4), the entity is permitted, but is not required, to report a gain or loss on settlement.

When an entity settles the entire accumulated postretirement benefit obligation (Block 5) the maximum gain or loss is computed as illustrated in Chart 7-13 (Block 4).

Chart 7-13 Computation of Settlement Gain or Loss[1]

Gains[2]

1. Gain = Net gain since transition to ASC 715-60 + transitional asset created at adoption of ASC 715-60, or
2. Gain = Net gain since transition to ASC 715-60 when a transitional asset was not established at date of adoption of ASC 715-60, or
3. Gain = Transitional asset created at adoption of ASC 715-60 – net loss since transition to ASC 715-60, when the transitional asset exceeds the net loss.

Losses

1. Loss = Net loss since transition to ASC 715-60 – transitional asset created at adoption of ASC 715-60, when the net loss exceeds the transitional asset, or
2. Loss = Net loss since transition to ASC 715-60, when a transitional asset was not established on adoption of ASC 715-60.

[1] Gains and losses include any gains and losses from remeasurement of plan assets and/or postretirement obligation at time of settlement.

[2] Gains first must be used to reduce any transitional obligation. The net loss, net gain, net transitional asset, and net transitional obligation amounts listed above are the balances included in accumulated other comprehensive income.

In Chart 7-13, the maximum gain or loss (assumes that entire obligation is settled) depends on the composition of the elements in the postretirement plan at date of settlement. If the plan has a net loss since adoption of the standard, but a transitional obligation was established at adoption, the maximum net loss is equal to the net loss. When the entire accumulated postretirement benefit obligation is not settled (Block 7), only part of the gain or loss in Chart 7-13 is recognized. The gain or loss recognized is equal to the percentage reduction in the accumulated postretirement benefit obligation times the gain or loss calculated in Chart 7-13.

If a qualifying participating annuity contract is used to effect the settlement (Block 6, Footnote 2), the gain (but not the loss) computed in Chart 7-13 is reduced, first, by the cost of the participation right. The cost of the right is the difference between the cost of a participating and a nonparticipating annuity. When only a percentage of the accumulated postretirement benefit obligation is settled, the cost of the participation right is used to reduce the gain before applying the percentage reduction in the postretirement obligation.

If a gain is reported for the settlement (Block 8) and a transitional obligation (Block 9) exists at date of settlement, the gain is used first to reduce the transitional obligation (Block 10). Any excess gain is reported in income (Block 12). If only part of the postretirement obligation is settled, the pro rata part of the gain is used to reduce the transitional obligation. If a loss is reported for the settlement, the entire loss is recognized in income (Block 11).

If, on the date of a settlement, an enterprise has a transitional obligation, the entity must determine if a portion of the obligation should be recognized prior to computing the settlement gain or loss. Cumulative benefit payments since transition to ASC 715-60 must be compared to cumulative postretirement cost since transition. If the benefit payments exceed the postretirement cost, an amount of the transitional obligation equal to the excess payments is recognized. Benefit payments used in the computation must be adjusted for the following: the fair value of plan assets on the date of transition adjusted for any balance sheet account and payments made for the settlement.

Next, gains and losses on curtailment of defined benefit postretirement benefit plans are considered (Block 13). The computation of the gain or loss on curtailment is divided into a three-step process as follows:

Step 1—Computation of Loss From Prior Service Cost. The first step, calculation of the loss from prior service cost (Block 14), involves the determination of prior service cost at the date of curtailment in accumulated other comprehensive income. For purposes of this computation, prior service cost consists of prior service cost from plan amendments and any transitional obligation. Because a curtailment generally will reduce the expected future years of service of participants terminated, the loss from prior service cost is the prior service cost times the percentage reduction in future years of service of terminated employees (Block 15). The percentage reduction in expected future years of service may be different for prior service cost from each plan amendment and for the transitional obligation because different employee groups exist on the date of adoption of ASC 715-60 and on each amendment date.

Step 2—Computation of Gain or Loss from Postretirement Obligation. The second step is calculation of the gain or loss resulting from the decrease or the increase in the accumulated postretirement benefit obligation (Blocks 16, 17, 20, and 21). A decrease in the obligation is a gain (Block 20) and an increase is a loss (Block 21). If the curtailment causes a decrease in the accumulated postretirement benefit obligation, the gain from the decrease is accounted for as follows:

- The gain is recognized in total, if the plan has no net loss since transition to ASC 715-60 (Blocks 23 and 26), or
- If the gain exceeds the net loss, the excess is recognized as a gain (Block 27), or
- If the gain is less than the net loss, no gain or loss is recognized (Blocks 25 and 26).

If the curtailment causes an increase in the accumulated postretirement benefit obligation, the loss from the increase is accounted for as follows:

- The loss is recognized in total, if the plan has no net gain since transition to ASC 715-60 (Blocks 35 and 36), or
- If the loss exceeds the net gain, the excess is recognized as a loss (Blocks 37 and 38), or
- If the loss is less than the net gain, no loss or gain is recognized (Block 39).

Step 3—Combination of Steps 1 and 2. The third step of the three-step process is combination of the loss from the decrease in employee service years with the gain or loss from the decrease or increase in the accumulated postretirement benefit obligation. Combination of Steps 1 and 2 will result in a final net gain or net loss (Blocks 18, 19, and 31–43). If the final gain or loss is a net gain, the gain is recognized in the income statement when the related employees terminate or the plan changes are adopted (Block 33). If the final gain or loss is a net loss, the loss is reported in the income statement when the curtailment is probable and the effects of the curtailment can be estimated (Blocks 34 and 43). The net gain or net loss is classified in the income statement using the provisions of ASC 225-20. Generally, the net gain or loss is classified as a line item in income from continuing operations.

Settlements and Curtailments of Postretirement Plans—Technical Considerations

Two examples are used to illustrate the technical considerations for settlements and curtailments of defined benefit postretirement plans. It is important to understand the technical provisions related to the computation of postretirement cost for defined benefit postretirement plans before reviewing examples on settlements and curtailments. Assumptions for Example 7-20 are presented below.

Example 7-20
Assumptions for Settlement of Defined Benefit Postretirement Plan

1. The Dixon Company and Fairwell Enterprises both have defined benefit postretirement plans that cover substantially all employees. Both companies adopted ASC 715-60 on January 1, 20X6.
2. During 20X7, both companies settled portions of the accumulated postretirement benefit obligation (the vested part) by entering into nonparticipating annuity contracts with insurance companies.
3. On the date of settlement, the following information relates to the postretirement plans of the companies. The net loss, net gain, transitional asset, transitional obligation, and prior service cost amounts listed below are the balances included in accumulated other comprehensive income.

	Dixon Company	Fairwell Enterprises
• Net loss		$500,000
• Net gain	$400,000	
• Transitional asset		380,000
• Transitional obligation	200,000	
• Prior service cost from plan amendment	100,000	200,000
• Percentage of accumulated postretirement benefit obligation settled	85%	70%

		Dixon Company	Fairwell Enterprises
•	Postretirement liability		180,000
•	Postretirement asset	200,000	

4. Since the date of transition to ASC 715-60, Dixon Company's cumulative postretirement cost has exceeded its cumulative benefit payments after adjusting the benefit payments for the fair value of plan assets at transition and payments made for the settlement.

The first step in the analysis of the postretirement plans in Example 7-20 is to determine whether the transactions for both companies qualify as postretirement plan settlements under the provisions of ASC 715-60. Both transactions qualify as settlements because the purchase of nonparticipating annuity contracts are irrevocable actions that transfer primary responsibility for the postretirement obligation to insurance companies and eliminates any significant risks to the plans for the accumulated postretirement benefit obligation.

The second step in the analysis is to compute any gain or loss on the postretirement plan settlement. The gain or loss for the companies is computed in Table 7-55.

Table 7-55 Computation of Postretirement Settlement Gain or Loss[1]

Dixon Company	
Net gain	$400,000
Percentage reduction in accumulated postretirement benefit obligation	85%
Gain on settlement	$340,000
Gain used to reduce transitional obligation	(200,000)
Gain reported in income	$140,000
Fairwell Enterprises	
Net loss	$500,000
Transitional asset	(380,000)
Excess of loss over asset	$120,000
Percentage reduction in accumulated postretirement benefit obligation	70%
Loss reported in income	$84,000

[1] Information for computation of gain or loss taken from Example 7-20, Item 3.

Because Dixon Company has a gain on settlement and a transitional obligation at date of settlement, $200,000 of the gain must first be used to reduce the transitional obligation. Only the excess gain of $140,000 is reported in the income statement. There is no entry for the part of the gain that offsets the transitional obligation, because the obligation was never recorded. In future computations of postretirement cost, there will be no amortization for the transitional obligation.

Dixon Company was not required to recognize a portion of the transitional obligation prior to computing the settlement gain or loss, because, since transition to ASC 715-60, the cumulative benefit payments did not exceed the cumulative postretirement cost.

Using information from Table 7-55, journal entries required for the settlements are as follows:

Dixon Company		
Other Comprehensive Income	140,000	
Gain on Settlement of Defined Benefit Postretirement Plan		140,000
Fairwell Enterprises		
Loss on Settlement of Defined Benefit Postretirement Plan	84,000	
Other Comprehensive Income		84,000

The prior service cost from the plan amendment and the transitional obligation are not used in the calculation of the settlement gain or loss.

Example 7-20 covered settlements of defined benefit postretirement plans. Example 7-21 illustrates curtailments of postretirement plans. Assumptions for Example 7-21 are as follows.

Example 7-21

Assumptions for the Curtailment of Defined Benefit Postretirement Plans

1. Bacon Enterprises and the Davis Company have defined benefit postretirement plans that cover substantially all employees. Both companies adopted the provisions of ASC 715-60 on January 1, 20X6.

2. On December 20, 20X7, both companies terminated a significant number of employees because of declining business. The following information is available on the date of termination. The net loss, net gain, transitional asset, transitional obligation, and prior service cost amounts listed below are the balances included in accumulated other comprehensive income.

	Bacon Enterprises	Davis Company
• Reduction in accumulated postretirement benefit obligation from terminated employees	$1,335,000	$897,000
• Transitional obligation	292,500	
• Transitional asset		195,000
• Net loss since adoption of ASC 715-60	390,000	
• Net gain since adoption of ASC 715-60		487,500
• Prior service cost from plan amendment	195,000	146,250
• Postretirement liability		
• Postretirement asset	585,000	487,500

	Bacon Enterprises	Davis Company
• Percentage reduction in service years of those employees present at date of adoption of ASC 715-60	35%	15%
• Percentage reduction in service years of those employees present at time of plan amendment	25%	20%

The termination of employees by both firms qualify as curtailments because the expected service years of the employee groups are significantly reduced.

Because the employee terminations are classified as curtailments the gain or loss on curtailment must be computed. The gain or loss for Bacon Enterprises is computed in Table 7-56.

Table 7-56 Computation of Gain or Loss on Curtailment for Bacon Enterprises

Transitional obligation	$(292,500)	
Percentage reduction in service years of those employees present at date of adoption of ASC 715-60	35%	$(102,375)
Prior service cost	$(195,000)	
Percentage reduction in service years of those employees present at date of plan amendment	25%	(48,750)
Prior service cost loss		$(151,125)
Gain from reduction in accumulated postretirement benefit obligation from terminated employees	$1,335,000	
Net loss since adoption of ASC 715-60	(390,000)	945,000
Gain on postretirement curtailment		$793,875

Table 7-56 is divided into two parts. First, a $151,125 loss on prior service cost is computed, because the years of service expected to be rendered by the employees has been reduced. For purposes of this computation, prior service cost includes prior service cost from plan amendments and any transitional obligation. If a transitional asset had been established, it would not be used in the computation. The reduction in the expected service years of the employee group existing at the adoption of ASC 715-60 as a result of the termination is 35%. Therefore, 35% or $102,375 of the transitional obligation is recognized as a loss, and the remaining $190,125 ($292,500 – $102,375) is amortized over the remaining service life of the employee group.

The reduction in the expected service years of the employee group existing at the date of amendment of the plan is 25%. Consequently, 25% of the prior service cost ($48,750) is recognized as a loss at the time of curtailment. The remaining $146,250 ($195,000 – $48,750) is amortized over the remaining employee service life.

The second part of Table 7-56 focuses on the possible gain from the reduction in the accumulated postretirement benefit obligation. The reduction in the accumulated postretirement benefit obligation creates a $1,335,000 gain for Bacon Enterprises because future benefits associated with the reduction of the obligation will not be paid in the future for the terminated employees who had not reached full eligibility on the date of settlement. Because a net loss is available, the loss is offset against the gain. The loss of $390,000 is less than the gain of $1,335,000 and the excess gain is recognized. If the $390,000 loss had been a gain, the entire $1,335,000 gain would have been recognized. The $151,125 prior service cost loss from reduction in service years is offset against the $945,000 net gain leaving a $793,875 gain on curtailment. The curtailment gain is recognized in earnings when the employees are terminated. The entry for the gain is made on December 20, 20X7 because the employees are terminated on this date. The following journal entry is required to record the gain on curtailment of the postretirement plan:

Other Comprehensive Income	793,875	
Gain on Postretirement Plan Curtailment		793,875

The account, Gain on Postretirement Plan Curtailment, is classified in the income statement using the provisions of ASC 225-20. Generally, the account is classified as a line item in the nonoperating section of income from continuing operations.

Next, the gain or loss on curtailment for the Davis Company is computed. Table 7-57 shows the gain or loss computation.

Table 7-57 Computation of Gain or Loss on Curtailment for Davis Company

Prior service cost	$(146,250)
Percentage reduction in service years of those employees present at date of plan amendment	20%
Loss on prior service cost	$(29,250)
Gain from reduction in accumulated postretirement benefit obligation from terminated employees	897,000
Gain on postretirement curtailment	$867,750

Computation of the gain on curtailment in Table 7-57 is similar to the computations in Table 7-56 and requires very little discussion. However, two points need to be noted. First, in the computation of the loss in the top part of Table 7-57, only prior service cost is used. At the date of transition to ASC 715-60 a transitional asset was established. The asset is not used in the computation of the loss. Last, because the Davis Company has a net gain of $487,500, the gain of $897,000 from the decrease in the accumulated postretirement benefit obligation is recognized in total and then offset against the loss from the prior service cost.

Using the information from Table 7-57, the following journal entry is required to record the gain on postretirement curtailment for the Davis Company:

Other Comprehensive Income	867,750	
Gain on Postretirement Plan Curtailment		867,750

This completes the explanation and analysis of settlements and curtailments of defined benefit postretirement plans. The next section covers termination benefits.

Termination Benefits

Postretirement benefits may be provided by an enterprise in the form of special or contractual termination benefits. Special termination benefits are benefits provided for a short period of time as an incentive for employees to terminate employment. Contractual termination benefits are contracts with selected employees who provide termination benefits in case of the occurrence of a specific event. Accounting and reporting requirements for termination benefits are provided by ASC 715-30. When postretirement benefits are used as termination benefits, the accounting specified in ASC 715-30 should be used. Special termination benefits should be recorded as a loss and a liability when the offer is accepted by the employee and the amount of the liability reasonably can be estimated. Contractual termination benefits should be recorded as a loss and a liability when it is probable the event that triggers the benefit will occur and the amount of the loss reasonably can be estimated.

When postretirement benefits are used as special termination benefits, the amount of the loss and liability is computed in the following manner: (1) adjust the accumulated postretirement benefit obligation for employees accepting the termination offer by assuming that the employees who have not reached full eligibility will retire upon reaching full eligibility and the employees who already have reached full eligibility will retire at once, but do not adjust the obligation for the special termination benefits, (2) take the accumulated postretirement benefit obligation as computed in (1) and adjust it for the impact of the special termination benefits, and (3) take the difference in (1) and (2) to compute the loss and liability.

Special or contractual termination benefits may cause a curtailment of a defined benefit postretirement plan. See a discussion of curtailments of postretirement plans in the preceding section. This completes the discussion of termination benefits. The next section covers disclosure requirements for postretirement benefit plans.

Disclosures

The disclosure requirements for postretirement plans are divided into the following categories: disclosures for defined contribution postretirement plans, disclosures for multiemployer postretirement plans, disclosures for multiemployer postretirement plans (multiemployer plans that provide pension benefits and multiemployer plans that provide benefits other than pensions), disclosures by public entities of defined benefit plans, disclosures for non-public entities of defined benefit plans, disclosures, when an entity has two or more plans, and disclosures for interim periods. Disclosures for both pensions and postretirement plans are essentially the same and disclosures for both plans are disclosed together in the financial statements, generally in a column format.

Disclosures for Defined Contribution Postretirement Plans

ASC 715-70-50 specifies that an employer shall disclose:

- The amount of cost recognized for defined contribution pension plans and for other defined contribution postretirement for all periods presented separately from the amount of cost recognized for defined benefit plans.
- A description of the nature and effect of any significant changes during the period affecting comparability, such as a change in the rate of employer contributions, a business combination, or a divestiture.

Disclosures for Multiemployer Postretirement Plans

ASC 715-80-50 covers disclosures for retirement benefits of multiemployer plans that provide pension benefits and postretirement benefits other than pensions.

Multiemployer Plans That Provide Pension Benefits

An employer shall provide the disclosures required in its annual financial statements. The disclosures based on the most recently available information shall be the most recently available through the date at which the employer has evaluated subsequent events.

An employer that participates in a multiemployer plan that provides pension benefits shall provide a narrative description both of the general nature of the multiemployer plans that provide pension benefits and of the employer's participation in the plans that would indicate how the risks of participating in these plans are different from single-employer plans.

When feasible, ASC 715-80-50-5 requires the employer to present the following information in a tabular format. Information that requires a greater narrative description may be provided outside the table. For each individually significant multiemployer plan that provides pension benefits, an employer shall disclose the following:

1. Legal name of the plan.
2. The plan's Employer Identification Number and, if available, its plan number.
3. For each statement of financial position presented, the most recently available certified zone status provided by the plan, as currently defined by the Pension Protection Act of 2006 or a subsequent amendment of that Act. The disclosure shall specify the date of the plan's year-end to which the zone status relates and whether the plan has utilized any extended amortization provisions that affect the calculation of the zone status. If the zone status is not available, an employer shall disclose, as of the most recent date available, on the basis of the financial statements

provided by the plan, the total plan assets and accumulated benefit obligations, whether the plan was:

a. Less than 65% funded

b. Between 65% and 80% funded

c. At least 80% funded.

4. The expiration date(s) of the collective-bargaining agreement(s) requiring contributions to the plan, if any. If more than one collective-bargaining agreement applies to the plan, the employer shall provide a range of the expiration dates of those agreements, supplemented with a qualitative description that identifies the significant collective-bargaining agreements within that range as well as other information to help investors understand the significance of the collective-bargaining agreements and when they expire (e.g., the portion of employees covered by each agreement or the portion of contributions required by each agreement).

5. For each period that a statement of income is presented:

   a. The employer's contributions made to the plan

   b. Whether the employer's contributions represent more than 5% of total contributions to the plan as indicated in the plan's most recently available annual report (Form 5500 for U.S. plans). The disclosure shall specify the year-end date of the plan to which the annual report relates.

6. As of the end of the most recent annual period presented:

   a. Whether a funding improvement plan or rehabilitation plan (e.g., as those terms are defined by the Employment Retirement Security Act of 1974) had been implemented or was pending

   b. Whether the employer paid a surcharge to the plan

   c. A description of any minimum contribution(s), required for future periods by the collective-bargaining agreement(s), statutory obligations, or other contractual obligations, if applicable.

Factors other than the amount of the employer's contribution to a plan, for example, the severity of the underfunded status of the plan, may need to be considered when determining whether a plan is significant.

ASC 715-80-50-6 requires that an employer provide a description of the nature and effect of any significant changes that affect comparability of total employer contributions from period to period. Significant changes may results from:

1. A business combination or a divestiture.
2. A change in the contractual employer contribution rate.
3. A change in the number of employees covered by the plan during each year.

The requirements in ASC 715-80-50-5 assume that the other information about the plan is available in the public domain. For example, for U.S. plans, the plan information in Form 5500 is publicly available. In circumstances in which plan level information is not available in the public domain, an employer shall disclose under ASC 715-80-50-7, in addition to the requirements of ASC 715-80-50-5 and 6, the following information about each significant plan:

1. A description of the nature of the plan benefits
2. A qualitative description of the extent to which the employer could be responsible for the obligations of the plan, including benefits earned by employees during employment with another employer
3. Other quantitative information, to the extent available, as of the most recent date available, to help users understand the financial information about the plan, such as total plan assets, actuarial present value of accumulated plan benefits, and total contributions received by the plan.

If such quantitative information cannot be obtained without undue cost and effort, that quantitative information may be omitted and the employer shall describe what information has been omitted and why. In that circumstance, the employer also shall provide any qualitative information as of the most recent date available that would help users understand the financial information that otherwise is required to be disclosed about the plan.

Disclosures about multiemployer plans that are subject to the guidance in the preceding paragraph shall be included in a separate section of the tabular disclosure required by ASC 715-80-50-5.

In addition to the information about the significant multiemployer plans that provide pension benefits required by ASC 715-80-50-5 and 7, an employer shall disclose in a tabular format for each annual period for which a statement of income is presented, both of the following:

1. Its total contributions made to all plans that are not individually significant
2. Its total contributions made to all plans.

Multiemployer Plans That Provide Postretirement Benefits Other Than Pensions

Under ASC 715-80-50-11, an employer shall disclose the amount of contributions to multiemployer plans that provide postretirement benefits other than pensions for each annual period for which a statement of income is presented. The disclosures shall include a description of the nature and effect of any changes that affect comparability of total employer contributions from period to period. Comparability may be effected by:

1. A business combination or a divestiture
2. A change in the contractual employer contribution rate
3. A change in the number of employees covered by the plan during each year.

The disclosures also shall include a description of the nature of the benefits and the types of employees covered by these benefits, such as medical benefits provided to active employees and retirees.

Disclosures by Public Entities of Defined Benefit Plans

An employer that sponsors one or more defined benefit pension plans or one or more defined benefit other postretirement plans shall provide information, separately for pension plans and other postretirement benefit plans. Amounts related to the employer's results of operations shall be disclosed for each period for which a statement of income is presented. Amounts related to the employer's statement of financial position shall be disclosed as of the date of each statement of financial position presented. All of the following shall be disclosed:

1. A reconciliation of beginning and ending balances of the benefit obligation showing separately, if applicable, the effects during the period attributable to each of the following:
   a. Service cost
   b. Interest cost
   c. Contributions by plan participants
   d. Actuarial gains and losses
   e. Foreign currency exchange rate changes. (The effects of foreign currency exchange rate changes that are to be disclosed are those applicable to plans of a foreign operation whose functional currency is not the reporting currency.)
   f. Benefits paid
   g. Plan amendments
   h. Business combinations
   i. Divestitures
   j. Curtailments, settlements, and special and contractual termination benefits

   For defined benefit pension plans, the benefit obligation is the projected benefit obligation. For defined benefit other postretirement plans, the benefit obligation is the accumulated postretirement benefit obligation.
2. A reconciliation of beginning and ending balances of the fair value of plan assets showing separately, if applicable, the effects during the period attributable to each of the following:
   a. Actual return on plan assets
   b. Foreign currency exchange rate changes (see (1)(e))
   c. Contributions by the employer
   d. Contributions by plan participants
   e. Benefits paid
   f. Business combinations
   g. Divestitures
   h. Settlements.
3. The funded status of the plans and the amounts recognized in the statement of financial position, showing separately the assets and current and noncurrent liabilities recognized.

4. The objectives of the disclosures about postretirement benefit plan assets are to provide users of financial statements with an understanding of:

   a. How investment allocation decisions are made, including the factors that are pertinent to an understanding of investment policies and strategies

   b. The classes of plan assets

   c. The inputs and valuation techniques used to measure the fair value of plan assets

   d. The effect of fair value measurements using significant unobservable inputs (Level 3) on changes in plan assets for the period

   e. Significant concentrations of risk within plan assets.

   An employer shall consider those overall objectives in providing the following information about plan assets:

   (1) A narrative description of investment policies and strategies, including target allocation percentages or range of percentages considering the classes of plan assets disclosed pursuant to (2) below, as of the latest statement of financial position presented (on a weighted-average basis for employers with more than one plan), and other factors that are pertinent to an understanding of those policies and strategies such as investment goals, risk management practices, permitted and prohibited investments including the use of derivatives, diversification, and the relationship between plan assets and benefit obligations. For investment funds disclosed as classes as described in (2) below, a description of the significant investment strategies of those funds shall be provided.

   (2) The fair value of each class of plan assets as of each date for which a statement of financial position is presented. Examples of classes of assets include: cash and cash equivalents; equity securities (segregated by industry type, company size, or investment objective); debt securities issued by national, state, and local governments; corporate debt securities; asset-backed securities; structured debt; derivatives on a gross basis (segregated by type of underlying risk in the contract, for example, interest rate contracts, foreign exchange contracts, equity contracts, commodity contracts, credit contracts, and other contracts); investment funds (segregated by type of fund); and real estate. An employer may determine the measurement date of plan assets as of a recent month-end that does not coincide with the sponsor's year end. If the employer contributes assets to the plan between that measurement date and its fiscal year-end, the employer shall not adjust the fair value of each class of plan assets for the effects of the contribution. Instead, the employer shall disclose the amount of the contribution to permit reconciliation of the total fair value of all the classes of plan assets to the ending balance of the fair value of plan assets.

(3) A narrative description of the basis used to determine the overall expected long-term rate-of-return-on-assets assumption, such as the general approach used, the extent to which the overall rate-of-return-on-assets assumption was based on historical returns, the extent to which adjustments were made to those historical returns in order to reflect expectations of future returns, and how those adjustments were determined. The description should consider the classes of assets as described in (2) above, as appropriate.

(4) Information that enables users of financial statements to assess the inputs and valuation techniques used to develop fair value measurements of plan assets at the reporting date. For fair value measurements using significant unobservable inputs, an employer shall disclose the effect of the measurements on changes in plan assets for the period. To meet those objectives, the employer shall disclose the following information for each class of plan assets disclosed pursuant to (2) above for each annual period:

   (a) The level of the fair value hierarchy within which the fair value measurements are categorized in their entirety, segregating fair value measurements using quoted prices in active markets for identical assets or liabilities (Level 1), significant other observable inputs (Level 2), and significant unobservable inputs (Level 3). Investments for which fair value is measured using the net asset value per share (or its equivalent) practical expedient in ASC 820-10-35-59 shall not be categorized within the fair value hierarchy. An employer may determine the measurement date of plan assets as of a recent month-end that does not coincide with the sponsor's year end. If the employer contributes assets to the plan between that measurement date and its fiscal year-end, the employer shall not adjust the fair value of each class of plan assets for the effects of the contribution. Instead, the employer shall disclose the amount of the contribution to permit reconciliation of the total fair value of all plan assets in the fair value hierarchy to the ending balance of the fair value of plan assets.

   (b) For fair value measurements of plan assets using significant unobservable inputs (Level 3), a reconciliation from the opening balances to the closing balances, disclosing separately changes during the period attributable to the following:

      i. Actual return on plan assets separately identifying the amount related to assets still held at the reporting date and the amount related to assets sold during the period.

      ii. Purchases, sales, and settlements, net.

      iii. The amounts of any transfers into or out of Level 3 (e.g., transfers due to changes in the observability of significant inputs).

(c) Information about the valuation technique(s) and inputs used to measure fair value and a discussion of changes in valuation techniques and inputs, if any, during the period.

5. For defined benefit pension plans, the accumulated benefit obligation.
6. The benefits (as of the date of the latest statement of financial position presented) expected to be paid in each of the next five fiscal years, and in the aggregate for the five fiscal years thereafter. The expected benefits shall be estimated based on the same assumptions used to measure the entity's benefit obligation at the end of the year and shall include benefits attributable to estimated future employee service.
7. The employer's best estimate, as soon as it can reasonably be determined, of contributions expected to be paid to the plan during the next fiscal year beginning after the date of the latest statement of financial position presented. Estimated contributions may be presented in the aggregate combining all of the following:
   a. Contributions required by funding regulations or laws
   b. Discretionary contributions
   c. Noncash contributions.
8. The amount of net benefit cost recognized, showing separately all of the following:
   a. The service cost component
   b. The interest cost component
   c. The expected return on plan assets for the period
   d. The gain or loss component
   e. The prior service cost or credit component
   f. The transition asset or obligation component
   g. The gain or loss recognized due to settlements or curtailments.
9. Separately the net gain or loss and net prior service cost or credit recognized in other comprehensive income for the period under paragraphs 715-30-35-11,715-30-35-21, 715-60-35-16, and 715-60-35-25, and reclassification adjustments of other comprehensive income for the period, as those amounts, including amortization of the net transition asset or obligation, are recognized as components of net periodic benefit cost.
10. The amounts in accumulated other comprehensive income that have not yet been recognized as components of net periodic benefit cost, showing separately the net gain or loss, net prior service cost or credit, and net-transition asset or obligation.
11. On a weighted-average basis, all of the following assumptions used in the accounting for the plans, specifying in a tabular format, the assumptions used to determine the benefit obligation and the assumptions used to determine net benefit cost:

a. Assumed discount rates
b. Rates of compensation increase for pay-related plans
c. Expected long-term rates of return on plan assets.

12. The assumed health care cost trend rate(s) for the next year used to measure the expected cost of benefits covered by the plan (gross eligible charges), and a general description of the direction and pattern of change in the assumed trend rates thereafter, together with the ultimate trend rate(s) and when that rate is expected to be achieved.
13. The effect of a one-percentage-point increase and the effect of a one-percentage-point decrease in the assumed health care cost trend rates on the aggregate of the service and interest cost components of net periodic postretirement health care benefit costs and the accumulated postretirement benefit obligation for health care benefits. Measuring the sensitivity of the accumulated postretirement benefit obligation and the combined service and interest cost components to a change in the assumed health care cost trend rates requires remeasuring the accumulated postretirement benefit obligation as of the beginning and end of the year. (For purposes of this disclosure, all other assumptions shall be held constant, and the effects shall be measured based on the substantive plan that is the basis for the accounting.)
14. The amounts and types of securities of the employer and related parties included in plan assets, the approximate amount of future annual benefits of plan participants covered by insurance contracts, including annuity contracts issued by the employer or related parties, and any significant transactions between the employer or related parties and the plan during the period.
15. Any alternative method used to amortize prior service amounts or net gains and losses pursuant to ASC paragraphs 715-30-35-13 and 715-30-35-25 or 715-60-35-18 and 715-60-35-31.
16. If applicable, any substantive commitment, such as past practice or a history of regular benefit increases, used as the basis for accounting for the benefit obligation.
17. If applicable, the cost of providing special or contractual termination benefits recognized during the period and a description of the nature of the event.
18. An explanation of any significant change in the benefit obligation or plan assets not otherwise apparent in the other disclosures required by this subtopic.
19. The amounts in accumulated other comprehensive income expected to be recognized as components of net periodic benefit cost over the fiscal year that follows the most recent annual statement of financial position presented, showing separately the net gain or loss, net prior service cost or credit, and net transition asset or obligation.
20. The amount and timing of any plan assets expected to be returned to the employer during the 12-month period, or operating cycle if longer, that follows the most recent annual statement of financial position presented.

21. The accounting policy, if elected under ASC paragraphs 715-30-35-63A or 715-60-35-123A, to measure plan assets and benefit obligations using the month-end that is closest to the employer's fiscal year-end and the month-end measurement date.

Disclosures for Non-Public Entities of Defined Benefit Plans

A nonpublic entity that sponsors one or more defined benefit pension plans or one or more other defined benefit postretirement plans shall provide all of the following information, separately for pension plans and other postretirement benefit plans. Amounts related to the employer's results of operations shall be disclosed for each period for which a statement of income is presented. Amounts related to the employer's statement of financial position shall be disclosed as of the date of each statement of financial position presented.

1. The benefit obligation, fair value of plan assets, and funded status of the plan.
2. Employer contributions, participant contributions, and benefits paid.
3. The objectives of the disclosures about postretirement benefit plan assets are to provide users of financial statements with an understanding of:
    a. How investment allocation decisions are made, including the factors that are pertinent to an understanding of investment policies and strategies
    b. The classes of plan assets
    c. The inputs and valuation techniques used to measure the fair value of plan assets
    d. The effect of fair value measurements using significant unobservable inputs (Level 3) on changes in plan assets for the period
    e. Significant concentrations of risk within plan assets.

    An employer shall consider those overall objectives in providing the following information about plan assets:

    (1) A narrative description of investment policies and strategies, including target allocation percentages or range of percentages considering the classes of plan assets disclosed pursuant to (2) below, as of the latest statement of financial position presented (on a weighted-average basis for employers with more than one plan), and other factors that are pertinent to an understanding of those policies and strategies such as investment goals, risk management practices, permitted and prohibited investments including the use of derivatives, diversification, and the relationship between plan assets and benefit obligations. For investment funds disclosed as classes as described in (2) below, a description of the significant investment strategies of those funds shall be provided.

    (2) The fair value of each class of plan assets as of each date for which a statement of financial position is presented. Examples of classes of assets could include, but are not limited to, the following: cash and

cash equivalents; equity securities (segregated by industry type, company size, or investment objective); debt securities issued by national, state, and local governments; corporate debt securities; asset-backed securities; structured debt; derivatives on a gross basis (segregated by type of underlying risk in the contract, for example, interest rate contracts, foreign exchange contracts, equity contracts, commodity contracts, credit contracts, and other contracts); investment funds (segregated by type of fund); and real estate. An employer may determine the measurement date of plan assets as of a recent month-end that does not coincide with the sponsor's year end as permitted under ASC 715-30-35-63A or ASC 715-30-35-123A. If the employer contributes assets to the plan between that measurement date and its fiscal year-end, the employer shall not adjust the fair value of each class of plan assets for the effects of the contribution. Instead, the employer shall disclose the amount of the contribution to permit reconciliation of the total fair value of all plan assets in the fair value hierarchy to the ending balance of the fair value of plan assets.

(3) A narrative description of the basis used to determine the overall expected long-term rate-of-return-on-assets assumption, such as the general approach used, the extent to which the overall rate-of-return-on-assets assumption was based on historical returns, the extent to which adjustments were made to those historical returns in order to reflect expectations of future returns, and how those adjustments were determined. The description should consider the classes of assets described in (2) above, as appropriate.

(4) Information that enables users of financial statements to assess the inputs and valuation techniques used to develop fair value measurements of plan assets at the reporting date. For fair value measurements using significant unobservable inputs, an employer shall disclose the effect of the measurements on changes in plan assets for the period. To meet those objectives, the employer shall disclose the following information for each class of plan assets disclosed pursuant to (2) above for each annual period:

(a) The level of the fair value hierarchy within which the fair value measurements are categorized in their entirety, segregating fair value measurements using quoted prices in active markets for identical assets or liabilities (Level 1), significant other observable inputs (Level 2), and significant unobservable inputs (Level 3). Investments for which fair value is measured using the net asset value per share (or its equivalent) practical expedient in ASC 820-10-35-59 shall not be categorized within the fair value hierarchy. An employer may determine the measurement date of plan assets as of a recent month-end that does not coincide with the sponsor's year end. If the employer contributes assets to the plan between that measurement date and its fiscal year-end, the employer shall not adjust the fair value of each class of plan assets for the effects of the contribution. Instead, the employer shall disclose the amount of the contribution to permit reconciliation of the total fair value of all plan assets in the fair value hierarchy to the ending balance of the fair value of plan assets.

(b) For fair value measurements of plan assets using significant unobservable inputs (Level 3), a reconciliation from the opening balances to the closing balances, disclosing separately changes during the period attributable to the following:

i. Actual return on plan assets, separately identifying the amount related to assets still held at the reporting date and the amount related to assets sold during the period

ii. Purchases, sales, and settlements, net

iii. The amounts of any transfers into or out of Level 3 (e.g., transfers due to changes in the observability of significant inputs).

(c) Information about the valuation technique(s) and inputs used to measure fair value and a discussion of changes in valuation techniques and inputs, if any, during the period.

4. For defined benefit pension plans, the accumulated benefit obligation.
5. The benefits (as of the date of the latest statement of financial position presented) expected to be paid in each of the next five fiscal years, and in the aggregate for the five fiscal years thereafter. The expected benefits shall be estimated based on the same assumptions used to measure the entity's benefit obligation at the end of the year and shall include benefits attributable to estimated future employee service.
6. The employer's best estimate, as soon as it can reasonably be determined, of contributions expected to be paid to the plan during the next fiscal year beginning after the date of the latest statement of financial position presented. Estimated contributions may be presented in the aggregate combining any of the following:

   a. Contributions required by funding regulations or laws

   b. Discretionary contributions

   c. Noncash contributions.
7. The amounts recognized in the statements of financial position, showing separately the postretirement benefit assets and current and noncurrent postretirement benefit liabilities.
8. Separately the net gain or loss and net prior service cost or credit recognized in other comprehensive income for the period under ASC paragraphs 715-30-35-11,715-30-35-21, 715-60-35-16, and 715-60-35-25, and reclassification adjustments of other comprehensive income for the period, as those amounts, including amortization of the net transition asset or obligation, are recognized as components of net periodic benefit cost.

9. The amounts in accumulated other comprehensive income that have not yet been recognized as components of net periodic benefit cost, showing separately the net gain or loss, net prior service cost or credit, and net transition asset or obligation.

10. On a weighted-average basis, all of the following assumptions used in the accounting for the plans, specifying in a tabular format, the assumptions used to determine the benefit obligation and the assumptions used to determine net benefit cost:

    a. Assumed discount rates

    b. Rates of compensation increase (for pay-related plans)

    c. Expected long-term rates of return on plan assets.

11. The assumed health care cost trend rate(s) for the next year used to measure the expected cost of benefits covered by the plan (gross eligible charges), and a general description of the direction and pattern of change in the assumed trend rates thereafter, together with the ultimate trend rate(s) and when that rate is expected to be achieved.

12. The amounts and types of securities of the employer and related parties included in plan assets, the approximate amount of future annual benefits of plan participants covered by insurance contracts, including annuity contracts, issued by the employer or related parties, and any significant transactions between the employer or related parties and the plan during the period.

13. The nature and effect of significant nonroutine events, such as amendments, combinations, divestitures, curtailments, and settlements.

14. The amounts in accumulated other comprehensive income expected to be recognized as components of net periodic benefit cost over the fiscal year that follows the most recent annual statement of financial position presented, showing separately the net gain or loss, net prior service cost or credit, and net transition asset or obligation.

15. The amount and timing of any plan assets expected to be returned to the employer during the 12-month period, or operating cycle if longer, that follows the most recent annual statement of financial position presented.

16. The accounting policy, if elected under ASC paragraphs 715-30-35-63A or 715-60-35-123A, to measure plan assets and benefit obligations using the month-end that is closest to the employer's fiscal year-end and the month-end measurement date.

17. The amount of net periodic benefit cost recognized.

Disclosures When an Entity Has Two or More Plans

ASC 715-20-50 specifies the following disclosures, presented as of the measurement date for each balance sheet presented, when an entity has two or more postretirement plans:

1. When an employer has two or more postretirement plans, aggregation is required for disclosure purposes. However, disaggregation of the plans may be appropriate if it provides more useful information.

2. Disclosures about pension plans with assets in excess of the accumulated benefit obligation generally may be aggregated with disclosures about pension plans with accumulated benefit obligations in excess of assets. The same aggregation is permitted for other postretirement benefit plans. If aggregate disclosures are presented, an employer shall disclose both of the following:

   a. The aggregate benefit obligation and aggregate fair value of plan assets for plans with benefit obligations in excess of plan assets as of the measurement date of each statement of financial position presented

   b. The aggregate pension accumulated benefit obligation and aggregate fair value of plan assets for pension plans with accumulated benefit obligations in excess of plan assets.

3. A U.S. reporting entity may combine disclosures about pension plans or other postretirement benefit plans outside the United States with those for U.S. plans unless the benefit obligations of the plans outside the United States are significant relative to the total benefit obligation and those plans use significantly different assumptions. A foreign reporting entity that prepares financial statements in conformity with U.S. generally accepted accounting principle shall apply the preceding guidance to its domestic and foreign plans.

Disclosures for Interim Accounting Periods

Paragraphs 6 and 7 of ASC 715-20-50 specify the disclosure requirements for interim accounting periods:

Public Entity (ASC 715-20-50-6)

A publicly traded entity shall disclose the following information for its interim financial statements that include a statement of income:

1. The amount of net benefit cost recognized, for each period for which a statement of income is presented, showing separately each of the following:

   a. The service cost component

   b. The interest cost component

   c. The expected return on plan assets for the period

   d. The gain or loss component

   e. The prior service cost or credit component

   f. The transition asset or obligation component

   g. The gain or loss recognized due to a settlement or curtailment.

The line item(s) used in the income statement to present the components other than the service cost component shall be disclosed if the other components are not presented in a separate line item or items in the income statement.

2. The total amount of the employer's contributions paid, and expected to be paid, during the current fiscal year, if significantly different from amounts previously disclosed pursuant to ASC paragraph 715-20-50-1(g). Estimated contributions may be presented in the aggregate combining all of the following:
    a. Contributions required by funding regulations or laws
    b. Discretionary contributions
    c. Noncash contributions.

Nonpublic Entity (ASC 715-20-50-7)

A nonpublic entity shall disclose in interim periods for which a complete set of financial statements is presented the total amount of the employer's contributions paid, and expected to be paid, during the current fiscal year, if significantly different from amounts previously disclosed pursuant to ASC paragraph 715-20-50-5(f). Estimated contributions may be presented in the aggregate combining all of the following:

1. Contributions required by funding regulations or laws
2. Discretionary contributions
3. Noncash contributions.

Recent Changes

ASU 2017-07, *Compensation—Retirement Benefits (Topic 715): Improving the Presentation of Net Periodic Pension Cost and Net Periodic Postretirement Benefit Cost*, was issued in March 2017 to provide consistency regarding how entities report the components of periodic pension and post-retirement benefit costs. Under U.S. GAAP, such costs include several components that reflect different aspects of an employer's financial arrangements as well as the cost of benefits provided to employees. Those components are aggregated for reporting in the financial statements. Topic 715, *Compensation—Retirement Benefits*, does not prescribe where the amount of net benefit cost should be presented in an employer's income statement and does not require entities to disclose by line item the amount of net benefit cost that is presented in the income statement or capitalized in assets.

ASU 2017-07 applies to all employers, including not-for-profit entities that offer defined benefit pension plans, other postretirement benefit plans, or other types of benefits accounted for under Topic 715 to their employees.

Under ASU 2017-07, all employers will report service cost component of such costs in the same financial statement line(s) as other compensation costs arising from services rendered by the pertinent employees during the period.

The other components of such cost, such as interest and amortization, etc., as defined in paragraphs 715-30-35-4 and 715-60-35-9, are required to be presented separately from service cost and outside a subtotal of income from operations. If the other components of benefit cost are presented in a separate line item, that line item should be described appropriately. If not separately presented, the entity must disclose the line item (or items) in the income statement where the entity presents the other components (of net periodic pension cost and net periodic postretirement benefit cost).

Under the amendments in ASU 2017-07, service cost would be the only component eligible for capitalization as part of the cost of an assets such as inventory or property, plant, and equipment.

ASU 2017-07 will be effective as follows:

- For public business entities for annual reporting periods beginning after December 15, 2017, including interim periods within that reporting period.
- For entities other than public business entities for annual reporting periods beginning after December 15, 2018, and interim periods beginning after December 15, 2019.

Early adoption will be permitted for all entities as of the beginning of an annual period for which financial statements (interim or annual) have not been issued or made available for issuance.

The amendments for the presentation in the income statement of the service cost component and other components of net periodic pension cost and net periodic postretirement benefit cost will be applied retrospectively. The amendments for the capitalization in assets of the service cost component of net periodic pension cost and net periodic postretirement benefit cost will be applied prospectively.

Lastly, entities should disclose the nature of and reason for the change in accounting principle in the first interim and annual reporting periods in which the entity adopts the amendments.

To ease transition, ASU 2017-07 provides a practical expedient to permit entities that have difficulty in determining the disaggregation of the service cost component and other components for the prior comparative periods to use the amounts previously disclosed in their pension and other postretirement benefit plan footnote(s) as the basis for applying retrospective presentation requirements. An entity is required to disclose that it is using the practical expedient.

Topic 718: Compensation—Stock Compensation

Topic 718, *Compensation—Stock Compensation,* contains six subtopics:

10 Overall

20 Awards Classified as Equity

30 Awards Classified as Liabilities

40 Employee Stock Ownership Plans

50 Employee Share Purchase Plans

740 Income Taxes

Introduction

ASC 718 specifies the accounting and reporting requirements for share-based transactions with employees. ASC 505-50 specifies the requirements for share-based transactions with parties other than employees.

When the share-based transaction involves employees, ASC 718 requires public companies to measure the cost of services provided by employees in exchange for the share-based grant using a date of grant fair value method. The cost of the award to the employees is recognized in the accounting periods that the employees provide the related services.

ASC 805 should be consulted to determine whether share-based awards provided in a business combination are for services that will be provided in the post-combination period or as part of the consideration in exchange for the acquired company (the acquiree). If the share-based awards are for consideration in exchange for the acquiree, the provisions of ASC 805 are applicable; however, if the awards are for post-combination services, the provisions of ASC 718 should be used.

Accounting for Share-Based Payment Plans Provided to Employees

Employee share-based payment plans should be classified as either noncompensatory or compensatory. A noncompensatory award (an employee share purchase plan) may be viewed as a plan or method for the enterprise to raise capital by selling stock to employees. A compensatory plan (an employee share-based payment arrangement), which is divided into either share-based payments classified as equity or share-based payments classified as liabilities, may be thought of as a plan to provide employees with compensation in addition to their salaries. It is an effort by the entity to report in the entity's financial statements services provided by the employee in exchange for equity instruments or liabilities issued by the enterprise, and to report the cost incurred by the entity in the accounting period that the services are consumed.

Accounting and reporting requirements for share-based payments made to employees is divided into the following six parts: (1) employee share purchase plans (noncompensatory arrangements)—general discussion; (2) employee share-based payments classified as equity (compensatory plans)—general discussion; (3) employee share-based payment plans classified as liabilities (compensatory plans)—general discussion; (4) technical considerations; (5) disclosure requirements; and (6) other applicable accounting standards.

Share Purchase Plans—General Discussion

An employee share purchase plan is an arrangement between the company and its employees whereby the employees may purchase equity instruments of the company for a specified price. Such plans are not intended to provide compensation in return for employee services and do not require computing or reporting of employee compensation expense. Therefore, such plans are classified as noncompensatory. For a given award plan to be classified as noncompensatory, the following four conditions must be met:

1. Participation in the award plan is open to most full-time employees who have met limited qualification for employment and the company uses an objective basis for participation in the plan.
2. The company allows only a short time period for employees to enroll in the award plan subsequent to the date that the purchase price has been established. This time period should not exceed 31 days.
3. Purchase price of the stock is determined using the selling price of the stock on the purchase date. In addition, employees may terminate participation in the plan and receive a refund of moneys paid when termination is made prior to purchase date.
4. The difference between the exercise price and the market price of the stock is not significant.

The share purchase plan contains no option feature other than conditions 2 and 3. The purchase price associated with the award plan in condition 4 should meet one of the following items: all holders of the same class of stock have the same terms as the employees in the employee purchase plan, that is the employees do not have more favorable plan terms or any discount from the market price of the stock provided under the employee share purchase plan is not greater than the costs incurred by the company on a per share basis in a public offering of a significant amount of stock. Generally, the discount should not exceed 5% of the market price of the stock. Should the discount exceed 5%, and if the greater discount cannot be justified, the entire discount would be considered compensation expense. If the share purchase plan provides a provision that determines the purchase price as the smaller of the market price on the date of grant or the market price on the date of purchase, the plan is assumed to have an option feature and the plan would be classified as a compensatory plan. The share purchase plan is considered a compensatory plan when the share price is based on the market price at the date of grant and the employee can cancel prior to the purchase date and receive a full refund of amounts paid. Should an employee share purchase plan result in compensation expense, the compensation expense should be reported in the requisite service period, which is the time period that the employee participates in the plan and pays for the shares. If the plan does not meet all four criteria, it is classified as compensatory.

The reason for classifying the award as a noncompensatory is that the plan involves no compensation to the employees who receive the right to purchase shares of stock. In addition, the entity reports no compensation expense for the award. No accounting is required at the time the stock options are issued. When the options are actually exercised (when the stock is purchased), an entry is made for the exercise of the award plan. Cash is increased by an amount equal to the purchase price multiplied by the number of options. The capital stock account is increased by the amount of the par value, in the case of par value stock, or by the purchase price if the shares are not par value stock. In the case of par value stock, the excess cash over the par value is used to increase paid-in-capital.

If an employee award plan does not meet the preceding four criteria to be classified as noncompensatory share-based purchase plan, it will be classified as a compensatory share-based payment plan. Compensatory share-based payment plans are divided into two broad categories: share-based payment plans classified as equity and share-based payment plans classified as liabilities.

Share-Based Payment Plans Classified as Equity—General Discussion

An award or share-based payment plan provided to employees that is classified as equity is measured at its fair value on the grant date of the equity instrument that the company is required to issue when the employee has provided the required service and satisfied any other required conditions. The part of the fair value of the equity instrument, such as stock options or similar instruments, that relates to employee service is the fair value of the instrument net of any amount that must be paid by the employee. For example, if an equity instrument has a grant-date fair value of $20 and the employee is required to pay $2 for the instrument, the amount related to employee service is $18 ($20 - $2). Fair value should be determined using quoted market prices of identical or similar items. When determining the fair value of equity options or similar instruments, fair value should be measured using market price, if available, of an option with the same or similar terms. However, in many cases, such prices are not available, and an entity must estimate fair market value. Fair market value may be estimated using an acceptable valuation technique consistent with (1) the fair value requirements of ASC 718, (2) established principles of financial economic theory, and (3) all substantive elements of the instrument. Fair value of employee share-based options and similar instruments can be estimated at the date of grant using an appropriate option pricing model, such as a lattice or closed-form model. A binomial model is an example of a lattice model and the Black-Scholes-Merton model is an example of a closed-form model. The model selected must consider the following factors as a minimum:

1. The stock's current market price.
2. The exercise price of the options.
3. The estimated term of the options.
4. The anticipated dividends over the estimated term of the options.
5. The interest rate that is considered risk free for the estimated term of the options.
6. The anticipated volatility of the stock that will be issued for the options for the estimated term of the options.

Once the fair value of the share-based options have been estimated on the date of grant using an acceptable valuation model that incorporates, as a minimum, the six criteria listed above, fair value should not be adjusted in future accounting periods because of future changes in those criteria. Some of the criteria require further explanation. The estimated term of the options is implicit in most of the minimum factors used in the valuation model. The estimated term of the option is the expected term that the option will be outstanding and will take into consideration the contractual option terms as well as the impact of the expected exercise and post-vesting employment termination behavior of the employees. The risk-free interest rate used in the computation when the options relate to U.S. stock using a closed-form model is the implied yield currently available on U.S. government zero coupon securities. The zero coupon securities should have a remaining life equal to the anticipated life of the options. When a lattice model is used, the risk-free rate is the implied yield from the U.S. Treasury zero-coupon yield curve on the option's contractual term. Companies based outside the U.S. should use the implied yield available currently on zero-coupon government securities denominated in the currency where the security trades. The anticipated volatility of the stock price is the amount that the price is anticipated to change over a specified period of time. The expected volatility of the stock must be computed and included in the option pricing model.

When an entity elects to use the Black-Scholes-Merton model when estimating fair value of share-based payments, certain adjustments must be made for the characteristics of the employee options that are not consistent with the assumptions used in the model. For example, the model assumes that the options are exercised at the end of the option term and volatility, anticipated dividends, and the risk free interest rate are constant over the life of the options. A lattice model can be designed to better accommodate the characteristics of employee option plans including the impact of blackout periods. A blackout period is a period of time when the options cannot be legally exercised. However, the entity must develop reasonable assumptions regardless of the model selected for estimating fair value, and it must change valuation models if there is information that indicates that one of the other models is better for estimating fair value. Factors other than the six listed above may have to be considered in estimating the fair value of share-based options on the date of grant.

Any restrictions or conditions in the share-based option award must be considered when estimating fair value of the options. Restrictions may be a governmental or contractual requirement preventing the sale of the equity instrument for a specified period of time. A restriction is factored into the computation of grant-date fair value, if the restriction continues after the instruments have been issued to the employees such as the inability to sell or transfer vested equity securities to third parties. However, inability to sell or transfer nonvested shares are not factored into the grant-date fair value computation, but are considered when determining the amount of compensation cost. Compensation cost is recognized only for the awards where the employees provide the required service.

Employee share-based award plans may contain performance, service, or market conditions that impact the vesting, exercise price, exercisability, or other factors related to the share-based plans. A performance condition is a condition that requires the attainment of a specific performance goal either inside the company or a comparison to external factors. For example, the performance goal may be related to a firm achieving a certain return on asset, a certain earnings per share, meeting or exceeding a specific industry average, or some other specified condition. A service condition is the condition that the employee provides the requisite service over some specified period of time. A market condition refers to, for example, the attainment of a specific price of the stock of the enterprise, a specific amount of intrinsic value indexed to the company's stock, or a specific stock price in relation to a similar security. If the required service is provided for either performance or service conditions, the appropriate compensation expense is recognized. However, if any of the equity instruments are forfeited because the appropriate performance or service condition is not satisfied, no compensation expense is reported for the forfeitures. The impact of market conditions should be reported in the grant-date fair value computation, and compensation expense should be reported for a market conditions if the required service is provided, even if the market condition is never achieved. A restricted equity share provided to an employee for requisite service is an equity instrument that is restricted by governmental or contractual requirements and is restricted after the employee has a vested right to the security. Vested indicates that the right to receive the equity instrument is not contingent on the achievement or maintenance of any requirement. Restricted equity shares are reported at fair value, the amount that third parties would pay for similar shares. Nonvested shares or share units are measured at fair value as if vested on the date of grant. A share unit allows the right of the holder of the share unit to convert the unit into a specified number of shares of the company issuing the share unit.

An award of share-based instruments may contain a reload feature or contingent features may be included in the award plan. A reload option is the automatic granting of additional options when previously granted options are exercised using equity shares of the entity instead of cash for the amount of the exercise price. The number of options issued in the reload feature generally are equal to the shares used in the exercise of the previously issued options. A share-based payment award may contain a contingent feature where the employee returns to the employer equity shares earned or the gains from shares sold for consideration that is less than fair value on the date of the return. In some cases, there is no consideration provided to the employee for the contingent feature. An example is a clawback feature where the employee takes a position with a competitor and returns any share-based payments to the former employer. Contingent features in share-based awards are not considered in the computation of the grant-date fair value of the awards, but are considered only when the contingent event occurs.

When a nonpublic company cannot estimate the fair value of share-based payments on the date of grant because of the inability to estimate the expected volatility of the stock price, the nonpublic company should determine the expected volatility of the stock using something other than the stock price volatility. The nonpublic company should estimate the grant-date fair value using a value computed using the volatility on a historical basis from an industry sector that is appropriate for the situation.

When it is not possible to estimate the fair value of the share-based payments because of the complexity of the terms of the equity instruments, the intrinsic model should be applied to such options. The options should be remeasured each balance sheet date until exercised or settled. The entity should continue to use the intrinsic model even if later the company decides it is possible to estimate fair value. Compensation cost each accounting period is based on the change in the intrinsic value and any amount reported based on the requisite service period. Once the service period is complete any compensation cost is equal to the change in the intrinsic value. Total compensation cost under the intrinsic model is the excess of the fair value of the stock over the option price. The final measure of compensation cost is the intrinsic value on the date of settlement.

Once fair value of the share options have been determined, the total compensation cost is computed, the requisite service period is determined, and the total compensation cost is amortized over the requisite service period. The total compensation cost is the fair value of the share options times the number of options for which the required service has been provided. Therefore, the initial estimate of compensation cost is based on the number of options less an estimate of the number of forfeitures. For example, if the share award is for 1,000,000 options with an expected forfeiture rate of 2% per year, the number of options that would be used in the estimate of compensation expense is 980,000 options (1,000,000 × .98). Assuming the grant-date fair value of each option is $10, the total estimated compensation expense is $9,800,000 (980,000 options × $10). If new information indicates that the forfeiture estimate needs to be changed, the change is accounted for as a change in estimate and the impact of the change is reported in the accounting period when the change is made. When an entity has a performance condition tied to a share-based award, the determination of total compensation cost is based on whether it is probable that the performance goal will be achieved. If it is probable that the goal will be achieved, the compensation cost should reflect the performance goal. However, if it is not probable that the performance goal will be achieved, the performance goal is not reflected in the computation of total compensation cost. Probable as used in the situation is the same probable concept reflected in ASC 450. To illustrate a performance goal or condition, assume that specific employees will receive 1,000 share options if the market price of the company stock increases by 5% over a two-year period, and will receive 2,000 share options if the market price increases by 10% over the same time period. The entity must determine if it is probable that the stock will increase by less than 5%, more than 5%, but less than 10% or more than 10% and incorporate this decision into the computation of the compensation cost by adjusting the number of share options used in the computation.

Once the total compensation cost is computed, it is amortized over the requisite service period. The requisite service period is the period of time that employees provide service in return for the share-based award. If the award is based only on a service condition, the requisite service period is assumed to be the vesting period. Generally the vesting period is the requisite service period; however, the vesting period could differ from the service period in some circumstances.

The service period may be explicit, implicit, or derived, and an award plan may have one or more of the different types of service periods. For accounting purposes, however, there can only be one service period unless the service period of the award plan is treated as an in-substance multiple award plan. An award plan with an explicit service period is a service period that is stated in the plan. For example, if an award plan states that the options in an award plan vest after four years of continuous service from the date of grant, the service period of four years is considered stated in the agreement and the award plan has an explicit service period of four years. An implicit service period is a service period that is not explicitly stated in the award plan, but can be inferred by reviewing the award plan agreement. For example, if an option in an award plan vest when a new airplane is certified and it is probable that the new airplane will be certified in three years, the implicit service period is three years. A derived service period, a service period tied to an award plan that contains a market condition, is inferred from the application of the valuation models when estimating grant-date fair value. To illustrate, assume that employees can exercise options awarded in a share-based award plan if the market price of the related stock increases by 30% over a four-year period of time. The service period for this award must be inferred from the valuation model used in determining the grant-date fair value of the options. If the derived service period is four years, the total compensation expense is reported over the four-year time period, unless the market condition is satisfied at a date prior to the end of the four-year time period.

The requisite service period begins at the service inception date, and total compensation cost is amortized to accounting periods over the service period beginning at the service inception date. The service inception date is the date that the required service period begins. The date of grant is defined as the date that the employee and the employer reach a mutual agreement as to the substantive terms of the award plan. In addition, it can also be defined as the date that the employee starts to benefit from the plan (i.e., the date the employee will be impacted by the change in the price of the equity shares of the employer). Generally, the service inception date is the date of grant. However, the service inception date may be prior to or subsequent to the date of grant of the award plan. The service inception date is prior to the date of grant when the following conditions are met: share-based award plan has been authorized, employee service starts prior to an understanding of the key conditions and terms, and one of the following conditions is satisfied: no substantive service is required subsequent to the grant date or there is a market or performance condition, that if not satisfied prior to the date of grant, will result in the forfeiture of the share-based award. To illustrate a service inception date that is prior to the date of grant, assume that on January 1, 20X6, an entity states that it will award an employee 2,000 fully vested share options on January 1, 20X7 with the exercise price equal to the market price on January 1, 20X7. All approvals for the award plan were obtained on January 1, 20X6 and the employee is not required to be employed after January 1, 20X7 to receive the award. The service inception date is January 1, 20X6 and the service period is one year and all compensation expense is reported in 20X6. When the service inception date precedes the date of grant, any compensation cost reported prior to the date of grant is based on the fair value of the share-based award on the reporting date. Cumulative compensation cost is adjusted in the accounting period that contains the date of grant based on the grant-date fair value computation of the share-based payment.

Once the total compensation expense is computed and the requisite service period is determined, the total compensation expense is amortized over the service period generally using a straight-line method. However, when an award plan with only a service condition provides for a graded vesting period, an entity may elect one of the following methods of amortization of total compensation expense: straight-line method over the required service period for each vesting part of the award as if the award is a multiple award or straight-line method over the service period of the entire award. An example of graded vesting award plan would be 30% of the awards vest at the end of the first year, 30% vest at the end of the second year, and the remaining 40% vest at the end of the third year. Assuming that an entity elected the first method of amortization, the total compensation cost for the 30% of the share-based award for year 1 is amortized all to year 1. The 30% that vests in year 2 is amortized to year 1 and year 2, and the 40% that vests in year 3 is amortized to year 1, year 2, and year 3. When an entity elects the second method of amortization, compensation expense for all three years is totaled and the total is amortized over the three-year time period using a straight-line method. Compensation expense amortized in prior accounting periods is not reversed if the employee receiving the share-based award fails to exercise the award once the employee provides the required service. For example, assume that an employee has options to purchase 100,000 shares of stock at $10 per share and the required service period is three years. In addition, assume that the required three-year service period is provided by the employee and compensation is reported over the three-year time period. The market price of the stock falls below the $10 exercise price and the employee does not exercise the options by the end of the expiration date. The compensation expense reported by the company for the three-year service period is not reversed as a result of the employee not exercising the options.

A share-based payment award with an exercise price denominated in the currency of a market in which a substantial portion of the company's equity securities trades shall not be considered to contain a condition that is not market, performance, or service condition. The award should not be classified as a liability if it otherwise qualifies for equity classification.

Share-Based Payment Plans Classified as Liabilities—General Discussion

A share-based award or stock plan may be classified as a liability instead of equity. When determining whether an award is a liability or equity, the substantive terms of the share-based award and any related agreements should be used. The written plan typically provides the best information as to the substantive terms; however, past practice must be reviewed to determine whether past practice causes the substantive terms to differ from the written plan. To illustrate, assume that an entity provides selected employees stock appreciation rights (SARs), which is a form of a variable or performance driven award plan where the total cost to the entity is unknown until the rights are actually exercised by the employee. The award plan specifies that the designated employees receive in cash the excess of the price of the company's stock over a predetermined (target) price using a designated number of shares. The predetermined price is usually the price of the stock on the date of grant. The employees are not receiving the base shares, but only a cash settlement based on the appreciation in price of the stock over the predetermined price, times the number of shares in the base at the time of exercise. Should the price of the stock fall below the predetermined price, the employees would receive nothing. In this case, the written plan and the substantive plan are the same and the award plan is classified as a liability. However, assume that the company grants a tandem plan of SARs where the employer can either settle in stock or cash. If the employee has the option to receive cash or stock, the award plan is classified as a liability, but if the choice is determined by the employer, the award plan generally is classified as equity because the employer can avoid transferring cash to the employee by settling the award in stock, unless past practice indicates cash settlement. When the employer generally settles awards in cash, the substantive plan indicates that the award plan should be classified as a liability. When making the decision of whether the substantive plan should be classified as equity or a liability, the company should consider the following: does it have the ability to provide the shares and if a contingent event occurs, does the company have to pay cash.

Generally, ASC 718 does not provide guidance as to what types of securities are classified as liabilities, but refers readers to other generally accepted accounting principles. For example, if a freestanding financial instrument is provided to employees in a share-based award plan, ASC 480-10 should be used to determine if the freestanding financial instruments is classified as a liability or equity. A callable or puttable share-based employee award plan is classified as a liability only if one of the following conditions is met: it is probable that the employee will be prevented by the employer from bearing the risk and rewards of ownership of the share for a reasonable period of time from the date that the share is issued or, for a reasonable period of time from the date that the share is issued and the service period is provided, the repurchase option prevents the employee from bearing the risks and rewards of ownership. An entity must classify options and similar instruments in a share-based award plan as liabilities when the underlying shares are classified as liabilities or the entity can be required to transfer cash or assets to settle the option. A share-based award that is indexed to a factor other than share price when the factor is not a service, market, or performance condition is classified as a liability. The factor or condition should be used when computing the fair value of the share-based award. A factor or condition that meets this requirement is a share-based award where the exercise price is indexed to the price of silver. A broker-assisted cashless exercise of a share-based award is not classified as a liability if the share-based award is normally classified as equity and the following two conditions are met: (1) there is a valid exercise of the options and (2) the legal owner of the shares subject to the options is the employee (this condition would be met even if the exercise price has not been paid by the employee prior to the sale). A broker-assisted cashless exercise is the exercise of the options by the employee and the sale of the shares by a broker at the same time. The broker pays the company for the exercise of the options and remits the remaining amount to the employees.

The measurement objective and approach to measurement of the share-based awards classified as liabilities is the same as discussed above for share-based awards classified as equity. However, the measurement date for share-based awards classified as liabilities is the settlement date instead of the date of grant. Consequently, the awards are remeasured at the end of each accounting period (balance sheet date) until the settlement date has been reached. A public company must measure the share-based liability using the fair value of the award by applying the same measurement procedures described above for share-based awards classified as equity. These same measurement procedures are reapplied at the end of each accounting period until settlement. Total and annual compensation expense for liability share-based awards is determined using the same procedures as for equity share-based awards discussed in the previous section, with one exception. The annual compensation expense is based on the change or a part of the change in the fair value of the award plan based on the remeasurement of the plan each accounting period. A nonpublic entity with share-based awards classified as liabilities can elect to either use the fair value method as discussed above for public companies or the intrinsic method when determining the amount of compensation cost. The intrinsic method computes the amount of compensation cost as the excess of the fair value of the stock over the exercise price. To illustrate, assume that a company grants to employees 100,000 SARs with a target price of $10. At the end of the accounting period, the stock price is $15. Compensation cost per SAR is $5 ($15-$10) and total compensation cost is $500,000 ($5 × 100,000 SARs). Compensation cost is remeasured at the end of each accounting period until settlement date. Time periods for amortization and methods of amortization except for the remeasurement and changes in fair value or intrinsic value for share-based awards classified as liabilities are the same as discussed above for share-based awards classified as equity.

Share-Based Compensation—Additional Considerations

U.S. tax law allows certain deductions for share-based compensation cost when computing federal tax liability. This deduction for share-based awards classified as equity is usually based on the intrinsic value of the award (excess of the selling price of the stock over the option price at a specified time period). The time period for the deduction and the amount of the deduction differs from the timing and amount of the deduction for financial accounting purposes. This cumulative difference in timing results in a deductible temporary difference equal to the amount deducted for financial accounting purposes and the tax impact of the deductible temporary difference gives rise to a deferred tax asset. Any increase or decrease in the temporary difference is reported in the income statement in the accounting period of the change. When recognition of compensation expense for financial accounting purposes does not result in a tax deduction, no temporary difference is reported and no deferred tax asset is recognized. When the share-based award is classified as a liability, the deductible temporary difference is based on the cumulative compensation cost reported for financial accounting purposes. An entity must evaluate the realizability of the deferred tax asset created for the cumulative compensation cost to determine the need for a valuation allowance account for the deferred tax asset. However, the difference between the temporary difference based on the preceding discussion and the tax deduction that would result using the current fair value of the equity shares is not used in the computation of the deferred tax asset or in the determination of the need for a valuation allowance account. When the compensation deduction reported on the tax return exceeds the compensation cost deduction reported for financial accounting purposes, the excess is reported as additional paid-in-capital. Any excess of a realized tax benefit in excess of the deferred tax asset is reported in the income statement only when the excess relates to circumstances other than an increase in the fair value of the stock from the financial accounting measurement date and the later tax measurement date. If the amount of compensation cost reported for financial accounting purposes exceeds the amount reported for tax purposes, the reduction in the deferred tax asset related to this difference is first used to offset any increase in additional paid-in-capital from the excess of tax deductions over financial accounting deductions previously reported. Any excess of the deferred tax asset reduction not used as a reduction to paid-in-capital is then reported in the income statement. When an entity is permitted to use the intrinsic method, the amount that is allowed as an offset is equal to the amount of net excess tax benefits that would have been computed if ASC 718 had been used.

Share-based equity instruments granted to employees are considered potential common shares when computing diluted earnings per share, and the treasury stock method should be applied to such securities. The number of share-based awards is based on the number granted and not forfeited.

In some situations, an employer may modify the terms of a share-based equity award. Any modification of the terms or conditions of the equity award is accounted for as an exchange of a new award for the existing award. It is assumed that the company repurchases the existing equity award by replacing it with a new award that is equal to or greater in value than the original award. Therefore, the company will incur additional compensation cost for any increase in value. Modifications of equity instruments should be accounted for as follows: any incremental compensation cost is determined as the excess of the fair value of the new award compared to the fair value of the original award measured just prior to its modification, total compensation cost is equal to the grant date fair value of the award for the service period that is expected to be satisfied and the incremental cost from the modification, and when an entity uses the intrinsic method, the change in compensation cost is measured by comparing the intrinsic value after the modification with the intrinsic value of the original award measured just prior to the modification. A short-term inducement is accounted for as a modification of terms for only the employees that accept the inducement. All other inducements are modifications of terms of all awards that are subject to the modification. Changes in the terms of equity awards or exchanges of share options in an equity restructuring or business combination are classified as modification of terms. Cancellation of an award with a concurrent grant of a replacement award is accounted for as a modification of the terms of the award that is cancelled. When an award is cancelled and there is no concurrent grant of a replacement award, the transaction is accounted for as a repurchase for no consideration and any unamortized compensation cost is reported at the date of repurchase.

When an entity repurchases an equity award, the cash or other assets used in the repurchase is charged to equity when the amount paid for the repurchase does not exceed the fair value of the equity instruments on the date of repurchase. When the repurchase price exceeds the fair value of the award, the excess is accounted for as compensation cost. When an entity repurchases an equity award prior to the time that the required service period has been satisfied, the unamortized compensation cost should be recognized at the date of repurchase.

Share-Based Payment Plans—Technical Considerations

Six examples are used to illustrate the technical aspects of share-based plans. Assumptions for Example 7-22 are as follows.

Example 7-22
Assumptions for Noncompensatory Stock Plan

1. On September 1, 20X6, Micro Enterprises, a December 31 year-end company, gave all its full-time employees the opportunity to buy 2,000 shares of its $5 par value common stock at a price that is 4% less than the market price of the stock on the purchase date.
2. The stock had to be purchased by September 25, 20X6. The market price of the stock on September 25 was $60.
3. Employees that enrolled in the plan could cancel their enrollment prior to September 25 and receive a full refund for any money paid in for the stock purchase.
4. Employees purchased 25,000 shares of common stock under the award or option plan by September 25.

The stock plan qualifies as noncompensatory because the following conditions are met:

1. Each full-time employee may buy 2,000 shares of stock.
2. The time period for exercise of the option is less than 31 days.
3. The exercise or purchase price is based on the market price of the stock, and employees may cancel enrollment in the plan prior to the stock purchase date.
4. The exercise or purchase price is discounted less than 5% from the market price of the stock on the date of purchase.

A journal entry is not required to show issuance of the options, but is required to reflect exercise of the options or purchase of the stock. Before the entry is made, the proceeds that will be received by the enterprise upon purchase of the 25,000 shares of stock (exercise of the options) under the award plan must be computed:

Market price of stock on purchase date	$60.00
Discount on stock ($60.00 × 4%)	(2.40)
Purchase price	$57.60
Number of shares purchased	25,000
Proceeds from award plan	$1,440,000

The receipt of the $1,440,000 proceeds and issuance of the common stock should be recorded. Common stock and paid-in capital are recorded at $125,000

($5 par value × 25,000 shares) and $1,315,000 ($1,440,000 – $125,000), respectively. The entry to record exercise of the award plan is presented as follows:

Cash	1,440,000	
Common Stock		125,000
Paid-in Capital in Excess of Par		1,315,000

This completes the discussion of noncompensatory stock plans in Example 7-22. To illustrate the accounting and reporting requirements for a share-based payment plan classified as a liability where the company qualifies to use the intrinsic method, the assumptions in Example 7-23 are used.

Example 7-23
Assumptions for Award Plan Classified as a Liability

1. Peterson Enterprises (Peterson), a non-public December 31 year-end company, offered an award plan that requires a cash settlement to four key management personnel on January 1, 20X6. The award plan gives the employees the right to share in stock appreciation (stock appreciation rights (SARs)) on 100,000 shares of common stock above a predetermined or target price.
2. The target price is $20, the market price of the stock on January 1, 20X6, the date of grant. The rights associated with the award plan can be exercised any time after December 31, 20X8, the date the rights are fully vested. The 100,000 SARs were actually exercised on December 31, 2010, and cash was paid to the employees for the difference between the market price of the stock and the target price of $20.
3. Peterson qualifies for and has elected to use the intrinsic method of accounting for the share-based payments. There were no forfeitures during the vesting period, and the example assumes no income tax implications.
4. The award plan expires on December 31, 2011. Quoted market prices of the common stock of Peterson are as follows:

   December 31, 20X6—$26

   December 31, 20X7—$32

   December 31, 20X8—$23

   December 31, 20X9—$35

   December 31, 2010—$40

   December 31, 2011—$45

The first step in the analysis of the assumptions in Example 7-23 is to determine the service period. Because the awards cliff vest at the end of three years, there is an explicit required service period of three years. In addition, because all the awards vest, there are no forfeitures to consider in the computation of the total compensation cost and share-based liability. Next, the compensation cost and share-based liability adjustment are computed for each accounting period until the awards are exercised using the intrinsic method. Compensation cost under the intrinsic method is computed as the excess of the selling price of the stock over the target price.

Because the service period is three years, one-third of the compensation expense is amortized each year. The compensation expense per option or SAR is computed as the difference between the balance sheet date market price and the target price. For example, at the end of 20X6, compensation expense per option is $6 ($26 market price – $20 target price). Next, the total number of SARs that are expected to vest multiplied by the compensation expense per SAR is the estimated total compensation expense at the end of that specific year. In this example, the company estimates that all SARs will vest, so 100,000 SARs are used in the initial computation. Because all 100,000 vested, no adjustment to compensation expense or liability for forfeitures is required subsequent to the grant date. All the rights were exercised on December 31, 2010; therefore, compensation expense and an estimated liability for the SARs is computed for the years 20X6–2010. The computation is presented in Table 7-58.

Table 7-58 Computation of Compensation Expense and Liability for Share-Based Plan Classified as a Liability

(a)	(b)	(c)	(d)=(b)–(c)	(e)	(f)=(d)×(e)	(g)	(h)=(f)×(g)	(i)	(j)=(h)–(i)
Year	Market Price on Balance Date[1]	Predetermined Price[2]	Excess	Number of Shares[3]	Total	Fraction Accrued[4]	Balance That Should Be in Liability	Balance in Liability Account[5]	Increase/ (Decrease) in Liability and Expense
20X6	$26	$20	$6	100,000	$600,000	1/3	$200,000	$0	$200,000
20X7	32	20	12	100,000	1,200,000	2/3	800,000	200,000	600,000
20X8	23	20	3	100,000	300,000	3/3	300,000	800,000	(500,000)
20X9	35	20	15	100,000	1,500,000	3/3	1,500,000	300,000	1,200,000
2010	40	20	20	100,000	2,000,000	3/3	2,000,000	1,500,000	500,000

1 Information taken from Example 7-23, Assumption 4.
2 Information taken from Example 7-23, Assumption 2.
3 Information taken from Example 7-23, Assumption 1.
4 Computed from three-year service period as follows: 1/3 for first year, 2/3 for second year, and 3/3 for third year.
5 Amount is balance from the prior year in the column titled, "Balance That Should Be in Liability."

In Table 7-58, column (g), the service period ends in 20X8. After the end of the service period, any change in the market price of the stock before exercise is recognized in total in the year of change. Also, the balance in the liability account in column (i) is taken from the prior year balance in column (h).

Using the information from Table 7-58, journal entries for 20X6–2010 to recognize accrual of the compensation expense and payment to the employees are presented below:

20X6

Estimated Compensation Expense	200,000	
Estimated Liability for Share-Based Award		200,000

20X7

Estimated Compensation Expense	600,000	
Estimated Liability for Share-Based Award		600,000

20X8		
Estimated Liability for Share-Based Award	500,000	
Estimated Compensation Expense		500,000
20X9		
Estimated Compensation Expense	1,200,000	
Estimated Liability for Share-Based Award		1,200,000
2010		
Estimated Compensation Expense	500,000	
Estimated Liability for Share-Based Award		500,000
Estimated Liability for Share-Based Award	2,000,000	
Cash		2,000,000

At the end of 2010, when the stock appreciation rights are exercised, there is a $2,000,000 balance in the liability account. This liability account is reduced by the $2,000,000 cash payment to the employees. The estimated liability for the share-based award plan is classified in the balance sheet as current or long-term, depending upon when it is estimated to be paid. The liability is current if it is expected to be paid within one year or within the normal operating cycle, whichever is longer. Otherwise, the estimated liability is classified as long-term.

The first example on cash award plans assumed that there were no forfeitures of SARs prior to the vesting date. Because it was assumed that no forfeitures would occur during the vesting period, and because none occurred, no adjustments to compensation expense or liability were required. The information in Example 7-24 is used to illustrate the proper accounting for forfeitures.

Example 7-24
Assumptions for Award Plan Classified as a Liability

1. The Jones Company (Jones), a December 31 year-end company, offered a share-based award plan that requires a cash settlement to four key management personnel on January 1, 20X6. The award plan give the employees the right to share in stock appreciation (stock appreciation right (SARs)) on 100,000 shares of common stock above a predetermined target price of $20, the market price of the stock on January 1, 20X6.
2. The rights associated with the award plan can be exercised any time after December 31, 20X8, the date the rights are fully vested. The SARs cliff vest at the end of the three-year time period. The 100,000 SARs were actually exercised on December 31, 2010 and cash was paid to the employees for the difference between the market price of the stock and the target price of $20. The market price of the stock on the date of exercise was $40.
3. On the date of grant, Jones estimates that the requisite service will be provided for all of the SARs except for 15,000 (85,000 is expected to vest). In 20X7, 10,000 of the SARs were forfeited and it is estimated that no additional SARs will be forfeited.
4. An appropriate option pricing model was used to compute the fair value of the SARs. The following fair values were computed:

Date of Grant—$10
December 31, 20X6—6
December 31, 20X7—12
December 31, 20X8—3
December 31, 20X9—15
December 31, 2010—20

5. Jones has a 40% tax rate.

The first step in the analysis of the assumptions in Example 7-24 is to determine the service period. Because the awards cliff vest at the end of three years, there is an explicit required service period of three years. In addition, because 15,000 of the SARs are expected to be forfeited, only 85,000 SARs are used in the computation of the total compensation cost and share-based liability. Using the grant-date fair value of the SARs, the total fair value of the SARs on the date of grant is $850,000 ($10 grant-date fair value × 85,000 SARs). The 20X6 compensation cost is based on the 85,000 SARs because it is assumed that 15,000 of the SARs will be forfeited. In 20X7, 10,000 SARs were actually forfeited and it is expected that no additional SARs will be forfeited. Therefore, for 20X6–2010, computation of compensation cost is based on 90,000 SARs. The SARs are revalued using an appropriate option pricing model each balance sheet date until the date of exercise. Annual compensation cost is based on the revalued SARs. The company has a 40% tax rate and deferred taxes are increased or decreased each accounting period based on the tax impact of the compensation cost. On December 31, 2010 when the market price of the stock is $40, the 90,000 SARs were exercised. Table 7-59 shows the computation of compensation cost and share-based liability adjustment for each accounting period until the awards are exercised using the end-of-period SAR value.

Table 7-59 Computation of Compensation Expense and Liability for Share-Based Plan Classified as a Liability

(a) Year	(b) Fair Value of Award on Balance Sheet Date	(c) Number of Shares[1]	(d)=(b)×(c) Total	(e) Fraction Accrued[2]	(f)=(d)×(e) Balance That Should Be in Liability	(g) Balance in Liability Account[3]	(h)=(f)–(g) Increase/ (Decrease) in Liability and Expense
20X6	$6	85,000	$510,000	1/3	$170,000	$0	$170,000
20X7	12	90,000	1,080,000	2/3	720,000	170,000	550,000
20X8	3	90,000	270,000	3/3	270,000	720,000	(450,000)
20X9	15	90,000	1,350,000	3/3	1,350,000	270,000	1,080,000
2010	20	90,000	1,800,000	3/3	1,800,000	1,350,000	450,000

[1] Information taken from Example 7-24, Assumptions 2 and 3.
[2] Computed from three-year service period as follows: 1/3 for first year, 2/3 for second year, and 3/3 for third year.
[3] Amount is balance from the prior year in the column titled, "Balance That Should Be in Liability."

Using the information from Table 7-59, journal entries for 20X6–2010 to recognize accrual of the compensation cost, tax impact, and payment to the employees is presented below.

20X6		
Estimated Compensation Expense	170,000	
Estimated Liability for Share-Based Awards		170,000
Deferred Tax Asset	68,000	
Deferred Tax Benefit		68,000
$170,000 × 40% Tax Rate = $68,000.		
20X7		
Estimated Compensation Expense	550,000	
Estimated Liability for Share-Based Awards		550,000
Deferred Tax Asset	220,000	
Deferred Tax Benefit		220,000
$550,000 × 40% Tax Rate = $220,000.		
20X8		
Estimated Liability for Share-Based Awards	450,000	
Estimated Compensation Expense		450,000
Deferred Tax Benefit	180,000	
Deferred Tax Asset		180,000
$450,000 × 40% Tax Rate = $180,000		
20X9		
Estimated Compensation Expense	1,080,000	
Estimated Liability for Share-Based Awards		1,080,000
Deferred Tax Asset	432,000	
Deferred Tax Benefit		432,000
$1,080,000 × 40% Tax Rate = $432,000.		
2010		
Estimated Compensation Expense	450,000	
Estimated Liability for Share-Based Awards		450,000
Deferred Tax Asset	180,000	
Deferred Tax Benefit		180,000
$450,000 × 40% Tax Rate = $180,000.		
Estimated Liability for Share-Based Awards	1,800,000	
Cash		1,800,000
Deferred Tax Expense	720,000	
Deferred Tax Asset		720,000
$1,800,000 × 40% Tax Rate = $720,000.		
Taxes Payable	720,000	
Tax Expense		720,000

At the end of 2010 when the stock appreciation rights are exercised, there is a $1,800,000 balance in the liability account. This liability account is reduced by the $1,800,000 cash payment to the employees. The $720,000 balance in the deferred tax asset account is reversed because there is no longer a temporary difference between the book and the tax share-based liability balance. In addition, taxes payable and tax expense is reduced by the tax effect of the $1,800,000 cash payment because the payment is deductible for tax purposes.

This completes the discussion of award plans classified as liabilities. The next section covers employee award plans involving the distribution of equity securities. Assumptions for Example 7-25 are as follows.

Example 7-25
Assumptions for Share-Based Award Classified as Equity

1. Jackson Enterprises, a December 31 year-end company, granted 400,000 share-based options to several top management personnel on January 1, 20X6. Under the share-based plan, those employees may purchase 400,000 shares of $5 par value common stock at $40 per share any time after December 31, 20X9 through December 31, 2013.
2. The market price of the stock on January 1, 20X6 is $40, the vesting period is four years, the life of the options is eight years, and the average number of forfeitures each year is estimated at 8,000. Actual forfeitures were as follows: 20X6—6,000, 20X7—9,000, 20X8—10,000, and 20X9—6,000. All of the options cliff vest on December 31, 20X9, four years after the date of grant.
3. Assume that the fair value of each option on the date of grant (January 1, 20X6) was $15, and assume that the $15 fair value was computed using an appropriate option pricing model.
4. On September 1, 2011, 359,000 options were exercised when the market price of the stock was $65. The remaining 10,000 options expired unexercised on December 31, 2013, the expiration date of the options. Assume income taxes for purposes of this example is 40% for current and future periods.

The first step in the analysis is to determine the grant-date fair value of the options using an appropriate option pricing model. In this example, $15 was computed as the fair value of each option on the date of grant using an option pricing model. The next step is to determine the number of options for which the requisite service will be provided (number of options that are expected to vest). Because 8,000 options are expected to be forfeited each year over the next four years, 32,000 (8,000 options × 4 years) total options are estimated to be forfeited over the four-year time period. Therefore, total compensation cost for the share-based plan is initially computed using the grant date fair value of $15 times 368,000 options (400,000 total options – 32,000 options expected to vest). Total compensation cost is initially computed as $5,520,000 ($15 × 368,000 options). Next, the requisite service period must be determined. Because all the options cliff vest at the end of four years, there is an explicit required service period of four years. Therefore, 25% of the $5,520,000 compensation expense, or $1,380,000, is amortized in 20X6. In 20X7, compensation expense of $1,380,000 is equal to 50% of the total compensation cost less the amount computed for 20X6 ($2,760,000 – $1,380,000). This procedure is continued until the service period ends. Because Jackson Enterprises' estimate of the number of forfeitures remained the same during the entire service period, a change in accounting estimate was not required. However, in the last year of the service period, the actual forfeitures differed from the estimated forfeitures by 1,000 options, and the number of options and the compensation expense for 20X9 is adjusted for the change. The compensation expense in years 20X6–20X8 is not changed for the change in estimate.

Table 7-60 Computation of Compensation Expense and Equity Balance

(a) Year	(b) Fair Value of Option on Grant Date[1]	(c) Number of Options[2]	(d) Adjustments for Forfeitures	(e)=(c)−(d) Adjusted Number of Options	(f)=(b)×(e) Total Compensation Expense	(g) Percentage of Amortization[4]	(h)=(f)×(g) Balance That Should Be in Equity	(i) Balance in Equity Account[5]	(j)=(h)−(i) Increase/ (Decrease) in Equity and Expense
20X6	$15	368,000	0	368,000	$5,520,000	25	$1,380,000	$ 0	$1,380,000
20X7	15	368,000	0	368,000	5,520,000	50	2,760,000	1,380,000	1,380,000
20X8	15	368,000	0	368,000	5,520,000	75	4,140,000	2,760,000	1,380,000
20X9	15	368,000	1,000[3]	369,000	5,535,000	100	5,535,000	4,140,000	1,395,000

[1] Information taken from Example 7-25, Assumption 3.

[2] 368,000 = 400,000 options granted – 32,000 estimated forfeitures (8,000 forfeitures per year × 4 years).

[3] 1,000 = 32,000 estimated forfeitures – 31,000 actual forfeitures (6,000 + 9,000 + 10,000 + 6,000). See Example 7-26, Assumption 2.

[4] Computed from four-year service period as follows: = 25%, = 50%, = 75%, and = 100%.

[5] Amount is the balance from the prior year in the column titled, "Balance That Should Be in Equity."

The compensation cost reported for financial accounting purposes, at this point, represents a deductible temporary difference for purposes of deferred tax computations. Because Jackson Enterprises has a current and future tax rate of 40%, a deferred tax asset is established each accounting period for an amount equal to the compensation cost times the amount of the change in the share-based equity balance. Table 7-60 shows the computation of the annual compensation cost and the balance in the stockholders' equity account. Computation of the amount of deferred tax is presented below the related journal entry.

Using the information from Table 7-60, journal entries for amortization of the annual compensation cost over the four-year service period and for the deferred tax computation are presented.

December 31, 20X6

Estimated Compensation Expense	1,380,000	
Common Stock Options—Share-Based Awards		1,380,000
Deferred Tax Asset	552,000	
Deferred Tax Benefit		552,000

$1,380,000 × 40% Tax Rate = $552,000.

December 31, 20X7

Estimated Compensation Expense	1,380,000	
Common Stock Options—Share-Based Awards		1,380,000
Deferred Tax Asset	552,000	
Deferred Tax Benefit		552,000

$1,380,000 × 40% Tax Rate = $552,000.

December 31, 20X8

Estimated Compensation Expense	1,380,000	
Common Stock Options—Share-Based Awards		1,380,000
Deferred Tax Asset	552,000	
Deferred Tax Benefit		552,000

$1,380,000 × 40% Tax Rate = $552,000.

December 31, 20X9

Estimated Compensation Expense	1,395,000	
Common Stock Options—Share-Based Awards		1,395,000
Deferred Tax Asset	558,000	
Deferred Tax Benefit		558,000

$1,395,000 × 40% Tax Rate = $552,000.

On September 1, 2011, employees exercised 359,000 of the options by paying Jackson Enterprises $40 per share. The entry to record that exercise is presented as follows:

September 1, 2011

Cash	14,360,000[a]	
Common Stock Options Outstanding—Share-Based Award	5,385,000[b]	
Common Stock		1,795,000[c]
Paid-in Capital in Excess of Par		17,950,000[d]

[a] $40 exercise price × 359,000 shares issued = $14,360,000.
[b] $15 fair value of option × 359,000 options = $5,385,000.
[c] $5 par value × 359,000 number of shares issued = $1,795,000.
[d] $14,360,000 + $5,385,000 – $1,795,000 = $17,950,000.

In addition to the entry for the actual exercise of the share-based award, entries are required to remove the deferred tax asset balance, the tax impact of the exercise, and the impact on additional paid-in capital. Table 7-61 shows the computation of all items needed for the tax entries related to the exercise of 359,000 share-based awards.

Table 7-61 Computation of Amounted Deducted for Tax Purposes and Reduction in Deferred Tax Asset from Exercise of Options

Amount Deducted for Tax Purposes	
Number of share-based awards that vested (Table 7-60)	369,000
Number of share-based awards not exercised (Assumption 4)	10,000
Number of share-based awards exercised	359,000
Difference between market price on date of exercise and exercise price ($65 – $40).	$25
Total expense deducted for tax purposes	$8,975,000
Tax rate (Assumption 4)	40%
Tax impact of exercise	$3,590,000
Amount of Reduction in Deferred Tax Asset Account	
Number of options exercised (from above)	359,000
Grant-date fair value (Assumption 3)	$15
Temporary differences	$5,385,000
Tax rate (Assumption 4)	40%
Reduction in deferred tax from exercise	$2,154,000

Amount of Adjustment to Paid-in Capital from Exercise of Share-Based Award	
Tax impact of exercise	$3,590,000
Reduction in deferred tax from exercise	2,154,000
Adjustment to paid-in capital	$1,436,000

Using the information from Table 7-61, the following entries are required at September 1, 2011 to show removal of the deferred tax asset and the tax impact of the exercise.

Deferred Tax Expense	2,154,000	
Deferred Tax Asset		2,154,000
Taxes Payable	3,590,000	
Tax Expense		2,154,000
Paid-In Capital From Share-Based Plan		1,436,000

At the end of 2013, 10,000 options expired because they had not been exercised. The $150,000 (10,000 expired options × $15 fair value of each option) remaining in the common stock options outstanding account should be transferred into paid-in capital from the expired stock options account to reflect the expiration of the options. In addition, the remaining balance in the deferred tax asset accounting of $60,000 (10,000 share-based awards × $15 grant date fair value = $150,000 × 40% = $60,000) must be removed for the share-based awards that expired. The required journal entries are presented below:

December 31, 2013

Common Stock Options Outstanding	150,000[a]	
Paid-in Capital from Expired Stock Options		150,000
Deferred Tax Expense	60,000	
Deferred Tax Asset		60,000

[a] 10,000 expired options × $15 fair value of options = $150,000.

This completes the analysis of Example 7-25. Example 7-26 covers the proper accounting when an entity offers employees a performance-based share-based award plan. Assumptions for Example 7-26 are as follows.

Example 7-26

Assumptions for Performance-Based Share-Based Award Plan

1. Assume the same information as in Example 7-25, except for the changes below.
2. The number of options to be granted to top management personnel depends on future earnings per share (EPS) during the service period as follows: 200,000 options will be granted if EPS exceeds $2.50, 300,000 options will be granted if EPS exceeds $3.50, and 400,000 options will be granted if EPS exceeds $4.00.
3. On the date of grant, it was probable that EPS would be between $2.50 and $3.00 during the service period. In 20X8, Jackson Enterprises changed its estimate of EPS to be between $3.50 and $3.75 during the remaining service period. During the service period, EPS actually exceeded $3.50, but never exceeded $4.00.

The fair value of each stock option under a performance-driven (variable stock) plan is computed on the date of grant using option pricing models the same as those used for a fixed stock option plan, as illustrated in Example 7-25. Generally, the fair value of the option does not change over the life of the option under a performance-driven plan. The difference in the computation between Example 7-25, using a fixed option plan, and Example 7-26, related to performance-based plans, centers on the number of options used in the computation. Table 7-62 provides computation of compensation expense for the assumptions in Example 7-26. Under the performance-driven plan in this example, the number of options that vest depends upon the company's EPS exceeding a specific amount. Because on the date of grant Jackson Enterprises thinks that it is probable that, during the service period, EPS will range between $2.50 and $3.00, 200,000 options are assumed to be granted under the stock agreement. Next, the 200,000 options assumed to be granted must be adjusted for estimated forfeitures. Therefore, the 200,000 options are adjusted for the 32,000 (8,000 × 4 years) options expected to be forfeited by employees. Of the 200,000 options, 168,000 (200,000 – 32,000) options are used in the computation until 20X8. In 20X8, Jackson Enterprises changed its estimate related to the number of options that will be granted because it was then probable that EPS will be between $3.50 and $3.75. Should this level of EPS be achieved, 300,000 options would be granted, and the number of options to use in the computation of compensation expense in 20X8 will increase to 268,000 (300,000 – 32,000). In 20X9, the end of the service period, the number of actual forfeitures was 1,000 less than estimated; therefore, the number of options used in the computation is increased by 1,000 to 269,000. Information and computations in Table 7-62 are the same as those in Table 7-60, except for the change in the number of options, as discussed above. The journal entries for Example 7-26 are not shown because they are the same as those in Example 7-25 except for the amounts. The reader may wish to review the discussion for Example 7-25, Table 7-60, including the journal entries, before proceeding with the analysis in Table 7-62.

Table 7-62 Computation of Compensation Expense and Equity Balance

(a) Year	(b) Fair Value of Option on Grant Date[1]	(c) Number of Options[2]	(d) Adjustments For Forfeitures	(e)=(c)–(d) Adjusted Number of Options	(f)=(b)×(e) Total Compensation Expense	(g) Percentage of Amortization[4]	(h)=(f)×(g) Balance That Should Be in Equity	(i) Balance in Equity Account[5]	(j)=(h)–(i) Increase/ (Decrease) in Equity and Expense
20X6	$15	168,000	0	168,000	$2,520,000	25	$630,000	$ 0	$630,000
20X7	15	168,000	0	168,000	2,520,000	50	1,260,000	630,000	630,000
20X8	15	268,000	0	268,000	4,020,000	75	3,015,000	1,260,000	1,755,000
20X9	15	268,000	1,000[3]	269,000	4,035,000	100	4,035,000	3,015,000	1,020,000

[1] Information taken from Example 7-25, Assumption 3.

[2] 168,000 = 200,000 options that are assumed to meet earnings requirement – 32,000 estimated forfeitures (8,000 forfeitures per year × 4 years). 268,000 = 300,000 options that now are assumed to meet earnings requirement because of change in estimate – 32,000 estimated forfeitures (8,000 forfeitures per year × 4 years).

[3] 1,000 = 32,000 estimated forfeitures – 31,000 actual forfeitures (6,000 + 9,000 + 10,000 + 6,000). See Example 7-25, Assumption 2.

[4] Computed from four-year service period as follows: 1/4= 25%, 2/4= 50%, 3/4= 75%, and 4/4= 100.

[5] Amount is the balance from the prior year in the column titled, "Balance That Should Be in Equity."

Disclosures

ASC 718-10-50 provides the disclosure requirements for share-based award plans. The disclosures are divided into general guidelines and specific minimum disclosure information. The following disclosures represent the basic general guidelines required for one or more share-based award plans:

1. Nature and terms of the share-based award plan and the impact of the plan on shareholders.
2. Impact on the income statement of compensation cost from share-based payment plans.
3. Method used to estimate fair value of instruments granted or offered to grant or the fair value of goods or services received.
4. Cash flow impact of share-based payment plans.

When an entity acquires goods or services from nonemployees, disclosures similar to those listed in items 1–4, above, should be provided if such disclosures are important to an understanding of the financial results. In addition, when an entity has multiple share-based plans, if the characteristics of the plans are different so that separate disclosures are needed for an understanding of the financial results of the transactions, separate disclosures should be provided.

ASC 718-10-50-2 provides minimum disclosure information for share-based plans that satisfy the general disclosure guidelines listed above, and ASC 718-10-55, paragraphs 134 through 137, provide illustrations of the minimum disclosure requirements. The minimum disclosures are as follows:

1. A general description of the share-based plan with disclosure of award terms such as maximum time period for options that have been granted, number of shares that have been authorized for grants of equity securities, required service period, and other important conditions such as vesting stipulations.
2. For the most recent accounting period that an income statement is presented, the following information should be disclosed:
   a. Number and exercise prices on a weighted-average basis for each of the following share options or share units granted, forfeited, exercised or converted, expired, options that could be exercised or converted at year end, and options outstanding at the beginning and the end of the accounting period.
   b. Grant-date fair value on a weighted-average basis and number of equity securities not covered in 2(a), above, divided into the following categories: securities that are nonvested at the beginning of the year, securities that are nonvested at the end of the year, securities forfeited, securities vested, and securities granted. If the entity is a nonpublic company that uses a calculated amount for fair value or the intrinsic method, the calculated amount or intrinsic value is presented.
3. For each annual accounting period that an income statement is presented, the following information is required:

a. Number and grant-date fair value on a weighted average basis of equity securities granted during the accounting period. If the entity is a nonpublic company that uses a calculated amount for fair value or the intrinsic method, the calculated amount or intrinsic value is presented.

b. The total intrinsic value of the following is required: options exercised or share units converted, share-based liabilities paid, and total fair value of shares that vested during the accounting period.

4. The following disclosures are required for fully vested share options or share units or those that are anticipated to vest by the date of the most recent balance sheet presented:

   a. For options or share units outstanding disclose the number, the exercise price or conversion ratio on a weighted average basis, remaining contractual term on a weighted average basis, and the intrinsic value (excluding nonpublic companies) on an aggregate basis.

   b. For options or share units that are currently exercisable or convertible disclose the number, the exercise price or conversion ratio on a weighted average basis, remaining contractual term on a weighted average basis, and the intrinsic value (excluding nonpublic companies) on an aggregate basis.

5. For each annual accounting period that an income statement is presented, the following information is required (these disclosures are not required for an entity that is allowed to use the intrinsic method under ASC 718:

   a. Description of method and important assumptions used in determining fair value or calculated value of share-based compensation arrangement. The important or significant assumptions should include, if applicable, the following:

      (1) Anticipated term of the award instruments with a discussion of how the entity incorporates the term and employee anticipated exercise and post vesting employment termination behavior into the computation of the valuation.

      (2) Anticipated volatility of the entity's shares and the method used when estimating the volatility. If an entity uses a range of volatility, disclose the range of anticipated volatilities and the weighted average anticipated volatility. When a nonpublic company uses a calculated amount disclosure should be provided as to why it is not practicable to estimate the expected volatility and the industry sector selected, reasons for that selection and how the historical volatility was computed.

      (3) Anticipated dividends and, if different dividend rates are used, the range and weighted-average anticipated dividends should be disclosed.

(4) Risk-free interest rate and if a range of rates are used, disclose the range of rates used.

(5) The discount and the method of estimating the discount for post-vesting restrictions.

6. Disclosures specified in items 1–5 should be provided separately for different types of awards for equity and liability instruments if characteristics of the awards make separate disclosures important.

7. For each annual accounting period that an income statement is provided, the following disclosures are required:

   a. Total compensation cost reported in the income statement, total compensation cost capitalized and total tax benefit recognized that is related to the compensation cost.

   b. Describe any significant modification and include in the description the terms, number of employees impacted, and the total incremental compensation cost resulting from the modification.

8. Total compensation cost for nonvested share-based awards that is unrecognized and the weighted-average period over which the cost will be recognized as of the most recent balance sheet date presented.

9. The amount of cash received from exercise of share-based awards and the tax benefits received from stock options exercised during the annual accounting period, if not disclosed elsewhere.

10. The amount of cash used to settle equity instruments from share-based agreements, if not disclosed elsewhere.

11. Describe the company's policy for issuing shares (such as issuing new shares or using treasury shares) when share options are exercised or when share units are converted. When a company expects to repurchase shares in the next annual accounting period to provide for share option exercise, the company must disclose the estimated number of shares or range of shares to be repurchased.

Employee Stock Ownership Plans (ESOPs)

ASC 718-40 provides the accounting and reporting requirements for employers when accounting for employee stock ownership plans (ESOPs). ASC 718-40 covers leveraged ESOPs, nonleveraged ESOPs, and pension plan asset reversion involving ESOPs. Accounting for leveraged ESOPs covers the following issues: the purchase and release of shares of stock by an ESOP; determination of fair value to use for the ESOP shares; reporting of dividends; share redemption; and interest, debt, and earnings-per-share reporting. Nonleveraged ESOP accounting covered includes the purchase and redemption of shares and dividend and earnings-per-share reporting. ASC 718-40 also covers the accounting for a pension plan asset reversion when assets from the pension plan termination are transferred to an ESOP.

Targeted Guidance for Performance Targets

ASU 2014-12, *Compensation—Stock Compensation (Topic 718): Accounting for Share-Based Payments When the Terms of an Award Provide That a Performance Target Could Be Achieved after the Requisite Service Period,* became effective for all entities for annual periods and interim periods within those annual periods beginning after December 15, 2015, with earlier adoption permitted. The effective date was the same for both public business entities and all other entities.

Entities commonly issue share-based payment awards that require a specific performance target to be achieved in order for employees to become eligible to vest in the awards.

In some cases, the terms of an award may provide that the performance target could be achieved after an employee completes the requisite service period (i.e., the employee would be eligible to vest in the award regardless of whether the employee is rendering service on the date the performance target is achieved).

Prior to ASU 2014-12, there was no explicit guidance on how to account for these types of awards.

Many reporting entities did not reflect the performance target in their estimate of the grant-date fair value of the award; other reporting entities did reflect them in the grant-date fair value of the award.

Under ASU 2014-12, the performance target should not be reflected in estimating the grant-date fair value of the award. Compensation cost should be recognized in the period in which it becomes probable that the performance target will be achieved and should represent the compensation cost attributable to the period(s) for which the requisite service has already been rendered.

Entities are now required to apply ASU 2014-12 to all new or modified awards after its effective date.

Recent Changes

ASU 2016-09, *Compensation—Stock Compensation (Topic 718): Improvements to Employee Share-Based Payment Accounting,* was issued in March 2016 under FASB's simplification initiative.

A summary of the amendments made under ASU 2016-09 follows:

1. All excess income tax benefits and tax deficiencies (including tax benefits of dividends on share-based payment awards) should be recognized in income tax expense or benefit in the income statement. The income tax effects of exercised or vested awards should be treated as discrete items in the reporting period in which they occur.
2. An entity also should recognize excess income tax benefits regardless of whether the benefit reduces income taxes payable in the current period.
3. Excess income tax benefits should be classified along with other income tax cash flows as an operating activity.

4. An entity can make an entity-wide accounting policy election to either estimate the number of awards that are expected to vest (current GAAP) or account for forfeitures when they occur.
5. The threshold to qualify for equity classification permits withholding up to the maximum statutory tax rates in the applicable jurisdictions.
6. Cash paid by an employer when directly withholding shares for tax withholding purposes should be classified as a financing activity.
7. A nonpublic entity can make an accounting policy election to apply a practical expedient to estimate the expected term for all awards with performance or service conditions that meet certain conditions.
8. A nonpublic entity can make a one-time accounting policy election to switch from measuring all liability-classified awards at fair value to intrinsic value.

For public business entities, the amendments in ASU 2016-09 are effective for annual periods beginning after December 15, 2016, and interim periods within those annual periods. For all other entities, the amendments are effective for annual periods beginning after December 15, 2017, and interim periods within annual periods beginning after December 15, 2018. Early adoption is permitted for any entity in any interim or annual period. If an entity early adopts the amendments in an interim period, any adjustments should be reflected as of the beginning of the fiscal year that includes that interim period. An entity that elects early adoption must adopt all of the amendments in the same period. Amendments related to the timing of when excess tax benefits are recognized, minimum statutory withholding requirements, forfeitures, and intrinsic value should be applied using a modified retrospective transition method by means of a cumulative-effect adjustment to equity as of the beginning of the period in which the guidance is adopted. Amendments related to the presentation of employee taxes paid on the statement of cash flows when an employer withholds shares to meet the minimum statutory withholding requirement should be applied retrospectively. Amendments requiring recognition of excess tax benefits and tax deficiencies in the income statement and the practical expedient for estimating expected term should be applied prospectively. An entity may elect to apply the amendments related to the presentation of excess tax benefits on the statement of cash flows using either a prospective transition method or a retrospective transition method.

ASU 2017-09, *Compensation—Stock Compensation (Topic 718): Scope of Modification Accounting,* was issued in May 2017. This ASU provides guidance about which changes to the terms or conditions of a share-based payment award require an entity to apply modification accounting in ASC Topic 718.

An entity should account for the effects of a modification unless all the following are met:

1. The fair value (or calculated value or intrinsic value, if such an alternative measurement method is used) of the modified award is the same as the fair value (or calculated value or intrinsic value, if such an alternative measurement method is used) of the original award immediately

before the original award is modified. If the modification does not affect any of the inputs to the valuation technique that the entity uses to value the award, the entity is not required to estimate the value immediately before and after the modification.

2. The vesting conditions of the modified award are the same as the vesting conditions of the original award immediately before the original award is modified.
3. The classification of the modified award as an equity instrument or a liability instrument is the same as the classification of the original award immediately before the original award is modified.

The current disclosure requirements in ASC Topic 718 apply regardless of whether an entity is required to apply modification accounting under the amendments in this ASU 2017-09.

The amendments in ASU 2017-09 are effective for all entities for annual periods, and interim periods within those annual periods, beginning after December 15, 2017. Early adoption is permitted, including adoption in any interim period, for (1) public business entities for reporting periods for which financial statements have not yet been issued; and (2) all other entities for reporting periods for which financial statements have not yet been made available for issuance.

The amendments in ASY 2017-09 should be applied prospectively to an award modified on or after the adoption date.

Topic 720: Other Expenses

Topic 720, *Other Expenses*, contains the following subtopics:

10 Overall

15 Start-Up Costs

20 Insurance Costs**

25 Contributions Made**

30 Real and Personal Property Taxes

35 Advertising Costs**

40 Electronic Equipment Waste Obligations**

45 Business and Technology Reengineering**

50 Fees Paid to the Federal Government by Pharmaceutical Manufacturers and Health Insurers

908 Airlines*

922 Entertainment—Cable Television*

924 Entertainment—Casinos*

926 Entertainment—Films*

928 Entertainment—Music*

932 Extractive Activities—Oil and Gas*

942 Financial Services—Depository and Lending*

944 Financial Services—Insurance*

948 Financial Services—Mortgage Banking*

952 Franchisors*

954 Health Care Entities*

958 Not-For-Profit Entities*

970 Real Estate—General*

972 Real Estate—Common Interest Realty Associations*

978 Real Estate—Time-Sharing Activities*

* See the corresponding topic in Chapter 9 for coverage of this shared subtopic.

** This topic is not covered in this book.

Overall

Each of the subtopics in the *Other Expenses* topic contains standalone guidance; there is no relationship between the individual subtopics within this *Other Expenses* topic. Each subtopic provides accounting and reporting guidance for the specific type of costs and expenses as indicated by the subtopic title.

Start-Up Costs

Costs of start-up activities, including organization costs, shall be expensed as incurred.

Real and Personal Property Taxes Subtopic

Real and personal property taxes are taxes assessed based on the value of real or personal property by a state or other legal authority at some specific point in time (ASC 720-30-25-1). Accounting for real and personal property taxes usually involves two issues: (1) when and what amount should the entity report as a liability for property taxes and (2) how much tax should be reported in the income statement.

Generally, two methods have evolved when accounting for property taxes. Under the first method, which is considered the most appropriate method under ASC 720-30, property tax is accrued monthly over the taxing authority's fiscal year. An enterprise should record a liability and an expense each month for that month's share of the total property tax. The second method requires an accrual of the total amount of property tax on the lien date by establishing a property tax asset and liability. The property tax asset is amortized to expense monthly using a straight-line method over the fiscal year of the taxing authority. The property tax liability is reported as a current liability in the balance sheet, and the amount expensed is reported in the income statement either as part of operating expenses, as a line item deducted from income, or as an allocation to various expenses or costs reported in the income statement.

To illustrate the accounting for real and personal property tax, assume the facts in Example 7-27.

Example 7-27
Assumptions for Property Taxes

1. Johnson Enterprises (Johnson), a December 31 year-end company, received a property tax bill on April 15, 20X6 for $600,000.
2. The taxing authority's fiscal year is from July 1–June 30, and the lien date is July 1.
3. Johnson can elect to pay for the tax bill in two equal installments on October 1 and January 1.

If Johnson elects to accrue the taxes on a monthly basis, no entry is required on April 15, the date that the tax bill was received by Johnson. The $600,000 is charged to expense at a rate of $50,000 ($600,000 ÷ 12 months) per month using a straight-line method from July 1–June 30, the fiscal year of the taxing authority. Journal entries required on July 31, August 31, and September 30, 20X6 to record accrual for the first three months are as follows:

July 31, August 31, and September 30 Entries

Property Tax Expense	50,000	
Property Tax Payable		50,000

On October 1, one-half or $300,000 ($600,000 × 1/2) of the property tax must be paid by Johnson. As of October 1, only $150,000 of the $300,000 payment has been accrued as a liability. Therefore, Johnson will establish an asset for $150,000 of the payment and reduce the accrued liability for the $150,000 ($50,000 × 3 months) balance. The entry required for the $300,000 payment is as follows:

October 1 Payment

Prepaid Property Tax	150,000	
Property Tax Payable	150,000	
Cash		300,000

The prepaid property tax is classified as a current asset in the balance sheet amortized to expense at a rate of $50,000 per month. Entries for October, November, and December are shown below:

October 31, November 30, and December 31 Entries

Property Tax Expense	50,000	
Prepaid Property Tax		50,000

On January 1, the second half of the property tax bill is due, and Johnson does not have a balance in the property tax liability account; therefore, the payment will be recorded in the prepaid property tax account and amortized over the six months remaining in the taxing authority's fiscal year. The entries to record the payment and amortization of the payment over the next six months are as follows:

January 1, 20X7 Payment

Prepaid Property Tax	300,000	
Cash		300,000

January 31–June 30 Amortization

Property Tax Expense	50,000	
Prepaid Property Tax		50,000

If Johnson elects to use the second method and accrue the total property tax on the lien date, an asset and liability is recorded for $600,000 on July 1, and the asset is amortized over the taxing authority's fiscal year using a straight-line method at an amount equal to $50,000 ($600,000 ÷ 12 months). Entries to record the liability and amortization of the asset are as follows:

July 1 Accrual of Liability

Deferred Property Tax	600,000	
Property Tax Payable		600,000

July 31, 20X6–June 30, 20X7 Amortization

Property Tax Expense	50,000	
Deferred Property Tax		50,000

Payments of the tax bill of $300,000 ($600,000 × 1/2) are required on October 1 and on January 1. Entries to show these two payments are presented below:

October 1, 20X6 and January 1, 20X7

Property Tax Payable	300,000	
Cash		300,000

Fees Paid to the Federal Government by Pharmaceutical Manufacturers and Health Insurers Subtopic

ASC 720-50 provides guidance on the annual fee paid by pharmaceutical manufacturers and health insurers to the U.S. Treasury in accordance with the Patient Protection and Affordable Care Act as amended by the Health Care and Education Reconciliation Act (the Acts). The Acts impose an annual fee on the pharmaceutical manufacturing industry for each calendar year beginning on or after January 1, 2011 and for health insurers for each calendar year beginning on or after 1, 2014. An entity's portion of the annual fee is payable no later than September 30 of the applicable calendar year and is not tax deductible.

For the pharmaceutical manufacturers industry, the annual fee will be allocated to individual pharmaceutical manufacturers on the basis of the amount of their branded prescription drug sales for the preceding year as a percentage of the industry's branded prescription drug sales for the same period. A pharmaceutical manufacturer's portion of the annual fee becomes payable once it has a gross receipt from branded prescription drug sales to any specified government program or in accordance with coverage under any government program for each calendar year beginning on or after January 1, 2011.

For the health insurance industry, the annual fee will be allocate to individual health insurers bases on the ratio of the amount of health insurance for any U.S. health risk that is written during the preceding calendar year. A health insurer's portion of the annual fee becomes payable once it provides health insurance for any U.S. health risk for each calendar year beginning on or after January 1, 2014.

Topic 730: Research and Development

Topic 730, *Research and Development*, contains four subtopics:

10 Overall

20 Research and Development Arrangements

912 Contractors—Federal Government*

985 Software*

* See the corresponding topic in Chapter 9 for coverage of this shared subtopic.

Overall Subtopic—Flowchart and General Discussion

ASC 730-10 requires two major decisions in assessing research and development activities for financial accounting and reporting purposes. First, a decision must be made as to whether a particular activity is considered "research and development," as defined in ASC 730-10-20. For those activities determined to be research and development, the second decision involves the proper recognition of the costs associated with the activity. Most types of research and development costs will be charged to income as incurred, while other costs (e.g., those for physical facilities used in the research and development process) will be capitalized and charged to current and future periods through amortization.

Flowchart 7-7 identifies the major decisions that must be made in determining which specific costs will be expensed as research and development costs and which costs will be capitalized. The costs capitalized may become research and development costs in some future period.

Flowchart 7-7

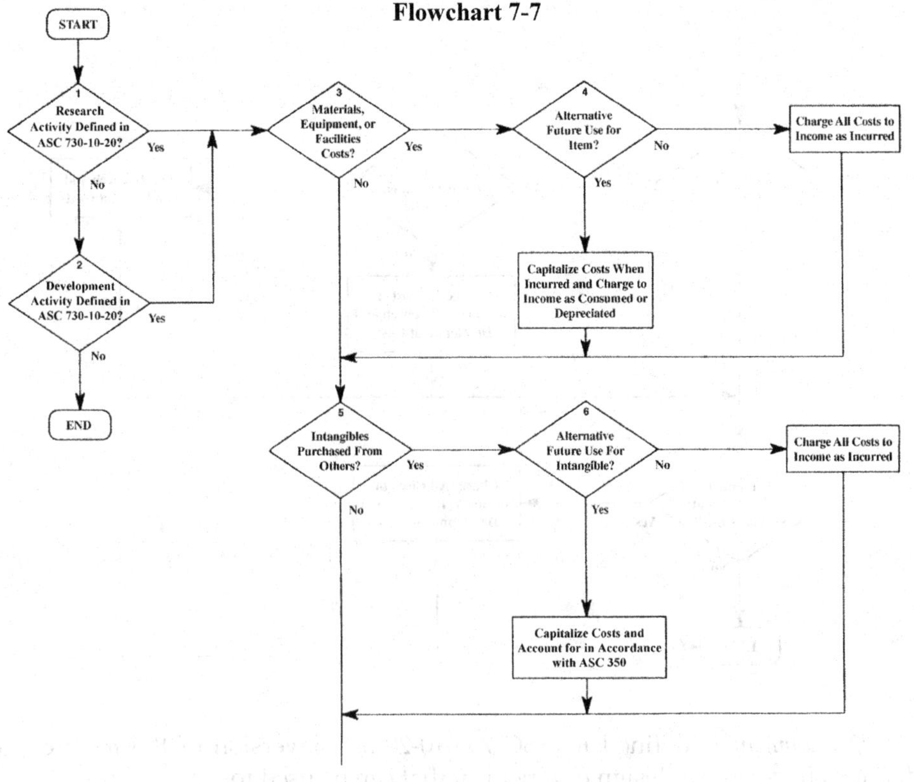

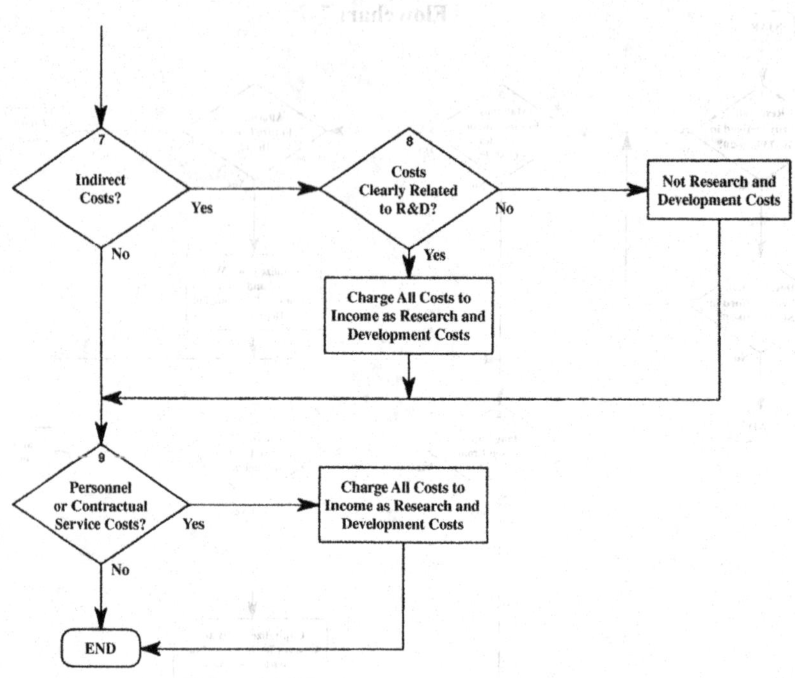

Development is defined in ASC 730-10-20 as conversion of the research, as defined above, into a design or blueprint that can be used for:

- A new service, product, technique, or process, or
- A notable improvement in an existing service, product, technique, or process.

The definitions of research and development specifically exclude the following types of activities:

- Changes of a routine nature in a currently available product or manufacturing process. Such activities are excluded even if the product or process is improved as a result of the change.
- Activities that involve market research and testing.

ASC 730-10-55-1 specifically identifies certain activities that are considered research and development for purposes of ASC 730-10. ASC 730-10-55-2 identifies activities that are *not* considered to represent research and development. Examples of both types of activities are shown in Chart 7-14.

Chart 7-14 Identifying Research and Development Activities[a]

Activities Considered to Be Research and Development (ASC 730-10-55-1)	Activities Not Considered to Be Research and Development (ASC 730-10-55-2)
1. Discovery of new information through laboratory research.	1. Changes in design of existing products that are considered periodic or seasonal.
2. A product or process design modification.	2. Activities during commercial production such as routine testing, trouble-shooting, and quality control.
3. Exploring for ways that new research or knowledge can be applied.	3. Activities, considered routine, to improve an existing product.
4. Testing that is used to evaluate or search for alternative processes or products.	4. Activities of a legal nature that are related to items such as application for patents.
5. Design of items, such as tools and dies, that relate to new technology.	5. Design of items, such as tools and dies, that are routine in nature.

[a] For information about computer software for selling and administrative activities as it relates to research and development, see ASC 730-10-15-4.

When faced with a specific cost, the first step in the decision process is to determine if the cost is related to research and development, as defined in ASC 730-10 (Blocks 1 and 2). If the cost is determined to be part of research and development, proper accounting depends upon the type of cost incurred. If the cost represents materials, equipment, or facilities that will be used in the research and development process (Block 3), and if these items have no alternative future use (Block 4), the costs will be considered research and development costs and should be expensed in the current period. This means that the cost of certain physical assets will be expensed as incurred rather than capitalized. If the materials, equipment, or other facilities have an alternative future use, their costs should be capitalized. The costs of materials used in the current period, along with the current period depreciation applicable to the equipment and facilities, will be research and development costs and will be expensed in the current period.

If the costs incurred represent an amount paid to some other entity or individual for the purchase of an intangible asset (Block 5), and if the intangible has no alternative future use (Block 6), the costs will be expensed in the current period. An intangible would have no alternative future use if it were purchased for a specific research and development project and could be used in no other project, or if it had no general use to the enterprise other than in the particular project. If the intangible had some alternative future use, it would be capitalized and accounted for in accordance with the provisions of ASC 350. The amortization expenses or impairment loss, if appropriate, for the current period would be classified as research and development costs and would be charged against current income.

If the costs represent indirect costs (Block 7), and if those costs clearly are related to research and development type activities (Block 8), they should be considered research and development costs and expensed in the current period. Research and development costs may include allocated indirect costs, but only if the costs are specifically identified with research and development activities.

The final category of costs represents personnel services or contractual services provided by others (Block 9). All of these types of costs are research and development costs and should be charged to expense as incurred. The contractual service costs referred to above represent services provided by some other organization for the company. It is a common practice to farm out part or all of a research project to an organization with expertise in a particular area.

If the entity provides research and development work for another organization under a contractual arrangement, costs incurred under the contract *do not* represent research and development, as defined in ASC 730-10. In this case, the entity conducting the research and development work would be doing so as a routine part of its revenue producing activities.

Overall Subtopic—Technical Considerations

To illustrate the technical considerations of accounting for research and development costs, one example will be used. The assumptions for Example 7-28 are as follows.

Example 7-28
Assumptions for Research and Development Costs

1. R&D, Inc., a December 31 calendar year-end company, was involved in research and development Project Number 3 during the year 20X6.
2. $1,000,000 of materials were used by R&D, Inc. in Project Number 3 during 20X6.
3. A patent was acquired at a cost of $100,000 on January 1, 20X6 for use in Project Number 3. The patent will have alternative future uses. It has a finite useful life of 10 years with no residual value.
4. Equipment was acquired on January 5, 20X6 at a cost of $30,000, for use in Research Project Number 3. The equipment has a useful life of five years, with no residual value. It has no alternative uses. Straight-line depreciation is used on all equipment.
5. Salaries of persons directly involved in Research Project Number 3 were $500,000 for 20X6.
6. Equipment was acquired on July 1, 20X6 at a cost of $1,500,000 for use in Research Project Number 3. The equipment has a 10-year useful life with no residual value. It can be used in other research and development activities and other activities not classified as research and development.
7. Consulting fees paid to persons or entities outside the firm for research and development projects amounted to $50,000.
8. Overhead allocated to research and development activities was $15,000. This was considered to be a reasonable allocation.

Given the information in Example 7-28, the research and development costs for 20X6 may be computed. The research and development costs are presented in Table 7-63.

Table 7-63 Research and Development Costs

Situation	Research and Development Costs
Material Used	$1,000,000
Amortization of Patent ($100,000/10 years)	10,000
Equipment Purchased on January 5	30,000
Personnel Salaries	500,000
Depreciation of Equipment Purchased on July 1 ($1,500,000/10 years)	150,000
Consulting Fees	50,000
Overhead Allocation	15,000
Total Research and Development Costs for Project Number 3	$1,755,000

As noted in Table 7-63, the materials used, personnel salaries, consulting fees, and overhead allocation were directly related to Project Number 3 and were incurred in 20X6. These costs are research and development costs and are charged to income in 20X6. The patent and the equipment purchased on July 1 have alternative uses after Project Number 3 is completed. Because the items have alternative uses, only the amortization of the patent of $10,000 and of the depreciation of $150,000 are considered research and development costs for 20X6 and accordingly charged to expense. The cost of the equipment purchased on January 5 was charged to research and development costs, instead of to depreciation for 20X6, as the equipment will not have any alternative uses after Project Number 3 is completed.

Overall Subtopic—Disclosures

The entity should disclose the total amount of research and development costs charged to income. If comparative financial statements are issued, total research and development costs charged to income should be disclosed for each period.

The disclosure may be made in the text of the income statement or in the footnotes to the financial statements.

Research and Development Arrangements Subtopic—General Discussion

Many research and development activities are carried out through venture arrangements between two or more entities. These ventures help to spread the risk of research and development among the parties and also allow each party to contribute different skills and assets. Some arrangements take the form of joint ventures, and others may be handled as limited partnerships. The form of the arrangement is of little consequence to the required accounting. ASC 730-20 provides guidance on the accounting for research and development costs in these types of arrangements.

The major accounting issue raised by such arrangements is the treatment of research and development costs. ASC 730 generally requires costs classified as research and development to be expensed in the current accounting period. Some expenditures relating to research and development activities may be capitalized, but this determination depends upon the alternative future use of the asset.

Accounting for assets received and costs incurred by an entity involved in a research and development arrangement depends upon whether the entity is obligated to repay monies received to the contributing parties. In some cases, the entity conducting the research and development is obligated to repay funds received, regardless of the outcome of the project. This type of arrangement might be viewed as a borrowing transaction where the entity obtains funds to conduct research and development and repays the amount from future cash inflows. If this is the case, a liability must be recognized in the amount of the advances received. The means used to repay the advances does not change the requirement to recognize a liability.

In some cases, the agreement between the parties to the venture does not require the repayment of funds advanced, but the entity conducting the research and development may be *committed* to repay part or all of the funds. If this is the case, the accounting described in the previous paragraph is appropriate. ASC 730-20-25-4 identifies three situations in which an enterprise is considered to be committed to repay the monies received. These situations are:

1. When the entity guarantees to repay or has a contract that commits it to repay the funds advanced.
2. When the contributing parties can require the entity to acquire their interest in the venture.
3. When the contributing parties will receive the entity's debt or equity securities at the conclusion of the venture.

In the most unstructured financial arrangement, the entity may not be obligated to repay amounts advanced, but conditions surrounding the project indicate that it is probable that the amounts will be repaid regardless of the outcome of the research and development. If the available evidence indicates that repayment is likely and the amount can be estimated, a liability should be recorded by the entity conducting the research and development. ASC 730-20-25-6 lists conditions that generally will lead one to assume that the amounts will not be repaid.

If the entity is required to record a liability for funds received, research and development costs are to be expensed as incurred. The provisions of ASC 730-10 would be applied by the entity conducting the research and development.

In other types of research and development arrangements, the repayment of funds advanced depends upon whether the project results in an asset that has future economic benefits to the parties. When this is the case, the entity conducting the research and development is merely performing contract services for the contributing parties. The amounts received would be treated as advances, and costs incurred would be charged against the advance account. The parties making the advance payments would account for them as research and development costs.

Research and Development Arrangements Subtopic—Technical Considerations

To illustrate the accounting requirements of ASC 730-20, two examples are developed that illustrate different aspects of the subtopic. Information for Example 7-29 is as follows.

Example 7-29
Research and Development Arrangements

1. During 20X6, Snider Company (Snider), a December 31 year-end entity, entered into a research and development arrangement in a joint venture with other entities.
2. Snider will perform all research and development activities other than outside contract services on the venture known as Research Project Number 5. The other entities transferred $1,500,000 in cash to Snider on February 15, 20X6. Snider has agreed to repay the $1,500,000 at the end of the project, regardless of the outcome of the research and development activities.
3. During 20X6, the following costs were incurred for research and development on Research Project Number 5:
   a. Equipment was acquired on March 1, 20X6 at a cost of $50,000. The equipment has a useful life of 10 years, with no residual value. The equipment has no alternative use other than Research Project Number 5, and will be abandoned upon completion.
   b. Additional equipment was acquired on April 1, 20X6 for $500,000 for use in Research Project Number 5. The equipment has a useful life of five years, with no residual value. The equipment can be used for purposes other than research and development.
   c. During 20X6, materials costing $100,000 were used.
   d. Salaries of employees directly associated with Research Project Number 5 were $200,000.
   e. During 20X6, fees of $150,000 were paid to outside consultants for research directly related to Research Project Number 5, and overhead of $10,000 was allocated to Research Project Number 5. This allocation was considered reasonable.
   f. All equipment is depreciated on a straight-line basis, and a full year's depreciation is taken in the year of purchase.
4. Research and development activities for Research Project Number 5 were not completed at December 31, 20X6.

Snider's involvement in research and development activities are subject to the provisions of ASC 730-20. Because Snider has agreed to repay the monies advanced by outside entities regardless of the outcome of the project, Snider must recognize a liability for $1,500,000. The journal entry needed on the date of the advance to record the liability is:

Cash	1,500,000	
Liability Under Research and Development Arrangements		1,500,000

Several different accounting procedures can be used to account for the advance. One alternative is for Snider to account for the advance as partner capital and recognize the liability as the advance is used for the research and development activities.

The next step in accounting for Research Project Number 5 is to determine the total research and development costs incurred in 20X6. The research and development costs are presented in Table 7-64.

Table 7-64 Research and Development Costs for 20X6

Transaction (from Example 7-29, Item 3)	R&D Cost
Equipment acquired on March 1	$50,000
Depreciation of equipment acquired on April 1 ($500,000 ÷ 5 years)	100,000
Materials used during 20X6	100,000
Salaries of employees	200,000
Consulting fees	150,000
Overhead	10,000
Total R&D costs for Research Project Number 5	$610,000

Depreciable assets with no alternative future use are not depreciated, but expensed when purchased. Therefore, the equipment acquired on March 1 is expensed in 20X6. Depreciation on the equipment acquired on April 1 is charged to research and development costs, because the equipment has an alternative future use. The materials, salaries, consulting fees, and overhead incurred in 20X6 are directly related to Research Project Number 5 and should be expensed as research and development costs. The reader is encouraged to review ASC 730-10 for a more complete analysis of basic research and development costs.

A journal entry can be made for all research and development costs incurred in 20X6. The entry required is shown below:

Research and Development Expense	610,000	
Cash		610,000

During 20X6, individual journal entries would have been made for the items composing the $610,000. The summary entry was used for illustrative purposes only.

This completes the analysis and discussion of Example 7-29. Example 7-30 involves multiple research and development arrangements. Information for Example 7-30 is as follows.

Example 7-30
Research and Development Arrangements

1. The Logan Company (Logan), a December 31 year-end entity, was involved in two research and development arrangements with other entities during 20X6.
2. In the first arrangement, Logan will perform all research and development activities for Project Number 7. The other entities involved in the venture transferred $2,500,000 in cash to Logan on January 1, 20X6. The research and development activities are expected to last two years. Repayment of any funds advanced to Logan is contingent on whether the research results in a successful patent.
3. Research and development costs incurred during 20X6 for Project Number 7 are:
   a. Materials costing $700,000 were used.
   b. Salaries of $500,000 were incurred by employees directly involved in the research activities.
   c. Outside consultants were paid $300,000 for work related to the research project.
   d. Overhead allocated to Project Number 7 during 20X6 was $20,000. This allocation was reasonable.
4. The second research and development arrangement is known as Project Number 11. Johnson Enterprises (Johnson), another entity, is responsible for conducting all research and development activities. On April 15, 20X6, Logan transferred to Johnson $750,000, which represents Logan's share of the estimated research and development costs. Repayment of the advance to Logan by Johnson depends on whether the research and development activity results in a successful patent. The $750,000 cannot be related to any activity other than research and development.

The first research and development arrangement is subject to the provisions of ASC 730-20. It is an arrangement entered into with outside entities for the sole purpose of conducting research and development activities. The other entities involved in the arrangement advanced Logan $2,500,000, contingent upon a successful patent resulting from the research activity. Therefore, Logan does not have a liability for the $2,500,000 advance.

The entry required on January 1, 20X6 to record receipt of the advance is:

Cash	2,500,000	
Advance Under R&D Arrangement		2,500,000

The Advance Under R&D Arrangement will be carried as a liability until the proceeds are used in the research activities. The liability will be reduced as the research costs are incurred for Project Number 7. The research and development costs for 20X6 are computed in Table 7-65.

Table 7-65 Computation of Research and Development Costs

Transaction (from Example 7-30, Item 3)	R&D Cost
Materials used during 20X6	$700,000
Salaries of employees	500,000
Consulting fees	300,000
Overhead	20,000
Total R & D costs for Project Number 7	$1,520,000

The research and development costs presented above are similar to the costs determined in the Example 7-29 material, and no further explanation is needed.

The summary entry needed to record the costs in Table 7-65 is presented below:

Advance under R&D Arrangement	1,520,000	
Cash		1,520,000

Because Logan is not required to repay the $2,500,000 advance unless the research results in a successful patent, costs incurred for research and development will *not* be expensed, but will be charged against the advance. Multiple journal entries normally would be made for the items included in R&D costs. The summary entry was made for illustrative purposes only. After the journal entry at December 31 of $1,520,000, the balance in the advance account is $980,000 ($2,500,000 advance – $1,520,000 R&D costs for 20X6).

In consideration of the second research and development arrangement, Project Number 11, Logan must account for the $750,000 advance made to the outside entity. The outside entity is responsible for conducting all research and development activities. Because repayment to Logan of the $750,000 advance depends on successful results from the research activity, the company's $750,000 advance must be accounted for as research and development costs at the time the advance is made.

The required journal entry by Logan on April 15 for the advance is:

Research and Development Expense	750,000	
Cash		750,000

This completes the discussion and analysis of Example 7-30. The next section describes the required disclosures for research and development arrangements.

Research and Development Arrangements Subtopic—Disclosures

The disclosure requirements for ASC 730-20 are specified in Section 50 and include the following:

1. For each balance sheet date, the significant terms of all agreements must be disclosed.
2. For each accounting period that an income statement is presented, the compensation earned and the costs incurred under research and development arrangements must be disclosed.

Topic 740: Income Taxes

Topic 740, *Income Taxes*, contains 18 subtopics:

10 Overall

20 Intraperiod Tax Allocation

30 Other Considerations or Special Areas

270 Interim Reporting

323 Investments—Equity Method and Joint Ventures [See the corresponding topic in Chapter 3 for coverage of this shared subtopic]

718 Compensation—Stock Compensation [See the corresponding topic in this chapter for coverage of this shared subtopic]

805 Business Combinations [See the corresponding topic in Chapter 8 for coverage of this shared subtopic]

830 Foreign Currency Matters [See the corresponding topic in Chapter 8 for coverage of this shared subtopic]

852 Reorganizations [See the corresponding topic in Chapter 8 for coverage of this shared subtopic]

924 Entertainment—Casinos*

932 Extractive Activities—Oil and Gas*

942 Financial Services—Depository and Lending*

944 Financial Services—Insurance*

946 Financial Services—Investment Companies*

954 Health Care Entities*

972 Real Estate—Common Interest Realty Associations*

980 Regulated Operations*

995 U.S. Steamship Entities*

* See the corresponding topic in Chapter 9 for coverage of this shared subtopic.

Introduction

ASC 740 addresses accounting for income taxes and intraperiod tax allocation. ASC 740 views differences between book and tax bases of asset and liabilities, caused either by differences between book and tax incomes or direct adjustments to asset and liabilities bases, as temporary differences that are taxable or deductible in future accounting periods when the book values of the assets or liabilities are recovered or settled. All taxable temporary differences are used to compute deferred tax liabilities and all deductible temporary differences are used to compute deferred tax assets. Operating loss carryforwards and tax credit carryforwards are also used in calculating deferred tax assets. Deferred tax assets are adjusted by a valuation allowance for the benefits that have a greater than 50% likelihood to not be realized.

A balance sheet approach was selected by the FASB for computing deferred taxes. That is, currently enacted future tax rates are applied to future taxable and deductible temporary differences to compute what the balance should be in the deferred tax asset account and the deferred tax liability account. The difference between the balances in the deferred tax accounts at the beginning of the period and the balances at the end of the period is the deferred tax expense or benefit for the accounting period. The deferred tax expense or benefit plus or minus current taxes payable is the income tax expense for the year under consideration.

The total income tax expense is then allocated to items on the income statement and balance sheet, that must be reported net of their related tax effects, using intraperiod tax allocation procedures specified in ASC 740.

Overview of Deferred Tax Accounting

Chart 7-15 provides a general overview of the deferred tax accounting requirements under ASC 740. In Chart 7-15, income for financial accounting purposes is determined through the application of U.S. generally accepted accounting principles (U.S. GAAP). Income for tax purposes is determined through the application of the rules and regulations contained in the Internal Revenue Code (IRC) and the rules specified by various other taxing authorities.

The reasons underlying U.S. GAAP are different from those supporting the various provisions specified by taxing authorities. For example, depreciation expense for financial accounting purposes represents a rational and systematic allocation of the cost of an asset over its estimated useful life, but depreciation deductions for tax purposes may be designed to serve as an incentive for investment in new assets.

The manner in which revenues and expenses are recognized for accounting and tax purposes may not always be the same. As a result there are likely to be some differences between accounting income and taxable income. These differences have tax consequences that are divided into differences that relate to assets and liabilities and, therefore, translate into a difference between book and tax bases of assets and liabilities and differences that do not relate to assets and liabilities and do not impact on the tax or book bases of assets and liabilities. Only differences between book and tax incomes that have tax consequences are considered temporary differences. Differences that do not have tax consequences, commonly referred to as permanent differences, are not considered in the computation of deferred taxes.

Chart 7-15

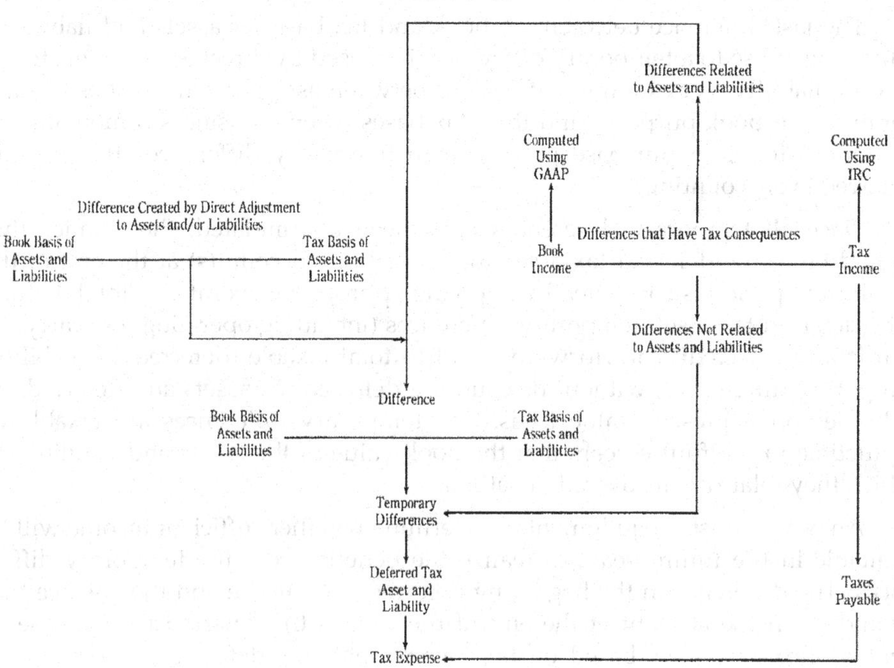

To illustrate a situation where there is a temporary difference related to an asset, assume straight-line depreciation is used for financial accounting and accelerated depreciation is used for tax purposes. When accelerated depreciation is used for tax purposes and straight-line depreciation is used for financial accounting purposes, a difference is created between book and tax incomes. In addition, because accelerated depreciation is used for tax, accumulated depreciation is greater for tax and, therefore, the tax basis is less than the book basis of the asset.

To illustrate a situation in which a difference between financial accounting income and tax income creates a difference between book and tax bases of liabilities, assume that a loss is accrued for the estimated future cost of litigation for financial accounting purposes and is deducted for tax when paid in a future accounting period. Because a liability is created in the year of accrual for financial accounting purposes and no liability is established for tax purposes, a difference exists between the book and tax bases of the liability.

Some differences between book and tax incomes do not relate to assets and liabilities and, therefore, do not cause a difference between book and tax bases of assets or liabilities. For example, the use of percentage-of-completion for financial accounting and modified percentage-of-completion for tax on long-term contracts causes a difference that has tax consequences between book and tax income. The difference between financial accounting income and tax income is a temporary difference requiring deferred tax computations, but the difference does not impact on the bases of assets or liabilities.

The last difference between the book and tax bases of assets and liabilities, which gives rise to a temporary difference, is caused by direct adjustments to the asset or liability. For example, differences between assigned values of assets and liabilities for book purposes and their tax bases when a business combination is accounted for as a purchase gives rise to temporary differences that require deferred tax accounting.

Once all temporary differences have been accumulated, the balance that should be in the deferred tax asset and/or liability account(s) at the end of the accounting period is computed by applying appropriate tax rates to total deductible (deferred tax asset) temporary differences (including operating loss carryforwards and tax credit carryforwards) and to total taxable (deferred tax liability) temporary differences, without discounting deferred tax assets and deferred tax liabilities on a present value basis. The temporary differences are taxable or deductible in the future years that the book value of the assets and liabilities to which they relate are recovered or settled.

An entity must use judgment to determine whether sufficient income will be available in the future years to realize the benefits from the temporary differences. The difference in the beginning deferred tax balance and the balance that should be in the account at the end of the year is the deferred tax expense or benefit. Taxes payable, based on tax income, and the deferred tax expense or benefit is added or deducted in computing tax expense. That is, deferred taxes and taxes payable are computed directly and tax expense is computed indirectly (or plugged) by combining taxes payable and the deferred tax expense or benefit. Therefore, a balance sheet approach is used because the balance sheet items are computed directly and the income statement item is computed indirectly.

The overview of interperiod tax allocation illustrates how temporary differences arise in the deferred tax computations. Temporary differences are discussed and illustrated in more detail in the following discussion.

Concept of Temporary Differences

Temporary differences are differences between book and tax bases of assets and liabilities at a particular point in time, plus cumulative temporary differences that arise in the current and prior years that are unrelated to assets and liabilities. Chart 7-16 contains types of temporary differences with examples for each type. In addition, Chart 7-16 indicates whether each example is taxable or deductible when the financial accounting basis of the asset or liability is recovered or settled.

Chart 7-16 shows that all currently existing temporary differences can be divided into nine types. The first four types relate to a difference in financial accounting and tax incomes. The fifth type of temporary difference also relates to a difference between financial accounting and tax income, but the difference does not cause a difference in book and tax basis of assets and/or liabilities. The remaining four types relate to situations where temporary differences are created when an asset or liability is directly adjusted. Temporary differences for all nine types will become taxable (revenue item) or deductible (expense item) for deferred tax calculations in future years when the book value of the asset or liability is recovered or settled. If the temporary difference does not relate to an asset or liability, the temporary difference is taxable or deductible in the future year(s) that the difference reverses.

For the first type of temporary difference, where revenues are included in financial accounting income after they are taxed, the temporary differences created are deductible in future years. The examples, subscriptions in advance and rent and royalties, are included in financial accounting income when earned and taxed when collected. Therefore, because a liability is created for financial accounting purposes, and there is no liability for tax purposes, a temporary difference between the tax and financial accounting basis of the liability that is deductible in future years is created. The temporary difference is deductible in the future years that the liability is settled. The liability is settled when the revenue is earned for financial accounting purposes. (See item 1 in Chart 7-16.)

The second type of temporary difference, where revenue and gains are included in financial accounting income before they are taxed, creates a temporary difference that relates to an asset. Revenue is recognized for financial accounting purposes when the sale is made and for tax purposes when the cash is collected. The temporary difference between the financial accounting basis and the tax basis of the asset is taxable in the future years that the cash is collected. This temporary difference is the gross profit that is deferred on the sale. (See item 2 in Chart 7-16.)

Two examples illustrate situations where temporary differences are created because expenses and losses are deducted in financial accounting income after deductions are taken for tax income. Using straight-line depreciation for financial accounting income and some form of accelerated depreciation for tax income causes the tax basis of the asset to be less than the financial accounting basis. Temporary differences between the tax and the financial accounting basis of the asset are taxable in future years when the book basis of the asset is recovered. The issue of when, in the future years, the book basis is recovered and temporary differences are taxable is covered in more detail after all of the types of temporary differences have been discussed. In the second example, where interest is capitalized as part of the cost of the asset for financial accounting, but expensed for tax, the financial accounting basis of the asset exceeds the tax basis by the amount of the interest capitalized. The temporary difference is taxable in the future years that the financial accounting basis of the asset is recovered. (See item 3 in Chart 7-16.)

For the fourth type of temporary difference, expenses for financial accounting are deducted before they are deducted in tax income. For financial accounting purposes, estimated costs for product warranties and litigation are treated as contingencies in accordance with ASC 450. ASC 450 requires contingent liabilities to be expensed in the accounting period that it is probable that an expense has been incurred and the entity can estimate the amount. For tax, warranties and litigation are deducted when paid. Because a financial accounting liability is recorded at the time of accrual and there is no liability for tax, a temporary difference between the financial accounting and tax basis of the liability is created. As the financial accounting liability is settled (paid), the temporary differences are deductible. (See item 4 in Chart 7-16.)

The next types of temporary differences, revenues or expenses reported on the tax balance sheet but not on the financial accounting balance sheet, are differences between financial accounting and tax income that do not have an impact on book asset or liability basis. Because the temporary differences do not relate to assets or liabilities, the differences are taxable in the future years that the temporary differences reverse. For the first example on long-term contracts, revenue from percentage of completion is included in financial accounting income as costs are incurred and in tax income using a modified percentage of completion method. Because income from long-term contracts is reported in financial accounting income before it is reported in tax income, the temporary differences are taxable when the long-term contract income is reported for tax purposes. The second example, organizational costs expensed for financial accounting and deferred for tax income, creates a temporary difference between the financial accounting and tax basis of the asset that is deductible in future years when the organizational costs are charged to tax income. (See item 5 in Chart 7-16.)

The last four types of temporary differences are caused by direct adjustments to the tax or financial accounting basis of the asset or liability. One type of direct adjustment covers situations where the tax basis of an asset is adjusted directly because of allowable tax credits. An example includes the reduction in the tax basis of an asset for 50% of the related investment tax credit as allowed under the Tax Act of 1982. The direct reduction in the tax basis of the asset creates a temporary difference that is taxable in future years as the book basis of the asset is recovered through depreciation or sale. (See item 6 in Chart 7-16.)

For Type 7 temporary differences, the use of the deferral method in accounting for the investment tax credit reduces the book basis of the related asset. For book purposes, the investment tax credit is deferred and offset against the related asset. For tax purposes, the investment tax credit is not deferred and there is no adjustment to the tax basis of the asset. The temporary difference between the book and tax basis of the asset is deductible when the book basis of the asset is recovered in future years. (See item 7 in Chart 7-16.)

The next type of temporary difference, Type 8, relates to the proposed indexing for inflation when the local currency is the functional currency. Indexing for inflation would increase the tax basis of assets for depreciation and gain and loss computations, but would not change the book basis of the related assets. The increase in the tax basis of the asset for inflation creates a temporary difference between the book and tax basis of the assets. The temporary difference is deductible in the future years that the book basis of the asset is recovered. (See item 8 in Chart 7-16.)

Chart 7-16 Temporary Differences

TYPES	EXAMPLES	TAXABLE/ DEDUCTIBLE IN FUTURE YEARS
DIFFERENCES BETWEEN FINANCIAL ACCOUNTING INCOME AND TAX INCOME THAT DIFFERENCES BETWEEN BOOK AND TAX BASIS OF ASSETS AND LIABILITIES		
1. Revenue and gains included in financial accounting income after including them in tax income.	• Subscription in advance. • Rent or royalties in advance.	Deductible Deductible
2. Revenue and gains included in financial accounting income before including them in tax income.	• Installment sales.	Taxable
3. Expenses and losses deducted in financial accounting income after deducting them in tax income.	• Straight-line depreciation for financial income and accelerated for tax income.	Taxable
	• Capitalization of interest.	Taxable
4. Expenses and losses deducted in financial accounting income before deducting them in tax income	• Product warranties. • Litigation losses.	Deductible Deductible
DIFFERENCES BETWEEN FINANCIAL ACCOUNTING INCOME AND TAX INCOME THAT DOES NOT CAUSE A DIFFERENCE BETWEEN BOOK AND TAX BASIS OF ASSETS AND LIABILITIES		
5. Revenue or expense reported on tax balance sheet but not on financial accounting balance sheet.	• Long-term contracts- Percentage of completion for financial and modified method for tax.	Taxable
	• Organizational costs expensed for financial and deferred for tax.	Deductible
DIRECT ADJUSTMENTS TO BOOK OR TAX ASSETS AND LIABILITIES THAT CAUSE A DIFFERENCE BETWEEN BOOK AND TAX BASIS OF ASSETS AND LIABILITIES		
6. Tax basis of assets reduced for tax credits.	• Full investment tax credit (ITC) taken by an entity and tax basis asset reduced by of ITC under Tax Act of 1982.	Taxable

TYPES	EXAMPLES	TAXABLE/ DEDUCTIBLE IN FUTURE YEARS
7. Deferral method used for ITC.	• Financial basis of asset reduced by ITC.	Deductible
8. Indexing for inflation when local currency is functional currency.	• Indexing causes tax basis of asset to increase.	Deductible
9. Business combination where tax and financial basis of assets and/or liabilities are different.	• Recognized value of assets and/or liabilities acquired or assumed may cause difference between financial basis and tax basis.	Taxable or[a] Deductible

[a] The temporary differences are deductible or taxable depending on whether the difference between the financial accounting basis and the tax basis of the acquired company is a net asset or net liability position and whether the tax basis is more or less than the financial accounting basis.

The last type of temporary difference, Type 9, relates to business combinations. When a business combination is accounted for in accordance with ASC 805, there may be a difference between the recognized value of the assets and liabilities acquired or assumed and the tax basis of the related assets and liabilities. Therefore, any differences between the tax and book bases of the assets and liabilities are taxable or deductible when the book value of the assets and liabilities are recovered or settled. For example, if the revalued net assets exceed the tax basis of the net assets, the temporary differences will be taxable in the future years that the book basis of the assets are recovered. However, if the revalued net assets are less than the tax basis of the net assets, the temporary differences will be deductible in the future years of recovery. (See item 9 in Chart 7-16.)

As indicated in the discussion of Type 3 temporary differences related to depreciation expense (See discussion of item 3 in Chart 7-16), some temporary differences may build up over a period of years and reverse out. Where accelerated depreciation is used for tax purposes and straight-line depreciation is used for financial accounting, temporary differences build up as long as, for any individual accounting period, accelerated depreciation exceeds straight-line depreciation. When straight-line depreciation exceeds accelerated depreciation for any individual future year, the book value of the asset is recovering (the temporary difference is reducing). These types of temporary differences are taxable in the future years that the differences are realized. The differences are realized in the future years that the book value of the asset is recovered.

Accounting for Deferred Taxes—General Discussion

After accumulating all temporary differences from the nine types illustrated in Chart 7-16, an entity should use the temporary differences in computing deferred taxes for the accounting period under consideration. The temporary differences used in the computation of deferred taxes consist of the temporary differences existing at the end of the current accounting period. These differences will be made up of the net differences arising in the current year and prior years. The balance that should be in the deferred tax asset and/or liability account at the end of the accounting period is the tax results of the temporary differences after incorporating the impact of tax operating loss carryforwards and tax credit carryforwards into the computation.

Several steps are involved in the computation of deferred taxes. An enterprise may use the following step process when computing deferred taxes. The step process should be applied on a separate basis for each tax jurisdiction and for each component within that jurisdiction subject to taxation (ASC 740-10-30-5).

Step 1: Divide the temporary differences into proper categories based on the type of income or expense and its tax implications.

Step 2: Divide each category of temporary differences from Step 1 into taxable and deductible differences.

Step 3: Accumulate all deductible temporary differences in each category.

Step 4: Determine enacted tax rates in future years under the regular tax system for each category.

Step 5: If tax rates are constant in future years, the deferred tax asset balance related to temporary differences is equal to the accumulated deductible temporary differences in Step 2 times the enacted rate.

Step 6: If tax rates are not constant in future years, the deductible temporary differences are scheduled to years in which the differences will be realized. Groups of years may be combined when the rates stay constant for two or more years. Apply the appropriate tax rates to the deductible temporary differences to compute the deferred tax asset balance related to temporary differences.

Step 7: Determine the amounts and expiration dates of all operating loss carryforwards.

Step 8: Apply the same procedures in Step 5 and 6 to the operating loss carryforwards to compute a deferred tax asset balance related to operating losses.

Step 9: Determine the amounts and expiration dates of tax credit carryforwards.

Step 10: Compute a deferred tax asset balance related to tax credit carryforwards.

Step 11: Determine if the entity will have sufficient income in future years to realize all benefits from the deferred tax assets.

Step 12: If there is a greater than 50% likelihood that the entity will have insufficient income in future years to realize all the deferred tax asset computed, establish a valuation allowance for the part of the deferred tax asset not expected to be realized.

Step 13: Accumulate all taxable temporary differences in each category.

Step 14: Apply the same procedures in Step 5 and 6 to the taxable temporary differences to compute the ending balance in the deferred tax liability account.

Step 15: Apply all appropriate tax planning strategies to adjust realization of benefits of deferred tax assets.

Step 16: If appropriate, measure the deferred tax asset for alternative minimum tax (AMT) credit carryforward.

Step 17: Compute a valuation allowance for the AMT deferred tax asset if there is more than a 50% likelihood that at least a part of the asset will not be realized.

Step 18: Accumulate all deferred tax assets and compute the deferred tax expense or benefit from deferred tax assets for the accounting period by taking the difference in the beginning and ending balances.

Step 19: Compute the deferred tax expense or benefit from deferred tax liabilities for the accounting period by taking the difference in the beginning and ending balances.

Step 20: Compute the change in the valuation allowance account by comparing the beginning and ending balances.

Step 21: Compute income tax expense for the accounting period by adding to or deducting from income taxes payable the amounts from Step 18, 19, and 20.

Step 22: Combine deferred tax assets and liabilities to report noncurrent deferred tax amount as required under ASU 2015-17, *Income Taxes (Topic 740): Balance Sheet Classification of Deferred Taxes*. (Note: For public business entities, ASU 2015-17 is effective for financial statements issued for annual periods beginning after December 15, 2016, and interim periods within those annual periods. For all other entities, ASU 2015-17 is effective for financial statements issued for annual periods beginning after December 15, 2017, and interim periods within annual periods beginning after December 15, 2018.)

Some of the steps in the step process require further explanation. As noted in Step 1, it is first necessary to divide temporary differences into appropriate categories because deductible and taxable differences are offset against income in future years and some types of incomes cannot be offset for tax purposes. For example, temporary differences related to capital gains and losses should be separated from temporary differences for ordinary income and losses. Capital losses can only be deducted up to the amount of capital gains; they cannot be offset against ordinary income. Whether temporary differences can be offset is a function of existing tax law.

Determining which of the temporary differences are taxable or deductible, as required in Step 2, may be determined by reviewing the discussion of Chart 7-16 related to temporary differences. Because a deferred tax asset is computed based on all deductible temporary differences, it is necessary to accumulate all differences that are deductible in each category (Step 3). This accumulation is necessary for each category because different tax rates and different types of incomes can exist in different categories. Once the deductible temporary differences have been accumulated, it is necessary to determine the appropriate tax rate or rates (based on existing tax law) to be used in the computation of the asset (Step 4). Notice that the tax rate(s) under the regular tax system is used and there is no direct interaction with the AMT system. If there are no changes in tax rates in future years, as noted in Step 5, it is not necessary to schedule deductible temporary differences to the future years that the differences are realized. All deductible temporary differences can be combined and one tax rate applied to the total differences to compute the deferred tax asset related to deductible temporary differences. However, if rates change in future years or if marginal tax rates are significant, some scheduling of temporary differences may be required. For example, assume an entity has a $100,000 temporary difference in which $20,000 will be deductible each year for the future years of 20X7–2011. Further assume that income is adequate in each of the future years to realize the benefit of the temporary differences, and the currently enacted tax rates are 30% for 20X7 and 20X8 and 40% for 20X9–2011. Using this information, $40,000 ($20,000 for 20X7 + $20,000 for 20X8) of the temporary difference will be combined and taxed at a rate of 30% to compute a deferred tax asset of $12,000 ($40,000 × 30%) and $60,000 of the temporary differences (20X9–2011 deductions) will be combined and taxed at a rate of 40% to compute a deferred tax asset of $24,000 ($60,000 × 40%) or a total deferred tax asset balance of $36,000 ($24,000 + $12,000). In addition, an entity may anticipate losses in some future years. The temporary differences that are deductible in the future years that have losses will not be realized in those years because operating losses are expected. Therefore, deferred taxes are computed on temporary differences using the tax rates in effect in the years in which the differences are realized (i.e., the years that encompass the operating loss carryback or carryforward.) For example, assume that at the end of 20X6 an entity has a $100,000 temporary difference that is deductible in 20X8, and also assume that the company anticipates a $200,000 loss in 20X4, which will be carried back to recapture taxes in 20X5. A deferred tax asset will be computed for the $100,000 deductible difference using the tax rate in effect in 20X5.

If graduated tax rates are not significant in the computation of deferred taxes, an entity should use the highest graduated rate. However, in some future years, income may be at varying levels, which would require different graduated tax rates. ASC 740-10-55, paragraphs 136 through 138, state that some form of an average graduated tax rate would be appropriate in order to eliminate a great deal of scheduling of temporary differences when graduated rates are significant. However, some scheduling of temporary differences may be required when computing deferred taxes.

Once deferred tax assets are computed for deductible temporary differences, it is necessary to compute deferred taxes for tax operating loss carryforwards (Step 7 and 8). The same procedures used in Step 5 and 6 for temporary differences related to scheduling and appropriate tax rates would be applicable to operating losses. Next, in Step 9 and 10, deferred tax assets are measured for tax credit carryforwards. The amount of the tax credit carryforward that can be used as a deferred tax asset depends on existing tax law and anticipation of future income.

As noted in Step 11, once an enterprise has computed a deferred tax asset, it is necessary to determine if all the benefit from the deferred tax asset will be realized. Because realization depends on future income, some assessment must be made as to whether, in the judgment of management, income in future years will be sufficient to realize all of the deferred tax asset. If it is likely (more than 50% so) that the entire deferred tax asset will not be realized, a valuation allowance must be established equal to the amount of the deferred tax asset that is not expected to be realized. The valuation allowance is a contra asset that is used to reduce the deferred tax asset account. Any change in the valuation account, generally, is an adjustment to income tax expense (Paragraph 17).

Both positive and negative information should be used when judging the likelihood of future income. Historical information about the operations of the entity provides management with some information about the probability of income in future years. In addition, ASC 740-10-30-18 provides selected guidelines for sources of income that an entity may use when judging if income is sufficient in future years to realize the benefits from deferred tax assets, including the following:

1. Taxable temporary differences that reverse in future years.
2. Taxable income in future years that does not include taxable temporary differences and loss carryforwards.
3. Taxable income available from prior years that encompass the carryback period under existing tax law.
4. Taxable income generated from tax planning strategies (discussed in Step 15).

After determining any required valuation allowance for the deferred tax asset, an entity must compute any required deferred tax liability (Step 14). The same procedures used in Step 5 and 6 for deferred tax assets are used to compute deferred tax liabilities.

While performing the computations of deferred tax assets and liabilities using Step 5–14, an enterprise should consider using all appropriate tax planning strategies (Step 15). A tax planning strategy is an action by an enterprise, meeting certain requirements, that allows it to take advantage of an operating loss carryforward or tax credit carryforward that otherwise would expire. A tax planning strategy must be possible and prudent; is an action that management might not otherwise undertake, that allows the use of a loss carryforward or tax credit carryforward that otherwise would be lost; and allows deferred tax assets to be realized (ASC 740-10-30-19). Examples of tax planning strategies include using loss carryforwards that would normally expire by expediting amounts taxable and changing from nontaxable to taxable income (ASC 740-10-30-18).

Deferred tax asset calculations are impacted when the alternative minimum tax (AMT) system is required to be used. When AMT is appropriate, a deferred tax asset is established for the AMT tax credit carryforward (Step 16). The AMT tax credit carryforward is the excess of the tentative minimum tax (TMT) over tax, computed by using the regular tax system. The TMT is the tax computed by using the AMT system and equals the tentative alternative minimum income times the AMT rate of 20%. The tentative alternative minimum income is taxable income under the regular tax system adjusted for AMT preference and adjustment items and the adjusted current earnings adjustment. If a deferred tax asset is computed for an AMT tax credit carryforward, an entity must determine if there is a greater than 50% likelihood that all of the deferred tax asset related to the AMT system will not be realized. If all of the deferred tax asset is not expected to be realized, a valuation allowance must be established for the part of the asset that the entity does not anticipate realizing (Step 17). The procedures used in Step 11, 12, and 15 to determine if future income is sufficient to realize the benefit of the deferred tax asset can be used in the determination of the AMT valuation allowance (ASC 740-10-55, paragraphs 31 through 33).

Once all deferred tax assets and liabilities have been computed, the deferred tax expense and/or benefit can be computed. In Step 18, all ending balances of deferred tax assets are accumulated and compared to the beginning balances. A deferred tax benefit exists if the deferred tax asset balance increases, and a deferred tax expense is created if the deferred tax asset balance decreases during the year. Step 19 requires a comparison of beginning and ending balances of the deferred tax liability account. If the liability balance increases, a deferred tax expense is created, and if the balance decreases, a deferred tax benefit is created. However, if a business combination occurred during the accounting period, the deferred tax expense or benefit for the acquisition is the change in the deferred tax asset or liability from the acquisition date to the end of the year (ASC 740-10-30-4). Next, Step 20 requires that the change in the valuation allowance be calculated by comparing the ending balance with the beginning balance. Any change in the account will be an adjustment to the valuation allowance account and, generally, to income tax expense. However, the adjustment to the allowance account may require an allocation between income from continuing operations and other components of the financial statements (ASC 740-10-45-20).

After computing the deferred tax expense and deferred tax benefit for the accounting period, income tax expense can be indirectly calculated by adding and/or deducting the deferred tax expense, the deferred tax benefit, and the change in the valuation allowance amounts to income taxes payable (Step 21).

Once the ending deferred tax asset and liability balances have been calculated, they are classified as current or long-term for presentation in the financial statements (Step 22). A deferred tax asset or liability is classified as current if it relates to a current asset or current liability. If a deferred tax asset relates to a warranty liability that is payable within one year, the deferred tax asset is classified as current because the warranty liability is classified as current. In addition, a deferred tax asset or liability is classified as noncurrent if it relates to a noncurrent asset or liability. For example, a deferred tax liability that relates to property, plant, and equipment is classified as long-term because the property, plant, and equipment are classified as long-term. Deferred tax assets from operating loss carryforwards, tax credit carryforwards, and certain other deferred tax assets and liabilities are not directly related to balance sheet assets and liabilities. These types of deferred tax assets and liabilities are classified as current or long-term based on when they are expected to be realized in future years. If they are expected to be realized within the next year, the deferred item is classified as current. However, if realization is anticipated in a period of time in excess of one year, the deferred item is classified as long-term. Once all deferred tax assets and liabilities have been classified as current or long-term, current assets must be netted against current liabilities and one net current amount reported in the financial statements (Step 23). In addition, noncurrent assets must be netted against noncurrent liabilities and one net noncurrent amount reported (ASC 740-10-45-6).

Accounting for Deferred Taxes—Technical Considerations

Four examples are used to illustrate the technical aspects of deferred tax calculations. Assumptions for Example 7-31 are as follows.

Example 7-31
Assumption for Deferred Tax Computations

1. Johnson Enterprises (Johnson) is computing deferred taxes for 20X6 and has accumulated the following information about financial accounting basis and tax basis of assets and liabilities:

	Tax Basis	Financial Basis	Temporary Difference
a. Litigation liability	$0	$105,000	$105,000
b. Warranty liability	0	38,000	38,000
c. Compensated absence liability	0	47,000	47,000
d. Rent in advance	0	60,000	60,000
e. Depreciable assets	600,000	920,000	320,000
f. Installment sales	0	180,000	180,000

2. There are no operating loss or tax credit carryforwards for tax purposes, and the alternative minimum tax is not applicable in this situation. Johnson meets the requirements for use of the installment sales basis, and the amount represents gross profit on the sale.

3. Based on all available information, Johnson estimates that it will have sufficient income in all future years to realize all benefits from the temporary differences.

4. The deferred tax asset balance at the beginning of 20X6 is $10,000, and the deferred liability balance is $25,000.

5. Warranty liability and compensated absence liability are classified as current liabilities in the 20X6 balance sheet and litigation liability and rent in advance are classified as long-term. Installment sales is classified as a current asset.

6. Tax income for 20X6 is $400,000 and tax income in all future years is expected to exceed $75,000. Currently enacted tax rates for 20X6 and all future years are as follows and graduated tax rates are not significant:

$0–$50,000	15%
$50,001–$75,000	25%
Over $75,000	34%

Using the information from Example 7-31, deferred taxes for Johnson can be computed using the step process illustrated in the general discussion. Table 7-66 illustrates calculation of the deferred tax asset and deferred tax liability balance at the end of 20X6, computation of the deferred tax benefit and deferred tax expense for 20X6, and calculation of income tax expense and income taxes payable for 20X6.

Table 7-66 Computation of Deferred Taxes, Taxes Payable and Tax Expense for 20X6

Temporary Differences:	Deductible Differences	Taxable Differences	Total
Litigation liability	$(105,000)		
Warranty liability	(38,000)		
Compensated absence liability	(47,000)		
Rent in advance	(60,000)		
Depreciable assets		$320,000	
Installment sales		180,000	
Total temporary differences	$(250,000)	$500,000	
Future enacted tax rates	34%	34%	
Ending deferred tax (asset)/liability balance	$(85,000)	$170,000	
Temporary Differences:	**Deductible Differences**	**Taxable Differences**	**Total**
Beginning deferred tax asset balance	10,000		
Beginning deferred tax liability balance		(25,000)	
Deferred tax (benefit) for 20X6	$(75,000)		$(75,000)
Deferred tax expense for 20X6		$145,000	145,000
Taxes payable computation (Example 7-31 assumptions):			
	$ 50,000 × 15% =	$7,500	
	25,000 × 25% =	6,250	
	325,000 × 34% =	110,500	
Taxes payable for 20X6			124,250
Tax expense for 20X6			$194,250

At the end of 20X6, all deductible temporary differences are aggregated into one total deductible amount to compute what the ending balance should be in the deferred tax asset account, and all taxable temporary differences are aggregated into one total taxable amount to calculate the ending balance in the deferred tax liability account. Scheduling over the future periods that the book basis of the asset or liability is recovered or settled is unnecessary in this situation because the currently enacted tax rate stays constant over the period of time that the temporary differences are recovered and graduated tax rates are not significant. It is only necessary to determine which temporary differences are deductible and which are taxable.

Temporary differences related to the litigation liability, the warranty liability, the liability for compensated absences (vacation pay), and the liability for rent in advance are deductible differences that can be combined as one total amount because benefit from the differences will be realized at the same tax rate regardless of which future years the liabilities are settled. Expenses related to all the liabilities, except for rent in advance, were accrued for financial accounting purposes in 20X6 or prior years and are deductible for tax purposes in the future years that the liability is paid or settled. Rent received in advance was recorded as a liability for financial accounting purposes when the cash was received. However, it will not be recognized as revenue for books until it is earned. The rent in advance was recognized as revenue and taxed in the accounting period that the cash was received. Therefore, the liability will be settled, and the temporary difference deductible, when the revenue is recognized for book purposes.

Temporary differences related to depreciation and installment sales are taxable amounts and are combined as one total to compute the deferred tax liability at the end of 20X6. Again, scheduling of the temporary differences to the future years that the book asset is recovered is unnecessary because the differences will be taxed at the same tax rate, regardless of the year of recovery. Temporary differences related to depreciation are taxable as the book value of the depreciable assets are recovered. Because accelerated depreciation is used by Johnson for tax purposes and straight-line is used for financial accounting purposes, the tax basis of the asset is less than the book basis and taxable temporary differences are created. The book basis of the asset recovers and temporary differences are taxable in the years when annual book depreciation exceeds annual tax depreciation.

Because there are no operating loss or tax credit carryforwards, only the deductible temporary differences are used in the computation of the deferred tax asset balance. In addition, no valuation allowance is required for the deferred tax asset because Assumption 3 from Example 7-31 indicates that the company estimates that income will be sufficient in future years to realize the benefits from all temporary differences. Also, the alternative minimum tax is not applicable to this situation, according to Assumption 2.

Using the information from Table 7-66, the balances that should be in the deferred tax asset and deferred tax liability at the end of 20X6 are $85,000 and $170,000, respectively. Because the beginning balance in the deferred tax asset account is $10,000, the change in the account for the year is a $75,000 increase. The deferred tax asset account increased during the year, and the increase will decrease income tax expense. The increase in the asset is a deferred tax benefit. If the deferred tax asset account had decreased during the year, the decrease would be a deferred tax expense because the change would cause income tax expense to increase. The beginning balance in the deferred tax liability account is $25,000, and the deferred tax liability account increased by $145,000. The $145,000 increase is a deferred tax expense because it increases income tax expense. If the change in the deferred tax liability account for the year had been a decrease, the change would be a deferred tax benefit because income tax expense would decrease. The deferred tax benefit of $75,000 and the deferred tax expense of $145,000 are combined with the $124,250 taxes payable to compute income tax expense of $194,250 for 20X6. The 34% tax rate, the highest graduated rate, is used in the computation of deferred taxes because income in all future years is expected to exceed the income that would be taxed at the highest graduated rate and the graduated rates are not significant. Using the information from Table 7-66, the required journal entry at the end of 20X6 can be prepared as follows:

Income Tax Expense	194,250	
Deferred Tax Asset	75,000	
Deferred Tax Liability		145,000
Income Taxes Payable		124,250

The deferred tax asset balance of $85,000 and the deferred tax liability balance of $170,000 are classified as current or long-term based on how the asset or liability to which they relate is classified. Because the warranty liability, compensated absence liability, and receivable from installment sales are classified as current, the tax effect of the temporary differences related to these three items are classified as current. The tax impact of the temporary differences related to depreciable assets and litigation liability are classified as long-term because both items are classified as long-term in the financial statements. The computation below shows the amounts of current and long-term deferred tax assets and liabilities.

	Temporary Difference		*Tax Rate*	*Current*	*Noncurrent*
Deferred Tax Assets:					
Litigation liability	$(105,000)	×	34%		$(35,700)
Rent in advance	(60,000)	×	34%		(20,400)
Warranty liability	(38,000)	×	34%	$(12,920)	
Compensated absences	(47,000)	×	34%	(15,980)	
Total deferred tax assets				$(28,900)	$(56,100)
Deferred Tax Liabilities:					
Depreciable assets	$320,000	×	34%		$108,800
Installment sales	180,000	×	34%	$61,200	
Total deferred tax liabilities				$61,200	$108,800

For financial statement disclosure purposes, current deferred tax assets are combined with current deferred tax liabilities, and a net current amount is presented in the financial statements. In addition, noncurrent deferred tax assets are combined with noncurrent deferred tax liabilities, and a net noncurrent amount is presented in the financial statements. For 20X6, a net current deferred tax liability of $32,300 ($61,200 current deferred tax liability – $28,900 current deferred tax asset), and a net noncurrent deferred tax liability of $52,700 ($108,800 noncurrent deferred tax liability – $56,100 noncurrent deferred tax asset) are reported in the financial statements.

This completes the analysis of Example 7-31. Example 7-31 assumed that the currently enacted tax rate stayed constant during the period of time that the temporary differences were taxable or deductible. Example 7-32 illustrates a situation where the currently enacted tax rates change over time. Assumptions for Example 7-32 are as follows.

Example 7-32
Assumptions for Deferred Tax Computations

1. Maxwell Enterprises (Maxwell) is computing deferred taxes for 20X6 and has accumulated all necessary information relative to temporary differences.

2. Maxwell purchased depreciable property in 20X5 at a cost of $300,000 and with a useful life of 10 years. Straight-line depreciation with a useful life of 10 years is used for financial accounting purposes and a five-year accelerated method is used for tax purposes. Depreciation expense for both book and tax purposes is reported as follows:

Year	Financial Accounting Depreciation	Tax Depreciation	Difference
20X5	$30,000	$60,000	$(30,000)
20X6	30,000	96,000	(66,000)
20X7	30,000	57,600	(27,600)
20X8	30,000	34,500	(4,500)
20X9	30,000	34,500	(4,500)
2010	30,000	17,400	12,600
2011	30,000		30,000
2012	30,000		30,000
2013	30,000		30,000
2014	30,000		30,000
Total	$300,000	$300,000	

3. Maxwell's differences between tax and book bases of assets and liabilities other than depreciable assets (above) are presented below. In addition, the future accounting periods that the temporary differences are estimated to be taxable or deductible are provided.

Difference	20X7	20X8	20X9	2010	2011	2012	2013	2014	Total
Installment sales	$20,000	$30,000	$75,000	$60,000	$80,000	$90,000	$70,000	$75,000	$500,000
Litigation liability	0	40,500	20,000	30,000	60,000	40,000	95,000	20,000	305,500
Warranty liability	10,000	15,000	16,000	20,000	25,000	20,000	25,000	30,000	161,000

Assume that the installment sales basis meets the limited exception for use for tax purposes and the amount shown is the gross profit on the sale.

4. There are no operating loss carryforwards or tax credit carryforwards for tax purposes, and the alternative minimum tax is not applicable in this situation.

5. The deferred tax asset balance at the beginning of 20X6 is $124,600, and the deferred liability balance is $122,000.

6. Taxable net incomes for 20X5 and 20X6 are $25,000 and $30,000, respectively. Reconciliation of taxable income to financial accounting income for 20X6 is as follows:

Financial accounting income before differences without tax consequences	$141,000
Goodwill impairment	(25,000)
Interest on nontaxable bonds	50,000
Financial accounting income	$166,000
Differences without tax consequences for 20X6:	
Goodwill impairment	25,000
Interest on nontaxable bonds	(50,000)
Temporary differences for 20X6:	
Depreciation	(66,000)
Installment	(200,000)
Litigation	100,000
Warranties	55,000
Taxable income	$30,000

7. Currently enacted tax rates are as follows: 30% for 20X5 and 20X6, 35% for 20X7–20X9, 40% for 2010–2012, and 45% for 2013–2014.

8. Based on all available information, Maxwell estimates that it will have sufficient income in all future years to realize all benefits from the temporary differences.

Using the information from Example 7-32, deferred tax asset and liability balances at the end of 20X6 can be computed for Maxwell. It is assumed that the alternative minimum tax is not applicable, and there are no operating loss or tax credit carryforwards to be considered in the computations. Calculations of the deferred tax asset and liability balances at the end of 20X6 are presented in Table 7-67.

Table 7-67 Computation of Deferred Taxes for 20X6

	Temporary Differences Recovered from Future Years			
	20X7/X9	**2010/11**	**2013/14**	**20X6 Balance**
Deductible Temporary Differences:[a]				
Litigation liability	$(60,500)	$(130,000)	$(115,000)	
Warranty liability	(41,000)	(65,000)	(55,000)	
Total deductible temporary differences	$(101,500)	$(195,000)	$(170,000)	

	Temporary Differences Recovered from Future Years			
	20X7/X9	**2010/11**	**2013/14**	**20X6 Balance**
Currently enacted future tax rates	35 %	40 %	45 %	
Deferred tax asset	$(35,525)	$(78,000)	$(76,500)	$(190,025)
Taxable Temporary Differences:[a]				
Installment receivable	$125,000	$230,000	$145,000	
Recovery of asset (depreciation)	0	72,600	23,400	
Total taxable temporary differences	$125,000	$302,600	$168,400	
Currently enacted future tax rates	35 %	40 %	45 %	
Deferred tax liability	$43,750	$121,040	$75,780	$240,570

[a] Unless otherwise indicated in the text of the material, the amount for each taxable or deductible temporary difference is the summation of the temporary differences that would be taxable or deductible in the years indicated. For example, the deductible temporary difference of litigation liability of $60,500 for 20X7/X9 is composed of the following: $0 from 20X7, $40,500 from 20X8, and $20,000 from 20X9.

Because currently enacted tax rates change in this example, some scheduling of temporary differences to future years is required. Assumption 8 in Example 7-32 indicates that income will be available in all future years to realize the benefit from all temporary differences. Therefore, all temporary differences will be realized in the future years that the temporary differences are estimated to be taxable or deductible. The tax rate remains the same (35%) from 20X7 to 20X9; therefore, all deductible differences expected to be realized during this time period are combined as one total amount, and all taxable differences are combined. The tax rate of 40% is applicable for 2010–2012 and all temporary differences estimated to be deductible during this time period are combined; all temporary differences expected to be taxable during this period are combined. Again, the tax rate changes and 45% is used for deductible and taxable temporary differences during 2013–2014, and the temporary differences during this time period are combined.

All the temporary differences were discussed in detail in Example 7-31 and require no further explanation, except for depreciation. Notice that the depreciation temporary difference at the end of 20X6 is $96,000 ($30,000 for 20X5 +

$66,000 for 20X6). The depreciation temporary difference will continue to build up through 20X9 and, in 2010, the temporary difference will start to be realized as the book basis of the asset begins to recover. Of the $96,000 in temporary differences, $12,600 is recovered in 2010, $30,000 in 2011, $30,000 in 2012, and the remaining $23,400 ($96,000 – $12,600 – $30,000 – $30,000) in 2013. Therefore, $72,600 ($12,600 + $30,000 + $30,000) of temporary differences related to depreciation is used in the 2010–2012 computation, and the remaining $23,400 ($96,000 – $72,600) is included in the 2013–2014 calculation.

No valuation allowance is required for the deferred tax asset because the company estimates that income in future years will be sufficient to realize all benefits from the reversing temporary differences.

Using the $190,025 ending deferred tax asset balance and the $240,570 ending deferred tax liability balance from Table 7-67, deferred tax expense, deferred tax benefit, and income tax expense for 20X6 are computed in Table 7-68.

Table 7-68 Computation of Deferred Tax Expense/Benefit, Taxes Payable, and Tax Expense for 20X6

Computation of Deferred Tax Benefit/Expense:		
Ending deferred tax asset balance (from Table 7-67)	$(190,025)	
Ending deferred tax liability balance (from Table 7-67)		$240,570
Beginning deferred tax asset balance	124,600	
Beginning deferred tax liability balance		(122,000)
Deferred tax benefit for 20X6	$(65,425)	
Deferred tax expense for 20X6		$118,570
Computation of Taxes Payable and Tax Expense:		
Taxable income (Example 7-32 assumptions)		$30,000
Tax rate in 20X6 (Example 7-32 assumptions)		30 %
Taxes payable for 20X6		$9,000
Deferred tax benefit for 20X6 (above)		(65,425)
Deferred tax expense for 20X6 (above)		118,570
Income tax expense for 20X6		$62,145

Using the information from Table 7-68, the required tax journal entry for 20X6 is presented as follows:

Income Tax Expense	62,145	
Deferred Tax Asset	65,425	
Income Taxes Payable		9,000
Deferred Tax Liability		118,570

The $190,025 deferred tax asset and the $240,570 deferred tax liability is reported as a net noncurrent liability in the balance sheet. The details of the components of the deferred tax assets and liabilities are shown in Table 7-69 below.

Table 7-69 Details of Deferred Tax Assets and Liabilities

	Temporary Difference		Tax Rate	Noncurrent
Deferred Tax Assets:				
Warranty liability—20X7	$(10,000)	×	35%	$(3,500)
Warranty liability—20X8/X9	(31,000)	×	35%	(10,850)
Warranty liability—2010/12	(65,000)	×	40%	(26,000)
Warranty liability—2013/14	(55,000)	×	45%	(24,750)
Litigation liability—20X8/X9	(60,500)	×	35%	(21,175)
Litigation liability 2010/12	(130,000)	×	40%	(52,000)
Litigation liability—2013/14	(115,000)	×	45%	(51,750)
Total Deferred Tax Assets				$(190,025)
Deferred Tax Liabilities:				
Installment sales—20X7	$20,000	×	35%	$7,000
Installment sales—20X8/X9	105,000	×	35%	36,750
Installment sales—2010/12	230,000	×	40%	92,000
Installment sales—2013/14	145,000	×	45%	65,250
Depreciable assets—2010/12	72,600	×	40%	29,040
Depreciable assets—2013/14	23,400	×	45%	10,530
Total Deferred Tax Liabilities				$240,570

Using the information from Assumption 6 of Example 7-32 and the preceding journal entry, a partial income statement may be presented for Maxwell for 20X6.

Maxwell Enterprises Partial Income Statement For the Year Ended December 31, 20X6

Income from continuing operations	$166,000
Income tax expense:	
Current	$9,000
Deferred	53,145
Income tax expense	62,145
Net Income	$103,855

The net deferred tax expense of $53,145 ($118,570 deferred tax expense for 20X6 - $65,425 deferred tax benefit for 20X6) reported as part of the income tax expense for 20X6 is the net impact of the deferred tax expense and deferred tax benefit for 20X6.

Goodwill impairment and interest on nontaxable bonds (Example 7-32, Assumption 6) are not used as temporary differences in the computation of deferred taxes. Only differences that have tax consequences are considered temporary differences for deferred tax computations. Because goodwill in this situation is not deductible for tax purposes, it does not have tax consequences and is not a temporary difference. Also, interest on nontaxable bonds does not have tax consequences and is not a temporary difference because it is not included in revenue for tax purposes.

Computation of deferred taxes becomes more complex when there is more than one enacted future tax rate and an entity assumes, based on available information, that losses will occur in one or more future years. The possibility of future losses creates problems as to when temporary differences will be realized. To illustrate, assume the same information in Example 7-32, except that Maxwell estimates that tax losses of about $55,000 will be incurred in years 20X7 and 20X8, and any losses will be used as carrybacks to 20X5 and 20X6. The company estimates that income in 20X9–2014 will be sufficiently large to utilize all deductible items. Using these changed assumptions, deferred tax assets and liabilities are computed in Table 7-70.

Table 7-70 Computation of Deferred Taxes for 20X6

	Prior and Current Year	Temporary Differences Recovered from Future Years			
	20X5/X6	20X9	2010/12	2013/14	20X6 Balance
Deductible Temporary Differences:[a]					
Litigation liability	$(40,500)	$(20,000)	$(130,000)	$(115,000)	
Warranty liability	(25,000)	(16,000)	(65,000)	(55,000)	
Total deductible temporary differences	$(65,500)	$(36,000)	$(195,000)	$(170,000)	
Currently enacted future tax rates	30 %	35 %	40 %	45 %	
Deferred tax asset	$(19,650)	$(12,600)	$(78,000)	$(76,500)	$(186,750)
Taxable Temporary Differences:[a]					
Installment receivable	$50,000	$75,000	$230,000	$145,000	
Recovery of asset (depreciation)	0	0	72,600	23,400	
Total taxable temporary differences	$50,000	$75,000	$302,600	$168,400	
Currently enacted future tax rates	30 %	35 %	40 %	45 %	
Deferred tax liability	$15,000	$26,250	$121,040	$75,780	$238,070

[a] Unless otherwise indicated in the text of the material, the amount for each taxable or deductible temporary difference is the summation of the temporary differences that would be taxable or deductible in the years indicated. For example, the deductible temporary difference of litigation liability of $40,500 that was deductible in 20X7 and 20X8 was recovered by a loss carryback to 20X5 (a prior year) and 20X6 (the current year). The $40,500 is composed of the following: $0 from 20X7 and $40,500 from 20X8.

All items in Table 7-70 have been explained in prior examples, except for the 20X7 and 20X8 temporary differences that are assumed to be recovered in 20X5 and 20X6. The $65,500 (20X8 litigation liability of $40,500 + 20X7 warranty liability of $10,000 + 20X8 warranty liability of $15,000) of temporary differences that are expected to be deducted in 20X7 and 20X8 when the book basis of the liabilities are settled will not be realized in those years, because losses are expected to be reported. Therefore, the benefit of the deductible differences will be realized in the years in which the loss is used to offset income. In Example 7-32, the losses that are estimated to occur in 20X7 and 20X8 are assumed to be carried back to 20X5 and 20X6 and offset against income in those years. As a result, the deductible differences are realized in 20X5 and 20X6 when the tax rate is 30%. The $50,000 ($20,000 in 20X7 + $30,000 in 20X8) in temporary differences expected to be taxable in 20X7 and 20X8 also are assumed to be realized in 20X5 and 20X6 as a result of the expected carryback of the 20X7 and 20X8 losses. If the $50,000 in temporary differences had not been taxable in 20X7 and 20X8 the $55,000 of losses would have been $50,000 more. The taxable temporary differences reduce the loss carryback from what it would have been without the differences. Therefore, the taxable temporary differences are realized in 20X5 and 20X6 using the 30% tax rate applicable to the years that offset the 20X7–20X8 losses.

Using the $186,750 deferred tax asset balance and the $238,070 deferred tax liability balance from Table 7-70, the deferred tax benefit, the deferred tax expense, income taxes payable, and tax expense are computed in Table 7-71.

Table 7-71 Computation of Deferred Tax Benefit/Expense, Taxes Payable, and Tax Expense for 20X6

Computation of Deferred Tax Benefit/Expense:		
Ending deferred tax asset balance (from Table 7-70)	$(186,750)	
Ending deferred tax liability balance (from Table 7-70)		$238,070
Beginning deferred tax asset balance	124,600	
Beginning deferred tax liability balance		(122,000)

Deferred tax benefit for 20X6	$(62,150)	
Deferred tax expense for 20X6		$116,070
Computation of Taxes Payable and Tax Expense:		
Taxable income (Example 7-32 assumptions)		$30,000
Tax rate in 20X6 (Example 7-32 assumptions)		30 %
Taxes payable for 20X6		$9,000
Deferred tax benefit for 20X6 (above)		(62,150)
Deferred tax expense for 20X6 (above)		116,070
Income tax expense for 20X6		$62,920

Using the information from Table 7-71, the required tax journal entry for 20X6 can be prepared.

Income Tax Expense	62,920	
Deferred Tax Asset	62,150	
Income Taxes Payable		9,000
Deferred Tax Liability		116,070

The income statement presentation of income tax expense and deferred taxes has been illustrated in Example 7-31. Refer to the prior solution for the presentation.

This completes the analysis of Example 7-32. Example 7-32 illustrated a situation where currently enacted tax rates changed over the time period that temporary differences were taxable or deductible. Example 7-33 illustrates a situation where a valuation allowance must be established for a deferred tax asset. The assumptions for Example 7-33 are as follows.

Example 7-33
Assumptions for Deferred Tax Computations

1. Clark Enterprises (Clark) is computing deferred taxes for 20X6 and has accumulated the following information about financial accounting basis and tax basis of assets and liabilities

	Tax Basis	Financial Basis	Temporary Difference
a. Litigation liability	$0	$350,000	$350,000
b. Depreciable assets	500,000	790,000	290,000
c. Rent in advance	0	200,000	200,000

2. Clark also has temporary differences of $170,000 related to long-term contracts that are a result of using percentage of completion for books and the modified method for tax purposes. Temporary differences related to the long-term contract are estimated to be realized as follows: $45,000 during 20X7, and $45,000 during 20X8, $50,000 during 20X9–2010, and $30,000 during 2011–2012. Temporary differences of $290,000 for depreciable assets relate to excess of accelerated depreciation for tax purposes over straight-line depreciation for books. For each of the future years 20X7–2012, book depreciation is exceeding tax depreciation and the book value of the assets is being recovered

during this time period. The recovery is estimated as follows: $65,000 during 20X7, and $65,000 during 20X8, $90,000 during 20X9–2010, and $70,000 during 2011–2012. Temporary differences of $350,000 related to the litigation liability were created when the expense was accrued for book purposes. It will be deducted for tax when paid. The litigation liability is estimated to be settled in the following time periods: $20,000 in 20X7, and $20,000 in 20X8, $100,000 in 20X9–2010, and $210,000 in 2011–2012. The $200,000 in temporary differences related to rent in advance was recorded as a liability when the cash was received. The liability is estimated to be settled as follows: $15,000 in 20X7, and $15,000 in 20X8, $75,000 during 20X9–2010, and $95,000 during 2011–2012.

3. There are no operating loss or tax credit carryforwards for tax purposes, and the alternative minimum tax is not applicable in this situation.
4. Taxable income for 20X6 is $500,000 and, based on all available information, Clark estimates that it will have sufficient income in all future years to realize all benefits from the temporary differences, except for $100,000 of deductible temporary differences in 2011 and 2012. There is a greater than 50% likelihood that the deferred tax asset related to these differences will not be realized.
5. The deferred tax asset balance at the beginning of 20X6 is $120,000 and the deferred liability balance is $116,000.
6. Currently enacted tax rates are as follows:

20X6	30%
20X7–20X8	35%
20X9–2010	40%
2011–2012	45%

Using the information from Example 7-33, the deferred tax asset balance and the deferred tax liability balance at the end of 20X6 are computed in Table 7-72.

Table 7-72 Computation of Deferred Taxes for 20X6 Temporary Differences Recovered from Future Years

Deductible Temporary Differences: [a]	**20X7/X8**	**20X9/10**	**2011/12**	**20X6 Balance**
Litigation liability	$(40,000)	$(100,000)	$(210,000)	
Rent in advance	(30,000)	(75,000)	(95,000)	
Total deductible temporary differences	$(70,000)	$(175,000)	$(305,000)	
Currently enacted future tax rates	35 %	40 %	45 %	
Deferred tax asset	$(24,500)	$(70,000)	$(137,250)	$(231,750)

Taxable Temporary Differences: [a]				
Long-term contracts	$90,000	$50,000	$30,000	
Recovery of asset (depreciation)	130,000	90,000	70,000	
Total taxable temporary differences	$220,000	$140,000	$100,000	
Currently enacted future tax rates	35 %	40 %	45 %	
Deferred tax liability	$77,000	$56,000	$45,000	$178,000

Unless otherwise indicated in the text of the material, the amount for each taxable or deductible temporary difference is the summation of the temporary differences that would be taxable or deductible in the years indicated. For example, the deductible temporary difference for litigation liability of $40,000 for 20X7/X8 is composed of the following: $20,000 from 20X7, and $20,000 from 20X8.

All temporary differences and change in tax rate computations used in Table 7-72, except for temporary differences related to long-term contracts, have been explained in detail in prior examples and will not be repeated in Example 7-33. Temporary differences related to long-term construction contracts do not cause a difference between the book and tax basis of an asset or liability because the differences are reported on the tax balance sheet, but not on the financial accounting balance sheet (see Chart 7-16). Revenues from the contracts are recognized for book purposes as costs are incurred and at a later date for tax purposes. Therefore, the temporary differences are taxable in the future years when the revenue is recognized for tax purposes. Refer to prior examples for a detailed review of other temporary differences. The information computed in Table 7-72 can now be used with other assumptions from Example 7-33 to compute the information for the tax journal entry for 20X6. The information for the 20X6 journal entry is computed in Table 7-73.

Table 7-73 Computation of Deferred Tax Benefit/Expense, Taxes Payable, Tax Expense, and Deferred Tax Asset Valuation Allowance for 20X6

Computation of Deferred Tax Benefit/Expense:		
Ending deferred tax asset balance (from Table 7-72)	$(231,750)	
Ending deferred tax liability balance (from Table 7-72)		$178,000
Beginning deferred tax asset balance	120,000	
Beginning deferred tax liability balance		(116,000)
Deferred tax benefit for 20X6	$(111,750)	
Deferred tax expense for 20X6		$62,000
Computation of Taxes Payable and Tax Expense:		
Taxable income (Example 7-33 assumptions)		$500,000
Tax rate in 20X6 (Example 7-33 assumptions)		30 %
Taxes payable for 20X6		$150,000

Deferred tax benefit for 20X6 (above)	(111,750)
Deferred tax expense for 20X6 (above)	62,000
Income tax expense for 20X6	$100,250
Computation of Valuation Allowance:	
Deductible temporary difference not expected to be realized	$100,000
Tax rate in 2011/12	45 %
Valuation allowance at the end of 20X6	$45,000
Valuation allowance at the end of 20X5	0
Increase/(decrease) in valuation allowance	$45,000

Because there is a greater than 50% likelihood that $100,000 of temporary differences expected to be deductible in 2011 and 2012 will not be realized because of the lack of income, a valuation allowance account must be established to reduce the deferred tax asset account, computed in Table 7-72, to the amount that is likely (more than 50%) to be realized. Because the temporary differences not expected to be realized are deductible in 2011 and 2012 when the tax rate is 45%, the valuation allowance will be established at the 45% tax rate. All calculations in Table 7-73 have been discussed in detail in prior examples and no further explanation is required.

Using information from Table 7-73, the tax journal entries required for 20X6 are as follows:

Income Tax Expense	100,250	
Deferred Tax Asset	111,750	
Income Taxes Payable		150,000
Deferred Tax Liability		62,000
Income Tax Expense	45,000	
Valuation Allowance to Reduce Deferred Tax Asset to Realizable Amounts		45,000

The Valuation Allowance to Reduce Deferred Tax Asset to Realizable Amounts account is a contra asset and will be offset against the deferred tax asset balance.

The deferred tax asset valuation allowance account may change from accounting period to accounting period as assumptions change relative to future income. To illustrate, assume the same information in Example 7-33, except for the following: Clark is computing deferred taxes for 20X7, taxable income for 20X7 is $400,000, taxable and deductible temporary differences reverse out in 20X7 as indicated in the Example 7-33 assumptions, and Clark estimates that there is a greater than 50% likelihood that only $20,000 of temporary differences expected to be deductible in 2011 and 2012 will not be realized because of the lack of income. Using these changed assumptions, deferred taxes are computed for 20X7 in Table 7-74.

Table 7-74 Computation of Deferred Taxes for 20X7

Temporary Differences Recovered from Future Years

	20X8	20X9/10	2011/12	20X7 Balance
Deductible Temporary Differences:[a]				
Litigation liability	$(20,000)	$(100,000)	$(210,000)	
Rent in advance	(15,000)	(75,000)	(95,000)	
Total deductible temporary differences	$(35,000)	$(175,000)	$(305,000)	
Currently enacted future tax rates	35 %	40 %	45 %	
Deferred tax asset	$(12,250)	$(70,000)	$(137,250)	$(219,500)
Taxable Temporary Differences:[a]				
Long-term contracts	$45,000	$50,000	$30,000	
Recovery of asset (depreciation)	65,000	90,000	70,000	
Total taxable temporary differences	$110,000	$140,000	$100,000	
Currently enacted future tax rates	35 %	40 %	45 %	
Deferred tax liability	$38,500	$56,000	$45,000	$139,500

[a] Temporary differences for construction of Table 7-74 were taken from Example 7-33, Assumption 1.

Using the deferred tax asset and liability balances from Table 7-74, the information needed for the tax journal entries at the end of 20X7 is computed in Table 7-75.

Table 7-75 Computation of Deferred Tax Benefit/Expense, Taxes Payable, Tax Expense, and Deferred Tax Asset Valuation Allowance for 20X7

Computation of Deferred Tax Benefit/Expense:		
Ending deferred tax asset balance (from Table 7-74)	$(219,500)	
Ending deferred tax liability balance (from Table 7-74)		$139,500
Beginning deferred tax asset balance (from Table 7-72)	231,750	
Beginning deferred tax liability balance (from Table 7-72)		(178,000)
Deferred tax expense for 20X7	$12,250	
Deferred tax benefit for 20X7		$(38,500)

Computation of Taxes Payable and Tax Expense:	
Taxable income (assumptions in text)	$400,000
Tax rate in 20X7 (Example 7-33 assumptions)	35 %
Taxes payable for 20X7	$140,000
Deferred tax benefit for 20X7 (above)	(38,500)
Deferred tax expense for 20X7 (above)	12,250
Income tax expense for 20X7	$113,750
Computation of Valuation Allowance:	
Deductible temporary difference not expected to be realized	$20,000
Tax rate in 2011/12	45 %
Valuation allowance at the end of 20X7	$9,000
Valuation allowance at the end of 20X6 (from Table 7-73)	(45,000)
Increase/(decrease) in valuation allowance	$(36,000)

From the Table 7-75 computations, because no temporary differences were added in 20X7 and the temporary differences at the end of 20X6 that were expected to be recovered in 20X7 were recovered as anticipated, both the deferred tax asset and liability balances decreased for 20X7. The decrease in the deferred tax asset is a deferred tax expense for 20X7, and the decrease in the deferred tax liability is a deferred tax benefit. In addition, Table 7-75 indicates that, because assumptions changed relative to the amount of deductible temporary differences that are estimated to be realized, the valuation allowance must be adjusted at the end of 20X7. At the end of 20X7, Clark estimates that there is a greater than 50% likelihood that $20,000 of the deductible temporary differences at the end of 20X7 will not be realized. Therefore, the valuation allowance account should only have a balance of $9,000, and it must be decreased by $36,000 to reflect the fact that more of the deferred tax asset is expected to be realized. Information from Table 7-75 can be used to prepare the tax journal entries at the end of 20X7.

Income Tax Expense	113,750	
Deferred Tax Liability	38,500	
Income Taxes Payable		140,000
Deferred Tax Asset		12,250
Valuation Allowance to Reduce Deferred Tax Asset to Realizable Amounts	36,000	
Income Tax Expense		36,000

This completes the analysis of Example 7-33 for 20X7. Example 7-34 illustrates the accounting for deferred taxes when an entity has an actual tax loss and investment tax credit carryforward. Assumptions for Example 7-34 are as follows.

Example 7-34
Assumptions for Deferred Tax Computations

1. Howard Enterprises (Howard) is computing deferred taxes for 20X6 and has accumulated the following information about financial accounting basis and tax basis of assets and liabilities as of the end of 20X6:

	Tax Basis	Financial Basis	Temporary Difference
a. Litigation liability	$0	$300,000	$300,000
b. Warranty liability	0	60,000	60,000
c. Compensated absence liability	0	40,000	40,000
d. Rent in advance	0	100,000	100,000
e. Depreciable assets	500,000	800,000	300,000
f. Installment sales	0	150,000	150,000

2. Howard meets the requirements for use of the installment sales basis, and the temporary difference represents gross profit from the sale.

3. In addition to the temporary differences listed above, Howard has $125,000 of temporary differences related to long-term construction contracts from using percentage-of-completion for financial accounting purposes and modified percentage-of-completion for tax purposes.

4. Howard has an investment tax credit carryforward of $50,000 at the end of 20X6. Assume there is no limitation on its use.

5. Tax income for 20X3, 20X4, and 20X5 is $70,000, $156,000, and $150,000, respectively. Howard reported a tax loss of $350,000 for 20X6 and elected to carry the loss back two years and forward twenty. In addition, assume that there is no limitation on the use of the loss.

6. At the beginning of 20X6, the deferred tax asset balance related to temporary differences is $75,000, the deferred tax asset balance related to the investment tax credit is $50,000, and the deferred tax liability balance is $55,000.

7. Based on all available information, Howard estimates that it will have sufficient income in all future years to realize all benefits from temporary differences, investment tax credits, and operating loss carryforwards.

8. Currently enacted tax rates are as follows:

20X3	20%
20X4	25%
20X5	30%
20X6	35%
20X7 and after	40%

Using the assumptions in Example 7-34, all information for the tax journal entry at the end of 20X6 is computed in Table 7-76.

Table 7-76 Computation of Receivable from Loss Carryback, Deferred Tax Asset/Liability, Deferred Tax Benefit/Expense, Taxes Payable, and Tax Expense for 20X6

Computation of Receivable from Loss Carryback:			
20X4 tax income	156,000 × 25% =	39,000	
20X5 tax income	150,000 × 30% =	45,000	
Total receivable from loss carryback			$84,000
Computation of Deferred Tax Asset:			
Deferred Tax Asset from Temporary Differences:			
Litigation liability		$(300,000)	
Warranty liability		(60,000)	
Compensated absence liability		(40,000)	
Rent in advance		(100,000)	
Total deductible temporary differences		$(500,000)	
Currently enacted tax rate		40 %	
Deferred tax balance at the end of 20X6		$(200,000)	
Beginning deferred tax asset balance		75,000	
Deferred tax benefit from temporary differences (20X6)			$(125,000)
Deferred Tax Asset from Operating Loss Carryforward:			
Operating loss carryforward		$(44,000)[a]	
Currently enacted tax rate		40 %	
Deferred tax asset balance at the end of 20X6		$(17,600)	
Beginning deferred tax asset balance		0	
Deferred tax benefit from operating loss carryforward			(17,600)
Deferred Tax Asset from Investment Tax Credit (ITC) Carryforward:			
ITC carryforward at the end of 20X6		$(50,000)	
Beginning deferred tax asset from ITC		50,000	
Deferred tax benefit from ITC carryforward			0

Computation of Deferred Tax Liability:		
Taxable Temporary Differences:		
Recovery of depreciable assets	$300,000	
Installment sales	150,000	
Long-term contracts	125,000	
Total taxable temporary differences	$575,000	
Currently enacted tax rate	40 %	
Deferred tax liability balance at end of 20X6	$230,000	
Beginning deferred tax liability balance	(55,000)	
Deferred tax expense for 20X6		175,000
Income tax expense for 20X6		$32,400

[a] The $44,000 operating loss carryforward is the $350,000 tax loss for 20X6 – $156,000 20X2 carryback– $150,000 20X5 carryback.

Howard had a tax operating loss during 20X6 and elected to first carry the loss back two years to 20X4 and 20X5 and recapture taxes actually paid in those years. $156,000 of the loss is used to recapture taxes of $39,000 in 20X4, and $45,000 of taxes is recaptured in 20X5 when the tax rate is 30%. Howard will record a receivable for $84,000, which is the amount of taxes recovered from prior years. Howard used $306,000 ($156,000 + $150,000) of the $350,000 operating loss as a carryback, leaving $44,000 of the loss that can be used as a loss carryforward in the computation of a deferred tax asset. The 20X6 ending deferred tax asset balance of $267,600 is composed of three parts as follows:

1. A $200,000 asset related to temporary differences,
2. A $17,600 asset related to the operating loss carryforward, and
3. A $50,000 asset related to the investment tax credit carryforward.

However, the change in the deferred tax asset account for 20X6 is only $142,600 (deferred tax asset benefit of $125,000 + $17,600 deferred tax benefit from the operating loss carryforward). All temporary differences can be combined when computing the deferred tax asset because the currently enacted tax rate of 40% is the same in all future years. The operating loss carryforward is used to compute a deferred tax asset because it can be used to offset taxable income in future years and reduce the amount of taxes paid. The deferred asset associated with the operating loss is computed by multiplying the appropriate tax rate by the operating loss. The appropriate tax rate or rates is the enacted future rate in the period that the operating loss is realized. Because the tax rate in Example 7-34 is constant, it is not necessary to determine when the operating loss carryforward is going to be realized. The investment tax credit carryforward is applied directly to reduce taxes payable; consequently, the amount of the credit is a deferred tax asset. The assumptions in Example 7-34 specify that Howard will have sufficient income in all future years to realize all benefits from the temporary differences, operating loss carryforward, and the investment tax credit carryforward; therefore, a valuation allowance for the deferred tax asset balance is unnecessary. The deferred tax asset related to the deductible temporary differences created a deferred tax benefit of $125,000 for 20X6, because there was a beginning balance in the asset account of $75,000. There is a $17,600 deferred tax benefit from the operating loss carryforward because there was no beginning deferred tax asset balance for the operating loss. There is no deferred tax benefit in 20X6 for the ITC carryforward because there is no change in the deferred tax asset balance related to the ITC. All deductible and taxable temporary differences have been discussed in detail in previous examples and will not be repeated.

By using the information from Table 7-76, the tax journal entry at the end of 20X6 can be prepared as follows:

Income Tax Expense	32,400	
Receivable from Loss Carryback	84,000	
Deferred Tax Asset	142,600	
Tax Effect of Loss Carryback		84,000
Deferred Tax Liability		175,000

The Receivable from Loss Carryback is classified as a current asset, and the Tax Effect of Loss Carryback is reported in the income statement following income tax expense. It will decrease the loss for 20X6 by $84,000.

Special Areas

ASC 740-30 covers the income tax accounting for special areas such as subsidiaries and corporate joint ventures. The central issue addressed by ASC 740-30 is the income tax accounting for undistributed earnings. Undistributed earnings of these companies are equal to the difference between the parent company's percentage share of the reported earnings and the dividends distributed. Under the equity method of accounting for investments in subsidiaries and corporate joint ventures, the parent company recognizes income as earned by the subsidiary or joint venture, rather than as it is received. (Topic 323 in Chapter 3 details the analysis of accounting for investments using the equity method.) Therefore, the parent would recognize income based upon the entire reported income, whether distributed or undistributed. The income thus recognized would be included in the parent company's income and enter into the computation of the deferred taxes of the parent. However, income is not recognized for tax purposes until such time as the dividends are received. The issue is whether the undistributed earnings of the subsidiary or corporate joint venture should be treated as a temporary difference.

Normally, undistributed earnings of a subsidiary or corporate joint venture should be treated as a temporary difference in the computation of deferred tax liabilities by the parent company. The reason for this treatment is based upon the assumption that eventually all earnings will be paid to the parent in the form of dividends. According to ASC 740-30-25-18, an exception to this general rule exists if a subsidiary or corporate joint venture (classified as domestic) had undistributed earnings that were earned on or prior to December 15, 1992, evidence to indicate that the subsidiary or joint venture has permanently invested or will permanently invest the undistributed earnings, or will pay out the undistributed earnings in the form of a tax-free liquidation (i.e., the difference is permanent in duration). The determination as to whether a company intends to indefinitely postpone the payment of undistributed earnings is largely a matter of managerial judgment. If undistributed earnings arise in a domestic subsidiary or domestic corporate joint venture in years beginning after December 15, 1992, the undistributed earnings are treated as temporary differences in the deferred tax computation, unless the temporary differences are nontaxable. The differences are considered nontaxable when the earnings can be recovered tax free according to tax law and the entity intends to use that method to recover the investment.

When a foreign company is taxed at a different rate on income that is not distributed to stockholders compared to income that is distributed to stockholders, a tax credit is given to the company for the tax difference when the company pays out dividends from undistributed income. Any tax benefit from the tax credit is used to reduce tax expense in the accounting period that the tax credit is used to reduce taxable income and, therefore, the tax impact of temporary differences should be computed using the rate that is applied to income not distributed to stockholders. Use by a parent company of a foreign subsidiary of either the rate for undistributed income or the rate for distributed income for the tax impact of the foreign company's operations depends upon the parent company's determination regarding indefinite reversal.

When undistributed earnings are treated as temporary differences, the differences should be included in the computation of deferred tax liabilities using the provisions of ASC 740.

If it was assumed previously that distribution of part or all of the undistributed earnings would be indefinitely postponed, but it now appears that these earnings will be distributed in the form of dividends, the deferred tax computation in the current period must include the temporary differences related to undistributed earnings.

The opposite situation would occur where deferred taxes were established for temporary differences related to undistributed earnings, but it now appears that those earnings will not be distributed. Rather, they will be permanently invested by the subsidiary or corporate joint venture. In this case, the parent company should remove the related temporary differences when computing the current year deferred taxes.

If the investment in a subsidiary decreases so that the investment is no longer accounted for as a subsidiary, the amount of the temporary differences and deferred tax liability will change. However, if an investment in an investee increases so that the investee becomes a subsidiary, any temporary differences for undistributed earnings prior to the date the investee becomes a subsidiary will continue to be treated as temporary differences unless cumulative dividends exceed cumulative earnings subsequent to the date of the change from investee to a subsidiary status.

ASC 740-30-25, paragraphs 5 and 18, cover two other areas related to subsidiaries—joint ventures and investee companies. If an entity has an investment of 50% or less in an investee company, the excess of book basis of the investment over its tax basis is treated as a temporary difference for purposes of computing a deferred tax liability, except for corporate joint ventures the duration of which is considered permanent (hereafter referred to as "considered permanent"). When an enterprise has an investment in a foreign subsidiary or foreign joint venture (considered permanent) and there is an excess of book basis over tax basis of the investment, the excess is not accounted for as a temporary difference.

An entity may have an investment in a subsidiary or corporate joint venture where the tax basis of the investment is in excess of the book basis. In this situation, the excess should be treated as a temporary difference and a deferred tax asset established (even for ventures considered permanent) if it appears that the difference will reverse in the future. When a deferred tax asset is established for this type of a situation, the entity must determine whether a valuation allowance is required for the asset.

ASC 740-10 together with ASC 810-10 prohibits the immediate recognition of the current and deferred income tax impact in the consolidated financial statements for intra-entity asset transfers. An entity is precluded from reflecting in its consolidated financial statements a tax benefit or expense from an intra-entity asset transfer between entities within the consolidation that file separate tax returns, whether or not such entities are in different tax jurisdictions, until the asset has been sold to a third party or otherwise recovered. Recognition of the deferred tax asset for the temporary difference arising from the excess of the buyer's tax basis over the cost to the seller is prohibited. The tax benefit from any step up in tax basis is recorded as it is realized each period, via a deduction in the tax return.

Uncertain Tax Positions

A *tax position* is a position that an entity took in a past tax return or that the entity expects to take in a future tax return that that has impacted or will impact the amounts and or timing of the entity's tax liabilities. A tax position taken by an entity may cause (1) income taxes to be permanently reduced, (2) income taxes that would be payable in the current year to be deferred to some future year, or (3) a change in the realizability of deferred tax assets. Taxpaying entities routinely take tax positions that they believe will minimize their tax liabilities in both the short-term and long-term. Under ASC 740, tax positions include, but are not limited to, the following: (1) an entity decides not to file a tax return, (2) an entity decides to classify as tax exempt a transaction, entity, or other tax position, (3) an entity decides to exclude income from the tax return, and (4) an entity decides to shift or allocate income between jurisdictions.

Because it is not always clear to taxpaying entities how they should apply provisions of tax law to the preparation of their tax returns, the validity of some tax positions that entities take is uncertain. ASC 740 contains specific provisions regarding how the degree of uncertainty associated with a tax position should be considered when recognizing and measuring current and deferred tax assets and liabilities for financial accounting purposes.

Once an entity decides that it has an uncertain tax position, the entity must apply a two-step process to determine the proper recognition and measurement of the tax position. First, the entity must determine whether a tax position should be recognized (the recognition criterion) and, second, the amount to be used in the measurement of the tax position (the measurement criteria). The recognition criterion includes a determination of two items, the appropriate unit of account and the recognition threshold.

ASC 740 provides little guidance on what constitutes the unit of account but indicates that the unit of account should be evaluated using individual facts and circumstances. In addition, ASC 740 states that the way that a tax return is prepared and supported by an entity, and the anticipated approach that a taxing authority will take on an audit, should be used by the entity when determining the unit of account. To illustrate the unit of account, assume that an entity expects to spend $400,000 on five research projects for a total of $2,000,000 and claim a $2,000,000 research experimentation credit on its tax return. The unit of account may be each individual research project or the total research projects. If management determines that the unit of account is each individual project, the credit for each individual project is to be evaluated to determine whether the expected benefit will be sustained.

Once an entity determines the unit of account, the next step is to determine the recognition threshold. The impact of the tax position should be recognized in the financial statements if it is more likely than not (likelihood is more than 50%) that the tax position will be sustained if it is examined by the appropriate taxing authority, based on all available information at the reporting date. The more-likely-than-not criterion should be assessed using the following factors: (1) the entity must assume that the tax return will be audited by the appropriate tax authority and the authority will have all appropriate information, (2) the entity should consider prior practices and precedents of the taxing authority with the entity or similar entities, and (3) the entity should evaluate each tax position separately, without consideration of any offsetting impacts of other tax positions.

Once the recognition criterion is met, the entity must measure the tax position. An entity should measure the benefit from a tax position at the largest amount that is in excess of 50% likely to be realized. This likely realization assumes effective settlement with the appropriate taxing authority that has full knowledge of the facts of the situation (ASC 740-10-25, paragraphs 9 through 12, provide conditions that may be used by an entity to evaluate whether a tax position has been effectively settled). The amounts and probabilities should be used when determining the amount of the tax position using all available information on the most recent balance sheet date (the reporting date). The measurement rules apply to both the initial and subsequent measurement of the tax position.

When realization of deferred tax assets is supported by future taxable income as a result of tax planning strategies, the rules for recognition and measurement of tax positions, as discussed above, should be used to determine the amount of future taxable income.

If a tax position that has been previously recognized no longer meets the more-likely-than-not criterion, the tax position should be removed or derecognized in the first accounting period that the more-likely-than-not criterion is no longer met. A valuation allowance cannot be used for the derecognition. The benefit of a tax position should be reported in the first interim period that meets one of the following conditions when the more-likely-than-not criterion is not met in the period that the tax position is taken or anticipated to be taken: (1) statute of limitations has expired for the examination and challenge of the tax position, (2) the tax issue has been settled, or (3) the recognition criterion has been met by the reporting date. An entity may have a change in judgment that requires a change in the tax position that was taken in a prior accounting period, such as a change in the measurement amount, recognition, or derecognition of the position. When there is a change in judgment, the impact of the change should be accounted for in the accounting period of the change as a discrete item. If the change in judgment is a result of a position taken in an interim accounting period of the same annual accounting period, the provisions of ASC 270-10 and ASC 740-270 should be used for the appropriate accounting.

The provisions of ASC 740 should be used when computing deferred tax assets, deferred tax liabilities, and amounts that are payable or due from the appropriate taxing authority for prior tax positions that existed on the date of a business combination. In addition, when there is a change in an acquired tax position or a tax position is changed as a result of an acquisition, the following process should be used: (1) goodwill should be adjusted for a corresponding amount for any changes that occur during the measurement period when the change is a result of new information about situations that existed on the date of acquisition. If such an adjustment reduces goodwill to zero, any additional adjustment is reported as a gain on a bargain purchase using the provisions of ASC 805-30. Any other change in a tax position acquired in a business combination is accounted for using the provisions of ASC 740.

An entity may incur interest and penalties as a result of the underpayment of taxes or failure of the tax position to meet the more-likely-than-not criterion. When interest is required to be reported, the entity should record an expense beginning in the first accounting period that tax law would require interest to be accrued by multiplying the appropriate statutory tax rate to the difference between the amount taken or expected to be taken in the tax return and the amount required to be reported using the provisions of ASC 740. Any required penalty should be reported by the entity as an expense in the period that the position is taken in the tax return. If conditions change where a penalty was reported but is no longer required, the penalty should be derecognized in the period that the conditions change. Interest recognized may be reported as either income tax expense or interest expense. The expense related to penalties may be reported as either income tax expense or another expense category.

An entity should classify a liability related to an unrecognized tax benefit as a result of applying the provisions of ASC 740 as a current liability if it meets the definition of a current liability (payment within one year or the normal operating cycle, whichever is longer). The liabilities related to unrecognized tax benefits should not be combined with deferred tax assets or deferred tax liabilities.

To illustrate the measurement of uncertain tax positions, assume the facts in Example 7-35.

Example 7-35
Uncertain Tax Position Assumptions

1. XYZ Company has met the recognition threshold for two different uncertain tax positions.
2. In the first uncertain tax position, the Company has a benefit of $2,000,000 that should be recognized and measured, and it has accumulated the following amounts and probabilities of possible outcomes for the benefit:

Anticipated Outcomes	Estimated Probabilities	Cumulative Probabilities
$2,000,000	20%	20%
1,500,000	40%	60%
1,000,000	30%	90%
500,000	10%	100%

3. In the second uncertain tax position, the Company has a benefit of $5,000,000 that should be recognized and measured, and it has accumulated the following amounts and probabilities of possible outcomes for the benefit:

Anticipated Outcomes	Estimated Probabilities	Cumulative Probabilities
$5,000,000	10%	10%
4,000,000	15%	25%
3,000,000	20%	45%
2,500,000	30%	75%
1,000,000	10%	85%
500,000	10%	95%
100,000	5%	100%

XYZ Company would report a tax benefit of $1,500,000 for the first uncertain tax position because $1,500,000 is the largest amount of benefit that exceeds 50% likely of being realized at the time of settlement. The estimated probability for $1,500,000 is 40%, but the cumulative probability is 60%, which exceeds 50%. No other amount below the $1,500,000 is greater than the $1,500,000 anticipated amount.

In the second uncertain tax position, XYZ Company should report a tax benefit of $2,500,000 because the $2,500,000 is the largest amount of benefit that exceeds 50% likely to be realized at the time of settlement. Note that the cumulative probability is 75% and the prior anticipated amount of $3,000,000 is only 45%. Therefore, the $3,000,000 does not meet the 50% threshold.

To illustrate journal entries for uncertain tax positions, assume the facts in Example 7-36.

Example 7-36
Uncertain Tax Position Assumptions

1. ABC Inc., a December 31 year-end company, is computing deferred taxes for 20X8 and has one uncertain tax position. ABC's current and currently enacted future tax rates are 40%.
2. ABC received notice in 20X8 from the appropriate federal agency that ABC may have to pay for certain environmental pollution problems. The following facts relate to this environmental issue:
   a. An expense and liability was recognized in 20X8 for $4,000,000 for financial accounting purposes because ABC determined that it is probable that $4,000,000 would be paid for the pollution problem.
   b. ABC did not intend to deduct the $4,000,000 in the 20X8 tax return. Subsequently, ABC entered into a contract that allowed them to deduct the $4,000,000 in the 20X8 tax return.
   c. ABC determines that the $4,000,000 tax deduction will not meet the recognition criterion for deduction in 20X8.
   d. ABC expects to have sufficient income in future accounting periods to realize the benefit from the $4,000,000 deduction.
   e. ABC expects to pay a penalty of $100,000 and interest of $200,000 as a result of underpayment of taxes from the tax position taken.
   f. The $4,000,000 is the largest amount of benefit that exceeds 50% likely to be realized at the time of settlement.

Because ABC reported a deduction of $4,000,000 for both financial accounting and tax purposes, initially there was no temporary difference created for the environmental pollution problem. However, a temporary difference of $4,000,000 is created because the $4,000,000 tax deduction did not meet the recognition criterion of ASC 740. Therefore, ABC must establish a deferred tax asset and a tax liability of $1,600,000 ($4,000,000 × 40%) for the uncertain tax position. The tax liability would be classified as a current liability if ABC expects to pay taxes to the taxing authority within one year or the normal operating cycle, whichever is longer, otherwise the liability would be classified as long-term in the statement of financial position. The journal entry to reflect this tax position is as follows:

Deferred Tax Asset	1,600,000	
Taxes Payable		1,600,000

Because ABC expects to pay a penalty of $100,000 as a result of the underpayment of taxes, the following entry is required:

Estimated Penalty for Underpayment of Taxes	100,000	
Estimated Liability for Underpayment of Taxes		100,000

An entity can elect to include the penalty for underpayment of taxes in income tax expense or treat it as a separate expense in the income statement. The estimated liability is classified as a current liability if ABC expects to pay the penalty to the taxing authority within one year or the normal operating cycle, whichever is longer, otherwise the liability would be classified as long-term in the statement of financial position. The entry for the $200,000 of accrued interest on the underpayment is presented as follows:

Interest Expense or Income Tax Expense	200,000	
Interest Payable		200,000

Specific Guidance for an Unrecognized Tax Benefit

ASU 2013-11, *Income Taxes (Topic 740): Presentation of an Unrecognized Tax Benefit When a Net Operating Loss Carryforward, a Similar Tax Loss, or a Tax Credit Carryforward Exists,* was issued to eliminate diversity in the presentation of unrecognized tax benefits when net operating loss or tax credit carryovers exist. Generally, in those situations, unrecognized benefits are reflected in the financial statements as reductions of deferred income tax assets. ASU 2013-11 provides for an exception as follows.

If the carryover is not available at the report date to settle any additional taxes that would result from the disallowance or the tax law does not require the entity to use, and the entity does not intend to use, the deferred tax asset, then the reporting entity would reflect the unrecognized benefit as a liability.

Other Considerations Related to Deferred Tax Calculations

This section covers several miscellaneous situations relating to deferred tax calculations that are specialized in nature such as business combinations, foreign assets and liabilities, interim accounting periods, changes in tax rates and laws, and leveraged leases.

An entity that enters into a business combination using the provisions of ASC 805 must recognize, on the date of acquisition, a deferred tax asset or deferred tax liability for the taxable or deductible differences, or the operating loss and tax credit carryforwards of the acquired company. However, deferred taxes should not be computed on differences related to goodwill amortization not deductible for tax purposes, leveraged leases, and other differences related to ASC 740-30.

When a business combination is accounted for under the provisions of ASC 805, the acquired company may have deductible temporary differences, operating loss carryforwards, or tax credit carryforwards that require an acquiring entity to recognize a deferred tax asset as a result of the acquisition. ASC 740 should be used to determine whether a valuation allowance is required by the acquirer for any deferred tax asset recognized. Circumstances may require a change in the valuation allowance account, and changes should be reported in the following manner:

1. Adjust goodwill for changes (changes that occurred within the measurement period) related to new information about circumstances existing on the date of acquisition. The measurement period is defined in ASC 805-10-25, paragraphs 13 through 19.
2. If goodwill in item 1, above, is reduced to zero, any additional decrease in the valuation allowance is reported as a bargain purchase using the provisions of ASC 805-30-30, paragraphs 4 through 6.
3. Other changes not covered in items 1 and 2, above, are accounted for as a change in income tax expense or, if appropriate, an adjustment to contributed capital.

When an entity is required to remeasure its foreign assets and liabilities from a local currency to a functional currency under ASC 830, there may be a difference between the historical rates and the rates used in the remeasurement process. This difference is not accounted for as a temporary difference.

When an enterprise prepares interim period reports, tax expense must be computed using the estimated annual effective tax rate applied on a year-to-date basis with taxes from prior quarters of the current year deducted from the year-to-date amount. This approach is consistent with the provisions of ASC 270-10 and ASC 740-270, except as noted below. Because ASC 740 requires that a balance sheet approach using an asset/liability method be used in the computation of deferred taxes, the calculation of the estimated annual effective tax rate is more complex. Under ASC 740, both the taxes payable (current part of tax expense) and the deferred tax expense or benefit (deferred part of tax expense) are computed directly and combined to indirectly compute income tax expense. Therefore, computing the effective annual tax rate for interim reporting purposes requires a two-step calculation. First, the part of the effective rate related to the current part of the tax expense can be computed based on the estimated annual tax liability. Second, the deferred part of the tax rate should be based on the estimated annual deferred tax provision. A combination of the two steps provides the annual effective tax rate for interim reporting purposes. The two-step process requires an estimate of the year-end taxes payable and the year-end deferred tax asset and liability computation.

Changes in tax laws and tax rates should be included in the interim period encompassing the enactment date, and adjustments to valuation allowance accounts as a result of changes in judgment should be included in the interim period when the judgments about the account change.

Because deferred tax assets and deferred tax liabilities are computed based on existing tax law, a change in tax law or a change in enacted tax rates will have an impact on the deferred tax asset and liability calculations. An adjustment is required for deferred tax assets and liabilities when changes in tax law or tax rates occur, and the impact of the adjustment should be included as a component of income from continuing operations in the accounting period that encompasses the date of enactment. In addition to the impact on deferred taxes from changes in tax laws or tax rates, deferred taxes may be impacted by a change in the tax status of an enterprise. For example, a corporation may change to a partnership or a partnership may change to a corporation. Deferred tax assets and/or liabilities should be added or eliminated when the tax status of the enterprise changes using the provisions of ASC 740. The impact of the change is included in income from continuing operations.

Deferred taxes related to leveraged leases should be accounted for using the provisions of ASC 840. In some cases, an integration of the temporary differences computed for leveraged leases using ASC 840 is required with other temporary differences computed using ASC 740.

Intraperiod Tax Allocation

Intraperiod tax allocation is the process of allocating the income tax expense or benefit computed using the deferred tax procedures, discussed in the preceding section, to individual items on the income statement and balance sheet that have individual tax consequences and are required to be reported separately and net of their related tax effect. ASC 225-20 requires that segment dispositions be reported as separate items in the income statement, net of the related tax effect.

ASC 740 requires that income tax expense/benefit computed using the deferred tax procedures be allocated within one accounting period among the following items when the income statement and balance sheet are prepared:

1. Income from continuing operations.
2. Gains and losses from discontinued operations.
3. Stockholders' equity items.

For a detailed analysis of the accounting and reporting requirements of items 1 through 4, see Topic 225 in Chapter 2. ASC 740-20-45-11 provides a listing of the types of items that are considered stockholders' equity items. A summary of the items is presented below:

1. Direct adjustments to beginning retained earnings for error corrections and changes in accounting principles that require a retrospective restatement of prior year financial statements.
2. Gains and losses from transactions where the gains and losses are not reported in net income but are reported in comprehensive income.
3. Costs that are reported differently for tax and book incomes for stock option plans under ASC 718-740.
4. Changes in paid-in-capital, such as reductions in paid-in-capital for expenses related to the issuance of stock.
5. Dividend payments charged to retained earnings for shares of stock related to an ESOP.
6. Temporary differences that are deductible and carryforwards on the date that an entity has a quasi-reorganization, unless exempt by ASC 852-740-45-3.

Some of the items listed above require further explanation. For example, gains and losses included in comprehensive income but excluded from net income (item 2) are unrealized gains and losses that are viewed as gains and losses, but are not reported in the income statement. For example, under ASC 320-10, an unrealized holding gain or loss from available-for-sale securities is viewed as a gain or loss, but the change in market value is reported in stockholders' equity and not in the income statement. The items that are included in comprehensive income but excluded from net income may change from time to time. Other examples are as follows:

- Foreign currency translation adjustments (ASC 830).
- Changes in prior service cost and net gains and losses from application of ASC 715.
- Prior service cost, net gains and losses, and transitional assets and obligations amortized to pension or postretirement cost using the provisions of ASC 715.

Under ASC 718, the amount of compensation expense deducted for book purposes may differ from the amount deducted for tax purposes. In some cases, this difference is an adjustment to the contributed capital of an enterprise and may require intraperiod tax allocation. A more detailed discussion of some of the other items in stockholders' equity that require intraperiod tax allocation may be found in ASC 718.

Income tax expense or tax benefit computed for the accounting period is applied to the items included in the income statement and balance sheet that are required to be reported net of tax using an incremental two-step approach. Under the first step, income tax expense or benefit is computed on income from continuing operations, assuming no other income or losses requiring intraperiod tax allocation. This amount reflects adjustments for the tax effect of changes in judgment about deferred tax asset realization, tax law or rate changes, tax status changes, uncertain tax positions, and dividends to stockholders that are tax deductible. Under the second step, the tax expense or benefit on total income including those other income or loss items requiring intraperiod tax allocation is determined. The difference between the tax expense or benefit under step 1 and step 2 is the total incremental tax expense or benefit. The incremental tax expense or benefit is allocated to all items requiring intraperiod tax allocation, except income from continuing operations. When the total incremental tax does not equal the sum of the incremental tax effects of two or more items, a formula basis is required in the allocation process. The following four-step process may be used in the allocation when a formula basis is required:

- **Step 1:** Compute the tax benefit of the total net loss items, other than loss from continuing operations.
- **Step 2:** Apportion ratably to each loss item the tax benefit.
- **Step 3:** Compute the tax impact of all gains and losses, other than income from continuing operations.
- **Step 4:** Compute the difference between Step 1 and Step 3 and ratably apportion the difference in each gain category.

Some intraperiod income and loss item categories may have two or more income and loss items within them such as two changes in accounting principles. When the individual items must be presented net of tax, the four-step process may be applied, if preferred, to the individual category.

One example is used to illustrate the technical application of intraperiod tax allocation. Assumptions for Example 7-37 are as follows.

Example 7-37
Assumptions for Intraperiod Tax Allocation

1. The following income, gain, loss, and equity items were reported by Love Enterprises during 20X6.

Income from continuing operations	$85,000
Loss from discontinued operations	(25,000)
Cumulative effect of change in accounting principle	(10,000)
Total before tax	$70,000

2. The company had the following tax rates during 20X6.

$ 0–$ 50,000	15%
$ 50,001–$75,000	25%
Over $75,000	35%
$100,000–$335,000	5% additional tax

Under the first step in applying the intraperiod tax allocation procedures compute the tax on income from continuing operations assuming no other intraperiod income or expense items. Under the second step compute the tax on total income including the intraperiod income and loss items. In addition, because graduated tax rates are used and income is not at the highest margin tax rate, the incremental tax on intraperiod items other than income from continuing operations will not equal the total computed incremental tax. The difference will be allocated proportionately. The calculation and intraperiod allocation of income taxes for the information shown in Example 7-37 is shown in Table 7-77.

Table 7-77 Computation of Tax for Continuing Operations and Incremental Tax

	Continuing Operations	Discontinued Operations	Accounting Change	Incremental Tax	Total
Income (loss) before tax	$85,000	$(25,000)	$10,000		$70,000
Tax	17,250	(3,750)	1,500	$(2,500)	12,500
Allocation of incremental tax		(1,775)	(725)	2,500	
Intraperiod tax allocation	17,250	(5,525)	775	-	12,500
Income (loss), net of tax	$67,750	$(19,475)	$9,225	-	$57,500

	Continuing Operations	Discontinued Operations	Accounting Change	Incremental Tax	Total
15% × first $50,000	7500	-3750	1500		7500
25% × next 25,000 up to $75,000	6250				5000
35% over $75,000	3500				
	17250	-3750	1500		12500

Allocation of incremental tax

Absolute Amounts	Percentage	Allocation
3,750	71	1775
1,500	29	725
5,250	100	2500

Table 7-78 Presentation of Allocation to Each Income, Gain, and Loss Item

	Income/(Loss)	(Expense)/ Benefit	Amounts After Tax
Income from continuing operations	$85,000	$(17,250)	$67,750
Discontinued operations	(25,000)	5,525	(19,475)
Accounting changes	10,000[a]	(775)	9,275[a]
Total income	$70,000	$12,500	$57,500

[a] Impact of the accounting change, after adjustment for the tax allocation, will be reported as a direct adjustment to beginning retained earnings in the retained earnings statement.

Using the summary information from Table 7-78, except for the accounting change, a partial income statement showing the intraperiod tax allocation is presented below. The cumulative effect, net of tax of the accounting change is not reported in the income statement but is included as a direct adjustment to beginning retained earnings in the retained earnings statement.

Love Enterprises Partial Income Statement For the Year Ended December 31, 20X6

Income from continuing operations before income taxes	$85,000
Income taxes	17,250
Income from continuing operations	$67,750
Loss on discontinued operations, net of tax benefit of $5,525	(19,475)
Cumulative effective of accounting changes, net of taxes of $775	9,275
Net income	$57,500

Disclosure Requirements

ASC 740-10-50 specifies the income statement, balance sheet, and related footnote disclosure requirements for deferred taxes. The disclosures are as follows:

1. For each accounting period presented, the amount of income tax expense or income tax benefit related to income from continuing operations divided into the following major categories should be disclosed:

   a. Amount of tax expense/benefit that is current.

   b. Amount of tax expense/benefit that is deferred. This excludes adjustments in c through h, below.

   c. Grants from the government, if used to reduce income tax expense.

   d. Investment tax credit.

   e. Changes in the deferred tax asset or deferred tax liability account that were caused by changes in the tax rate, tax status, and tax law.

   f. Changes in the valuation allowance account at the beginning of the accounting period that was caused by a change in estimate related to ability of the entity to realize the deferred tax asset.

   g. Benefit that an entity receives from an operating loss carryforward.

   h. Income tax expense impact from the allocation of selected income tax benefits to capital.

2. The total tax expense or tax benefit should be allocated among the following items on the income statement and balance sheet for each accounting period that the items are presented using intraperiod tax allocation procedures:

   a. Income from continuing operations.

   b. Gains and losses from discontinued operations.

   c. Retrospective impact of a change in accounting principle reported in the retained earnings statement.

   d. Other stockholders' equity items.

3. Within each tax jurisdiction, deferred tax assets should be netted against deferred tax liabilities, and the net deferred tax asset or liability should be reported as a noncurrent asset or liability in the balance sheet. The deferred tax asset should be reduced for any valuation allowance.

4. The following elements of deferred taxes and temporary differences must be disclosed:

   a. Total deferred tax assets, total deferred tax liabilities, and total valuation allowance account must be disclosed.

   b. Net change in the valuation allowance for the accounting period.

   c. Significant types of temporary differences and carryforwards that create the deferred tax assets and liabilities, and for public companies, the tax impact of each type.

5. The amount of tax operating loss carryforwards and tax credit carryforwards and the expiration dates of each. Also, the amount of the valuation allowance for which tax benefits will be allocated to capital.

6. The amount of tax expense reported for income from continuing operations must be reconciled with what tax expense would be for income from continuing operations if the domestic statutory tax rate (regular tax system) was used. Either percentages or dollars may be used in the reconciliation. The amount and nature of each significant item used in the reconciliation must be disclosed, unless the enterprise is a nonpublic company. Nonpublic companies do not have to present the numerical reconciliation, but must disclose significant items used in the reconciliation.

7. All significant items that impact interperiod comparability between or among the periods presented must be disclosed.

8. When a deferred tax liability is not reported for areas covered by the provisions of ASC 740-30 or ASC 995, the following selected disclosures are required:

   a. Description of the types of temporary differences and the events that would make these differences taxable.

   b. Deferred tax liability amount not recorded that relates to permanent duration investments in foreign joint ventures and subsidiaries, if practicable to determine. If not practicable, so state.

   c. Each type of temporary difference disclosed in cumulative amounts.

   d. Deferred tax liability amount (excluding items in b, above) not reported using the provisions of ASC 740-30.

9. The following disclosures are required by an enterprise that is part of a group that files a consolidated tax return and issues separate financial statements:

   a. For each period that an income statement is presented, the current tax expense and the deferred tax expense.

   b. For each period that a balance sheet is presented, the tax-related balances payable to or receivable from affiliates.

   c. Provisions used to allocate current and deferred tax expense to members of the group and the impact of changes in methods on disclosures in a. and b.

10. Disclose when the owners of a public company are taxed directly on the income of the company, and the difference in book and tax bases of assets and liabilities.

ASC 740-10-50, paragraphs 15, 15A, and 19, specify required disclosures for uncertain tax positions. The disclosures are as follows:

1. The entity must disclose the policy that is used for classifying interest and penalties in the income statement.
2. The entity must reconcile the beginning and ending balance in the unrecognized tax benefit. The following should be provided, as a minimum, in the reconciliation:
   a. Disclose, as a result of tax positions taken during the current period, the gross increase or decrease in the unrecognized tax benefit.
   b. Disclose, as a result of tax positions taken during a prior period, the gross increase or decrease in the unrecognized tax benefit.
   c. Disclose the decrease in the unrecognized tax position from lapse of the statute of limitations and from settlements during the period with the taxing authority.
3. Disclose the impact on the effective income tax rate if the unrecognized tax benefits were actually recognized.
4. Disclose penalties and interest recognized in the income statement and in the statement of financial position.
5. Disclose a description of the remaining tax years that are subject to examination by the appropriate taxing authority.
6. Disclose the following information when it is reasonably possible that unrecognized tax benefits will significantly change over the next 12 months:
   a. Nature of the uncertainty and nature of the event that could occur in the next 12 months that causes the increase or decrease.
   b. Provide an estimate of the range of the possible increase or decrease or specify that an estimate cannot be made.

Investment Tax Credit—Flowchart and General Discussion

ASC 740-10-25-46 specifies two acceptable methods of accounting for the investment tax credit. The preferable method is referred to as the deferral method (or the cost reduction method). The alternative method is known as the flow-through method (or the tax reduction method).

A reporting entity's management is free to choose between the deferral and the flow-through methods. Each method has a different impact on the balance sheet and income statement in any given year, but, in the long-run, the effects are identical. The situation is similar to selecting straight-line or accelerated depreciation.

The investment tax credit first was introduced in the Revenue Act of 1962, and was designed as an incentive for businesses to invest in productive assets. For tax purposes, the investment tax credit is a reduction in the current taxes payable by a company.

For financial accounting purposes, the deferral method treats the investment tax credit as a reduction in the cost of the equipment acquired. The amount of the credit is not used to reduce the cost basis of the property for accounting purposes, but is treated as a contra asset or a deferred credit. The investment tax credit established is amortized each period, as a reduction in income tax expense, in relation to the benefits received from the use of the asset (i.e., over the useful life of the asset acquired). The effects of the credit are recognized over the life of the asset and not just in the year the asset was purchased.

The flow-through method treats the entire investment tax credit as a reduction in income tax expense in the year the asset is acquired. The entire benefit of the credit is recognized in one year. This is similar to the income tax treatment of the credit. The primary advantage of the flow-through method is that it will increase income in the year an asset is acquired, whereas the deferral method recognizes the tax saving gradually.

Flowchart 7-8 identifies the major decisions required for the application of either the deferral or the flow-through method. Once it has been determined that the acquired asset qualifies for the investment tax credit (Block 1), and the amount of the credit has been determined, the company must then determine which of the two accounting methods to use (Block 2).

Flowchart 7-8

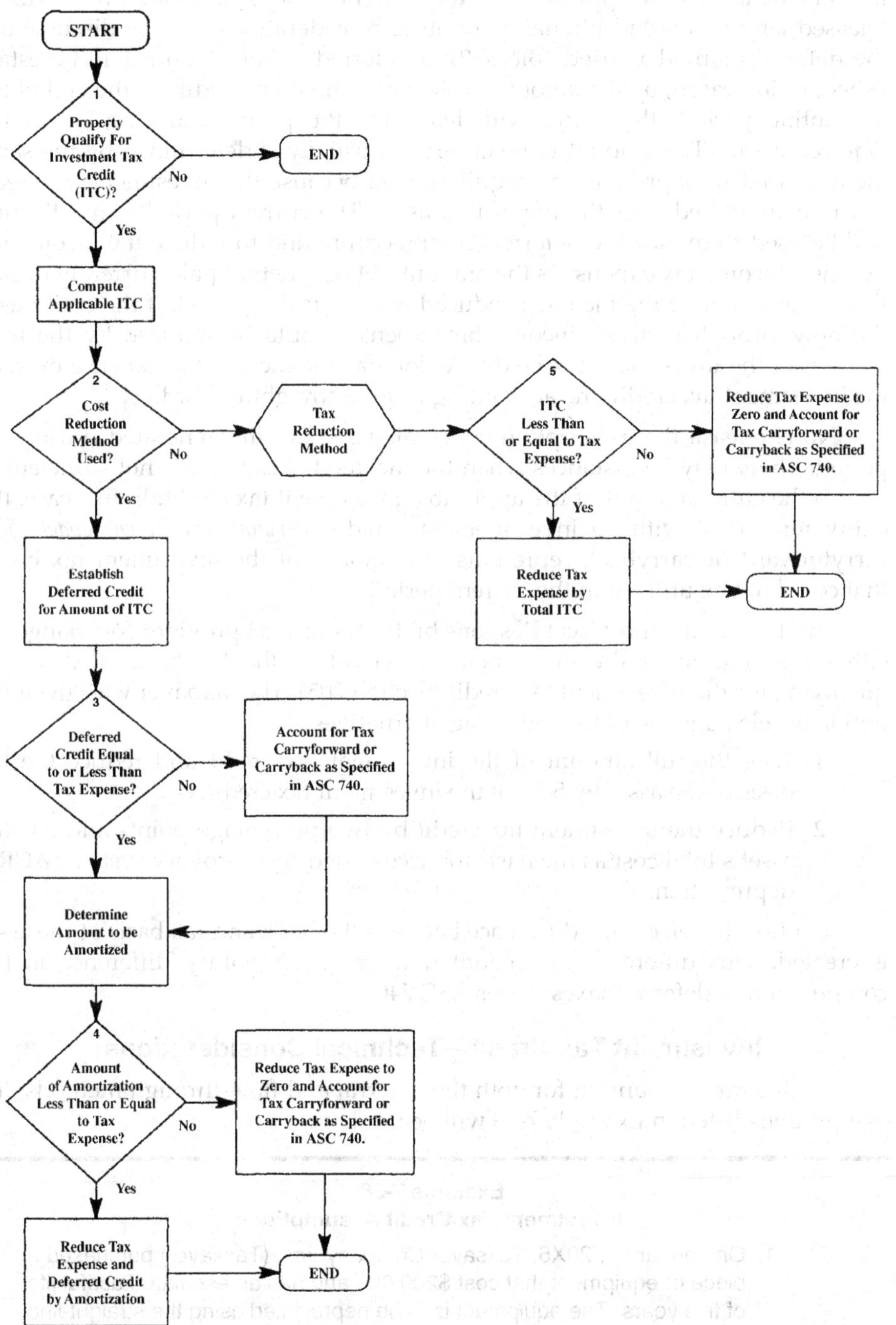

Assume that an entity has income enough to allow it to utilize the entire investment tax credit applicable to the current year. This assumption will be released later so that additional accounting considerations may be discussed. If the deferral method is used (Block 2), a deferred credit account will be established, or increased, by the amount of the investment tax credit. At the end of the accounting period, the entity will determine the proper amortization of the deferred credit. The amount to be amortized usually is determined by the same method used to depreciate the acquired asset because the investment tax credit must be amortized over the life of that asset. The current period's amortization will be used to reduce the deferred credit account and to reduce the income tax expense. Income tax expense is the amount of tax, whether paid currently or not, that is applicable to the income produced in the current period. If the entity uses the flow-through method, income tax expense would be reduced by the total amount of the investment tax credit. As long as the income tax expense exceeds the investment tax credit, the accounting is quite straightforward.

Now, release the assumption concerning the income generated during the period. There may be instances when the income tax expense is not sufficient to absorb the entire amount of the applicable investment tax credit. In this case, the entity must deal with an investment tax credit *carryforward* or *carryback*. The carryforward or carryback represents the amount of the investment tax credit that could not be utilized in the current period.

The Tax Equity and Fiscal Responsibility Act of 1982 provides for changes in either the amount of the investment tax credit or the tax basis of the asset qualifying for the investment tax credit (Section 205). The taxpayer was given the option of selecting one of the following alternatives:

1. Take the full amount of the investment tax credit and reduce the tax basis of the asset by 50% of the investment tax credit, or
2. Reduce the investment tax credit by two percentage points and use the asset's total cost as the basis for accelerated cost recovery system (ACRS) depreciation.

If option 1 is elected, a difference between the book and tax basis of the asset is created. This difference is accounted for as a temporary difference in the computation of deferred taxes under ASC 740.

Investment Tax Credit—Technical Considerations

To illustrate accounting for both the deferral and flow-through methods, the assumptions listed in Example 7-38 will be used.

Example 7-38
Investment Tax Credit Assumptions

1. On January 1, 20X6, Taxsaver Company, Inc. (Taxsaver) purchased a piece of equipment that cost $200,000 and has an estimated useful life of five years. The equipment is to be depreciated using the straight-line method with a zero salvage value.
2. Taxsaver has elected to reduce the investment tax credit from 10% to 8% instead of reducing the cost basis of the equipment for tax purposes.

3. Accounting income before taxes for the year ended December 31, 20X6 is $100,000. Taxable income is also equal to $100,000 and the tax rate applicable is 40%.
4. Taxsaver has had no deferred tax items since beginning business several years ago.

The property acquired qualifies for the investment tax credit of 8%, or $16,000 ($200,000 × .08). Assume that Taxsaver uses the deferral method of accounting for the investment tax credit. A deferred credit will be established for the amount of the investment tax credit. The first step is to determine if the transaction will result in an investment tax credit carryforward or carryback. To make this determination, income tax expense must be compared with the amount of the investment tax credit. This comparison is shown below:

Net Income Before Income Taxes	$100,000
Tax Rate	×.40
Income Tax Expense	$40,000
Investment Tax Credit	16,000
Excess of Expense over Tax Credit	$24,000

The investment tax credit is less than income tax expense, so it appears that no carryforward or carryback will be recognized. The income taxes payable for 20X6 would be determined as follows:

Taxable Income	$100,000
Tax Rate	×.40
Income Taxes Payable Before Credits	$40,000
Investment Tax Credit	(16,000)
Income Taxes Payable	$24,000

For tax purposes, the investment tax credit is treated as a reduction in taxes payable in the year the asset is acquired, subject to certain limitations. Based upon the information developed above, the entry required to record the income tax expense, deferred credit, and income taxes payable would be:

Income Tax Expense	40,000	
Deferred Investment Tax Credit		16,000
Income Taxes Payable		24,000

Next, the entry to amortize the investment tax credit must be prepared. The investment tax credit will be recognized over the life of the asset, using the straight-line method of amortization. The amount of the amortization for 20X6 would be $3,200 ($16,000 ÷ 5 years). The amount of the amortization is less than the income tax expense for the period and, therefore, the entire amount of the amortization will be recognized. The entry to record the amortization is shown below:

Deferred Investment Tax Credit	3,200	
Income Tax Expense		3,200

As a result of the entries prepared above, the income tax expense for 20X6 will be $36,800 ($40,000 – $3,200). The balance in the deferred investment tax credit account is $12,800 ($16,000 – $3,200). The deferred investment tax credit account may be treated as a contra asset account in property, plant, and equipment, but more commonly is carried as a deferred credit.

The investment tax credit did not affect the cost basis of the equipment purchased. Depreciation expense recorded on the asset during 20X6 would be $40,000 ($200,000 ÷ 5 years).

Assume the same facts as in Example 7-38, except that Taxsaver uses the flow-through method of accounting for the investment tax credit. In addition, Taxsaver elects to take the full 10% investment tax credit and reduce the asset's cost basis for tax purposes by 50% of the investment tax credit. The total investment tax credit of $20,000 ($200,000 × .10) is used to reduce both income tax expense and income tax payable because it is less than the $40,000 tax expense. However, because the tax basis of the asset is reduced by 50% of the ITC to $190,000 ($200,000 – ($20,000 × .50)), the $10,000 difference in asset basis between book and tax is accounted for as a temporary difference. The $4,000 tax effect ($10,000 × .40) of the $10,000 temporary difference is recorded as a deferred tax liability, assuming no other temporary differences. The $4,000 temporary difference is taxable in the future years that the book value of the asset recovers. The adjustments to income tax expense and tax payable are summarized below:

	Income Tax Expense	*Income Tax Payable*
Total tax before Investment Tax Credit	$40,000	$40,000
Reduction for Investment Tax Credit ($200,000 × 10%)	(20,000)	(20,000)
Tax effect of temporary difference ($10,000 × 40%)	4,000	
Total	$24,000	$20,000

The entry required to record the impact of the investment tax credit and the taxes payable for 20X6 would be:

Income Tax Expense	24,000	
Income Tax Payable		20,000
Deferred Tax Liability		4,000

Partial income statements for 20X6 under the deferral and the flow-through methods are compared below:

	Deferral Method	*Flow-Through Method*
Income Before Income Taxes	$100,000	$100,000
Income Tax Expense	36,800	24,000
Net Income	$63,200	$76,000

ASC 740-10-50-20 specifies that the entity's method of accounting for the investment credit (deferral or flow-through) must be disclosed, along with the amounts involved, when material.

Recent Changes

ASU 2016-16, *Income Taxes (Topic 740): Intra-Entity Transfers of Assets Other Than Inventory,* was issued in October 2016 under the "Simplification Initiative" to reduce complexity in accounting standards. Under current guidance, ASC 810-10-45-8 and ASC 740-10-25-3(e) prohibit immediate recognition of the current and deferred income tax impact on intra-entity asset transfers. The ASU eliminates this prohibition for all intra-entity asset transfers, except for inventory.

The new guidance will be effective for public business entities in fiscal years beginning after December 15, 2017. For all other entities, the new guidance will be effective for fiscal years beginning after December 15, 2018. Early adoption is only permitted as of the beginning of an annual reporting period. The new guidance must be adopted using a modified retrospective transition.

CHAPTER 8
BROAD TRANSACTIONS

CONTENTS

The *Broad Transactions* area of the FASB *Accounting Standards Codification* contains the following topics:

805	Business Combinations
808	Collaborative Arrangements
810	Consolidation
815	Derivatives and Hedging
820	Fair Value Measurements and Disclosures
825	Financial Instruments
830	Foreign Currency Matters
835	Interest
840	Leases
842	Leases
845	Nonmonetary Transactions
850	Related Party Disclosures
852	Reorganizations
853	Service Concession Arrangements
855	Subsequent Events
860	Transfers and Servicing

Topic 805: Business Combinations

Topic 805, *Business Combinations*, contains 11 subtopics:

10 Overall

20 Identifiable Assets and Liabilities, and Any Noncontrolling Interest

30 Goodwill or Gain from Bargain Purchase, Including Consideration Transferred

40 Reverse Acquisitions

50 Related Issues

740 Income Taxes

930 Extractive Activities—Mining*

942 Financial Services—Depository and Lending*

944 Financial Services—Insurance*

954 Health Care Entities*

958 Not-For-Profit Entities*

* See the corresponding topic in Chapter 9 for coverage of this shared subtopic.

General Discussion

ASC 805 specifies the accounting and reporting requirements for business combinations. Under ASC 805, all business combinations are accounted for using the acquisition method. However, the provisions of ASC 805 do not apply to (1) the formation of a joint venture, (2) a combination where the businesses or entities are under common control, (3) the acquisition of a for-profit entity by a not-for-profit entity or a combination of not-for-profit entities, and (4) an asset acquisition not considered a business.

What Is a Business Combination?

A business combination is a transaction or event whereby an entity (the acquirer) gets control of one or more businesses of another entity (the acquiree). An acquirer may gain control of the acquiree in several ways, including transferring cash or other assets, issuing equity interests, or incurring liabilities. The acquirer in a business combination is the entity that gets control of the acquiree, and the acquiree is the business or businesses that are controlled by the acquirer. A business in a business combination is defined as a set of assets and activities that can be used to provide a return to owners and investors. Control used in the definition of a business combination has the same meaning as used in ASC 810 for a controlling financial interest. As noted in the definition of a business combination, the acquisition must be a business for the acquisition to be treated as a business combination. If the acquisition is not considered a business, the transaction is accounted for as an asset acquisition.

Business combinations may be structured in various ways. Examples follow: (1) a business becomes a subsidiary of an acquirer, (2) the net assets of an acquiree business are merged (legally) into those of the acquirer entity, or (3) all of the combining companies transfer their net assets to a newly formed entity.

Steps in the Acquisition Process

Once a transaction is classified as a business combination, the combination should be accounted for using the acquisition method. The acquisition method involves the following steps: (1) identify the acquirer; (2) determine the acquisition date; (3) recognize and measure the identifiable assets acquired, liabilities assumed, and noncontrolling interests; and (4) determine the amount of goodwill or any bargain purchase gain to be recognized. The acquirer is the entity that gets control of the acquiree.

Step 1: Identify the Acquirer

The provisions of ASC 810 are used to determine which entity in the business combination is the acquirer. For example, when cash or other assets are transferred or liabilities incurred to consummate the business combination, the entity that transfers the assets or incurs the liabilities generally is the acquirer. In addition, when equity interests are exchanged in the business combination, the entity that transfers the equity interest is the acquirer entity. The primary beneficiary is the acquirer entity when the business combination involves a variable interest entity.

Step 2: Determine the Acquisition Date

The second step in the business combination process is to identify the acquisition date. The acquisition date is the date on which control of the acquiree is obtained by the acquirer entity. The acquisition date is generally the closing date of the business combination; in other words the date that consideration is legally transferred and the acquirer entity acquires the assets and assumes the liabilities of the acquiree. The closing date may be before or after the closing date if the acquirer entity obtains control of the acquiree before or after the closing date.

Step 3: Recognize and Measure Assets Acquired, Liabilities Assumed and Noncontrolling Interests

The identifiable assets acquired in a business combination as well as liabilities assumed and any noncontrolling interest in the acquiree must be recognized and measured by the acquirer entity as of the acquisition date. Identifiable assets are those that meet one of the following criteria: (1) the assets can be separated or divided from the enterprise and can be either individually or as a group sold, rented, licensed, etc. (referred to as the "separability" criteria) or (2) the assets are a result of a contract or other legal rights, even if the rights cannot be separated from the entity or from other rights (referred to as the "contractual/legal" criteria). The identifiable assets should be recognized and measured separately from any goodwill in the business combination. Acquired assets and assumed liabilities in a business combination should only be recognized by the acquirer entity on the date of acquisition when they meet the definitions of assets and liabilities in FASB Statement of Financial Accounting Concepts No. 6. Some assets and liabilities acquired and recognized by the acquirer entity in the combination may not have been recognized by the acquiree entity prior to the business combination. For example, some assets may have been developed internally by the acquiree, such as customer relationships, patents, and brand names, and were not reported in the acquiree financial statements prior to the combination. However, such assets are identifiable assets and must be recognized by the acquirer entity. All identifiable assets, including both tangible and intangible assets, should be recognized. Identifiable intangible assets should be reported separately from goodwill in a business combination. Intangible assets, which are assets with no physical substance, are separately identifiable when one of the following criteria is met: (1) contractual/legal or (2) separability. The contractual/legal criterion is described above in the discussion of identifiable assets. An intangible asset meeting the contractual/legal criterion is considered an identifiable asset regardless of whether it can be separated or transferred from the acquiree or from other obligations or rights. An intangible asset meets the separability criterion when it can be separated or divided from the acquiree and can be either individually or as a group sold, rented, licensed, etc., regardless of whether the acquirer entity expects or intends to sell, rent, or license the intangible. In addition, the separability criterion is met when there are exchange transactions for that intangible asset type or similar intangible asset types. ASC 805 divides identifiable intangible assets into different types of intangible assets and provides examples of the different types of identifiable intangibles that may be acquired in a business combination. Table 8-1 lists types of intangibles, examples of each type and whether the intangible meets the contractual/legal or separability criterion.

Table 8-1 Types and Examples of Identifiable Intangible Assets

Type of Identifiable Intangible	Example	Contractual/Legal or Separable
Market-related	Trademarks, trade dress, service marks, trade names, certification marks, Internet domain names, and noncompetition agreements	Contractual/legal
Customer related	Customer lists, customer contracts, and customer relationships	Contractual/legal
Customer related	Non-contractual customer relationships and order backlogs	Separable
Artistic related	Plays, operas, books, newspapers, musical works, pictures, and video material	Contractual/legal
Contract related	Licensing agreements, royalty agreements, advertising contracts, lease agreements, franchise agreements, employment contracts, and use rights	Contractual/legal
Technology related	Patents, computer software, and trade secrets	Contractual/legal
Technology related	Databases and unpatented technology	Separable

More information about the types and examples of intangible assets is covered in ASC 805. Once an identifiable intangible asset is recognized in a business combination using the provisions of ASC 805, subsequent accounting for the intangible is provided for by ASC 350 and ASC 360.

The acquirer entity should not recognize assets and liabilities of the acquiree as part of the combination if they relate to separate transactions between the acquiree and acquirer entity. Only assets and liabilities acquired as part of the exchange should be recognized as part of the business combination. The acquirer entity should not recognize as part of a business combination costs that the acquirer does not have an obligation to pay on the date of acquisition but expects to pay at some future date. These costs should be reported as liabilities in financial statements subsequent to the date of the combination using generally accepted accounting standards that apply to such costs.

Some assets acquired or liabilities assumed in a business combination require the acquirer entity to either classify or designate them on the acquisition date for purposes of future accounting because different accounting may be required depending on the classification or designation of the asset or liability. The acquirer entity should determine the classification or designation using factors existing on the date of acquisition, such as terms of contracts, economic conditions, accounting and operating policies, and other factors that may be relevant to the situation. Examples of assets and liabilities that require classification or designation include (1) investments covered by ASC 320 that are divided into either trading, available for sale, or held to maturity; (2) derivative instruments under ASC 815 designated as hedges; and (3) embedded derivatives separated using the provisions of ASC 815. However, ASC 805 provides an exception to the classification or designation for two items: (1) classification of leases as operating or capital using the provisions of ASC 840 and (2) classification of contracts covered by the provisions of ASC 944. Contracts covered by ASC 944 should be classified by the acquirer entity using the contractual terms and other factors at contract inception.

Generally, an asset or liability should not be reported for an operating lease when the acquiree entity is the lessee. However, when the acquiree entity is the lessee or lessor in an operating lease, the acquirer entity should report an intangible asset if the terms of the acquired leases are favorable on the date of acquisition compared to the market terms of leases with items that are similar or the same. When the market terms of the lease are unfavorable as compared to market terms, the acquirer entity should report a liability. In some cases the operating lease terms are equivalent to market terms at the date of acquisition, but the acquirer entity records an intangible asset for the lease, because market participants will pay a price for the lease such as retail space in a prime shopping area.

The identifiable assets acquired, the liabilities assumed, and the noncontrolling interest, if any, in a business combination should be measured by the acquirer entity at their fair values on the date of acquisition. Fair value is the amount that would be received on the measurement date from the sale of property or the amount paid to transfer a liability between seller and buyers (market participants) in an orderly transaction.

Exceptions to Recognition and Measurement Principles

ASC 805 provides for certain exceptions to the recognition and measurement principles discussed above for identifiable assets acquired and liabilities assumed in the business combination. These exceptions include contingent assets and liabilities, income taxes, employee benefit arrangements, and indemnification of assets.

First, assets acquired and liabilities assumed in a business combination that arise from contingencies (as defined in ASC 450) are accounted for using the provisions of ASC 805 rather than the provisions of ASC 450. An asset or liability arising from a contingency is to be recognized at the acquisition date if the acquisition-date fair value can be determined during the measurement period or if both of the following criteria are met: (1) information available before the end of the measurement period indicates that it is probable that an asset existed or that a liability had been incurred at the acquisition date and (2) the amount of the asset or liability can be reasonably estimated. If the acquisition-date fair value of a recognized asset or liability can be determined during the measurement period, the asset or liability is to be measured at its acquisition-date fair value. Otherwise, the recognized asset or liability is to be measured using an estimated amount. Any asset or liability arising from a contingency that does not meet the recognition criteria at the acquisition date is to be accounted for by the acquirer in periods after the acquisition date in accordance with other applicable GAAP (e.g., ASC 450) as appropriate.

Next, the deferred tax assets, deferred tax liabilities, and tax uncertainties of an acquiree should be recognized and measured on the date of acquisition by the acquirer entity using the provisions of ASC 740.

Another exception relates to employee benefits. Any liabilities or assets related to employee benefit agreements of the acquiree entity should be reported and measured using other appropriate accounting standards. See ASC 805 for examples of other accounting standards that apply to employee benefit agreements.

Another recognition and measurement exception relates to an asset indemnification by the seller in a business combination. An indemnification asset exists when the seller in the business combination contractually indemnifies the acquirer entity against the outcome, for example, of a contingency or uncertainty related to assets and liabilities. For example, the seller may provide a guarantee that the liability of the acquirer entity will not exceed a specified amount. The acquirer entity should report an indemnification asset at the time that the item that is indemnified is reported. In addition, the indemnification asset should be reported using the same measurement process as used for the indemnified item. For example, if the indemnified item is reported at the date of acquisition using fair value on the date of acquisition, the indemnification asset is also reported at fair value on the date of acquisition. In some cases, a valuation allowance may be needed for the uncertainty regarding uncollectible amounts. However, when fair value is used in the measurement of the indemnification asset, uncertainty is included in the fair value measurement and a valuation allowance is not needed. In some cases an indemnification by the seller relates to assets and liabilities that are exceptions to the general recognition and measurement principles specified in ASC 805. In these cases, any recognition and measurement of the indemnification asset should be consistent with recognition and measurement of the indemnified items.

In addition to the exceptions noted above, ASC 805 provides several exceptions related exclusively to the general measurement principle of fair value. These exceptions relate to reacquired rights, share-based payments, and assets held for sale.

A reacquired right is a right that the acquirer entity provides to the acquiree entity, such as the right to use a trade name, that the acquirer entity receives in the business combination. The acquirer entity should recognize the reacquired right as an identifiable intangible asset at fair value. A settlement gain or loss may be reported when the contract terms of the reacquired right are favorable or unfavorable comparable to the current market for such transactions.

The next exception relates to share-based payment awards. When the acquirer entity replaces share-based award payments of the acquiree with share-based award payments of the acquirer entity, a liability should be measured by the acquirer entity using the method provided in ASC 718. However, ASC 805 provides additional guidelines when accounting for share-based award payments in a business combination.

When an acquirer entity acquires in a business combination long-lived assets that are classified as held for sale by the acquiree entity, the acquirer entity should measure the held for sale assets at fair value less the cost of the sale using the provisions of ASC 360.

Step 4: Determine the Amount of Goodwill

After the acquirer entity measures identifiable assets, assumed liabilities, and any noncontrolling interests, the amount of goodwill or gain from a bargain purchase, if any, should be determined. Goodwill is defined in ASC 350, as an asset acquired in a business combination that has future economic benefit and is a result of acquired assets that could not be separately recognized and identified individually. The amount of goodwill should be reported as of the date of acquisition is the difference between (1) the aggregate fair value of the consideration transferred and (2) the net amount of the assets acquired and liabilities assumed.

The aggregate amount of consideration transferred in the business combination, includes the fair value of any noncontrolling interest plus the fair value of the equity interest in the acquiree held prior to the combination by the acquirer.

The net amount of the identifiable assets or liabilities on the date of acquisition is the difference between the identifiable assets acquired and the liabilities assumed in the business combination measured using ASC 805.

In some cases, a business combination may be consummated by exchanging equity interests, and the equity interest of the acquiree may be a better indicator of the fair value of the equity interest transferred on the date of acquisition than the fair value of the equity interest of the acquirer entity. In this case, any goodwill should be determined by using the fair value of the acquiree equity interest. In some cases, no consideration is exchanged in a business combination. When no consideration is exchanged, the acquirer entity should use a valuation technique, as illustrated in ASC 805, to compute goodwill in place of the fair value of the consideration transferred, as indicated above.

If the amount of (2), above, exceeds the amount of (1), above, the acquirer entity has made a bargain purchase and a gain should be reported on the date of acquisition for the amount that (2) exceeds (1). The gain from the bargain purchase is related to the acquirer entity. However, before the gain from the bargain purchase can be reported, the acquirer entity must reevaluate the recognition and measurement process used when determining the following to determine that all items that should be recognized have been recognized and that all items have been measured properly: (1) identifiable assets and liabilities, (2) noncontrolling interest, (3) transferred consideration, and (4) fair value of the equity interest in the acquiree held prior to the combination by the acquirer when the business combination occurs in stages. If the reassessment indicates that no changes should be made, the gain from the bargain purchase should not be adjusted. However, if changes are indicated the gain should be adjusted for any required changes.

This completes the general discussion of business combinations; however, several additional issues require discussion: (1) form of consideration transferred in a business combination, (2) achievement of a combination without the transfer of consideration, (3) measurement period for the business combination, (4) business combination achieved in stages, (5) transactions that are not part of the business combination, and (6) accounting subsequent to the date of the business combination.

Form of Consideration Transferred

Consideration transferred by the acquirer entity may consist of many forms of financial and nonfinancial assets, such as cash, other types of assets, equity instruments, options, warrants, contingent consideration, a business of the acquirer, or other consideration. When there is a difference in the carrying amounts and fair values of the assets or liabilities of the acquirer entity transferred as consideration in a business combination, the acquirer entity should report a gain or loss in income for such differences, unless the acquirer entity has control of the assets or liabilities before and after the business combination. Therefore, any assets or liabilities that the acquirer entity controls before and after the combination should be measured at the carrying amounts just before the combination and no gain or loss is reported. When contingent consideration is transferred by the acquirer entity in the combination, the contingent consideration should be reported at fair value for purposes of determining the amount of consideration transferred in the combination. When there is an obligation to pay contingent consideration, the acquirer entity should use the provisions of appropriate accounting standards to determine whether the obligation should be classified as debt or equity.

Achieving a Business Combination without Transferring Consideration

In some cases, a business combination may be achieved without the acquirer entity transferring consideration to the acquiree. Examples of situations where no consideration is required to achieve a business combination follow: (1) the acquirer entity and the acquiree entity enter into a contract to combine their businesses, (2) the acquiree repurchases its own shares that allow the acquirer, which is an existing investor, to gain control of the acquiree entity, or (3) the acquirer entity gains control as a result of the lapse of minority veto rights. When a business combination is achieved by entering into a contract and the acquirer entity holds no equity interest before or after the acquisition, the net assets of the acquiree, using the provisions of ASC 805, should be attributed to the acquiree equity holders (the noncontrolling interest).

Measurement Period

The measurement period is the time period after the date of acquisition that the acquirer entity has to obtain the necessary information to adjust any provisional amounts reported for the business combination and to record any additional assets or liabilities based on facts that existed at the date of acquisition. The time period should not be greater than one year from the date of acquisition. All pertinent information should be used to determine whether the information acquired after the date of acquisition results from events that occurred after the acquisition date and would not require an adjustment to any provisional amounts reported or whether the information relates to events on the acquisition date that require an adjustment to provisional amounts reported.

When additional information is obtained during the measurement period that requires an adjustment to any provisional amounts, increases or decreases in assets or liabilities should be reported as an increase or decrease in goodwill. Adjustments to provisional amounts as a result of additional information should be reported as if the combination had been completed on the date of acquisition. Any changes in provisional amounts after the end of the measurement period should only be made to correct an error. The provisions of ASC 250 should be used for any error correction.

An acquirer reporting entity may consummate a business acquisition and issue financial statements when the measurements of the assets and liabilities of the acquired business are incomplete as of the end of the reporting period covering the business combination. Prior to the effective date of ASU 2015-16, *Business Combinations (Topic 805): Simplifying the Accounting for Measurement-Period Adjustments,* the acquirer reporting entity was required to adjust such provisional amounts by restating prior-period financial statements as long as the information necessary to complete the measurement was received within the measurement period. The measurement period is the timeframe within one year from acquisition date. Adjustments to provisional amounts within the measurement period are referred to as "measurement period adjustments."

New guidance under ASU 2015-16 eliminates the requirement to restate prior-period financial statements for measurement-period adjustments. Instead, ASU 2015-16 requires that the cumulative impact of a measurement-period adjustment be recognized in the reporting period in which the adjustment is determined. Further, the acquirer reporting entity reflects the cumulative adjustment within the respective financial statement line items affected (e.g., the cumulative change in amortization expense would be recognized in the income statement in the financial statement line item that includes amortization expense). The acquirer reporting entity is required to disclose the nature and amount of such measurement-period adjustments. Also, the acquirer reporting entity is required to present separately on the face of the statement of operations or disclose in the notes the portion of the adjustment recorded in current-period earnings by line item that would have been recorded in previous reporting periods if the adjustment to the provisional amounts had been recognized as of the acquisition date.

For public entities, ASU 2015-16 is effective for interim and annual periods beginning after December 15, 2015. For nonpublic entities it is effective for annual periods beginning after December 15, 2016 and interim periods beginning after December 15, 2017. Early adoption permitted for all entities.

ASU 2015-16 is to be applied prospectively to measurement period adjustments that occur after the standards effective date.

Acquisition in Stages

When an acquirer entity holds an equity interest in an acquiree prior to the acquisition date and on the acquisition date purchases an additional equity interest that provides it with control to the acquirer entity, the business combination is assumed to have occurred in stages. For example, prior to January 1, 20X8, XYZ Company holds a 45% interest in the equity of ABC Company. On January 1, 20X8, XYZ purchases an additional 50% interest in the equity of ABC. XYZ Company now holds a 95% interest in ABC and is assume to control ABC. ASC 805 states that when an acquirer entity acquires another entity in stages, the equity interest held prior to the acquisition date must be revalued to fair value on the acquisition date and any gain or loss from the revaluation should be reported as part of income. When an equity interest is revalued to acquisition-date fair value, any unrealized gain or losses included in other comprehensive income in prior accounting periods should be included in the computation of the gain or loss on the revaluation on the date of acquisition.

Transactions That Are Not Part of a Business Combination

Some transactions may appear to relate to the business combination but are actually part of a preexisting relationship prior to the beginning of negotiations for the business combination. An acquirer entity must determine which amounts relate to the preexisting relationship and which actually relate to the business combination. Only the amounts exchanged between the acquirer entity and the acquiree in the business combination for the acquisition of the acquiree entity should be treated as consideration transferred for the acquiree. Other transactions should be treated as separate transactions and accounted for using other appropriate accounting principles. A separate transaction is likely to be one that is entered into for the benefit of the acquirer entity or the combined entity as opposed to a transaction entered into for the benefit of the acquiree or the former owners of the acquiree. Examples of separate transactions include the following: (1) transactions that result in the settlement of a relationship between the acquirer entity and the acquiree that existed prior to the business combination, (2) transactions that provide payments to former owners or employees of the acquiree entity for future services, and (3) reimbursements to the former owners of the acquiree entity or the acquiree for payments of acquisition-related costs of the acquirer entity. Any costs that the acquirer entity incurs for the business combination are referred to as acquisition-related costs and are generally expensed in the accounting periods in which the costs are incurred or the services are received. However, other appropriate accounting principles should be used to account for costs related to the issuance of debt and equity securities. Examples of acquisition-related costs include the following: accounting, legal, finder's fees, valuation fees, and other professional fees.

Subsequent Accounting

Subsequent to a business combination, other appropriate accounting standards generally should be used for the accounting and reporting of the assets acquired, liabilities and noncontrolling assumed, and equity interests issued in the business combination. For example, ASC 350 should be used in the accounting for goodwill and intangible assets, ASC 740 should be used when accounting for deferred taxes, and ASC 718 is used for share-based payment awards. However, ASC 805 provides subsequent accounting requirements for specific items. The specific items are (1) reacquired rights, (2) assets and liabilities resulting from contingencies, (3) indemnification assets, (4) contingent consideration, and (5) contingent consideration arrangements of an acquiree assumed by the acquirer.

Technical Considerations

The following five examples illustrate the technical considerations of business combinations. Example 8-1 illustrates a situation in which intangible assets are identifiable and are reported separately from any goodwill computations. Assumptions for Example 8-1 are as follows.

Example 8-1
Assumptions for Identifiable Intangible Assets

1. XYZ (the acquirer entity) acquired 100% of ABC (the acquiree entity) in a business combination.
2. The following intangible assets were acquired by XYZ in the business combination:
    a. ABC has an operating lease that cannot be transferred via sublease or sale, but has terms that are favorable when compared to market terms.
    b. ABC has a license to operate a power plant that ABC owns.
    c. ABC has licensed a patent that it owns to foreign entities where ABC receives a percentage of revenue from the foreign entities.
    d. ABC owns both a trademark that is registered and the technical expertise (that is not patented but is documented) to produce the product that is trademarked. Transfer of the trademark also requires a transfer of the technical expertise.
    e. ABC has a workforce that will continue to operate the entity acquired by XYZ in the business combination.
    f. ABC has potential contracts with possible new customers that are under negotiation on the acquisition date. None of the contracts are consummated shortly after the date of consummation of the business combination.

The first intangible asset, the operating lease, cannot be sold or transferred by the acquirer entity. However, a separately identifiable intangible asset should be established for the amount that the operating lease has favorable terms as compared to current market terms for items that are the same or similar. The favorable terms of the operating lease are assumed to meet the contractual/legal requirements of ASC 805 for separately identifiable intangible assets.

The second possible identifiable intangible asset is the license to operate a power plant. The license is accounted for as an identifiable intangible asset separate from any goodwill measurement at its acquisition-date fair value because it meets the contractual/legal requirements of ASC 805 even if the license cannot be separated and sold separate from the power plant.

The third possible identifiable intangible asset is the license for a patent that is provided to foreign entities for a percentage of the revenue received by the foreign enterprises. The license is considered an identifiable intangible asset separate from a measurement of goodwill because it meets the contractual/legal requirement of ASC 805 even if it is not practical or is difficult to separate the license and the patent in a sale or other transfer.

The fourth possible identifiable intangible asset is the registered trademark with the documented technical expertise. Because the documented technical expertise must be separated from the entity and sold when and if the trademark is sold, the documented but unpatented technical expertise is accounted for as an identifiable intangible asset separate from the measurement of goodwill because it meets the separability requirement of ASC 805.

The fifth possible identifiable intangible asset is the workforce acquired in the business combination. An assembled workforce is not considered under ASC 805 to be a separately identifiable intangible asset. Any value related to an assembled workforce acquired in a business combination is measured as part of any goodwill.

The last possible identifiable intangible asset is potential contracts under negotiation at the date of acquisition of the business combination. The potential contracts are not considered assets at the date of acquisition; therefore the acquirer entity should not treat them as identifiable intangible assets. The value of any potential contracts would be included in any measurement of goodwill.

Example 8-2 illustrates the computation of goodwill and recording of a business combination by the acquirer entity when the acquirer pays more than the acquisition-date fair value of the assets acquired and the liabilities assumed. Assumptions for Example 8-2 are presented as follows.

Example 8-2
Assumptions for Computation of Goodwill

1. Peterson Enterprises acquired 100% of the Johnson Company on January 1, 20X8, for $2,000,000.
2. Acquisition-date fair value of the assets acquired and the liabilities assumed in the business combination are as follows:

Current assets	$ 500,000
Property, plant, and equipment	2,500,000
Intangible assets	400,000
Current liabilities	(500,000)
Long-term liabilities	(1,500,000)
Fair value of net assets	$1,400,000

3. The fair value and tax bases of the assets and liabilities listed above are the same.

Because Peterson acquired 100% of Johnson Company, there is no noncontrolling interest. Therefore, the fair value of the consideration transferred to Johnson on the date of acquisition is the $2,000,000 cash payment. Because there is no difference between the acquisition-date fair values and the tax bases of assets acquired and liabilities assumed, no deferred taxes should be computed by Peterson. Goodwill is computed as the excess of the acquisition-date fair value of the consideration of $2,000,000 over the acquisition-date fair value of the assets acquired and the liabilities assumed in the business combination. Goodwill of $600,000 is computed as follows:

Consideration paid for Johnson Company		$2,000,000
Acquisition-date fair value of assets and liabilities		
Current assets	$ 500,000	
Property, plant, and equipment	2,500,000	
Intangible assets	400,000	
Current liabilities	(500,000)	
Long-term liabilities	(1,500,000)	
Net assets		1,400,000
Goodwill		$ 600,000

Using the information from the above calculation of goodwill, the journal required by Peterson on the date of the business combination is as follows:

Current assets	500,000	
Property, plant, and equipment	2,500,000	
Intangible assets	400,000	
Goodwill	600,000	
Current liabilities		500,000
Long-term liabilities		1,500,000
Cash		2,000,000

The information in Example 8-2 illustrates the computation of goodwill when an acquirer entity transfers consideration to the acquiree entity in excess of the acquisition-date fair value of the assets acquired and liabilities assumed. Example 8-3 illustrates a situation where the amount of consideration transferred to the acquiree entity by the acquirer entity is less than the acquisition-date fair value of the assets acquired and liabilities assumed, a bargain purchase. Assumptions for Example 8-3 are presented as follows.

Example 8-3
Assumptions for Computation of a Bargain Purchase

1. Jones Enterprises acquired 100% of the Masters Company on January 1, 20X8, for $1,500,000.

2. Acquisition-date fair value of the assets acquired and the liabilities assumed in the business combination are as follows:

Current assets	$ 600,000
Property, plant, and equipment	2,700,000
Intangible assets	300,000
Current liabilities	(400,000)
Long-term liabilities	(1,200,000)
Fair value of net assets	$ 2,000,000

3. The fair value and tax bases of the assets and liabilities listed above are the same.

Because Jones acquired 100% of Masters Company, there is no noncontrolling interest and, therefore, the fair value of the consideration transferred to Masters on the date of acquisition is the $1,500,000 cash payment. Because there is no difference between the acquisition-date fair values and the tax bases of assets acquired and liabilities assumed, no deferred taxes should be computed by Jones. Because the fair value of the net assets exceeds the fair value of the consideration transferred, Jones has a bargain purchase. A bargain purchase gain is computed as the excess of the acquisition-date fair value of the assets acquired and the liabilities assumed in the business combination (net assets) over the acquisition-date fair value of the consideration of $1,500,000 transferred. The gain on the bargain purchase of $500,000 is computed as follows:

Consideration paid for Masters Company		$1,500,000
Acquisition-date fair value of assets and liabilities		
Current assets	$ 600,000	
Property, plant, and equipment	2,700,000	
Intangible assets	300,000	
Current liabilities	(400,000)	
Long-term liabilities	(1,200,000)	
Net Assets		2,000,000
Gain on bargain purchase		$ 500,000

Using the information from the above calculation of the gain on the bargain purchase, the journal required by Jones on the date of the business combination is as follows:

Current assets	600,000	
Property, plant, and equipment	2,700,000	
Intangible assets	300,000	
Current liabilities		400,000
Long-term liabilities		1,200,000
Cash		1,500,000
Gain on bargain purchase		500,000

In Examples 8-2 and 8-3 the assumption was made that there was no difference between the acquisition-date fair value and the tax bases of the assets acquired and the liabilities assumed in the business combination. However, in many cases when assets and liabilities of an acquiree entity are revalued to acquisition-date fair value in accordance with the provisions of ASC 805, a difference is created between the acquisition-date fair value (book basis) and the tax bases of the assets and liabilities. Under ASC 740, this difference is a temporary difference for which a deferred tax asset or liability must be recognized. However, deferred taxes should not be computed for the difference between the book and tax bases of items such as goodwill (not deductible for tax) and leveraged leases. See ASC 740 for more exceptions and more details of the exceptions.

To illustrate the computation of deferred tax assets or liabilities and the impact on goodwill of the deferred taxes in a business combination, when a difference exists between the acquisition-date fair value and the tax bases of assets and liabilities, assume the facts in Example 8-4.

Example 8-4
Assumptions for Computation of Deferred Taxes

1. Financial Enterprises acquired 100% of the White Company on January 1, 20X8, for $3,000,000.

2. The acquisition-date fair value of the assets acquired and the liabilities assumed in the business combination are as follows:

Current assets	$ 500,000
Property, plant, and equipment	2,700,000
Intangible assets	400,000
Current liabilities	(300,000)
Long-term liabilities	(1,100,000)
Fair value of net assets	$ 2,200,000

3. The tax bases of the assets and liabilities listed above are the same except for property, plant, and equipment. The tax bases for property, plant, and equipment acquired by Financial Enterprises is $2,200,000.

4. The current enacted tax rate for current and future accounting periods is 40%.

The only difference between acquisition-date fair value and the tax bases of assets and liabilities is the $500,000 ($2,700,000 – $2,200,000) related to property, plant, and equipment. Because the acquisition-date fair value of the assets exceeds the tax basis, a deferred tax liability is reported for the temporary difference between acquisition-date fair value and tax. When tax bases of assets exceed acquisition-date fair values, a deferred tax asset is computed. The deferred tax liability is computed as follows:

Acquisition-date fair value of property, plant, and equipment	$2,700,000
Tax basis of property, plant, and equipment	2,200,000
Temporary difference	$ 500,000
Tax rate	40%
Deferred tax liability	$ 200,000

Because the $200,000 deferred tax liability is included as part of the liabilities assumed in the acquisition, goodwill is increased by the amount of the deferred taxes. The amount of goodwill reported in the acquisition by the acquirer entity is computed as follows:

Consideration paid for White Company		$3,000,000
Acquisition-date fair value of assets and liabilities		
Current assets	$ 500,000	
Property, plant, and equipment	2,700,000	
Intangible assets	400,000	
Current liabilities	(300,000)	
Long-term liabilities	(1,100,000)	
Deferred tax liability	(200,000)	
Net assets		2,000,000
Goodwill		$1,000,000

If the deferred tax liability of $200,000 had not been recorded, goodwill would have been reported by the acquirer entity at $800,000. The journal entry to record the acquisition is presented as follows:

Current assets	500,000	
Property, plant, and equipment	2,700,000	
Intangible assets	400,000	
Goodwill	1,000,000	
Current liabilities		300,000
Long-term liabilities		1,100,000
Deferred tax liability		200,000
Cash		3,000,000

Examples 8-2 through 8-4 illustrate situations where the acquirer entity acquired 100% of the acquiree entity. Example 8-5 illustrates the acquisition of less than 100% of the acquiree entity.

Example 8-5
Assumptions for Computation of Deferred Taxes

1. Robinson Enterprises acquired 80% of the Wild Company on January 1, 20X8, for $1,500,000.
2. Acquisition-date fair value of the assets acquired and the liabilities assumed in the business combination are as follows:

Current assets	$ 400,000
Property, plant, and equipment	2,300,000
Intangible assets	500,000
Current liabilities	(400,000)
Long-term liabilities	(1,800,000)
Fair value of net assets	$ 1,000,000

3. The fair value and tax bases of the assets and liabilities listed above are the same.
4. The fair value of the 20% noncontrolling interest is $375,000.

Because Robinson Enterprises only acquired 80% of Wild Company, there is a 20% noncontrolling interest. Therefore, the fair value of the consideration used in the computation of either goodwill or a bargain purchase on the date of acquisition is the $1,500,000 cash payment plus the $375,000 fair value of the noncontrolling interest. There is no difference between the acquisition-date fair values and the tax bases of assets acquired and liabilities assumed, therefore, no deferred taxes should be computed by Robinson. Because the fair value of the consideration used to complete the business combination exceeds the fair value of the net assets acquired, goodwill is computed as the excess of the acquisition-date fair value of the consideration of $1,875,000 and the acquisition-date fair value of the assets acquired and the liabilities assumed in the business combination. Goodwill of $875,000 is computed as follows:

Fair value of consideration transferred:		
Fair value of cash transferred		$1,500,000
Fair value of noncontrolling interest		375,000
Total fair value of consideration transferred		$1,875,000
Acquisition-date fair value of assets and liabilities		
Current assets	$ 400,000	
Property, plant, and equipment	2,300,000	
Intangible assets	500,000	
Current liabilities	(400,000)	
Long-term liabilities	(1,800,000)	
Net assets acquired		1,000,000
Goodwill		$ 875,000

The journal entry to record the acquisition is presented as follows:

Current assets	400,000	
Property, plant, and equipment	2,300,000	
Intangible assets	500,000	
Goodwill	875,000	
Current liabilities		400,000
Long-term liabilities		1,800,000
Noncontrolling interest		375,000
Cash		1,500,000

The noncontrolling interest of $375,000 is reported in the equity section of the consolidated financial statements of Robinson.

This completes the discussion of the technical aspects of business combinations. The next section covers the disclosure requirements.

Disclosure Requirements

ASC 805-10-50, ASC 805-20-50, and ASC 805-30-50 specify the disclosure requirements for the acquirer of a business combination that occurred during the current accounting reporting period or that occurred before the release date of the financial statements but after the reporting date. These disclosures should allow users of the financial statements to evaluate the financial impact and nature of the business combinations. The required disclosures are as follows:

1. Provide a description and name of the acquiree, the acquisition date, and percent of voting equity securities obtained in the acquisition.
2. Provide a description of how control of the acquiree was obtained by the acquirer and explain the primary reasons for the combination.
3. Qualitatively describe the factors that compose the amount of recognized goodwill.
4. Provide fair value on the date of acquisition for the following: (a) total transferred consideration and (b) each major class of consideration. Examples include cash, other tangible and intangible assets, liabilities, and acquirer equity interest.
5. Provide the following information for indemnification assets and contingent consideration: (a) acquisition-date amount recognized, (b) describe the arrangement and how the amount of payment was determined, and (c) provide an estimate of the range of undiscounted outcomes (when the amount is unlimited, disclose this fact) and when no range can be estimated, disclose the reason that a range cannot be estimated and the fact that it cannot be estimated.
6. Disclose the following information by major class of receivables when receivables that are acquired are not covered by ASC 310-30: (a) the receivable fair value, (b) contractual receivable amounts using gross amounts, and (c) an estimate of the contractual cash flows on the date of acquisition not anticipated to be collected.
7. Disclose the amounts reported for each major class of acquired assets and liabilities assumed on the date of acquisition.

8. For assets and liabilities arising from contingencies recognized at the acquisition date, disclose (a) the amount recognized on the date of acquisition and the measurement basis applied (that is, at fair value or at an amount recognized in accordance with ASC 450) and (b) the nature of the contingencies (aggregation can be elected when assets and liabilities arising from contingencies are similar in nature). For assets and liabilities arising from contingencies that have not been recognized at the acquisition date, provide the disclosures required by ASC 450 if the criteria for disclosures in ASC 450 are met. Required disclosures for assets and liabilities arising from contingencies both recognized at the acquisition date and not are to be included in the business-combination footnote.

9. Disclose total goodwill that is anticipated to be deductible for tax purposes.

10. Disclose the amount of goodwill by reportable segment when the acquirer is required to present segment information in accordance with the provisions of ASC 280 and, when the acquirer has not made the assignment of the goodwill to reporting units using the provisions of ASC 350, disclose the fact that goodwill has not been assigned to reporting units.

11. Disclose the following information for transactions that are separately reported from the assets and liabilities acquired or assumed in a combination: (a) each transaction should be described, (b) how each transaction was accounted for by the acquirer, (c) amount reported for each transaction and the location, by line item, in the financial statements where the transaction is reported, (d) method used to determine amount of settlement for transactions that are preexisting relationships. Any acquisition-related cost should be disclosed, the amount should be reported, as well as the location, by line item, in the income statement where the cost is reported. If the costs are not reported as an expense, disclose how the cost is reported.

12. Disclose the following when a bargain purchase is reported for a business combination: (a) amount reported and the location, by line item, in the income statement where the gain is reported and (b) describe why a gain was reported.

13. Disclose the following information when the acquirer entity has less than 100% of the equity of the acquiree entity on the date of acquisition date: (a) acquisition-date fair value of the noncontrolling interest and (b) significant inputs and valuation methods used to determine noncontrolling interest fair value.

14. Disclose the following information when the acquisition of a business combination is in stages: (a) fair value of the equity interest in the acquiree entity on the date of acquisition held by the acquirer entity just prior to the date of acquisition and (b) amount reported and the location, by line item, in the income statement where any gain or loss is reported as a result of the remeasurement to fair value of the equity interest in the acquiree held by the acquirer entity prior to the business combination.

15. Disclose the following information when the acquirer entity is a public business enterprise in accordance with the provisions of ASC 280: (a) for the reporting period, acquiree revenues and earnings subsequent to the date of acquisition included in the consolidated income statement, (b) for the current reporting period, combined entity revenues and earnings as if the acquisition date of the combination was at the beginning of the annual accounting period, and (c) for the prior comparable reporting period, combined entity revenues and earnings as if the acquisition date of the combination was at the beginning of the prior annual accounting period, if comparable financial statements are presented. When disclosure information is not practicable (ASC 250 defines impracticable), disclose this fact and why the disclosures are not practicable.

16. Certain disclosure requirements when business combinations are individually immaterial but collectively material.

17. Disclose why disclosures are not made and which disclosures could not be made for business combinations occurring after the reporting date but prior to the release of the financial statements when the initial accounting for the business combination is incomplete on the release date of the financial statements.

Provide information about business combinations that occurred in current and previous accounting periods that allow financial statement users to determine the financial impact of adjustments reported in the current reporting period. The following disclosures should be presented for each business combination that is material and in the aggregate for business combinations that are individually immaterial but collectively material:

1. Disclose the following when the initial accounting for a business combination is incomplete or the amounts reported in the financial statements have been provisionally determined: (a) reasons why there is incomplete initial accounting, (b) the items for which there is incomplete initial accounting, such as assets, liabilities, and equity interest, and (c) measurement period adjustments (amount and nature) recognized during the reporting period using the provisions of ASC 805-10-25-17.

2. Disclose the following for each reporting period subsequent to the date of acquisition until the date that a contingent asset is sold, collected, or the right to the asset is lost or until a contingent liability expires or is cancelled by the entity: (a) changes in recognized amounts, including differences upon settlement, (b) changes in undiscounted range of outcomes and provide reasons for any changes, and (c) disclosures required by ASC 820.

3. Disclose the following for each reporting period subsequent to the date of acquisition until the date that a contingent asset is sold, collected, or the right to the asset is lost or until a contingent liability expires or is cancelled by the acquirer: (a) changes in recognized amounts of assets and liabilities from contingences and (b) changes in undiscounted range

of outcomes for assets and liabilities (both unrecognized and recognized) related to contingencies and provide reasons for any changes.

4. Disclose a reconciliation of the beginning and ending carrying amount of goodwill using the provisions of ASC 350.

An acquirer entity should provide any additional disclosure information needed to meet the required reporting objectives for business combinations when the required disclosures presented above do not meet the objectives specified in ASC 805-10-50, paragraphs 1 and 5. The amendments in ASU 2010-29, *Business Combinations (Topic 805): Disclosure of Supplementary Pro Forma Information for Business Combinations*, specify that when a public company presents comparative financial statements, the entity should disclose revenue and earnings of the combined entity as though the business combination that occurred during the current year had occurred as of the beginning of the comparable prior annual reporting period only. The entity should also expand supplemental pro-forma disclosures to include a description of the nature and amount of material, nonrecurring pro-forma adjustments directly attributable to the business combination included in pro-forma revenue and earnings.

Pushdown Accounting

ASU 2014-17, *Business Combinations (Topic 805): Pushdown Accounting*, allows acquired companies to irrevocably elect whether to apply fair value pushdown accounting in their separate financials, on a transaction-by-transaction basis resulting in a change in control. The option to use pushdown accounting became available for changes in control after November 4, 2014. Prior to ASU 2014-17 very limited guidance was available. ASU 2015-08, *Business Combinations (Topic 805): Pushdown Accounting*, amended or superseded various SEC paragraphs in ASC 805-50, *Business Combinations–Related Issues*, resulting from issuance of SEC Staff Accounting Bulletin 115 in November 2014. The SEC issued SAB 115 in connection with the release of ASU 2014-17.

Under pushdown accounting the buyer's basis is "pushed down" to the acquired entity resulting in the acquired entity "stepping up" the basis of its assets and liabilities to fair value and recording goodwill. Example 8-6 illustrates how the buyer's basis is pushed down to the acquired entity.

Example 8-6
Applying Pushdown Accounting

An investment company purchases 90% of Company S for $900. To better evaluate Company S's performance, the investment company instructs Company S to use pushdown accounting. As of the closing date, the fair value of Company S's inventory was—$250, equipment was $460, and other intangible assets (OIA) was $100. Further, the fair value of the noncontrolling interest was $80. The historical cost of Company S's net assets was $700, including inventory—$200, OIA—$10, and equipment, net— $400.

What is the implied fair value of Company S?

Answer: $1,000 ($900/90%)

What is the implied fair value of the noncontrolling interest?

Answer: $100 ($1,000 × 10%)

What is the amount of goodwill to push-down?

Answer: $80 - ($900 + $80) – ([700 + ($250 - $200) + ($460 - $400) + ($100-$10)]

Company S's historical cost balance sheet as of the closing date is presented below along with the adjustments to apply pushdown accounting. Note the elimination of retained earnings.

S's Historical Cost	Adjustments	Pushdown	Fair Value
Cash	$125	$0	$125
Accounts receivable	190	0	190
Inventory	200	50	250
Equipment, net of accumulated depreciation	400	60	460
Other intangible assets	10	90	100
Goodwill	0	80	80
Total assets	$925	$280	$1,205
Accounts payable and accrued expenses	$225	$0	$225
Noncontrolling interests	0	80	80
Capital stock	300	0	300
Additional paid-in capital	0	600	600
Retained earnings	400	(400)	0
Total liabilities and equity	$925	$280	$1,205

What consolidating journal entry would the Parent Company make assuming:

Company S did not apply pushdown accounting?

Company S did apply pushdown accounting?

Parent's Consolidating Entry:

	Without Pushdown		With Pushdown	
Inventory	$50			
Equipment, net	60			
Other intangible assets	90			
Goodwill	80			
Investment in S		$900		$900
Noncontrolling interest		80		
Capital stock	300		$300	
Additional paid-in capital		0	600	
Retained earnings	400			
	$980	$980	$900	$900

Pushdown Accounting Disclosures

If an acquiree elects the option to apply pushdown accounting in its separate financial statements, it shall disclose information in the period in which the pushdown accounting was applied that enables users of financial statements to evaluate the effect of pushdown accounting. To meet this disclosure objective, the acquiree shall consider the disclosure requirements in other subtopics of Topic 805.

Private Company Business Acquisition Accounting Alternative

ASU 2014-18, *Business Combinations (Topic 805): Accounting for Identifiable Intangible Assets in a Business Combination*, is applicable to private entities. It applies when a private entity is required to recognize or consider the fair value of intangible assets as a result of any one of the following:

- Applying the acquisition method;
- Assessing the nature of the difference between the carrying amount of an investment and the amount of underlying equity in net assets of an investee when applying the equity method of accounting; and
- Adopting fresh-start reporting.

This accounting alternative permits a private entity acquirer to not recognize separately from goodwill the following intangible assets:

- Customer-related intangible assets unless they are capable of being sold or licensed independently from other assets of a business; and
- Non-competition agreements.

  Customer-related intangibles include mortgage servicing rights, commodity supply contracts, core deposits, and customer information, e.g., names and contact information.

Once the accounting alternative is elected, it shall be applied to all future transactions. Entities that elect this alternative must also adopt the accounting alternative for amortizing goodwill in the accounting alternative subsections of FASB ASC Topic 350-20 on intangibles—goodwill and other. If the accounting alternative for amortizing goodwill was not adopted previously, it should be adopted on a prospective basis as of the adoption of this accounting alternative under ASU 2014-18.

ASU 2016-03, *Intangibles—Goodwill and Other (Topic 350), Business Combinations (Topic 805), Consolidation (Topic 810), Derivatives and Hedging (Topic 815): Effective Date and Transition Guidance (a consensus of the Private Company Council)*, makes the guidance in ASU 2014-18 and others effective immediately by removing their effective dates. The amendments also include transition provisions that provide that private companies are able to forgo a "preferability" assessment the first time they elect the accounting alternatives within the scope of ASU 2016-03. Any subsequent change to an accounting policy election requires justification that the change is preferable under Topic 250, *Accounting Changes and Error Corrections*.

Recent Changes

ASU 2017-01, *Business Combinations (Topic 805): Clarifying the Definition of a Business*, was issued in January 2017. Prior guidance to determine whether an acquisition or disposal transaction involved a business was very broad, resulting in the treatment of many transactions being accounted for as business acquisitions that will be accounted for as asset acquisitions under the new guidance. ASU 2017-01 is intended to clarify the definition of a business with the objective of adding guidance to assist entities with evaluating whether transactions should be accounted for as acquisitions (or disposals) of assets or businesses.

The clarified definition is complex and will be difficult to apply in practice. The entity should consult, as amended by ASU 2017-01, paragraphs ASC 805-10-55-3A, 805-10-55-4 through 55-6, and 805-10-55-8 and 9.

The definition of a business affects many areas of accounting including acquisitions, disposals, goodwill, and consolidation. Any entity must determine whether it has acquired or sold a business under the entered transaction.

Under current guidance, there are three elements of a business—inputs, processes, and outputs. While an integrated set of assets and activities (a "set") that is a business usually has outputs, outputs are not required to be present. In addition, all the inputs and processes used in operating a set are not required if market participants can acquire the set and continue to produce outputs by integrating the acquired set with their own inputs and processes. ASU 2017-01 provides a screen to determine if an acquired set is a business. When substantially all of the fair value of the gross assets acquired (or disposed) is concentrated in a single, identifiable asset or group of similarly identifiable assets, the set would not be considered a business. If the set fails the screen, an entity must perform further analysis to determine if the acquisition should be accounted for as a business combination. For that analysis, a set must include, at a minimum, an input and a substantive process that together significantly contribute to the ability to create output to be considered a business. If the set has no outputs, there must be an organized workforce and an input that that workforce could develop or convert into output for the set to be classified as a business.

Under ASU 2017-01 outputs result from inputs and substantive processes that provide goods or services to customers, other revenue or investment income.

Lastly, ASU 2017-01 removes the evaluation of whether a market participant could replace missing elements (as referred to above) from the determination of whether the transaction is a business combination or an asset acquisition.

ASU 2017-01 is effective for public entities in fiscal years beginning after December 15, 2017, including interim periods. For all other entities it is effective in fiscal years beginning after December 15, 2018, and interim periods beginning one year later.

The adoption of ASU 2017-01 is required to be on a prospective basis. Early adoption is permitted for transactions:

- With an acquisition date before the issuance date or effective date of this ASU only if the transaction has not been reported in financial statements that have been issued or made available for issuance.
- In which a subsidiary is deconsolidated or a group of assets is derecognized before the issuance date or effective date of this ASU, only if the transaction has not been reported in financial statements that have been issued or made available for issuance.

Topic 808: Collaborative Arrangements

Topic 808, *Collaborative Arrangements,* contains one subtopic:

10 Overall

This topic is not covered in this book.

Topic 810: Consolidation

Topic 810, *Consolidation,* contains 18 subtopics:

10 Overall

20 Control of Partnerships and Similar Entities

30 Research and Development Arrangements

910 Contractors—Construction*

915 Development Stage Entities*

930 Extractive Activities—Mining*

932 Extractive Activities—Oil and Gas*

940 Financial Services—Brokers and Dealers*

942 Financial Services—Depository and Lending*

946 Financial Services—Investment Companies*

948 Financial Services—Mortgage Banking*

952 Franchisors*

954 Health Care Entities*

958 Not-For-Profit Entities*

970 Real Estate—General*

974 Real Estate—Real Estate Investment Trusts*

978 Real Estate—Time-Sharing Activities*

980 Regulated Operations*

* See the corresponding topic in Chapter 9 for coverage of this shared subtopic.

Introduction

ASC 810 specifies the requirements for consolidated financial statements.

Under ASC 810, a reporting entity is required to consolidate certain legal entities under circumstances described below. Legal entities include, among others, corporations, limited liability companies, partnerships, and trusts. Since consolidation is only assessed for legal entities, the determination of whether an entity is a legal entity is important.

A reporting entity that has a controlling financial interest in one or more subsidiaries as well as a reporting entity that is the primary beneficiary of a variable interest entity (discussed below) is referred to as the parent. An entity in which the reporting entity holds a controlling financial interest and a variable interest entity that is consolidated by a primary beneficiary are both referred to as a subsidiary.

A reporting entity is required to consolidate a majority-owned subsidiary but there are some exceptions to this requirement. Such exceptions include situations where the reporting entity does not control the majority-owned subsidiary. Examples of exceptions include, among others, a subsidiary in bankruptcy or under legal reorganization. Also, if the reporting entity is a broker-dealer it shall not consolidate a subsidiary if control of that subsidiary is likely to be temporary. Further, a reporting entity may be required to apply consolidation accounting to a research and development agreement and to consolidate a "rabbi trust" under certain deferred compensation arrangements.

Certain legal entities shall not be consolidated under ASC 810-10-15-12 as follows:

1. A reporting entity employer shall not consolidate an employee benefit plan.
2. An investment company reporting entity shall not consolidate an investee that is not an investment company.
3. A reporting entity shall not consolidate a governmental organization and shall not consolidate a financing entity established by a governmental organization unless the financing entity meets specified conditions.
4. A reporting entity shall not consolidate a legal entity that is required to comply with or operate in accordance with requirements that are similar to those included in Rule 2a-7 of the Investment Company Act of 1940 for registered money market funds, under ASU 2015-02.

A reporting entity is also required to consolidate a variable interest entity (VIE) if the reporting entity is the primary beneficiary. This requirement applies to all legal entities except:

1. Not-for-profit (NFP) entities. (However, a NFP used by the reporting entity in a manner similar to a VIE in an effort to circumvent the VIE consolidation requirements is not exempted from VIE accounting.)
2. Separate accounts of life insurance entities.
3. A reporting entity with an interest in a VIE or potential VIE created before December 31, 2003, is not required to apply the VIE guidance in ASC 810 to that VIE or legal entity if the reporting entity, after making an exhaustive effort, is unable to obtain the information necessary to:

   a. Determine whether the legal entity is a VIE; or
   b. Determine whether the reporting entity is the VIE's primary beneficiary; or
   c. Perform the accounting required to consolidate the VIE for which it is determined to be the primary beneficiary.
4. A legal entity that is deemed to be a business need not be evaluated by a reporting entity to determine if the legal entity is a VIE under the requirements of the VIE subsections of ASC 810 unless:
   a. The reporting entity, its related parties, or both participated significantly in the design or redesign of the legal entity; or
   b. The legal entity is designed so that substantially all of its activities either involve or are conducted on behalf of the reporting entity and its related parties; or
   c. The reporting entity and its related parties provide more than half of the total of the equity, subordinated debt, and other forms of subordinated financial support to the legal entity based on an analysis of the fair values of the interests in the legal entity; or
   d. The activities of the legal entity are primarily related to securitizations or other forms of asset-backed financings or single-lessee leasing arrangements. (ASU 2014-07, *Consolidation (Topic 810): Applying Variable Interest Entities Guidance to Common Control Leasing Arrangements*, provides that a private lessee reporting entity may elect not to apply VIE accounting to a VIE lessor entity under specified circumstances as discussed below.)

There are two primary models for determining whether consolidation is appropriate for legal entities not scoped out of the consolidation or variable interest entity requirements as referred to above:

1. The voting interest entity model; and
2. The variable interest entity (VIE) model.

To determine which model applies the reporting entity first determines whether it holds an economic interest in or is otherwise involved with the legal entity that is being evaluated for consolidation. The reporting entity then determines if the legal entity is a VIE. If it is a VIE, then the VIE model is applied. If it is not a VIE, then the voting interest entity model is applied.

Consolidated financial statements are required for the reporting entity and all other entities in which it has financial control attained by majority ownership, or as primary beneficiary or under contractual arrangements.

Consolidation Policy

Consolidated financial statements include the accounts of the reporting entity and:

- The reporting entity's majority-owned subsidiaries (with certain exceptions);
- VIEs of which the reporting entity is the primary beneficiary; and

- Entities controlled by the reporting entity via contractual arrangements. (e.g., consolidation may be required under contractual arrangements between physician practices and physician practice management entities.)

Under the voting interest model, the usual condition for a controlling financial interest is ownership by the reporting entity (directly or indirectly) of more than 50% of the outstanding voting shares of another entity.

Under the VIE model, a reporting entity with a controlling financial interest in a VIE is referred to as the primary beneficiary. To have a controlling financial interest in a VIE, the reporting entity must:

- Have the power to direct the activities that most significantly impact the VIE's economic performance; and
- Be obligated to absorb the losses of or the right to receive the benefits from the VIE that could potentially be significant to the VIE.

The consolidation policy used by the parent must be disclosed in the financial statements. This disclosure is usually made in the summary of significant accounting policies.

The remainder of this section addresses:

- Procedures for Consolidation
- Accounting for VIEs—The VIE model, and Recent Changes in VIE Accounting
- Accounting for Majority-owned Subsidiaries—The Voting Interest Model
- Disclosure Requirements

Procedures for Consolidation

Different Fiscal Years

A parent and a subsidiary's fiscal years may differ as long as the time-period difference does not exceed three months. The subsidiary's financial statements for its accounting period may be consolidated with the parent's financial statements with disclosure of any material events that occur in the time period between the two fiscal year-ends. If the time period between the fiscal year-ends of the parent and subsidiary exceeds three months, the subsidiary may have to prepare financial statements for a time period that corresponds with the parent company's year-end. A change in fiscal years of either the parent or subsidiary is accounted for as a change in accounting principle.

Eliminations

Consolidation procedures involve eliminating all intercompany transactions and balances since the consolidated financial statements are intended to be those of a single entity. Therefore, intercompany transactions, such sales/purchases between the parent and the subsidiary, should be eliminated; otherwise, sales and expenses for the consolidated group would be overstated. Similarly, intercompany asset and liability balances should also be eliminated to preclude overstating the consolidated amounts. For example, an intercompany account receivable from a subsidiary in the parent's accounts and an intercompany account payable to the parent in the subsidiary's accounts would be eliminated when preparing the consolidated financial statements.

When a subsidiary is acquired and included in the consolidated financial statements, the retained earnings of the subsidiary existing at the acquisition date are also eliminated. The revenues, gains, expenses, and losses of an acquired subsidiary are included in the consolidated financial statements only from the date of the subsidiary's acquisition.

When intercompany profits on assets are still within the group of entities that will be consolidated, for which income taxes have been paid on those intercompany profits, the income taxes paid are deferred or the amount of any intercompany profits eliminated in the consolidation are reduced by an appropriate amount for such taxes.

When a subsidiary holds shares of the stock of the parent such shares shall not be treated as outstanding and thereby eliminated in consolidation and accounted for as the parent's treasury shares in the statement of financial position.

When a subsidiary issues a stock dividend or effects a similar transaction after its acquisition that requires retained earnings to be capitalized, a transfer to additional paid-in capital is not required when the entities are consolidated.

Parent Financial Statements

Separate financial information for the parent may be desired for various reasons. One way to provide such information may be to present "consolidating" financial statements with separate columns for the parent, each subsidiary or subsidiary group, eliminations and consolidated totals. Parent-only financial statements cannot be substituted for consolidated financial statements, because the consolidated financial statements are considered general purpose financial statements for the reporting group.

Combined Financial Statements

In some cases the combined financial statements of a group of entities under common control may be more appropriate and informative than the separate stand-alone financial statements of each entity within that group. When combined financial statements for a group of related entities are prepared, intercompany profits and losses and intercompany transactions and balances are eliminated. Further, if the entities have income taxes, foreign operations, noncontrolling interests, or different fiscal year ends, the procedures for consolidated financial statements apply.

Proportionate Consolidation

Proportion consolidation is limited to investors in unincorporated entities in the construction and extraction industries in which the investor (reporting entity) owns an undivided interest in each asset and is proportionately liable for its share of each liability. Under proportionate consolidation the reporting entity reports its share of each asset and liability of the investee as well as its pro rata share of the investee's revenue and expenses. Although ASU 2015-02, *Consolidation (Topic 810): Amendments to the Consolidation Analysis*, removes the separate consolidation model for limited partnerships and similar entities that are voting interest entities, the previous exception in that model is generally retained. Accordingly, a general partner may continue to apply the proportionate consolidation method rather than consolidating the entity and reflecting a noncontrolling interest.

Noncontrolling Interest

A noncontrolling interest in a subsidiary (commonly referred to as a minority interest) represent the net assets of the subsidiary that the parent does not control; it is the interest held by other than the parent. The noncontrolling interest is considered equity and is reported in the equity section of the consolidated statement of financial position separately from the equity of the parent. If there are noncontrolling interests in two or more subsidiaries, the noncontrolling interests may be presented in the consolidated statement of financial position in the aggregate.

When a subsidiary issues a financial instrument, the instrument may be classified as equity or a liability depending on the circumstances. The instrument (or an embedded feature) can be a noncontrolling interest if it is classified by the subsidiary as equity. Alternatively, a financial instrument (or an embedded feature) issued by a parent or a subsidiary can be a noncontrolling interest if (1) the instrument's (or embedded feature's) payoff to the counterparty is based, in whole or in part, on the stock of a consolidated subsidiary; (2) the payoff is considered indexed to the entity's own stock in the consolidated financial statements of the parent; and (3) the instrument is classified by the subsidiary as equity. However, no instrument can be a noncontrolling interest if it is classified as a liability.

A noncontrolling interest does not change the amount of intercompany transactions or the intercompany gain and loss eliminated in consolidation. The amount of intercompany gain and loss eliminated is allocated between the parent and the noncontrolling interest as applicable. The consolidated amounts of income, gains, revenues, expenses, losses, and other comprehensive income reported in the consolidated financial statements reflect transactions between the consolidated group and entities outside the consolidated group. The parent and the noncontrolling interest will receive an assignment of net income or loss, and comprehensive income or loss as specified in ASC 220. In some cases, losses of the subsidiary exceed its equity. If a subsidiary's losses cause it to have a deficiency in assets, those losses should continue to be allocated between the parent and noncontrolling interest even if the parent or noncontrolling equity interest becomes negative.

A parent's equity interest in a subsidiary may increase or decrease resulting from a variety of reasons. For example, the parent may purchase or sell equity securities in the subsidiary or the subsidiary may sell additional equity shares to entities other than the parent or the subsidiary may repurchase its equity shares. The accounting for such changes is dependent on whether there is a change in control.

Changes in a Parent's Ownership Interest in a Subsidiary

Control Retained—Changes in the parent's ownership interest in a subsidiary is treated as an equity transaction (no gain or loss is reported on change) when the parent keeps a controlling financial interest in the subsidiary. Because the parent's ownership has changed, the noncontrolling interest also changes. The change in the noncontrolling interest in the subsidiary will be reflected by adjusting the carrying amount of the equity interest of the noncontrolling interest. In addition, any difference in the adjustment to the noncontrolling interest and the fair value of the consideration exchanged in the transaction is accounted for as an adjustment of equity assigned to the parent. When there is accumulated other comprehensive income in the equity section of the subsidiary's financial statements, any change in ownership interest requires that an adjustment be made to the carrying amount of the accumulated other comprehensive income assigned to the parent.

Control Lost—Subsidiary Deconsolidated—When a parent no longer retains a controlling financial interest in a subsidiary, the parent should deconsolidate the subsidiary. A loss of a controlling financial interest by the parent may occur as a result of several factors. Events that may cause a loss of controlling financial interest by the parent include the following: (1) the subsidiary issues additional shares to entities other than the parent, (2) the parent sells part or all of its equity ownership interest in the subsidiary, or (3) a contract giving the parent control expires.

When a parent deconsolidates a subsidiary (other than through a nonreciprocal transfer such as a spin-off), it should report a gain or loss determined as follows:

1. Determine the carrying amount of the assets and liabilities of the subsidiary.

2. Determine consideration received adjusted for noncontrolling interest by aggregating the fair value of consideration received and the retained noncontrolling interest and the carrying amount of the noncontrolling interest.

3. Compute the gain or loss as the difference between (1) and (2).

The noncontrolling interest of the deconsolidated subsidiary is the parent's interest on the date of deconsolidation. If the subsidiary is deconsolidated as a result of a nonreciprocal transfer, the parent should apply the accounting and reporting requirements of ASC 845 related to nonmonetary transactions. When a parent no longer has a controlling financial interest in a subsidiary resulting from multiple transactions (two or more), the parent must determine whether the multiple transactions are considered a single transaction for purposes of the applying the deconsolidation rules. All the conditions and terms of the transactions should be analyzed by the parent when making the determination of whether the transactions should be treated as one transaction. The parent should consult additional guidelines in ASC 810 to help make a decision on whether multiple transactions or arrangements are to be accounted for as a single transaction.

When a parent deconsolidates a former consolidated foreign subsidiary because it ceases to control it, it removes the amount of accumulated foreign currency translation adjustment related to that foreign entity and includes it in the determination of any gain or loss upon deconsolidation as described in this chapter under Topic 830, *Foreign Currency Matters*.

Accounting for Variable Interest Entities—The VIE Model

ASC 810 specifies when a variable interest entity (VIE) must be consolidated. A reporting entity must consolidate a VIE when that reporting entity has a variable interest in the VIE that provides the reporting entity with a controlling financial interest in the VIE. A variable interest is one that changes with the VIE's fair value. A VIE is an entity that is subject to consolidation under the provisions of ASC 810. A VIE may be any legal entity that can hold assets or conduct activities. Examples include partnerships, corporations, trusts, limited liability companies, special purpose entities, and majority-owned subsidiaries. ASC 810 applies to all entities except as noted above.

Where to Begin

After determining that a scope exception does not apply, there are four steps to determining whether VIE accounting applies to the reporting entity:

Step 1: Does the reporting entity have a relationship with another legal entity that could trigger VIE accounting?

Step 2: Does the reporting entity have a variable interest in that legal entity?

Step 3: Is that legal entity a VIE?

Step 4: Is the reporting entity the primary beneficiary?

Each of the four steps is discussed below.

Step 1: Does the Reporting Entity Have a Relationship with Another Legal Entity that Could Trigger VIE Accounting?

The reporting entity considers four factors in evaluating its relationship with another entity that could trigger VIE accounting. If the answer to any one of the following four questions is "yes," then the reporting entity would proceed to Step 2:

1. Did the reporting entity participate significantly in the other entity's design?
2. Is the design of the other entity such that substantially all of its activities involve or are conducted on behalf of the reporting entity?
3. Does the reporting entity provide more than half of the subordinated financial support of the other entity?
4. Are the activities of the other entity related to securitizations or single-lessee leasing arrangements?

Design of the Other Entity:

The review of the design of the entity involves a two-step process: (1) risk analysis and (2) entity purpose and variability creation, and variability distribution. Examples of risk that should be considered under the Step 1 risk analysis include credit, operations, equity price, interest rate, foreign currency, and commodity price. Examples of factors that should be considered in the evaluation of Step 2 are (1) entity activity, (2) contract terms related to entity contracts, (3) when the entity was designed or redesigned and which parties were significantly involved in the process, (4) the nature of the interest of the entity that was issued, and (5) how the interests with possible investors were negotiated or marketed. In some cases, a contract or an arrangement may seem to both create and distribute variability. In such cases, the contract or arrangement should be reviewed as to whether it creates or distributes variability using the design of the entity instead of its legal form. A qualitative analysis using the provisions of ASC 810 would be considered conclusive when determining variability and the primary beneficiary.

Step 2: Does the Reporting Entity Have a Variable Interest in that legal entity?

A variable interest is one that changes with the legal entity's fair value. A variable interest may be an ownership, contractual, or other monetary interest that will change with a change in the net asset value of the legal entity. The variable interest may be explicit in the form of a financial instrument or implicit resulting from a relationship. Examples of variable interests include operating leases, service contracts, equity investments, debt instruments, and guarantees.

Decision Making Services:

The reporting entity may provide decision making services to another entity under a contractual arrangement. ASU 2015-02 removes three of the six criteria that must be considered when determining whether the decision maker fee arrangement is a variable interest. Briefly, if the decision maker fee arrangement is arms-length and contains customary terms and conditions and represents compensation that is considered fair value for the services provided then the decision making arrangement would not be a variable interest provided the decision maker and its related parties have no other interests. ASU 2015-02 notes that the magnitude of the fee does not on its own mean that the fee arrangement is not at market or commensurate.

Interests in Specific Assets:

A reporting entity may hold an interest in specific assets of a VIE. If the fair value of the specific assets is greater than 50% of the fair value of the total assets, or if the reporting entity has other variable interests in the entity, the interest in specific assets is considered to be a variable interest. This requirement is necessary to prevent a reporting entity that would otherwise be the primary beneficiary of a VIE from circumventing the requirement for consolidation simply by arranging for other parties with interests in certain assets to hold small or inconsequential interests in the VIE as a whole. The expected losses and expected residual returns applicable to variable interests in specified assets of a VIE shall be deemed to be expected losses and expected residual returns of the VIE only if that variable interest is deemed to be a variable interest in the VIE.

Step 3: Is that Legal Entity a VIE?

If a VIE is covered by ASC 810-10-15, then it is subject to consolidation by the reporting entity using the provisions of ASC 810. If the answer to any one of the following questions is "no," then the other entity is a VIE by its design:

1. Can the other entity's activities be financed with the total equity investment at risk without other subordinated financial help from other parties, including the equity holders? (Note: The total equity investment at risk is the "equity" section of its balance sheet. See the "Equity Investment at Risk" caption below.)
2. Do the equity holders as a group have the right to receive anticipated residual returns from the other entity should they be available? (Note: The equity holders as a group do not have that right if their return is capped by the other entity's governing documents or arrangements with other variable interest holders in the other entity or the other entity itself.)
3. Do the equity holders as a group have the requirement to absorb the expected losses of the other entity should they occur? (Note: The equity holders do not have that obligation if they are directly or indirectly protected from the expected losses or are guaranteed a return by the other entity or other parties involved with the other entity.)
4. Do the equity holders as a group in the other entity have the power, through voting or similar rights, to direct the activities of the other entity that most significantly impact its economic performance? (Note: More than one reporting entity may have the right to receive anticipated residual returns referred to in 2 above and obligation to absorb losses referred to in 3 above but only one reporting entity will have the power to direct the activities of the other entity that most significantly impact its economic performance. See the "Power to Direct" caption below.)

Questions 2 and 3 above are sometimes referred to as the "economics test" and question 4 is sometimes referred to as the "power test."

Equity Investment at Risk:

Under ASC 810-10-15-14, the total equity investment at risk:

1. Significantly participates, regardless of voting rights, in the losses and profits of the other entity.
2. Excludes equity issued for subordinated interests in other VIEs.
3. Excludes amounts received (either directly or indirectly) by the investor from the other entity or others involved with the other entity, unless the provider of the amounts is required to be included in the same consolidated financial statements of the investor as a parent, subsidiary, or affiliate of the investor.
4. Excludes amounts financed for the equity investor by the other entity or others involved with the other entity, unless the provider of the amounts is required to be included in the same consolidated financial statements of the investor, as a parent, subsidiary, or affiliate of the investor.

ASC 810-10-25-45 through ASC 810-10-25-47 provide guidelines as to the sufficiency of the equity investment at risk. The sufficiency test is made at the time the reporting entity first becomes involved with the other entity. An equity investment at risk of less than 10% of the assets of the other entity is presumed not sufficient. This presumption may be overcome with qualitative or quantitative analyses, or both. Generally, a qualitative analysis would be used first followed by a quantitative analysis. Together the combination of analyses may demonstrate that equity investment at risk of less than 10% is sufficient when neither of the separate analysis could demonstrate sufficiency. Qualitative analysis may include:

- Demonstrating that the other entity does not need additional subordinated financial support to finance its activities.
- Comparing the equivalent equity investment of other entities that hold similar assets of similar quality in a similar amount and operate with no additional subordinated financial support.

A quantitative analysis may include showing that the investment equity exceeds estimated expected losses based on reasonable quantitative information.

An equity investment at risk of more than 10% does not automatically mean that the equity investment at risk is sufficient. Judgment and analysis is required to determine if the entity can finance its activities without subordinated financial support in addition to the equity investment. This analysis applies to an entity involved in high-risk activities, holds high-risk assets, or has exposure to risks that are not reflected in the reported amounts of the entity's assets or liabilities.

Power to Direct (Power Test):

Analysis for Entities Other than Limited Partnerships:

The equity holders as a group do not have the power to direct the activities of the other entity that most significantly impact its economic performance if:

- They hold no voting right or similar rights.
- Their voting rights are not proportional to their obligations to absorb expected losses, rights to receive residual returns, or both.
- Substantially all of the other entity's activities are conducted on behalf of or involve an equity holder that has disproportionately few voting rights.

Legal entities that are not controlled by the holder of a majority voting interest because of noncontrolling shareholder veto rights (participating rights) are not VIEs if the holders of the equity investment at risk as a group have the power to control the entity and the equity investment meets the other VIE requirements.

If no owners hold voting rights or similar rights (such as those of a common shareholder in a corporation) over the activities of a legal entity that most significantly impact the entity's economic performance, kick-out rights or participating rights held by the holders of the equity investment at risk shall not prevent interests other than the equity investment from having this characteristic unless a single equity holder (including its related parties and de facto agents) has the unilateral ability to exercise such rights. Alternatively, interests other than the equity investment at risk that provide the holders of those interests with kick-out rights or participating rights shall not prevent the equity holders from having this characteristic unless a single reporting entity (including its related parties and de facto agents) has the unilateral ability to exercise those rights. A decision maker also shall not prevent the equity holders from having this characteristic unless the fees paid to the decision maker represent a variable interest.

If a reporting entity determines that power is shared among multiple unrelated parties such that no one party has the power to direct the activities that most significantly impact the other entity's economic performance, then no party would consolidate the other entity.

Analysis Specific to Limited Partnerships:

ASU 2015-02 introduces a new requirement to determine the existence of the power to direct the activities of the other entity that most significantly impact its economic performance to be applied only to limited partnerships and similar entities. For example, a limited liability company governed by a managing member rather than a board of directors.

ASU 2015-02 requires limited partners of a limited partnership, or the members of a limited liability company that is similar to a limited partnership, to have, at minimum, kick-out or participating rights to demonstrate that the partnership is a voting entity. Any of these rights, if present, are considered analogous to voting rights held by corporate shareholders that provide those shareholders with power over the entity being evaluated for consolidation. A limited partnership may be a VIE under one of the other characteristics even if these rights are present.

The definition of kick-out rights is amended by ASU 2015-02 to include both removal and liquidation rights. Liquidation rights are now broadly defined as the ability to dissolve the entity.

The kick-out rights must be substantive to demonstrate that the limited partnership (or similar entity) is not a VIE. Kick-out rights will only be considered substantive if they are exercisable by a simple majority vote of the entity's limited partners (exclusive of the general partner, parties under common control with the general partner, and other parties acting on behalf of the general partner) or a lower threshold (i.e., as low as a single limited partner). The substance of kick-out rights granted to an entity's limited partners may be called into question when there are economic or operational barriers such as:

- Conditions that make it unlikely that the rights will be exercised;
- The kick-out rights are subject to financial penalties or operational barriers to exercise;
- There is an inadequate number of qualified replacements, or the level of compensation paid to the decision maker is inadequate to attract a qualified replacement; and

- No explicit mechanism exists, by matter of contract or law, that would allow the holder to exercise the rights or obtain the information necessary to exercise the rights.

Substantive participating rights held by one or more of the limited partners would also demonstrate that the partnership is a voting entity. For this purpose, ASU 2015-02 defines participating rights as rights to block or participate in significant financial and operating decisions that are made in the ordinary course of business, consistent with the definition in the voting interest model. There were no other changes to extant guidance for assessing whether these rights are substantive.

Redemption rights held by the limited partners are not considered equivalent to kick-out or participation rights under ASU 2015-02. The ability of an individual investor to require a limited partnership to redeem its interest is not considered to provide the holder with the ability to remove the decision maker or liquidate the partnership.

If a limited partnership is determined to be a variable interest entity and the general partner meets both the "power" and "economics" tests (discussed elsewhere herein), then a single party kick-out or participating right over all of the entity's most significant activities would be needed for the general partner to avoid consolidation, i.e., the right must be unilaterally exercisable and not exercisable solely by a simple majority of limited partners.

Step 4: Is the Reporting Entity the Primary Beneficiary?

A reporting entity that holds a variable interest in a VIE and is the primary beneficiary must consolidate the VIE. The reporting entity is the primary beneficiary if it has (1) the power to direct the VIE's most significant economic activities (power test) and (2) is either obligated to absorb the VIE's losses or has the right to receive the benefits significant to the VIE or both (economic test).

If a reporting entity does not meet both the power and economics tests on a standalone basis, it must consider whether, together with its related parties, the group collectively meets both tests. If the related party group has both characteristics of a primary beneficiary, the "related party tiebreaker" test is performed to identify the variable interest holder within that related party group that is "most closely associated" with the VIE when the entities are under common control or power is shared. The party most closely associated with the VIE consolidates it.

ASU 2015-02 introduces the indirect interest concept that effectively accelerates the consideration of related party interests by incorporating them into the reporting entity's assessment of whether it is the primary beneficiary on a standalone basis in situations where the power test is met by a single party. However, consistent with extant requirements, all variable interests must be considered when assessing whether the related party group has the characteristics of a primary beneficiary.

ASU 2015-02 limits application of the related party tiebreaker test to two circumstances:

1. If no single party in the related party group has unilateral power (i.e., power is shared), then the related party tiebreaker should be applied to identify the related party that consolidates the entity.
2. If a single party in the related party group has unilateral power, and entities in the related party group are under common control, then the related party tiebreaker should be applied to identify the related party within the common control group that consolidates the entity.

If a single party within a related party group has unilateral power and the related party group is not under common control, the related party tiebreaker would not apply. However, ASU 2015-02 requires that if "substantially all" of the VIE's activities involve or are conducted on behalf of any party within the related party group, then that party is required to consolidate the VIE.

Determination of VIE Status

The determination for VIE accounting must be made at the time that the reporting entity (i.e., potential variable interest holder) becomes involved with the other entity (i.e., potential VIE) and subsequently at the end of each reporting period. Changes in interests by variable interest holders may also require a reconsideration of who is the primary beneficiary. All aspects of rights of the variable interest holders should be considered when determining which entity must consolidate the VIE. If one entity has a majority of the expected losses and another entity will receive a majority of the expected residual returns, the entity that will absorb the losses is considered the primary beneficiary and must consolidate the VIE. Variable interests in a VIE held by related parties should be treated as one interest for purposes of determining who is the primary beneficiary. ASC 810 provides guidelines as to which related party should consolidate the VIE.

Consolidating a VIE

How a reporting entity parent consolidates a VIE depends on whether or not the VIE is under common control with the reporting entity parent.

Under Common Control:

Once a reporting entity is classified as the primary beneficiary of a VIE, the reporting entity must initially measure the assets, liabilities, and noncontrolling interest of the VIE that are to be consolidated. The assets, liabilities, and noncontrolling interest in a VIE should initially be measured by the primary beneficiary at the same amounts in the accounts of the reporting entity that controls the VIE, or the same amounts that would be reported if statements were prepared using U.S. GAAP, when the VIE and the primary beneficiary of the VIE are under common control.

Not Under Common Control:

ASC 805 should be used to account for the initial consolidation of a VIE that is classified as a business and is not under common control. When the VIE is not a business, the assets, excluding goodwill, and liabilities should initially be measured by the primary beneficiary using ASC 805. If the transfer occurred before, shortly after, or at the time the entity became the primary beneficiary, any assets or liabilities transferred by the primary beneficiary to a VIE should initially be measured at the same amounts as if the transfer had not occurred. A gain or loss should not be reported on the transfer.

Any difference between (1) the sum of the fair value of consideration paid, the reported amount of prior held interests, and the fair value of noncontrolling interest and (2) the net amount of identifiable assets and liabilities of the VIE reported (recognized and measured) using the provisions of ASC 805 should be reported as a gain or loss by the primary beneficiary. The primary beneficiary should not report goodwill when the VIE is not classified as a business. Subsequent to initial measurement, the provisions of ASC 810 should be used to account for the VIE as if the VIE were consolidated using equity voting interests.

ASC 810 discusses other considerations related to variable interest entities such as development stage enterprises discussed below under ASU 2014-10, *Development Stage Entities (Topic 915): Elimination of Certain Financial Reporting Requirements, Including an Amendment to Variable Interest Entities Guidance in Topic 810, Consolidation*, and interests in specific assets of a variable interest entity.

Election to Not Apply VIE Accounting

As originally issued, ASU 2014-07, *Consolidation (Topic 810): Applying Variable Interest Entities Guidance to Common Control Leasing Arrangements*, was effective for annual periods beginning after December 15, 2014, and interim periods within annual periods beginning after December 15, 2015. ASU 2016-03, *Intangibles—Goodwill and Other (Topic 350), Business Combinations (Topic 805), Consolidation (Topic 810), Derivatives and Hedging (Topic 815): Effective Date and Transition Guidance (a consensus of the Private Company Council)*, makes the guidance in ASU 2014-07 and certain other ASUs effective immediately by removing their effective dates. The amendments also include transition provisions that provide that private companies are able to forgo a "preferability" assessment the first time they elect the accounting alternatives within the scope of ASU 2016-03. Any subsequent change to an accounting policy election requires justification that the change is preferable under Topic 250, *Accounting Changes and Error Corrections*.

Early application of ASU 2014-07 is permitted if financial statements are not yet available for issuance.

Under ASU 2014-07, a private lessee reporting entity may elect not to apply VIE accounting to a VIE lessor entity if:

- There is a lease agreement between the reporting entity as lessee and the VIE as lessor;
- All activities between the reporting entity lessee and lessor relate to leasing arrangements between them;
- The lessee and lessor are under common control; and
- The lessee's amount of guarantee or collateral at inception does not exceed the value of the asset leased.

This accounting policy election applies to all entities except public entities, employee benefit plans, and not-for-profit entities.

The disclosures unique to ASU 2014-07 include:

- The amount and key terms of the lessor's recognized liability that expose lessee to providing financial support to lessee.
- A qualitative description of circumstances not recognized in the lessor's financial statements that expose the lessee to providing financial support to lessee (e.g., commitments and contingencies).
- Disclosures as required by other U.S. GAAP related to guarantees (ASC 460), related party transactions (ASC 850), and leases (ASC 840).

Investments in Development Stage Entities and VIE Accounting

Among other matters, ASU 2014-10 eliminates the concept of a development stage entity. For purposes of this section on consolidation, entities that have not commenced planned principal operations are referred to as DSEs. ASU 2014-10 impacts all companies that invest in DSEs. As such, the investor entity is required to determine if it should consolidate a DSE as a VIE. Prior to ASU 2014-10, development stage entities were excluded from VIE accounting.

Investor entities that have a variable interest in a DSE are now required to:

- Perform a consolidation analysis under the VIE model;
- Accumulate the information needed to meet the extensive VIE disclosure requirements; and
- Perform the required reassessments each reporting period.

Public entities are required to develop, document, and test internal controls over these processes.

When does that portion of ASU 2014-10 applicable to DSEs/VIEs become effective?

- For public business entities, the amendment eliminating the exception to the sufficiency-of-equity-at-risk criterion for development stage entities in ASC 810-10-15-16 should be applied retrospectively for annual reporting periods beginning after December 15, 2015, and interim periods therein.
- For all other entities, the amendments to Topic 810 should be applied retrospectively for annual reporting periods beginning after December 15, 2016, and interim reporting periods beginning after December 15, 2017.
- Early application of each of the amendments is permitted for any annual reporting period or interim period for which the entity's financial statements have not yet been issued (public business entities) or made available for issuance (other entities).

Investments in a VIE Collateralized Financing Entity

ASU 2014-13, *Consolidation (Topic 810): Measuring the Financial Assets and the Financial Liabilities of a Consolidated Collateralized Financing Entity*, requires a reporting entity to consolidate in its financial statements a VIE collateralized financing entity, such as a CDO or CLO entity, when it is the primary beneficiary. Many reporting entities currently elect or are required to account for the financial assets and the financial liabilities of a consolidated collateralized financing entity at fair value. Fair value, determined under U.S. GAAP, of a collateralized financing entity's financial assets may differ from the fair value of its financial liabilities even when the financial liabilities have recourse only to the financial assets. ASU 2014-13 provides an alternative for measuring the financial assets and the financial liabilities of a consolidated collateralized financing entity to eliminate that difference.

ASU 2014-13 is effective for public business entities for annual periods, and interim periods within those annual periods, beginning after December 15, 2015. For other entities, it is effective for annual periods ending after December 15, 2016, and interim periods beginning after December 15, 2016. Early adoption is permitted as of the beginning of an annual period.

Entities transitioning to ASU 2014-13 may use either a retrospective or modified retrospective method.

Recent Changes in Consolidation Accounting

ASU 2016-17, *Consolidation (Topic 810): Interests Held through Related Parties That Are under Common Control*, was issued in October 2016. Under this ASU, a single decision maker of a variable interest entity (VIE) is required to consider indirect economic interests in the entity held through related parties on a proportionate basis when determining whether it is the primary beneficiary of that VIE unless the single decision maker and its related parties are under common control. However, if a single decision maker and its related parties are under common control, the single decision maker is required to consider indirect interests in the entity held through those related parties to be the equivalent of direct interests in their entirety.

ASU 2016-17 does not change the characteristics of a primary beneficiary in current U.S. GAAP. Therefore, a primary beneficiary of a VIE has both of the following characteristics:

- The power to direct the activities of a VIE that most significantly impact the VIE's economic performance, and
- The obligation to absorb losses of the VIE that could potentially be significant to the VIE or the right to receive benefits from the VIE that could potentially be significant to the VIE.

If a reporting entity satisfies the first characteristic of a primary beneficiary (such that it is the single decision maker of a VIE), this update requires that reporting entity, in determining whether it satisfies the second characteristic of a primary beneficiary, to include all of its direct variable interests in the VIE and, on a proportionate basis, its indirect variable interests in the VIE held through related parties, including related parties that are under common control with the reporting entity. Further, under this ASU, a single decision maker is not required to consider indirect interests held through related parties that are under common control with the single decision maker to be the equivalent of direct interests in their entirety. Instead, a single decision maker is required to include those interests on a proportionate basis consistent with indirect interests held through other related parties. However, if, after performing that assessment, a reporting entity that is the single decision maker of a VIE concludes that it does not have the characteristics of a primary beneficiary, this update continues to require that reporting entity to evaluate whether it and one or more of its related parties under common control, as a group, have the characteristics of a primary beneficiary. If the single decision maker and its related parties that are under common control, as a group, have the characteristics of a primary beneficiary, then the party within that related party group that is most closely associated with the VIE is the primary beneficiary.

ASU 2016-17 is effective for public entities for fiscal years beginning after December 15, 2016, and interim periods within those fiscal years. For all other entities, the ASU is effective for fiscal years beginning after December 15, 2016, and interim periods for fiscal years beginning after December 15, 2017. Early adoption is permitted, including adoption in any interim period. As for transition, entities who have not yet adopted ASU 2015-02 should adopt the amendments in this ASU in the same method in which they adopt ASU 2015-02. Entities that have adopted ASU 2015-02 should adopt the amendments in this ASU retrospectively, to all relevant prior periods beginning in the fiscal year in which ASU 2015-02 was initially applied.

Accounting for Majority-owned Subsidiaries—The Voting Interest Model

ASU 2015-02 creates single model for all voting interest entities regardless of their legal form of governance structure. As such, this ASU removes the voting model specific to limited partnerships and similar entities under ASC 810-20. That guidance is effectively incorporated into the VIE determination in assessing whether the equity investment at risk has decision making rights. In addition, the rebuttable presumption that a general partner unilaterally controls a limited partnership has been eliminated.

The single voting interest model under ASU 2015-02 focuses on relative voting rights and considers other rights that enable a noncontrolling equity investor to participate in an entity's ordinary course operating and/or financial decisions. Such voting rights may be in the form of kick-out or participating rights. In the absence of such rights, a majority investor would be expected to control an entity unilaterally and consolidate the entity under the voting model.

ASU 2015-02 also clarifies that a single investor's ability to exercise a kick-out right (e.g., a limited partner that holds the majority of the kick-out rights) may convey unilateral control to the holder in the voting model, assuming another limited partner does not hold a substantive participating right. Accordingly, the investor with the kick-out right may be required to consolidate the entity under the revised voting model. This represents a change in current practice as the holder of a single party kick-out right typically accounts for its interest in a partnership that is a voting interest entity using the equity method of accounting, as opposed to consolidation.

The voting interest model applies to a reporting entity that has a variable interest in a legal entity that is not scoped out of consolidation under the exceptions for consolidation or VIE accounting. (Note: The reporting entity may have a variable interest in a legal entity that is not a VIE.) If consolidation is not otherwise required under the VIE model, the reporting entity evaluates whether consolidation is required under the voting interest model as follows.

- If the reporting entity owns a majority of the voting rights (shares) in a legal entity (other than a limited partnership or similar entity) and the noncontrolling shareholders do not hold "substantive participating rights" then consolidation is required.
- If the reporting entity owns a majority of the limited partnership's kick-out rights through voting interests and the noncontrolling partners do not hold substantive participating rights then consolidation is required.

Disclosure Requirements

ASC 810-10-50 specifies the disclosure requirements for a reporting entity presenting consolidated financial statements.

Consolidation Policy

The consolidated financial statements shall disclose the consolidation policy that is being followed.

Parent with a Less-Than-Wholly-Owned Subsidiary

A parent with one or more less-than-wholly-owned subsidiaries shall disclose all of the following for each reporting period:

1. Separately, on the face of the consolidated financial statements the:
   a. Amounts of consolidated net income and consolidated comprehensive income; and
   b. Related amounts of each attributable to the parent and the noncontrolling interest.
2. Either in the notes or on the face of the consolidated income statement, amounts attributable to the parent for any of the following, if reported in the consolidated financial statements:
   a. Income from continuing operations; or
   b. Discontinued operations
3. Either in the consolidated statement of changes in equity, if presented, or in the notes to consolidated financial statements, a reconciliation at the beginning and the end of the period of the carrying amount of total equity (net assets), equity (net assets) attributable to the parent, and equity (net assets) attributable to the noncontrolling interest. That reconciliation shall separately disclose:
   a. Net income;
   b. Transactions with owners acting in their capacity as owners, showing separately contributions from and distributions to owners; and
   c. Each component of other comprehensive income.
4. In notes to the consolidated financial statements, a separate schedule that shows the effects of any changes in a parent's ownership interest in a subsidiary on the equity attributable to the parent.

In the period that either a subsidiary is deconsolidated or a group of assets is derecognized in accordance the parent shall disclose:

1. The amount of any gain or loss recognized.
2. The portion of any gain or loss related to the remeasurement of any retained investment in the former subsidiary or group of assets to its fair value.
3. The caption in the income statement in which the gain or loss is recognized unless separately presented on the face of the income statement.
4. A description of the valuation technique(s) used to measure the fair value of any direct or indirect retained investment in the former subsidiary or group of assets.
5. Information that enables users of the parent's financial statements to assess the inputs used to develop the fair value in item (4).
6. The nature of continuing involvement with the subsidiary or entity acquiring the group of assets after it has been deconsolidated or derecognized.
7. Whether the transaction that resulted in the deconsolidation or derecognition was with a related party.
8. Whether the former subsidiary or entity acquiring a group of assets will be a related party after deconsolidation.

Variable Interest Entities

The principal objectives of the VIE disclosure requirements are to provide financial statement users with an understanding of:

1. The significant judgments and assumptions made by a reporting entity in determining whether it must:
   a. Consolidate a VIE and/or
   b. Disclose information about its involvement in a VIE.
2. The nature of restrictions on a consolidated VIE's assets and on the settlement of its liabilities reported by a reporting entity in its statement of financial position, including the carrying amounts of such assets and liabilities.
3. The nature of, and changes in, the risks associated with a reporting entity's involvement with the VIE.
4. How a reporting entity's involvement with the VIE affects the reporting entity's financial position, financial performance, and cash flows.

A reporting entity shall consider the overall objectives in providing the disclosures specifically required. To achieve those objectives, a reporting entity may need to supplement the disclosures otherwise required, depending on the facts and circumstances surrounding the VIE and a reporting entity's interest in that VIE.

Disclosures related to VIEs under ASC 810-10-50 that a reporting entity shall make as (1) a primary beneficiary; or (2) as a nonprimary beneficiary holder of a variable interest in a VIE; or (3) as primary beneficiaries or other holders of interests in VIEs follow.

Primary Beneficiary Holder of a Variable Interest in a VIE

The primary beneficiary of a VIE shall disclose:

1. The carrying amounts and classification of the VIE's assets and liabilities in the statement of financial position that are consolidated, including qualitative information about the relationship(s) between those assets and liabilities. For example, if the VIE's assets can be used only to settle obligations of the VIE, the reporting entity shall disclose qualitative information about the nature of the restrictions on those assets.*

2. The lack of recourse if creditors (or beneficial interest holders) of a consolidated VIE have no recourse to the general credit of the primary beneficiary.*

3. The terms of arrangements, giving consideration to both explicit arrangements and implicit variable interests that could require the reporting entity to provide financial support (e.g., liquidity arrangements and obligations to purchase assets) to the VIE, including events or circumstances that could expose the reporting entity to a loss.*

*A VIE may issue voting equity interests, and the entity that holds a majority voting interest also may be the primary beneficiary of the VIE. If so, and if the VIE meets the definition of a business and the VIE's assets can be used for purposes other than the settlement of the VIE's obligations, then this disclosure is not required.

Nonprimary Beneficiary Holder of a Variable Interest in a VIE

A reporting entity that holds a variable interest in a VIE, but is not the VIE's primary beneficiary, shall disclose:

1. The carrying amounts and classification of the assets and liabilities in the reporting entity's statement of financial position that relate to the reporting entity's variable interest in the VIE.

2. The reporting entity's maximum exposure to loss as a result of its involvement with the VIE, including how the maximum exposure is determined and the significant sources of the reporting entity's exposure to the VIE. If the reporting entity's maximum exposure to loss as a result of its involvement with the VIE cannot be quantified, that fact shall be disclosed.

3. A tabular comparison of the carrying amounts of the assets and liabilities, as required by 1 above, and the reporting entity's maximum exposure to loss, as required by 2 above. A reporting entity shall provide qualitative and quantitative information to allow financial statement users to understand the differences between the two amounts. That discussion shall include, but is not limited to, the terms of arrangements, giving consideration to both explicit arrangements and implicit variable interests, that could require the reporting entity to provide financial

support (e.g., liquidity arrangements and obligations to purchase assets) to the VIE, including events or circumstances that could expose the reporting entity to a loss.

4. Information about any liquidity arrangements, guarantees, and/or other commitments by third parties that may affect the fair value or risk of the reporting entity's variable interest in the VIE is encouraged.
5. If applicable, significant factors considered and judgments made in determining that the power to direct the activities of a VIE that most significantly impact the VIE's economic performance is shared.

Primary Beneficiaries or Other Holders of Interests in VIEs

A reporting entity that is a primary beneficiary of a VIE or a reporting entity that holds a variable interest in a VIE but is not the entity's primary beneficiary shall disclose all of the following:

1. Its methodology for determining whether the reporting entity is the primary beneficiary of a VIE, including, but not limited to, significant judgments and assumptions made. One way to meet this disclosure requirement would be to provide information about the types of involvements a reporting entity considers significant, supplemented with information about how the significant involvements were considered in determining whether the reporting entity is the primary beneficiary.
2. If facts and circumstances change such that the conclusion to consolidate a VIE has changed in the most recent financial statements (e.g., the VIE was previously consolidated and is not currently consolidated), the primary factors that caused the change and the effect on the reporting entity's financial statements.
3. Whether the reporting entity has provided financial or other support (explicitly or implicitly) during the periods presented to the VIE that it was not previously contractually required to provide or whether the reporting entity intends to provide that support, including both of the following:
   a. The type and amount of support, including situations in which the reporting entity assisted the VIE in obtaining another type of support.
   b. The primary reasons for providing the support.
4. Qualitative and quantitative information about the reporting entity's involvement (giving consideration to both explicit arrangements and implicit variable interests) with the VIE, including, but not limited to, the nature, purpose, size, and activities of the VIE, including how the VIE is financed.

Accounting Alternative

If a private lessee reporting entity elects not to apply VIE accounting to a VIE lessor entity under ASU 2014-07, it shall disclose:

1. The amount and key terms of liabilities (e.g., debt, environmental liabilities, and asset retirement obligations) recognized by the lessor entity that expose the lessee entity to providing financial support to the lessor entity. For example, a lessee exposed to debt of the lessor should disclose information such as the amount of debt, interest rate, maturity, pledged collateral, and guarantees associated with the debt.
2. A qualitative description of circumstances (e.g., certain commitments and contingencies) not recognized in the financial statements of the lessor that expose the lessee to providing financial support to the lessor.

Disclosures required in 1 and 2 above may be presented in combination with the disclosures required by other guidance (e.g., in Topics 460 on guarantees, 850 on related party disclosures, and 840 on leases).

Topic 815: Derivatives and Hedging

Topic 815, *Derivatives and Hedging,* contains 12 subtopics:

10 Overall

15 Embedded Derivatives

20 Hedging—General

25 Fair Value Hedges

30 Cash Flow Hedges

35 Net Investment Hedges

40 Contracts in Entity's Own Equity

45 Weather Derivatives

932 Extractive Activities—Oil and Gas*

944 Financial Services—Insurance*

954 Health Care Entities*

958 Not-For-Profit Entities*

* See the corresponding topic in Chapter 9 for coverage of this shared subtopic.

Flowchart and General Discussion

ASC 815 provides the accounting and reporting requirements for derivative financial instruments and for derivative instruments used as hedges. Derivative financial instruments must be reported as assets or liabilities in the balance sheet at fair value. If the derivative is not used as a hedge, the change in its fair value for the accounting period under consideration is reported as a component of income from continuing operations. If the derivative is used as a hedge, accounting for the change in value depends on the type of hedge. There are three types of derivative hedges: (1) fair value, (2) cash flow, and (3) foreign currency.

With fair value hedges, both the derivative instrument and the hedged item are reported at fair value with changes in fair value of both the derivative and the hedged item reported as a component of income from continuing operations. With cash flow hedges, the derivative instrument is reported at fair value and changes in its fair value reported as a component of other comprehensive income. ASC 815 does not require the hedged item in a cash flow hedge to be reported at fair value.

Foreign currency hedges are divided into unrecognized firm commitments, available-for-sale securities, foreign currency transactions, and net investments in foreign operations. Hedges related to unrecognized firm commitments and available-for-sale securities are classified as fair value hedges and accounted for as described above for fair value hedges. Hedges related to foreign currency transactions are classified as cash flow hedges and accounted for as specified above for such hedges. A derivative that is a hedge of a net investment in foreign operations is reported at fair value, and changes in its fair value reported as a component of other comprehensive income.

The major provisions of ASC 815 are illustrated in Flowchart 8-1. The decision blocks numbered and are referred to in the discussion.

Flowchart 8-1

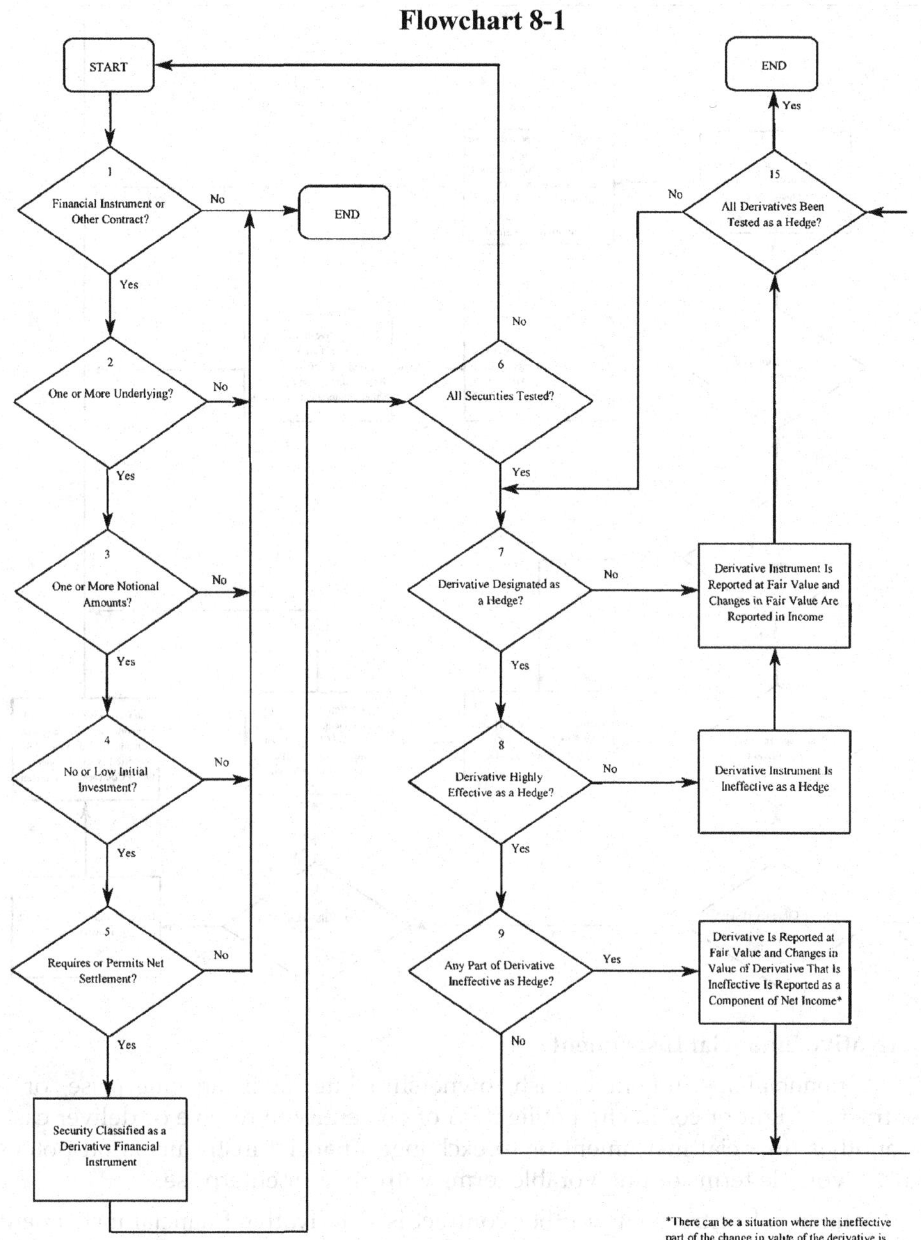

*There can be a situation where the ineffective part of the change in value of the derivative is not reported in income. See the discussion for details.

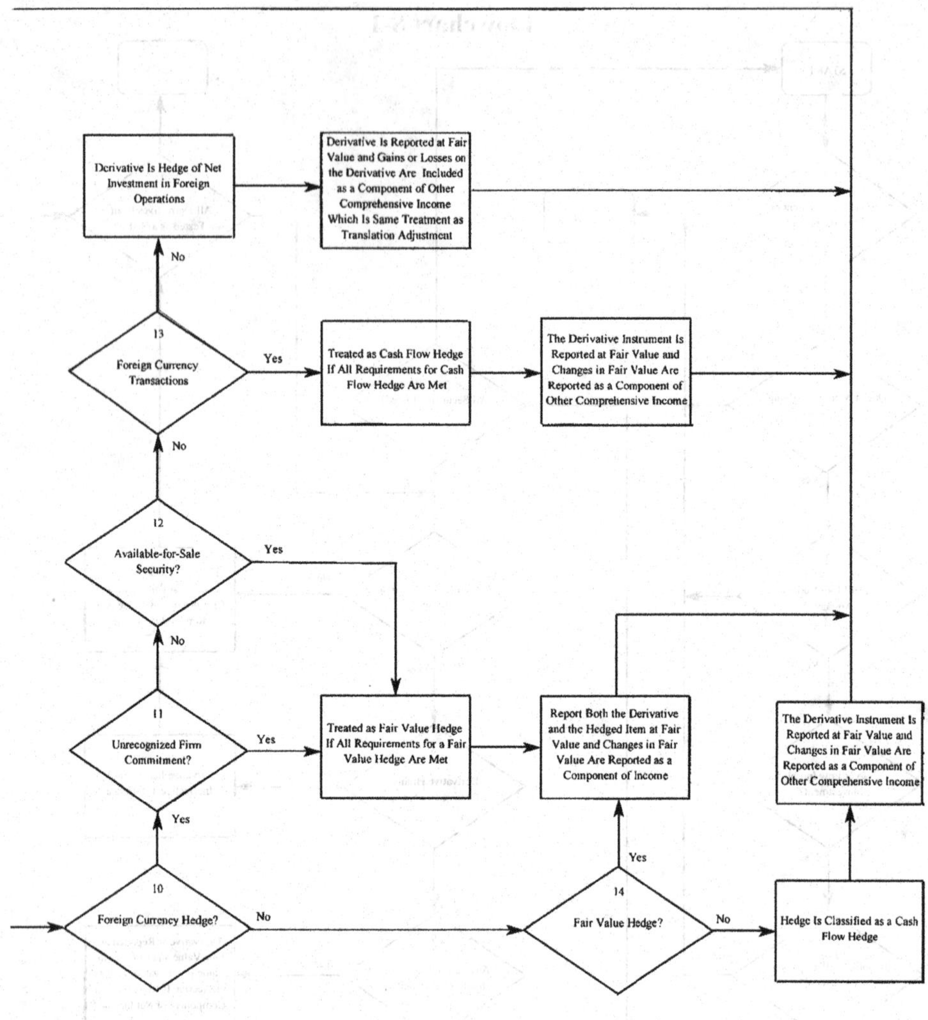

Derivative Financial Instrument

A financial instrument is cash, ownership interest in an enterprise, or a contractual right or contractual obligation of one entity to receive or deliver cash or another financial instrument or to exchange financial instruments on potentially favorable terms or unfavorable terms with another enterprise.

A financial instrument or other contract is a derivative financial instrument (Block 1) if it meets the following four requirements:

1. Has one or more underlyings (Block 2).
2. Has one or more settlement provisions, notional amounts, or combination of notional amounts and settlement provisions (Block 3).
3. Either has an initial investment that is lower than required for similar contracts with a similar response to market changes or no initial investment (Block 4).
4. Either permits or requires net settlement (Block 5).

Underlying

The first requirement for a financial instrument to be classified as a derivative is that the instrument must have one or more underlyings. An underlying is a variable factor that causes a financial instrument's fair value or cash flow to change. The underlying coupled with the payment requirements or notional amount indicates the settlement amount. Underlyings may include one or a combination of variable factors. Examples of underlyings include prices of securities, interest rates, prices of commodities, foreign currency exchange rates, credit ratings, geological or climatic conditions (such as the amount of rain), or an index of any of the preceding items. To illustrate an underlying, assume that an entity enters into a contract to sell a specified amount of gold at a specified price at a specified future date. Changes in the price of gold impact the value of the contract and, therefore, the underlying for this transaction is the price of gold. Another illustration of an underlying involves an interest rate swap. Assume that an enterprise enters into an agreement to exchange a variable rate interest stream for a fixed rate stream on a specified amount of debt. The value of the interest rate swap changes as interest rates increase or decrease and, therefore, the variable factor or underlying is the interest rate.

Settlement Provisions or Notional Amounts

The second requirement for a financial instrument to be classified as a derivative is that the instrument must have one or more settlement provisions or notional amounts. A settlement provision or notional amount is the amount or quantity specified in the agreement. For example, an entity might enter into an interest rate swap to swap a fixed interest stream for a variable interest stream on $20,000,000 of debt. The $20,000,000 is the notional amount used in the agreement. The $20,000,000 notional amount coupled with the interest rate indicates the settlement amount of the derivative. An example of a payment provision in a derivative is the requirement that an entity pay $2,000,000 if tornado damage in Kansas exceeds $150 million. Other examples of notional amounts or settlement provisions include dollars, barrels, pounds, bushels, ounces, currency units, or other units.

Initial Investment

The third requirement for a financial instrument to be classified as a derivative is that the financial instrument have an initial investment that is lower than required for similar contracts with a similar response to market factors. This indicates that an initial investment equal to the notional amount or payment provision of the contract is not required. Therefore, there generally is no initial cash exchanged by the parties to the derivative transaction.

To illustrate, assume that an entity enters into an interest rate swap to swap a fixed interest stream for a variable interest stream on $20,000,000 of debt. In this case, the parties to the transaction do not exchange the $20,000,000 debt, only the right to the interest streams is exchanged. Generally, the amount of cash that is exchanged between the parties at future dates is the difference in the fixed and variable interest rates times the $20,000,000 notional amount of the swap. However, some derivative agreements may require a specified initial investment. To illustrate a second situation related to net investment requirements, assume an entity enters into a gold futures contract to purchase gold at a specified price at a specified future date. This agreement, which is a commodity contract, generally requires no initial investment. However, if the same entity purchased the same amount of gold, an initial investment equal to the purchase price would be required. The illustrations provided above generally require no initial investment; however, there are situations where an initial investment may be required, such as remuneration for differences in asset fair values when such assets are exchanged at inception of a contract, premium associated with a forward purchase contract that is a payment for terms that are different from current market conditions, and option premium to cover remuneration for time value.

The initial net investment requirement is met if the initial net investment is less than what would be incurred to acquire the asset or incur the obligation. When making this determination, the initial net investment should be adjusted for the time value of money and the initial net investment must be less by more than a nominal amount.

Net Settlement

The fourth and last requirement for classifying a financial instrument as a derivative is that it either permit or require net settlement. A general definition of net settlement implies that a derivative contract may be settled at maturity by exchanging cash or another asset that easily can be convertible into cash instead of delivering the related item. Specifically, a derivative contract satisfies this last requirement if one of the following three conditions are met:

1. An asset equal to the notional amount or other amounts related to the underlying does not have to be delivered by either party to the agreement. Therefore, net settlement is permitted or required under the contract either in explicit or implicit terms. The delivery of cash or other assets will satisfy the net settlement requirements.

2. There is an established external market mechanism that allows the contracting parties to sell contracts or to enter into offsetting contracts as opposed to asset delivery by one of the parties to the agreement. This determination must be made at inception and on an on-going basis.

3. Delivery of an asset that is easily convertible into cash or a security classified as a derivative is required by one of the parties to the agreement. This requirement should be applied during the life of the contract.

Financial instruments or other contracts meeting all four requirements (Blocks 2-5) as discussed above are classified as derivative financial instruments and the accounting and reporting requirements in ASC 815 are applicable. Examples of financial instruments or other contracts meeting the definition of a derivative include futures contracts, currency swaps, interest rate caps, interest rate collars, interest rate floors, interest rate swaps, and forward exchange contracts.

Exclusions from ASC 815

Regardless of the classification requirements specified above, there are some financial instruments or other contracts that are specifically excluded from the provisions of ASC 815. These include the following:

1. Normal sales and purchases—A normal sale or purchase is a contract not involving the sale or purchase of a financial instrument or a derivative. A normal sale or purchase is the sale or purchase of something that will be used or sold by the entity in the normal course of business during a reasonable period of time. Certain securities qualify for normal sales and purchases. Forward contracts, freestanding option contracts, forward contracts with optionality features, and power purchase or sale agreements may qualify to be classified as normal sales and purchases. In addition, power purchase or sales agreements related to the sale or purchase of electricity meet the normal sale or purchase requirements if certain criteria are met.

2. Specific insurance contracts—covered by the provisions of ASC 944.

3. Security trades classified as regular way—buying and selling of publicly traded securities where the transaction generally is settled and delivered using customary market requirements and, therefore, the security trade does not meet the settlement and external market mechanism requirements. However, the regular-way security exception is not met if a contract for an existing security permits or requires net settlement of the security or if net settlement is facilitated by a market mechanism. An exception to this rule exists if an entity must use a trade-date instead of a settlement-basis for purchases and sales. In addition, there are exceptions to regular-way security trades.

4. Selected agreements that are not exchange traded.

5. Selected financial guarantees—are not derivatives if the agreement is not tied to an underlying and only requires payment to a creditor in case of debtor default. Additional requirements must be met for a financial guarantee to be excluded from derivative classification.

6. Derivative that impedes classifying a transaction as a sale—such as a residual value guarantee that prevents the lessor from classifying the lease agreement as a sale-type lease.

7. Registration payment arrangements within the scope of ASC 825-20.

8. Agreements related to stock compensation under ASC 718 issued by the reporting enterprise. If such contracts ceased to be covered by the provisions of ASC 718, the contracts should be reviewed to determine if ASC 815 should be applied.

9. Contracts between an acquirer and a seller to enter into a future business combination.

10. Agreements included in stockholders' equity and indexed to the stock of the reporting entity when the agreement is issued by the reporting entity.

11. Certain investment contracts covered by ASC 960.
12. Holders of loan commitments and issuers of loan commitments for other than mortgage loans.
13. Forward contracts that require cash settlement by the reporting entity for the acquisition of a fixed number of its equity shares and that are accounted for under ASC 480-10.

The exceptions noted in items 8–13, above, normally do not apply to the counterparty of the agreement.

Hybrid Contracts

The discussion above indicates the requirements that must be met by a financial instrument or other contract to be classified as a derivative instrument. In some situations, a financial instrument or contract in total may not meet ASC 815 requirements, but certain segments or parts meet the requirements. This type of financial instrument or contract is a hybrid contract consisting of a host contract and an embedded derivative. For example, a debt instrument with interest payments tied to an interest rate index would be classified as a hybrid contract where the debt instrument is the host contract and the underlying interest rate index is the embedded derivative. Another example of a hybrid contract is convertible debt that is convertible into a specified number of common shares of company stock. The host contract is the debt instrument and the embedded derivative is the conversion feature. An entity must determine if a hybrid contract should be separated into the host contract and the embedded derivative. If the embedded derivative is separated from the host contract, the embedded derivative should be accounted for separately using the accounting and reporting requirements of ASC 815. The embedded derivative should be separated from the host contract and accounted for separately when the contract meets all of the following requirements:

1. Fair value changes in the hybrid instrument or contract are not reported in the financial statements under accounting principles that normally would apply to the instrument.
2. If the embedded derivative was a separate instrument or contract with the same terms and conditions, it would be accounted for as a derivative in accordance with ASC 815.
3. The risks and economic attributes of the embedded derivative and the host contract are not closely and clearly related.

In the first requirement, the condition is met if the hybrid instrument or contract would not be remeasured to fair value each accounting period with the change in fair value reported in the income statement if the instrument was accounted for by an accounting principle other than ASC 815. The second requirement is a straightforward requirement needing no additional explanation. The third requirement is the most difficult to apply in practice and requires further explanation. To illustrate, assume that an entity has leased equipment with future lease payments tied to an interest rate index that is variable. The embedded derivative, which is the contingent rental, is closely and clearly related to the host contract, which is the lease contract. Therefore, the embedded derivative and the host contract would not be separated in this situation. To illustrate a situation where the embedded derivative would be separated from the host contract, assume that an entity has convertible debt that is convertible into common stock of the entity at a specified conversion rate. The debt issue, which is the host contract, would change in value as a result of changes in interest rates. However, changes in the fair value of the embedded derivative, which is the conversion feature or equity interest, would not be closely and clearly related to the change in interest rates. As a result, the embedded derivative would be separated from the host contract and accounted for using the provisions of ASC 815. To illustrate another situation, assume that an entity has convertible preferred stock that is convertible into common stock of the entity. If the preferred stock is viewed more as a debt, the embedded derivative and the host contract would be separated, but if the preferred stock is viewed more as equity, the host contract and the embedded derivative would be considered to be closely and clearly related and an entity would not separate the two.

When an entity has hybrid instruments that meet the requirements for separation under the provisions of ASC 815-15, an entity may elect to measure the entire hybrid instrument at fair value and report changes in fair value in income. This would be an initial irrevocable election that requires documentation. The hybrid instrument could be an asset or a liability and it may be issued or acquired by an entity. The election is made on an instrument-by-instrument basis. However, the instrument may not be used for hedging purposes. Any difference in fair value and transaction price at the inception of the instrument may not be reported in income, unless the fair value was estimated by using active market quoted prices, by using valuation methods that incorporated market data that was observable, or by using other comparable market transactions that were observable. Hybrid financial instruments where the entire instrument is reported at fair value should be presented separately in the statement of financial position either by actual separate reporting or by parenthetically disclosing the fair value of the instruments.

Entities with an interest in securitized assets (excluding interest and principal-only strips) must determine if the instrument contains an embedded derivative and is subject to the accounting requirements of ASC 815. However, in some cases, changes in cash flows related to changes in creditworthiness related to securitized financial assets and credit risk concentration related to the subordination of financial instruments may not be considered embedded derivatives. In addition, interest-only and principal-only strips may meet the requirements for embedded derivative accounting.

Classifying Derivatives

Once an entity determines that all financial instruments have been tested for derivative classification (Block 6) and if one or more of the financial instruments or contracts meet all requirements for accounting as a derivative, the enterprise then must determine if each derivative is classified as a non-hedge derivative or a derivative that is designated as a hedge (Block 7). Derivatives that are not accounted for as hedges should be included in the statement of financial position as assets or liabilities and reported at fair value. Changes in fair value are reported in the income statement in the accounting period in which the change occurs.

Hedge Effectiveness

If a derivative instrument is designated as a hedge (Block 7), the accounting requirements depend on whether the derivative is effective or ineffective as a hedge and the type of hedge. For an entity to use the accounting provisions of ASC 815 to account for a derivative instrument as a hedge, the derivative must be highly effective as a hedge (Block 8). The derivative instrument is assumed to be highly effective if changes in fair value of the derivative are highly effective in offsetting changes in fair value or cash flows of the hedged item. The ASC provides little guidance in determining if a derivative instrument is highly effective as a hedge and the decision is somewhat left to the judgment of the entity to make the determination.

To illustrate the highly effective offsetting issue, assume that an entity enters into a gold futures contract to hedge changes in the value of existing gold inventory. The value of the futures contracts increases by $100,000 and the value of the inventory decreases by $100,000. The futures contract would not only be highly effective, but would also be perfectly effective. In this situation, the gain of $100,000 from the derivative perfectly offsets the $100,000 loss from the decline in the value of the inventory. However, if the value of the futures contract increased by $90,000 and the value of the inventory decreased by $100,000, the hedge would not be perfectly effective, but generally would be highly effective and would qualify for hedge accounting under ASC 815, assuming all other requirements for hedge accounting are met. Accounting for the change in value of the derivative depends on the type of hedge. However, the $10,000 ($90,000 gain – $100,000 loss) ineffective part of the derivative would generally be reported as a component of income in the accounting period in which the change occurs. An exception to this accounting for the ineffective part of a derivative exists for one specific situation related to a cash flow hedge that is discussed in detail in the cash flow hedge discussion.

When assessing the effectiveness of a derivative instrument, an entity may elect, in some situations, to exclude part of the change in value of the derivative in the assessment process. These exclusions are allowed because the part of the change in value of the derivative that can be excluded generally would not be effective at offsetting changes in the value or cash flows of the hedged item. Any change in value of a derivative excluded from the assessment process is included as a component of income. The part of the change in value of the derivative that may be excluded in the assessment process includes the following:

1. Change in the time value of an option contract when the contract is assessed using changes in intrinsic value of the option.
2. Change in the difference in the spot and forward rate on a futures contract when the assessment of effectiveness is based on the change in the spot rate.

3. Change in the volatility value of an option contract when the assessment of effectiveness is based on a combination of the intrinsic value and impact of discounting.

If a derivative instrument does not meet the highly effective assessment process discussed above, the derivative is reported at fair value in the financial statements and all changes in fair value of the derivative are reported as a component of income.

Summary of Non-Hedge Accounting Requirements

Before proceeding to the hedge accounting requirements, the non-hedge accounting requirements discussed to this point are summarized as follows:

1. *A derivative instrument that is not designated as a hedge or does not meet the requirements for a hedge:* The derivative is stated at fair value with changes in fair value are reported as a component of income.
2. *A derivative instrument that is designated as a hedge and meets requirements for a hedge, but part of the change in value of the derivative is ineffective as a hedge:* The change in value of that part of the derivative that is ineffective as a hedge generally is reported as a component of income. An exception exists in a specific situation related to cash flow hedges that is discussed later.
3. *A derivative instrument where part of the change in value of the derivative is excluded in the highly effective assessment process:* The change in value of the derivative that is excluded is included as a component of income.
4. *A derivative does not meet the highly effective assessment process:* The derivative is accounted for at fair value and the changes in fair value are reported as a component of income.

Hedge Accounting Requirements

Once it has been determined that a derivative meets the highly effective assessment process, accounting requirements for the different types of hedges can be addressed. Derivatives that are designated as hedges may be divided into three basic types: foreign currency hedges (Block 10), fair value hedges (Block 14), and cash flow hedges. Foreign currency hedges may be either fair value or cash flow hedges. Fair value hedges and cash flow hedges are discussed below.

Fair Value Hedges

A derivative instrument or contract is classified as a fair value hedge when the instrument hedges risk as a result of an exposure to potential changes in an asset or liability's fair value resulting from fixed provisions such as interest rates or prices. Fair value hedges may be hedges of existing assets, existing liabilities, or firm commitments.

Assume an entity has an existing inventory of wheat at a specified price and the value of the wheat could increase or decrease prior to the time that it is sold. The entity could enter into a futures contract to hedge the change in value of the wheat inventory.

An entity may hedge an existing liability. Assume an entity has fixed rate debt. It could hedge the existing liability for that fixed rate debt issue by entering into an interest rate swap to swap the fixed rate interest stream of interest payments for a variable stream of interest payments.

A firm commitment is a binding agreement between unrelated parties that generally can be enforced at law and meets both of the following criteria: (1) all significant terms of the agreement are specified and (2) there is a penalty sufficiently large to ensure performance. A hedge of a firm commitment might exist when an entity enters into a fixed purchase commitment to acquire inventory at a specified future date at a specified future price. The entity then enters into a futures contract to hedge the change in the value of the inventory.

A derivative instrument must meet specific requirements to be accounted for as a fair value hedge. The requirements are as follows:

1. Formal documentation is available at the inception of the hedge stating the objective and strategy for risk management and for the hedging relationship.
2. The entity has a reasonable hedge effectiveness assessment plan that is used to assess the effectiveness of the hedge at the inception and on a periodic basis thereafter.
3. The relationship between the derivative and the hedged item is anticipated to be highly effective both at the inception of the hedge and on an ongoing basis.
4. The combination of both the hedge and the hedged item produce similar possibilities for both gains and losses when a reported asset or liability is hedged by a written option.
5. The hedged item is all or part of an existing asset, all or part of an existing liability, all or part of a group of similar assets, all or part of a group of similar liabilities, or all or part of a firm commitment.
6. Earnings reported in the financial statements may be affected by risk exposure of the item hedged.
7. The hedged item is not excluded from the scope of ASC 815.
8. The risk exposure of a hedged item that is a debt security classified as held-to-maturity relates to the change in the credit worthiness of the obligator of the debt, foreign exchange risk or both credit risk and foreign exchange risk.
9. The risk exposure of a hedged item that is an option on a held-to-maturity security relates to the change in the value of the option.
10. The risk exposure on a hedged item that is a nonfinancial asset or liability relates to the total asset or liability.
11. The risk exposure of a hedged item that is a financial asset, financial liability, nonfinancial firm commitment, or loan servicing right may relate to changes in interest rates. When there is a hedge of interest rate risk, the benchmark interest rate being hedged must be documented and designated at inception. The benchmark interest rate is, in theory, a risk

free rate that indicates high quality and is widely quoted in active financial markets. Benchmark interest rates include the interest rates on direct Treasury obligations of the U.S. government, the London Interbank Offered Rate (LIBOR), and the "Overnight Index Swap Rate," which is also referred to as the "Fed Funds Effective Swap Rate."

When a derivative instrument meets the requirements for a fair value hedge as discussed above, and the derivative is considered highly effective as a hedge. As such, the derivative is reported at fair value and the changes in its fair value are reported as a component of income. In addition, changes in the fair value of the hedged item are used to adjust the carrying value of the hedged item, such changes are reported as a component of income. If any part of the derivative is ineffective as a hedge, any change in fair value of the derivative related to the ineffective part is reported as a component of income. If a gain or loss on a hedged item is normally reported as a component of other comprehensive income because the hedged item is normally reported at fair value, the change in value subsequent to the time that the item is hedged using a fair value hedge is no longer reported as other comprehensive income, but as a component of income. An example of such a situation is an available-for-sale security where the security is carried at fair value and changes in fair value are reported as a component of other comprehensive income.

Impairment issues should be considered when accounting for fair value hedges. ASC 815 provides guidance on applications related to these issues.

The accounting described above for fair value hedges should be discontinued on a prospective basis when the derivative instrument is exercised, sold, terminated or expires, the fair value hedge designation has been removed by the enterprise, or the fair value hedge no longer meets the requirements for a fair value hedge as discussed above. This completes the discussion of fair value hedges. The next section covers cash flow hedges.

Cash Flow Hedges

A derivative instrument or contract is classified as a cash flow hedge when the instrument hedges risk as a result of an exposure to potential changes in anticipated cash flows from possible increases or decreases in items such as prices or interest rates. Cash flow hedges may be hedges of existing assets, existing liabilities, or forecasted transactions. To illustrate a cash flow hedge of an existing asset, assume that an entity has reported inventory that is to be sold in the future. Because the future selling price may be more or less than the current selling price, the entity faces risk related to the possible change in selling price. The entity can hedge this variability in future cash flows by entering into a futures contract that is designated as a hedge of the expected sale of the inventory. Please note that the entity is hedging the variability of the anticipated selling price and not the change in value of the underlying inventory, which is a fair value hedge.

For a cash flow hedge of an existing liability, assume an entity has a $20,000,000 debt issue with a variable interest rate. As such, the entity has risk associated with the expected future cash flows of the possible variable interest payments. The entity can hedge this variability in future cash flows resulting from possible changes in interest rates by entering into an interest rate swap that swaps the variable rate stream of interest payments for a fixed rate stream of interest payments.

The last type of cash flow hedge is a hedge of a forecasted transaction. A forecasted transaction is an anticipated future transaction that does not have a firm commitment. Because the forecasted transaction will be consummated at future prices or rates, the entity currently does not have any rights or obligations regarding the future transaction. Examples of forecasted transactions include an anticipated sale of inventory in two months, the anticipated purchase of equipment at the end of four months, or the expected issuance of five-year debt in two months. Because the amount of cash flow associated with the forecasted transaction may change as a result of change in prices or interest rates, any hedge of a forecasted transaction is classified as a cash flow hedge.

To illustrate a cash flow hedge of a forecasted transaction, assume an entity expects to purchase 100 ounces of gold in three months to use in its product manufacturing process. To hedge this forecasted transaction, the entity could enter into a three-month futures contract to purchase 100 ounces of gold at a specified price to hedge possible changes in the price of gold.

To qualify as a cash flow hedge, the transaction must meet the following criteria:

1. Formal documentation is created at the inception of the hedge stating the objective and strategy for risk management and for the hedging relationship.
2. The entity has a reasonable hedge effectiveness assessment plan that is used to assess the effectiveness of the hedge at the inception of the hedge and on a periodic basis thereafter.
3. The relationship between the derivative and the hedged item is anticipated to be highly effective both at the inception of the hedge and on an ongoing basis.
4. The combination of both the hedge and the hedged item produce similar possibilities for both positive and negative cash flows when the variability in future cash flows of a reported asset or liability is hedged by a written option.
5. The modification by a hedge instrument of a variable interest payment or interest receipt to another variable interest payment or interest receipt for existing assets or liabilities requires that the instrument must link a designated liability with variable cash flows with a designated asset with variable cash flows.
6. If the hedging transaction is a forecasted transaction, the following requirements must be met:

    a. It is probable that the forecasted transaction will occur.

    b. The forecasted transaction is either an individual transaction or group of individual transactions.

c. The other party to the transaction is external to the entity and the transaction is exposed to cash flow variations that could impact earnings, unless otherwise allowed by ASC 815.

d. An asset is not acquired or a liability incurred in the transaction that will later be remeasured for changes in fair value related to the hedged risk that is reported in earnings.

e. The forecasted transaction is not associated with a business combination, other consolidated transaction, or equity transaction.

f. Risk of credit worthiness or default is the risk hedged in a forecasted transaction involving a held-to-maturity debt security.

g. If a sale or purchase of a financial asset or liability or an existing asset or liability's variable cash flows is the forecasted transaction, ASC 815 describes the risk hedged in such transactions.

h. If a sale or purchase of a nonfinancial asset is the forecasted transaction, ASC 815 describes the risk hedged in such a transaction.

A derivative instrument or contract classified as a cash flow hedge is reported at fair value. Changes in fair value should be divided between the part of the change that is effective as a hedge and any part that is ineffective as a hedge. Any change in fair value of the derivative that is considered effective as a hedge is reported as a component of other comprehensive income in accordance with the provisions of ASC 220. The change in fair value, if any, that is considered ineffective as a hedge is generally reported as a component of income. The specific accounting requirements are as follows:

1. Any gain or loss excluded from the hedge effectiveness assessment process is reported as a component of income.
2. The balance in accumulated other comprehensive income should be adjusted for gains and losses from the hedged transaction in such a way that the balance at the end of the period equals the smaller of the following, assuming absolute numbers in the comparison:

   a. The derivative's cumulative gain or loss from inception after removing the gain or loss excluded from the hedge effectiveness assessment process described in 1, above, and any amounts reclassified to income from accumulated other comprehensive income.

   b. The portion of the derivative's cumulative gain or loss from inception that is required to offset the cumulative anticipated future cash flows of the transaction that is hedged, less any amounts reclassified to income from accumulated other comprehensive income.

3. Include in other comprehensive income an amount of the gain or loss needed to adjust accumulated other comprehensive income as indicated in 2, above.
4. Include as a component of income any gain or loss required as a result of the accounting prescribed in 2, above, or for any required adjustments to other comprehensive income. An amount equal to the related gain or loss from remeasurement in a foreign-currency-denominated asset or liability may be required to be reclassified to or from other comprehensive income depending on the circumstances.

The information in Tables 8-2 and 8-3 illustrates the income recognition requirements for cash flow hedges as discussed above. Table 8-2 shows two different situations over two time periods. In Situation 1, Period 1, the cumulative change in fair value of the derivative exceeds the cumulative change in cash flows; therefore, the smaller $2,000,000 cumulative change in cash flows is used as the balance that should be in the accumulated other comprehensive income account. Because the account had a zero balance at the beginning of the period, the change in the account for the period is $2,000,000, which is the amount reported as other comprehensive income. In addition, a $500,000 gain is reported in income for the excess of the cumulative change in fair value over the cumulative change in cash flows and the derivative is increased by $2,500,000. Notice in Period 2 that the cumulative change in fair value still exceeds the cumulative change in cash flows. Again, the smaller amount should be the ending balance in the accumulated other comprehensive income and other comprehensive income is increased by another $1,100,000, the amount needed to bring accumulated other comprehensive income to the $3,100,000 required balance. Also notice that a gain of $400,000 ($4,000,000 – $3,100,000 = $900,000 – $500,000 reported in prior accounting period) is reported in the income statement for the excess of the cumulative change in fair value in excess of the cumulative change in cash flows not already recognized and the derivative is increased by $1,500,000.

In Situation 2, the cumulative change in cash flows exceeds the cumulative change in fair value of the derivative. Again, the smaller of the two, in this case the cumulative change in fair value of $2,000,000, is selected as the balance that should be in the accumulated other comprehensive income. In addition, the process for adjusting the accumulated other comprehensive income and other comprehensive income is the same as discussed in Situation 1. The difference in the second situation relates to the recognition of gains or losses in the income statement. Notice that because the cumulative cash flows exceed the fair value amount, none of the difference is reported in the income statement, because only the derivative is reported at fair value. The derivative instrument and other comprehensive income are both increased by $2,000,000 in Period 1. In Period 2, the cumulative fair value of the derivative still exceeds the cumulative cash flow amounts and the accumulated other comprehensive income is increased by $2,000,000. Again, both the derivative instrument and other comprehensive income are increased by $2,000,000.

To illustrate a second situation for income recognition related to cash flow hedges, assume the information in Table 8-3 associated with an option that is used as a cash flow hedge. Notice that the same process used for adjusting accumulated other comprehensive income and determining the amount reported in other comprehensive income is the same as discussed in Table 8-2. However, one item added in this situation is the change in time value associated with the option that was not included in the illustration in Table 8-2. The change in time value is the amount of gain or loss reported in the income statement. The adjustment to the derivative for the change in fair value is the combination of the amount reported in other comprehensive income and the amount reported in the income statement. For example, in Period 1, the derivative would increase by $2.75 ($11.00 gain in other comprehensive income – $8.25 loss reported in other income).

Table 8-2 Illustration of Income Recognition Requirements for Cash Flow Hedges

Situation	Cumulative Change in Fair Value of Derivative	Cumulative Change in Cash Flows of Hedged Transaction	Balance That Should Be in Accumulated Other Comprehensive Income	Existing Balance in Accumulated Other Comprehensive Income	Amount of Gain/(Loss) Included in Other Comprehensive Income	Gain/Loss Included in Income
1-Period 1	$2,500,000	$2,000,000	$2,000,000	$0	$2,000,000	$500,000
1-Period 2	$4,000,000	$3,100,000	$3,100,000	$2,000,000	$1,100,000	$400,000
2-Period 1	$2,000,000	$2,500,000	$2,000,000	$0	$2,000,000	$0
2-Period 2	$4,000,000	$4,500,000	$4,000,000	$2,000,000	$2,000,000	$0

Table 8-3 Illustration of Income Recognition Requirements for Cash Flow Hedges

Time Period	Cumulative Change in Fair Value of Derivative Excluding Time Value Component	Cumulative Change in Cash Flows of Hedged Transaction	Change in Time Value	Balance That Should Be in Accumulated Other Comprehensive Income	Existing Balance in Accumulated Other Comprehensive Income	Amount Of Gain/(Loss) Included in Other Comprehensive Income	Gain/(Loss) Included in Income
1	$11.00	$11.00	$(8.25)	$11.00	$0	$11.00	$(8.25)
2	$2.10	$(2.10)	$(9.50)	$2.10	$11.00	$(8.90)	$(9.50)
3	$0	$3.20	$(11.90)	$0	$2.10	$(2.10)	$(11.90)
4	$28.00	$28.00	$(14.50)	$28.00	$0	$28.00	$(14.50)

When a cash flow hedge relates to a forecasted transaction, the gain or loss included in accumulated other comprehensive income is reclassified into income in the accounting period in which the forecasted transaction impacts earnings. If the forecasted transaction is a sale, it impacts earnings at the time of sale and reclassification would occur in the accounting period of sale. However, if the forecasted transaction relates to the acquisition of an asset or the incurrence of a liability, the gain or loss in the accumulated other comprehensive income is reclassified when the asset or liability impacts the earnings process. For example, an asset impacts the earnings process through periodic depreciation expense. If an overall loss is anticipated in the hedging transaction, the loss should be reclassified to income in the accounting period that an overall loss is determined. When it is probable that a forecasted transaction will not be completed and discontinuation of the cash flow hedge will occur, any gain or loss in accumulated other comprehensive income should be reclassified to income in the accounting period that it is determined that the forecasted transaction will not occur.

Impairment issues should be considered when accounting for cash flow hedges.

The accounting described above for cash flow hedges should be discontinued on a prospective basis when the derivative instrument is exercised, sold, terminated, or expires, the cash flow hedge designation has been removed by the enterprise, or the cash flow hedge no longer meets the requirements for a cash flow hedge as discussed above.

Simplified Hedge Accounting for Private Entities

Under ASU 2014-03, *Derivatives and Hedging (Topic 815): Accounting for Certain Receive-Variable, Pay-Fixed Interest Rate Swaps—Simplified Hedge Accounting Approach*, private entities (excluding employee benefit plans, not-for-profit entities, and financial institutions) are allow to use simplified hedge accounting for certain "plain vanilla interest rate swaps" if six criteria are met:

1. The rate for both the interest rate swap and the borrowing are based on the same index (e.g., LIBOR) and reset period (e.g., six months).
2. The terms of the interest rate swap are typical, or "plain vanilla."
3. The repricing and settlement dates are the same or close. (The term "close" is not defined, but at least one national firm has stated it considers a time period of seven days to be close.)
4. The fair value of the interest rate swap at time of execution is at or near zero.
5. The notional amount of the interest rate swap matches or is less than the principal amount of the borrowing.
6. All interest payments are designated as "hedged" in total or in proportion to principal amount of borrowing.

Simplified hedge accounting under ASU 2014-03 assumes there is no hedge ineffectiveness. Also the documentation of the nature and intent of the interest rate swap (e.g., cash flow hedge to address risk with a change in interest rates) may be delayed until the reporting entities financial statements are available for issuance. Lastly, the reporting entity recognizes the interest rate swap in its financial statements at settlement value rather than fair value. The difference between the two is applicable to the risk of non-performance.

As originally issued, ASU 2014-03 was effective for fiscal years beginning after December 31, 2014, with early adoption permitted. AUS 2014-03 may be adopted using either the modified retrospective approach or full retrospective approach.

ASU 2016-03, *Intangibles—Goodwill and Other (Topic 350), Business Combinations (Topic 805), Consolidation (Topic 810), Derivatives and Hedging (Topic 815): Effective Date and Transition Guidance (a consensus of the Private Company Council)*, makes the guidance in ASU 2014-03 and certain other ASUs effective immediately by removing their effective dates. The amendments also include transition provisions that provide that private companies are able to forgo a preferability assessment the first time they elect the accounting alternatives within the scope of ASU 2016-03. Any subsequent change to an accounting policy election requires justification that the change is preferable under Topic 250, *Accounting Changes and Error Corrections*.

This completes the discussion of cash flow hedges. The next section covers accounting and reporting requirements for foreign currency hedges.

A derivative instrument or contract is classified as a foreign currency hedge when the instrument hedges risk as a result of exposure to possible changes in foreign currency exchange rates. ASC 815 divides foreign currency hedges into the following types:

1. Hedges of unrecognized firm commitments (Block 11).
2. Hedges of available-for-sale securities (Block 12).
3. Hedges of forecasted transactions (Block 13).
4. Hedges related to net investments in foreign operations.

Foreign currency hedges of unrecognized firm commitments and available-for-sale securities are classified as fair value hedges and are accounted for the same as fair value hedges described above, assuming the transaction meets the criteria for a fair value hedge. A nonderivative financial instrument may be used to hedge an unrecognized firm commitment related to foreign currency exchange rates; however, a nonderivative instrument cannot be used to hedge foreign currency exchange rate risk related to available-for-sale securities. If the available-for-sale securities to be hedged are classified as equity securities, the hedge qualifies for fair value hedge accounting, if all requirements for fair value hedges are met and the equity security also meets the following two criteria:

1. The available-for-sale equity security is not traded on an exchange with trades denominated in the functional currency of the investor.
2. Anticipated cash flows from the sale of the security are denominated in the same currency as dividends or other items received by the security investors.

In a fair value hedge a nonderivative instrument cannot be a hedging instrument in a foreign currency exposure related to a liability or asset that is recognized.

As noted above, accounting for changes in value of derivatives and hedged items related to foreign currency firm commitments and available-for-sale securities are accounted for the same as described for fair value hedges. Please note that the change in value of an available-for-sale security hedged as a result of foreign currency exchange risk is included in income and not other comprehensive income. In addition, any gain or loss on a nonderivative financial instrument used in a hedge of a firm commitment is computed using the procedures to compute foreign currency transaction gains and losses as specified in ASC 830.

Hedges of foreign currency forecasted transactions, unrecognized firm commitments, and recognized assets or liabilities are classified as cash flow hedges and are accounted for the same as cash flow hedges described above, assuming the transaction meets the criteria for a cash flow hedge and the four requirements specified below:

1. The entity that is party to the hedging instrument is also the entity with the foreign currency exposure.
2. The entity's functional currency and the hedged transaction are denominated in different currencies.

3. The one criterion for a forecasted transaction that states that the transaction must be with an external party is not met, because the foreign currency forecasted transaction may be with related parties, such as a parent and a subsidiary.

4. Forecasted foreign inflows and outflows may not be combined in the same group if the hedged transaction involves a group of individual foreign currency forecasted transactions.

A nonderivative instrument may not be used to hedge a forecasted transaction related to foreign currency exchange risk.

Hedges related to net investments in foreign operations retain most of the accounting requirements specified under ASC 830. The amount of the translation adjustment (gain or loss) created when consolidating parent and foreign subsidiary statements is included as a component of other comprehensive income as required by ASC 830. Therefore, gains and losses from hedging foreign currency net investments by either derivative or nonderivative instruments are reported as a component of other comprehensive income to the extent that they are effective as a hedge. This means that as long as the gain or loss from the derivative or nonderivative instrument is equal to or less than the translation gain or loss, the total amount of the gain or loss on the hedge is assumed to be effective and all the gain or loss is included in other comprehensive income. However, if the hedge gain or loss on a cumulative basis exceeds the translation gain or loss on a cumulative basis, the excess gain or loss is considered ineffective as a hedge and is reported as a component of income. Any discount or premium (difference between forward and spot rates at inception of the contract) related to the hedge is not excluded from the determination of hedge effectiveness. Therefore, the discount or premium is included in hedge effectiveness and all hedge gain and losses are included as a component of other comprehensive income as long as the hedge gain or loss is equal to or less than the translation gain or loss as described above.

ASC 815 does not directly cover hedges of existing assets or liabilities that are denominated in a foreign currency. These types of transactions are not considered fair value or cash flow hedges. The gains or losses from remeasurement of the asset or liability denominated in a foreign currency will be reported as a component of income, and gains and losses from the change in the value of the derivative that is undesignated by ASC 815 also will be reported as a component of income. As a result, no special accounting is required of such transactions because the gains and losses from the asset or liability remeasurement tend to be offset by gains and losses from changes in fair value of the derivative.

An entity, such as a not-for-profit enterprise, where earnings are not reported separately in an income statement should report gains and losses from hedging and nonhedging instruments as a change in net assets in the accounting period when the gain or loss occurs. An exception exists if the gain or loss relates to a hedge of a net investment with a foreign currency exposure. In this situation, the accounting and reporting requirements discussed above for hedges of foreign currency net investments should apply. Changes in hedged items should be accounted for as changes in net assets in accordance with the requirements for fair value hedges as discussed above. Cash flow hedges are not allowed for entities that do not separately report income.

Technical Considerations

Four examples are used to illustrate the technical aspects of derivative accounting. Assumptions for Example 8-7 are presented below and cover the accounting for a derivative not classified as a hedge.

Example 8-7
Assumptions for a Derivative Not Accounted for as a Hedge

1. On November 1, 20X6, Speculation Inc. (Speculation), a December 31 year-end company, purchases 50 March 1, 20X7, wheat futures contracts when the quoted market price is $3.50 per bushel. Each wheat futures contract is for 5,000 bushels. Assume away any margin deposit in the example.
2. On December 31, Speculation's year-end, the quoted market price of the futures contract is $3.20 per bushel.
3. Speculation closes out the 50 March 1 futures contracts on February 5, 20X7, when the quoted market price is $2.98.

Speculation has entered into a contract that is classified as a derivative financial instrument not accounted for as a hedge because the contract does not relate to a hedged item. The derivative should be reported at fair value and classified as an asset or liability in the balance sheet. Any changes in fair value should be reported in the income statement generally as other income or expense.

Speculation has a December 31 year-end and the financial statements are prepared prior to the consummation of the derivative, the derivative must be adjusted to fair value and a gain or loss reported in the December 31, 20X6 statements. The gain or loss is computed as follows:

November 1 quoted market price	$3.50
December 31 quoted market price	3.20
Decrease in market price of contract	$.30
Size of contract (5,000 bushels × 50 contracts)	250,000
Loss on futures contracts at December 31, 20X6	$75,000

The entry required on December 31, 20X6 is:

Loss on Derivative Contract	75,000	
Derivative Instrument—Wheat Futures		75,000

The Loss on Derivative Contract account is classified in the income statement generally as other income and expense and the Derivative Instrument—

Wheat Futures account is included in the balance sheet and classified as a current liability because it is expected to be settled within one year or normal operating cycle.

On February 1, 20X7, the derivative instrument is closed and Speculation reports a loss of $55,000 from the change in market prices of the contracts from December 31, 20X6 to February 5, 20X7. The $55,000 loss for 20X7 is computed as follows:

December 31 quoted market price	$3.20
February 5 quoted market price	2.98
Decrease in market price of contract	$.22
Size of contract (5,000 bushels × 50 contracts)	250,000
Loss on futures contracts at February 5, 20X7	$55,000

The total loss reported by Speculation for the derivative instrument is $130,000 ($75,000 for 20 × 1 + $55,000 for 20 × 2). The entries required on February 5 to adjust the derivative to fair value and report the loss is:

Loss on Derivative Contract	55,000	
Derivative Instrument—Wheat Futures		55,000

Next, Speculation closes the contract and pays the broker for the $130,000 loss on the contract. The entry is as follows:

Derivative Instrument—Wheat Futures	130,000	
Cash		130,000

This completes the discussion of Example 8-7. Example 8-8 illustrates the accounting for a fair value hedge. Assumptions for Example 8-8 are as follows:

Example 8-8
Assumptions for a Derivative Accounted for as a Fair Value Hedge

1. On January 1, 20X6, Stone Enterprises (Stone) issued a $4,000,000, 6%, two-year fixed rate debt issue at par. Interest is paid at the end of each quarter. On the same date Stone entered into a two-year interest rate swap with a $4,000,000 notional amount. Stone is swapping the fixed rate interest stream for a variable rate interest stream (a receive-fixed pay-variable swap).

2. Stone pays a variable rate equal to the three-month LIBOR rate and settlement dates are at the end of each quarter. LIBOR rates for the two-year time period are as follows: January 1, 20X6—6%; March 31, 20X6—6.2%; June 30, 20X6—6.5%; September 30, 20X6—6.7%; December 31, 20X6—6.8%; March 31, 20X7—7.0%; June 30, 20X7—7.3%; September 30, 20X7—7.6%; and December 31, 20X7—8.0%.

3. Stone has designated the interest rate swap as a fair value hedge to hedge the changes in fair value of the fixed-rate debt as a result of changes in interest rates.

4. Changes in the value of the swap are assumed to be totally effective in offsetting changes in the value of the debt. Therefore, there is assumed

to be no ineffectiveness in the hedge and there is no premium exchanged at the beginning of the swap.

5. There is no difference between the fixed interest received from the interest rate swap and the fixed rate paid on the debt issue.

Stone has designated the interest rate swap as a fair value hedge of the possible change in value of the debt from changes in interest rates. Because there is assumed to be no ineffectiveness in the hedge, the short-cut method can be used to compute the amount of interest expense, the change in value of the interest rate swap and the value of the debt issue. The short-cut method involves the following process: compute the amount of interest expense incurred by the enterprise by adding any difference between the fixed rate paid on the debt issue and the fixed rate received in the swap with the variable interest rate, compute the change in value of the interest rate swap by computing the present value using the variable interest rate of the difference in cash flows between the fixed and variable interest rates, adjust the interest rate swap by the change in the present value from time period to time period, and adjust the debt issue by the same amount that was used for the interest rate swap. The value computed in this example is assumed to be in accordance with the fair value requirements of ASC 820. Table 8-4 shows the computation of the value of the interest rate swap. Notice that the present value is computed using the variable interest rate at the end of the quarter under consideration and for the time period remaining from the end of that specific quarter to the expiration of the interest rate swap. For example, the $13,171 value computed at the end of Quarter 1, 20X6 is the present value of $2,000 for 7 periods using the variable rate of 6.2% adjusted to a quarterly rate of 1.55% (6.2% ÷ 4 quarters). In addition, the $28,365 value at the end of Quarter 2, 20X6 is the present value of $5,000 for 6 periods using the variable interest rate of 6.5% adjusted to a quarterly rate of 1.62% (6.5% ÷ 4 quarters).

Table 8-4 Computation of Value of Interest Rate Swap

	20X6				20X7			
	Quarter 1	Quarter 2	Quarter 3	Quarter 4	Quarter 1	Quarter 2	Quarter 3	Quarter 4
Cash Flows Using Quarterly Fixed Interest Rate ($4,000,000 × 6% = $240,000 ÷ 4 Quarters)	$60,000	$60,000	$60,000	$60,000	$60,000	$60,000	$60,000	
Cash Flows Using Variable Interest Rate:								
Q 1—$4,000,000 × 6.2%/4	62,000							
Q 2—$4,000,000 × 6.5%/4		65,000						
Q 3—$4,000,000 × 6.7%/4			67,000					
Q 4—$4,000,000 × 6.8%/4				68,000				
Q 1—$4,000,000 × 7.0%/4					70,000			
Q 2—$4,000,000 × 7.3%/4						73,000		
Q 3—$4,000,000 × 7.6%/4							76,000	
Q 4—$4,000,000 × 8.0%/4								

	20X6				20X7			
	Quarter 1	Quarter 2	Quarter 3	Quarter 4	Quarter 1	Quarter 2	Quarter 3	Quarter 4
Difference in Cash Flows Using Fixed and Variable Rates	$2,000	$5,000	$7,000	$8,000	$10,000	$13,000	$16,000	
Present Value of Cash Flow Differences Using Variable Interest Rates (Fair Value of Interest Rate Swap)	$13,171	$28,365	$33,308	$30,685	$28,980	$25,305	$15,702	$0

Table 8-5 shows the computation of the change in value of the interest rate swap for each quarter. The change is value is the amount used in the journal entry to reflect the gain or loss on the swap and the change in value of the derivative. In addition, the same amount is used to adjust the value of the debt issue.

Table 8-5 Computation of Change in Value of Interest Rate Swap

Time Period	Beginning Balance in Interest Rate Swap (Table 8-4) (a)	Ending Balance in Interest Rate Swap (Table 8-4) (b)	Increase/(Decrease) in Interest Rate Swap (c) = (a) – (b)
20X6, Quarter 1	$0	$13,171	$(13,171)
20X6, Quarter 2	13,171	28,365	(15,194)
20X6, Quarter 3	28,365	33,308	(4,943)
20X6, Quarter 4	33,308	30,685	2,623
20X7, Quarter 1	30,685	28,980	1,705
20X7, Quarter 2	28,980	25,305	3,675
20X7, Quarter 3	25,305	15,702	9,603
20X7, Quarter 4	15,702	0	15,702

Table 8-6 shows the computation of the interest expense and the cash interest payment each quarter. Notice there is no fixed rate difference, because the fixed interest rate paid on the debt issue and the fixed rate from the interest rate swap are the same.

Table 8-6 Computation of Quarterly Interest Expense Using Short-Cut Method

Time Period	Fixed Rate Differences	Debt Maturity Amount	Quarterly Variable Interest Rate	Interest Expense
20X6, Quarter 1	0%	$4,000,000	6.2%/4	$62,000
20X6, Quarter 2	0%	$4,000,000	6.5%/4	$65,000
20X6, Quarter 3	0%	$4,000,000	6.7%/4	$67,000
20X6, Quarter 4	0%	$4,000,000	6.8%/4	$68,000
20X7, Quarter 1	0%	$4,000,000	7.0%/4	$70,000
20X7, Quarter 2	0%	$4,000,000	7.3%/4	$73,000

Time Period	Fixed Rate Differences	Debt Maturity Amount	Quarterly Variable Interest Rate	Interest Expense
20X7, Quarter 3	0%	$4,000,000	7.6%/4	$76,000
20X7, Quarter 4	0%	$4,000,000	8.0%/4	$80,000

Using information from Tables 8-5 and 8-6, and the assumptions in Example 8-8, journal entries can be prepared for the debt and the interest rate swap. The first entry is for the January 1, 20X6 issuance of the debt. Notice that there is no entry for the interest rate swap on January 1, because the interest rate swap has no value on this date.

January 1, 20X6—Record Issuance of $4,000,000, Fixed Interest Note

	Debit	Credit
Cash	4,000,000	
Notes Payable		4,000,000

Next, journal entries for the end of the first quarter are prepared showing the adjustment for the change in fair value of the interest rate swap and the debt issue, and the first quarter interest payment. Because this is a fair value hedge, both the debt issue and the interest rate swap are reported at fair value on the financial statements.

March 30, 20X6—Record Change in Value of Interest Rate Swap, Debt Issue and Interest Payment

	Debit	Credit
Loss on Interest Rate Swap	13,171	
Interest Rate Swap		13,171
Notes Payable	13,171	
Gain from Adjustment of Debt to Fair Value		13,171
Interest Expense	62,000	
Cash		62,000

Notice there is a loss on the interest rate swap of $13,171 as a result of the increase in the variable interest rate from 6.0% to 6.2%. Therefore, the interest rate swap is recorded as a liability with a corresponding amount reported in the income statement. The loss would normally be reported as a component of other income and expensed. An adjustment equal to the change in the value of the interest rate swap is made to the debt issue. The $13,171 change in value of the debt issue results in a decrease in the debt carrying value because the increase in the variable interest rate causes the debt's value to decline. A corresponding amount will be reported as a gain and classified in the income statement the same as the loss on the interest rate swap. Notice that the net impact on the income statement is zero because the gain and loss are equal offsetting amounts. Next, the interest expense of $62,000 is composed of the following two parts: the $60,000 interest expense related to the fixed interest rate that Stone Enterprises still remits to its lending agency and the $2,000 interest amount that Stone remits to the counterparty to the interest rate swap because Stone is exchanging only interest streams. Stone had to pay the counterparty the $2,000 because Stone receives the fixed rate of 6% and pays the variable rate that increased from 6.0% to 6.2%. The .2% increase (6.2% – 6.0%) accounts for the $2,000 ($4,000,000 × .2% = $8,000 ÷ 4 quarters) that Stone remits to the counterparty.

The entries for quarters two and three are the same as presented for March 30 except for the amounts and therefore are not shown. The appropriate amounts to use for the second and third quarters are shown in Tables 8-5 and 8-6. In quarter four, the value of the interest rate swap changes and the interest rate swap liability declines and the value of the debt issue increases. To illustrate this change, journal entries for quarter four are prepared for the interest rate swap and the change in value of the debt issue.

December 31, 20X6—Record Change in Value of Interest Rate Swap and Debt Issue

Interest Rate Swap	2,623	
Gain on Interest Rate Swap		2,623
Loss from Adjustment of Debt to Fair Value	2,623	
Notes Payable		2,623

Notice there is gain on the interest rate swap of $2,623 and a corresponding loss on the increase in value of the debt issue of $2,623. The entries for the swap and the debt issue are the same for the remaining quarters, except for amounts.

At the end of quarter four, 20X7, the debt issue is repaid, the last interest payment is made, and the interest rate swap expires and these events are reflected in the following journal entries. Information for the journal entries is taken from Tables 8-5 and 8-6 and the assumptions to Example 8-8.

Interest Expense	80,000	
Cash		80,000
Notes Payable	3,984,298	
Interest Rate Swap	15,702	
Cash		4,000,000

The Notes Payable balance of $3,984,298 is computed by taking the beginning balance of $4,000,000 and adjusting for all changes in value of the debt during the two-year time period. The computation is as follows: $3,984,298 = $4,000,000 – $13,171 – $15,194 – $4,943 + $2,623 + $1,705 + $3,675 + $9,603.

This completes the discussion of the solution to Example 8-8. Example 8-9 illustrates a cash flow hedge. Assumptions for Example 8-9 are as follows.

Example 8-9
Assumptions for a Derivative Accounted for as a Cash Flow Hedge

1. Baxter, Inc. (Baxter), a December 31 year-end enterprise, has 50,000 bushels of soybeans in its inventory that are held for resale and are expected to be sold on March 1, 20X7. The cost basis of the inventory is $4.20 a bushel.
2. To hedge the risk from a possible change in market prices for the soybeans, Baxter sells 10 March 1, 20X7 futures contracts on November 20, 20X6 at $5.75 per bushel. Each contract is for 5,000 bushels. The soybean contracts are designated as a cash flow hedge of the possible change in selling prices in future periods. Assume away any margin deposit.
3. On December 31, 20X6, March futures contracts were quoted at $5.95 per bushel. On March 1, 20X7, Baxter sold the 50,000 bushels of soybeans for $6.25 and closed out the 10 futures contracts at $6.25 per bushel.
4. Changes in the value of the futures contracts are assumed to be totally effective in offsetting changes in the selling price of the soybeans. Therefore, there is assumed to be no ineffectiveness in the hedge.
5. Assume there is no settlement of the contract until the end of the contract period.

Because the futures contract is designated as a cash flow hedge of the possible change in selling price in future accounting periods of the existing asset, soybean inventory, and the hedge is assumed to be totally effective in offsetting changes in the selling price of the soybeans, all changes in value of the derivative instrument will be charged to other comprehensive income. In addition, there is no adjustment to fair value for the soybean inventory because this is a cash flow hedge. There is no entry to record the derivative at the inception of the futures contract on November 20 because the value on that date is zero. Because Baxter's year-end is prior to the close of the futures contract, accounting must be provided for the change in market value of the contracts from November 20 to December 31, 20X6. Changes in market value of the contracts are computed as follows using futures prices for March delivery:

December 31 market value of futures contracts	$5.95
November 20 market value of futures contracts	5.75
Increase in market value of futures contracts	$.20
Size of contract (5,000 bushels × 10 contracts)	50,000
Total change in market value of contracts	$10,000

Because the futures prices increased from $5.75 to $5.95 a bushel from November 20 to December 31, the change in the market value of the futures contracts of $10,000 is a loss because Baxter sold the soybean contract at $5.75 a bushel and would currently have to buy at $5.95 to offset the contract that was sold. However, the loss is not reported in income, but is recognized as a component of other comprehensive income. In addition, the derivative instrument is reported as a current liability in the balance sheet at an amount equal to $10,000. The entry required for the change in market value of the derivative on December 31, 20X6 is as follows:

Loss on Futures Contracts—Other Comprehensive	10,000	
Income Derivative Instrument—Futures Contract		10,000

The futures contracts are closed on March 1, 20X7, by entering into corresponding contracts to purchase 10 March 1 soybean contracts at $6.25 per bushel. The change in value of the contracts from December 31, 20X6 to March 1, 20X7, is computed as follows:

March 1 market value of futures contracts	$6.25
December 31 market value of futures contracts	5.95
Decrease in market value of futures contracts	$.30
Size of contract (5,000 bushels × 10 contracts)	50,000
Total change in market value of contracts	$15,000

Because the futures prices per bushel of soybeans increased from $5.95 to $6.25, Baxter again has a loss on the transaction. However, the loss again is reported as a component of other comprehensive income. The entry required for the change in the value of the futures contract is presented below:

Loss on Futures Contracts—Other Comprehensive Income	15,000	
Derivative Instrument—Futures Contract		15,000

Next, Baxter records the settlement of the futures contracts by paying the broker an amount equal to $25,000 ($10,000 + $15,000), the decline in the value of the derivative from November 20 to March 1. The entry to record the settlement is as follows:

Derivative Instrument—Futures Contract	25,000	
Cash		25,000

The inventory is sold to normal customers on March 1 at the market price of $6.25 or a total price of $312,500 (50,000 bushels × $6.25), and the cost of the inventory of $4.20 per bushel or a total cost of $210,000 (50,000 bushels × $4.20) is removed from Baxter's records. The entries to show the sale of the inventory and to report cost of sales is as follows:

Cash	312,500	
Sales-Soybeans		312,500
Cost of Sales	210,000	
Soybean Inventory		210,000

Last, the $25,000 ($10,000 + $15,000) loss on the futures contract that has been deferred in other comprehensive income is reclassified as an adjustment to sales. Baxter locked in a selling price per bushel of $5.75 on November 20, 20X6, but the inventory was sold to normal customers for $6.25 per bushel. Therefore, sales must be reduced using the reclassification adjustment from other comprehensive income in order that sales reflect the $5.75 selling price locked in by the futures contract. The entry to reclassify the $25,000 loss deferred in other comprehensive income is shown below:

Sales—Soybeans	25,000	
Loss on Futures Contract—Other Comprehensive Income		25,000

This completes the discussion of Example 8-9. Example 8-10 covers a hedge of foreign currency net investment. Assumptions for Example 8-10 are as follows.

Example 8-10
Assumptions for a Derivative Accounted for as a Hedge of a Foreign Currency Net Investment

1. Johnson Enterprises (Johnson), a December 31 year-end company, has a net investment in Peterson Enterprises (Peterson), a Canadian subsidiary, of $50,000,000 at December 31, 20X6. The functional currency of the subsidiary is the Canadian dollar. Johnson's net investment in Peterson at December 31, 20X5, was also $50,000,000. The exchange rate between the U.S. dollar and the Canadian dollar is as follows: December 31, 20X5—$1.68 Canadian to $1 U.S. (.5952) and December 31, 20X6—$1.85 Canadian to $1 U.S. (.5405).
2. To hedge the net investment in the Canadian subsidiary as a result of the risk from changes in foreign currency exchange rates, Johnson issues on January 1, 20X6, a $50,000,000 debt issue denominated in Canadian dollars. The $50,000,000 debt issue is designated by Johnson as a hedge of the net investment in Peterson.
3. Changes in the value of the debt issue are assumed to be totally effective in offsetting changes in the translation adjustment. Therefore, there is assumed to be no ineffectiveness in the hedge.

Because Johnson has a net investment in a Canadian foreign subsidiary with a functional currency that is the Canadian dollar, Johnson must translate the net investment at the end of the accounting period to its reporting currency (the U.S. dollar) using the exchange rate between the U.S. and Canadian dollars. The translation of the net investment from Canadian dollars to U.S. dollars will result in a gain or loss on translation, which is reported as a component of other comprehensive income. Johnson has elected to hedge the risk associated with possible changing exchange rates by issuing debt of $50,000,000 denominated in Canadian dollars, which is equal to the $50,000,000 balance in the net investment account. The hedge is designated as a hedge of a foreign currency net investment and the debt issue used as the hedging instrument is assumed to be effective in offsetting changes in the translation adjustment. Therefore, there is no hedge ineffectiveness in the transaction.

The first step is to compute the amount of the translation adjustment for the net investment and the change in debt issue as a result of the change in exchange rates on December 31, 20X6. The exchange rate on December 31, 20X5, was 1.68 Canadian dollars per 1 U.S. dollar or .5952 U.S. dollars to 1 Canadian dollar. This exchange rate declined to .5405 U.S. dollars to 1 Canadian dollar at December 31, 20X6. The amount of the translation adjustment and the change in the debt issue is computed below:

Translated Investment Account—12/31/20X5 ($50,000,000 × .5952)	$29,760,000
Translated Investment Account—12/31/20X6 ($50,000,000 × .5405)	27,025,000
Translation Loss on Net Investment	$2,735,000

Using the translation loss of $2,735,000, the entry to record the translation loss at December 31, 20X6, is:

Translation Adjustment—Other Comprehensive Income	2,735,000	
Investment in Peterson Enterprises		2,735,000

Next, the gain on the hedging instrument, the $50,000,000 debt issue, can be computed. Notice that it is computed using the same exchange rates used in the translation adjustment for the net investment. Because a loss is computed on the net investment translation, there is an offsetting gain of $2,735,000 on the remeasurement of the debt issue. The gain on the debt issue is computed as follows:

Translated Debt Issue—12/31/20X5 ($50,000,000 × .5952)	$29,760,000
Translated Debt Issue—12/31/20X6 ($50,000,000 × .5405)	27,025,000
Translation Gain on Debt Issue	$2,735,000

Using the $2,735,000 gain, the entry to record the gain on the debt remeasurement is as follows:

Notes Payable	2,735,000	
Translation Adjustment—Other Comprehensive Income		2,735,000

The debt issue is decreased by the amount of the gain and the gain is reported as a component of other comprehensive income.

This completes the discussion of the technical issues related to derivative instruments and hedges. The next section covers disclosure requirements.

Disclosure Requirements

ASC 815 provides disclosure requirements for derivative instruments. Some of the disclosures are common disclosures for all derivatives and other specific disclosures are required for each type of hedge (fair value, cash flow and foreign currency net investments). First, the common disclosures for all derivatives are presented:

1. Information should be disclosed by an entity with derivative instruments so that the readers of the statements will understand the following:
    a. Why and how derivative instruments are used by an enterprise.
    b. Using ASC 815 and related statements, the accounting for derivatives and related hedges.
    c. The impact of derivatives and related hedges on an entity's financial position and financial performance.

2. For derivatives (and nonderivatives used as hedges), the entity that issues or holds the instrument must describe the following for each interim and annual accounting period that a balance sheet and income statement (financial position statement and financial performance statement) are provided:

   a. Entity objective for issuing or holding the security or contract.

   b. Context required to understand the entity's objective.

   c. The strategies required to accomplish the objective.

   d. Disclose information related to the primary underlying risk exposure of each instrument (such as credit, interest rate, and foreign exchange risk).

   e. Distinguish between instruments that are used for risk management (includes instruments designated as hedges under ASC 815, as amended, and instruments used as economic hedges and other purposes related to the risk exposure of the entity) and instruments that are for purposes other than risk management.

   f. For ASC 815, as amended, derivatives designated as hedges, disclosures should make a distinction between cash flow hedging instruments, fair value hedging instruments, and foreign currency net investment hedging instruments.

   g. Describe the purpose of any derivative situation when the derivative is not designated as a hedge instrument under ASC 815.

   h. Disclose information about the volume of an entity's derivative activity that would allow readers to understand derivative activity volume, and the entity should use individual facts and circumstances to select the appropriate format and specifics of disclosures that would be most relevant and practicable.

3. An entity is encouraged to include additional qualitative disclosure information about the objectives and strategies of its derivative activity related to risk exposure and how it is managed. If the qualitative disclosures are made, the disclosures should also include information about exposures that may not be managed by derivative instruments.

4. For derivative (and nonderivatives used as hedges), the entity that issues or holds the instrument must disclose the following for each interim and annual accounting period that a balance sheet and income statement (financial position statement and financial performance statement) are provided:

   a. The fair value amount and location of derivatives reported in the balance sheet (statement of financial position). A gross basis should be used for the fair value even if the instruments qualify for netting under a master netting agreement. Fair value amounts should not be adjusted for cash collateral payables and receivables. Derivative instruments should be divided into two categories: (1) instruments that are designated and qualify as hedging instruments under ASC 815, as amended, and (2) instruments that are not hedges. For each category, a separate asset or liability should be presented for the fair value amounts separately presented for each type of derivative contract (such as credit contracts or interest rate contracts). In addition, the disclosure should state the location in the statement of financial position, by line item, of the fair value amounts by categories of instruments.

b. The amount and location of gains and losses in the income statement or, if appropriate, the statement of financial position with the gains and losses separately presented for the following:

   (1) Designated and qualifying hedging derivative instruments in fair value hedges and related hedged items that are qualifying and designated in fair value hedges.

   (2) The part of the gain and loss on derivative instruments considered effective that qualifies and is designated in cash flow hedges and net investment hedges reported during the current accounting period in other comprehensive income.

   (3) The part of the gain and loss on derivative instruments considered effective that qualifies and is designated in cash flow hedges and net investment hedges reported during the term of the hedging relationship reported in accumulated other comprehensive income and the amount treated as a reclassification adjustment (reclassified into income) during the current accounting period.

   (4) The part of the gain and loss on derivative instruments considered ineffective and amounts not included in hedge effectiveness assignment that qualifies and is designated in cash flow hedges and net investment hedges.

   (5) Derivative instruments under ASC 815, as amended, that are not effective or designated as hedging instruments.

Information in b(1)–b(5) should be separately presented in the financial statements by type of contract, such as credit contracts, interest rate contracts, and so on. In addition, an entity should disclose the location in the statement of financial performance, by line item, of the gain and loss amounts by categories of instruments.

5. A tabular format should be used for the quantitative information required by 4(a) and 4(b), above, except for the disclosure requirement in 4(b)(1), above. The entity may elect a tabular or nontabular format for this disclosure.

6. An entity may elect not to separately disclose gains and losses in accordance with 4(b)(5), above, when it includes in its trading activities derivative instruments that are not qualifying or designated as hedging instruments. When the entity elects not to separately disclose such gains

and losses, the following disclosures are required: (a) provide a description of the nature and related risks of the trading activities and describe how those risks are managed by the entity, (b) disclose trading activity (both derivative and nonderivative instruments) gains and losses reported in the statement of financial performance by major item type, and (c) location, by line item, of the trading gains and losses in the statement of financial performance.

7. For derivatives (and nonderivatives used as hedges), an entity that issues or holds an instrument must disclose the following for each interim and annual accounting period for which a statement of financial position is provided:

   a. Nature and existence of credit-risk-related contingent features and, for derivative instruments that are in a net liability position at the end of the accounting period, circumstances when the features could be triggered.

   b. For derivative instruments in a net liability position at the end of the accounting period, fair value amounts on an aggregate basis of derivative instruments that have credit-risk-contingent features.

   c. Aggregate fair value of the following: (1) asset posted as collateral at the end of the accounting period and (2) additional assets needed to settle the instrument if credit-risk-related contingent features were triggered at the end of the accounting period.

8. To enable users of financial statements to assess the potential effects of credit derivatives (e.g., credit default swaps, credit spread options, credit index products) on the reporting entity's financial position, financial performance, and cash flows, a seller of credit derivatives must disclose certain information for each credit derivative (or each group of similar credit derivatives), even if the likelihood of the seller's having to make any payments under the credit derivative is remote, for each statement of financial position presented. For purposes of this requirement, credit derivatives include hybrid instruments that have embedded credit derivatives, for which the seller of an embedded credit derivative must disclose the required information for the entire hybrid instrument (e.g., a credit-linked note), not just the embedded credit derivative. The required disclosures include the following:

   a. The nature of the credit derivative, including the approximate term of the credit derivative, the reasons for entering into the credit derivative, the events or circumstances that would require the seller to perform under the credit derivative, and the current status (as of the date of the statement of financial position) of the payment/performance risk of the credit derivative. If the current status of the payment/performance risk of a credit derivative is based on internal groupings used by the seller to manage its risk, the seller must disclose how those groupings are determined and used for managing risk.

b. The maximum potential amount of undiscounted future payments the seller could be required to make under the credit derivative without reduction for the effect of any amounts that may possibly be recovered under recourse or collateralization provisions in the credit derivative (which are addressed under 8d, below). If the maximum potential future payments under the contract are unlimited, that fact must be disclosed. If the seller is unable to develop an estimate of the maximum potential amount of future payments under the credit derivative, the seller must disclose the reasons why.

c. The current fair value of the credit derivative (as of the date of the statement of financial position).

d. The nature of any recourse provisions that would enable the seller to recover from third parties any of the amounts paid under the credit derivative, the nature of any assets held as collateral, and the nature of any assets held by third parties that upon the occurrence of any specified triggering event or condition under the credit derivative the seller can obtain and liquidate to recover all or a portion of the amounts paid under the credit derivative. If estimable, the seller must state the approximate extent to which the proceeds from liquidation of such assets would be expected to cover the maximum potential amount of future payments under the credit derivative. If a seller of credit protection has purchased credit protection with identical underlying(s), the seller must consider the effect of the purchased credit protection in estimating potential recoveries.

9. Cross-referencing of footnote disclosures is required when derivative (and nonderivatives used as hedges) disclosures are presented in more than a single footnote.

Next, additional disclosures required only for fair value hedges are presented below:

1. For derivatives and nonderivatives used as fair value hedges where gains and losses from foreign currency transactions have been produced using ASC 830, the following information should be disclosed for the instrument and the related hedged items:

   a. Net gain or loss reported as a component of income during the accounting period under consideration that is composed of the gain or loss that relates to the ineffectiveness of the hedge and the amount of the gain or loss that was not used when evaluating hedge effectiveness.

   b. Gain or loss reported in income when a firm commitment that is hedged loses its designation as a fair value hedge.

2. The disclosures in 1, above, should be made for each interim and annual accounting period in which a statement of financial performance and a statement of financial position are issued.

The following information represents disclosures required only for derivative instruments classified (designated and qualified) as cash flow hedges:

1. For gains and losses that will be reclassified from accumulated other comprehensive income to net income, describe the transactions or events that will cause the reclassification.
2. Disclose the amount of gains and losses, as of the reporting date, anticipated to be reclassified into net income within the next year.
3. Other than forecasted transactions associated with variable interest payments on existing instruments, disclose the maximum time period for which the enterprise is hedging future cash flow risk for forecasted transactions.
4. The amount of the reclassification of gains and losses to net income from accumulated other comprehensive income when a cash flow hedge is discontinued because the entity has determined that it is not probable that the forecasted transaction will occur.

The information, above, is required for both the instrument and the hedged transaction.

The following disclosure information related to presentation of comprehensive income and accumulated other comprehensive income is required:

1. The net gain or loss from instruments classified as cash flow hedges should be disclosed separately in other comprehensive income when the gains and losses qualify for presentation in other comprehensive income.
2. The following should be disclosed in accumulated other comprehensive income from derivative gains and losses:
   a. Beginning and ending accumulated gain or loss from derivative activity.
   b. Net change in the gain or loss from hedges during the current accounting period.
   c. Amount of any reclassifications from accumulated other comprehensive income to net income on a net basis.

In addition to the preceding disclosures, the FASB encourages entities to disclose similar quantitative information about nonfinancial liabilities and assets and financial instruments that are related to the derivative instrument by activity. Certain derivatives that include items such as up-front cash payments or off-market terms may have a financing component that should be included in the cash flow statement as a financing activity using the provisions of ASC 230.

This completes the disclosures required by ASC 815. However, ASC 825 requires additional disclosures for all financial instruments.

Specialized Topics Related to Derivatives and Hedging

ASU 2015-13, *Derivatives and Hedging (Topic 815): Application of the Normal Purchases and Normal Sales Scope Exception to Certain Electricity Contracts within Nodal Energy Markets,* applies to entities that enter into contracts for the purchase or sale of electricity on a forward basis and arrange for transmission through, or delivery to a location within, a nodal energy market whereby one of the contracting parties incurs charges (or credits) for the transmission of that electricity based in part on locational marginal pricing differences payable to (or receivable from) an independent system operator. Entities with such contracts should refer to the complete text of ASU 2015-13.

Other Recent Changes

In addition to ASU 2015-13, Topic 815 is also being effected by other recent ASUs, namely:

1. ASU 2014-16, *Derivatives and Hedging (Topic 815): Determining Whether the Host Contract in a Hybrid Financial Instrument Issued in the Form of a Share Is More Akin to Debt or to Equity (a consensus of the FASB Emerging Issues Task Force)*
2. ASU 2016-05, *Derivatives and Hedging (Topic 815): Effect of Derivative Contract Novations on Existing Hedge Accounting Relationships (a consensus of the FASB Emerging Issues Task Force)*
3. ASU 2016-06, *Derivatives and Hedging (Topic 815): Contingent Put and Call Options in Debt Instruments (a consensus of the FASB Emerging Issues Task Force)*

A brief summary of these recent pronouncements is presented below.

ASU 2014-16, *Derivatives and Hedging (Topic 815): Determining Whether the Host Contract in a Hybrid Financial Instrument Issued in the Form of a Share Is More Akin to Debt or to Equity (a consensus of the FASB Emerging Issues Task Force)*, was issued in November 2014. ASU 2014-16 eliminates the use of different methods in the accounting for hybrid financial instruments issued in the form of a share. ASU 2014-16 applies to all entities that are issuers of, or investors in, hybrid financial instruments that are issued in the form of a share.

For hybrid financial instruments issued in the form of a share, the issuer or the investor should determine the nature of the host contract by considering all stated and implied substantive terms and features of the hybrid financial instrument, weighing each term and feature on the basis of relevant facts and circumstances. That is, such entity should determine the nature of the host contract by considering the economic characteristics and risks of the entire hybrid financial instrument, including the embedded derivative feature that is being evaluated for separate accounting from the host contract. In evaluating the stated and implied substantive terms and features, the existence or omission of any single term or feature does not necessarily determine the economic characteristics and risks of the host contract. Although an individual term or feature may weigh more heavily in the evaluation on the basis of facts and circumstances, an entity should use judgment based on an evaluation of all the relevant terms and features. ASU 2014-16 does not change the current criteria for determining when separation of certain embedded derivative features in a hybrid financial instrument is required. So an entity will continue to evaluate whether the economic characteristics and risks of the embedded derivative feature are clearly and closely related to those of the host contract, among other relevant criteria. ASU 2014-16 does provide clarification in evaluating the economic characteristics and risks of a host contract in a hybrid financial instrument that is issued in the form of a share. Specifically, it clarifies that an entity should consider all relevant terms and features—including the embedded derivative feature being evaluated for bifurcation—in evaluating the nature of the host contract. Furthermore, it clarifies that no single term or feature would necessarily determine the economic characteristics and risks of the host contract. Rather, the nature of the host contract depends upon the economic characteristics and risks of the entire hybrid financial instrument. In addition, ASU 2014-16 clarifies that, in evaluating the nature of a host contract, an entity should assess the substance of the relevant terms and features (i.e., the relative strength of the debt-like or equity-like terms and features given the facts and circumstances) when considering how to weight those terms and features. Specifically, the assessment of the substance of the relevant terms and features should incorporate a consideration of (1) the characteristics of the terms and features themselves (e.g., contingent versus noncontingent, in-the-money versus out-of-the-money), (2) the circumstances under which the hybrid financial instrument was issued or acquired (e.g., issuer-specific characteristics, such as whether the issuer is thinly capitalized or profitable and well-capitalized), and (3) the potential outcomes of the hybrid financial instrument (e.g., the instrument may be settled by the issuer issuing a fixed number of shares; the instrument may be settled by the issuer transferring a specified amount of cash; or the instrument may remain legal-form equity), as well as the likelihood of those potential outcomes.

The effects of initially adopting ASU 2014-16 should be applied on a modified retrospective basis to existing hybrid financial instruments issued in the form of a share as of the beginning of the fiscal year for which the amendments are effective. Retrospective application is permitted to all relevant prior periods.

ASU 2014-16 is effective for public business entities for fiscal years, and interim periods within those fiscal years, beginning after December15, 2015. For all other entities, ASU 2014-16 is effective for fiscal years beginning after December 15, 2015, and interim periods within fiscal years beginning after December 15, 2016. Early adoption, including adoption in an interim period, is permitted. If an entity early adopts the amendments in an interim period, any adjustments shall be reflected as of the beginning of the fiscal year that includes that interim period.

ASU 2016-05, *Derivatives and Hedging (Topic 815): Effect of Derivative Contract Novations on Existing Hedge Accounting Relationships (a consensus of the FASB Emerging Issues Task Force),* was issued in March 2016. Under the context of Topic 815, the term novation, as it relates to derivative instruments, refers to replacing one of the parties to a derivative instrument with a new party. In practice, derivative instrument novations may occur for a variety of reasons, including financial institution mergers. The derivative instrument that is the subject of a novation may be the hedging instrument in a hedging relationship that has been designated under Topic 815, *Derivatives and Hedging*.

Prior to ASU 2016-05, guidance in Topic 815 was not explicitly clear about the effect on an existing hedging relationship, if any, of a change in the counterparty to a derivative instrument that has been designated as a hedging instrument.

ASU 2016-05 clarifies that a change in the counterparty to a derivative instrument that has been designated as the hedging instrument under Topic 815 does not, in and of itself, require dedesignation of that hedging relationship, provided that all other hedge accounting criteria (including those in paragraphs 815-20-35-14 through 35-18) continue to be met.

For public business entities, ASU 2016-05 is effective for financial statements issued for fiscal years beginning after December 15, 2016, and interim periods within those fiscal years.

For all other entities, ASU 2016-05 is effective for financial statements issued for fiscal years beginning after December 15, 2017, and interim periods within fiscal years beginning after December 15, 2018.

An entity has an option to apply ASU 2016-05 on either a prospective basis or a modified retrospective basis.

For entities electing the prospective approach, this ASU should be applied to all existing hedging relationships in which a change in the counterparty to a derivative instrument occurs after the date an entity adopts the amendments.

For entities electing the modified retrospective approach, this ASU should be applied to all derivative instruments that meet all of the following conditions:

1. The derivative instrument was outstanding during all or a portion of the periods presented in the financial statements.
2. The derivative instrument was previously designated as a hedging instrument in a hedging relationship.
3. The hedging relationship was dedesignated solely due to a novation of the derivative instrument, and all other hedge accounting criteria would have otherwise continued to be met.

Under the modified retrospective approach, an entity should not revise its financial statements for derivative instruments that were not outstanding as of the beginning of the earliest period presented in the financial statements.

Under the modified retrospective approach, derivative instruments that were dedesignated from hedging relationships during a period presented in the financial statements should have:

1. The effect of the hedge dedesignation removed from the financial statements for each period presented.

Under the modified retrospective approach, derivative instruments that were dedesignated from hedging relationships before the beginning of the earliest period presented that remain outstanding during all or a portion of the periods presented should have:

1. The effect of the hedge dedesignation removed from the financial statements for each period presented.
2. Beginning retained earnings reflect a cumulative-effect adjustment for effects to financial statements before the beginning of the earliest period presented.

Under the modified retrospective approach, assessments of effectiveness and measurements of ineffectiveness required by the original hedge documentation should be performed for all periods between the date on which the hedging relationship was dedesignated due solely to a novation and the date on which an entity adopts this ASU.

Early adoption is permitted, including adoption in an interim period.

ASU 2016-06, *Derivatives and Hedging (Topic 815): Contingent Put and Call Options in Debt Instruments (a consensus of the FASB Emerging Issues Task Force),* was issued in March 2016. Topic 815, *Derivatives and Hedging* under the ASC, requires that embedded derivatives be separated from the host contract and accounted for separately as derivatives if certain criteria are met. One of those criteria is that the economic characteristics and risks of the embedded derivatives are not clearly and closely related to the economic characteristics and risks of the host contract (the "clearly and closely related" criterion).

The ASC provides specific guidance for assessing whether call (put) options that can accelerate the repayment of principal on a debt instrument meet the clearly and closely related criterion. The guidance states that for contingent call (put) options to be considered clearly and closely related, they can be indexed only to interest rates or credit risk. A four-step decision sequence is provided, which applies to all call (put) options. The four-step decision sequence requires an entity to consider whether (1) the payoff is adjusted based on changes in an index, (2) the payoff is indexed to an underlying other than interest rates or credit risk, (3) the debt involves a substantial premium or discount, and (4) the call (put) option is contingently exercisable.

Questions emerged about how the four-step decision sequence interacts with the original guidance for assessing embedded contingent call (put) options in debt instruments. Two divergent approaches developed in practice. Under the first approach, the assessment of whether contingent call (put) options are clearly and closely related to the debt host only requires an analysis of the four-step decision sequence. Under the second approach, an assessment of whether the event that triggers the ability to exercise the call (put) option is indexed only to interest rates or credit risk is required in addition to the four-step decision sequence.

Those two approaches, which resulted from different interpretations of the intent of the four–step decision sequence, may result in different conclusions about whether the embedded call (put) option is clearly and closely related to its debt host, and, thus, may result in different conclusions about which call (put) options should be bifurcated and accounted for separately as derivatives.

ASU 2016-06 applies to all entities that are issuers of or investors in debt instruments (or hybrid financial instruments that are determined to have a debt host) with embedded call (put) options. It clarifies the requirements for assessing whether contingent call (put) options that can accelerate the payment of principal on debt instruments are clearly and closely related to their debt hosts. An entity performing the assessment under ASU 2016-06 is required to assess the embedded call (put) options solely in accordance with the four-step decision sequence discussed above.

For public business entities, ASU 2016-06 is effective for financial statements issued for fiscal years beginning after December 15, 2016, and interim periods within those fiscal years. For entities other than public business entities, it is effective for financial statements issued for fiscal years beginning after December 15, 2017, and interim periods within fiscal years beginning after December 15, 2018.

An entity should apply ASU 2016-06 on a modified retrospective basis to existing debt instruments as of the beginning of the fiscal year of adoption. If an entity had bifurcated an embedded derivative aggregate of the carrying amount of the debt host contract and the fair value of the previously bifurcated embedded derivative will become the carrying amount of the debt instrument at the date of adoption. If an entity is no longer required to bifurcate an embedded derivative as a result of applying ASU 2016-06, the entity has a one-time option, as of the beginning of the fiscal year of adoption, to irrevocably elect to measure that debt instrument in its entirety at fair value with changes in fair value recognized in earnings. For those instruments for which the entity elects fair value, the effects of initially complying with this standard as of the effective date should be reported as a cumulative-effect adjustment directly to retained earnings as of the beginning of the fiscal year of adoption. The entity should elect fair value on an instrument-by-instrument basis.

Early adoption is permitted, including adoption in an interim period. If an entity early adopts this standard in an interim period, any adjustments should be reflected as of the beginning of the fiscal year that includes that interim period.

Topic 820: Fair Value Measurements and Disclosures

Topic 820, *Fair Value Measurements and Disclosures*, contains two subtopics:

10 Overall

940 Financial Services—Brokers and Dealers [See the corresponding topic in Chapter 9 for coverage of this shared subtopic]

Introduction

ASC 820 provides a definition of fair value and a framework for determining or measuring fair value. In addition, ASC 820 specifies disclosures requirements for fair value. The fair value framework of ASC 820 should be used in conjunction with other accounting pronouncements that permit or require the use of fair values. However, the following items are excluded from the provisions of ASC 820: (1) share-based payment transactions covered by ASC 718 and any related accounting pronouncements, (2) any practicability exception rule to fair value contained in other accounting pronouncements, and (3) any accounting pronouncement that has a measurement that is not intended to determine fair value but is similar to a fair value measurement (such as inventory valuations and evidence of fair value that is vendor specific).

Fair Value Measurement

Fair value is defined as the amount that would be received on the measurement date from the sale of property, or the amount paid to transfer a liability between sellers and buyers (market participants) in an orderly transaction, an exit price. The fair value measurement is based on a hypothetical transaction from the view of market participants and the assumptions that market participants would use in the valuation process. The fair value measurement process involves several steps, one of which is the determination of the asset or liability subject to measurement. Consideration should be given to any restrictions related to sale or use, the location and condition of the asset or liability, and whether the asset or liability is viewed as a stand-alone or as part of a group. Whether the asset or liability is measured at fair value as a stand-alone (such as a financial instrument) or as a group of assets or liabilities (such as a business or an asset group) depends upon the unit of account. The unit of account should be determined using the provisions of other accounting pronouncements. The unit of account indicates what is being measured relative to the aggregation or disaggregation of the asset or liability.

The next step in the fair value measurement process is to determine the appropriate valuation premise. This aspect of the measurement approach is based on the market participants highest and best use of the asset. The highest and best use by market participants may be different from the current use of the asset by the entity. The issue is where the asset provides maximum value: Does the asset provide maximum value in use with other assets or as a stand-alone in an exchange transaction? If it is determined that the asset provides maximum value in use, the entity should use an in-use valuation concept, and the asset is valued assuming that it is used with the other asset group and the other assets are available in the assumed sale. If it is determined that the asset provides maximum value as a stand-alone asset, an in-exchange valuation concept is used to determine the asset's fair value. An in-exchange valuation concept assumes that the fair value of the asset is based on the amount that would be received in a stand-alone exchange transaction. When considering liabilities, the fair value measurement process assumes a transfer of liabilities to market participants, and any risk related to nonperformance does not change as a result of the assumed transfer. The risk of nonperformance includes credit risk of the entity, and the fair value measurement of the liability considers the risk of nonperformance and the credit risk of the entity. The impact of the entity's credit risk depends on the type of liability, such as a liability to provide cash or a liability to provide services.

After determining the highest and best use of an asset, the next step in the fair value measurement process is to determine the appropriate market for the asset or liability. The measurement process assumes that the sale or transfer of the asset or liability occurs in the principal market. If there is no principal market for the asset or liability, the most advantageous market is used. The market with the greater level of activity or volume for the sale or transfer of the asset or liability is the principal market, and the market that would maximize the price received from the sale of the asset or minimize the cost paid to transfer the liability is the most advantageous market. When there is a principal market, the fair value measurement is based on the price in the principal market even when there may be a more advantageous price in another market. Transaction costs, which are direct costs incurred to transfer the liability or sell the asset, should not be used to adjust the price in the principal or most advantageous market. But, costs incurred to move an asset or liability to the principal or most advantageous market should be used to adjust the fair value measurement. The entity should use the assumptions that market participants (buyers and seller) would use when determining the fair value measurement for assets and liabilities in the principal or most advantageous market.

Market participants have the following characteristics: (1) are not parties related to the reporting entity (independent), (2) using available information, are knowledgeable about the asset or liability and the transaction, (3) have the ability to enter into a transaction for the asset or liability, and (4) are willing to enter into a transaction for the asset or liability.

The price paid to initially acquire an asset or assume a liability is a transaction price and is considered an entry price. However, fair value under ASC 820 is the price received from the sale of property, or the amount paid to transfer a liability, which is an exit price. Therefore, the entry price may or may not be the same as the exit price at the date of initial recognition of the asset or liability. Some of the factors that may cause the entry and exit price to differ on the date of initial recognition are as follows: (1) related parties are involved in the transaction, (2) the seller is in financial difficulty and the sale is made under duress, (3) the unit of account for the entry and exit price are different, and (4) the markets where the transactions takes place differ for the entry price and the exit price.

Fair Value Valuation Techniques

Once an entity determines that an asset or liability is to be measured at fair value and considers all the appropriate measurement aspects, as discussed above, the valuation technique must be determined. ASC 820 states that three valuation techniques are available to use to measure fair value; they are the market approach, the income approach, and the cost approach.

The market approach uses prices from market transactions related to assets and liabilities that are identical or comparable. An entity may use methods that are consistent with the market approach, such as market multiples and the matrix pricing method. Market multiples resulting from a set of comparables may be used to determine fair value. Judgment may be required using qualitative and quantitative factors to make an appropriate selection when there are ranges of multiples. The matrix pricing method may be used to determine the fair value of debt securities. The matrix pricing method is used to determine fair value without exclusively using quoted market prices.

The income approach computes a present value or discounted value using future amounts, such as earnings or cash flows, consistent with market expectations about those future amounts. Examples of methods that may be used in the income approach include present value models, multiperiod excess earnings models, and option pricing models.

The cost approach measures fair value by determining the cost to replace the asset's service capacity. The cost to replace the asset's service capacity is based on what it would cost to buy or construct a comparable asset adjusted for deterioration and obsolescence.

When valuing assets and liabilities, an entity should select the most appropriate valuation technique based on available data. The method selected should be consistently applied. However, the technique or method of application may be changed when circumstances indicate a change should be made. An entity may find that only one valuation technique, such as the market approach, is appropriate. However, in some cases, the valuation process may indicate that more than one valuation technique, such as the market approach and the income approach, could be appropriate when determining the fair value of an asset or liability.

When using the valuation techniques, assumptions that market participants would use in the measurement of fair value are referred to as inputs in ASC 820. Inputs used in the valuation models include observable inputs and unobservable inputs. Observable inputs are market participant assumptions derived from sources independent of the entity that are used in the determination of the fair value of the assets and liabilities. Assumptions that the entity determines that market participants will use as assumptions in the determination of the fair value of assets and liabilities are unobservable inputs. ASC 820 states that unobservable inputs should be minimized and relevant observable inputs should be maximized when using inputs in the valuation techniques.

Once the valuation techniques and inputs are determined, the entity must prioritize the inputs using a fair value hierarchy or an input hierarchy that divides inputs into three levels, Level 1, Level 2, and Level 3. Level 1 inputs have the highest priority and Level 3 inputs have the lowest priority.

Level 1 inputs are quoted market prices of identical assets and liabilities. Quoted market prices must be in active markets and the entity must have the ability on the measurement date to obtain the quoted market prices. An active market is one that has enough volume and frequency of trading to produce a reliable fair value amount. Generally, quoted market prices should be used to measure fair value when available because quoted prices usually provide the most reliable measure of fair value. However, there are exceptions to and variations of the quoted market price rule. For example, assume an entity owns a large position in a financial asset, e.g., common stock that is traded in an active market with a quoted market price. Also, assume that the normal trading volume of the common stock is not large enough to absorb the entity's position if the entity's entire position were held for sale in a single transaction without impacting its market price. In this situation, the quoted market price on the measurement date should be used without adjusting the market price for the size of the entity's position in the financial asset. When an entity owns a large number of assets (or liabilities) that are similar in nature and a quoted market price is available but cannot be readily accessed by the entity for each individual security, an alternative method, such as the matrix pricing method, may be used to measure fair value. In some cases, a quoted market price may not reflect fair value. For example, a significant event may occur, such as the release of new information that requires an entity to adjust the quoted market price for that information. Any adjustments to the quoted market price or the use of an alternative method create a lower level measurement of fair value.

Level 2 inputs are direct or indirect observable inputs excluding quoted market prices. When there is a specified term for an asset or liability, the inputs from Level 2 must be available for substantially all of the specified term. Examples of items that are included in Level 2 inputs include (1) quoted market prices in nonactive markets for assets and liabilities that are the same or similar, (2) quoted market prices in active markets for assets and liabilities that are similar, (3) observable inputs, excluding quoted market prices, for assets and liabilities, and (4) inputs that are not observable but are derived from market data that is observable. Level 2 inputs may require adjustments when determining fair value for items such as the location and condition of the asset, asset and liability comparability, and market activity and volume. Significant adjustments to an otherwise Level 2 measurement may cause it to be categorized as a Level 3 measurement. Examples of Level 2 inputs include a royalty rate for a licensing agreement obtained in a business combination that is a result of a recent negotiation by an unrelated party when valuing a licensing agreement, price per square foot of a building that is obtained from market data that is observable when valuing a building in use, or retail prices in a retail market adjusted for location, condition, or comparability differences when valuing inventory acquired in a business combination.

Unobservable inputs for asset and liability fair value measurement are classified as Level 3 inputs. Unobservable inputs should be used in the valuation process when relevant observable inputs are unavailable. Assumptions that the enterprise determines that market participants will use as assumptions in the determination of the fair value of assets and liabilities are unobservable inputs. Examples of Level 3 inputs include cash flows computed by the entity related to the measurement of an asset retirement obligation or a cash flow or earnings forecast developed by an entity when trying to measure the fair value of an entity.

ASC 820 should be applied at the beginning of the fiscal year in the year that ASC 820 is adopted using a prospective method. However, certain financial instruments require retrospective application on the date of initial adoption. Included are certain financial instruments held by broker-dealers or investment companies and certain financial instruments covered by ASC 815. When the statement is applied to these instruments retrospectively, the difference between the fair value and the carrying amounts of the instruments is reported as a cumulative adjustment to beginning retained earnings. The disclosure requirement for a change in principle under ASC 250 is not applicable. However, the disclosure requirements in ASC 820 are required for the first interim accounting period (including annual disclosure requirements) that ASC 820 is applied.

Disclosure Requirements

ASC 820-10-50 specifies the disclosure requirements for assets and liabilities measured at fair value using the provisions of ASC 820. The disclosure requirements presented below reflect amendments through ASU 2013-09, *Fair Value*

Measurement (Topic 820): Deferral of the Effective Date of Certain Disclosures for Nonpublic Employee Benefit Plans in Update No. 2011-04. Quantitative disclosures should be presented in a tabular format.

For each major class of assets and liabilities in the balance sheet measured at fair value disclosures for both annual and interim reporting dates are required, as follows:

1. Disclose the fair value measurements at the end of the reporting period for recurring and nonrecurring fair value measurements.
2. Disclose the reasons for the nonrecurring fair value measurements.
3. Disclose the hierarchy levels within which the fair value measurements are categorized in their entirety (Level 1, Level 2, and Level 3). (Note: The requirement to disclose "the level of the fair value hierarchy within which the fair value measurements are categorized in their entirety," e.g., Level 3 does *not* apply to private companies, including those with derivatives and assets greater than $100 million, for items that are not measured at fair value in the statement of financial position, but for which fair value is disclosed for such items under ASU 2013-03, *Financial Instruments (Topic 825): Clarifying the Scope and Applicability of a Particular Disclosure to Nonpublic Entities*.)
4. Disclose, *for public entities only*, for assets and liabilities held at the end of the reporting period that are measured on a recurring basis, (a) the amount of any transfers between Level 1 and Level 2, (b) the reasons for such transfers, and (c) the policy for determining when such transfers have occurred. (Note: Transfers in and out should be reported separately.)
5. Disclose, for Level 2 and Level 3 fair value measurements, (a) the valuation technique(s) and inputs used in the measurement and (b) any change in valuation techniques and the reasons. Also, disclose for Level 3 fair value measurements, quantified information about the significant unobservable inputs used in the measurement. The requirements to disclose quantitative information about significant unobservable inputs used in Level 3 fair value measurements for investments held by a nonpublic employee benefit plan in its plan sponsor's own nonpublic equity securities are deferred indefinitely under ASU 2013-09.
6. For recurring Level 3 fair value measurements, provide a reconciliation from the beginning to the ending balances with separate disclosure in the reconciliation of (a) gross transfers in and out; (b) sales, settlements, purchases, and issuances; (c) realized and unrealized gains and losses recognized in earnings and the line item in the income statement in which those gains or losses are recognized; and (d) gains and losses recognized in the other comprehensive income and the line item in other comprehensive income in which those gains or losses are recognized. Disclose the policy for determining when transfers in (a) are deemed to have occurred.

7. Provide, *for public entities only*, for recurring fair value measurements categorized within Level 3 a description of the sensitivity of the fair value measurement to changes in unobservable inputs if a change in those inputs to a different amount might result in a significantly different fair value measurement.
8. Disclose for recurring and nonrecurring fair value measurements, if the highest and best use of a nonfinancial asset differs from its current use and why the asset is being used in such a manner.
9. Disclose the accounting policy exception for fair value measurement, if used, under ASC 820-10-35-18D for a group of financial assets and financial liabilities with offsetting positions in market risks or counterparty credit risk.
10. Disclose, *for public entities only*, for each class of assets and liabilities not measured at fair value in the balance sheet but for which fair value information is required to be disclosed (a) the level of fair value hierarchy within which it is categorized, (b) the valuation techniques and inputs, (c) any changes in valuation techniques and the reasons, and (d) any departure from the highest and best use of a nonfinancial asset and why the asset is being used in such a manner.
11. Disclose for derivative assets and liabilities the matters discussed in 1, 2, and 6, above.
12. Disclose the existence of credit enhancement liabilities issued with an inseparable third party.
13. Numerous additional disclosures are required under ASC 820-10-50-6A for investments in entities that calculate net asset value per share.

Topic 825: Financial Instruments

Topic 825, *Financial Instruments*, contains five subtopics:

10 Overall

20 Registration Payment Arrangements

942 Financial Services—Depository and Lending*

944 Financial Services—Insurance*

954 Health Care Entities*

* See the corresponding topic in Chapter 9 for coverage of this shared subtopic.

Disclosure Requirements

ASC 825 specifies disclosure requirements for all financial instruments. The disclosure requirements relate to fair value and those associated with a concentration of credit risk.

When an enterprise discloses fair value information, the fair value of one instrument should not be netted with the fair value of another instrument, unless netting or offsetting is allowed under current accounting standards. Fair value and carrying amounts should be presented in a summary table and cross referenced to other fair value information if presented in separate footnotes. In addition, the fair value and carrying amounts of financial instruments should be divided into assets and liabilities so that it is clear to the reader of the statements as to which fair values and carrying amounts represent assets and liabilities and the relationship of the carrying amounts to the amounts reported in the balance sheet.

In some cases, it may not be practicable to determine the fair value of some financial instruments. It may not be practicable to estimate or determine fair value when an enterprise has to incur excessive costs to determine the fair value amount. It also may not be practicable to determine fair value on an individual security basis, but it may be cost effective to estimate fair value on a group basis. In some cases, it may be practicable to determine fair value for only a part of a class of financial instruments. In such cases, fair value for the part should be disclosed. Therefore, the precision of fair value estimates and the actual practicability of determining fair value are affected by the costs that would be incurred to estimate the required information. When it is not practicable to estimate fair value, the enterprise must provide specific disclosure requirements.

Some financial instruments are excluded from the disclosure requirements of ASC 825. The following financial instruments are not required to present fair value disclosures in accordance with ASC 825:

1. Pension, postretirement, and post-employment obligations of employers and pension plans.
2. Stock purchase plans, share-based payment plans, and deferred compensation plans.
3. Debt that is substantively extinguished.
4. Insurance contracts (including financial guarantee insurance contracts). Investment contracts and financial guarantees are not excluded from ASC 825.
5. Leases under the provisions of ASC 840. Lease obligations guaranteed by a third party and canceled lease contingent obligations are covered by ASC 825.
6. Unconditional purchase obligations under ASC 440.
7. Obligations and rights under warranties.
8. Investments in investees accounted for using the equity method, as specified in ASC 323.
9. Equity investments and noncontrolling interest in subsidiaries that are consolidated.
10. Equity securities issued by the enterprise and reported in the stockholders' equity section of the balance sheet.

Certain entities have the option to elect not to report fair value information in accordance with the provisions of ASC 825. When the following conditions are met, an enterprise may elect not to present fair value disclosures:

1. The company is classified as a nonpublic enterprise.
2. The company has total assets of less than $100 million on the balance sheet date.
3. The company, during the accounting period under consideration, did not have a derivative financial instrument that was in total or in part covered by the provisions of ASC 815.

A nonpublic enterprise is a company that (1) does not have debt or equity securities traded in a public market, (2) has not filed with a regulatory authority in preparation for a sale of debt or equity securities in a public market, or (3) is not controlled by an enterprise that meets the requirements in (1) or (2), above.

When ASC 825 is applied and current-year financial statements are included in prior-year comparative financial statements, the following procedures are appropriate: ASC 825 requirements are applied to the most recent financial statements included in the comparative group, when market value disclosures are not required for the current financial statements, such disclosures may be excluded for prior comparative years if presented; and when market value disclosures are required in current-year financial statements, such disclosures, if not included in prior-year comparative statements, are not required for such prior years.

When a nonpublic entity, meeting the exclusion requirements of ASC 825, elects to present market value information, as required by ASC 825, the provisions of ASC 825 must be used.

In addition to fair value disclosure requirements, an entity must disclose any concentration of credit risk. Credit risk is the risk that the other party to a contract will not perform according to the terms of the contract, even if the possibility of loss is assessed to be remote. To illustrate, assume that XYZ Company guarantees a $1,000,000 note of ABC Company and does not record a loss under the provisions of ASC 450 because it is remote that ABC Company will default on future payments. In this situation, XYZ Company has a credit risk of $1,000,000. To illustrate another example of credit risk, assume that Company A has a receivable balance of $2,000,000. Company A has a $2,000,000 credit risk because the counterparty to the receivable could fail to pay the $2,000,000 debt. ASC 460 may require a liability to be recorded for a guarantee.

An enterprise may have significant financial instruments with credit risk with firms that have similar economic characteristics, that operate in the same region, that are in the same industry, that are involved in a similar activity, or have characteristics such that changes in economic conditions may prevent the firms from performing according to the terms of the contracts. The shared characteristics of such firms may create a group concentration of credit risk for the enterprise. In addition, an enterprise may have a concentration of credit risk with one firm. If an enterprise has significant financial instruments with credit risk with one entity, or a group of entities, disclosures of the concentration must be provided. ASC 825 does not provide guidelines as to what constitutes significant concentration of credit risk, but allows the enterprise to use judgment in making the decision. To illustrate a concentration of credit risk, assume that Company X has an account receivable balance of $5,000,000 all from customers in the oil and gas industry. In this case, because the $5,000,000 receivable balance is concentrated only in the oil and gas industry, Company X has a $5,000,000 concentration of credit risk that must be disclosed. To illustrate another situation, assume that Company Z has $20,000,000 of investments, which constitutes 100% of its investments, in the utility industry. In this case, because Company Z has all of its investments in one industry, it has a concentration of credit risk for the $20,000,000.

ASC 825-10-55 states that terms of some loan products may increase a concentration of credit risk. Certain shared characteristics may increase the credit risk, such as negative amortization loans, high loan-to-value ratios, and loans where payments can increase significantly.

Concentrations of credit risk disclosures required by ASC 825 exclude the following:

1. Pension plan financial instruments.
2. Pension, postretirement, and post-employment obligations of employers and pension plans.
3. Stock purchase plans, stock option plans, and deferred compensation plans.
4. Insurance contracts. Prepaid reinsurance premiums and reinsurance receivables are not excluded from the credit risk disclosures.
5. Unconditional purchase obligations under ASC 440.
6. Obligations and rights under warranties.

The following fair value and concentration of credit risk disclosures are required for all financial instruments, unless specifically exempt by ASC 825. (See ASC 820 for additional fair value disclosures.)

Fair Value Disclosure Requirements

The following fair value disclosures may be presented directly in the statement of financial position or in related notes to the financial statements. In addition, the disclosures are divided into situations when it is practicable to determine fair value and situations when it is not practicable to estimate fair value information.

When it is practicable to estimate fair value, the following information must be disclosed:

1. Fair value of financial instruments.
2. Methods used to estimate fair value.
3. Significant assumptions used in the fair value estimate.

When it is not practicable to estimate fair value, the following information must be disclosed:

1. Why fair value is not estimated.
2. Information that is useful in estimating fair value, such as maturity, carrying amount, and effective interest of the financial instrument.

Fair value disclosure is not required for trade receivables and payables when the fair value and the carrying amount are approximately equal.

Concentration of Credit Risk Disclosures

The following disclosures are required for significant concentrations of credit risk (ASC 825-10-50, paragraphs 20–22):

1. Economic characteristics, region, or activity that identifies the concentration.
2. Company policy for financial instrument collateral, nature, and description of such collateral and company access to the collateral.
3. Maximum accounting loss that an enterprise would suffer if counterparties to the concentration totally default and any collateral related to the contracts is worthless. This determination is made using the gross fair value of the instruments.
4. Company policy related to master netting arrangements that are used to reduce credit risk and the following information for any arrangement with which the enterprise is currently involved:
   a. The terms of the arrangement.
   b. The extent the arrangement reduces the credit loss of the enterprise.

This completes the fair value and concentration of credit risk disclosures required by ASC 825. However, ASC 825 encourages entities to disclose certain market risk information about financial instruments. Market risk is the risk that a financial instrument will be more onerous or less valuable because of future changes in the market of the instrument. To illustrate market risk, assume that a financial institution enters into a loan commitment agreement at a fixed rate. The financial institution has market risk from the possible future change in interest rates. The FASB suggests, but does not require, the disclosure of quantitative information about market risk consistent with an entity's risk management policies. Methods of presenting the information may be different for different enterprises and will most likely change over time as measurement techniques and risk management policies change. Possible information that might be disclosed includes the following:

1. Information about financial instrument activity and current positions.
2. Possible impacts on net assets, comprehensive income, and net income, from assumed changes in market prices.
3. Length of the financial instruments.
4. Value at risk on the balance sheet date and an average value at risk during the accounting period under consideration.
5. Gap analysis related to maturity dates or repricing of interest rates.

Disclosures other than the items listed above may be appropriate. An enterprise is encouraged to develop other disclosure information that may be appropriate in the circumstances.

Accounting for Financial Assets and Financial Liabilities Using the Fair Value Option

ASC 825-10 allows an entity to elect to use fair value in reporting certain financial assets and financial liabilities. ASC 825-10 also specifies the accounting and reporting requirements when an entity elects to use the fair value option. ASC 820 specifies how fair value is to be determined for items that are reported at fair value. Fair value is the amount that would be received on the measurement date from the sale of an asset, or the amount paid to transfer a liability between sellers and buyers (market participants) in an orderly transaction. In addition, it is assumed that the sellers and buyers are unrelated parties on the measurement date.

A financial asset is cash, ownership interest in an enterprise, or a contractual right to receive cash or another financial instrument or to exchange financial instruments on potentially favorable terms with the other enterprise. A financial liability is a contractual obligation to deliver cash or another financial instrument or to exchange financial instruments on potentially unfavorable terms with the other enterprise. Table 8-7 lists financial assets and financial liabilities that are and are not eligible for the fair value option.

Table 8-7 Eligible and Ineligible Financial Assets and Financial Liabilities

Assets and Liabilities Eligible for the Fair Value Option (ASC 825-10-15-4)	Assets and Liabilities Not Eligible for the Fair Value Option (ASC 825-10-15-5)
1. Any financial asset or financial liability that has been recognized in the financial statements, except for those specified in ASC 825-10-15-4.	1. Investment in a subsidiary that would be consolidated.
2. A firm commitment that involves only a financial instrument that at inception would not otherwise be recognized.	2. Variable interest entities that would be consolidated.
3. Written loan commitment.	3. Plan obligations and employer obligations or assets from overfunding related to pension plans, postretirement plans, post-employment plans, employee stock option and purchase plans, and other types of deferred compensation.
4. Obligations and rights related to an insurance contract that has terms that allow a third party paid by the insurer to provide specific goods and services but is not classified as a financial instrument.	4. Financial assets and financial liabilities covered by the provisions of ASC 840 related to lease accounting. This does not apply to contingent obligations related to lease cancellations and third-party lease obligation guarantees.

Assets and Liabilities Eligible for the Fair Value Option (ASC 825-10-15-4)	Assets and Liabilities Not Eligible for the Fair Value Option (ASC 825-10-15-5)
5. Obligations and rights related to a warranty that has terms that allow a third party paid by the warranty party to provide specific goods and services but is not classified as a financial instrument.	5. Withdrawals on demand and deposit liabilities of depository entities such as credit unions, banks, and savings and loans.
6. A host financial instrument that arose from the separation of an embedded derivative nonfinancial instrument from a hybrid nonfinancial instrument.	6. Financial instruments classified as stockholders' equity. This also includes temporary equity.

In particular, ASC 825-10 allows an entity to elect fair value reporting for available-for-sale securities and held-to-maturity securities covered by ASC 320 and investments accounted for under the equity method covered by the provisions of ASC 323. Note that trading securities accounted for under ASC 320 already use fair value for accounting and reporting requirements.

Once an entity determines that a financial asset or financial liability qualifies for the fair value option, the fair value option can only be elected on an appropriate election date. Listed below are the elections dates (ASC 825-10-25-4):

1. The eligible item is first recognized by the entity.
2. Financial assets that were subject to specialized industry accounting where the unrealized gains and losses were reported in income are no longer subject to the specialized accounting requirements.
3. The investment accounting requirements change because either
   a. The investment is now subject to equity method accounting under ASC 323 or
   b. A subsidiary or variable interest entity is no longer subject to consolidation, but the investor company retains an interest.
4. An investment initially requires fair value measurement but fair value measurement in subsequent accounting periods is not required.
5. An eligible firm commitment is entered into by the entity.

When an entity elects the fair value option for an eligible asset or liability, the option generally must be applied on an instrument-by-instrument basis, the option is generally irrevocable, and the option must be applied to the entire instrument (ASC 825-10-25-2). When applying the instrument-by-instrument basis, whether to investments or other financial assets or financial liabilities, an entity can elect the fair value option for a specific item without applying the election to other identical items unless one of the following is met (ASC 825-10-25-7):

1. The fair value option is applied only to the larger balance when multiple advances are made to a single borrower under a single contract and each advance loses its identity when it becomes part of the larger loan balance.

2. The fair value option must be applied to all financial interest in an entity, such as equity, debt, and guarantees, when the fair value option is elected for an investment that meets the requirement for equity method accounting under ASC 323.
3. The fair value option is applied to all claims and obligations when the fair value option is elected for insurance or reinsurance contracts.
4. The fair value option must be applied to both the integrated and nonintegrated features of a contact when the fair value option is elected for an insurance contract with integrated and nonintegrated features.

When several financial assets and/or financial liabilities are acquired in a single transaction, the fair value option does not have to be applied to all the items unless it is one of the four items noted above. For example, when an entity acquires shares of stock, the fair value option can be applied to some of the shares. If an entity acquires bonds and stock, the fair value option may be applied to some of the shares and some of the bonds or only some of the shares or only some of the bonds. A single bond for purposes of applying the fair value option is the lowest denomination of the bond issue, such as $1,000. However, an instrument may not be divided into parts for application of the fair value option if the instrument legally is considered a single contract. The fair value option may be elected for an entire investment in an equity security by an equity security investor, including fractional shares of the equity security (ASC 825-10-25, paragraphs 7 through 11).

When the fair value option is elected for a financial asset or a financial liability, any change in fair value at each reporting date is determined and is included in income. "Income" is used in this discussion to mean income or some other performance measure when an entity has a performance measure other than income (ASC 825-10-35-4). When an entity elects the fair value option, any cost or fees incurred up front are expensed in the accounting period during which they are incurred.

When an entity elects the fair value option for one or more of its financial assets and financial liabilities, the fair value amount reported under ASC 825-10 should be reported in the statement of financial position separately from amounts reported using non-fair-value measurement attributes, such as cost or carrying value. This separate presentation may be accomplished by one of two methods. First, two separate line items may be presented, one for the fair value amounts and one for the non-fair-value amounts. The other alternative is to present one aggregate amount for both fair value and non-fair-value amounts and disclose parenthetically the fair value amount reported in the total. Any cash flows related to items where the fair value option is elected are reported in the cash flow statement based on the nature and purpose of the cash flow (ASC 825-10-45).

Not-for-profit entities may also apply the provisions of ASC 825-10; however, certain modifications must be made. First, the term "statement of activities," "statement of operations," or "statement of changes in net assets" replaces the term "income statement" as it is used in discussions of business entities. Second, the term "changes in net assets" should replace the word "earnings" as used in the discussion related to business entities, except for health care entities. Unrealized gains and losses from the election of the fair value option are reported as part of discontinued operations or within the appropriate performance indicators, whichever is the appropriate location, for health care entities covered by the provisions of ASC 954. The performance indicators for organizations covered by ASC 954 are similar to income from continuing operations. In addition, not-for-profit entities may report unrealized gains and losses that are not part of discontinued operations, outside or within an intermediate indicator of operations. The disclosures, discussed below, related to the income statement should not only apply to the performance indicators for not-for-profit entities, but also, when appropriate, to the impact on the change related to each net asset class, such as permanently restricted, temporarily restricted, and unrestricted.

Accounting for Investments Using the Fair Value Option—Technical Considerations

An example to illustrate the fair value option specified by ASC 825-10 follows.

Example 8-11
Assumptions for Fair Value Option

ACE Enterprises, a December 31 year-end company, purchased XXX Bonds and XYZ Bonds at their fair value, which was the same as par value on January 1, 20X8. Fair values on the date of purchase and at the end of the accounting period as presented were determined using quoted market prices. Fair value and cost on the date of acquisition (1/1/X8) are the same.

	Fair Value 1/1/X8	Fair Value 12/31/X8
Investment in XXX Bonds	800,000	825,000
Investment in XYZ Bonds	200,000	240,000

ACE has elected the fair value option for the XYZ bond investment but has not elected it for the XXX bond investment. Therefore, the XXX bond investment will be accounted for using amortized cost under ASC 320-10 and the XYZ bond investment will be accounted for using fair value under ASC 825-10. The XXX bond investment is reported at its carrying value and no change in fair value is reported. However, the XYZ bond investment is reported at fair value, and the change in fair value of $40,000 ($240,000 – $200,000) is reported as a component of income from continuing operations. The journal entry for the change in fair value of the XYZ bond investment as follows:

Investment in XYZ Bonds	40,000	
Unrealized Investment Holding Gain on XYZ Bonds		40,000

Disclosure Requirements

ASC 825-10 requires certain disclosures for financial assets and financial liabilities that allow a comparison between entities that elect different measurement attributes. Entities that report financial assets and financial liabilities at fair value using the provisions of ASC 825-10 are required to provide disclosures in accordance with ASC 825-10-50 for both annual and interim accounting periods presented. An entity is encouraged to combine the ASC 825-10 disclosures with the required fair value disclosures of other standards such as ASC 820. The disclosures in are not required for the following: (1) trading securities accounted for using ASC 320 and (2) life settlement contracts. The following are the required disclosures for each period that a statement of position is presented by an entity:

1. The reason that management elected the fair value option for each item or group of items that is eligible for election.
2. When fair value is not elected for all items in a similar eligible group of items, describe the similar items and the reason for electing fair value for only part of the items and provide information that will allow readers of the financial statements to understand how the individual line items in the statement of financial position relate to the group of similar items.
3. Report the aggregate carrying amount of items included in each line item in the statement of financial position when the items are not eligible for fair value accounting and provide information that allows readers of the financial statements to understand the relationship of each line item in the balance sheet and major classes of assets and liabilities presented using the provisions of ASC 820 when an entity elects fair value reporting for an item or group of items that is presented within a line item in the statement of financial position.
4. For loans, long-term receivables, and long-term debt instruments, excluding ASC 320 securities that have contractual principal amounts and where the entity has elected fair value accounting, disclose the difference between the unpaid principal balances and the fair value on an aggregate basis.
5. When an entity elects fair value accounting for loans that are held as assets, disclose the following: (1) fair value of loans on an aggregate basis that are past due by 90 days or more, (2) fair value of nonaccrual loans on an aggregate basis when interest income is reported separately from the change in fair value, and (3) the difference between the unpaid principal balance and the fair value on an aggregate basis of loans, in nonaccrual status or both, that is past due by 90 days or more.
6. Disclose most of the information required by ASC 323 for investments where the entity would have used equity method accounting if the entity had not elected the fair value option.

The following disclosures, for items for which the fair value option has been elected, are required by an entity for each accounting period that an income statement is presented:

1. Disclose the line item in the income statement where the gains and losses from changes in fair value are reported, and the amount of those gains and losses for each line item reported in the statement of financial position.

2. Describe where dividends and interest are reported in the income statement and how they are measured.
3. Disclose the amount of estimated gains and losses reported in income related to instrument-specific credit risk changes, and how the gains and losses were determined for loans and other receivables held as assets.
4. Disclose the amount of estimated gains and losses from fair value changes reported in income related to instrument-specific credit risk changes, how such gains and losses were determined, and qualitative disclosures providing reasons for the changes for liabilities where fair values have been significantly impacted by instrument-specific credit risk changes.

An entity should disclose, in annual reports only, the methods and any significant assumptions that were used to determine fair value for items for which the company elects fair value.

When accounting requirements change for an investment, because the investment is now required to be accounted for using the equity method or consolidation is no longer required for a subsidiary or a variable interest entity and the entity elects the fair value option, qualitative information should be disclosed in the accounting period that the fair value option is elected. Disclosure includes qualitative information (1) about the nature of the event and (2) by statement of financial position line item specifying which income statement line item contains the impact of the initial fair value election.

Recent Changes

Topic 825, *Financial Instruments,* will be amended by ASU 2016-01, *Financial Instruments—Overall (Subtopic 825-10): Recognition and Measurement of Financial Assets and Financial Liabilities.*

Some of the key provisions of ASU 2016-01 follow.

1. Equity investments (except those accounted for under the equity method of accounting or those that result in consolidation of the investee) are required to be measured at fair value with changes in fair value recognized in net income. However, an entity may choose to measure equity investments that do not have readily determinable fair values at cost minus impairment, if any, plus or minus changes resulting from observable price changes in orderly transactions for the identical or a similar investment of the same issuer.
2. The impairment assessment of equity investments without readily determinable fair values has been simplified by requiring a qualitative assessment to identify impairment. When a qualitative assessment indicates that impairment exists, an entity is required to measure the investment at fair value.
3. Entities that are not public business entities are no longer required to disclose the fair value of financial instruments measured at amortized cost.

4. The requirement for public business entities to disclose the method(s) and significant assumptions used to estimate the fair value that is required to be disclosed for financial instruments measured at amortized cost on the balance sheet has been eliminated.
5. Require public business entities to use the exit price notion when measuring the fair value of financial instruments for disclosure purposes.
6. Require an entity to present separately in other comprehensive income the portion of the total change in the fair value of a liability resulting from a change in the instrument-specific credit risk when the entity has elected to measure the liability at fair value in accordance with the fair value option for financial instruments.
7. Require separate presentation of financial assets and financial liabilities by measurement category and form of financial asset on the balance sheet or the accompanying notes to the financial statements.
8. Clarify that an entity should evaluate the need for a valuation allowance on a deferred tax asset related to available-for-sale securities in conjunction with the entity's other deferred tax assets.

For public business entities, the amendments in ASU 2016-01 are effective for fiscal years beginning after December 15, 2017, including interim periods within those fiscal years. For all other entities, including not-for-profit entities and employee benefit plans within the scope of Topics 960 through 965 on plan accounting, the amendments in ASU 2016-01 are effective for fiscal years beginning after December 15, 2018, and interim periods within fiscal years beginning after December 15, 2019. All entities that are not public business entities may adopt the amendments in ASU 2016-01 earlier, as of the fiscal years beginning after December 15, 2017, including interim periods with those fiscal years. The standards under ASU 2016-01 are not reflected in the discussion of Topic 825: *Financial Instruments* above.

Early application by public business entities to financial statements of fiscal years or interim periods that have not yet been issued or, by all other entities, that have not yet been made available for issuance, of the following amendments in ASU 2016-01 are permitted as of the beginning of the fiscal year of adoption. In connection therewith:

1. An entity should present separately in other comprehensive income the portion of the total change in the fair value of a liability resulting from a change in the instrument-specific credit risk if the entity has elected to measure the liability at fair value in accordance with the fair value option for financial instruments.
2. Entities that are not public business entities are not required to apply the fair value of financial instruments disclosure guidance in the General subsection of Section 825-10-50.

Except for the early application guidance discussed above, early adoption of ASU 2016-01 is not permitted.

An entity should apply ASU 2016-01 by means of a cumulative-effect adjustment to the balance sheet as of the beginning of the fiscal year of adoption.

Further, for equity securities without readily determinable fair values, the standard should be applied prospectively to equity investments that exist as of the date of adoption of ASU 2016-01.

Topic 830: Foreign Currency Matters

Topic 830, *Foreign Currency Matters*, contains six subtopics:

10 Overall

20 Foreign Currency Transactions

30 Translation of Financial Statements

230 Statement of Cash Flows

740 Income Taxes

946 Financial Services—Investment Companies [See the corresponding topic in Chapter 9 for coverage of this shared subtopic]

ASC 830 divides foreign currency accounting into two major categories. The first is the accounting for foreign currency transactions and the second is the translation of foreign currency financial statements.

Foreign Currency Transactions That Are Not the Result of Derivative Instruments Flowchart and General Discussion

Accounting for a foreign currency transaction that is not related to a derivative instrument requires the use of the current exchange rate. Flowchart 8-2 outlines the major decisions and accounting related to these types of transactions. On the date of the foreign currency transaction (Block 3), the asset, liability, revenue, or expense arising from the transaction is to be measured and recorded in the functional currency of the entity, using the current exchange rate on that date. After the date of the transaction, there are two dates of significance. If there is a balance sheet date between the date of the transaction and the date of settlement of the transaction, the balance in the foreign currency transaction account must be adjusted to reflect the current rate on the balance sheet date. Any gain or loss resulting from the restatement will be reflected in the current period income statement.

Flowchart 8-2

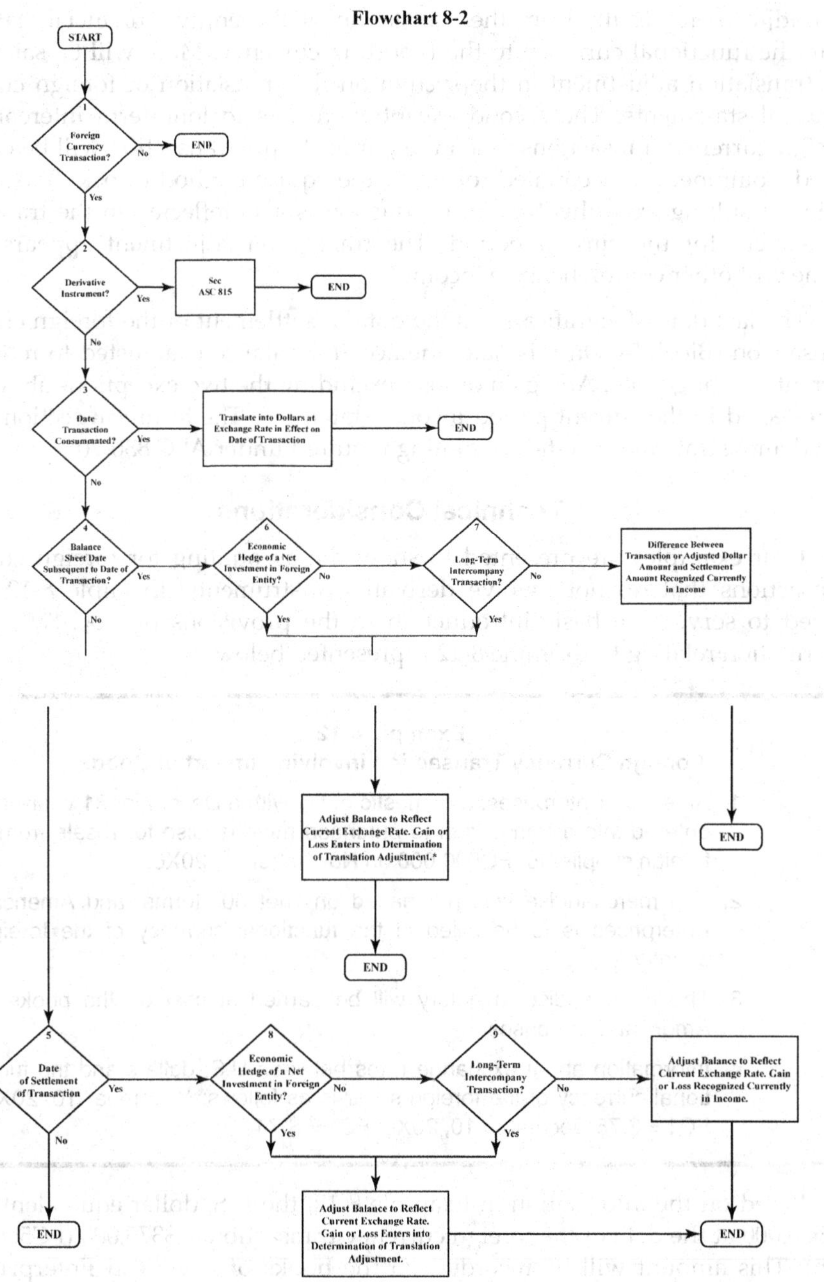

* Reported as a component of other comprehensive income in accordance with the provisions of ASC 220.

There are two exceptions to this accounting. First, if the foreign currency transaction is the result of an economic hedge of a net investment in a foreign entity, the gain or loss resulting from the restatement will be reflected in the determination of the translation adjustment for the period (Block 6). The translation adjustment results from the translation of the entity's financial statement from the functional currency to the reporting currency. More will be said about the translation adjustment in the section on the translation of foreign currency financial statements. The second exception relates to long-term intercompany foreign currency transactions when the parties to the transaction will be consolidated, combined, or accounted for using the equity method (Block 7). Any gain or loss resulting from this type of transaction is also reflected in the translation adjustment for the current period. The translation adjustment appears as an element of other comprehensive income.

The last date of significance is the date of settlement of the foreign currency transaction (Block 5). On this date, the account balance is adjusted to reflect the current exchange rate. Any gain or loss, excluding the two exceptions above, will be reflected in the current period income statement. The technical section below will demonstrate the specific accounting required under ASC 830-20.

Technical Considerations

Four examples are presented to show the accounting for foreign currency transactions that do not involve derivative instruments. Example 8-12 is designed to serve as a basic introduction to the provisions of ASC 830-20. The information relating to Example 8-12 is presented below.

Example 8-12
Foreign Currency Transaction Involving Import of Goods

1. American Enterprises, a domestic entity with a December 31 year-end, entered into a transaction to purchase merchandise for resale from a foreign supplier for FC500,000 on November 10, 20X6.
2. The merchandise was purchased on "net 30" terms, and American Enterprises is to be billed in the functional currency of the foreign country.
3. The merchandise inventory will be carried at cost on the books of American Enterprises.
4. Information about exchange rates between U.S. dollars and the functional currency of the foreign seller is as follows: November 10, 20X6: FC1 = $.75 December 10, 20X6: FC1 = $.74

Based on the information in Example 8-12, the U.S. dollar equivalent of the FC500,000 at the date of the foreign currency transaction is $375,000 (FC500,000 × $.75). This amount will be recorded on the books of American Enterprises on November 10, 20X6 as shown in the following journal entry:

Inventory	375,000	
Accounts Payable		375,000

The date of settlement of the foreign currency transaction is December 10, 20X6, which is prior to the balance sheet date of American Enterprises. On the settlement date, December 10, 20X6, the current exchange rate is FC1 = $.74. Therefore, American Enterprises would pay $370,000 (FC500,000 × $.74) to the bank to purchase a draft for FC500,000. The journal entry to record the settlement of the payable at December 10, 20X6 is as follows:

Accounts Payable	375,000	
Cash		370,000
Exchange Gain		5,000

The transaction results in an exchange gain to American Enterprises, because it takes fewer dollars to purchase the same number of units of foreign currency. The amount of the gain may be computed by multiplying the amount of the obligation by the difference between the exchange rates on November 10, 20X6, and December 10, 20X6 (FC500,000 × $.01 = $5,000). The gain will be reported in the current period income statement as a nonoperating item. Had it cost more dollars to purchase the same number of units of foreign currency (e.g., if FC1 = $.77), the transaction would have resulted in an exchange loss to American Enterprises.

Example 8-12 dealt with the import of goods by a U.S. company where the date of transaction and date of settlement occurred in the same accounting period. Example 8-13 deals with the export of goods and illustrates the accounting when the date of transaction and date of settlement occur in different accounting periods. The information relating to Example 8-13 is presented below.

Example 8-13
Foreign Currency Transactions Involving Export of Goods

1. American Enterprises, a domestic entity with a December 31 year-end, sells merchandise to a foreign customer for FC500,000 on December 18, 20X6.
2. The terms of the sale are "net 30" and American Enterprises will bill and be paid in the functional currency of the foreign customer.
3. The following exchange rates are in effect on the dates indicated: December 18, 20X6- FC1 = $.75 December 31, 20X6- FC1 = $.72 January 17, 20X7- FC1 = $.74.

On December 18, 20X6, the date of the transaction the dollar equivalent of FC500,000 is $375,000 (FC500,000 × $.75), and the following journal entry would be made on the books of American Enterprises:

Accounts Receivable	375,000	
Sales		375,000

The next date of significance is December 31, 20X6, the balance sheet date of American Enterprises. The balance sheet date falls between the date of the transaction and the date of settlement. In this case, the accounts receivable must be adjusted to represent the dollar equivalent of the amount receivable on that date. On December 31, 20X6, the exchange rate is FC1 = $.72; therefore, the balance in the receivable account should be $360,000 (FC500,000 × $.72). The difference between the current balance in the receivable ($375,000) and the new balance to be reflected ($360,000) is the amount of the exchange loss for the period ($15,000). This amount is a loss because on December 31, 20X6 FC500,000 could be converted into fewer dollars than reflected on the date of the transaction. If the FC500,000, could have been converted into more dollars on December 31, 20X6 (e.g., FC1 = $.80, the transaction would have resulted in a gain for the period). The general journal entry to record the exchange loss for the period on the books of American Enterprises would be:

Exchange Loss	15,000	
Accounts Receivable		15,000

The carrying value of the account receivable is now $360,000 ($375,000 – $15,000) as a result of the recognition of the exchange loss. The exchange loss account will be included in the 20X6 income statement as a nonoperating item.

The last date of significance is the settlement date of January 17, 20X7. On this date, American Enterprises will receive FC500,000 that can be converted into $370,000 (FC500,000 × $.74). The account receivable is currently carried at $360,000, so the settlement will result in a gain. The gain or loss is determined by comparing the adjusted receivable balance with the proceeds from liquidation of the receivable. The gain or loss would be calculated as follows:

Amount received on settlement	$370,000
Adjusted amount of the receivable	360,000
Exchange gain	$10,000

Assuming that the foreign customer purchases a bank draft to settle the account, the journal entry on the books of American Enterprises on January 17, 20X7, would be:

Cash	370,000	
Accounts Receivable		360,000
Exchange Gain		10,000

The exchange gain of $10,000 would be included in the 20X7 income statement as a nonoperating item. In summary, the above transaction resulted in an exchange loss of $15,000 in 20X6 and an exchange gain of $10,000 in 20X7. On a net basis, there has been a $5,000 exchange loss resulting from the transaction. Part of the loss was recognized in one accounting period and the remainder in another accounting period. The net loss can be computed by taking the difference in the exchange rate on the date of the sale (FC1 = $.75) and the exchange rate on the date of settlement (FC1 = $.74), multiplied by the face amount of the transaction (FC500,000).

The first two examples dealt with the purchase or sale of merchandise between a domestic and foreign entity. Example 8-14 is designed to illustrate the accounting required when a domestic entity invests in the marketable securities of a foreign entity. The information relating to Example 8-14 is given below.

Example 8-14
Foreign Currency Transaction Involving Investments

1. American Enterprises, a domestic entity with a December 31 year-end, purchased marketable securities in a foreign company for FC1,500,000, on October 29, 20X6.
2. The management of American Enterprises intends to convert the marketable securities, which are measured in the functional currency of the foreign entity, into cash within the normal operating cycle of the company.
3. Exchange rates in effect on selected dates are shown below: October 29, 20X6- FC1 = $.90 December 31, 20X6- FC1 = $.95
4. The fair value of the marketable securities of the foreign company in FC units is the same on October 29, 20X6 and December 31, 20X6.

The marketable securities described above will be classified as current assets because management intends to convert them into cash within the next operating cycle of the company. The dollar equivalent of the FC1,500,000 paid for the securities is $1,350,000 (FC1,500,000 × $.90) on the date of acquisition. The journal entry to record the purchase of the securities on October 29, 20X6 would be:

Marketable Securities	1,350,000	
Cash		1,350,000

On December 31, 20X6, the year-end for American Enterprises, the exchange rate is FC1 = $.95. Any gain or loss created by a change in the exchange rate will be reflected in the income statement for 20X6. The FC1,500,000 is to be converted into dollars using the exchange rate in effect on December 31, 20X6. The gain or loss resulting from the change in the exchange rate is computed as follows:

Marketable Securities—December 31, 20X6 (FC1,500,000 × $.95)	$1,425,000
Marketable Securities—October 29, 20X6 (FC1,500,000 × $.90)	1,350,000
Exchange Gain	$75,000

The journal entry at December 31, 20X6, to record the exchange gain is:

Marketable Securities	75,000	
Exchange Gain		75,000

The $75,000 exchange gain will be included in the nonoperating section of the 20X6 income statement. This completes the explanation and analysis of Example 8-14. Example 8-15 illustrates the proper accounting for long-term intercompany transactions.

Example 8-15
Foreign Currency Transactions Involving Intercompany Items

1. On March 29, 20X6, American Enterprises, a domestic entity with a December 31 year-end, made an advance to London, Ltd., a subsidiary located in a foreign country, of FC4,000,000 for plant expansion.

2. The management of American Enterprises considers the advance to be long-term in nature and repayment is not expected in the foreseeable future.
3. Exchange rates in effect on selected dates are as follows: March 29, 20X6- FC1 = $.82 December 31, 20X6- FC1 = $.90

The dollar equivalent of FC4,000,000 on the date of the advance is $3,280,000 (FC4,000,000 × $.82). This amount will be recorded as an investment in London, Ltd. on March 29, 20X6. The journal entry to record the investment would be:

Investment in London, Ltd.	3,280,000	
Cash		3,280,000

The next date of significance is December 31, 20X6, the year-end for American Enterprises. Because the advance by American Enterprises is a long-term intercompany transaction, any gain or loss resulting from changes in the exchange rate will be used in the determination of the translation adjustment for the year. The amount of the gain or loss is determined by comparing the exchange rate in effect on the transaction date (March 29, 20X6) with the rate in effect at the balance sheet date (December 31, 20X6). The difference will enter into the determination of the translation adjustment and be reflected in other comprehensive income on December 31, 20X6. The amount to be included in the translation adjustment from this particular transaction would be determined as follows:

Advance on March 29, 20X6 (FC 4,000,000 × $.82)	$3,280,000
Advance on December 31, 20X6 (FC 4,000,000 × $.90)	3,600,000
Amount used in Translation Adjustment	$320,000

The four examples just discussed were relatively straightforward in nature and serve as a good introduction to the section on foreign currency derivatives covered in this chapter.

Translating Foreign Currency Financial Statements

General Discussion

The most critical step in the process of translating foreign currency financial statements is the proper determination of the *functional currency*. The concept of functional currency is central to ASC 830-30.

The financial statements of a foreign entity should be measured in terms of that entity's functional currency. The functional currency of the enterprise is the currency in use in the operations of the enterprise that reflects the economic environment. It may be thought of as the currency in which the enterprise primarily produces its cash inflows and disburses its cash outflows. In its most straightforward form, the functional currency of an entity that operates as an independent enterprise in one particular country would be the currency of that country. For example, if there were a company that operated in Great Britain as an independent entity and generated its cash and incurred its expenses in this country, the functional currency would be the British pound. On the other hand, if the British company were merely an extension of a French parent company, the functional currency of the company would be the euro. The location of the company does not always indicate the functional currency. In any particular situation it may be very difficult to determine the functional currency to be used in the process of translating foreign currency financial statements.

ASC 830-30 provides guidance for determining the functional currency. Management of a company must consider the following indicators in its determination of the functional currency: cash flows, sales price, sales market, expense, financing, and transactions and arrangements that are of an intercompany nature.

When considering the cash flow indicators, the accountant would want to be sure that the cash inflows from the foreign company were denominated in that entity's currency, and that the cash flow of the parent company was not directly affected. In some cases, the cash collected by the foreign company will be denominated in the local currency, but will be directly transferred to the parent company. In effect, the foreign operation is merely an extension of the parent company located in another country. The foreign entity may be nothing more than an agent for the parent company. In this case, the functional currency would be the currency of the parent company. The fact that the money collected by the entity is denominated in a foreign currency is not the main factor to consider when deciding on the functional currency.

Once the functional currency has been determined, the books and records of a business entity must be measured in that currency. This measurement of assets and liabilities into the functional currency must be done before there is any translation into the reporting currency for a group of related companies. If the functional currency and the reporting currency are the same, no translation is required. However, remeasurement into the functional currency must be completed. The goal of remeasurement is to reflect the entity's books in the functional currency. One major exception to this general rule exists when the functional currency is that of a highly inflationary economy. A highly inflationary economy is one where inflation on a cumulative basis equals or exceeds 100% in the last three years. If the functional currency is that of a highly inflationary economy, the reporting currency should be used as the functional currency.

The objectives of the translation process are listed below (Paragraph 4):

1. Furnish financial information that agrees with the economic impact of changes in currency rates of exchange on the equity and cash flows of an entity.
2. Report in consolidated statements, in accordance with U.S. GAAP, financial information, and affiliations of the entities that are consolidated, as originally reported in their functional currencies.

The financial statements of a foreign enterprise are expected to be prepared in accordance with generally accepted accounting principles and to be denominated in the entity's functional currency. If these conditions are not met, adjustments must be made by the foreign enterprise. First, if the financial statements of the foreign enterprise are not stated in terms of its functional currency, they must be *remeasured* into the functional currency. The remeasurement process must take place prior to the translation of the financial statements into the reporting currency. If the financial statements of the foreign entity are not prepared in accordance with U.S. GAAP, they must be adjusted to U.S. GAAP before the remaining provisions of ASC 830-30 can be appropriately applied. In the most complex situation, a foreign enterprise might have financial statements that are not measured in its functional currency and are not prepared in accordance with U.S. GAAP. In this case, considerable effort will be required before the translation process can begin.

The remeasurement and translation process will result in gains or losses depending upon the differences in exchange rates used in the process. The gains or losses from the remeasurement process are reported in the income statement as a component of income from continuing operations. Any gains or losses from translation are reported as a component of other comprehensive income and are included in accumulated other comprehensive income in the balance sheet. The gains and losses included in accumulated other comprehensive income will be reclassified and reported in the income statement when realized.

The problem of translating foreign currency financial statements can be divided into two major categories. The first case would be where the U.S. dollar is considered to be the functional currency. The second case would be where a foreign currency would be considered to be the functional currency. The exchange rate to use to translate a particular account balance will depend on whether the functional currency is the U.S. dollar or a foreign currency. Once the foreign currency financial statements have been measured in the functional currency and prepared in accordance with U.S. GAAP, the translation process can begin.

The translation process generally proceeds on an account-by-account basis. The author believes that it is best to begin the translation with the balance sheet. One should proceed down the asset and liability sides of the balance sheet, translating one account at a time. The retained earnings account should not be translated until after the translation of the income statement is completed. The reason for this approach is that income or loss may be the single largest element of retained earnings. Once income has been successfully translated, the remaining elements of retained earnings may be translated.

Chart 8-1 has been developed to indicate the proper exchange rate to use in the translation of specific balance sheet and income statement accounts. Notice that one set of exchange rates applies to financial statements where the U.S. dollar is the functional currency, or where financial statements must be remeasured from the books of record to the functional currency, and another set of rates applies when a foreign currency is considered to be the functional currency. The column headings for the exchange rates refer to the current rate, the historical rate, and the average rate. The current rate is defined as the exchange rate in effect as of the end of the period covered by the financial statements. The historical rate is the rate that was in effect on the date the transaction took place. For example, when U.S. dollars are the functional currency, or where financial statements must be remeasured from the books of record to the functional currency, inventories carried at cost should be translated at the historical rate in effect when each item in the inventory was purchased. In most cases, this type of information requires excessive bookkeeping and clerical efforts. ASC 830-30 suggests that, in cases where the cost of obtaining the detail information exceeds the benefit derived, appropriate averages or weighted averages may be used. Revenue and expenses should be translated using either a current or an average for the period exchange rate, except for those expenses relating to assets translated at the historical rate. For example, depreciation expense should be based on the translated value of the property, plant, and equipment. Because property, plant, and equipment is translated at historical rates, depreciation will be expressed in terms of those rates.

When the financial statements are translated and the foreign currency is determined to be the functional currency, the current exchange rate is used for all balance sheet accounts. Revenue and expenses should be translated using either current or average exchange rates in effect for the period covered by the financial statements. Chart 8-1 contains a sample of exchange rates for different balance sheet and income statement accounts.

Chart 8-1 Translation and Remeasurement Rates Used for Balance Sheet and Income Statement

	U.S. Dollar Is Functional Currency or Remeasurement from Books of Record to Functional Currency — Translation or Remeasurement Rates			Foreign Currency Is Functional Currency — Translation Rates		
	Current	Historical	Average	Current	Historical	Average
ASSETS						
Cash	X			X		
Marketable securities:						
Reported at fair value	X			X		
Reported at cost		X		X		
Accounts receivable	X			X		
Notes receivable	X			X		
Allowance for bad debts	X			X		
Inventory:						
Reported at other than cost	X			X		
Reported at cost		X		X		
Prepaid rent and other short-term prepaid items	X		X			
Cash surrender value of life insurance	X					

	U.S. Dollar Is Functional Currency or Remeasurement from Books of Record to Functional Currency Translation or Remeasurement Rates			Foreign Currency Is Functional Currency Translation Rates		
	Current	**Historical**	**Average**	**Current**	**Historical**	**Average**
Long-term debt and equity investments:						
Reported at fair value	X			X		
Reported at cost or equity method		X		X		
Advances to subsidiaries not consolidated	X			X		
Property, plant, and equipment	X		X			
Accumulated depreciation	X		X			
Intangible assets	X		X			
Long-term prepayments	X		X			
LIABILITIES						
Accounts payable	X			X		
Notes payable	X			X		
Salaries payable and other similar accrued expenses	X			X		
Deposits that are refundable	X			X		
Rent in advance and similar deferred income items		X		X		
Warranty liabilities	X			X		
Premium liabilities	X			X		
Noncurrent debt	X			X		
Convertible debt	X			X		
Discounts and premiums on noncurrent debt that has not been amortized	X			X		
INCOME STATEMENT[1]						
Sales	X		X	X		X
Cost of sales		X		X		X
Salary expense	X		X	X		X
Advertising expense	X		X	X		X

	U.S. Dollar Is Functional Currency or Remeasurement from Books of Record to Functional Currency			Foreign Currency Is Functional Currency		
	Translation or Remeasurement Rates			Translation Rates		
	Current	Historical	Average	Current	Historical	Average
General and administrative expense	X		X	X		X
Depreciation expense		X		X		X
Amortization of intangibles		X		X		X
Interest expense	X		X	X		X
Interest income	X		X	X		X

[1] If there is an X in both the current and average columns, either rate may be used. But an entity should be consistent and use either all current or all average where both are appropriate. In the remeasurement from books of record to functional currency, if the income statement item relates to a nonmonetary balance sheet item, the historical rate used for the balance sheet item should be used for the related income statement item.

Technical Considerations

Because the translation process is linked to the determination of the functional currency, two examples illustrate foreign currency financial statement translation. The first assumes that the U.S. dollar is the functional currency, and the second assumes that the foreign currency is the functional currency and the U.S. dollar is the reporting currency.

To begin, assume that American Manufacturing Company, Inc., a parent company, wishes to translate the financial statements of its subsidiary, Foreign Enterprise, Ltd. The functional currency is determined to be the U.S. dollar. The balance sheet, income statement, and statement of retained earnings of Foreign Enterprise, Ltd. for the years 20X7 and 20X6 are shown in Tables 8-8 through 8-10, respectively. The statement of cash flow has been omitted for sake of simplicity; however, American Manufacturing plans to prepare such a statement after the translation has been completed. The financial statements of Foreign Enterprise are prepared in accordance with U.S. generally accepted accounting principles, so no adjustment to the account balances is required prior to translation.

The financial statements presented for Foreign Enterprise are from the date of inception of the company. This has been done to illustrate the accumulation of certain important information relating to balance sheet translation. Table 8-11 contains selected exchange rate information that will aid the process of translation. Each of the quotations shown in Table 8-11 represents the dollar equivalent of one unit of foreign currency of Foreign Enterprises. The translation will begin with the 20X6 (oldest) statements and move forward to the 20X7 statements. The actual translation process is quite lengthy, and the reader is encouraged to make frequent references to Tables 8-8 through 8-11.

Table 8-8 Balance Sheet in Foreign Currency Foreign Enterprise, Ltd.
December 31, 20X7 and 20X6

	20X7	20X6
Current Assets:		
Cash	1,250,000	956,300
Accounts receivable—trade	3,902,500	2,443,700
Accounts receivable—intercompany	942,500	—0—
Notes receivable	2,970,000	1,000,000
Inventories	9,100,000	7,900,500
Prepaid expenses	425,300	—0—
Accrued interest on notes receivable	35,800	11,400
Total Current Assets	18,626,100	12,311,900
Long-Term Notes Receivable	6,000,000	6,000,000
Property, Plant, and Equipment:		
Land	17,000,000	17,000,000
Buildings	156,768,000	149,811,000
Fixtures and equipment	39,932,000	32,626,000
Total Property, Plant, and Equipment	213,700,000	199,437,000
Accumulated depreciation	(23,267,200)	(11,265,200)
Net Property, Plant, and Equipment	190,432,800	188,171,800
Total Assets	215,058,900	206,483,700
Current Liabilities:		
Accounts payable	2,774,550	3,628,000
Accrued interest on long-term debt	510,000	450,000
Income taxes payable	763,250	766,500
Dividends payable	500,000	250,000
Current maturities on long-term debt	2,500,000	2,500,000
Total Current Liabilities	7,047,800	7,594,500
Long-Term Debt	75,000,000	67,500,000
Deferred Income Taxes	1,858,900	1,096,200
Stockholders' Equity		
Common stock	50,000,000	50,000,000
Contributed capital in excess of par	77,182,400	77,182,400
Retained earnings	3,969,800	3,110,600
Total Stockholders' Equity	131,152,200	130,293,000
Total Liabilities and Stockholders' Equity	215,058,900	206,483,700

Table 8-9 Income Statement in Foreign Currency Foreign Enterprise, Ltd. Years Ended December 31, 20X7 and 20X6

	20X7	20X6
Sales	84,075,500	73,376,000
Costs and Expenses:		
Cost of goods sold:		
Inventory—January 1	7,900,500	—0—
Production costs	48,462,500	49,965,600
Goods available for sale	56,363,000	49,965,600
Inventory—December 31	(9,100,000)	(7,900,500)
Cost of goods sold	47,263,000	42,065,100
General and administrative	9,731,400	8,245,000
Advertising and selling	7,326,000	4,671,500
Depreciation	12,002,000	11,265,200
Total costs and expenses	76,322,400	66,246,800
Income from operations	7,753,100	7,029,200
Other income (expenses)	(2,987,500)	(678,200)
Income before taxes	4,765,600	6,351,000
Income taxes:		
Current	1,143,700	1,144,200
Deferred	762,700	1,096,200
Total taxes	1,906,400	2,240,400
Net income	2,859,200	4,110,600

Table 8-10 Statement of Retained Earnings in Foreign Currency Foreign Enterprise, Ltd. Years Ended December 31, 20X7 and 20X6

	20X7	20X6
Retained earnings—January 1	3,110,600	—0—
Add net income for the year	2,859,200	4,110,600
Deduct dividends for the year	(2,000,000)	(1,000,000)
Retained earnings—December 31	3,969,800	3,110,600

Table 8-11 Foreign Currency Rates

	U.S. Dollar Is Functional Currency FC1		Foreign Currency Is Functional Currency FC1	
Explanation of Rates	**20X7**	**20X6**	**20X7**	**20X6**
Conversion rate at March 31	$.245	$.25	N/A[1]	N/A
Conversion rate at June 30	$.25	$.2475	N/A	N/A
Conversion rate at September 30	$.25	$.245	N/A	N/A
Conversion rate at December 31	$.245	$.24	$.245	$.24
Average conversion rate for the year	$.2475	$.2455	$.2475	$.2455
Historical conversion rate when stock was issued and land purchased		$.255		$.255
Historical conversion rate when buildings, fixtures and equipment were purchased	$.245	$.25	N/A	N/A
Average historical rate applicable to inventories on hand at December 31	$.25	$.2425	N/A	N/A

[1] N/A is not applicable.

First Example: Translation Process When U.S. Dollar Is Functional Currency

The translation of the 20X6 financial statements will begin by concentrating on as many balance sheet accounts as is possible in the circumstances. At this point, translation of an income statement account will be postponed, unless the translation is needed to complete the translation of a particular balance sheet account.

A logical place to begin is with the translation of current assets. Foreign Enterprise, Ltd. carries its inventories at cost. All current assets except inventories will be translated at the current exchange rate of $.24, because these accounts represent cash or amounts receivable. Foreign Enterprise has determined that the average historical rate applicable to inventories is $.2425. This average rate may have been determined on the basis of inventory turnover or the use of some weighted, average rate based upon the age of the inventory. Again, an average rate was used because it would be very expensive and time-consuming to maintain records of all of the actual exchange rates in effect at each inventory transaction date. The translation of the current asset section of the balance sheet for the year 20X6 is accomplished as follows:

	Foreign Currency Balance	Translation Rate	Dollar Balance
Cash	956,300	$.24	$229,512
Accounts receivable-trade	2,443,700	$.24	586,488
Notes receivable	1,000,000	$.24	240,000

	Foreign Currency Balance	Translation Rate	Dollar Balance
Inventories	7,900,500	$.2425	1,915,871
Accrued interest	11,400	$.24	2,736
Total current assets	12,311,900		$2,974,607

The next item to be translated on the balance sheet is the long-term note receivable. Because this account represents an amount receivable, it should be translated at the current exchange rate in effect on December 31, 20X6, which is the balance sheet date. The FC6,000,000 would translate into $1,440,000 (FC6,000,000 × $.24 = $1,440,000).

The next major section of the balance sheet to be translated consists of property, plant, and equipment. Because all accounts in this section are carried at historical cost, the historical rate in effect when the land, building, fixtures, and equipment were purchased should be used to translate the accounts. Table 8-11 indicates that the land was purchased when the common stock originally was issued. At that date, the exchange rate was FC1 = $.255; therefore, the land account should be translated at this rate. The building, fixtures, and equipment were purchased when the exchange rate was different, and should be translated at the rate of FC1 = $.25. Because this is the initial year of operations for the company, the balance in the accumulated depreciation account is equal to the depreciation expense for the year. The accumulated depreciation balance should be translated at the historical rate applicable to the building, fixtures, and equipment accounts, because that would be the rate used to translate depreciation expense for the period. The translation of the property, plant, and equipment section of the balance sheet for 20X6 is shown below:

	Foreign Currency Balance	Translation Rate	Dollar Balance
Land	17,000,000	$.255	$4,335,000
Buildings	149,811,000	$.25	37,452,750
Fixtures and equipment	32,626,000	$.25	8,156,500
Total property, plant, and equipment	199,437,000		$49,944,250
Accumulated depreciation	(11,265,200)	$.25	(2,816,300)
Net property, plant, and equipment	188,171,800		$47,127,950

The translation of the asset side of the balance sheet now is completed. The total assets, expressed in dollars, is shown below:

Current assets	$2,974,607
Long-term notes receivable	1,440,000
Property, plant, and equipment	47,127,950
Total assets	$51,542,557

The accounts that make up the current liability section of the balance sheet for 20X6 all represent amounts payable and should be translated at the current exchange rate at December 31, 20X6. The translation of current liabilities is shown below:

	Foreign Currency Balance	Translation Rate	Dollar Balance
Accounts payable	3,628,000	$.24	$870,720
Accrued interest	450,000	$.24	108,000
Income taxes payable	766,500	$.24	183,960
Dividends payable	250,000	$.24	60,000
Current maturities	2,500,000	$.24	600,000
Total current liabilities	7,594,500		$1,822,680

Long-term debt represents amounts payable and, therefore, is translated at the current exchange rate at December 31, 20X6. The foreign currency balance in long-term debt would be translated into $16,200,000 (FC67,500,000 × $.24 = $16,200,000).

Because this is the first year of operations for the company, the balance in the deferred income taxes account on the balance sheet is equal to the deferred tax portion of the income tax expense reported on the income statement. However, even though the two amounts are the same, different exchange rates are used in the translation process. The average exchange rate is used to translate the deferred portion of the income tax expense (computed in the income statement below), and the current exchange rate is used to translate the deferred tax account in the balance sheet. The difference is an adjustment to the translation gain or loss. Therefore, the foreign currency balance in the deferred income taxes account would translate into $263,088 (FC1,096,200 × $.24 = $263,088).

The stockholders' equity section of the balance sheet is the last set of accounts that must be translated. Common stock and contributed capital in excess of par are carried at historical cost on the balance sheet. These accounts should be translated at the exchange rate in effect on the date the stock was issued. Table 8-11 shows that the appropriate rate to use is FC1 = $.255. Using this rate, common stock would translate into $12,750,000 (FC50,000,000 × $.255 = $12,750,000), and the contributed capital would translate into $19,681,512 (FC77,182,400 × $.255 = $19,681,512).

No information has been given concerning the translation of the retained earnings account. In the initial year, the account balance will represent the difference between the income earned and the dividends paid. Direct translation of the retained earnings account is usually not possible. However, it is known that the retained earnings account represents a residual value on the balance sheet. Because all asset, liability, and owners' equity accounts have been translated, except for retained earnings, it is possible to determine the balance in the retained earnings account by comparison of all asset, liability, and equity accounts translated. To begin the process, first recap the liability and equity accounts that have been translated into dollars. This computation is shown below:

Current liabilities	$1,822,680
Long-term debt	16,200,000
Deferred income taxes	263,088
Common stock	12,750,000
Contributed capital in excess of par	19,681,512
Total liabilities and equities translated	$50,717,280

This total amount now may be compared with the total dollar value of the assets translated. The difference between the two balances must represent the balance in the retained earnings account. The computation is made as follows:

Total dollar value of assets translated	$51,542,557
Total dollar value of liabilities and equity accounts (other than retained earnings) translated	50,717,280
Retained earnings balance 12/31/X6	$825,277

This residual value assigned to retained earnings is correct because it causes the translated dollar value of the assets to equal the liabilities and stockholders' equity. With this final determination completed, the translation of the income statement accounts can be started. Recall that during the discussion of translating accumulated depreciation and deferred income taxes, reference has been made to related income statement accounts.

Most items on the income statement will be translated at the average exchange rate during the period. Remember that this is allowed because the cost of keeping track of the historical rate for each income statement item is prohibitive. Income statement accounts that are directly related to balance sheet accounts that were translated at historical rates should be translated at the same historical rates.

The only accounts on the 20X6 income statement (Table 8-9) that would be translated at historical rates are depreciation expense and the December 31 inventory. All the other accounts would be translated at the average rate during the period. The complete translation of the income statement is shown below:

Table 8-12 Income Statement Foreign Enterprise, Ltd. Year Ended December 31, 20X6

	Foreign Currency Balance	Translation Rate	Dollar Balance
Sales	73,276,000	$.2455	$17,989,258
Costs and Expenses:			
Cost of goods sold:			
Inventory—January 1	-0-		-0-
Production costs	49,965,600	$.2455	$12,266,554
Inventory—December 31	(7,900,500)	$.2425*	(1,915,871)
Cost of goods sold	42,065,100		$10,350,683

	Foreign Currency Balance	Translation Rate	Dollar Balance
General and administrative expenses	8,245,000	$.2455	2,024,148
Advertising and selling	4,671,500	$.2455	1,146,853
Depreciation	11,265,200	$.25*	2,816,300
Total costs and expenses	66,246,800		$16,337,984
Income from operations	7,029,200		$1,651,274
Other income (expense)	(678,200)	$.2455	(166,498)
Income before taxes	6,351,000		$1,484,776
Income taxes:			
Current	1,144,200	$.2455	$280,901
Deferred	1,096,200	$.2455*	269,117
Total income taxes	2,240,400		$550,018
Net income	4,110,600		$934,758

* See balance sheet translation.

The income statement translation above ignores the possibility of any translation gains or losses resulting from fluctuations in the exchange rate between the foreign currency and the dollar. Before the translation process is complete, consideration must be given to such gains or losses. To begin this determination, the balance in the retained earnings account must be reviewed (Table 8-10).

The two elements that make up the retained earnings balance are net income for the year and dividends paid. Assume that dividends of FC250,000 were declared at the end of each quarter (FC250,000 × 4 = $1,000,000). The translation of the dividends for 20X6 would be accomplished by applying the exchange rate in effect at the end of each quarter to the dividends declared. The translation is shown below:

March 31 dividend (FC250,000 × $.25)	$62,500
June 30 dividend (FC250,000 × $.2475)	61,875
September 30 dividend (FC250,000 × $.245)	61,250
December 31 dividend (FC250,000 × $.24)	60,000
Translated dividends for 20X6	$245,625

After the dividends have been translated, a detailed analysis of the components of retained earnings can be made. With the information developed to this point, a reconstructed retained earnings account would appear as follows:

Retained earnings—January 1, 20X6	$-0-
Add net income for the year (see income statement above)	934,758
Deduct dividends for the year	(245,625)
Retained earnings—December 31, 20X6	$689,133

Refer to the computation of retained earnings required during the translation of the balance sheet. Notice that the retained earnings balance previously determined is $825,277, and the retained earnings balance computed above is $689,133. Recall that, when the income statement was translated, no recognition was given to possible translation gains or losses. Therefore, the difference between the two calculations of retained earnings must be the translation gain or loss for the period. In 20X6, there was a gain from translation in the amount of $136,144 ($825,277 – $689,133). With the gain determined, the income statement for 20X6 may be recast to reflect the translation gain as follows:

Income from operations		$1,651,274
Nonoperating items:		
Other income (expense)	$(166,498)	
Translation gain	136,144	(30,354)
Income before taxes		$1,620,920
Income taxes:		
Current	$280,901	
Deferred	269,117	550,018
Net income		$1,070,902

Once the income statement has been recast to reflect the translation gain, the statement of retained earnings would appear as follows:

Retained earnings—January 1, 20X6	$-0-
Add net income for the year	1,070,902
Deduct dividends for the year	(245,625)
Retained earnings—December 31, 20X6	$825,277

With this final step, the translation of the 20X6 financial statements is complete. It should be mentioned that there are alternative ways to compute the translation gain or loss. One method commonly used is to determine the net exposed asset or liability position in foreign currency and translate the detail causes of changes in the position from one year to the next. The author has decided to use the method shown above because it is simple and efficient.

Although somewhat lengthy, the translation of the 20X6 financial statements was relatively straightforward. Some new complexities are added when the translation of the 20X7 financial statements is undertaken.

The translation of the 20X7 financial statements will follow the same pattern as was used for the 20X6 statements. A review of the 20X7 current assets indicates two new accounts: Intercompany accounts receivable and Prepaid expenses (Table 8-8). The intercompany receivable should be translated at the reciprocal dollar balance on the parent's financial statement. In this case, American Manufacturing Company's payable is carried at $210,000, so this amount will be used to convert from the foreign currency to dollars. Prepaid expenses represent amounts carried at past exchange prices, and should be translated at the historical exchange rate in effect when the prepaid expense was incurred. For purposes of translation, assume that all the prepaid items were incurred on September 30, 20X7, when the exchange rate was FC1 = $.25. Inventories will be translated at historical rates, as in the previous translation. All other current assets represent cash or amounts receivable and will be translated at the current exchange rate on December 31, 20X7. The translation of the current assets for 20X7 is shown below:

	Foreign Currency Balance	Translation Rate	Dollar Balance
Cash	1,250,000	$ .245	$306,250
Accounts receivable—trade	3,902,500	$ .245	956,113
Accounts receivable—intercompany	942,500	–	210,000
Notes receivable	2,970,000	$ .245	727,650
Inventories	9,100,000	$ .25	2,275,000
Prepaid expenses	425,300	$ .25	106,325
Accrued interest	35,800	$ .245	8,771
Total current assets	18,626,100		$4,590,109

The long-term note receivable represents an amount receivable and will be translated at the current rate of FC1 = $.245. Recall that, in the 20X6 balance sheet, the long-term note was translated at the then current rate of FC1 = $.24. This is the type of exchange rate change that gives rise to the translation gains and losses. The long-term note will be translated into $1,470,000 (FC6,000,000 × $.245 = $1,470,000).

Although property, plant, and equipment will still be translated at the historical rate, notice that Foreign Enterprise has purchased some additional buildings, fixtures, and equipment during 20X7. These additions will be translated at a different historical rate than that used to translate the original acquisitions. The historical rate applicable to the new purchases of property, plant, and equipment is FC1 = $.245. The schedule below shows the detail translation of the buildings account:

Buildings Acquired in 20X6 (FC149,811,000 × $.25)	$37,452,750
Buildings Acquired in 20X7 (FC6,957,000 × $.245)	1,704,465
Translated Building Account	$39,157,215

The translated value of the fixtures and equipment would be determined in a similar manner, and is shown below:

Fixtures and Equipment Acquired in 20X6 (FC32,626,000 × $.25)	$8,156,500
Fixtures and Equipment Acquired in 20X7 (FC7,306,000 × $.245)	1,789,970
Translated Fixtures and Equipment Account	$9,946,470

Land would continue to be translated at the same rate used in 20X6.

The calculation of the proper dollar balance in the accumulated depreciation account is somewhat more complex than the procedure used for 20X6. For purposes of illustration, assume that Foreign Enterprise is using straight-line depreciation, and that there has been no plant retirement during 20X7. Under this set of assumptions, the balance in the accumulated depreciation account must be made up of the following elements:

Straight-line depreciation for 20X6	FC11,265,200
Straight-line depreciation for 20X7 on those assets acquired in 20X6	11,265,200
Straight-line depreciation for 20X7 on those assets acquired in 20X7	736,800
Foreign Currency Balance in Accumulated Depreciation	FC23,267,200

The depreciation associated with those assets acquired in 20X6 will be translated into dollars at the 20X6 exchange rate of FC1 = $.25, and the depreciation associated with the assets acquired in 20X7 will be translated at the historical rate of FC1 = $.245 (Table 8-11). Depreciation would be translated as follows:

Depreciation on Assets Acquired in 20X6 (FC11,265,200 × 2 years × $.25)	$5,632,600
Depreciation on Assets Acquired in 20X7 (FC736,800 × 1 year × $.245)	180,516
Accumulated Depreciation	$5,813,116

Based upon the above information, the property, plant, and equipment section of the 20X7 balance sheet would carry the following dollar values:

Land	$4,335,000
Buildings	39,157,215
Fixtures and equipment	9,946,470
Total property, plant, and equipment	$53,438,685
Accumulated depreciation	(5,813,116)
Net property, plant, and equipment	$47,625,569

Total assets, in dollars, can be determined by putting together the individual balance sheet sections.

Current assets	$4,590,109
Long-term notes receivable	1,470,000
Property, plant, and equipment	47,625,569
Total assets	$53,685,678

Maintaining records on plant additions and retirements is critical to the successful translation of property, plant, and equipment. The process of translation will become more complex as time passes.

All current liability accounts represent amounts payable, and are to be translated at the current exchange rate at December 31, 20X7. The conversion is shown below:

	Foreign Currency Balance	Translation Rate	Dollar Balance
Accounts payable	2,774,550	$.245	$679,765
Accrued interest	510,000	$.245	124,950
Income taxes payable	763,250	$.245	186,996
Dividends payable	500,000	$.245	122,500
Current maturities	2,500,000	$.245	612,500
Total current liabilities	7,047,800		$1,726,711

The long-term debt represents an amount payable, and is translated at the current exchange rate at December 31, 20X7. The foreign currency amount translates into $18,375,000 (FC75,000,000 × $.245 = $18,375,000).

The balance in the deferred income taxes account is made up of the carry-over from year 20X6 and the additional deferral recorded in the 20X7 income statement (FC762,700). The computations below show the proper method of translating the deferred income taxes account:

Deferred taxes resulting from 20X6 operations (FC1,096,200 × $.24)	$263,088
Deferred increase resulting from 20X7 operations (FC762,700 × $.245)	186,862
Deferred income taxes in dollars	$449,950

The final section of the 20X7 balance sheet to be translated is the stockholders' equity section. Because there have been no additional sales of common stock, the 20X7 balances will be the same as the 20X6 balances. Recall that the common stock was translated at $12,750,000, and the contributed capital in excess of par was translated at $19,681,512. It is now time to determine the residual value that will be assigned to the retained earnings account. The recap of liabilities and equities translated appears below:

Current liabilities	$1,726,711
Long-term debt	18,375,000
Deferred income taxes	449,950
Common stock	12,750,000
Contributed capital in excess of par	19,681,512
Total liabilities and equities translated	$52,983,173

This total now is compared with the total translated value of the assets to determine the balance in the retained earnings account. The comparison is shown below:

Translated value of assets	$53,685,678
Translated value of liabilities and equity accounts other than retained earnings	52,983,173
Retained earnings balance—12/31/X7	$702,505

Again, this is the residual value that is needed to equate total assets with total liabilities and stockholders' equity. This computation will be revisited when it comes time to consider any translation gains or losses.

The translation of the 20X7 income statement is shown below. The procedures for translation are similar to those used to translate the 20X6 income statements. Any difference will be explained.

Table 8-13 Income Statement Foreign Enterprise, Ltd. Year Ended December 31, 20X7

	Foreign Currency Balance	Translation Rate	Dollar Balance
Sales	84,075,500	$.2475	$20,808,686
Costs and Expenses:			
Cost of goods sold:			
Inventory—January 1	7,900,500	$.2425*	$1,915,871
Production costs	48,462,500	$.2475	11,994,468
Cost of goods available	56,363,000		$13,910,339
Inventory—December 31	(9,100,000)	$.25**	(2,275,000)
Cost of goods sold	47,263,000		$11,635,339
General and Administrative expense	9,731,400	$.2475	2,408,522
Advertising and selling	7,326,000	$.2475	1,813,185
Depreciation (see Schedule 1 below)	12,002,000		2,996,816
Total costs and expenses	76,322,400		$18,853,862
Income from operations	7,753,100		$1,954,824
Other income (expense)	(2,987,500)	$.2475	(739,406)
Income before taxes	4,765,600		$1,215,418
Income taxes:			
Current	1,143,700	$.2475	$283,066
Deferred	762,700	$.2475	188,768
Total taxes	1,906,400		$471,834
Net income	2,859,200		$743,584

* See 20X6 income statement

** See 20X7 balance sheet translation

Schedule 1 Calculation of Depreciation Expense for 20X7

Straight-line depreciation in 20X7 on assets acquired in 20X6 (FC11,265,200 × $.25)	$2,816,300
Straight-line depreciation in 20X7 on assets acquired in 20X7 (FC736,800 × $.245)	180,516
Depreciation expense—20X7	$2,996,816

As part of the detailed analysis of the statement of retained earnings for 20X7, it is necessary to translate the dividend in a manner similar to that used in 20X6. Assuming that FC500,000 of dividends are declared quarterly, the following computations are needed to translate the 20X7 dividends:

March 31 dividend (FC500,000 × $.245)	$122,500
June 30 dividend (FC500,000 × $.25)	125,000
September 30 dividend (FC500,000 × $.25)	125,000
December 31 dividend (FC500,000 × $.245)	122,500
Dividends for 20X7	$495,000

Based upon the information generated thus far for 20X7, the retained earnings account appears as follows:

Retained earnings—January 1	$825,277
Add net income for the year	743,584
Deduct dividends for the year	(495,000)
Retained earnings—December 31	$1,073,861

However, the retained earnings balance determined during the translation of the balance sheet was $702,505. Once again, the difference between the two balances must be the exchange gain or loss for the period. In this particular year, Foreign Enterprise experienced an exchange loss in the amount of $371,356 ($1,073,861 – $702,505). Once the loss has been determined, the income statement for 20X7 must be recast. The partial income statement is shown below:

Income from operations		$1,954,824
Nonoperating items:		
Other income (expense)	$(739,406)	
Translation loss	(371,356)	(1,110,762)
Income before taxes		$844,062
Income taxes		
Current	$283,066	
Deferred	188,768	471,834
Net income		$372,228

The final step is to restate net income in the statement of retained earnings for 20X7. This would be accomplished as follows:

Retained earnings—January 1	$825,277
Add net income for the year	372,228
Deduct dividends for the year	(495,000)
Retained earnings—December 31	$702,505

Tables 8-14 through 8-16 show the translated balance sheets, income statements, and statements of retained earnings for Foreign Enterprise, Ltd.

Table 8-14 Balance Sheet Foreign Enterprise, Ltd.
December 31, 20X7 and 20X6

	20X7	20X6
Current Assets:		
Cash	$306,250	$229,512
Accounts receivable—trade	956,113	586,488
Accounts receivable—intercompany	210,000	-0-
Notes receivable	727,650	240,000
Inventories	2,275,000	1,915,871
Prepaid expenses	106,325	-0-
Accrued interest on notes receivable	8,771	2,736
Total Current Assets	$4,590,109	$2,974,607
Long-Term Notes Receivable	$1,470,000	$1,440,000
Property, Plant, and Equipment:		
Land	$4,335,000	$4,335,000
Buildings	39,157,215	37,452,750
Fixtures and equipment	9,946,470	8,156,500
Total Property, Plant, and Equipment	$53,438,685	$49,944,250
Accumulated depreciation	(5,813,116)	(2,816,300)
Net Property, Plant, and Equipment	$47,625,569	$47,127,950
Total Assets	$53,685,678	$51,542,557
Current Liabilities:		
Accounts payable	$679,765	$870,720
Accrued interest on long-term debt	124,950	108,000
Income taxes payable	186,996	183,960
Dividends payable	122,500	60,000
Current maturities on long-term debt	612,500	600,000
Total Current Liabilities	$1,726,711	$1,822,680

	20X7	20X6
Long-Term Debt	$18,375,000	$16,200,000
Deferred Income Taxes	$449,950	$263,088
Stockholders' Equity		
Common stock	$12,750,000	$12,750,000
Contributed capital in excess of par	19,681,512	19,681,512
Retained earnings	702,505	825,277
Total Stockholders' Equity	$33,134,017	$33,256,789
Total Liabilities and Stockholders' Equity	$53,685,678	$51,542,557

Table 8-15 Income Statement Foreign Enterprise, Ltd. Years Ended December 31, 20X7 and 20X6

	20X7	20X6
Sales	$20,808,686	$17,989,258
Costs and Expenses:		
Cost of goods sold:		
Inventory—January 1	$1,915,871	$-0-
Production costs	11,994,468	12,266,554
Cost of goods available for sale	$13,910,339	$12,266,554
Inventory—December 31	(2,275,000)	(1,915,871)
Cost of goods sold	$11,635,339	$10,350,683
General and administrative	2,408,522	2,024,148
Advertising and selling	1,813,185	1,146,853
Depreciation	2,996,816	2,816,300
Total costs and expenses	$18,853,862	$16,337,984
Income from operations	$1,954,824	$1,651,274
Nonoperating items:		
Other income (expense)	$(739,406)	$(166,498)
Translation gain (loss)	(371,356)	136,144
Total nonoperating items	$(1,110,762)	$(30,354)
Income before income taxes	$844,062	$1,620,920
Income Taxes:		
Current	$283,066	$280,901
Deferred	188,768	269,117
Total Taxes	$471,834	$550,018
Net Income	$372,228	$1,070,902

Table 8-16 Statement of Retained Earnings Foreign Enterprise, Ltd. Years Ended December 31, 20X7 and 20X6

	20X7	20X6
Retained earnings—January 1	$825,277	$-0-
Add net income for the year	372,228	1,070,902
Deduct dividends for the year	(495,000)	(245,625)
Retained earnings—December 31	$702,505	$825,277

With some supplemental information and the translated financial statements, American Manufacturing Company, the parent, could prepare the necessary statement of cash flow for Foreign Enterprise, Ltd.

Second Example: Translation Process When Foreign Currency Is the Functional Currency

The first example illustrated the translation process when the U.S. dollar was determined to be the functional currency. This second example is designed to illustrate the translation of foreign currency financial statements when the local foreign currency is determined to be the functional currency, and the U.S. dollar is to be the reporting currency. The basic information to be translated is the same as shown in Tables 8-8 through 8-10. The exchange rate information is located in Table 8-11 and Chart 8-1 provides information as to the appropriate exchange rate to use when translating specific accounts. Before going on with this second example, take a few moments and review the information found in these Tables 8-8 through 8-10 and Chart 8-1.

As the translation process progresses, it will prove very beneficial to refer back to the previous example to note any significant differences or similarities in the translated amounts. Remember that the current exchange rate will be used to translate most balance sheet accounts, and the average for the period rate will be used to translate most revenues and expenses. From this standpoint, the translation process is much easier to follow.

Once again, the translation will begin with the 20X6 financial statements of Foreign Enterprises, Ltd. To provide the reader with new insights, the income statement (see Table 8-17) is translated first.

Table 8-17 Income Statement Foreign Enterprise, Ltd. Year Ended December 31, 20X6

	Foreign Currency Balance	Translation Rate	Dollar Balance
Sales	73,276,000	.2455	$17,989,258
Costs and Expenses:			
Cost of Goods Sold:			
Inventory—January 1	0		0
Production costs	49,965,600	.2455	12,266,554
Cost of goods available for sale	49,965,600		$12,266,554
Inventory—December 31	(7,900,500)	.2455	(1,939,573)
Cost of goods sold	42,065,100		$10,326,981
General and administrative	8,245,000	.2455	2,024,148
Advertising and selling	4,671,500	.2455	1,146,853
Depreciation	11,265,200	.2455	2,765,607
Total costs and expenses	66,246,800		$16,263,589
Net income from operations	7,029,200		$1,725,669
Nonoperating items:			
Other income (expense)	(678,200)	.2455	(166,498)
Other income (expense)			
Net income before income taxes	6,351,000		$1,559,171
Income Taxes:			
Current	1,144,200	.2455	$280,901
Deferred	1,096,200	.2455	269,117
Total Taxes	2,240,400		$550,018
Net Income	4,110,600		$1,009,153

The translated income statement does not contain a translation gain or loss line-item. When the local foreign currency is determined to be the functional currency, translation gains and losses are reported as an element of other comprehensive income. All items on the income statement have been translated at the average for the period exchange rate. Historical rates did not enter into the translation process. As a result of these differences, income is translated at $1,009,153, rather than $1,070,902 when the U.S. dollar was considered the functional currency.

Next, the retained earnings statement is translated. Table 8-18 reflects the translated amounts for 20X6. The only item that needs to be discussed is the translation of the dividend payment. Dividends are to be translated using the exchange rate in effect on the date of declaration, so dividends are translated at the same amount regardless of the functional currency used. Some accountants have suggested that dividends be translated at the average for the period exchange rate, while others advocate using the rate in effect on the date of declaration.

Table 8-18 Statement of Retained Earnings Foreign Enterprises, Ltd. Year Ended December 31, 20X6

Retained earnings—January 1	$0
Add net income for the year	1,009,153
Deduct dividends for the year	(245,625)
Retained earnings—December 31	$763,528

Once the translation of the retained earnings statement has been completed, the December 31, 20X6 balance can be transferred to the balance sheet. The next step in the translation process is to complete the translation of the 20X6 balance sheet. This translation is shown in Table 8-19.

Table 8-19 Balance Sheet Foreign Enterprise, Ltd. December 31, 20X6

	Foreign Currency Balance	Translation Rate	Dollar Balance
Current Assets:			
Cash	956,300	.24	$229,512
Accounts receivable—trade	2,443,700	.24	586,488
Notes receivable	1,000,000	.24	240,000
Inventories	7,900,500	.24	1,896,120
Accrued interest on notes receivable	11,400	.24	2,736
Total Current Assets	12,311,900		$2,954,856
Long-Term Notes Receivable	6,000,000	.24	$1,440,000
Property, Plant, and Equipment:			
Land	17,000,000	.24	$4,080,000
Buildings	149,811,000	.24	35,954,640
Fixtures and equipment	32,626,000	.24	7,830,240
Total Property, Plant, and Equipment	199,437,000	.24	$47,864,880
Accumulated depreciation	(11,265,200)	.24	(2,703,648)
Net Property, Plant, and Equipment	188,171,800		$45,161,232
Total Assets	206,483,700		$49,556,088
Current Liabilities:			
Accounts payable	3,628,000	.24	$870,720
Accrued interest on long-term debt	450,000	.24	108,000
Income taxes payable	766,500	.24	183,960
Dividends payable	250,000	.24	60,000
Current maturities on long-term debt	2,500,000	.24	600,000
Total Current Liabilities	7,594,500		$1,822,680

	Foreign Currency Balance	Translation Rate	Dollar Balance
Long-Term Debt	67,500,000	.24	$16,200,000
Deferred Income Taxes	1,096,200	.24	$263,088
Stockholders' Equity			
Common Stock	50,000,000	.255	$12,750,000
Contributed capital in excess of par	77,182,400	.255	19,681,512
Retained Earnings	3,110,600		763,528[1]
Translation adjustment[2]			(1,924,720)
Total Stockholders' Equity	130,293,000		$31,270,320
Total Liabilities and Stockholders' Equity	206,483,700		$49,556,088

[1] Taken from the retained earnings statement, Table 8-18.
[2] Translation adjustment would first be included in other comprehensive income prior to closing to stockholders' equity.

The translation adjustment of $(1,924,720) shown in Table 8-19 was determined by plugging the difference between total assets and total liabilities plus stockholders' equity, except for the translation adjustment. The translation adjustment may be computed directly by using the process presented in Table 8-20.

Table 8-20 Computation of Translation Adjustment[1] for 20X6

Total Assets—Foreign Currency	206,483,700
Total Liabilities—Foreign Currency	
Current	7,594,500
Long-term Debt	67,500,000
Deferred Income Taxes	1,096,200
Total Liabilities	76,190,700
Net Assets—Foreign Currency	130,293,000
End of Period Exchange Rate	.24
Net Assets in Dollars	$31,270,320
Stockholders' Equity—Dollars	
Common Stock	$12,750,000
Contributed Capital in Excess of Par	19,681,512
Retained Earnings	763,528
Total Stockholders' Equity in Dollars	33,195,040
Translation Adjustment	$1,924,720

[1] All information for the translation adjustment was taken from the balance sheet in Table 8-19.

This completes the translation process for Foreign Enterprise's 20X6 financial statements. The entity's 20X7 statements are translated in Tables 8-21 through 8-24. No new items, needing explanation, appear in the statements. Because the 20X7 statements are translated in the same manner as the 20X6 statements, no discussion is necessary. The reader is encouraged to work through the computations in the 20X7 translation and compare translated amounts to the 20X7 statements translated using the U.S. dollar as the functional currency.

Table 8-21 Income Statement Foreign Enterprise, Ltd. Year Ended December 31, 20X7

	Foreign Currency Balance	Translation Rate	Dollar Balance
Sales	84,075,500	.2475	$20,808,686
Costs and Expenses:			
Cost of goods sold:			
Inventory—January 1	7,900,500	.2475	$1,955,374
Production Costs	48,462,500	.2475	11,994,468
Cost of goods available for sale	56,363,000		$13,949,842
Inventory—December 31	(9,100,000)	.2475	(2,252,250)
Cost of goods sold	47,263,000		$11,697,592
General and administrative	9,731,400	.2475	2,408,522
Advertising and selling	7,326,000	.2475	1,813,185
Depreciation	12,002,000	.2475	2,970,495
Total costs and expenses	76,322,400		$18,889,794
Income from operations	7,753,100		$1,918,892
Nonoperating items:			
Other income (expense)	(2,987,500)	.2475	(739,406)
Income before income taxes	4,765,600		$1,179,486
Income Taxes:			
Current	1,143,700	.2475	$283,066
Deferred	762,700	.2475	188,768
Total Taxes	1,906,400		$471,834
Net Income	2,859,200	.2475	$707,652

Table 8-22 Statement of Retained Earnings Foreign Enterprise, Ltd. Year Ended December 31, 20X7

Retained earnings—January 1	$763,528[1]
Add net income for the year	707,652[2]
Deduct dividends for the year	(495,000)[3]
Retained earnings—December 31	$976,180

[1] Taken from the 20X6 retained earnings statement, Table 8-14.
[2] See the 20X7 income in Table 8-21.
[3] Dividends are computed in the same manner as in the section using the dollar as the functional currency. See the previous section for the $495,000 dividend payment.

Table 8-23 Balance Sheet Foreign Enterprise, Ltd. December 31, 20X7

	Foreign Currency Balance	Translation Rate	Dollar Balance
Current Assets:			
Cash	1,250,000	.245	$306,250
Accounts receivable—trade	3,902,500	.245	956,113
Accounts receivable—intercompany	942,500	.245	230,913
Notes receivable	2,970,000	.245	727,650
Inventories	9,100,000	.245	2,229,500
Prepaid expenses	425,300	.245	104,199
Accrued interest on notes receivable	35,800	.245	8,771
Total Current Assets	18,626,100		$4,563,396
Long-Term Notes Receivable	6,000,000		$1,470,000
Property, Plant, and Equipment:			
Land	17,000,000	.245	$4,165,000
Buildings	156,768,000	.245	38,408,160
Fixtures and equipment	39,932,000	.245	9,783,340
Total Property, Plant, and Equipment	213,700,000		$52,356,500
Accumulated depreciation	(23,267,200)	.245	(5,700,464)
Net Property, Plant, and Equipment	190,432,800		$46,656,036
Total Assets	215,058,900		$52,689,432
Current Liabilities:			
Accounts payable	2,774,550	.245	$679,765
Accrued interest on long-term debt	510,000	.245	124,950

	Foreign Currency Balance	Translation Rate	Dollar Balance
Income taxes payable	763,250	.245	186,996
Dividends payable	500,000	.245	122,500
Current maturities on long-term debt	2,500,000	.245	612,500
Total Current Liabilities	7,047,800		$1,726,711
Long-Term Debt	75,000,000	.245	$18,375,000
Deferred Income Taxes	1,858,900	.245	$455,432
Stockholders' Equity			
Common stock	50,000,000	.255	$12,750,000
Contributed capital in excess of par	77,182,400	.255	19,681,512
Retained earnings	3,969,800		976,180[1]
Translation adjustment[2]			(1,275,403)
Total Stockholders' Equity	131,152,200		$32,132,289
Total Liabilities and Stockholders' Equity	215,058,900		$52,689,432

[1] Taken from the retained earnings statement, Table 8-22.
[2] See Footnote 2 in Table 8-19.

Table 8-24 Computation of Translation Adjustment[1] for 20X7

Total Assets—Foreign Currency	215,058,900
Total Liabilities—Foreign Currency	
Current	7,047,800
Long-term Debt	75,000,000
Deferred Income Taxes	1,858,900
Total Liabilities	83,906,700
Net Assets—Foreign Currency	131,152,200
End of period exchange rate	.245
Net assets in dollars	$32,132,298
Stockholders' Equity—Dollars	
Common Stock	$12,750,000
Contributed Capital in Excess of Par	19,681,512
Retained Earnings	976,180
Total Stockholders' Equity in Dollars	33,407,692
Translation Adjustment	$1,275,403

[1] All information for the translation adjustment was taken from the 20X7 balance sheet in Table 8-23.

Derecognition from Sale or Liquidation of an Investment in a Foreign Entity

ASU 2013-05, *Foreign Currency Matters (Topic 830): Parent's Accounting for the Cumulative Translation Adjustment upon Derecognition of Certain Subsidiaries or Groups of Assets within a Foreign Entity or of an Investment in a Foreign Entity,* provides that upon sale or upon complete or substantially complete liquidation of an investment in a foreign entity, the reporting entity should remove the cumulative currency translation adjustment attributable to that investment from the reporting entity's separate component of equity and include that amount as part of the gain or loss on sale or liquidation of the investment in the period the sale or liquidation occurs. Under the requirements of ASU 2013-05 the parent recognizes the cumulative translation adjustment (CTA) when it ceases to have a controlling financial interest in a foreign subsidiary. Further, upon the sale of a portion of an investment accounted for by the equity method, the investor reporting entity would recognize in operations the pro rata portion of the CTA.

Disclosures

ASC 830-20-50 and ASC 830-30-50 specify the disclosure requirements for foreign currency transactions and financial statement translations. The required disclosures include:

1. The aggregate gains or losses from foreign currency transactions used in determining net income for the period.
2. A rate change that occurs after the date of the reporting entity's financial statements or after the date of the foreign currency statements of a foreign entity if they are consolidated, combined, or accounted for by the equity method in the financial statements of the reporting entity and its effects on unsettled balances pertaining to foreign currency transactions, if significant. (If disclosed, include consideration of changes in unsettled transactions from the date of the financial statements to the date the rate changed. In some cases it may not be practicable to determine these changes; if so, that fact shall be stated.)
3. The changes during the period in the accumulated amount of translation adjustments reported in equity including:
   a. The beginning and ending amount of the cumulative translation adjustments;
   b. The aggregate adjustment for the period resulting from translation adjustments and gains and losses from certain hedges and intra-entity balances;
   c. The amount of income taxes for the period allocated to translation adjustments; and
   d. The amounts transferred from cumulative translation adjustments and included in determining net income for the period as a result of the sale or complete or substantially complete liquidation of an investment in a foreign entity.

Topic 835: Interest

Topic 835, *Interest*, contains 10 subtopics:

10 Overall

20 Capitalization of Interest

30 Imputation of Interest

912 Contractors—Federal Government*

922 Entertainment—Cable Television*

926 Entertainment—Films*

932 Extractive Activities—Oil and Gas*

970 Real Estate—General*

974 Real Estate—Real Estate Investment Trusts*

980 Regulated Operations*

* See the corresponding topic in Chapter 9 for coverage of this shared subtopic.

Capitalization of Interest—Introduction

Under certain defined circumstances, it is appropriate to capitalize interest cost (i.e., the cost of debt) rather than to treat it as a period cost. When capitalized, interest cost is treated as part of the cost of an asset acquired or constructed.

ASC 835-20 defines certain key terms, some of which are as follows (and others will be introduced during the discussion of Flowchart 8-3, later in this chapter):

1. **Interest Cost (ASC 835-20-20):** The term interest cost is meant to include the following:

    a. Interest expense computed on liabilities that have interest rates that are explicit,

    b. Interest expense imputed on liabilities in accordance with the provisions of ASC 835-30,

    c. Interest expense computed on obligations of capital leases in accordance with ASC 840-30.

2. **Qualifying Asset (ASC 835-20-15-5):** A qualifying asset is one for which interest capitalization is appropriate. Qualifying assets include:

    a. Assets that an entity constructs or produces for its own use, including those assets that others construct or produce for use by the entity, assuming the entity has made progress payments or deposits.

    b. Assets resulting from discrete activities (such as the construction of a major shopping center) that the entity expects to lease or sell.

c. Investments subject to equity method accounting if the investee company meets the following two requirements: (1) activities that will start planned operations are ongoing and (2) such activities include using funds for qualifying asset acquisitions.

ASC 932-835-25-1 identifies qualifying assets for oil and gas producing companies using the full cost accounting method. Assets not qualifying for interest capitalization include assets currently being depreciated, depleted, or amortized. Qualifying assets are: significant development ventures and significant unproved property investments where activities (development and exploration) are ongoing, but the properties are not currently subject to depletion, amortization, or depreciation and significant projects where activities (development and exploration) are ongoing, but there is no production in the cost center.

3. **Capitalization Period:** The capitalization period represents the length of time during which it is appropriate to capitalize interest on a qualifying asset. This time period encompasses all the activities required to bring a qualifying asset to the condition and location necessary for its intended use. A problem is created for accountants because the capitalization period may include several fiscal periods or merely a part of one fiscal period. Interest capitalization will require the same type of allocations as accountants often make for other costs that do not coincide with a company's accounting period. In the technical examples that appear later in this section, interest capitalization may require certain estimations and/or allocations depending upon the circumstances faced in a given case.

The capitalization period does not begin until the following three conditions have been met (ASC 835-20-25-3):

1. Expenditures have been made for a qualifying asset.
2. Necessary activities have started to prepare the asset for its use.
3. Interest expense has been incurred.

Remember that all three of these conditions must be met before it is appropriate to begin the capitalization of interest.

The capitalization period ends when a qualifying asset is substantially complete and ready for its intended use. More will be said about the capitalization period during the discussion of Flowchart 8-3.

4. **Capitalization Rate (ASC 835-20-20):** The amount of interest to be capitalized during any given accounting period is determined by multiplying the capitalization rate times the *average accumulated expenditures* made on a qualifying asset. The amount of the average accumulated expenditures would be determined from the beginning of the capitalization period until the date the asset was complete and ready for use. Recall from the previous discussion that interest may be capitalized for more than one accounting period if the qualifying asset is not ready for its intended use.

If an enterprise borrowed money specifically for the construction or production of a qualifying asset, the rate of interest on the specific borrowing should be used as the capitalization rate for the qualifying asset in question. If the company incurred no specific new borrowing for the qualifying asset, the weighted average rate of interest on all borrowed funds should be used as the capitalization rate. A more refined definition of the capitalization rate is provided in the discussion of Flowchart 8-3.

5. **Expenditures (ASC 835-20-20):** For an amount to qualify as an expenditure on a qualifying asset, the amount expended must be in the form of cash, an asset transfer other than cash, or a liability that requires recognition of interest expense. Liabilities, such as trade payables and accruals, are not qualifying expenditures. They become qualifying expenditures when the trade payable or accrual is settled by transferring cash or another asset in settlement of the trade payable or accrual.

With this introduction to some of the key terms of ASC 835-20, attention may be turned to an examination of Flowchart 8-3, which is designed to demonstrate how each of the terms defined above impact the accountant's decision-making process.

Capitalization of Interest—Flowchart and General Discussion

The first step in the decision-making process is for the accountant to determine whether the asset acquired or constructed by the entity is one that qualifies for interest capitalization (i.e., a qualifying asset) (Block 1). A description of qualifying assets has been given previously and no additional discussion is necessary. Once it has been determined that the entity has a qualifying asset, the next step is to determine if the capitalization period has begun. Identification of the proper capitalization period is a complex process and requires several blocks in Flowchart 8-3. Before it is appropriate to capitalize interest in the current accounting period, three conditions must be met.

Flowchart 8-3

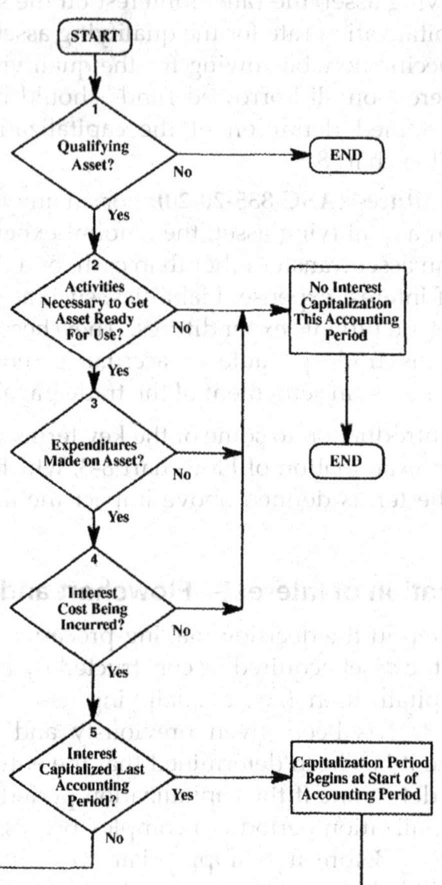

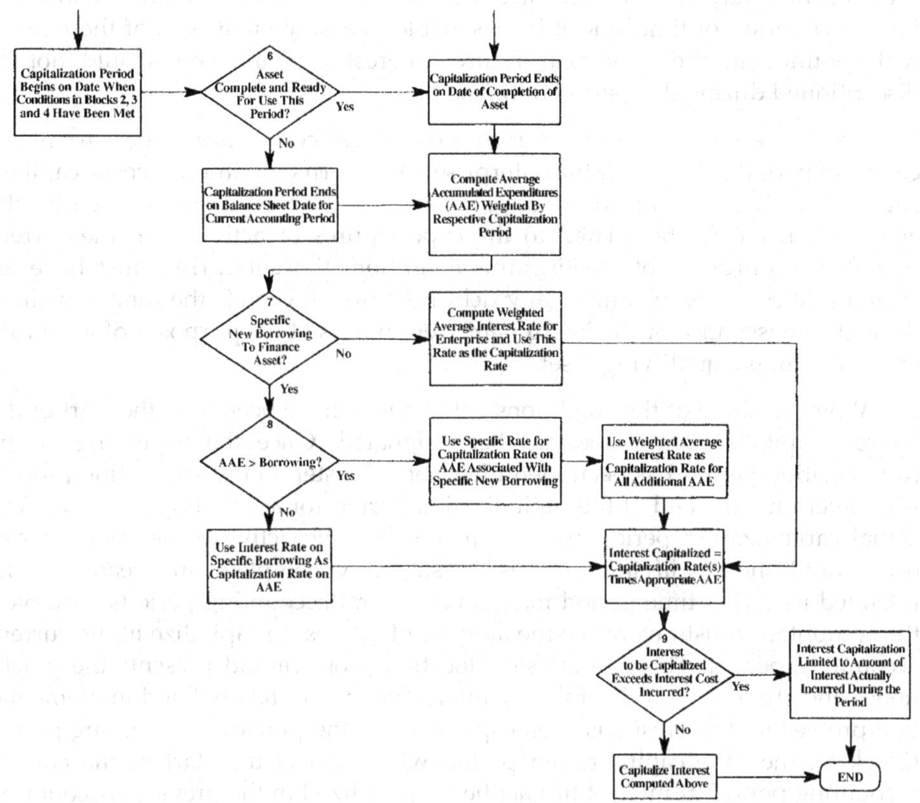

First, the entity must have undertaken activities that are necessary to make the qualifying asset ready for its intended use (Block 2). The word "activities" is meant to encompass a broad range of functions that relate to the asset and includes any steps needed to get the asset ready for its use (ASC 835-20-20). In addition to physical construction, the following items are considered activities for purposes of meeting the first condition:

1. Preconstruction period activities of a technical or administrative nature, such as plan development and securing permits from governmental agencies.
2. Activities subsequent to the start of construction to overcome situations, such as technical and labor problems, that were not anticipated at the inception of the project.

"Activities" includes work during the preconstruction stage, work during the construction phase, and some post-construction work. Certainly the construction of a nuclear power plant would involve substantial costs of obtaining governmental permits and costs relating to unforeseen obstacles.

Second, the entity must have incurred qualifying expenditures in connection with a qualifying asset (Block 3). If an enterprise has ceased activities or expenditures on a qualifying asset, no interest should be capitalized in that particular accounting period. When activities and expenditures have started again, interest capitalization may resume. If the activities or expenditures have been suspended for a *brief* period of time, and it is reasonable to assume that both of these items will continue in the very near future, interest capitalization should not be discontinued during this period of time.

Third, the entity must have incurred interest costs during the current accounting period (Block 4). If the enterprise has incurred no interest costs, capitalization of interest would not be appropriate. The interest costs incurred by the enterprise need not be related to the expenditures or activities in the current period. For purposes of meeting this condition, the enterprise must have incurred interest costs relating to any debt instrument, even if the funds obtained through the issuance of the instrument were not used for purposes of acquiring or constructing a qualifying asset.

When all three of the conditions listed above have been met, the start of the interest capitalization period has been signaled. Once the beginning of the capitalization period has been identified, the next step in the accounting process is to determine the end of the capitalization period for accounting purposes. The actual capitalization period runs from the date the activities described above occur until the qualifying asset is substantially complete and ready for its intended use. This time period may cover several accounting periods; however, the accountant must determine the amount of interest to capitalize in the current accounting period. This is a classic allocation problem and presents the practitioner and student with several very interesting computational and implementation problems. If interest has been capitalized in the previous accounting period (Block 5), then the capitalization period will begin at the start of the current accounting period. If interest has *not* been capitalized in the previous accounting period, the capitalization period will begin on the date when the three conditions discussed above have been met (i.e., activities undertaken, expenditures made, and interest costs incurred).

To identify the end of the capitalization period for current accounting purposes it is necessary to determine whether the asset has been substantially completed and made ready for use in the current period (Block 6). If the qualifying asset has been completed in the current period, the capitalization period ends on the date of completion of the asset. If the asset has not been completed in the current accounting period, the capitalization period ends on the balance sheet date of the current period. It is important to determine the appropriate capitalization period for accounting purposes. If interest is to be capitalized in the current accounting period, the accountant must know the proper time period for which capitalization is appropriate.

Once the proper capitalization period has been determined, the accountant must next compute the *average accumulated expenditures* that have been made on the qualifying asset. Although ASC 835-20 does not provide specific guidance as to the computation of the average accumulated expenditures, the author believes that a weighted average is the appropriate technique to apply. Practitioners are free to choose other techniques for computing the average accumulated expenditures; the final method adopted should be rational and provide a reasonable basis for interest capitalization. By selecting a weighted average technique for this computation, the author has provided some flexibility in terms of the time period to use in the weighting process (i.e., the expenditures may be weighted on a daily, weekly, monthly, or some other periodic basis depending upon the materiality of the expenditures incurred by the enterprise). Computation of the weighted average accumulated expenditures will be shown in detail in the example material that follows.

For discussion purposes, it is sufficient to say that each individual expenditure should be weighted for its *unique* capitalization period. Each expenditure made on a qualifying asset will have its own capitalization period. If the entity elects to weight the expenditures on a daily basis, all expenditures incurred on any given day will be weighted from that date to the end of the capitalization period. Expenditures made on the following day would have a different capitalization period. This same logic applies for weekly or monthly weighting. Once the capitalization period has been determined and the amount of the expenditures subject to capitalization has been calculated, the final step in the accounting process is to determine the proper capitalization rate.

If the entity has incurred specific new borrowings to finance the acquisition or construction of the qualifying asset, the interest rate associated with the new borrowing *may* be selected as the capitalization rate (Block 7). The interest rate on the new borrowing will be used as the capitalization rate as long as the average accumulated expenditures associated with the new borrowing *do not* exceed the amount of the new borrowing (Block 8). If the average accumulated expenditures exceed the amount of the new borrowing, the entity will have two capitalization rates. The rate of interest on the new borrowings will be used as the capitalization rate for the average accumulated expenditures associated with the new borrowing and the weighted average interest rate from all borrowings will be used as the capitalization rate for all other average accumulated expenditures. In this case, it is necessary for the entity to compute the weighted average interest rate on all borrowings.

If the entity has not incurred any new borrowing specifically for the purpose of financing the qualifying asset, the weighted average interest rate will be used as the capitalization rate (Block 7). ASC 835-20-30-2 states that the interest to be capitalized should be an amount that would not have been incurred if the entity had not made the asset expenditures. This conclusion leads the author to believe that the weighted average interest rate should be reflective of the current interest costs the enterprise *might* incur if it borrowed funds to finance the acquisition of the qualifying asset. Therefore, some judgment is required when calculating the weighted average interest rate. This interest rate must reflect only current interest rates if the requirements of ASC 835-20-30-2 are to be met.

Once the capitalization period has been determined, the average accumulated expenditures calculated, and the capitalization rate(s) identified, the final step in the computational process is to compute the interest to be capitalized. When this amount has been computed, the final decision in the accounting process involves a comparison of the interest capitalized with the actual interest costs incurred during the period (Block 9). The amount of interest that may be capitalized during any accounting period is limited to the amount of interest actually incurred. If the amount of interest capitalized is less than the actual interest incurred, there are no further decisions or entries to be made. If the amount of interest capitalized is greater than the interest incurred, the amount capitalized must be adjusted to the amount of interest incurred. In this case, all interest incurred will be capitalized and there will be no interest charged to income. The capitalized interest is charged to depreciation expense over the life of the asset in the same manner as the other cost components of the asset.

This general discussion of Flowchart 8-3 was designed to aid in the understanding of the nature of the interest capitalization process. However, as is seen in the technical material that follows, many new and difficult accounting problems must be solved before a complete understanding of the process can be obtained.

Technical Considerations Involved in the Interest Capitalization Process

To illustrate the specific computational and accounting problems associated with interest capitalization, five examples will be fully developed. Assumptions for Example 8-16 are as follows.

Example 8-16
Interest Capitalization Assumptions

1. Maddan, Inc., a December 31 year-end company, was involved in several long-term construction or asset purchase activities during 20X6.

2. On January 1, 20X6, a $500,000 advance payment was made to Clair Company for equipment to be delivered to Maddan, Inc. on July 1, 20X6. The equipment was delivered as scheduled and the final $500,000 payment was made on that date. Maddan, Inc. borrowed the $500,000 advance payment and the $500,000 final payment. The rate of interest associated with these borrowings was 12%.

3. On April 1, 20X6, construction was started on an addition to the current plant facilities. The addition was to be completed on March 1, 20X7 at an estimated cost of $10,000,000. Cash payments made during 20X6 relating to the construction project were as follows:

May 1, 20X6	$1,200,000
July 1, 20X6	400,000
August 1, 20X6	900,000
October 1, 20X6	5,000,000
November 1, 20X6	600,000
	$8,100,000

Maddan, Inc. had established a line of credit for the construction project that allowed the company to borrow up to $10,000,000 anytime during 20X6 and 20X7. The rate of interest associated with the line of credit was 13%.

4. Total interest costs incurred during 20X6 amounted to $500,000.

The first problem associated with the material presented in Example 8-16 is to determine whether the assets described are qualifying assets as defined in ASC 835-20. The equipment purchased on July 1, 20X6, is a qualifying asset because it is an asset that was produced by an outside entity for Maddan, Inc.'s use, and thus qualifies under ASC 835-20-15-5(a). The fact that an entity has acquired a qualifying asset does not mean that interest will be capitalized. Before it is appropriate to capitalize interest, the accountant must determine whether the qualifying asset meets the conditions specified for the capitalization period to begin. The plant facilities being constructed for Maddan, Inc.'s use also qualify under ASC 835-20-15-5(a). In this particular example, both of the assets described are qualifying assets.

The next step in the analysis of Example 8-16 is to determine if the conditions needed for interest capitalization have been met. Maddan, Inc. has undertaken activities necessary to make both assets ready for their intended use (i.e., the construction or purchase of the asset has begun). In addition, Maddan, Inc. has incurred expenditures in connection with both of the assets *and* the company has incurred interest during the current accounting period. All three of the conditions necessary to begin the capitalization of interest have been met.

Next, the proper capitalization period must be determined. This is a complex problem and will be discussed in some detail. Because the acquisition of both assets was started this accounting period, no interest was capitalized last period. The capitalization period will begin on a qualifying asset on the date the three conditions described above—activities undertaken, expenditures incurred, and interest incurred—have been met.

In the case of the equipment acquired on July 1, 20X6, the capitalization period begins on January 1, 20X6 and ends on July 1, 20X6, the date the asset was delivered and made ready for its intended use. Thus the capitalization period for the equipment is one-half of the current accounting period (January 1 through July 1, 20X6).

The equipment will be analyzed first. To compute the average accumulated expenditures, each individual expenditure must be weighted from the date it was incurred until the end of the capitalization period. The $500,000 expenditure made on January 1, 20X6 has been outstanding from the beginning of the capitalization period to the end of the period (six months) and should be weighted accordingly. The $500,000 final payment was made on the date the equipment was delivered and made ready for use. The average accumulated expenditures would be computed as follows:

Date of Expenditure[a]	*Amount*[a]	*Capitalization Period*[b]	*Average Expenditure*
January 1	$500,000	6/12	$250,000[c]
July 1	500,000	0/12	—0—
			$250,000

[a] See Example 8-17, Item 2.
[b] Period from date of expenditure to July 1, 20X6.
[c] $500,000 × 6/12 = $250,000.

After the amount of the average accumulated expenditures has been computed, the appropriate capitalization rate must be selected. Because Maddan, Inc. entered into a specific new borrowing agreement for the acquisition of the equipment, the capitalization rate *may* be the rate of interest associated with the new borrowing. The average accumulated expenditures of $250,000 are less than the amount of the new borrowing of $1,000,000, therefore, the 12% interest rate on the borrowing should be used as the capitalization rate.

The final step in the computational process is to calculate the amount of interest to capitalize in relation to the equipment. The calculation would be made as follows:

Average Accumulated Expenditures	$250,000
Capitalization Rate	× 12%
Interest to be Capitalized	$30,000

The journal entries to record the progress payment on January 1, 20X6, would be as follows:

Progress Payment on Constructed Asset	500,000	
Cash		500,000

The journal entry to record the final payment for the equipment of July 1, 20X6 would be:

Progress Payment on Constructed Asset	500,000	
Cash		500,000

The journal entry to record the interest to be capitalized and to transfer the asset into service would be:

Equipment	1,030,000	
Progress Payment on Constructed Asset		1,000,000
Interest Incurred		30,000

The author believes that it is important for an enterprise to use an interest suspense or clearing account as a result of ASC 835-20. The Interest Incurred account is such a suspense account. All interest incurred during the period should be charged to the suspense account instead of interest expense. The account will be cleared by debits to either an asset account (as shown above) or to interest expense and a credit to the suspense account. This type of accounting facilitates the allocation procedures required by ASC 835-20. The use of a suspense account should prove very beneficial if the entity prepares interim financial statements and capitalizes interest in the interim period.

This last set of journal entries completes the analysis of the equipment described in Example 8-16. The remaining item requiring analysis is the expansion of the existing plant facilities of Maddan, Inc. Once again, the company has undertaken activities to make the asset ready for its intended use, made expenditures in connection with the plant facilities, and incurred interest during the period. Because all three conditions required for interest capitalization have been met, interest capitalization is appropriate in the current accounting period (20X6). Because there was no interest capitalized on the plant construction last period, the capitalization period begins on the first date that all the conditions described above have been met.

In this case, there will be a different capitalization period for each individual expenditure incurred. When thinking about the capitalization period, it is important to remember that each individual expenditure has its own unique capitalization period. These differing capitalization periods will impact the computation of the average accumulated expenditures on the project. Because the construction has not been completed by the end of the current accounting period, the capitalization period for all expenditures will end on the balance sheet date (December 31, 20X6).

In the computation of the average accumulated expenditures relating to the plant facilities, each individual expenditure will be weighted from the date it was incurred to the balance sheet date. For example, the first expenditure was incurred on May 1, 20X6 and amounted to $1,200,000. This expenditure must be weighted from May 1 to December 31, 20X6, or a period of eight months. The computation of the average accumulated expenditures for the plant facilities is shown below:

Date of Expenditure[a]	*Amount*[a]	*Capitalization Period*[b]	*Average Expenditure*
May 1, 20X6	$1,200,000	8/12	$800,000[c]
July 1, 20X6	400,000	6/12	200,000
August 1, 20X6	900,000	5/12	375,000
October 1, 20X6	5,000,000	3/12	1,250,000
November 1, 20X6	600,000	2/12	100,000
	$8,100,000		$2,725,000

[a] See Example 8-17, Item 3.
[b] Period from date of expenditure to December 31, 20X6.
[c] $1,200,000 × 8/12 = $800,000.

Once the average accumulated expenditures have been calculated, the next step is to determine the proper capitalization rate(s). Maddan, Inc.'s line of credit for the construction of the plant facility represents a specific new borrowing intended to finance the asset. The amount of the new borrowing ($8,100,000) is more than the amount of the average accumulated expenditures ($2,725,000); therefore, the capitalization rate will be the 13% associated with the line of credit. The amount of interest capitalized in connection with the plant facilities in 20X6 would be computed in the following manner:

Average Accumulated Expenditures	$2,725,000
Capitalization Rate	× 13%
Interest Capitalized	$354,250

The journal entry necessary to record the interest computed above would be:

Construction in Progress-Plant Facility	354,250	
Interest Incurred		354,250

The balance in the construction in progress-plant facility account at December 31, 20X6 is $8,454,250 ($8,100,000 expenditures + $354,250 interest).

The total amount of interest capitalized during 20X6 was $384,250 ($354,250 on plant facility + $30,000 on equipment). The total amount of interest incurred in 20X6 by Maddan, Inc. was $500,000. Therefore, the interest incurred was greater than the interest capitalized and no adjustment to the amounts capitalized is required. The balance in the interest incurred account at December 31, 20X6 is $115,750 ($500,000 incurred – $384,250 capitalized). Because no additional interest will be capitalized in 20X6, the balance in the suspense account would be cleared through a charge to interest expense for the period. The journal entry necessary to clear the suspense account at the end of the accounting period would be:

Interest Expense	115,750	
Interest Incurred		115,750

Of the $500,000 interest incurred during 20X6, $384,250 has been capitalized as part of the cost of qualifying assets and $115,750 has been charged to income as interest expense.

The assumptions established for Example 8-16 were designed to be relatively straightforward. The primary concerns of the material were to introduce the concept of the capitalization period, the computation of the average accumulated expenditures, and the selection of the appropriate capitalization rate where the enterprise financed the construction or purchase of the asset through the issuance of new borrowings. There are several complicating factors that have not been discussed. Example 8-17 is designed to introduce some additional new concepts and computations required of accountants under the provisions of ASC 835-20. The new decision requirements introduced in Example 8-17 deal with the following problems:

1. Interest capitalization on land.
2. The impact of issuing noninterest-bearing notes in exchange for qualifying assets.
3. Selection of the proper capitalization rate when qualifying assets are purchased with the proceeds from the sale of stock.
4. Accounting for interest to be capitalized when the amount of interest capitalized exceeds the amount of interest actually incurred during the period.

Assumptions for Example 8-17 are as follows.

Example 8-17
Interest Capitalization Assumptions

1. Tract Development Corporation (Tract), a December 31 year-end company, was involved in certain construction and development activities during 20X7.

2. A parcel of land was purchased on January 1, 20X7 for $3,000,000 cash. The land is being held for a future plant site. During 20X7, no activities were performed on the land to make it ready for its intended use.

3. On April 1, 20X7, Tract purchased another parcel of land for $5,000,000 cash and a noninterest-bearing note for $4,000,000. The note is to be repaid in full at the end of 10 years. Tract would normally have to pay 10% for similar financing. The land purchased was to be subdivided and sold as developed lots in the near future. Tract incurred the following *cash* expenditures during 20X7 for the development of the land.

May 1, 20X7	$120,000
July 1, 20X7	300,000
December 1, 20X7	48,000
	$468,000

The land development was incomplete at December 31, 20X7.

4. Tract contracted for the construction of a building for its use on July 1, 20X6. Estimated total expenditures were $4,000,000, which were financed through the issuance of common stock. The building is to be constructed on a site purchased on July 1, 20X6 for $500,000 cash. Actual cash expenditures for the building during 20X6 and 20X7 were:

July 1, 20X6	$100,000
September 1, 20X6	300,000
December 1, 20X6	400,000
February 1, 20X7	500,000
March 1, 20X7	400,000
May 1, 20X7	500,000
July 1, 20X7	800,000
	$3,000,000

The building was completed and ready for use on August 1, 20X7.

5. In addition to the financing discussed above, Tract's debt structure at December 31, 20X7 is presented below:

Debt	*Interest Rate*
$500,000	10%
50,000	5%
1,000,000	11%
2,000,000	12%
$3,550,000	

6. Total interest incurred by Tract during 20X7 amounted to $598,500.

Because the assumptions for Example 8-17 are complex and detailed, each asset will be discussed individually and a summary of all the assets will be prepared at the end of the discussion.

To begin the analysis of the information presented in Example 8-17, consider the land purchased on January 1, 20X7 for $3,000,000 cash. Technically, the land may be considered a qualifying asset; however, there will be no interest capitalization in the current accounting period because no activities are in progress to make the land ready for its intended use. If some activities were under way and expenditures were incurred in connection with the land, interest capitalization would be proper because Tract did incur interest during the accounting period. Because interest will not be capitalized on the land in the current period, no further consideration will be given to this asset.

The next asset, described in Item 3, is the land purchased on April 1, 20X7 that is to be subdivided and sold as developed lots. This land is a qualifying asset as defined in ASC 835-20-15-5(b). Tract is in the process of making the land ready for its intended use, has incurred expenditures in connection with the property, and has incurred interest costs during the current accounting period. Once it has been determined that interest capitalization is proper, the next step in the accounting process is to determine the appropriate capitalization period for the asset.

The capitalization period for the land begins on April 1, 20X7 because that is the first date on which activities were underway to develop the property, expenditures have been incurred in connection with the purchase price and development activities, and Tract has incurred interest during the period of $598,500. The capitalization period ends on December 31, 20X7 because at the balance sheet date, the development of the land was still not complete. Therefore, the capitalization period runs from April 1 to December 31, 20X7.

Once the capitalization period has been determined, the next step is to compute the average accumulated expenditures relating to the land. The first problem encountered in the computation is related to the issuance of the $4,000,000 noninterest-bearing note. ASC 835-20 specifies that the provisions of ASC 310 apply in the process of interest capitalization. The noninterest-bearing note issued for land would fall under the provisions of ASC 310. With this in mind, Tract would have to pay 10% interest for financing similar to the noninterest-bearing note and no information is available about the fair value of the land or the market value of the note. Under these circumstances, it is assumed under ASC 820 that it is appropriate to use the 10% interest rate to *impute* interest on the note. The $4,000,000 face amount of the note must be divided into its principal and interest elements. This calculation is made below:

Face Amount of the Note	$4,000,000
Present Value Factor for $1 for 10 Years at 10%—Appendix E	× .38554
Principal Amount of the Note	$1,542,160

The principal amount of the note is equal to $1,542,160; therefore, the interest component would be equal to $2,457,840 ($4,000,000 Face Amount less $1,542,160 Principal Amount). Once the principal component of the note has been determined, the amount of the average accumulated expenditures may be calculated.

Each individual expenditure associated with the land will be weighted in the computation from the date the expenditure is incurred to the balance sheet date (the end of the capitalization period). The computation of the average accumulated expenditures for 20X7 is shown below:

Date of Expenditure[a]	*Amount*[a]	*Capitalization Period*[b]	*Average Expenditure*
April 1, 20X7 (Principal Amount of Note)	$1,542,160	9/12	$1,156,620[c]
April 1, 20X7 (Cash Down payment)	5,000,000	9/12	3,750,000
May 1, 20X7	120,000	8/12	80,000
July 1, 20X7	300,000	6/12	150,000
December 1, 20X7	48,000	1/12	4,000
	$7,010,160		$5,140,620

[a] See Example 8-18, Item 3.
[b] Period from date of expenditure to December 31, 20X7.
[c] $1,542,160 × 9/12 = $1,156,620.

Each expenditure has been weighted from the date it was incurred to the end of the accounting period. Because the expenditures were incurred on the first of each month, the author has decided to use a monthly weighting for the expenditures. If the expenditures had been incurred at various times during the month and the amounts were material, a daily or weekly weighting may be appropriate. This is a judgment that management must make.

The entry to record the original purchase of the land would be:

Land Under Development	6,542,160[a]	
Discount on Notes Payable	2,457,840	
Notes Payable		4,000,000
Cash		5,000,000

[a] $5,000,000 cash down payment + $1,542,160 principal of note = $6,542,160.

There would have been three separate journal entries to record the development expenditures incurred in connection with the land; however, the entry below represents a summary of all three of those entries and has been prepared for illustration purposes only.

Land Under Development	[a]468,000	
Cash		468,000

[a] $120,000 + $300,000 + $48,000 = $468,000.

The balance in the land under development account prior to interest capitalization is $7,010,160 ($6,542,160 + $468,000) and appears in the schedule showing the computation of the average accumulated expenditures.

Now that the proper amounts have been recorded for the land, the next step is to select the proper capitalization rate(s). The $4,000,000 face amount noninterest-bearing note represents a specific new borrowing in connection with the land. The $5,000,000 cash down payment and the $468,000 development expenditures incurred during the period will be capitalized at the weighted average interest rate because no new borrowings were incurred to finance these expenditures.

Average accumulated expenditures in an *amount equal to the principal amount* of the noninterest-bearing note will be capitalized at the rate of 10%—the rate used to impute interest. Average accumulated expenditures in excess of the amount specified above will be capitalized at the weighted average capitalization rate. Before the computation of the interest to be capitalized in this particular example can be completed, the weighted average capitalization rate must be calculated. The author's computation of this rate is shown below:

Selected Debt[a]	Interest Rate[a]	Interest Cost
$ 500,000	10%	$50,000
1,000,000	11%	110,000
2,000,000	12%	240,000
$3,500,000		$400,000

[a] See Example 8-18, Item 5.

The weighted average capitalization rate would be computed by dividing the total interest cost on the *selected* debt by the amount of the debt. In the above computation, the weighted average capitalization rate is equal to 11.43% ($400,000 ÷ $3,500,000). The author has omitted the $50,000, 5% debt listed in Example 8-17 from the computation of the weighted average capitalization rate. ASC 835-20 requires that the accountant exercise judgment in determining the debt to include and exclude in the calculation of the proper weighted average capitalization rate, and the author believes that the $50,000, 5% debt represents an obsolete interest rate that does not reflect the realities of any current borrowing by Tract. The objective of the computation is to attempt to estimate a reasonable measure of the acquisition cost of the asset by determining the interest cost that could be *avoided* if the asset had not been purchased and developed. The author feels that inclusion of the $50,000, 5% debt would distort the determination of the weighted average capitalization rate. Judgments similar to this will have to be made in most cases where the weighted average capitalization rate must be calculated.

Now that the two interest rates associated with the acquisition and development of the land have been determined, the amount of interest to be capitalized may be computed. This computation is shown below:

Average Accumulated Expenditures	$5,140,620
Average Accumulated Expenditures Equal to Principal Amount of the Noninterest Bearing Note	1,156,620
Average Accumulated Expenditures in Excess of the Principal Amount of the Note	$3,984,000

Although the principal amount of the new borrowing ($1,542,160) is in excess of the average accumulated expenditures associated with the new borrowing ($1,156,620), the difference between these two amounts cannot be used to apply to other average accumulated expenditures. The reason for this is that the note was issued only for the purchase price of the land and cannot be used for the payment of development expenditures. The remainder of the purchase price of the land was paid for in cash and this amount did not come from a new borrowing. The 10% interest rate on the noninterest-bearing note will be used as the capitalization rate for the average accumulated expenditures associated with the principal amount of the note and the weighted average interest rate will be used as the capitalization rate for all other average accumulated expenditures. The computation of the interest to be capitalized in connection with the land development is shown below:

Average Expenditure	*Capitalization Rate*	*Interest Capitalization*
$1,156,620	10%	$115,662
3,984,000	11.43%	455,371
$5,140,620		$571,033

The reason for the use of two capitalization rates was the fact that the average accumulated expenditures exceeded the amount of the specific new borrowing associated with the purchase price of the land.

The journal entry necessary to capitalize the interest relating to the land would be as follows:

Land Under Development	571,033	
Interest Incurred		571,033

The Interest Incurred account is a clearing account that facilitates the accounting problems encountered in ASC 835-20. The interest capitalized above does not exceed the actual interest incurred by the company of $598,500. However, if any additional interest is to be capitalized, the entry just completed may require an adjustment. This part of the accounting process will be addressed in the summary part of the analysis.

The final assets that need to be analyzed from the Example 8-17 material are the building that is currently being constructed for Tract and the land that was purchased as the site for the building. The building and land are both qualifying assets because they represent assets that are being constructed by an outside enterprise for use by Tract. It is appropriate to capitalize interest on the land and building because activities are currently underway to make the assets ready for their intended use, expenditures have been incurred on both the land and the building, and Tract has incurred interest during the current accounting period. Because interest capitalization is proper, the next step is to determine the capitalization period for the assets.

The capitalization period for the building being constructed begins on January 1, 20X7 because interest has been capitalized during 20X6 and the construction was not complete on December 31, 20X6. During 20X7, construction is still in progress, expenditures are being made and interest is being incurred by Tract. The capitalization period ends on August 1, 20X7, the date the building is completed and ready for its intended use. Now that the proper capitalization period has been determined, the average accumulated expenditures may be computed.

The average accumulated expenditures during 20X7 are calculated below. Each individual expenditure must be weighted for the length of time it has been outstanding during the capitalization period.

Date of Expenditure[a]	*Amount*[a]	*Capitalization Period*[b]	*Average Expenditure*
July 1, 20X6 (Land Purchase)	$500,000	7/12	$291,667[c]
July 1, 20X6	100,000	7/12	58,333
September 1, 20X6	300,000	7/12	175,000
December 1, 20X6	400,000	7/12	233,333
February 1, 20X7	500,000	6/12	250,000
March 1, 20X7	400,000	5/12	166,667
May 1, 20X7	500,000	3/12	125,000
July 1, 20X7	800,000	1/12	66,667
	$3,500,000		$1,366,667

[a] See Example 8-18, Item 4.
[b] Period from January 1, 20X7 or date of expenditure to August 1, 20X7.
[c] $500,000 × 7/12 = $291,667.

Two important points need to be made about the calculations shown above. First, interest will be capitalized on the land that was purchased on July 1, 20X6. The interest associated with the land expenditure *will not* be charged to the land account, instead, it will be added to the cost of the facility that is constructed on the land. Second, the expenditures for 20X6 are included as part of the base for computation of the interest to be capitalized in 20X7. ASC 835-20 requires the accountant to compute the average *accumulated* expenditures, and these would include expenditures incurred in prior accounting periods. However, the capitalization period relating to these expenditures would run only from the beginning of the current accounting period (January 1, 20X7) to the date the assets are completed and made ready for use (August 1, 20X7).

Once the capitalization period has been identified and the average accumulated expenditures have been calculated, the proper capitalization rate(s) must be selected. Because the land was acquired for cash and the construction of the building is being financed through the sale of stock, no specific new borrowing can be related to the expenditures incurred. Because no new borrowing can be identified, the weighted average capitalization rate is the appropriate rate to use. The weighted average capitalization rate has been previously calculated to be 11.43%. The amount of interest to be capitalized on the plant construction for 20X7 would be:

Average Accumulated Expenditures	$1,366,667
Weighted Average Capitalization Rate	× 11.43%
Interest Capitalization on Plant Facility	$156,210

Some of the expenditures associated with the plant site and facilities were recorded in 20X6. There would have been several entries to record the 20X7 expenditures; however, a summary of the entries is shown below:

Progress Payments on Construction	2,200,000[a]	
Cash		2,200,000

[a] $500,000 + $400,000 + $500,000 + $800,000.

Finally, the journal entry to record the interest capitalization on the land and plant facilities for 20X7 would be:

Progress Payments on Construction	156,210	
Interest Incurred		156,210

At this point in the accounting process it is necessary to summarize the information developed during the analysis of the information from Example 8-17. Total interest capitalized is equal to $727,243 ($571,033 from the purchase of the land to be subdivided + $156,210 from the building facilities constructed for Tract). The total interest incurred during 20X7 was $598,500 as shown in Example 8-17. The interest capitalized of $727,243 *exceeds* the interest actually incurred during the period of $598,500. ASC 835-20-30-6 prohibits the capitalization of interest in excess of the amount of interest incurred during the period. The total amount of interest to capitalize is *limited* to $598,500. In this case, it is necessary to correct the journal entries previously made.

When the interest capitalized exceeds the interest incurred, an additional allocation problem is created. The interest capitalized must be allocated to the various assets that qualify for capitalization on some rational basis. ASC 835-20 provides no specific guidance in the implementation of the allocation process, but it would seem logical to allocate the interest on the basis of the relative value of the interest that was capitalized. Although other allocation procedures may be acceptable (e.g., on the basis of the average accumulated expenditures on the assets involved), the author believes that the process described above is rational and systematic. In the case of the Example 8-17 material, the allocation would be accomplished as follows:

Interest Capitalized on Land to be Subdivided	$571,033
Interest Capitalized on Land and Plant Facilities	156,210
Total Interest Capitalized	$727,243

$$\frac{\$571,033}{\$727,243} \times \$598,500 = \$469,944 \text{ Allocate to Land Development}$$

$$\frac{\$156,210}{\$727,243} \times \$598,500 = \$128,556 \text{ Allocate to Land and Plant Facility}$$

As a result of the above allocation process, an adjusting journal entry is required to properly state the amount of interest capitalized. In the case of the land development, interest of $571,033 has been capitalized and only $469,944 should be capitalized. The difference of $101,089 should be used to reduce the Land under Development account. For the land and plant facility, interest of $156,210 has been capitalized, and $128,556 should have been capitalized. The difference of $27,654 should be used to reduce the Progress Payments on Construction account. As a result of the allocation process the following journal entry is needed to restate the interest capitalized:

Interest Incurred	128,743	
Land Under Development		101,089
Progress Payments on Construction		27,654

This completes the discussion and analysis of the Example 8-17 material. The reader may wish to take a few minutes to review both the information given in Example 8-17 and the solution offered on the preceding pages before moving on to the next example. The Example 8-17 material was much more complex than Example 8-16 and may require some additional time to digest. Example 8-18 is designed to extend the reader's understanding of ASC 835-20.

The assumptions for Example 8-18 are outlined below. Specifically, Example 8-18 is designed to illustrate the following problem areas:

1. Temporary interruptions in the construction process of a qualifying asset;
2. Accounting for self-constructed qualifying assets where the construction costs exceed the fair market value of the asset constructed;
3. Accounting for the discontinuation of a land development project; and
4. Distinction between cost incurred and expenditure as defined in the Statement.

Example 8-18
Interest Capitalization Assumptions

1. Dyer, Inc., a December 31 year-end company, was involved in several specific construction and purchase activities during 20X6.

2. On January 1, 20X6, Dyer, Inc. began construction on a new coal burning generator designed to reduce its utility costs. When completed, the generator would provide all electrical needs of Dyer, Inc. Dyer, Inc. was forced to shut down construction of the generator from May 1, 20X6 to June 1, 20X6 as the result of a governmental injunction that grew out of public concern about the pollution potential of the generating facility. This interruption was considered only

temporary in nature. Construction materials for the entire project were purchased on January 1, 20X6 for $400,000 cash. Other cash expenditures during 20X6 were as follows:

February 1, 20X6	$100,000
March 1, 20X6	150,000
April 1, 20X6	200,000
May 1, 20X6	150,000
June 1, 20X6	200,000
	$800,000

The generator was completed and placed in service on July 1, 20X6. Dyer, Inc. financed the construction of the generator through the use of a line of credit that allowed it to borrow any amount up to $1,500,000 throughout 20X6. The line of credit carried an interest rate of 12%. The generator could be constructed by an outside contractor for a purchase price of $1,150,000.

3. On April 1, 20X6, Dyer, Inc. purchased land that cost $1,000,000 with the intent of subdividing the parcel and selling it as developed lots. A note was issued for the entire purchase price of the land. The note bears interest at the rate of 11%, which is assumed to be a reasonable interest rate for this type of project. Dyer incurred costs of $20,000 on April 1, 20X6 and $30,000 on May 1, 20X6 relating to the development of the property. Dyer, Inc. financed the expenditures by borrowing funds with a stated interest rate of 13%. On June 1, 20X6, Dyer, Inc. determined that it was not economically feasible to develop the land for sale as lots, so it discontinued the development project. Dyer, Inc. decided to retain the land as a possible future plant site.

4. On November 1, 20X6, Dyer, Inc. began construction on a new piece of equipment. Materials for the construction cost $150,000 and were purchased on November 1 on credit terms of net-90 days (no interest). Labor costs of $25,000 were incurred during November and paid on December 1, 20X6. Additional labor costs were incurred during December in the amount of $40,000, and were paid on January 1, 20X7. In addition to the materials described above, Dyer, Inc. purchased materials on November 1, for $50,000. In payment of this purchase, the seller required that Dyer, Inc. sign a 10%, 90-day note for the entire purchase price.

5. Total interest costs incurred during 20X6 amounted to $210,500.

6. Dyer computed its weighted average capitalization rate to be 12.2%.

Because Example 8-18 contains several different assets, the analysis of the information presented will be on a piecemeal basis taking one asset at a time. Towards the end of the analysis, information about each individual asset will be summarized to determine if the total interest capitalized is less than the interest costs incurred by Dyer, Inc. during 20X6.

The analysis will start with the coal burning generator described in Item 2 of Example 8-18. The generator is a qualifying asset according to the provisions of ASC 835-20-15-5(a). The capitalization period for this asset begins on January 1, 20X6 because that is the first date that activities are underway on the construction project, expenditures have been made for construction materials, and interest has been incurred by Dyer, Inc. The capitalization period ends on July 1, 20X6 because this is the date the generator is complete and ready for use. Interest capitalization would not be suspended during the month of May because the interruption in construction is deemed to be temporary in nature. Interest capitalization will be suspended only when there has been a prolonged or permanent interruption in the construction or purchase of a qualifying asset (i.e., an extended period of time when no activities were being carried out and no expenditures were being made in connection with the project).

Once the capitalization period has been determined, the average accumulated expenditures must be calculated. This computation is shown below. Each individual expenditure must be weighted from the date it was incurred to the end of the capitalization period.

Date of Expenditure[a]	*Amount*[a]	*Capitalization Period*[b]	*Average Expenditure*
January 1, 20X6	$400,000	6/12	$200,000[c]
February 1, 20X6	100,000	5/12	41,667
March 1, 20X6	150,000	4/12	50,000
April 1, 20X6	200,000	3/12	50,000
May 1, 20X6	150,000	2/12	25,000
June 1, 20X6	200,000	1/12	16,667
	$1,200,000		$383,334

[a] See Example 8-19, Item 2.
[b] Period from date of expenditure to July 1, 20X6.
[c] $400,000 × 6/12 = $200,000

Because the average accumulated expenditures of $383,334 do not exceed the $1,200,000 amount of new borrowing, the interest rate associated with the line of credit will become the capitalization rate. The final step in the accounting process is to compute the amount of interest to capitalize. This computation is shown below:

Average Accumulated Expenditures	$383,334
Capitalization Rate	× 12%
Interest to Be Capitalized	$46,000

There would have been several journal entries during 20X6 to record the expenditures associated with the generator; however, the entry below represents a summary of those entries.

Construction in Progress—Generator	1,200,000	
Cash		1,200,000

The journal entry required to capitalize the interest relating to the generator would be as follows:

Construction in Progress—Generator	46,000	
Interest incurred		46,000

The amount of interest capitalized thus far does not exceed the interest incurred during the accounting period. However, if the total interest capitalized exceeds the interest incurred, some adjustment will be required for the entry above. This comparison will be made in the summary phase of the analysis.

Before the amount shown in the Construction in Progress—Generator account can be transferred to the Equipment account and placed in service, the cost of the asset ($1,246,000) must be compared with the fair market value of the generator. Based upon the information in Example 8-18, the fair value of the generator as measured by the price quote from an outside contractor is $1,150,000. Because the fair market value is $96,000 ($1,246,000 – $1,150,000) less than the amount currently recorded in the Construction in Progress account, a loss must be recognized in the period of construction. The loss will be equal to the $96,000 necessary to reduce cost to market value. ASC 835-20-25-7 requires that interest be capitalized during the construction period even though cost will exceed fair market value of the asset. As a result of this requirement, the entry necessary to transfer the amount currently in Construction in Progress to the proper Equipment account would be:

Equipment	1,150,000	
Provision to Reduce Construction Cost to Fair Value	96,000	
Construction in Progress—Generator		1,246,000

The Provision to Reduce Construction Cost to Fair Value account should be shown on the income statement as a line item in the nonoperating section. Another point must be made about the construction of the generator. Materials for the entire construction of the generator were purchased on January 1, 20X6 for cash. This expenditure is weighted from the date of purchase *rather than* the date the materials were actually used on the project.

The second asset to be considered from the Example 8-18 material is the purchase of land for subdivision and development. The land is a qualifying asset for at least part of the year because it was purchased for the purpose of development. However, when development was discontinued on June 1, 20X6, the land no longer qualified for interest capitalization. The capitalization period for the land development project begins on April 1, 20X6 because that is the first date that activities were undertaken to develop the property, expenditures have been made on the land, and interest was incurred by Dyer, Inc. The capitalization period ends on June 1, 20X6 because this is the date that Dyer, Inc. determined that it was not economically feasible to continue the development of the land. When it was decided that the land would be held for a future plant site, the amount of the expenditures incurred represent an investment rather than an inventory item. Interest capitalization is not considered proper for assets classified as investments. In the case of the land, the interest capitalization period runs from April 1, 20X6 to June 1, 20X6.

The next step in the accounting process is to compute the average accumulated expenditures on the land while it was a qualifying asset. The computation of the average accumulated expenditures is shown below. Each individual expenditure must be weighted from the date it was incurred to the end of the capitalization period.

Date of Expenditure[a]	Amount[a]	Capitalization Period[b]	Average Expenditure
April 1, 20X6 (Purchase Price)	$1,000,000	2/12	$166,667[c]
April 1, 20X6 (Development Cost)	20,000	2/12	3,333
May 1, 20X6	30,000	1/12	2,500
	$1,050,000		$172,500

[a] See Example 8-19, Item 3.
[b] Period from date of expenditure to June 1, 20X6.
[c] $1,000,000 × 2/12 = $166,667.

Both the purchase of the tract of land and the payment of the development costs were made through specific new borrowings. The purchase price of the *land* was financed through the issuance of an 11% note and the development costs were financed by borrowed funds bearing interest at the rate of 13%. Because the amount of the new borrowings ($1,050,000) is greater than the amount of the average accumulated expenditures ($172,500), the interest rates on the new borrowings will be used as the capitalization rates. The 11% interest rate will be used for the average accumulated expenditures associated with the purchase price of the land and the 13% interest rate will apply to the average accumulated expenditures associated with the development costs. The computation of the interest to be capitalized during 20X6 on the land development project is shown below:

Type of Expenditure	Average Expenditure	Capitalization Rate	Interest Capitalized
Land-Purchase Price	$166,667	11%	$18,333[a]
Development Cost	3,333	13%	433
Development Cost	2,500	13%	325
	$172,500		$19,091

[a] $166,667 × 11% = $18,333

A summary of the journal entries necessary to record the initial purchase of the land, the subsequent development expenditures, and interest capitalization would be:

	Debit	Credit
Land Under Development	1,069,091	
Cash		1,050,000
Interest Incurred		19,091

At this point in the analysis, it is not known if the interest capitalized is greater than the interest incurred by Dyer, Inc. in the current accounting period. As a consequence, the journal entry shown above may require some adjustment during the summary phase of the analysis.

Because Dyer, Inc. discontinued development of the land on June 1, 20X6 and decided to hold it as a possible future plant site, it must transfer the balance in the Land under Development account to an appropriate investment account. The land is no longer held for development and is therefore no longer a qualifying asset. The cost basis of the land is now $1,069,091, even though the original purchase price was only $1,000,000. The journal entry to transfer the balance in the Land under Development account would be:

Land Held for Plant Site	1,069,091	
Land Under Development		1,069,091

In the case of the land development, two different capitalization rates were used. It would not be unusual to find multiple interest rates from specific new borrowings being used as capitalization rates.

Attention is now turned to the last asset from the Example 8-18 material. Dyer, Inc. is in the process of constructing a piece of equipment for its own use. This is a qualifying asset as defined in ASC 835-20-15-5(a). The capitalization period for the equipment begins on November 1, 20X6 because that is the first date that activities have been started to construct the asset, expenditures have been made in connection with the project, and interest has been incurred by Dyer, Inc. The capitalization period ends on December 31, 20X6 because this is the balance sheet date and construction has not been completed. After the capitalization period has been determined, the average accumulated expenditures may be calculated. This calculation is shown below:

Date of Expenditure[a]	*Amount*[a]	*Capitalization Period*[b]	*Average Expenditure*
November 1, 20X6	$50,000	2/12	$8,333[c]
December 1, 20X6	25,000	1/12	2,083
	$75,000		$10,416

[a] See Example 8-19, Item 4.
[b] Period from date of expenditure to December 31, 20X6.
[c] $50,000 × 2/12 = $8,333.

Recall from Example 8-18 that the following costs were incurred by Dyer, Inc. in connection with the construction project:

Materials (Purchased on net-90 day basis)	$150,000
Labor for November (Paid December 1, 20X6)	25,000
Labor for December (Paid January 1, 20X7)	40,000
Materials (Purchased by issuing note payable)	50,000
	$265,000

Of the $265,000 total costs incurred in connection with the project, only $75,000 qualifies as expenditures according to the provisions of ASC 835-20. For purposes of interest capitalization, an expenditure exists when cash has been paid, an asset transferred, or a liability incurred that requires the recognition of interest. In the case of the materials purchased on November 1, 20X6 on a net-90 day basis, no payment will be made until the end of January 20X7; therefore, the cost cannot be considered an expenditure. The labor costs incurred during December were not paid until January 20X7 and cannot be included in the expenditures for purposes of interest capitalization. The labor costs for November were actually weighted from December 1, 20X6, the date of payment. The materials that were purchased on November 1, 20X6 by issuing a note payable qualify as expenditures because the liability created bears interest. Now that the average accumulated expenditures have been computed, the next step in the capitalization process is to select the proper capitalization rate(s).

For the information being analyzed, two capitalization rates will be used. The expenditure for the acquisition of materials on November 1, 20X6 was accomplished by issuing a 10% note payable. The 10% rate will be applied to the average accumulated expenditures associated with the $50,000 purchase of materials. No specific new borrowing is related to the labor costs paid on December 1, 20X6; therefore, the company's weighted average capitalization rate of 12.2% applies to these expenditures. The computation of the interest to be capitalized is shown below:

Type of Expenditure	*Average Expenditure*	*Capitalization Rate*	*Interest Capitalized*
Materials purchased	$8,333	10%	$833
Labor costs	2,083	12.2%	254
	$10,416		$1,087

The journal entry to record the interest to be capitalized would be:

Construction in Progress—Equipment	1,087	
Interest Incurred		1,087

Once again, two capitalization rates were used to determine the proper amount of interest to be capitalized. The analysis of all assets listed in the Example 8-18 material has been completed and one final test is required.

The final step is to compare the interest capitalized in connection with all the assets listed above with the actual interest incurred by Dyer, Inc. during 20X6. The summary below shows the amount of interest that has been capitalized.

Qualifying Asset	*Interest Capitalized*
Generator Construction	$46,000
Land Development	19,091
Equipment Construction	1,087
	$66,178

The actual interest incurred by Dyer in 20X6 amounted to $210,500 (see Example 8-18), which is in excess of the amount of interest capitalized; therefore, no adjustment is required to the journal entries prepared for each asset. The final entry required by Dyer, Inc. is to clear the suspense account Interest Incurred. The balance in the suspense account is $144,322 ($210,500 actual interest costs – $66,178 interest capitalized) and must be closed to interest expense for 20X6. The entry to accomplish this would be:

Interest Expense	144,322	
Interest Incurred		144,322

This last entry completes the analysis of the Example 8-18 material. Example 8-19 is designed to demonstrate some refinements of ASC 835-20. Specifically, Example 8-19 deals with interest capitalization on certain leasing transactions and with the problem of project completion in stages rather than as one discrete event. Assumptions for Example 8-19 are as follows.

Example 8-19
Interest Capitalization Assumptions

1. Eagle, Inc. (Eagle), a December 31 year-end company, signed a lease agreement on January 1, 20X6 requiring the payment of $100,000 at the beginning of each of the next five years. Eagle's incremental borrowing rate is 12%, which is approximately equal to the lessor's implicit rate on the leased property. The property has a fair market value of $403,735 and an estimated economic life of five years. Eagle depreciates similar owned property on the straight-line basis. The equipment was installed on January 1, 20X6, and Eagle made the first lease payment on this date; however, problems soon developed with the installation and Eagle could not use the equipment until April 1, 20X6.

2. Eagle contracted with Hayes Company (Hayes) to construct an apartment complex consisting of 10 units with a total estimated cost of $1,000,000. Hayes began construction on January 1, 20X6 and completed two of the 10 units on August 1, 20X6. Eagle was able to rent these two units during the month of August. The remaining units were still not completed at December 31, 20X6. Advance payments were made by Eagle for the units under construction in the following amounts:

March 1, 20X6	$150,000
May 1, 20X6	150,000
June 1, 20X6	170,000
July 1, 20X6	180,000
September 1, 20X6	80,000
December 1, 20X6	70,000
	$800,000

Of the payments made between March 1 and July 1, 20X6, $200,000 represents payments for the two units that have been completed. These payments were incurred uniformly during the period (i.e., at the rate of $50,000 for each payment made). Eagle obtained a loan from a local bank in connection with the construction project. The borrowing bears interest at the rate of 12%.

3. Eagle contracted with Owens Contractor, Inc. (Owens) to construct a plant facility consisting of three separate processes: a metal stamping process facility, a cleaning and painting process facility, and an assembly facility. The production facility requires that the incoming metal be stamped first, then sent to the cleaning and painting facility, and finally to the assembly room. The estimated cost of the facility is $3,000,000. Construction was started by Owens on January 1, 20X6. The metal stamping facility was completed on September 1, 20X6; however, the cleaning and painting and assembly facilities were not completed by December 31, 20X6. Advanced payments were made by Eagle to Owens in the following amounts:

January 1, 20X6	$200,000
March 1, 20X6	500,000
June 1, 20X6	500,000
September 1, 20X6	400,000
November 1, 20X6	360,000
	$1,960,000

Eagle obtained a bank loan to finance the construction of the plant facility and is required to pay 13% on the borrowed funds.

4. Interest costs incurred during 20X6 amounted to $245,600.

5. For the sake of simplicity, the land that would be associated with the apartment complex in 2, above, and the land portion of the plant facility in 3, above, have been ignored. Detailed information about interest capitalization on land was shown in the Example 8-17 material and need not be repeated in Example 8-19.

Once again, the analysis of the information in Example 8-19 is carried out on each individual asset and a summary of the individual considerations will be prepared towards the end of the discussion. The first asset identified in Example 8-19 is the leased property, and the analysis will begin by examining the terms of the lease agreement in detail.

The lease agreement creates a unique problem for Eagle in the interest capitalization process. Because the lease described in Item 1 of Example 8-19 is a capital lease, an obligation on which interest accrues is created on January 1, 20X6, the date of the lease agreement (see Topic 840 in this chapter for a complete discussion of lease accounting). Because Eagle was not able to use the property until April 1, 20X6, the leased asset is a qualifying asset as defined by ASC 835-20. The capitalization period begins on January 1, 20X6 because this is the first date that activities have begun in connection with the leased property, expenditures have been made in the form of the lease payment, and Eagle has incurred interest costs. The capitalization period ends on April 1, 20X6, the date the equipment is ready for its intended use. The capitalization period will be for three months of 20X6. Before the average accumulated expenditures can be computed, the entry to record the capital lease property and related obligation must be made. The journal entry is shown below:

Leased Property under Capital Lease	403,735	
Obligation under Capital Lease		403,735

The amount recorded as the leased asset and obligation is the present value of the minimum lease payments required by the lease agreement. The calculation of this amount is shown below:

Lease Payment	$100,000
Present Value Factor for an Annuity Due at 12% for Five Years (Appendix E)	4.03735
Present Value of the Minimum Lease Payment	$403,735

The present value of the minimum lease payment is equal to the fair value of the leased asset at the inception, and is used to record the leased asset and obligation. The discount rate of 12% is used because it is equal to Eagle's incremental borrowing rate and the rate implicit in the lease.

Given the journal entry to record the capital lease, the average accumulated expenditures would be calculated as follows:

Total Expenditures—January 1, 20X6	$403,735
Capitalization Period (January 1–April 1)	× 3/12
Average Accumulated Expenditures	$100,934

Expenditures, as defined in ASC 835-20-20, are made when cash is paid, assets transferred, or liabilities incurred that normally bear interest. In the case of the leased asset, the obligation of $403,735 was incurred on January 1, 20X6, and this obligation bears interest at the rate of 12%. The expenditure for 20X6 is equal to $403,735, the amount of the lease obligation.

Now that the average accumulated expenditures have been computed, the proper capitalization rate must be determined. Eagle assumed a specific new borrowing in connection with the leased property (i.e., the lease obligation), and because this amount is greater than the average accumulated expenditures of $100,934, the 12% interest rate implicit in the lease will be used as the capitalization rate. The computation of the interest to be capitalized is shown below:

Average Accumulated Expenditures	$100,934
Capitalization Rate	× 12%
Interest to be Capitalized	$12,112

The journal entry necessary to record the interest would be:

Leased Property Under Capital Lease	12,112	
Interest Incurred		12,112

Because it is not yet known if the interest capitalized on all qualifying assets will exceed the amount of interest actually incurred, this journal entry may require some adjustment in the summary phase of the analysis. The next asset to be reviewed is the apartment complex under construction. The land portion of the project has been intentionally left out of the analysis in order to simplify the accounting process.

In connection with the apartment project, two units were completed and placed in service before the entire complex was completed. This is an example of a qualifying asset being completed in stages rather than all at one time. The construction of the apartment complex is a qualifying asset as specified in ASC 835-20-15-5(a). The new problem created in this example is that ASC 835-20-25-5 requires that interest capitalization cease on the part of the asset that has been substantially completed as long as the use of the asset is not dependent upon the completion of the entire project. In this example there will be one capitalization period for the two units completed during 20X6 and another capitalization period for the uncompleted units.

The capitalization period for all of the units begins on March 1, 20X6 because this is the first date that activities were started on the apartment complex, expenditures in the form of advanced payments were made by Eagle to Hayes and interest was incurred by Eagle. Even though construction began on January 1, 20X6, the capitalization period did not begin on this date because no expenditures have been made. The capitalization period ends on two different dates. For the two units completed during 20X6, the capitalization period ends on August 1, 20X6, the date the units were placed in service. For the eight units that were not completed during 20X6, the capitalization period ends on December 31, 20X6, the balance sheet date of Eagle.

After the capitalization periods have been determined, the average accumulated expenditures may be computed. The expenditures on the apartment complex must be divided between the completed units and the uncompleted units. Recall from the information in Example 8-19 that the $200,000 total expenditures associated with the completed units were incurred at the rate of $50,000 for each of the following dates: March 1, May 1, June 1, and July 1, 20X6. The remainder of the expenditures made on these dates were associated with the uncompleted units. The computation of the average accumulated expenditures for the two completed units would be as follows:

Date of Expenditure[a]	*Amount*[a]	*Capitalization Period*[b]	*Average Expenditure*
March 1, 20X6	$50,000	5/12	$20,833[c]
May 1, 20X6	50,000	3/12	12,500
June 1, 20X6	50,000	2/12	8,333
July 1, 20X6	50,000	1/12	4,167
	$200,000		$45,833

[a] See Example 8-20, Item 2.
[b] Period from date of expenditure to August 1, 20X6.
[c] $50,000 × 5/12 = $20,833.

The computation of the average accumulated expenditures relating to the eight units that were not completed during 20X6 would be accomplished as follows:

Date of Expenditure[a]	*Total Expenditure*[a]	*Applicable to Completed Units*	*Applicable to Uncompleted Units*	*Capitalization Period*[b]	*Average Expenditure*
March 1	$150,000	$50,000	$100,000	10/12	$83,333[c]
May 1	150,000	50,000	100,000	8/12	66,667
June 1	170,000	50,000	120,000	7/12	70,000
July 1	180,000	50,000	130,000	6/12	65,000
September 1	80,000	-0-	80,000	4/12	26,667
December 1	70,000	-0-	70,000	1/12	5,833
	$800,000	$200,000	$600,000		$317,500

[a] See Example 8-20, Item 2.
[b] Period from date of expenditure to December 31, 20X6.
[c] $100,000 × 10/12 = $83,333.

The average accumulated expenditures for the completed and uncompleted units have been calculated and the next step is to determine the appropriate capitalization rate to apply to these expenditures.

Eagle financed the expenditures on the apartment complex through a specific new borrowing. The bank loan bears interest at the rate of 12%. Because the average accumulated expenditures of $363,333 ($45,833 + $317,500) do not exceed the $800,000 amount of the new borrowing, the interest rate associated with the bank loan will be used as the capitalization rate for both the completed and the uncompleted units. The computation of the amount of interest to be capitalized in connection with the construction of the apartment complex is shown below:

	Completed Units	*Uncompleted Units*	*Total*
Average Accumulated Expenditures	$45,833	$317,500	$363,333
Capitalization Rate	× 12%	× 12%	× 12%
Interest Capitalization	$5,500	$38,100	$43,600

The journal entry to record the capitalization of interest and the cost of the completed units would be:

Rental Property—Apartment	205,500	
Cash		200,000
Interest Incurred		5,500

The journal entry to record the capitalization of interest and the costs of the uncompleted units would be:

Progress Payments on Constructed Assets	638,100	
Cash		600,000
Interest Incurred		38,100

Once again, it is not known if the amount of interest capitalized on all assets exceeds the amount of interest incurred by Eagle during the current accounting period. The journal entries made above may require some adjustment in the summary phase of the analysis. The final asset to be considered is the plant facility being constructed.

The plant facility is a qualifying asset according to ASC 835-20-15-5(a). The plant is being constructed to produce a product by a sequential process. The metal stamping process is complete and ready for use, but cannot be used until the entire plant is complete. No single process will stand alone. ASC 835-20-25-5 requires that, until all of the parts or processes have been completed and can be used, interest capitalization should continue on the entire plant facility. Accounting for interest capitalization on the construction of the plant will *not* require the determination of two or more separate capitalization periods as was the case with the apartment complex.

The capitalization period begins on January 1, 20X6 because this is the first date that activities were started to construct the facility, expenditures were made on the plant in the form of advanced payments to Owens, and Eagle has incurred interest costs. The capitalization period ends on December 31, 20X6, the balance sheet date of the company. The construction of the entire facility is not complete at December 31, 20X6. Once the capitalization period has been determined, the average accumulated expenditures may be computed. The computation would be made as follows:

Date of Expenditure[a]	*Expenditure*[a]	*Capitalization Period*[b]	*Average Expenditure*
January 1, 20X6	$200,000	12/12	$200,000[c]
March 1, 20X6	500,000	10/12	416,667
June 1, 20X6	500,000	7/12	291,667
September 1, 20X6	400,000	4/12	133,333
November 1, 20X6	360,000	2/12	60,000
	$1,960,000		$1,101,667

[a] See Example 8-20, Item 3.
[b] Period from date of expenditure to December 31, 20X6.
[c] $200,000 × 12/12 = $200,000.

As in Examples 8-16, 8-17, and 8-18, each individual expenditure must be weighted for the length of time it has been outstanding during the capitalization period. Now that the average accumulated expenditures have been calculated the proper capitalization rate must be selected.

Eagle has financed the construction of the plant through a specific new borrowing at the bank. Because the average accumulated expenditures of $1,101,667 are less than the amount of the new borrowings of $1,960,000, the rate of interest on the new borrowing will be used as the capitalization rate. The computation of the interest to be capitalized would be made as follows:

Average Accumulated Expenditures	$1,101,667
Capitalization Rate	× 13%
Interest to Be Capitalized	$143,217

A summary journal entry to record the costs of the plant facility and the interest capitalization would be:

Progress Payments on Constructed Asset	2,103,217	
Cash		1,960,000
Interest Incurred		143,217

After this entry has been made it is time to summarize the results of the interest capitalization on the various assets in Example 8-19. The total interest capitalized is computed below:

Leased Property	$12,112
Completed Apartment Units	5,500
Uncompleted Apartment Units	38,100
Plant Facility	143,217
Total Interest Capitalized	$198,929

The total interest incurred by Eagle during 20X6 amounted to $245,600 as shown in Example 8-19. The total amount of interest incurred of $245,600 exceeds the total amount of interest capitalized of $198,929; therefore, the interest capitalization shown in the various journal entries will not require adjustment.

The final problem to be solved in connection with the information in Example 8-19 is to clear the suspense account Interest Incurred. The balance in the account is $46,671 ($245,600 incurred – $198,929 capitalized) and will be closed to interest expense at December 31, 20X6. The journal entry to clear the suspense account would be:

Interest Expense	46,671	
Interest Incurred		46,671

As a result of this entry, it is now known that Eagle has capitalized interest of $198,929 during 20X6 and expensed interest of $46,671 during the same period.

ASC 835-20-30, paragraphs 8 through 12, deal with interest capitalization where the transaction involves certain tax-exempt borrowing or gifts and grants. As a general rule, the Board has not permitted the offsetting of interest income against interest expense when applying the provisions of ASC 835-20. However, the FASB concluded that, in certain well-defined situations, this offsetting process would be appropriate.

The first situation for which ASC 835-20-30 permits an exception to the general rule relates to tax-exempt borrowings that are restricted for use in the acquisition of an asset that qualifies for interest capitalization. The basic accounting provisions permit a company to offset the interest income earned on investments made with the proceeds of the tax-exempt borrowing against the interest expense related to that borrowing. The offsetting of interest begins on the date the funds are borrowed, and ends when the qualifying asset is ready for its intended use.

Regarding the second major issue addressed in ASC 835-20-30, interest capitalization is not appropriate for assets acquired with funds received from gifts and grants that are restricted for that purpose.

The technical example presented below demonstrates the major provisions of ASC 835-20-30. Assumptions for Example 8-20 are as follows.

Example 8-20
Interest Capitalization Assumptions

1. Smith Enterprises (Smith), a December 31 year-end company, was involved in two construction activities during 20X6.
2. On January 1, 20X6, Smith received $5,000,000 of 9% tax-exempt debt for the purpose of constructing a building. The funds are restricted to the financing of the building or the servicing of the related debt. The $5,000,000 was immediately invested, earning a rate of return of 12%. Smith contracted for the construction of the building on January 1, 20X6 and incurred the following cash expenditures during 20X6 for the construction of the building:

January 1, 20X6	$400,000
March 1, 20X6	600,000
May 1, 20X6	500,000
August 1, 20X6	200,000
September 1, 20X6	300,000
November 1, 20X6	500,000
December 1, 20X6	500,000
	$3,000,000

The construction was in process on December 31, 20X6.

3. On July 1, 20X6, Smith received a restricted gift of $2,000,000 for the construction of an addition to an existing building. The $2,000,000 was immediately invested at a rate of 12%. On August 1, 20X6, Smith contracted for the construction of the building addition. Actual cash expenditures for the addition during 20X6 are:

August 1, 20X6	$500,000
October 1, 20X6	400,000
December 1, 20X6	600,000
	$1,500,000

The construction was in process on December 31, 20X6.

4. Smith had no other debt during 20X6.
5. The land that would be associated with the buildings has been ignored. Detailed information about interest capitalization on land was illustrated in Example 8-17.

The first requirement is to determine if the assets described are qualifying assets. The building is a qualifying asset because it is being constructed by an outside party for Smith's own use. The fact that tax-exempt debt is used to construct the facility does *not* disqualify the asset. The building addition being constructed with the gift of $2,000,000 may or may not be classified as a qualifying asset. Assets acquired as gifts restricted by the donor are disqualified from interest capitalization, in most cases. An exception is made when qualifying expenditures incurred exceed the restricted gifts and earnings on the gifts. Expenditures incurred in excess of the sum of the gifts and gift earnings *are* subject to interest capitalization.

To determine what portion of the addition is a qualifying asset, the gift, plus the 20X6 earnings from the gift, must be compared to expenditures incurred in 20X6. The sum of the gift and gift earnings is computed below:

Gift	$2,000,000
20X6 Earnings from Gift ($2,000,000 × 12% × 1/2 Year)[1]	120,000
Total	$2,120,000

[1] This information was taken from Example 8-21, Item 3.

The sum of the gift and 20X6 earnings from the gift of $2,120,000 exceeds expenditures incurred of $1,500,000 in 20X6. No portion of the expenditures qualifies for interest capitalization in 20X6. This test is repeated each year to determine whether any expenditures related to restricted gifts qualify for capitalization of interest.

Once it has been determined which construction activity represents qualifying assets, the capitalization period must be determined.

The capitalization period begins on January 1, 20X6. That is the first date on which activities were underway to construct the building, expenditures have been incurred in connection with the construction, and interest has been incurred from January 1 to December 31.

The next step in the capitalization process is to determine the amount of interest to be capitalized from the tax-exempt borrowing. Interest income earned on the temporary investment of the borrowed funds must be offset against the interest expense on the tax-exempt debt. The asset value may increase or decrease by the capitalized amount when tax-exempt debt is used. If interest income exceeds interest expense, the asset value is reduced by the excess. If interest expense exceeds interest income, the asset value is increased by the excess expense. The excess expense cannot exceed the total interest that can be capitalized using the provisions of ASC 835-20.

Before the excess interest can be computed, the amount of interest income from the temporary investment must be determined. Table 8-25 presents the interest income for the temporary investment for 20X6.

Table 8-25 Computation of Interest Income for 20X6

	Balance Before Expenditure (a)	Expenditure[1] (b)	Balance (c)=(a)–(b)	Monthly Interest Rate[2] (d)	Monthly Interest Income (e) = (c) × (d)
January	$5,000,000[3]	$400,000	$4,600,000	1%	$46,000
February	4,600,000	0	4,600,000	1%	46,000
March	4,600,000	600,000	4,000,000	1%	40,000
April	4,000,000	0	4,000,000	1%	40,000
May	4,000,000	500,000	3,500,000	1%	35,000
June	3,500,000	0	3,500,000	1%	35,000
July	3,500,000	0	3,500,000	1%	35,000
August	3,500,000	200,000	3,300,000	1%	33,000
September	3,300,000	300,000	3,000,000	1%	30,000
October	3,000,000	0	3,000,000	1%	30,000

	Balance Before Expenditure (a)	Expenditure[1] (b)	Balance (c)=(a)–(b)	Monthly Interest Rate[2] (d)	Monthly Interest Income (e) = (c) × (d)
November	3,000,000	500,000	2,500,000	1%	25,000
December	2,500,000	500,000	2,000,000	1%	20,000
Total interest income for 20X6					$415,000

[1] This information came from Example 8-21, Item 2.
[2] Annual interest rate of 12% is from Example 8-21, Item 2; 12% ÷ 12 months = 1%.
[3] This information is from Example 8-21, Item 2.

The interest income for 20X6 is compared to the interest expense paid on the tax-exempt debt. The difference is the excess interest available for use in the capitalization process. The excess interest is computed in Table 8-26.

Table 8-26 Computation of Excess Interest for 20X6

Year (a)	Interest Expense (b)	Interest Income (c)	Excess Expense (Income) (d) = (b) – (c)
20X6	$450,000[1]	$415,000[2]	$35,000

[1]$5,000,000 × 9% = $450,000.
[2]Taken from Table 8-25.

Because the excess interest is an expense, any capitalization of interest will be an addition to the asset account. As shown in Table 8-26, the maximum interest available for capitalization from the tax-exempt debt is $35,000. Interest will not be capitalized on the project because excess interest expense is available for capitalization using the provisions of ASC 835-20-30. Before any interest is capitalized, the provisions of ASC 835-20 must be consulted to determine if and how much interest expense can be capitalized on the qualifying asset. The total amount of interest that can be capitalized under ASC 835-20 is computed in Table 8-27. The amount of interest that can be capitalized using ASC 835-20 is subject to the availability of interest expense.

Table 8-27 Possible Interest Capitalization under SFAS No. 34

Date of Expenditure[1]	Amount[1]	Capitalization Period[2]	Average Expenditure
January 1	$400,000	12/12	$400,000[3]
March 1	600,000	10/12	500,000
May 1	500,000	8/12	333,333
August 1	200,000	5/12	83,333
September 1	300,000	4/12	100,000
November 1	500,000	2/12	83,333
December 1	500,000	1/12	41,667
Total Average Accumulated Expenditures			$1,541,666

Date of Expenditure[1]	Amount[1]	Capitalization Period[2]	Average Expenditure
Capitalization Rate			9%[4]
Possible Interest Capitalization on Building			$138,750

[1] See Example 8-21, Item 2.
[2] Period from date of expenditure to December 31, 20X6.
[3] $400,000 × 12/12 = $400,000.
[4] See Example 8-21, Item 2.

The 9% capitalization rate is the interest rate on the tax-exempt borrowing. Because a specific borrowing was used to finance the construction of the building, its rate is used to compute the possible interest to capitalize. Because tax-exempt debt was issued, the excess interest available for interest capitalization of $35,000 (Table 8-26) must be compared to the possible interest to capitalize under ASC 835-20 of $138,750 (Table 8-27). The smaller of these two amounts is the interest to be capitalized. Therefore, $35,000 is capitalized for 20X6.

Journal entries are not illustrated in the solution to Example 8-20. The entries would be the same as presented for the contracted building in Example 8-17. The reader is encouraged to review the detailed journal entries illustrated in the solution of Example 8-17.

This completes the analysis of all five examples relating to interest capitalization. However, there are some additional matters that must be mentioned before the discussion of ASC 835-20 is complete.

Capitalization of Interest—Other Considerations

ASC 835-20 provides no guidelines for the accounting and reporting of interest capitalization in interim reports; however, ASC 270-10 states that the interim period should apply the same accounting principles that were applied in the last annual period (with certain modifications). Interest capitalization in the interim period may present a serious problem in the computation of the weighted average capitalization rate. The author feels that using an effective weighted rate, where it is required, would be an appropriate procedure. Applying this effective rate to the year-to-date average accumulated expenditures and subtracting previous interest capitalized during the current fiscal year appears to be a procedure that will meet the requirements of interim reporting.

Capitalization of Interest—Disclosures

ASC 835-20-50-1 specifies the disclosure requirements during the period of interest capitalization. These disclosures include:

1. Distinction between cost incurred and expenditure as defined in the Statement.
2. The total amount of interest incurred and the amount capitalized, if any interest has been capitalized in the current period.

Imputation of Interest—Flowchart and General Discussion

ASC 835-30 specifies the accounting treatment for a receivable or payable when the present value and face amount are not equal. ASC 835-30 applies to receivables and payables that are either: a right under contract to receive an amount of money on a specified date or a date that can be determined or an obligation under contract to pay an amount of money on a specified date or a date that can be determined. The contractual right or obligation may or may not have a stated requirement for interest.

ASC 835-30-15-2 specifically identifies the following receivables and payables as being subject to the provisions of ASC 835-30:

1. Notes that are secured or unsecured.
2. Bonds, mortgage notes, and debenture bonds.
3. Obligations supported by equipment.
4. Selected accounts receivable and payable.

ASC 835-30-15-3 identifies specific receivables and payables that are exempt from the provisions of ASC 835-30. These include the following:

1. Current receivables and payables arising from the normal course of business and on normal terms of trade;
2. Amounts that will be applied to the future purchase price of property, goods, or services;
3. Amounts representing security for one party to a transaction, such as a security deposit;
4. Cash lending activities of financial entities such as banks and savings and loans; and
5. Transactions between a subsidiary and parent or subsidiaries of the same parent.

Flowchart 8-4 identifies the general accounting and reporting requirements established by ASC 835-30. The decision blocks have been numbered for referencing in the discussion below.

Flowchart 8-4

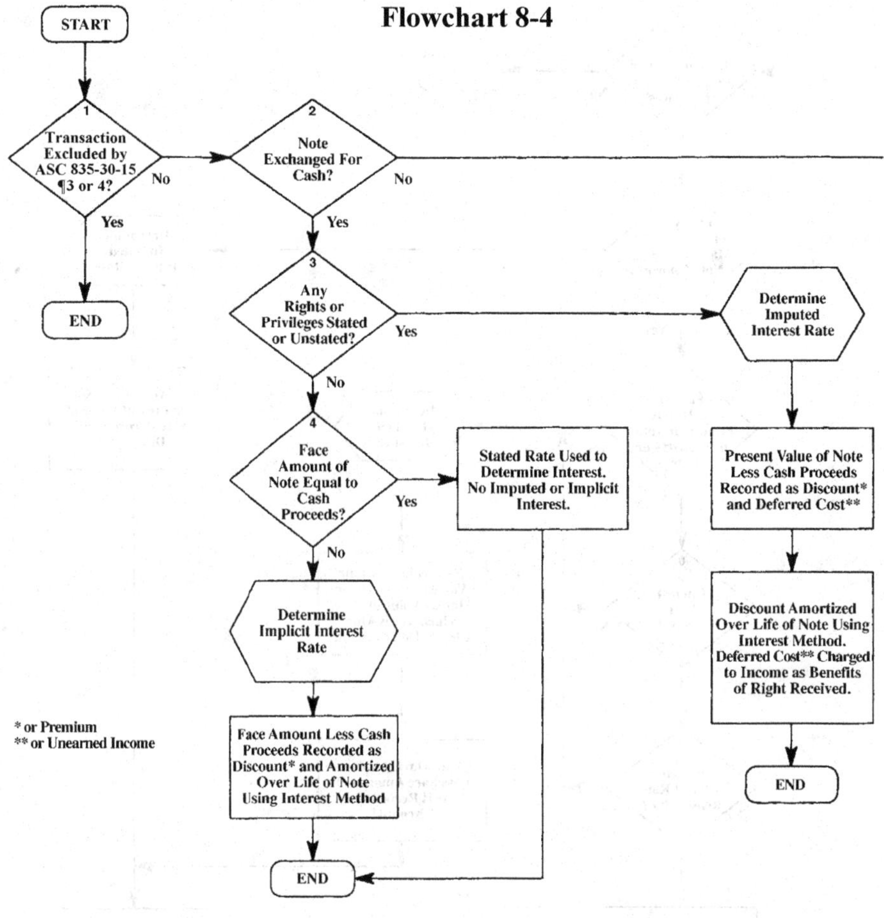

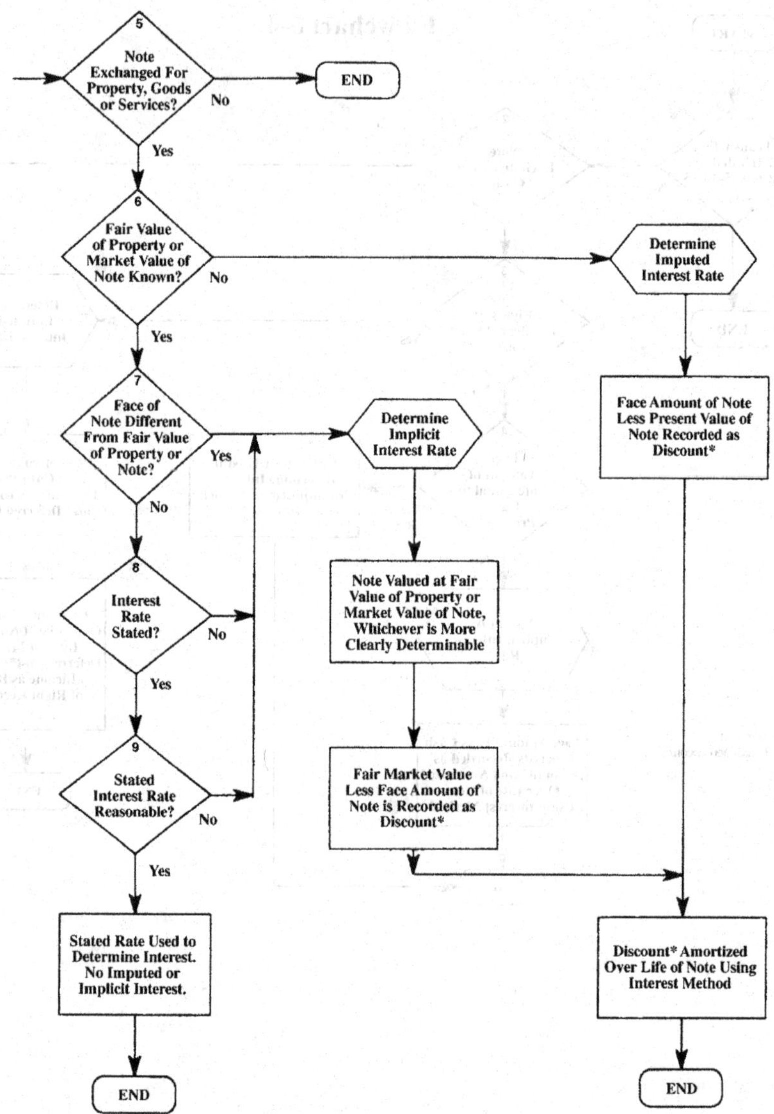

The receivables and payables identified as being subject to the provisions of ASC 835-30 will be referred to as "notes" in the remainder of this discussion. The general types of notes identified in ASC 835-30 are notes exchanged for cash only, notes exchanged for cash *and* a right or privilege, and notes exchanged for property, goods, or services. In the discussion below, a general outline of each type of note will be presented first, followed by the technical considerations involved in accounting for the note.

Notes Exchanged for Cash Only—General Considerations

A note issued or received for cash only (Block 2), and not containing stated or unstated rights or privileges (Block 3), is recorded at an amount equal to the face of the note. The note has a value equal to its present value. The present value on the date of exchange is equal to the cash proceeds given or received. If there is a difference between the cash proceeds and the face of the note (Block 4), the amount is recorded as a discount or premium, whichever is appropriate. When a discount or premium is recorded, it is amortized over the life of the note, using the interest method. (The interest method is the application of the effective interest rate to the unrecovered obligation balance—face of the note, plus or minus the unamortized premium or discount.) The premium and discount amortization process described above does not apply when the liabilities are reported at fair value using the provisions of ASC 825-10. In addition, the interest method does not apply to amortization procedures for unamortized issue cost when liabilities are reported at fair value using ASC 825-10. If a right or privilege is not associated with a note exchanged for cash, interest will be calculated at either the stated rate or the implicit rate. It is never appropriate to recognize imputed interest in the case outlined above.

The stated interest rate is commonly understood, and no explanation is necessary. However, an explanation of implicit and imputed interest may prove beneficial. The implicit interest rate is the rate that equates the present value of the note with the face of the note and is determined by factors directly associated with the note transaction. The imputed interest rate is also a rate that equates the present value of the note with the face of the note, but it may be determined by factors not associated with the note transaction. The imputed interest rate would approximate the rate that would be negotiated by independent borrowers and lenders for a note having similar characteristics and a similar degree of risk. Implicit interest always may be determined mathematically, but imputed interest requires judgment on the part of the accountant.

Where a note is issued solely for cash (no rights or privileges associated with the note), the implicit interest rate will be used to determine interest if the face is different than the proceeds. If the face of the note is equal to the proceeds, and the interest rate is zero, no interest will be recognized from the transaction. It is appropriate to have a true non-interest bearing note under the provisions of ASC 835-30.

Notes Exchanged for Cash Only—Technical Considerations

To illustrate the technical aspects of a note issued or received for cash only, assume that Borrower, Inc. borrows $10,000 from Lender Company, with no stated interest. The agreement requires Borrower, Inc. to repay $10,000 at the end of four years. There are no rights or privileges associated with the agreement.

By following Flowchart 8-4, it can be determined that the stated rate of interest should be used to determine interest expense or income in the example. This note qualifies as a true non-interest bearing note, because the face amount ($10,000) is not greater than the proceeds ($10,000). ASC 835-30 prohibits *imputing* interest where a note is exchanged for cash only; therefore, no interest will be recognized over the four-year period. The journal entries necessary to record the note for Borrower, Inc. and Lender Company are shown below:

	Borrower, Inc.	
Cash	10,000	
Notes Payable		10,000
	Lender Company	
Notes Receivable	10,000	
Cash		10,000

Because interest will not be recognized on this note, the only other entry required is for the payment of the principal amount at the end of the four-year period. The entries would be merely a reversal of the ones shown above.

This first example represents a very straightforward exchange of a note for cash only. A more complex example is presented below. In this case, assume that Borrower, Inc. borrows $300,000 from Lender Company and that, once again, there is no stated interest rate. The agreement requires Borrower, Inc. to repay $710,210 at the end of 10 years. There are no rights or privileges associated with the agreement.

Because the face amount of the note ($710,210) is greater than the cash proceeds ($300,000), the *implicit* interest rate must be determined. Since Borrower, Inc. is receiving only $300,000 in cash and is required to repay $710,210, interest of $410,210 ($710,210 – $300,000) is implicit in the transaction.

At inception of the agreement, Borrower, Inc. and Lender Company should record the note at its face amount and recognize the implicit interest as a discount on the note. The following entries reflect the proper accounting at the date of the transaction:

	Borrower, Inc.	
Cash	300,000	
Discount on Notes Payable	410,210	
Notes Payable		710,210
	Lender Company	
Notes Receivable	710,210	
Cash		300,000
Discount on Notes Receivable		410,210

The total interest has been determined above; however, the implicit rate of interest has yet to be determined. To calculate the implicit rate, the trial-and-error method, a computer program or the procedure outlined below may be used.

The following formula will provide the *present value factor* that is associated with the effective interest rate implicit in the transaction:

$$F = \frac{C}{N}$$

Where: F = Present value factor of $1

C = Cash proceeds received or given on exchange

N = Face of the note

Using this formula and the information given above, the following answer is generated:

$$F = \frac{\$300,00}{\$710,210}$$

$$F = .42241$$

The answer of .42241 represents the present value factor for $1 for 10 periods at a yet-to-be-determined interest rate. Given this information, turn to the present value table for $1, Appendix E, Table I. Start in the 10 periods row, and go across the columns until the factor of .42241 is found. This present value factor corresponds to an interest rate of 9%. Therefore, 9% is the effective interest rate that will be used to recognize interest expense or income, using the interest method. The exact present value factor may not always be found in the table. Interpolation of an interest rate between two factors may be required. This was not an installment note. In the case of installment notes, it will be necessary to use an annuity table, rather than merely a present value table. Even with these restrictions, the technique described above is more efficient than the trial-and-error method.

Once the effective rate has been determined, an amortization schedule can be prepared. Table 8-28 shows the amortization necessary for the example.

Table 8-28 Discount Amortization Schedule

	Period	Discount Amortization	Carrying Value of Note
Initial Value			$300,000
	1	[a]$27,000	[b]327,000
	2	29,430	356,430
	3	32,079	388,509
	4	34,966	423,475
	5	38,113	461,588
	6	41,543	503,131
	7	45,282	548,413
	8	49,357	597,770
	9	53,799	651,569
	10	58,641	[c]710,210
		$410,210	

[a] $300,000 × 9% = $27,000.
[b] $300,000 + $27,000 = $327,000.
[c] Amount equals the face of the note at maturity.

Even though the note is non-interest bearing, implicit interest will be recognized. The entries to record the first year's amortization of the discount are as follows:

Borrower, Inc.

Interest Expense	27,000	
Discount on Notes Payable		27,000

Lender Company

Discount on Notes Receivable	27,000	
Interest Income		27,000

Amounts for subsequent amortization are found in Table 8-28.

Notes Exchanged for Cash and a Right or Privilege—General Considerations

A note may be exchanged for cash and also have a stated or unstated right or privilege associated (Block 3). For example, a company may loan money to a major supplier with no stated interest, but with a provision that the supplier allow the company to purchase products in the future at less than the prevailing market price. Obtaining this right may be the primary reason for the loan. If such a right or privilege exists, recognition must be given to the value of the right by establishing a discount or premium on the note. In this case, the discount or premium is not the result of implicit interest, but must be the result of imputed interest. Interest associated with the right must be imputed by using an assumed interest rate. The imputed interest rate is based largely on judgments made by the user, but ASC 835-30 does provide some guidance in the selection of an appropriate rate. The rate should be equal to the rate that the debtor would have to pay on the date of the transaction for similar financing with a similar degree of risk from an independent source. Selection of an appropriate interest rate may be influenced by factors such as terms of the agreement, collateral provided by the debtor, creditor risk of the debtor, and any restrictive covenants. The selection of the appropriate imputed interest is discussed in detail in ASC 835-30-25, paragraphs 12 and 13.

Once the appropriate rate has been selected, the present value of the note is calculated. The difference between the present value of the note and the face amount is the discount or premium. In most cases, the face of the note is equal to the amount disbursed or received; therefore, it is necessary to establish a deferred asset or unearned income account to offset the discount or premium recorded.

The discount or premium is amortized over the life of the note, using the interest method. The imputed interest rate is used in the amortization process. The deferred asset or unearned income account is amortized over the life of the note in proportion to the benefits received from the right or privilege. For example, for the right described above, the lender would amortize the deferred asset to cost of goods sold, based on the relationship between the current period purchases and the estimated total purchases from the supplier over the life of the note. The supplier would amortize the unearned income, based on the relationship between the current sales to the customer and estimated total sales over the life of the note.

Notes Exchanged for Cash and a Right or Privilege—Technical Considerations

To illustrate the somewhat complex technical aspects of accounting for a note exchanged for cash and a right or privilege, assume that Lender Company loans $3,000,000 to Borrower, Inc., a supplier of products to Lender Company. The $3,000,000 is to be repaid in four years, with no interest. Borrower, Inc. agrees to allow Lender Company to purchase merchandise at less than prevailing market prices during the next four years. Assume further that Borrower, Inc. would have to pay 12% interest for similar financing.

Flowchart 8-4 (Block 3), shows that interest must be imputed on this loan agreement. For this example, the imputed interest rate was given at 12%. The right to purchase merchandise at less than the prevailing market price must be given accounting recognition. To accomplish this, the present value of the note must be determined, using the imputed interest rate. Because this is a lump-sum payment, the present value of $1 must be used (see Appendix E, Table I). The present value factor for four periods at 12% is .63552, which leads to the following computation:

$3,000,00 × .63552 = $1,906,560

The present value of the note is, therefore, $1,906,560 and the difference between the face of the note ($3,000,000) and the present value is the imputed interest of $1,093,440.

Given this information, the entries required at the date the loan agreement was consummated are as follows:

Borrower, Inc.		
Cash	3,000,000	
Discount on Notes Payable	1,093,440	
Notes Payable		3,000,000
Unearned Income		1,093,440
Lender Company		
Deferred Cost of Purchases	1,093,440	
Notes Receivable	3,000,000	
Cash		3,000,000
Discount on Notes Receivable		1,093,440

The next step involves the determination of the proper amortization of both the discount and the unearned income and deferred cost of purchases. The discount is amortized using the interest method, but the unearned income and deferred cost of purchases are amortized using the relationship between annual purchases/sales of merchandise and total expected purchases/sales of merchandise. The expected purchases/sales of merchandise, for purposes of the example, are presented in Table 8-29.

Table 8-29 Schedule of Purchases/Sales

Year	Purchases/Sales
1	$500,000
2	600,000
3	800,000
4	1,000,000
Total	$2,900,000

Table 8-30 develops the calculation necessary to amortize the discount, as well as the amortization of the unearned income and deferred cost of purchases.

Table 8-30 Amortization Schedule for Note Exchanged for Cash and a Right

	Period	Deferred Cost or Unearned Income Amortization	Deferred Cost or Unearned Income Balance	Discount Amortization	Carrying Value of Note
Initial Value	—	—	$1,093,440	—	$1,906,560
	1	[a]$188,524	[b]904,916	[c]$228,787	[d]2,135,347
	2	[e]226,229	678,687	256,242	2,391,589
	3	[f]301,639	377,048	286,991	2,678,580
	4	377,048	—0—	*321,420	[h]3,000,000
		$1,093,440	$1,093,440		

[a] $500,000/$2,900,000 × $1,093,440 = $188,524.
[b] $1,093,440 – $188,524 = $904,916.
[c] $1,906,560 × 12% = $228,787.
[d] $1,906,560 + $228,787 = $2,135,347.
[e] $600,000/$2,900,000 × $1,093,440 = $226,229.
[f] $800,000/$2,900,000 × $1,093,440 = $301,639.
[g] $1,000,000/$2,900,000 × $1,093,440 = $377,048.
[h] Amount represents the face of the note at the maturity date.
* Rounded.

Information from Table 8-30 is used to prepare the required journal entries for Year 1:

Borrower, Inc.

Unearned Income	188,524	
Sales		188,524
Interest Expense	228,787	
Discount on Notes Payable		228,787

Lender Company

Cost of Goods Sold	188,524	
Deferred Cost of Purchases		188,524
Discount on Notes Receivable	228,787	
Interest Income		228,787

In the example just completed, several assumptions were made to limit the complexity of the problem. Some of the complicating factors will now be discussed (though they do not change the basic accounting presented above).

Because the effective interest rate is imputed, it is possible for the borrower and lender to have a different perception of the borrower's imputed interest rate. If this were the case, the borrower and lender would use a different interest rate to determine the value of the right or privilege. By using a different rate, different amounts may be charged to sales and cost of sales over the life of the note.

In addition to this problem, the periodic amortization of the right or privilege by the lender and the borrower may not be the same. This would be the case where the two parties had different expectations concerning the total and annual sales/purchases between them. Thus, the combination of using different imputed interest rates and also different estimations of sales/purchases may complicate the analysis necessary to arrive at a correct solution to the problem.

Notes Exchanged for Property, Goods, or Services—General Considerations

In most cases, a note issued or received for property, goods, or services (Block 5) is valued at the present value of the consideration given or, if more clearly determinable, the present value of the consideration received. The consideration exchanged for the property, goods, or services (hereafter referred to as property) consists of two components. One component is the purchase price in an arm's length cash transaction. The second component is the interest factor or the return to the seller for accepting the note instead of receiving cash at the time the exchange is made. If the fair value of the property (or market value of the note) is known (Block 6), the transaction may involve the use of the stated rate or the implicit rate, but interest may not be imputed. Assuming these values are known, if the face of the note is equal to the fair value of the property (Block 7), if the note contains a stated interest rate (Block 8) and if the stated rate is reasonable (Block 9), no new accounting problems are created. However, if any of these conditions are not met, special accounting treatment is required.

If the fair value of the property or the fair value of the note is known, any implicit interest in the exchange can be determined and a discount or premium established for the difference between the fair value of the property and the face of the note. If, however, the fair value of the property and the fair value of the note are not known, interest must be imputed. The discount or premium established by imputing the interest or by recognizing the implicit interest is amortized, using the interest method over the life of the note. Generally, the use of imputed interest is a last resort for the accountant.

Notes Exchanged for Property, Goods, or Services—Technical Considerations

To illustrate the accounting for a note exchanged for property, assume that Borrower, Inc. purchased equipment from Lender Company and was unable to pay cash. Lender Company agreed to accept Borrower's five-year, non-interest bearing note with payments of $54,114 payable at the end of each year. The total amount to be repaid is $270,570 (5 × $54,114). Lender Company normally purchases the equipment for $150,000, and resells it for $200,000.

Because the fair value of the property ($200,000) is known, the only applicable interest rates are the stated rate or the implicit rate. The face amount of the note ($270,570) is greater than the fair value of the property; therefore, this note requires the calculation of implicit interest. Borrower, Inc. is receiving equipment with a fair value of $200,000, but is required to pay $270,570, so there is $70,570 ($270,570 – $200,000) interest implicit in the transaction. The entries below are required to record the note at the date the agreement is consummated:

Borrower, Inc.		
Equipment	200,000	
Discount on Notes Payable	70,570	
Notes Payable		270,570

Lender Company		
Notes Receivable	270,570	
Sales		200,000
Discount on Notes Receivable		70,570
Cost of Goods Sold	150,000	
Inventory		150,000

The discount of $70,570 must be amortized over the life of the note, using the appropriate effective interest rate. The effective interest rate necessary to amortize the discount is unknown and must be computed. The *present value factor* corresponding to the effective interest rate is determined using the following formula:

$$F = \frac{P}{C}$$

Where:

F = Present value factor of an annuity
P = Fair Value of Property or market value of the note
C = Periodic cash payment

Based upon the information in the example transaction, the formula yields the following results:

$$F = \frac{\$200,000}{\$54,114} = 3.69590$$

The answer of 3.69590 represents the present value factor for an ordinary annuity for five years at a yet-to-be-determined interest rate. Turn to the present value table for an ordinary annuity, Appendix E, Table II. Start in the five periods row, and go across the columns until the factor of 3.69590 is found. This present value factor corresponds to an interest rate of 11%, which is the effective rate that will be used to amortize the discount.

Once the appropriate implicit interest rate has been determined, an amortization schedule may be prepared. Table 8-31 shows the calculation of the amortization of the discount for the example note.

Table 8-31 Schedule of Discount Amortization and Principal Repayment

Period	Principal Payment	Discount Amortization	Reduction in Note Carrying Value	Carrying Value of Note
Initial Value	—	—	—	$200,000
1	$54,114	[a]$22,000	[b]$32,114	[c]167,886
2	54,114	18,467	35,647	132,239
3	54,114	14,546	39,568	92,671
4	54,114	10,194	43,920	48,751
5	54,114	5,363	48,751	—0—
	$270,570	$70,570	$200,000	

[a] $200,000 × 11% = $22,000.
[b] $54,114 – $22,000 = $32,114.
[c] $200,000 – $32,114 = $167,886.

Based upon the information generated in Table 8-31, the entries to reflect the discount amortization and the note principal reduction for Year 1 of the note are presented below:

Borrower, Inc.

Notes Payable	54,114	
Interest Expense	22,000	
Discount on Notes Payable		22,000
Cash		54,114

Lender Company

Cash	54,114	
Discount on Notes Receivable	22,000	
Notes Receivable		54,114
Interest Income		22,000

This completes the example of accounting for a note exchanged for property where the interest is *implicit* in the transaction. To illustrate a situation where interest is not implicit in the contract, but must be *imputed,* assume that Borrower, Inc. purchased equipment from Lender Company. Lender agrees to accept a noninterest bearing note for the equipment, with annual year-end payments of $150,000 for six years. Assume that Borrower, Inc. normally would have to pay 12% for a similar financing arrangement. Due to the unique nature of the property, its fair value is not known. The fair value of the note cannot be determined, but the cost of the equipment to Lender is $500,000.

Because neither the fair market value of the equipment nor the fair value of the note is known, interest on the loan must be imputed to determine the present value of the note. The present value calculation would be based on the 12% interest rate that Borrower, Inc. would have to pay for similar financing. The present value of the note (using the 4.11141 present value factor for an ordinary annuity for six periods at 12%) would be determined as follows:

$150,000 × 4.11141 = $616,712

The difference between the present value of the note ($616,712) and the total payments of $900,000 ($150,000 × 6) is the imputed interest on the note ($900,000 – $616,712 = $283,288 imputed interest). The entries required to record the note and equipment are as follows:

Borrower, Inc.

Equipment	616,712	
Discount on Notes Payable	283,288	
Notes Payable		900,000

Lender Company

Notes Receivable	900,000	
Equipment		500,000
Discount on Notes Receivable		283,288
Gain on Sale of Equipment		116,712

The gain on the sale is a residual value, resulting from the fact that the seller of the equipment did not know the fair market value of the equipment sold.

The next step involves the amortization of the discount, using the interest method. Table 8-32 shows the principal reduction, discount amortization and carrying value of the note, using the imputed interest rate of 12%.

Table 8-32 Schedule of Discount and Principal Amortization

Period	Principal Payment	Discount Amortization	Reduction in Note Carrying Value	Carrying Value of Note
Initial Value	—	—	—	$616,712
1	$150,000	[a]$74,005	[b]$75,995	[c]540,717
2	150,000	64,886	85,114	455,603
3	150,000	54,672	95,328	360,275
4	150,000	43,233	106,767	253,508
5	150,000	30,421	119,579	133,929
6	150,000	16,071	133,929	—0—
	$900,000	$283,288	$616,712	

[a] $616,712 × 12% = $74,005.
[b] $150,000 – $74,005 = $75,995.
[c] $616,712 – $75,995 = $540,717.

The entries required to amortize the discount and record the principal reduction are the same as shown in the previous example, except for the amounts, and will not be repeated at this point.

The preceding two examples illustrated the accounting for a non-interest bearing note. However, the situation could occur where the note had a stated interest rate, but the stated rate was considered to be unreasonable in light of the transaction. To illustrate this situation, assume that Borrower, Inc. purchased equipment from Lender Company and issued a note, instead of cash. Assume that Lender Company paid $300,000 for the equipment, and that Borrower, Inc. agrees to a 12% note for $500,000. The note is to be paid in full at the end of five years. Borrower, Inc. normally would have to pay 10% interest for similar financing, and it is determined that the 12% stated rate is clearly unreasonable.

When it has been determined that the stated interest rate is unreasonable, the appropriate rate may be an implicit rate or an imputed rate. If the fair value of the property or the fair value of the note are known, implicit interest will be calculated; otherwise, interest must be imputed. For purposes of this example, assume that the fair value of the property and the fair value of the note are not known. Therefore, interest will have to be imputed at the 10% rate (the rate assumed to be reasonable). The present value of the note may be calculated using the following formula:

$$PVN = (MV \times SR)(PVA) + (MV)(PV)$$

Where:
PVN = Present value of the note
MV = Maturity value of the note
SR = Stated interest rate
PVA = Present value factor for an annuity, using the imputed rate
PV = Present value factor for $1, using the imputed rate

Given the information in the above example—and using 3.79079 as the present value factor for an ordinary annuity for five periods at 10% and .62092 as the present value factor for $1 for five periods at 10%—the formula would provide the following results:

PVN = ($500,000 × .12)(3.79079) + ($500,000)(.62092) = $537,907

The difference between the present value of the note ($537,907) and the total proceeds ($500,000) is the discount or premium. In this case, the amount is a premium of $37,907.

The entries to record the note at inception of the agreement are as follows:

Borrower, Inc.

Equipment	537,907	
Notes Payable		500,000
Premium on Notes Payable		37,907

Lender Company

Notes Receivable	500,000	
Premium on Notes Receivable	37,907	
Equipment		300,000
Gain on Sale of Equipment		237,907

After determining the appropriate present value, an amortization schedule similar to Table 8-33 can be prepared.

Table 8-33 Schedule of Interest and Premium Amortization

Period	Stated Interest	Interest Expense or Income	Premium Amortization	Carrying Value of Note
Initial Value	—	—	—	$537,907
1	[a]$60,000	[b]$53,791	[c]$6,209	[d]531,698
2	60,000	53,170	6,830	524,868
3	60,000	52,487	7,513	517,355
4	60,000	51,736	8,264	509,091
5	60,000	50,909	9,091	[e]500,000
	$300,000	$262,093	$37,907	

[a] $500,000 × 12% = $60,000.
[b] $537,907 × 10% = $53,791.
[c] $60,000 – $53,791 = $6,209.
[d] $537,907 – $6,209 = $531,698.
[e] Represents the maturity value of the note.

Using the information in Table 8-33, the journal entries required for Year 1 to record the interest payment and premium amortization would be as follows:

Borrower, Inc.

Interest Expense	53,791	
Premium on Notes Payable	6,209	
Cash		60,000

Lender Company

Cash	60,000	
Interest Income		53,791
Premium on Notes Receivable		6,209

Income Tax Considerations

A difference may exist between the financial and tax reporting of interest expense and interest income when implicit or imputed interest must be used. Any difference is considered to be a temporary difference and is to be handled in accordance with the provisions of ASC 740.

Presentation Requirements

Certain presentation requirements are specified in ASC 835-30-45. They include the following items:

- The discount or premium should be shown as a contra or adjunct account to the related receivable or payable;
- The effective interest rate should be specified, and any unamortized issue costs should be carried as an asset properly classified as a deferred charge; and
- The maturity or face amount of the receivable or payable should be reported.

Recent Changes

ASU 2015-03, *Interest—Imputation of Interest (Subtopic 835-30): Simplifying the Presentation of Debt Issuance Costs,* and ASU 2015-15, *Interest—Imputation of Interest (Subtopic 835-30): Presentation and Subsequent Measurement of Debt Issuance Costs Associated with Line-of-Credit Arrangements,* were issued in 2015.

Under ASU 2015-03, the reporting entity is required to report debt issuance costs in its balance sheet as direct deduction from carrying amount of the debt liability that such costs relate to consistent with the reporting of debt discounts. This accounting increases the reporting entity's effective interest rate with the amortization of the debt costs, using the effective interest rate method, included in interest expense. ASU 2015-03 is effective for annual periods for all entities with years beginning after December 15, 2015. And public entities are required to apply ASU 2015-03 to interim periods within that year, while nonpublic entities are required to apply it to interim periods within years beginning after December 15, 2016. Early adoption is permitted. ASU 2015-03 is applied retrospectively resulting in a restatement of the prior year's comparative balance sheet. Customary disclosures related to a change in accounting principle are required.

ASU 2015-03 does not address the presentation or subsequent measurement of debt-issuance costs related to line-of-credit arrangements. ASU 2015-15 reflects the views of the SEC staff that they would not object to deferring and presenting debt issuance costs as an asset and subsequently amortizing them ratably over the term of the line-of-credit arrangement, regardless of whether there are any outstanding borrowings on the line.

Topic 840: Leases

Topic 840, *Leases,* contains eight subtopics:

10 Overall

20 Operating Leases

30 Capital Leases

40 Sale-Leaseback Transactions

958 Not-For-Profit Entities*

974 Real Estate—Real Estate Investment Trusts*

978 Real Estate—Time-Sharing Activities*

980 Regulated Operations*

ASC 840 provides financial accounting guidance for leases from the perspectives of both the lessee and the lessor. The following material on ASC 840 is divided into lessee accounting and lessor accounting.

---

* See the corresponding topic in Chapter 9 for coverage of this shared subtopic.

Defining Some Important Terms

At the outset, it is important to define some of the terms that will appear first in the flowcharts and later in the example material presented. ASC 840 defines several terms; some will be defined below and others will be introduced at a more appropriate time. The full meaning of each of these terms cannot be conveyed easily, but, with some explanation and the support of illustrations, the reader will have a good understanding of the specific meaning of the following terms contained in ASC 840:

1. *Minimum Rental Payment* (MRP). The MRP consists of the minimum payments required to be made under the lease agreement by the lessee to the lessor. The term indicates that additional payments above the minimum might be involved in the lease agreement, but most of the major decisions required are concerned with the MRP.

2. *Minimum Lease Payments* (MLP). The MLP may be different from the MRP; in some cases, it may be the same. The MLP always will include the MRP, but also can include other items, if specified in the lease. In addition to the MRP, the MLP may include:

   a. *Guarantee of residual value by the lessee.* This represents an amount guaranteed by the lessee to the lessor for a portion or all of the estimated residual value of the asset at the end of the lease term. If, at the termination of the lease, the actual residual value received by the lessor is less than the guaranteed residual value, the lessee may have to make up the deficiency by a payment to the lessor.

   b. *Payment required for failure to renew or extend the lease.* A penalty payment may be required of the lessee if the agreement specifies that the lease must be renewed or extended, or grants the lessee the right to renew or extend the lease. This part of the agreement is present to protect the rights of both the lessee and the lessor.

   c. *Bargain purchase option payment.* This represents a payment by the lessee to the lessor at the end of the lease term that will allow the lessee to obtain title to the leased property. The bargain purchase price usually is substantially below the estimated fair value of the property; therefore, it is reasonable to assume that the lessee will exercise the bargain purchase payment.

3. *Lessor's Implicit Interest Rate.* In general terms, this can be thought of as the lessor's rate of return on the leased property; more specifically, it is the rate of interest that will equate the present value of the MLP (after certain deductions) with the fair value of the leased property, less the investment tax credit at the inception of the lease.

4. *Lessee's Incremental Borrowing Rate.* This is the rate of interest that the lessee would have to pay to borrow the funds necessary to purchase the leased property rather than enter into the lease agreement. This is an opportunity cost rate of interest, rather than a real interest cost. The determination of the incremental borrowing rate requires a series of

reasoned judgments. Basically, the lessee is attempting to determine the terms of borrowing *if* the asset were purchased rather than leased.

5. *Fair Value.* Fair value is defined as the amount that would be received on the measurement date from the sale of property between sellers and buyers (market participants) in an orderly transaction. In addition, on the measurement date, the sellers and buyers are unrelated parties. The fair value provisions of ASC 820 do not apply to ASC 840. However, this exception does not apply to assets and liabilities acquired in a business combination using the provisions of ASC 805 even if the assets or liabilities are related to leases.

Flowchart and Discussion of General Lease Agreement—Lessee

Flowchart 8-5 depicts the classification and accounting for general lease agreements from the standpoint of the lessee. The left side of Flowchart 8-5 deals with the problem of lease classification, and the right side addresses the major accounting problems. The decision blocks are numbered and are referred to in this section.

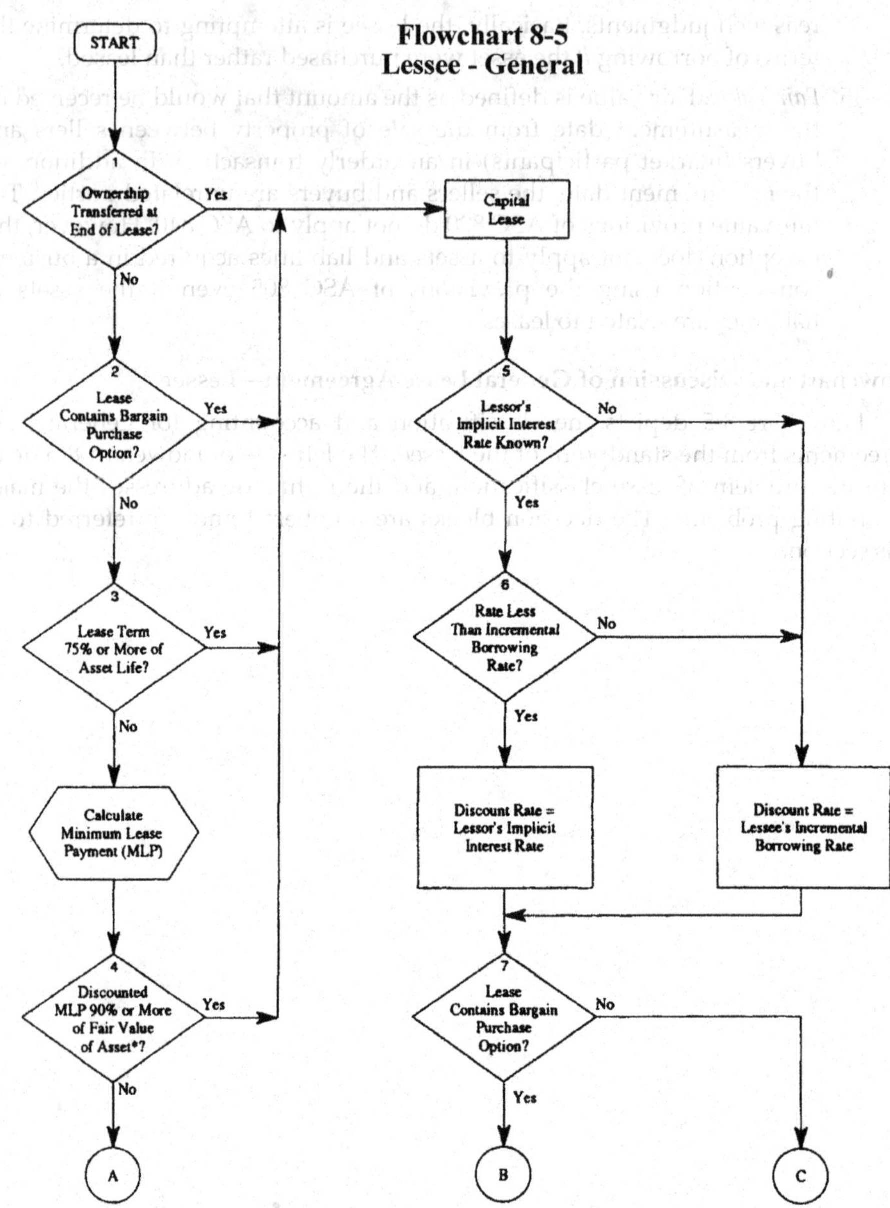

Flowchart 8-5
Lessee - General
START
1
Ownership Transferred at End of Lease?
Yes
No
Capital Lease
2
Lease Contains Bargain Purchase Option?
Yes
No
3
Lease Term 75% or More of Asset Life?
Yes
No
Calculate Minimum Lease Payment (MLP)
4
Discounted MLP 90% or More of Fair Value of Asset*?
Yes
No
A
5
Lessor's Implicit Interest Rate Known?
No
Yes
6
Rate Less Than Incremental Borrowing Rate?
No
Yes
Discount Rate = Lessor's Implicit Interest Rate
Discount Rate = Lessee's Incremental Borrowing Rate
7
Lease Contains Bargain Purchase Option?
No
Yes
B
C

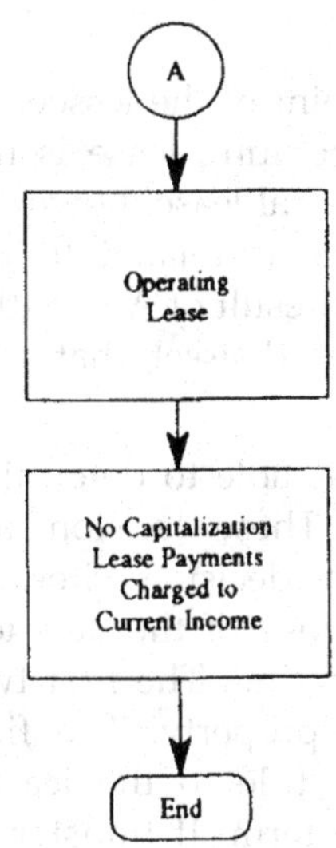

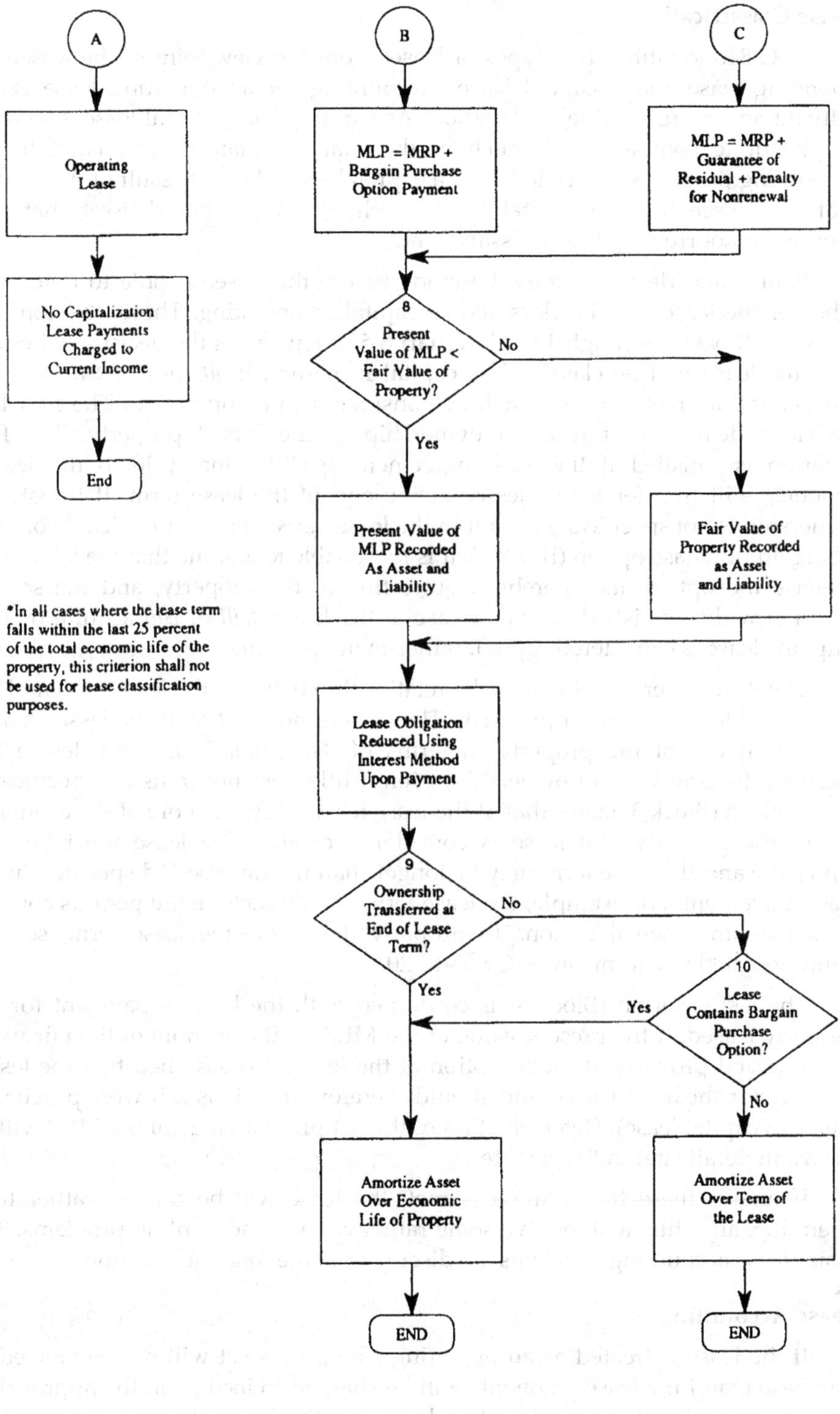

A
Operating Lease
No Capitalization Lease Payments Charged to Current Income
End
B
MLP = MRP + Bargain Purchase Option Payment
C
MLP = MRP + Guarantee of Residual + Penalty for Nonrenewal
8
Present Value of MLP < Fair Value of Property?
No
Yes
Present Value of MLP Recorded As Asset and Liability
Fair Value of Property Recorded as Asset and Liability
*In all cases where the lease term falls within the last 25 percent of the total economic life of the property, this criterion shall not be used for lease classification purposes.
Lease Obligation Reduced Using Interest Method Upon Payment
9
Ownership Transferred at End of Lease Term?
No
Yes
10
Lease Contains Bargain Purchase Option?
Yes
No
Amortize Asset Over Economic Life of Property
Amortize Asset Over Term of the Lease
END
END

Lease Classification

ASC 840 identifies two types of leases from the viewpoint of the lessee: an operating lease and a capital lease. Accounting for an operating lease is not difficult and requires little explanation. Accounting for a capital lease, however, can be quite complex, and much of the example material is related to the accounting problems associated with a capital lease. The end result of ASC 840 is that the lessee treats a capital lease much like a purchased asset that was acquired by borrowing the necessary funds.

Four major decisions must be made before the lessee is able to determine whether the lease is to be classified as capital or operating. These decisions are shown in Blocks 1 through 4 of Flowchart 8-5. If any *one* of the decision criteria is met, the lease will be classified as capital in nature. If *all* four of the decision criteria are *not* met, the lease will be considered to be operating. The first two decisions deal with transfer of ownership to the leased property. The first criterion is satisfied if the lease agreement specifies that title to the leased property will transfer to the lessee at the end of the lease term. If transfer of ownership is not specifically set out in the lease agreement, but the lease contains a bargain purchase option (Block 2), it is reasonable to assume that the lessee will exercise the option and thereby acquire title to the property, and the second criterion will be satisfied. In either case, if the lessee *will* or *can* acquire ownership, the lease is considered capital, rather than operating.

The third criterion addresses the relationship between the lease term and the economic life of the leased property. The assumption is that, if the lessee makes substantial use of the property in terms of its economic life, the lessee has received the privileges of ownership, even if title does not transfer. Specifically, the criterion (Block 3) states that, if the lease term is 75% or more of the economic life of the property, the lease is considered capital. The lease must be *non-cancellable* and the lease term may be longer than the time period specified in the lease agreement. For example, the lease term should include the periods covered by a bargain renewal option. To properly determine the lease term, see the definition of "lease term" in ASC 840-10-20.

The last criterion (Block 4) is concerned with the lessee's payment for the property leased. If the present value of the MLP is 90% or more of the fair value of the leased property at the inception of the lease, it is assumed that the lessee will pay for the asset leased and should therefore treat it as if it were purchased (i.e., as a capital lease). Determination of the net present value of the MLP will be shown in detail later in this chapter.

If one of these four criteria is met, the lease will be capital, rather than operating, and thus will involve some rather complex accounting problems. The major lease accounting problems are discussed in the following section.

Lease Accounting

If the lease is treated as an operating lease, the asset will not be viewed as purchased, and the lease payments will be charged to income in the appropriate accounting period. In general, a straight-line method over the lease term should be used by both the lessor and lessee for operating leases with scheduled rent increases. Another method, as long as it is systematic and rational, may be applied if it better represents the time pattern when the leased property is actually used.

If the lease is classified as capital, the lessee must determine the present value of the MLP. For any present value computation, the number of periods involved, the appropriate interest rate, and the dollar amount to be discounted need to be known. For a capital lease transaction, the number of periods will be determined by the lease term. The selection of the appropriate interest rate will depend upon several factors. The rate to be used will be the lessor's implicit interest rate if it is known (Block 5) *and* if it is less than the lessee's incremental borrowing rate (Block 6).

If the lessor's implicit rate is not known, the lessee's incremental rate must be used. The determination of the appropriate amount to use in the discounting process will depend on whether the lease contains a bargain purchase option (Block 7). If the lease does contain a bargain purchase option, the MLP will be equal to the MRP, plus the amount of the bargain purchase payment. For the present value computation, the MRP is an annuity and the bargain purchase option payment is a lump-sum payment at the end of the lease term. If present value tables are used, it will be necessary to have a table for the present value of $1 and the present value of an ordinary annuity of $1. (If payments are made at the beginning of each period, a table for the present value of an annuity due of $1 would replace the ordinary annuity table. Present value tables are provided in Appendix E.) If the lease does not contain a bargain purchase option, the MLP will be equal to the MRP, plus any guarantee of residual value and plus any penalty for nonrenewal of the lease. Again, the MRP is an annuity, and the other two items *generally* represent lump-sum payments at the end of the lease term.

As in the case of any purchased asset, the recorded value of the asset must not exceed the fair value at the date of acquisition. Therefore, it is necessary to record the asset acquired through the lease agreement at the lower of the present value of the MLP or the fair value of the leased property (Block 8). The liability owed to the lessor will be recorded at the same amount.

The lease obligation will be reduced as the lease payments are made, using the interest method. (The interest method is the application of the discount rate against the unrecovered obligation balance, and is used extensively in this chapter.) The asset recorded will be amortized over its economic life, if ownership transfers or if there is a bargain purchase option (Blocks 9 and 10), or over the lease term, in the absence of either of these two provisions. The depreciation method used should be consistent with the method used for owned assets of a similar nature.

The lessee or a third party may acquire from the lessor the right to own a leased asset, or the right to receive the proceeds from the sale of the asset at the end of the lease term. A transaction of this nature is referred to as acquiring an interest in the residual value of the leased asset. Such a transaction should be accounted for as an acquisition of an asset. The asset acquired should be recorded at an amount equal to one or more of the following: cash paid, fair value of other assets exchanged, and/or liabilities accepted computed on a present value basis, unless the fair value of the asset received is a better estimate. The guarantee of a residual value by the lessee or a third party does not change the preceding accounting for the acquisition of an interest in the residual value of a leased asset. If the residual value of a leased asset should change over time, the entity acquiring an interest in the residual value should not adjust the cost of the interest for the change in residual value.

Technical Considerations for Lessee Accounting—General

Two examples will illustrate the specific provisions of ASC 840 as they apply to the lessee.

Example 8-21
Lease Assumptions

1. Lessee enters into a 10-year, non-cancellable lease that requires year-end payments of $53,000 ($3,000 of which represent executory costs).
2. Lessee's incremental borrowing rate is 8%, and the lessor's implicit interest rate is unknown.
3. Ownership transfers to the lessee at the end of the lease term. The lease does not contain a bargain purchase option.
4. The leased property has a fair value of $340,000 and an estimated economic life of 12 years.

The major problems outlined in the above discussion deal with proper classification of the lease, determination of the appropriate interest rate for calculating the present value of the MLP, determining the proper MLP, and selecting the proper amortization technique for the asset recorded and the related obligation. The technical aspects of the general discussion will be shown through the solution to the example problem presented.

The Example 8-21 lease qualifies as a capital lease. The lease agreement actually meets three of the four basic criteria, although only one criterion need be met. First, ownership to the property transfers to the lessee at the end of the lease term. Also, the lease term of 10 years is more than 75% of the asset's economic life (12 years × .75 = 9 years), and the present value of the MLP is more than 90% of the fair value of the leased property. The computation of the MLP is shown after selection of the proper interest rate.

Determination of the proper interest rate in this particular example is quite easy, because the lessor's implicit rate is not known. Therefore, the only possible rate to use in the discounting process is the lessee's incremental borrowing rate of 8%.

Because the lease does not contain a bargain purchase option, the MLP will be equal to the MRP, plus any guaranteed residual value plus any penalty for nonrenewal. In the Example 8-21 lease, there is no guaranteed residual value or penalty for nonrenewal, so the MLP will be equal to the MRP. To calculate the proper MRP, the lessee must exclude executory costs, such as insurance, maintenance, and taxes, from the required payments. In the example problem, $3,000 of the total MRP of $53,000 represents executory costs, and must be removed and treated as a separate component of the lease. The MLP therefore is equal to $50,000 per year.

There is now enough information to calculate the present value of the MLP, which is determined as follows:

Lease Payment Required	$53,000
Less: Executory Costs	3,000
	$50,000
Present Value Factor	[a]6.71008
Present Value of MLP	$335,504

[a] Present value factor for an ordinary annuity for 10 periods at 8%, see Appendix E, Table II.

The fair value of the leased property is equal to $340,000, and 90% of the amount is $306,000. Therefore, the present value of the MLP ($335,504) is more than 90% of the fair value of the property ($306,000), and the fourth general criterion is met.

Once the lease has been identified as a capital lease, it is necessary to determine the proper amount to capitalize and record as a lease obligation. This determination involves a comparison of the present value of the MLP with the fair value of the leased property. The recorded value of the asset and the obligation will be the smaller of the two. In this particular case, the present value of the MLP is $335,504, and the fair value of the property is $340,000. Therefore, the appropriate amount to use would be $335,504 (the present value of the MLP). The journal entry necessary to record the asset and obligation at the inception of the lease would be:

	Debit	Credit
Leased Property Under Capital Lease	335,504	
Obligation Under Capital Lease		335,504

The next major problem involves the amortization of the asset and the obligation. The lease obligation is amortized each interest payment period, using the interest method. Table 8-34 shows the complete determination of the amortization of the obligation and the classification of all lease expenses. It will prove beneficial to take a few minutes and recompute some of the values in Table 8-34.

Table 8-34 Lease Amortization and Expenses Amortization Schedule for Capital Lease

	Period	Annual Payment	Annual Interest Expense	Obligation Reduction	Present Value of Obligation at Year-End
Initial Value	—	—	—	—	$335,504
	1	$50,000	[a]$26,840	[b]$23,160	[c]312,344
	2	50,000	24,988	25,012	287,332
	3	50,000	22,987	27,013	260,319
	4	50,000	20,826	29,174	231,145
	5	50,000	18,492	31,508	199,637

Period	Annual Payment	Annual Interest Expense	Obligation Reduction	Present Value of Obligation at Year-End
6	50,000	15,971	34,029	165,608
7	50,000	13,249	36,751	128,857
8	50,000	10,309	39,691	89,166
9	50,000	7,132	42,868	46,298
10	50,000	3,702	46,298	-0-
	$500,000	$164,496	$335,504	

Schedule of Recorded Expenses for Capital Lease

Period	Amortization	Interest	Executory Costs	Total	Annual Lease Payment
1	[d]$27,959	$26,840	$3,000	$57,799	$53,000
2	27,959	24,988	3,000	55,947	53,000
3	27,959	22,987	3,000	53,946	53,000
4	27,959	20,826	3,000	51,785	53,000
5	27,959	18,492	3,000	49,451	53,000
6	27,959	15,971	3,000	46,930	53,000
7	27,959	13,249	3,000	44,208	53,000
8	27,959	10,309	3,000	41,268	53,000
9	27,959	7,132	3,000	38,091	53,000
10	27,959	3,702	3,000	34,661	53,000
11	27,959			27,959	
12	*27,955			27,955	
	$335,504	$164,496	$30,000	$530,000	$530,000

[a] $335,504 × 8% = $26,840.
[b] $50,000 – $26,840 = $23,160.
[c] $335,504 – $23,160 = $312,344.
[d] Assuming that straight-line depreciation is used for owned assets ($335,504/12 years = $27,959).
* Rounded.

By using Table 8-34, it can be determined that the proper accounting for the year-end payment of $53,000 would be as follows:

Obligation Under Capital Lease	23,160	
Interest Expense	26,840	
Executory Costs	3,000	
Cash		53,000

At the end of the year, an adjusting entry is necessary to record the amortization of the leased property. Because ownership to the property transfers to the lessee at the end of the lease term, the asset should be amortized over the economic life of the property, using the depreciation method commonly used for similar owned assets. In the example problem, assume that straight-line depreciation is the appropriate method to use. The following adjusting entry would be required to complete the recording of lease expenses:

Amortization of Leased Property	27,959	
Accumulated Amortization—Leased Property		27,959

The Example 8-21 lease is relatively straightforward, and it demonstrates the basic considerations of capital lease accounting. Example 8-22 is somewhat more complex and requires additional decisions and computations. A complete understanding of Example 8-21 is necessary before proceeding to Example 8-22.

Example 8-22
Lease Assumptions

1. The lessee enters into a five-year non-cancellable lease that requires payments of $100,000 at the beginning of each of the five years. The lease agreement further specifies that the lessee will guarantee the residual value of the property in the amount of $10,000, which also is equal to the estimated residual value at the end of the lease term.
2. The lessee's incremental borrowing rate is 8% and the lessor's implicit rate is known to be 10%.
3. The leased property has a fair value of $423,196 and an estimated economic life of five years. The lessee depreciates similar assets using the straight-line method.
4. In the third year of the lease term, the estimated residual value declines to $8,000.

On the face of these assumptions, the Example 8-22 lease qualifies as a capital lease. As will be shown, the lease agreement meets two of the four basic criteria for classification as a capital lease, either of which is sufficient to classify the lease as capital. First, the lease term of five years is more than 75% of the economic life of the leased property (5 years × .75 = 3.75 years). Second, as the computations below will show, the present value of the MLP is more than 90% of the fair value of the leased property.

Selection of the proper interest rate to use in discounting the MLP requires a comparison of the lessee's incremental borrowing rate with the lessor's implicit rate, because both are known in this example. The lessee's incremental borrowing rate of 8% will be used in this case, because it is less than the lessor's implicit rate.

As before, the lease does not contain a bargain purchase option and the MLP will be equal to the MRP, plus any guaranteed residual value and plus any penalty for nonrenewal. In the Example 8-22 lease, the MRP is equal to $100,000, and there is a guarantee of residual value of $10,000. To determine the present value of the MLP, the lessee must compute the present value of an annuity due (the MRP) and the present value of an amount (the guarantee of residual value). Determination of the present value of the MLP is as follows:

Lease Payment Required	$100,000	
Less: Executory Costs	-0-	
	$100,000	
Present Value Factor	[a]4.31213	
Present Value of Rental Payment		$431,213

Guarantee of Residual Value	$10,000	
Present Value Factor	[b].68058	
Present Value of Residual		6,806
Present Value of MLP		$438,019

[a] Present value factor for an annuity due for five periods at 8%. See Appendix E, Table III.
[b] Present value factor for $1 for five periods at 8%. See Appendix E, Table I.

The fair value of the leased property is equal to $423,196, and 90% of the amount is $380,876. Therefore, the present value of the MLP is more than 90% of the fair value of the leased property.

The present value of the MLP ($438,019) is greater than the fair value of the leased property ($423,196), so the leased property will be recorded at fair value of $423,196, the lesser of the two amounts. At the inception of the lease, the required journal entry would be:

Leased Property under Capital Lease	423,196	
Obligation under Capital Lease		423,196

Table 8-35 shows the computations for the amortization of the obligation and the asset, along with the determination of the expenses related to the lease transaction. Following are several important points about the computations shown in Table 8-35. First, because the fair value of the leased property is recorded as the asset and obligation, the interest rate that must be used in the amortization of the obligation is the *lessor's implicit rate* of 10%. Recall that the lessee's incremental borrowing rate was used to determine the present value of the MLP, but this amount was never used in the capitalization process. Therefore, the 8% rate will not be used when applying the interest method. Second, because the lease did not transfer ownership or contain a bargain purchase option, the asset recorded will be amortized over the lease term, rather than over the economic life of the property.

Table 8-35 Lease Amortization and Expenses Amortization Schedule for Capital Lease

Period	Annual Payment	Annual Interest Expense	Obligation Reduction	Present Value of Obligation at Year-End
Initial Value	—	—	—	$423,196
1	$100,000	[a]$32,320	$67,680	355,516
2	100,000	25,552	74,448	281,068
3	100,000	18,107	81,893	199,175
4	100,000	9,917	90,083	109,092
5	100,000	[b]908	99,092	[c]10,000
	$500,000	$86,804	$413,196	

Schedule of Recorded Expenses for Capital Lease

Period	Amortization	Interest	Total	Annual Lease Payment
1	[d]$82,639	$32,320	$114,959	$100,000
2	82,639	25,552	108,191	100,000
3	[e]83,306	18,107	101,413	100,000
4	83,306	9,917	93,223	100,000
5	83,306	908	84,214	100,000
Payment for Residual Value				2,000
	$415,196	$86,804	$502,000	$502,000

[a] ($423,196 – $100,000) × 10% = $32,320.

[b] Interest on the guaranteed residual value.

[c] Guaranteed residual value.

[d] $423,196 – $10,000 = $413,196 ÷ 5 years = $82,639.

[e] Annual depreciation expense	$82,639
Number of years prior to change in residual value	× 2
Accumulated depreciation	$165,278
Recorded value of leased property	$423,196
Accumulated depreciation	(165,278)
Revised estimated residual value	(8,000)
Amount remaining to depreciate	$249,918
Remaining useful life	÷ 3
Current depreciation	$83,306

Given this information, the entries to record the lease expenses for the first year would be as follows:

Obligation under Capital Lease	67,680	
Interest Expense	32,320	
Cash		100,000
Amortization of Leased Property	82,639	
Accumulated Amortization—Leased Property		82,639

The last significant point in Table 8-35 relates to the $2,000 decline in residual value, which occurred in the third year of the lease term. This decline in residual value is a change in an accounting estimate and is treated in a prospective manner, as prescribed in ASC 250. The effect of the change in accounting estimate is charged to current and future periods. This is illustrated by the change in the amount of amortization of the asset account, from $82,639 in Year 2 to $83,306 in Year 3. In all future years, $83,306 will be charged to income as amortization.

The decline in residual value increased the ultimate cash outflow to the lessee by $2,000. Because the lessee guaranteed the residual value of $10,000, any decline would require the lessee to pay an amount equal to the decline to the lessor at the end of the lease term. The entry necessary to remove the asset and obligation balances at the end of the lease term would be as follows:

Accumulated Amortization—Leased Property	415,196	
Obligation under Capital Lease	10,000	
Leased Property under Capital Lease		423,196
Cash		2,000

The $2,000 payment by the lessee to the lessor represents the decline in the residual value below the amount guaranteed.

Operating Leases

If a lease agreement fails to meet any of the lease criteria necessary to qualify as a capital lease, the accounting is quite simple. To illustrate, assume a five-year lease, with annual payments of $75,000. Further assume that the criteria necessary for classification as a capital lease are not met. The only entry that is necessary is the annual or periodic lease payment shown below:

Lease Rental Expense	75,000	
Cash		75,000

This completes the discussion of the technical aspect of accounting for general type leases. The remaining sections will deal with accounting problems associated with special lease situations faced by a lessee.

Flowchart and General Discussion of Sale-Leaseback Transactions

A sale and leaseback transaction is a sale of property by Entity 1 to Entity 2 and leaseback of the property by Entity 1. In this type of transaction, Entity 1 is the seller/lessee and Entity 2 is the buyer/lessor. ASC 840-40 identifies three types of sale-leaseback transactions that are of importance from an accounting perspective. The first type of transaction is referred to as a "minor" leaseback because the seller-lessee retains only a minor interest in the property sold. The second type of sale-leaseback transaction is referred to as a "more than minor but less than substantially all" leaseback. Although the wording associated with this type of sale-leaseback is cumbersome, it is very descriptive of the transaction and is used throughout the remainder of this discussion. The third type of sale-leaseback transaction is referred to as a "substantially all" leaseback because the seller/lessee retains substantially all of the ownership interest in the property sold. Additionally, special provisions of ASC 840-40 apply to sale-leasebacks involving real estate.

Flowchart 8-6 depicts the major decisions involved in classification and accounting for the three main types of sale-leaseback transactions identified in ASC 840-40. Flowchart 8-7 illustrates the proper accounting for sale-leasebacks involving real estate. The information presented in the flowcharts provides an overview of the accounting treatment associated with the various sale-leaseback transactions.

Flowchart 8-6 Sale and Leaseback

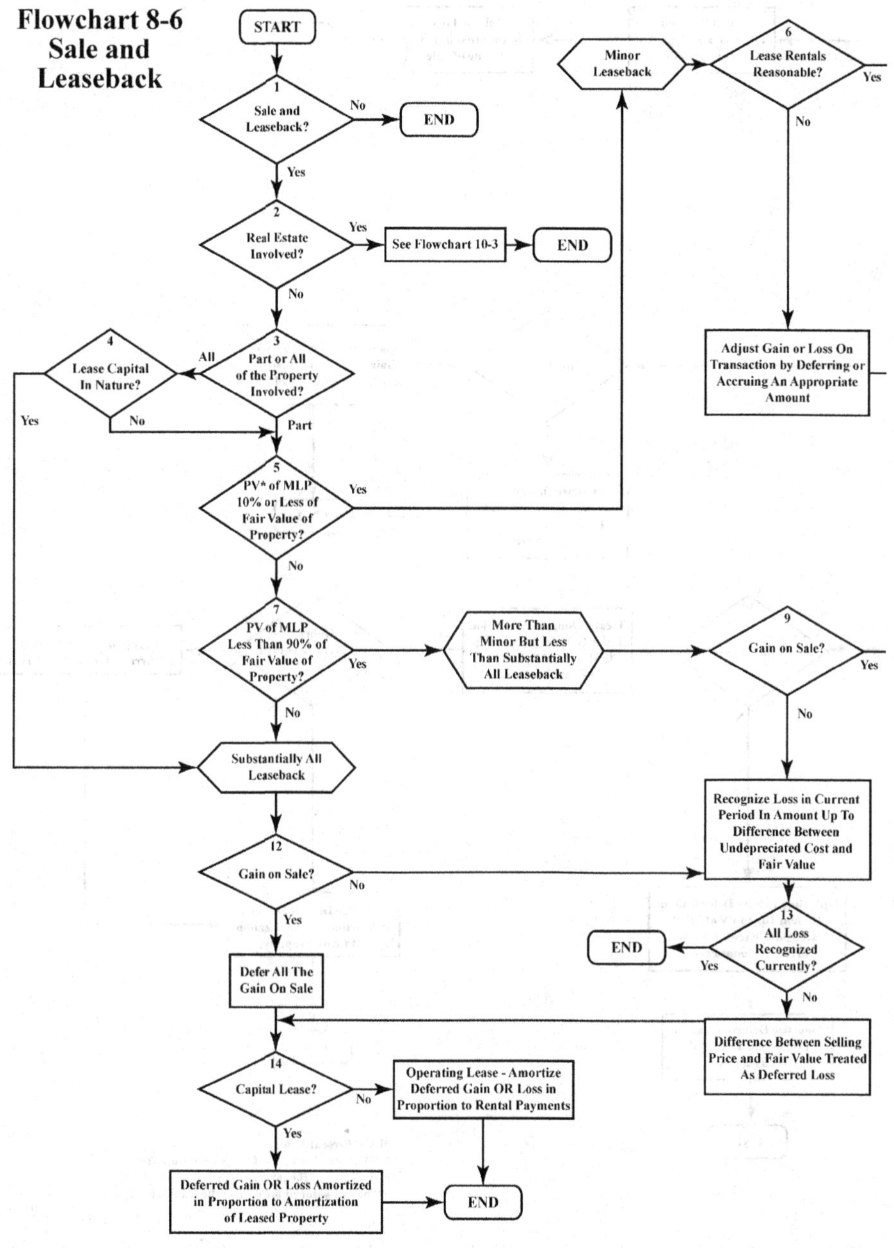

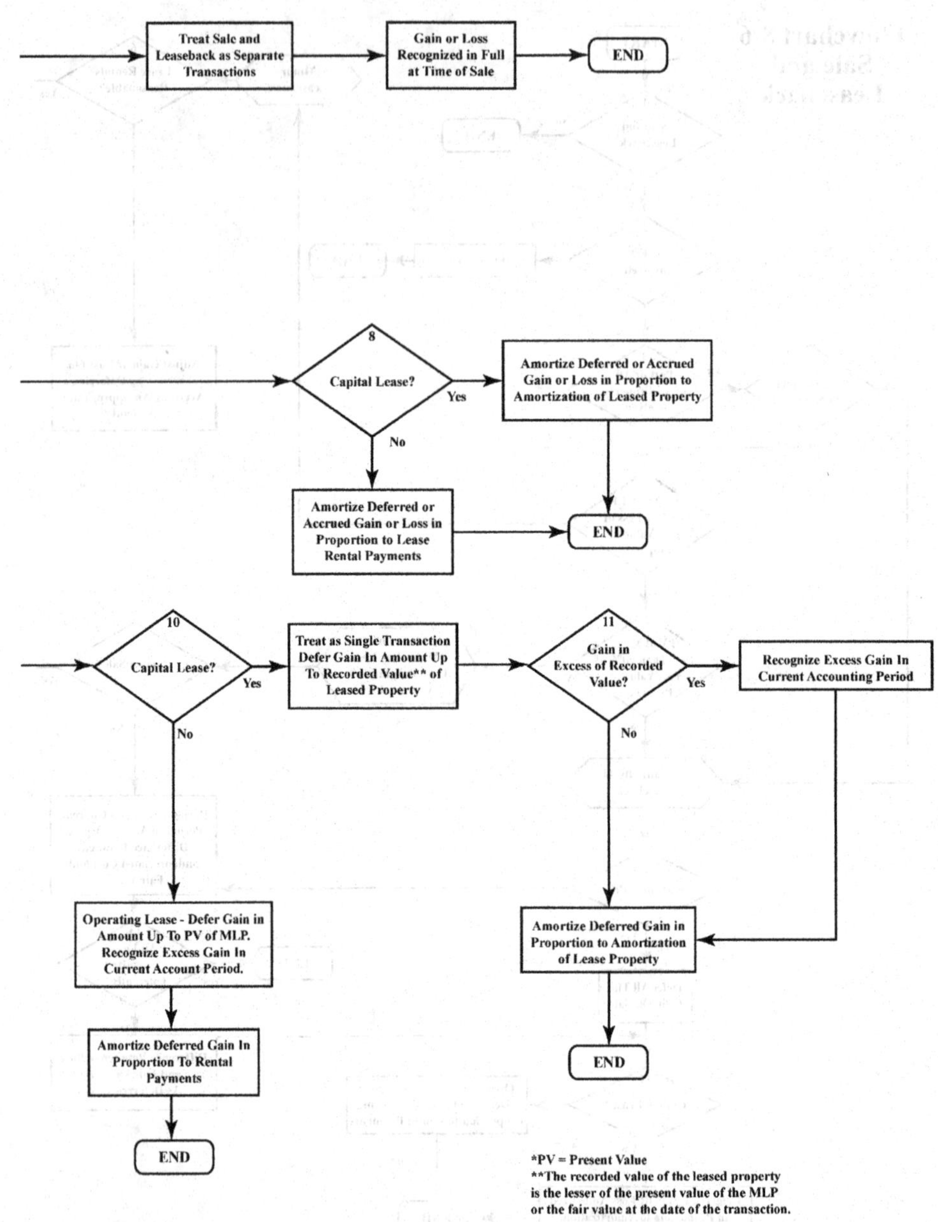

Once it has been determined that a sale and leaseback transaction has occurred (Block 1), the next step is to determine if the sale-leaseback involves real estate (Block 2). If real estate is involved, the provisions illustrated in Flowchart 8-7 should be used to determine the proper accounting. However, if real estate is not involved, the next step is to determine if all or only a part of the property sold has been involved in the transaction (Block 3). If all of the property is involved in the leaseback and the agreement qualifies as a capital lease (Block 4), the leaseback will be classified as a "substantially all" leaseback. If the sale and leaseback involves all the property sold, but the leaseback does not qualify as a capital lease, test the transaction as a leaseback involving only part of the property sold. If the leaseback involves only part of the property, the next test is to make a comparison between the present value of the minimum lease payments required under the leaseback agreement and the fair market value of the property sold (Block 5). If the present value of the minimum lease payments is 10% or less of the fair value of the property sold, the transaction must be classified as a "minor" leaseback. If the present value of the minimum lease payments is greater than 10%, but less than 90% of the fair value of the property sold, the transaction must be classified as a "more than minor but less than substantially all" leaseback (Block 7). Finally, if the present value of the minimum lease payments is 90% or more of the fair value of the property sold, the transaction must be classified as a "substantially all" leaseback. Chart 8-2 clearly illustrates the classification problems shown in Flowchart 8-6 Blocks 3, 5, and 7.

Chart 8-2
Sale-Leaseback Classification

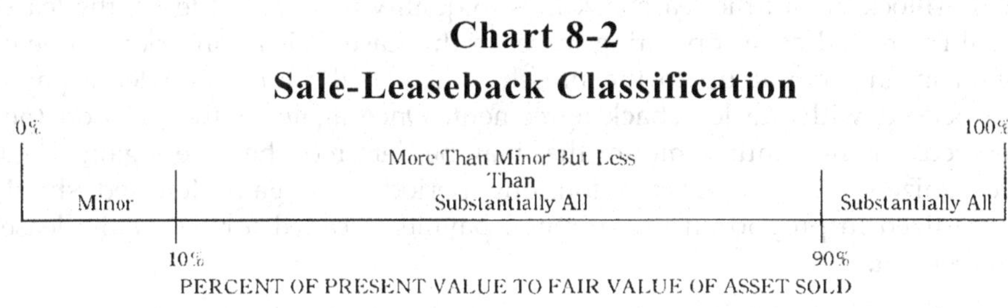

Once a sale-leaseback transaction has been properly classified, the appropriate accounting procedures may be determined. If the sale-leaseback transaction is determined to be "minor," and the lease rentals are reasonable in light of the current market for the property (Block 6), the sale of the property and subsequent leaseback should be treated as two separate transactions. Any gain or loss resulting from the transaction should be recognized in full in the current accounting period. On the other hand, if the transaction has been classified as a minor leaseback, *and* the lease rentals are clearly not reasonable given current market conditions, the gain or loss resulting from the sale will not be recognized in full in the current period. Instead, the gain or loss on the sale must be adjusted by deferring or accruing an appropriate amount of the gain or loss and amortizing this amount over future periods. The amount to be amortized in any period will depend on whether the leaseback is classified as a capital or an operating lease (Block 8). If the leaseback is classified as an operating lease, the amortization will be made in proportion to the rental payments made by the seller-lessee. If the leaseback is classified as a capital lease, the amortization will be in proportion to the amortization of the lease property. Under normal circumstances, the gain or loss resulting from a minor sale-leaseback transaction will be recognized in the current accounting period. Only in unusual circumstances would there be any deferred or accrued gain or loss.

If the sale-leaseback transaction is classified as "more than minor but less than substantially all," the next step is to determine if the sale part of the transaction resulted in a gain (Block 9). If the sale of the property results in a gain, and the leaseback meets the criteria for classification as a capital lease (Block 10), the sale and leaseback will be treated as a single transaction. The seller-lessee will defer all or part of the gain and amortize it in proportion to the amortization of the leased property. The amount of the gain that may be deferred is an amount equal to the recorded value of the property (recall from previous discussions that the recorded value of the property under a capital lease is the lesser of the present value of the minimum lease payment *or* the fair value of the property at the date of the lease agreement). If the total gain from the sale of the property is greater than the recorded value of the asset, the excess gain will be recognized in the current accounting period. In this latter case, part of the gain would be deferred, and part would be recognized in the current period.

If a sale-leaseback transaction results in a "more than minor but less than substantially all" leaseback, and the sale portion of the transaction results in a gain (Block 9), but the leaseback fails to qualify as a capital lease, the leaseback will be treated as an operating lease. In this case, it is appropriate to defer the gain in an amount up to the present value of the minimum lease payments associated with the leaseback agreement. Once again, if the gain on the sale exceeds the maximum amount that may be deferred, the excess gain should be recognized in the current accounting period. Any gain deferred should be amortized in proportion to the rental payments called for under the leaseback agreement.

In the cases discussed thus far, the "more than minor but less than substantially all" leaseback resulted in a gain on the sale portion of the transaction. Different accounting procedures are required in the cases where the sale results in a loss to the seller-lessee. When the sale-leaseback transaction results in a loss on the sale of the property (Block 9), the seller-lessee should recognize a loss in the current period in an amount up to the *difference* between the undepreciated cost of the property and its fair value. If the sales transaction results in a loss that exceeds the amount defined above, the seller-lessee should defer any excess loss. The excess loss will be equal to the difference between the selling price of the property and its fair value. The amortization of the deferred loss would depend on whether the leaseback is a capital or operating lease. If the leaseback qualifies for capital lease treatment, the deferred loss would be amortized in proportion to the amortization of the leased property. If the leaseback is to be treated as an operating lease, the deferred loss would be amortized in proportion to the rental payments made by the seller-lessee.

The final type of sale-leaseback results in a "substantially all" leaseback agreement. This type of leaseback results when the leaseback involves all the property sold and the leaseback is a capital lease or when the present value of the minimum lease payments is 90% or more of the fair value of the property subject to the agreement (Block 7). When a "substantially all" leaseback transaction occurs, and the sale portion of the transaction results in a gain (Block 12), the entire gain should be deferred. Once again, the amortization of the deferred gain will depend on whether the leaseback is treated as a capital lease or an operating lease. The deferred gain will be amortized in the same manner described for the "more than minor but less than substantially all" leaseback. If a "substantially all" leaseback transaction results in a loss on the sale portion of the transaction, the loss should be handled in the same manner described for the "more than minor but less than substantially all" leaseback transaction. Because this accounting has been described above it is not necessary to repeat the details.

Flowchart 8-7 depicts the major decisions involved in classification and accounting for sale-leaseback involving real estate. Once it has been determined that a sale-leaseback involves real estate (Block 1), the sale-leaseback will be accounted for as a sale-leaseback transaction using the special provisions of ASC 840-40, as discussed in Flowchart 8-6, only if the following three conditions are met:

1. The leaseback is classified as a normal leaseback (Block 2).
2. The initial investment (down payment) is adequate, and the buyer/lessor has a continuing investment (such as periodic payments that reduce some portion of the principal) in the property (Block 3).
3. The buyer/lessor receives all ownership risks and rewards, and the seller/lessee has no additional involvement in the property (Block 4).

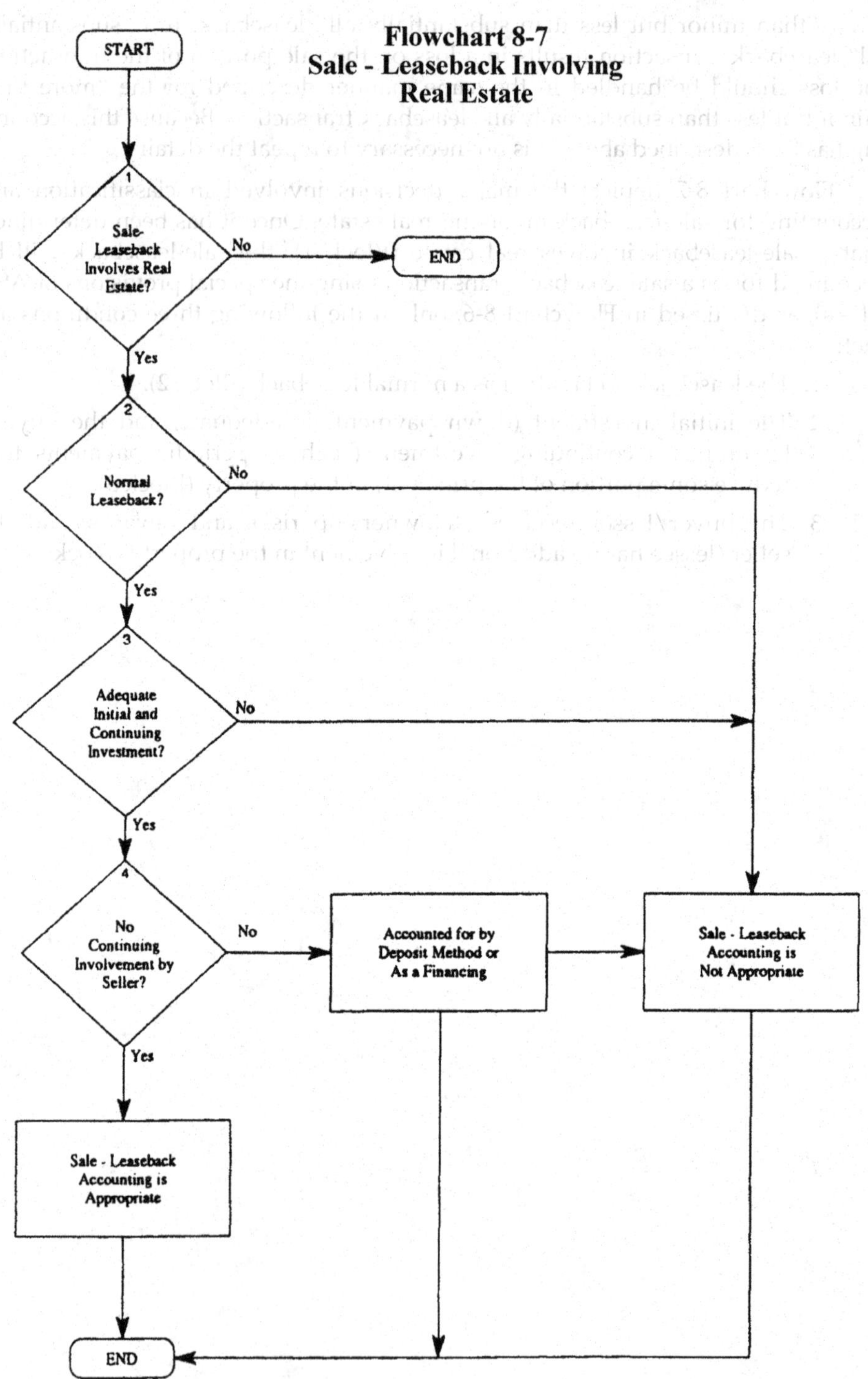

A normal leaseback is a situation where the seller/lessee actively uses the property leased back in its trade or business, and any sublease of the leased property by the seller/lessee is minor. The sublease is considered minor when the sublease constitutes 10% or less of the lease. In addition, in a normal leaseback there would be no continuing involvement in the property by the seller/lessee as described in 3, above. However, the use of the leased property for short-term services, such as a hotel or a golf course, is considered active use. Sale-leaseback accounting would not be appropriate if condition 1, above, is not met, because the seller/lessor has continuing involvement in the property equivalent to an investor or developer.

To determine if the buyer/lessor down payment is adequate and if there is continuing investment in the purchased property, the provisions of ASC 360-20 must be consulted. ASC 360-20-40-9 specifies the size and composition of a down payment that is considered adequate. The size and composition is as follows:

1. The size of the initial investment should meet the following conditions:
   a. The down payment should range from 10% to 25% of the sales price depending upon the type of real estate property.
   b. The down payment should be equal to a major portion of the difference between the sales price and the normal loan limits.
2. The composition of the down payment is made up of one or more of the following items:
   a. Cash.
   b. A note from the buyer, backed by an independent financial institution's letter of credit that is irrevocable.
   c. A reduction of existing debt on the property by payments to third parties by the buyer.
   d. Other payments that are considered components of the sales price.

In addition to having an adequate initial investment, the buyer/lessor must have a continuing investment in the property. The buyer/lessor is considered to have a continuing investment in the property when the buyer is required by contract to make annual payments that, as a minimum, would be required to pay off the principal and interest over a period of time not longer than 20 years for land or the normal lending time for a first mortgage from a financial entity for similar real estate. If the initial and continuing investment, as discussed above, is not adequate, the sale-leaseback is accounted for by integrating the provisions of ASC 360-20 on real estate and ASC 840-40 on sale-leasebacks.

In some cases, a seller/lessee may not transfer all the rewards and risks of ownership to the buyer/lessor by maintaining some form of continuing involvement in the property sold, other than the normal leaseback. When the seller/lessee maintains some form of continuing involvement, the sale-leaseback is accounted for using the deposit method or as a financing, whichever is appropriate using the provisions of ASC 360-20.

Examples of continuing involvement by the seller/lessee include, but are not limited to, the following:

1. The buyer/lessor's investment or investment return is assured by the seller/lessee for a period of time.
2. The buyer/lessor can force the seller/lessee to buy the property back, or the seller/lessee has an option to do so.

3. The lease payment is based on some future level of operations of the buyer/lessor that is predetermined or is determinable.
4. The seller/lessee shares in the property's appreciation.
5. Nonrecourse financing is provided to the buyer/lessor by the seller/lessee for some part of the sales price.

Disclosures must be provided for sale-leaseback transactions involving real estate. The disclosures are specified in ASC 840-40-50 and include the following:

1. Terms of the sale-leaseback must be described, including any requirements that result in or require continuing involvement by the seller/lessee.
2. If a sale-leaseback transaction is accounted for using the deposit method or as a financing, the following additional disclosures are required:
   a. On the last balance sheet date presented, the aggregate liability for future minimum lease payments and the payments for each of the five years subsequent to the last balance sheet date.
   b. The aggregate amount of sublease rentals to be received and the rentals for each of the five years subsequent to the date of the latest balance sheet that are from non-cancellable subleases.

Technical Considerations of a Sale-Leaseback Transaction

To illustrate the technical provisions of ASC 840-40, six comprehensive examples are developed. Each example builds on the previous material, so it is important to review the examples in order. The assumptions for Example 8-23 are set out below.

Example 8-23
Sale-Leaseback Assumptions

1. On January 1, 20X6, Cites Corporation (Cites) sold equipment to Sanders, Inc. (Sanders) for $12,000,000, and immediately leased *all* of the property back for a period of three years. The leaseback agreement requires Cites to make annual year-end rental payments of $400,000. Cites Corporation has a December 31 year end for accounting purposes.
2. The property subject to the sale-leaseback has a cost basis to Cites of $9,000,000, and an estimated economic life of 30 years. The fair market value of the property on January 1, 20X6 was $12,000,000.
3. The seller-lessee's incremental borrowing rate is 10%, and the interest rate implicit in the leaseback agreement is known by Cites to be 12%. The leaseback agreement *does not* contain a bargain purchase option, and title to the property will be retained by Sanders at the end of the lease term.
4. The lease payments are considered reasonable in relation to the current market for similar types of property and similar lease terms.

The first step in the solution to Example 8-23 is to recognize that the two companies have entered into a sale and leaseback agreement not involving real estate. Before the leaseback can be properly classified, the accountant must determine if the leaseback transaction will be treated as an operating or a capital lease. In this case, the leaseback is properly classified as an operating lease because ownership does not transfer to Cites at the end of the lease term, the leaseback does not contain a bargain purchase option, the lease term is less than 75% of the economic life of the property (3 year lease term ÷ 30 year life = 10%), and the present value of the MLP is less than 90% of the fair value of the leased property at the inception of the leaseback agreement, as computed below. Therefore, the leaseback fails to meet any of the criteria necessary for classification as a capital lease. The next major computational problem facing the accountant is to compute the present value of the minimum lease payments (MLP) required in the leaseback agreement. The purpose of this computation is to aid the accountant in the proper classification of the transaction. The present value of the MLP is calculated below:

Lease Payments Required	$400,000
Present Value Factor for an Ordinary Annuity for 3 Periods at 10% (Appendix E)	× 2.48685
Present Value of MLP	$994,740

The present value of the MLP was calculated using the 10% incremental borrowing rate of Cites because the implicit rate of 12% is known and it is greater than the incremental borrowing rate.

To properly classify the leaseback, the present value of the MLP must be compared to the fair value of the property on the date of the leaseback agreement. The present value of the MLP is 8.3% of the fair value of the leased property ($994,740 ÷ $12,000,000 = 8.3%). Because the present value of the MLP is 10% or less of the fair market value of the property, the leaseback should be classified as "minor."

Because the transaction is classified as a minor leaseback, and the lease payments are considered to be reasonable, no profit or loss resulting from the original sale will be deferred or accrued. The sale and leaseback must be treated as two separate transactions, and any gain or loss will be recognized in full in 20X6, the period in which the sale took place. The gain on the sale of the equipment is computed below:

Selling Price	$12,000,000
Cost Basis	9,000,000
Gain on Sale	$3,000,000

The journal entry required on January 1, 20X6, to record the sale portion of the sale-leaseback transaction is:

Cash	12,000,000	
Equipment		9,000,000
Gain on Sale-Leaseback		3,000,000

The gain on sale-leaseback account would be classified on the income statement in accordance with the provisions of ASC 225-20.

Because the leaseback will be treated as an operating lease, the only entry required in connection with the leaseback is to record the year-end lease payment. The entry on December 31, 20X6, is shown below:

Lease Rental Payment	400,000	
Cash		400,000

This last entry completes the analysis of the Example 8-23 material.

Example 8-23 was designed to be straightforward and to serve as an introduction to the problems associated with a sale-leaseback transaction. Example 8-24 is somewhat more complex than Example 8-23. The assumptions relating to Example 8-24 are listed below.

Example 8-24
Sale-Leaseback Assumptions

1. On January 1, 20X6, the Hunt Company (Hunt), a December 31 year-end company, sold equipment with an estimated economic life of five years to the Thomas Company (Thomas) for $400,000 cash, and immediately leased *part of* the equipment from Thomas for four years. The leaseback agreement requires Hunt to pay $100,000 at the beginning of each of the next four years to Thomas.
2. The equipment involved in the sale and leaseback transaction has a cost to Hunt of $300,000, and a fair market value on the date of the sale of $400,000.
3. Hunt's incremental borrowing rate is 12%, and the rate implicit in the leaseback agreement is unknown.
4. Title to the equipment transfers to Hunt at the end of the lease term, and Hunt uses straight-line depreciation for similar owned assets.

After recognizing this as a sale-leaseback transaction not involving real estate, the first step in the accounting process is to determine the proper classification of the partial leaseback. To accomplish this, the present value of the MLP must be computed. This calculation is shown below:

Lease Payment Required	$100,000
Present Value Factor for an Annuity Due for 4 Periods at 12% (Appendix E)	×3.40183
Present Value of MLP	$340,183

Next, the present value of the MLP must be compared to the fair value of the property sold. In this example, the present value of the MLP is 85% of the fair value of the equipment ($340,183 present value of MLP – $400,000 fair value of equipment = 85%). This sale-leaseback would be classified as "more than minor but less than substantially all" because the percentage relationship calculated above is more than 10%, but less than 90%, of the fair market value of the equipment.

After the sale-leaseback has been properly classified, the next step is to determine the type of lease involved in the transaction. The lease in this example must be classified as a capital lease because title to the property transfers to the seller-lessee at the end of the lease term. All or part of the gain will be deferred because the leaseback qualified as a capital lease and there is a gain on the sale portion of the transaction. The amount to be deferred may not exceed the recorded amount of the leased property, and the amount deferred should be amortized in proportion to the amortization of the leased asset. These accounting procedures apply only if there is a *gain* associated with the sale portion of the sale-leaseback transaction. Other accounting procedures will be applied in cases where the sale results in a loss to the seller-lessee. If the amount of gain on the sale is greater than the recorded value of the property, this excess gain will be recognized in the current accounting period.

Before the amount of the gain to defer can be determined, the recorded value of the leased property must be computed. Under normal capital lease accounting, the recorded value of the property will be the smaller of the present value of the MLP or the fair market value of the asset on the date of the lease agreement. In this particular example, the present value of the MLP was calculated to be $340,183, which is less than the fair value of the property at the inception of the leaseback ($400,000). Therefore, the recorded value of the property will be $340,183. The maximum gain that could be deferred is limited to $340,183, the recorded value of the asset. The next step in the accounting process is to calculate the actual gain from the sale portion of the transaction. The amount of the gain is computed below:

Selling Price	$400,000
Cost Basis	300,000
Gain on Sale	$100,000

Because the gain on the sale of $100,000 is less than the recorded amount of the property ($340,183), the entire gain will be deferred, and the sale-leaseback will be treated as a single transaction. The entries necessary to record the initial sale and subsequent leaseback of the equipment are as follows:

Cash	400,000	
Equipment		300,000
Deferred Gain on Sale-Leaseback		100,000
Leased Property under Capital Lease	340,183	
Obligation under Capital Lease		340,183

Table 8-36 shows the computation of the amortization schedule and the determination of the expenses to be recorded under the lease assumptions used in Example 8-24.

Table 8-36 Amortization Schedule for Sale-Leaseback

Amortization Period	Annual Payment	Annual Interest Expense	Obligation Reduction	Present Value of Obligation at Year-End
Initial Value				$340,183
1	$100,000	[a]$28,822	$71,178	269,005
2	100,000	20,281	79,719	189,286
3	100,000	10,714	89,286	100,000
4	100,000	-0-	100,000	-0-
	$400,000	$59,817	$340,183	

Schedule of Recorded Expenses for Capital Lease

Period	Amortization	Deferred Gain	Amortization After Gain	Interest Expense	Total Expense
1	[b]$68,037	[c]$20,000	[d]$48,037	$28,822	$76,859
2	68,037	20,000	48,037	20,281	68,318
3	68,037	20,000	48,037	10,714	58,751
4	68,036	20,000	48,036	-0-	48,036
5	68,036	20,000	48,036	-0-	48,036
	$340,183	$100,000	$240,183	$59,817	$300,000

[a] $340,183 – $100,000 = $240,183 × .12 = $28,822.

[b] $340,183/5 years = $68,037.
[c] $100,000 gain/5 years = $20,000.
[d] $68,037 – $20,000 = $48,037.

Given the information generated in Table 8-36, the entry for the first year is presented below:

Interest Expense	28,822	
Obligation under Capital Lease	71,178	
Cash		100,000

The final entry required is to amortize the leased asset and to amortize a portion of the deferred gain on the sale portion of the transaction. The gain should be amortized in proportion to the amortization of the leased property. Because the leased property is amortized using the straight-line method, the deferred gain should be amortized using the same accounting method. The amortization period should be that period considered appropriate for the leased asset (economic life of the property or the term of the lease). In this example, title to the property transferred to the seller-lessee at the end of the lease term, and the appropriate amortization period is the economic life of the asset. Given this information, the deferred gain should be amortized using the straight-line method over the economic life of the leased property. The journal entry necessary to record the depreciation of the leased asset and the amortization of the deferred gain would be as follows:

Amortization of Leased Property	48,037	
Deferred Gain on Sale-Leaseback	20,000	
Leased Property under Capital Lease		68,037

Information required to make the journal entries for the remainder of the life of the property can be found in Table 8-36.

Had the leaseback in this example been classified as an operating lease, the maximum gain that could have been deferred would be equal to the present value of the MLP, which may or may not be equal to the fair value of the property. The fair value of the leased property would be of no consequence in the case of an operating lease classified as "more than minor but less than substantially all."

This completes the analysis of the Example 8-24 material. This material required a more complex decision-making process on the part of the accountant. Example 8-25, which follows, will build on some of the material just presented.

Example 8-25
Sale-Leaseback Assumptions

1. On January 1, 20X6, Western Industries (Western), a December 31 year-end company, sold equipment to Mills Company (Mills) for $600,000, and immediately leased *part of* the equipment back for a period of five years. The leaseback agreement requires Western to make annual year-end rental payments of $158,278 for each of the next five years.
2. The equipment subject to the sale-leaseback has a cost basis to Western of $500,000, and an estimated useful life of five years. The fair market value of the equipment on January 1, 20X6 is $600,000.
3. Western's incremental borrowing rate is 10%, and the lessor's implicit interest rate is not known.
4. The leaseback agreement is non-cancellable, and ownership to the leased equipment transfers to Western at the end of the lease term. Western uses the sum-of-the-years' digits method to depreciate similar owned assets.

After recognizing that the transaction between Western and Mills is a sale and leaseback that does not involve real estate, the next step is to properly classify the partial leaseback. To accomplish this, the accountant must compute the present value of the MLP. This computation is shown below:

Lease Payments Required	$158,278
Present Value Factor for an Ordinary Annuity for 5 Periods at 10% (Appendix E)	× 3.79079
Present Value of MLP	$600,000

The present value of the MLP must now be compared to the fair market value of the equipment to determine the proper classification of the leaseback. The present value of the MLP is 100% ($600,000 ÷ $600,000) of the fair value of the equipment. Therefore, the leaseback qualifies as a "substantially all" leaseback.

Once the leaseback has been properly classified, the next step is to determine the type of lease involved in the transaction. The lease described in Example 8-25 qualifies as a capital lease because ownership to the equipment transfers at the end of the lease term. Also, the lease term of five years is more than 75% of the economic life of the asset, and the present value of the MLP is more than 90% of the fair value of the leased property. Table 8-37 shows the computations of the amortization schedule and the determination of the expenses to be recorded under the lease assumptions specified. Meeting one of the four basic criteria is sufficient to classify the lease as a capital lease.

Table 8-37 Amortization Schedule for Sale-Leaseback

Amortization Period	Annual Payment	Annual Interest Expense	Obligation Reduction	Present Value of Obligation at Year-End
Initial Value				$600,000
1	$158,278	[a]$60,000	$98,278	501,722
2	158,278	50,172	108,106	393,616
3	158,278	39,362	118,916	274,700
4	158,278	27,470	130,808	143,892
5	158,278	*14,386	143,892	—0—
	$791,390	$191,390	$600,000	

Schedule of Recorded Expenses for Capital Lease

Period	Amortization	Deferred Gain	Amortization After Gain	Interest Expense	Total Expense
1	[b]$200,000	[c]$33,333	[d]$166,667	$60,000	$226,667
2	160,000	26,667	133,333	50,172	183,505
3	120,000	20,000	100,000	39,362	139,362
4	80,000	13,333	66,667	27,470	94,137
5	40,000	6,667	33,333	14,386	47,719
	$600,000	$100,000	$500,000	$191,390	$691,390

[a] $600,000 × .10 = $60,000.

[b] 5/15 × $600,000 = $200,000 for 20X1.
[c] 5/15 × $100,000 = $33,333.
[d] $200,000 – $33,333 = $166,667.
* Rounded.

Because the present value of the MLP is equal to the fair value of the equipment, the asset and obligation will be recorded at $600,000. The journal entries to record the initial sale and subsequent leaseback of the equipment are as follows:

Cash	600,000	
Equipment		500,000
Deferred Gain on Sale-Leaseback		100,000
Leased Property under Capital Lease	600,000	
Obligation under Capital Lease		600,000

The entire gain on the sale portion of the transaction was deferred because the leaseback was classified as "substantially all."

Because ownership of the equipment transfers to the seller-lessee at the end of the lease term, the asset will be amortized over its economic life of five years. The seller-lessee uses the sum-of-the-years' digits method to depreciate similar owned assets, and will use this method for assets recorded under capital lease agreements. The obligation is amortized using the interest method at the rate of 10%, the seller-lessee's incremental borrowing rate. The deferred gain must be amortized consistent with the amortization of the asset. The journal entries necessary to record the first annual leaseback payment and the amortization of the equipment and deferred gain would be as follows:

Obligation under Capital Lease	98,278	
Interest Expense	60,000	
Cash		158,278
Amortization of Leased Property	166,667	
Deferred Gain on Sale-Leaseback	33,333	
Leased Property under Capital Lease		200,000

The amortization of the deferred gain reduces the total amortization expense charged to income during the period. Rather than a direct reduction of the leased property account, as shown above, the accountant may elect to utilize an accumulated amortization account that would serve as a contra asset account.

This completes the analysis of the Example 8-25 material. All examples to this point have resulted in a gain to the seller-lessee, so the final example is designed to demonstrate the proper accounting when a loss results from the sale portions of a sale-leaseback.

The relevant information relating to Example 8-26 is presented below.

Example 8-26
Sale-Leaseback Assumptions

1. Johnson, Inc. (Johnson), a December 31 year-end company, sold equipment to the Great Northern Company (Great Northern) on January 1, 20X6 for $290,000, and immediately leased *part of* the property back for a period of four years. The leaseback agreement requires that Johnson make annual year-end rental payments in the amount of $100,000 for each of the next four years.

2. The equipment sold has an undepreciated cost basis to Johnson of $350,000, and an estimated economic life of five years. The fair value of the equipment on January 1, 20X6 is $310,245.

3. Johnson's incremental borrowing rate is 11%, and the implicit rate used by Great Northern is unknown.
4. Johnson uses straight-line depreciation for similar owned assets.

Because the transaction is obviously a partial sale-leaseback agreement not involving real estate, the first step is to compute the present value of the MLP. This computation is shown below:

Lease Payment Required	$100,000
Present Value Factor for an Ordinary Annuity at 11% for 4 Periods (Appendix E)	× 3.10245
Present Value of MLP	$310,245

Next, the present value of the MLP must be compared to the fair market value of the leased equipment to determine the proper classification of the leaseback. The present value of the MLP is 100% ($310,245 ÷ $310,245) of the fair value of the leased equipment. Therefore, the leaseback qualifies as "substantially all."

The leaseback agreement in this example qualifies as a capital lease because the lease term of four years is more than 75% of the economic life of the equipment (4 years ÷ 5 years = 80%). The sale portion of the transaction results in a loss to the seller-lessee. The amount of the loss is computed below:

Selling Price of Equipment	$290,000
Cost Basis of Equipment	350,000
Loss on Sale of Equipment	$60,000

Because the leaseback results in a loss of $60,000, the next step is to determine if any of the loss will be deferred or if the entire loss will be recognized in the current period.

The amount of the loss that must be recognized in the current accounting period is equal to the difference between the undepreciated cost basis of the asset and its fair value. The computation of the amount of loss to be *recognized* in 20X6 is shown below:

Undepreciated Cost Basis of the Equipment	$350,000
Fair Market Value of Equipment	310,245
Loss Recognized in 20X6	$39,755

Of the total loss of $60,000, only $39,755 will be recognized in the period of the sale. The difference of $20,245 ($60,000 total loss – $39,755 recognized loss = $20,245) will be deferred. The deferred loss will be amortized in proportion to the amortization of the leased property under the capital lease. In effect, the deferred loss represents a prepayment of lease payments relating to the leaseback. In this particular example, the deferred loss will be amortized over a period of four years using the straight-line method, because the leaseback is a capital lease and the straight-line method is used for similar owned assets.

The entries necessary to record the initial sales transaction and the related leaseback are as follows.

Cash	290,000	
Loss on Sale-Leaseback	39,755	
Deferred Loss on Sale-Leaseback	20,245	
Equipment		350,000
Leased Property under Capital Lease	310,245	
Obligation under Capital Lease		310,245

Table 8-38 shows the computation of the amortization schedule and the determination of the expenses to be recorded under the leaseback assumptions specified.

Table 8-38 Amortization Schedule for Sale-Leaseback

Amortization Period	**Annual *Payment***	**Annual Interest Expense**	**Obligation Reduction**	**Present Value of Obligation at Year-End**
Initial Value				310,245
1	$100,000	[a]$34,127	$65,873	$244,372
2	100,000	26,881	73,119	171,253
3	100,000	18,838	81,162	90,091
4	100,000	9,909	90,091	-0-
	$400,000	$89,755	$310,245	

Schedule of Recorded Expenses for Capital Lease

Period	***Amortization***	***Deferred Loss***	***Amortization After Loss***	***Interest Expense***	***Total Expense***
1	[b]$77,561	[c]$5,061	[d]$82,622	$34,127	$116,749
2	77,561	5,061	82,622	26,881	109,503
3	77,561	5,061	82,622	18,838	101,460
4	*77,562	*5,062	82,624	9,909	92,533
	$310,245	$20,245	$330,490	$89,755	$420,245

[a] $310,245 × .11 = $34,127.

[b] $310,245/4 years = $77,561.
[c] $20,245/4 years = $5,061.
[d] $77,561 ÷ $5,061 = $82,622.
* Rounded.

Because the leaseback agreement does not contain a bargain purchase option and the equipment title does not transfer to the seller-lessee at the end of the lease term, the equipment will be amortized over the life of the leaseback term using the straight-line method. The deferred loss must be amortized in a like manner. With the information provided in Table 8-38, the entries to record the year-end lease rental payment and the amortization expense relating to the equipment and the deferred loss can be made. These entries appear below:

Interest Expense	34,127	
Obligation under Capital Lease	65,873	
Cash		100,000
Amortization of Leased Property	82,622	
Deferred Loss on Sale-Leaseback		5,061
Leased Property under Capital Lease		77,561

The first four examples related to sale-leaseback transactions did not involve real estate. Examples 8-27 and 8-28 cover sale-leasebacks of real estate. Assumptions for Example 8-27 are as follows.

Example 8-27
Assumptions for Sale-Leaseback of Real Estate

1. On January 1, 20X6, the Smith Company (Smith) sold a building to Bryant Enterprises (Bryant) for $1,600,000, and immediately leased the building back for a period of seven years. The book and fair value of the building is $1,280,000 and $1,600,000, respectively. The building has a useful life of 13 years. The building had an original cost of $1,500,000 and accumulated depreciation at time of sale of $220,000.
2. The seven-year lease requires beginning of year annual payments of $160,000. The rate implicit in the lease is unknown by Smith, and the incremental borrowing rate is 10%. The lease has no bargain purchase option or transfer of ownership.
3. Bryant, the buyer, finances the purchase by making a down payment of $128,000 and issuing a seven-year, 10% note for $1,472,000. The annual payment on the note is $302,357.
4. The installment method of recognizing revenue is appropriate because the down payment is not adequate. However, Smith changes to full accrual accounting at the end of 20X8 because the initial and continuing investment is adequate on that date.

The first step in analyzing the Example 8-27 assumptions is to determine the amount of profit recognition using the provisions of ASC 360-20 as if there is no leaseback. The gross profit percentage on the sale is 20% ($1,600,000 selling price – $1,280,000 cost = $320,000 profit ÷ $1,600,000 = 20%). Because the installment method is used for 20X6–20X8 and a change is made to full accrual at the end of 20X8, Table 8-39 shows the profit that would be recognized, assuming no leaseback.

Table 8-39 Profit Recognition under the Installment Method

20X6	
Down payment	$128,000
Gross profit percentage	20 %
Profit for 20X6, assuming no leaseback	$25,600

20X7	
Receivable balance at beginning of 20X6	$1,472,000
Interest rate	10 %
Interest income	$147,200
Annual payment	$302,357
Interest income	$147,200
Receivable reduction at end of 20X6	$155,157
Gross profit percentage	20 %
Profit for 20X7, assuming no leaseback	$31,031
20X8	
Receivable balance at beginning of 20X7 ($1,472,000 – $155,157)	$1,316,843
Interest rate	10 %
Interest income	$131,684
Annual payment	$302,357
Interest income	131,684
Receivable reduction at end of 20X6	$170,673
Gross profit percentage	20 %
Profit for 20X8, assuming no leaseback	$34,135
20X9	
Total gain to be recognized ($1,600,000 – $1,280,000)	$320,000
Gain recognized in 20X6–20X8 ($25,600 + $31,031 + $34,135)	90,766
Gain recognized in 20X9 under full accrual	$229,234

The next step in the analysis is to determine the type of lease, because this is a leaseback of all the property. The leaseback agreement does not contain a transfer of ownership or bargain purchase option, the 75% rule is not met (7 year lease term ÷ 13-year life = 53.85%), and the 90% rule is not met. The 90% rule is computed as follows:

Lease payment	$160,000
Present value factor for annuity due at 10% for 7 years (Appendix E)	5.35526
Present value of the lease payments	$856,842
Fair value of property	÷ 1,600,000
Percentage	53.55 %

Because the present value of the lease payments is only 53.55% of the fair value of the property, the 90% rule is not met, and the lease is classified as an operating lease. The present value of the lease payments in relationship to the fair value of the property is used to determine the type of leaseback because the lease is classified as an operating lease. The leaseback is classified as "more than minor but less than substantially all" because the present value of the lease payments is between 10% and 90% of the fair value of the property. The gain of $320,000 on the sale of the property is less than the $856,842 present value of the lease payments; therefore, all the gain recognized is deferred and amortized in proportion to the rental expense.

Next, recognition of the gain under ASC 360-20 using the installment method is integrated with the leaseback provisions of ASC 840-40. The gain recognized each year under the installment method is deferred and amortized over the remaining life of the lease. Table 8-40 shows the integration of the installment method with the leaseback provisions.

Table 8-40 Amount of Gain Recognized Each Year of Leaseback

Year	Down payment	20X7 Gain	20X8 Gain	20X9 Gain	Total
20X6	[a]$3,657				$3,657
20X7	3,657	[b]$5,172			8,829
20X8	3,657	5,172	[c]$6,827		15,656
20X9	3,657	5,172	6,827	[d]$57,308	72,964
2010	3,657	5,172	6,827	57,308	72,964
2011	3,657	5,172	6,827	57,309	72,965
2012	3,658	5,171	6,827	57,309	72,965
Total	$25,600	$31,031	$34,135	$229,234	$320,000

[a] $25,600 profit from down payment (Table 8-39)/7-year lease term = $3,657.
[b] $31,031 profit in 20X7 (Table 8-39)/6-year remaining lease term = $5,172.
[c] $34,135 profit in 20X8 (Table 8-39)/5-year remaining lease term = $6,827.
[d] $229,234 profit in 20X9 full accrual (Table 8-39)/4-year remaining lease term = $57,308.

The rental expense on the operating lease is reduced each year by the amount in the Total column of Table 8-40. Journal entries for the sale-leaseback are not presented for this example because they are the same as presented in earlier examples. If the full accrual method had been used at the beginning of the lease, the accounting would be the same as in Examples 8-23 through 8-26.

The next example on sale-leaseback of real estate illustrates the deposit method. Assumptions for Example 8-28 are as follows.

Example 8-28
Assumptions for the Deposit Method

1. On January 1, 20X6, Johnson Enterprises (Johnson) sold a building to the Peterson Company (Peterson) for $1,425,000, and immediately leased the building back for a period of 10 years. The book and fair values of the building are $1,350,000 and $1,425,000, respectively. The building has a useful life of 13 years. The building has an original

cost of $1,950,000 and accumulated depreciation at time of sale is $600,000. The building is depreciated at a rate of $120,000 per year.

2. The 10-year lease requires beginning-of-year annual payments of $225,000. The interest rate appropriate for the lease is 10%. The lease is classified as a capital lease and is recorded by the lessee at fair market value.
3. Peterson, the buyer, finances the purchase by making a down payment of $75,000 and issuing a 10-year, 10% note for $1,350,000. The annual payment on the note is $219,706.
4. The deposit method of recognizing revenue is appropriate because the down payment is not adequate and Peterson's credit standing is in question. However, Peterson changes to full accrual accounting at the end of 20X8 because the initial and continuing investment is adequate on that date.

The deposit method requires a credit to a deposit account for the receipt of payments from the buyer and a debit to the deposit account for lease payments. At the end of 20X8 when the change is made to the full accrual method, the building is removed from Johnson's books and the remaining gain is deferred and amortized over the remaining lease term. The following entries are required for the deposit method.

January 1, 20X6: To Record Down Payment

Cash	75,000	
Deposit		75,000

January 1, 20X6–20X8: To Record Lease Payments

	20X6		20X7		20X8	
Deposit	225,000		225,000		225,000	
Cash		225,000		225,000		225,000

December 31, 20X6–20X8: To Record Note Payments

	20X6		20X7		20X8	
Cash	219,706		219,706		219,706	
Deposit		219,706		219,706		219,706

December 31, 20X6–20X7: To Record Annual Depreciation

	20X6		20X7	
Depreciation Expense	120,000		120,000	
Accumulated Depreciation		120,000		120,000

December 31, 20X8: To Record Annual Depreciation

Depreciation Expense	120,000	
Accumulated Depreciation		120,000

At the end of 20X8, after all necessary journal entries for 20X8 are recorded, Johnson changes to the full accrual method of recognizing revenue from the sale of the building. When the change is made from the deposit method to full accrual, the sale of the building and the lease is recorded. Because the lease is classified as a capital lease and the leaseback is for all of the property sold, the leaseback is classified as a substantially all leaseback. Therefore, the gain on the sale is deferred and amortized over the remaining life of the lease in proportion to the amortization of the leased asset. The deferred gain recorded on the date of change to full accrual accounting is computed in Table 8-41.

Table 8-41 Computation of Deferred Gain

Sales price of building	$1,425,000
Carrying value of building on date of change to full accrual method	990,000
Excess of sales price over carrying value	$435,000
Adjustments to Change from Deposit to Full Accrual:	
Interest income on note included in deposit account (Table 8-42)	378,741
Interest expense on capital lease included in deposit account (Table 8-43)	(327,450)
Amortization of leased asset ($1,425,000/10 years × 3 years)	(427,500)
Deferred Gain at December 31, 20X8	$58,791

The interest income and interest expense components used in the computation of the deferred gain in Table 8-41 are computed in Table 8-42.

Table 8-42 Computation of Income and Expense Components

Interest Income on Note

Time Period	Cash	Interest Income	Note Receivable Reduction	Note Receivable Balance
				$1,350,000
20X6	$219,706	[a]$135,000	[b]$84,706	1,265,294
20X7	219,706	126,529	93,177	1,172,117
20X8	219,706	117,212	102,494	1,069,623
		$378,741		

Interest Expense on Capital Lease

Time Period	Cash	Interest Expense	Lease Obligation Reduction	Lease Obligation Balance
				$1,425,000
20X6	$225,000	[c]$120,000	[d]$105,000	1,320,000
20X7	225,000	109,500	115,500	1,204,500
20X8	225,000	97,950	127,050	1,077,450
		$327,450		

---

[a] $1,350,000 × 10% = $135,000.
[b] $219,706 – $135,000 = $84,706.
[c] $1,425,000 – $225,000 = $1,200,000 × 10% = $120,000.
[d] $225,000 – $120,000 = $105,000.

Using the information from Tables 8-41 and 8-42 and assumptions in Example 8-28, the following journal entry is prepared to change from the deposit method to full accrual on December 31, 20X8.

Leased Asset under Capital Lease	1,425,000[a]	
Note Receivable	1,069,623	
Accumulated Depreciation	960,000[b]	
Deposit	59,118[c]	
Building		1,950,000
Obligation under Capital Lease		1,077,450
Accumulated Amortization of Leased Asset		427,500[d]
Deferred Gain on Sale-Leaseback		58,791

---

[a] The leased asset is recorded at fair market value based on assumptions in Example 8-28.
[b] $120,000 × 3 years = $360,000 depreciation for 20X6–20X8 + $600,000 accumulated depreciation at time of sale.
[c] Represents balance in deposit account at the end of 20X8.
[d] $1,425,000/10 years = $142,500 × 3 years = $427,500. Assume that title to asset will return to lessor at end of lease.

The $58,791 deferred gain is amortized over the seven-year remaining lease term using a straight-line method because straight line is used for the leased asset. The amortization and entries are similar to those in Examples 8-23–8-26 and are not repeated.

Example 8-28 completes the discussion and example material for sale and leaseback transactions for the seller-lessee. The next specialized area deals with real estate leasing. Much of the previous material will prove helpful during the discussion of leases involving real estate.

Flowcharts and Discussion of Leases Involving Real Estate—Lessee

Flowcharts 8-8 and 8-9 illustrate the classification and some of the accounting problems associated with real estate leases. All of the basic concepts discussed in the preceding section apply to real estate leases; however, there are some cases where only a limited number of criteria apply or where additional computations may be required. The calculation of the MLP and the present value of the MLP for real estate leases is the same as previously discussed. The real estate flowcharts refer the reader back to the general flowchart (Flowchart 8-5) for specifics on the computation of the MLP.

Flowchart 8-8
Lessee - Real Estate

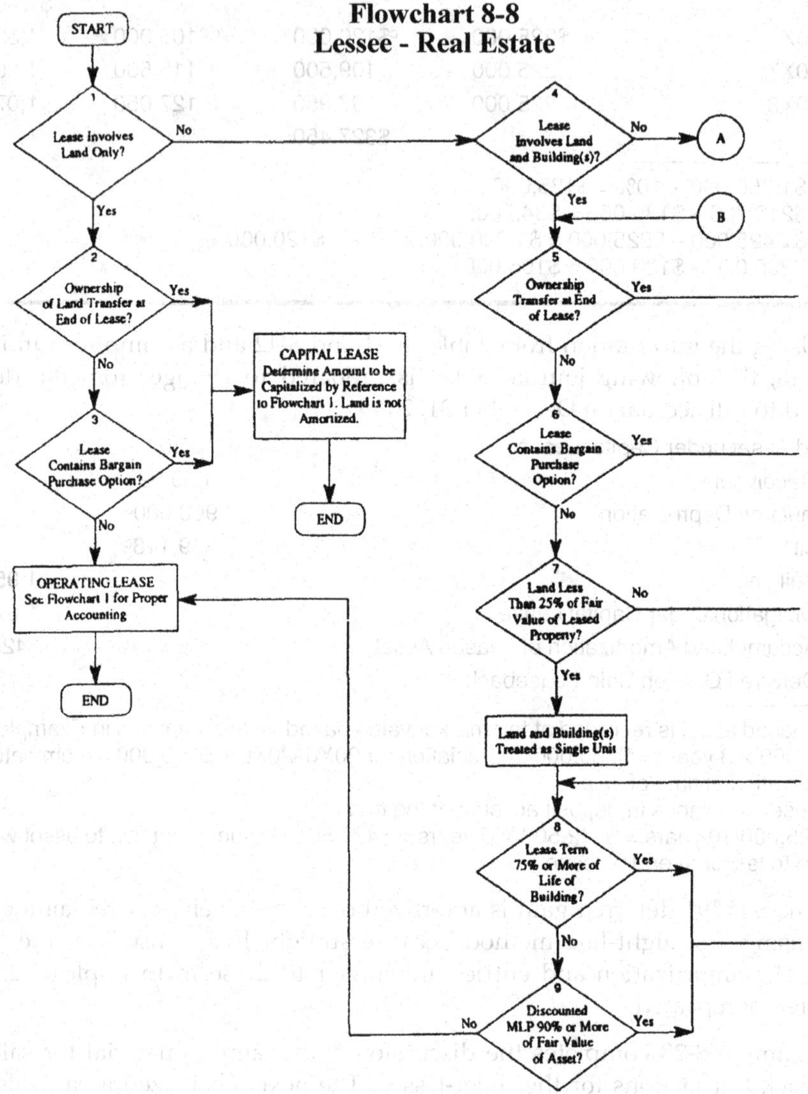

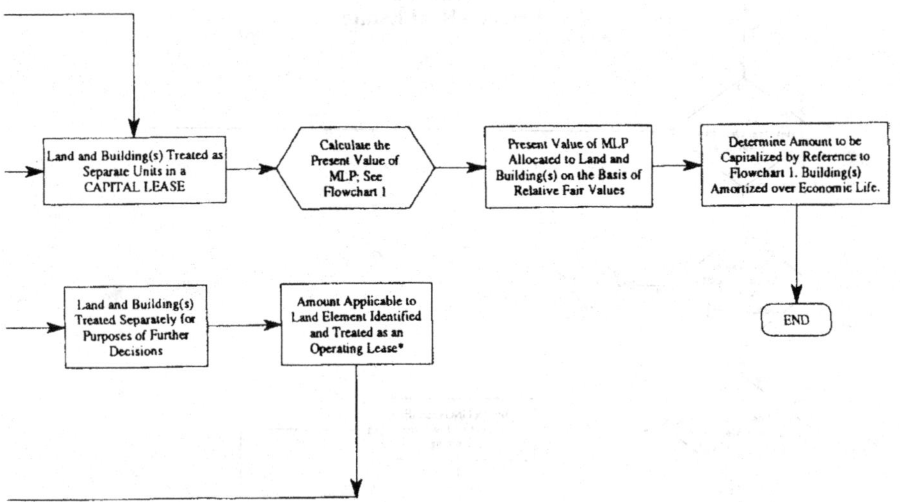

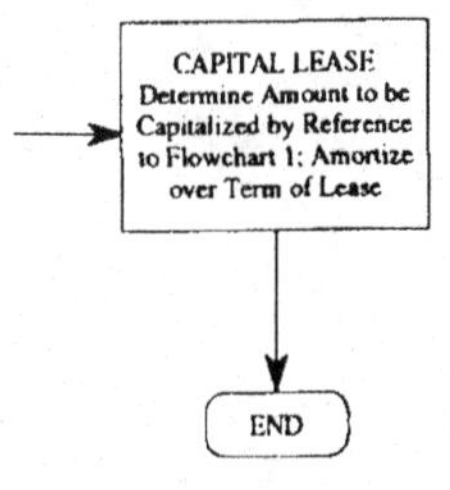

*Fair value of the land discounted at the lessee's incremental borrowing rate is equal to the MLP allocated to the land. Total MLP less MLP allocated to land is equal to MLP allocated to building(s).

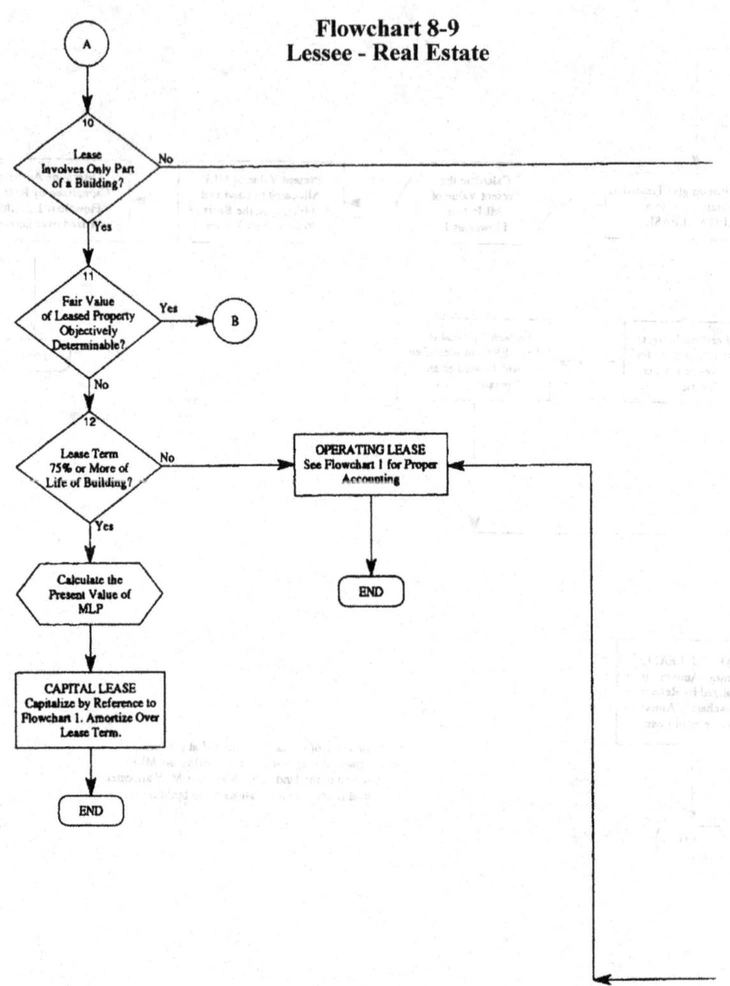
Flowchart 8-9
Lessee - Real Estate
A
10
Lease Involves Only Part of a Building?
No
Yes
11
Fair Value of Leased Property Objectively Determinable?
Yes
B
No
12
Lease Term 75% or More of Life of Building?
No
OPERATING LEASE See Flowchart 1 for Proper Accounting
END
Yes
Calculate the Present Value of MLP
CAPITAL LEASE Capitalize by Reference to Flowchart 1. Amortize Over Lease Term.
END

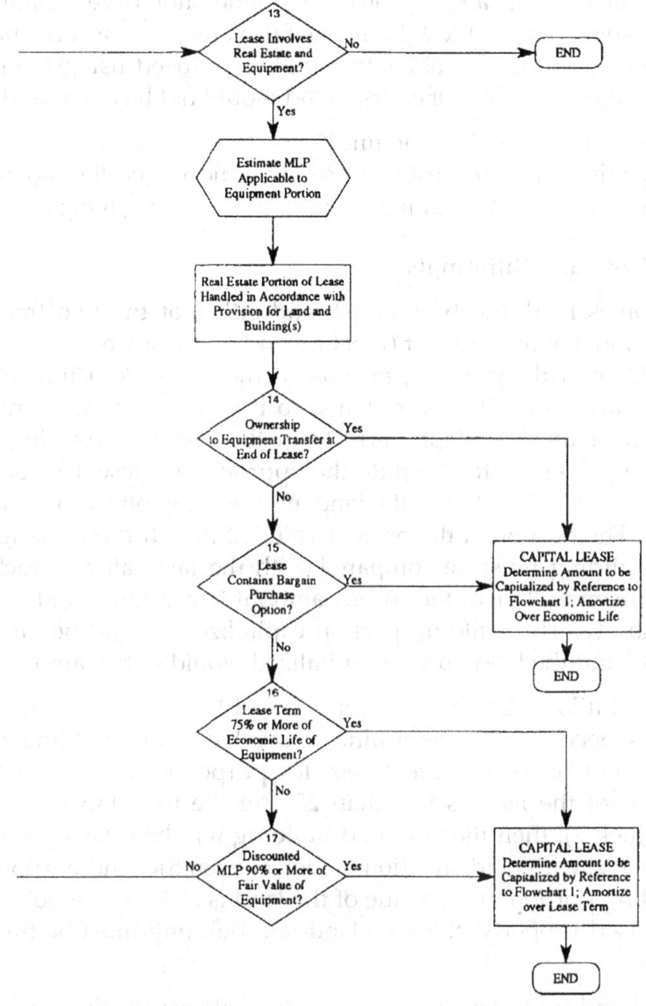

As indicated in Flowcharts 8-8 and 8-9, there are four types of real estate lease transactions. These include leases involving: land only, land and building(s), part of a building, and real estate and equipment. The discussion is organized to follow the flowcharts. Of the four types of leases, only leases involving land and building(s) require the presentation of new example materials. The other types of real estate leases either are handled in the same way as are general leases or are merely an extension of the land and building(s) lease accounting.

Leases Involving Land Only

For leases involving land only, the relevant criteria are those dealing with transfer of ownership. If the ownership transfers *or* the lease contains a bargain purchase option, the lease will be classified as a capital lease (Blocks 2 and 3). In the absence of either of these two criteria, the lease will be accounted for as an operating lease. If classified as a capital lease, the land should be capitalized at the lesser of the present value of the MLP or the fair value, with a corresponding liability for the same amount. The obligation will be reduced using the interest method over the term of the lease. Of course, land would not be amortized.

Other than the fact that land is not amortized, there are no new accounting problems posed by this type of real estate lease. As indicated earlier, no example material is presented to show the technical aspects of leases involving only land.

Leases Involving Land and Building(s)

If a lease involves land and building(s), and either of the two transfer of ownership criteria noted above are met (Blocks 5 and 6), the lessee must separate the MLP associated with the building portion of the lease. Both the land and building will be treated as capital lease items, so it is necessary to identify the amortizable portion of the leased property from the non-amortizable portion. The first step in the process is to compute the appropriate present value of the MLP. This amount will be allocated to the land and building on the basis of their relative fair values. The portion of the present value of the MLP thus assigned to the land and the building must be compared with the fair value of each asset leased. This comparison will yield the correct amount to capitalize and record as an asset(s) and liability. The building portion capitalized should be amortized over its *economic life*, and the land portion capitalized would not be amortized.

If the land and building(s) do not meet *either* of the transfer of ownership criteria, it becomes necessary to determine if the land and building will be treated as a single unit or as separate assets, for purposes of applying further criteria. If the value of the land is less than 25% of the total fair value of the leased property (Block 7), then the land and building will be treated as a single unit of leased property, with no distinction made between the land portion of the lease and the building portion. If the value of the land is 25% or more of the total fair value of the leased property, then the land and building must be treated as two separate assets.

When the land and building are treated as separate assets, the land will be accounted for as an operating lease, and the building portion will be tested against additional criteria before a proper classification can be made. To determine the part of the MLP that will be associated with the land (and treated as an operating lease), the lessee must discount the fair value of the land at the incremental borrowing rate applicable to the lessee. The discounted amount determined in this manner will represent the portion of the MLP identified with the land. The difference between the total MLP and the MLP attributed to the land will be the MLP associated with the building. The amount applicable to the building portion will be used to determine if the lease should be classified as operating or capital.

In cases where land and building are treated as a single unit or where the MLP associated with the building portion of a land and building lease has been determined, two additional criteria must be considered (Blocks 8 and 9). If *either* of the two criteria are met, the lease will be classified as capital; and if neither criterion is met, it will be classified as operating. The first criterion is the 75% test, and the second is that the discounted value of the MLP is 90% or more of the fair value of the asset decision. (For a more explicit discussion of these two criteria, see Lease Classification.) The amount capitalized, if either criterion is met, will be amortized over the lease term.

Technical Considerations for Leases Involving Land and Building(s)

From an accounting standpoint, land and building(s) leases are, perhaps, the most complex type of real estate leases. The technical accounting and classification problems can be simplified by subdividing the land and building (s) category into four sections. The four sections are: leases containing transfer of ownership or bargain purchase option provisions; leases where the land element comprises less than 25% of the total fair value of the leased assets; leases where the land element comprises 25% or more of the total fair value of the leased property; and operating leases.

Leases Meeting the Transfer of Ownership Criteria

If the lease agreement meets either of the transfer of ownership criteria, the present value of the MLP must be divided into a land element and a building element. The Example 8-29 lease will be used to illustrate the separation of the two elements and the subsequent accounting. The Example 8-29 lease contains the following assumptions.

Example 8-29
Lease Assumptions—Land and Building Lease

1. The lessee enters into a five-year, noncancelable lease for land and renovated building that requires payments of $155,000 at the beginning of each of the five years. $5,000 of the payments are for executory costs. The lease specifies that ownership will transfer to the lessee at the end of the leased term.
2. The lessee's incremental borrowing rate is 11%, and the lessor's implicit rate is 10%.
3. The leased building has an estimated economic life of five years. The fair value of the land is $100,000, and the fair value of the building is $550,000 at the inception of the lease.
4. The lessee uses the straight-line depreciation method for all existing owned assets.

The present value of the MLP is determined as follows:

Rental Payments Required	$155,000
Less: Executory Costs	5,000
	$150,000
Present Value Factor	[a]4.16987
Present Value of MLP	$625,481

[a] Present value factor for an annuity due for five periods at 10%. See Appendix E, Table III. The lessor's implicit rate is used, because it is known and is less than the lessee's incremental borrowing rate.

Once the present value of the MLP has been determined, it is divided between the building and land elements, using the relative fair values at the inception of the lease. The disaggregation process is illustrated below:

Fair Value of the Land	$100,000
Fair Value of the Building	550,000
Total Fair Value of Leased Property	$650,000

MLP Allocated to Land	=	$96,228 ($100,000 ÷ $650,000 × $625,481)
MLP Allocated to Building	=	529,253 ($550,000 ÷ $650,000 × $625,481)
Total MLP		$625,481

The present value of the MLP assigned to the land and to the building is less than the fair value of the respective assets, so the assets and obligation will be recorded at the present value of the MLP assigned. The entry to record the assets and obligation at inception of the lease is:

Leased Property Capital Lease-Land	96,228	
Leased Property Capital Lease-Building	529,253	
Obligation under Capital Lease		625,481

The obligation would be reduced using the interest method, which has been described extensively in the preceding pages. The entry to reduce the obligation and record the interest expense is the same as previously shown and will not be repeated here. Because ownership to the leased property transfers to the lessee at the end of the lease, the building will be amortized over its economic life. Land is not amortized. The entry to record the amortization of the building portion of the leased property is:

Amortization of Leased Property	105,851	
Accumulated Amortization of Leased Property—Building		105,851

The amount is determined on a straight-line basis as follows:

$529,253 ÷ 5 years = $105,851.

Land Element Less Than 25% of Fair Value

A lease agreement for land and building(s) may be classified as a capital lease without a transfer of ownership or a bargain purchase option. When the land element of the leased property is less than 25% of the total fair value, land and building will be combined and treated as a single unit of leased property for purposes of testing further criteria. If the lease term is 75% or more of the economic life of the *building,* or if the present value of the MLP of the combined land and building is 90% or more of the combined fair value, the lease will qualify as a capital lease. If neither of these criteria is met, the lease will be classified as an operating lease.

To illustrate capital lease accounting, assume the same facts as in the Example 8-29 lease, except that ownership of the leased property *does not* transfer to the lessee at the end of the lease term. In the Example 8-29 lease, the fair value of the land is 15% of the total fair value of both land and building ($100,000 ÷ $650,000 = 15%). However, the lease term of five years is more than 75% of the economic life of the building (5 years × .75 = 3.75 years), and the present value of the MLP ($625,481) is more than 90% of the fair value of the combined land and building ($650,000 × .90 = $585,000). Because the lease agreement meets *at least one* of the criteria, it qualifies as a capital lease.

Because the fair value of the land element is less than 25% of the total fair value, the land and building are treated as a single unit under a capital lease. The single unit (both land and building) will be amortized over the lease term, using the straight-line method. The entries necessary at inception of the lease and the subsequent amortization are presented below (amortization of the lease obligation is not shown):

Leased Property under Capital Lease	625,481	
Obligation under Capital Lease		625,481
Amortization of Leased Property	[a]125,096	
Accumulated Amortization of Leased Property		125,096

[a] $625,481/5 years = $125,096 per year.

The amortization schedule for the obligation would be consistent with those previously shown.

Land Element 25% or More of Fair Value

To illustrate the accounting for a land and building lease, where the fair value of the land element is 25% or more of the total fair value of the leased property, it is necessary to change two of the assumptions of the Example 8-29 lease. First, assume that ownership does not transfer to the lessee at the end of the lease term. Second, assume that the fair value of the land is $200,000 and the fair value of the building is $450,000 at the inception of the lease. With these modified assumptions, the land element is now 31% of the total fair value of the leased assets ($200,000 ÷ $650,000 = 31%). The lease still qualifies as a capital lease, because the lease term of five years is more than 75% of the economic life of the building.

Because the lease is a capital lease, and the land element is 25% or more of the total fair value of the assets, the present value of the MLP must be divided between the land element and the building element. The procedure for dividing the MLP requires that the MLP associated with the land be determined by discounting the fair value of the land at the lessee's incremental borrowing rate. This is accomplished as follows:

$$\frac{\text{Fair Value of Land}}{\text{Present Value Factor}^{a}} \qquad \frac{\$200{,}000}{4.10245} = \$48{,}751 \text{ MLP assigned to land}$$

[a] Present value factor for an annuity due at 11% for five periods. See Appendix E, Table III.

The difference between the MLP assigned to land and the total MLP will be the MLP assigned to the building. This amount would be determined as follows:

Rental Payment Required	$155,000
Less: Executory Costs	5,000
	$150,000
MLP Assigned to Land	(48,751)
MLP Assigned to Building	$101,249

Once the MLP associated with the building element has been calculated, the next step is to determine the present value of the MLP, using the implicit interest rate of 10%. The present value of the MLP is calculated below:

MLP Assigned to Building	$101,249
Present Value Factor	[a]4.16987
Present Value of MLP Assigned to Building	$422,195

[a] Present value factor for an annuity due at 10% for 5 periods. See Appendix E, Table III.

The present value ($422,195) of the MLP assigned to the building element is less than the fair value ($450,000) of the building; therefore, the building would be recorded at the present value of the MLP. The entry required at the inception of the lease would be:

Leased Property under Capital Lease—Building	422,195	
Obligation under Capital Lease		422,195

The land element would be treated as a separate *operating lease.*

The entry to record the first lease payment is shown below:

Lease Rental Expense—Land	[a]48,751	
Interest Expense	[b]32,095	
Obligation under Capital Lease	[c]69,154	
Executory Costs	5,000	
Cash		155,000

[a] Annual lease payment assigned to land per computation.
[b] ($422,195 – $101,249) × 10% = $32,095.
[c] $101,249 – $32,095 = $69,154.

The only amortization required would be for the building element of the lease. Assuming straight-line depreciation, the entry would be:

Amortization of Leased Property—Building	[a]84,439	
Accumulated Amortization of Leased Property—Building		84,439

[a] $422,195/5 years = $84,439 per year.

This last set of entries completes the illustrations of accounting for leases involving land and building(s). If any of the above lease examples had been classified as an operating lease, the only entry required would have been a record of the annual or interim rental expense.

Leases Involving Part of a Building

Where a lease agreement involves only part of a building, proper classification depends largely upon whether the lessee can determine the fair value of the leased asset (Block 11). If the fair value of the property can be *objectively* determined, the lessee would account for the lease as if it were the building portion of a lease involving land and building(s). (See the preceding section for a complete discussion of proper classification and accounting for land and building(s) leases.) If the fair value *cannot* be determined, the only relevant criterion is the 75% test. If the lease term is 75% or more of the building's economic life, the lease will be classified as capital, and will be treated as if it were the building portion of a lease involving land and building(s). If the lease qualifies as a capital lease under the 75% test, the asset recorded will be amortized over the lease term. The determination of the MLP and the amortization of the obligation are consistent with the method used for the general lease agreement (see Flowchart 8-5). If the fair value of the leased property is not known, *and* the lease term is less than 75% of the economic life of the building, the lease will be classified and accounted for as an operating lease.

Leases Involving Real Estate and Equipment

If the lease agreement involves both real estate and equipment, the lessee must separate the real estate portion of the MLP from the portion of the MLP applicable to the equipment. The separation of the minimum lease payments for real estate and equipment should be made by using the most appropriate method for the situation. It would appear that an allocation on the basis of fair values or appraisal values would be appropriate in most cases.

Once the allocation of the MLP has been completed, the real estate portion will be classified and accounted for according to the provisions specified for leases involving land and building(s).

The portion of the MLP allocated to the equipment must meet one of the four basic criteria—ownership transfer, bargain purchase option, 75% or more of economic life, or discounted MLP 90% or more of fair value of the equipment—to be classified as a capital lease. If the equipment portion qualifies as a capital lease, the provisions described in Flowchart 8-5 would apply. If none of the four basic criteria are met, the lease is an operating lease.

When the equipment is classified as a capital lease, the asset recorded will be amortized over its economic life, if either of the two transfer-of-ownership criteria is met, and over the lease term, if neither of these criteria is met.

This completes the discussion and illustration of accounting for real estate leases. The last type of lease that needs to be explored is the *sublease.* Because a sublease involves accounting from the standpoints of both the lessee and the lessor, complete discussion of the topic is deferred until after the lessor's accounting has been examined in full. Here leases are discussed from the viewpoint of the lessor.

There are many new and interesting problems associated with the lessor's accounting for capital leases. These new problems result primarily from the more sophisticated classification of various types of capital leases, which requires the knowledge of new terminology.

Defining Some Additional Terms

Additional new terms that are important for a complete understanding of lessor accounting are defined below:

1. *Unguaranteed residual value:* The difference between the leased property's estimated salvage or residual value and the guaranteed amount of the residual value.

2. *Initial direct costs:* Costs that the lessor incurs to complete a lease agreement. These costs include the following items: costs to acquire lease agreements with third parties that are independent, where the costs were necessary to acquire the lease and where, without the lease, the costs would not have been incurred and costs incurred for certain lease activities, such as evaluating the lessee's financial ability to perform according to the lease terms, working out the terms of the lease, and closing the deal.

Flowcharts and Discussion of General Lease Agreement—Lessor Lease Classification

Flowchart 8-10 depicts the classification of various types of leases for the lessor and Flowcharts 8-10 (A), 8-10 (B), and 8-10 (C) show the proper accounting treatment for the different types of capital leases.

As stated in the discussion of the lessee, it is necessary to determine only if a particular lease is an operating or a capital lease to determine the appropriate accounting; however, in the case of the lessor, it also is necessary to determine the proper type of capital lease. ASC 840-30 identifies three types of capital leases: sales-type, direct financing, and leveraged. All three of these capital leases present different accounting problems to the lessor.

Flowchart 8-10, the classification flowchart, starts with the same four criteria as the lessee flowchart, and the decision process for these criteria is identical. If none of the four criteria (Blocks 1 through 4) are met, the lease would be classified as operating, and the accounting would be quite simple. If any one of the four criteria is met, there are two additional criteria that must be met before the lease will qualify as a capital lease. First, the lessor must be reasonably certain about the ability to collect the MLP (Block 5), and the lessor must have no significant unreimbursable costs (Block 6). If *both* these criteria are met, the lease will be classified as capital; if either one fails to be met, the lease will be classified as operating. These two additional criteria are often referred to in the discussion that follows as the "risk transfer criteria," because they deal with the certainty of the future income stream from the lease.

Flowchart 8-10
Lessor - General Classification

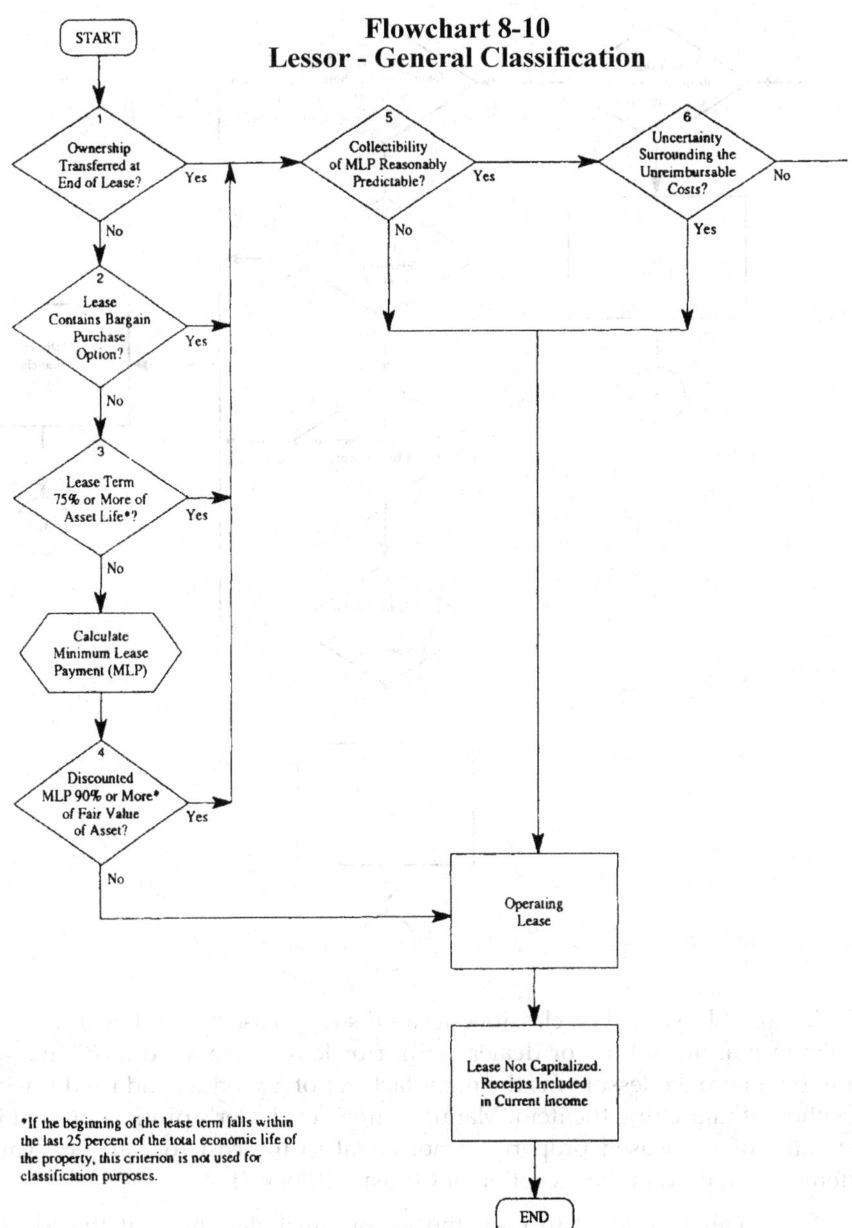

*If the beginning of the lease term falls within the last 25 percent of the total economic life of the property, this criterion is not used for classification purposes.

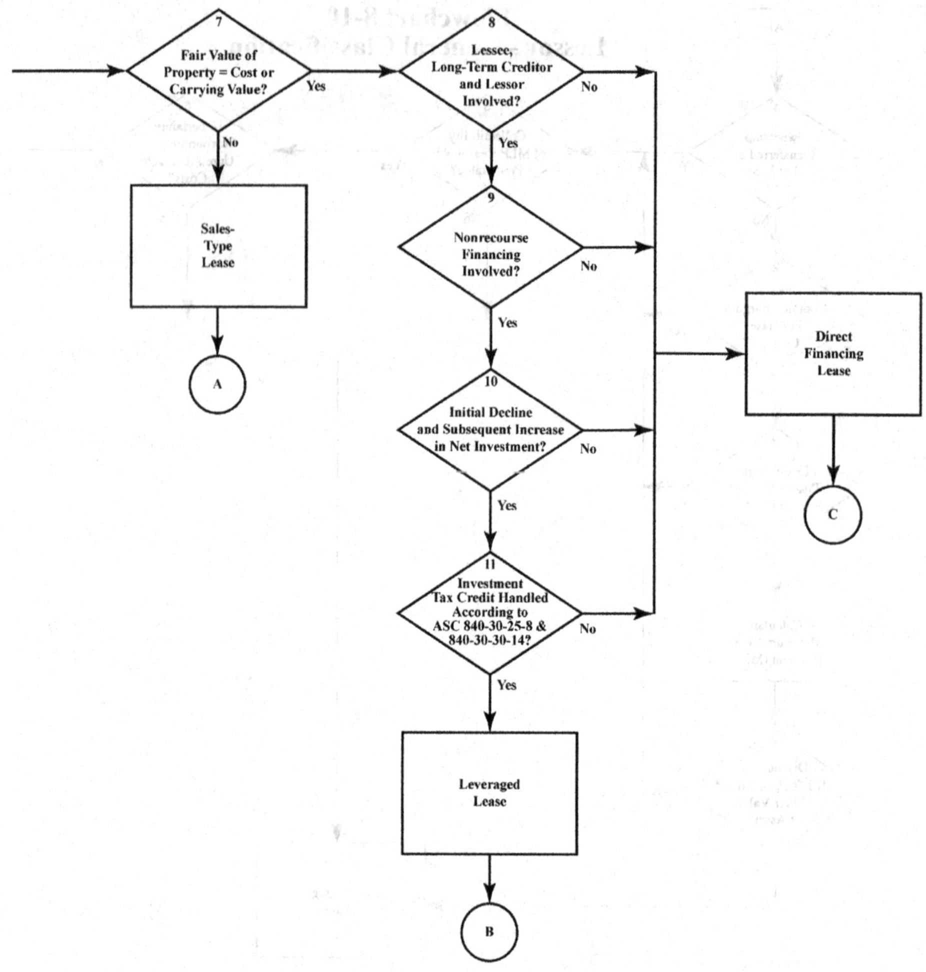

A capital lease will be classified as a *sales-type* lease by the lessor if the lease results in manufacturer's or dealer's profit or loss to the lessor. This would be common where the lessor was the manufacturer of a product and used leasing as a method of marketing the item. Manufacturer's or dealer's profit is present if the fair value of the leased property is not equal to the cost (or carrying value if different from cost) at the inception of the lease (Block 7).

If fair value is equal to cost, the lessor must determine if the lease is a leveraged or a direct financing lease. At this stage of Flowchart 8-10, if a lease does not qualify as a leveraged lease, then, by default, it will be classified as a direct financing lease.

As the name leveraged lease implies, the lessor is attempting to take advantage of the financial concept of leverage. Four criteria must be met before a lease can be identified as leveraged. The first criterion (Block 8) indicates that three parties must be involved in the lease agreement: the lessee, the lessor, and a long-term creditor. The funds borrowed from the long-term creditor should allow the lessor to have leverage that is considered substantial. After it has been determined that the three parties are involved, the next criterion (Block 9) states that the financing arrangement between the lessor and the third-party creditor must be a nonrecourse agreement to the lessor's general credit. The third criterion (Block 10) results from the unusual pattern of the lessor's net investment in the lease over time. In a typical leveraged lease, the value of the lessor's net investment will decline in the early years of the lease, may become *negative* for a while, then turn positive and increase in the latter years. To be classified as a leveraged lease, the lessor's net investment must follow this pattern. Finally, the lessor must establish a receivable for the amount of the investment tax credit to be realized and recognize the benefits of the investment tax credit over the life of the lease as an element of income. If the accounting for the investment tax credit is handled differently, the lease will not qualify as a leveraged lease (Block 11).

A lease that does not qualify as a sales-type or leveraged lease is accounted for as a *direct financing* type lease. In the following sections, discussion of accounting for sales-type leases will be addressed first, followed by leveraged leases and direct financing leases.

Accounting for a Sales-Type Lease

Once it has been determined that a particular lease is a sales-type lease, the lessor must capitalize the leased property as an investment. Proper accounting for both the date of inception of the lease and subsequent periods is shown in Flowchart 8-10 (A).

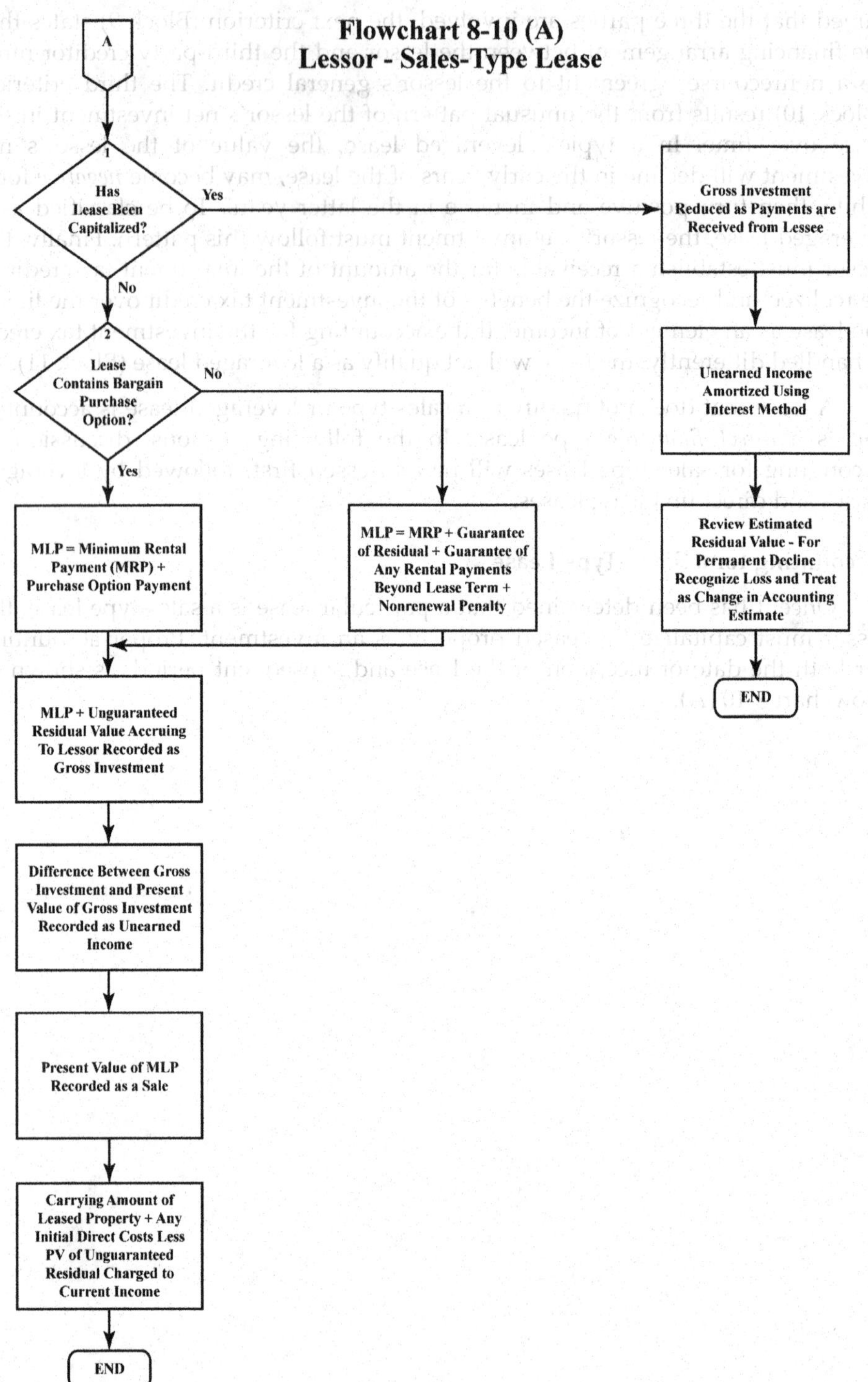
Flowchart 8-10 (A)
Lessor - Sales-Type Lease
A
1
Has Lease Been Capitalized?
Yes
No
Gross Investment Reduced as Payments are Received from Lessee
Unearned Income Amortized Using Interest Method
Review Estimated Residual Value - For Permanent Decline Recognize Loss and Treat as Change in Accounting Estimate
END
2
Lease Contains Bargain Purchase Option?
No
Yes
MLP = Minimum Rental Payment (MRP) + Purchase Option Payment
MLP = MRP + Guarantee of Residual + Guarantee of Any Rental Payments Beyond Lease Term + Nonrenewal Penalty
MLP + Unguaranteed Residual Value Accruing To Lessor Recorded as Gross Investment
Difference Between Gross Investment and Present Value of Gross Investment Recorded as Unearned Income
Present Value of MLP Recorded as a Sale
Carrying Amount of Leased Property + Any Initial Direct Costs Less PV of Unguaranteed Residual Charged to Current Income
END

At the date of inception of the lease, the lessor must determine the proper value of the gross investment. The value of the gross investment depends on whether the lease agreement contains a bargain purchase option. If a bargain purchase option is specified, the MLP will be computed as follows (Block 2):

MLP = Minimum Rental Payments (MRP) +Purchase Option Payment

If the lease does not contain a bargain purchase option, the MLP would consist of one or more of the following:

MLP = Minimum Rental Payments (MRP)
+Guaranteed residual value (if any)
+Penalty payment for nonrenewal (if any)
+Guarantee of any rental payments beyond the lease term (if any)

The appropriate MLP will be added to any unguaranteed residual value retained by lessor, and this total will constitute the lessor's gross investment in the lease.

The difference between the gross investment computed above, and the present value of the gross investment, will be recorded as *unearned income* resulting from a capital lease.

The final part of the initial accounting process is the recording of the sale and cost of sale of the property. As indicated in Flowchart 8-10 (A), the present value of the MLP would be recorded as the sales price, and the cost of the property sold would be determined as follows:

Cost of Sales = Carrying value of property
+ Initial direct costs (if any)
– Present value of unguaranteed residual value (if any).

The difference between the sales price and the cost of the sale would represent the profit resulting from the sales-type lease.

In subsequent periods, the value of the gross investment would be reduced as lease payments are received. The unearned income would be recognized using the interest method. As a result, part of each lease receipt would be a recovery of investment, and the other part would be income from the lease of property.

Technical Considerations for a Sales-Type Lease

To illustrate the technical aspects of accounting for a sales-type lease, two example leases will be presented, along with solutions. The Example 8-30 lease assumptions are listed below.

Example 8-30
Lease Assumptions

1. The lessor enters into a five-year, non-cancellable lease with a lessee that requires annual advance payments of $50,000. Title to the leased property does not pass to the lessee at the end of the lease term, and there is no bargain purchase option in the lease agreement.
2. The implicit interest rate is 10%.
3. The collectibility of the MLP is reasonably predictable, and there are no unreimbursable costs associated with the lease.

4. The cost of the leased property is $200,000, and the fair value at inception of the lease is $208,494. The property has an estimated economic life of five years and zero estimated residual value.

The lessor must begin by determining the proper classification of the lease. Because ownership does not transfer, and the lease does not contain a bargain purchase option, the lease agreement fails to meet the first two general criteria. However, the lease term of five years is more than 75% of the economic life of the leased property (five-year economic life × .75 = 3.75 years).

Because the third general criterion is met, *and* the collectibility of the MLP is reasonably certain and there are no unreimbursable costs associated with the lease, the Example 8-30 lease qualifies as a capital lease.

Although not required for proper classification of the Example 8-30 lease, the lease agreement also meets the fourth general criterion. The present value of the MLP would be calculated as follows:

Required rental payments	$50,000
Present value factor	[a]4.16987
Present value of MLP	$208,494

[a] Present value factor for an annuity due at 10% for five periods. See Appendix E, Table III.

The present value of the MLP ($208,494) is more than 90% of the fair value of the leased property at inception of the lease ($208,494 fair value × .90 = $187,645). The above computations show that the fourth general criterion also has been met.

Next, the lessor must determine the appropriate type of capital lease (i.e., sales-type, leveraged, or direct financing). For the Example 8-30 lease, cost ($200,000) is different from fair value ($208,494); therefore, the lease properly is classified as a sales-type lease.

Because the lease does not contain a bargain purchase option, and there is no guarantee of residual value or penalty for nonrenewal or guarantee of rentals beyond the lease term, the MLP will be equal to the required minimum rental payments. The MLP is referred to as the lessor's gross investment in the lease, and is determined as follows:

Required rental payments	$50,000
Number of annual payments required	× 5
Gross investment in lease	$250,000

The value of the gross investment will be recorded as an asset under a sales-type lease. In addition, a sale will be recorded in an amount equal to the present value of the gross investment. In the Example 8-30 lease, the present value of the gross investment is equal to the present value of the MLP ($208,494). The difference between the gross investment ($250,000) and the present value of the gross investment ($208,494) is recorded as unearned income under a capital lease. When a sale is recorded, it also is necessary to record the cost of the sale, which, in this case, is $200,000. Given this information, the entry to record the capital lease at date of inception would be as follows:

Minimum Lease Payment Receivable	250,000	
Sales		208,494
Unearned Income		41,506
Cost of Goods Sold	200,000	
Inventory		200,000

Under a sales-type lease, there are two elements of profit: one from the sale of the property ($208,494 – $200,000 = $8,494) and the second from the financing of the sale through the lease agreement ($41,506 recognized over the five-year lease term).

Table 8-43 shows the computation of the lease amortization and the income recognition over the lease term.

Table 8-43 Amortization Schedule for Example 8-30 Lease

	Period	Annual Payment	Annual Interest Income	Principal Reduction	Present Value of Principal
Initial Value	—	—	—	—	$208,494
	1	$50,000	[a]$15,849	[b]$34,151	[c]174,343
	2	50,000	12,434	37,566	136,777
	3	50,000	8,678	41,322	95,455
	4	50,000	4,545	45,455	50,000
	5	50,000	-0-	50,000	-0-
		$250,000	$41,506	$208,494	

[a] ($208,494 – $50,000) × 10% = $15,849.
[b] $50,000 – $15,849 = $34,151.
[c] $208,494 – $34,151 = $174,343.

The lease agreement requires advance rental payments (payment made at the beginning of each year); therefore, in Year 5, there would be no interest, because the last rental payment is made at the beginning of the year. Immediately after recording the investment in the lease, the lessor would record the receipt of the first rental payment and, at the end of Year 1, would record the income earned. The following entries reflect these two events.

Cash	50,000	
Minimum Lease Payment Receivable		50,000
Unearned Income	15,849	
Income From Capital Lease		15,849

Table 8-43 states the amounts that would be used for the above entries for the remainder of the lease term. At the end of the lease, the minimum lease payment receivable account would have a zero balance, and all of the unearned income would have been recognized.

The Example 8-30 lease served as an introduction to accounting for sales-type leases. Example 8-31 builds on the Example 8-30 lease, and incorporates more complex material.

The Example 8-31 lease assumptions are listed below. (Many of the features of the Example 8-31 lease are the same as the Example 8-30 lease.)

Example 8-31
Lease Assumptions

1. The lessor enters into a five-year, non-cancellable lease with a lessee that requires annual advance payments of $50,000. Title to the leased property does not pass to the lessee at the end of the lease term, and there is no bargain purchase option in the lease agreement.
2. The implicit interest rate is 10%.
3. The collectibility of the MLP is reasonably predictable, and there are no unreimbursable costs associated with the lease.
4. The cost of the leased property is $200,000, and the fair value at inception of the lease is $214,703. The property has an estimated economic life of five years and an unguaranteed residual value of $10,000.
5. The lessor incurred $5,000 of initial direct costs to consummate the lease agreement.

The Example 8-31 lease is also a capital lease, because the lease term of five years is more than 75% of the economic life of the property *and* because the collectibility of the MLP is reasonably predictable *and* there are no unreimbursable costs. The lease is a sales-type lease, because cost ($200,000) is not equal to fair value ($214,703) at the inception of the lease. The new variables added to this lease agreement are the unguaranteed residual value and the initial direct costs.

The gross investment in the lease is equal to the total rental payments required in the lease agreement, plus the unguaranteed residual value, and is computed below:

Annual Required Rental Payments	$50,000
Number of Rental Payments Required	× 5
Total Rental Payments	$250,000
Unguaranteed Residual Value	10,000
Gross Investment in Lease	$260,000

From Example 8-30, it is known that the difference between the gross investment and the present value of the gross investment is the amount of unearned income to be recognized over the lease term. The calculation of the present value of the gross investment would be as follows:

Annual Required Rental Payments	$50,000
Present Value Factor	[a]4.16987
Present Value of MLP	$208,494
Unguaranteed Residual Value	$10,000

Present Value Factor	[b].62092
Present Value of Unguaranteed Residual Value	6,209
Present Value of Gross Investment	$214,703

[a] Present value factor for an annuity due at 10% for five periods. See Appendix E, Table III.
[b] Present value factor for $1 at 10% for five periods. See Appendix E, Table I.

After this computation has been made, unearned income is determined to be $45,297 ($260,000 – $214,703). The present value of the gross investment is equal to the fair value of the leased property at inception of the lease. To continue the initial entry required to record the gross investment, the amount of the sale has to be determined. The value of the sale is equal to the present value of the minimum rental payments, and was computed above to be $208,494.

The unguaranteed residual value affected both the computation of the gross investment and the present value of the gross investment. Both the unguaranteed residual value and the initial direct costs will affect the determination of cost of goods sold. Cost of sales is equal to the cost or carrying value of the leased property, plus any initial direct costs, less the present value of the unguaranteed residual value. The value of the cost of sales would be computed as follows:

Cost of Leased Property	$200,000
Initial Direct Costs	5,000
Present Value of Unguaranteed Residual Value	(6,209)
Cost of Goods Sold	$198,791

Based on the information developed above, the entries at inception of the lease would be:

Minimum Lease Payment Receivable	260,000	
Sales		208,494
Unearned Income		45,297
Inventory		6,209
Cost of Goods Sold	198,791	
Inventory		193,791
Cash		5,000

Inventory was reduced by $200,000 ($6,209 + $193,791 = $200,000) and the initial direct costs were assumed to be fully paid in cash. The entries shown above are quite different from the basic entries made for the Example 8-30 lease. It is worth the reader's time to spend a few minutes analyzing and comparing the sets of entries under the Example 8-30 and Example 8-31 leases.

Once the initial entry to record the lease has been made, the lessor must prepare an amortization schedule to determine the income to be recognized in each of the five years of the lease term. Table 8-44 develops the required information.

Table 8-44 Amortization Schedule for Example 8-31

	Period	Annual Payment	Annual Interest Income	Principal Reduction	Present Value of Principal
Initial Value	—	—	—	—	[a]$214,703
	1	$50,000	[b]$16,470	[c]$33,530	[d]181,173
	2	50,000	13,117	36,883	144,290
	3	50,000	9,429	40,571	103,719
	4	50,000	5,372	44,628	59,091
	5	50,000	[e]909	49,091	[e]10,000
		$250,000	$45,297	$204,703	

[a] The initial value is the present value of the gross investment.
[b] ($214,703 – $50,000) × 10% = $16,470.
[c] $50,000 – $16,470 = $33,530.
[d] $214,703 – $33,530 = $181,173.
[e] Interest on the unguaranteed residual value.
[f] Unguaranteed residual value.

From the information in Table 8-44, the lessor would make the following journal entries to record the first advance rental payment and to record income under the capital lease in the first year:

Cash	50,000	
Minimum Lease Payment Receivable		50,000
Unearned Income	16,470	
Income from Capital Lease		16,470

The amounts shown on Table 8-44 would be used for all subsequent entries involving receipt of rental payments and recognition of income.

Assuming that the estimated residual value turned out to be the actual residual value at the end of the lease, and that the lessor sold the property for $10,000, the following entry would be made:

Cash	10,000	
Minimum Lease Payment Receivable		10,000

Flowchart 8-10 (A) indicates that the lessor must review the estimated residual value on a periodic basis and prepare an adjusting entry when it has been determined that there has been a permanent decline in the residual value. Illustration of accounting for a permanent decline in residual value will be deferred at this point, but will be shown in the accounting for direct financing leases. The accounting is identical and need not be repeated.

This completes the discussion and illustration of accounting for sales-type leases. Attention will now be focused on accounting for leveraged leases. Leveraged leases present many new and challenging problems, in the areas of both lease classification and lease accounting.

Accounting for Leveraged Leases

Flowchart 8-10 (B) indicates the proper accounting for a lease classified as leveraged. The accounting at inception of the lease is shown on the left side of Flowchart 8-10 (B), and subsequent accounting is shown on the right.

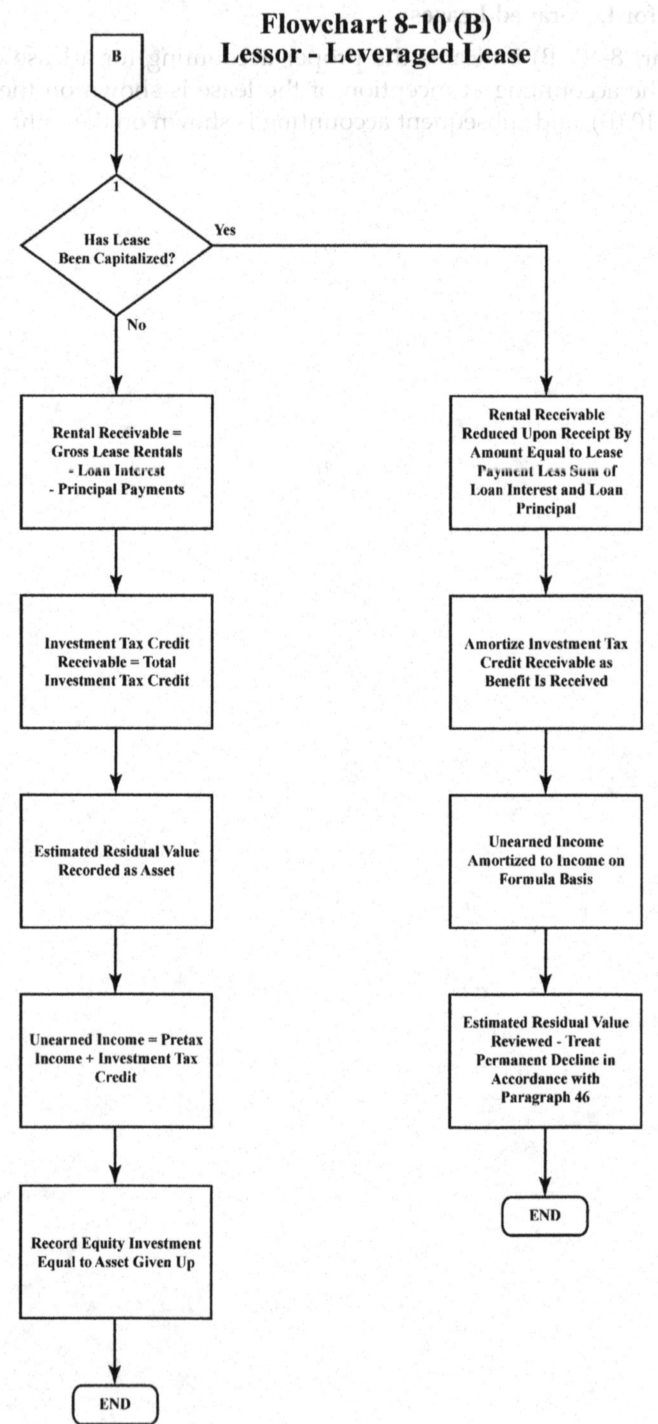
Flowchart 8-10 (B)
Lessor - Leveraged Lease
B
1
Has Lease Been Capitalized?
Yes
No
Rental Receivable = Gross Lease Rentals - Loan Interest - Principal Payments
Investment Tax Credit Receivable = Total Investment Tax Credit
Estimated Residual Value Recorded as Asset
Unearned Income = Pretax Income + Investment Tax Credit
Record Equity Investment Equal to Asset Given Up
END
Rental Receivable Reduced Upon Receipt By Amount Equal to Lease Payment Less Sum of Loan Interest and Loan Principal
Amortize Investment Tax Credit Receivable as Benefit Is Received
Unearned Income Amortized to Income on Formula Basis
Estimated Residual Value Reviewed - Treat Permanent Decline in Accordance with Paragraph 46
END

At date of inception, the lessor will establish three asset accounts. First, a receivable will be set up for the gross rentals identified in the lease agreement, less the total principal and interest payments called for by the third-party creditor. Next, a receivable will be established for the total investment tax credit applicable to the leased property, if available. Finally, the estimated residual value will be recorded as an asset. The lessor also will record the equity investment in the property (i.e., the funds committed to the property by the lessor). Given the nature of a leveraged lease, the lessor's equity investment always will be less than the cost of the property, because the third-party creditor also will be investing in the property. Unearned and deferred income will be recorded in an amount equal to the estimated pretax income expected to be earned, plus the investment tax credit to be received by the lessor.

In subsequent periods, the rental receivable will be reduced by the difference between the gross rental received and the total payment made to the third-party creditor. The investment tax credit receivable (if available) will be amortized as the benefits are received, usually in the year of inception. The unearned and deferred income will be recognized under a complex formula that requires the allocation of expected cash flows to income and to the investment made by the lessor. Income is recognized on the basis of the cash flows allocated to income. The examples that follow will demonstrate this allocation process.

Technical Considerations for a Leveraged Lease

To illustrate technical considerations of leveraged leases, two examples are used. The first example (Example 8-32) assumes the leveraged lease is entered into prior to 1986; therefore, accelerated depreciation for tax purposes prior to 1986 and the investment tax credit are used in the solution. The second example (Example 8-33) assumes use of current accelerated depreciation for tax purposes and no investment tax credit. Assumptions for Example 8-32 are as follows.

Example 8-32
Lease Assumptions—Lease Prior to 1986

1. Cost of the leased equipment is equal to $500,000. The equipment has an estimated residual value of $50,000, which will be realized at the end of the first year, after the termination of the lease.
2. The lessor finances the equipment by investing $50,000, and securing $450,000 worth of 8%, 10-year nonrecourse financing from a third-party creditor. The financing agreement calls for payments of $67,063 to be made at the end of each year.
3. The lease term is 10 years and requires that lease payments of $70,000 be made at the end of each of the 10 years. The lessor is certain about the collectibility of the lease payments and there are no unreimbursable costs associated with the lease agreement.
4. Relevant income tax information includes the facts that the equipment qualifies for a 10% investment tax credit, that this credit will be retained by the lessor, and the benefit from the tax credit will be received in year 1. Due to the special nature of the equipment, a 10-year accelerated depreciation method life is used. It is assumed that the lessor's tax rate throughout the lease term will be 50%.

First, the proper classification of the lease must be determined. Because ownership to the property does not pass, and the lease does not contain a bargain purchase option, the agreement fails to meet the first two criteria for a capital lease. However, the lease term is 10 years, and the economic life of the equipment also is 10 years; therefore, the lease meets the criterion that specifies that the lease term must be 75% or more of the economic life of the property. Further, Assumption 3, above, indicates that there are no unreimbursable costs and that the lessor is certain of the collectibility of the lease payments. On the basis of these facts it can be determined that the lease is a capital lease.

The lease is not a sales-type because cost ($500,000) can be assumed to be equal to fair value, as the property was purchased and immediately leased. The lease appears to be a leveraged lease, because there are three parties involved and the financing secured by the lessor is nonrecourse. However, before it can be correctly classified, the pattern of the net investment must be determined. Assume that the lessor has agreed to account for the investment tax credit in accordance with ASC 840-30, requiring a receivable for the amount of the credit and requiring recognition as part of unearned and deferred income.

To begin the process of computing the value of the lessor's net investment in the equipment, it is necessary to calculate the expected taxable income from the lease and the expected cash flows. Table 8-45 shows the computation of estimated taxable income and Table 8-46 shows the expected cash flows.

Table 8-45 Computation of Taxable Income

Year	Rentals Due	Depreciation for Tax Purposes	Loan Interest Paid	Taxable Income (Loss)
1	$70,000	$36,000	[a]$36,000	$(2,000)
2	70,000	63,000	33,515	(26,515)
3	70,000	54,000	30,831	(14,831)
4	70,000	45,000	27,933	(2,933)
5	70,000	45,000	24,802	198
6	70,000	45,000	21,421	3,579
7	70,000	40,500	17,769	11,731
8	70,000	40,500	13,827	15,673
9	70,000	40,500	9,567	19,933
10	70,000	40,500	4,968	24,532
	$700,000	$450,000	$220,633	$29,367

[a] $450,000 × .08 = $36,000 interest element of payment.

Table 8-46 Computation of Cash Flow

Year	Rentals and Residual Value	Loan Principal and Interest	Tax (Expense) or Credits	Investment Tax Credit	Cash Inflows (Outflows)
1	$70,000	$(67,063)	$(1,000)[a]	$50,000[b]	$53,937
2	70,000	(67,063)	(13,258)	-0-	16,195
3	70,000	(67,063)	(7,416)	-0-	10,353
4	70,000	(67,063)	(1,467)	-0-	4,404
5	70,000	(67,063)	99	-0-	2,838
6	70,000	(67,063)	1,790	-0-	1,147
7	70,000	(67,063)	5,866	-0-	(2,929)
8	70,000	(67,063)	7,837	-0-	(4,900)
9	70,000	(67,063)	9,967	-0-	(7,030)
10	70,000	(67,063)	12,266	-0-	(9,329)
11	50,000	-0-	-0-	-0-	50,000
	$750,000	$(670,630)	$14,684	$50,000	$114,686

[a] 50% of taxable income or loss from Table 8-45.
[b] 10% × $500,000 = $50,000. The investment tax credit (ITC) is applicable only to qualifying property placed in service prior to 1986. The ITC is retained in this example to illustrate its impact on existing property.

The total cash flow of $114,686 will be allocated $50,000 to investment and $64,686 to income. The specific amounts to be allocated to investment and income in a particular year are calculated by use of the interest method. Allocations to *income* will be made only in those years when the net investment balance is positive. In years when the investment is negative, the entire cash flow will be allocated to the investment. This method of allocation causes a new problem in the implementation of the interest method.

After determining the cash flow, the next step is to determine the appropriate rate for the allocation process. Perhaps the most efficient method of estimating the rate is through the use of a computer application, but the rate also can be estimated on a trial-and-error basis. When the trial-and-error method is used, if the amount allocated to income is too high (more than $64,686 in this case), then the interest rate used is too high; and, conversely, if the amount allocated to income is too low (less than $64,686), then the interest rate is too low. The trial-and-error method can be very time-consuming, because the interest rate used in the allocation process has no obvious connection with the rate of return from the leased property.

For the Example 8-32 lease, the appropriate interest rate to use to allocate the cash flow to income in the years when the net investment is positive is 44.399%. Table 8-47 shows the proper allocation of the estimated cash flows to income and investment over the life of the leased property. It would be worth the reader's time to take a few minutes and recompute the values shown Table 8-47.

Table 8-47 shows that the value of the investment is declining in the early years of the lease, turns negative in Years 5 and 6, again becomes positive, and continues to increase in the later years. This is the typical pattern described earlier and indicates that the example meets this criterion (Block 10 of Flowchart 8-9) for a leveraged lease. Assuming that the lessor agrees to account for the investment tax credit as described in ASC 840-30, the lease would qualify as a leveraged lease.

Table 8-47[a]

ALLOCATION OF CASH FLOW TO INVESTMENT AND INCOME				INCOME RECOGNIZED ON BASIS OF CASH FLOW ALLOCATION			
End of Year	Cash Inflows and (Outflows)	Investment Balance	Allocate to Investment	Allocate to Income	Accounting Income Recognized	Income Tax Effect	Investment Tax Credit Recognized
—	—	$50,000	—	—	—	—	—
1	$53,937	18,263	$31,737	[b]$22,200	[c]$10,078	[d]$5,039	$17,159
2	16,195	10,176	8,086	8,108	3,681	1,841	6,268
3	10,353	4,342	5,835	4,518	2,051	1,026	3,492
4	4,404	1,865	2,476	1,928	875	437	1,490
5	2,838	(145)	2,010	828	376	188	640
6	1,147	(1,292)	1,147	—0—	—0—	—0—	—0—
7	(2,929)	1,637	(2,929)	—0—	—0—	—0—	—0—
8	(4,900)	7,264	(5,626)	727	330	165	562
9	(7,030)	17,520	(10,255)	3,225	1,464	732	2,493
10	(9,329)	34,626	(17,107)	7,778	3,532	1,765	6,012
11	50,000	—0—	34,626	15,374	6,980	3,490	11,884
	$114,686		$50,000	$64,686	$29,367	$14,684	$50,000

[a] All columns rounded to nearest dollar.

[b] The appropriate rate to use to allocate the cash flows was determined through the use of a computer application and is equal to 44.399%. The allocation is based on the beginning investment balance and the income allocation is determined as follows: $50,000 × .44399 = $22,200 allocation to income. $53,937 cash inflow – $22,200 allocation to income = $31,737 allocation to investment. If the investment account balance is negative at the beginning of the year the entire allocation is to the investment account and no allocation is made to income.

[c] The income to be recognized for accounting purposes is determined as follows:

$$\frac{\$22,200}{\$64,686} = .34319 \times \$29,367 = \$10,078 \text{ income recognized.}$$

$$.34319 \times \$50,000 = \$17,159 \text{ investment tax credit recognized.}$$

[d] 50% of the income recognized in the period.

In Table 8-47 the entire cash flow in Years 6 and 7 is allocated to the investment account. This is because the value of the investment is $(145) at the *beginning* of Year 6 and is $(1,292) at the beginning of Year 7. The amounts shown in Table 8-47 are *end-of-year* balances and the allocation process is based upon the investment balance at the beginning of the year.

Table 8-47 also incorporates the calculation of income to be recognized in each year. The income recognized in a particular year is determined by multiplying the *total* pretax income by the percentage relationship between the cash flow allocated to that year and the total cash flow over the entire life. In Years 6 and 7, when no cash flow is allocated to income, no income can be recognized, because the numerator of the equation would be zero. The total income to be recognized can be found on Table 8-45, and the total tax effect of that income and the investment tax credit can be found on Table 8-46.

Using information from the tables, journal entries for the inception of the leveraged lease and entries for the first year are presented below:

Inception of Lease:

Rentals Receivable	[a]29,367	
Investment Tax Credit Receivable	50,000	
Estimated Residual Value	50,000	
Cash		50,000
Unearned and Deferred Income		[b]79,367
[a]Total Rental Payments ($70,000 × 10)	$700,000	
Debt Principal Repayment	(450,000)	
Total Debt Interest Payment	(220,633)	
Rental Receivable	$29,367	
[b]Pretax Accounting Income	$29,367	
Investment Tax Credit	50,000	
Unearned and Deferred Income	$79,367	

Receipt of Lease Rental and Payment of Debt:

Cash	2,937	
Rentals Receivable		[c]2,937
Income Taxes Payable	50,000	
Investment Tax Credit Receivable		50,000
Unearned and Deferred Income	10,078	
Income from Leveraged Lease		[d]10,078
Unearned and Deferred Income	17,159	
Investment Tax Credit Recognized		[e]17,159
[c] Rental Payment Received		$70,000
Debt Payment Incurred		(67,063)
Net Cash Received from Lease		$2,937

[d] See Table 8-47.

[e] See Table 8-47.

This completes the analysis of Example 8-32. Example 8-33, uses the same facts in Example 8-32 except that there is no investment tax credit, tax depreciation for property placed in service after 1986 is used, and the tax rate is assumed to be 34%. Assumptions for Example 8-33 are as follows.

Example 8-33
Lease Assumptions—Lease after 1986

1. Cost of the leased equipment is equal to $500,000. The equipment has an estimated residual value of $50,000, which will be realized at the end of the first year, after the termination of the lease.
2. The lessor finances the equipment by investing $50,000, and securing $450,000 worth of 8%, 10-year nonrecourse financing from a third-party creditor. The financing agreement calls for payments of $67,063 to be made at the end of each year.
3. The lease term is 10 years and requires that lease payments of $70,000 be made at the end of each of the 10 years. The lessor is certain about the collectibility of the lease payments and there are no unreimbursable costs associated with the lease agreement.
4. Relevant income tax information includes the facts that there is no investment tax credit. Tax depreciation for property placed in service after 1986 is used. It is assumed that the lessor's tax rate throughout the lease term will be 34%.

The same procedures used in the Example 8-32 solution are used for Example 8-33. The estimated taxable income is computed in Table 8-48, and Table 8-49 shows the expected cash flows. The cash flows from Table 8-49 are allocated to income and the investment balance over the life of the lease using 7.6459%. The investment balance is declining until Year 7, then it begins to recover. Because the computations were explained in detail in Example 8-32, no additional explanation is required for Example 8-33. Tables 8-48 through 8-50, which show the computations, follow.

Table 8-48 Computation of Taxable Income

Year	Rentals & Residual Value	Depreciation for Tax Purposes	Loan Interest Paid	Taxable Income (Loss)
1	$70,000	$50,000	$36,000[a]	($16,000)
2	70,000	90,000	33,515	(53,515)
3	70,000	72,000	30,831	(32,831)
4	70,000	57,600	27,933	(15,533)
5	70,000	46,100	24,802	(902)
6	70,000	36,850	21,421	11,729
7	70,000	32,750	17,769	19,481
8	70,000	32,750	13,827	23,423
9	70,000	32,800	9,567	27,633
10	70,000	32,750	4,968	32,282
11	50,000	16,400		33,600
	$750,000	$500,000	$220,633	$29,367

[a] $450,000 × .08 = $36,000 interest element of payment.

Table 8-49 Computation of Cash Flow

Year	Rentals & Value	Loan Principal & Interest Expense	34% Tax (Expense) or Credits	Cash Inflows (Outflows)
1	$70,000	($67,063)	($5,440)[a]	$8,377
2	70,000	(67,063)	(18,195)	21,132
3	70,000	(67,063)	(11,163)	14,100
4	70,000	(67,063)	(5,281)	8,218
5	70,000	(67,063)	(307)	3,244
6	70,000	(67,063)	3,988	(1,051)
7	70,000	(67,063)	6,624	(3,687)
8	70,000	(67,063)	7,964	(5,027)
9	70,000	(67,063)	9,395	(6,458)
10	70,000	(67,063)	10,976	(8,039)
11	50,000	0	11,424	38,576
	$750,000	($670,630)	$9,985	$69,385

[a] 34% of taxable income or loss from Table 8-48.

Table 8-50[a]

	Allocation of Cash Flow to Investment and Income		Income Recognized on Basis of Cash Flow Allocation			
Year End	Cash Inflows (Outflows)	Investment Balance	Allocate to Investment	Allocate to Income	Accounting Income Recognized	Income Tax (34%) Effect
		$50,000				
1	$8,377	45,446	$4,554	$3,823[b]	$5,791[c]	$1,969[d]
2	21,132	27,789	17,657	3,475	5,264	1,790
3	14,100	15,814	11,975	2,125	3,219	1,094
4	8,218	8,805	7,009	1,209	1,832	623
5	3,244	6,234	2,571	673	1,020	347
6	(1,051)	7,762	(1,528)	477	722	246
7	(3,687)	12,042	(4,280)	593	899	306
8	(5,027)	17,990	(5,948)	921	1,395	474
9	(6,458)	25,824	(7,834)	1,376	2,084	708
10	(8,039)	35,837	(10,013)	1,974	2,991	1,017
11	38,576	0	35,837	2,739	4,151	1,411
	$69,385		$50,000	$19,385	$29,367	$9,985

[a] All columns rounded to nearest dollar.
[b] The appropriate rate to use to allocate the cash flow is 7.6459%.
The allocation is determined as follows:
$50,000 × .076459 = $3,823 allocation to income.
$8,377 cash inflow – $3,823 = $4,554 allocation to investment.
If the investment account balance is negative at the beginning of the year the entire allocation is to the investment account and no allocation is made to income.
[c] The income to be recognized for accounting purposes is determined as follows:
$3,823/$19,385 = .1972 × $29,367 = $5,791.
[d] 34% of the income recognized in the period.

The information developed in the tables can be used as a basis for the journal entries. Journal entries are not shown for Example 8-33, because they are the same as in Example 8-32, except for removal of the investment tax credit. This completes the discussion of leveraged leases. The next section covers direct financing leases.

Accounting for a Direct Financing Lease

Flowchart 8-10 (C) shows the proper accounting for a direct financing lease, with accounting at date of inception on the left, and subsequent accounting on the right.

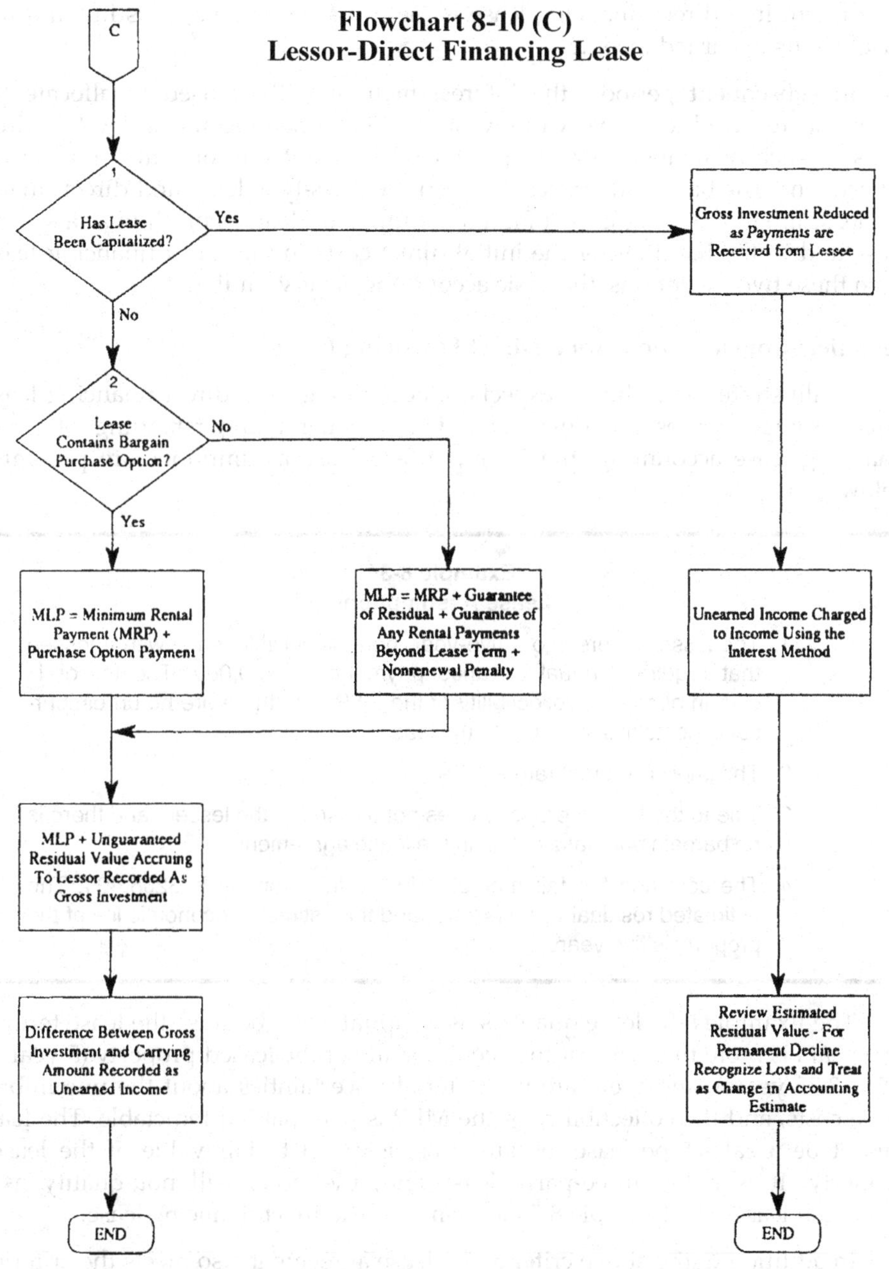
Flowchart 8-10 (C)
Lessor-Direct Financing Lease
C
1
Has Lease Been Capitalized?
Yes
No
Gross Investment Reduced as Payments are Received from Lessee
2
Lease Contains Bargain Purchase Option?
No
Yes
MLP = Minimum Rental Payment (MRP) + Purchase Option Payment
MLP = MRP + Guarantee of Residual + Guarantee of Any Rental Payments Beyond Lease Term + Nonrenewal Penalty
Unearned Income Charged to Income Using the Interest Method
MLP + Unguaranteed Residual Value Accruing To Lessor Recorded As Gross Investment
Difference Between Gross Investment and Carrying Amount Recorded as Unearned Income
Review Estimated Residual Value - For Permanent Decline Recognize Loss and Treat as Change in Accounting Estimate
END
END

The gross investment in the lease is determined in much the same manner as for the sales-type lease (i.e., the value of the MLP depends on the existence of a bargain purchase option). The individual elements of the MLP are the same as those of the sales-type lease. The gross investment for the direct financing lease is recorded at an amount equal to the MLP, plus any unguaranteed residual value accruing to the lessor. Unearned income is the difference between the gross investment and the cost or carrying amount of the leased property. The net investment in a direct financing lease is the gross investment, plus initial direct costs minus unearned income.

In subsequent periods, the interest method will be used to allocate the payments received to recovery of investment, unearned income and initial direct costs in such a manner so as to produce a constant rate of return on the net investment. The basic differences between the sales-type lease and direct financing lease are in the recognition of manufacturer's or dealer's profit in a sales-type lease and in the handling of the initial direct costs in the direct financing lease. With these two exceptions, the basic accounting is very similar.

Technical Considerations for a Direct Financing Lease

To illustrate the technical aspects of accounting for a direct financing lease, three example leases are developed. For a general understanding of direct financing lease accounting, the Example 8-35 lease assumptions are presented below.

Example 8-34
Lease Assumptions

1. The lessor enters into a five-year, non-cancellable lease with a lessee that requires annual advance payments of $50,000. The lessor is certain about the collectibility of the MLP, and there are no unreimbursable costs associated with the lease.
2. The implicit interest rate is 10%.
3. Title to the leased property does not transfer to the lessee, and there is no bargain purchase option in the lease agreement.
4. The cost and the fair market value of the property is $208,494. The estimated residual value is zero, and the estimated economic life of the property is five years.

The Example 8-34 lease qualifies as a capital lease, because the lease term of five years is more than 75% of the economic life of the leased property (5 years × .75 = 3.75 years), and there are no material uncertainties about the unreimbursable costs, and the collectibility of the MLP is reasonably predictable. The lease cannot be a sales-type lease, because cost is equal to fair value of the leased property. It is not a three-party lease and, therefore, will not qualify as a leveraged lease. The Example 8-34 lease must be a direct financing lease.

In addition to the above criteria, the lease agreement also meets the criterion concerning the discounted value of the MLP being 90% or more of the fair value of the property. The present value of the MLP is determined as follows:

Lease Payments Required	$50,000
Present Value Factor	[a]4.16987
Present Value of MLP	$208,494

[a] Present value factor for an annuity due at 10% for 5 periods. See Appendix E, Table III.

The $208,494 present value of the MLP is more than 90% of the fair value of the leased property ($208,494 Fair Value × .90 = $187,645).

Under a direct financing lease, the asset recorded—called the gross investment in the lease—is equal to the *total* rentals receivable. In this case, the gross investment would be $250,000 ($50,000 × 5 = $250,000). The difference between the gross investment and the cost of the asset leased is recorded as unearned income, and would be determined as follows:

Gross Investment	$250,000
Cost of Asset Leased	208,494
Unearned Income	$41,506

Table 8-51 below shows the calculation of the lease amortization that is necessary to determine the pattern of income recognition.

Table 8-51 Lease Amortization and Income—Lessor-Direct Financing

	Period	Annual Payment	Annual Interest Income	Principal Reduction	Present Value of Principal
Initial Value	—	—	—	—	[a]$208,494
	1	$50,000	[b]$15,849	[c]$34,151	[d]174,343
	2	50,000	12,434	37,566	136,777
	3	50,000	8,678	41,322	95,455
	4	50,000	4,545	45,455	50,000
	5	50,000	-0-	50,000	-0-
		$250,000	$41,506	$208,494	

[a] The cost and fair value of the property at the inception of the lease.
[b] ($208,494 – $50,000) × 10% = $15,849.
[c] $50,000 – $15,849 = $34,151.
[d] $208,494 – $34,151 = $174,343.

Because the lease requires advanced payments, the entry to record the asset at inception of the lease will be followed by the entry to record the receipt of the first payment and the recognition of income. The required entries are as follows:

Minimum Lease Payments Receivable	250,000	
Equipment		208,494
Unearned Income		41,506
Cash	50,000	
Minimum Lease Payments Receivable		50,000
Unearned Income	15,849	
Income from Capital Lease		15,849

For a direct financing lease, the lessor must calculate the present value of the MLP for *classification* purposes only. The present value of the MLP does not enter into the accounting for direct financing leases. The Example 8-34 lease illustrated the basic accounting for a direct financing lease. The Example 8-35 lease builds on the basic example by incorporating new variables into the computation of the lease payments receivable.

The assumptions of the Example 8-35 lease are as follows.

Example 8-35
Lease Assumptions

1. The lessor enters into a five-year, non-cancellable lease with a lessee that requires annual year-end payments of $30,000. The lessor is certain about the collectibility of the MLP, and there are no unreimbursable costs associated with the lease.
2. The implicit interest rate is 10%.
3. Title to the leased property does not transfer to the lessee, and the lease agreement contains a guaranteed residual value of $10,000.
4. The cost and the fair market value of the property each are $126,142 at the inception of the lease. The property has an estimated economic life of five years, and an *unguaranteed* residual value of $10,000 at the end of its useful life.

The new items for consideration are the guaranteed residual value of $10,000, and the unguaranteed residual value of $10,000. Both of these amounts will influence the accounting for a direct financing lease.

The Example 8-35 lease qualifies as a capital lease because the lease agreement meets the 75% test, there are no uncertainties regarding the unreimbursable costs, and the collectibility of the MLP is predictable. Cost of the property is equal to fair value at inception of the lease; therefore, the Example 8-35 lease is not a sale-type lease. There are only two parties to the lease agreement, so the lease is not a leveraged lease. By process of elimination, the lease is a direct financing lease.

The lease agreement meets the 75% test because the lease term of five years is more than 75% of the economic life (5 years × .75 = 3.75 years). The calculation of the present value of the MLP, which is needed for lease classification purposes only, is shown below:

Lease Payment Required	$30,000
Present Value Factor	[a]3.79079
Present Value of Lease Payments	$113,724
Guaranteed Residual Value	$10,000
Present Value Factor	[b].62092
Present Value of Guaranteed Residual Value	6,209
Present Value of MLP	$119,933

[a] Present value factor for ordinary annuity at 10% for 5 periods. See Appendix E, Table II.
[b] Present value factor for $1 at 10% for 5 periods. See Appendix E, Table I.

The present value of the MLP ($119,933) is more than 90% of the fair value of the leased property ($126,142 × .90 = $113,528), and the fourth basic criterion also is met. The calculation of the present value of the MLP does not include the $10,000 unguaranteed residual value.

The gross investment in the lease is $170,000 and is determined as follows:

Lease Payments Required ($30,000 × 5)	$150,000
Guaranteed Residual Value	10,000
Unguaranteed Residual Value	10,000
	$170,000

The $170,000 gross investment is the recorded value of the asset under a direct financing lease. The difference between the gross investment and the cost of the leased property ($170,000 – $126,142 = $43,858) is recorded as unearned income. The entry at inception of the lease would be as follows:

Minimum Lease Payments Receivable	170,000	
Equipment		126,142
Unearned Income		43,858

Table 8-52 develops the amortization schedule necessary to determine the income to be recognized in Years 1 through 5.

Table 8-52 Lease Amortization and Income—Lessor-Direct Financing

	Period	Annual Payment	Annual Interest Income	Principal Reduction	Present Value of Principal
Initial Value	—	—	—	—	[a]$126,142
	1	$30,000	[b]$12,614	[c]$17,386	[d]108,756
	2	30,000	10,876	19,124	89,632
	3	30,000	8,963	21,037	68,595
	4	30,000	6,860	23,140	45,455
	5	30,000	4,545	25,455	[e]20,000
		$150,000	$43,858	$106,142	

[a] Cost and fair value of the property.
[b] $126,142 × 10% = $12,614.
[c] $30,000 – $12,614 = $17,386.
[d] $126,142 – $17,386 = $108,756.
[e] Represents an unguaranteed residual value of $10,000 and a guaranteed residual value of $10,000.

The entry to record the first rental payment and the income for the year would be as follows:

Cash	30,000	
Minimum Lease Payments Receivable		30,000
Unearned Income	12,614	
Income from Capital Lease		12,614

As indicated in Flowchart 8-10 (C), the lessor must periodically review the estimated residual value and be prepared to account for a permanent decline in the residual value. In the case of a permanent decline in the estimated residual value, a loss must be recognized, and the amortization of the unearned income must be treated as a change in an accounting estimate, in accordance with ASC 250.

The third example lease is used to illustrate the accounting for a permanent decline in the estimated residual value. Assume the lessor has entered into a direct financing capital lease that requires five annual year-end payments of $100,000, with an implicit interest rate of 10% and an unguaranteed residual value of $20,000. The cost and fair market value of the property leased each are $391,497. Also assume that, at the beginning of the second year of the lease term, a permanent decline of $2,000 in the residual value occurred. The decline in the residual value will affect the unearned income over the life of the lease and the minimum lease payment receivable account. The calculation of the income adjustment is as follows:

Unguaranteed Residual Value	$20,000	
Present Value Factor (four remaining periods)	[a].68301	
Present Value of Unguaranteed Residual Beginning of Year 2		$13,660
Unguaranteed Residual Value—Revised	$18,000	
Present Value Factor	[a].68301	
Present Value of Revised Residual Value Beginning of Year 2		12,294
Unearned Income Adjustment		$1,366

[a] Present value factor for $1 at 10% for four periods. See Appendix E, Table I.

The journal entry necessary to reflect the permanent decline in residual value is:

Loss on Decline in Estimated Residual Value	634	
Unearned Income	1,366	
Minimum Lease Payment Receivable		2,000

Table 8-53 illustrates the effect of the change in residual value on the capital lease amortization.

Table 8-53 Lease Amortization and Income—Decline in Residual Value

	Period	Annual Payment	Annual Interest Income	Principal Reduction	Present Value of Principal
Initial Value	—	—	—	—	[a]$391,497
	1	$100,000	[b]$ 39,150	[c]$60,850	[d]329,281
	2	100,000	32,928	67,072	262,209
	3	100,000	26,221	73,779	188,430
	4	100,000	18,843	81,157	107,273
	5	100,000	10,727	89,273	[e]18,000
		$500,000	$127,869	$372,131	

[a] The cost and fair value of the leased property at the inception of the lease.
[b] \$391,497 × 10% = \$39,150.
[c] \$100,000 – \$39,150 = \$60,850.

[d]Cost and Fair Value at Inception of Lease	\$391,497
Principal Amortization Period 1	(60,850)
Adjustment to Unearned Income for Change in Residual Value	(1,366)
Present Value of Principal in Year 2	\$329,281

[e]Unguaranteed residual value at the end of Year 5.

Once the adjusting entry has been recorded, and a new amortization table prepared, subsequent accounting would be identical to that previously described. Table 8-53 would be used for income recognition purposes for Years 2 through 5.

An entity may assign or sell a lease or the leased property to another enterprise, or lease payments or residual values may be transferred to another enterprise. When the lease agreement is classified as either a direct financing or sales-type, and the lease of the leased property is sold or assigned, the original direct financing or sales-type accounting is not changed. In addition, if an entity transfers the minimum lease payments or the guaranteed residual value to another party from a lease agreement classified as a direct financing or sales-type lease, the transfer is accounted for using the provisions of ASC 860. However, ASC 860 accounting is not appropriate when unguaranteed residual values are transferred to third parties.

This completes the discussion of direct financing, sales-type and leverage leases, other than real estate. The next section of this chapter deals with real estate leasing from the viewpoint of the lessor.

Flowcharts and Discussion of Leases Involving Real Estate—Lessor

Flowcharts 8-11 and 8-12 illustrate the classification and accounting for real estate leases from the standpoint of the lessor. All of the basic classification and accounting concepts discussed previously apply to real estate leases. There are, however, certain cases where only a limited number of criteria apply or where additional computations may be required. The computation of the MLP, the gross investment, and the present value of both is the same as discussed in the general lessor flowcharts (Flowcharts 8-10, 8-10 (A), 8-10 (B), and 8-10 (C)). Real estate leases involving initial direct costs or a permanent decline in the estimated residual value will be treated in a manner similar to that discussed in the preceding sections. The real estate flowcharts make reference to the general lessor flowcharts for specifics on accounting procedures.

Flowchart 8-11
Lessor - Real Estate

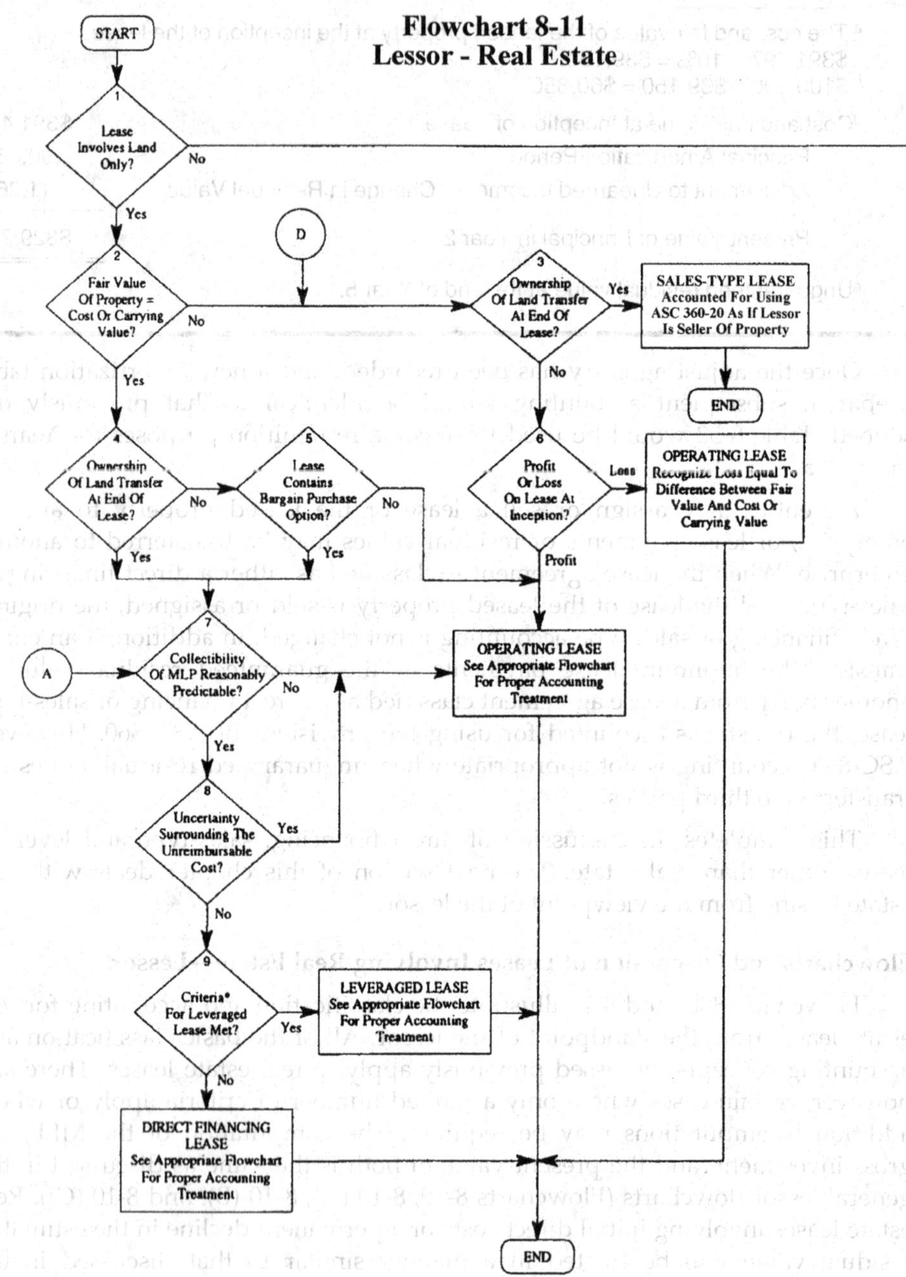

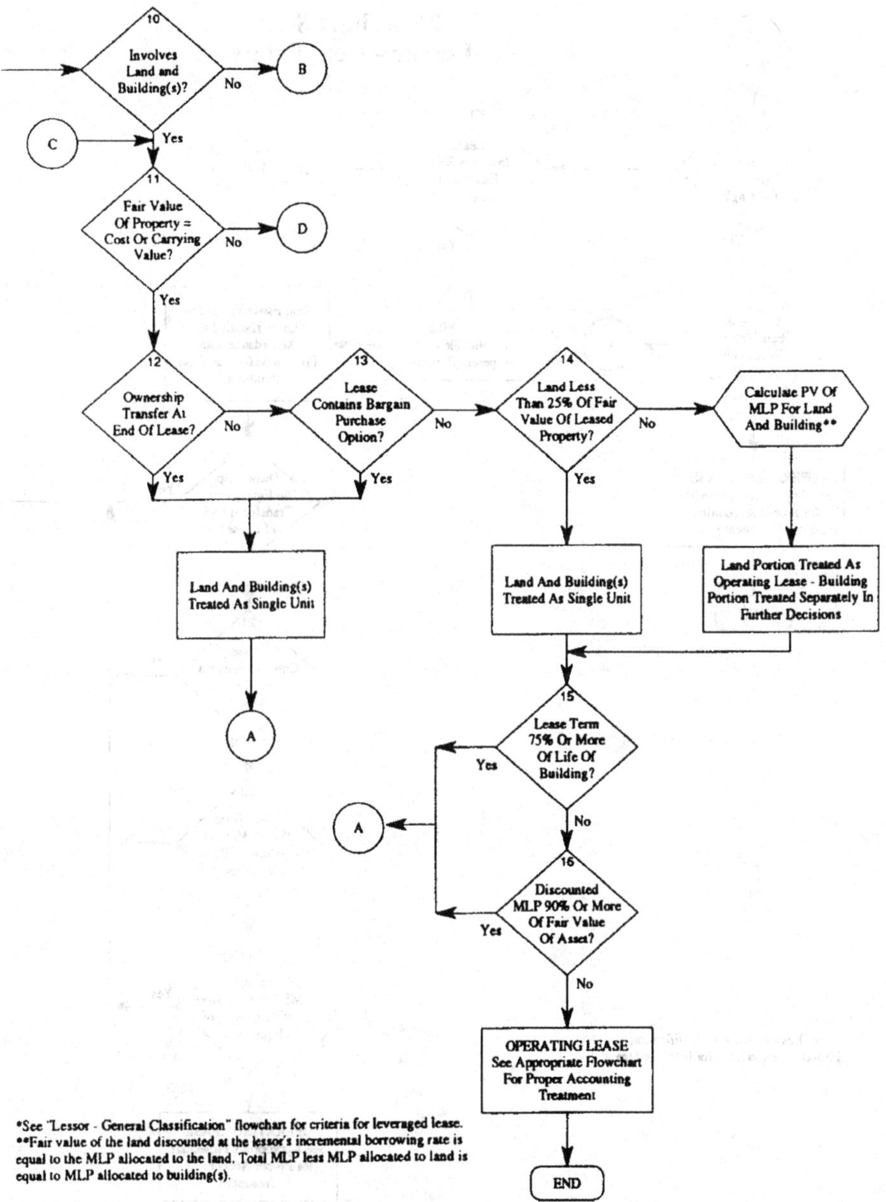

*See "Lessor - General Classification" flowchart for criteria for leveraged lease.
**Fair value of the land discounted at the lessor's incremental borrowing rate is equal to the MLP allocated to the land. Total MLP less MLP allocated to land is equal to MLP allocated to building(s).

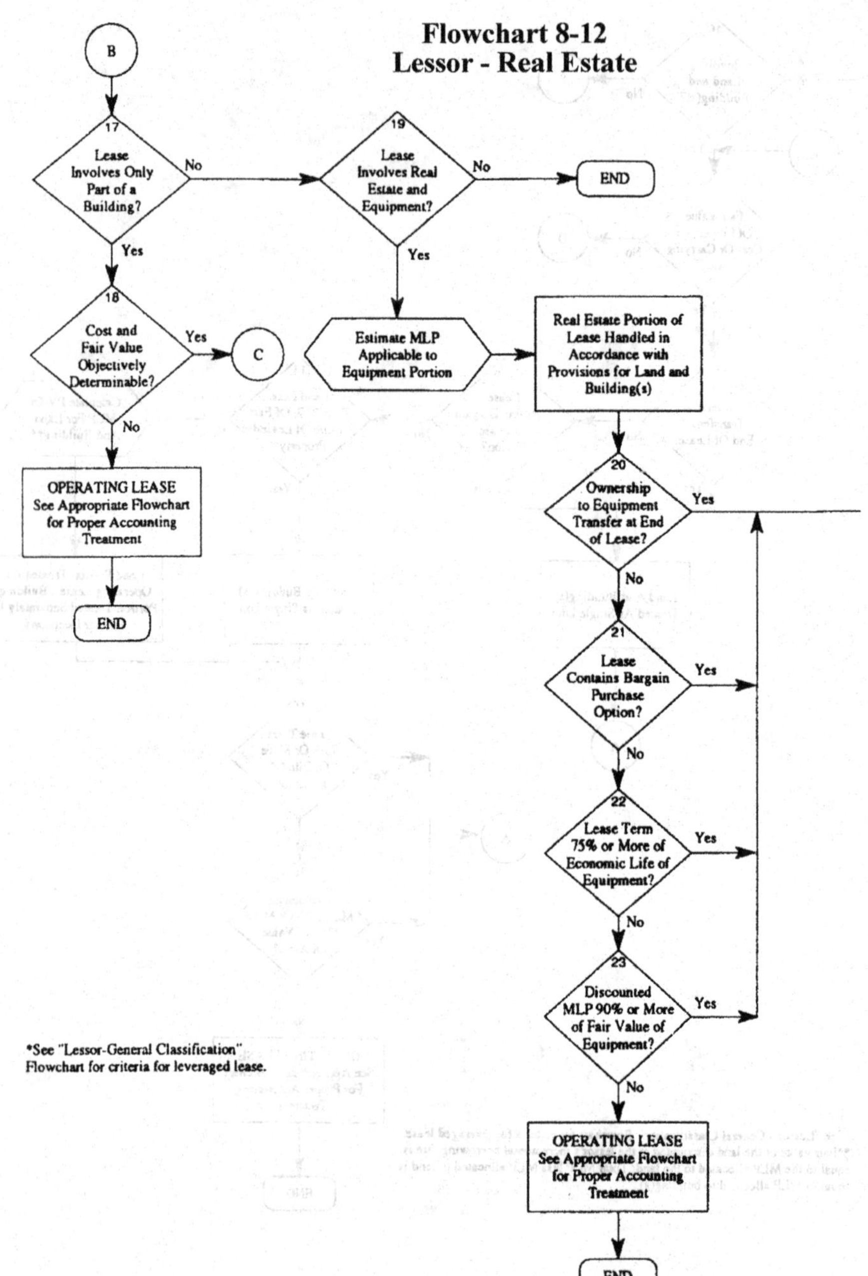

*See "Lessor-General Classification" Flowchart for criteria for leveraged lease.

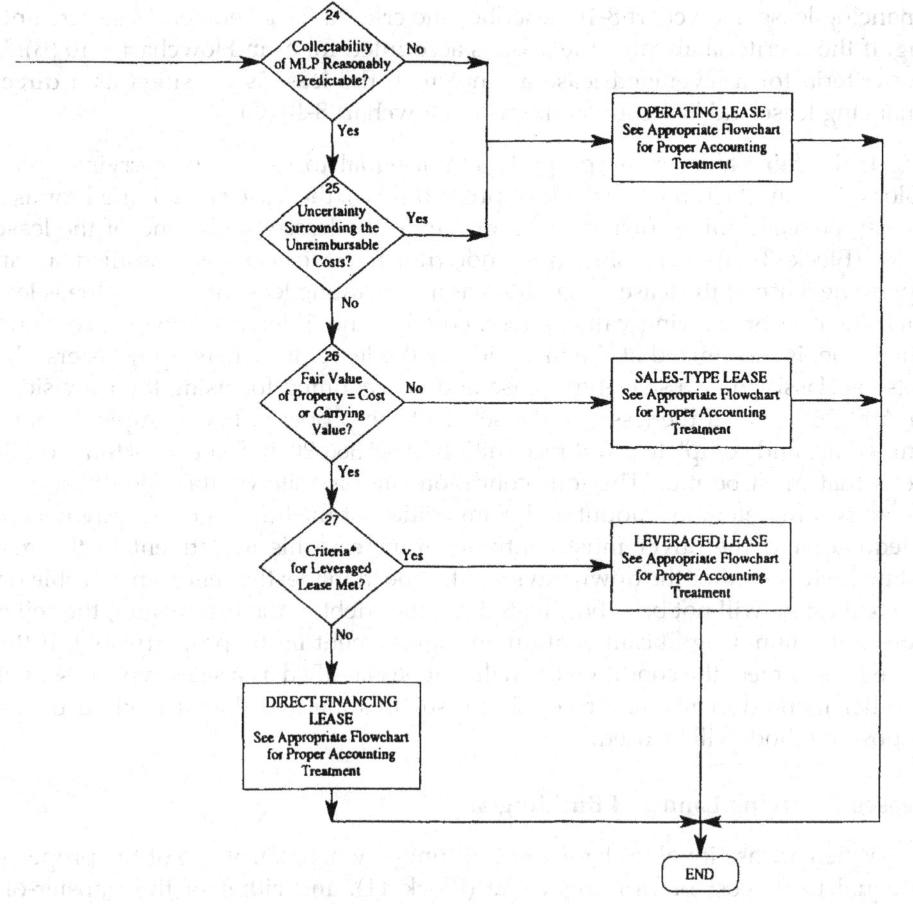

The discussion that follows will include all four types of real estate leases (land only, land and building(s), part of a building, and real estate and equipment) covered in ASC 840. However, new example material will be developed only for leases involving land and building(s). As discussed earlier, leases other than those involving land and building(s) are either handled in a conventional manner or are merely extensions of the land and building(s) category.

Leases Involving Land Only

When a lease involves land only, it may be classified as an operating, direct financing, leveraged, or sales-type lease. If there is no manufacturers' or dealers' profit or loss indicated in the lease agreement (Block 2), the lease is a capital lease if it meets one of the transfer-of-ownership tests (Blocks 4 and 5), and both of the risk-transfer tests (Blocks 7 and 8). If the lease agreement fails to meet one of the transfer-of-ownership tests and either of the risk-transfer tests, it will be treated as an operating lease for financial accounting purposes.

Once it has been determined that the lease agreement meets the conditions for a capital lease (other than when there is manufacturers' or dealers' profit or loss), the capital lease is classified as either a leveraged lease (Block 9) or a direct financing lease. Flowchart 8-10 describes the criteria for leveraged lease accounting. If those criteria are met, the lease is accounted for as in Flowchart 8-10 (B). If the criteria for a leveraged lease are not met, the lease is classified as a direct financing lease and is accounted for as in Flowchart 8-10 (C).

If the fair value of the property is not equal to its cost or carrying value (Block 2) (manufacturers' or dealers' profit or loss), the lease is accounted for as a sales-type lease only if ownership transfers to the lessee by the end of the lease term (Block 3). If ownership does not transfer, the lease is classified as an operating lease. If the lease is classified as an operating lease and fair value is less than the cost or carrying value, a loss, equal to the difference between cost and fair value, is recognized at the inception of the lease. If ownership transfers, the lease is classified as a sales-type lease and is accounted for using the provisions of ASC 360-20 as if the lessor is the seller of the property. For example, to have immediate and complete profit recognition, ASC 360-20-40-5 specifies four conditions that must be met. The four conditions are as follows: the sale of the real estate is complete; the amount and composition of the buyer's down payment is adequate, and the buyer must continue to increase his investment in the real estate each year after the down payment has been made; the seller's receivable on the real estate will not be subordinated to other debt in the future; and, the seller does not retain a significant continuing involvement in the property sold. If the lease fails to meet the conditions, it will still be classified as a sales-type lease, but another method of revenue recognition, such as the installment method or the deposit method, will be used.

Leases Involving Land and Building(s)

When a lease involves land and building(s) where fair value of the property is equal to its cost or carrying value (Block 11), and either of the transfer-of-ownership criteria and both of the risk-transfer tests (Blocks 7, 8, 10, 12, and 13) are met, the lease is classified as a capital lease, and the land and building(s) are treated as a single unit of leased property. If the lease fails to meet either of the two transfer-of-ownership criteria, it still may qualify for capital lease accounting if certain other conditions are met. Before these additional tests can be met, the lessor must determine the relative values of the land and building portions of the leased property. If the land portion of the leased property constitutes less than 25% of the total fair value, land and building(s) will be treated as a single unit of leased property for purposes of subsequent tests (Block 13). If the land element is 25% or more of the total value of the leased property, the lessor must separate the portion of the MLP applicable to land and to building and treat each as a separate unit of leased property.

When land and building(s) are treated as a single unit for purposes of subsequent testing, the lease term must be 75% or more of the economic life of the building, *or* the present value of the MLP must be 90% or more of the fair value of both the land and building (Blocks 15 and 16), and *both* risk-transfer tests must be met before the lease will qualify for capital lease treatment. When the land and building are treated as separate units of leased property, the land will be accounted for as an operating lease, and the building portion will be tested as indicated in the previous sentence.

To determine the portion of the MLP that will be associated with the land (and treated as an operating lease), the lessor must discount the fair value of the land at the incremental borrowing rate of the *lessee.* The discounted amount determined in this manner will represent the portion of the MLP identified with the land. The difference between the total MLP and the MLP attributed to the land will be the MLP associated with the building portion of the leased property. The amount thus associated with the building portion will be used to determine if the lease should be classified as operating or capital.

Once it has been determined that a lease is a capital lease (when cost equals fair value), it must be classified as either a leveraged or direct financing lease. If the criteria for a leveraged lease are met (Block 9), the building part of the lease is classified as leveraged. If the criteria are not met, the lease is classified as direct financing.

If fair value of the lease property is not equal to its cost or carrying value (Block 11), the lease is classified as a sales-type or operating based on the same procedures discussed, above, for land only.

Technical Considerations for Leases Involving Land and Building(s)

From an accounting standpoint, real estate leases involving land and building(s) can become quite complex. The complexity of the technical problems can be simplified by subdividing the land and building category into three sections: leases meeting the transfer-of-ownership criteria, leases where the land element comprises 25% or more of the total fair value of the leased property, and operating leases. The discussion that follows is organized around these three categories.

Leases Meeting the Transfer-of-Ownership Criteria

The Example 8-36 lease assumptions listed below are designed to show the accounting for a lease agreement that meets the transfer-of-ownership or bargain-purchase-option criteria.

Example 8-36
Lease Assumptions

1. The lessor enters into a five-year, non-cancellable lease for land and building that requires annual payments of $78,000 at the beginning of each of the next five years. $3,000 of the payments is for executory costs. The lease specifies that ownership will transfer to the lessee at the end of the lease term.
2. The lessee's incremental borrowing rate is 9% and the lessor's implicit rate is 10%.
3. The cost and fair value of the land is $100,000, and the cost and fair value of the building is $211,240 at the inception of the lease.
4. The collectibility of the MLP is reasonably predictable, and there are no unreimbursable costs associated with the lease.

Example 8-36 lease meets the criteria necessary for classification as a capital lease (ownership transfers, collectibility of the MLP is reasonably predictable and no unreimbursable costs). Because the lease meets the transfer-of-ownership criterion, the land and building are treated as a single unit of leased property for accounting purposes (the same accounting treatment will apply to land and building leases where the land element is less than 25% of the total fair value of the leased property). Because cost of the asset is equal to fair value at inception of the lease, the Example 8-36 lease is a direct financing lease. If necessary, refer to Flowchart 8-10 (C) for a review of accounting for direct financing leases.

The gross investment in the lease is $375,000 ($78,000 – $3,000 = $75,000 × 5 payments = $375,000), and the cost of the leased property is $311,240 ($100,000 for land + $211,240 for building). The difference between the gross investment and the cost of the leased assets is unearned income of $63,760 ($375,000 – $311,240 = $63,760). Given this information, the following journal entry to record the direct financing lease can be made:

Minimum Lease Payments Receivable	375,000	
Unearned Income		63,760
Land		100,000
Building		211,240

Because the entries to record the receipt of the rental payments and the recognition of income were discussed in detail in the section dealing with direct financing leases, they will not be repeated at this point.

Recall that if the lease agreement does not transfer ownership or contain a bargain purchase option, land and building will be treated as a single unit if the land element is less than 25% of the total fair value. If, in this case, the lease qualifies for capital lease treatment, the accounting will be the same as that described above.

Lease Agreements Where Land Element Is 25% or More of Fair Value

If a lease agreement qualifies for capital lease accounting, and the land element is 25% or more of the fair value of both the land and building, the present value of the MLP must be divided into a land element and a building element. This accounting problem would develop if a lease agreement involving land and building failed to meet the transfer of ownership criteria, but the lease term was 75% or more of the economic life of the asset *or* the present value of the MLP was 90% or more of the fair value of the leased asset(s).

To illustrate this accounting problem, assume an Example 8-37 lease with the same facts as in the Example 8-36 lease, except that ownership of the leased property does not transfer to the lessee and the implicit interest rate is not known.

Example 8-37
Lease Assumptions

1. The lessor enters into a five-year, non-cancellable lease for land and building that requires annual payments of $78,000 at the beginning of each of the next five years. $3,000 of the payments is for executory costs. Ownership does not transfer to the lessee at the end of the lease term.
2. The lessee's incremental borrowing rate is 9% and the lessor's implicit rate is not known.
3. The cost and fair value of the land is $100,000, and the cost and fair value of the building is $211,240 at the inception of the lease.
4. The collectibility of the MLP is reasonably predictable, and there are no unreimbursable costs associated with the lease.

When ownership to the leased property does not transfer, the lessor first must determine the relative fair values of the land and building elements of the lease. In this case, the land is more than 25% of the fair value of both land and building ($100,000 fair value of land ÷ $311,240 total fair value = 32%). When the land element is 25% or more of the total fair value of the leased property, the land element and the building element will be treated as separate units of leased property.

Even though ownership does not transfer to the lessee, the Example 8-37 lease qualifies as a capital lease because the lease term of five years is more than 75% of the economic life of the building *and* the two risk-transfer criteria are met. Cost is equal to fair value of the property at inception of the lease; therefore, the Example 8-37 lease is a direct financing lease.

Because the lease is a capital lease, and the land element is 25% or more of the total fair value of the assets, the MLP must be divided between the land element and the building element. The procedure for dividing the MLP requires that the fair value of the land be discounted at the lessee's incremental borrowing rate to determine the portion of the MLP that will be associated with the land. This is accomplished as follows:

Fair Value of Land	$100,000	=	$23,586
Present Value Factor[a]	4.23972		

[a] Present value factor for an annuity due at 9% for five periods. See Appendix E, Table III.

The $23,586 will be the portion of the total MLP associated with the land element of the lease. The difference between the MLP assigned to the land and the total MLP will be the MLP assigned to the building portion of the lease. The difference is determined in the following manner:

Rental Payment Required	$78,000
Less: Executory Costs	3,000
	$75,000
MLP Assigned to Land	(23,586)
MLP Assigned to Building	$51,414

Once the MLP associated with the building element has been determined, the next step is to calculate the gross investment and unearned income. These two amounts are determined as follows:

MLP Assigned to Building	$51,414
Number of Lease Payments	× 5
Gross Investment in Lease	$257,070
Less: Fair Value of Building	211,240
Unearned Income	$45,830

Based upon the information developed above, the following entry would be required at inception of the lease:

Minimum Lease Payment Receivable	257,070	
Unearned Income		45,830
Building		211,240

The land element of the lease is treated as an operating lease. Income would be recognized as the periodic rental payment is received.

To amortize the unearned income over the lease term, using the interest method, the implicit interest rate relating to the building portion of the lease must be determined. In the absence of a computer program to calculate the interest rate, the following formula will provide the *present value factor* that corresponds with the new effective rate:

$$X = \frac{M - UI}{P}$$

Where: X = Present value factor of an annuity
M = Total minimum rental payments applicable to building
UI = Unearned income
P = Periodic minimum rental payment applicable to building.

Given the information above, the formula will provide the following results:

$$X = \frac{\$257{,}070 - \$45{,}830}{\$51{,}414} = 4.10861$$

The answer of 4.10861 represents the present value factor for an annuity due for five periods. Using Table III in Appendix E, move across the 5 periods row until a present value factor close to 4.10861 is found. The actual implicit interest rate is somewhere between 10% and 11%. To obtain the exact rate, it will be necessary to interpolate or to use the trial-and-error method. For the Example 8-37 lease, the implicit interest rate is 10.9069%, which was derived through the use of a computer program. Given this interest rate, Table 8-54 shows the proper income recognition for the lease.

Table 8-54 Lease Amortization Schedule

	Period	Annual Rental	Annual Interest Income	Principal Reduction	Present Value of Year-End Balance
Initial Value	—	—	—	—	[a]$211,240
	1	$51,414	[b]$17,432	[c]$33,982	[d]177,258
	2	51,414	13,726	37,688	139,570
	3	51,414	9,615	41,799	97,771
	4	51,414	5,057	46,357	51,414
	5	51,414	-0-	51,414	-0-
		$257,070	$45,830	$211,240	

[a] Fair value and cost of building at inception of lease.
[b] ($211,240 – $51,414) × 10.9069% = $17,432.
[c] $51,414 – $17,432 = $33,982.
[d] $211,240 – $33,982 = $177,258.

The entry to record the first annual lease rental payment would be as follows:

Cash	78,000	
Minimum Lease Payment Receivable		51,414
Rental Income—Operating Lease		23,586
Executory Costs Clearing Account		3,000
Unearned Income	17,432	
Income from Capital Lease		17,432

Table 8-54 would be used for income recognition purposes under the capital lease for Years 1 through 5. The Example 8-37 lease completes the discussion of accounting for capital leases involving land and building(s).

Operating Leases

If any of the above lease examples had been classified as an operating lease, the only entry required would be the annual or interim rental income recognition. This was illustrated in the preceding section, for the land element of the Example 8-37 lease. The next major area of real estate leasing—leases involving part of a building—will now be discussed.

Leases Involving Part of a Building

A lease agreement may involve part of a building, such as an office or a complete floor(s) of a building. If both the fair value and the cost (or carrying value, if different from cost) can be objectively determined (Block 18), the lessor would account for the lease as if it were the building portion of a lease involving land and building. If either the fair value or the cost cannot be objectively determined, the lease will be classified as an operating lease. If the lease qualifies as a capital lease, refer to the preceding section on accounting for leases involving land and building for a complete technical review.

Leases Involving Real Estate and Equipment

If the lease agreement involves both real estate and equipment, the lessor must separate the real estate portion of the MLP from the portion of the MLP applicable to the equipment. The separation of the minimum lease payments for real estate and equipment should be made by using the most appropriate method for the situation. It would appear that an allocation on the basis of fair values or appraisal values would be appropriate in most cases.

Once the allocation of the MLP to real estate and equipment has been accomplished, the real estate portion will be classified and accounted for in the manner specified for leases involving land and building(s). Refer to the preceding discussion and technical review of land and building(s) for specifics.

The equipment must meet one of the four basic criteria (Blocks 20 through 23), and *both* of the risk-transfer criteria (Blocks 24 and 25), to be considered for capital lease treatment. The next step in the classification process is to compare the cost of the equipment portion of the leased property with its fair value (Block 26). If cost and fair value are not equal, the equipment part is classified as a sales-type lease. If fair value and cost or carrying value are equal, the lease is classified as either a leveraged or direct financing lease. If the criteria for a leveraged lease are met (Block 27), the lease is classified as leveraged, otherwise as direct financing. Refer to Flowcharts 8-10 (A)–(C) for detailed information about accounting for the different types of capital leases.

This concludes the discussion of lessor accounting for real estate leasing transactions. The next section of this chapter addresses the problems of *sublease* classification and accounting. Subleases deal with accounting for both the lessor and the lessee, so the material examined above will be most helpful in the discussion that follows.

Subleases

The area of subleases is an excellent way to complete the technical discussion of ASC 840, because subleases involve both lessee and lessor accounting. A sublease is a transaction where the property that has been leased is released by the lessee to another party. The original lease is intact between the original lessor and the original lessee; therefore, the original lessee is both a lessee and a lessor. There are three parties involved in the sublease agreement: the original lessor, the original lessee/sublessor, and the sublessee. To avoid any confusion that may result from the dual role played by the original lessee (i.e., both lessee and sublessor), the lessee is referred to as the sublessor in the discussion that follows.

Flowchart and Discussion of Subleases—Sublessor

Flowchart 8-13 depicts the lease classification problems inherent in the sublease process, and it refers the reader to previous flowcharts for specific accounting treatment once the sublease has been properly classified. As indicated by the first major decision in Flowchart 8-13, the broad area of sublease accounting can be divided into two manageable sections: when the sublessor is relieved of primary obligation under the original lease and when the sublessor is not relieved of such obligation. The left-hand column of Flowchart 8-13 addresses the former problem, and the rest of the flowchart deals with the latter.

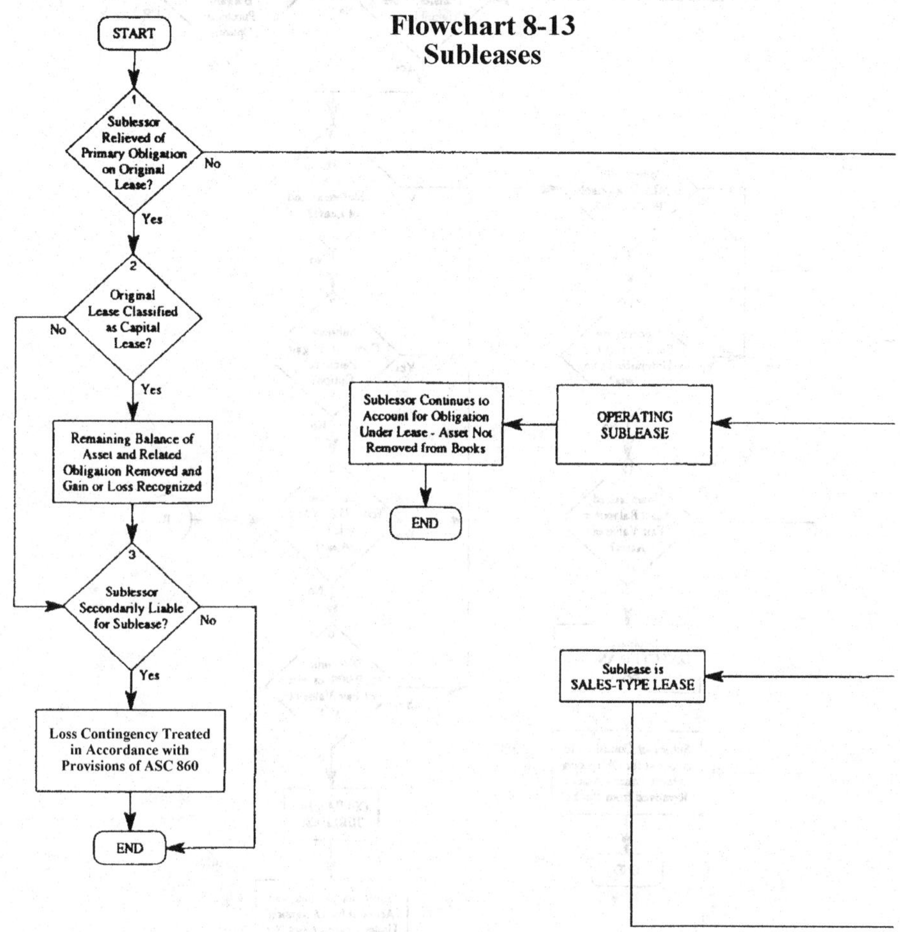

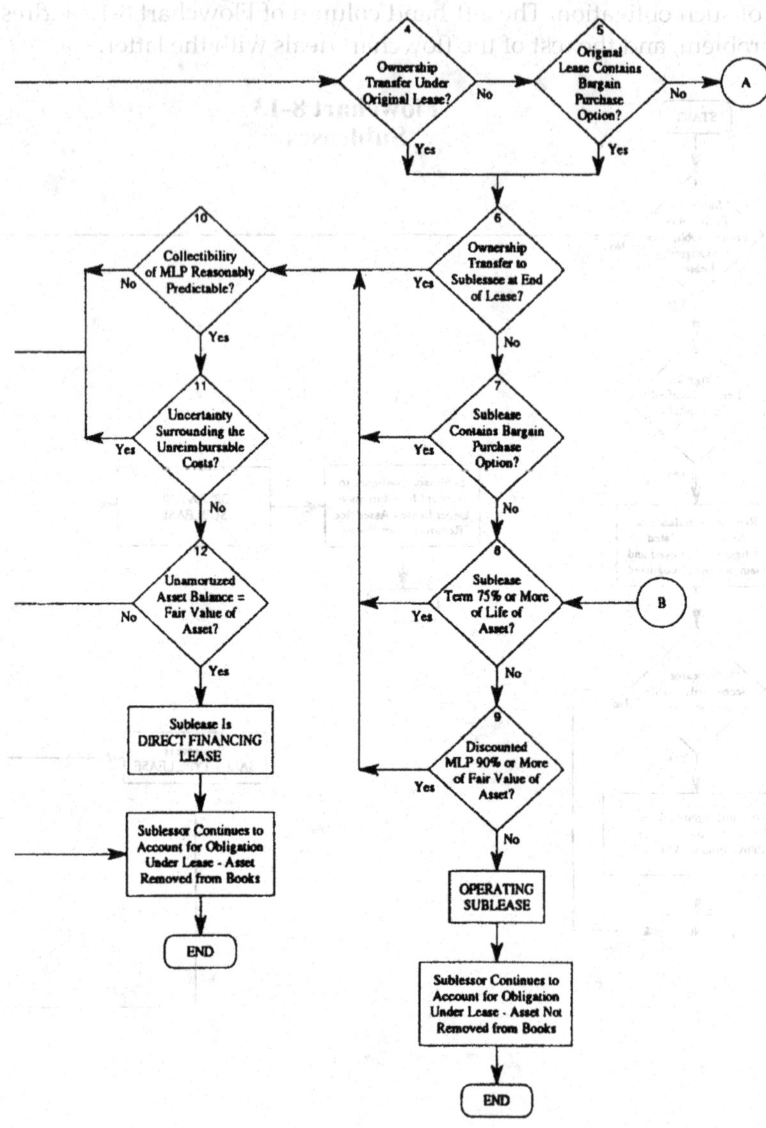

4
Ownership Transfer Under Original Lease?
No
Yes
5
Original Lease Contains Bargain Purchase Option?
No
Yes
A
6
Ownership Transfer to Sublessee at End of Lease?
Yes
No
10
Collectibility of MLP Reasonably Predictable?
No
Yes
11
Uncertainty Surrounding the Unreimbursable Costs?
Yes
No
7
Sublease Contains Bargain Purchase Option?
Yes
No
12
Unamortized Asset Balance = Fair Value of Asset?
No
Yes
8
Sublease Term 75% or More of Life of Asset?
Yes
No
B
9
Discounted MLP 90% or More of Fair Value of Asset?
Yes
No
Sublease Is DIRECT FINANCING LEASE
Sublessor Continues to Account for Obligation Under Lease - Asset Removed from Books
END
OPERATING SUBLEASE
Sublessor Continues to Account for Obligation Under Lease - Asset Not Removed from Books
END

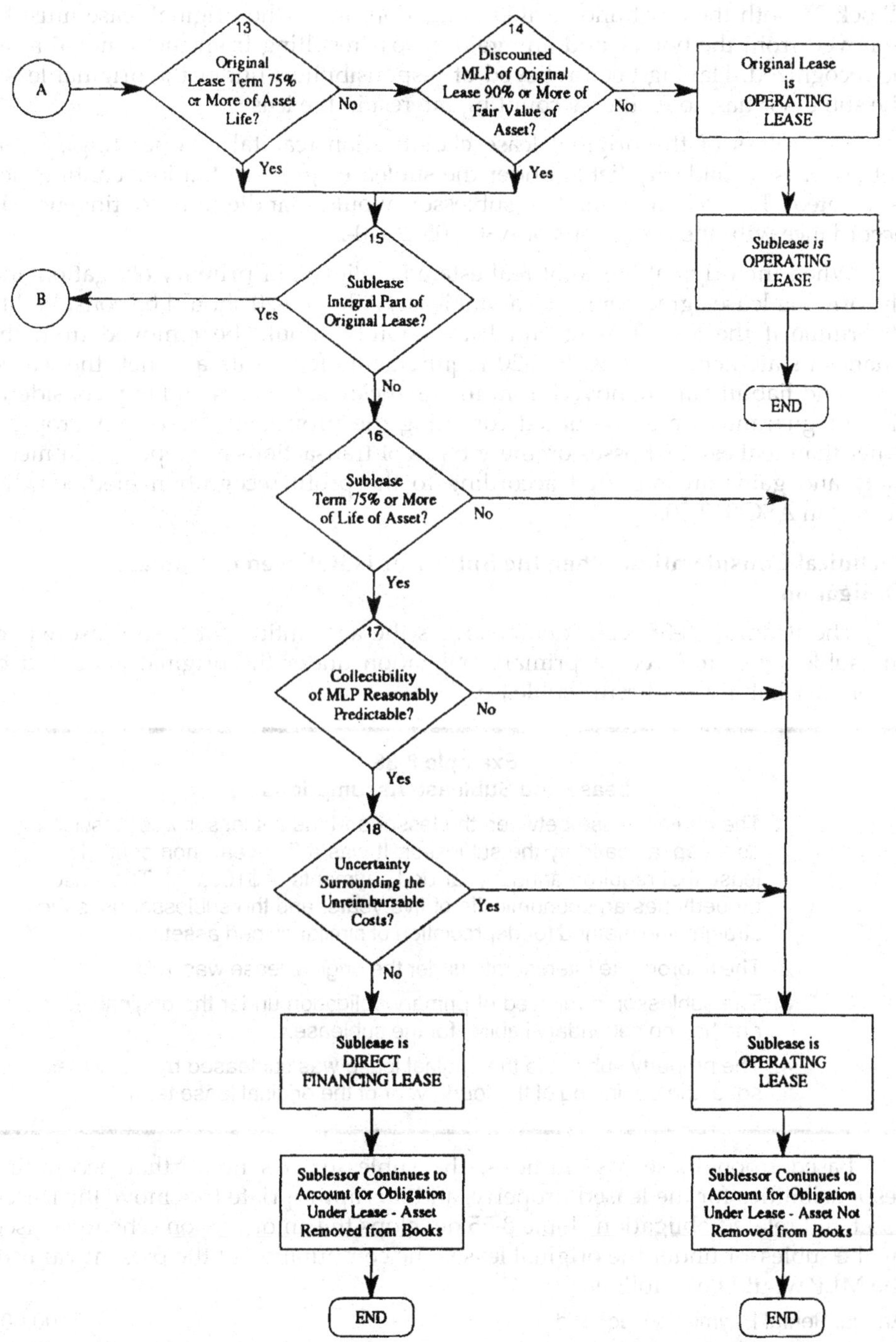

Accounting When the Sublessor Is Relieved of Primary Obligation

If the sublessor has been relieved of primary obligation under the original lease, *and* the original lease was classified as a capital lease by the sublessor

(Block 2), both the asset and related obligation under the original lease must be removed from the books, and any gain or loss resulting from the removal must be recognized. Having been relieved of responsibilities under the original lease, the sublessor has no further accounting interest in the lease.

Regardless of the original lease classification (capital or operating), if the sublessor is secondarily liable under the sublease agreement, a loss contingency is created. In such a case, the sublessor would handle the contingency in accordance with the provisions of ASC 405-20-40-2.

When the original lessee of real estate is relieved of primary obligation and the original lease agreement is a capital lease, ASC 360-20 should be consulted to determine if the leased asset and lease liability should be removed from the financial statements. If ASC 360-20 requirements for a sale are met, the leased asset and liability are removed from the financial statements and any consideration or guarantees are accounted for using the provisions for leased property other than real estate. Losses on these types of transactions are reported immediately and gains are reported according to the profit recognition methods discussed in ASC 360-20.

Technical Consideration When the Sublessor Is Relieved of Primary Obligation

The Example 8-38 lease demonstrates the accounting for a sublease where the sublessor is relieved of primary obligation under the original lease and of secondary liability under the sublease.

Example 8-38
Lease and Sublease Assumptions

1. The original lease between the lessor and the sublessor was classified as a capital lease by the sublessor. It was a five-year, non-cancellable lease that required annual year-end payments of $100,000. The leased property has an economic life of five years, and the sublessor uses the straight-line method for depreciation of similar owned assets.
2. The appropriate interest rate under the original lease was 10%.
3. The sublessor is relieved of primary obligation under the original lease and has no secondary liability for the sublease.
4. The property subject to the original lease was subleased by the sublessor at the beginning of the fourth year of the original lease term.

Based upon these assumptions, the sublessor has no further accounting responsibilities for the leased property, and it is appropriate to remove the leased asset and related obligation. Table 8-55 develops the amortization schedules used by the sublessor under the original lease. The computation of the present value of the MLP would be as follows:

Annual Rental Payments Required	$100,000
Present Value Factor	[a]3.79079
Present Value of MLP	$379,079

[a] Present value factor for an ordinary annuity at 10% for 5 periods. See Appendix E, Table II.

Under the terms of the original lease, the present value of the MLP was recorded as the value of the leased asset and related obligation.

Table 8-55 Amortization Schedules—Original Lease

Amortization Schedule for Lease Obligation

	Period	Annual Payment	Annual Interest Expense	Obligation Reduction	Present Value of Obligation at Year-End
Initial Value	—	—	—	—	$379,079
	1	$100,000	[a]$37,908	[b]$62,092	[c]316,987
	2	100,000	31,699	68,301	248,686
	3	100,000	24,869	75,131	173,555
	4	100,000	17,355	82,645	90,910
	5	100,000	9,090	90,910	-0-
		$500,000	$120,921	$379,079	

Schedule of Amortization of Leased Asset

	Period	Amortization	Cumulative Amortization	Unamortized Asset Balance at Year-End
Initial Value	—	—	—	$379,079
	1	[d]$75,816	$75,816	303,263
	2	75,816	151,632	227,447
	3	75,816	227,448	151,631
	4	75,816	303,264	75,815
	5	*75,815	379,079	-0-
		$379,079		

[a]$379,079 × 10% = $37,908.

[b]$100,000 – $37,908 = $62,092.

[c]$379,079 – $62,092 = $316,987.

[d] Assuming straight-line depreciation is used for owned assets ($379,079/5 years = $75,816).

* Rounded.

At the date of inception of the sublease, the sublessor must determine the unamortized balance in the asset and obligation accounts and remove them from the books. At the beginning of Year 4, the unamortized obligation balance was $173,555, and the unamortized asset balance was $151,631. The difference between the two balances indicates that a $21,924 gain ($173,555 - $151,631 = $21,924) will be recognized. Given this information, the following journal entry is required at the date of inception of the sublease:

Accumulated Amortization of Leased Property	227,448	
Obligation under Capital Lease	173,555	
Leased Asset under Capital Lease		379,079
Gain on Capital Lease Transaction		[a]21,924

[a] Gains or losses on lease transactions are handled in accordance with ASC 225-20.

No further entries would be required by the sublessor. A *loss* on the sublease should be recognized if the recorded amount of the property exceeds the gross investment. In addition, any loss on a sublease that is a component of a discontinued operation should be treated as part of the gain or loss on the discontinued operation.

If the sublessor is secondarily liable under a capital lease or an operating lease, additional accounting or footnote disclosures may be necessary.

Accounting When the Sublessor Is Not Relieved of Primary Obligation

The classification and accounting problems are much more interesting and complex when the sublessor is not relieved of primary obligation under the original lease agreement. When this occurs, the relationships between the parties to the lease and sublease become involved. First, there is the relationship between the original lessor and the sublessor (which has remained intact), and, next, there is the new relationship between the sublessor and the sublessee. One important point to keep in mind throughout the following discussion is that if the sublessor is not relieved of primary obligation under the original lease, he or she must continue to account for the obligation that resulted if the original lease qualified as a capital lease; however, the unamortized balance of the leased asset will be removed. In effect, the sublessor is both lessee and lessor.

If, under the terms of the original lease, ownership transferred or there was a bargain purchase option (Blocks 4 and 5), the sublease will be classified as either a sales-type or direct financing capital lease or as an operating lease. For the *sublease* to qualify as a capital lease, it must meet *one* of the four general criteria—(transfer of ownership, bargain purchase option, 75% of economic life, or 90% of fair value (Blocks 6 through 9)—*and* both of the risk-transfer criteria (collectibility of MLP and no uncertainties about unreimbursable costs (Blocks 10 and 11). If the sublease qualifies as a capital lease, it will be classified as a sales-type lease if the unamortized asset balance is different from fair value of the asset. If the unamortized asset balance is equal to fair value, the lease will be classified as a direct financing lease. Finally, if *none* of the general criteria and risk transfer criteria are met, the sublease will be accounted for as an operating lease by the sublessor.

If the original lease did not transfer ownership or contain a bargain purchase option, the sublease still may qualify as a capital lease. If the *original* lease term was 75% or more of the economic life of the property, or if the discounted value of the MLP under the *original* lease was 90% or more of the fair value of the property, the sublessor is faced with two separate sets of classification problems.

First, when the sublease is an integral part of the original lease agreement (Block 15) the sublease must meet either the 75% test *or* the discounted-

MLP-90%-or-more-of-fair value test, *and* both of the risk-transfer tests, before it may be classified as a capital lease. If these tests are met, the sublease will be classified as either a sales-type or direct financing lease on the same basis as previously discussed. If the sublease fails these tests, it will be treated as an operating lease.

Second, when the sublease is *not* an integral part of the original lease agreement, it must meet the 75% test and both of the risk-transfer tests to qualify as a direct financing lease. Under these conditions, the sublease cannot be a sales-type lease. As before, if the sublease fails to meet these tests, it will be treated as an operating lease.

If the original lease failed to meet the four general criteria, it would have been classified as an operating lease. If the original lease was classified as operating, then the sublease would be classified the same.

Technical Considerations When the Sublessor Is Not Relieved of Primary Obligation

To illustrate the accounting aspects inherent in the situation where the sublessor is not relieved of primary obligation under the original lease agreement, it is necessary to develop assumptions for both the original lease and the sublease. Listed below are the assumptions relating to the original lease between the lessor and the sublessor.

Example 8-39
Lease Assumptions—Original Lease

1. The sublessor and lessor entered into a five-year, non-cancellable lease that required annual year-end payments of $150,000.
2. Ownership to the property does not transfer at the end of the lease term, and the lease does not contain a bargain purchase option.
3. The sublessor's (original lessee's) incremental borrowing rate is 10%, and the lessor's implicit rate is not known.
4. The leased property has a fair value of $568,619. The estimated economic life is five years, and the estimated residual value is zero.

The original lease is a capital lease, because the lease term of five years is more than 75% of the economic life of the property (5 year economic life × .75 = 3.75 years). In addition, the present value of the MLP is more than 90% of the fair value of the property. This is shown through the following computations:

Fair Value of Property	$568,619
	× .90
90 % of Fair Value of Property	$511,757
Annual Rental Payment Required	$150,000
Present Value Factor	[a]3.79079
Present Value of MLP	$568,619

[a] Present value factor for an ordinary annuity at 10% for 5 periods. See Appendix E, Table II.

Therefore, the present value of the MLP of $568,619 is more than 90% of the fair value of the property ($511,757).

Table 8-56 prepares the amortization schedule used by the sublessor under the original lease agreement.

Table 8-56 Amortization Schedule for Original Lease

Period	Amortization	Annual Payment	Annual Interest Expense	Obligation Reduction	Present Value of Obligation at Year-End
Initial Value —	—	—	—	—	$ 568,619
1	[a]$113,724	$150,000	[b]$56,862	[c]$93,138	[d]475,481
2	113,724	150,000	47,548	102,452	373,029
3	113,724	150,000	37,303	112,697	260,332
4	113,724	150,000	26,032	123,968	136,364
5	*113,723	150,000	13,636	136,364	-0-
	$568,619	$750,000	$181,381	$568,619	

[a] Assuming that straight-line depreciation is used for owned assets ($568,619/5 years = $113,724).
[b] $568,619 × 10% = $56,862.
[c] $150,000 – $56,862 = $93,138.
[d] $568,619 – $93,138 = $475,481.
* Rounded.

The sublessor (original lessee) would use the values shown on Table 8-56 to account for a capital lease as discussed in the section dealing with lessee accounting. The second assumptions in Example 8-40 relate to the sublease agreement.

Example 8-40
Lease Assumptions—Sublease

1. At the beginning of the second year of the original lease, the sublessor entered into a four-year, non-cancellable *sublease* with a sublessee. The sublease requires annual year-end payments of $150,000.
2. The sublessor is not relieved of primary obligation under the original lease agreement.
3. The implicit interest rate on the sublease is the rate that equates the present value of the lease payments with the unamortized asset balance. (The calculation of the implicit rate will be shown in the material that follows.) The sublessee's incremental borrowing rate is 11%, and the implicit rate is unknown to the sublessee.
4. Ownership does not transfer to the sublessee at the end of the lease term, and the sublease does not contain a bargain purchase option.
5. The collectibility of the MLP is reasonably predictable, and there are no unreimbursable costs associated with the sublease.

Neither the original lease nor the sublease allowed for the transfer of ownership, and neither contained a bargain purchase option. If we assume further that the sublease was not an integral part of the original lease, then the sublease must be either a direct financing lease or an operating lease. Because the sublease term of four years is more than 75% of the economic life of the property (5-year economic life × .75 = 3.75 years), and the two risk-transfer criteria are met, the sublease qualifies as a direct financing lease.

To begin the process of determining the implicit interest rate under the sublease agreement, the sublessor must determine the unamortized asset balance. The computation is shown below:

Capitalized Value of Leased Property (Table 8-56)	$568,619
Year 1 Amortization (Table 8-56)	(113,724)
Unamortized Asset Balance	$454,895

The difference between the $600,000 ($150,000 × 4 = $600,000) minimum rental payments (also called gross investment) required and the unamortized asset balance of $454,895 represents unearned income of the sublessor. In this example, the unearned income is $145,105 ($600,000 – $454,895). Next, the rate that will equate the rental payment stream with the unamortized asset balance must be determined.

For a relatively simple example, like the one presented, the following equation will compute the *present value factor* that can be used to determine the appropriate interest rate.

$$X = \frac{T - UI}{P}$$

Where: X = Present value factor of an annuity
T = Total minimum rental payments required
UI = Unearned income
P = Periodic minimum rental payment

By applying the above information to this equation, the following results are obtained:

$$X = \frac{\$600,000 - \$145,105}{\$150,000} = 3.03263$$

The answer developed represents the present value factor for an ordinary annuity for four periods. Turn to the present value of an ordinary annuity table, Appendix E, Table II; move across the four-period row until the value 3.03263 is found. The exact value is not on the table. However, it can be determined that the actual interest rate is between 12% and 13%. Using interpolation, it can be seen that the value is actually closer to 12% than to 13%. From this point forward, the trial-and-error method or a computer application must be used to achieve the exact answer. The correct implicit interest rate for this example is 12.0738%, which will be used to amortize the obligation of $454,895 and is illustrated in Table 8-57.

Table 8-57 Sublessor Amortization Schedule under Sublease

	Period	Payment	Annual Interest Income	Principal Reduction	Present Value of Principal
Initial Value	—	—	—	—	[a]$454,895
	2	$150,000	[b]$54,923	[c]$95,077	[d]359,818
	3	150,000	43,444	106,556	253,262
	4	150,000	30,578	119,422	133,840
	5	150,000	16,160	133,840	-0-
		$600,000	$145,105	$454,895	

[a] Unamortized lease asset balance at date of sublease.
[b] $454,895 × 12.0738% = $54,923.
[c] $150,000 - $54,923 = $95,077.
[d] $454,895 - $95,077 = $359,818.

Using Tables 8-56 and 8-57, the journal entries for the sublessor can be made for the original lease and the sublease. Recall that the sublessor must continue to account for the obligation under the original lease, as well as that under the new sublease. The journal entries required during Year 1 for the original lease are as follows (all amounts are from Table 8-56):

Leased Asset under Capital Lease	568,619	
Obligation under Capital Lease		568,619
Interest Expense	56,862	
Obligation under Capital Lease	93,138	
Cash		150,000
Amortization of Leased Property	113,724	
Accumulated Amortization—Leased Property		113,724

The first entry is to record the value of the leased property and related obligation under the original lease assumptions. The second entry is to record the first annual lease payment from the sublessor to the lessor, and the third entry is to record the amortization of the leased asset, assuming straight-line depreciation is used for similar owned assets.

The required journal entries for Year 2, the first year of the sublease, necessitate the use of both Tables 8-56 and 8-57. The entry to record the payment for the second year from the sublessor to the lessor under the original lease is as follows (amounts from Table 8-56):

Interest Expense	47,548	
Obligation under Capital Lease	102,452	
Cash		150,000

For the sublease example, the sublessor would record the gross investment in the direct financing lease, remove the asset account and record the unearned income. The entry to accomplish this at date of inception of the sublease would be (amounts from Tables 8-56 and 8-57):

Accumulated Amortization—Leased Property	113,724	
Minimum Lease Payments Receivable	600,000	
Unearned Income		145,105
Leased Property under Capital Lease		568,619

The entry to record the receipt of the first lease payment from the sublessee and the recognition of income would be as follows:

Cash	150,000	
Minimum Lease Payments Receivable		150,000
Unearned Income	54,923	
Income from Sublease		54,923

The sublessor would need the information contained in both Tables 8-56 and 8-57 to determine the proper journal entries and amounts for Years 3 through 5. At the end of Year 5, both the original lease and the sublease will terminate, and no further accounting is required.

To complete the cycle of sublease accounting, information is developed below relating to proper classification and accounting from the viewpoint of the *sublessee*. The sublessee would use Flowchart 8-5 to classify the lease as capital or operating.

The Example 8-40 sublease qualifies as a capital lease for the sublessee, because the lease term of four years is more than 75% of the economic life of the asset (5-year economic life × .75 = 3.75 years).

Table 8-58 shows the amortization and expense schedule for the sublessee. The present value of the minimum lease payments is computed using the sublessee's incremental borrowing rate of 11% because the implicit rate is not known to the sublessee. The present value of the MLP is determined as follows:

Annual Rental Payments Required	$150,000
Less: Executory Costs	-0-
	$150,000
Present Value Factor	[a]3.10245
Present Value of MLP	$465,368

[a] Present value factor for an ordinary annuity at 11% for four periods. See Appendix E, Table II.

At inception of the sublease, the sublessee would record the asset and related obligation as follows:

Leased Asset under Capital Lease	465,368	
Obligation under Capital Lease		465,368

The payment of the first year-end lease payment and amortization of the leased asset would require the following entries:

Interest Expense	51,190	
Obligation under Capital Lease	98,810	
Cash		150,000
Amortization of Leased Asset	116,342	
Accumulated Amortization—Leased Asset		116,342

Table 8-58 would be used by the sublessee to record expenses and amortization for Years 2 through 4 of the sublease.

This completes the discussion of subleases. The reader should now begin to see the differences and similarities that exist for lessee and lessor lease accounting.

Table 8-58 Amortization and Expense Schedule—Sublessee

Schedule of Lease Amortization

	Period	Amortization	Annual Payment	Annual Interest Expense	Obligation Reduction	Present Value of Obligation at Year-End
Initial Value	—	—	—	—	—	$465,368
	1	[a]$116,342	$150,000	[b]$51,190	[c]$98,810	[d]366,558
	2	116,342	150,000	40,321	109,679	256,879
	3	116,342	150,000	28,257	121,743	135,136
	4	116,342	150,000	14,864	135,136	-0-
		$465,368	$600,000	$134,632	$465,368	

[a] Assuming that straight-line depreciation is used for owned assets ($465,368/4 years = $116,342).
[b] $465,368 × 11% = $51,190.
[c] $150,000 - $51,190 = $98,810.
[d] $465,368 - $98,810 = $366,558.

Disclosures Required for Lessee

Disclosure requirements for lessees can be divided into the following three categories:

1. A description of the leasing activities of the lessee, including such items as restrictions, purchase option payments, renewal payments, and contingent rentals.
2. Capital leases require disclosure of: the gross value of the assets leased, shown by major classes or combined with owned assets; the minimum rental payments, less executory costs and interest, for each of the five years subsequent to the balance sheet date, and the aggregate payments for the years thereafter; and minimum sublease rentals and contingent rentals.

3. Operating leases require disclosure of: the minimum rental payments for each of the five years subsequent to the balance sheet date, and the aggregate payments for years thereafter; the aggregate amount of all future minimum rentals; and lease expense for each income statement period. Separate disclosures are necessary for minimum rentals, contingent, and sublease rentals.

Disclosures Required for Lessor

Disclosure requirements for lessors may be divided into the following four categories:

1. A description of the leasing activities of the lessor.
2. Direct financing and sales-type leases require disclosure of: the composition of the investment account, including presentation of the minimum lease payments, with deductions shown separately for executory costs, any profit on the executory costs, allowance for uncollectibles, unguaranteed residual values that go to the lessor, unearned income, and initial direct costs for direct financing leases; the minimum rental payments for each of the five years subsequent to the balance sheet date; and any contingent rentals included in income.
3. The composition of the investment account for leveraged leases. This would include the presentation of the receivable, residual value, unearned and deferred income, and deferred taxes.
4. Operating leases require disclosure of: cost and carrying value of leased assets by major class and total accumulated depreciation; minimum rental payments for each of the five years subsequent to the balance sheet date, and the aggregate amount for years thereafter; and contingent rentals for each income statement period.

Refunding Tax-Exempt Debt—Flowchart and General Discussion

ASC 840-30-35, paragraphs 10 and 31, apply to a specific type of lease agreement. Many governmental units or agencies have issued tax-exempt obligations to finance the construction of physical facilities that are to be leased to a user entity. This type of lease agreement might be undertaken to attract new industry to a particular locale, or to finance community facilities, such as hospitals. The governmental unit becomes the lessor, and the user entity is the lessee in the lease agreement. Generally, the lease payments are set at an amount equal to the debt service costs (i.e., the lease payments would be equal to the principal and interest payments on the tax-exempt obligations).

In recent years, the lessor (governmental unit) often has refunded the obligations through the issue of a new obligation that contains more favorable terms. The economic advantage of the refunding may be passed through to the lessee in the form of lower lease payments. Such a refunding poses two problems from an accounting viewpoint. First, there has been a change in the terms of the lease agreement, and the general provisions of ASC 840 would be applicable. Second, the refunding may be viewed as an extinguishment of debt, and the provisions of ASC 470-50 would be applicable.

Where the revised lease agreement qualifies as a capital lease, the asset recorded under the lease agreement, or the obligation recorded, should be adjusted for the amount of the change. A gain or loss resulting from a revision in the terms of a capital lease would not be recognized in the current period, but would be treated as an adjustment to the asset or liability account.

If the refunding is viewed as an extinguishment of debt, the provisions of ASC 470-50 specify that any gain or loss resulting from the extinguishment should be recognized currently.

The accounting treatment of the gain or loss is not consistent in these two standards. ASC 840-30-35, paragraphs 10 and 31, resolve this conflict in accounting treatment for lease agreements involving the refunding of tax-exempt obligations.

Flowchart 8-14 outlines the major decisions and resultant accounting required by ASC 840-30-35, paragraphs 10 and 31. For the provisions of ASC 840-30-35, paragraphs 10 and 31, to be applicable, the transaction must involve the refunding of tax-exempt obligation by the lessor (Block 1), and the perceived economic advantage of the refunding must be passed through to the lessee (Block 2). The specific accounting treatment required will depend upon whether the entity under consideration is the lessor or the lessee (Block 3).

Flowchart 8-14

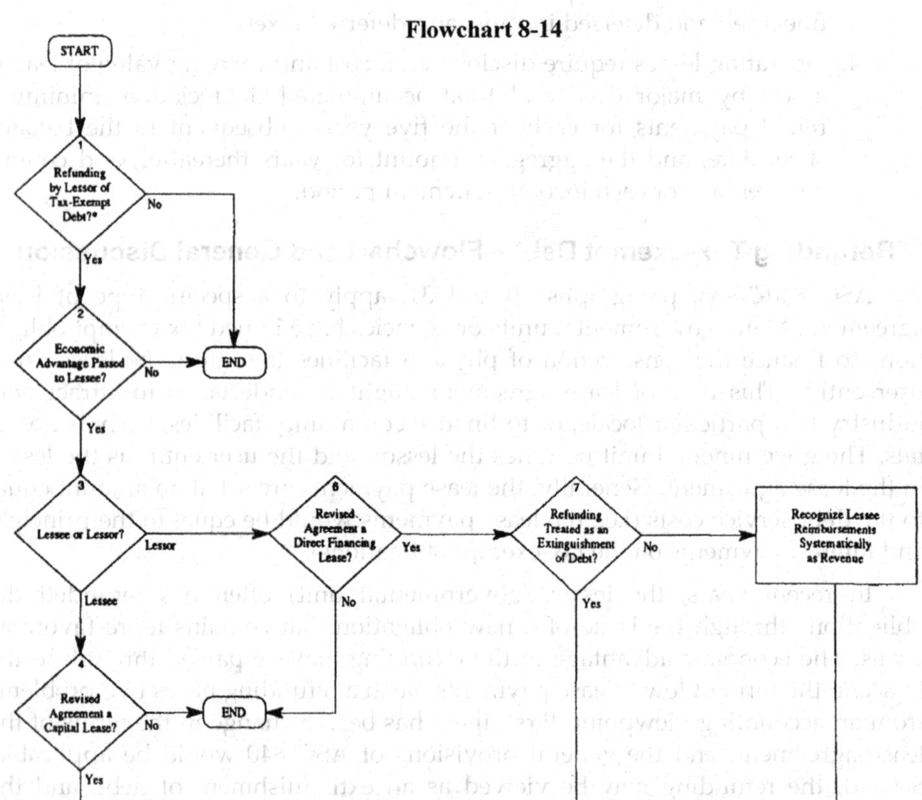

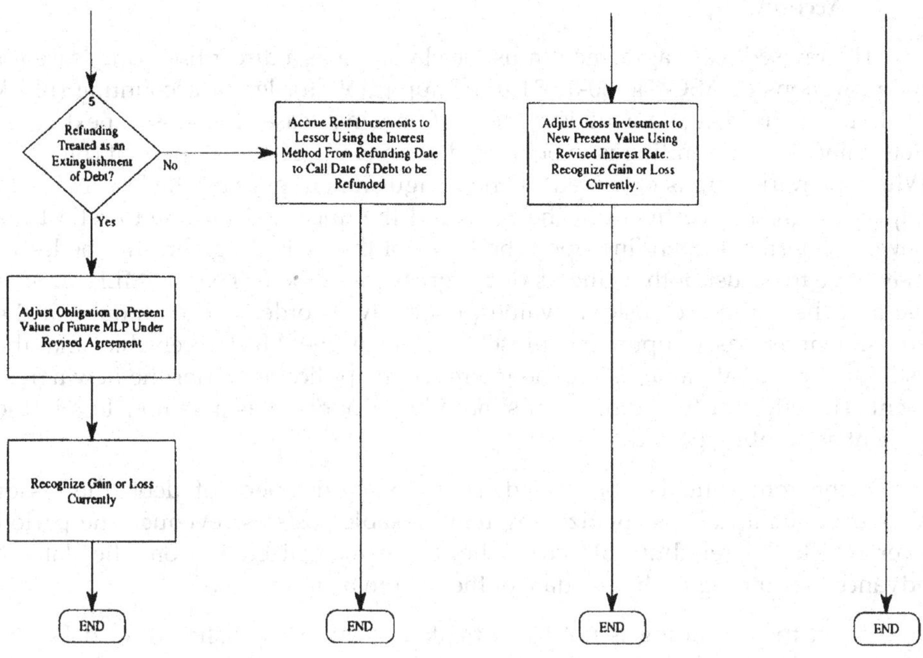

Lessee Accounting

The new lease agreement resulting from the revised terms of the refunding must meet the conditions necessary to be classified as a capital lease in order for the provisions of ASC 840-30-35-10 to be applicable (Block 4). If the revised terms qualify the agreement for treatment as a capital lease, the lessee must determine if the transaction is to be treated as an extinguishment of debt (Block 5). If the refunding is an extinguishment of debt, the lessee must adjust the obligation under the capital lease to reflect the new terms. The lease obligation should be adjusted to an amount equal to the present value of the MLP under the new terms. The present value computation should be based upon the effective interest rate under the revised agreement. Any gain or loss resulting from the adjustment will be *recognized currently.* It is important to remember that the recognition of the gain or loss is applicable only to revised lease agreements resulting from tax-exempt refunding, and does not apply to all refunding that relates to lease agreements.

If the refunding does not qualify as an extinguishment of debt, but the lessee is obligated to reimburse the lessor for any costs associated with the refunding, an alternative accounting treatment is required. Costs of the refunding that may be reimbursed by the lessee would include unamortized discount or debt issue costs or any call premium required to be paid. These costs should be accrued by the lessee using the interest method, from the date of the advanced refunding to the call date of the obligations to be refunded.

Lessor Accounting

The revised lease agreement must be classified as a direct financing lease for the provisions of ASC 840-30-35-31 to be applicable for lessor accounting (Block 6). If the revised agreement is a direct financing lease, the lessor next must determine if the refunding is to be treated as an extinguishment of debt (Block 7). When the refunding is classified as an extinguishment of debt, the lessor should adjust the gross investment in the lease and the unearned income to reflect the new lease terms. Depending upon the terms of the revised agreement, the lessor may have to adjust both elements of the gross investment (i.e., the MLP receivable and the estimated residual value previously recorded). The amount of the adjustment is based upon the present value of the MLP receivable and the estimated residual value, using the interest rate applicable under the new agreement. The effect of the adjustment should be recognized as a gain or loss in the current accounting period.

If the refunding is not treated as an extinguishment of debt, the lessor should systematically recognize any reimbursable costs as revenue. The period over which the reimbursable costs should be recognized is from the date of advanced refunding to the call date of the debt to be refinanced.

When the refunding is not to be treated as an extinguishment of debt, the lessee and lessor are, in effect, systematically recognizing the gain or loss over future periods rather than in the current period.

Refunding of Tax-Exempt Debt Involving a Lease—An Example

To illustrate the technical aspects of ASC 840-30-35, paragraphs 10 and 31, the assumptions listed in Example 8-41 are used.

Example 8-41
Assumptions for Refunding of Tax-Exempt Debt

1. Fastgrow City financed the construction of a $10,000,000 physical facility by issuing tax-exempt obligations. The debt bears interest at the rate of 8%, and $1,000,000 in principal is to be repaid at the end of each of the next 10 years.
2. Fastgrow City leased the facility to Lessee, Inc. for a period of 10 years. The lease payments were set equal to the loan principal and interest payments of the lessor. The lease was appropriately classified as a capital lease for the lessee and a direct financing lease for the lessor.
3. At the beginning of Year 3, Fastgrow City refunded the 8%, $10,000,000 serial obligations by issuing 5% serial obligations that require a $1,012,500 principal payment at the end of each of the next eight years.
4. The refunding is treated as an extinguishment of debt.
5. The economic advantage associated with the refunding (lower interest payments and therefore, lower lease payments) are passed through to Lessee, Inc.

6. The lease agreement under the revised terms is properly classified as a capital lease for the lessee and as a direct financing lease for the lessor.

The appropriate accounting for the lease transaction will be illustrated from the standpoint of both the lessee and the lessor.

Lessee Accounting

Based upon the assumptions listed above, the provisions of ASC 840-30-35-10 apply to the transaction. Before the proper accounting for the lessee can be determined, it is necessary to calculate the balance in the obligation account of the lessee at the date of the refunding. The present value and fair value of the original leased property and obligation was $10,000,000. Table 8-59 shows the amortization of the $10,000,000 obligation under the original lease agreement.

Table 8-59 Amortization of Lease Obligation

Period	Annual[a] Payment	Annual Interest Expense	Obligation Reduction	Obligation Balance End of Year
Initial Value				[b]$10,000,000
1	$1,800,000	[c]$800,000	[d]$1,000,000	[e]9,000,000
2	1,720,000	720,000	1,000,000	8,000,000
3	1,640,000	640,000	1,000,000	7,000,000
4	1,560,000	560,000	1,000,000	6,000,000
5	1,480,000	480,000	1,000,000	5,000,000
6	1,400,000	400,000	1,000,000	4,000,000
7	1,320,000	320,000	1,000,000	3,000,000
8	1,240,000	240,000	1,000,000	2,000,000
9	1,160,000	160,000	1,000,000	1,000,000
10	1,080,000	80,000	1,000,000	-0-
	$14,400,000	$4,400,000	$10,000,000	

[a] The annual payment is equal to the $1,000,000 principal payment plus the annual interest computed at 8% of the obligation balance.

[b] The $10,000,000 initial value is equal to the amount recorded as the lease obligation at the beginning of the lease term.

[c] $10,000,000 × .08 = $800,000.

[d] The annual principal payment.

[e] $10,000,000 - $1,000,000 = $9,000,000.

At the beginning of Year 3, the date of the refunding, the unamortized obligation balance is equal to $8,000,000. Because the economic advantage of the refunding is to be passed through to the lessee, and the revised lease agreement is classified as a capital lease, the lessee is required to adjust the lease obligation account. The amount of the adjustment will be recognized currently as a gain or loss, in accordance with the provisions of ASC 470-50.

The calculation of the gain or loss resulting from the revised lease terms is shown below:

8% Obligations to Be Refunded	$8,000,000
Premium Required to Refund the Issue	100,000
5% Obligation to Be Issued	$8,100,000
Unamortized Obligation—Lessee	8,000,000
Loss on Lease Revision	$100,000

The premium required to refund the 8% obligations is equal to the difference between the unamortized obligation balance for the 8% debt of $8,000,000, and the face amount of the 5% refunding issue of $8,100,000 ($1,012,500 × 8 years = $8,100,000).

The journal entry necessary to reflect the loss and to adjust the balance in the lessee's obligation account would be:

Loss on Revised Lease Agreement	100,000	
Obligation under Capital Lease		100,000

As a result of this adjustment, the new obligation balance will be $8,100,000, and will be reduced each period by the principal payment of $1,012,500. Interest will be recognized in subsequent periods, using the interest method. The new effective interest rate is 5%.

Table 8-60 shows the amortization of the lease obligation under the revised lease agreement.

Table 8-60 Amortization of Lease Obligation under Revised Agreement

Period	Annual[a] Payment	Annual Interest Expense	Obligation Reduction	Obligation Balance End of Year
Initial Value				[b]$8,100,000
3	$1,417,500	[c]$405,000	[d]$1,012,500	[e]7,087,500
4	1,366,875	354,375	1,012,500	6,075,000
5	1,316,250	303,750	1,012,500	5,062,500
6	1,265,625	253,125	1,012,500	4,050,000
7	1,215,000	202,500	1,012,500	3,037,500
8	1,164,375	151,875	1,012,500	2,025,000
9	1,113,750	101,250	1,012,500	1,012,500
10	1,063,125	50,625	1,012,500	-0-
	$9,922,500	$1,822,500	$8,100,000	

[a] The annual payment is equal to the $1,012,500 principal payment plus the annual interest computed at 5% on the obligation balance.

[b] The $8,100,000 initial value at the beginning of Year 3 is equal to the balance in the obligation account under the prior lease agreement, plus the $100,000 loss recognized as a result of the lease revision.

[c] $8,100,000 × .05 = $405,000.

[d] The annual principal payment.

[e] $8,100,000 - $1,012,500 = $7,087,500.

The economic advantage of the revised agreement has resulted in lower lease payments in each of the Years 3 through 10. Under the original agreement, the lease payment in Year 3 would have been $1,640,000. However, under the revised agreement, the required lease payment in Year 3 is $1,417,500.

This completes the discussion of the lessee accounting. Tables 8-59 and 8-60 are used in connection with the lessor accounting under the refunding.

Lessor Accounting

Fastgrow City, the lessor, must reduce the minimum lease payment receivable by an amount equal to the difference between the remaining principal and interest payments on the 8% obligations and the 5% obligations. The principal and interest payments are computed from the date of refunding to the maturity date of the respective issues. As shown in Table 8-59, Fastgrow City recorded the minimum lease payment receivable of $14,400,000, and unearned income of $4,400,000, at the inception of the original lease. At the beginning of Year 3, the date of the refunding, the minimum lease payment receivable would have been reduced by $3,520,000 ($1,800,000 in Year 1, and $1,720,000 in Year 2), and the unearned income account would have been reduced by $1,520,000 ($800,000 in Year 1, and $720,000 in Year 2). Therefore, the remaining balance in the minimum lease payment receivable is $10,880,000, and the balance in the unearned income account is $2,880,000, just prior to the refunding.

Table 8-60 shows that the total minimum lease payment receivable under the revised agreement will be $9,922,500, and the unearned income will be $1,822,500.

Given this information, the lessor could compute the amount of the adjustment required in the following manner:

	8% Obligation	5% Obligation	Difference
Principal Payment	$8,000,000	$8,100,000	$100,000
Interest Payment	2,880,000	1,822,500	(1,057,500)
Total	$10,880,000	$9,922,500	$(957,500)

The adjustment required to reflect the revised lease terms will reduce the unearned income account by $1,057,500, and the minimum lease payment receivable will be reduced by $957,500. The difference between these two amounts ($100,000) will be recognized as a *loss* on the refunding of debt *and* as a *gain* from the revised lease agreement. The entry to record the refunding of the debt is as follows:

	Debit	Credit
Long-Term Debt—8%	8,000,000	
Loss on Refunding of Tax-Exempt Debt	100,000	
Long-Term Debt—5%		8,100,000

The entry required to reflect the revised lease agreement is as follows:

	Debit	Credit
Unearned Income	1,057,500	
Minimum Lease Payment Receivable		957,500
Gain from Lease Revision		100,000

The amortization of the unearned income for Years 3 through 10 is shown in Table 8-60, in the column for interest expense. The minimum lease payment receivable would be reduced each year by the amounts shown in the Annual Payment column of Table 8-60.

Date of Inception of the Lease

The date of inception of the lease is important, because it is on this date that the classification of the lease is made. If an improper date of inception exists, the lease classification made on that date may not reflect the economic substance of the transaction. ASC 840 specifies that the date of inception of the lease is the *lease agreement date,* unless a commitment to lease the property has been made prior to the lease agreement. If such a commitment exists, the date of the commitment, rather than the agreement date, is considered the date of inception of the lease. The date of commitment is earlier than the date of lease agreement.

Risk-Transfer Criterion

For the lessor to classify a lease agreement as a capital lease, in accordance with the provisions of ASC 840, the agreement must meet a risk-transfer test, in addition to other criteria. One part of the risk-transfer test specifies that the lessor will have no significant unreimbursable costs or there will be no significant uncertainties about any such costs. This risk-transfer test normally would be applied at the date of inception of the lease, however, for property that is acquired or constructed subsequent to the date of the lease agreement or the commitment date, the risk-transfer test is to be applied on the date of acquisition of the property, if purchased, or on the date that construction is completed.

Determination of Fair Value of the Leased Property

ASC 840 requires that the lessee compare the present value of the minimum lease payments with the fair value of the leased property. The lesser of the two amounts should be recorded as the value of the leased property and the obligation under the capital lease. If a lease agreement involves both land and building(s), and also contains either a provision for transfer of ownership or a bargain purchase option, the lessee must account separately for the land and building elements. The separation of the land and building elements is made on the basis of the relative fair values of the two elements. Fair value must be adjusted for cost increases during the construction of a leased asset or during the time period prior to acquisition.

Unguaranteed Residual Value

ASC 840 specifies that the lessor's gross investment in both a direct financing and a sales-type lease consists of the summation of the minimum lease payments and the unguaranteed residual value. The total residual value used to determine the amount of any unguaranteed residual value cannot be greater than the estimated residual value on the lease agreement or commitment date. However, if the agreement provides for the escalation of rental payments due to cost increases for leased property that is to be acquired at a later date or for property to be constructed, the effect of the increases are to be used in computing the estimated residual value.

Estimated Residual Value in a Leveraged Lease Agreement

ASC 840 requires that, at the inception of a leveraged lease agreement, the lessor must record the estimated residual value of the leased property as an asset. The amount of the estimated residual value recorded as an asset cannot exceed the residual value estimated at the lease inception date. However, if the agreement provides for the escalation of rental payments, due to cost increases for leased property that is to be acquired at a later date or that is to be constructed subsequent to the lease inception date, the effect of the increases should be used in computing the estimated residual value.

Recent Changes

ASU 2016-02, *Leases (Topic 842),* was issued in February 2016. ASU 2016-02 affects any entity that enters into a lease (as defined), with some specified scope exemptions. Topic 842 in ASU 2016-02 supersedes Topic 840, *Leases,* in the ASC.

The amendments in ASU 2016-02 are effective for fiscal years beginning after December 15, 2018, including interim periods within those fiscal years, for:

1. A public business entity;
2. A not-for-profit entity that has issued, or is a conduit bond obligor for, securities that are traded, listed, or quoted on an exchange or an over-the-counter market; and
3. An employee benefit plan that files financial statements with the U.S. Securities and Exchange Commission.

For all other entities, the amendments in ASU 2016-02 are effective for fiscal years beginning after December 15, 2019, and interim periods within fiscal years beginning after December 15, 2020.

Early application of the amendments in ASU 2016-02 is permitted for all entities.

A brief overview of the accounting requirements under ASU 2016-02 follows.

Changes in the accounting requirements relate mainly to lessees. Limited changes have been made to lessor accounting. Those changes relate to conforming and aligning lessor guidance with the lessee guidance and other areas within generally accepted accounting principles, such as Topic 606, *Revenue from Contracts with Customers.*

The main difference between extant generally accepted accounting standards and newly created ASC Topic 842 resulting from ASU 2016-02 is the recognition of lease assets and lease liabilities by lessees for those leases classified as operating leases under extant standards.

New Topic 842 retains a distinction between finance leases and operating leases. The classification criteria for distinguishing between such leases are substantially similar to the classification criteria for distinguishing between capital leases and operating leases in the extant leases guidance. The result of retaining a distinction between finance leases and operating leases is that under the lessee accounting model in Topic 842, the effect of leases in the statement of comprehensive income and the statement of cash flows is largely unchanged from extant standards. Other differences between the previous lease guidance and Topic 842 are described below.

Lessee Accounting

All leases create an asset and a liability for the lessee in accordance with FASB Concepts Statement No. 6, Elements of Financial Statements. As such, under Topic 842, a lessee should recognize in the balance sheet a liability to make lease payments (the lease liability) and a right-of-use asset representing its right to use the underlying asset for the lease term. When measuring assets and liabilities arising from a lease, a lessee (and a lessor) should include payments to be made in optional periods only if the lessee is reasonably certain to exercise an option to extend the lease or not to exercise an option to terminate the lease.

Similarly, optional payments to purchase the underlying asset should be included in the measurement of lease assets and lease liabilities only if the lessee is reasonably certain to exercise that purchase option. Reasonably certain is a high threshold that is consistent with and intended to be applied in the same way as the reasonably assured threshold in the previous leases guidance. In addition, also consistent with the previous leases guidance, a lessee (and a lessor) should exclude most variable lease payments in measuring lease assets and lease liabilities, other than those that depend on an index or a rate or are in substance fixed payments.

For leases with a term of 12 months or less, a lessee is permitted to make an accounting policy election by class of underlying asset not to recognize lease assets and lease liabilities. If a lessee makes this election, it should recognize lease expense for such leases generally on a straight-line basis over the lease term.

The recognition, measurement, and presentation of expenses and cash flows arising from a lease by a lessee have not significantly changed from extant standards. There continues to be a differentiation between financing leases and operating leases. However, the principal difference from extant guidance is that the lease assets and lease liabilities arising from operating leases should be recognized in the balance sheet.

For finance leases, a lessee is required to:

1. Recognize a right-of-use asset and a lease liability, initially measured at the present value of the lease payments, in the balance sheet.
2. Recognize interest expense on the lease liability separately from the amortization of the right-of-use asset in the income statement.
3. Classify repayments of the principal portion of the lease liability within financing activities and payments of interest on the lease liability and variable lease payments within operating activities in the statement of cash flows.

For operating leases, a lessee is required to:

1. Recognize a right-of-use asset and a lease liability, initially measured at the present value of the lease payments, in the balance sheet.
2. Recognize a single lease cost, calculated so that the cost of the lease is allocated over the lease term generally on a straight-line basis.
3. Classify all cash payments within operating activities in the statement of cash flows.

Lessor Accounting

The accounting applied by a lessor is largely unchanged from that under extant standards. For example, the vast majority of operating leases should remain classified as operating leases, and lessors should continue to recognize lease income for those leases generally on a straight-line basis over the lease term. However, some changes to lessor accounting guidance were made to align both:

1. The lessor accounting guidance with specific changes made to the lessee accounting guidance. For example, certain glossary terms that are applied by lessees and lessors and that will affect a lessee applying the lessor guidance as a sublessor were updated so that lessees and lessors apply the same terms.
2. Key aspects of the lessor accounting model with the revenue recognition guidance in Topic 606. Leasing is fundamentally a revenue-generating activity for lessors, and many aspects of the previous lessor accounting guidance aligned with, or were derived from, the revenue recognition guidance that preceded Topic 606 (e.g., specific aspects of the lessor accounting guidance for real estate assets were designed to conform with the revenue recognition guidance specific to sales of real estate, and both the previous leasing and certain revenue recognition guidance in extant standards utilized a risk-and-rewards principle for determining when the sale of an asset occurred). Topic 842 retains alignment in key respects between the lessor accounting guidance and the revenue recognition guidance in Topic 606. For example, whether a lease is similar to a sale of the underlying asset depends on whether the lessee, in effect, obtains control of the underlying asset as a result of the lease (consistent with the transfer-of-control principle for a sale in Topic 606), and a lessor is precluded from recognizing selling profit or sales revenue at lease commencement for a lease that does not transfer control of the underlying asset to the lessee. Also consistent with the guidance in Topic 606, the lessor accounting model in Topic 842 does not differentiate between leases of real estate and leases of other assets.

Leveraged Leases

In addition to the changes outlined above, the previous accounting model for leveraged leases continues to apply only to those leveraged leases that commenced before the effective date of the guidance in ASU 2016-02. The accounting model for leveraged leases in extant ASC Topic 840 is not retained for leases that commence after the effective date of the guidance in ASU 2016-02.

Definition of a Lease

At the inception of a contract, an entity should determine whether the contract is or contains a lease. Topic 842 defines a lease as a contract, or part of a contract, that conveys the right to control the use of identified property, plant, or equipment (an identified asset) for a period of time in exchange for consideration. Control over the use of the identified asset means that the customer has both (1) the right to obtain substantially all of the economic benefits from the use of the asset and (2) the right to direct the use of the asset.

Under the lessee accounting model in extant standards, the critical determination was whether a lease was a capital lease or an operating lease because lease assets and lease liabilities were recognized only for capital leases. Under Topic 842, the critical determination is whether a contract is or contains a lease because lessees are required to recognize lease assets and lease liabilities for all leases other than those that are "short-term," as defined and for which the entity has elected the short-term lease recognition and measurement exemption. Topic 842 provides detailed guidance and several examples to illustrate the application of the definition of a lease.

Components

Topic 842 requires an entity to separate the lease components from the nonlease components (e.g., maintenance services or other activities that transfer a good or service to the customer) in a contract. Although this was a requirement in extant standards, Topic 842 provides more guidance on how to identify and separate components. Only the lease components must be accounted for in accordance with Topic 842. The consideration in the contract is allocated to the lease and nonlease components on a relative standalone price basis (for lessees) or in accordance with the allocation guidance in Topic 606 (for lessors).

Consideration attributable to nonlease components is not a lease payment and, therefore, is not included in the measurement of lease assets or lease liabilities. Entities should account for nonlease components in accordance with other applicable ASU topics. Activities that do not transfer a good or service to the lessee or amounts paid solely to reimburse costs of the lessor are not components in a contract and are not allocated any of the consideration in the contract.

The above notwithstanding, Topic 842 provides a practical expedient for lessees as it relates to separating lease components from nonlease components. Lessees may make an accounting policy election by class of underlying asset not to separate lease components from nonlease components. If an entity makes that accounting policy election, it is required to account for the nonlease components together with the related lease components as a single lease component.

Sale and Leaseback Transactions

For a sale to occur in the context of a sale and leaseback transaction, the transfer of the asset must meet the requirements for a sale in Topic 606. If there is no sale for the seller-lessee, the buyer-lessor also does not account for a purchase. Any consideration paid for the asset is accounted for as a financing transaction by both the seller-lessee and the buyer-lessor. There could be circumstances in which a transaction would have qualified for a sale under the previous lease accounting guidance but will not qualify for a sale under Topic 606, or vice versa. In particular, many sale and leaseback transactions involving real estate will qualify for sale and leaseback accounting that would not have qualified for sale and leaseback accounting under extant lease accounting guidance. In contrast, some sale and leaseback transactions involving assets other than real estate that previously would have qualified for sale and leaseback accounting will not qualify for sale and leaseback accounting under Topic 842. Topic 842 includes implementation guidance to assist entities in determining whether the transfer of an asset in the context of a sale and leaseback transaction is a sale. In particular, Topic 842 specifies that if the leaseback is classified as a finance/sales-type lease, no sale has occurred. Topic 842 also specifies that a repurchase option (i.e., for the seller-lessee to repurchase the asset from the buyer-lessor) precludes sale accounting unless (1) the asset is nonspecialized and (2) the exercise price of the option is the fair value of the asset on the date the option is exercised. For transactions previously accounted for as a sale and a leaseback under extant standards, the transition guidance in Topic 842 does not require an entity to reassess whether the transaction would have qualified as a sale and a leaseback in accordance with Topic 842.

Disclosures

Disclosures are required by lessees and lessors to meet the objective of enabling users of financial statements to assess the amount, timing, and uncertainty of cash flows arising from leases. As such, both qualitative and specific quantitative disclosures are required to enable users to understand more about the nature of an entity's leasing activities.

Transition

In transition, lessees and lessors are required to recognize and measure leases at the beginning of the earliest period presented using a modified retrospective approach. The modified retrospective approach includes a number of optional practical expedients that entities may elect to apply. These practical expedients relate to the identification and classification of leases that commenced before the effective date, initial direct costs for leases that commenced before the effective date, and the ability to use hindsight in evaluating lessee options to extend or terminate a lease or to purchase the underlying asset.

An entity that elects to apply the practical expedients will, in effect, continue to account for leases that commence before the effective date in accordance with previous standards unless the lease is modified, except that lessees are required to recognize a right-of-use asset and a lease liability for all operating leases at each reporting date based on the present value of the remaining minimum rental payments that were disclosed under previous standards.

The transition guidance in Topic 842 also provides specific guidance for sale and leaseback transactions, build-to-suit leases, leveraged leases, and amounts previously recognized in accordance with the business combinations guidance for leases.

Topic 842: Leases

Topic 842, *Leases*, contains the following subtopics:

10 Overall

20 Lessee

30 Lessor

40 Sale and Leaseback Transactions

50 Leverage Lease Arrangements

Overview of New Topic 842

ASC 842, *Leases*, supersedes the guidance in ASC 840, *Leases*. ASC 842 was created under ASU 2016-02, *Leases* which was issued in February 2016. Topic 842 affects any entity that enters into a lease (as defined), with specific exemptions. The new guidance is intended to improve the quality and comparability of financial reporting by providing greater transparency about leverage, the assets an entity uses in its operations, and its risks related to leasing transactions. In general, the new accounting guidance for leases is applicable to public and nonpublic entities.

Improvements contemplated by ASU 2016-02 include:

- A more faithful representation of lessee's rights and obligations arising from leases.
- Better comparability of lessee's financial statements.
- Reduced opportunities to structure contracts to avoid balance sheet recognition.
- Clarification of the definition of a lease.

The core principle of the new lessee accounting model is that a lessee entity should recognize "right-of-use" (ROU) assets and liabilities for lease obligations arising from leases with a lease term of more than 12 months. A lessee will recognize a ROU asset (representing its right to use the leased asset for the lease term) and a liability for its obligation to make lease payments. The recognition, measurement, and presentation of expenses and cash flows arising from a lease by a lessee depends on its classification as either a financing lease or operating lease.

Lessor accounting is mostly unchanged. Lessors will continue to classify a lease as either sales-type, direct financing, or operating.

Leverage leases have been eliminated, but existing ones are grandfathered under the new standard if they commenced before the new standard's effective date. This classification of a lease is made by the lessor at the lease commencement date and is not reassessed unless the lease is modified and not accounted for as a new lease.

The new lease accounting standard as codified in ASC 842, *Leases*, is effective for public entities in fiscal years beginning after December 15, 2018, and for nonpublic entities in fiscal years beginning after December 15, 2019. Early implementation is permitted. All entities transitioning to the new standard are required to use the modified retrospective method.

Scope Exclusions

Excluded from scope of ASU 2016-02 are:

- Leases to explore for or use oil, gas, minerals, and other non-regenerative resources.
- Leases of biological assets, including plants and living animals.
- Leases of intangible assets (including licenses of internal-use software).
- Leases of inventory.
- Leases of assets under construction.

Arrangements

Vendors and customers enter into numerous types of arrangements. The nature and substance of these arrangements may be for services, or for leases, or a combination of both. The reporting entity must evaluate its arrangements with its vendors and customers to determine which ones include a lease.

Lease Definition

A lease is a contract or part of a contract between entities that conveys the right to control the use of specific property, plant, or equipment (i.e., an identifiable asset) for a period of time in exchange for consideration.

Key Terms

Some key terms under ASC 842 follow:

- Lease commencement date—Date the lessor makes an underlying identifiable asset available for use by a lessee.
- Incremental borrowing rate—Rate of interest lessee would have to pay to borrow an amount equal to the lease payments in a similar economic environment on collateralized basis over a term similar to the lease term.
- Lease modification—Change to the terms and conditions that results in a change in the scope of or consideration for a lease. (For example, a change to the contract that adds or terminates the right to use one or more underlying assets or extends or shortens the contractual lease term.)
- Residual guarantee—A guarantee made to a lessor that the value of an underlying asset returned to the lessor at the end of a lease will be at least a specified amount.
- Right-of-use asset—An asset that represents a lessee's right to use an underlying asset for the lease term.

- Short-term lease—A lease that, at the commencement date, has a lease term of 12 months or less and does not include an option to purchase the underlying asset that the lessee is reasonably certain to exercise.

Steps in Accounting for a Lease

Steps in the accounting model for a lease follow:

Step 1: Identify the lease.

Step 2: Classify the lease.

Step 3: Measure and recognize the lease asset and liability.

Step 4: Meet continuing requirements (e.g., modifications, terminations, etc.).

Step 1: Identify the Lease

A lease is present in a contract if the contract includes both:

- An identified asset, and
- The customer has the right to control the use of the identified asset during the lease term.

The identified asset may be explicitly or implicitly specified in the contract. Also, the supplier has no practical ability to substitute or would not economically benefit from substituting another asset. If the supplier has a substantive right to substitute another asset, then the arrangement does not contain an identified asset. A substitution right is substantive if the supplier can practically use another asset to fulfill the arrangement, and it is economically beneficial for the supplier to do so.

Right to Direct Control and the Use of the Asset

To determine if the arrangement contains a lease, entities must now consider both power and benefits.

An entity has the right to direct the use of an asset if:

- It either has he right to direct how and for what purpose the asset is used, or
- If decisions about how and for what purpose the asset is used are predetermined (i.e., they are part of the contract).

To control use on the asset, the entity must have:

- Decision making rights (authority) over the use of the asset, and
- The ability to obtain substantially all economic benefits from the use of the asset.

Examples of decision making rights include the:

- Right to change the type of output,
- Right to change when the output is produced,
- Right to change where the output is produced, and
- Right to change whether the output is produced.

Does the Arrangement Contain a Lease?

Background: A customer enters into a contract with manufacturer to purchase a particular type, quality, and quantity of product for a three-year period, all of which are specified within an executed contract. The manufacturer has only one factory that can meet the needs of the customer. The manufacturer is unable to supply the product from another factory or source the product from a third-party supplier. The capacity of the factory exceeds the required output for the customer under the arrangement. The manufacturer makes all decisions about the operations of the factory.

Questions: Does the arrangement contain a lease? Why?

Answer: No. Key consideration is that the customer does not control the factory.

Background: A customer enters into a contract with a supplier for the use of a truck for one year to transport cargo between two locations. The supplier does not have substitution rights and only cargo specified in the contract is permitted to be transported on this truck for the period of the contract. The contract specifies a maximum distance that the truck can be driven but the customer is able to choose the details of the journey. The customer does not have the right to continue using the truck after the specified trip is complete and the cargo to be transported and the timing and location of pickup and delivery in are specified in the contract. The customer is responsible for driving the truck between locations.

Questions: Does the arrangement contain a lease? Why?

Answer: Yes. The key consideration includes the following: The customer has use of a specific truck for a specified time. Further, the customer gets benefits from using the truck which is, under the customer's control. Lastly, the supplier not allowed to substitute another truck.

Multiple other examples are included in ASU 2016-02 within the implementation guidance for different industries and types of contracts, including those for rail cars, retail units, and energy/power.

Lessee Accounting

The lessee classifies leases as either financing or operating.

Step 2: Classify the Lease

Under the lessee accounting model, a lessee classifies a lease as either a finance or operating lease. The lease is classified as a finance lease if:

1. Ownership of the underlying asset transfers to the lessee;
2. The lessee is reasonably certain to exercise an embedded purchase option;
3. The lease term is for the major part of the remaining economic life of the underlying asset;

4. The present value of lease payments plus any residual value guaranteed equals or exceeds substantially all of the fair value of the underlying asset (no longer a 90% test but 90% considered substantially all); or
5. The underlying asset is specialized for lessee with no alternative use to the lessor.

Under criteria (3) above, the major part of the remaining economic life is considered to be 75%. Also, if the commencement date of the lease falls at or near the end of the economic life of the underlying asset then this criteria does not apply.

Under criteria (4) above, substantially all is considered to be 90%.

If none of the five criteria above is met, then the lease is classified as an operating lease.

Step 3: Measure and Recognize the Lease Asset and Liability

The lessee recognizes assets and liabilities for both finance and operating leases. The lessee also recognizes interest and amortization for finance leases and straight-line lease expense for operating leases. Straight-line leases expense consists of interest expense on the lease liability and amortization expense on the lease asset.

Lessee Recording of Finance Leases

The lessee recognizes:

1. An intangible right-of-use (ROU) asset underlying physical leased asset;
2. A liability for its obligation to make lease payments;
3. Amortization expense on ROU asset using the straight-line or another method that reflects the pattern of consumption of the future economic benefits; and
4. Interest expense (using effective interest rate method) on its obligation to make lease payments.

Interest and amortization expense are shown separately in statement of operations or otherwise disclosed in the financial statements.

Lessee Recording of Operating Leases

The lessee recognizes:

1. A ROU asset underlying leased asset;
2. A liability for its obligation to make lease payments;
3. Interest expense on obligation to make lease payments; and
4. Amortization of the ROU asset to reflect straight-line lease expense (i.e., the sum of interest in "c" and amortization in "d" would be a level amount over the lease term).

Lease expense (interest—3 and amortization—4) is presented as one amount in the statement of operations and classified and disclosed as "lease expense."

Lessee ROU Asset

At the initial measurement, the lessee records a ROU asset at the present value of the lease payments it is obligated to make over the lease term. The initial measurement is made as of the lease commencement date. The ROU asset also includes initial direct costs and is amortized. Similar to other long-lived assets, a ROU asset is also reviewed for potential impairment when a triggering event suggests that the carrying cost of the asset may not be recovered. In such cases, an impairment loss would be determined and recognized using ASC 360, *Property, Plant, and Equipment*. Following an impairment write down, the lessee amortizes the remaining carrying amount of the ROU asset on a straight-line basis. For operating leases, the lessee will continue to reflect a single lease expense in the income statement.

Lessee Discount Rate to Calculate Present Value

The lessee uses the interest rate the lessor charges the lessee (i.e., the implicit rate), if available; otherwise the lessee uses its incremental borrowing rate to determine the present value of its payments under the lease obligation. Nonpublic entities may use a risk-free discount rate for a term comparable to the lease term. A nonpublic entity lessee may use the risk-free discount rate as an accounting policy election, as such an election must be applied to all leases. The interest rate should not be reassessed if there is no change in lease payments.

Lessee Lease Term

The lease term includes:

- Non-cancellable periods;
- Periods under options that a lessee is reasonably certain to exercise; and
- Periods under options controlled by lessor.

The lease term begins at the lease commencement date and includes rent-free periods.

For example: A lessee has entered into a contract to lease a specialized piece of equipment for use in its operations. The lease includes an initial noncancelable term of five years. During the fourth year of the lease, the lessor has the unilateral ability to extend the lease for another two years at the conclusion of the initial five-year term. In addition, the lessee is provided with two three-year options to extend the lease. At the lease commencement date, the lessee is not sure whether it will extend the lease.

In this situation, the total lease term for measurement purposes is seven years (5 +2).

Initial Direct Costs

Initial direct costs are those that result directly from originating a lease and that would not have been otherwise incurred. Examples of initial direct costs include commissions and fees paid to an existing tenant to incentivize that tenant to terminate its lease.

Examples of certain costs that are not identified as initial direct costs for lessees and/or lessors under ASC 842 follow:

- General overhead costs such as depreciation, occupancy and equipment repairs and maintenance, unsuccessful origination efforts, and idle time.
- Costs related to activities performed by the lessor for advertising, soliciting potential lessees, servicing existing leases, or other ancillary activities.

Costs related to activities that occur before the lease is obtained, such as costs of obtaining tax or legal advice, negotiating lease terms and conditions, or evaluating a prospective lessee's or lessor's financial condition.The examples of the costs shown above are expensed as incurred.

An example applying the accounting follows:

Background: A lessee enters into a 10-year lease for office space. In connection with this lease, the lessee pays a commission of $10,000 to a real estate agent who identified the property for the lessee and legal fees of $5,000 for assistance provided to the lessee in negotiating the lease terms.

Question: How would lessee account for these costs?

Answer: Capitalize and amortize commission which was paid only because the lease agreement was executed for the suitable property the agent identified. Expense the legal fees since such fees would have been incurred even if the lease agreement was not consummated.

Lessee Lease Payment Obligation

The initial measurement of the lessee's obligation is the present value of the lease payment over lease term (as previously discussed). The lease payment obligation includes:

- Fixed payments, including in-substance fixed payments (i.e., variable payments that lack commercial substance), less any lease incentives paid or payable to the lessee;
- Variable lease payments tied to an index or a rate based on the index/rate at inception of the lease;
- The exercise price of an option to purchase the underlying asset if the lessee is reasonably certain to exercise that option;
- Payments for penalties for terminating the lease, if the lease term reflects the lessee exercising an option to terminate the lease;
- Fees paid by the lessee to the owners of a special-purpose entity for structuring the transaction; and
- For a lessee only, amounts probable of being owed by the lessee under residual value guarantees.

Certain payments that the lessee makes to or on behalf of the lessor are not included in the lease obligation liability. These include variable lease payments not tied to a rate or index and payments under a guarantee by the lessee of the lessor's debt. Lastly, the lessee may make an accounting policy election not to separate the nonlease component for a portion of the lease payment for a given class of underlying assets and account for the whole contract payment as a lease. This latter matter is discussed further below.

Lessee Amortization of ROU Asset

The lessee amortizes the ROU asset on straight-line or other systemic basis that reflects the pattern of consumption of future economic benefits of the asset. The amortization period is the shorter of the lease term or useful life of underlying asset. However, if the lease agreement includes a significant economic incentive to exercise a purchase option, then the lessee amortizes the ROU asset over its economic life rather than lease term.

Lessee Accounting for a Finance Lease

Assume the follow facts:

- A lease term of five years for equipment (1.1.X1 to 12.31.X5).
- Annual payments of $10,000 payable in advance (annuity due).
- Discount rate—6%.
- Initial direct costs—$6,644.
- Probable amount of residual guarantee—$5,000.
- Lease commencement date—1.1.X1.
- Lastly, assume that one or more of the five finance criteria is met.

A table summarizing the above information follows:

	Right-to-Use Asset
Present value of lease payments	$ 44,651
Present value of probable residual guaranty	3,705
Initial direct costs	6,644
	$ 55,000

		Interest		
	Amortization Expense	Residual Guaranty	Lease Obligation	Payments Principal
X1	$11,000	$229		$10,000
X2	11,000	243	$2,079	7,921
X3	11,000	258	1,604	8,396
X4	11,000	275	1,100	8,900
X5	11,000	290	566	9,434
	$55,000	$1,295	$5,349	$44,651

The lessee would record the following journal entries for years one and two based on the information immediately above for a finance lease.

First Year:

Right-of-use asset	$44,651	
Lease obligation		$44,651

To record present value of lease payments at lease commencement.

Right-of-use asset	$3,705	
Probable residual lease obligation guaranty		$3,705

To record present value of residual guarantee at lease commencement.

Right-of-use asset	$6,644	
Cash		$6,644

To record initial direct costs.

Lease obligation	$10,000	
Cash		$10,000

To record initial lease payment on 1/1/x1.

Amortization expense	$11,000	
Accumulated amortization?—Right-of-use asset		$11,000

To record amortization for X1

Interest expense	$2,308	
Accrued interest		$2,079
Probable residual lease obligation guaranty		229

To record interest on lease obligation and residual guaranty for X1.

Second Year:

Accrued interest	$2,079	
Lease obligation	7,921	
Cash		$10,000

To record lease payment on 1/1/X2.

Amortization expense	$11,000	
Accumulated amortization—Right-of-use asset		$11,000

To record amortization for X2.

Interest expense	$1,847	
Accrued interest		$1,604
Probable residual lease obligation guaranty		243

To record interest on lease obligation and residual guaranty for X2.

Lessee Accounting for an Operating Lease

Assume the follow facts which are the same as those above except for the "bolded" portion.

- A lease term of five years for equipment (1.1.X1 to 12.31.X5).
- Annual payments of $10,000 payable in advance (annuity due).
- Discount rate—6%.
- Initial direct costs—$6,644.
- Probable amount of residual guarantee—$5,000.
- Lease commencement date—1.1.X1.
- Lastly, assume that none of the five finance criteria is met.

The lessee would record the following journal entries for years one and two based on the information immediately above for the operating lease. Note the similarity of these entries with those for the finance lease.

First Year:

Right-of-use asset	$44,651	
Lease obligation		$44,651

To record present value of lease payments at lease commencement.

Right-of-use asset	$3,705	
Probable residual lease obligation guaranty		$3,705

To record present value of residual guarantee at lease commencement.

Right-of-use asset	$6,644	
Cash		$6,644

To record initial direct costs.

Lease obligation	$10,000	
Cash		$10,000

To record initial lease payment on 1/1/x1.

Lease expense	$12,328	
Accumulated amortization - Right-of-use asset		$10,020
Accrued interest		2,079
Probable residual lease obligation guaranty		229

To record lease expense, interest on lease obligation and residual guarantee, and amortization for X1.

Second Year:

Accrued interest	$2,079	
Lease obligation	7,921	
Cash		$10,000

To record lease payment on 1/1/X2.

Lease expense	$12,238	
Accumulated amortization - Right-of-use asset		$10,481
Accrued interest		1,604
Probable residual lease obligation guaranty		243

To record lease expense, interest on lease obligation and residual guarantee, and amortization for X2.

The chart presented below shows how the amount of straight line lease expense (including the amount for amortization of the ROU asset) was determined.

	Straight-Line Lease Expense	Interest – Probable Residual Guaranty	Interest – Lease Obligation	Total Interest	Calculated Amortization
	$12,328	$229	$2,079	$2,308	$10,020
	12,328	243	1,604	1,847	10,481
	12,328	258	1,100	1,358	10,970
	12,328	275	566	841	11,487
	12,332	290		290	12,042
Totals	$61,644	$1,295	$5,349	$6,644	$55,000

Separate Lease and Nonlease Components

A lease may include lease and nonlease components, e.g., a lease for equipment that includes maintenance services.

Lessee treatment:

The lessee separates lease components from nonlease components and allocates the consideration for the components on a relative standalone basis. The allocation should maximize the use of observable standalone prices. In addition, the lessee may make an accounting policy election not to separate the nonlease component for a given class of underlying assets and account for the whole contract as a lease.

Lessor treatment:

The lessor allocates the transaction price to the separate performance obligations consistent with the new revenue standard.

An example of separating the lease and nonlease components follows. A lessee leases a copier with lease and nonlease components. Assume the lease is properly classified as an operating lease by lessee. Selected information about the lease follows:

- Annual lease payments are $500, including maintenance.
- The lessor normally leases the same copier for $475 per year and offers a maintenance contract for $75 per year.
- The lessee has not made an accounting policy election to not separate the lease and nonlease components for this class of asset.

Question: How should the lessee separate the contract into its lease and nonlease components?

Answer: The lessee should allocate the consideration in the contract to the lease and nonlease components based on their relative standalone price as shown below.

	Selling Price	Allocation %	Payment	As Allocated
Copier (Lease component)	$475	86.36	$500	$432
Maintenance (Nonlease component)	75	13.64	500	68
	$550	100.00		$500

Lessee Short-Term Leases

A lease with a term of 12 months or less is a short-term lease. A lessee can make an accounting policy election to not apply the balance sheet recognition requirements to such short-term leases. A lease will no longer meet the definition of a short-term lease if either: (a) the lease term changes and the remaining lease term is greater than 12 months from the end of the previously determined lease term; or (b) contrary to its earlier determination, the lessee becomes reasonably certain of exercising a purchase option.

A lessee recognizes expense under a short-term lease on a straight-line basis. Further, a lessee is required to disclose the amount of expense under short-term leases. However, the lessee is not required to disclose amount of expense for leases of a month or less. Lastly, the lessee is required to disclose its accounting policy election to not apply the balance sheet recognition requirements to short-term leases.

Entities that structure leases as short-term with the intent of not recording ROU assets and liabilities for lease obligations may be disincentivized to do so by being charged higher rental rates.

Lessor Accounting

Lessor accounting under ASC 842 is substantially unchanged compared to the lessor accounting model under ASC 840. As such, the extant lease classifications by lessors are retained. Namely, lessors will continue to classify leases as either:

1. sales-type, or
2. direct financing, or
3. operating.

Lessor Sales-Type Leases

Lessors use the same criteria used for finance lease. Accordingly, a lease is a sales-type if it meets any one of the following:

1. Transfers ownership of the leased assets;
2. The lease includes an option to purchase that is reasonably certain to be exercised;
3. The lease term for a major part of the remaining economic life of underlying asset;
4. The present value of the lease payments and residual guaranty equals or exceeds substantially all of fair value of the underlying asset; or
5. The underlying asset so specialized that it is expected to have no alternative use to lessor at the end of the lease term.

Lessor Accounting for a Sales-Type Lease

For a sales-type lease, the lessor derecognize the underlying asset at the commencement date and recognizes its net investment in the lease, a selling profit or loss, and the initial direct costs incurred in entering into the sales-type lease.

Subsequently, the lessor recognizes interest income on the net investment in the lease (and the accretion of residual asset) and variable lease payments in the income statement for those payments not included in the net investment of the lease. The net investment in lease is evaluated for impairment.

An example of the accounting for a sales-type lease follows.

A lessor enters into a lease of non-specialized equipment. The lessor manufactures that equipment and uses both direct sales and leases for selling its equipment.

Summarized information about the lease and the leased equipment follows:

- The lease term is five years with no renewal option.
- The economic life of the leased equipment is six years.
- The lease does not include a purchase option.
- Annual lease payments are $1,100.
- Lease payments are due on January 1.
- The fair value of the leased equipment is $5,000.
- The lessor's carrying value of the leased equipment is $4,500.
- The implicit interest rate in the lease is 7.04%.
- Title to the equipment remains with the lessor upon expiration of the lease.
- The lessee does not guarantee the residual value of the equipment.
- The estimated fair value of the equipment at the end of the lease term is $250.
- The lessee pays for all equipment maintenance separately from the lease.
- The lessor incurred no initial direct costs.
- The lessor did not provide any incentives.

The lessor determines that the lease is a sales-type lease. As such, its initial net investment in the lease is the present value of the lease receivable and the unguaranteed residual asset.

The present value of the lease receivable is equal to the present value of the lease payments discounted at 7.04% or $4,822. And, the present value of the unguaranteed residual asset discounted at 7.04% is $178.

The carrying value of leased asset is $4,500, net of the unguaranteed residual asset of $178 or $4,322. The lessor's selling profit is $500 ($4,822 minus $4,322).

The lessor records revenue at the lease commencement date equal to the lease receivable amount ($4,822). Cost of sales is recorded as the difference between the carrying value of the leased asset ($4,500) and the discounted value of the unguaranteed residual asset ($178).

Following is the journal entry the lessor makes to record this sales-type lease on the lease commencement date.

Lease receivable	$4,822	
Unguaranteed residual asset	178	
Cost of sales	4,322	
Inventory (Equipment)		$4,500
Sales		4,822

A roll-forward of the above lease receivable follows.

	Payment	Principal	Interest	Lease A/R
Commencement				
Year 1	$1,100	$1,100	$262	$4,822
Year 2	1,100	838	203	3,984
Year 3	1,100	897	140	3,087
Year 4	1,100	960	73	2,127
Year 5	1,100	1,027	0	1,100
	$5,500	$4,822	$678	

Lastly, a roll-forward of the above residual asset follows.

	Accretion	Residual Asset
Commencement		$178
Year 1	$13	191
Year 2	13	204
Year 3	14	218
Year 4	15	233
Year 5	17	250
	$72	

At end of year 5 the lessor reclassifies residual asset of $250 to inventory or property, plant and equipment as appropriate under its business model.

Lessor Accounting for a Direct Financing Lease

If the lease is not a sales-type lease and meets two conditions, the lessor will account for the lease as a direct financing lease. The two conditions follow:

1. The present value of the sum of the lease payments and any residual value guaranteed by the lessee that is not already reflected in the lease payments and/or any other third party unrelated to the lessor equals or exceeds substantially all of the fair value of the underlying asset; and
2. It is probable that the lessor will collect the lease payments plus any amounts necessary to satisfy a residual value guarantee.

For a direct financing lease, the lessor derecognizes the underlying asset at the commencement date similar to a sales-type lease. The lessor also recognizes both its net investment in in the lease and any selling loss arising from lease. Selling profit, if any, is deferred and amortized over the lease term as an adjustment of interest income.

Subsequently, the lessor recognizes interest income on the net investment in the lease and variable lease payments in the income statement for those payments not included in the net investment of the lease. The net investment in lease is evaluated for impairment.

Lessor Accounting for an Operating Lease

The classification of leases as operating is similar for both lessors and lessees. A lease that is not classified as a sales-type or direct financing by the lessor is classified as an operating lease.

For an operating lease, the lessor does not derecognize the underlying leased asset at the commencement date. The lessor does continue to recognize depreciation on the underlying leased asset over its estimated economic useful life. Any initial direct costs of obtaining the lease are deferred as of commencement date and amortized over the lease term.

The lessor recognizes lease payments received or receivable under the operating lease, including variable lease payments, as income in the statement of operations using the straight-line method.

Lessor Lease Terminations

The lessor's net investment in a lease is assessed for impairment immediately before the return of the underlying asset. The lessor accounts for the returned asset as a reclassification of the net investment in the lease and measures the asset returned at the carrying value of the net investment in the lease asset.

Lessee Lease Modifications

A lease modification is "[a] change to the terms and conditions of a contract that results in a change in the scope of or the consideration for a lease." The lessee must determine whether a modification results in new lease contract or a change to existing lease contract.

A modification results in a separate contract if:

- It grants the lessee an addition right of use not in the original contract, and
- The lease payments are commensurate with the standalone price of the additional right of use.

If the modification does not result in separate contract, the entity is required to reassess the classification of the lease as of the effective date of the modification.

Following is a common lease modification. A lessee enters into a 10-year lease for 10,000 square feet of office space. At the beginning of Year 6, the lessee and lessor agree to modify the lease for the remaining five years to include an additional 10,000 square feet of office space in the same building. The increase in the lease payments is commensurate with the market rate at the date the modification is agreed for the additional 10,000 square feet of office space. The lessee accounts for the modification as a new contract, separate from the original contract because the modification grants the lessee an additional right of use not part of the original contract, and the increase in the lease payments is commensurate with the standalone price of the additional right of use. Accordingly, from the effective date of the modification, the lessee would have two separate contracts.

The following four lease modifications require the lessee to remeasure the ROU asset and lease liability:

1. The lessee is granted an additional right to use one or more underlying assets that were not in the original contract.
2. The term of the existing lease is extended or terminated other than by exercising a contractual option to extend or terminate the lease.
3. The consideration only in the contract is changed.
4. The existing lease is fully or partially terminated.

Numbers 1 through 3 result in adjustments to the ROU asset and lease liability for the same amount. Under number 4 the amount of the adjustment to the ROU asset and lease liability may differ and result in gain or loss for the difference between reduction in lease liability and the reduction in ROU asset.

An illustration for accounting for lease modification that changes only consideration with no change in the classification of the lease is presented next.

A lessee entered into a 10-year lease which commenced on January 1, 2001 for 10,000 square feet of office space. Under this lease annual lease payments of $95,000 increasing $1,000 a year starting in 2002 payable in arrears were required. At the lease commencement the lessee's incremental borrowing rate was 6%. The lease was properly classified as an operating lease.

As of December 31, 2005, the lease liability was $429,171 and the ROU asset was $416,671.

Effective January 1, 2006, the lease is modified. As modified, the annual lease payments are reduced for 2006 by $7,000. As such, the lease payment for 2006 is $93,000. Thereafter, the lease payments are increased by $1,000 a year payable in arrears through 2010. The lessee's incremental borrowing rate on the effective date of the modification was 7%.

The lease continues to be properly classified as an operating lease as of January 1, 2006; the remeasured lease liability on that date was $388,965.

The lessee makes the following entry to give effect to the lease modification.

Lease obligation (Pre - $429,171 minus Post - $388,965)	$40,206	
ROU asset		$40,206

Another illustration for accounting for lease modification that changes only consideration with no change in the classification of the lease is presented next.

The lessee entered into a five year lease agreement which commenced on January 1, 2001 to for retain store property. Annual lease payments of $100,000 a year commencing January 1, 2001 were required. At the lease commencement date, the lessee's incremental borrowing rate was 5%. The lease was properly classified as an operating lease.

The present value of an annuity due of $100,000 for five years at 5% is $454,595. This amount represents both the initial lease obligation and ROU asset as of January 1, 2001.

On January 1, 2004, the lessee considers terminating the lease and relocating. To entice the lessee to remain, the lessor agreed to amend the original lease contract by reducing the annual lease payments to $90,000. The lessee determines that the lease should continue to be classified as an operating lease upon modification. On January 1, 2004 the lessee's incremental borrowing rate was 4%.

The present value of an annuity due of $90,000 for two years is $176,538.

As of December 31, 2003, the lease liability was $195,238, including accrued interest of $9,297 and the ROU asset was also $195,238 (Cost - $454,595 less accumulated amortization of $259,357).

The lessee makes the following entry on January 1, 2004 to give effect to the lease modification.

The lessee makes the following entry to give effect to the lease modification.

Lease obligation (Pre - $195,238 minus Post - $176,538)	$18,700	
ROU asset		$18,700

Under the modified lease, the lessee record $90,000 as straight-line lease expense for both for 2004 and 2005.

The chart which follows provides the information used to determine the amounts shown above.

	Payments Straight-Line Expense	Interest Paid	Lease Obligation	Interest Expense	Accrued Interest EOY	EOY Liability	ROU Asset	Amortization
P.V. at commencement date			$454,595				$454,595	
1/1/2001	$100,000	0	354,595	$17,730	$17,730	$372,325	82,270	$82,270
1/1/2002	100,000	$17,730	272,325	13,616	13,616	285,941	86,384	86,384
1/1/2003	100,000	13,616	185,941	9,297	9,297	195,238	90,703	90,703
	300,000			40,643			259,357	259,357
Balance before modification			185,941		9,297	195,238	195,238	
Modification Adjustment			-9,403		-9297	-18,700	-18,700	
P.V. balance after modification			176,538		0	176,538	176,538	
1/1/2004	90,000	0	86,538	3,462	3462	93,462	86,538	86,538
1/1/2005	90,000	3,462	0	0	0	0	90,000	90,000
	180,000			3462			176,538	176,538
	$480,000			$44,105			0	$435,895

Legend: BOY – Beginning of Year; EOY – End of Year; ROU – Right-of-Use

A lease modification may result in a full or partial termination of the lease. For a termination, the lessee decreases the carrying amount of the ROU asset on a basis proportionate to the full or partial termination of the existing lease. Any difference between the reduction in the lease liability and the proportionate reduction in the ROU asset is recognized as either a gain or loss as of the effective date of the termination modification.

An example of the accounting for a lease modification that results in a decrease in the scope and partial termination of the lease is shown next.

Lessee entered into a 10-year lease which commenced on January 1, 2001 for 10,000 square feet of office space. Under this lease annual lease payments of $100,000 increasing by 5% a year payable in arrears were required. At the lease commencement the Lessee's incremental borrowing rate was 6%. The lease was properly classified as an operating lease.

As of December 31, 2005, the lease liability was $590,767 and the ROU asset was $514,436.

Effective January 1, 2006 the lease is modified. As modified the leased footage is reduced to 5,000 square feet and the annual lease payments are reduced to $68,000 for 2006 increasing by 5% a year payable in arrears through 2010. The lessee's incremental borrowing rate on the effective date of the modification was 7%.

The lease continues to be properly classified as an operating lease as of January 1, 2006; the remeasured lease liability as of that date was $306,098.

The lessee makes the following entry to give effect to the lease modification.

Lease obligation	$284,669	
Right-of-use asset		$247,888
Gain on partial lease termination		36,781

The gain on the difference between the decrease of the lease obligation and the decrease in the ROU asset on the partial lease termination was calculated as follows:

Lease liability pre termination	$590,767	
Lease liability post termination	306,098	
Decrease	$284,669	or 48.2%

Decrease in right-of-use asset: 48.2% × $514,436 - $247,888

Lessor Lease Modifications

Accounting for a lease modification by the lessor depends on type of lease modified (operating, direct financing, or sales-type)

Lessor guidance is consistent with lessee guidance on lease modifications. Under such guidance, the lessor assesses whether to account for modification as a separate contract. If modification not accounted for as a separate contract, the lessor is required to account for it as if it were a termination of the existing lease and the creation of a new lease that commences on the effective date of the modification.

Operating

If the new lease is considered an operating lease, the lessor should consider any prepaid or accrued lease rentals relating the original lease as part of the lease payments for the modified lease.

If the modified lease results in a sales-type or direct financing classification, the lessor is required to derecognize any deferred rent liability or accrued rent asset and adjust the selling profit or loss accordingly. If the modified lease continues to be a direct financing lease, the lessor should adjust the discount rate for the modified lease so that the initial net investment in the modified lease equals the carrying amount of the net investment in the original lease immediately before the effective date of the modification.

Direct Financing

If the newly modified direct financing lease is now classified as a sales-type lease, the lessor should account for the modified lease in accordance with overall lease guidance applicable to sales-type leases and use the effective date of the modification as the commencement date.

If the newly modified financing lease is now classified as an operating lease, the carrying amount of the underlying asset equals the net investment in the original lease immediately before the effective date of the modification.

Sales-Type

If the newly modified sales-type lease now results in either a sales-type or direct financing lease classification, the lessor is required to adjust the discount rate for the modified lease so that the initial net investment in the modified lease equals the carrying amount of the net investment in the original lease immediately before the effective date of the modification.

If the newly modified sales-type lease results in an operating lease classification, the carrying amount of the underlying asset equals the net investment in the original lease immediately before the effective date of the modification.

Sale and Leaseback Transactions and Leveraged Leases

A sale of an asset in accordance with ASC 606, *Revenue from Contracts with Customers,* must occur before the reporting entity may have a sale and leaseback transaction. To have a sale, there must be a contract and satisfaction of a performance obligation, i.e., the transfer of control of the asset.

All of the following characteristics must be present to have a contract.

- The parties to the contract have approved the contract and are committed to perform their respective obligations.
- Each party can identify its rights regarding the goods or services to be transferred.
- The payment terms for the asset or services to be transferred can be identified.
- The contract has commercial substance.
- Collection of the contract consideration is probable.

To satisfy its performance obligation, the transferee (seller) must transfer control of the asset to the buyer. The existence of a leaseback does not, in isolation, prevent the buyer-lessor from obtaining control of asset. However, the buyer-lessor cannot obtain control if the leaseback is a sales-type or direct financing lease.

Indicators that control of the asset have been transferred to the buyer-lessor follow:

- The buyer/lessor has legal title to asset.
- The seller/lessee has a right to payment for the asset's selling price.
- The buyer/lessor has the significant risks and rewards of ownership.

So in summary, a sale-leaseback transaction will qualify as a sale only if:

- The transaction meets the sale guidance in the new revenue recognition standard, and
- The leaseback is not a financing or a sales-type lease.

Repurchase Options

A seller-lessee option to repurchase the asset prevents sale treatment unless:

- The exercise price of the option is for the fair value of the asset at the time the option is exercised, and
- There are substantially similar alternative assets readily available in the marketplace.

Accounting for a Sale and Leaseback Transaction

When a sale does occur, the seller-lessee recognizes the transaction price for the sale when buyer-lessor obtains control of asset. Also, the seller-lessee derecognizes the carrying amount of asset and accounts for the leaseback lease in accordance with ASC 842. The leaseback lease must be an operating lease.

An example of sale and leaseback transaction which results in a gain on the sale is presented next. Background information follows:

- A seller-lessee enters into a sale and leaseback transaction of its corporate headquarters with a buyer-lessor for a market value sales price of $20 million.
- The seller-lessee leases back the asset for 10 years in exchange for $200,000 per year in rental payments.
- The seller-lessee's net carrying amount of the asset at the date of sale is $15 million.
- Assume the leaseback is classified as an operating lease for purposes of this example.

The seller-lessee accounts for the transaction as a sale and leaseback. The sale results in a gain on sale of $5 million ($20 million sales price minus the $15 million carrying amount of asset). Since the sale and leaseback transaction is at market value and the leaseback lease is classified as an operating lease, the seller-lessee should recognize the gain on sale of $5 million in the period in which the sale is recognized.

An example of sale and leaseback transaction which results in a loss on the sale is presented next. Background information follows:

- A seller-lessee enters into a sale and leaseback transaction of its corporate headquarters with a buyer-lessor for a market value sales price of $20 million.
- The seller-lessee leases back the asset for 10 years in exchange for $200,000 per year in rental payments.
- The seller-lessee's net carrying amount of the asset at the date of sale is $25 million.
- Assume the leaseback is classified as an operating lease for purposes of this example.

The seller-lessee accounts for the transaction as a sale and leaseback. The sale results in a loss on sale of $5 million ($20 million sales price minus the $25 million carrying amount of asset). Since the sale and leaseback transaction is at market value and the leaseback lease is classified as an operating lease, the seller-lessee should recognize the loss on the sale of $5 million in the period in which the sale is recognized (assuming an impairment of the asset was not required to be recorded in an earlier period).

If a Sale Does Not Occur

If a sale does not occur, then the seller-lessee should not derecognize transferred asset. Also, the seller-lessee accounts for any amounts received as a financial liability

Assets under Construction

When a lessee controls an asset before the lease commencement date (e.g., an asset under construction), the transaction is accounted for as a sale and lease-back. Under ASC 842, the lessee is deemed the owner of an asset under construction if the lessee controls that asset during the construction period. Following are indicators that the lessee has control.

1. The lessee has the right to obtain the partially constructed underlying asset at any point during the construction period.
2. The lessor has an enforceable right to payment for its performance to date, and the asset does not have an alternative use to the owner-lessor.
3. The lessee legally owns either both the land and the property improvements or the non-real-estate asset under construction.
4. The lessee controls the land that property improvements will be constructed upon to transfer the land to the lessor, but the transfer does not qualify as a sale and does not enter into a lease of the land before the beginning of construction that, together with renewal options, permits the lessor or another unrelated third party to lease the land for substantially all of the economic life of the property improvements.
5. The lessee is leasing the land that property improvements will be constructed upon, the term of which, together with lessee renewal options, is for substantially all of the economic life of the property improvements, and does not enter into a sublease of the land before the beginning of construction that, together with renewal options, permits the lessor or another unrelated third party to sublease the land for substantially all of the economic life of the property improvements.

The above list of circumstances in which a lessee controls an underlying asset that is under construction before the commencement date is not all-inclusive. There may be other circumstances that individually or in combination demonstrate that a lessee controls an underlying asset that is under construction before the commencement date.

If a lessee incurs costs relating to the construction of an asset it does not control, it accounts for those costs in accordance with other ASC guidance. As such, some or all of such costs may qualify for recognition as an asset.

An example of accounting by a lessee for an asset under construction is presented next.

A university ("University") would like to construct a new library on a parcel of land next to its campus. The University acquires the parcel of land and enters into an agreement with an independent third-party developer ("Developer"). The Developer will lease the parcel of land from University, construct the library, and lease the completed library to University. Both the ground leased to the Developer and the library leased to University have 20-year lease terms. The rental rates on both leases are consistent with prevailing market rents for similar leased assets. The economic life of the library is 40 years.

The University controls the underlying asset during the construction period because the ground leased to the Developer is for a term that is less than substantially all of the economic life of the property improvements. Accordingly, the University accounts for the underlying asset during the construction period similar to any other owned asset under construction (i.e., under ASC 360, *Property, Plant, and Equipment*). Additionally, any construction costs paid for by the Developer are recorded as a financial liability and asset by the University. Consistent with the University's accounting, the Developer does not recognize the asset under construction. Rather, it accounts for any payments it makes during the construction period as a collateralized loan to the lessee in accordance with ASC 310, *Receivables*.

Leveraged Leases

A leveraged lease reflects certain characteristics. A leveraged lease:

- Does not give rise to a manufacturer's or dealer's profit (or loss) to the lessor.
- Involves at least three parties: a lessee, a long-term creditor, and a lessor (equity participant).
- Includes nonrecourse financing as to the general credit of the lessor. Also, the lessor's net investment declines during the early years once the investment has been completed and rises during the later years of the lease before its final elimination.

The existing accounting model for leveraged leases under ASC 840 has not been retained under ASC 842. However, existing leveraged leases are "grandfathered" during transition.

Financial Reporting of Leases

A summary of financial statement presentation matters follows:

Balance Sheet

Lessee

- Present financing and operating lease right-of-use assets and liabilities separately from other assets and liabilities or otherwise disclose which financial statement line term (FSLI) contains them.
- Do not present financing lease and operating lease assets and liabilities within the same FSLI.

Lessor

- There are no changes from previous lease requirements.
- Present lease assets separately from other assets.
- Lease assets are classified as current or noncurrent based on traditional classification concepts.

Income Statement

Lessee

- Finance leases: Present both the amortization of a right-of-use asset and interest on a lease liability consistently with presentation of the amortization of other assets and other interest expense.
- Operating leases: Present as a single lease cost consistent with previous lease standards.

Lessor

- All leases: Lessor has an option to present lease income separately or disclose within the notes to the financial statements which FSLIs includes lease income.
- Present the profit or loss from leases in a manner that best reflects lessor's business model. For example, report sales and cost of sales for sales-type leases and interest income for financing leases.

Statement of Cash Flows

Lessee

- Operating activities: This classification is for operating lease payments, variable lease payments, and short-term lease payments.
- Investing activities: This classification is for payments to bring an asset to the condition necessary for its intended use.
- Financing activities: This classification is for the repayment of principal portion of lease liability.

Lessor

- Operating activities: This classification is for all cash receipts from a lease.

Disclosures of Leases

Lessees and lessors are required to make qualitative and quantitative disclosures. Following is an overview of the required disclosures of leases for lessees and lessors.

Lessee and Lessor

Both lessees and lessors are required to disclose information about:

- The nature of entity's leasing activities;
- The existence of options to extend or terminate leases;
- The significant assumptions and judgments made in accounting for leases; and
- Lease transactions with related parties.

The overall guidance for disclosure and accounting requirements for related party transactions is included in ASC 850, *Related Party Disclosures*. Disclosures of related party transactions (e.g., leases) are required even when the transactions are not documented and/or the terms and conditions are not at arm's length.

Lessee Only

Lessees are required to provide certain disclosures, including information about:

- Residual value guarantees;
- Restrictions or covenants imposed by leases;
- Discount rate determination (including its accounting policy to elect to use the risk free rate of return);
- Lease maturities;
- If elected, accounting policy for short-term leases; and
- Lease cost, sublease income, any gain or loss on sale and leaseback transactions.

Lessor Only

Lessors are required to provide certain disclosures, including information about:

- Options held by a lessee to purchase a leased asset;
- It manages risk with residual value of assets;
- Lease maturities; and
- Lease income and the components of its aggregate net investment in leases.

Transitioning

All entities are required to use the modified retrospective approach when adopting the new lease guidance. As of the effective date of adoption, the reporting entity need not reassess:

- Whether any expired or existing contracts are or contain leases;
- The lease classification (e.g., capital or operating) of any expired or existing leases; and
- Initial direct costs for existing leases.

Also, the reporting entity may use hindsight in determining lease term and assessing impairment of ROU assets.

So no changes required for existing capital leases except for the nomenclature. Capital lease obligations under extant U.S. GAAP are labelled lease obligations and the related assets are labelled ROU assets under the new standards. Operating leases require changes. The lessee will recognize a lease obligation and a ROU asset at the present value of remaining lease payments for each operating lease using incremental borrowing rate as of effective date of adoption.

Lastly, lessors can continue to account for leveraged leases existing as of the effective date of the adoption of ASU 2016-02 (ASC 840).

Topic 845: Nonmonetary Transactions

Topic 845, *Nonmonetary Transactions*, contains five subtopics:

10 Overall

908 Airlines*

920 Entertainment—Broadcasters*

926 Entertainment—Films*

985 Software*

Flowchart and General Discussion

Before a meaningful discussion of ASC 845-10 can be started, it is important to define several terms that have special meaning for purposes of this subtopic. Although it is always difficult to convey the significance of a term in words, the following definitions (from ASC 845-10-20), along with the example material presented later in the discussion, should give the reader an appreciation of the terms:

1. **Monetary Assets and Liabilities:** Those assets and liabilities whose value is expressed in a fixed amount of purchasing power (e.g., cash, receivables, and payables).
2. **Nonmonetary Assets and Liabilities:** Those assets and liabilities whose value is not expressed in a fixed amount of purchasing power (e.g., inventories, land, and equipment).
3. **Exchange (or Exchange Transaction):** A transfer between two entities. Each entity receives a benefit in the form of an asset and each entity gives up an asset or incurs a liability.
4. **Nonreciprocal Transfer:** A one-directional transfer. It involves a transfer of assets or a receipt of assets or services, but not both. The payment of a property dividend by an entity to its stockholders would be an example of a nonreciprocal transfer.
5. **Productive Assets:** Assets used in the production process (e.g., equipment, buildings, land, and investments accounted for using the equity method).
6. **Similar Productive Assets:** Assets used in the production process that are of the same general category, are used in the same business line, or perform the same job.

ASC 845-10 specifies the accounting for exchange transactions and nonreciprocal transfers of nonmonetary assets and liabilities. It also covers exchanges and transfers that are primarily, but not exclusively, nonmonetary transactions. An exchange transaction or nonreciprocal transfer may include nonmonetary assets and liabilities, as well as a small amount of monetary assets or liabilities. The amount of the monetary assets or liabilities involved in the transaction is referred to as "boot."

---

* See the corresponding topic in Chapter 9 for coverage of this shared subtopic.

ASC 845-10-15-4 identifies the following nine specific transactions that are exempt from the general provisions of ASC 845-10:

1. Business combinations reported in accordance with ASC 805. A business-for-business exchange is a business combination.
2. Nonmonetary asset transfers between companies under the same control.
3. Exchange of capital stock for nonmonetary assets or services (covered by ASC 718-10 and 505-50).
4. Receipt or issuance of stock resulting from a stock split or stock dividend.
5. Receipt of an equity interest in an entity from a transfer of asset to the entity.
6. A joint undertaking where assets are pooled to find, develop, or produce oil and gas from a specific property or a specific group of properties as described in ASC 932-360-40-7.
7. An entity exchanges part of one operating interest for a part of another operating interest owned by another entity and covered by the provisions of ASC 932-360-55-6.
8. Financial asset transferred to another entity as covered by the provisions of ASC 860-10.
9. Nonmonetary assets converted involuntarily to monetary assets with a subsequent reinvestment in nonmonetary assets.

When an entity has an involuntary conversion of a nonmonetary asset to a monetary asset, the general provisions of ASC 845-10 do not apply (see ASC 605-40). The gain or loss resulting from the involuntary conversion must be recognized currently. However, if the involuntary conversion resulted in damage or destruction to the asset, and the amount to be received cannot be determined, the provisions of ASC 450 are applicable. The gain or loss that must be recognized currently must be disclosed.

This introduction to the terms used in ASC 845-10 should assist in the understanding of the essential features of Flowchart 8-15 and example material.

Flowchart 8-15

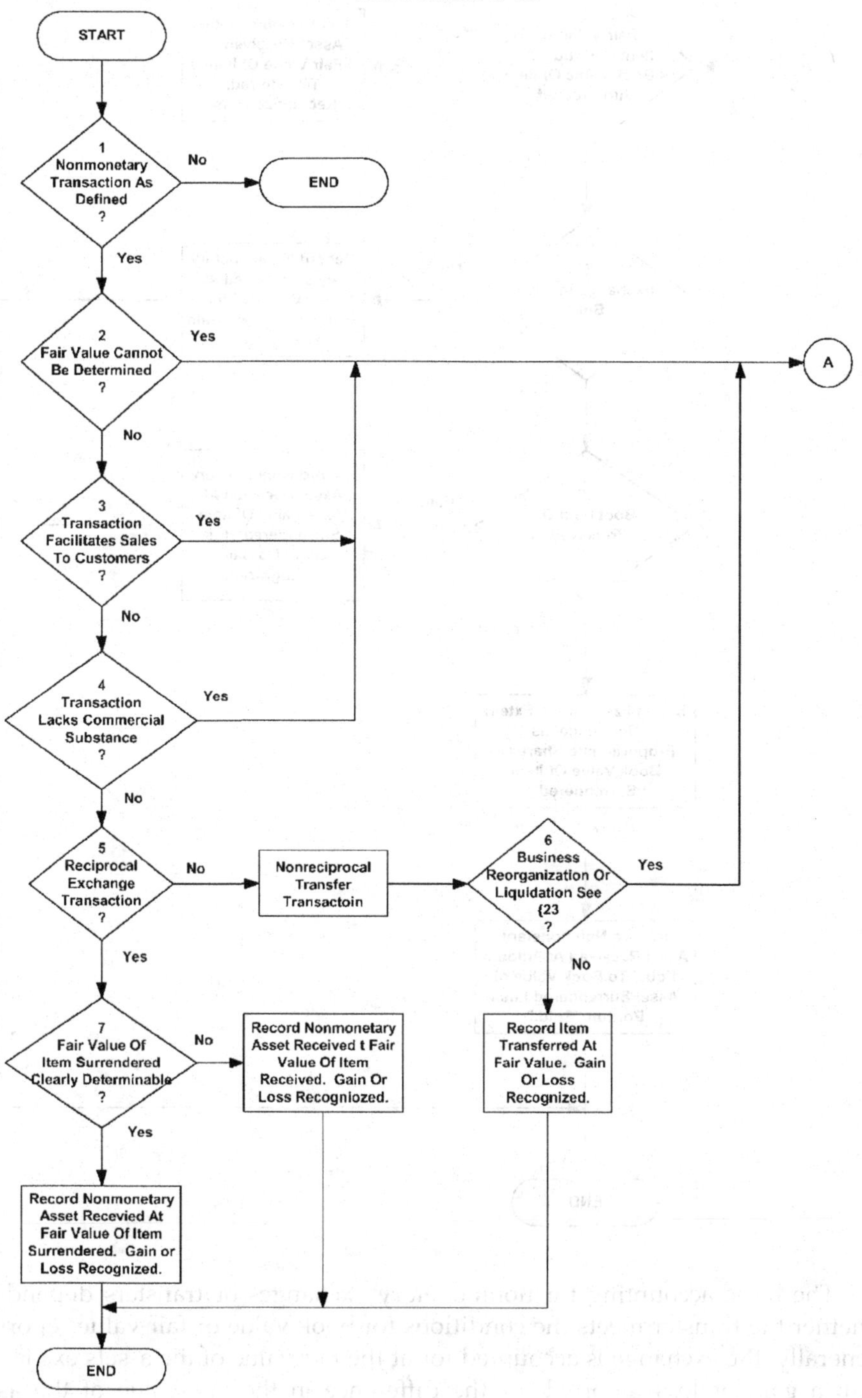

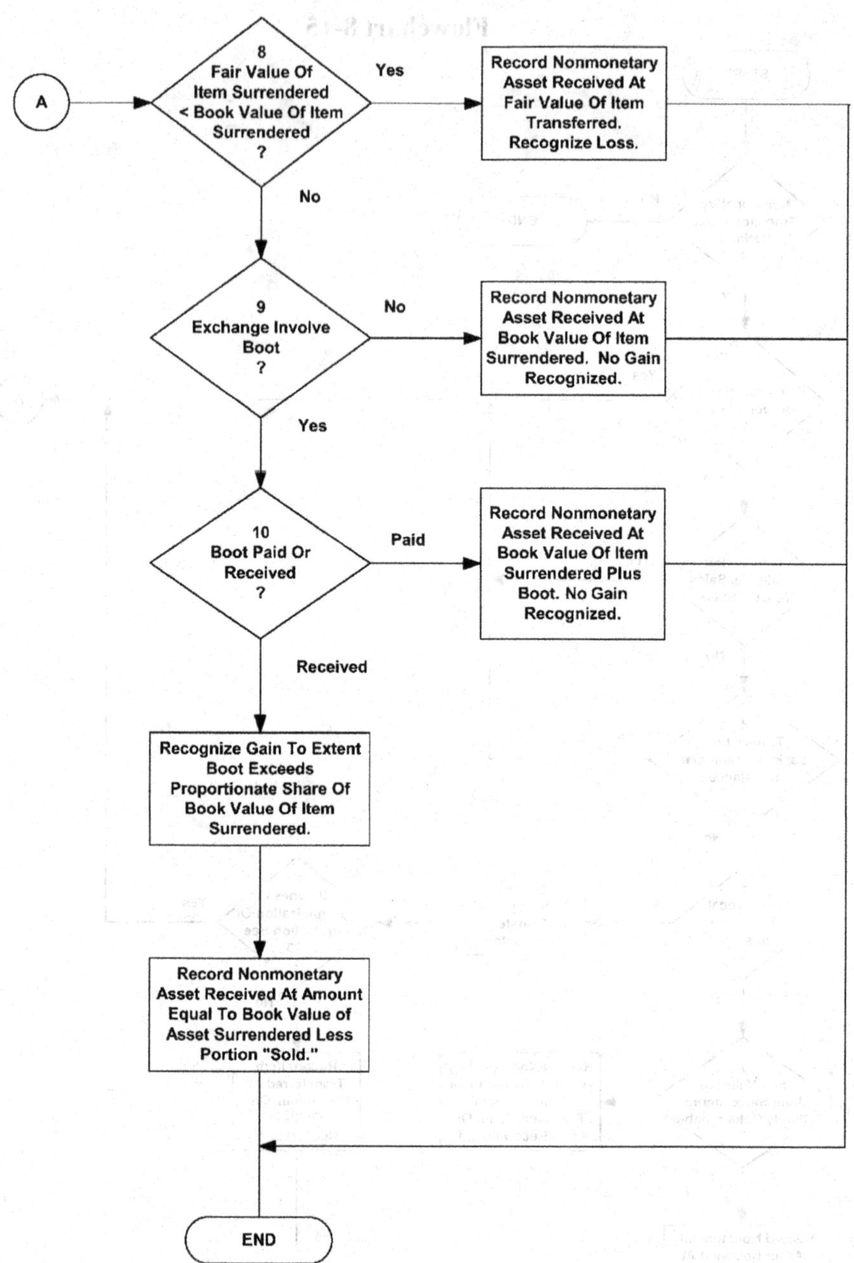

The basic accounting for nonmonetary exchanges or transfers depends on whether the transfer meets the conditions for book value or fair value reporting. Generally, the exchange is accounted for at the fair value of the assets exchanged with a gain or loss reported for the difference in the fair value of the assets transferred. However, if any of the three following conditions are met, the nonmonetary exchange is accounted for using the recorded amount of the asset given up less an indicated impairment of value (ASC 845-10-30-3):

1. Fair value cannot be determined.
2. The exchange is for the purpose of facilitating sales to customers.
3. The exchange lacks commercial substance.

In the first situation, neither the fair value of the asset received nor the fair value of the asset given up can be determined. The second situation might represent the exchange of inventory for inventory. An exchange lacks commercial substance if the entity's future cash flows are not expected to significantly change as a result of the exchange transaction.

Flowchart 8-15 can be divided into two major sections: the left half deals with the accounting problems faced when fair value accounting is required for the exchange transaction and the right side assumes that the recorded amount of the asset exchanged is used in the accounting process. The following discussion is organized along this major division in Flowchart 8-15.

Exchanges and Transfers When Fair Value Accounting Is Required

This portion of the material is divided into nonmonetary exchanges—general considerations, nonmonetary exchanges—technical considerations, nonreciprocal transfers—general considerations, and nonreciprocal transfers—technical considerations.

Nonmonetary Exchanges—General Considerations

If an entity is involved in a nonmonetary transaction (Block 1), and fair value is determinable (Block 2), the transaction is not to facilitate a sale to customers (Block 3), and the transaction has commercial substance (Block 4), the exchange is accounted for using fair value. The nonmonetary asset received generally is recorded at the fair value of the nonmonetary item given up. If the fair value of the item given up cannot be determined (Block 7), the nonmonetary item received should be recorded at the fair value of the item received. However, ASC 845-10 states that when one party to the transaction can elect to receive cash in place of the nonmonetary asset, the best estimate of fair value may be the amount of cash that could be received. A gain or loss should be recognized in an amount equal to the difference between the amount recorded for the asset received and the book value of the asset given up. Fair value is not determinable if fair value of either the item received or the item surrendered cannot be determined within reasonable limits. The determination of fair value is discussed in more detail below. A nonmonetary exchange is a transaction to facilitate a sale to customers when an asset that is to be sold in the normal course of business is exchanged for an asset held for sale in the same business line in an effort to aid customer sales other than the parties involved in the exchange. This type of transaction might be an exchange of inventory for inventory. In a situation where inventory is purchased from and sold to the same counterparty, the issues are whether a transaction that involves two or more purchases and sales to the same counterparty should be accounted for as a single transaction and when fair value accounting is appropriate for an inventory exchange treated as a nonmonetary exchange in the same line of business. An entity should account for two or more purchases or sales of inventory with the same counterparty as a single exchange transaction under the provisions of ASC 845-10 when one of the inventory transactions is contingent upon the performance of the other inventory transaction (i.e., the transactions are in contemplation of one other). Even if one of the purchase and sales transactions is not legally contingent upon the performance of the other inventory transaction, the transactions may be in contemplation of one another when certain indicators are met. The following are examples of indicators that may be used in the evaluation:

1. There is a legal right of offset for the sale and purchase transactions.
2. The counterparties entered into the purchase and sale transactions simultaneously.
3. The terms of the transactions were off-market at the time of the arrangement.
4. The transactions with the same counterparties are relatively certain.

When an entity exchanges finished goods inventory for work-in-process inventory or raw materials inventory in the same line of business, the exchange transaction is reported at fair value, if the fair value requirements are met. However, book value reporting is required when an entity in the same line of business exchanges work-in-process inventory or raw materials inventory for raw materials inventory, work-in-process inventory, or finished goods inventory or when the entity exchanges finished goods inventory for finished goods inventory. The definitions used in financial reporting for raw material, work-in-process, and finished goods should be used for purposes of applying these provisions.

A nonmonetary exchange has commercial substance when future cash flows of the entity are anticipated to significantly change as a result of the transaction. When one of the following conditions is met, the future cash flows of the entity are expected to significantly change as a result of the exchange:

- The configuration of the future cash flows of the assets received and surrendered differ significantly.
- There is a significant difference between the entity-specific fair values of the asset received and the asset surrendered.

Configuration of future cash flows refers to risk, timing, and amounts of cash flows; a change in any one of these items is considered a change in configuration. An entity-specific value of the assets exchanged refers to the valuation of the asset in the context of a specific entity. The entity would determine the entity-specific value of the asset using the expected use of the asset rather than the use assumed by the market place. When tax cash flows are a result of a tax business purpose that is to achieve a specific financial reporting goal, those cash flows should not be used when determining commercial substance.

A small amount of boot (cash or other monetary consideration) may be given or received in connection with a nonmonetary exchange. The fact that boot is involved does not change the general principle that the asset received should be recorded at the fair value of the item given up. If the fair value of the item given up cannot be determined, the decision process described above should be followed.

ASC 845-10 does not define the meaning of "small" as it relates to the boot given or received. The question that must be answered by the accountant's judgment is: What is the maximum boot that can be given or received in an exchange transaction and still have that transaction qualify as a nonmonetary exchange? If the boot were to exceed 25% of the total fair value, the transaction could not be classified as nonmonetary.

The determination of fair value in an exchange transaction can pose difficult problems for the accountant. ASC 820 provides guidance on the determination of fair value. Fair value is the amount that would be received on the measurement date from the sale of property or the amount paid to transfer a liability between sellers and buyers (market participants) in an orderly transaction. In addition, it is assumed that the sellers and buyers are unrelated parties on the measurement date.

It is not appropriate to use estimated fair value in an exchange transaction unless the fair value can be estimated within reasonable limits. When there are major uncertainties regarding whether the value assigned to an asset will be realized, it is assumed that fair value cannot be estimated within reasonable limits. As indicated above, if it is not appropriate to use fair value, the asset received should be recorded at the book value of the item given up.

Nonmonetary Exchanges—Technical Considerations

To illustrate the technical aspects of nonmonetary exchanges where the requirements for book value accounting are not met, assume that Book-It, Inc. exchanged a piece of equipment that had an appraised value of $30,000 for inventory to be resold. The equipment had a cost basis of $100,000; and, at the date of exchange, accumulated depreciation was $75,000. None of the requirements for book value accounting have been met. The exchange of equipment for inventory represents an exchange of dissimilar assets; therefore, fair value will be used for the exchange transaction because none of the requirements for book value reporting have been met. In this example, the fair value of the item surrendered is known to be $30,000, and this amount should be used to record the value of the inventory received. The next step is to determine whether there is a gain or loss on the transaction that must be recognized. The gain or loss is determined by comparing the fair value of the asset given up with the book value of that asset, and is computed as follows:

Cost of Equipment	$100,000
Less: Accumulated Depreciation	75,000
Book Value of Equipment	$25,000
Fair Value of Equipment	30,000
Gain on Exchange	$5,000

Because the fair value assigned to the asset received is greater than the book value of the asset given up, a gain resulted from the exchange. The entry to record the exchange of equipment for inventory would be as follows:

Inventory	30,000	
Accumulated Depreciation—Equipment	75,000	
Equipment		100,000
Gain on Nonmonetary Exchange		5,000

The preceding example depicted a situation where the fair value of the item surrendered in the exchange transaction was known. In many nonmonetary exchanges, the fair value of the item given up may not be known, or the fair value of the item received may be more evident than the fair value of the item given up. To illustrate this situation, assume the same facts as in the above example, except that the fair value of the equipment is not known and the normal selling price of the inventory items was $20,000. In this case, the value assigned to the inventory received would be $20,000, and the gain or loss would be determined as follows:

Cost of Equipment	$100,000
Less: Accumulated Depreciation	75,000
Book Value of Equipment	$25,000
Fair Value of Inventory	20,000
Loss on Exchange	$5,000

The fair value of the inventory received is less than the book value of the equipment; therefore, a loss will be recognized. The entry required to record the exchange in this case would be:

Inventory	20,000	
Accumulated Depreciation—Equipment	75,000	
Loss on Nonmonetary Exchange	5,000	
Equipment		100,000

The two preceding examples involved exchanges of nonmonetary assets where no boot was given or received. To show the effect of the boot on a nonmonetary exchange, assume that Book-It, Inc. exchanges equipment with a fair value of $100,000, plus $10,000 in cash, for some inventory items. The equipment given up has a cost basis of $95,000 and, at the date of the exchange, accumulated depreciation of $20,000 has been recorded. The assets exchanged are dissimilar (equipment and cash for inventory) and none of the requirements for book value accounting are met. The inventory acquired should be recorded at the fair value of the items given up ($100,000 + $10,000). The calculation of gain or loss on the exchange is shown below.

Fair Value of Equipment	$100,000
Cash Paid	10,000
Total Fair Value of Assets Surrendered	$110,000

Book Value of Equipment ($95,000 – $20,000)	(75,000)
Book Value of Cash	(10,000)
Gain on Exchange	$25,000

Because the fair value ($110,000) assigned to the asset received is greater than the book value ($85,000) of the assets given up, a gain on the exchange will be recognized. The entry required to record the exchange transaction is as follows:

Inventory	110,000	
Accumulated Depreciation—Equipment	20,000	
Equipment		95,000
Cash		10,000
Gain on Nonmonetary Exchange		25,000

Because the fair value of the cash paid always is equal to the book value, a boot paid in cash will not affect the determination of the gain or loss. However, if the boot were paid in some other monetary asset, such as a receivable, there could be a difference between fair value and book value that would impact the gain or loss.

Nonreciprocal Transfers—General Considerations

If an entity enters into a nonmonetary transaction (Block 1), if none of the conditions for book value accounting are met (Blocks 2–4), and if the transaction does not qualify as an exchange transaction (Block 5), it will be classified as a nonreciprocal transfer between owners or between an owner and another entity. Nonreciprocal transfers include property dividends to owners, gifts from municipalities, gifts to other entities, and reacquisitions of an enterprise's stock by transfer of nonmonetary assets rather than cash.

Generally, nonmonetary items involved in a nonreciprocal transfer should be recorded at their fair value, and any resulting gain or loss would be recognized. The gain or loss is measured by the difference between the fair value and the book value of the nonmonetary asset transferred. However, there are exceptions to this general rule. The exceptions include nonreciprocal transfers of nonmonetary assets to owners in a liquidation or reorganization, such as a spin-off, or in a plan that repeals, in substance, a business combination consummated prior to the transfer (Block 6—ASC 845-10-30-10). For these exceptions, the item(s) transferred should be accounted for at book value, rather than at fair value. If it can be demonstrated that the item transferred has suffered an impairment in value below book value, it would be appropriate to recognize a loss on the transfer. However, it is never appropriate to recognize a gain from these nonreciprocal transfers considered to be exceptions to the general rule.

Nonreciprocal Transfers—Technical Considerations

To illustrate the technical aspects of accounting for nonreciprocal transfers, assume that Book-It, Inc. distributes its investment in the shares of Speculation Company as a property dividend to existing stockholders. The investment in

Speculation Company was accounted for using the cost method. The stock to be distributed currently is selling for $75,000 and has a book value to Book-It, Inc., of $60,000.

This transaction involves a nonmonetary asset (investment) and because none of the requirements for book value accounting are met (Blocks 2–4), fair value accounting is appropriate. Because this is a one-way transfer, the transaction cannot be classified as an exchange transaction. Therefore, the transaction must represent a nonreciprocal transfer. Because the investment is carried on the cost basis, the transaction should be accounted for using fair value of the item transferred. In this particular case, the recorded value of the dividend should be $75,000. The difference between the fair value ($75,000) and the book value ($60,000) of the stock represents a gain of $15,000 to be recognized. Based upon this information, the following journal entries are required.

Investment in Speculation Company Stock	15,000	
Gain Due to Market Increase of Investment		15,000
Retained Earnings	75,000	
Property Dividend Payable		75,000
Property Dividend Payable	75,000	
Investment in Speculation Company Stock		75,000

Had the investment in Speculation Company been carried on the equity basis rather than on the cost basis, the transaction would have been treated as a spin-off and book value would have been the appropriate accounting value to use.

A second example of a nonreciprocal transfer would result from the assumptions that Book-It, Inc. wants to construct a plant in the town of Rogers; to induce Book-It to locate in Rogers, the city government has agreed to donate land with a fair value of $200,000 to the company for use as a plant site; and to secure the land, Book-It, Inc. agreed that it will hire at least 100 residents of Rogers in the next five years. This example represents a nonreciprocal transfer (only Book-It, Inc. received an asset) with a performance agreement. The presence of a performance agreement does not alter the general rule for recording nonreciprocal transfers. Therefore, Book-It, Inc. would record the value of the plant site at $200,000. The following journal entry is needed to record the transfer:

Land Held for Future Plant Site	200,000	
Revenue From Plant Site Donation		200,000

Exchanges and Transfers When Book Value Accounting Is Required

This portion of the material focuses on the problems of accounting for nonmonetary exchanges where the earnings process is *not* culminated. It is divided into nonmonetary exchanges not involving boot and nonmonetary exchanges involving boot.

Nonmonetary Exchanges Not Involving Boot

Book value accounting for nonmonetary transactions not involving boot is required for the following situations: fair value cannot be determined (Block 2), the transaction is for the purpose of facilitating sales to customers, the transaction lacks commercial substance (Block 4), or the transaction is a business reorganization or liquidation (Block 6). When accounting for nonmonetary exchanges at book value, the first step is to determine if there is any impairment in book value of the item surrendered. The entity should first compare the fair value of the item surrendered with the book value of the item surrendered (Block 8). If fair value is less than book value, an impairment of the asset is indicated, the item received is recorded at the fair value of the item surrendered, and a loss is reported on the transaction. However, if fair value is equal to or greater than book value, the item received is recorded at the book value of the item surrendered.

To illustrate a situation where both the fair value of the item given up and the fair value of the item received cannot be determined within reasonable limits, assume that Jones, Inc. exchanged inventory with a book value of $50,000 for a parcel of land. Because the fair value of either item is reasonably determinable, the land would be recorded at the book value of the inventory and no gain or loss is reported on the exchange. The entry to reflect the exchange would be:

Land	50,000	
Inventory		50,000

To illustrate a situation where the nonmonetary exchange is a transaction for the purpose of facilitating sales to customers, assume that Eric Enterprises exchanges inventory with a recorded value of $150,000 for other inventory with a current selling price of $135,000 and no boot is involved in the transaction. Because this is an exchange of inventory with no boot to facilitate sales to customers other than the parties to the transaction, the first step is to determine if a loss is indicated from any impairment of book value of the inventory exchanged. Because the fair value of the inventory received is less than the book value of the inventory surrendered, a loss of $15,000 ($150,000 - $135,000) is indicated and must be recognized. The entry necessary to record this exchange of inventory is as follows:

Inventory	135,000	
Loss on nonmonetary exchange	15,000	
Inventory		150,000

If the nonmonetary exchange does not indicate a loss, and there is no boot involved in the transaction (Block 9), the nonmonetary asset received is recorded at the book value of the item surrendered. If the asset received is assigned the book value of the asset surrendered, no gain will result (and the possibility of a loss has been ruled out). To illustrate, assume the same facts in the prior example of an exchange of inventory for inventory to facilitate sales to customers, except assume the inventory received has a current selling price of $160,000. Because the fair value of the inventory received is greater that the book value of the inventory surrendered, no loss is indicated, and because a gain cannot be recognized, the inventory received is reported at the book value of the inventory surrendered. The entry to report this exchange is presented as follows:

Inventory	150,000	
Inventory		150,000

To illustrate another transaction that requires book value accounting, assume that Price Enterprises exchanges Equipment A, a productive asset, for similar Equipment B. The exchange lacks commercial substance. Equipment A has a cost basis of $100,000; and, at the date of exchange, accumulated depreciation of $50,000 had been recorded. Equipment A currently has a fair value of $75,000. Equipment B also has a fair value of $75,000.

Because this transaction lacks commercial substance, the first step is to determine if the exchange transaction indicates a loss. The fair market value of the asset transferred ($75,000) is greater than the book value of $50,000 ($100,000 - $50,000), and therefore a gain, not a loss, is indicated. Because the transaction lacks commercial substance, the gain cannot be recognized, and the asset received is recorded at the book value of the asset surrendered. The entry required to reflect this exchange is as follows:

Equipment B	50,000	
Accumulated depreciation—equipment A	50,000	
Equipment A		100,000

Equipment B now has a depreciable cost basis of $50,000, which is the book value of Equipment A.

Nonmonetary items involved in a nonreciprocal transfer should be recorded at their book values, after any indicated impairment, with no gain reported when the nonreciprocal transfer is a spin-off or other business reorganization or liquidation (Block 8). A distribution of stock to owners from an investment in a company that is either consolidated or accounted for using the equity method is considered a spin-off for purposes of accounting for such distributions.

To illustrate the technical aspects of a nonreciprocal transfer accounted for using book value, assume that Johnson Enterprises distributes its investment in the shares of Enterprise, Inc. as a property dividend to existing stockholders. The investment in Enterprise, Inc. is accounted for using the equity method because Johnson Enterprises has a 35% ownership in Enterprise, Inc. The stock to be distributed currently is selling for $100,000 and has a book value to Johnson Enterprises of $75,000. Because this investment is accounted for using the equity method and there is an indicated gain of $25,000 ($100,000 - $75,000), the gain is not reported and the distribution is made at the book value of $75,000. The following entries illustrate the declaration of the dividend and the transfer of the stock.

Retained earnings	75,000	
Property dividend payable		75,000
Property dividend payable	75,000	
Investment in Enterprise, Inc.		75,000

Assume the same information as above, except that Enterprise, Inc. stock is currently selling for $60,000. An impairment of $15,000 ($75,000 - $60,000) is indicated and a $15,000 loss must be reported on the nonreciprocal transfer. The entries to record the declaration and payment of the property dividend are shown below:

Loss on decline in market value	15,000	
Investment in Enterprise, Inc.		15,000
Retained earnings	60,000	
Property dividend payable		60,000
Property dividend payable	60,000	
Investment in Enterprise, Inc.		60,000

Nonmonetary Exchanges Involving Boot

When a company enters into a nonmonetary transaction (Block 1) where book value accounting is required (Blocks 2, 3, and 4) and boot is involved (Block 9), the test to determine if a loss is indicated (Block 8) is still applicable. Once it has been determined that a loss is not indicated, the accounting for the transaction depends on whether the company paid or received the boot (Block 10).

The entity paying the boot is required to record the asset received at an amount equal to the monetary consideration paid, plus the book value of the item surrendered. Accordingly, a gain would not be recognized on this type of exchange. As before, if a loss is indicated, it should be recognized in full at the date of the exchange.

The entity receiving the boot is considered to have sold a portion of the asset exchanged; therefore, it is appropriate to recognize a gain on the portion sold. The gain is limited to the extent that the boot received exceeds the proportionate share of the asset sold. The asset received by the entity is recorded at an amount equal to the book value of the item surrendered, less the portion of the book value sold. Any indicated losses would be recognized in full.

To illustrate the technical aspects of nonmonetary exchanges involving monetary consideration, assume that Book-It, Inc. and Jar, Inc. exchange nonmonetary assets where the transaction lacks commercial substance. Book-It, Inc. surrenders Equipment A and $5,000 cash for Equipment B, which is held by Jar, Inc. Specific information about the two pieces of equipment is shown in Example 8-42.

Example 8-42
Exchange Assumptions

	Equipment A (Book-It, Inc.)	Equipment B (Jar, Inc.)
Cost	$100,000	$90,000
Accumulated Depreciation	20,000	15,000
Book Value	$80,000	$75,000
Fair Market Value	$65,000	$70,000

Because the transaction lacks commercial substance, book value accounting with any indicated impairment of book value is appropriate. The first test is to determine if a loss on the exchange is indicated. Considering Book-It, Inc. first, the loss would be determined as follows:

Book Value of Equipment	$80,000
Book Value of Cash	5,000
Total Book Value	$85,000
Fair Value of Equipment Surrendered	(65,000)
Fair Value of Cash Surrendered	(5,000)
Loss on Exchange	$15,000

Because the fair value ($70,000) of the items surrendered is less than the book value ($85,000) of the equipment and cash, a loss of $15,000 is indicated. When a loss is indicated, the value assigned to the nonmonetary asset received is the fair value ($70,000) of the items surrendered. The loss must be recognized in full. The entry necessary to record the exchange is:

Equipment B	70,000	
Accumulated Depreciation—Equipment A	20,000	
Loss on Nonmonetary Exchange	15,000	
Equipment A		100,000
Cash		5,000

In the situation described above, the asset received must be recorded at fair value because generally accepted accounting principles prohibit recording assets at more than fair value on the date of the transaction.

Next, an analysis of the effect of the transaction on Jar, Inc. must be made. For the same reasons stated above, book value accounting with a possible indicated impairment of book value is appropriate with the possible loss test being applied. The determination of the loss would be accomplished as follows:

Book Value of Equipment Surrendered	$75,000
Fair Value of Equipment Surrendered	70,000
Loss on Exchange	$5,000

Because fair value is less than book value, a loss is indicated on the exchange. The value of the nonmonetary asset received should be equal to its fair value of $65,000. The $5,000 loss should be recognized in full. The necessary journal entry is presented below.

Cash	5,000	
Equipment A	65,000	
Accumulated Depreciation—Equipment B	15,000	
Loss on Nonmonetary Exchange	5,000	
Equipment B		90,000

The preceding example illustrated the accounting for a nonmonetary exchange where a loss was indicated. To depict a similar exchange where a gain is present, assume that Book-It, Inc. and Jar, Inc. exchange nonmonetary assets in a transaction that lacks commercial substance. Book-It, Inc. exchanges Equipment A and $5,000 cash for Equipment B, which is held by Jar, Inc. Specific information relating to the two pieces of equipment is shown in Example 8-43.

Example 8-43
Exchange Assumptions

	Equipment A (Book-It, Inc.)	Equipment B (Jar, Inc.)
Cost	$100,000	$90,000
Accumulated Depreciation	20,000	15,000
Book Value	$80,000	$75,000
Fair Market Value	$95,000	$100,000

Again, the first step is to determine whether a loss is indicated. Turning first to Book-It, Inc., the fair value of $95,000 is greater than the book value of $80,000; therefore, no loss is indicated. Because Book-It, Inc. is the payer of the boot, no gain can be recognized on the exchange (Block 10). The asset received, Equipment B, is recorded at an amount equal to the book value of the asset surrendered, Equipment A, plus the boot paid. In this particular case, the amount assigned to Equipment B would be calculated as follows:

Book Value of Asset Surrendered	$80,000
Cash Paid	5,000
Amount Assigned to Equipment B	$85,000

The following journal entry is required on the books of Book-It, Inc. to record the nonmonetary exchange.

Equipment B	85,000	
Accumulated Depreciation—Equipment A	20,000	
Equipment A		100,000
Cash		5,000

For Jar, Inc., the fair market value of $100,000 is greater than the $75,000 book value of the asset. Therefore, no loss is indicated. On the contrary, a gain is indicated and Jar, Inc., as recipient of the boot, must recognize a portion of the gain. The amount of gain to be recognized is determined by the following formula:

$$G = MC - \left[\left(\frac{MC}{MC + FAR}\right)(BV)\right]$$

Where:	G	=	Gain to be recognized.
	MC	=	Monetary consideration received.

FAR	=	Fair value of asset received (or, if more clearly determinable, the fair value of the asset surrendered).
BV	=	Book value of the asset surrendered.

Using this formula and the information given above, the gain to be recognized is calculated as follows:

$$G = \$5{,}000 - [(\frac{\$\,5{,}000}{\$\,5{,}000 + 95{,}000})\ (\$75{,}000)]$$

$$G = \$1,\,250$$

The expression is used to determine the percentage of the book value of the asset considered to be sold is:

$$MC = MC + FAR$$

Next, the amount to be recorded as the value of the asset received must be calculated, using a similar formula. The formula used for this purpose is presented below.

$$A = BV - [(\frac{MC}{MC + FAR})\ (BV)]$$

Where:			
	A	=	Amount recorded for the asset received.
	BV	=	Book value of asset surrendered.
	MC	=	Monetary consideration received.
	FAR	=	Fair value of asset received (or, if more clearly determinable, the fair value of the asset surrendered).

Using this formula and the related information, the amount to be used for the asset received can be calculated as follows:

$$A = \$75{,}000 - [(\frac{\$5{,}000}{\$5{,}000 + \$95{,}000})\ (\$75{,}000)]$$

$$A = \$71{,}250$$

Based upon the information generated from the two formulas, the following journal entry is required by Jar, Inc. to record the exchange:

Equipment A	71,250	
Accumulated Depreciation—Equipment B	15,000	
Cash	5,000	
Equipment B		90,000
Gain on Nonmonetary Exchange		1,250

Income Tax Considerations

A difference may exist between the financial reporting and tax reporting of gains and losses on nonmonetary transactions. Any difference is considered to be a temporary difference and is accounted for in accordance with the provisions of ASC 740.

Disclosure Requirements

The disclosure requirements of ASC 845-10 are minor in nature and include the following items:

1. A description of the nature of the nonmonetary transactions, as well as of the accounting basis used for the transferred assets, must be disclosed; and
2. Gains and losses on nonmonetary exchanges must be disclosed.

Recent Changes

The guidance in ASC 845, *Nonmonetary Transactions,* as discussed above is substantially reduced under ASU 2017-05, *Other Income—Gains and Losses from the Derecognition of Nonfinancial Assets (Subtopic 610-20): Clarifying the Scope of Asset Derecognition Guidance and Accounting for Partial Sales of Nonfinancial Assets.* ASU 2017-05 was issued in February 2017 as complementary update to ASU 2017-01, *Business Combinations (Topic 805): Clarifying the Definition of a Business.* ASU 2017-05, which updates ASC 610-20, provides guidance for most nonmonetary transactions with noncustomers. As such, refer to Chapter 6 above. However, purchases and sales of inventory with the same counterparty and barter transactions when the counterparty is not a customer continue to be in the scope of ASC 845 discussed above.

The amendments in ASU 2017-05 are effective at the same time an entity adopts the new revenue guidance in ASC 606. Therefore, for public business entities with calendar year-ends, the standard is effective on January 1, 2018. All other entities have an additional year to adopt the guidance. Early adoption is permitted beginning January 1, 2017, for calendar year-end entities, provided adoption coincides with the adoption of the revenue standards. Entities may transition to ASU 2017-05 using either the full retrospective approach or the modified retrospective approach, regardless of the transition approach elected for the new revenue standard.

Topic 850: Related Party Disclosures

Topic 850, *Related Party Disclosures,* contains two subtopics:

10 Overall

972 Real Estate—Common Interest Realty Associations [See the corresponding topic in Chapter 9 for coverage of this shared subtopic]

ASC 850-10 specifies the disclosure requirements for related-party transactions. Transactions involving related parties typically are not conducted on an arm's-length basis. Generally, all transactions and events reported in financial statements are presumed to be completed on an arm's-length basis, unless otherwise indicated. Without disclosure of related-party transactions, users of financial information may be misled to believe that such transactions are consummated on an arm's-length basis. Consequently, the FASB feels that financial reports are more informative and reliable if related-party disclosures are required.

To better understand related parties and related-party transactions, a definition and examples are provided. Related parties represent a relationship where one party has the ability to influence the decisions of the other party. Examples of related-party transactions include transactions between affiliated companies, parent and subsidiary companies, companies under common control, pension plans and other such plans of an enterprise that are controlled by an entity's management, and entities and their principal owners, management, or immediate family members. (See ASC 850-10-05, paragraphs 3 through 5, for a more detailed description of related-party transactions.)

Several terms having special meaning were used in the examples above and must be defined for complete comprehension. The definitions below (from ASC 850-10-20) should aid in the understanding of related-party transactions and disclosure requirements contained in ASC 850-10:

1. **Affiliate:** A party that, directly or indirectly through one or more intermediaries, controls, is controlled by, or is under common control with an entity.
2. **Control:** The possession, direct or indirect, of the power to direct or cause the direction of the management and policies of an entity through ownership, by contract, or otherwise.
3. **Management:** Persons who are responsible for achieving the objectives of the entity and who have the authority to establish policies and make decisions by which those objectives are to be pursued.
4. **Principal owners:** Owners of record or known beneficial owners of more than 10 percent of the voting interests of the entity.
5. **Immediate family:** Family members who might control or influence a principal owner or a member of management, or who might be controlled or influenced by a principal owner or a member of management, because of the family relationship.

ASC 850-10-50 requires disclosure of all material related-party transactions. The following disclosures are required:

1. Nature of the related-party relationship.
2. Receivables or payables associated with related-party transactions for each date that a balance sheet is presented and, if not clearly determinable, the conditions and methods of settlement.
3. For each period that an income statement is presented, the following is required:
   a. A description of transactions and other necessary information needed for an understanding of the impact of the transactions.
   b. Dollar amounts assigned to transactions and the impact of determining the terms of the transactions if different from prior periods.
4. A company that is part of a group of entities that files a consolidated tax return must disclose the following information in financial statements issued separately (see ASC 740-10-50-17).

a. For each period that an income statement is presented, the amount of current and deferred tax expense.

b. For each date that a balance sheet is prepared, the amount of any tax-related balances due to or from affiliates.

c. The provisions of the method, and any changes in the method, used to allocate current and deferred tax expense to members of the consolidated group.

If two or more companies are under common control via ownership or management, the disclosure in item 1, above, is required, even though no transaction occurred, if the common control could have a material impact on the financial statements of the reporting company.

The preceding disclosures are not required for transactions eliminated in consolidated or combined reports and transactions such as compensation and expense allowance arrangements.

ASC 460-10 requires disclosures in addition to the disclosures required in ASC 850-10 for entities that meet the definition of a related party where controlling interest cannot be determined by reviewing voting interests. See detailed disclosure requirements specified by ASC 460-10 in Chapter 4.

Topic 852: Reorganizations

Topic 852, *Reorganizations*, contains three subtopics:

10 Overall

20 Quasi-Reorganizations

740 Income Taxes

ASC 852-10 provides financial accounting and reporting guidelines for entities involved in reorganization proceedings under bankruptcy. The subtopic indicates how the basic financial statements should be presented to reflect the reorganization proceedings and provides examples of such statements.

ASC 852-20 provides financial accounting and reporting guidelines for entities involved in quasi-reorganizations. A quasi-reorganization is a restatement of assets, capital, and retained earnings generally effected to correct the over valuation of company assets that may have resulted in a retained earnings deficit. Generally, the assets are adjusted to fair value, and the loss is written off to retained earnings. If retained earnings is reduced to zero, the remaining loss reduces paid-in-capital. A new retained earnings account should be established and dated as of the date of the quasi-reorganization. This dating of retained earnings should continue until it is no longer important, which is usually within 10 years of the quasi-reorganization (ASC 852-20-50-2).

Topic 853: Service Concession Arrangement

ASC Topic 853 contains a single Subtopic, ASC 853-10, *Overall.*

ASC 853 provides guidance for private entities engaged by governmental entities to operate government-owned airports, toll roads, bridges, etc. under "concession arrangements." Previously, U.S. GAAP did not contain specific guidance for such concession arrangements. Under the added guidance, concession arrangements should not be accounted for as leases by the private operating entity nor should the private operating entity recognize the infrastructure used under the concession arrangement as its property, plant, and equipment.

Recent Changes

ASU 2017-10, *Service Concession Arrangements (Topic 853): Determining the Customer of the Operation Services*, was issued in May 2017 to address disparity in practice of determining who the customer in a service concession arrangement is. Under this Update, the grantor (government) is the customer, in all instances when Topic 853 applies.

The new guidance will be effective at the time the reporting entity adopts Topic 606 if it has not already adopted Topic 606. A public business entity which has already adopted Topic 606 is required to apply this Update in its fiscal year beginning after December 15, 2017. A non-public entity which has already adopted Topic 606 is required to apply this Update in its fiscal year beginning after December 15, 2018. Lastly, this Update can be adopted on a full or modified retrospective basis

Topic 855: Subsequent Events

Topic 855, *Subsequent Events*, contains two subtopics:

10 Overall

926 Entertainment—Films [See the corresponding topic in Chapter 9 for coverage of this shared subtopic]

ASC 855-10-20 requires non-public companies to disclose the date through which subsequent events have been evaluated and whether the date is either the date the financial statements were issued or the date the financial statements were available to be issued.

ASC 855-10-S99-2 states that "financial statements are 'issued' as of the date they are distributed for general use and reliance in a form and format that complies with U.S. generally accepted accounting principles (U.S. GAAP) and, in the case of annual financial statements, that contain an audit report that indicates that the auditors have complied with generally accepted auditing standards (GAAS) in completing their audit."

Topic 860: Transfers and Servicing

Topic 860, *Transfers and Servicing*, contains five subtopics:

10 Overall

20 Sales of Financial Assets

30 Secured Borrowing and Collateral

40 Transfers to Qualifying Special Purpose Entities

50 Servicing Assets and Liabilities

Introduction

ASC 860 covers the accounting and reporting requirements for the transfer and servicing of financial assets. The discussion of ASC 860 is divided into the following five areas: (1) accounting for the transfer of financial assets, (2) accounting for servicing of assets and liabilities and prepayment of securities, (3) accounting for secured debt and collateral, (4) other considerations, and (5) disclosure requirements.

ASC 860-10-40-24 provides clarification for determining when two debt securities are essentially the same instruments. It lists six criteria that must be met for the securities to be essentially the same instrument. This issue is important when an entity is attempting to determine whether the exchange of debt instruments should be accounted for as a financing or a sale.

Accounting for the Transfer of Financial Assets

Financial assets are cash, an ownership interest in another entity, and the contractual right of one enterprise to receive cash, or another financial instrument, or to exchange financial instruments on potentially favorable terms with another enterprise. When financial assets are transferred, the transfer is treated as a sale when the entity (the transferor or seller) transferring the assets relinquishes control over them assuming consideration, exclusive of beneficial interest, is received in the transfer. A transfer of financial assets is assumed to be a sale (the seller has surrendered control) if all the criteria below are met:

1. The entity transferring the assets and its creditors do not have access to the assets transferred (i.e., the transferred assets have been isolated and are beyond the reach of the transferor and its creditors).
2. The buyer or transferee, or holders of an interest in a qualifying special purpose entity (SPE) (the transferee) have the right to exchange or pledge the assets or interest and there are no conditions that would prevent the transferee from exercising the right and provide a benefit to the transferor other than a trivial benefit.
3. The entity transferring the assets does not maintain effective control of the assets by means of one of the following: (a) an agreement that both entitles and obligates the transferor to repurchase or redeem the assets prior to their maturity; (b) an agreement that provides the transferor with the unilateral ability to cause the holder to return specific financial assets and a more than trivial benefit; and (c) an agreement that permits the transferee to require the transferor to repurchase the transferred assets at a price that is so favorable to the transferee that it is probable that the transferee will require the transferor to repurchase them.

If the transfer of financial assets is classified as a sale, the assets sold should be removed from the books (i.e., derecognized). However, if the transferor continues to hold any interest in the assets sold, the cost or carrying basis of the assets should be allocated between the assets sold and the assets that continue to be held by the transferor. The allocation of the carrying basis of the assets is based on their fair values on the transfer date. The assets that continue to be held by the transferor would be reported in the balance sheet equal to the amount computed in the allocation process. Record any assets received and any liabilities incurred in the exchange at fair value. Any difference between the carrying value of the assets transferred and the fair value of the assets received and liabilities incurred in the transaction would be reported as a gain or loss. If the seller (transferor) in the transaction is unable to estimate the fair value of the assets received as consideration in the exchange, such assets should be reported at zero. When the seller is unable to determine the fair value of any liabilities incurred in the transaction, a gain should not be reported on the exchange, and the liabilities should be reported at the larger of the amount reported using ASC 450, or the amount that the assets received less other liabilities incurred on a fair value basis exceeds the total of the carrying amounts of the transferred assets. When practicable, any servicing assets and servicing liabilities should be initially measured and reported at fair value when the provisions of ASC 860-50 require recognition (see the section on accounting of servicing assets and liabilities for a complete discussion).

The buyer (transferee) of assets in a transfer of financial assets should report the assets received and any liabilities incurred at fair value in the statement of financial position.

A transfer of financial assets is treated as a secured obligation with collateral pledged by both the buyer and seller when the transaction does not meet the requirements for treatment as a sale.

Fair values used in ASC 860 are determined using the provisions of ASC 820.

Accounting for Secured Debt and Collateral

This situation exists when a debtor (transferor) gives to the secured party (hereafter the creditor or transferee) a security interest in assets that is used as collateral for a debt. If the debtor transfers the collateral to the secured party, the debtor has pledged the property and the secured party in some cases may repledge or sell the pledged property. The accounting requirements for such a noncash transaction depend on the content of the agreement.

If the transferee can repledge or sell the collateral, the asset should be reclassified by the transferor and reported as a separate asset in its balance sheet. Should the transferee or creditor sell the pledged property, the transferee should report, as an asset, the consideration received from the transaction and a liability for the commitment to return the property to the debtor. The sale is considered a transfer and the appropriate accounting would be determined using the accounting and reporting requirements of ASC 860. If the debtor should default on the terms of the agreement and cannot redeem the asset pledged, the collateral should be removed from the books of the debtor and reported as an asset on the books of the transferee or creditor at fair value. If the collateral has been sold, the transferee should remove its liability to return the asset. Unless the transferor defaults on the terms of the agreement, as noted above, the debtor should continue to report the pledged property in its balance sheet, and the creditor or transferee should not report the property in its balance sheet.

Accounting for Servicing of Assets and Liabilities and Prepayments of Securities

This section of material covers the servicing of financial assets and prepayments of financial assets. Servicing of financial assets involves several functions such as interest and principal collections, payment of insurance and taxes, and handling foreclosures. When an enterprise enters into a contract to service financial assets, a servicing asset or a servicing liability is initially measured at fair value, when practicable. (See the section on transfer of financial assets for a discussion of methods used to measure the assets and liabilities when it is not practicable to determine fair value.) An entity generally enters into a servicing contact in one of the following situations:

- When the financial assets of the servicer are transferred and the transfer qualifies as a sale (see the section on accounting for the transfer of financial assets);
- When the financial assets of the servicer are transferred to a qualifying SPE in a guaranteed mortgage securitization and all the securities are retained by the transferor and the securities retained are classified using ASC 320 as trading securities or available-for-sale securities; or
- When a servicing obligation unrelated to the financial assets of the servicer or consolidated affiliates of the servicer is assumed or acquired.

When the financial assets of the servicer are transferred to a qualifying SPE in a guaranteed mortgage securitization and all the securities are retained by the transferor and the securities retained are classified using ASC 320 as held-to-maturity securities, the entity may elect to report the securities separately as servicing assets or servicing liabilities or to include them with the serviced asset.

Once servicing assets and servicing liabilities are reported, an enterprise may elect to use either the amortization method or the fair value measurement method when measuring each class of servicing assets and servicing liabilities subsequent to the initial measurement. The method chosen for each class of servicing assets and servicing liabilities must subsequently be applied to the class. That is, if the fair value measurement method is elected in year one for a class, the amortization method cannot be elected for the same class in year two.

Once an election is made, servicing assets and servicing liabilities cannot be moved from a class or group where the fair value measurement method was elected to a group that elected the amortization method. Servicing assets and servicing liabilities should be identified with classes based on the following criteria: (1) market input availability for determining fair value, (2) method of risk management related to its servicing assets and servicing liabilities, or (3) both (1) and (2).

When an entity elects the amortization method for a class of servicing assets and servicing liabilities, the assets and liabilities are written off (amortized) over the period of time of and in proportion to the net servicing income or loss. Net servicing income exists when servicing revenues are greater than servicing costs. Net servicing loss exists when servicing costs are greater than servicing revenues. When the amortization method is elected, servicing assets and servicing liabilities are assessed at each financial accounting reporting date using fair value on that date. If an entity elects the fair value measurement method, the servicing assets and servicing liabilities are reported at fair value on each financial reporting date and changes in fair value are reported in income in that accounting period. When an entity cannot determine fair value for its servicing assets and servicing liabilities because it is impracticable, the assets and liabilities should initially be measured as discussed in the transfer of financial assets section and included in a class that is measured using the amortization method.

An entity should report servicing assets and servicing liabilities separately in the statement of financial position. Separate reporting must be provided for classes of servicing assets and servicing liabilities electing the amortization method and for classes of servicing assets and servicing liabilities electing the fair value measurement method. The FASB allows two methods for the separate reporting: (1) report classes of assets and liabilities electing fair value as a line item and report classes of assets and liabilities electing the amortization method as a separate line item in the financial statements or (2) report one total amount for fair value and amortization methods and report, parenthetically, the amount of the assets and liabilities reported at fair value.

When an entity elects the amortization method for servicing assets and servicing liabilities, impairment on servicing assets should be measured for each class that is separately reported using the following evaluation and measurement method: (1) divide each class of servicing assets into individual stratum using one or more of the underlying risk characteristics (such as type, size, or interest rate) of the assets; (2) use a valuation allowance by individual stratum to recognize impairment equal to the excess of the carrying amount over the fair value of the servicing assets; and (3) change the valuation allowance to report changes in impairment measurement but do not recognize an excess of fair value over the carrying amount of the servicing assets.

A contractual agreement may allow for the prepayment of a security prior to its maturity date. When a security can be prepaid prior to maturity and the security holder cannot recoup most of the investment recorded in the financial statements, the security cannot be reported in the financial statements as held-to-maturity in accordance with ASC 320. However, such securities may be reported as available-for-sale or trading unless the provisions of ASC 815 cover the securities.

Disclosures under ASC 860

ASC 860 specifies the disclosure requirements for transfers and servicing of a nonpublic entity's financial assets.

Sales or Transfers of Financial Assets

The disclosures may be reported in the aggregate for similar transfers if separate reporting of each transfer would not provide more useful information. A transferor shall disclose how similar transfers are aggregated; and distinguish transfers that are accounted for as sales from those accounted for as secured borrowings.

1. For securitizations, asset-backed financing arrangements, and similar transfers accounted for as sales when the transferor has continuing involvement with the transferred financial assets:

   a. For each period for which an income statement is presented disclose:

      (1) The characteristics of the transfer, including (i) a description of the transferor's continuing involvement, (ii) the nature and initial fair value of the assets obtained as proceeds and the liabilities incurred in the transfer, and (iii) the gain or loss from the sales of transferred assets.

      (2) For initial fair value measurements in (1) the (i) level within the fair value hierarchy that the fair value of the measurement in their entirety fall segregating fair value measurements using quoted prices in active markets for identical assets or liabilities (Level 1), significant other observable inputs (Level 2), and significant unobservable inputs (Level 3); (ii) the key inputs and assumptions (including but not limited to discount rates, expected payments, and anticipated credit losses); and (iii) the valuation techniques used.

      (3) Cash flows between the transferor and transferee, including proceeds from new transfers, proceeds collected on reinvested revolving-period transfers, purchases of previously transferred financial assets, servicing fees and proceeds received from the transferor's interests.

   b. For each period for which a balance sheet is presented disclose:

      (1) Qualitative and quantitative information about the transferor's continuing involvement with the transferred financial assets so users may assess the reasons for the continuing involvement and the related thereto, including (i) the principal amount outstanding, the amount derecognized, and the amount continued to be recognized in the balance sheet; (ii) the terms of any arrangement that could require the transferor to provide financial support; (iii) the type and amount and reasons the transferor has provided financial or other support during the periods presented; (iv) information about any liquidity arrangements, guarantees, or other commitments provided by third parties related to the transferred financial assets that may affect their fair value or the transferor's risk.

      (2) The transferor's accounting policies for subsequently measuring assets and liabilities for which the transferor has continuing involvement.

      (3) The key inputs and assumptions used to measure the fair value of the assets and liabilities in (2), above (including but not limited to discount rates, expected payments, and anticipated credit losses).

(4) For the transferor's interest in the transferred financial assets, a sensitivity analysis or stress test showing the hypothetical effect on the fair value for the key assumptions.

(5) Information about the quality of transferred financial assets and any other financial assets that the transferor manages separated between assets that have been derecognized and those that continue to be recognized in the balance sheet.

2. For sales of loans and trade receivables, disclose the aggregate amount of gains or losses.

Secured Borrowings and Collateral

1. If the secured party (transferee) has the right to sell or repledge the collateral, the obligor (transferor) should report the collateral separately in its balance sheet.
2. Liabilities incurred by either the secured party or obligor in connection with securities borrowing or resale transactions are required to be separately classified in the balance sheet.
3. If the entity has entered into repurchase agreements or securities lending transactions, disclose its policy for requiring collateral or other security.
4. If the entity has pledged any of its assets as collateral that are not reclassified and separately reported in the balance sheet, disclose as of the date of the latest balance sheet presented (i) the carrying amounts and classifications of those pledged assets and associated liabilities and (ii) qualitative information about the relationship between the pledged assets and associated liabilities.
5. If the entity has accepted collateral that it is permitted to sell or pledge, disclose (i) the fair value of the collateral and (ii) the fair value of that portion of the collateral sold or repledged as of each balance sheet date and (iii) information about the sources and uses of that collateral.
6. Disclose the information required by paragraphs ASC 210-20-50-1 through 50-6 for (a) recognized repurchase agreements and reverse sale and repurchase agreements and (b) recognized securities borrowing and securities lending transactions that are either offset in accordance with ASC 210-20-45 or subject to an enforceable master netting arrangement or similar agreement.

Servicing Assets and Liabilities

1. If an entity subsequently measures separately recognized servicing assets and servicing liabilities using the fair value measurement method and presents the aggregate of (a) those amounts that are subsequently measured at fair value and (b) those other amounts that are separately recognized and subsequently measured using the amortization method, disclose parenthetically on the face of the balance sheet the amount that is subsequently measured at fair value that is included in the aggregate amount.

2. For all servicing assets and servicing liabilities disclose (i) management's basis for determining its classes of servicing assets and servicing liabilities; (ii) a description of the risks inherent in servicing assets and servicing liabilities and the instruments used to mitigate the income statement effect of changes in fair value of the servicing assets and servicing liabilities; (iii) the amount of contractually specified servicing fees, late fees, and ancillary fees earned for each period for which an income statement is presented, including where each amount is reported in the income statement; and (iv) quantitative and qualitative information about the assumptions used to estimate fair value.

3. For each class of servicing assets and servicing liabilities subsequently measured at fair value disclose for each period presented (i) where changes in fair value are reported in the income statement and (ii) the activity in the servicing assets and liabilities, including but not limited to (a) beginning and ending balances, (b) additions, (c) disposals, (d) changes in fair value resulting from changes in inputs or assumptions used in the valuation model and other changes in fair value, and (e) other changes that affect the balance.

4. For each class of servicing assets and servicing liabilities subsequently measured using the amortization method disclose for each period presented (i) where changes in the carrying amount are reported in the income statement; (ii) the activity in the servicing assets and liabilities, including but not limited to (a) beginning and ending balances, (b) additions, (c) disposals, (d) amortization, (e) valuation allowance adjustments, (f) other-than-temporary impairments, and (g) other changes that affect the balance; (iii) the fair value of recognized servicing assets and servicing liabilities at the beginning and end of the periods presented; (iv) the risk characteristics of the underlying financial assets used to stratify recognized servicing assets for purposes of measuring impairment in accordance with ASC 860-35-9; and (v) changes in the valuation allowance for impairment of recognized assets, including (a) beginning and ending balances, (b) aggregate additions charged to operations, (c) aggregate recoveries credited to operations, and (d) aggregate write-downs charged to the allowance.

5. If the entity makes an irrevocable decision at the beginning of the fiscal year to subsequently measure a class of servicing assets and servicing liabilities at fair value, disclose the amount of the cumulative-effect adjustment to retained earnings.

Recent Changes

ASU 2014-11, *Transfers and Servicing (Topic 860): Repurchase-to-Maturity Transactions, Repurchase Financings, and Disclosures,* amended the accounting guidance for "repo-to-maturity" transactions and repurchase agreements executed as repurchase financings. Under ASU 2014-11, repo-to-maturity transactions are reported as secured borrowings. Under prior standards, these transactions may have qualified for sale accounting if certain conditions were met. Transferors will no longer apply the current "linked" accounting model to repurchase agreements executed contemporaneously with the initial transfer of the underlying financial asset with the same counterparty. Under ASU 2014-11, the accounting for each transaction is instead evaluated on a standalone basis. As a result many of these repurchase agreements will be reported as secured borrowings.

CHAPTER 9
INDUSTRY

CONTENTS

The *Industry* area of the FASB *Accounting Standards Codification* contains the following topics:

905 Agriculture
908 Airlines
910 Contractors—Construction
912 Contractors—Federal Government
915 Development Stage Entities
920 Entertainment—Broadcasters
922 Entertainment—Cable Television
924 Entertainment—Casinos
926 Entertainment—Films
928 Entertainment—Music
930 Extractive Activities—Mining
932 Extractive Activities—Oil and Gas
940 Financial Services—Broker and Dealers
942 Financial Services—Depository and Lending
944 Financial Services—Insurance
946 Financial Services—Investment Companies
948 Financial Services—Mortgage Banking
950 Financial Services—Title Plant
952 Franchisors
954 Health Care Entities
958 Not-for-Profit Entities
960 Plan Accounting—Defined Benefit Pension Plans
962 Plan Accounting—Defined Contribution Pension Plans
965 Plan Accounting—Health and Welfare Benefit Plans
970 Real Estate—General
972 Real Estate—Common Interest Realty Associations
974 Real Estate—Real Estate Investment Trusts
976 Real Estate—Retail Land
978 Real Estate—Time-Sharing Activities
980 Regulated Operations
985 Software
995 U.S. Steamship Entities

Topic 905: Agriculture

Topic 905, *Agriculture*, contains 10 subtopics:

10 Overall

205 Presentation of Financial Statements

310 Receivables

325 Investments—Other

330 Inventory

360 Property, Plant, and Equipment

405 Liabilities

505 Equity

605 Revenue Recognition

705 Cost of Sales and Services

This topic is not covered in this book.

Topic 908: Airlines

Topic 908, *Airlines*, contains nine subtopics:

10 Overall

280 Segment Reporting

330 Inventory

350 Intangibles—Takeoff and Landing Slots

360 Property, Plant, and Equipment

605 Revenue Recognition

710 Compensation—General

720 Other Expenses

845 Nonmonetary Transactions

This topic is not covered in this book.

Topic 910: Contractors—Construction

Topic 910, *Contractors—Construction*, contains 10 subtopics:

10 Overall

20 Contract Costs

235 Notes to Financial Statements

310 Receivables

330 Inventory

340 Other Assets and Deferred Costs

360 Property, Plant, and Equipment

405 Liabilities

605 Revenue Recognition

810 Consolidation

This topic is not covered in this book.

Topic 912: Contractors—Federal Government

Topic 912, *Contractors—Federal Government*, contains 16 subtopics:

10 Overall

20 Contract Costs

210 Balance Sheet

225 Income Statement

235 Notes to Financial Statements

255 Changing Prices

275 Risks and Uncertainties

310 Receivables

330 Inventory

405 Liabilities

450 Contingencies

605 Revenue Recognition

705 Cost of Sales and Services

715 Compensation—Retirement Benefits

730 Research and Development

835 Interest

ASC 912 contains accounting and reporting requirements for government contracts. The material on government contracts covers issues related to cost-plus-fixed-fee contracts. Fees from contracts generally are reported in the financial statements as work is performed, using some acceptable basis such as recognition as items are delivered or as fees are billable. In addition, how the fees and reimbursable costs are included in the income statement depends on the type of contract. Some contracts are for the manufacturing of a product and others are service-related. Generally, when the contract is a manufacturing contract, both fees and reimbursable costs are included in some type of revenue account, such as sales, and reported in the income statement. When the contract is a service contract, only the fees are reported as part of revenue. Fees and costs that are not billed should be reported as receivables, separately from billed receivables. Amounts due from government contracts may only be offset against advances when such amounts can be used to offset at the time of settlement.

Topic 915: Development Stage Entities

Recent Change

In June 2014, ASU 2014-10, *Development Stage Entities (Topic 915): Elimination of Certain Financial Reporting Requirements, Including an Amendment to Variable Interest Entities Guidance in Topic 810, Consolidation*, eliminated the concept of development stage entities effective for annual reporting periods beginning after December 15, 2014. However, please see Chapter 2 (section 275-10-05-2, Risks and Uncertainties), for a discussion of amended disclosures for the nature of an entity's operations.

Topic 920: Entertainment—Broadcasters

Topic 920, *Entertainment—Broadcasters*, contains seven subtopics:

10 Overall

310 Receivables

350 Intangibles—Goodwill and Other

405 Liabilities

440 Commitments

605 Revenue Recognition

845 Nonmonetary Transactions

Discussion

ASC 920 is very narrow in scope, but it does propose some interesting accounting for license agreements relating to program material.

For purposes of ASC 920, a broadcaster may be viewed as an enterprise that transmits radio programs or television shows. A local station, as opposed to a network, would be defined as a broadcaster and is typically the licensee of radio or television materials. The entity providing programs to the broadcaster is the licensor in the license agreement. The broadcaster pays a fee to the licensor for the right to transmit one or more programs. The normal license agreement usually covers several programs and specifies the period of time during which the programs may be broadcast. The license period may cover more than one accounting period, and the broadcaster may have the right to transmit the programs several times. Payments for the license fee usually are made using an installment basis over a time period that is less than the license period.

Local stations may affiliate with a network or choose to remain independent. When dealing with a network, the affiliate is able to obtain programming at a lower cost than would the independent, because of the compensation system between a network and its affiliates.

ASC 920 requires the broadcaster to recognize an asset for the value of the right to acquire programming under a license agreement. In addition, the broadcaster is to recognize a liability for the obligation payable to the licensor. The asset and liability are to be recorded on the books of the broadcaster when the criteria listed below are met:

1. The license period has begun;
2. The broadcaster knows or can estimate each program's cost in the license package;
3. The licensee has accepted the programs; and
4. The programs are ready for showing for the first time.

The asset and liability should be valued at either the fair value of the liability or the liability's gross amount. When fair value is used, the provisions of ASC 820 on fair value accounting should be used to determine the appropriate fair value amount. When a present value is used to determine fair value, the difference between the net liability and the gross liability is considered interest. Any interest is accounted for using the provisions of ASC 835-30, *Imputation of Interest*.

Once the fair value or gross value of the program or package of programs has been determined, the cost should be apportioned to each program using relative fair values. In most cases, the relative value of each program is specified in the license agreement. The costs that are capitalized should be written off using the estimated number of showings in the future and the relative revenue produced by each showing. For example, a program may be broadcast three times, with the first broadcast producing 75% of the total expected revenue, the second broadcast producing 15%, and the final broadcast producing the remaining 10%. In this case, 75% of the capitalized cost should be amortized during the accounting period covering the first broadcast. If it is not possible to determine the number of future broadcasts, the capitalized costs should be amortized over the license period using the straight-line method. When earlier broadcasts produce more revenue than later broadcasts, an accelerated method may be used to amortize the capitalized costs. It would be difficult to determine the relative value of a program when one is unable to estimate the number of future broadcasts.

Capitalized costs are to be valued in the balance sheet at unamortized cost (if the gross value method is used) or net realizable value (if the present value method is used). Costs should be shown on a program-by-program or package basis and separated between current and noncurrent assets. If the value of these assets has been impaired, a loss should be recognized and a new cost basis established.

The costs associated with network affiliation agreements are classified as intangible assets by the broadcaster, and should be amortized according to the provisions of ASC 350, *Intangibles—Goodwill and Other*. If a broadcaster ends a network affiliation agreement, and does not intend to replace the agreement immediately, the unamortized cost of the intangible asset should be charged to income as an ordinary expense. If the agreement is to be replaced by another, a loss may be recognized to the extent that the unamortized intangible costs exceed the fair value of the new affiliation agreement.

It is a common industry practice for broadcasters to exchange advertising time that has not been sold for services or products that are of value to the station. These transactions should be reported at the anticipated fair value of the goods and services received using the fair value rules in ASC 820, *Fair Value Measurement*.

Revenue from these nonmonetary exchanges should be recognized when the advertising is aired, and the value of the assets received should be recorded as received. If the exchange is not completed at one time, a receivable or payable must be recorded until such time as the transaction is finalized.

The broadcaster is required to disclose any license agreement that was entered into but was not reported in the financial statements because it failed to meet the four criteria specified above.

Topic 922: Entertainment—Cable Television

Topic 922, *Entertainment—Cable Television*, contains seven subtopics:

10 Overall

350 Intangibles—Goodwill and Other

360 Property, Plant, and Equipment

430 Deferred Revenue

605 Revenue Recognition

720 Other Expenses

835 Interest

Discussion of the Standard

The cable television industry has experienced tremendous growth. In all but the smallest cable systems, heavy initial costs are incurred before significant revenue is produced. In addition, the cable system comes on-line or is energized in stages. It is likely that the entire system will not be energized for an extended period of time. During this preliminary or prematurity period, the company continues to incur substantial capital costs.

ASC 922 addresses the appropriate accounting for costs incurred in the preliminary or prematurity period, and the subsequent disposition of those costs. The prematurity period is defined in the pronouncement as the period of time during which part of the system is in service and part is under construction. The prematurity period begins when the first subscriber revenue is received. This is evidence that part of the system is in service. The end of the prematurity period will vary. It is obviously over when the entire system is in service and no additional capital expenditures are anticipated. However, the prematurity period may end coincidentally with the end of the first major construction period or when a certain predetermined number of subscribers have been obtained. In any case, it is assumed that the prematurity period will not be greater than two years from beginning to end. The prematurity period may be more than two years for cable companies that operate in major urban markets, where construction efforts may continue for a number of years. Management of the company must make a reasoned determination of the prematurity period at the time the first subscriber revenue is received. ASC 922 provides little guidance as to the determination of the prematurity period.

Proper accounting for cable television companies requires that the accountant be able to determine major portions or segments of the entire system. Proper recognition of a portion or segment of the system requires consideration of the following items:

1. Geographic area served;
2. Mechanical differences, such as different types of equipment used to receive signals or different types of studio facilities;
3. Construction or marketing differences;
4. Differences in the investment decisions affecting the segment, such as different break-even and return-on-investment analyses; and
5. Different accounting records, budgets, and forecasts.

Once a portion or segment of the system has been identified, proper accounting procedures may be implemented. Although charged to the segment should be specifically identified with that segment. While the system is in the prematurity period, costs of the cable television plant should be capitalized in full. Such costs would include materials, direct labor, and construction overhead. Subscriber-related costs and general and administrative expenses are charged to income in the current accounting period. Subscriber-related costs include all costs to obtain and keep subscribers on the system and would include billing and collection, mailing, repairs and maintenance, bad debts and franchise fees related to revenues or number of subscribers, and direct selling costs.

Remaining costs may be divided between programming-related costs and system costs. System costs would include such things as poles, underground duct, antenna site, microwave rental for the entire system, local origination programming, and property taxes based on valuation of the total system. Of these costs, those that will not vary significantly regardless of the number of subscribers should be allocated between current and future periods. A portion of programming and system costs will be expensed in the current period and the remainder will be capitalized and expensed in future periods. ASC 922 provides specific guidance in the determination and amount to be charged to income in the current period.

Each month the cable television company must compute the fractions shown in equations (1), (2), and (3) below.

$$(1)\quad \frac{\text{Average Number of Subscribers in Month as Estimated at Start of Prematurity Period}}{\text{Estimated Total Number of Subscribers at End of Prematurity Period}}$$

$$(2)\quad \frac{\text{Estimated Total Number of Subscribers} \div \text{Number of Months in Prematurity Period}}{\text{Estimated Total Number of Subscribers at End of Prematurity Period}}$$

$$(3)\quad \frac{\text{Average Number of Actual Subscribers in Month}}{\text{Estimated Total Number of Subscribers at End of Prematurity Period}}$$

One of these fractions is selected and used as a basis for determining depreciation and amortization of capitalized costs of the system. All three of the fractions are based on the relationship between the number of subscribers in the current month (either estimated or actual) and the total anticipated number of subscribers at the end of the prematurity period. The first equation, (1), uses the average month number of subscribers as estimated at the start of the prematurity period in the numerator. The second equation, (2), assumes that the number of subscribers will be added on a straight-line basis. The first step is to determine the average number of subscribers that will be added each month of the prematurity period and to use this number in the numerator of the equation to determine the fraction for the month. In the third equation, (3), the actual average number of monthly subscribers is used in the numerator. The accountant is required to select the fraction that results in the greatest percentage for the month. The equation that would be selected would be the one with the largest numerator, because it will yield the greatest percentage answer.

The fraction calculated is used to amortize the programming and system costs. The amount of these costs to be expensed in the current period is determined by multiplying the fraction, as determined above, by the total of such costs for the month. The computation of monthly depreciation will use the fraction developed above. The cable television company will calculate monthly depreciation on total costs expected to be capitalized during the prematurity period. This expected monthly depreciation will be reduced by the fraction selected that month. Programming and system costs that are capitalized should be depreciated in the same manner as other cable plant assets.

Cable television companies incur substantial costs to hook up the system in subscriber locations. There is usually a charge for installation of the cable system. The monies received for installation should be reported as revenue at an amount up to, but not to exceed, the direct selling costs. Any amount in excess of the direct selling costs should be deferred and recognized in income over the expected period of time the subscriber is estimated to stay on the system. Direct selling costs include commissions, the portion of a salesperson's compensation other than commissions for obtaining new subscribers, local advertising targeted for acquisition of new subscribers, the costs of processing documents related to new subscribers acquired. Direct selling costs do not include supervisory and administrative expenses or indirect expenses such as rent and costs of facilities.

Franchise costs incurred will be accounted for under the provisions of ASC 350, *Intangibles—Goodwill and Other*. The system must determine if the plant and intangible asset costs will be recoverable in the future. These assets should never be stated at more than the recoverable amount.

Topic 924: Entertainment—Casinos

Topic 924, *Entertainment—Casinos*, contains six subtopics:

10 Overall

280 Segment Reporting

405 Liabilities

605 Revenue Recognition

720 Other Expenses

740 Income Taxes

This topic is not covered in this book.

Topic 926: Entertainment—Films

Topic 926, *Entertainment—Films*, contains 12 subtopics:

10 Overall

20 Other Assets—Film Costs

230 Statement of Cash Flows

330 Inventory

405 Liabilities

430 Deferred Revenue

605 Revenue Recognition

705 Cost of Sales and Services

720 Other Expenses

835 Interest

845 Nonmonetary Transactions

855 Subsequent Events

This topic is not covered in this book.

Topic 928: Entertainment—Music

Topic 928, *Entertainment—Music*, contains seven subtopics:

10 Overall

340 Other Assets and Deferred Costs

405 Liabilities

430 Deferred Revenue

440 Commitments

605 Revenue Recognition

720 Other Expenses

Flowchart and General Discussion

ASC 928 deals with specialized accounting practices in the record and music industry. The accounting standards in ASC 928 are not complex, but the terminology of the record and music industry may prove confusing at first. ASC 928 is concerned with the recognition of revenues and expenses by record and music licensors and licensees. The license agreement is between the owner of the music or record (licensor) and the party seeking to sell or distribute the record or music (licensee). Of course, in some cases, the owner and distributor may be the same party. These agreements often involve the payment of royalties from the distributor to the owner. In other cases, the owner may make a sale of the music or record to the distributor, with no provision for future royalty payments.

Flowchart 9-1 depicts the accounting required for some common situations faced by the licensor of music or records. The first part of Flowchart 9-1, Blocks 2 through 5, indicates the conditions that must exist before it can be determined that the licensor has sold the rights to records or music owned. Given the existence of a license agreement (Block 1), the licensor must demonstrate that a non-cancellable contract has been signed (Block 2) and that the licensor has accepted a fixed fee, as opposed to a royalty, for the record or music (Block 3), has given the licensee the right to exercise the license (Block 4), and has no further obligation to furnish music or records under the agreement (Block 5), before the agreement will be viewed as a sale of the rights to the music or record. If all these conditions have been met, the licensor will record the fee received as revenue. If the fee is yet to be received, the licensor will recognize revenue to the extent that the collectibility of the fee is reasonably assured.

Flowchart 9-1

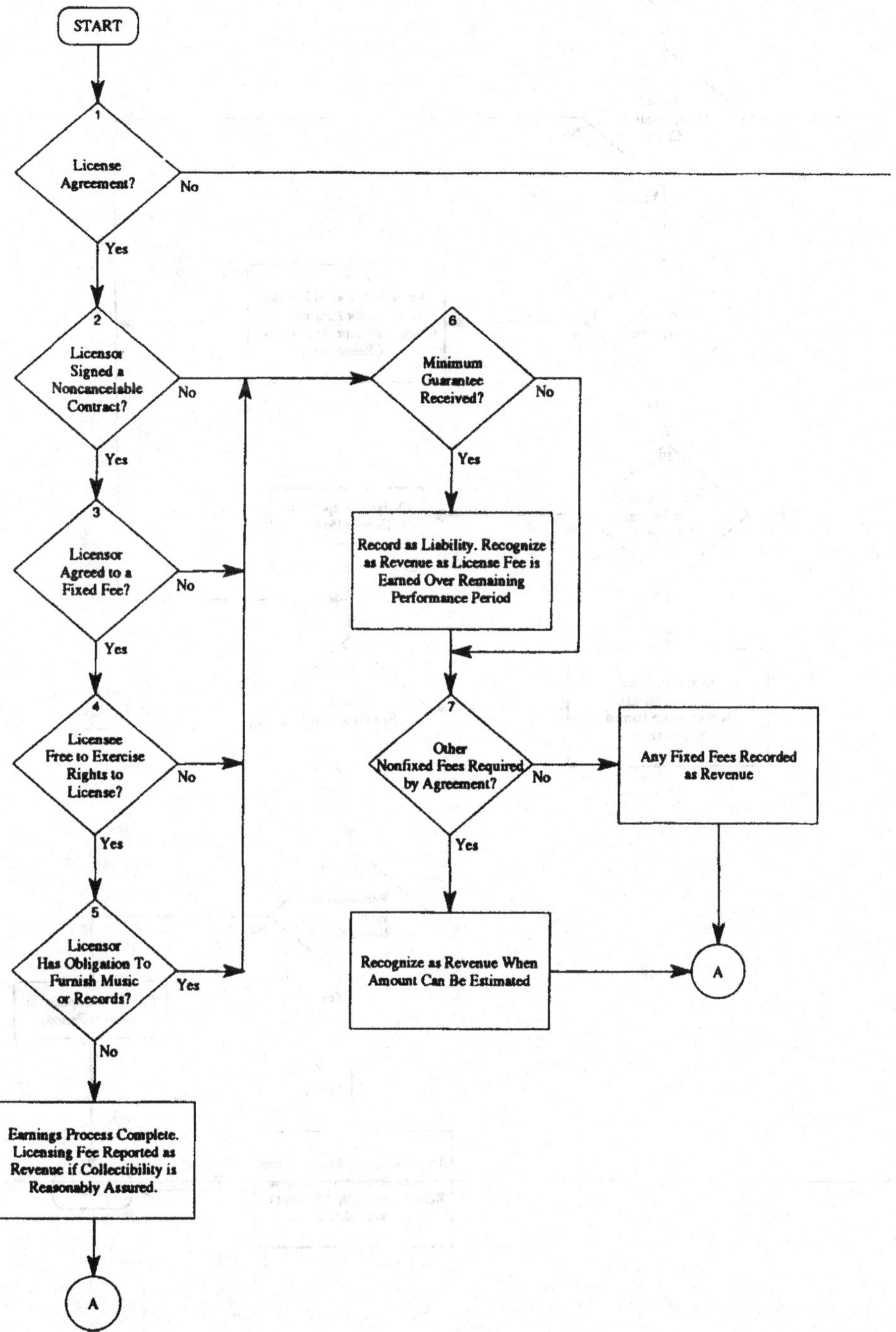

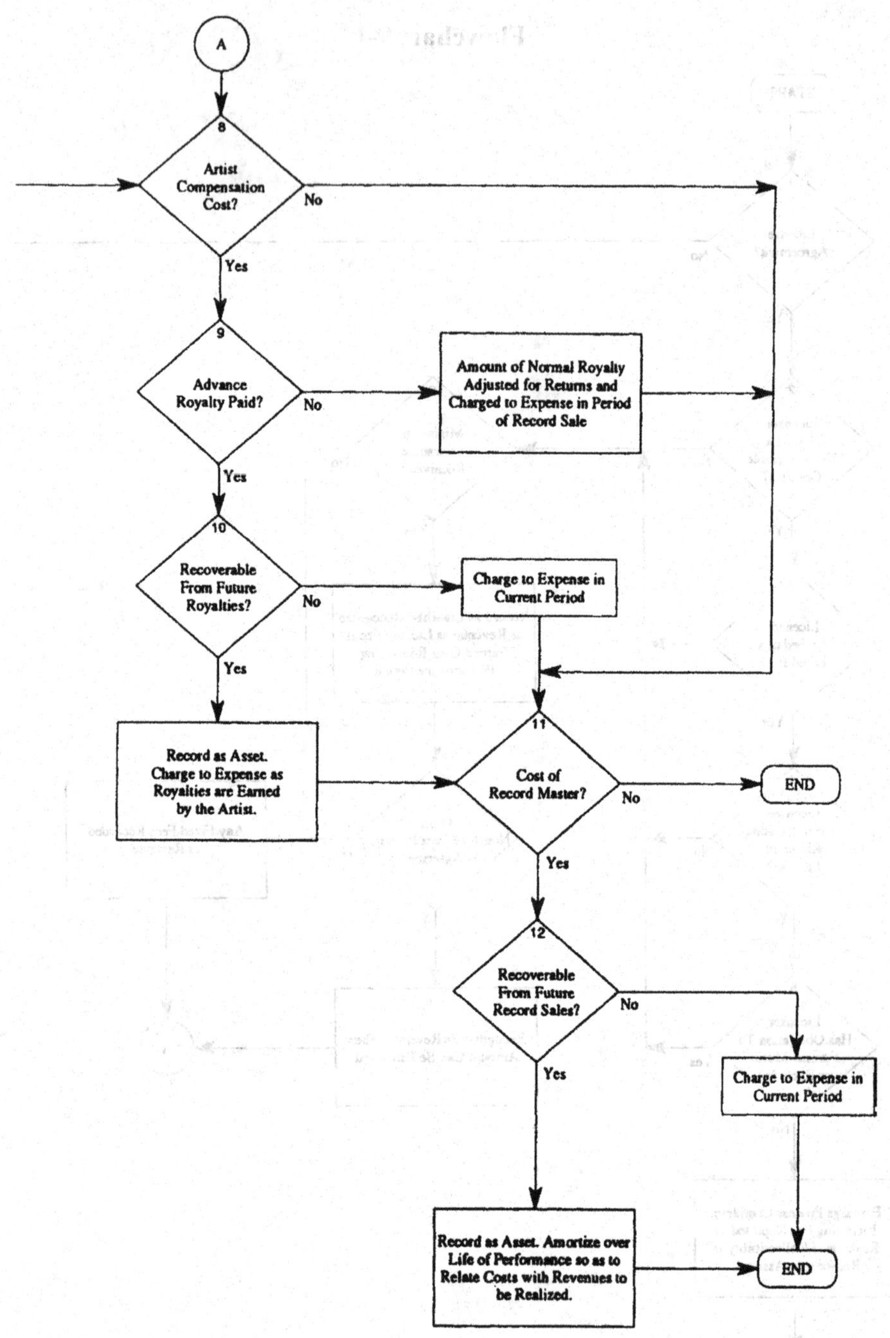

The license agreement may provide for the payment of a minimum guaranteed fee by the licensee (Block 6). This minimum guarantee would be paid for the right to sell or distribute records or music owned by the licensor. The licensor may earn fees in excess of the minimum guarantee, but accounting for the excess will be different. The amount of the minimum guarantee fee should be recorded initially as a liability by the licensor and recognized as revenue as any licensee fee is earned. If the license fees to be earned cannot be determined, the licensor should recognize the liability as revenue over the remaining performance period, which is usually the period covered by the license agreement.

Other fees that are not fixed in nature may be required by the license agreement (Block 7). These fees should be recognized as revenue only if a reasonable estimate of their amount can be made. If it is not possible to estimate the amount of the fees, the revenue should be recognized when the license agreement has expired. Any fixed fees to be received should be recorded as revenue when earned.

The licensor may incur certain artist compensation costs in connection with the production of the music or record (Block 8). In certain cases, the licensor may be required to pay the artist an advance royalty (Block 9). These payments generally are nonrefundable. The question that must be answered by the licensor is whether the advance royalty will be recovered from future record or music sales (Block 10). If it is reasonable to assume that the advance payment will be recovered from future sales, the payment should be recorded as an asset and charged to expense as normal royalties are earned by the artist. If, at some point, it appears that the advance payment will not be recovered from future sales, the unamortized amount should be charged to expense in the current period.

The licensor may incur costs to produce a record master (Block 11). These costs would generally include the cost of musical talent, engineering and other technical talent, equipment costs, and studio facility charges. If these costs will be recouped from sales in the future (Block 12), they should be recorded initially as an asset and amortized over the estimated life of the recorded performance. The licensor should use a method of amortization that will reasonably relate the amount expensed to the net revenue expected to be realized. When it appears that the costs will not be recovered from future revenues, they should be charged to income in the current period.

Accounting by the licensee for minimum guarantees paid and other fees to be paid under the terms of a license agreement are very similar to the licensor accounting described above. Additional explanation is not necessary.

The disclosures required in the record and music industry are specified in ASC 928-340-50 and ASC 928-440-50 and are listed below:

1. Guarantees of future royalties.
2. Liabilities for future advanced royalty payments.
3. Record master costs recorded as assets.

Topic 930: Extractive Activities—Mining

Topic 930, *Extractive Activities—Mining*, contains six subtopics:

10 Overall

330 Inventory

360 Property, Plant, and Equipment

715 Compensation—Retirement Benefits

805 Business Combinations

810 Consolidation

This topic is not covered in this book.

Topic 932: Extractive Activities—Oil and Gas

Topic 932, *Extractive Activities—Oil and Gas,* contains 16 subtopics:

10 Overall

225 Income Statement

235 Notes to Financial Statements

270 Interim Reporting

280 Segment Reporting

323 Investments—Equity Method and Joint Ventures

330 Inventory

350 Intangibles—Goodwill and Other

360 Property, Plant, and Equipment

470 Debt

605 Revenue Recognition

720 Other Expenses

740 Income Taxes

810 Consolidation

815 Derivatives and Hedging

835 Interest

ASC 932 provides accounting and reporting requirements for oil and gas producing companies.

ASC 932-360-40-4 and ASC 932-470-25-1 cover issues related to the conveyances of mineral properties. Some of the conveyance transactions are considered borrowings. ASC 932 also covers the issue of tax allocation within the oil and gas industry and states that there will be differences between book and tax basis of assets and liabilities in the oil and gas industry. According to ASC 932, ASC 740 should be used in the computation of any deferred tax assets and liabilities. ASC 932 specifies the disclosure requirements for oil and gas producing activities that are significant. The required disclosures are divided into five categories: information about quantities of proved oil and gas reserves; information about capitalized costs; information about acquisition, development, and exploration costs; information about operating results; and information about cash flow of reserves on a discounted basis presented using a standard measure. There are a large number of detailed disclosures related to information about quantities of proved oil and gas reserves. The required disclosures for oil and gas producing activities are as follows:

1. Capitalized costs and related amortization, depletion, valuation allowance, and depreciation on an aggregate basis divided into classes of assets.
2. Capitalized costs related to properties that are unproved, if significant.
3. Investors' share of investee's capitalized cost for oil and gas producing activities when investments are accounted for using the equity method.

The required disclosures related to costs for development, acquisition, and exploration are as follows:

1. Costs for development, acquisition of property, and exploration.
2. Certain information pertaining to costs incurred in foreign countries.
3. Certain cost information related to investments accounted for using the equity method.

Required disclosure information about the results of operations for oil and gas producing companies includes: revenue; costs of production; exploration costs; income tax expense; depletion, depreciation, valuations, and amortization; and operation results. There are a large number of detailed disclosures related to information on cash flow of reserves on a discounted basis presented using a standard measure.

Topic 940: Financial Services—Broker and Dealers

Topic 940, *Financial Services—Broker and Dealers,* contains 10 subtopics:

10 Overall

20 Broker-Dealer Activities

310 Receivables

320 Investments—Debt and Equity Securities

325 Investments—Other

340 Other Assets and Deferred Costs

405 Liabilities

605 Revenue Recognition

810 Consolidation

820 Fair Value Measurements and Disclosures

This topic is not covered in this book.

Topic 942: Financial Services—Depository and Lending

Topic 942, *Financial Services—Depository and Lending,* contains 19 subtopics:

10 Overall

210 Balance Sheet

225 Income Statement

230 Statement of Cash Flows

235 Notes to Financial Statements

305 Cash and Cash Equivalents

310 Receivables

320 Investments—Debt and Equity Securities

325 Investments—Other

360 Property, Plant, and Equipment

405 Liabilities

470 Debt

505 Equity

605 Revenue Recognition

720 Other Expenses

740 Income Taxes

805 Business Combinations

810 Consolidation

825 Financial Instruments

This topic is not covered in this book.

Topic 944: Financial Services—Insurance

Topic 944, *Financial Services—Insurance,* contains 24 subtopics:

10 Overall

20 Insurance Activities

30 Acquisition Costs

40 Claim Costs and Liabilities for Future Policy Benefits

50 Policyholder Dividends

60 Premium Deficiency and Loss Recognition

80 Separate Accounts

210 Balance Sheet

225 Income Statement

235 Notes to Financial Statements

310 Receivables

320 Investments—Debt and Equity Securities

325 Investments—Other

340 Other Assets and Deferred Costs

360 Property, Plant, and Equipment

405 Liabilities

470 Debt

505 Equity

605 Revenue Recognition

720 Other Expenses

740 Income Taxes

805 Business Combinations

815 Derivatives and Hedging

825 Financial Instruments

Overview

Accounting and reporting by insurance enterprises are covered by ASC 944, which divides insurance contracts into two major categories: short-duration contracts and long-duration contracts. The proper accounting for assets, liabilities, revenues, and expenses depends upon whether the contract is classified as short-duration or long-duration. As with most industries, the insurance business has developed its own unique terminology. The reader may find it difficult to follow the narrative of these pronouncements if he or she is not familiar with the terminology of the industry. Before reading the text of ASC 944, it would prove very helpful to read through the definitions of terms located in Section 20 of each subtopic of ASC 944.

Provisions of ASC 944 generally apply to mutual life insurance companies. Mutual life insurance companies include the following: mutual life insurance entities, fraternal benefit societies, and assessment entities. When mutual life insurance companies present financial reports in accordance with generally accepted accounting principles, reinsurance and insurance transactions should be accounted for using the provisions of ASC 944. In addition, ASC 944 should be used to account for participating life insurance contracts of mutual life insurance companies.

The item scope of ASC 944 includes financial guarantee insurance contracts if those contracts (1) are issued by entities that are within the scope of ASC 944 and (2) are not derivative instruments that fall within the scope of ASC 815. Additionally, ASC 944 specifies how premium revenue and claim liabilities are to be recognized and measured for such contracts. ASC 944 also requires specific disclosures about financial guarantee insurance contracts.

In an effort to simplify the presentation in ASC 944, the following discussion will be divided into six sections. The accounting related to short-duration and long-duration contracts under ASC 944 will be covered in the first two sections. The third section covers accounting for long-duration contracts as required by ASC 944, and section four covers reinsurance of both short-duration and long-duration contracts. The final two sections discuss accounting that is common to both classifications of insurance contracts. This presentation is designed to assist the reader in understanding the decision process presented by ASC 944.

Most accounting problems relating to insurance contracts are due to the uncertain nature of the basic transaction. The typical insurance transaction requires the purchaser to make an initial payment followed by periodic premium payments. The payment is made in advance of the actual service to be received from the insurance company. The insurance company receives the periodic payments, but is uncertain when, if, or how much might be paid to the insured on any particular contract. From the insurance company's perspective, the uncertainty of any individual transaction is reduced by the law of large numbers and past experience.

Short-Duration Insurance Contracts

Short-duration contracts provide protection for a short period of time and permit the insurer to cancel the policy or adjust its terms at the end of the contract period. Almost all property and liability insurance and credit life insurance is classified as short-duration. Accident and health insurance may be classified as short-duration if the policy is not expected to be in force for an extended period of time.

Premiums received from short-duration contracts generally are recognized as revenue over the contract period in the same manner and time period as those in which the insurance is provided. For example, the amount of insurance in force on a credit life policy may decrease as the amount of the loan declines. In this case, the revenue recognized would be greater during the early part of the contract and less towards the end. However, in most cases, the revenue will be recognized evenly over the contract period.

In addition to the revenue recognized on short-duration contracts, liabilities must be established for unpaid claims and claim adjustment expenses. The liability for unpaid claims represents an estimate of the amount of future payments that will have to be made in connection with claims that have been reported to the insurer on the balance sheet date and claims relating to events that have occurred but have not been reported. Obviously, the estimate of the liability relating to the unreported claims is extremely difficult and must be closely linked to past experience of the company. The liability for claim adjustment expenses is an estimate of the costs that will be incurred to investigate and settle claims that have occurred at the balance sheet date. This is another difficult estimate, because it will be composed of both reported claims and unreported occurrences.

For some types of short-duration contracts, the premium paid may be adjusted based upon actual costs and payments made during the period of coverage. The AICPA group life insurance policy is an excellent example of this type of arrangement. Under these types of contracts, the actual premium earned by the company will not be known until the adjustment is determined. In this case, revenue recognized depends upon the company's ability to estimate the ultimate premium. When the premium can be estimated, revenue should be recognized over the contract period, based upon the estimate. The estimate may be revised as additional information becomes available, and any revision will change future revenue recognition. Revenue recognition becomes much more complex when the ultimate premium cannot be estimated. In this latter case, revenue will be recognized using the cost recovery or deposit method. Both of these accounting techniques have special meaning in the insurance industry.

When the cost recovery method is used, and until the premium can be estimated, premiums are reported as revenue based on the expected claim costs as events that are insured arise. Premiums received will be established as deferred income and used to offset estimated claim costs from insured events. Revenue recognition is postponed until the company is able to estimate the ultimate premium. Until the ultimate premium can be estimated, the deposit method does not report revenue or recognize claim costs. Premiums received will be treated as deferred income, and claim costs will be treated as deferred expenses, until some reasonable estimate of the premium can be made.

All insurance contracts incur acquisition costs. These are costs directly relating to the successful acquisition of new or renewed policies, including commissions, costs related to underwriting and policy issue, medical and investigation fees paid, and similar costs. Generally, acquisition costs are capitalized and charged to income in relation to revenue recognized. However, some acquisition costs on short-duration contracts are determined on a percentage basis between incurred costs and premiums that are received. If acquisition costs are determined in this manner, they should be accounted for in relation to unearned premiums over the entire contract period.

In some cases, the unearned premiums may not be sufficient to cover expected claim costs, claim adjustment expenses, policy dividends, unamortized acquisition costs, and policy serving costs. In this case, the contract has a premium deficiency. The amount of the premium deficiency is to be charged to income through a reduction of any acquisition costs that are not amortized. When the acquisition costs that are not amortized are less than the premium deficiency, the company should establish a liability for the difference.

Long-Duration Insurance Contracts

Long-duration contracts are characterized by the facts that the terms of the contract generally are not subject to change and the relationship between the insured and the company covers an extended period of time. Long-duration contracts include whole-life policies, guaranteed renewable term policies, endowment contracts, annuity contracts, and title insurance. Accident and health insurance policies may be considered long-duration if the contract is non-cancellable or guaranteed renewable.

Revenue is reported when premiums are due from the insured. In addition to the recognition of revenue, the company is to establish a liability for estimated costs associated with the current and future contract periods. The company is to accrue the difference between the net present value of estimated future costs and premiums when premium revenue is recognized. The present value computations are subject to all the actuarial assumptions used in the industry and are referred to as the liability for future policy benefits. Liabilities for claims that are unpaid and claim adjustment expenses should be established in a manner consistent with the accounting required for short-duration contracts.

Policy acquisition costs generally are capitalized and charged to income as revenue is recognized. On long-duration contracts, when gross premiums are sufficient to cover actual acquisition costs, the actual costs are to be capitalized.

The capitalized costs should be charged to income in a manner consistent with the assumptions used to calculate the liability for future policy benefits.

The determination of a premium deficiency is more complex for long-duration than for short-duration contracts. The liability for policy benefits is determined as of some specified valuation date. If there is a change in the assumptions used to calculate the liability, a new calculation is required. The revised liability for policy benefits is used to determine the premium deficiency.

An example of a calculation of premium deficiency is as follows:

Previously determined liability	$10,000,000
Less: unamortized acquisition costs	500,000
Net liability	$9,500.000
Newly determined liability	12,000,000
Premium deficiency	$2,500,000

The premium deficiency is charged to income through a reduction of the acquisition costs that have not been amortized or reported as an increase in liability. The premium deficiency should be recognized as an aggregate liability for the entire insurance business. In some cases, the deficiency may be disaggregated by product line.

Accounting for Long-Duration Insurance Contracts

Contracts covered by ASC 944 include universal life-type contracts, limited-payment contracts, and investment contracts.

Definition of Long-Duration Contracts

Long-duration insurance contracts with terms that are *not* guaranteed and fixed are classified as universal life-type contracts. Such contracts may provide either annuity benefits or death benefits and, generally, the following policyholder items are not guaranteed or fixed: assessments, accruals, and premiums.

Limited-payment contracts are insurance contracts that meet the following criteria: benefits provided to the policyholder are received over a longer period of time than the premiums are paid and the terms of the contract are guaranteed and fixed.

Long-duration insurance contracts where the insurance company is not exposed to insurance risk (risk of morbidity or mortality) are classified as investment contracts and not accounted for as insurance contracts.

Accounting for Long-Duration Contracts

When an entity has a universal life-type long-duration contract, a liability is recognized at an amount equal to the combined total of the following items: (1) the loss commonly referred to as a premium deficiency, as specified in ASC 944; (2) assessments for services to be provided by the insurer in the future; (3) refundable assessments if the insurance contract is discontinued; and (4) accumulated balance for policyholder benefit on the statement of financial position date. The part of the liability described in (4), above, is equal to the cash value upon surrender of the policy on the date of the statement of financial position if no contract value or account balance is stated.

Several types of expenses are recognized by an insurance company when accounting for universal life-type long-duration contracts. Examples of items included in expenses are contract administration expense, capitalized acquisition costs amortization, and accrual of interest to the insured party.

One of the expenses, capitalized acquisition cost amortization, requires additional explanation. The amount of the amortization reported each accounting period is based on an interest method approach, which is the application of a constant interest rate to the estimated gross profit expected over the life of a book of universal life-type contracts expressed on a present value basis. The expected gross profit's present value is calculated by applying the contract rate to the estimated future gross profit amounts. The rate of interest that relates to policyholders' balances is the contract rate used in the present value computations. If estimated future gross profits are anticipated to be negative for any future periods, other items may be substituted for the gross profit, such as gross revenues or gross costs.

The expected gross profit used in the computation of amortization of capitalized acquisition cost is composed of the following elements:

1. Anticipated assessments against policyholder balances for contracts that have been terminated.
2. Anticipated assessments for mortality minus claims of benefits greater than associated policyholder balances.
3. Anticipated assessments for contract administration in excess of related costs.
4. Anticipated income on investments of policyholder balances in excess of interest provided on such balances.
5. Amounts from other anticipated credits or assessments.

Each of the preceding elements of estimated gross profits is determined based on an estimate of that item individually over the life of the book of contracts.

Revenue for a universal life-type long-duration contract is recognized in the income statement equal to the amount that the policyholders are assessed on the assessment date. However, revenue should be deferred and reported in future accounting periods when the assessment, if any, is for future services that are to be provided by the insurance company. The amortization method should encompass the same factors and assumptions used in capitalized acquisition cost amortization.

Revenue is not recognized for limited-payment insurance contracts when the premiums are collected by the insurance company because the earnings process is assumed not to be completed on that date. Therefore, for limited-payment insurance contracts, revenue recognition involves the comparison of the premiums charged to the policyholder (gross premiums) with the premiums that are necessary for all benefits and expenses (net premiums). Any excess of gross premiums over net premiums is recognized as unearned revenue and reported in income over future accounting periods. The method of reporting revenue in future periods depends on whether the accounting is for life insurance contracts or annuity contracts.

An insurance company should use the accounting and reporting requirements specified in ASC 944 to account for any liability required for limited-payment insurance contracts.

Investment contracts are not accounted for as insurance contracts, and premium payments received by an insurance company are not accounted for as revenue. However, premium payments received by the insurance company are recorded as liabilities. The liabilities are accounted for in the same manner as other liabilities of the enterprise.

Accounting for Reinsurance of Short-Duration and Long-Duration Contracts

Insurance companies provide indemnification to policyholders for losses that might occur in future periods in return for a premium payment. In addition, an insurance company (ceding company) may indemnify itself against losses from claims that might be filed by policyholders by entering into a contract with another insurance company (assuming company or reinsurer). The contract with another insurance company is commonly referred to as reinsurance. ASC 944 specifies the proper accounting and reporting for reinsurance of short- and long-duration contracts.

Before discussing the proper accounting requirements for reinsurance, it must be determined if a contract with another insurance company qualifies for reinsurance accounting. If a contract indemnifies a ceding company against loss or liability for an insurance risk, the contract is accounted for using ASC 944. A short-duration contract meets the requirements for reinsurance when one of the two following conditions is met:

1. Reinsurance accounting requires both of the following two conditions:
   a. Significant risk related to the insurance contract is assumed by the reinsurer.
   b. There is a reasonable probability that a major loss will be realized by the reinsurer from the reinsurance.
2. If condition 1(a. above) is not met, reinsurance is still appropriate if the reinsurer assumes the risk associated with reinsured parts of the insurance contracts.

A long-duration contract meets the requirements for reinsurance when it is reasonably possible that a significant loss could be realized by the reinsurer from the insurance contract.

When an insurance contract qualifies as reinsurance, the ceding entity must determine the proper accounting for assets, liabilities, revenues, and costs related to the reinsurance. Proper accounting depends on whether the existing contract is a short-duration or long-duration insurance contract.

Accounting for short-duration contracts depends on whether the reinsurance is prospective or retroactive. Prospective reinsurance exists when a reinsurer agrees to pay the ceding company for losses that might be incurred in the future from events that are insured under the contract. Retroactive reinsurance exists when a reinsurer agrees to pay the ceding company for liabilities from past events that were insured and covered by the reinsurance contract.

When a reinsurance is classified as prospective, the ceding company should record an asset, Prepaid Reinsurance Premium, for an amount equal to the amounts paid for the reinsurance. The asset recorded should be amortized over the remaining life of the contract using the same method as the protection amount granted by the insurance contract. When the amount paid by the ceding company can be adjusted, any amortization should be based on an estimate of what will actually be paid.

Payments for retroactive reinsurance are recorded as reinsurance recoverables. However, the amount of the payments may be less than or exceed the amount of liabilities reported by the contract that is subject to reinsurance. When there is a difference between the receivable and the liability at date of reinsurance, one or both of the accounts must be adjusted for the difference. When the reinsurance receivable exceeds the recorded liability, either the receivable should be reduced, the liability increased for the difference, or both should be adjusted to account for the difference. The adjustment is charged to income in the accounting period that encompasses the reinsurance. If the receivable is less than the liability, increase the receivable to equal the liability and recognize a deferred gain for the difference. The amount of the gain that is deferred should be written off over the settlement period that remains, using either the interest method or the recovery method, whichever is most appropriate under the circumstances. Any changes in the liability or the reinsurance recoverables should be adjusted in the accounting period of change and accounted for according to ASC 944.

Accounting for long-duration contracts depends on whether the contract for reinsurance is classified as long- or short-duration. Such classification depends on the judgment of the ceding enterprise. If the reinsurance contract is classified as short-duration, the cost paid for the reinsurance is written off over the period of the contract. However, if the reinsurance is a long-duration contract, the cost is amortized over the remaining life of the contract that is reinsured. Included in the cost of reinsured contracts subject to amortization is the difference between the amount paid to the reinsurer and the liability related to the contract reinsured.

Receivables and payables between the reinsurer and the ceding company should not be offset unless the company has the right of offset.

Accounting for Investment Gains and Losses

ASC 944 requires insurance companies to report investment gains and losses as a part of other income from continuing operations. Such gains and losses are presented before tax.

Other Accounting Considerations

Insurance companies have significant investments in stocks and bonds, mortgage loans, and real estate. The valuation procedures below should be followed for such investments:

1. Long-Term Investment in Bonds.
2. Short-Term Investment in Bonds.
3. Common and Nonredeemable Preferred Stock.
4. Preferred Stock Redeemable by Issuer.
5. Mortgage Loans—principal balance that is outstanding or amortized cost.
6. Real Estate Investments—costs less accumulated depreciation and adjusted for any impairment considered permanent.

Some real estate owned by insurance companies is used in their own operations. Real estate predominantly used in its business should result in operating expenses to the company rather than in investment expenses.

Insurance companies often maintain separate accounts for the funding of, for example, fixed or variable annuity contracts and pension plans. Investments maintained in these separate accounts should be valued in a manner consistent with that discussed above.

The disclosure requirements of ASC 944 are extensive.

Recent Change

ASU 2015-09, *Financial Services—Insurance (Topic 944): Disclosures about Short-Duration Contracts,* requires insurance entities to disclose extensive information concerning unpaid claims and claim adjustment expenses.

Topic 946: Financial Services—Investment Companies

Topic 946, *Financial Services—Investment Companies*, contains 17 subtopics:

10 Overall

20 Investment Company Activities

205 Presentation of Financial Statements

210 Balance Sheet

225 Income Statement

230 Statement of Cash Flows

235 Notes to Financial Statements

305 Cash and Cash Equivalents

310 Receivables

320 Investments—Debt and Equity Securities

323 Investments—Equity Method and Joint Ventures

405 Liabilities

505 Equity

605 Revenue Recognition

740 Income Taxes

810 Consolidation

830 Foreign Currency Matters

If an entity is covered by ASC 946, the topic specifies the requirements that must be met when investment company accounting is to be retained in the statements of an investor using the equity method or a parent company in consolidation. ASC 946 also provides disclosure requirements for parent companies and investor companies using the equity method subject to investment company accounting. In addition, ASC 946 is applicable to the separate statements of companies subject to the Investment Companies Act of 1940, and companies with separate legal status whose purpose is to invest in multiple substantive investments for income and appreciation of capital.

Topic 948: Financial Services—Mortgage Banking

Topic 948, *Financial Services—Mortgage Banking*, contains six subtopics:

10 Overall

310 Receivables

340 Other Assets and Deferred Costs

605 Revenue Recognition

720 Other Expenses

810 Consolidation

Overview of the Industry

ASC 948 deals with the mortgage banking industry. ASC 948 is very limited in scope and will have little meaning to those outside the industry. Most have been exposed to the mortgage banking industry when purchasing homes. Even this brief exposure to the industry will make reading ASC 948 more meaningful. It may be helpful to the reader to read the definitions in ASC 948-10-20 first and then turn to the remainder of the topic.

The mortgage banking industry represents an extremely complex mixture of private and public institutions. An individual's first reaction to the industry is usually naive, in that the thought is of going to the local savings and loan to borrow money to purchase a home. In many cases, the local financial institution serves as an intermediary between the borrower and a permanent investor in mortgage loans or securities. In addition to savings and loans, insurance companies, pension plans, real estate investment trusts, and other organizations participate in long-term mortgage investments. Besides these private enterprises, government agencies and government-initiated/privately operated organizations are active in the mortgage banking industry. For example, the Federal Home Loan Mortgage Corporation, the Federal National Mortgage Association, and the Government National Mortgage Association are involved in some aspect of the mortgage banking industry. Generally, these organizations encourage stability and security in the marketplace for mortgage loans.

The major activities of the mortgage banking industry can be divided between those activities relating to placement of a mortgage and those involved in servicing the mortgage. Mortgage loans are placed with permanent investors, but the mortgage banking enterprise usually retains the right to service the loan. Loan servicing includes processing the periodic payments and handling the escrow accounts for insurance and taxes. Of course, the permanent investor receives the principal and interest payments from the institution servicing the mortgage. The company servicing the mortgage receives a fee. When the fee for loan servicing is greater than cost, the right to service the loan has value and can be sold to, or purchased from, other mortgage banking enterprises.

The mortgage banking industry deals in mortgage loans and mortgage-backed securities. Mortgage-backed securities are securities that generally represent an interest that is undivided in a group of designated mortgage loans that are issued by either corporations or an agency of the government. Principal and interest payments are guaranteed by the issuing entity and make the securities marketable. Mortgage-backed securities are issued by the Federal Home Loan Mortgage Corporation (referred to as Freddie Mac), the Federal National Mortgage Association (Fannie Mae), and the Government National Mortgage Association (Ginnie Mae). The securities are known as participation certificates, because the investor is participating in a group of mortgage loans.

Discussion of Accounting Standards

Reporting of Mortgage Loans and Mortgage-Backed Securities

A mortgage banking institution may hold mortgage-backed securities or mortgage loans for sale or as a long-term investment. The appropriate accounting depends upon whether the loan will be sold or held.

Mortgage-backed securities should be categorized as trading securities and classified as current assets and carried at fair value if the securities are held for sale and relate to the activities of the mortgage banking business.

Mortgage loans that are for sale should be recorded using the lower of cost or fair value rule. Fair value is determined by reference to the nature of the loan or security. The portfolio of loans or securities should first be divided into residential and commercial loans. Next, the accountant must determine if the loan is committed or uncommitted. A committed loan is one that is subject to an investor's purchase commitment. The value of a committed loan is based on fair value. For uncommitted loans, fair value is determined through reference to market prices and returns from the typical market outlet and quotes from the Government National Mortgage Association or current prices from the Federal Home Loan Mortgage Corporation and the Federal National Mortgage Association. The determination of fair value on uncommitted mortgage-backed securities is based on published yields for these securities.

The ultimate determination of lower of cost or fair value can be made on the basis of individual loans or by the aggregate loans in the commercial and residential categories. Any decrease in fair value below cost should be accounted for using a valuation allowance. Changes in the valuation allowance between accounting periods are to be reflected in income.

Any discounts relating to mortgage loans should not be amortized as long as the loans or securities are being held for sale.

As a method of raising funds for a short period of time, a mortgage banking institution may temporarily transfer mortgage loans to another financial institution with a formal or informal repurchase agreement. Such transfers should be accounted for as collateralized financing arrangements, with the loan or securities still reported by the mortgage banking institution as being held for sale.

If an entity has the intent and the ability to keep mortgage loans until they mature, or at least for the foreseeable future, the loans may be classified as long-term investments. The ability and intent criteria are determined by management action. A loan classified as a long-term investment should be transferred to this category at lower of cost or fair value on the date of classification. The value assigned to the loan or security on the date of transfer becomes the new cost basis. Recovery in value above the newly established basis is not recognized until the instrument is sold or matures.

The interest method is used to adjust the yield on the loan for the difference between the balance of the principal payments of the loan and the carrying value of the loan.

If the carrying value of a mortgage loan or security classified as a long-term investment is permanently impaired, it should be reduced to the expected collectible amount. This reduction in value establishes a new cost basis, and the associated loss should be reflected in the current income statement.

Accounting for Other Loan Fees

Most are familiar with other types of fees that are paid in connection with mortgage loans. For example, most mortgage banking institutions charge a loan origination fee designed to cover the administrative costs incurred in preparing all necessary loan documentation. These fees are deferred, and appropriate accounting for the fees deferred depends on whether the loan is held for sale or held as an investment by the entity. If the loan is held for sale, the deferred fees are recognized when the loan is sold. If the loan is held as an investment, the deferred fees are accounted for as a yield adjustment.

Often, other types of fees are paid for loans that are held for sale to a permanent investor. In almost all cases, these fees should be reported as an expense when the loans are sold. Although the type of fee may vary, the accounting is relatively straightforward.

It is common to pay a fee to receive a guarantee that funding of a mortgage loan for the development of real estate will be made. Generally, this fee is deferred and reported as a yield adjustment.

Financial Reporting and Disclosures

A mortgage banking entity is required to report mortgage loans held for sale in a separate category from those loans held as long-term investments. In addition, the notes to the financial statements should disclose the method used to determine lower of cost or market.

Topic 950: Financial Services—Title Plant

Topic 950, *Financial Services—Title Plant*, contains one subtopic:

350 Intangibles—Goodwill and Other

Discussion

ASC 950 specifies accounting for title plant. The word "plant," as commonly used in accounting, refers to a tangible asset that would be classified in the property, plant, and equipment section of the balance sheet. However, the word "plant," as used in ASC 950, takes on a different meaning. Title plant is composed of the historical record of all matters affecting title to parcels of land in a particular geographic area. The number of years covered by a title plant varies depending on regulatory requirements and the minimum information period considered necessary to efficiently issue title insurance policies. The documents may include evidence of ownership and encumbrances on, for example, a parcel of land, maps and plants, copies of title insurance policies, and lists of prior owners. Title plants are used by title insurance companies, title abstract companies, and title agents so that information regarding a parcel of land is readily available at a reasonable cost.

Although the concept of a title plant is easy to understand, the accounting for that plant is somewhat unusual. All costs incurred to develop the title plant should be capitalized until such time as the company can use the plant to conduct title searches. A company may develop its own title plant or purchase an existing one from another enterprise. In either case, all costs directly associated with the title plant should be capitalized. So far, the accounting is fairly direct and not out of the ordinary. However, ASC 950 specifies that the capitalized costs identified above should *not* be depreciated or charged to income, unless there has been an impairment in value. The following five circumstances indicate an impairment in value:

1. Legal or statutory changes;
2. Impact of demand, obsolescence, and other economic considerations;
3. Impact on the entity's competitive advantage from competition and other sources;
4. Lack of current maintenance of the title plant; or
5. Title plant abandonment or situations that imply obsolescence.

If there is impairment to the title plant below its cost basis, the amount of the impairment should be charged to income. Rather than depreciating title plant through a systematic and rational allocation of cost, the asset will be depreciated through analysis of impaired value. Such an analysis should be conducted periodically. In some cases, an enterprise with an established title plant may decide to extend the period of time covered by the documents. Development of an extension that goes back in time is referred to as a backplant. The costs directly associated with developing the backplant should be capitalized and accounted for as previously discussed.

Once a title plant becomes operational, costs may be incurred to modernize the plant in light of new technology. For example, management may decide to use microfilm to store records that were previously filed in hard-copy form. The costs incurred to modernize the title plant should be separately capitalized and depreciated.

Once a title plant has been established, an enterprise will incur costs to maintain and keep the plant current. Title plant maintenance costs, as well as the costs associated with conducting title searches, should be charged to income as incurred.

A title plant, like any asset, has a market value and may be sold to another party. If the title plant is sold and the seller gives up all rights for use of the plant in the future, the gain or loss on the sale is determined by comparing the cost basis of the plant to the proceeds received. The determination of gain or loss is complicated when the enterprise sells an interest in the title plant that is undivided. When this is done, the proceeds from the sale should be compared with a pro rata part of the cost basis of the title plant. ASC 950 does not provide guidance as to how to determine the appropriate pro rata amount, but it seems logical that, before the sales price could be determined, the seller would have to consider the allocation of pro rata costs. Because the title plant is composed of documents, an enterprise could sell a copy of the current plant with no future update service. In this case, no cost should be associated with the sale, and the total proceeds would represent a gain on the transaction. The only exception to this general rule would be in the case where the title plant decreased in value as a result of the sale. When this happens, the amount of the decrease below cost would be used to determine gain or loss.

Topic 952: Franchisors

Topic 952, *Franchisors*, contains six subtopics:

10 Overall

340 Other Assets and Deferred Costs

440 Commitments

605 Revenue Recognition

720 Other Expenses

810 Consolidation

Flowchart and General Discussion

ASC 952 deals with the proper accounting for franchise fee revenue by a franchisor. There are two major considerations when dealing with the franchise fees earned by the franchisor. The first consideration is related to accounting for the initial franchise fee, and the second consideration is related to accounting for any continuing franchise fees earned by the franchisor. Before a meaningful discussion of accounting by the franchisor can be started, certain key terms found in ASC 952 must be defined.

The franchisee and franchisor enter into a franchise agreement. The franchise agreement must be in writing and must contain the following conditions:

1. There is a contractual relationship between the parties that is for a specific time period,
2. The purpose of the agreement is to distribute a service or product in a specific market,
3. The franchise is organized from resources from both parties,
4. The agreement identifies the market to be served and the contribution of each party to the operations of the franchise,
5. The franchisee generally must devote full time to the establishment of the business entity, and
6. Both parties have a familiar public name.

Before one can determine whether the provisions of ASC 952 are applicable to a specific situation, it must be established that the parties to an arrangement have, in fact, entered into a franchising agreement. This determination would be made by comparing the franchise agreement to the conditions listed above.

The initial franchise fee is the amount paid to create the franchise affiliation and to provide some beginning assistance. The beginning assistance mentioned might include any or all of the following:

1. Help in site selection;
2. Help in facility acquisition;
3. Help in advertising;
4. Help in training employees;
5. Development of books for such things as operations and administration;
6. Accounting and advisory assistance;
7. Programs that relate to inspection and to controlling quality; and
8. Other services.

The continuing franchise fee is an amount paid for the ongoing rights that the agreement specifies and for specific or general assistance during the period of the agreement.

With these definitions in mind, attention can be turned to Flowchart 9-2, which represents the decision process and general accounting requirements relating to the initial franchise fee. A discussion of the proper accounting for the continuing franchise fee appears after Flowchart 9-2 has been examined in some detail.

The basic problem facing the franchisor is when to recognize the initial franchise fee as revenue. It would be reasonable to assume that the franchisor would have to provide the franchisee with some service before the initial fee could be recorded as a revenue. Even though the initial franchise fee is collected in advance, the test of realization would be the rendering of services by the franchisor. Flowchart 9-2 outlines the rather complex process that could develop in common franchise agreements.

Flowchart 9-2

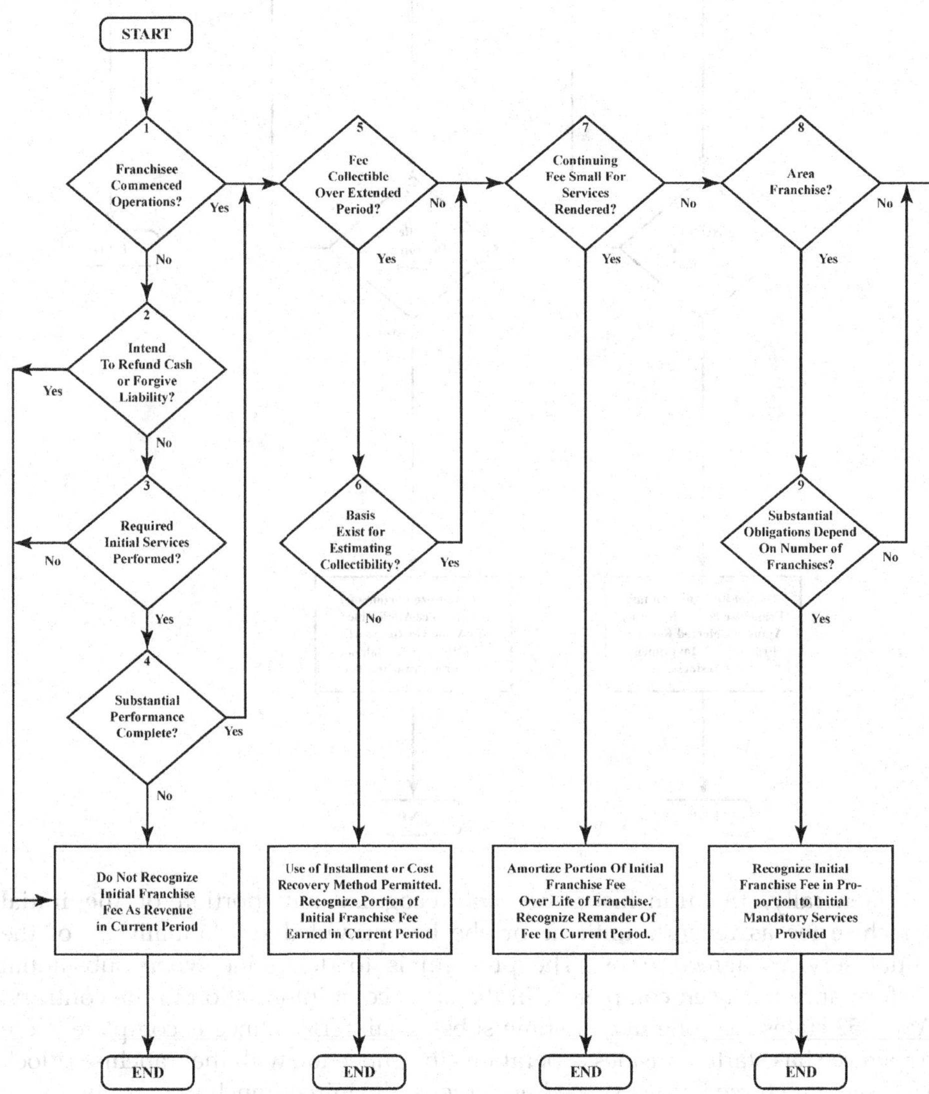
START
1 Franchisee Commenced Operations?
Yes
No
2 Intend To Refund Cash or Forgive Liability?
Yes
No
3 Required Initial Services Performed?
No
Yes
4 Substantial Performance Complete?
Yes
No
Do Not Recognize Initial Franchise Fee As Revenue in Current Period
END
5 Fee Collectible Over Extended Period?
No
Yes
6 Basis Exist for Estimating Collectibility?
Yes
No
Use of Installment or Cost Recovery Method Permitted. Recognize Portion of Initial Franchise Fee Earned in Current Period
END
7 Continuing Fee Small For Services Rendered?
No
Yes
Amortize Portion Of Initial Franchise Fee Over Life of Franchise. Recognize Remander Of Fee In Current Period.
END
8 Area Franchise?
No
Yes
9 Substantial Obligations Depend On Number of Franchises?
No
Yes
Recognize Initial Franchise Fee in Proportion to Initial Mandatory Services Provided
END

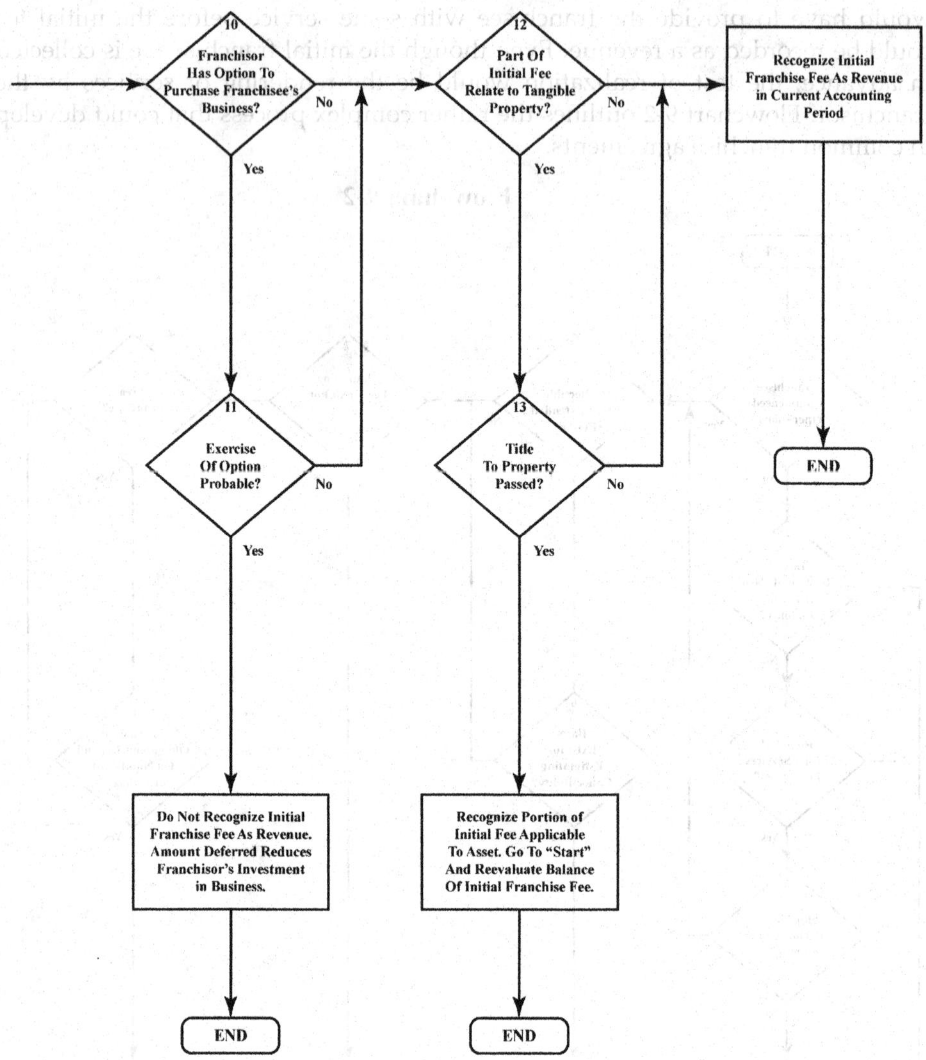

Generally, the franchisor *may not* recognize any portion of the initial franchise fee as revenue until he or she has provided substantially all of the initial services agreed upon. The problem is to determine when substantial performance has been completed. In the absence of information to the contrary, ASC 952 states that one may assume substantial performance is complete if the franchisee has started business operations in connection with the franchise (Block 1). If the franchisee has *not* started operations, the initial franchise fee may not be recognized as revenue unless:

1. The franchisor meets the following requirements relating to the franchisee: cash is not expected to be repaid to the franchisee; notes that have not been paid, or receivables that have not been collected, are not expected to be forgiven by the franchisor; and there is no obligation to the franchisee (Block 2),

2. Most of the beginning services have been performed (Block 3), and

3. There are no major requirements or obligations associated with substantial performance (Block 4).

If all these conditions have been met, the assumption is that the franchisor has substantially completed all obligations required by the franchise agreement, and may recognize the initial franchise fee as revenue if certain other conditions have been met.

In the vast majority of cases, the initial franchise fee is collected in advance by the franchisor. However, in those rare situations where the fee is received over a period of time (Block 5), and the franchisor has no reasonable basis for estimating the collectibility of the fee (Block 6), the installment or cost recovery method may be used to recognize the initial franchise fee as revenue. In this rare case, the fee would be recognized over a period of time rather than in the period when substantial performance of the initial services has been completed. Remember that this is the exception rather than the general rule for revenue recognition.

In some franchise agreements, the initial franchise fee is very large, and the continuing franchise fee is small in comparison to the services to be performed by the franchisor (Block 7). If this is the case, a part of the initial franchise fee should be deferred and reported in future periods. The continuing franchise fee, in these cases, is probably not sufficient to provide the franchisor with a reasonable profit on the services to be provided. The amount of the initial franchise fee to be deferred must be the estimated amount in excess of the stated continuing fee that is necessary to provide a reasonable profit for the franchisor on those continuing services to be provided. Determination of the amount to be deferred may prove to be a very difficult problem in cost estimation.

Some franchise agreements are for area franchises rather than individual franchises. An area franchise relates to a specific geographical region and may allow the franchisee to open a number of stores within that region. The franchisee will take a more active role in site selection and other matters in an area franchise than in an individual franchise. If the franchisor has entered into an area franchise (Block 8) *and* the determination of substantial performance depends upon the number of stores opened in the region (Block 9), the initial franchise fee should be reported as revenue based on a percentage of the initial services furnished. If the determination of substantial performance does not depend upon the number of stores opened in the region, the initial franchise fee will be recognized as revenue when substantial performance is complete.

In still other cases, the franchisor may be permitted an option to purchase the franchise from the franchisee (Block 10). Such a condition may exist in the case where the franchisee appears to be unable to continue the operations of the franchise. If it is probable that the franchisor will exercise the option to purchase the franchise, the initial franchise fee should not be recognized as revenue. Rather, the fee should be treated as a reduction in the cost basis of the investment recorded by the franchisor.

In yet other circumstances, the initial franchise fee may, in fact, represent payment for items other than the establishment of the franchise relationship. Part of the initial franchise may be payment for certain tangible assets to be received by the franchisee (Block 12). This type of arrangement is referred to as a commingled revenue situation. The tangible assets acquired by the franchisee may include signs, inventory, equipment, and the like. When faced with this situation, the accountant should allocate a portion of the initial franchise fee to the tangible assets. The amount so allocated should be based on the fair value of the assets acquired by the franchisee. The amount allocated to the tangible assets should be recognized when title to the assets is passed to the franchisee (Block 13). This may be before or after the recognition of the remaining portion of the initial franchise fee as revenue.

If none of these special situations is faced by the franchisor, the initial franchise fee will be recognized as revenue when the franchisee has commenced operations or substantial performance of the initial services are complete, whichever comes first. This completes the discussion of accounting for the initial franchise fee. The remaining general discussion will relate to the continuing franchise fee paid by the franchisee to the franchisor.

Generally, continuing franchise fees are recognized as revenue when they have been earned/received. Costs associated with earning these fees should be charged to expense as the costs are incurred. There are some important exceptions to this general rule. An unusual accounting situation arises when the franchisor agrees to sell equipment or supplies to the franchisee at bargain purchase prices for a certain period of time. The bargain purchase price must be less than the price charged to other customers of the franchisor, or must be such that the franchisor does not earn a reasonable profit from the sale of the item. In this situation, a part of the initial franchise fee is not recognized immediately, but is used to adjust the selling price of the item sold to the franchisee. The amount of the deferral should be equal to the difference between the selling price and the price charged by the franchisor to other customers, or the amount that is required to permit the franchisor to earn a reasonable profit on the item sold.

If the franchisor has incurred direct costs relating to franchise sales, but no revenue has been reported, the direct costs should not be recognized until the revenue is reported. Any normal and recurring indirect costs incurred in relation to franchise sales should be expensed. These indirect costs would include general, selling, and administrative costs of the franchisor.

This completes the general discussion of the accounting for both initial franchise fees and continuing franchise fees. The technical material presented in the next section is designed to illustrate the specific accounting problems encountered.

Franchise Fee Revenue—Technical Considerations

Two examples will be developed to show the more important provisions of ASC 952. Example 9-1 serves as an introduction to Example 9-2 and it is important to review them in order.

Example 9-1
Franchise Agreement

1. On November 15, 20X6, the Franchisor Company (Franchisor), a December 31 year-end enterprise, entered into a franchise agreement with Franchisee, Inc. (Franchisee), that meets all of the conditions outlined in ASC 952 for such an agreement.
2. The agreement specifies that Franchisor will provide the following initial and continuing services and advice to Franchisee:
   a. Assistance in selection of location and acquisition of necessary facilities;
   b. Training of Franchisee's personnel and preparation of manuals for operations, administration, and recordkeeping; and
   c. Advertising and quality control programs.
3. On November 15, 20X6, Franchisee paid $100,000 cash to Franchisor as an initial franchise fee and agreed to pay a continuing franchise fee of 4% of its gross revenues.
4. On January 15, 20X7, Franchisee commenced operations, and, on this same date, it was determined that Franchisor had performed all initial services outlined in the agreement.
5. During 20X7, Franchisee earned gross revenues of $300,000. The continuing franchise fee is to be paid to Franchisor no later than January 15, 20X8.
6. Franchisor incurred direct costs relating to the franchise of $4,000 in November and December 20X6. Administrative costs relating to the franchise agreement amounted to $1,500 for the same period.

Franchisor has entered into a franchise agreement as defined in ASC 952, and received an initial franchise fee of $100,000. Substantial performance of the initial services was not completed on the day that Franchisee paid the initial franchise fee to Franchisor. The initial franchise fee cannot be recognized as revenue, so the following journal entry would be required to reflect the transfer of funds from Franchisee to Franchisor on November 15, 20X6:

Cash	100,000	
Deferred Initial Franchise Fee		100,000

The deferred initial franchise fee account will be classified as a liability on the balance sheet of Franchisor until the related services have been substantially performed. Substantial performance of the initial services was not complete in 20X6; therefore, none of the initial franchise fee can be recognized as revenue during this year. In addition, Franchisee did not earn revenue during 20X6, so no continuing franchise fee is receivable.

Franchisor incurred certain direct and indirect costs relating to the franchise agreement during 20X6. The direct costs incurred must be deferred until such time as revenue relating to those agreements is recognized. However, the indirect costs incurred should be expensed in 20X6. The journal entry necessary to record the distribution of costs would be:

Prepaid Franchise Costs	4,000	
Administrative Expenses	1,500	
Cash		5,500

On January 15, 20X7, the initial services offered by Franchisor were substantially completed. Once the initial services were substantially completed, Franchisor could recognize the initial franchise fee received. The journal entry to reflect the revenue is as follows:

Deferred Initial Franchise Fee	100,000	
Initial Franchise Fee Revenue		100,000

Now that the initial franchise fee has been recognized as revenue, the deferred direct costs may be charged to expense. The following journal entry is needed to accomplish this transfer:

Franchise Expense	4,000	
Prepaid Franchise Costs		4,000

In addition to accounting for the initial franchise fee, Franchisee has agreed to pay a 4% continuing franchise fee to Franchisor. Franchisee reported gross revenue of $300,000 for 20X7. The continuing franchise fee would be $12,000 ($300,000 × .04) and would be accrued by Franchisor at December 31, 20X7 with the following journal entry:

Receivable from Franchisee, Inc.	12,000	
Franchise Fee Revenue		12,000

This last journal entry completes the accounting required by the Example 9-1 material. Example 9-2 builds upon this solution and introduces additional complexities.

Example 9-2
Franchise Agreement

1. The Franchisor Company (Franchisor), a December 31 year-end enterprise, entered into a franchise agreement with Franchisee, Inc. (Franchisee) on March 15, 20X6 that meets all the conditions specified in ASC 952.
2. Franchisor agreed to provide certain initial and continuing services and advice to Franchisee.
3. On March 15, 20X6, Franchisee paid $350,000 to Franchisor as an initial franchise fee and agreed to pay a continuing franchise fee of 3% of gross revenues. The initial franchise fee included the payment for certain tangible assets. The fair value of the tangible assets covered by the initial fee is shown below:

Buildings	$130,000
Land	45,000
Equipment	20,000
Signs	5,000
	$200,000

4. The franchise agreement permits Franchisee to purchase from Franchisor supplies at 10% below the price paid by other customers of Franchisor. The agreement is to end on March 15, 20X7. Franchisor has estimated that the total amount of the discount to be realized by Franchisee is $10,000 and that $7,500 will be realized in 20X6.

5. Franchisee reported gross revenues of $450,000 for 20X6. The continuing franchise fee is to be paid to Franchisor no later than January 10, 20X7.

6. It has been determined that Franchisor completed all initial services and advice on May 1, 20X6.

Franchisor has entered into a franchise agreement as described in ASC 952, and an initial franchise fee was paid by Franchisee to Franchisor on March 15, 20X6. The initial franchise fee contains commingled revenues because it includes payments for certain specified tangible assets. The $350,000 initial franchise fee must be allocated to the various assets involved on the basis of fair market value. Any residual, after the allocation is complete, will be assigned to the initial franchise fee. Franchisor also granted Franchisee the right to purchase supplies at a bargain purchase price. When this situation exists, a portion of the initial franchise fee must be deferred and treated as an adjustment to the selling price of the supplies when purchased by Franchisee. Franchisor has estimated that the savings to Franchisee will amount to $10,000 over the one-year agreement period. This $10,000 will be included in the initial franchise fee and recognized as purchases of supplies are made by Franchisee. The allocation of the initial franchise fee would be accomplished as follows:

Building	$130,000
Land	45,000
Equipment	20,000
Signs	5,000
Deferred Fee—Product Sales	10,000
Total	$210,000
Total Initial Franchise Fee	$350,000
Total Allocation	210,000
Initial Franchise Fee	$140,000

The journal entry required on March 15, 20X6 to reflect the receipt of the initial franchise fee by Franchisor would be as follows:

Cash	350,000	
Building		130,000
Land		45,000
Equipment		20,000
Signs		5,000
Deferred Fee—Product Sales		10,000
Deferred Initial Franchise Fee		140,000

This journal entry assumes that title to the tangible assets effectively transferred to Franchisee on March 15, 20X6. If this were not the case, the allocation would take place on the date of transfer of title to the tangible assets.

On May 1, 20X6, Franchisor completed all initial services and advice. The following journal entry would be required on that date to record the revenue associated with the initial franchise fee:

Deferred Initial Franchise Fee	140,000	
Initial Franchise Fee Revenue		140,000

Franchisor estimated that Franchisee would realize $7,500 in benefits under the bargain purchase agreement during 20X6. In practice, a journal entry would be required each time Franchisee purchased supplies subject to the agreement. For illustrative purposes, one journal entry is shown to reflect the benefits received by Franchisee during 20X6. Remember that Franchisor must adjust the selling price of each item of supplies sold to Franchisee.

Deferred Fee—Product Sales	7,500	
Sales		7,500

The remaining balance in the deferred fee—product sales account is $2,500 ($10,000 – $7,500). This amount will be recognized prior to March 15, 20X7, the expiration date of the agreement relating to the bargain purchase of supplies.

In addition to the initial franchise fee, the franchise agreement contains a provision for a continuing franchise fee. Franchisee has agreed to pay Franchisor a continuing fee of 3% of gross sales. Gross sales during 20X6 amounted to $450,000; therefore, the continuing franchise fee for 20X6 would be $13,500 ($450,000 × .03). The journal entry to reflect the earned franchise fee on the books of Franchisor at December 31, 20X6 would be:

Receivable from Franchisee, Inc.	13,500	
Franchise Fee Revenue		13,500

This completes the journal entries for 20X6 and the analysis of the information contained in the Example 9-2 material.

Disclosures

ASC 952-605-50 specifies the following disclosures relating to franchise agreements:

1. The nature of major obligations and commitments.
2. Description of the remaining services to be provided relating to agreements not substantially completed at the balance sheet date.
3. The method (cost recovery or installment) used for fees when collectibility cannot be estimated. The sales price, revenues, and costs deferred and the periods when fees are payable by the franchisee. Franchise fees deferred and later collected.
4. Separation of franchise fees and other franchise revenues, if significant.
5. Whether initial franchise fees are expected to decline because of a saturation of sales.

6. The relative contribution of initial franchise fees to income, if not apparent.
7. Distinction of revenues and costs related to outlets owned by franchisee and others.
8. The number of franchises sold, purchased, in operation, and franchisor-owned outlets, if significant changes have occurred during the year.

Topic 954: Health Care Entities

Topic 954, *Health Care Entities*, contains 24 subtopics:

10 Overall
205 Presentation of Financial Statements
210 Balance Sheet
225 Income Statement
280 Segment Reporting
305 Cash and Cash Equivalents
310 Receivables
320 Investments—Debt and Equity Securities
325 Investments—Other
340 Other Assets and Deferred Costs
360 Property, Plant, and Equipment
405 Liabilities
430 Deferred Revenue
440 Commitments
450 Contingencies
460 Guarantees
470 Debt
605 Revenue Recognition
720 Other Expenses
740 Income Taxes
805 Business Combinations
810 Consolidation
815 Derivatives and Hedging
825 Financial Instruments

This topic is not covered in this book.

Topic 958: Not-for-Profit Entities

Topic 958, *Not-for-Profit Entities*, contains 19 subtopics:

10 Overall

20 Financially Interrelated Entities

30 Split-Interest Agreements

205 Presentation of Financial Statements

210 Balance Sheet

225 Income Statement

230 Statement of Cash Flows

310 Receivables

320 Investments—Debt Securities

321 Investments—Equity Securities

325 Investments—Other

360 Property, Plant, and Equipment

405 Liabilities

450 Contingencies

605 Revenue Recognition—Contributions

715 Compensation—Retirement Benefits

720 Other Expenses

805 Business Combinations—Mergers and Acquisitions

810 Consolidation

Overview

ASC 958 establishes accounting standards for the form and content of general purpose external financial statements presented by not-for-profit entities that are nongovernmental entities. It specifies which financial statements must be presented as basic financial statements and the content of each statement. The basic financial statements required are a statement of financial position as of the end of the reporting period, a statement of activities and statement of cash flows for the reporting period, and accompanying notes to the financial statements. Reporting of amounts of expenses by both their natural classification and their functional classification is also required. That analysis of expenses is to be provided in one location, which could be on the face of the statement of activities, as a separate statement, or in notes to financial statements.

Each of the financial statements is discussed in detail below.

Statement of Financial Position

A statement of financial position reports the entire organization's assets, liabilities and net assets as of a specified date. The statement provides users with information about the entity's liquidity, ability to provide service on a continuing basis, flexibility from a financial standpoint, ability to settle obligations when due, and external financing needs. In providing information about assets and liabilities in a statement of financial position, assets and liabilities with similar characteristics should be combined into reasonably homogeneous groups. Examples include cash and cash equivalents; notes and accounts receivable; inventory; prepayments; investments on a long-term basis; and property, plant, and equipment. Assets should not be included in a category, such as cash available for current use, if those assets are restricted for long-term use. Assets and liabilities should be included in the statement of financial position in such a way as to provide information about liquidity. The FASB suggests that this may be accomplished by using one or more of the following methods:

1. Use the provisions of ASC 210-10 to divide assets and liabilities into a current or noncurrent classification.
2. Place assets in order of liquidity by putting first the asset expected to be converted to cash first.
3. Place liabilities in order of expected maturity with the one having the shortest maturity listed first.
4. Disclose restrictions and liquidity information in the notes to the statements.

Net assets in the statement of financial position must be divided into two categories, in accordance with the recent ASU 2016-14, *Not-for-Profit Entities (Topic 958): Presentation of Financial Statements of Not-for-Profit Entities*. The categories are Net Assets with Donor Restrictions and Net Assets without Donor Restrictions. Net Assets with Donor Restrictions represent those portions of net assets of the not-for-profit entity that are subject to donor-imposed restrictions, while Net Assets without Donor Restrictions are those net assets that are not subject to donor restrictions. "Donors" include makers of certain grants as well as other types of contributors.

Any significant information that limits the use of net assets without donor restrictions, such as contractual limits or limits imposed by the enterprise, should be disclosed in related note disclosures or, if appropriate, the information can be reported on the face of the statement.

Statement of Activities

A statement of activities should provide users with information about the amount of change in net assets for the entire organization for a specified period of time. The change in net assets reported in the statement of activities plus or minus the beginning net asset balance should equal the ending net asset balance reported in the statement of financial position. The statement of activities should present the net change in both categories of net assets: net assets with donor restrictions and net assets without donor restrictions. The total change in net assets is also required to be shown. Net assets in the statement of activities will be either increased or decreased by revenues, expenses, gains and losses, and these items should be classified in the statement according to the provisions of ASC 958.

Revenues generally will be reported as increases in net assets that are unrestricted. However, in some situations, donor-imposed restrictions require the revenue to be reported as an increase in net assets with donor restrictions. The revenue generally is reported on a gross basis; however, revenue may be reported on a net basis if the related expenses are disclosed either in the statement or in related notes. Contributions received are reported as an increase in net assets without donor restrictions, unless the contributions are donor restricted. Gains should be reported as increases in net assets without donor restrictions unless restrictions require the gains to be reported in net assets with donor restrictions.

Expenses should be reported as reductions in net assets without donor restrictions in the statement of activities. Losses should be reported as decreases in net assets without donor restrictions unless restrictions require the losses to be reported in net assets with donor restrictions. In some cases, gains and losses may be reported as net amounts in the statement of activities. For example, gains and losses may be netted when they are a result of incidental transactions not within the control of management or the entity.

Not-for-profit entities may classify revenues, gains, expenses, and losses within each category of net assets such as, for example, operating or nonoperating or earned or unearned. The use of further classifications within each net asset category is a decision that is left to the individual entity.

A not-for-profit recognizes the expiration of a donor-imposed restriction on a contribution when the restriction expires. A restriction expires when the stipulated time has elapsed, when the stipulated purpose for which the resource was restricted has been fulfilled, or both. If two or more temporary restrictions are imposed on a contribution, the effect of the expiration of those restrictions shall be recognized in the period in which the last remaining restriction has expired.

As an example, a gift of a term endowment that is to be invested for five years has two temporary restrictions—a purpose restriction (to be invested) and a time restriction (for a period of five years). After five years of investing, the purpose restriction will be met and the time restriction will lapse. In Year 5, when that term endowment becomes unrestricted, a reclassification shall be reported to reflect the decrease in net assets with donor restrictions and the increase in net assets without donor restrictions.

In determining when the last of two or more temporary restrictions has expired, explicit donor stipulations generally carry more weight than implied restrictions. For example, assume in Year 1 that an entity receives an unconditional promise to give that is payable in two equal installments in Years 2 and 3 with an explicit donor stipulation that its gift is to cover purchases of new equipment for the new School of Chemistry, which is expected to be completed in Year 3. That gift would have a purpose restriction (to be used to acquire new equipment to be housed in the new building), and because the unconditional promise is payable in Years 2 and 3, an entity generally would imply a time restriction. If, however, the building was completed early and opened in Year 2, and all of the needed equipment was purchased in Year 2 and exceeded the promised amount, absent an explicit stipulation to the contrary, it would be reasonable to conclude that those purchases fulfilled the donor restriction on the promised gift. Because the entity did not adopt a policy of implying time restrictions on long-lived assets, the restriction for the purchase of the equipment expires when the equipment is placed in service. In addition, a reclassification would be reported to reflect the decrease in net assets with donor restrictions and the increase in net assets without donor restrictions in Year 2.

ASC 958 specifies disclosure information for not-for-profit organizations that will provide users with information about the entity's service efforts. This information may be reported in the statement of activities or in related note disclosures. ASU 2016-14 now requires amounts of expenses to be disclosed by both their natural classification and their functional classification. That analysis of expenses is to be provided in one location, which could be on the face of the statement of activities, as a separate statement, or in notes to financial statements. Natural classifications would include categories such as rent, depreciation, professional fees, and others.

Statement of Cash Flows

The statement of cash flows should provide users with information about the entity's cash receipts and cash payments. The cash flow statement should be divided into the following three sections: operating, investing, and financing. In addition to cash flow information reported in these three sections, the entity must also report as supplemental data information about noncash investing and financing activities.

The operating section of the statement can be prepared using either the direct or indirect approach and should include cash flow information that impacts net assets of the entity. Unlike the requirements for business entities, if a not-for-profit entity uses the direct method of reporting operating cash flows, the entity is no longer required to include a reconciliation between the net change in cash and cash equivalents and the change in net assets. This amendment to the Codification was effective with ASU 2016-14 and applies to not-for-profit entities for fiscal years ending after December 15, 2017. Examples of items that would be reported in the operating section of the statement include cash from interest and dividends, from contributions, from service recipients, paid to suppliers and employees, and paid for interest.

The investing section includes cash receipts and payments of an investing nature. Examples of items included in the investing section include cash from sale of an investment, paid for equipment, and from sale of a building.

The financing section of the cash flow statement includes all transactions of a financing nature. Examples of items included in the financing section include cash payments on notes and cash flows from contributions that are restricted for investments in endowments. Supplemental information about noncash investing and financing activities would include transactions such as equipment received as a gift.

The cash proceeds from the sale of donated financial assets shall be classified as operating activity in the statement of cash flows if the financial assets were (1) received without any not-for-profit imposed limitations on sale, (2) converted into cash almost immediately, and (3) not restricted by the donor for long-term purposes. If these three conditions do not apply, the cash received from the sale should be classified as an investing activity. If (1) and (2) apply but the donor restricts the donation for long-term purposes, the proceeds should be classified as a financing activity.

In addition to the three basic financial statements discussed above, the entity must present appropriate note disclosures required by generally accepted accounting principles, unless an accounting principle exempts not-for-profit entities. For example, not-for-profit entities, like other business entities must report disclosures related to accounting changes and loss contingencies.

Recent changes to disclosure requirements for not-for-profits (ASU 2016-14) include all of the following: governing board actions that result in self-imposed limits on the use of resources that are not donor restricted; composition of net assets with donor restrictions; qualitative information that communicates how the entity manages its liquid resources to meet cash needs within one year of the balance sheet date; quantitative information that communicates the availability of an entity's financial assets to meet cash needs within one year of the balance sheet date; cost allocation methods among programs and support functions; "underwater" endowment funds disclosures.

Debt and Equity Securities—Flowchart and General Discussion

ASC 958-320 specifies the accounting and reporting requirements for all debt securities and ASC 958-321 covers most equity securities for which fair values can be easily determined that are held by not-for-profit organizations (Flowchart 9-3, Block 1).

Flowchart 9-3

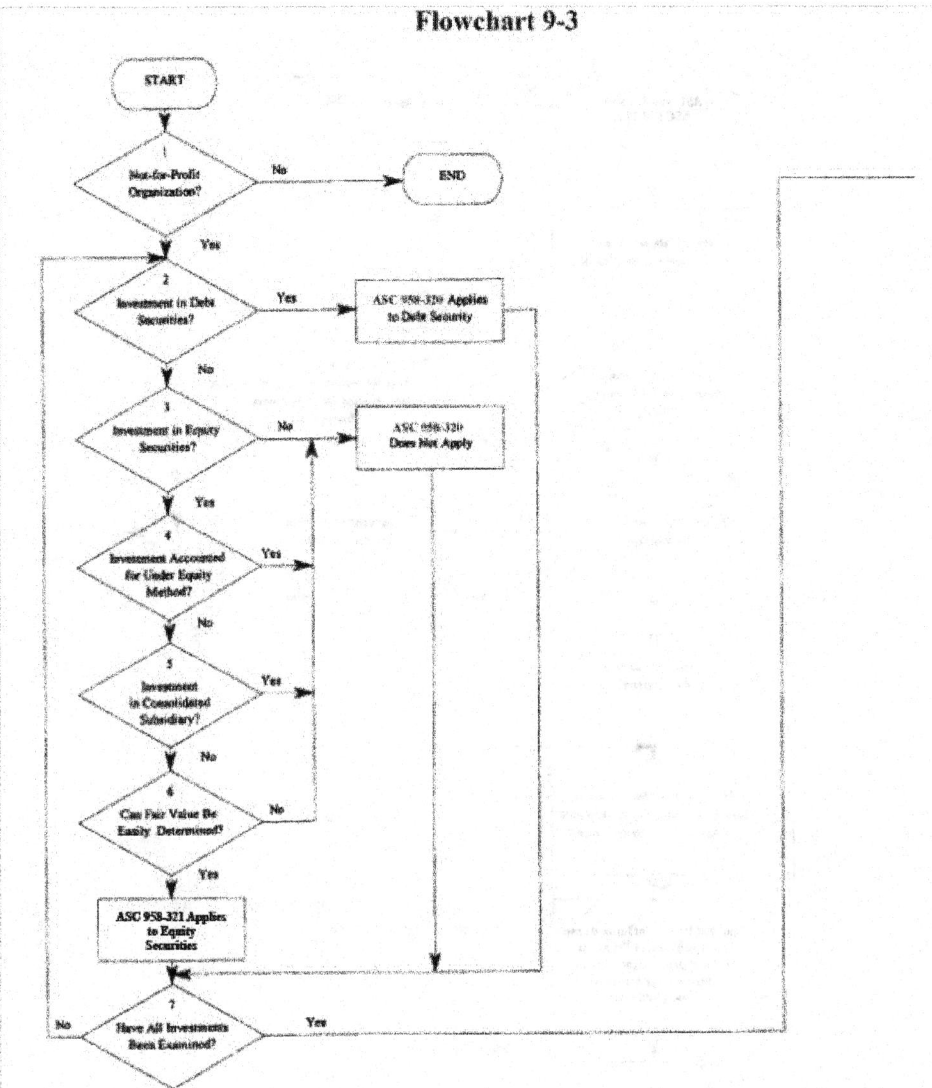

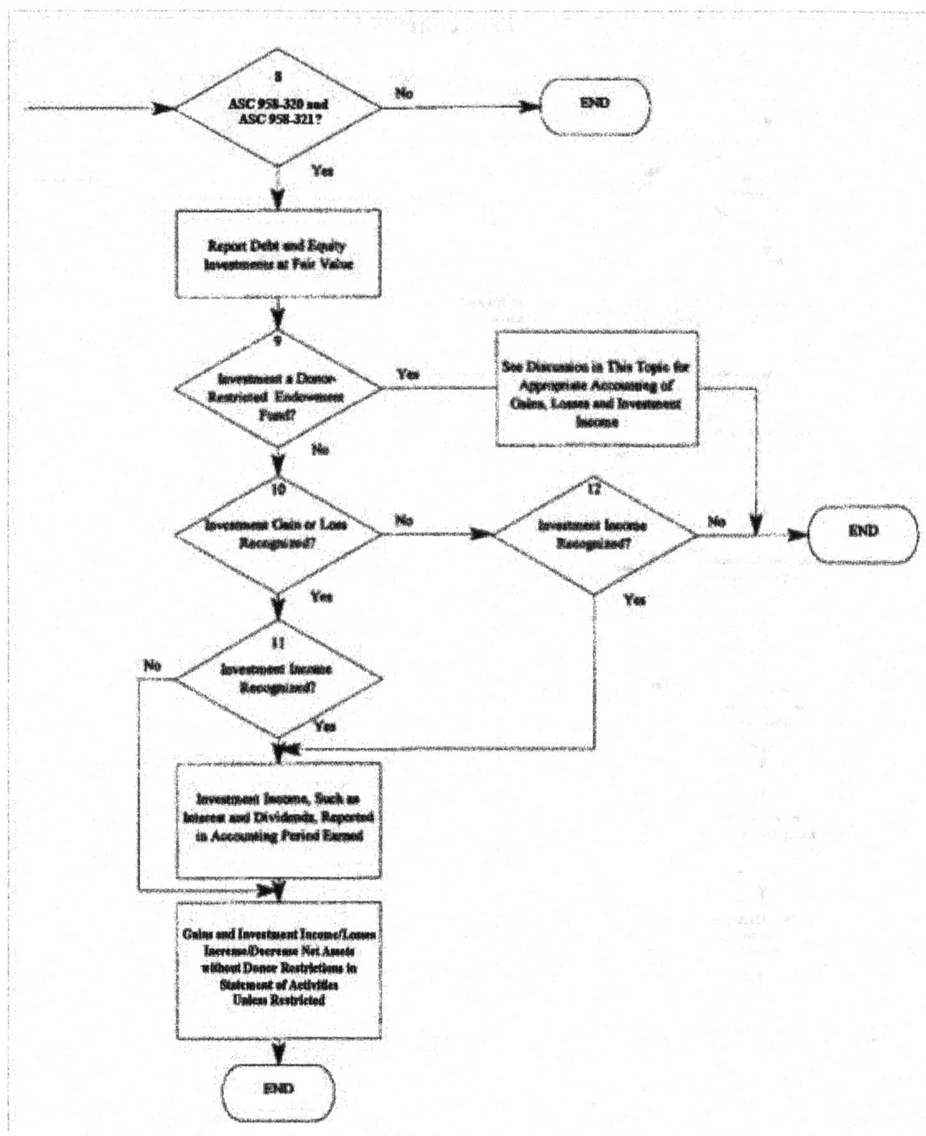

A debt security (Block 2) under ASC 958-320 is a security for which the not-for-profit organization is the debtor and the counterparty to the transaction is the creditor. Therefore, the not-for-profit organization has a creditor affiliation with the entity. Examples of debt securities include: corporate bonds, debt convertible into other securities, preferred stock that is redeemable, and securities of the U.S. Treasury. Examples of instruments not accounted for as debt securities are: leases, trade accounts receivable, forward contracts, and option contracts.

An equity security (Block 3) is a security that meets one of the following conditions: the security represents an interest in the ownership of an entity, the security represents a right of disposition of an interest in the ownership of an entity at an amount that is either fixed or can be determined, or the security represents a right of acquisition of an interest in the ownership of an entity at an amount that is either fixed or can be determined. Examples of equity securities include: common and preferred stock, options, rights, and warrants.

ASC 958-321 does not apply to all equity securities. Investments accounted for under the equity method of accounting (Block 4), as prescribed in ASC 323, are excluded from the scope of ASC 958-321. Therefore, ASC 958-321 would apply to equity securities accounted for under the cost method (i.e., to those signifying ownership interest of less than 20% and absence of significant influence over the operating policies of the investee company). However, ASC 958-321 does not apply to investments in equity securities of consolidated subsidiaries (Block 5) or to equity securities where the fair value of the securities cannot be easily determined (Block 6). In addition, ASC 958-321 does not apply to derivative instruments covered by ASC 815.

ASC 958-321 does apply to equity securities where fair value can be easily determined. It is assumed that fair value can be easily determined if the securities are quoted on a U.S. exchange or on a foreign exchange that is equivalent to a U.S. exchange. In addition, fair value can be easily determined for mutual funds that have published quotes and ready markets. The accounting requirements for fair value accounting and reporting are covered by ASC 820 and ASC 325.

Debt and equity securities covered by ASC 958-320 or ASC 958-321 (Block 8) are reported in the statement of financial position at fair market value and changes in value are reported as gains and losses. A not-for-profit organization may receive a gift that has no legal or donor requirements or stipulations or that has donor stipulations that require the gift to be invested for a specific period of time or in perpetuity (i.e., an endowment fund that is donor restricted (Block 9)). When there are no legal or donor requirements for the investment, the gain or loss from the change in value of the investment (Block 10) is an increase or decrease in net assets without donor restrictions in the statement of activities (Paragraph 8). When the not-for-profit organization has income from the investment (Blocks 11 and 12), such as dividends and interest, the investment income is reported in the accounting period that the income is earned. The investment income increases net assets without donor restrictions in the statement of activities, as long as the investment income has no restrictions placed on it by the donor.

The investment may be classified as an endowment fund that is donor restricted (Block 9) because of donor stipulations and requirements. Gains and losses from changes in the value of the investment are subject to the restrictions stipulated by the donor. When stipulations or restrictions are met in the same accounting period that the restricted gains are reported, the gains may be used to increase net assets without donor restrictions when these conditions are met: the accounting procedure used is disclosed, the procedure is applied on a consistent basis from accounting period to accounting period, and contributions received are accounted for using a similar policy. If there are no legal or donor stipulations or restrictions placed on the change in investment value, losses should be accounted for in the following manner: net assets with donor restrictions are reduced to the degree that the net increase in the investment from restrictions stipulated by the donor has not been achieved prior to the time of the loss and the excess loss, if any, remaining after meeting the first condition, decreases net assets without donor restrictions.

In some cases, losses from endowment funds that are donor restricted reduce the funds below levels required by legal or donor stipulations or requirements. In such cases, subsequent gains that reinstate asset fair value to specified amounts are accounted for as an increase in net assets classified as without donor restrictions.

Investment income related to restricted investments increases net assets that are donor restricted. When stipulations or restrictions are met in the same accounting period that the restricted investment income is reported, the income may be used to increase net assets without restrictions when the following conditions are met: the accounting procedure used is disclosed, the procedure is applied on a consistent basis from accounting period to accounting period, and contributions received are accounted for using a similar policy.

This completes the general discussion of Flowchart 9-3 and the accounting requirements for investments in debt and equity securities. The next section covers the disclosure requirements for such investments.

Debt and Equity Securities—Disclosure Requirements

ASC 958-320-50 and ASC 958-321-50 require specific disclosures for not-for-profit organizations that have investments in debt and equity securities, as follows:

1. Disclose the nature and carrying amount of investments, on either a group or individual basis, that have a market risk concentration considered significant. This information is disclosed for the latest accounting period that a statement of financial position is provided.
2. Disclose the following information for each accounting period that a statement of financial position is prepared:
   a. The investment carrying amount, on an aggregate basis, reported by major type of investments.
   b. For investments not covered by the accounting requirements of ASC 958-320 or ASC 958-321, the basis used for ascertaining investment carrying amount.
   c. When investments that are not classified as financial instruments are reported on a fair value basis, the assumptions and methods used for estimating fair value.
   d. The amount of deficiencies, on an aggregate basis, for endowment funds that are donor restricted, when asset fair values are below stipulated levels.
3. Disclose the following information for each accounting period that a statement of activities is prepared:
   a. The elements of return on investment, with the following items reported as a minimum: gains and losses on a net basis when fair

value is used for investments, realized gains and losses on a net basis when fair value is not used for investments, and income from investments.

b. When the return on investment is divided into nonoperating and operating elements, a reconciliation of amounts in the statement of activities with the return on investment.

c. A description of the policy for determining the amount of the investment return that is included in operations and, if the policy changed, the conditions that caused the change.

Depreciation

ASC 958-360 requires that not-for-profit entities report depreciation expense on long-lived tangible assets in general purpose financial statements issued to external parties. In addition, it requires that ASC 360-10, covering issues related to depreciation expense and depreciation disclosures, be applied to not-for-profit organizations.

An entity is classified as not-for-profit if it meets the following criteria: the entity does not have ownership interest as in a profit-directed enterprise, the purpose of the entity is not profit-directed, and individuals and entities that make contributions to the not-for-profit entity do not expect commensurate returns. As noted above, an entity classified as not-for-profit in accordance with the provisions of ASC 958-360 must report depreciation expense on tangible assets that are long-lived, except historical treasures and works of art. In addition, the entity also must disclose the following selected depreciation information:

1. As of the date of the statement of financial position, the balance of major classes of assets subject to depreciation either by function or by nature.
2. As of the date of the statement of financial position, the amount of accumulated depreciation disclosed in total or by major classes.
3. The amount of depreciation expense included in the financial statements for the current accounting period.
4. For major classes of assets, a description of the method(s) used in the calculation of depreciation expense.

Services

ASU 2013-06, *Not-for-Profit Entities (Topic 958): Services Received from Personnel of an Affiliate*, effective for fiscal years beginning after June 15, 2014, amended the accounting for services received from personnel of affiliate entities. The amendment requires a recipient not-for-profit to recognize all services received from personnel of an affiliate that directly benefit the recipient not-for-profit entity. Although the recognition will usually be at the cost recognized by the affiliate for the personnel providing the services, the recipient not-for-profit entity may elect to recognize the services at the fair value of that service if using the cost would significantly over-or understate the value of the service received.

Recent Changes

ASU 2016-14, *Not-for-Profit Entities (Topic 958): Presentation of Financial Statements of Not-for-Profit Entities,* changes some of the aspects of presentation and disclosures of not-for-profit entities. The Update changes the requirement for the entity to present only two classes of net assets rather than three classes of net assets. The two classes of net assets will be "with donor restrictions" and "without donor restrictions." Further, the Update requires enhanced disclosures removes the requirement to present the indirect method of operating cash flows when choosing to use the direct method of reporting operating cash flow. In addition, the Update eliminated the option to release the donor-imposed restriction over the estimated useful life of the acquired asset, so that now only the "placed-in-service" approach can be used on gifts to acquire or construct long-lived assets. These changes are effective for annual financial statements issued for fiscal years beginning after December 15, 2017 and for interim periods within fiscal years beginning after December 15, 2018.

ASU 2017-02, *Not-for-Profit Entities—Consolidation (Subtopic 958-810): Clarifying When a Not-for-Profit Entity That Is a General Partner or a Limited Partner Should Consolidate a For-Profit Limited Partnership or Similar Entity,* retains the consolidation guidance that was in Subtopic 810-20 for not-for-profit (NFP) entities by including it within Subtopic 958-810. The amendments in this Update are effective for NFP entities for fiscal years beginning after December 15, 2016, and interim periods within fiscal years beginning after December 15, 2017. Early adoption is permitted, including adoption in an interim period. If an NFP entity early adopts the amendments in an interim period, any adjustments should be reflected as of the beginning of the fiscal year that includes that interim period.

Topic 960: Plan Accounting—Defined Benefit Pension Plans

Topic 960, *Plan Accounting—Defined Benefit Pension Plans,* contains eight subtopics:

10 Overall

20 Accumulated Plan Benefits

30 Net Assets Available for Plan Benefits

40 Terminating Plans

205 Presentation of Financial Statements

310 Receivables

325 Investments—Other

360 Property, Plant, and Equipment

ASC 960 deals with the financial presentation of information developed by a defined benefit pension plan. A defined benefit plan is one in which the benefits payable to the employee are determinable at any given point in time. ASC 960 applies to pension plans of private enterprises.

When considering the accounting that should be followed by a pension plan, there are several viable reporting alternatives available. One alternative is to permit pension plans to report their financial position and results of operations in the same manner as any business enterprise (i.e., prepare an income statement, balance sheet, and statement of changes in financial position using conventional U.S. GAAP). This alternative may be referred to as the general purpose financial statement approach. The FASB rejected this approach by deciding that financial statements of pension plans should benefit the participants of the plan and, therefore, should be directed to the needs of the participants. Rather than the general purpose approach, the FASB decided that, if a pension plan issues financial statements, those statements should serve the special purpose described above.

ASC 960 *does not* require pension plans to issue financial statements, but provides guidance for those plans that do wish to issue statements to participants and other interested parties. When a defined benefit pension plan decides to issue financial statements, the ASC 960 suggests the following be issued:

1. Statement of Net Assets Available for Benefits;
2. Statement of Changes in Net Assets Available for Benefits;
3. Statement of Accumulated Plan Benefits; and
4. Statement of Changes in Accumulated Plan Benefits.

ASC 960 provides alternatives to these four basic financial statements, but the alternatives are merely combinations of the statements listed above.

The financial statements listed may seem foreign to accountants not accustomed to working with pension plan information. The remainder of the discussion relating to ASC 960 will be directed toward defining the information content of each statement in sufficient detail to allow areas of interest to be pursued in an informed manner. The discussion will begin with a general description of the information content of each statement and proceed to specific examples of the financial presentation and related notes. Many of the specialized terms associated with pension plan accounting will be introduced and defined as necessary for a clear understanding of the content of the financial statements.

The Recommended Financial Statements

The recommended financial statements should be prepared at (as of) the end of the plan year. The date of the financial statements is referred to as the benefit information date. If information is not available at the end of the plan year, it may be necessary to use information at the beginning of the year. In this case, additional disclosures are required. The FASB has encouraged pension plans to adopt methods and procedures that will enable it to present financial information at the end of the plan year. These procedures may require the use of estimates or allocations to adjust information from beginning-of-year to end-of-year amounts. More will be said about the specific additional disclosures required when beginning-of-year information is used by the pension plan.

Statement of Net Assets Available for Benefits

This financial statement should be prepared on the accrual basis and should contain information about the pension plan's resources available for the payment of benefits to participants. The statement begins with a listing of the pension plan assets, carried for the most part at fair value, and subtracts total liabilities showing a residual amount for net assets available for the payment of benefits. The net asset amount is the bottom line in this financial statement. In the typical case, pension plan asset amounts are substantially in excess of plan liability amounts. One would expect to find substantial asset amounts available for payment of plan benefits.

The typical statement of net assets available for benefits would be prepared in the following form:

XYZ Company Pension Plan Statement of Net Assets Available for Benefits
December 31, 20X6

Assets:	
Investments	$00,000
Deposit administration contract	00,000
Receivables	00,000
Cash	00,000
Total assets	$000,000
Liabilities:	
Accounts payable	$0,000
Accrued expenses	0,000
Total liabilities	$0,000
Net assets available for benefits	$000,000

Most of the accounts shown in the example statement are familiar to accountants. The deposit administration contract account represents transactions between the company and an insurance company involved in the pension plan. Funds are deposited with the company, earn interest, and can be used to provide for the benefits due to retiring employees. Generally, the funds deposited are used to purchase annuity contracts for retiring employees. With minor exceptions, the assets and liabilities of the pension plan are stated at fair value. This can result in valuations that are different from the traditional historical cost basis used for general purpose financial statements.

Chart 9-1 details the common pension plan assets and the valuation basis that should be used in the preparation of the statement of net assets available for benefits.

Chart 9-1 Assets Available for Benefits and Valuation Basis

Assets Available for Benefits	Valuation Basis
Investments:	
Equity securities	Fair value
Debt securities	Fair value
Real estate	Fair value
Mortgages	Fair value
Other investments	Fair value
Insurance Contracts	Same basis as under ERISA*

Assets Available for Benefits	**Valuation Basis**
Investment Contracts	Fair value
Receivables:	
Contributions from the employer	Net realizable value
Contributions from the employer	Net realizable value
Funding from state subsidies or federal grants	Net realizable value
Dividends receivable	Net realizable value
Accrued interest	Net realizable value
Receivable from sale of securities	Net realizable value
Other receivables	Net realizable value
Cash	Net realizable value

* ERISA stands for the Employee Retirement Income Security Act of 1974. An adjustment is reflected on the financial statements for fully benefit-responsive contracts that are recorded at fair value and adjusted to cost for financial reporting purposes.

Investments. Plan investments should be shown in the statement at fair value. Fair value is defined as the amount that would be received on the measurement date from the sale of property between sellers and buyers (market participants) in an orderly transaction. In addition, the sellers and buyers are unrelated parties on the measurement date. The provisions of ASC 820 should be consulted to determine how fair value should be computed and what methods are appropriate.

Mortgages and debt securities that are not traded could be valued at the present value of future cash flows. The following formula may be used to value mortgages and debt securities when the valuation date and the interest payment date are the same:

$$FV = (PP)(PA) + (MV)(PV)$$

Where: FV = Fair value of mortgage or debt security on interest payment date.

PP = Amount of periodic interest payment.

PA = Present value factor for an ordinary annuity using the effective interest rate per interest payment period.

MV = Maturity value of the mortgage or security.

PV = Present value factor for $1, using the effective interest rate per interest payment period.

If the valuation date and the interest payment date are not the same, the formula given above must be adjusted as follows:

$$VFV = FV + AD - AP$$

Where: VFV = Fair value on valuation date.

AD = Discount amortization from last interest payment date to date of valuation.

AP = Premium amortization from last interest payment date to date of valuation.

The information presented in Example 9-3 was developed to demonstrate the computations associated with mortgages and debt securities.

Example 9-3
Bond Valuation Information

1. Western Enterprises (Western) has elected to present financial statements for its pension plan for the year ended December 31, 20X6.
2. Western's pension plan had an investment in a $500,000 face value, 10% bond due in 10 years from October 1, 20X6. There was no quoted market price associated with this investment.
3. Interest of $25,000 was received on April 1 and October 1 of each year.
4. At December 31, 20X6, Western determined that an appropriate effective interest rate for similar bonds was 12%.

There is no market quotation for the bonds, so Western has decided to determine fair value by computing the discounted future cash flows for the bond. The first step in the process is to calculate the fair value at October 1, 20X6, the interest payment date. The equation requires the use of the effective interest rate per interest payment period. The effective annual interest rate is known to be 12%, and interest is paid semiannually. There are 20 semiannual interest payment periods from October 1, 20X6. Therefore, the interest factors used in the equation will be based on a 6% interest rate for 20 periods. The fair value is determined as follows:

FV = ($25,000)(11.46992[1]) + ($500,000)(.31180[2])
FV = ($286,748 + $155,900)
FV = $442,648

[1] Present value factor for an ordinary annuity.
[2] Present value factor $1.

The calculated amount of $442,648 represents the fair value of the bonds on October 1, 20X6, the last interest payment date. This amount must be adjusted to determine the fair value of the bonds on December 31, 20X6, the valuation date of the pension plan financial statements. The required adjustment is shown below:

VFV = $442,648 + $780
VFV = $443,428

The amount of the adjustment, $780, represents the amortization of the discount created from the use of the 12% effective interest rate. The discount amortization period was from October 1, 20X6 to December 31, 20X6 and is computed as follows:

Fair value of the bonds	$442,648
Semiannual effective interest rate	× .06
Semiannual interest income	$26,559
Semiannual cash interest income	25,000
Semiannual discount amortization	$1,559
Amortization period (10/1-12/31)	× 3/6
Required adjustment for amortization	$780

In addition to the investments itemized in Chart 9-1, a pension plan may have an investment in leased property. Determining the fair value of a leased asset may prove to be a difficult problem. The pension plan may elect to value the leased asset at the discounted amount of the future cash flows. If this is the case, the formula shown below may be used to compute the discounted amount:

	V	=	(R)(A) + (RV)(P)
Where:	V	=	Fair value of the leased property at rental payment date.
	R	=	Periodic rental payment received.
	A	=	Present value factor of an annuity using the interest rate representative of the risk involved in the lease.
	RV	=	Residual value of the leased asset.
	P	=	Present value factor for $1 using an interest rate representative of the risk involved in the lease.

To illustrate the valuation of a leased asset using the discounted value of the future cash flows, the information in Example 9-4 is used.

Example 9-4
Leased Asset Information

1. Stanley Company (Stanley) has an investment in an asset that is subject to a long-term lease agreement with a lessee. Stanley, a December 31 year-end enterprise, plans to determine the fair value of the leased asset using the discounted value of the future cash flows.

2. The original lease agreement specified a 10-year lease term. On December 31, 20X6, the remaining lease term is five years.

3. The lease agreement requires the lessee to pay Stanley a $100,000 lease payment each December 31. Stanley has estimated that the leased asset will have a residual value of $50,000 at the end of the lease term.

4. At December 31, 20X6, the valuation date, Stanley estimated that an appropriate rate of interest, considering all the risk factors, is 12%.

The lease agreement specifies annual payments; therefore, the present value computation will be based on the five-year remaining lease term. The appropriate annual interest rate to use in the discounting process is known to be 12%. The present value factors to be used will be for five periods at 12%. The computation of the fair value of the future cash payments would be determined as follows:

V = ($100,000)(3.60478[1]) + ($50,000)(.56743[2])
V = $360,478 + $28,372
V = $388,850

[1] Present value factor for an ordinary annuity.
[2] Present value factor $1.

The present value of the future lease payment is $360,478, and the present value of the estimated residual is $28,372. The lease payment is an annuity for five years, and the residual is a lump-sum amount at the end of the five-year period. The total of these two amounts, $388,850, is the fair value of the future cash flows resulting from the lease agreement.

Insurance contracts, as defined in ASC 944, should be reported the same way they are reported for purposes of the Employee Retirement Income Security Act of 1974 (ERISA), which is either fair value or contract value. Investment contracts, even if the contracts are with insurance companies, should be reported at fair market value. Investment contracts are defined in ASC 944.

Any investment of the pension plan that constitutes 5% or more of the net assets available for benefit must be disclosed. In addition, significant related party transactions must be disclosed. Related-party transactions are indicated when the pension plan has transactions with the employer company (or other sponsor, if not the employer) or an employee or employee organization. (See Topic 850 in Chapter 8 for a discussion of related-party transactions.)

Receivables: Example 9-5 indicates the variety of items that may be identified as receivables by the pension plan, one of which is contributions receivable. Contributions receivable are amounts that a plan expects to receive from parties such as employers, participants of the plan, and others. Amounts due to the plan from these sources may be evidenced by formal contracts or other legal requirements. In addition, a formal commitment by the employer(s) may be sufficient evidence to support the creation of a receivable. This latter event assumes that the accountant is able to determine what constitutes a formal commitment. A formal commitment may exist if any of the following situations can be identified:

1. The body that governs the employer approves a designated contribution;
2. The employer has a constant policy of making contributions to the plan subsequent to year end according to a funding plan that relates the payments to the prior year;
3. The payment is deducted for federal income taxes on or prior to the date that the employer reports to the pension plan;
4. As of the date that the employer reports to the pension plan, a contribution is reported on the books of the employer.

Contributions receivable normally will be valued at their cash equivalent amount. The remaining receivables are self-explanatory and require no further discussion.

Cash: Cash is shown in the financial statement at fair value.

Operating assets: ASC 960 requires that assets used in the operations of the plan be reported at cost net of accumulated depreciation or amortization. Operating assets would include such items as equipment, buildings used in the pension plan's operations, furniture, and fixtures.

Liabilities of the fund: ASC 960 does not include a discussion of the presentation of liabilities in the statement of net assets available for benefits. However, ASC 960 defines net assets available for benefits and provides for a deduction for liabilities, but it notes that accumulated plan benefits of plan participants are not considered liabilities for purposes of the pension plan. It may be reasonably inferred that the FASB intended the pension plan's net assets available for benefits to be reduced by certain plan liabilities such as accounts payable and accrued expenses.

End-of-period versus beginning-of-period information date: Recall from the previous discussion that a complete set of pension plan financial statements includes the Statement of Accumulated Plan Benefits. This statement shows the actuarial present value of the accumulated plan benefits as determined by the plan's actuary using end-of-period or beginning-of-period information date.

The FASB has encouraged the use of end-of-period benefit information dates and would like to have accountants and actuaries use this date for valuation purposes. At the current time, most actuarial computations are made sometime during the year and are based upon beginning-of-the-year data.

If a pension plan finds it necessary to use beginning-of-year benefit information in the preparation of the statement of net assets, ASC 960 requires additional financial presentation. When beginning-of-year benefit information is used, the pension plan should prepare both a statement of net assets and a statement of change in net assets for the prior year. Information relating to the prior period must be disclosed, along with the current period financial statements.

To illustrate the preparation of the Statement of Net Assets Available for Benefits, the information in Example 9-5 is used.

Example 9-5
Financial Statement Preparation

1. Parker Enterprises, a December 31 year-end company, has elected to present financial information relating to its pension plan, in accordance with the provisions of ASC 960, for the year ended December 31, 20X6.

2. The pension plan is using an end-of-year benefit information date and has the following investments on December 31, 20X6:

	Cost	Fair Value
U.S. Government Bonds	$2,800,000	$3,500,000
Bonds and notes	6,350,000	7,300,000
Preferred stocks:		
Parker Enterprises	1,800,000	2,100,000
Other	4,300,000	4,800,000
Common stock:		
Parker Enterprises	2,300,000	2,900,000
Other	8,950,000	9,550,000
Mortgages	1,500,000	1,600,000
Real estate	1,600,000	2,500,000
	$29,600,000	$34,250,000

3. Receivables of the pension plan on December 31, 20X6 were as follows:

Employer contributions	$300,000
Employee contributions	100,000

Receivable from sale of securities	500,000
Funding from federal grant	150,000
Dividends receivable	50,000
Accrued interest	125,000
Total	$1,225,000

4. Pension plan cash on hand and in the bank amounted to $300,000 at December 31, 20X6.
5. The pension plan had an insurance contract with the First Warranty Insurance Company with a contract value of $3,500,000 on December 31, 20X6.
6. Liabilities of the pension plan on December 31, 20X6 were:

Accounts payable	$80,500
Accrued expenses	44,500
Total	$125,000

ASC 960 suggests that the statement of net assets begin with investments, followed by deposit administration contracts, receivables, cash, and other assets. Subtotals should be taken where appropriate. Using the information developed in Example 9-5, the statement of net assets would appear as follows:

Parker Enterprises Pension Plan Statement of Net Assets Available for Benefits December 31, 20X6

ASSETS:		
Investments, at fair value:		
U.S. government securities	$3,500,000	
Bonds and notes—corporate	7,300,000	
Preferred stock:		
Parker Enterprises	2,100,000	
Other	4,800,000	
Common stock:		
Parker Enterprises	2,900,000	
Other	9,550,000	
Mortgages	1,600,000	
Insurance Contract	6,000,000	
Total investments, at fair value		$34,250,000
Receivables:		
Employer contributions	$300,000	
Employee contributions	100,000	
Receivable from sale of securities	500,000	
Funding from federal grant	150,000	
Dividends receivable	50,000	
Accrued interest	125,000	
Total receivables		1,225,000
Cash		300,000
TOTAL ASSETS		$39,275,000

LIABILITIES:		
Accounts payable	$80,500	
Accrued expenses	44,500	
TOTAL LIABILITIES		125,000
Adjustment from fair value to contract value for fully benefit-responsive investment contract		
NET ASSETS AVAILABLE FOR BENEFITS		$39,150,000

Because end-of-year benefit information was used in the preparation of the statements, comparative information is not required. However, if beginning-of-year benefit information had been used, information for both December 31, 20X6 and 20X5 would be required to be presented in the format shown.

This completes the discussion and examples relating to the Statement of Net Assets Available for Benefits.

Statement of Changes in Net Assets Available for Benefits

The Statement of Changes in Net Assets Available for Benefits is designed to inform the reader as to the major causes of changes in net assets of the pension plan from the beginning to the end of the current accounting period. This statement is similar in nature to the statement of changes in financial position prepared by most profit-directed enterprises.

The major causes of changes in net assets available for benefits are income from investments (less expenses associated with the investing activity), contributions from employers and employees during the period, payment of benefits to retired employees, and expenditures associated with the purchase of retirement annuities and other retirement benefits. The net increase (decrease) is added to (subtracted from) the beginning net asset balance to determine the ending net assets available for benefits.

ASC 960 requires that the statement of changes in net assets be presented in sufficient detail so that the user can identify the significant changes occurring during the period. The precise format of the statement is not dictated to the accountant, but is to remain flexible. At a minimum, the following information should be disclosed:

1. The net appreciation (depreciation) in fair value. Net appreciation or depreciation includes realized gains and losses on investment that were both purchased and sold during the period, as well as unrealized appreciation or depreciation of the investments held at year-end.
2. Investment income not considering the net change in fair value described in 1, above.
3. The amount of cash and non-cash contributions made by the employer. All non-cash contributions should be appropriately described and reported at fair value.
4. Employee (participant) contributions, including contributions from a sponsor for the employee. Refunds of employee contributions may be reported separately, may be netted against the contribution, or may be included in the benefits paid.

5. Other identified contributions.
6. Amount of benefits distributed to employees (participants).
7. Payments on insurance contracts not included in pension plan assets. Dividend income relating to these contracts may be netted against payments to the insurance company for contracts purchased. If this latter practice is followed, the amount of the dividends must be disclosed.
8. Expenses related to administration of the plan.
9. Other charges should also be presented if significant

Given these required disclosures and the intent of the statement of changes in net assets, a format can be developed. One approach may be called the reconciliation format, because it would begin with the net asset balance at the beginning of the period and show the required additions and subtractions to arrive at the ending balance of net assets available for benefits. A second approach may be called the net change method and would begin with the required increases and decreases in net assets during the period and combine the net increase or decrease with the balance at the beginning of the period to produce the balance at the end of the period. The second, or net change, approach is used in the example material below.

The material presented in Example 9-6 is merely an extension of the material used in Example 9-5. The same company, Parker Enterprises, will be used throughout the remaining examples. The only difference between the Example 9-6 information and the Example 9-5 information is the intent of the company to prepare the Statement of Changes in Net Assets Available for Benefits. Review the material in Example 9-6 before proceeding to the financial statement.

Example 9-6

Statement of Changes in Net Assets Available for Benefits

1. Parker Enterprises' pension plan has developed the following information for the preparation of the statement of changes in net assets for the year ended December 31, 20X6. The statement is to be prepared in accordance with the provisions of ASC 960.

2. The pension plan is using an end-of-year benefit information date and has determined that the following items will explain the change in net assets for the year ended December 31, 20X6:

(1)	Net appreciation in fair value of investments	$1,370,000
(2)	Interest income from investments	987,040
(3)	Dividend income from investments	1,064,250
(4)	Rental income from real estate	509,250
(5)	Employer contributions during the year	6,000,000
(6)	Employee contributions during the year	1,000,000
(7)	Benefits paid directly to participants	3,897,206
(8)	Purchase of insurance contracts	875,000
(9)	Administrative expenses of the plan	393,069

(10)	Investment expenses	196,527
(11)	Funding from federal grants during the period	300,000

3. Last year's statement of changes in net assets showed a balance of $33,281,262 at December 31, 20X5.

Using the information from Example 9-6, the following statement of changes in net assets can be prepared.

Parker Enterprises Pension Plan Statement of Changes in Net Assets Available for Benefits for the Year Ended December 31, 20X6

Investment Income		
Net appreciation in fair value of investments	$1,370,000	
Interest	987,040	
Dividends	1,064,250	
Rents	509,250	
Total	$3,930,540	
Less: investment expenses	196,527	
Net Investment Income Contributions		$3,734,013
Employer	$6,000,000	
Employee	1,000,000	
Funding from federal grants	300,000	
Total		7,300,000
Total Additions to Net Assets		$11,034,013
Benefits paid directly to plan participants	$3,897,206	
Purchase of insurance contracts	875,000	
Administrative expenses	393,069	
Total Reduction in Net Assets	(5,165,275)	
Increase in Net Assets During Period	$5,868,738	
Net Assets Available for Benefits at Beginning of the Period	33,281,262	
Net Assets Available for Benefits at End of the Period	$39,150,000	

Because an end-of-year benefit information date was used in the preparation of the statement, comparative financial information is not required. Refer to the Statement of Net Assets Available for Benefits for Parker's pension plan and notice that the net assets shown above tie into the balance of the net asset statement.

Statement of Accumulated Plan Benefits

The statement of net assets was designed to inform the reader about the ability of the plan to meet its obligations to participants. The statement of accumulated benefits is designed to describe to the reader the benefits that will have to be paid to participants. Information about the pension plan's assets would be meaningless without information about the benefits that will have to be paid to the plan participants in the future.

Accumulated plan benefits are benefits that a pension plan estimates it will have to pay to the following groups: (1) participants who have terminated employment or retired, (2) participants who are deceased, (3) current participants, and (4) beneficiaries of the groups in (1)–(3), above. Accountants deal with historical information for the most part, but accumulated plan benefit information is concerned with forecasting future payments. Determination of accumulated plan benefits is beyond the scope of the accountant's function. The FASB has recognized the need for actuaries to develop information about accumulated plan benefits. The statement of accumulated plan benefits must disclose the actuarially determined present value of the benefits. This means that the amounts shown as plan benefits must be based upon actuarial assumptions about the future payment of the benefits. The present value of the benefits merely recognized the time value of money from the benefit information date to the expected benefit payment date.

At a minimum, the actuarial present value of the plan benefits must be divided into: (1) vested benefits due and payable on the benefit information date, (2) vested benefits other than in (1), and (3) nonvested benefits.

Vested benefits are those that are not contingent upon future services of the employee. Employees are entitled to their vested benefits, even if they leave their current employer. The basic format of the statement of accumulated plan benefits will contain the three line-items described above.

In addition to the financial information presented in the statement, certain disclosures at the benefit information date are required. The disclosures should include the current employees' accumulated contributions to the plan, including interest credited to the contributions. If the contributions earn interest, the rate should be disclosed.

Measurement of accumulated benefits: The first step in the accounting process is to ensure the proper determination of the pension plan's accumulated benefits. If possible, the benefits should be determined for each year of service, using the current plan provisions. If application of this method is not possible, the ASC 960 states that the plan's benefits should accumulate using one of the following formulas:

Formula 1—Assumes that this benefit type is in vested benefits:

$$\text{MAB} = \frac{\text{SYBID}}{\text{SYFV}}$$

MAB	=	Method of accumulating pension plan benefits.
SYBID	=	Years of service to the benefit information date.
SYFV	=	Years of service completed to date that participant is fully vested.

Formula 2—Assumes that this benefit type is not in vested benefits:

$$\text{MAB} = \frac{\text{YSC}}{\text{YSP}}$$

MAB	=	Method of accumulating pension plan benefits.
YSC	=	Years of service completed.
YSP	=	Years of service projected to date employment ceases.

When attempting to measure the accumulated plan benefits, the following items should be given appropriate consideration:

1. History of the employee's service, pay and other items should be used as a basis for the accumulated plan benefits.
2. Projected years of service should be used only to determine benefits such as disability, death, early retirement, and increased benefits due to the employee working a specified number of years.
3. Recognition should be given to automatic increases in benefits estimated to happen subsequent to the benefit information date. This would include items such as cost-of-living adjustments.
4. Benefits to be paid by outside sources, such as insurance companies when the insurance contract is not included in net assets available for benefits, should be excluded.
5. No consideration should be given to plan amendments subsequent to the benefit information date.
6. Employee compensation is assumed to be stable when it becomes necessary to project future earnings for the determination of Social Security benefits.

Actuarial assumptions: Once the accumulated benefits have been determined, it becomes necessary to compute the actuarial present value of the benefits. All actuarial computations are based upon assumptions about the future. ASC 960-20-35-1 specifies certain requirements concerning the assumptions to be used in computing the present value of the accumulated benefits. These requirements include:

1. The pension plan is assumed to be ongoing.
2. The rate of return assumed by the actuary should be reflective of the rate of return that could be earned by the plan's assets. If this rate is based on existing plan assets, the value of the plan assets should be the same as that used in the Statement of Net Assets Available for Benefits.
3. Assumed rates of inflation and rates of return should be consistent.
4. Administrative expenses paid by the pension plan should be accounted for in either of the following ways: an adjustment to the assumed rate of return, or assign expenses to future periods and discount them back to the benefit information date.

As an alternative to the assumptions shown above, the actuary may elect to estimate the cost of benefits by determining the expenses involved in obtaining an insurance contract to pay the plan benefits on the benefit information date. Additional assumptions by the actuary may be needed and should be consistent with the assumptions given in ASC 960.

Because the FASB did not resolve the issue of whether accumulated plan benefits were liabilities, the presentation of this information has been made flexible. The FASB suggests that the accumulated benefits be shown in a *separate statement,* disclosed in a statement with net assets available for benefits, or disclosed in a note to the financial statements. If the separate financial statement option is selected, information similar to that shown in Example 9-7 must be generated.

Example 9-7
Accumulated Plan Benefit Information

1. Parker Enterprises, the same company used in the Examples 9-5 and 9-6 financial statements, has a pension plan that will issue financial statements recommended by ASC 960.
2. The pension plan has employed an actuary to compute the present value of accumulated plan benefits, using an end-of-year benefit information date, consistent with the assumptions specified by ASC 960.
3. The actuary provides the pension plan with the following information about the accumulated plan benefits on December 31, 20X6:
   a. Vested benefits of participants currently receiving payment amounted to $13,264,020.
   b. Vested benefits relating to all other participants amounted to $35,571,690.
   c. Nonvested benefits amounted to $11,455,290.

Using the information presented in Example 9-7, the following financial statement may be prepared:

Parker Enterprises Pension Plan Statement of Accumulated Plan Benefits
December 31, 20X6

Actuarial present value of accumulated plan benefits		
Vested benefits:		
Participants receiving benefits	$13,264,020	
Other participants	35,571,690	
		$48,835,710
Nonvested benefits		11,455,290
Total actuarial present value of accumulated plan benefits		$60,291,000

The final statement recommended by ASC 960 is the Statement of Changes in Accumulated Plan Benefits.

Statement of Changes in Accumulated Plan Benefits

The purpose of the statement of changes in plan benefits is to provide information that will explain any increase or decrease in plan benefits from one period to the next. The following items can cause a change in the accumulated plan benefits from one benefit information period to the next:

1. The pension plan is amended;
2. The nature of the plan changes (i.e., one employee plan merges with another);
3. The actuarial assumptions used to estimate the accumulated benefits change; and
4. Other significant events, such as the benefits accumulated, actuarial experience gains or losses, benefits paid, and others, occur.

The plan may elect to combine actuarial experience gains and losses with the additional benefits accumulated during the period, rather than disclosing them separately. If benefits paid during the period are disclosed in this financial statement as a significant event, payments made by insurance companies should be disclosed if the insurance contract has been excluded from the pension plan assets. In addition, payments made to an insurance company for contracts should be included in benefits paid during the period.

Information relating to the changes in accumulated plan benefits may be disclosed in the form of financial statements *or* notes. If the note disclosure approach is selected, the pension plan must disclose the present value of the plan benefits on the preceding benefit information date.

The financial statement presented may take the reconciliation form by starting with accumulated benefits at the beginning of the period and adjusting this amount for the net increase or decrease for the period to arrive at the ending balance. An alternative approach would be to use the net change method. Under this method, the net change in accumulated benefits would be shown first and this calculated amount would serve as an adjustment to the beginning amount to arrive at the ending balance. The net change approach in the statement of changes in net assets has been demonstrated and the reconciliation approach will be demonstrated using the information in Example 9-8.

Example 9-8
Changes in Accumulated Plan Benefit Information

1. Parker Enterprises, the same company used in the previous examples of financial presentation, has a pension plan that prepares its financial statements in accordance with the provisions of ASC 960.
2. The pension plan employs an actuary to determine the present value of accumulated plan benefits using an end-of-year benefit information date. Assumptions made by the actuary are consistent with those described in ASC 960.
3. For the year ended December 31, 20X6, the actuary provides the pension plan with the following information regarding changes in the accumulated benefits of the plan during the period:
   a. The plan was amended during the year, resulting in an increase in the present value of accumulated plan benefits of $10,490,634;
   b. Changes in the underlying actuarial assumptions previously used resulted in a decrease in the present value of accumulated plan benefits of $4,521,825;

c. Benefits accumulated during the year amounted to $3,858,624;

d. Benefits paid during the year amounted to $4,340,952; and

e. The present value of the accumulated plan benefits at December 31, 20X5, amounted to $54,804,519.

Assuming the pension plan elects to use the financial statement form, the statement of changes in accumulated plan benefits would appear as shown below.

Parker Enterprises Pension Plan Statement of Changes in Accumulated Plan Benefits for the Year Ended December 31, 20X6

Actuarial present value of accumulated plan benefits at beginning of year		$54,804,519
Increases (decreases) related to:		
Amendment of plan	$10,490,634	
Changes in actuarial assumptions	(4,521,825)	
Benefits accumulated	3,858,624	
Benefits paid	(4,340,952)	
Net increase during the year		5,486,481
Actuarial present value of accumulated plan benefits at end of year		$60,291,000

The statement of changes in accumulated benefits is the final recommended financial statement presented in ASC 960.

ASC 965 covers the accounting and reporting requirements for the 401(h) elements of post-retirement medical benefits contained in a defined benefit pension plan. It states that a defined benefit pension plan should include both assets and liabilities associated with health and welfare obligation on the face of the statement of net assets available for benefits when computing net assets available for benefits.

Additional Note Disclosures

ASC 960-20-50, ASC 960-205-50, and ASC 960-325-50 specify additional disclosures that may be required of a defined benefit pension plan. Some disclosures deal with the accounting policies of the pension plan. The plan should disclose any assumptions made and the methods used to value investments at fair value and insurance contracts at their reported value. In addition, assumptions made and methods used to value accumulated plan benefits should be disclosed. This disclosure should include changes in assumptions or methods between benefit information dates.

Other disclosures relating to the pension plan include:

1. Description of the pension plan, including benefit and vesting requirements;
2. Major amendments to the pension plan;
3. The order of priority of claims of participants should the plan terminate;

4. Guarantee of both pension plan amendments and benefits by the Pension Benefit Guaranty Corporation (PBGC);
5. Policy for funding and any changes in this policy;
6. Method used to compute contributions of participants;
7. Statement as to whether the plan meets the minimum requirements for funding specified by ERISA;
8. Status of any request for a waiver of minimum funding from the Internal Revenue Service;
9. Insurance company contracts not included in plan assets and any dividend income relating to these contracts;
10. Tax status of plan if no letter of determination has been issued;
11. Investments equal to 5% or more of the net assets available for benefits;
12. Real estate and other transactions between the plan and related parties; and
13. Significant events occurring after the benefit information date but prior to the issuance of the plan's financial statements.

See ASC 960 for a detailed discussion and examples of the disclosure requirements for pension plans.

Recent Changes

ASU 2017-06, *Plan Accounting: Defined Benefit Pension Plans (Topic 960), Defined Contribution Pension Plans (Topic 962), Health and Welfare Benefit Plans (Topic 965): Employee Benefit Plan Master Trust Reporting*, specifies accounting and disclosure requirements for defined benefit pension plans, defined contribution plans, and health and welfare plans. The amendments in this Update are effective for fiscal years beginning after December 15, 2018. Early adoption is permitted. An entity should apply the amendments in this Update retrospectively to each period for which financial statements are presented.

Topic 962: Plan Accounting—Defined Contribution Pension Plans

Topic 962, *Plan Accounting—Defined Contribution Pension Plans*, contains six subtopics:

10 Overall

40 Terminating Plans

205 Presentation of Financial Statements

235 Notes to Financial Statements

310 Receivables

325 Investments—Other

ASC 962 covers the accounting, reporting and, disclosure requirements for insurance contracts and investments that are held by defined contribution pension plans. Generally, insurance contracts should be reported using the same procedures as would be used under the Employee Retirement Income Security Act of 1974 (ERISA). Investment contracts should be reported at contract value.

The financial statements of a defined contribution plan shall be prepared on the accrual basis of accounting and include both a statement of net assets available for benefits of the plan as of the end of the plan year that includes amounts for total assets, total liabilities and net assets available for benefits, and a statement of changes in net assets available for benefits of the plan for the year then ended.

Effective for fiscal years ending after December 15, 2010, and prior year(s) presented retrospectively, all participant loans are classified as notes receivable from participants, which are segregated from plan investments and measured at their unpaid principal balance plus any accrued but unpaid interest.

Recent Changes

ASU 2017-06 specifies accounting and disclosure requirements for defined benefit pension plans, defined contribution plans, and health and welfare plans. The amendments in this Update are effective for fiscal years beginning after December 15, 2018. Early adoption is permitted. An entity should apply the amendments in this Update retrospectively to each period for which financial statements are presented.

Topic 965: Plan Accounting—Health and Welfare Benefit Plans

Topic 965, *Plan Accounting—Health and Welfare Benefit Plans,* contains nine subtopics:

10 Overall

20 Net Assets Available for Plan Benefits

30 Plan Benefit Obligations

40 Terminating Plans

205 Presentation of Financial Statements

310 Receivables

320 Investments—Debt and Equity Securities

325 Investments—Other

360 Property, Plant, and Equipment

ASC 965 addresses the accounting and reporting requirements for health and welfare benefit plans. It explains which kinds of plans are considered to be health and welfare plans and describes the two basic types of plans (i.e., defined benefit plans and defined contribution plans). The financial statements that should be issued by a defined benefit plan and the basic content of such statements are discussed. Such statements include a statement of net assets available for benefits of the plan as of the end of the plan year that includes amounts for total assets, total liabilities, and net assets available for benefits, as well as a statement of changes in net assets available for benefits of the plan for the year then ended. In addition, required note disclosures are specified and illustrations of note disclosures and statement formats are provided.

ASC 965 covers the accounting and reporting requirements for the 401(h) elements of post-retirement medical benefits contained in a defined benefit pension plan. It states that the statement for health and welfare benefit plan should contain the 401(h) assets and the changes in such assets used for health benefits.

ASC 965-325 covers the accounting, reporting, and disclosure requirements for insurance contracts and investments that are held by health and welfare benefit plans. Generally, insurance contracts should be reported using the same procedures as would be used under the Employee Retirement Income Security Act of 1974 (ERISA). Investment contracts should be reported at contract value, and investments held by defined benefit health and welfare plans should be reported at fair value.

Recent Changes

ASU 2017-06 specifies accounting and disclosure requirements for defined benefit pension plans, defined contribution plans and health and welfare plans. The amendments in this Update are effective for fiscal years beginning after December 15, 2018. Early adoption is permitted. An entity should apply the amendments in this Update retrospectively to each period for which financial statements are presented.

Topic 970: Real Estate—General

Topic 970, *Real Estate—General,* contains 10 subtopics:

10 Overall

230 Statement of Cash Flows

323 Investments—Equity Method and Joint Ventures

340 Other Assets and Deferred Costs

360 Property, Plant, and Equipment

470 Debt

605 Revenue Recognition

720 Other Expenses

810 Consolidation

835 Interest

Scope of the Pronouncement

ASC 970 identifies accounting principles that are applicable to a specific segment of the real estate industry. The entities affected by ASC 970 are those that are engaged in the development, construction, selling, and rental of real estate projects.

The initial phases of any real estate project involve the acquisition and development of the site and the construction of the dwelling units. Upon completion, the units may be sold or treated as rental property. A good place to begin an examination of the accounting described in ASC 970 is to look at the provisions associated with real estate acquisition and development.

Accounting for Real Estate Acquisition, Development, and Construction

Initially, the business entity locates property that it wishes to purchase. Costs are incurred to locate the property and prepare an option or other form of purchase offer. Generally, the preacquisition costs should be capitalized if they meet the following three conditions:

1. Costs are related to a designated property;
2. Costs are generally capitalized on the acquired property; and
3. The property is likely to be acquired.

The third condition requires that the potential purchaser demonstrate the ability to acquire the property by arranging for proper financing and making a determination that the property is actually for sale.

These initial costs are referred to as preacquisition costs, and will be charged to income only if it is likely that the property in question will not be acquired. Costs such as property taxes and insurance are to be capitalized until such time as the property is ready for its intended use. Insurance and property taxes incurred after the property is ready for use are to be charged to income. These types of costs can be described as direct costs because they can be identified with a particular parcel of real estate. Real estate companies also will incur costs that apply to several projects. These costs are indirect in nature and should be allocated to appropriate projects. If the indirect costs cannot be associated with any particular project or projects, they should be expensed in the current accounting period.

In many apartment and condominium units, costs are incurred to provide routine amenities such as swimming pools, tennis courts, and recreational facilities. The costs incurred to develop these amenities are not associated with any specific unit within the complex. The accounting for the costs of amenities depends upon whether the developer plans to sell the facilities as part of the purchase of individual units within the complex. If the amenities are to be sold to the buyers of the units in the project, the buyers will assume full financial responsibility for the amenities. The developer's costs of furnishing the amenities are included in the purchase price of the individual unit. If costs are incurred in excess of those anticipated, they should be allocated to all units in the project as a common cost.

The developer may plan on the separate sale of the amenities or may retain and operate them as a business venture. In this case, the costs of the amenities should be capitalized in the same manner as any other productive assets. If the amenities are sold at some later date, the gain or loss is to be included in income.

ASC 970 states that amenity costs are allocated to the parcels of land that will benefit from the amenities and to those parcels of land where development is probable. A parcel of land may consist of an amenity, a phase, a unit, or an individual lot. Fair value of the parcel of land can be impacted by several factors such as physical characteristics, best use, and time and cost associated with completing items for development.

Capitalized costs associated with the real estate projects are to be allocated to individual units within the project on a specific identification basis. In cases where specific identification is not appropriate, the cost of land may be allocated on the basis of relative fair value prior to construction. This method of allocation is based solely on the relative value of the land element of the project and does not take into consideration any of the additional costs that will be incurred. Construction costs may be allocated on the basis of relative sales value of each unit constructed. If these allocation methods cannot be used, the developer is to allocate capitalizable costs on an area method that takes into consideration the relative size of each unit or parcel of land. For example, the allocation may be made on the basis of the square footage in each of the units offered for rent or sale.

Accounting for the Sale or Rental of Real Estate

The seller of real estate projects is likely to incur substantial costs in the process of selling the units. These costs would include, for example, those for brochures, legal fees, signs, advertising, sales salaries or commissions, and the cost of sales facilities. Those costs estimated to be recovered from the units sold should be capitalized and included in the cost basis. These costs also must be incurred for tangible assets that will be used during the selling period or must be related to services required to obtain necessary regulatory approval of the sale. These capitalized costs will be charged to income in the period in which the property is sold and revenue is recognized.

The initial direct costs of renting units that will likely be recovered from future rental operations should be capitalized. These costs include furnishings for a model unit, cost of maintaining rental facilities, signs, and brochures. The capitalized costs should be amortized over the lease term, if they are directly related to revenues from specific operations, or over the period to be benefited, if they are not related to these revenues. Initial direct costs that do not meet the conditions for capitalization should be expensed in the current accounting period.

Once the project is significantly complete and ready for occupancy, the rental property is considered to be in its operational phase. Costs incurred and revenues received are to be accounted for as with any other business enterprise. As with other productive assets, if the net realizable value falls below the unamortized cost, an allowance should be established to reduce cost to fair value. One piece of evidence that fair value is below cost would be if there is not sufficient rental demand for the project.

Abandonment of Real Estate Projects

In the unlikely event that a real estate project or an option to purchase real estate is abandoned, all capitalized costs should be charged to expense. Real estate projects that are donated to governmental agencies are not considered abandoned, and costs capitalized in connection with the donated property should be allocated to remaining units in the project.

Topic 972: Real Estate—Common Interest Realty Associations

Topic 972, *Real Estate—Common Interest Realty Associations*, contains nine subtopics:

10 Overall

205 Presentation of Financial Statements

235 Notes to Financial Statements

360 Property, Plant, and Equipment

430 Deferred Revenue

605 Revenue Recognition

720 Other Expenses

740 Income Taxes

850 Related Party Disclosures

This topic is not covered in this book.

Topic 974: Real Estate—Real Estate Investment Trusts

Topic 974, *Real Estate—Real Estate Investment Trusts*, contains six subtopics:

10 Overall

323 Investments—Equity Method and Joint Ventures

605 Revenue Recognition

810 Consolidation

835 Interest

840 Leases

This topic is not covered in this book.

Topic 976: Real Estate—Retail Land

Topic 976, *Real Estate—Retail Land*, contains five subtopics:

10 Overall

310 Receivables

330 Inventory

605 Revenue Recognition

705 Cost of Sales and Services

General Discussion

ASC 976 divides real estate sales into two broad categories: accounting for retail land sales and accounting for real estate sales other than retail land sales. During the remainder of the discussion, category will be referred to as retail land sales and the second category as other real estate sales. The first step in the accounting process is to determine if the transaction under consideration is a retail land sale or other real estate sale. Once this has been accomplished, the accountant will find it necessary to analyze the conditions surrounding the sale to determine which specific accounting method should be applied.

To demonstrate the complexity of the accounting for these two types of transactions, the accounting methods that may be applied to each major category are listed below.

Retail Land Sales

1. Full accrual method
2. Deposit method
3. Installment method
4. Percentage of completion method

Other Real Estate Sales

1. Full accrual method
2. Deposit method
3. Installment method
4. Percentage of completion method
5. Cost recovery method
6. Reduced-profit method
7. Other methods—generally variations of above

The selection of the specific accounting method from the lists presented above depends upon the conditions associated with the basic transaction. The approach offered below deals with the accounting methods in some detail and then relates the particular method to the conditions of a real estate sale. It is hoped that the reader will find this approach useful when reading the text of ASC 976.

Full Accrual Accounting

This accounting method is that most frequently used in accounting today. Basically, the method requires that a sale be recorded when the product is sold or the service rendered. In the real estate area, the sale and related profit should be recognized when the sales price and profit element are known and the earnings process has been completed. The earnings process has been completed when the seller has no further obligations relating to the real estate sold. If the conditions relating to determination of sales price (and related profit) and culmination of the earnings process have not been met, it is not appropriate to recognize profit from the sale. The details of how one determines the existence of a sale and the culmination of the earnings process are interesting, but do not alter the basic idea of profit recognition under the accrual method. The specific details involved in making an appropriate determination will be discussed later in this section.

Profit under the full accrual method is determined by comparing the sales price with the cost basis of the asset sold or service provided. In many real estate transactions, the buyer is required to make an initial down payment and a series of periodic payments. The seller may receive the full selling price from the buyer and/or the buyer's lending institution. In this case, the determination of the selling price is quite straightforward. If the seller finances the periodic payments, the interest element must be separated from the principal element of the payments. The cost of the real estate sold includes all capitalizable costs incurred plus the cost to sell the property.

Deposit Method

When the full accrual method is not appropriate, the accountant may be required to use the deposit method to account for the real estate sale. Accounting under the deposit method gives the appearance that a sale has **not** taken place and, therefore, profit will not be recognized. The seller of the real estate continues to carry the property and any related debt on his or her balance sheet. No receivables from the buyer are recorded on the seller's books. The seller continues to account for the property as if it were his or hers. The seller may be required to place nonrecourse debt of the buyer on his or her balance sheet as a liability.

The cash received by the seller from the buyer is reported as a deposit and is not used as an offset against the property subject to their contract. The payments received from the buyer include both a principal and interest portion. If the interest portion is not subject to refund in the event of default on the contract, the seller may apply that interest as an offset against the carrying costs of the property. Normally, the carrying costs include property taxes and interest on existing debt. If the interest is subject to refund, the interest is added to the deposit account on the books of the seller. If the buyer's payments include a portion that is to be applied to existing debt of the seller, this portion of the payment should be used to reduce the debt and related interest expense, rather than placed in the deposit account.

When a sale is finally recognized under the deposit method, the deposit account will be eliminated, and any interest accumulated in the account will be recognized as interest income rather than as profit from the sale of the property.

The deposit method would be appropriate when there are major uncertainties surrounding the sale of real estate. For example, the buyer may be unable to make a sufficient down payment on the property, or the conditions required to demonstrate that the sale has been consummated have not been met. In any event, the accountant is so uncertain about the transaction between the buyer and the seller that it would not be appropriate to recognize profit.

Cost Recovery Method

When the cost recovery method is used, there is no immediate recognition of profits. Instead, profits are recognized only when the cash payments received by the seller are greater than the cost of the property sold. The initial payments received from the buyer are viewed as recovery of the cost of the property, and, once cost has been recovered, profit may be recognized. A simple example of how this method works may be useful. Assume that a buyer issues a note for $20,000 to the seller of real estate. The seller's cost of the real estate sold is $15,000. The buyer agrees to make monthly payments of $1,000, which represent principal payments and interest on the unpaid balance at 12% per year. Under the cost recovery method, the following journal entry would be made on the date of the sale:

Notes receivable	20,000	
Inventory of real estate		15,000
Deferred profit on sale		5,000

The Deferred profit on sale account would be used as an offset against the notes receivable on the balance sheet. In effect, there would be no gross profit recognized in the income statement prepared on the date of the sale.

The first $1,000 payment would be divided into a principal payment of $800 and interest of $200 ($20,000 × .12 = $2,400 ÷ 12 months = $200). The following journal entry would be prepared:

Cash	1,000	
Deferred profit on sale		200
Notes receivable		800

Prior to the collection of the cash, the receivable would be reported at $15,000 ($20,000 face amount – $5,000 deferred profit). After the first payment, the receivable would be reported as $14,000, determined as follows:

Previous balance		$20,000
Less: principal reduction		(800)
Unpaid balance		$19,200
Deferred profit on sale	$5,000	
Interest payment received	200	
Revised deferred profit		(5,200)
Reported amount of the note		$14,000

The reported amount of the note would be $14,000, but the unpaid balance of the note is $19,200. As subsequent payments are received, the reported amount of the note will reach zero, and the unpaid balance will be some positive value. It is at this stage that the seller will begin to recognize profit on the sale of the real estate.

Reduced-Profit Method

This method is appropriate when the buyer has made an adequate initial investment in the real estate, but there is some question about the nature of the buyer's continuing investment because of the nature of the terms of settlement. The method permits immediate recognition of profit from the sale of the real estate, but only at a reduced amount. The amount by which profit is reduced in the initial year of the sale will be recovered in later years.

An illustration of the accounting required by this method will aid in the understanding of how the initial profits will be reduced. Assume that a buyer has made an initial down payment of $25,000 on real estate that has a selling price of $100,000. The seller has agreed to finance the remaining balance of $75,000 for 40 years at an interest rate of 10%. The cost of the land to the seller is $10,000. These facts imply that the seller will recognize a profit of $90,000 ($100,000 – $10,000) in the year of the sale. However, one of the conditions of the sale specified in ASC 976 is that the buyer's continuing investment in the real estate be amortized over 20 years for land, at the normal terms from lending institutions for other types of real estate. At the time of this sale, independent lending institutions required an interest rate of 16% and an amortization period of 30 years. This indicates that the buyer's continuing investment in the real estate does not meet the conditions specified in ASC 976 and the reduced-profit method should be used.

Under the agreement between the buyer and the seller, the buyer will make annual payments of $7,669.46 (the payment required to amortize $75,000 at 10% for 40 years). The lending institution would require annual payments of $12,141.43, for a 30-year, 16% loan for $75,000. This transaction would require that the profit from the sale of the real estate be reduced by the present value of the different terms.

The seller will make annual payments of $7,669.46 for the next 40 years. The present value of these payments at 16% for 30 years would be $47,375.78 ($7,669.46 × 6.1772 present value factor for 30 years at 16%). The profit reduction would be determined as follows:

Face amount of receivable	$75,000.00
Present value of receivable	47,375.78
Profit reduction	$27,624.22

The journal entries to record the sale would be as follows:

Cash	25,000.00	
Notes receivable	47,375.78	
Sales of real estate		72,375.78
Cost of real estate sold	10,000.00	
Inventory of real estate		10,000.00

If the reduced profit method were not required, the seller would have recognized $90,000 profit in the year of sale ($25,000 cash + $75,000 notes receivable – $10,000 cost of the real estate). The amount of the profit reduction of $27,624.22 will be recognized by the seller in years 31 through 40, when the buyer is making periodic payments of $7,669.46, but the present value of the note will be fully amortized.

Installment Method

The installment method is understood by most accountants, because it can be applied in a variety of circumstances. Basically, the installment method requires that all cash received from the buyer be allocated between cost recovery and profit. ASC 976 requires that the allocation be made using the percentage of total cost and profit to sales. Under this type of allocation, if real estate is sold for

$100,000, and has a cost basis to the seller of $75,000, each dollar of cash received in payment of the real estate from the buyer would be allocated $.75 to cost recovery and $.25 to profit. The method is quite simple and easy to follow. The example below illustrates the basic accounting.

Assume a buyer makes a $10,000 down payment on real estate that has a selling price of $60,000, and issues a note to the seller for the remaining $50,000. The note is payable in 10 years, with interest at 15%. The annual note payment would be $9,962.60. The real estate has a cost basis to the seller of $40,000, so the gross profit involved in the transaction is $20,000 ($60,000 selling price – $40,000 cost).

Under this set of assumptions, each dollar of payment for the real estate received from the buyer would be allocated—($40,000 ÷ $60,000) to cost recovery and—to profit recognition. The journal entry to record an initial sale could be made as follows:

Account	Debit	Credit
Notes receivable	50,000.00	
Cash	10,000.00	
Net sale of real estate		40,000.00
Deferred profit on sale		20,000.00

The cash received as down payment on the real estate represents a payment towards the property and should be divided between cost recovery and profit. One-third of the amount received represents profit, so the following entry should be made:

Account	Debit	Credit
Deferred profit on sale	3,333.33	
Profit on installment sale		3,333.33

The first $9,962.60 note payment received must be divided between the interest and principal elements. The interest element would be $7,500 ($50,000 × .15), so the principal element would be $2,462.60 ($9,962.60 – $7,500.00). One-third of the principal element would represent profit received by the seller; therefore, $820.87 ($2,462.60 × 1/3) would be recognized as profit. The following journal entry is needed to record the first note payment:

Account	Debit	Credit
Cash	9,962.60	
Interest income		7,500.00
Notes receivable		2,462.60
Deferred profit on sale	820.87	
Profit on installment sale		820.87

On the income statement, in the period in which the property was sold, the seller is to report the sales value of the transaction, the gross profit not recognized, and the cost of the real estate sold. The disclosure may be made in the notes to the income statement.

Percentage-of-Completion Method—This method is widely understood in accounting and taxation because of its use in the construction industry. The earning process cannot be complete if the seller of the goods or services must perform substantial services to complete the project. Many real estate projects take a substantial period of time to complete and are excellent candidates for the percentage-of-completion method of accounting. In general, revenue is recognized under the percentage-of-completion method in the ratio of costs incurred to total estimated costs to complete the project. Because the method is so widely used in accounting, no example is developed here. The reader is advised to refresh his or her memory as to the specific accounting under this method by reference to any standard intermediate accounting textbook.

Application of Accounting Methods

Situations that require the application of the accounting methods illustrated above are identified in this section. The reader should refer to the flowchart located in the final appendix to ASC 976 for general guidance in the accounting decision process.

The full accrual method of accounting should be used when the real estate transaction represents a normal sales event (i.e., when the selling price and profit can be determined) and the earnings process has been completed. The other accounting methods discussed above will be used when there are exceptions to this general rule.

The **deposit** method generally is used in the following circumstances:

1. During the construction phase of the development of condominiums, office buildings, and similar types of projects.
2. When the buyer has made a sufficient initial investment (generally between 5% and 25% of the selling price), but the seller is not certain that the cost of the real estate sold will be recovered.
3. When an investment return is guaranteed by the seller for a short time period and there is uncertainty as to whether the return will be realized.
4. In a retail land sale where the seller is obligated to refund the payment made by the buyer or when the initial and subsequent payments are less than 10% of the selling price.
5. Where there is substantial uncertainty concerning the ability of the buyer to make all payments required.

The **cost recovery** method generally is used in the following circumstances:

1. When the buyer has made a sufficient initial and continuing investment in the real estate, but the buyer's obligation is subordinated beyond that of a first mortgage.
2. When a real estate transaction involves an option to purchase, and the buyer has not made a sufficient initial and continuing investment in the real estate.

The **reduced-profit** method generally is used in the following circumstance:

1. Where the buyer has made a sufficient initial, but not a sufficient continuing, investment in the real estate and the land payments are amortized over a period other than 20 years, and the loan terms for the remainder of the property are materially different from those currently offered by an independent lending institution.

The **installment** method generally is used in the following circumstances:

1. In retail land sales, where there is some question about the ability of the buyer to pay for the land or for the seller to complete the sale, but it is known that the seller has the financial ability to meet his or her obligations.
2. If there is a partial sale of the real estate, and collection from the buyer is not assured.
3. When the buyer has made a sufficient initial investment, but not a sufficient continuing investment, but the obligation terms are consistent with those relating to the 20-year loan amortization period for land and normal amortization period for the remainder of the transaction.
4. Where all the risks and rewards of ownership have not been passed to the buyer.

The **percentage-of-completion** method generally is used in the following circumstance:

1. Where the real estate development project takes some time to complete and there has been the sale of one or more units in the project, construction has begun, and the buyer is committed to the purchase.

ASC 976 contains more detail on the application of the various accounting techniques to specific transactions. The transactions covered are so specialized that additional analysis will not prove beneficial.

Disclosures

The following disclosures are described in ASC 976-310-50 and ASC 976-330-50 for those enterprises having retail land sale operations:

1. For each of the five years subsequent to the balance sheet date, the maturities of the accounts receivable;
2. Accounts receivable that are delinquent;
3. The range of interest rates and weighted average rates for the receivables;
4. Expected costs in total and time frames for projects to be sold in the next five years; and
5. Obligations for improvements that have been recorded.

Topic 978: Real Estate—Time-Sharing Activities

Topic 978, *Real Estate—Time-Sharing Activities*, contains 10 subtopics:

10 Overall

230 Statement of Cash Flows

250 Accounting Changes and Error Corrections

310 Receivables

330 Inventory

340 Other Assets and Deferred Costs

605 Revenue Recognition

720 Other Expenses

810 Consolidation

840 Leases

This topic is not covered in this book.

Topic 980: Regulated Operations

Topic 980, *Regulated Operations*, contains 17 subtopics:

10 Overall

20 Discontinuation of Rate-Regulated Accounting

250 Accounting Changes and Error Corrections

340 Other Assets and Deferred Costs

350 Intangibles—Goodwill and Other

360 Property, Plant, and Equipment

405 Liabilities

410 Asset Retirement and Environmental Obligations

450 Contingencies

470 Debt

605 Revenue Recognition

710 Compensation—General

715 Compensation—Retirement Benefits

740 Income Taxes

810 Consolidation

835 Interest

840 Leases

Background and Discussion

ASC 980 addresses the accounting treatment for regulated companies.

Reporting Requirements

ASC 980 relates to general purpose financial statements of certain types of regulated enterprises. For the accounting and reporting provisions of ASC 980 to be applicable, all of the following conditions must be met:

1. Rates are established by an independent third party or by a governing board established by statute;
2. The rate structure is designed to recover the costs of providing services; and
3. It is likely that regulated costs will be recovered.

If an enterprise has regulated operations that meet these conditions, the provisions of ASC 980 are applicable. In general, ASC 980 requires that accounting principles promulgated by the FASB apply to regulated companies, but only when the accounting does not conflict with accounting directed by the regulator. The area of most concern revolves around the question of capital expenditures. In many cases, a regulated company will be required to capitalize certain costs that have been incurred, while generally accepted accounting principles require that the costs be expensed. Careful attention must be given to the nature of the accounting requirements specified by regulatory agencies, so that conflicts can be kept to a minimum.

Along these lines, ASC 980 recognizes that certain costs may be capitalized that would otherwise be expensed, but two preconditions must exist. These conditions are:

1. It is probable that revenues in the future will be at least equal to the costs that are capitalized.
2. The revenues are intended to recover incurred costs, rather than anticipated future costs.

The costs incurred should be expensed when conditions 1 and 2, above, are no longer met.

This rather straightforward requirement addresses the question of whether to record a cost as an asset or an expense. If it can be demonstrated that, because of actions of the regulatory body, future revenues will not recover a capitalized cost, the enterprise should recognize the impairment in the value of the asset equal to the amount of the cost excluded. Any loss in value is to be reflected in current period income. The provisions of ASC 360 should apply to the impairment issue.

When costs have not been included initially in allowable costs for rate purposes, but the regulator subsequently allows such costs to be included, the entity should record an asset for such costs and classify it the same way that it would have been classified initially.

Just as regulatory authorities are involved in the determination of costs as assets or expenses, they are active in the determination of when to recognize liabilities and revenues. For example, a regulatory agency may require an enterprise to refund specified amounts to customers. If the refunds meet the conditions set out in ASC 450 (i.e., if the refund is probable and the amount can be reasonably estimated), the regulated enterprise must record a liability and related reduction in revenue (or increase in expense). There are other ways for the regulator to establish liabilities for the regulated enterprise, and ASC 980 lists several specific conditions and the accounting that should result.

In addition to the general standard that certain regulated companies follow generally accepted accounting principles and the exceptions noted for the creation of assets, liabilities, expenses, and revenue, ASC 980 itemizes a number of specific accounting standards. These specific standards are discussed below.

Allowance for Funds Used During Construction

Most utility companies are allowed to capitalize the costs associated with funds used in major construction projects, if it is probable that the capitalized cost will be allowable for rate-making purposes. This allowance includes the costs of debt as well as equity securities. The amount capitalized is not consistent with the provisions of ASC 835-20. The FASB concluded that the amount capitalized for rate-making purposes also should be disclosed in the general purpose financial statements. Subsequent accounting for funds used during construction and interest capitalized under ASC 835-20 are consistent and will not create any future reporting problems.

Intercompany Profit

It is generally accepted accounting practice to eliminate profits on sales to affiliated companies. However, ASC 980 provides that profits on such sales to regulated affiliates should not be eliminated if there is a reasonable sales price, and that the regulated company will recover the selling price from future revenue. ASC 980 lacks both theoretical and practical support in the accounting community and can be justified on the basis of being a common industry practice.

Accounting Disclosures

When refunds are required to be paid in an accounting period other than the one in which the related revenue was earned, the regulated company must disclose the impact on income of the refund and the years during which the revenue was received. The FASB suggests that the dollar impact of the refund be shown as a separate line item on the income statement net of tax.

Accounting Requirements for Regulated Entities When the Provisions of ASC 980 Are Discontinued

A regulated enterprise that has met the requirements to use the provisions of ASC 980 in prior periods may not currently meet the specific requirements and must discontinue use of ASC 980 provisions. ASC 980 provides the proper accounting for the discontinuation process.

Before proceeding with this material, the reader is encouraged to review (in the preceding discussion) the requirements that must be met to use ASC 980. The accounting and reporting requirements of ASC 980 should no longer be applied when an entity determines that all or a portion of its operations in a particular jurisdiction no longer meet the requirements specified in ASC 980. When a part (but not all) of an entity's operations fails to meet the requirements of ASC 980, it is assumed that all operations in that jurisdiction fail to meet the requirements. However, this assumption may be overcome by demonstrating that a separable part of the operations continues to meet the requirements of ASC 980.

When ASC 980 is no longer applicable to the operations of a regulated company, certain assets and liabilities may have to be eliminated from the statement of financial position when it is included in general-purpose external reports. The assets and/or liabilities to be eliminated are those recognized when using the provisions of ASC 980 that would not have been recorded by entities in general. After discontinuation of ASC 980, assets and liabilities will no longer be recorded for actions of regulators, except where the asset (right to receive payment) or liability (obligation to pay) is a result of prior transactions and events.

Inventory and property, plant, and equipment recorded when using the provisions of ASC 980 are the same as for enterprises in general except for the following: intercompany profit, costs disallowed for plants completed recently, allowance for funds while construction is in progress, and operating costs capitalized during postconstruction. Generally, the recorded amount of inventory and property, plant, and equipment should not be adjusted for the discontinuation of ASC 980. However, any costs included in these assets as a result of actions of a regulator are to be accounted for, as described above (for actions of a regulator). If evidence indicates an impairment in value of the inventory, property, plant, and equipment, the impairment should be accounted for using the provisions of ASC 360. Any write-off of assets and liabilities as a result of actions of the regulator and any write-down in assets for impairment of value should be netted and reported in income in the accounting period that ASC 980 is discontinued.

The following disclosures are required when ASC 980 is discontinued for all or a portion of an entity's operations (Paragraph 8):

1. Specify the reason that the operations are discontinued.
2. Identify the operations of the entity that is discontinued.

Plant Costs and Abandonments

ASC 980 provides guidance on accounting for costs that are disallowed for plants that have been completed recently and for plant abandonments. In addition, ASC 980 provides specific guidelines for the capitalization of cost of funds during construction of plant assets.

Accounting for Costs Disallowed on Plants Completed Recently

In many cases, a regulator will not allow all costs incurred in constructing a plant to be recovered in the rate-making process. When some of the costs recorded as assets are disallowed on recently constructed plants, the enterprise may have to write down the plant asset and report a loss. The loss should be reported in the accounting period when an enterprise determines that it is probable that a loss will occur (i.e., costs will be disallowed) and the amount of the costs disallowed can be estimated. ASC 450 is used to assess the probability of disallowance, and ASC 450 should be used to determine whether the amount can reasonably be estimated.

Accounting for Costs of Funds During Construction

In some situations, the provisions of ASC 980 require that an entity include in the cost of a plant asset the cost of funds used during construction of the plant. Whether the cost of funds should be capitalized as part of the cost of the asset depends on the probability of the cost of funds being used in the ratemaking process. The cost of funds should be included as part of the asset cost when it is probable that the cost of funds will be an allowable cost in the ratemaking process.

Accounting for Plant Abandonment

A utility company may abandon a plant after it has been constructed (an operating asset) or during construction. Until recently, most plants abandoned during construction were abandoned prior to the time that significant costs were incurred. More recently, entities have tended to abandon plants later in the construction process, after more significant costs have been incurred. ASC 980 specifies the accounting and reporting requirements for plant abandonments during and after construction. A plant asset where construction is either completed or is ongoing is accounted for as a plant asset abandonment when it is probable (likely to occur) that the asset will be abandoned.

Once it is probable that an entity's plant asset will be abandoned, appropriate accounting is governed by whether the entity anticipates receiving a full return or less than a full return on its investment. The time period for determination of the amount of return is the period from the date it is probable that the asset will be abandoned to the recovery date. The entity should use all facts available, as well as historical experience, when determining the amount of return anticipated from the abandonment.

When an entity abandons an operating asset, or an asset under construction, and expects to receive less than a full return on the asset, the following accounting is appropriate: The anticipated future revenue to recover allowable cost and investment return from the abandoned plant is computed on a present value basis. The present value of the expected future revenue is compared to the cost basis of the plant asset. The excess of the cost of the plant asset over the present value of the future revenue stream is reported as a loss on the income statement in the accounting period that it is probable that an abandonment will occur and the amount can be estimated. The cost basis of the plant asset is removed from the books and a new asset is established equal to the present value computed above. The loss computed above may be composed of two parts as follows: the amount of plant costs that is disallowed when it is probable and can be estimated and the plant asset after adjustment for (1) in excess of the present value of the future revenue computed above. When computing the present value of the anticipated future revenue, the time period used may create a problem for the entity. The company will have to address the following issues: the estimated period of time before plant asset recovery starts and the estimated period of time over which the asset will be recovered. If the enterprise can estimate only a range of time periods, ASC 450 should be consulted for guidance. ASC 450 states that when a range is estimated, the best estimate within the range should be used as the appropriate period of time. However, if there is no best estimate within the range, the lower end of the range should be used as the appropriate period of time for present value calculations. The interest rate that should be used in the present value computations is the rate that the entity would have to pay for similar financing with a similar degree of risk.

The entity must accrue a service charge on the carrying value of the abandoned asset from the date that the asset is recognized to the date that recovery starts. The carrying charge increases the carrying value of the asset and is calculated using the interest rate that was used to compute the present value of the abandoned asset. The abandoned asset should be written off using a method that will provide a constant return on the asset equal to the rate that was used to calculate the present value of the asset.

When an entity abandons an operating asset or an asset under construction and expects to receive a full return on the asset, the following accounting is appropriate: First, the entity should determine if all of the costs of the asset recorded are allowable costs for rate-making purposes. When it is probable that a part of the asset cost will be disallowed, and the entity can estimate the amount, the costs expected to be disallowed should be reported as a loss in the income statement of the current accounting period and the plant asset should be reduced by the amount of the loss. The cost of the plant asset remaining after reduction for the disallowed costs, if any, should be transferred to a new asset account.

The entity must accrue a service charge on the carrying value of the abandoned asset from the date that the new asset is recognized to the date that recovery starts. The carrying charge increases the asset balance by using an interest rate that is equivalent to the entity's capital cost in the same jurisdiction as the anticipated recovery. The carrying value of the abandoned asset is written off over the period of recovery using the same procedure as is used for purposes of rate making.

Phase-In Plans—Introduction

ASC 980-340 provides the proper accounting and reporting requirements for phase-in plans of utility companies.

A phase-in plan is a method or procedure of including all allowable costs incurred in constructing a utility plan in current or future rates in such a way as to allow customer rates to increase gradually rather than suddenly. Allowable costs included in the phase-in plan are all costs that are expected to be recovered through future revenue. Phase-in plans have been developed so that significant costs incurred in the construction process of a new utility plant can be recovered. Generally, from a utility company standpoint, the costs are recovered using the normal rate-making process. Recently, because of the significant increase in the cost of construction, utilities have developed phase-in plans that allow the increased costs to be absorbed into customer rates without causing significant increases in rates that would occur from the normal rate-making policies.

Phase-In Plans—Accounting

A phase-in plan, as defined above, is any procedure that includes construction costs that are allowable in rates that customers pay for utilities and that meets all of the criteria listed below:

1. The phase-in plan is accepted by a regulator, and the plan relates to a major new plant of the utility company or to a plant of a supplier of the utility company, or the plan relates to a major plant that is estimated to be finished soon.

2. The phase-in plan allows a longer time to recover allowable costs than is acceptable for entities in general under current generally accepted accounting principles.

3. The phase-in plan permits rate increases that permit allowable costs to be deferred over a time period longer than would have been allowed using procedures that were available before 1982.

The proper accounting for phase-in plans for general purpose financial statements depends on when the plant is completed or when substantial progress has been made on the plant. If the plant is not completed or if significant physical construction has not been made before January 1, 1988, allowable costs under the phase-in plan are reported as a deferred charge (asset) if the plant is completed or if significant physical construction has been made on the plant before January 1, 1988 and the phase-in plan meets all of the following criteria:

1. From the date of deferral, the costs deferred should be recovered within 10 years.

2. The plan must have a specified time period for deferred cost recovery.

3. A formal phase-in plan is approved by a regulator for deferral of allowable costs.

4. The phase-in plan's specified percentage rate increase in each future year does not exceed the percentage increase in the year that precedes a particular future year. That is, the percentage increase in 20X6 does not exceed the percentage increase in 20X5.

The amount on a cumulative basis of all allowable costs recorded as assets using phase-in plans are presented in the statement of financial position as a separate line item. The amount of allowable costs capitalized in a specific accounting period is classified in the income statement as a separate item. In addition, the recovered amount of allowable costs that were capitalized in years prior to the current year is reported in the income statement as a separate item. Capitalized costs using phase-in plans should not be used to reduce other expenses.

When a phase-in plan is modified, replaced, or supplemented, except for existing plans that were amended to meet the requirements of ASC 980-340, the preceding criteria related to capitalization of allowable costs should be applied to a combination of the new plan and the existing plan. The 10-year-or-less recovery period required for capitalization for amended plans is modified as follows:

1. The beginning of the deferral date is the earliest date of deferral on the old or new plan.

2. The latest date of recovery for deferred amounts is considered the date of final recovery.

When a phase-in plan that meets the requirements of ASC 980-340 has a disallowance of plant costs included, the disallowance should be accounted for in accordance with the provisions of ASC 980-360.

Phase-In Plans—Accounting for Allowances for Earnings on Shareholders' Investments

A cost incurred may be capitalized rather than expensed when specific situations are met. The issue related to the allowance for earnings on shareholders' investment, also referred to as a specified cost of equity funds, is whether the allowance or cost is an incurred cost and should be capitalized or whether the cost should be expensed. The FASB concluded in ASC 980-340 that the allowance should be expensed and not accounted for as a capitalized incurred cost. However, under certain situations, the cost of equity funds may be capitalized during the construction phase. In addition, the cost may be capitalized for phase-in plans that meet specific qualifications.

Phase-In Plans—Disclosure Requirements

The disclosures required by ASC 980-340 involve the issues of phase-in plans and the cost of equity funds. For any current or ordered future phase-in plans, an entity should disclose the terms of such plans. In addition, as of the date of the statement of financial position, the entity should disclose the net change in and the balance of deferred allowable costs. In addition to disclosures related to phase-in plans, the utility must disclose information related to the cost of funds. When the cost of funds is capitalized for rate-making reasons, but not for financial reporting, the utility should disclose the amount and nature capitalized.

Topic 985: Software

Topic 985, *Software*, contains eight subtopics:

10 Overall

20 Costs of Software to Be Sold, Leased, or Marketed

330 Inventory

350 Intangibles—Goodwill and Other

605 Revenue Recognition

705 Cost of Sales and Services

730 Research and Development

845 Nonmonetary Transactions

Costs of Software to Be Sold, Leased, or Marketed Subtopic—Introduction

ASC 985-20 specifies the proper accounting and reporting requirements for software developed internally and purchased from outside entities that is to be sold, leased, or otherwise marketed. The software product may include a software program, a group of computer programs, or computer product enhancement. In addition, the software product may be marketed individually or included as a part of another product or process.

ASC 985-20 does not cover software developed or purchased for internal use or software developed for other entities based on a contractual agreement.

Costs of Software to Be Sold, Leased, or Marketed Subtopic—Definition of Important Terms

At the outset it is important to define some of the terms that will be used in the discussion and in the example material. The full meaning of each of these terms cannot be conveyed easily, but, some explanation and will aid in the understanding of the specific meaning of the terms in ASC 985-20. Some of the more important terms are as follows:

1. *Coding.* Producing, in a computer language, instructions in such detail that the requirements specified in the detailed program design are met.
2. *Detailed Program Design.* A software product that is ready for coding and represents a detail design that takes all requirements to the most detailed form.
3. *Product Design.* A logical depiction of the software functions in enough detail to meet the qualifications of the software.
4. *Testing.* Performing procedures needed to make sure the computer software in coded form meets the requirements specified by the product design.
5. *Working Model.* A computer product that is ready for customer testing. The product is in the same computer language and contains the same major functions that will be used in the final product.

Costs of Software to Be Sold, Leased, or Marketed Subtopic—General Discussion

Generally, two problems are encountered in accounting for and reporting computer software costs when the software is internally developed. First, the computer software costs must be classified into four different categories, and second, any capitalized software costs must be amortized. Chart 9-2 illustrates the classification of software costs and indicates the proper accounting for each type.

Chart 9-2
Classification and Accounting for Computer Software Costs

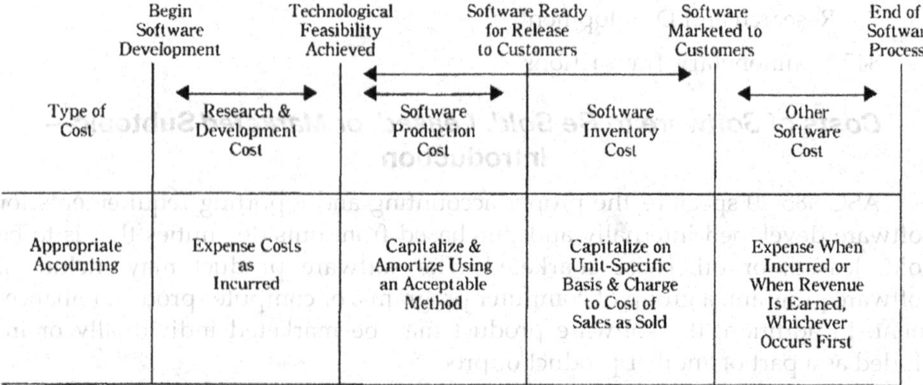

Begin Software Development
Technological Feasibility Achieved
Software Ready for Release to Customers
Software Marketed to Customers
End of Software Process
Type of Cost
Research & Development Cost
Software Production Cost
Software Inventory Cost
Other Software Cost
Appropriate Accounting
Expense Costs as Incurred
Capitalize & Amortize Using an Acceptable Method
Capitalize on Unit-Specific Basis & Charge to Cost of Sales as Sold
Expense When Incurred or When Revenue Is Earned, Whichever Occurs First

Chart 9-2 shows that costs incurred from the beginning of the software project to the date that technological feasibility is achieved are classified as research and development costs. Research and development costs are expensed as incurred using the provisions of ASC 730-10. ASC 982-20-25-2 states that technological feasibility is achieved when all activities necessary for the entity to determine that the software product can be produced to meet all specifications have been completed. Included in activities are such items as coding, testing, and designing. From a practical standpoint, if the software package has a detail program design, technological feasibility is achieved when the three conditions in Chart 9-3 are met.

Chart 9-3 Conditions for Establishing Technological Feasibility When Product Has Detail Program Design

1. Both the product design and the detail program design have been finished by the entity and all requirements, such as skill and technology, are available to produce the software.
2. The entity has verified, by documenting and comparing detail product design and product specifications, that the detail program design is complete and compatible with the product design.
3. Either the entity has determined that there are no uncertainties concerning development issues of a high risk nature, such as novel and unique functions and technological innovations, or such uncertainties have been resolved.

If the software product does not have a detail program design, technological feasibility is established when the two conditions in Chart 9-4 are met.

Chart 9-4 Conditions for Establishing Technological Feasibility When Product Has No Detail Program Design

1. The entity has finished a product design and a working model of the software.
2. The entity has verified, by testing, that the product design and the working model are complete and compatible.

If the software is to be used as an integral part of a software process or product, software costs are classified as research and development costs until both of the following conditions are met (Paragraph 5):

1. Achievement of technological feasibility for the product.
2. Completion of all research and development activities associated with the remaining components (other than software) of the product.

Chart 9-2 shows that all software costs incurred after the date that technological feasibility is achieved to produce the product masters are classified as production costs. Software production costs are capitalized as assets and amortized using an appropriate amortization method. Software production costs are classified on the balance sheet as long-term assets until amortized. If the software is to be used as an integral part of a software product or process, software costs are not classified as production costs until both technological feasibility is achieved and all research and development activities have been completed.

In Chart 9-2, production costs and inventory costs may overlap. The enterprise could be incurring inventory costs and production costs at the same time. Production costs will stop at the time the product is ready for general customer release and inventory costs will stop at the time the software is sold, leased, or otherwise marketed.

Inventory costs are costs, other than research and development and production costs, that are incurred to get the software product ready for general customer release. Included are costs of duplicating software masters, documenting software, developing training material, and packaging the software product. Software inventory costs are capitalized as assets on a unit-specific basis and charged to the cost of sales as the product is sold.

After the software product is marketed to customers and until the end of the software process, Chart 9-2 shows that other software costs are expensed as incurred or as the related revenue is earned, whichever occurs first. Included in other software costs are software maintenance and software support.

Chart 9-5 provides examples of the types of software costs discussed in Chart 9-2.

Chart 9-5 Examples of Types of Computer Software Costs

Research and Development Costs

- Cost of planning
- Cost of product design
- Cost of detail program design
- Cost of achieving technological feasibility
- Cost of testing software prior to achieving technological feasibility
- Cost of coding software prior to achieving technological feasibility

Production Costs

- Cost of coding after achieving technological feasibility
- Cost of testing after achieving technological feasibility

Inventory Costs

- Cost of duplicating software
- Cost of software documentation
- Cost of developing software training materials
- Cost of physically packaging software for distribution

Other Software Costs

- Cost of software maintenance
- Cost of software support

As was noted in Chart 9-2 and in the subsequent discussion, production costs are capitalized as an asset and amortized on a product-by-product basis using an appropriate method. Annual amortization of production costs is equal to the greater of the amounts computed using the following two methods:

1. The straight-line method over the useful life of the software product.
2. The gross revenue ratio method.

Amortization under the gross revenue ratio method may be computed using the following formula:

$$\text{PCAE} = \frac{\text{ASR}}{\text{ASR+ESR}} \times \text{TPC}$$

PCAE	=	Annual production cost amortization expense.
ASR	=	Actual software revenue recorded for the current year.
ESR	=	Estimated remaining software revenue to be recorded in future years.
TPC	=	The smaller of total production costs or net realizable value of the software.

The balance in the unamortized production cost account must be compared to the net realizable value of the software product on each balance sheet date. If the net realizable value is less than the unamortized production cost balance, a loss is recognized for the difference and the unamortized production cost is written down to equal net realizable value. Net realizable value is considered the new cost basis for the production costs and future amortization is computed using the net realizable value. Net realizable value is equal to the future gross revenues from the sale of the software product less any costs to complete and dispose of the product. Cost to complete and dispose includes cost of customer support and cost of software maintenance.

The preceding discussion has been directed to the accounting of a software product that is developed internally. However, a company may purchase software that is to be marketed to outside customers. The purchased software may be marketed as purchased, modified and then marketed, or used as an integral part of a product or process. In addition, the purchased software may have an alternative future use (i.e., the software may be used for something besides the software product). Most of the accounting described above for internally developed software is applicable to purchased software. However, some classification questions are unique to the purchased software. Chart 9-6 illustrates how the costs of purchased software are classified when the purchased software is not used as an integral part of a software product or process.

Chart 9-6 Classification of Costs of Purchased Software That Is Not Used as an Integral Part of a Product or Process

Situation	Accounting Requirements When Technological Feasibility Achieved	Accounting Requirements When Technological Feasibility Not Achieved[1]
Purchased software has no alternative use.	The purchase price of the software is capitalized as production costs.	The purchase price of the software is accounted for as research and development costs and expensed as incurred.
Purchased software has an alternative use.	The purchase price of the software is capitalized as production costs.	The purchase price of the software is capitalized at the date of purchase and accounted for based on its use.

[1] The column headings refer to whether or not technological feasibility is achieved on the date of purchase of the software.

After the purchase price is properly classified, the accounting for purchased software is the same as that for internally developed software and requires no further discussion. However, two aspects of Chart 9-6 are unique to purchased software. First, the concept of alternative future use as developed in ASC 730-10 on accounting for research and development costs is applied to purchased computer software. Alternative future use means that the software product purchased is used for a project in addition to the software product under current consideration. Second, as noted in Chart 9-6, when purchased software has an alternative use and technological feasibility is not achieved on the date of purchase, the cost of the software is capitalized and accounted for based on its use. This means that part of the cost of the software is charged to research and development costs of the current software product, and the remaining cost is accounted for in accordance with how the product is used in the future.

Charts 9-7 and 9-8 provide the proper classification of purchased software costs when a software product is used as an integral part of a product or process.

Chart 9-7 Classification of Costs of Purchased Software That Is Used as an Integral Part of a Product or Process

Situation	Accounting Requirements When Both Technological Feasibility Is Achieved and All Research and Development Activities Are Completed
• The software *has no* alternative future use.	The cost of buying the software is accounted for as a production cost, capitalized and amortized using an acceptable method.
• The software *has an* alternative future use.	The cost of buying the software is accounted for as a production cost, capitalized and amortized using an acceptable method.

Chart 9-7 illustrates that both technological feasibility of the computer software purchased must be achieved, and all research and development activities related to the remaining components of the product or process must be complete on the date of purchase for the purchase price to be accounted for as production costs.

Chart 9-8 Classification of Costs of Purchased Software That Is Used as an Integral Part of a Product or Process

Situation	Accounting Requirements When Both Technological Feasibility Is Achieved and All Research and Development Activities Are Completed
• The software *has no* alternative future use.	The cost of buying the software is accounted for as a research and development cost and expensed when incurred.
• The software *has an* alternative future use.	The cost of buying the software is capitalized at the date of purchase and accounted for based on its use.

Costs of Software to Be Sold, Leased, or Marketed Subtopic—Technical Considerations

Two examples are used to illustrate the technical aspects of computer software. Assumptions for Example 9-9 are as follows.

Example 9-9
Assumptions for Internally Developed Computer Software

1. Howard Enterprises (Howard), a December 31 calendar year-end company, is involved in the development of computer software that is to be sold to outside customers.

2. During 20X6, the company was involved in two different computer software projects—Computer Software A and Computer Software B. The company incurred the following costs for the two projects during 20X6.

Computer Software A:

Costs Incurred Before May 1, 20X6:	
• Cost of coding software	$40,000
• Cost of testing software	20,000
• Cost of planning	30,000
• Cost of achieving technological feasibility of the software	10,000
• Cost of developing a product design	80,000
• Cost of developing a detailed program design	65,000
Costs Incurred After May 1, 20X6:	
• Cost of coding software	50,000
• Cost of testing software	30,000
• Cost of software documentation	20,000
• Cost of developing training materials for the software	60,000
• Cost of duplicating software	20,000
• Cost of packaging the software for customer distribution	25,000

Computer Software B:	
Costs Incurred Before September 1, 20X6:	
• Cost of coding software before June 1, 20X6	25,000
• Cost of testing software before June 1, 20X6	15,000
• Cost of coding software between June 1 and September 1, 20X6	40,000
• Cost of testing software between June 1 and September 1, 20X6	25,000
• Cost of planning	15,000
• Cost of achieving technological feasibility of the software	5,000
• Cost of developing a product design	30,000
• Cost of developing a detailed program design	25,000
Costs Incurred After September 1, 20X6:	
• Cost of coding software	60,000
• Cost of testing software	40,000
• Cost of software documentation	25,000
• Cost of developing training materials for the software	50,000
• Cost of duplicating software	30,000
• Cost of packaging the software for customer distribution	15,000

3. Computer Software A is to be marketed as developed, but Computer Software B is to be used as an integral part of a software product. Technological feasibility was achieved on May 1 for Computer Software A and on June 1 for Computer Software B. All research and development activities for the remaining components related to Computer Software B were not completed until September 1, 20X6.

4. By January 1, 20X7, both software products were available for general release to customers, and all inventory costs were incurred by this date.

5. During 20X7, the company incurred the following costs for both computer software products.

	Computer Software A	**Computer Software B**
• Cost of customer support	$25,000	$35,000
• Cost of software maintenance	20,000	30,000
• Miscellaneous software costs	5,000	2,000

6. Net realizable value for Computer Software A exceeds the unamortized production cost balance for each year. The net realizable value for Computer Software B for each balance sheet date is provided below:

December 31	**Computer Software B**
20X7	$800,000
20X8	500,000
20X9	20,000
2010	49,000
2011	0

7. Computer Software A has a useful life of four years and Computer Software B has a useful life of five years. Actual and estimated revenues from the products are as follows:

Actual Revenues:	**Computer Software A**	**Computer Software B**
20X7	$300,000	$100,000
20X8	400,000	200,000
20X9	300,000	150,000
2010	600,000	200,000
2011		50,000

Estimated Revenues Remaining at End of Year:	**Computer Software A**	**Computer Software B**
20X7	$1,200,000	$900,000
20X8	800,000	600,000

Estimated Revenues Remaining at End of Year:	**Computer Software A**	**Computer Software B**
20X9	500,000	400,000
2010	0	100,000
2011		0

The first step in the analysis of the Example 9-9 assumptions is to classify the various software costs into research and development costs, production costs, inventory costs, and other software costs. Before the costs can be classified, the date at which technological feasibility is achieved must be determined. Technological feasibility is achieved for Computer Software A on May 1 as noted in Example 9-9, Item 3. Therefore, all costs incurred prior to May 1 are classified as research and development costs and expensed as incurred. The costs incurred after technological feasibility is achieved to produce the product masters are classified as production costs and capitalized on a product-by-product basis. Other costs incurred to get the product ready for sale, such as those for preparing training materials and documenting and duplicating the software master, are inventory costs and are capitalized on a unit-specific basis. Costs incurred after the product is sold are classified as other software costs and expensed as incurred or when the related revenue is recognized, whichever occurs first. Table 9-1 presents the classification of software costs for Computer Software A.

Table 9-1 Calculation of Computer Software Costs for Computer Software A

Type of Software Cost	**Research and Development Costs**	**Production Costs**	**Inventory Costs**	**Other Software Costs**
Cost of Planning	$30,000			
Cost of developing a product design	80,000			
Cost of developing a detail program design	65,000			

Type of Software Cost	Research and Development Costs	Production Costs	Inventory Costs	Other Software Costs
Cost of achieving technological feasibility	10,000			
Cost of coding before May 1, 20X6	40,000			
Cost of testing before May 1, 20X6	20,000			
Cost of coding software after May 1, 20X6		$50,000		
Cost of testing software after May 1, 20X6		30,000		
Cost of software documentation			$20,000	
Cost of developing training materials			60,000	
Cost of duplicating software			20,000	
Cost of software packaging			25,000	
Cost of customer support				$25,000
Cost of software maintenance				20,000
Miscellaneous software costs				5,000
Total costs	$245,000	$80,000	$125,000	$50,000

Using the information in Table 9-1, the following two summary journal entries are prepared for computer software costs. The first entry is for software costs incurred in 20X6 and the second entry is for costs incurred in 20X7.

Costs Incurred in 20X6:

Research and Development Expense	245,000	
Computer Software Production Costs	80,000	
Computer Software Inventory	125,000	
Cash		450,000

Costs Incurred in 20X7:

Computer Software Expense	50,000	
Cash		50,000

The two preceding entries are summary entries that are used only for illustrative purposes. In reality, several entries would be made for each class of costs.

Research and development expenses and computer software expenses are classified as normal operating expenses on the income statement. Computer software production costs are classified as long-term assets on the balance sheet and amortized using an appropriate method. Computer software inventory is classified as a current asset and charged to cost of sales as the software is sold.

This completes the discussion of Computer Software A. Computer Software B is similar to Computer Software A and will require very little discussion. However, Computer Software B is to be used as an integral part of a software product. Therefore, all costs incurred to the date that both technological feasibility is achieved for the software and all research and development activities related to the remaining product are completed and classified as research and development costs. Because both technological feasibility and all research and development activities are completed on September 1, all costs incurred prior to September 1 are classified as research and development costs. Classification of the software costs is presented in Table 9-2.

Table 9-2 Calculation of Computer Software Costs for Computer Software B

Type of Software Cost	Research and Development Costs	Production Costs	Inventory Costs	Other Software Costs
Cost of planning	$15,000			
Cost of developing a product design	30,000			
Cost of developing a detail program design	25,000			
Cost of achieving technological feasibility	5,000			
Cost of coding before June 1, 20X6	25,000			
Cost of testing before June 1, 20X6	15,000			
Cost of coding between June 1 and September 1, 20X6	40,000			
Cost of testing between June 1 and September 1, 20X6	25,000			
Cost of coding software after September 1, 20X6		$60,000		
Cost of testing software after September 1, 20X6		40,000		
Cost of software documentation			$25,000	
Cost of developing training materials			50,000	

Type of Software Cost	Research and Development Costs	Production Costs	Inventory Costs	Other Software Costs
Cost of duplicating software			30,000	
Cost of software packaging			15,000	
Cost of customer support				$35,000
Cost of software maintenance				30,000
Miscellaneous software costs				2,000
Total costs	$180,000	$100,000	$120,000	$67,000

Using the information in Table 9-2, the following two journal entries can be prepared for Computer Software B.

Costs Incurred in 20X6:

Research and Development Expense	180,000	
Computer Software Production Costs	100,000	
Computer Software Inventory	120,000	
Cash		400,000

Costs Incurred in 20X7:

Computer Software Expense	67,000	
Cash		67,000

The second step in the analysis of the Example 9-9 assumptions is to amortize the software costs classified as production costs using an acceptable method. Amortization begins on January 1, 20X7, because the software is ready for customer use on this date. Annual amortization is the larger of the amount computed using the straight-line method over the useful life of the software or the amount computed using the gross revenue ratio method. First, annual amortization using the gross revenue ratio method is computed in Table 9-3 for Computer Software A.

Table 9-3 Calculation of Annual Amortization Using Gross Revenue Ratio Method for Computer Software A

(a) Year	(b) Current Year Revenue	(c) Current + Estimated Remaining Revenue	(d) = (b) ÷ (c) Revenue Ratio	(e) Production Costs	(f) = (d) × (e) Annual Amortization
20X7	$300,000	$300,000 + $1,200,000	20.0%	$80,000	$16,000
20X8	400,000	400,000 +800,000	33.0%	80,000	26,400
20X9	300,000	300,000 +500,000	37.5%	80,000	30,000

(a) Year	(b) Current Year Revenue	(c) Current + Estimated Remaining Revenue	(d) = (b) + (c) Revenue Ratio	(e) Production Costs	(f) = (d) × (e) Annual Amortization
Total Before 2010					$72,400
2010	—		—		7,600[1]
Total					$80,000

[1]Total production costs $80,000
Amortization for 20X7-20X9 ($16,000 + $26,400 + $30,000) 72,400
Amortization for 2010 $7,600

Table 9-3 shows that the amortization for 2010 (the last year of the product's life) is not computed directly, but is a plug number representing the balance in the production costs account.

Using the information computed in Table 9-3 and information provided in Example 9-9, Items 6 and 7, the annual amortization for Computer Software A can be computed. The calculation for 20X7–2010 is made in Table 9-4.

Table 9-4 Calculation of Amortization of Production Costs for Computer Software

Year	Straight-Line Method[1]	Gross Revenue Ratio Method[2]	Actual Annual Amortization[3]	Unamortized Balance of Production Costs[4]
				$80,000
20X7	$20,000	$16,000	$20,000	60,000
20X8	20,000	26,400	26,400	33,600
20X9	20,000	30,000	30,000	3,600
2010	20,000	7,600	3,600[5]	0
Total	$80,000	$80,000	$80,000	

[1] $80,000 Production costs ÷ 4-year useful life = $20,000 amortization per year.
[2] Information taken from Table 9-3.
[3] The actual annual amortization reported on the income statement is the larger of the amounts computed by the straight-line method and the gross revenue ratio method.
[4] The original $80,000 production cost balance less actual annual amortization.
[5] $20,000 + $26,400 + $30,000 = $76,400 20X7–20X9 production cost amortization. Total production costs of $80,000 – $76,400 = $3,600 amortization for 2010.

As noted in Example 9-9, Item 6 net realizable value is greater than the unamortized production cost balance for each of the years 20X7–2010. Therefore, no write-down of production costs is required and the amortization is based on the $80,000 original production costs balance.

Using the information in Table 9-4, the journal entry for 20X7 for production cost amortization is as follows:

Amortization of Computer Software Production Costs	20,000	
Computer Software Production Costs		20,000

The account Amortization of Computer Software Production Costs is classified on the income statement as an operating expense. Journal entries for years 20X8–2010 are not prepared because they are the same as above except for amounts.

Next, amortization of production costs for Computer Software B is computed. The amortization for Computer Software B is similar to that for Computer Software A except that net realizable value is less than the unamortized balance of production costs in one year. Amortization of Computer Software B production costs begins on January 1, 20X7. First, the annual amortization using the gross revenue ratio method is computed in Table 9-5.

Table 9-5 Calculation of Annual Amortization Using Gross Revenue Ratio Method for Computer Software B

(a) Year	(b) Current Year Revenue	(c) Current+ Estimated Remaining Revenue	(d) = (b)/ (c) Revenue Ratio	(e) Production Costs	(f) = (d) × (e) Annual Amortization
20X7	$100,000	$100,000 + $900,000	10.00%	$100,000	$10,000
20X8	200,000	200,000 + 600,000	25.00%	100,000	25,000
20X9	150,000	150,000 + 400,000	27.27%	100,000	27,273
2010	200,000	200,000 + 100,000	66.67%	20,000[1]	13,333
Total Before 2011					$75,606
2011	—	—	—	—	16,667[2]
Total amortization					$92,273
Write-down					7,727[3]
Total					$100,000

[1] For 2010 amortization, the net realizable value of $20,000 is used in the computation because the production cost balance was written down to equal the $20,000 net realizable value at end of 20X9.

[2] Total production costs subject to amortization

($100,000 production costs - $7,727 write-down)	$92,273
Amortization for 20X7–2010	
($10,000 + $25,000 + $27,273 + $13,333)	75,606
Amortization for 2011	$16,667

[3] Unamortized production cost balance at the end of 20X9 (Table 9-6) $27,727

Net realizable value at the end of 20X9	20,000
Loss on write-down of production costs to net realizable value	$ 7,727

Table 9-5 shows that for 20X7-20X9 annual production cost amortization is based on the $100,000 original production costs. However, at the end of 20X9, net realizable value of $20,000 is less than the $27,727 (Table 9-6) unamortized production costs balance and production costs are written down by $7,727. The 2010 amortization is computed using the $20,000 net cost basis. Amortization expense of $16,667 for 2011 is a plug number and represents the balance in the production costs account at the end of 2011.

Using the information in Table 9-5 and information from Example 9-9, Items 6 and 7, the annual amortization for production costs for Computer Software B is computed in Table 9-6.

Table 9-6 Calculation of Amortization of Production Cost for Computer Software B

Year	Straight-Line Method[1]	Gross Revenue Ratio Method[2]	Actual Annual Amortization[3]	Unamortized Balance of Production Costs[4]
				$100,000
20X7	$20,000	$10,000	$20,000	80,000
20X8	20,000	25,000	25,000	55,000
20X9	20,000	27,273	27,273	27,727
2010	16,137[5]	13,333	16,137	3,863[6]
2011	16,136[7]	16,667	3,863[8]	0
Total	$92,273	$92,273	$92,273	
Write-down	7,727[9]	7,727	7,727	
Total	$100,000	$100,000	$100,000	

[1] Production costs of $100,000 ÷ 5-year useful life = $20,000 amortization per year.

[2] Information taken from Table 9-5.

[3] The actual annual amortization reported on the income statement is the larger of the amounts computed by the straight-line method and the gross revenue ratio method.

[4] The original $100,000 production cost balance less actual annual amortization.

[5] Original production cost balance of $100,000 - $20,000 amortization for 20X7 - $20,000 amortization for 20X8 - $20,000 amortization for 20X9 = $40,000 - $7,727 write-down of production cost to net realizable value (see Table 9-5, note 3) = $32,272/2-year remaining useful life = $16,137.

[6] 20X9 production cost balance of $27,727 - $7,727 loss from write-down to net realizable value - $16,137 2010 amortization = $3,863.

[7] Rounded.

[8] $20,000 + $25,000 + $27,273 + $16,137 = $88,410 20X7 - 2010 production cost amortization. Total production costs of $92,273 - $88,410 = $3,863 amortization for 2010.

[9] See Table 9-5, note 3 for computation of write-down.

Net realizable value of the computer software must be compared to the unamortized production cost account balance on each balance sheet date. If net realizable value is less than the unamortized balance, unamortized production costs must be written down to equal net realizable value. Net realizable value is less than unamortized production costs in only one year, 20X9. In 20X9, production costs were written down by $7,727 ($27,727 - $20,000).

Using the information in Table 9-6, journal entries can be prepared for 20X7–2011 to record the annual amortization of production costs. In addition, information from Table 9-6 can be used to record the entry for the write-down of production costs to net realizable value in 20X9. The entry for 20X7 amortization and the write-down to net realizable value in 20X9 are presented below:

20X7 Amortization of Production Costs:

Amortization of Computer Software Production Costs	20,000	
Computer Software Production Costs		20,000

20X9 Write-down of Production Costs to Net Realizable Value:

Loss on Write-down of Production Costs	7,727	
Computer Software Production Costs		7,727

The account Loss on Write-down of Production Costs is classified in the income statement in accordance with the provisions of ASC 225-20, which generally requires the loss to be reported in the nonoperating section of the statement as a line item in income from continuing operation. Journal entries for the annual amortization of production costs for 20X8–2011 are not presented because they are the same as above except for amounts.

This completes the analysis of Example 9-9. Example 9-10 illustrates the technical aspects related to purchases of computer software. Assumptions for Example 9-10 are as follows.

Example 9-10
Assumptions for Purchase of Computer Software

1. Software Enterprises, Inc. (Software), a December 31 calendar year-end company, is in the business of purchasing, modifying, and marketing computer software.
2. During 20X6, the company purchased computer software for the purpose of resale, modification and resale, and use as an integral part of a product or process. The following costs were incurred for purchases of computer software during 20X6:

Software	Cost
Software Product 1	$200,000
Software Product 2	160,000
Software Product 3	300,000
Software Product 4	250,000

3. Information about each software purchase is as follows:
   - Software Product 1—Technological feasibility is established at the date of purchase and the product has an alternative future use.
   - Software Product 2—The product will require modifications prior to sale. Technological feasibility is not achieved at the date of purchase and the product has no alternative future use.
   - Software Product 3—The product has an alternative future use and technological feasibility is not achieved at the date of purchase. Of the $300,000 purchase price, $200,000 relates to the software purchased.
   - Software Product 4—The software product is to be used as an integral part of a software process and has no alternative future use. Technological feasibility was achieved for the software on

the date of purchase. In addition, all research and development activities related to the remaining components of the software process are complete.

4. In addition to the purchase cost of the software, the company incurred additional costs in getting the software ready for general customer use. The costs are as follows:

	Software			
	1	**2**	**3**	**4**
Research and Development	$0	$30,000	$40,000	$0
Production	20,000	25,000	30,000	15,000
Inventory	30,000	28,000	35,000	20,000

5. All software products were available for general use by customers on December 31, 20X6.

The first step in analyzing the assumptions in Example 9-10 is to classify the cost of the software on the date of purchase. Proper classification of the software costs is presented in Table 9-7.

Table 9-7 Classification of Cost of Purchased Software

Purchased Software	Research and Development Cost	Production Cost	Other Capitalized Cost
Software Product 1		$200,000	
Software Product 2	$160,000		
Software Product 3			$300,000
Software Product 4		250,000	
Total	$160,000	$450,000	$300,000

The cost of Software Product 1 is classified as a production cost because technological feasibility is achieved at date of purchase. The fact that the software has an alternative use does not affect the classification, because technological feasibility is established at date of purchase. The $160,000 cost of Software Product 2 is considered research and development cost because technological feasibility is not achieved at date of purchase and the product has no alternative future use. The $300,000 cost of Software Product 3 is charged to other capitalized software costs because the software has an alternative future use and technological feasibility is not achieved at date of purchase. Of the $300,000, $200,000 will be amortized to research and development expense during 20X6 because it relates to the development of Software Product 3. Because both technological feasibility and all research and development activities related to the software process are complete at the date of purchase, the $250,000 cost of Software Product 4 is classified as production costs. The entry to record the purchase of the software products is as follows:

Research and Development Expense	160,000	
Computer Software Production Costs	450,000	

Other Computer Software Costs	300,000	
Cash		910,000

The account Other Computer Software Costs is an asset and its balance is amortized based on its use.

In addition to the purchase price of the software, the company incurred certain software costs during 20X6 in getting the software products ready for customer use. The additional software costs are computed in Table 9-8.

Table 9-8 Computation of Additional Software Costs[1]

Product or Transaction	Research and Development Cost	Production Cost	Inventory Cost
Software Product 1	$ 0	$20,000	$30,000
Software Product 2	30,000	25,000	28,000
Software Product 3	40,000	30,000	35,000
Software Product 4	0	15,000	20,000
Amortization of other capitalized costs to research and development	200,000		
Total	$270,000	$90,000	$113,000

[1] Information taken from Example 9-10, Items 2 and 3.

Using the information from Table 9-8, the following journal entry can be made to record the additional software costs incurred and amortization of $200,000 of the other computer software costs (Software Product 3) to research and development expense:

Research and Development Expense	270,000	
Computer Software Production Costs	90,000	
Computer Software Inventory	113,000	
Cash		273,000
Other Computer Software Costs		200,000

This completes the discussion of Example 9-10.

Costs of Software to Be Sold, Leased, or Marketed Subtopic—Disclosures

The disclosure requirements for ASC 985-20 are specified in Section 50 and include the following:

1. For each date that a balance sheet is presented, the balance in the unamortized computer software costs account is disclosed.
2. For each period that an income statement is presented, the following information is disclosed:

a. The amount of amortization of capitalized computer software costs charged to expense.

b. The amount of any losses incurred from the write-down of computer software costs to net realizable value.

c. The total research and development costs charged to expense.

Topic 995: U.S. Steamship Entities

Topic 995, *U.S. Steamship Entities*, contains one subtopic:

740 Income Taxes

This topic is not covered in this book.

APPENDIX A
CONCEPTUAL FRAMEWORK

The Conceptual Framework that underlies U.S. Generally Accepted Accounting Principles (GAAP) is documented in a series of Statements of Financial Accounting Concepts (SFACs) issued by the FASB. This Appendix summarizes the SFACs.

FASB Statement of Financial Accounting Concepts No. 1 (November 1978)

Objectives of Financial Reporting by Business Enterprises

SFAC No. 1 addresses the objectives of financial reporting by business entities. The objectives are based on the assumption that entities are producing financial statements that provide general purpose financial information. The objectives covered in SFAC No. 1 include objectives indicating that information provided should be useful to both direct and indirect users of the statements, objectives indicating that information provided should be useful to financial statement users in making decisions about potential cash flows, and objectives indicating that financial statements produce information about the entity's economic resources.

FASB Statement of Financial Accounting Concepts No. 2 (May 1980)

Qualitative Characteristics of Accounting Information

SFAC No. 2 covers issues that make financial statement information useful to direct and indirect users of such information. It addresses both user-specific qualities of information as well as primary decision-specific qualities. These qualities of information would include items such as understandability of information, relevance and reliability of information, and consistency and comparability of information. In addition, the information should be evaluated using the concepts of materiality and cost versus benefit analysis.

FASB Statement of Financial Accounting Concepts No. 4 (December 1980)

Objectives of Financial Reporting by Nonbusiness Organizations

SFAC No. 4 addresses the objectives of financial reporting by nonbusiness entities. The objectives are based on the assumption that nonbusiness entities are producing statements that provide general purpose information. The objectives covered in SFAC No. 4 address issues related to information provided to actual and potential providers of resources and other users of the information about making decisions relative to resource allocation, making decisions about services of the nonbusiness organization, making decisions about stewardship of the organization, the economic resources of the entity, changes in net resources of the entity, receipts and uses of cash, and explanations designed to help users understand the statements.

FASB Statement of Financial Accounting Concepts No. 5 (December 1984)

Recognition and Measurement in Financial Statements of Business Enterprises

SFAC No. 5 addresses what type of information should be reported in financial statements and when such information should be reported. The financial statements of an enterprise are the main means of financial reporting. The following financial statements should be presented during the accounting period to achieve proper recognition: earnings, comprehensive income, owner investments, and distributions to owners. In addition, a statement of financial position should be presented as of the end of the accounting period. Each of the statements is discussed in detail.

FASB Statement of Financial Accounting Concepts No. 6 (December 1985)

Elements of Financial Statements

SFAC No. 6 replaces SFAC No. 3 and supersedes Paragraph 4 and the second footnote in SFAC No. 2. SFAC No. 6 addresses 10 elements that are interrelated and important to the performance of an entity: assets, liabilities, equity, owner investments, distributions to owners, revenues, expenses, gains, losses, and comprehensive income. Each of these elements is defined and discussed in detail in SFAC No. 6. In addition to these ten elements, SFAC No. 6 also defines and discusses three elements that relate to nonbusiness entities (i.e., changes in permanently restricted net assets, temporarily restricted net assets, and unrestricted net assets).

FASB Statement of Financial Accounting Concepts No. 7 (February 2000)

Using Cash Flow Information and Present Value in Accounting Measurements

SFAC No. 7 provides a structure for the use of cash flows in the measurement of accounting issues. The structure or framework specified by the FASB includes general principles for using present value and an understanding of the objectives of present value in measurement of accounting issues. SFAC No. 7 provides general guidelines when using present value of cash flows in the measurement of both assets and liabilities but does not deal with recognition issues. Present value concepts attempt to capture the differences in sets of future cash flows. SFAC No. 7 states that an adjustment for uncertainty and risk should be incorporated into the present value computations and that an approach using expected cash flows would be more appropriate when calculating present value amounts. Expected cash flows incorporate the concept of an average using probability weighted cash flows using a range of estimated amounts (Paragraph 46). SFAC No. 7 applies to the measurement of both assets and liabilities, but measurement of liabilities may require an entity to use different techniques in the measurement process. In addition, measurement of liabilities should incorporate the credit standing of the party that has the obligation to pay (Paragraphs 75 and 78). In addition to present value concepts, SFAC No. 7 also addresses issues related to the interest method of amortization.

APPENDIX B ACCOUNTING STANDARDS UPDATES

The following Accounting Standards Updates (ASUs) to the Accounting Standards Codification have been issued by the FASB since the publication of the 2017 edition CCH's *U.S. Master™ GAAP Guide*. Each has been categorized according to the source of the update (FASB Non-EITF, FASB EITF, Private Company Council, or SEC) and the type of update (Substantive Amendment, Technical Amendment, or Technical Correction).

ASU No. 2016-09: Improvements to Employee Share-Based Payment Accounting
Primary Topic: 718 *Compensation—Stock Compensation*
Issued: March 2016
Category: FASB (non-EITF) Consensus

ASU No. 2016-10: Identifying Performance Obligations with Customers
Primary Topic: 606 *Revenue from Contracts with Customers*
Issued: April 2016
Category: FASB (non-EITF) Amendment

ASU No. 2016-11: Rescission of SEC Guidance Because of Accounting Standards Updates 2014-09 and 2014-16 Pursuant to Staff Announcements at the March 3, 2016 EITF Meeting
Primary Topics: 605 *Revenue Recognition* and 815 *Derivatives and Hedging*
Issued: May 2016
Category: FASB (non-EITF) Amendment

ASU No. 2016-12: Narrow-Scope Improvements and Practical Expedients
Primary Topic: 606 *Revenue from Contracts with Customers*
Issued: May 2016
Category: FASB (non-EITF) Amendment

ASU No. 2016-13: Measurement of Credit Losses on Financial Instruments
Primary Topic: 326 *Financial Instruments—Credit Losses*
Issued: June 2016
Category: FASB (non-EITF) Amendment

ASU 2016-14: Presentation of Financial Statements of Not-for-Profit Entities
Primary Topic: 958 *Not-for Profit Entities*
Issued: August 2016
Category: FASB (non-EITF) Consensus

ASU 2016-15: Classification of Certain Cash Receipts and Payments
Primary Topic: 230 *Statement of Cash Flow*
Issued: August 2016
Category: FASB (EITF) Consensus

ASU 2016-16: Intra-Entity Transfers of Assets Other Than Inventory
Primary Topic: 740 *Income Taxes*
Issued: October 2016
Category: FASB (non-EITF) Amendment

ASU 2016-17: Interests Held through Related Parties That are under Common Control
Primary Topic: 810 *Consolidation*
Issued: October 2016
Category: FASB (non-EITF) Amendment

ASU 2016-18: Restricted Cash
Primary Topic: 230 *Statement of Cash Flows*
Issued: November 2016
Category: FASB (EITF) Consensus

ASU 2016-19: Technical Corrections and Improvements
Primary Topic: *(VARIOUS)*
Issued: December 2016
Category: FASB (non-EITF) Amendment

ASU 2016-20: Technical Corrections and Improvements to Topic 606, Revenue from Contracts with Customers
Primary Topic: 606 *Revenue from Contracts with Customers*
Issued: December 2016
Category: FASB (non-EITF) Amendment

ASU 2017-01: Clarifying the Definition of a Business
Primary Topic: 805 *Business Combinations*
Issued: January 2017
Category: FASB (non-EITF) Amendment

ASU 2017-02: Clarifying When a Not-for-Profit Entity That is a General Partner or a Limited Partner Should Consolidate a For-Profit Limited Partnership or Similar Entity
Primary Topic: 958-810 *Not-for-Profit Entities—Consolidations*
Issued: January 2017
Category: FASB (non-EITF) Amendment

ASU 2017-03: Amendments to SEC Paragraphs Pursuant to Staff Announcements at the September 22, 2016 and November 17, 2016 EITF Meetings
Primary Topics: 250 *Accounting Changes and Error Corrections* and 323 *Investments—Equity Method and Joint Ventures*
Issued: January 2017
Category: FASB (non-EITF) Amendment

ASU 2017-04: Simplifying the Test for Goodwill Impairment
Primary Topic: 350 *Intangibles—Goodwill and Other*
Issued: January 2017
Category: FASB (non-EITF) Amendment

ASU 2017-05: Clarifying the Scope of Asset Derecognition Guidance and Accounting for Partial Sales of Nonfinancial Assets
Primary Topic: 610-20 *Other Income—Gains and Losses from the Derecognition of Nonfinancial Assets*
Issued: February 2017
Category: FASB (non-EITF) Amendment

ASU 2017-06: Employee Benefit Plan Master Trust Reporting
Primary Topics: 960 *Plan Accounting—Defined Benefit Pension Plans,* 962 *Plan Accounting—Defined Contribution Pension Plans,* and 965 *Plan Accounting—Health and Welfare Benefit Plans*
Issued: February 2017
Category: FASB (EITF) Consensus

ASU 2017-07: Improving the Presentation of Net Periodic Pension Cost and Net Periodic Postretirement Benefit Cost
Primary Topic: 715 *Compensation—Retirement Benefits*
Issued: March 2017
Category: FASB (non-EITF) Amendment

ASU 2017-08: Premium Amortization on Purchased Callable Debt Securities
Primary Topic: 310-20 *Receivables—Nonrefundable Fees and Other Costs*
Issued: March 2017
Category: FASB (non-EITF) Amendment

ASU 2017-09: Scope Modification of Accounting
Primary Topic: 718 *Compensation—Stock Compensation*
Issued: May 2017
Category: FASB (non-EITF) Amendment

ASU 2017-10: Determining the Customer of the Operation Services
Primary Topic: 853 *Service Concession Arrangement*
Issued: May 2017
Category: FASB (non-EITF) Amendment

APPENDIX C EXPOSURE DRAFTS

The following Exposure Drafts (EDs) of proposed Accounting Standards Updates (ASUs) have been issued by the FASB and are outstanding as of the publication of this edition of CCH's *U.S. Master™ GAAP Guide.*

Insurance: Targeted Improvements to the Accounting for Long-Duration Contracts
Primary Topic: 944, Financial Services—Insurance
Issued: September 29, 2016

Targeted Improvements to Accounting for Hedging Activities
Primary Topic: 815, Derivatives and Hedging
Issued: September 8, 2016

APPENDIX D CROSS-REFERENCING THE CODIFICATION AND PRE-CODIFICATION STANDARDS

Prior to July 1, 2009, most U.S. generally accepted accounting principles (GAAP) were documented in a diverse collection of pronouncements that had been issued by many different standard-setters over many decades. The initial content of the FASB *Accounting Standards Codification* was derived mainly from those pre-Codification pronouncements. Specifically, the pre-Codification pronouncements were disassembled into tens of thousands of text fragments, which were then reorganized in a topical manner and assembled to form the Codification.

Because the Codification changes continually, current Codification content increasingly differs from the pre-Codification standards from which it was originally derived. Nevertheless, specific Codification content can often be traced back to its pre-Codification sources. Similarly, specific content in pre-Codification standards can often be traced to its present location in the Codification.

Even though pre-Codification pronouncements are no longer authoritative, they still serve as meaningful points of reference for the many accounting professionals who became well acquainted with them when they were authoritative. For such individuals, the FASB's online Codification Research System (http://asc.fasb.org) has a Cross Reference feature that enables users to trace specific Codification content back to its pre-Codification sources and vice versa.

Access to the Codification Research System is available by subscription. A "Basic View" subscription, which includes access to the Cross Reference feature, is available at no cost. Similar functionality is provided by third-party research services, such as CCH's *Accounting Research Manager*®.

APPENDIX E
PRESENT VALUE FACTORS

Table I—Part A
Present Value of $1 Interest Rates

Periods	1%	2%	3%	4%	5%	6%	7%	8%	9%	10%
1	.9900990	.9803922	.9708738	.9615385	.9523810	.9433962	.9345794	.9259259	.9174312	.9090909
2	.9802960	.9611688	.9425959	.9245562	.9070295	.8899964	.8734387	.8573388	.8416800	.8264463
3	.9705901	.9423223	.9151417	.8889964	.8638376	.8396193	.8162979	.7938322	.7721835	.7513148
4	.9609803	.9238454	.8884870	.8548042	.8227025	.7920937	.7628952	.7350299	.7084252	.6830135
5	.9514657	.9057308	.8626088	.8219271	.7835262	.7472582	.7129862	.6805832	.6499314	.6209213
6	.9420452	.8879714	.8374843	.7903145	.7462154	.7049605	.6663422	.6301696	.5962673	.5644739
7	.9327181	.8705602	.8130915	.7599178	.7106813	.6650571	.6227497	.5834904	.5470342	.5131581
8	.9234832	.8534904	.7894092	.7306902	.6768394	.6274124	.5820091	.5402689	.5018663	.4665074
9	.9143398	.8367553	.7664167	.7025867	.6446089	.5918985	.5439337	.5002490	.4604278	.4240976
10	.9052870	.8203483	.7440939	.6755642	.6139133	.5583948	.5083493	.4631935	.4224108	.3855433
11	.8963237	.8042630	.7224213	.6495809	.5846793	.5267875	.4750928	.4288829	.3875329	.3504939
12	.8874492	.7884932	.7013799	.6245970	.5568374	.4969694	.4440120	.3971138	.3555347	.3186308
13	.8786626	.7730325	.6809513	.6005741	.5303214	.4688390	.4149644	.3676979	.3261786	.2896644
14	.8699630	.7578750	.6611178	.5774751	.5050680	.4423010	.3878172	.3404610	.2992465	.2633313
15	.8613495	.7430147	.6418619	.5552645	.4810171	.4172651	.3624460	.3152417	.2745380	.2393920
16	.8528213	.7284458	.6231669	.5339082	.4581115	.3936463	.3387346	.2918905	.2518698	.2176291
17	.8443775	.7141626	.6050164	.5133732	.4362967	.3713644	.3165744	.2702690	.2310732	.1978447
18	.8360173	.7001594	.5873946	.4936281	.4155207	.3503438	.2958639	.2502490	.2119937	.1798588
19	.8277399	.6864308	.5702860	.4746424	.3957340	.3305130	.2765083	.2317121	.1944897	.1635080
20	.8195445	.6729713	.5536758	.4563869	.3768895	.3118047	.2584190	.2145482	.1784309	.1486436
21	.8114302	.6597758	.5375493	.4388336	.3589424	.2941554	.2415131	.1986557	.1636981	.1351306
22	.8033962	.6468390	.5218925	.4219554	.3418499	.2775051	.2257132	.1839405	.1501817	.1228460
23	.7954418	.6341559	.5066917	.4057263	.3255713	.2617973	.2109469	.1703153	.1377814	.1116782
24	.7875661	.6217215	.4919337	.3901215	.3100679	.2469785	.1971466	.1576993	.1264049	.1015256
25	.7797684	.6095309	.4776056	.3751168	.2953028	.2329986	.1842492	.1460179	.1159678	.0922960
26	.7720480	.5975793	.4636947	.3606892	.2812407	.2198100	.1721955	.1352018	.1063925	.0839055
27	.7644039	.5858620	.4501891	.3468166	.2678483	.2073680	.1609304	.1251868	.0976078	.0762777
28	.7568356	.5743746	.4370768	.3334775	.2550936	.1956301	.1504022	.1159137	.0895484	.0693433
29	.7493421	.5631123	.4243464	.3206514	.2429463	.1845567	.1405628	.1073275	.0821545	.0630394
30	.7419229	.5520709	.4119868	.3083187	.2313774	.1741101	.1313671	.0993773	.0753711	.0573086
31	.7345771	.5412460	.3999871	.2964603	.2203595	.1642548	.1227730	.0920160	.0691478	.0520987
32	.7273041	.5306333	.3883370	.2850579	.2098662	.1549574	.1147411	.0852000	.0634384	.0473624

Periods	1%	2%	3%	4%	5%	6%	7%	8%	9%	10%
33	.7201031	.5202287	.3770262	.2740942	.1998725	.1461862	.1072347	.0788889	.0582003	.0430568
34	.7129733	.5100282	.3660449	.2635521	.1903548	.1379115	.1002193	.0730453	.0533948	.0391425
35	.7059142	.5000276	.3553834	.2534155	.1812903	.1301052	.0936629	.0676345	.0489861	.0355841
36	.6989249	.4902232	.3450324	.2436687	.1726574	.1227408	.0875355	.0626246	.0449413	.0323492
37	.6920049	.4806109	.3349829	.2342968	.1644356	.1157932	.0818088	.0579857	.0412306	.0294083
38	.6851534	.4711872	.3252262	.2252854	.1566054	.1092389	.0764569	.0536905	.0378262	.0267349
39	.6783697	.4619482	.3157535	.2166206	.1491480	.1030555	.0714550	.0497134	.0347030	.0243044
40	.6716531	.4528904	.3065568	.2082890	.1420457	.0972222	.0667804	.0460309	.0318376	.0220949
41	.6650031	.4440102	.2976280	.2002779	.1352816	.0917190	.0624116	.0426212	.0292088	.0200863
42	.6584189	.4353041	.2889592	.1925749	.1288396	.0865274	.0583286	.0394641	.0267971	.0182603
43	.6518999	.4267688	.2805429	.1851682	.1227044	.0816296	.0545127	.0365408	.0245845	.0166002
44	.6454455	.4184007	.2723718	.1780463	.1168613	.0770091	.0509464	.0338341	.0225545	.0150911
45	.6390549	.4101968	.2644386	.1711984	.1112965	.0726501	.0476135	.0313279	.0206922	.0137192
46	.6327276	.4021537	.2567365	.1646139	.1059967	.0685378	.0444986	.0290073	.0189837	.0124720
47	.6264630	.3942684	.2492588	.1582826	.1009492	.0646583	.0415875	.0268586	.0174162	.0113382
48	.6202604	.3865376	.2419988	.1521948	.0961421	.0609984	.0388668	.0248691	.0159782	.0103074
49	.6141192	.3789584	.2349503	.1463411	.0915639	.0575457	.0363241	.0230269	.0146589	.0093704
50	.6080388	.3715279	.2281071	.1407126	.0872037	.0542884	.0339478	.0213212	.0134485	.0085186
51	.6020186	.3642430	.2214632	.1353006	.0830512	.0512154	.0317269	.0197419	.0123381	.0077441
52	.5960581	.3571010	.2150128	.1300967	.0790964	.0483164	.0296513	.0182795	.0113194	.0070401
53	.5901565	.3500990	.2087503	.1250930	.0753299	.0455816	.0277115	.0169255	.0103847	.0064001
54	.5843134	.3432343	.2026702	.1202817	.0717427	.0430015	.0258986	.0156717	.0095273	.0058183
55	.5785281	.3365042	.1967672	.1156555	.0683264	.0405674	.0242043	.0145109	.0087406	.0052894
56	.5728001	.3299061	.1910361	.1112072	.0650728	.0382712	.0226208	.0134360	.0080189	.0048085
57	.5671288	.3234374	.1854719	.1069300	.0619741	.0361049	.0211410	.0124407	.0073568	.0043714
58	.5615137	.3170955	.1800698	.1028173	.0590229	.0340612	.0197579	.0115192	.0067494	.0039740
59	.5559541	.3108779	.1748251	.0988628	.0562123	.0321332	.0184653	.0106659	.0061921	.0036127
60	.5504496	.3047823	.1697331	.0950604	.0535355	.0303143	.0172573	.0098759	.0056808	.0032843

Table I—Part B
Present Value of $1 Interest Rates

Periods	11%	12%	13%	14%	15%	16%	17%	18%	19%	20%
1	.9009009	.8928571	.8849558	.8771930	.8695652	.8620690	.8547009	.8474576	.8403361	.8333333
2	.8116224	.7971939	.7831467	.7694675	.7561437	.7431629	.7305136	.7181844	.7061648	.6944444
3	.7311914	.7117802	.6930502	.6749715	.6575162	.6406577	.6243706	.6086309	.5934158	.5787037
4	.6587310	.6355181	.6133187	.5920803	.5717532	.5522911	.5336500	.5157889	.4986688	.4822531
5	.5934513	.5674269	.5427599	.5193687	.4971767	.4761130	.4561112	.4371092	.4190494	.4018776
6	.5346408	.5066311	.4803185	.4555865	.4323276	.4104423	.3898386	.3704315	.3521423	.3348980
7	.4816584	.4523492	.4250606	.3996373	.3759370	.3538295	.3331954	.3139250	.2959179	.2790816
8	.4339265	.4038832	.3761599	.3505591	.3269018	.3050255	.2847824	.2660382	.2486705	.2325680
9	.3909248	.3606100	.3328848	.3075079	.2842624	.2629530	.2434037	.2254561	.2089668	.1938067
10	.3521845	.3219732	.2945883	.2697438	.2471847	.2266836	.2080374	.1910645	.1756024	.1615056
11	.3172833	.2874761	.2606977	.2366174	.2149432	.1954169	.1778097	.1619190	.1475650	.1345880
12	.2858408	.2566751	.2307059	.2075591	.1869072	.1684628	.1519741	.1372195	.1240042	.1121567
13	.2575143	.2291742	.2041645	.1820694	.1625280	.1452266	.1298924	.1162877	.1042052	.0934639
14	.2319948	.2046198	.1806766	.1597100	.1413287	.1251953	.1110192	.0985489	.0875674	.0778866
15	.2090043	.1826963	.1598908	.1400965	.1228945	.1079270	.0948882	.0835160	.0735861	.0649055
16	.1882922	.1631217	.1414962	.1228917	.1068648	.0930405	.0811010	.0707763	.0618370	.0540879
17	.1696326	.1456443	.1252179	.1077997	.0929259	.0802074	.0693171	.0599799	.0519639	.0450732
18	.1528222	.1300396	.1108123	.0945611	.0808051	.0691443	.0592454	.0508304	.0436671	.0375610
19	.1376776	.1161068	.0980640	.0829484	.0702653	.0596071	.0506371	.0430766	.0366951	.0313009
20	.1240339	.1036668	.0867823	.0727617	.0611003	.0513855	.0432796	.0365056	.0308362	.0260841
21	.1117423	.0925596	.0767985	.0638261	.0531307	.0442978	.0369911	.0309370	.0259128	.0217367
22	.1006687	.0826425	.0679633	.0559878	.0462006	.0381878	.0316163	.0262178	.0217754	.0181139
23	.0906925	.0737880	.0601445	.0491121	.0401744	.0329205	.0270225	.0222185	.0182987	.0150949
24	.0817050	.0658821	.0532252	.0430808	.0349343	.0283797	.0230961	.0188292	.0153770	.0125791
25	.0736081	.0588233	.0471020	.0377902	.0303776	.0244653	.0197403	.0159569	.0129219	.0104826
26	.0663136	.0525208	.0416831	.0331493	.0264153	.0210908	.0168720	.0135228	.0108587	.0087355
27	.0597420	.0468936	.0368877	.0290783	.0229699	.0181817	.0144205	.0114600	.0091250	.0072796
28	.0538216	.0418693	.0326440	.0255073	.0199738	.0156739	.0123253	.0097119	.0076681	.0060663
29	.0484879	.0373833	.0288885	.0223748	.0173685	.0135120	.0105344	.0082304	.0064437	.0050553
30	.0436828	.0333779	.0255651	.0196270	.0151031	.0116482	.0090038	.0069749	.0054149	.0042127
31	.0393539	.0298017	.0226239	.0172167	.0131331	.0100416	.0076955	.0059110	.0045503	.0035106
32	.0354540	.0266087	.0200212	.0151024	.0114201	.0086565	.0065774	.0050093	.0038238	.0029255

Periods	11%	12%	13%	14%	15%	16%	17%	18%	19%	20%
33	.0319405	.0237577	.0177179	.0132477	.0099305	.0074625	.0056217	.0042452	.0032133	.0024379
34	.0287752	.0212123	.0156795	.0116208	.0086352	.0064332	.0048049	.0035976	.0027002	.0020316
35	.0259236	.0189395	.0138757	.0101937	.0075089	.0055459	.0041067	.0030488	.0022691	.0016930
36	.0233546	.0169103	.0122794	.0089418	.0065295	.0047809	.0035100	.0025837	.0019068	.0014108
37	.0210402	.0150985	.0108667	.0078437	.0056778	.0041215	.0030000	.0021896	.0016024	.0011757
38	.0189551	.0134808	.0096165	.0068804	.0049372	.0035530	.0025641	.0018556	.0013465	.0009797
39	.0170767	.0120364	.0085102	.0060355	.0042932	.0030629	.0021916	.0015725	.0011315	.0008165
40	.0153844	.0107468	.0075312	.0052943	.0037332	.0026405	.0018731	.0013327	.0009509	.0006804
41	.0138598	.0095954	.0066647	.0046441	.0032463	.0022763	.0016010	.0011294	.0007991	.0005670
42	.0124863	.0085673	.0058980	.0040738	.0028229	.0019623	.0013683	.0009571	.0006715	.0004725
43	.0112489	.0076494	.0052195	.0035735	.0024547	.0016916	.0011695	.0008111	.0005643	.0003937
44	.0101342	.0068298	.0046190	.0031346	.0021345	.0014583	.0009996	.0006874	.0004742	.0003281
45	.0091299	.0060980	.0040876	.0027497	.0018561	.0012572	.0008544	.0005825	.0003985	.0002734
46	.0082251	.0054447	.0036174	.0024120	.0016140	.0010838	.0007302	.0004937	.0003348	.0002279
47	.0074100	.0048613	.0032012	.0021158	.0014035	.0009343	.0006241	.0004184	.0002814	.0001899
48	.0066757	.0043405	.0028329	.0018560	.0012204	.0008054	.0005334	.0003545	.0002365	.0001582
49	.0060141	.0038754	.0025070	.0016280	.0010612	.0006943	.0004559	.0003005	.0001987	.0001319
50	.0054182	.0034602	.0022186	.0014281	.0009228	.0005986	.0003897	.0002546	.0001670	.0001099
51	.0048812	.0030894	.0019634	.0012527	.0008024	.0005160	.0003331	.0002158	.0001403	.0000916
52	.0043975	.0027584	.0017375	.0010989	.0006978	.0004448	.0002847	.0001829	.0001179	.0000763
53	.0039617	.0024629	.0015376	.0009639	.0006068	.0003835	.0002433	.0001550	.0000991	.0000636
54	.0035691	.0021990	.0013607	.0008455	.0005276	.0003306	.0002080	.0001313	.0000833	.0000530
55	.0032154	.0019634	.0012042	.0007417	.0004588	.0002850	.0001777	.0001113	.0000700	.0000442
56	.0028968	.0017530	.0010656	.0006506	.0003990	.0002457	.0001519	.0000943	.0000588	.0000368
57	.0026097	.0015652	.0009430	.0005707	.0003469	.0002118	.0001298	.0000799	.0000494	.0000307
58	.0023511	.0013975	.0008345	.0005006	.0003017	.0001826	.0001110	.0000677	.0000415	.0000256
59	.0021181	.0012478	.0007385	.0004392	.0002623	.0001574	.0000948	.0000574	.0000349	.0000213
60	.0019082	.0011141	.0006536	.0003852	.0002281	.0001357	.0000811	.0000486	.0000293	.0000177

Table II—Part A
Present Value of an Ordinary Annuity of $1 Interest Rates

Periods	1%	2%	3%	4%	5%	6%	7%	8%	9%	10%
1	.9900990	.9803922	.9708738	.9615385	.9523810	.9433962	.9345794	.9259259	.9174312	.9090909
2	1.970395	1.941561	1.913470	1.886095	1.859410	1.833393	1.808018	1.783265	1.759111	1.735537
3	2.940985	2.883883	2.828611	2.775091	2.723248	2.673012	2.624316	2.577097	2.531295	2.486852
4	3.901966	3.807729	3.717098	3.629895	3.545951	3.465106	3.387211	3.312127	3.239720	3.169865
5	4.853431	4.713460	4.579707	4.451822	4.329477	4.212364	4.100197	3.992710	3.889651	3.790787
6	5.795476	5.601431	5.417191	5.242137	5.075692	4.917324	4.766540	4.622880	4.485919	4.355261
7	6.728195	6.471991	6.230283	6.002055	5.786373	5.582381	5.389289	5.206370	5.032953	4.868419
8	7.651678	7.325481	7.019692	6.732745	6.463213	6.209794	5.971299	5.746639	5.534819	5.334926
9	8.566018	8.162237	7.786109	7.435332	7.107822	6.801692	6.515232	6.246888	5.995247	5.759024
10	9.471305	8.982585	8.530203	8.110896	7.721735	7.360087	7.023582	6.710081	6.417658	6.144567
11	10.36763	9.786848	9.252624	8.760477	8.306414	7.886875	7.498674	7.138964	6.805191	6.495061
12	11.25508	10.57534	9.954004	9.385074	8.863252	8.383844	7.942686	7.536078	7.160725	6.813692
13	12.13374	11.34837	10.63496	9.985648	9.393573	8.852683	8.357651	7.903776	7.486904	7.103356
14	13.00370	12.10625	11.29607	10.56312	9.898641	9.294984	8.745468	8.244237	7.786150	7.366687
15	13.86505	12.84926	11.93794	11.11839	10.37966	9.712249	9.107914	8.559479	8.060688	7.606080
16	14.71787	13.57771	12.56110	11.65230	10.83777	10.10590	9.446649	8.851369	8.312558	7.823709
17	15.56225	14.29187	13.16612	12.16567	11.27407	10.47726	9.763223	9.121638	8.543631	8.021553
18	16.39827	14.99203	13.75351	12.65930	11.68959	10.82760	10.05909	9.371887	8.755625	8.201412
19	17.22601	15.67846	14.32380	13.13394	12.08532	11.15812	10.33560	9.603599	8.950115	8.364920
20	18.04555	16.35143	14.87747	13.59033	12.46221	11.46992	10.59401	9.818147	9.128546	8.513564
21	18.85698	17.01121	15.41502	14.02916	12.82115	11.76408	10.83553	10.01680	9.292244	8.648694
22	19.66038	17.65805	15.93692	14.45112	13.16300	12.04158	11.06124	10.20074	9.442425	8.771540
23	20.45582	18.29220	16.44361	14.85684	13.48857	12.30338	11.27219	10.37106	9.580207	8.883218
24	21.24339	18.91393	16.93554	15.24696	13.79864	12.55036	11.46933	10.52876	9.706612	8.984744
25	22.02316	19.52346	17.41315	15.62208	14.09394	12.78336	11.65358	10.67478	9.822580	9.077040
26	22.79520	20.12104	17.87684	15.98277	14.37519	13.00317	11.82578	10.80998	9.928972	9.160945
27	23.55961	20.70690	18.32703	16.32959	14.64303	13.21053	11.98671	10.93516	10.02658	9.237223
28	24.31644	21.28127	18.76411	16.66306	14.89813	13.40616	12.13711	11.05108	10.11613	9.306567
29	25.06579	21.84438	19.18845	16.98371	15.14107	13.59072	12.27767	11.15841	10.19828	9.369606
30	25.80771	22.39646	19.60044	17.29203	15.37245	13.76483	12.40904	11.25778	10.27365	9.426914
31	26.54229	22.93770	20.00043	17.58849	15.59281	13.92909	12.53181	11.34980	10.34280	9.479013
32	27.26959	23.46833	20.38877	17.87355	15.80268	14.08404	12.64656	11.43500	10.40624	9.526376

Periods	1%	2%	3%	4%	5%	6%	7%	8%	9%	10%
33	27.98969	23.98856	20.76579	18.14765	16.00255	14.23023	12.75379	11.51389	10.46444	9.569432
34	28.70267	24.49859	21.13184	18.41120	16.19290	14.36814	12.85401	11.58693	10.51784	9.608575
35	29.40858	24.99862	21.48722	18.66461	16.37419	14.49825	12.94767	11.65457	10.56682	9.644159
36	30.10751	25.48884	21.83225	18.90828	16.54685	14.62099	13.03521	11.71719	10.61176	9.676508
37	30.79951	25.96945	22.16724	19.14258	16.71129	14.73678	13.11702	11.77518	10.65299	9.705917
38	31.48466	26.44064	22.49246	19.36786	16.86789	14.84602	13.19347	11.82887	10.69082	9.732651
39	32.16303	26.90259	22.80822	19.58448	17.01704	14.94907	13.26493	11.87858	10.72552	9.756956
40	32.83469	27.35548	23.11477	19.79277	17.15909	15.04630	13.33171	11.92461	10.75736	9.779051
41	33.49969	27.79949	23.41240	19.99305	17.29437	15.13802	13.39412	11.96723	10.78657	9.799137
42	34.15811	28.23479	23.70136	20.18563	17.42321	15.22454	13.45245	12.00670	10.81337	9.817397
43	34.81001	28.66156	23.98190	20.37079	17.54591	15.30617	13.50696	12.04324	10.83795	9.833998
44	35.45545	29.07996	24.25427	20.54884	17.66277	15.38318	13.55791	12.07707	10.86051	9.849089
45	36.09451	29.49016	24.51871	20.72004	17.77407	15.45583	13.60552	12.10840	10.88120	9.862808
46	36.72724	29.89231	24.77545	20.88465	17.88007	15.52437	13.65002	12.13741	10.90018	9.875280
47	37.35370	30.28658	25.02471	21.04294	17.98102	15.58903	13.69161	12.16427	10.91760	9.886618
48	37.97396	30.67312	25.26671	21.19513	18.07716	15.65003	13.73047	12.18914	10.93358	9.896926
49	38.58808	31.05208	25.50166	21.34147	18.16872	15.70757	13.76680	12.21216	10.94823	9.906296
50	39.19612	31.42361	25.72976	21.48218	18.25593	15.76186	13.80075	12.23348	10.96168	9.914814
51	39.79814	31.78785	25.95123	21.61749	18.33898	15.81308	13.83247	12.25323	10.97402	9.922559
52	40.39419	32.14495	26.16624	21.74758	18.41807	15.86139	13.86212	12.27151	10.98534	9.929599
53	40.98435	32.49505	26.37499	21.87267	18.49340	15.90697	13.88984	12.28843	10.99573	9.935999
54	41.56866	32.83828	26.57766	21.99296	18.56515	15.94998	13.91573	12.30410	11.00525	9.941817
55	42.14719	33.17479	26.77443	22.10861	18.63347	15.99054	13.93994	12.31861	11.01399	9.947106
56	42.71999	33.50469	26.96546	22.21982	18.69854	16.02881	13.96256	12.33205	11.02201	9.951915
57	43.28712	33.82813	27.15094	22.32675	18.76052	16.06492	13.98370	12.34449	11.02937	9.956286
58	43.84863	34.14523	27.33101	22.42957	18.81954	16.09898	14.00346	12.35601	11.03612	9.960260
59	44.40459	34.45610	27.50583	22.52843	18.87575	16.13111	14.02192	12.36668	11.04231	9.963873
60	44.95504	34.76089	27.67556	22.62349	18.92929	16.16143	14.03918	12.37655	11.04799	9.967157

Table II—Part B
Present Value of an Ordinary Annuity of $1 Interest Rates

Periods	11%	12%	13%	14%	15%	16%	17%	18%	19%	20%
1	.9009009	.8928571	.8849558	.8771930	.8695652	.8620690	.8547009	.8474576	.8403361	.8333333
2	1.712523	1.690051	1.668102	1.646661	1.625709	1.605232	1.585214	1.565642	1.546501	1.527778
3	2.443715	2.401831	2.361153	2.321632	2.283225	2.245890	2.209585	2.174273	2.139917	2.106481
4	3.102446	3.037349	2.974471	2.913712	2.854978	2.798181	2.743235	2.690062	2.638586	2.588735
5	3.695897	3.604776	3.517231	3.433081	3.352155	3.274294	3.199346	3.127171	3.057635	2.990612
6	4.230538	4.111407	3.997550	3.888668	3.784483	3.684736	3.589185	3.497603	3.409777	3.325510
7	4.712196	4.563757	4.422610	4.288305	4.160420	4.038565	3.922380	3.811528	3.705695	3.604592
8	5.146123	4.967640	4.798770	4.638864	4.487322	4.343591	4.207163	4.077566	3.954366	3.837160
9	5.537048	5.328250	5.131655	4.946372	4.771584	4.606544	4.450566	4.303022	4.163332	4.030967
10	5.889232	5.650223	5.426243	5.216116	5.018769	4.833227	4.658604	4.494086	4.338935	4.192472
11	6.206515	5.937699	5.686941	5.452733	5.233712	5.028644	4.836413	4.656005	4.486500	4.327060
12	6.492356	6.194374	5.917647	5.660292	5.420619	5.197107	4.988387	4.793225	4.610504	4.439217
13	6.749870	6.423548	6.121812	5.842362	5.583147	5.342334	5.118280	4.909513	4.714709	4.532681
14	6.981865	6.628168	6.302488	6.002072	5.724476	5.467529	5.229299	5.008062	4.802277	4.610567
15	7.190870	6.810864	6.462379	6.142168	5.847370	5.575456	5.324187	5.091578	4.875863	4.675473
16	7.379162	6.973986	6.603875	6.265060	5.954235	5.668497	5.405288	5.162354	4.937700	4.729561
17	7.548794	7.119630	6.729093	6.372859	6.047161	5.748704	5.474605	5.222334	4.989664	4.774634
18	7.701617	7.249670	6.839905	6.467420	6.127966	5.817848	5.533851	5.273164	5.033331	4.812195
19	7.839294	7.365777	6.937969	6.550369	6.198231	5.877455	5.584488	5.316241	5.070026	4.843496
20	7.963328	7.469444	7.024752	6.623131	6.259331	5.928841	5.627767	5.352746	5.100862	4.869580
21	8.075070	7.562003	7.101550	6.686957	6.312462	5.973139	5.664758	5.383683	5.126775	4.891316
22	8.175739	7.644646	7.169513	6.742944	6.358663	6.011326	5.696375	5.409901	5.148550	4.909430
23	8.266432	7.718434	7.229658	6.792056	6.398837	6.044247	5.723397	5.432120	5.166849	4.924525
24	8.348137	7.784316	7.282883	6.835137	6.433771	6.072627	5.746493	5.450949	5.182226	4.937104
25	8.421745	7.843139	7.329985	6.872927	6.464149	6.097092	5.766234	5.466906	5.195148	4.947587
26	8.488058	7.895660	7.371668	6.906077	6.490564	6.118183	5.783106	5.480429	5.206007	4.956323
27	8.547800	7.942554	7.408556	6.935155	6.513534	6.136364	5.797526	5.491889	5.215132	4.963602
28	8.601622	7.984423	7.441200	6.960662	6.533508	6.152038	5.809851	5.501601	5.222800	4.969668
29	8.650110	8.021806	7.470088	6.983037	6.550877	6.165550	5.820386	5.509831	5.229243	4.974724
30	8.693793	8.055184	7.495653	7.002664	6.565980	6.177198	5.829390	5.516806	5.234658	4.978936
31	8.733146	8.084986	7.518277	7.019881	6.579113	6.187240	5.837085	5.522717	5.239209	4.982447
32	8.768600	8.111594	7.538299	7.034983	6.590533	6.195897	5.843663	5.527726	5.243033	4.985372
33	8.800541	8.135352	7.556016	7.048231	6.600463	6.203359	5.849284	5.531971	5.246246	4.987810
34	8.829316	8.156564	7.571696	7.059852	6.609099	6.209792	5.854089	5.535569	5.248946	4.989842
35	8.855240	8.175504	7.585572	7.070045	6.616607	6.215338	5.858196	5.538618	5.251215	4.991535
36	8.878594	8.192414	7.597851	7.078987	6.623137	6.220119	5.861706	5.541201	5.253122	4.992946

Periods	11%	12%	13%	14%	15%	16%	17%	18%	19%	20%
37	8.899635	8.207513	7.608718	7.086831	6.628815	6.224241	5.864706	5.543391	5.254724	4.994122
38	8.918590	8.220993	7.618334	7.093711	6.633752	6.227794	5.867270	5.545247	5.256071	4.995101
39	8.935666	8.233030	7.626844	7.099747	6.638045	6.230857	5.869461	5.546819	5.257202	4.995918
40	8.951051	8.243777	7.634376	7.105041	6.641778	6.233497	5.871335	5.548152	5.258153	4.996598
41	8.964911	8.253372	7.641040	7.109685	6.645025	6.235773	5.872936	5.549281	5.258952	4.997165
42	8.977397	8.261939	7.646938	7.113759	6.647848	6.237736	5.874304	5.550238	5.259624	4.997638
43	8.988646	8.269589	7.652158	7.117332	6.650302	6.239427	5.875473	5.551049	5.260188	4.998031
44	8.998780	8.276418	7.656777	7.120467	6.652437	6.240886	5.876473	5.551737	5.260662	4.998359
45	9.007910	8.282516	7.660864	7.123217	6.654293	6.242143	5.877327	5.552319	5.261061	4.998633
46	9.016135	8.287961	7.664482	7.125629	6.655907	6.243227	5.878058	5.552813	5.261396	4.998861
47	9.023545	8.292822	7.667683	7.127744	6.657310	6.244161	5.878682	5.553231	5.261677	4.999051
48	9.030221	8.297163	7.670516	7.129600	6.658531	6.244966	5.879215	5.553586	5.261913	4.999209
49	9.036235	8.301038	7.673023	7.131228	6.659592	6.245661	5.879671	5.553886	5.262112	4.999341
50	9.041653	8.304498	7.675242	7.132656	6.660515	6.246259	5.880061	5.554141	5.262279	4.999451
51	9.046534	8.307588	7.677205	7.133909	6.661317	6.246775	5.880394	5.554357	5.262419	4.999542
52	9.050932	8.310346	7.678942	7.135008	6.662015	6.247220	5.880678	5.554540	5.262537	4.999618
53	9.054894	8.312809	7.680480	7.135972	6.662622	6.247603	5.880922	5.554695	5.262636	4.999682
54	9.058463	8.315008	7.681841	7.136818	6.663149	6.247934	5.881130	5.554826	5.262720	4.999735
55	9.061678	8.316972	7.683045	7.137559	6.663608	6.248219	5.881307	5.554937	5.262790	4.999779
56	9.064575	8.318725	7.684111	7.138210	6.664007	6.248465	5.881459	5.555032	5.262848	4.999816
57	9.067185	8.320290	7.685054	7.138781	6.664354	6.248676	5.881589	5.555111	5.262898	4.999847
58	9.069536	8.321687	7.685888	7.139281	6.664656	6.248859	5.881700	5.555179	5.262939	4.999872
59	9.071654	8.322935	7.686627	7.139720	6.664918	6.249016	5.881795	5.555237	5.262974	4.999894
60	9.073562	8.324049	7.687280	7.140106	6.665146	6.249152	5.881876	5.555285	5.263004	4.999911

Table III—Part A
Present Value of an Annuity Due of $1 Interest Rates

Periods	1%	2%	3%	4%	5%	6%	7%	8%	9%	10%
1	1.000000	1.000000	1.000000	1.000000	1.000000	1.000000	1.000000	1.000000	1.000000	1.000000
2	1.990099	1.980392	1.970874	1.961538	1.952381	1.943396	1.934579	1.925926	1.917431	1.909091
3	2.970395	2.941561	2.913470	2.886095	2.859410	2.833393	2.808018	2.783265	2.759111	2.735537
4	3.940985	3.883883	3.828611	3.775091	3.723248	3.673012	3.624316	3.577097	3.531295	3.486852
5	4.901966	4.807729	4.717098	4.629895	4.545951	4.465106	4.387211	4.312127	4.239720	4.169865
6	5.853431	5.713460	5.579707	5.451822	5.329477	5.212364	5.100197	4.992710	4.889651	4.790787
7	6.795476	6.601431	6.417191	6.242137	6.075692	5.917324	5.766540	5.622880	5.485919	5.355261
8	7.728195	7.471991	7.230283	7.002055	6.786373	6.582381	6.389289	6.206370	6.032953	5.868419
9	8.651678	8.325481	8.019692	7.732745	7.463213	7.209794	6.971299	6.746639	6.534819	6.334926
10	9.566018	9.162237	8.786109	8.435332	8.107822	7.801692	7.515232	7.246888	6.995247	6.759024
11	10.47130	9.982585	9.530203	9.110896	8.721735	8.360087	8.023582	7.710081	7.417658	7.144567
12	11.36763	10.78685	10.25262	9.760477	9.306414	8.886875	8.498674	8.138964	7.805191	7.495061
13	12.25508	11.57534	10.95400	10.38507	9.863252	9.383844	8.942686	8.536078	8.160725	7.813692
14	13.13374	12.34837	11.63496	10.98565	10.39357	9.852683	9.357651	8.903776	8.486904	8.103356
15	14.00370	13.10625	12.29607	11.56312	10.89864	10.29498	9.745468	9.244237	8.786150	8.366687
16	14.86505	13.84926	12.93794	12.11839	11.37966	10.71225	10.10791	9.559479	9.060688	8.606080
17	15.71787	14.57771	13.56110	12.65230	11.83777	11.10590	10.44665	9.851369	9.312558	8.823709
18	16.56225	15.29187	14.16612	13.16567	12.27407	11.47726	10.76322	10.12164	9.543631	9.021553
19	17.39827	15.99203	14.75351	13.65930	12.68959	11.82760	11.05909	10.37189	9.755625	9.201412
20	18.22601	16.67846	15.32380	14.13394	13.08532	12.15812	11.33560	10.60360	9.950115	9.364920
21	19.04555	17.35143	15.87747	14.59033	13.46221	12.46992	11.59401	10.81815	10.12855	9.513564
22	19.85698	18.01121	16.41502	15.02916	13.82115	12.76408	11.83553	11.01680	10.29224	9.648694
23	20.66038	18.65805	16.93692	15.45112	14.16300	13.04158	12.06124	11.20074	10.44243	9.771540
24	21.45582	19.29220	17.44361	15.85684	14.48857	13.30338	12.27219	11.37106	10.58021	9.883218
25	22.24339	19.91393	17.93554	16.24696	14.79864	13.55036	12.46933	11.52876	10.70661	9.984744
26	23.02316	20.52346	18.41315	16.62208	15.09394	13.78336	12.65358	11.67478	10.82258	10.07704
27	23.79520	21.12104	18.87684	16.98277	15.37519	14.00317	12.82578	11.80998	10.92897	10.16095
28	24.55961	21.70690	19.32703	17.32959	15.64303	14.21053	12.98671	11.93516	11.02658	10.23722
29	25.31644	22.28127	19.76411	17.66306	15.89813	14.40616	13.13711	12.05108	11.11613	10.30657
30	26.06579	22.84438	20.18845	17.98371	16.14107	14.59072	13.27767	12.15841	11.19828	10.36961
31	26.80771	23.39646	20.60044	18.29203	16.37245	14.76483	13.40904	12.25778	11.27365	10.42691
32	27.54229	23.93770	21.00043	18.58849	16.59281	14.92909	13.53181	12.34980	11.34280	10.47901

Periods	1%	2%	3%	4%	5%	6%	7%	8%	9%	10%
33	28.26959	24.46833	21.38877	18.87355	16.80268	15.08404	13.64656	12.43500	11.40624	10.52638
34	28.98969	24.98856	21.76579	19.14765	17.00255	15.23023	13.75379	12.51389	11.46444	10.56943
35	29.70267	25.49859	22.13184	19.41120	17.19290	15.36814	13.85401	12.58693	11.51784	10.60857
36	30.40858	25.99862	22.48722	19.66461	17.37419	15.49825	13.94767	12.65457	11.56682	10.64416
37	31.10751	26.48884	22.83225	19.90828	17.54685	15.62099	14.03521	12.71719	11.61176	10.67651
38	31.79951	26.96945	23.16724	20.14258	17.71129	15.73678	14.11702	12.77518	11.65299	10.70592
39	32.48466	27.44064	23.49246	20.36786	17.86789	15.84602	14.19347	12.82887	11.69082	10.73265
40	33.16303	27.90259	23.80822	20.58448	18.01704	15.94907	14.26493	12.87858	11.72552	10.75696
41	33.83469	28.35548	24.11477	20.79277	18.15909	16.04630	14.33171	12.92461	11.75736	10.77905
42	34.49969	28.79949	24.41240	20.99305	18.29437	16.13802	14.39412	12.96723	11.78657	10.79914
43	35.15811	29.23479	24.70136	21.18563	18.42321	16.22454	14.45245	13.00670	11.81337	10.81740
44	35.81001	29.66156	24.98190	21.37079	18.54591	16.30617	14.50696	13.04324	11.83795	10.83400
45	36.45545	30.07996	25.25427	21.54884	18.66277	16.38318	14.55791	13.07707	11.86051	10.84909
46	37.09451	30.49016	25.51871	21.72004	18.77407	16.45583	14.60552	13.10840	11.88120	10.86281
47	37.72724	30.89231	25.77545	21.88465	18.88007	16.52437	14.65002	13.13741	11.90018	10.87528
48	38.35370	31.28658	26.02471	22.04294	18.98102	16.58903	14.69161	13.16427	11.91760	10.88662
49	38.97396	31.67312	26.26671	22.19513	19.07716	16.65003	14.73047	13.18914	11.93358	10.89693
50	39.58808	32.05208	26.50166	22.34147	19.16872	16.70757	14.76680	13.21216	11.94823	10.90630
51	40.19612	32.42361	26.72976	22.48218	19.25593	16.76186	14.80075	13.23348	11.96168	10.91481
52	40.79814	32.78785	26.95123	22.61749	19.33898	16.81308	14.83247	13.25323	11.97402	10.92256
53	41.39419	33.14495	27.16624	22.74758	19.41807	16.86139	14.86212	13.27151	11.98534	10.92960
54	41.98435	33.49505	27.37499	22.87267	19.49340	16.90697	14.88984	13.28843	11.99573	10.93600
55	42.56866	33.83828	27.57766	22.99296	19.56515	16.94998	14.91573	13.30410	12.00525	10.94182
56	43.14719	34.17479	27.77443	23.10861	19.63347	16.99054	14.93994	13.31861	12.01399	10.94711
57	43.71999	34.50469	27.96546	23.21982	19.69854	17.02881	14.96256	13.33205	12.02201	10.95191
58	44.28712	34.82813	28.15094	23.32675	19.76052	17.06492	14.98370	13.34449	12.02937	10.95629
59	44.84863	35.14523	28.33101	23.42957	19.81954	17.09898	15.00346	13.35601	12.03612	10.96026
60	45.40459	35.45610	28.50583	23.52843	19.87575	17.13111	15.02192	13.36668	12.04231	10.96387

Table III—Part B
Present Value of an Annuity Due of $1 Interest Rates

Periods	11%	12%	13%	14%	15%	16%	17%	18%	19%	20%
1	1.000000	1.000000	1.000000	1.000000	1.000000	1.000000	1.000000	1.000000	1.000000	1.000000
2	1.900901	1.892857	1.884956	1.877193	1.869565	1.862069	1.854701	1.847458	1.840336	1.833333
3	2.712523	2.690051	2.668102	2.646661	2.625709	2.605232	2.585214	2.565642	2.546501	2.527778
4	3.443715	3.401831	3.361153	3.321632	3.283225	3.245890	3.209585	3.174273	3.139917	3.106481
5	4.102446	4.037349	3.974471	3.913712	3.854978	3.798181	3.743235	3.690062	3.638586	3.588735
6	4.695897	4.604776	4.517231	4.433081	4.352155	4.274294	4.199346	4.127171	4.057635	3.990612
7	5.230538	5.111407	4.997550	4.888668	4.784483	4.684736	4.589185	4.497603	4.409777	4.325510
8	5.712196	5.563757	5.422610	5.288305	5.160420	5.038565	4.922380	4.811528	4.705695	4.604592
9	6.146123	5.967640	5.798770	5.638864	5.487322	5.343591	5.207163	5.077566	4.954366	4.837160
10	6.537048	6.328250	6.131655	5.946372	5.771584	5.606544	5.450566	5.303022	5.163332	5.030967
11	6.889232	6.650223	6.426243	6.216116	6.018769	5.833227	5.658604	5.494086	5.338935	5.192472
12	7.206515	6.937699	6.686941	6.452733	6.233712	6.028644	5.836413	5.656005	5.486500	5.327060
13	7.492356	7.194374	6.917647	6.660292	6.420619	6.197107	5.988387	5.793225	5.610504	5.439217
14	7.749870	7.423548	7.121812	6.842362	6.583147	6.342334	6.118280	5.909513	5.714709	5.532681
15	7.981865	7.628168	7.302488	7.002072	6.724476	6.467529	6.229299	6.008062	5.802277	5.610567
16	8.190870	7.810864	7.462379	7.142168	6.847370	6.575456	6.324187	6.091578	5.875863	5.675473
17	8.379162	7.973986	7.603875	7.265060	6.954235	6.668497	6.405288	6.162354	5.937700	5.729561
18	8.548794	8.119630	7.729093	7.372859	7.047161	6.748704	6.474605	6.222334	5.989664	5.774634
19	8.701617	8.249670	7.839905	7.467420	7.127966	6.817848	6.533851	6.273164	6.033331	5.812195
20	8.839294	8.365777	7.937969	7.550369	7.198231	6.877455	6.584488	6.316241	6.070026	5.843496
21	8.963328	8.469444	8.024752	7.623131	7.259331	6.928841	6.627767	6.352746	6.100862	5.869580
22	9.075070	8.562003	8.101550	7.686957	7.312462	6.973139	6.664758	6.383683	6.126775	5.891316
23	9.175739	8.644646	8.169513	7.742944	7.358663	7.011326	6.696375	6.409901	6.148550	5.909430
24	9.266432	8.718434	8.229658	7.792056	7.398837	7.044247	6.723397	6.432120	6.166849	5.924525
25	9.348137	8.784316	8.282883	7.835137	7.433771	7.072627	6.746493	6.450949	6.182226	5.937104
26	9.421745	8.843139	8.329985	7.872927	7.464149	7.097092	6.766234	6.466906	6.195148	5.947587
27	9.488058	8.895660	8.371668	7.906077	7.490564	7.118183	6.783106	6.480429	6.206007	5.956323
28	9.547800	8.942554	8.408556	7.935155	7.513534	7.136364	6.797526	6.491889	6.215132	5.963602
29	9.601622	8.984423	8.441200	7.960662	7.533508	7.152038	6.809851	6.501601	6.222800	5.969668
30	9.650110	9.021806	8.470088	7.983037	7.550877	7.165550	6.820386	6.509831	6.229243	5.974724
31	9.693793	9.055184	8.495653	8.002664	7.565980	7.177198	6.829390	6.516806	6.234658	5.978936
32	9.733146	9.084986	8.518277	8.019881	7.579113	7.187240	6.837085	6.522717	6.239209	5.982447

Periods	11%	12%	13%	14%	15%	16%	17%	18%	19%	20%
33	9.768600	9.111594	8.538299	8.034983	7.590533	7.195897	6.843663	6.527726	6.243033	5.985372
34	9.800541	9.135352	8.556016	8.048231	7.600463	7.203359	6.849284	6.531971	6.246246	5.987810
35	9.829316	9.156564	8.571696	8.059852	7.609099	7.209792	6.854089	6.535569	6.248946	5.989842
36	9.855240	9.175504	8.585572	8.070045	7.616607	7.215338	6.858196	6.538618	6.251215	5.991535
37	9.878594	9.192414	8.597851	8.078987	7.623137	7.220119	6.861706	6.541201	6.253122	5.992946
38	9.899635	9.207513	8.608718	8.086831	7.628815	7.224241	6.864706	6.543391	6.254724	5.994122
39	9.918590	9.220993	8.618334	8.093711	7.633752	7.227794	6.867270	6.545247	6.256071	5.995101
40	9.935666	9.233030	8.626844	8.099747	7.638045	7.230857	6.869461	6.546819	6.257202	5.995918
41	9.951051	9.243777	8.634376	8.105041	7.641778	7.233497	6.871335	6.548152	6.258153	5.996598
42	9.964911	9.253372	8.641040	8.109685	7.645025	7.235773	6.872936	6.549281	6.258952	5.997165
43	9.977397	9.261939	8.646938	8.113759	7.647848	7.237736	6.874304	6.550238	6.259624	5.997638
44	9.988646	9.269589	8.652158	8.117332	7.650302	7.239427	6.875473	6.551049	6.260188	5.998031
45	9.998780	9.276418	8.656777	8.120467	7.652437	7.240886	6.876473	6.551737	6.260662	5.998359
46	10.00791	9.282516	8.660864	8.123217	7.654293	7.242143	6.877327	6.552319	6.261061	5.998633
47	10.01614	9.287961	8.664482	8.125629	7.655907	7.243227	6.878058	6.552813	6.261396	5.998861
48	10.02355	9.292822	8.667683	8.127744	7.657310	7.244161	6.878682	6.553231	6.261677	5.999051
49	10.03022	9.297163	8.670516	8.129600	7.658531	7.244966	6.879215	6.553586	6.261913	5.999209
50	10.03624	9.301038	8.673023	8.131228	7.659592	7.245661	6.879671	6.553886	6.262112	5.999341
51	10.04165	9.304498	8.675242	8.132656	7.660515	7.246259	6.880061	6.554141	6.262279	5.999451
52	10.04653	9.307588	8.677205	8.133909	7.661317	7.246775	6.880394	6.554357	6.262419	5.999542
53	10.05093	9.310346	8.678942	8.135008	7.662015	7.247220	6.880678	6.554540	6.262537	5.999618
54	10.05489	9.312809	8.680480	8.135972	7.662622	7.247603	6.880922	6.554695	6.262636	5.999682
55	10.05846	9.315008	8.681841	8.136818	7.663149	7.247934	6.881130	6.554826	6.262720	5.999735
56	10.06168	9.316972	8.683045	8.137559	7.663608	7.248219	6.881307	6.554937	6.262790	5.999779
57	10.06457	9.318725	8.684111	8.138210	7.664007	7.248465	6.881459	6.555032	6.262848	5.999816
58	10.06718	9.320290	8.685054	8.138781	7.664354	7.248676	6.881589	6.555111	6.262898	5.999847
59	10.06954	9.321687	8.685888	8.139281	7.664656	7.248859	6.881700	6.555179	6.262939	5.999872
60	10.07165	9.322935	8.686627	8.139720	7.664918	7.249016	6.881795	6.555237	6.262974	5.999894

Index

References are to page numbers.

A

Accounting changes and error corrections, . . . 2079-2100
. accounting errors
. . disclosure requirements, . . . 2095-2096
. . generally, . . . 2093-2094
. . interim period adjustments, . . . 2098-2100
. . prior period adjustments, . . . 2096-2098
. . recent changes, . . . 2100
. . technical considerations, . . . 2094-2095
. accounting estimates, changes in
. . disclosure requirements, . . . 2092
. . generally, . . . 2089
. . technical considerations, . . . 2090-2092
. accounting principles, changes in
. . disclosure requirements, . . . 2088-2089
. . generally, . . . 2080-2083
. . technical considerations, . . . 2083-2088
. reporting entities, changes in
. . disclosure requirements, . . . 2093
. . generally, . . . 2092-2093

Accounting Standards Codification, . . . 13,001

Accounting Standards Updates, . . . 11,001-11,003

Accumulated benefit obligation, . . . 7015, 7083

Agriculture, . . . 9001-9002

Airlines, . . . 9002

Allocation of intraperiod tax, . . . 7237-7241

Assets, . . . 3001-3136
. accounting for servicing of, . . . 8349-8350
. accounting for, using the fair value option, . . . 8100
. cash and cash equivalents, . . . 3001
. current assets, balance sheet presentation, . . . 2010-2011
. intangibles, . . . 3096-3113
. inventory, . . . 3083-3095
. investments
. . equity securities, . . . 3041-3064
. . equity method and joint ventures, . . . 3064-3081
. . financial instruments—credit losses, . . . 3083
. . other, . . . 3081-3083
. market-related value of plan assets, . . . 7083
. offsetting, . . . 2011-2022
. other assets and deferred costs, . . . 3095
. property, plant, and equipment, . . . 3113-3136
. receivables, . . . 3001-3040
. . received in full settlement, . . . 3025-3040
. retirement of, . . . 4009-4021
. transfer in full settlement of debt, . . . 4087-4088
. transfer of financial assets, accounting for, . . . 8347-8348

B

Balance sheet, . . . 2009-2022
. comparative information, . . . 2022
. current assets and liabilities, . . . 2010-2011
. offsetting, . . . 2011-2022

Basic earnings per share, . . . 2105-2114

Boot, . . . 8336-8342

Broad transactions, . . . 8001-8354
. business combinations, . . . 8001-8025
. collaborative arrangements, . . . 8025
. consolidation, . . . 8025-8047
. derivatives and hedging, . . . 8047-8086
. fair value measurements and disclosures, . . . 8086-8092
. financial instruments, . . . 8092-8104
. foreign currency matters, . . . 8104-8139
. interest, . . . 8139-8190
. leases, . . . 8191-8326
. nonmonetary transactions, . . . 8327-8343
. related party disclosures, . . . 8343-8345
. reorganizations, . . . 8345
. service concession arrangement, . . . 8345-8346
. subsequent events, . . . 8346
. transfers and servicing, . . . 8346-8354

Broadcasters, . . . 9004-9006

Broker services, . . . 9015

Business combinations, . . . 8001-8025
. acquisition accounting alternative, . . . 8023
. disclosure requirements, . . . 8018-8021
. overview, . . . 8002-8011
. pushdown accounting, . . . 8021-8023
. recent changes, . . . 8024-8025
. technical considerations, . . . 8011-8018

Business interruption insurance, . . . 2043-2044

C

Cable television, . . . 9006-9008

Cash and cash equivalents
. statement of cash flows, . . . 2045-2046
. overview, . . . 3001

Casinos, . . . 9008-9009

Changing prices, . . . 2100

Codification standards, . . . 13,001

Collaborative arrangements, . . . 8025

Commitments, . . . 4027-4035
. fees and costs, . . . 3018-3019
. overview, . . . 4027-4031
. unconditional purchase obligations, . . . 4031-4035

Common interest realty associations, . . . 9072

Compensation
. compensated absences, . . . 7006-7008
. nonretirement postemployment benefits, . . . 7009-7014
. overview, . . . 7002-7008
. retirement benefits, *See also* Retirement benefits 7014-7152.
. stock, . . . 7152-7177
. . disclosures, . . . 7175-7177
. . employee stock ownership plans, . . . 7177
. . overview, . . . 7152-7174
. . performance targets, targeted guidance for, . . . 7178
. . share purchase plans, . . . 7153-7155
. . share-based payment plans, 7153, . . . 7155-7174

Comprehensive income, . . . 2022-2043
. generally, . . . 2024-2026
. introduction, . . . 2022-2023
. recent changes, . . . 2022
. reclassifications, . . . 2026-2027
. technical considerations, . . . 2027-2043

Concentration of credit risk disclosures, . . . 8096

Conceptual Framework, . . . 10,001-10,003

Consolidation, . . . 8025-8047

Consolidation,—continued
. accounting alternative, . . . 8046-8047
. combined financial statements, . . . 8029
. consolidation policy, . . . 8027-8028
. disclosure requirements, . . . 8043-8047
. eliminations, . . . 8028-8029
. fiscal year, . . . 8028
. majority-owned subsidiaries, accounting for, . . . 8042-8043
. noncontrolling interest, . . . 8030-8031
. overview, . . . 8025-8027
. parent company financial statements, . . . 8029
. parent's ownership interest changes, . . . 8031-8032
. procedures for consolidation, . . . 8028-8032
. proportionate consolidation, . . . 8029-8030
. variable interest entities, . . . 8032-8043

Construction contractors, . . . 9002

Contingencies
. convertible securities, . . . 2137-2139
. loss contingencies, . . . 4035-4041
. . classification and accounting, . . . 4038-4041
. . disclosures, . . . 4040
. overview, . . . 4035-4038

Contractors
. construction, . . . 9002
. federal government, . . . 9003

Convertible securities, . . . 2131-2141
. contingent agreements, . . . 2137-2139

Corporate capital structure, . . . 2104

Costs. *See also* Expenses
. deferred, . . . 3095
. disposal cost obligations, . . . 4021-4026
. exit cost obligations, . . . 4021-4026
. interim period, . . . 2152

Costs.—continued
. leases, initial direct costs, . . . 3021
. lending activity fees and costs, . . . 3018-3020
. . commitment fees and costs, . . . 3018-3019
. . loan or group of loans, purchase of, . . . 3020-3021
. . origination fees and costs, . . . 3019
. . restructuring and refinancing fees and costs, . . . 3020
. . syndication fees, . . . 3019
. nonrefundable fees and other costs, . . . 3018, 3021
. plant costs and abandonments, . . . 9083-9085
. sales, . . . 7001-7002
. services, . . . 7001-7002
. software, . . . 9087-9105

Credit risk, concentration of, . . . 8096

Currency. *See* Foreign currency matters

Curtailments. *See* Settlements and curtailments

D

Dealer services, . . . 9015

Debt, *See also* Liabilities; Receivables 4043-4104.
. additional considerations, . . . 4047-4048
. callable or due on demand, . . . 4051-4053
. with conversion and other options, . . . 4055-4057
. convertible debt, . . . 4057-4060
. disclosures, . . . 4050-4051, 4055, 4083, 4104
. financing agreement, . . . 4046-4047, 4049-4051
. induced conversions, . . . 4066
. lending services, . . . 9015-9016

Debt,—continued
. modifications and extinguishments, . . . 4076-4083
. . accounting for, . . . 4078
. . classification, . . . 4077-4078
. . disclosure requirements, . . . 4083
. . technical considerations, . . . 4078-4083
. not-for-profit entity securities, . . . 9044-9049
. overview, . . . 4043-4047
. partial income statement, . . . 4084
. post-balance sheet-date issuance, . . . 4046, 4048-4049
. product financing arrangements, . . . 4069-4076
. secured debt and collateral, accounting for, . . . 8348
. short-term consideration, . . . 4044
. stock purchase warrants, . . . 4060-4066
. technical considerations, . . . 4049-4051, 4053-4055, 4066-4069, 4071-4076, 4078-4083
. troubled debt restructuring, . . . 4084-4104
. . debtor accounting, . . . 4086-4104
. . modification of terms, . . . 4090-4100
. . other considerations, . . . 4100-4104
. . overview, . . . 4084-4086
. . partial settlement, . . . 4093-4100
. . transfer of assets in full settlement, . . . 4087-4088
. . transfer of equity interest in full settlement, . . . 4089-4090

Deferred revenue, . . . 4026-4027

Deferred tax accounting, . . . 7196-7249
. calculations, . . . 7235-7237
. disclosure requirements, . . . 7241-7243
. intraperiod tax allocation, . . . 7237-7241
. investment tax credit, . . . 7243-7249
. overview, . . . 7195-7198, 7202-7207
. recent changes, . . . 7249
. special areas, . . . 7228-7230

Deferred tax accounting,—continued
. technical considerations, . . . 7208-7228
. temporary differences, . . . 7198-7202
. uncertain tax positions, . . . 7230-7235

Defined benefit pension plan
. defined, . . . 7015
. disclosures, . . . 7053-7062, 7137-7151
. plan accounting, . . . 9050-9067
. . financial statements, . . . 9051-9064
. . note disclosures, . . . 9066-9067
. . overview, . . . 9050-9051
. . recent changes, . . . 9067
. . statement of accumulated plan benefits, . . . 9061-9064
. . statement of changes in accumulated plan benefits, . . . 9064-9066
. . statement of changes in net assets available for benefits, . . . 9059-9061
. . statement of net assets available for benefits, . . . 9051-9059
. settlements and curtailments, . . . 7125-7137

Defined benefit postretirement plans, . . . 7082, 7125-7137

Defined contribution pension plan
. defined, . . . 7015, 7082
. disclosures, . . . 7053, 7138
. plan accounting, . . . 9067-9068

Depository services, . . . 9015-9016

Depreciation
. not-for-profit entities, . . . 9049
. property, plant, and equipment, . . . 3113-3117

Derivatives and hedging, . . . 8047-8086
. disclosure requirements, . . . 8076-8081
. foreign currency matters, . . . 8104-8106
. overview, . . . 8047-8064, 8081-8082
. recent changes, . . . 8082-8086

Derivatives and hedging,—continued
. simplified hedge accounting for private entities, ... 8064-8067
. technical considerations, ... 8067-8076

Development stage entities, ... 9003-9004

Diluted earnings per share, ... 2114-2131

Discontinued operations, ... 2001-2009
. accounting and disclosure requirements, ... 2003-2007
. going concern disclosures, ... 2008-2009
. "held for sale" classification, ... 2002-2003
. liquidation basis of accounting, ... 2007-2008
. recent changes, ... 2009
. strategic shift, ... 2002

Disposal cost obligations, ... 4021-4026

E

Earnings per share, ... 2100-2148
. basic earnings per share, ... 2105-2114
. calculating, ... 2100-2104
. convertible securities, ... 2131-2141
. corporate capital structure, ... 2104
. diluted earnings per share, ... 2114-2131
. disclosures, ... 2141-2147
. recent changes, ... 2147-2148

Employee stock ownership plan (ESOP), ... 7177

Entertainment
. broadcasters, ... 9004-9006
. cable television, ... 9006-9008
. casinos, ... 9008-9009
. films, ... 9009
. music, ... 9009-9013

Environmental obligations, ... 4009-4021

Equity, ... 5001-5006
. liabilities vs., ... 4104-4110

Equity,—continued
. not-for-profit entity securities, ... 9044-9049
. overview, ... 5001-5002
. share-based payment plans classified as, ... 7155-7160
. share-based transactions, accounting for, ... 5004-5006
. stock dividends and stock splits, ... 5002-5003
. transfer of equity interest in full settlement of debt, ... 4089-4090
. treasury stock, ... 5003-5004

Equity method
. disclosures, ... 3080-3081
. overview, ... 3064-3071
. recent changes, ... 3081
. technical considerations, ... 3071-3080

Error corrections. *See* Accounting changes and error corrections

Exit cost obligations, ... 4021-4026

Expenses, *See also* Costs 7001-7249.
. compensation
. . compensated absences, ... 7006-7008
. . nonretirement postemployment benefits, ... 7009-7014
. . overview, ... 7002-7008
. . retirement benefits, *See also* Retirement benefits 7014-7152.
. . stock compensation, ... 7152-7180
. deferred costs, ... 3095
. income taxes, *See also* Income taxes 7195-7249.
. interim period, ... 2152
. inventory period costs or expenses, ... 2154-2158
. other expenses, ... 7180-7184
. . pharmaceutical manufacturer fees, ... 7183-7184
. . property taxes, ... 7181-7183

Expenses,—continued
. product costs and expenses, . . . 2152-2153
. research and development, . . . 7184-7195
. sales and services, . . . 7001-7002

Exposure Drafts, . . . 12,001

Extractive activities
. mining, . . . 9013-9014
. oil and gas, . . . 9014-9015

F

Fair value measurements and disclosures, . . . 8086-8092
. disclosure requirements, . . . 8090-8092, 8095-8096
. fair value defined, . . . 8087-8088
. overview, . . . 8086
. valuation techniques, . . . 8088-8090

Federal government contractors, . . . 9003

Films, . . . 9009

Financial instruments, . . . 8092-8104
. disclosure requirements, . . . 8092-8104
. . accounting for investments, . . . 8100
. . concentration of credit risk, . . . 8096
. . fair value, . . . 8097-8100
. . financial assets and financial liabilities, . . . 8097-8100
. . generally, . . . 8092-8096
. overview, . . . 8092

Financial services
. broker and dealers, . . . 9015
. depository and lending, . . . 9015-9016
. insurance, . . . 9016-9024
. investment companies, . . . 9024-9025
. mortgage banking, . . . 9025-9028
. title plant, . . . 9028-9029

Financial statements
. combined, . . . 8029

Financial statements—continued
. defined benefit pension plan, . . . 9051-9064
. notes to financial statements, . . . 2073-2079
. parent company, . . . 8029
. personal financial statements, . . . 2160

Foreign currency matters, . . . 8104-8139
. disclosures, . . . 8138-8139
. overview, . . . 8104-8106
. technical considerations, . . . 8106-8138
. . translating financial statements, . . . 8110-8118
. . translation when foreign currency is functional currency, . . . 8131-8138
. . translation when U.S. dollar is functional currency, . . . 8118-8131
. transactions that are not the result of derivative instruments, . . . 8104-8106

Franchisors, . . . 9029-9039
. disclosures, . . . 9038-9039
. franchise fee revenue, . . . 9034-9038
. overview, . . . 9029-9034

G

Gas and oil activities, . . . 9014-9015

General principles, . . . 1001

Going concern
. disclosures, . . . 2008-2009

Goodwill
. accounting for, . . . 3100-3104, 3111
. financial statement presentation and disclosures, . . . 3109-3111
. other considerations, . . . 3104-3105
. technical consideration, . . . 3105-3109

Guarantees, . . . 4041-4043

Guaranty funds, . . . 4003-4005

Guaranty funds,—continued
. recognition of liability for assessments, . . . 4005-4006

H

Health and welfare benefit plan, accounting for, . . . 9068-9069

Health care entities, . . . 9039

Hedging. *See* Derivatives and hedging

I

Income. *See* Comprehensive income

Income statement, . . . 2043-2044
. business interruption insurance, . . . 2043-2044
. recent changes, . . . 2044
. unusual or infrequent occurring items, . . . 2043

Income taxes, . . . 7195-7249
. deferred tax accounting, . . . 7195-7249
. . calculations, . . . 7235-7237
. . disclosure requirements, . . . 7241-7243
. . intraperiod tax allocation, . . . 7237-7241
. . investment tax credit, . . . 7243-7249
. . overview, . . . 7195-7198, 7202-7207
. . recent changes, . . . 7249
. . special areas, . . . 7228-7230
. . technical considerations, . . . 7208-7228
. . temporary differences, . . . 7198-7202
. . uncertain tax positions, . . . 7230-7235
. interest, . . . 8190
. interim period, . . . 2159
. nonmonetary transactions, . . . 8342
. overview, . . . 7195-7196

Industry, . . . 9001-9105
. agriculture, . . . 9001-9002

Industry,—continued
. airlines, . . . 9002
. contractors
. . construction, . . . 9002
. . federal government, . . . 9003
. development stage entities, . . . 9003-9004
. entertainment
. . broadcasters, . . . 9004-9006
. . cable television, . . . 9006-9008
. . casinos, . . . 9008-9009
. . films, . . . 9009
. . music, . . . 9009-9013
. extractive activities
. . mining, . . . 9013-9014
. . oil and gas, . . . 9014-9015
. financial services
. . broker and dealers, . . . 9015
. . depository and lending, . . . 9015-9016
. . insurance, . . . 9016-9024
. . investment companies, . . . 9024-9025
. . mortgage banking, . . . 9025-9028
. . title plant, . . . 9028-9029
. franchisors, . . . 9029-9039
. health care entities, . . . 9039
. notes to financial statements, . . . 2077
. not-for-profit entities, . . . 9039-9050
. plan accounting
. . defined benefit pension plans, . . . 9050-9067
. . defined contribution pension plans, . . . 9067-9068
. . health and welfare benefit plans, . . . 9068-9069
. real estate
. . common interest realty associations, . . . 9072
. . general, . . . 9069-9071
. . real estate investment trusts, . . . 9072
. . retail land, . . . 9072-9079
. . time-sharing activities, . . . 9079-9080
. regulated operations, . . . 9080-9087
. software, . . . 9087-9105

Industry,—continued
. U.S. steamship entities, . . . 9105

Infrequent occurring items, . . . 2043

Insurance
. accounting for, . . . 9024
. business interruption, . . . 2043-2044
. investment gains and losses, . . . 9023
. life insurance, accounting for purchases, . . . 3082-3083
. long-duration contracts, . . . 9019-9023
. . accounting for, . . . 9020-9023
. . definition of, . . . 9020
. . overview, . . . 9019-9020
. . reinsurance, . . . 9022-9023
. recent change, . . . 9024
. services, . . . 9016-9024
. short-duration contracts
. . overview, . . . 9018-9019
. . reinsurance, . . . 9022-9023

Intangibles, . . . 3096-3113
. acquired individually or in a group, . . . 3096-3100
. financial statement presentation and disclosures, . . . 3109-3111
. goodwill, . . . 3100-3103, 3111
. internally generated, . . . 3100
. internal-use software, . . . 3112
. other considerations, . . . 3104-3105
. overview, . . . 3096
. recent changes, . . . 3112-3113
. technical considerations, . . . 3105-3109
. testing for impairment, . . . 3098-3100

Interest, . . . 8139-8191
. capitalization of
. . disclosures, . . . 8175
. . flowchart and general discussion, . . . 8141-8146
. . other considerations, . . . 8175
. . overview, . . . 8139-8141
. . technical considerations, . . . 8146-8175

Interest,—continued
. imputation of, . . . 8176-8178
. income tax considerations, . . . 8190
. notes exchanged for cash and a right or privilege, . . . 8182-8185
. . general considerations, . . . 8182
. . technical considerations, . . . 8183-8185
. notes exchanged for cash only, . . . 8178-8182
. . general considerations, . . . 8178-8179
. . technical considerations, . . . 8179-8182
. notes exchanged for property, goods, or services, . . . 8185-8190
. . general considerations, . . . 8185
. . technical considerations, . . . 8185-8190
. overview, . . . 8139-8141
. presentation requirements, . . . 8190
. recent changes, . . . 8191

Interim reporting, . . . 2148-2160
. accounting changes, . . . 2159
. disclosures, . . . 2160
. gains and losses, . . . 2158
. generally, . . . 2148-2151
. income taxes, . . . 2159
. inventory value, decline during interim period, . . . 2154-2158
. pension plans, . . . 7061-7062
. postretirement plans, . . . 7150-7151
. product costs and expenses, . . . 2152-2153
. revenues, . . . 2152
. seasonal influences, . . . 2158

Inventory
. accounting approaches, . . . 3085
. cost flow assumptions, . . . 3085
. . computations under, . . . 3085-3088
. . illustrations of, . . . 3088-3092
. interim period
. . decline in value, . . . 2154-2158
. . LIFO, . . . 2152-2153
. . period costs or expenses, . . . 2157-2158
. . standard cost systems, . . . 2156-2157

Inventory—continued
. interim period—continued
. . valuation procedures, . . . 2152-2153
. overview, . . . 3083-3084
. recent changes, . . . 3095
. subsequent measurement of, . . . 3092-3095

Investments
. accounting for, using the fair value option, . . . 8100
. debt securities, . . . 3043-3044
. equity method and joint ventures, . . . 3064-3081
. . disclosures, . . . 3080-3081
. . overview, . . . 3064-3071
. . recent changes, . . . 3081
. . technical considerations, . . . 3071-3080
. equity securities, . . . 3041-3064
. . disclosures, . . . 3048-3064
. . recent changes, . . . 3041-3048
. financial instruments—credit losses, . . . 3083
. financial services companies, . . . 9024-9025
. investment tax credit, deferred tax accounting, . . . 7243-7249
. life insurance purchases, . . . 3082-3083
. other, . . . 3081-3083

J

Joint ventures, . . . 3064-3081
. disclosures, . . . 3080-3081
. overview, . . . 3064-3071
. recent changes, . . . 3081
. technical considerations, . . . 3071-3080

L

Land
. land and building(s) leases, . . . 8232-8236, 8270-8275
. land only leases, . . . 8231-8232, 8269-8270

Land—continued
. retail land, . . . 9072-9079

Leases, . . . 8191-8326
. accounting model for, steps in, . . . 8304-8325
. arrangements, . . . 8303
. components, . . . 8300
. date of inception, . . . 8296
. definition of, . . . 8303
. definition of terms, . . . 8192-8193, 8238, 8300
. disclosures, 8301, . . . 8325-8326
. fair value, determination of, . . . 8296
. financial reporting of, . . . 8324-8325
. initial direct costs, . . . 3021, 8307-8308
. key terms, . . . 8303-8304
. lessee
. . accounting, . . . 8196-8204, 8291, 8293-8295, 8298-8299, 8305-8306
. . amortization of ROU asset, . . . 8309
. . building, part of, . . . 8237
. . classification, . . . 8196
. . disclosure requirements, . . . 8288-8289
. . discount rate to calculate present value, . . . 8307
. . finance leases, accounting for, . . . 8306
. . finance leases, recording of, . . . 8306
. . general lease agreement, . . . 8193-8195
. . land and building(s), . . . 8232-8236
. . land only leases, . . . 8231-8232
. . lease modifications, . . . 8316-8319
. . lease payment obligation, . . . 8308-8309
. . lease term, . . . 8307
. . operating lease, . . . 8204
. . operating lease, accounting for, . . . 8310-8312
. . operating lease, recording of, . . . 8306
. . real estate and equipment, . . . 8237-8238
. . real estate leases, . . . 8227-8231
. . ROU asset, . . . 8307
. . separate lease and nonlease components, . . . 8312

Leases,—continued
. lessee—continued
. . short-term leases, . . . 8313
. . tax-exempt debt, refunding of, . . . 8289-8291, 8292-8295
. lessor
. . accounting, . . . 8292, 8295-8296, 8299, 8313
. . building, part of, . . . 8275
. . definition of terms, . . . 8238
. . direct financing lease, . . . 8258-8265
. . direct financing lease, accounting for, . . . 8315-8316
. . disclosure requirements, . . . 8289
. . general lease agreement, . . . 8238-8241
. . land and building(s), . . . 8270-8275
. . land only leases, . . . 8269-8270
. . lease modifications, . . . 8320-8321
. . lease terminations, . . . 8316
. . leveraged leases, . . . 8249-8258
. . operating lease, . . . 8275
. . operating lease, accounting for, . . . 8316
. . real estate and equipment, . . . 8276
. . real estate leases, . . . 8265-8269
. . sales-type lease, . . . 8313
. . sales-type lease, accounting for, . . . 8241-8243, 8313-8315
. . sales-type lease, technical considerations, . . . 8243-8248
. . tax-exempt debt, refunding of, . . . 8289-8291, 8292-8293, 8295-8296
. leveraged lease, . . . 8321-8324
. leveraged lease agreement, estimated residual value, . . . 8297, 8299
. operating lease, accounting for, . . . 8204, 8275
. overview, . . . 8191, 8302-8303
. recent changes, . . . 8297-8302
. right to direct control and use of asset, . . . 8304
. risk-transfer criterion, . . . 8296

Leases,—continued
. sale-leaseback transactions, . . . 8204-8231, 8300-8302, 8321-8324
. . classification, . . . 8204-8212
. . overview, . . . 8204-8212
. . real estate, 8210, . . . 8227-8231
. . technical considerations, . . . 8212-8227
. scope exclusions, . . . 8303
. subleases, . . . 8276-8288
. . overview, . . . 8276-8279
. . sublessor not relieved of primary obligation, . . . 8282-8288
. . sublessor relieved of primary obligation, . . . 8279-8282
. tax-exempt debt, refunding of, . . . 8289-8296
. . example, . . . 8292-8293
. . lessee accounting, . . . 8291, 8293-8295
. . lessor accounting, . . . 8292, 8295-8296
. . overview, . . . 8289-8291
. transition, . . . 8301-8302, 8326
. unguaranteed residual value, . . . 8296-8297

Lending services, . . . 9015-9016

Liabilities, . . . 4001-4110
. accounting for servicing of, . . . 8349-8350
. accounting for, using the fair value option, . . . 8100
. asset retirement, . . . 4009-4021
. commitments, . . . 4027-4035
. contingencies, . . . 4035-4041
. current liabilities, balance sheet liabilities, . . . 2010-2011
. debt, *See also* Debt 4043-4104.
. deferred revenue, . . . 4026-4027
. disclosures, . . . 4008-4009
. environmental obligations, . . . 4009-4021
. equity vs., . . . 4104-4110
. estimation of, . . . 4006-4008
. exit or disposal cost obligations, . . . 4021-4026

Liabilities,—continued
. extinguishment of, . . . 4002
. guarantees, . . . 4041-4043
. guaranty funds, . . . 4003-4005
. insurance-related assessments, . . . 4003
. offsetting, . . . 2011-2022
. overview, . . . 4001-4002
. policy surcharges, . . . 4006, 4008
. premium tax offsets, . . . 4006, 4008
. present value measurement of obligation, . . . 4008
. recent update to ASC . . . 405-20, 4003
. recognition of liability for assessments, . . . 4005-4006
. share-based payment plans classified as, . . . 7160-7162
. state guaranty funds, . . . 4003-4005

Limited liability entities, . . . 2160

Loans. *See also* Debt; Receivables
. acquired with deteriorated credit quality, . . . 3021
. fees, accounting for, . . . 9027
. impairment
. . accounting and reporting, . . . 3002-3017
. . disclosures, . . . 3017
. mortgage banking financial services, . . . 9025-9028

M

Measurement date, . . . 7015, 7083

Mining activities, . . . 9013-9014

Mortgage banking financial services, . . . 9025-9028

Multiemployer pension plan
. defined, . . . 7015, 7082
. disclosures, . . . 7053-7054
. postretirement plans, . . . 7138, 7140
. provide pension benefits, . . . 7138-7140

Multiple-employer pension plan, defined, . . . 7015, 7082-7083

Music, . . . 9009-9013

N

Nonmonetary transactions, . . . 8327-8343
. book value accounting required, . . . 8336-8342
. . boot, exchanges involving, . . . 8339-8342
. . boot, exchanges not involving, . . . 8336-8339
. disclosure requirements, . . . 8343
. fair value accounting required, . . . 8331-8336
. . general considerations, . . . 8331-8333, 8335
. . technical considerations, . . . 8333-8336
. income tax considerations, . . . 8342
. nonreciprocal transfers, . . . 8335-8336
. overview, . . . 8327-8331

Non-public companies
. pension plans, . . . 7058-7061

Notes, . . . 8178-8191
. exchanged for cash and a right or privilege, . . . 8182-8185
. . general considerations, . . . 8182
. . technical considerations, . . . 8183-8185
. exchanged for cash only, . . . 8178-8182
. . general considerations, . . . 8178-8179
. . technical considerations, . . . 8179-8182
. exchanged for property, goods, or services, . . . 8185-8190
. . general considerations, . . . 8185
. . technical considerations, . . . 8185-8190

Notes to financial statements, . . . 2073-2079
. accounting policy application, . . . 2078
. accounting principles, alternative, . . . 2077
. format of disclosures, . . . 2078

Notes to financial statements,—continued
. generally, . . . 2073-2077
. industry policies, . . . 2077
. recent changes, . . . 2078-2079

Not-for-profit entities, . . . 9039-9050
. debt and equity securities, . . . 9044-9049
. depreciation, . . . 9049
. overview, . . . 9040
. pension plan disclosures, . . . 7062
. recent changes, . . . 9050
. services, . . . 9049
. statement of activities, . . . 9041-9043
. statement of cash flows, . . . 9043-9044
. statement of financial position, . . . 9040-9041

O

Offsetting of assets and liabilities, . . . 2011-2022

Oil and gas activities, . . . 9014-9015

Options, . . . 2119-2131

Origination fees and costs, . . . 3019

P

Pension plan assets, market-related value of, . . . 7015

Personal financial statements, . . . 2160

Pharmaceutical manufacturer fees paid to the federal government, . . . 7183-7184

Phase-in plans, . . . 9085-9087

Plan accounting
. defined benefit pension plans, . . . 9050-9067
. defined contribution pension plans, . . . 9067-9068

Plan accounting—continued
. health and welfare benefit plans, . . . 9068-9069

Plants. *See also* Property, plant, and equipment
. costs and abandonments, . . . 9083-9085
. title plant, . . . 9028-9029

Postemployment benefits
. overview, . . . 7009-7014
. technical considerations, . . . 7012-7014

Postretirement benefits. *See also* Retirement benefits
. definition of terms, . . . 7081-7083
. disclosures, . . . 7053-7061, 7081, 7137-7152
. . defined benefit postretirement plans, . . . 7054-7057
. . defined contribution postretirement plans, . . . 7053, 7138
. . entity has two or more plans, . . . 7057-7058, 7149-7150
. . interim accounting periods, . . . 7061-7062, 7150-7151
. . multiemployer postretirement plans, . . . 7053-7054, 7138, 7140
. . non-public companies, . . . 7058-7061
. . non-public entities of defined benefit plans, . . . 7146-7149
. . not-for-profit entities, . . . 7062
. . public entities of defined benefit plans, . . . 7141-7146
. overview, . . . 7084-7102
. settlements and curtailments, . . . 7125-7137
. . defined benefit postretirement plans, . . . 7125-7132
. . technical considerations, . . . 7132-7137
. technical considerations, . . . 7102-7125
. termination benefits, . . . 7137

Present value factors, . . . 14,001-14,013

Presentation, . . . 2001-2181

Presentation,—continued
. accounting changes and error corrections, ... 2079-2100
. balance sheet, ... 2009-2022
. changing prices, ... 2100
. comprehensive income, ... 2022-2043
. discontinued operations, ... 2001-2009
. earnings per share, ... 2100-2148
. of financial statements, ... 2001-2009
. income statement, ... 2043-2044
. interim reporting, ... 2148-2160
. limited liability entities, ... 2160
. notes to financial statements, ... 2073-2079
. overview, ... 2001
. personal financial statements, ... 2160
. risks and uncertainties, ... 2161-2162
. segment reporting, ... 2162-2181
. statement of cash flows, ... 2044-2073
. statement of shareholder equity, ... 2022

Prices, changing, ... 2100

Prior service cost, ... 7015, 7083

Products, revenue recognition of, ... 6001-6006

Projected benefit obligation, ... 7015

Property, plant, and equipment, ... 3113-3136
. depreciation, ... 3113-3117
. . disclosure requirements, ... 3117
. . methods, ... 3113-3117
. impairment and disposal
. . disclosure requirements, ... 3122-3126, 3135-3136
. . generally, ... 3118-3122
. . planned major maintenance, ... 3136
. . technical considerations, ... 3126-3135

Property taxes, ... 7181-7183

R

Real estate
. common interest realty associations, ... 9072
. general, ... 9069-9071
. . abandonment of real estate projects, ... 9072
. . accounting for acquisition, development, and construction, ... 9070-9071
. . accounting for sale or rental, ... 9071
. leases, ... 8210, 8227-8231, 8237-8238, 8265-8269, 8276
. real estate investment trusts, ... 9072
. retail land, ... 9072-9079
. sale-leaseback transactions, ... 8204-8231
. time-sharing activities, ... 9079-9080

Receivables, *See also* Debt; Loans 3001-3040.
. assets received in full settlement, ... 3025-3040
. . modification of terms, ... 3027-3037
. . overview, ... 3025-3027
. . recent changes, ... 3040
. . troubled debt restructuring, ... 3038-3040
. disclosure, ... 3017-3018
. leases, initial direct costs, ... 3021
. lending activity fees and costs, ... 3018-3020
. . commitment fees and costs, ... 3018-3019
. . loan or group of loans, purchase of, ... 3020-3021
. . origination fees and costs, ... 3019
. . restructuring and refinancing fees and costs, ... 3020
. . syndication fees, ... 3019
. loan impairment
. . accounting and reporting, ... 3002-3017
. . disclosures, ... 3017

Receivables,—continued
. loans and debt securities acquired with deteriorated credit quality, . . . 3021
. nonrefundable fees and other costs
. . disclosure requirements, . . . 3021
. . overview, . . . 3018
. troubled debt restructuring, . . . 3021-3024
. . creditor accounting, . . . 3024

Regulated operations, . . . 9080-9087
. accounting disclosures, . . . 9082
. accounting requirements, . . . 9082-9083
. funds used during construction, . . . 9082
. intercompany profit, . . . 9082
. overview, . . . 9080-9082
. phase-in plans, . . . 9085-9087
. plant costs and abandonments, . . . 9083-9085
. reporting requirements, . . . 9080-9081

Related party disclosures, . . . 8343-8345

Reorganizations, . . . 8345

Research and development, . . . 7184-7195
. arrangements, . . . 7189-7195
. . disclosures, . . . 7194-7195
. . technical considerations, . . . 7191-7194
. disclosures, . . . 7189
. overview, . . . 7184-7188
. technical considerations, . . . 7188-7189

Restructuring and refinancing fees and costs, . . . 3020

Retail land, . . . 9072-9079

Retirement benefits, . . . 7014-7079
. definition of terms, . . . 7014-7015
. disclosures, . . . 7053-7062
. . defined benefit pension plans, . . . 7054-7057
. . defined contribution pension plans, . . . 7053
. . entity has two or more plans, . . . 7057-7058

Retirement benefits,—continued
. disclosures,—continued
. . interim accounting periods, . . . 7061-7062
. . multiemployer pension plans, . . . 7053-7054
. . non-public companies, . . . 7058-7061
. . not-for-profit entities, . . . 7062
. overview, . . . 7016-7032
. postretirement benefits. *See* Postretirement benefits
. recent changes, . . . 7151-7152
. settlements and curtailments
. . overview, . . . 7062-7070
. . technical considerations, . . . 7070-7079
. technical considerations, . . . 7032-7053
. termination benefits. *See* Termination benefits, settlements and curtailments

Revenue, . . . 6001-6040
. contracts with customers, from
. . amortization and impairment, . . . 6031-6032
. . bill-and-hold arrangements, . . . 6029-6030
. . breakage, . . . 6027-6028
. . consignment arrangements, . . . 6029
. . core principle, . . . 6011
. . disclosure requirements, . . . 6032-6038
. . effective dates, . . . 6010-6011
. . incremental, fulfillment, and contract costs, . . . 6030-6032
. . issues of revenue recognition, . . . 6027-6030
. . key terms, . . . 6011
. . nonrefundable upfront fees, . . . 6028
. . overview, . . . 6009-6010
. . principal and agent considerations, . . . 6028-6029
. . recent changes, . . . 6040
. . recognizing revenue, steps to, . . . 6011-6027
. . repurchase agreements, . . . 6029

Revenue,—continued
. contracts with customers, from—continued
. . sales and similar taxes, . . . 6030
. . shipping and handling, . . . 6030
. . transitioning to ASU . . . 2014-09, 6038-6040
. . warranties, . . . 6030
. deferred, . . . 4026-4027
. interim period, . . . 2152
. other income . . . 6040-6043
. . derecognition models, categories of, . . . 6040-6041
. . effective dates of and transitioning to ASU . . . 2017-05, 6043
. . recognizing and measuring gain or loss, . . . 6041-6042
. recognition of
. . long-term contracts, . . . 6007-6008
. . milestone method, . . . 6007
. . multiple-element arrangements, . . . 6007
. . principal-agent considerations, . . . 6008-6009
. . products, . . . 6001-6006
. . services, . . . 6007

Risks and uncertainties, . . . 2161-2162
. disclosures, . . . 2161
. recent changes, . . . 2161-2162

S

Sale-leaseback transactions, . . . 8204-8227
. classification, . . . 8204-8212
. overview, . . . 8204-8212
. real estate, . . . 8210, 8227-8231
. technical considerations, . . . 8212-8227

Sales, cost of, . . . 7001-7002

Securities
. convertible securities, . . . 2131-2141
. . cash or stock settlement, . . . 2137
. . contingent agreements, . . . 2137-2139

Securities—continued
. convertible securities,—continued
. . other considerations, . . . 2139-2141
. debt securities, . . . 3043-3044
. equity securities, . . . 3041-3064
. . disclosures, . . . 3048-3064
. . recent changes, . . . 3041-3048
. not-for-profit debt and equity securities, . . . 9044-9050
. options, . . . 2119-2131
. prepayments, accounting for servicing of, . . . 8349-8350
. warrants, . . . 2119-2131

Segment reporting, . . . 2162-2181
. disclosure requirements, . . . 2173-2174
. generally, . . . 2162-2172
. technical considerations, . . . 2174-2181

Service concession arrangement, . . . 8345-8346

Services
. cost of, . . . 7001-7002, 7015, 7083
. expenses, . . . 7001-7002
. financial services
. . broker and dealers, . . . 9015
. . depository and lending, . . . 9015-9016
. . insurance, . . . 9016-9024
. . investment companies, . . . 9024-9025
. . mortgage banking, . . . 9025-9028
. . title plant, . . . 9028-9029
. insurance, . . . 9016-9024
. notes exchanged for, . . . 8185-8190
. revenue recognition, . . . 6007

Servicing. *See* Transfers and servicing

Settlements and curtailments
. disclosures, . . . 7081
. overview, . . . 7062-7070, 7125-7132
. postretirement benefits, . . . 7125-7137
. technical considerations, . . . 7070-7079, 7132-7137
. termination benefits, . . . 7079-7081

Shares. *See* Stock

Software
. costs of, . . . 9087-9105
. definition of terms, . . . 9088
. disclosures, . . . 9104-9105
. overview, 9087, . . . 9088-9093
. technical considerations, . . . 9093-9104

Statement of activities, not-for-profit entities, . . . 9041-9043

Statement of cash flows, . . . 2044-2073
. cash and cash equivalents, . . . 2045-2046
. financing section, . . . 2050-2052, 2054
. generally, . . . 2044-2045
. gross vs. net amounts, . . . 2046
. investing section, . . . 2049-2050
. noncash investing, . . . 2054
. not-for-profit entities, . . . 9043-9044
. operating section, . . . 2046-2049
. organization/structure, . . . 2046
. recent changes, . . . 2073
. summary of amendments, . . . 2052-2054
. technical considerations, . . . 2054-2073

Statement of financial position, not-for-profit entities, . . . 9040-9041

Statement of shareholder equity, . . . 2022

Statements of Financial Accounting Concepts (SFACs), . . . 10,001-10,003

Stock
. accounting for share-based transactions, . . . 5004-5006
. compensation, . . . 7152-7180
. . disclosures, . . . 7175-7177
. . employee stock ownership plans, . . . 7177
. . overview, . . . 7152-7175
. . performance targets, targeted guidance for, . . . 7178
. . recent changes, . . . 7178-7180

Stock—continued
. compensation,—continued
. . share purchase plans, . . . 7153-7155
. . share-based payment plans, . . . 7153, 7155-7175
. dividends, . . . 5002-5003
. splits, . . . 5002-5003
. treasury, . . . 5003-5004

Strategic shift, . . . 2002

Subsequent events, . . . 8346

Substantive postretirement plan, . . . 7083

Syndication fees, . . . 3019

T

Tax positions, uncertain, . . . 7230-7235

Taxes
. income taxes. *See* Income taxes
. property, . . . 7181-7183

Television, cable, . . . 9006-9008

Temporary differences, . . . 7198-7202

Termination benefits, settlements and curtailments
. disclosures, . . . 7079-7080
. overview, . . . 7137
. technical considerations, . . . 7080-7081

Time-sharing activities, . . . 9079-9080

Title plant financial services, . . . 9028-9029

Transfers and servicing, . . . 8346-8353
. assets, accounting for servicing of, . . . 8347-8348
. disclosures under ASC 860, . . . 8350-8353
. financial assets, accounting for, . . . 8347-8348
. liabilities, accounting for servicing of, . . . 8349-8350

Transfers and servicing,—continued
. overview, . . . 8347
. prepayments of securities, accounting for servicing of, . . . 8349-8350
. recent changes, . . . 8353-8354
. secured debt and collateral, accounting for, . . . 8348

Treasury stock, . . . 5003-5004

Troubled debt restructuring, . . . 4084-4104
. considerations, . . . 3038
. creditor accounting, . . . 3024
. debtor accounting, . . . 4086-4104
. disclosures, . . . 3039-3040
. foreclosures, . . . 3038-3039
. modification of terms, . . . 4090-4100
. other considerations, . . . 4100-4104
. overview, . . . 3021-3024, 4084-4086
. partial settlement, . . . 3034-3037, 4093-4100
. transfer of assets in full settlement, . . . 4087-4088

Troubled debt restructuring,—continued
. transfer of equity interest in full settlement, . . . 4089-4090

U

Uncertain tax positions, . . . 7230-7235

Unusual occurring items, . . . 2043

U.S. steamship entities, . . . 9105

V

Variable interest entities, accounting for, . . . 8032-8043

W

Warrants, . . . 2119-2131, 6030